6. **Negotiable Deductions: Publication expenses should be paid by the publisher.**

7. **Royalty Statements and Audit Provision: You should be entitled to periodic royalty statements and audits of the company.**

8. **Writer's Credit: You should receive credit for all uses of your song.**

9. **Arbitration: An arbitration clause should be included to avoid large legal costs.**

10. **Future Uses: Any right to a future use should be held by you until negotiations take place.**

For more information on single song contracts. See Randy Poe's article on page 4.

1993
Songwriter's Market

Where & How to Market Your Songs

Edited by
Michael Oxley

Assisted by
Anne M. Bowling

Writer's
Digest
Books

Cincinnati, Ohio

Distributed in Canada by McGraw-Hill,
300 Water Street,
Whitby Ontario L1N 9B6.
Also distributed in Australia by Kirby Books, Private Bag No. 19, P.O. Alexandria NSW 2015.

Managing Editor, Market Books Department:
Constance J. Achabal; Assistant Managing
Editor: Glenda Tennant Neff

International Standard Serial Number
0161-5971
International Standard Book Number
0-89879-581-8

Contents

Resources

From the Editor

The first year of any new undertaking is a learning experience. My first year editing *Songwriter's Market* (*SM*) has been that. The information I've gained as a part of editing this book has even impacted life outside *SM*.

As a member of a group seeking distribution for its first album, I've begun to understand the frustrations felt by many aspiring musical artists. Finding a market for one's work is a big task, and one that only the bravest and most dedicated attempt. It requires searching for and absorbing a great deal of information. I've tried to make that information easier to grasp in this edition.

The upfront material features very useful information regarding "nuts-and-bolts," practical matters of marketing music. Understanding song contracts can be one of the most confusing aspects of an aspiring songwriter's career. We offer an in-depth look at the contract most unpublished songwriters will first be offered: the single song contract.

Many beginning songwriters ask, "What are performing rights organizations? What do they do, and how could they help me?" The Songwriters' Roundtable features representatives of ASCAP, BMI, and SESAC, the three American performing rights societies. They describe their organizations, their function and the benefits of membership. Songwriters can't collect a large portion of royalties due them without the aid of these societies, so this feature should go a long way toward explaining the importance of membership.

The Business of Songwriting is a brief but detailed look at the internal workings of the music industry. It provides up-to-date information for the songwriter trying to get his work heard. We include a special piece by Walter Carter, who reduces to the essentials just what a musical artist should be paying for.

We're especially proud of our 1993 line-up of Close-up personalities. Women and men involved in folk, country, rock, rap, audiovisual, and concert music are included. Songwriters who have taken the path you and I are experiencing now, as well as industry executives who evaluate music every day provide not only good, solid advice, but an encouraging word about continuing the quest for an audience.

Finally and most importantly, the markets. This year's edition contains 550 new listings of music publishers, record companies and producers, performing groups and others seeking new music. You'll find that the geographical indexes at the end of the Music Publishers and Record Companies have been expanded to include firms not only in but near the music hub cities. The Play Publishers and Producers section has been subdivided into separate sections for publishers and producers. We're also pleased about the increase in theater and fine arts listings; it was an important goal to provide increased performing opportunities to the composers of musical theater and concert music.

Many of the changes and features you'll find in the 1993 *Songwriter's Market* were requested by you. In a survey we conducted just after the publication of the 1992 edition, we asked readers of *Songwriter's Market* what they liked about the book and what they would like to change. We hope that you will continue to send us your feedback about this and future editions. It's your input above all that will continue to improve this book, and to provide new and better opportunities for the musical artist.

How to Use Your Songwriter's Market

The hardest task for you, the aspiring songwriter, is deciding where and to whom to submit your music. You're reading this book in the hope of finding information on good potential markets for your work. You may be seeking a publisher who will pitch your music, a record company that will offer you a recording contract, or a chamber music group or theater company to produce and perform your music live. *Songwriter's Market* is designed to be a tool to help you make those submission decisions. Read the informational articles, Close-up interviews and section introductions for an overview of the industry. With careful research you can target your submissions and move toward achieving your goals.

Where do you start?

It's easiest to move from the very general to the very specific. The book is divided into Markets and Services. The Services section contains listings and information on organizations, workshops, contests and publications to help you learn more about the music industry and the craft of songwriting. The Markets portion contains all the markets seeking new material and is the part of the book you will need to concentrate on for submissions.

Markets is further divided into chapters corresponding to specific segments of the industry. This is of particular help to composers of music for the theater and concert hall, who can find prospective markets in the Play Producers & Publishers and Fine Arts chapters, respectively. Composers of audiovisual (film and TV) and commercial music will also find a chapter of the book, Advertising, AV and Commercial Music Firms, devoted to these possibilities.

The general markets

If you don't fall into these specific areas, you will need a little more work to target markets. Questions you need to ask are: Who am I writing this music for? Are these songs that I have written for an act I now belong to? Am I a songwriter sending my music to someone hoping to have it accepted and recorded by an artist?

If you fall into the first category, writing songs for an existing group, you're probably trying to advance the career of the group as a whole. Your demo is a promotional tool for your group as well as your songs. Because you're seeking to further the group's career, recordings are a goal. They represent a documentation of the group's abilities as well as an opportunity to make money and build an audience. If you're seeking a recording contract for your act, the Record Companies section may be the place to start. Look also at the Record Producers section. Independent record producers are constantly on the lookout for up-and-coming groups. They may also have strong connections with record companies looking for acts, and will pass your demo on or recommend the act to a record company. And if your group doesn't yet have representation, your demo submission may be included as part of a promotional kit sent to a prospective manager listed in Managers and Booking Agents.

If you are a songwriter seeking to have your songs recorded by other artists, you may submit to some of these same markets, but for different reasons. The Record Producers section contains mostly independent producers who work regularly with particular groups, rather than working full-time for one record company. Because they work closely with a limited number of clients, they may be the place to send songs written with a specific act in mind. The independent producer may be responsible for picking cuts for a recording project. The Managers and Booking Agents section may be useful for the same reason. A good personal manager is constantly seeking new song material for the acts he represents, and a good song sent at the right time can mean a valuable cut for the songwriter.

The primary market for songwriters not writing with particular artists in mind will be found in the Music Publishers section. Music publishers are the jacks-of-all-trades in the industry, having knowledge about and keeping abreast of developments in all other segments of the music business. They act as the first line of contact between the songwriter and the music industry.

If you're uncertain about which markets will have the most interest in your material, review the introductory explanations at the beginning of each section. It will aid in explaining the various functions of each segment of the music industry, and will help you narrow your list of possible submissions.

Now what?

You've identified the market categories you're thinking about sending demos to. The next step is to research within each section to find the individual markets that will be the most interested in your work.

Most users of *Songwriter's Market* should check three items in the listings: location of the firm, the type of music the firm is interested in hearing, and the submission policy of the firm. Depending on your personal concerns, any of these items could be considered a point of departure for you as you determine which markets to send your music to.

If it's important to send your work to a company close to your home for more opportunities for face-to-face contact, location should be checked first. Each section contains listings from all over the U.S. as well as the rest of the world. You may be interested in submitting to firms in the music hub cities (Nashville, Los Angeles and New York). If you're looking in the Music Publisher or Record Company sections, go first to the back of the sections for geographical listings of music publishers and record companies in or near the music hubs.

Your music isn't going to be appropriate for submission to all companies. Most music industry firms have specific music interests and needs, and you also need to do your homework in this area in order to be sure that your submissions are actually being seen and heard by companies who have a genuine interest in them. To find this information, go to the Music subheading in a listing. Pay particular attention to the information at the beginning of this subheading. It will contain the styles of music a listing is seeking. The music styles are listed in descending order of importance; so if your particular specialty is country music, you may want to search out those listings that list country as their first priority as your primary targets for submissions.

Finally, when you've placed the listings geographically and identified their music preferences, read the How to Contact subheading. This will give you all pertinent information about what to send as part of a demo submission and how to go about sending it. Not all of the markets listed in *Songwriter's Market* accept unsolicited submissions, so it's important to read this information carefully. Most companies have carefully considered their submission policy, and packages that do not follow their directions are returned or discarded without evaluation. Follow the instructions: it will impress upon the market your seriousness about getting your work heard and purchased.

You've now identified markets you feel will have the most interest in your work. Read the complete listing carefully before proceeding. Many of the listings have individualized information important for the submitting songwriter. Then, it's time for you to begin preparing your demo submission package to get your work before the people in the industry. For further information on that process, turn to The Business of Songwriting.

Understanding the Single Song Contract

by Randy Poe

Every published songwriter I have ever known has regretted at least one publishing agreement he or she has signed. In a lot of cases that regret is justified. In others, if the writer hadn't signed the contract as written (or with a minimum of changes), the song probably wouldn't have been recorded at all, and the songwriter's career might not have gotten off the ground.

The fact is, if you are an unknown, never-had-a-song-recorded songwriter, it is highly unlikely that the first agreement you sign is going to be as favorable as the agreement a songwriter with several hits to his credit is going to sign. Keep in mind that you shouldn't necessarily expect to start your career at the top. But getting there is still probably going to require some compromises on your part. Your advantage will be that you will know what compromises you are making because you are about to learn what your options are. And even the subtlest difference in the type of agreement you sign can mean a significant difference in royalties earned on a hit song.

Throughout this article we'll discuss the most common type of agreement between a beginning songwriter and a publisher that exists today: the single song contract.

The single song contract is an agreement between a music publisher and a songwriter in which the songwriter grants certain rights to a publisher for one or more songs. In acquiring these rights the music publisher usually provides an advance against future royalties and agrees to attempt to cause the song to be used in one or more ways that will cause both parties to receive income from such uses. (The phrase "single song contract" is a music publishing misnomer. One single song contract can include several songs, all of which are individually subject to the clauses in the agreement.)

Many single song contracts today consist of over 20 paragraphs that attempt to cover all possible types of royalties from all sources "now known or later developed." Many songwriters complain about the length and complexities of today's single song contracts. However, all of the provisions that now exist in these contracts evolved out of technological advances and precedent-setting situations that transpired over the decades.

So, rather than complain about the length and technical wording of a contract, the songwriter is better off learning what the single song contract is all about. A properly constructed agreement can protect both the writer and the publisher in any given situation. Although the wording differs from one single song contract to another, most of the contracts have basic paragraphs in common regarding the advance, royalty payments, copyright ownership, writer's warrant (that a song is an original work), and so on.

There is no such thing as a "Standard Song Contract," despite the fact that many publishers have contracts with the word "standard" in the heading. Any time a publisher offers a "standard contract" without allowing the songwriter the right to negotiate certain points of the agreement, it's time for the songwriter to seriously question the intentions of

Randy Poe *is currently executive vice-president and general manager of Leiber & Stoller, a music publishing company whose copyrights include "Jailhouse Rock," "Kansas City" and "Stand By Me." For five years Poe was executive director of the Songwriter's Hall of Fame and now serves on that organization's board of trustees. He frequently writes and speaks about music business topics and is the author of* Music Publishing: a Songwriter's Guide *(Writer's Digest Books).*

the publisher. When I use the term "standard contract," I am merely referring to a contract that has elements in common with other contracts of that type. Here are some characteristics common to all legitimate single song contracts.

Advances

The reason a publisher wants a songwriter to sign a single song contract is because the publisher believes that he can earn income on the song through successful exploitation. In exchange for attaining certain rights to that song, the publisher should be willing to offer an advance.

An advance is an amount of money paid to the songwriter by the publisher for allowing the publisher to own rights to a song and to share in the future royalties the song might be due. The actual amount of the advance varies widely among publishers, so it's impossible for me to tell you a specific dollar figure. Sometimes it's $250; other times it's $500 or more, depending on the publisher in question and the publisher's belief in the song's hit potential. By offering an advance, the publisher is showing that he is willing to gamble real money on his ability to get your song recorded.

Whatever the amount of the advance, the total sum is recoupable according to most song contracts. In fact, the actual phrase is usually along the lines of "a non-returnable, recoupable advance in the amount of $_____." Although that phrase seems contradictory, what it actually means is that the songwriter will receive an advance of x dollars. If the song doesn't earn any royalties for the duration of the agreement, the songwriter doesn't pay the amount of the advance back to the publisher when the agreement expires. If, on the other hand, the song gets recorded and earns back the amount of the advance or more, the publisher gets to recoup the advance, after which all other monies earned on the song are split between the publisher and the songwriter according to their agreement.

The only songwriter's royalty that the publisher can't recoup is performance royalty income, which is paid directly to the songwriter by his performing rights society. Of course, the publishing company is receiving its share of performance royalties directly as well. However, the single song contract usually states that the advance is to be recouped from the songwriter's share of income. Therefore, the publisher usually doesn't count his own performance royalty income as money earned back by the songwriter against the songwriter's advance.

Some exceptions

This is not to say that every single song contract offers an advance to the songwriter. A new publishing company may be too small to offer an advance. The publisher's argument may be that, since the publisher is small and "hungry," the publisher is going to work much harder to get the song cut than would a giant company that has to deal with thousands of songs and songwriters. Such an argument may be viable. Under such circumstances, the new publisher should be willing to offer a better overall deal than the more established publisher who is willing to write an advance check.

If, on the other hand, the publisher asks that the songwriter pay him, then the songwriter isn't dealing with a true publisher. Anyone who demands money from a songwriter to acquire publishing rights to a song is known in the industry as a "song shark." Therefore, any agreement that demands payment rather than offering an advance is not a legitimate song contract.

Transfer of rights

The U.S. Copyright Act grants five exclusive rights to the copyright owner:
1. [The right] "to reproduce the copyrighted work in copies or phonorecords";
2. [The right] "to prepare derivative works based upon the copyrighted work";

3. [The right] "to distribute copies or phonorecords of the copyrighted work by sale or other transfer of ownership, or by rental, lease, or lending";

4. [The right] "to perform the copyrighted work publicly, in the case of literary, musical, dramatic, and choreographic works, pantomimes, and motion pictures and other audiovisual works";

5. [The right] "to display the copyrighted work publicly, in the case of literary, musical, dramatic, and choreographic works, pantomimes, and pictorial, graphic, or sculptural works, including the audiovisual images of a motion picture or other audiovisual work."

Generally, in a single song contract these are the rights the songwriter transfers to the music publisher in exchange for an advance, a guarantee that the publisher will make a best effort to exploit the song, and a share of approximately 50 percent of all royalties actually earned by the song.

One of the phrases commonly used in a single song contract is "The writer hereby sells, assigns, transfers, and delivers" the copyright to the publisher. Theoretically, the writer could sell, assign, and transfer each of his five exclusive rights to five separate parties. However, since massive confusion would reign in such a situation, a writer usually transfers all of his rights in a song to one particular publisher. The exception to this rule would arise in the case of a songwriter who co-publishes a song with another co-publisher or assigns administration rights to an administrator.

The songwriter's royalties

It has generally been common practice among music publishers to offer single song contracts to a songwriter without a track record. Songwriters who are already successful to some degree are usually offered other types of agreements at higher royalty rates. The royalties that are shared between the publisher and the songwriter signing the single song contract are usually split 50/50.

In the case of mechanical royalties, synchronization royalties, and royalties received by the publisher from foreign sources, the single song contract generally calls for the songwriter to receive 50 percent of all such income. In no case should a songwriter agree to accept less than 50 percent of the income received by the publisher from these sources.

There is one area in which the publisher will usually end up with more than 50 percent of the income received. This royalty source is printed editions, in which case the songwriter is paid at one of a variety of rates depending on the type of edition in question and on whether or not the publisher also makes the printed editions or licenses rights to a print publisher. Sheet music royalties, for example, are usually paid in amounts of x cents for each copy sold. Although the percentage will vary according to the deal the music publisher has with the print publisher, if the single song contract calls for the writer to receive 12 cents per copy sold, and the publisher receives 50 cents per copy sold from the print publisher, then the songwriter is going to be paid substantially less than 50 percent on sheet music royalties.

The same is true of other printed editions as well. The single song contract may offer the songwriter 10 percent of the wholesale selling price of other printed editions of the composition (such as band, orchestra and choral arrangements) when, in fact, the publisher may be making a profit of 25 percent or more of the wholesale price.

Royalties for folios can become even more confusing, since the amount paid to the writer will depend on several factors. If the publisher prints his own folios, the royalty due the writer will be based on a percentage (usually 10 to 12½ percent) of the wholesale selling price. If the publisher allows someone else to print a folio that includes the song referred to in the single song contract, the songwriter's royalties will be based on a percentage (usually 50 percent) of what the publisher receives. In either case, the amount paid to the writer will be on a pro rata basis (determined by the number of songs in the folio).

Territory covered

As long as the songwriter hasn't already made a deal of some kind with one or more music publishers outside of the United States, the single song contract almost always calls for the publisher to acquire worldwide rights to the song in question. This gives the publisher the greatest possible chance of earning income on the song by either adding to the songs that are already part of a subpublishing agreement or by assigning the song to various subpublishers throughout the world.

Term of the contract

The term of the single song contract is the specific amount of time that the contract will be in effect. This length of time will be determined by several factors.

The act of signing a contract with a music publisher doesn't mean a song is now considered to be published. When a songwriter signs a single song contract, he is allowing one publisher to acquire the rights to one or more songs for a period of time.

Before the 1976 Copyright Law went into effect, there were generally two possible terms of contract a songwriter could agree to: the first term of U. S copyright (28 years) or the life of copyright including the renewal term (56 years). The 1976 law changed the life of copyright to the life of the author plus 50 years, while at the same time saying that a writer can terminate an agreement with a publisher at the end of 35 years if the song has been published or after 40 years from the date of the agreement, whichever is shorter. If the writer and/or his heirs wish, however, the song may remain with the original publisher for the rest of the copyright's life ("life-plus-50"). In such a case, the publisher would usually have to pay an advance or bonus (a bonus is nonrecoupable) in order to get to retain the copyright.

Of course, in a single song contract, the writer and publisher can agree to whatever amount of time they wish, up to the maximum allowed by copyright law. If Wanda the writer can convince Pete the publisher that Pete should have the song only for a decade, then the term of the single song contract would be ten years. If the contract included a "reversion clause" (see below), then the term of the contract might be even shorter.

The reversion clause

In a single song contract there is sometimes a specified amount of time in which the publisher is allowed to attempt to acquire a recording of the song in question. For instance, the songwriter may agree that the publisher has, say, one year to get the song cut. At the end of one year from the date of the contract, if the publisher is not successful in his efforts, all rights in the song revert to the writer. The portion of the single song contract that spells out the songwriter's right to regain the copyright is called the reversion clause. If the reversion becomes effective because the publisher hasn't caused the song to be recorded, some reversion clauses stipulate that the writer has to return the advance and/or the amount the publisher's demo costs.

It's also important to note that the amount of the advance might depend on the length of time the publisher is allowed to try to get the song recorded. For instance, a publisher who has only six months before a reversion clause goes into effect is probably going to offer a lower advance (if any) than a publisher would who has a year or 18 months to try to get the song used.

Another possible cause for a copyright to revert to a songwriter would be if a publisher fails to pay royalties properly or on time. Some single song contracts include this kind of language as well. Once the song is recorded and released (and, therefore, "published" as defined by copyright law), the copyright remains with the publisher unless some action (or inaction) takes place that causes the reversion clause to go into effect.

Accounting and audit clauses

Earlier we covered the topic of royalties to be paid to the writer by the publisher. Elsewhere in the single song contract there is a paragraph that explains how often and at what time during the fiscal or calendar year the publisher will make these royalty payments. Generally, royalty payments will be made twice a year at six-month intervals, usually within 45 days after the end of each six-month period. Assuming the publisher pays based on the calendar year, the writer should expect to be paid around August 14th (45 days after June 30th) and around February 14th (45 days after December 31st).

For the songwriter's protection there should also be an audit clause that allows the writer (or his financial representative) to examine the publisher's books once a year to make certain the royalty payments are accurate. Many publishers honestly attempt to make accurate payments. Those that don't make payments on time usually develop a reputation that prevents writers from wanting to sign agreements with them in the future. Sometimes, though, publishers or their royalty departments do make mistakes, so even the most honest of publishers can, on occasion, pay a writer less than he is actually due. For this reason, a publisher should be willing to include an audit clause in the single song contract.

Warranty, indemnity and disputes

These three topics are all a part of the common single song contract. The "warranty" section applies to the writer, who is required to warrant (or guarantee) that he is transferring the rights in an original work of authorship to the publisher, and that he hasn't already transferred those rights to any other publisher or third party.

The indemnity clause relates directly to the warranty clause. The indemnity clause says the writer will be held financially responsible for any lawsuits that might arise in case it turns out that, in fact, the song was actually written by someone else, or that the writer had already assigned the song to another publisher.

The "disputes" clause, on the other hand, refers to possible clashes between the writer and the publisher. Usually such disputes will transpire sometime shortly after the songwriter has had the publisher's books audited. Normally this kind of dispute will be resolved by proper payment from the publisher.

But what if the publisher refuses to pay what is actually owed? Or what if the publisher refuses to grant an audit at all, even though the contract clearly states that he must? The disputes clause is included in the single song contract to clarify how an internal disagreement will be resolved. Usually it will state that, rather than allowing actual lawsuits to be filed, the writer and publisher will agree to a resolution of any disputes through binding arbitration. Binding arbitration is the act of settling a dispute by putting the problem before a qualified, disinterested third party who will decide how the dispute will be resolved.

The entertainment lawyer

Throughout the centuries lawyers have been dealt with rather harshly. A common complaint in the music industry has been that lawyers have taken over the business — either by running the business from behind the scenes or by actually being the heads of major music publishing and record companies. Although the fact that lawyers seem to have too much control over the industry may anger some, it is advantageous to the songwriter who is trying to get the best possible protection and the best possible deal.

No matter what stage in his career a songwriter has reached, it is absolutely imperative that he have a good entertainment lawyer on his side. Real estate and divorce lawyers won't do in the music business game. An experienced entertainment lawyer knows what standard practices are in the music industry and is able to help his clients through every legal aspect of a music publishing deal.

In an ideal world (to use a common lawyer's phrase) there would be no need for lawyers.

But almost everyone involved in the music business would agree that things aren't exactly ideal out there. I cannot overemphasize the lawyer's importance.

Explaining how to choose the right entertainment lawyer for you isn't an easy task. The best advice I can give is to get recommendations from songwriters who are happy with their legal representation. If you don't know any successful songwriters, you should attend music industry workshops and seminars and ask the panelists for the names of respected lawyers in the business. Rupert Holmes, one of the most successful songwriters you could ever hope to meet, has strong feelings about the importance of entertainment lawyers: "I had a tendency in my first few years in the business to literally sign anything that was put in front of me. I was so afraid that I would offend someone by asking to read the contract or by taking it to a lawyer.

"I was so terrified that publishers might forever ignore me and that I would insult them so much. And, frankly, most of the time publishers have said, 'Oh, why do you want to take it to a lawyer? Lawyers cause trouble.'

"There's usually a reason why publishers say that. If someone says, 'Ah, don't bring a lawyer into this thing because it'll just get so complicated and it'll cause problems'—it means that in some way you're getting ripped off.

"If people object to you taking a contract to a lawyer, it isn't just because lawyers make things complicated. It's because lawyers have a tendency to ask for things that might be appropriate.

"But there's still always the pressure to sign because you're afraid that the publisher will vanish. In this day and age, though, there really is no reason to rush that signature. If someone asks my advice, I just tell them to go slow in terms of signing because when you sign contracts, those signatures don't go away—and they can loom large later on."

Rupert says there is another important reason to have a good entertainment lawyer: "Most of my best breaks in the business have come from attorneys and recording engineers. Choose your attorney carefully. If you choose an attorney who's already negotiating with a major record label or publisher for five other artists that they want, and he says, 'By the way, while I'm here, would you listen to this cassette?', it can be a real good 'in' for you."

Lawyers aren't cheap. Perhaps that's one of the reasons they have to endure so much criticism. However, the amount of money they can keep you from losing will usually justify the expense of their fees.

If you think legal advice isn't an option because of cost, here are several options. The Songwriter's Guild of America offers free contract review to its members. Volunteer Lawyers for the Arts also provides legal advice and other services to those unable to afford legal help. For further information on these useful organizations, see the listings for both groups in the Organizations chapter of *Songwriter's Market*.

Songwriters' Roundtable: The Performing Rights Societies

Royalties are the main source of income for songwriters and composers. The music industry provides many types of royalties, but none are as important as the performance royalties from live performance and media presentation of music. Songwriters can try to collect these royalties themselves, but organizations called performing rights societies exist to collect this money for songwriters.

We spoke with representatives of the American performing rights societies to learn more about these groups and their function in the music industry. These organizations are an important link in the music industry and provide more than just money for their members. If you don't already belong to one of these organizations, we hope this roundtable discussion provides information about what these societies can do for you. Here are a brief history and the addresses for each group, followed by our roundtable discussion.

ASCAP—The American Society of Composers, Authors and Publishers was founded in 1914 by composers and publishers of music to carry out the intent of the American Copyright Law of 1909. ASCAP currently has approximately 55,000 writer and publisher members in all musical styles. The main offices: 1 Lincoln Plaza, New York NY 10023; 6430 Sunset Blvd., Los Angeles CA 90028; 66 Music Square West, Nashville TN 37203; and Kingsbury Center, 350 W. Hubbard St., Chicago IL 60610. *Songwriter's Market* questioned Lisa Schmidt, Eastern Regional Executive Director of Membership and Jeff Sapan, Public Relations, for this article.

BMI—BMI was founded in 1940 as Broadcast Music, Inc. to help represent the growing repertoire of popular music and provide competition in the performing rights arena. BMI now represents the music catalogs of 95,000 members in all musical styles. The main offices: 320 W. 57th St., New York NY 10019; 8730 Sunset Blvd., Los Angeles, CA 90069; and 10 Music Square West, Nashville TN 37203. Clay Bradley, Associate Director, Writer/Publisher Relations represented BMI in this roundtable discussion.

SESAC—The third American performing rights organization began in 1930 as the Society of European Stage Authors and Composers. Now officially named SESAC, the smallest American performing rights society collects royalties for the catalogs of approximately 5,000 members. The main offices: 55 Music Square West, Nashville TN 37203; and 156 W. 56th St., New York NY 10019. Vice President C. Dianne Petty was SESAC's representative for this discussion.

SOCAN—The Canadian performing rights society came into existence as a result of the merger of two smaller organizations, CAPAC and PROCAN, in 1990. SOCAN offers many of the same services that American performing rights societies provide. The main office: 41 Valleybrook Dr., Don Mills ON M3B 2S6 Canada. Unfortunately, we were not able to include SOCAN in this discussion of performing rights societies.

What is your organization's main purpose?

ASCAP: The main goal is to maximize the income to the organization which also maximizes the income to the songwriter and publisher members. A sub-goal would be also to provide services to our members, supplying things like educational seminars about the industry, about performing rights, workshops to help songwriters perfect their craft and to help songwriters get exposure.

BMI: BMI's main purpose, I believe, is to license songwriter's copyrights, and to pay those songwriters when those copyrights are played on radio and TV. That's our main purpose, to collect performance royalties for songwriters.

SESAC: SESAC's main purpose is to be a creative, innovative alternative to what songwriters and publishers have known in the performing rights industry in the past. It's a family business built on one writer relationship at a time. The purpose behind what we do is to find natural raw talent with the potential for brilliance and to invest ourselves and our knowledge and our network into assisting to dream their dreams and reach their goals.

Who owns or operates your organization? How does this affect how your organization is operated?

ASCAP: It's owned by the songwriter and publisher members. We have about 55,000 songwriter and publisher members. The board of directors is comprised of 12 writers and 12 publishers who are elected by the membership. Everything that the organization does has the songwriter's and the publisher's interests at heart. It is completely run by songwriter peers, publisher peers. Any decisions that are made are for the benefit of its members.

BMI: BMI is a nonprofit organization. We have a board of directors that operates our company. This board of directors is made up of people in the media industry, from television and radio station owners. That board is selected by previous board members.

SESAC: The chairman of the board of SESAC is the daughter of our founder. Her name is Alice Prager. She is very receptive to new thinking. She's been the enabler in our growth and our diversity. Our president and CEO is Vincent Candilora. He's a 20-year veteran who literally grew up in the company. He first worked in the broadcast licensing division and has a hands-on working knowledge of every area here. The writers who come here, stay here. There's no short term in developing talent, no way to anticipate that this is going to hit here and this here. You have to continue to nurture it and focus it, nurture it and direct it. Being small and having direct access to upper management without a doubt allows us to move more quickly and more efficiently. If you're a writer with one of the other societies there are no short terms; you can't make decisions in any of those companies in a day. I can, and that gives me leverage.

What does your organization not do?

ASCAP: We do not collect mechanical royalties. We do not copyright works or administer copyrights; a lot of writers think that we do and send copyright forms or send their song and say, "Copyright this for me." We're not a record company; we're not a publishing company. We don't license "grand" rights, which are Broadway [musical theater] and opera. It's not ASCAP's place to exploit the works of the writer and publisher members. Although we may help to open doors for people, we're solely for performing rights.

BMI: BMI does not publish songs. BMI is not a profit-making organization; we are not out to make money. BMI does not license such things as the making of phonograph records or the printing of sheet music. The right to perform shows—known as the "grand right" — on the legitimate stage must be obtained directly from the producers or publishers of the show.

SESAC: We're not publishers. We are not managers. We are an ancillary support system in the creative process. We are a conduit between the writer and the publisher many times, not for negotiating their deals, but for networking them into the creative community. In reality, we're strictly a performing rights organization. Our job is to collect from the user of music and make sure that the writers and publishers are compensated for their talent.

How do writers go about becoming members of your organization?

ASCAP: The criteria are actually pretty easy. If someone has a commercially released LP, CD, cassette, that's criteria for membership. If someone has a performance in an ASCAP-licensable venue such as a night club, radio station, television station, cable station, that's also criteria for membership. If someone has printed sheet music that's commercially available, that's also criteria for membership. If they have a performance in a club or concert setting, we would require a letter from the venue confirming that material of that writer or publisher had performance on that particular date at a particular time. Then they just fill out the application and list the works, sign the agreement.

BMI: To become a member of BMI, what you need to do is set up an appointment with a performing rights employee who works with writers and publishers. If you cannot do that, make a phone call or write one of these people; they are located in New York, London, Nashville and Los Angeles. There are many people like myself who can help you become affiliated. All you need to do is fill out an application, sign your name to it, fill out a contract that says that BMI will license all the works that you write that are recorded, and you become affiliated. You don't have to have songs published or recorded to become a member. We do not discriminate against anyone; if we think you have the potential as a songwriter we will ask you to become affiliated and we will try to further your career. No fees or dues.

SESAC: It's slightly different from ASCAP and BMI, because of the fact that we took this selective approach to our business, recognizing that there are two ways to go; that you can sign everybody that walks in the door on the whim that maybe some of them will hit or you can take the time up front to go through the music, which is the product we license. When I meet with the publisher, one of the first things I do is explain to them the approach that we have to our business. The fact that we want to have excellence in all areas of music, that the quality of what we do is directly related to the number of people we commit ourselves to. So, I explain and ask their indulgence when I say that I want to see any writer that they're excited about. With the songwriters, if it's a new songwriter, just someone who calls with an enquiry, we will ask that writer to submit three songs. Those three songs are reviewed by a screening committee in the creative department. And if there is merit in what we hear in those three songs then we will set an appointment and sit with that writer in person, or we will communicate through the mail or on the phone with that writer. I get a lot of direct referrals. I have publishers who bring me talent who know I'm going to roll up my sleeves and get involved too. And you can only give yourself to so much as I said, so we're real selective about the writers we commit to, and then we really give them a wonderful business support system.

What rights, if any, are your members giving to you?

ASCAP: They're giving us the nonexclusive right for ASCAP to collect the performing rights royalties. At any point a member can license their works directly, as long as they tell us and there's no double payment. Someone could go to a radio station and say, "Pay me directly," and then they tell ASCAP, "Don't pay me on this particular performance or this particular media because I license them directly." They can do this at any time. We also license the nondramatic rights to our members' works.

BMI: What writers give to BMI when they join our organization is the ability to go out and log their works if they're performed on radio and TV and pay them [the songwriters] for them. That right is exclusive; no other performing rights organization can collect your royalties. You are giving BMI the exclusive right to license your musical works.

SESAC: Prior to January 1, 1992 our standard publishing agreement was not only for performing rights, but also for mechanical, synchronization and subpublishing. When I first came to SESAC, I was well aware that the major publishers were not going to work with us under those multiple restraints. As of January 1, 1992, we are very proud to have a new SESAC writer and publisher agreement, and these agreements go into effect as each writer's term or publisher's term comes up. And this agreement is strictly a performing rights agreement. So as of 1992, the only rights that the publisher or writer grants to SESAC is the right of public performance. We are no longer involved in mechanical, subpublishing and synchronization.

For what period of time do your members commit their catalog to the organization?

ASCAP: The agreements run for 10 years, but you can resign from ASCAP at the end of any year, giving 3 months advance notice. So it's essentially a year-to-year contract. The current agreement is from 1986 to 1995.

BMI: It's a two year deal. At the end of the two year period, if they decide to stay with us it automatically renews for two years. [To leave BMI] members have to send us a certified letter no later than 60 days before their termination date. Their termination date is the same day they became affiliated. BMI publishers are a little different. You're charged a $50 administration fee for paperwork, and then you become a member. We clear the [publisher's] name through BMI, check with ASCAP, and if you want to end that publisher contract with BMI, you have to notify us no less than 60 days before your termination date.

SESAC: We have three-year writer agreements and five-year publishing agreements. When we represent a copyright on behalf of a writer or publisher that copyright has been licensed to the user for a period of five years, so to delete it from the repertory would be taking away something we had already granted the right to. So the five-year publisher agreement is certainly in line with that; the publisher is the one who's granting us the rights to license it for the world.

What types of music does the organization's catalog contain? In what types of music is the catalog strongest?

ASCAP: Our catalog contains everything. It ranges from classical to jazz to theater to polkas to barber shop quartets to rock 'n' roll to thrash to punk. I think we cover every type of music. It's not a matter of strength, it's a matter of diversity, because we really do have a very open criteria for membership and the way we pay is completely genre-blind, so we represent every type of music there is.

BMI: We have a very interesting history. We were started in 1940 basically out of the necessity of ethnic music not being licensed by our competitors. Things like R&B, folk, country, blues. That's how BMI started, because all these types of ethnic genres of music were popping up, and these people could not join a performing rights organization. We license everything, we do not discriminate. We have a policy at BMI called the "Open Door" policy. That "Open Door" policy says that if you are a writer of music or a composer of music, you can become a member of BMI. I think the strength in BMI's musical catalog is probably its rock 'n' roll, especially the beginnings of rock 'n' roll. Almost every songwriter and performer from 1940 to 1970 were BMI. And we're a stronghold in country music.

SESAC: You'll see copyright in all genres, in every diverse category. But we focused on young talent in some areas early on in my tenure, and we are very strong in the New Age and new A/C marketplace. There's a great strength in the jazz area. Of course country, I'm very proud of what we've done there because mostly those writers are the kids who I started with when I first came. The classical field, because of the age of our repertory (We're 61 years old . . .), there are certain works that are here that are known internationally for their value. The gospel market certainly. We're very strong in the contemporary Christian marketplace, especially in the rock arena. We're growing and developing in the adult AOR arena, in the rock area. So you can sort of get the idea that we have diversified and grown. You don't need bulk; you need a continually active and vital repertory that we like to think has some distinction because of the way we're building it.

What types of businesses are required to be licensed by your organization?

ASCAP: Any place that plays the music for the public excluding churches and grammar schools has to pay a license fee to ASCAP to play ASCAP music. Even the airlines pay a fee, because they're using ASCAP music. Muzak, which supplies elevator music and music for shopping areas has to pay a license fee. Any place that plays music has to pay ASCAP a fee. Funeral parlors now have to pay an ASCAP fee because they use music. They're using music to enhance their services, so it's a license fee situation. Also, radio stations, television stations, nightclubs, restaurants.

BMI: TV stations, including network and cable, radio stations, nightclubs, hotels, dance clubs, restaurants, health clubs, aerobics centers, department stores. Anyone that uses music has to pay a fee. That's [music] an intellectual property, and if businesses are using this intellectual property you own to gain business in their realm of operation, if they're making money, our writers want to be compensated. So we license everybody that uses music.

SESAC: Everything in the general licensing arena. Broadcast licensing; we've been in a fairly constant relationship with them for many, many years. We're everywhere that radio and television are. We've got an entire floor of people, using telemarketing as their vehicle, on the phone with every type of general licensee, from hotels and nightclubs and dancing schools and colleges and funeral homes and everywhere that music is licensable, we're on that trail and after the dollar for our writers and publishers.

How does your organization sample your licensees in order to determine number of performances?

ASCAP: On radio, we sample 60,000 hours of radio time. There are people who tape 6-hour segments of radio stations that are determined by outside statistics based on the amount of the license fees they pay us. The tapes that are made are sent back to the New York headquarters where tape monitors listen to the tapes and identify the songs on those tapes. The songs on those tapes then get paid from license fees to the member songwriters and the member publishers of ASCAP. On network television we pay on all performances under the agreement we have with the networks. They are required to send us a cue sheet which itemizes the name of the show, the episode, the writer of the music, the publisher of the music, the use: is it a theme, a feature or background? Local television is very complicated. Essentially right now we survey a total of 127,000 hours of local television time. It's a little more complicated than that, but the basic sample is 30,000 hours of time. Again, the stations are determined by the license fees and statistics used in determining which stations we pick. We also include all syndicated performances on the top 50 paying stations to ASCAP. So when you add those performances to the 30,000 hours, that's essentially how you get the 127,000 hours. On cable, the only cable station we pay on a complete calendar census basis is HBO; all the other cable networks are on a survey basis. A certain amount of hours per year are surveyed. We do also survey some ice shows.

BMI: We send out a log book to radio stations all over the country. The log books are returned and the songs are put through mathematical equations and that says how often we think the song was played nationwide that week. In TV, it's different. It's a census; we pay on everything that's played on TV. Every producer of TV programs has to fill out a cue sheet for BMI. It says what songs were used, who wrote them, who performed them, if it was background or feature performance. Money collected from department stores and clubs and motels [for background music] is a different process. That money is collected, then it is paid to the songwriters based on who had the most performances in that given quarter. They will get the biggest chunk of that money, based on the radio and TV media.

SESAC: Our premise is basically that if you've got a hit song, it's that "pebbles-in-the-pond" effect. If it's out there, and it's a significant copyright you can almost anticipate how that song works its way down to the live arena. The copyrights are paid out on a chart payment system. We use the *Billboard* singles charts and album charts in all formats. We use *Radio & Records*; we use *Gavin Report*. And this gives us, at no expense to us, and in a way that is completely out of our control, a line on what is getting played at radio. As a song moves up the charts, its performances increase. We know that the value of that copyright and that record can be told at the radio level. On top of that there are television rates, which we pay for national television, syndicated television, local, cable. Those are done through logs. We use TV listings and satellite guides. There are several publications that come into our building that are surveyed looking for performances.

How does your organization determine the distribution of license fees? How often are royalties distributed?

ASCAP: We get the money in from the places who play the music, and based on very complicated formulas [ASCAP pays its members]. It's basically a mathematical formula using different multipliers that comes up with a pre-dollar value of one particular performance. The things taken into consideration of that performance are: kind of media, size of the particular station that the performance is picked up on, the use of music; was it a feature, was it a jingle, was it theme or background? When we get into television there are other determinations; how many days a week is this show on? What time of day was the show? Was the show on a weekend? Was the show during prime time? Was the show in the morning? All these different factors come into play to get the pre-dollar value of a particular performance. When we have a distribution, we take all the money that's available for that distribution, we divide it in half. Half goes to the writers, half goes to the publishers. We take the total pre-dollar value, which we call credits, and we divide into the total amount of dollars available for distribution. You get a dollar per credit value. For each member, each dollar value is multiplied times however many credits that have accumulated up to that quarter; that's essentially our distribution. ASCAP pays four times a year on domestic performances, 3 times a year on foreign performances. We have agreements with performing rights and licensing organizations all around the world that we will collect on behalf of their members and they will collect on behalf of ours.

BMI: BMI publishes a payment schedule of performance royalties. A copy of this schedule is given to members when they become a BMI writer. If the payment schedule should be changed, a revised copy will be sent to BMI writers and publishers. We have [payment schedules for] Radio 1, Radio 2 and TV. When you become a writer or publisher member of BMI, you receive a payment schedule and you can sit down with a director and they will explain to you how you are getting paid. That's an interesting process. It's complex. Especially at BMI, because we like to pay on hit songs and catalog. So we have a system called the "bonus" system. The bonus system kicks in when a song is performed over 150,000 times in a quarter. Once a song achieves that level, we call it bonus. It begins to be paid double. If it doesn't reach that level, it remains on what we call "entry" level. We pay royalties four times a year.

SESAC: We allocate quarterly. The wonderful thing about our system is, we are able, again because size is in our favor, to pay our writers their income sooner. If a writer in my organization has a hit record January through March, in that first quarter, he's going to get his first performance activity check in June, within six months of the activity. So that's a real important factor. You know what you get before you get it, and you're going to get it sooner. A writer can literally sit down with his payment schedule and know what he's going to get based on his hard work and his effort, before he gets the check.

What special services does your organization provide?

ASCAP: There's actually a lot of services that we provide. A very important one is our legislative lobbying efforts in Washington to support all aspects of the copyright law. We lobbied very heavily for the United States to join the Berne Convention. They're lobbying right now for the DAT code. There was also a source licensing bill that was introduced by the broadcasters which basically would have circumvented ASCAP and BMI license fees and that would have required producers of television shows to acquire licenses for performing rights directly from the writer or publisher and substantially bring down the performing rights royalty in the television medium. We're always trying to uphold every aspect of the copyright law and help the creators of music. The other things we do are education programs. We have seminars around the country about the music business. In our New York office, we have a monthly seminar called "Songwriters' Source," where we talk about ASCAP. We have songwriter workshops, which are basically critique sessions. We have showcase programs around the country, where we showcase local artists and get the industry involved. We've been successful getting some artists signed to record labels and publishing deals with the showcase program. We do have grants and scholarship programs. There's the [ASCAP Foundation] Grants to Young Composers, and there's the Rudolph Nissom award. We also have what's called the ASCAP awards panel. There are a group of people outside of ASCAP's employ, journalists, critics, D.J.'s, who review applications by the rider members. The awards are for people that, during the normal course of the ASCAP distribution may not see money, like jazz composers. There's not a lot of jazz stations around the countries so they wouldn't normally give a lot of money for performing rights. It's just people that have a lot of activity that wouldn't normally have been picked up in the ASCAP survey. They fill out the application. Then, if they (the panel) think that someone has a significant amount of material, they are awarded from $100 up to $3,000, which is just another way of ASCAP saying, "This music is important, and we feel that these people should be compensated in some way."

BMI: We market, plug, we actually sit down with writers to help in any way, shape or form we can. Sometimes acting as managers, songpluggers, songwriters. We provide a support to the songwriter, which is a very important ingredient in a songwriter's career. They need someone to support them because creative people are not a dime a dozen, they're very special people. They need a lot of help, they need to be guided. That's kind of an intangible thing to measure. We provide "BMI Live" performances, where members are put on in front of music industry professionals and play their music live for them. We do that at South by Southwest and New Music Seminar. We sponsor these events as well. We hold workshops all over the country for new songwriters. New York City holds a jazz workshop every other Sunday. BMI does have grant and scholarship programs. I think this all goes back to support.

SESAC: Because the music is where we start, it gives us an innate opportunity to assist that writer in his development. Sometimes a writer will come to me, and he's not very objective, and it's easy to understand why. It's hard to be objective about something that comes through you, something that's literally a product of you. Many times I will be able to identify what that writer's innate sense and strengths are. Now, no third person can predict who will work together well, because this is an intimate relationship to begin to co-write. But I have enough seasoning now, and I'm aware of my own writers' talents, so that now I'm able to mix it up inside [find SESAC collaborators] on a regular basis. We do whatever is necessary. If it's a writer/artist who has talent we believe we can assist in getting that writer placed, we put our energies behind that. We've done showcases where we've shopped talent and secured recording contracts. Many times when I'm working with a writer who is interested in networking into publishing, I'm able, through my awareness in the publishing community, to know right where I ought to send that writer. That's a real personal service in this arena. I have a writer's room right across the hall from me that's booked every day of the week, all day long. We have a small piano in there. The writers seem to love that room.

What do you think your organization does best?

ASCAP: We are the best at collecting monies that are due to writers and publishers. We're always analyzing new technologies and new forms of maximizing income for writers whether that be dealing with the foreign societies and trying to help them better identify the songs of our members. Whether it's the licensing people coming up with new and better ideas on how we can license some new music user that hasn't been licensed in the past or a new technology that hasn't been licensed. We're really good at meeting our goal. We have the largest income of any licensing organization in the world.

BMI: The best thing BMI does is give exposure to new, up-and-coming songwriters. We are the largest performing rights organization in the world. It's real easy to get lost when you're the biggest. We pride ourselves on exposing the new songwriters. Our competition focuses on established stars. We feel like we're a much better organization for new song-writers. It goes back to support. We support these people. The guy that comes through my office on Monday morning may come back a year later with the biggest hit song of the year. We want to do everything we can to help get songwriters to that stage in their career. Once they start receiving payment from BMI for hit songs, they no longer need to be on a "BMI Live" or go to a workshop. They've already done that, they've met with other songwriters. We might sit in our offices and talk all day, everything about business, the music business. From producers to record deals to publishing deals. And any insight we can give these people whatsoever is vital. And that's hard to measure.

SESAC: Serve songwriters. We take care of them; we care about them. We get involved with them; we reveal ourselves to them. We're not operating at arm's length; we're right up in their faces. They're the most important personality in this whole structure. Anybody who loses sight of that is not only losing sight of the way to do business, they're losing sight of, and pleasure in, being part of the process.

The Business of Songwriting

The music industry is a confusing and ever-changing place, with its own language, contracts and technology. There's a major label market and an independent market. The music "hub" cities, New York, Los Angeles and Nashville, all have different ways of operating and different expectations. To exist and thrive in this marketplace without being overwhelmed is one of the major challenges to the aspiring songwriter. Songwriters who not only survive but succeed are those who have taken time before entering the market to learn as much as they can about the music industry and how it works.

Educating yourself can be done two ways: study or experience. Experience is an effective teacher; unfortunately it can also be a cruel and costly one. The music business is impersonal despite the sometimes very personal output produced by it. The bottom line for the music publishers, record companies, and all others involved is this: They are in business to make money. The current state of the economy has created an adversarial artist/business relationship. Music industry contracts are an example of this; the language is generally intended to minimize the firm's expenses while maximizing profit, usually at the expense of the artists. Terms like "work for hire" and "cross-collateralization" can mean the difference between success or little or no return for your work.

The other teacher is study. Many sources exist to help you educate yourself about the intricacies of the music industry *before* diving in. Local and national songwriter groups and performing rights societies can be a source of information. Reading, studying and learning to use the information contained in source books like *Songwriter's Market* expand your understanding of the marketplace and make you a better business person. Recently an industry official at a regional music conference summarized the importance of educating oneself about the music industry in three words: "Forewarned is forearmed." Have an idea of what might happen before it does, and you will be the better for it. Experience will augment your knowledge rather than block it. You will be able to more effectively market yourself and your work in a highly competitive business, and do it in a professional manner.

Getting started

The music industry wouldn't exist without music—your songs. Your artistic vision and output are what appears on recordings, radio and in concerts. There are no patterns, forms, or paths that will guarantee success in songwriting. It's important to develop a personal vision and stick with it. Finding your personal way of working and allowing it to stand on its own will display your individuality and make your work interesting to those listening.

When working on songs, look for feedback everywhere. Collaborators, song critique sessions with your local songwriting group and submissions to publishers will help you to identify strenghts and weaknesses in your music and give you guidance in how to improve your craft. Improving your songwriting technique is important; it will free you to write songs you'll be happy with. Feedback will also create connections within the industry and continue your education, not only in the craft of songwriting, but in the business as well. You must never stop being a student when working in the music industry.

The structure of the music business

The music industry in the United States traditionally revolves around three hub cities: New York, Los Angeles and Nashville. Power is concentrated in those areas because that is where most of the record companies, publishers, songwriters and performers are. Many people who are trying to break into the music business—in whatever capacity—move to one of those three cities in order to be close to the people and companies they want to contact. From time to time a regional music scene will heat up in a non-hub city such as Austin, Seattle or Atlanta. When this happens, songwriters and performers in that city experience a kind of musical Renaissance complete with better paying gigs, a creatively charged atmosphere in which to work and active interest from the major labels. All this is not to say that a successful career cannot be nurtured from any city in the country. It can be, particularly if you are a songwriter. The disadvantages one faces by not being in a major music center can be offset somewhat by phone and mail contact with industry people and, if possible, occasional trips to the music hub nearest you. For the serious songwriter, a well-planned, once-a-year trip to New York, Los Angeles or Nashville to attend a seminar or to call on record companies and music publishers can be of immense value in expanding music industry contacts and learning how the business operates. There are, of course, many smaller, independent companies located in cities across the country. A career of international scope can be started on the local level, and some may find a local career more satisfying, in its own way, than the constant striving to gain the attention of a major label.

The perspective of any company, big or small, must begin with the buying public. Their support, in the form of money spent on records and other kinds of musical entertainment, keeps the record companies in business. Because of that, record companies are anxious to give the public what they want. In an attempt to stay one step ahead of public tastes, the record companies hire people who have a facility for spotting musical talent and anticipating trends and put them in charge of finding and developing new recording acts. These talent scouts are called "A&R representatives." "A&R" stands for artist and repertoire, which simply means they are responsible for finding new artists and matching songs to artists. The person responsible for the recording artist's finished product—the record—is called the producer. It is the producer's job to bring the recording artist out of the studio with a good-sounding, saleable product. His duties often involve choosing the songs to be included on the album, so record producers are great contacts for songwriters. Some A&R reps produce the bands they discover.

The A&R reps and the producers are helped in their search for songs (and sometimes artists) by the music publisher. A publisher is really a songwriter's representative who, for a percentage of the profits (typically 50% of all publisher/songwriter earnings), tries to find commercially profitable uses for the songs in his catalog. A good publisher stays in close contact with several A&R reps, trying to find out what kinds of projects are coming up at the record companies and whether any songs in his catalog might be of use.

When a song is recorded and commercially released, the record company, the recording artist, the producer, the publisher and the songwriter all stand to profit. Recording artists earn a negotiated royalty from their record company based on the number of records sold. Publishers and songwriters earn mechanical royalties (based on records sold) and performance royalties (based on radio air play). Producers are usually paid either a negotiated royalty based on sales or a flat fee.

Until you establish relationships with specific professionals in the industry who appreciate your music and are willing to work with you on a regular basis, you should submit your material to as many appropriate contacts as you can find. Based on what we've just discussed, you can see that appropriate contacts would include A&R reps, producers and publishers. You can add managers to that list. Depending on how "big" the artist is, he may have a personal and/or road manager. These people have direct access to the artists they manage, and they're always on the lookout for hit songs for them.

Any method of getting your song heard, published, recorded and released is the best way if it works for you. In this book music publishers, record companies, record producers and managers are listed with specifications on how to submit your material to each. If you can't find the person or company you're looking for, there are other sources of information you can try. Check trade publications such as *Billboard* or *Cash Box*, available at most local libraries. These periodicals list new companies as well as the artists, labels, producers and publishers for each song on the charts. There are several tipsheets available that name producers, managers and artists currently looking for new material. Album covers and cassette j-cards can be excellent sources of information. They give the name of the record company, producer, and usually the manager of the artist or group, and reveal who publishes the songs on the album. Liner notes can be revealing as well, telling how a song came to someone's attention, how a musical style evolved or what changes or new projects lie ahead for the artist. Be creative in your research—any clue you uncover may give you an edge over your competition.

Submitting your songs

When it comes to showing people what you have to offer, the tool of the music industry is a demonstration recording—a demo. Most people prefer cassettes because they're so convenient. Songwriters make demos showcasing their songs and musicians make demos of their performances. These demos are then submitted to various professionals in the industry. It's acceptable to submit your songs to more than one person at a time (this is called simultaneous submission). Most people try their best to return tapes if a self-addressed, stamped envelope is included in the submission, but even with the best intentions in the world sometimes it just doesn't happen. (A person screening tapes might open dozens of packages, take the tapes out and put them all in a bag or box, and listen to them in the car on his way to and from the office, thus separating the tapes from their SASEs. *Always* put your name, address and phone number on every item in your submission package, including the tape itself.)

The one exception to simultaneous submissions is when someone asks if he may put a song of yours on "hold." This means he intends to record it, and he doesn't want you to give the song to anyone else. Sometimes he'll give a song back to you without recording it, even if it's been on hold for months. Sometimes he'll record your song but decide that it's not as strong as his other material and so he won't include your song on his album. If either of these things happens, you're free to pitch that song to other people again. (You can protect yourself from having a song on hold indefinitely. Either establish a deadline for the person who asks for the hold, i.e., "You can put my song on hold for x number of months." Or modify the hold to specify that you will pitch the song to other people, but you will not sign a deal without allowing the person who has the song "on hold" to make you an offer.) When someone publishes your song, you grant that publisher exclusive rights to your song and you may not pitch it to other publishers (though you *may* pitch it to artists or producers who are interested in recording the song without publishing it themselves).

The production quality of demos can vary widely, but even simple demos with just piano/vocal or guitar/vocal need to sound clean, with the instrument in tune and the lyrics sung clearly with no background noise. Many songwriters are investing in equipment such as four- or eight-track recorders, keyboards and drum machines—for recording demos at home. Other writers like to book studio time, use live musicians, and get professional input from an engineer and/or producer. It's also possible to hire a demo service to do it all for you. Ultimately, you'll have to go with what you can afford and what you feel best represents your song. Once you have a master recording of your song, you're ready to make cassette copies and pitch your song to the contacts you've researched.

Some markets indicate that you may send for evaluation a video of your act in performance or a group doing your songs, in lieu of a standard cassette or reel-to-reel demo. Most of our listers have indicated that a videocassette is not required, but told us the format of their VCR should a songwriter or artist want to send one. It's always a good idea to check with the company first for appropriate video format and television system, especially if it's an international market. Be aware that the television systems vary from country to country. For example, a Beta or VHS format tape recorded using the U.S. system (called NTSC) will not play back on a standard English VCR (using the PAL system) even if the recorder formats are identical. It is possible to transfer a video demo from one system to another, but the expense in both time and money may outweigh its usefulness as opposed to a standard audio demo. Systems for some countries include: NTSC—U.S., Canada and Japan; PAL—United Kingdom, Australia and West Germany; and SECAM—France.

Submitting by mail

Here are guidelines to follow when submitting material to companies listed in this book:

• Read the listing and submit exactly what a company asks for and exactly how it asks that it be submitted.

• Listen to each demo before submitting to make sure the quality is satisfactory.

• Enclose a brief, neat cover letter of introduction. Indicate the types of songs you're submitting and recording artists you think they might suit. If you are a writer/artist looking for a record deal yourself, or pitching your demo for some reason other than for another artist to record your songs, you should say so in your letter. Have specific goals.

• Include typed or legibly printed lyric sheets. If requested, include a lead sheet. Place your name, address and phone number on each lead or lyric sheet.

• Neatly label each tape and tape box with your name, address, phone number and the names of the songs on the tape in the sequence in which they are recorded.

• Keep records of the dates, songs and companies you submit to.

• Include a SASE for the return of your material. Your return envelope to companies based in countries other than your own should contain a self-addressed envelope (SAE) and International Reply Coupons (IRC). Be certain the return envelope is large enough to accommodate your material, and include sufficient postage for the weight of the package.

• Wrap the package neatly and write (or type on a shipping label) the company's address and your return address so they are clearly visible. Your package is the first impression a company has of you and your songs, so neatness is very important.

• Mail first class. Stamp or write "First Class Mail" on the package and on the SASE you enclose. Don't send by registered mail unless the listing specifically requests it. The recipient must interrupt his day to sign for it and many companies refuse all registered mail.

If you are writing to inquire about a company's current needs or to request permission to submit, your query letter should be neat (preferably typed), brief and pleasant. Explain the type of material you have and ask for their needs and current submission policy.

To expedite a reply, you should enclose a self-addressed, stamped postcard asking the information you need to know. Your typed questions (see the Sample Reply Form) should be direct and easy to answer. Also remember to place the company's name and address in the upper lefthand space on the front of the postcard so you'll know which company you queried. Keep a record of queries, like tape submissions, for future reference.

If a market doesn't respond within several weeks after sending your demo, don't despair. As long as your submission is in the possession of a market there is a chance someone is reviewing it. That opportunity ends when your demo is returned to you. If after a reasonable length of time you still haven't received word on your submission, follow up with a friendly letter giving detailed information about your demo package.

Submitting in person

A trip to Los Angeles, Nashville or New York will give you insight as to how the music industry functions. You should plan ahead and schedule appointments to make the most of your time while you're there. It will be difficult to get in to see some people, as many professionals are extremely busy and may not feel meeting out-of-town writers is their highest priority. Other people are more open to, and even encourage, face-to-face meetings. They may feel that if you take the time to travel to where they are, and you're organized and persistent enough to schedule meetings, you're more advanced and more professional than many aspiring songwriters who blindly submit inappropriate songs through the mail.

You should take several cassette copies and lyric sheets of each of your songs. More than one of the companies you visit may ask that you leave a copy. If the person who's reviewing material likes a song, he may want to play it for someone else. There's also a good chance the person you have the appointment with will have to cancel (expect that occasionally), but wants you to leave a copy of your songs so he can listen and contact you later. *Never* give someone the last or only copy of your material—if it is not returned to you, all the effort and money that went into your demo will be lost.

Many good songs have been rejected simply because they weren't deemed appropriate by one listener at one particular time, so don't take rejection personally. Realize that if one or two people didn't like your songs, they just could have been having a bad day. However, if there seems to be a consensus about your work, like the feel of the song isn't quite right or a lyric needs work, you should probably give the advice some serious thought. Listen attentively to what the reviewers say and summarize their comments when you return home. That information will be invaluable as you continue to submit material to those people who now know you personally.

Contracts

The Songwriter's Guild of America (SGA) has drawn up a Popular Songwriter's Contract which it believes to be the best minimum songwriter contract available. The Guild will send a copy of the contract at no charge to any interested songwriter upon request (they do ask that you include a self-addressed stamped envelope with your request). SGA will also review free of charge any contract offered to its members, checking it for fairness and completeness. (See the Guild's listings in the Organizations section.)

The following list, taken from a Songwriter's Guild of America publication entitled "10 Basic Points Your Contract Should Include" enumerates the basic features of an acceptable songwriting contract:

1. Work for Hire. When you receive a contract covering just one composition you should

---

Sample Reply Form

I would like to hear:
(   ) "Name of Song" (   ) "Name of Song" (   ) "Name of Song"
I prefer:
(   ) reel-to-reel (   ) cassette (   ) videocassette
                              (   ) Beta (   ) VHS
    With:
(   ) lyric sheet (   ) lead sheet (   ) either (   ) both
(   ) I am not looking for material at this time, try me later.
(   ) I am not interested.

Name   *Title*

make sure that the phrases "employment for hire" and "exclusive writer agreement" are not included. Also, there should be no options for future songs.

2. Performing Rights Affiliation. If you previously signed publishing contracts, you should be affiliated with either ASCAP, BMI or SESAC. All performance royalties must be received directly by you from your performing rights organization and this should be written into your song contract. (The same goes for any third party licensing organization mutually agreed upon.)

3. Reversion Clause. The contract should include a provision that if the publisher does not secure a release of a commercial sound recording within a specified time (one year, two years, etc.) the contract can be terminated by you.

4. Changes in the Composition. If the contract includes a provision that the publisher can change the title, lyrics or music, this should be amended so that only with your previous consent can such changes be made.

5. Royalty Provisions. Basically, you should receive fifty percent (50%) of all publisher's income on all licenses issued. If the publisher prints and sells his own sheet music and folios, your royalty should be ten percent (10%) of the wholesale selling price. The royalty should not be stated in the contract as a flat rate ($.05, $.07, etc.).

6. Negotiable Deductions. Ideally, demos and all other expenses of publication should be paid 100% by the publisher. The only allowable fee is for the Harry Fox Agency collection fee, whereby the writer pays one half of the amount charged to the publisher. Today's rate charged by the Harry Fox Agency is 4.5%.

7. Royalty Statements and Audit Provision. Once the song is recorded and printed, you are entitled to receive royalty statements at least once every six months. In addition, an audit provision with no time restriction should be included in every contract.

8. Writer's Credit. The publisher should make sure that you receive proper credit on all uses of the composition.

9. Arbitration. In order to avoid large legal fees in case of a dispute with your publisher, the contract should include an arbitration clause.

10. Future Uses. Any use not specifically covered by the contract should be retained by the writer to be negotiated as it comes up.

For a more thorough discussion of the somewhat complicated subject of contracts, see Understanding the Single Song Contract, page 4, and these two books published by Writer's Digest Books: *The Craft and Business of Songwriting*, by John Braheny and *Music Publishing: A Songwriter's Guide*, by Randy Poe.

Copyright

When you create a song and put it down in some fixed or tangible form it is a property you own, and it is automatically protected by copyright. This protection lasts for your lifetime (or the lifetime of the last surviving author, if you co-wrote the song) plus 50 years. When you prepare demos, lyric sheets and lead sheets of your songs, you should put notification of copyright on all the copies of your song (on the lyric or lead sheet and on the label of a cassette). The notice is simply the word "copyright" or the symbol © followed by the year the song was created (or published) and your name: © 1992 by John L. Public.

For the best protection, you can register your copyright with the Library of Congress. Although a song is copyrighted whether or not it is registered, such registration establishes a public record of your claim to copyright that could prove useful in any future litigation involving the song. Registration also entitles you to a potentially greater settlement in a copyright infringement suit. To register your song, request a government form PA, available on request from the Copyright Office. Call (202)707-9100 to order forms. It is possible to register groups of songs for one fee, but you cannot add future songs to that particular collection.

Once you receive the PA form, you will be required to return it, along with a registration fee and a tape or lead sheet of your song, to the Register of Copyrights, Library of Congress, Washington DC 20559.

It may take as long as four months to receive your certificate of registration from the Copyright Office, but your songs are protected from the date of creation, and the date of registration will reflect the date you applied for registration.

If you ever feel that one of your songs has been stolen—that someone has unlawfully infringed on your copyright—you will need to have proof that you were the original creator of the work. Copyright registration is the best method of creating proof of a date of creation. You *must* have your copyright registered in order to file a copyright infringement lawsuit. One important way people prove a work is original is to keep their rough drafts and revisions of songs, either on paper or on tape, if they record different versions of the song as they go along.

True copyright infringement is rarer than many people think. For one thing, a title cannot be copyrighted, nor can an idea, nor can a chord progression. Only specific, fixed melodies and lyrics can be copyrighted. Second, a successful infringement suit would have to prove that another songwriter had access to your completed song and that he deliberately copied it, which is difficult to do and not really worthwhile unless the song is a smash hit. Song theft sometimes happens, but not often enough to allow yourself to become paranoid. Don't be afraid to play your songs for people or worry about creating a song that might sound similar to someone else's. Better to spend your time creating original songs, register the copyrights you intend to actively pitch to music professionals, and go ahead and make contacts to get your material heard.

Record keeping

It is a good idea to keep a ledger or notebook containing all financial transactions related to your songwriting. Your record keeping should include a list of income from royalty checks as well as expenses incurred as a result of your songwriting business: cost of tapes, demo sessions, office supplies, postage, traveling expenses, dues to songwriting organizations, class and workshop fees and publications of interest. It's also advisable to open a checking account exclusively for your songwriting activities, not only to make record keeping easier, but to establish your identity as a business for tax purposes.

Your royalties will not reflect tax or other mandatory deductions. It is the songwriter's responsibility to keep track of income and file appropriate tax forms. Contact the IRS or an accountant who serves music industry clients, for specific information.

International markets

Everyone talks about the world getting smaller, and it's true. Modern communication technology has brought us to the point at which media events and information can be transmitted around the globe instantly. No business has enjoyed the fruits of this progress more than the music industry. The music business of the 1990s is truly an international industry. American music is heard in virtually every country in the world, and music from all over the world has taken a firm hold on America's imagination over the past few years.

Those of you who have been buying *Songwriter's Market* over the years may have noticed a steady increase in the number of international companies listed. We believe these listings, though they may be a bit more challenging to deal with than domestic companies, provide additional opportunities for songwriters to achieve success with their music, and it is obvious from the response we get to our listing questionnaires that companies all over the world are very interested in music.

If you consider signing a contract with an enthusiastic publisher from a country outside the United States, use the same criteria that we referred to earlier when making a decision as to the acceptability of the contract.

Co-writing

Co-writing affects the creative side of your songwriting, and it also affects the business side. Many songwriters choose to collaborate because they like the instant feedback a writing partner can provide; they feel they are stronger in lyric or music writing skills and they seek someone whose talents will complement their own; they want to write in a style of music somewhat unfamiliar to them and so they seek someone more experienced in that genre. Or they feel the final outcome of two or more writers' experiences and creative input will be greater than the sum of its parts. While co-writing can be a boon to your creative output, you should think about how it will affect your business. You'll have to share the writer's royalties which means less money for you. On the other hand, your co-writer will be pitching your song to people you may not even know, thus expanding your network of contacts and increasing the possibilities for your song to get recorded.

Where do you find collaborators? Check the bulletin board at your local musician's union hall. If you don't see an advertisement that seems suitable for you, ask if you can post your own ad telling what type of writer you're looking for, what styles of music you're interested in, what experience you've had, what your goals are, etc. Other places to advertise are at music stores and college and university music departments, if they allow it.

Professional organizations like The National Academy of Songwriters, The Songwriters Guild of America, The Nashville Songwriters Association International and the Los Angeles Songwriters Showcase offer opportunities to meet collaborators or correspond with them through the mail. Check the Organizations section for addresses. Most local songwriters associations also provide names of potential co-writers. See if there's an organization in your area.

If there's not, why not start one? Having a local songwriting organization can be a great way to pool resources, critique each other's songs, help each other on demos and cooperate in many other ways. For more information on starting a local group, read the introduction to the Organizations section. As you use *Songwriter's Market* and learn more about the music industry, you'll have much to share with the songwriters in your area.

When to Pay: Songwriter Services

by Walter Carter

Just as you hire a mechanic or a tax accountant for your personal needs, you will want to hire specialists in the music business to take care of the things that you don't have the expertise or time to do yourself. As in the real world, the songwriter's world has a variety of services available, from legitimate and necessary professionals to con artists preying on egos and dreams. For every facet of songwriting—even the writing of the song—there is someone out there willing to take your money or your rights in exchange for providing a service. Some services have a clearcut value; some are clearly worthless. In some areas, however, the line between a legitimate service and a scam is determined only by the personal integrity of the people offering the service.

In hiring, contracting or subscribing to any services, never assume anything. Always ask these questions, and beware of anyone who acts insulted or avoids answering them:

- Exactly what is provided and exactly what is the cost?
- What is the value of this service to me as a songwriter?
- What is promised in writing and what is only a possibility?
- What recourse do I have if the service is not delivered satisfactorily?
- Do you have samples of your work, personal or professional references, examples of success as a result of your service?

Compared to the fee you'd pay a mechanic or accountant, few of these services are relatively high-priced—as long as you don't give up part of the rights to your song in the process. If your service doesn't deliver up to your expectations, write it off to experience and find a better one. After all, if you aren't satisfied with your mechanic's work, you complain, you try to get restitution, then you find another mechanic; you don't quit driving cars. The same goes for songwriter services.

Collaboration services

Legitimate songwriters do not charge a collaboration fee, nor do they work for collaboration services. If they think the song is worth working on they do it in exchange for a percentage of the writer's share. Never pay anyone to "put your songpoems to music" or to do any other type of work on your song. Never ever.

Consultation

You send in your song and, for a fee, someone tells you what he thinks about it. No successful songwriter or publisher wastes his time or his integrity doing this. Most successful songwriters are willing to help out an aspiring writer (within limits) by listening to a few songs and offering an opinion. The writers and publishers who serve on panels at seminars

---

Walter Carter *has been a part of the Nashville music scene since 1975. He is the co-author of Kathy Mattea's "Life As We Knew It,"* Gruhn's Guide to Vintage Guitars, *and the author of* The Songwriter's Guide to Collaboration *(Writer's Digest Books).*

are volunteering their time. You'll get a much greater return on your money by attending a critique session at a songwriting seminar—even if someone else's songs are being critiqued—than by sending off a song and a check.

Songplugging

In addition to consultation, some services offer to demo and pitch your song, if it is deemed worthy. At this point, the service begins to look more like a publishing company, and the lines of legitimacy get hazy. Publishers don't work for a fee, nor do independent songpluggers. Publishers work for half the royalty. Professional independent songpluggers work for a percentage of the publisher's royalty. Neither the publisher nor the plugger gets paid unless the song is cut. If someone is interested in pitching your songs, it should be for a percentage of the royalties made as a result of his pitches—not a piece of the publishing and not a flat fee. On the other hand, a service might be worth trying if, and only if, all three of these conditions apply: 1) the only fee is for a demo and that fee is comparable to those charged by demo services, 2) the service has a track record of getting songs cut (ask for references), and 3) you don't give away any rights unless your song is cut.

Publishing

Do not pay to have your song published. Do not pay a demo fee if it is tied in with publishing. "Publishing" does not mean having sheet music printed. It means you sign a publishing agreement giving the publisher all the rights to your song in exchange for half the royalty. It is common in writer-publisher contracts today for demo costs to be deducted from the writer's royalties, so the writer eventually does pay for demo costs, but not up front. If the song is worth publishing, the publisher should pay you an advance against future royalties.

Publishing services should not be confused with administration services, which take care of publishing paperwork—copyrights, licensing, collection and in some cases further exploitation of recorded works. Administration services charge a relatively small percentage of what they collect, and you won't need them (and vice versa) until you have a publishing company that is generating some income.

Demo services

With the development of cheap synthesizers, sequencers, samplers and recording equipment, many people have set up small home studios and offer demo services (not to be confused with custom recording services). You send in a guitar-vocal tape and a fee, and the service sends you back a professional demo. Demo services usually have one or more standard instrumentation packages—bass, drums, guitar, keyboard and vocal, for example—with add-ons, such as a female lead vocal or extra guitars or background vocals, available a la carte.

For the songwriter with little studio experience, no studio or no professional musicians in his area, the advantages of a demo service are obvious. The cost is also an advantage. Depending on how elaborate a demo you need, a service may charge anywhere from $50 to $200 per song. That still comes out less than the average per-song cost of a full session with union musicians.

Most services should provide samples, possibly at a nominal charge ($5) to cover tape cost. If the service has a good track record, if any of their demos have eventually been recorded, you can be sure they will let you know about it. To get the best results from a service it's important to be specific as to the style of music you want and the artists you're aiming for.

Custom recordings

You want to be a star, so you give someone a fee to produce a record with you singing. For more money, the service will send out your records to radio stations and promote the record. Your single might even show up on "independent" charts in an obscure music business publication. This is the classic, time-proven method of parting a fool from his money.

"Promotional" CDs

This is a new twist to the custom recording service. You provide a finished master recording of one song. The service collects 20 masters from various wanna-be's, puts them all on a CD, gives you a hundred copies and maybe even sends copies out to a list of big-time producers—all for a fee of $500.

First of all, the guy who puts this CD together is making a lot of money. His total expense for mastering, pressing and mailing is not going to be any more than $5,000. With 20 cuts at $500 each, he's taking in $10,000. Second, assuming anyone is going to listen through 20 cuts before tossing this CD in the trash, you don't want to pitch yourself in a package with 19 other artists. No matter what kind of bogus "Best of" title this CD comes with, it's not going to be any more impressive than a professional tape. A tape copy costs quite a bit less than $500. If you want to look really professional, use DAT (digital) tape.

Lead sheets

Lead sheets are copies of songs—melody, lyrics and chords—done by hand or, increasingly, by computer. There are only two uses for lead sheets: 1) for singers who read music and prefer to have music written out, and 2) as a guide for the preparation of a published piano arrangement (sheet music). You don't need a lead sheet to copyright a song; you can furnish a tape instead. You don't need a lead sheet to pitch a song; a lyric sheet will do just fine. If you do need one, look around wherever music-related services are advertised. Before you hire anyone, get a sample. Prices start around $35 for a song. Rates will be higher for longer songs.

Producers

If you need help running a demo session, look first to the engineer or the lead musician. Everybody wants to be a producer, so their assistance may not cost anything. If it means getting together an hour or two before a session to plan thing out, pay for the extra time at whatever rate you're paying for session time.

If you want to be a recording star as well as a successful songwriter, then you need a super demo (a master, really) with a production that showcases you as a singer. If you're very talented as a singer-songwriter, you might attract an independent producer who, if he's legitimate, pays for the sessions in exchange for a percentage of your future record royalties or publishing rights. (This would be a good time to call your lawyer.) Some successful, legitimate independent producers will work for a flat fee, providing they believe they can create a quality product that will not undermine their integrity. Others will work for a fee with anyone who will pay.

Whether it's a simple demo or a master-demo, if you hire a producer you entrust your music to someone else. Making sure the producer understands and agrees with your ideas about your music is as important as his credentials.

Tip sheets

Tip sheets tell you which artists are looking for songs, what style of songs, how to submit songs, etc. They are not cheap—expect to pay $50, $75 a year or more—and they do provide information that may not be readily available to writers who are not signed with major publishing companies. Some tip sheets have a preponderance of unknown artists. This does not necessarily mean they are less valuable or less legitimate than those with more major-label artists. You may be able to make a stronger pitch to a new artist on an independent label because you will probably have better access to the producer.

A tip sheet's success is based on accuracy and on cuts. If songs have been recorded as a result of pitches from the sheet, you can bet the people who publish the sheet will let you know about it.

Important information on market listings

● *Although every listing in* Songwriter's Market *is updated, verified or researched prior to publication, some changes are bound to occur between publication and the time you contact any listing.*

● *Listings are based on interviews and questionnaires. They are not advertisements, nor are markets reported here necessarily endorsed by the editor.*

● *A word about style: This book is edited (except for quoted material) in the masculine gender because we think "he/she," "she/he," "he or she," "him or her" or "they" in copy is distracting. We bow to tradition for the sake of readability.*

● *Looking for a particular market? Check the Index. If you don't find it there, it is because 1) It's not interested in receiving material at this time. 2) It's no longer in business or has merged with another company. 3) It charges (counter to our criteria for inclusion) for services a songwriter should receive free. 4) It has failed to verify or update its listing annually. 5) It has requested that it not be listed. 6) We have received reports from songwriters about unresolved problems they've had with the company. Check the '92-93 Changes list at the end of each section to find why some markets appearing in the 1992 edition do not appear in this edition.*

● *A word of warning. Don't pay to have your song published and/or recorded or to have your lyrics—or a poem—set to music. Read Walter Carter's article on songwriter services to learn how to recognize and protect yourself from the "song shark."*

● Songwriter's Market *reserves the right to exclude any listing which does not meet its requirements.*

Key to Symbols and Abbreviations

* *new listing in all sections*
SASE self-addressed, stamped envelope
SAE self-addressed envelope
IRC International Reply Coupon, for use on reply mail in countries other than your own.

(For definitions of terms and abbreviations relating specifically to the music industry, see the Glossary in the back of the book.)

The Markets

Music Publishers

The music publisher is the first link in the chain between the songwriter and the music industry. The publisher represents you not only as song plugger, but as networking resource, collaborator contact, administrator and more. The range of knowledge and personal contacts available to the good music publisher can be the most valuable resource to an aspiring songwriter beginning to learn about the music industry.

A music "publisher" doesn't actually publish a song; the firms that handle sheet music publication are called *music print publishers* and can be found in a separate section. The firms listed in this section are responsible for taking the product provided (your songs) and attempting to maximize the potential income of the song through recordings, use in the media, and other areas. Although this is his primary task, the music publisher may also handle administrative matters such as copyrighting music, collecting royalties for the songwriter, arranging and administering foreign rights and arranging and producing new demos of the music submitted to him. In order to be successful, the music publisher must be able to deal with the other segments of the music industry: producers, personal managers, A&R personnel, distributors and lawyers. In other words, the good music publisher is a generalist in an industry of specialists.

How can you find a music publisher that will work for you? First, you need to know about the music the publisher actually handles. Each listing will provide information about the type of music that publisher is most interested in. This is an important area to consider as you do research to identify companies to submit to. "Shotgunning" (sending out many packages without regard for music preference or submission policy) your demo packages is rarely a successful marketing technique and often may damage your reputation if you resubmit to that publisher.

Next, find out what songs have been successfully handled by the publisher. Most music publishers are glad to provide this information in order to attract quality material. Use this information; contact the songwriters already working with the company to get an opinion of how the publisher works and if they're successful. What is the publisher like? An important question to keep in mind as you're researching music publishers is this: Would you work with them if they weren't in the position they are in? If you can't work with a music publisher on a personal level, chances are your material won't be represented as you would like it to be.

Another issue to be addressed is the size of the publisher. The publishing affiliates of the major music conglomerates are huge, handling catalogs of thousands of songs by hundreds of songwriters. Unless you are an established talent, your songs won't receive enough attention. The smaller independent publisher offers several advantages. First, independent music publishers are located all over the country, offering you the chance to work with a publisher face-to-face rather than by mail or phone. Independent publishers often aren't affiliated with a record company but pitch to many different labels and acts; working with a publisher not affiliated with a record company adds another member to the team promoting your music. Indies are usually interested in a smaller range of music, thus allowing you to target your submissions more accurately. The most obvious advantage: working with a smaller publisher guarantees a certain amount of personal attention to your songs. The smaller publisher will work harder to maximize income not only for you but for himself.

If you've found a publisher you like, and he would like to shop your work, the next thing to check is the publishing contract. Most industry officials recommend having any music business contract reviewed by a competent entertainment lawyer. Especially with your first contract, it's important to ask questions about language and concepts you don't understand. Contract review services are also provided by many songwriter organizations such as The Songwriter's Guild of America. Use these resources to help you gain knowledge about music business language and what constitutes a fair publishing contract. (For more on song contracts, see the upfront article Understanding the Single Song Contract.)

The knowledge you gain from contract review may help you in identifying the music industry's unethical practitioners. The "song shark," as he's called, makes his living by asking a songwriter to pay to have a song published, will ask for more than the statutory royalties and may even ask you to give up all rights in a song in order to have it published. If you're asked about these "options" by a potential publisher, don't do it. Although none of these practices is illegal, it's certainly not ethical, and no successful publisher uses these methods. *Songwriter's Market*, to the best of our knowledge, contains only honest companies interested in hearing new material. (For more on "song sharks," see Walter Carter's article on songwriter services.)

With each company you choose to submit to, remember that a professional, courteous approach goes a long way in making a good impression. When you submit through the mail, make sure your package is neat and meets the particular publisher's submission specifications. This section is filled with helpful information and reflects the need for every conceivable style of music, from traditional country to rap to thrash to gospel. It's all here — remember to be selective.

Listings of companies in countries other than the U.S. will have the name of the country in bold type. You will find an alphabetical list of these companies at the end of this section. Also at the end of this section is an index of publishers in the New York, Los Angeles and Nashville metropolitan areas, which might prove helpful in planning a trip to one of the major music centers.

A STREET MUSIC, 445 W. 45th St., New York NY 10036. (212)903-4773. FAX: (513)531-4744. A&R Director: K. Hall. Music publisher and record producer (A Street Music). ASCAP. Estab. 1986. Publishes 25-30 songs/year; publishes 5 new songwriters/year. Receives 25-50 submissions/week. Works with composers. Pays standard royalty.
How to Contact: Submit demo tape—unsolicited submissions are OK. Prefers cassette or DAT with 3 songs. Lyric sheets optional. "SASE *only* will receive reply; for tape return include adequate postage."
Music: Mostly rock (heavy to pop/radio oriented); will listen to R&B (dance-oriented, radio/pop oriented). Published "Feeding Time at the Zoo" (by Nicarry/Strauss), recorded by Ripper Jack (heavy rock); "Zeudus" (by Weikle), recorded by Zeudus (heavy instrumental rock); and "When My Thoughts Return to You" (by Brad Mason), recorded by Debbie O. (pop/blues), all on A Street Records.
Tips: "Don't send sloppy, first-draft, off-the-cuff demos. Put your best foot forward. If you cannot sell it to us, then how can we hope to place it with an artist?"

ABINGDON PRESS, 201 8th Avenue, South, Nashville TN 37203. (615)749-6158. Music Editor: Gary Alan Smith. Music publisher. ASCAP. Publishes approximately 100 songs/year; publishes as many new songwriters as possible. Receives 20 submissions/month.
How to Contact: Submit a manuscript and/or a demo tape by mail—unsolicited submissions are OK. "Unsolicited material must be addressed with Gary Alan Smith's name on the first line." Prefers cassette with no more than 4 songs and lyric sheet. "Please assure name and address are on tapes and/ or manuscripts, lyric sheets, etc." SASE. Reports in 1 month.

Music: Mostly "sacred choral and instrumental; we do not publish separate octavos currently."
Tips: "Focus material on mid-size, volunteer church choirs and musicians."

*ACCENT PUBLISHING CO., 3955 Fold-ream Rd., Springfield OH 45502. (513)325-5767. President/ Owner: Dave Jordan. Music publisher, record company (Dove Song Records). Estab. 1989. Publishes 4-6 songs/year; publishes 3 new songwriters/year. Works with composers and lyricists; teams collaborators. Pays negotiable royalty.
How to Contact: Submit demo tape—unsolicited submissions are OK. Prefers cassette (or VHS videocassette) with 2 songs and lyric or lead sheet. Does return unsolicited material. Reports in 6-8 weeks.
Music: Mostly country, gospel and R&B; also pop, soft rock and rap. Published "Tell an Old Story" (by Joy Jordan), recorded by Carl Pinderman; "Without a Home," written and recorded by Dale Briggs; and "To Be Free" (by Gloria Wilson), recorded by Poor Boys, all on Dove Song Records (all singles).
Tips: "Write with feeling, catchy title and hook. Be willing to re-write until the song is good! Send a well-recorded demo."

AEROSCORE MUSIC CO., P.O. Box 179, Westminster MA 01473. (508)852-8600. Publisher: J.P. MacKay. Music publisher. BMI. Estab. 1989. Publishes 20 songs/year; publishes 4 new songwriters/ year. Works with composers and lyricists; teams collaborators. Pays standard royalty.
How to Contact: Submit a demo tape by mail—unsolicited submissions are OK. Prefers cassette or VHS videocassette. "Put name and how to contact on everything." Does not return unsolicited material. Reports "only if interested."
Music: Mostly A/C, orchestrated rock; also "any potential standards regardless of musical lineage. We are not interested in rap unless it's interspersed with singing."
Tips: "Put best songs first. If you have good songs, then a simple but clean recording is fine."

 AIM HIGH MUSIC COMPANY (ASCAP), 1300 Division St., Nashville TN 37203. (615)242-4722. FAX: (615)242-1177. Producer: Robert Metzgar. Music publisher and record company (Stop Hunger Records International). Estab. 1971. Publishes 250 songs/year; publishes 5-6 new songwriters/year. Hires staff writers. Works with composers and lyricists; teams collaborators. "Our company pays 100% to all songwriters."
Affiliate(s): Aim High Music (ASCAP), Bobby & Billy Music (BMI).
How to Contact: Submit a demo tape by mail—unsolicited submissions arc OK. Prefers cassette or VHS videocassette with 5-10 songs and lyric sheet. "I like to get to know songwriters personally prior to recording their songs." Does not return unsolicited material. Reports in 2 weeks.
Music: Mostly country, traditional country and pop country; also gospel, southern gospel and contemporary Christian. Publishes "Just the Two of Us" (by Metzgar/Patterson), recorded by Conway Twitty on MCA Records (country); "Stranger In My Arms" (by Curtis Wayne), recorded by George Strait on MCA Records (country); and "Standin' In the Shadows," written and recorded by Hank Williams, Jr. on Polygram International Records (country).
Tips: "Never write songs that have already been written a thousand times. Come to us with fresh, new and different material."

AKRANA MUSIC, P.O. Box 535, College Place WA 99324. (509)529-4649. Vice President/Publishing: Benjamin Fenton. Music publisher and record company (Akrana Country, Akrana Visions, Tin Soldier Songs). ASCAP. Estab. 1989. Pays standard royalty.
How to Contact: Submit a demo tape by mail—unsolicited submissions are OK. Prefers cassette with 1-4 songs and lyric sheet. SASE. Reports in 2 weeks.
Music: Mostly contemporary Christian country, gospel and children's music.
Tips: "We want music with Christian values for today's country market. Write lyrics that paint graphic word pictures and tell a compelling story (i.e. Kathy Mattea's 'Where've You Been?'). The most successful songs seem to be those that reflect or address the needs of the heart."

ALEXIS, P.O. Box 532, Malibu CA 90265. (213)463-5998. President: Lee Magid. Music publisher, record company, personal management firm, and record and video producer. ASCAP. Member AIMP. Estab. 1950. Publishes 50 songs/year; publishes 20-50 new songwriters/year. Receives 500 submissions/ year. Works with composers. Pays standard royalty.

* *The asterisk before a listing indicates that the listing is new in this edition. New markets are often the most receptive to unsolicited submissions.*

Affiliate(s): Marvelle (BMI), Lou-Lee (BMI), D.R. Music (ASCAP) and Gabal (SESAC).
How to Contact: Submit a demo tape—unsolicited submissions are OK. Prefers cassette (or VHS videocassette of writer/artist if available) with 1-3 songs and lyric sheet. "Try to make demo as clear as possible—guitar or piano should be sufficient. A full rhythm and vocal demo is always better." SASE. Reports in 1 month "if interested."
Music: Mostly R&B, jazz, MOR, pop and gospel; also blues, church/religious, country, dance-oriented, folk and Latin. Published "Jesus is Just Alright" (by Art Reynolds), recorded by Doobie Brothers on W/B Records (gospel rock); "What Shall I Do?" (by Quincy Fielding), recorded by Tramaine Hawkins on Sparrow Records (gospel); and "I Played the Fool" (by D. Alexis), recorded by The Clovers on Atlantic Records (R&B).
Tips: "Create a good melody-lyric and a good clean demo tape. A home recording will do."

ALHART MUSIC PUBLISHING, P.O. Box 1593, Lakeside CA 92040. (619)443-2170. President: Richard Phipps. Music publisher. BMI. Estab. 1981. Releases 4 singles/year. Receives 35-60 submissions/month. Works with songwriters on contract. Pays statutory royalty.
How to Contact: Submit demo tape—unsolicited submissions are OK. Prefers cassette with 2 songs and lyric or lead sheets. SASE. Reports in 2-3 weeks.
Music: Mostly country; also R&B. Released "Party For One," "Don't Turn My Gold To Blue," and "Blue Lady" (by Dan Michaels), on Alhart Records (country).

*ALJONI MUSIC CO., 8010 International Village Dr., Jacksonville FL 32211. (904)745-0897. Creative Manager: Ronnie Hall. Director/Producer: Al Hall, Jr. Music publisher, record producer (Hallways to Fame Productions). BMI. Estab. 1971. Publishes 4-8 songs/year; publishes 1-2 new songwriters/year. Teams collaborators. Pays standard royalty.
Affiliates: Hallmarque Musical Works Ltd. (ASCAP).
How to Contact: Submit demo tape—unsolicited submissions are OK. Prefers cassette (or VHS videocassette) with no more than 3 songs and lead sheet. SASE. Reports in 6-8 weeks.
Music: Mostly rap, dance/R&B and jazz. Published "Coast 2 Coast" (by R. Hall), recorded by Cosmos on 1st Coast Records; "The Intelligent Rapper," written and recorded by MC Power; and "All Hall," written and recorded by Al Hall, Jr., both on Hallway International Records.
Tips: "Rap—rise above the rest! Dance/R&B—songs should have a good hook and a meaningful story line. Jazz—send solid straight ahead stuff as well as electronically oriented material."

ALL ROCK MUSIC, P.O. Box 2296, Rotterdam 3000 CG **Holland.** Phone: (31) 1862-4266. FAX: (32) 1862-4366. President: Cees Klop. Music publisher, record company (Collector Records) and record producer. Estab. 1967. Publishes 50-60 songs/year; publishes several new songwriters/year. Pays standard royalty.
Affiliate(s): All Rock Music (England) and All Rock Music (Belgium).
How to Contact: Submit demo tape by mail. Prefers cassette. SAE and IRC. Reports in 4 weeks.
Music: Mostly 50s rock, rockabilly and country rock; also piano boogie woogie. Published "Loving Wanting You," by R. Scott (country rock) and "Ditch Digger" by D. Mote (rock), both recorded by Cees Klop on White Label Records; "Bumper Boogie" (by R. Hoeke), recorded by Cees Klop on Downsouth Records (boogie); and "Spring In April" by H. Pepping (rock).

ALLEGED IGUANA MUSIC, 44 Archdekin Dr., Brampton ON L6V 1Y4 **Canada.** President: Randall Cousins. Music publisher and record producer (Randall Cousins Productions). SOCAN. Estab. 1984. Publishes 80 songs/year. Works with composers and lyricists; teams collaborators.
Affiliate(s): Alleged Iguana (SOCAN), Secret Agency (SOCAN) and AAA Aardvark Music (SOCAN).
How to Contact: Write first and obtain permission to submit a tape. Prefers cassette or VHS videocassette with 3 songs and lyric sheet. SASE. Reports in 8 weeks.
Music: Mostly country, country-rock and A/C; also pop and rock. Published "Take Me in Your Arms" (by R. Cousins), recorded by Diane Raeside (country-rock); "Unfortunately" (by R. Materick), recorded by True Spirit (A/C); and "For Always" (by Hotchkiss-Terry), recorded by Lisa Logan (country); all on Roto Noto Records.

ALLISONGS INC., 1603 Horton Ave., Nashville TN 37212. (615)292-9899. President: Jim Allison. Music publisher, record company (ARIA Records), record producer (Jim Allison, AlliSongs Inc.) BMI, ASCAP. Estab. 1985. Publishes more than 50 songs/year. Receives 100 submissions/month. Works with composers and lyricists. 5 staff writers.

Affiliate(s): Jims' Allisongs (BMI), d.c. Radio-Active Music (ASCAP) and Annie Green Eyes Music (BMI).
How to Contact: Call or write first for permission to submit. Prefers cassette and lyric sheet. *Does not return* material. Will call or write if interested.
Music: Mostly country, pop and R&B. Published "What Am I Gonna Do About You" (by Allison/Simon/Gilmore), recorded by Reba McEntire on MCA Records (country); "Preservation of the Wild Life" (by Allison/Young), recorded by Earl Thomas Conley on RCA Records (country); and "Against My Will" (by Hogan), recorded by Brenda Lee on Warner Bros. Records (pop).

ALTERNATIVE DIRECTION MUSIC PUBLISHERS, Box 3278, Station D, Ottawa, Ontario K1P 6H8 Canada. (613)225-6100. President and Director of Publishing: David Stein. Music publisher, record company (Parade Records), record producer and management firm (Alternative Direction Management). SOCAN. Estab. 1980. Publishes 5-10 songs/year; publishes 2-3 new songwriters/year. Works with composers; teams collaborators. Pays standard royalty.
How to Contact: Submit demo tape—unsolicited submissions are OK. Prefers cassette (or VHS videocassette) with 2-4 songs. SASE if sent from within Canada; American songwriters send SAE and $2 for postage and handling. Reports in 1 month.
Music: Uptempo rock, uptempo R&B and uptempo pop. Published "Big Kiss" (by David Ray), recorded by Theresa Bazaar on MCA Records (pop/dance) and Cindy Valentine on CBS Records (rock), Kyana on Parade Records (R&B); The edge on Parade Records (rock) and "Paris in Red" on Parade Records.
Tips: "Make certain your vocals are up front in the mix in the demos you submit. I am looking only for uptempo R&B and pop songs with a strong chorus and killer hooks. Don't send me any MOR, country, blues or folk music. I don't publish that kind of material."

AMALGAMATED TULIP CORP., 117 W. Rockland Rd., Box 615, Libertyville IL 60048. (708)362-4060. President: Perry Johnson. Music publisher, record company and record producer. BMI. Estab. 1968. Publishes 12 songs/year; publishes 3-6 new songwriters/year. Pays standard royalty.
Affiliate(s): Mo Fo Music.
How to Contact: Submit a demo tape—unsolicited submissions are OK. Prefers cassette with 3-5 songs and lyric sheet. SASE. Prefers studio produced demos. Reports in 6 months.
Music: Mostly rock, top 40/pop, dance and R&B; also country, MOR, blues and easy listening progressive. Published "This Feels Like Love to Me" (by Charles Sermay), recorded by Sacha Distel (pop); "Stop Wastin' Time" (by Tom Gallagher), recorded by Orjan (country); and "In the Middle of the Night," recorded by Oh Boy (pop).
Tips: "Send commercial material."

AMERICATONE MUSIC INTERNATIONAL, 1817 Loch Lomond Way, Las Vegas NV 89102-4437. (702)384-0030. FAX: (702) 382-1926. President: Joe Jan Jaros. Estab. 1975. Publishes 5-10 songs/year. Receives 50 submissions/month. Pays standard royalty.
Affiliate(s): Americatone Records International, Christy Records International USA.
How to Contact: Submit demo tape—unsolicited submissions OK. Prefers cassettes, "studio production with top sound recordings," and lyric sheets. SASE. Reports in 4 weeks.
Music: Mostly country, jazz, R&R, Spanish, classic ballads. Published *The Ice Princess*, recorded by Sunset; *Goodbye Again*, recorded by Patrick McElhoes; *Going On, Going On* recorded by Penelope; all on Americatone Records (country). Other artists include Mark Masters Jazz Orchestra, Best of Benelope, Johnny by the Way and Santa Ana Winds.

AMIRON MUSIC, 20531 Plummer St., Chatsworth CA 91311. (818)998-0443. Manager: A. Sullivan. Music publisher, record company, record producer and manager. ASCAP. Estab. 1970. Publishes 2-4 songs/year; publishes 1-2 new songwriters/year. Pays standard royalty.
Affiliate(s): Aztex Productions, and Copan Music (BMI).
How to Contact: Prefers cassette (or Beta or VHS videocassette) with any number songs and lyric sheet. SASE. Reports in 10 weeks.
Music: Easy listening, MOR, progressive, R&B, rock and top 40/pop. Published "Lies in Disguise," "Rapid," and "Let's Work It Out" (by F. Cruz), recorded by Gangs Back; and "Try Me," written and recorded by Sana Christian; all on AKO Records (all pop). Also "Boys Take Your Mind Off Things" (by G. Litvak), recorded by Staunton on Les Disques Records (pop).
Tips: Send songs with "good story-lyrics."

ANGELSONG PUBLISHING CO., 2714 Westwood Dr., Nashville TN 37204. (615)297-2246. President: Mabel Birdsong. BMI, ASCAP. Music publisher and record company (Birdsong Records). Publishes 2 albums/year; publishes 2 new songwriters/year.

How to Contact: Prefers cassette with maximum 4 songs and lyric sheet. Does not return unsolicited material. Reports in 2 weeks, "if requested."
Music: Mostly gospel, country and MOR; also pop. Published *Bless This House* by Junior Rutty; and *Go Where The Peace Is*, by the Songwriters.

ANOTHER AMETHYST SONG, 273 Chippewa Dr., Columbia SC 29210-6508. (803)750-5391. Contact: Manager. Music publisher, record company (Amethyst Group). BMI. Estab. 1985. Publishes 40 songs/year; publishes 20 new songwriters/year. Works with composers. Pays standard royalty.
How to Contact: Prefers cassette (or VHS videocassette) with 3-7 songs and lyric sheet; include any photos, biographical information. SASE. Reports in 5 weeks.
Music: Mostly metal, rock, pop, new wave and eclectic styles. Recently published "Complicated Love" and "Back in the Race" (by C. Sargent and C. Hamblin), recorded by True Identity; "If You Had Your Mind Made Up," written and recorded by Kourtesy; "Surrender To The Order" (by U.S. Steel); and "Get to the Point" (by Synthetic Meat), all on Antithesis Records.
Tips: "Simplicity is the key. A hit is a hit regardless of the production. Don't 'overkill' the song! We mainly sign artist/writers. Get ready to cooperate and sign what's necessary."

ANOTHER EAR MUSIC, Box 110142, Nashville TN 37222-0142. General Manager: T.J. Kirby. BMI, ASCAP. Music publisher, record company (T.J. Records), record producer (T.J. Productions) and management firm (T.J. Productions). Publishes 2 songs/year; publishes 2 new songwriters/year. Works with composers and lyricists; teams collaborators. Pays standard royalty.
Affiliate(s): Peppermint Rainbow Music (ASCAP).
How to Contact: Submit a demo tape with 1-2 songs (or VHS videocassette) by mail. One song only on video with lyric sheets.
Music: Mostly country/pop and R&B; also gospel, rock and "concept songs." Published "Let it Be Me Tonight" (by Tom Douglas/Bob Lee/T.J. Kirby), recorded by Kathy Ford on Prerie Dust Records; and "Don't Take a Heart" (by Kirby/Lapp/Smith) and "Faster than a Speeding Bullet" (by Paul Hotchkiss), recorded by Deb Merrit on T.J. Records (both country/pop).
Tips: "Videos are great to help present a writer's concept but don't let the ideas of what you would put in a video stand in the way of writing a great song."

ART AUDIO PUBLISHING COMPANY/TIGHT HI-FI SOUL MUSIC, 9706 Cameron Ave., Detroit MI 48211. (313)893-3406. President: Albert M. Leigh. Professional Manager: Dolores M. Leigh. Music publisher and record company. BMI, ASCAP. Pays standard royalty.
Affiliates: Leopard Music (London), Pierre Jaubert, Topomic Music (France), ALPHABET (West Germany), KMW Publishing (South Africa).
How to Contact: Submit demo tape—unsolicited submissions are OK. Prefers cassette with 1-3 songs and lyric or lead sheets. "Keep lyrics up front on your demo." SASE. Reports in 2 weeks.
Music: House, dance, movie sound tracks and songs for TV specials for the younger generation, uptempo pop rock, mellow R&B dance, uptempo country, uptempo gospel, rap, soul, hip hop. Published "Jesus Showed Us the Way" (by Willie Ayers), recorded by The Morning Echoes of Detroit on Nashboro Records; "I'm Singing Lord," written and recorded by Willie Ayers on X-Tone Records; and "Twon Special" (by Jesse Taylor), recorded by Rock and Roll Sextet on Echoic High Fidelity Records.
Tips: "Basically we are interested only in a new product with a strong sexual uptempo title with a (hook) story. Base it on the good part of your life—no sad songs; we want hot dance and rap. Arrange your songs to match the professional recording artist."

*ART OF CONCEPT MUSIC, P.O. Box 40128, San Francisco CA 94140. (415)641-6235. General Manager: Trevor Levine. Music publisher, record company (Fountainhead Records). BMI. Estab. 1989. Publishes 6 songs/year; publishes 1 new songwriter/year. Works with composers and lyricists. Pays standard royalty.
How to Contact: Submit a demo tape by mail—unsolicited submissions are OK. Prefers cassette with 3-6 songs, lyric or lead sheet (if possible). Does not return unsolicited material. Reports in 1 month.
Music: Mostly pop/rock ballads, "moderate-paced meaningful rock (not 'good time rock and roll' or dance music)"; also rock operas, New Age music, synthesizer-oriented music. Published "Spare Me Now" (art-rock); "Winds of Change" (art-rock); "Don't Say You Love Me" (pop ballad); all written and recorded by Trevor Levine on Fountainhead Records.
Tips: "We are interested in songs with powerful melodic and lyrical hooks—songs that are beautiful, expressive and meaningful with uniquely dissonant or dramatic qualities that really *move* the listener. Our songs deal with serious topics, from inner conflicts and troubled relationships to anthems, story songs and message songs which address social and political issues, government corruption, women's and minority issues and human and animal rights. Keep the song's vocal range within an octave, if possible, and no more than 1½ octaves. The music should convey the meaning of the words."

ASSOCIATED ARTISTS MUSIC INTERNATIONAL (AAMI), Maarschalklaan 47, 3417 SE Montfoort, **The Netherlands.** Phone: (0)3484-2860. FAX: (31)3484-2860. General Manager: Joop Gerrits. Music publisher, record company (Associated Artists Records), record producer (Associated Artists Productions) and radio and TV promoters. BUMA. Estab. 1975. Publishes 200 songs/year; publishes 50 new songwriters/year. Receives 100 submissions/month. Works with composers; teams collaborators. Pays by agreement.
Affiliate(s): BMC Publishing Holland (BUMA); Hilversum Happy Music (BUMA); Intermelodie and Holland Glorie Productions.
How to Contact: Submit demo tape by mail—unsolicited submissions are OK. Prefers compact cassette (or VHS videocassette). SAE and IRC. Reports in 6 weeks.
Music: Mostly disco, pop and Italian disco; also rock, gospel (evangelical), musicals, MOR and country. Works with Electra Salsa, who "reached the top 40 in the Benelux countries, and the disco dance top 50." Older copyrights recorded by the Tremeloes, Whamm, Kayak and John Mackenzie. Published "Deep in My Heart" (by Bortolotti), recorded by Clubhouse on Media Records (house/techno); "Esa Chica es Mia" (by Anjurez), recorded by Sergio Dalma on Armada Records (ballad); and "Feel Allright" (by Leoni), recorded by Katherine E on Underground Records (dance).
Tips: "In a competive and hard market as Europe we need very good products written-composed and produced by talented people and artists."

ASTRODISQUE PUBLISHING, 6453 Conroy Rd, #1001, Orlando FL 32811. (407)295-6311. President: Richard Tiegen. Music publisher, record company (Plum Records) and record producer (Richard Tiegen/Magic Sound Productions). BMI. Estab. 1980. Publishes 15 songs/year; publishes 10 new songwriters/year. Works with composers and lyricists; teams collaborators. Pays standard royalty. "Charges recording and production fees."
How to Contact: Write or call first to obtain permission to submit. Prefers cassette (or VHS videocassette). SASE. Reports in 3 weeks.
Music: Rock, R&B and country; also New Age and acoustic. Published "Star Train Express," "Too Hot to Handle" and "I Need Your Love," (all by Letourneau), recorded by Dixie Train on Plum Records (all country singles).

***ASTRON MUSIC PUBLISHING**, 4746 Bowes Ave., P.O. Box 22174, Pittsburgh PA 15122. Director, A&R Manager: Renee Asher. Music publisher, record company. Estab. 1991. Publishes 20 songs/year. Works with composers and lyricists. Pays standard royalty.
How to Contact: Submit demo tape by mail—unsolicited submissions are OK.
Prefers cassette (or VHS videocassette if available) with 3-5 songs and lyric sheet. "Include promotional packages for artists and list of any credits." SASE. Reports in 2 months.
Music: Mostly rock, pop, heavy metal; also alternative, reggae and country. Published "Treats of the Mystery Sky" and "Another Frame of Mind" both written and recorded by Stream on Byron Records (progressive metal); and "Wild-Fire" written and recorded by Steve Cicone on Astron Records (rock).
Tips: "Be as professional as possible. We are looking for the same things record labels are looking for. Prefer groups with established base and strong independent release status. NO PHONE CALLS."

AUDIO MUSIC PUBLISHERS, 449 N. Vista St., Los Angeles CA 90036. (213)653-0693. Contact: Ben Weisman. Music publisher, record company and record producer. ASCAP. Estab. 1962. Publishes 25 songs/year; publishes 10-15 new songwriters/year. Receives 100 submissions/month. Works with composers and lyricists; teams collaborators. Pays standard royalty.
How to Contact: Submit a demo tape—unsolicited submissions are OK. "No permission needed." Prefers cassette with 3-10 songs and lyric sheet. "We do not return unsolicited material without SASE. Don't query first; just send tape." Reports in 2 weeks.
Music: Mostly pop, R&B, rap, dance, funk, soul and rock (all types).

AVC MUSIC, #200, 6201 Sunset Blvd., Los Angeles CA 90028. (213)461-9001. President: James Warsinske. Music publisher. ASCAP. Estab. 1988. Publishes 30-60 songs/year; publishes 10-20 new songwriters/year. Works with composers and lyricists; teams collaborators. Pays standard royalty.
Affiliate(s): AVC Music (ASCAP) and Harmonious Music (BMI).
How to Contact: Submit demo tape—unsolicited submissions OK. Prefers cassette or VHS videocassette with 2-5 songs and lyric sheet. "Clearly labelled tapes with phone numbers." SASE. Reports in 1 month.
Music: Mostly R&B/soul, pop and rock; also rap, metal and dance. Published "Let It Be Right," written and recorded by Duncan Faure on AVC Records (pop /rock); "Melissa Mainframe" (by Hohl/Rocca), recorded by Rocca on Life Records (pop/rap) and "In Service" (by Michael Williams), recorded by Madrok on AVC Records (rap).
Tips: "Be yourself, let your talents shine regardless of radio trends."

B. SHARP MUSIC, 24 rue Gachard, 1050 Brussels **Belgium**. Phone: (02)241-41-86. Music publisher, record company (B. Sharp, Selection Records) and record producer (Pletinckx). Estab. 1950. Works with composers. Pays standard royalty.
Affiliate(s): Prestation Music and Multi Sound.
How to Contact: Submit demo tape—unsolicited submissions are OK. Prefers cassette. SASE. Reports in 1 month.
Music: Jazz, rock and instrumental music. Published "After Touch," written and recorded by Ivan Podisort, (jazz fusion); and "Picture A View," written and recorded by Frank Vogonée (jazz), both on B. Sharp Records.

*BABY HUEY MUSIC, P.O. Box 121616, Nashville TN 37212. (615)269-9958. President: Mark Stephens. Music publisher, record company. BMI. Estab. 1969. Publishes 50-100 songs/year; publishes 4-5 new songwriters/year. Hires staff writers; works with composers and lyricists. Pays standard royalty.
Affiliates: Krimson Hues Music (BMI).
How to Contact: Submit demo tape—unsolicited submissions are OK. Prefers cassette (or VHS videocassette) with 3 songs and lyric sheet. SASE. Reports in 3 months.
Music: Mostly Christian; also pop, rock and R&B. Published "Jesus Says," written and recorded by Lanier Ferguson; "He'll Make a Way," written and recorded by Kathy Davis; and "Be Thou Exalted," written and recorded by Mark Stephen Hughes, all on Fresh Start Records.
Tips: "Make a demo worthy of your song."

BAD GRAMMAR MUSIC, Suite 306, 35918 Union-Lake Rd., Mt. Clemens MI 48043. Music Director: Joe Trupiano. Music publisher, record company (Rockit Records), record producer (Bad Grammar Enterprises) and management company. Estab. 1982. BMI. Publishes 10-20 songs/year; publishes 10-20 new songwriters/year. Receives 250 submissions/year. Works with composers and lyricists; teams collaborators. Pays standard royalty.
How to Contact: Submit a demo tape—unsolicited submissions are OK if submitting according to listing. Prefers cassette (or VHS videocassette) with 3-4 songs and lyric sheet. SASE. Reports in 6 weeks.
Music: Mostly dance-oriented, pop/rock and rock; also A/C, top 40/ballads and country. Published "Is Love Enough" (by Joey Harlow and JD Ruffcut) and "Passion's Fire" (by W. Bradley), both recorded by Hot Rod Hearts (country/pop); and "Choose Life" (by L. Phelps) recorded by Laya Phelps, all on Rockit Records (rock).
Tips: "Tell a definite story using plenty of nouns and verbs to add color and paint a distinct picture in the listener's mind."

BAGATELLE MUSIC PUBLISHING CO., 400 San Jacinto St., Houston TX 77002. (713)225-6654. President: Byron Benton. BMI. Music publisher, record company and record producer. Publishes 40 songs/year; publishes 2 new songwriters/year. Pays standard royalty.
Affiliate(s): Floyd Tillman Publishing Co.
How to Contact: Prefers cassette (or videocassette) with any number of songs and lyric sheet.
Music: Mostly country; also gospel and blues. Published "Everything You Touch," written and recorded by Johnny Nelms; "If I Could Do It All Over Again," written and recorded by Floyd Tillman; and "Mona from Daytona" (by Byron Benton), recorded by F. Tillman; all on Bagatelle Records (country).

BAL & BAL MUSIC PUBLISHING CO., P.O. Box 369, LaCanada CA 91012-0369. (818)548-1116. President: Adrian P. Bal. Music publisher, record company (Bal Records) and record producer. ASCAP. Member AGAC and AIMP. Estab. 1965. Publishes 2-6 songs/year; publishes 2-4 new songwriters/year. Receives 50 submissions/month. Works with composers; teams collaborators. Pays standard royalty.
Affiliate(s): Bal West Music Publishing Co. (BMI).
How to Contact: Submit a demo tape—unsolicited submissions are OK. Prefers cassette with 3 songs and lyric sheet. SASE. Reports in 1-3 months.
Music: Mostly MOR, country, rock and gospel; also blues, church/religious, easy listening, jazz, R&B, soul and top 40/pop. Published "Right To Know" and "Fragile" (by James Jackson), recorded by Kathy Simmons; "You're a Part of Me," "Can't We Have Some Time Together," "You and Me" and "Circles of Time," all written and recorded by Paul Richards (A/C); "Dance to the Beat of My Heart" (by Dan Gertz) recorded by Ace Baker (medium rock); all on Bal Records.

*BALANCE OF POWER MUSIC, 199 N. El Camino Real, #F402, Encinitas CA 92024. (619)436-1193. President: Mark Allyn. Music publisher. BMI. Estab. 1988. Publishes 10-20 songs/year; publishes 2-3 new songwriters/year. Works with composers and lyricists. Pays standard royalty.

How to Contact: Submit demo tape by mail—unsolicited submissions are OK. Prefers cassette (or VHS videocassette if available) with 1-3 songs, lyric or lead sheets (if possible). "Name and address on cassette tape. Tapes will not be returned to songwriter. Send SASE for response." Does not return unsolicited material. Reports in 1-2 months.
Music: Mostly rock, pop and alternative; also country-rock, R&B and A/C. Published "Alone" written and recorded by The Cry on B.O.P. Records (alternative); 'Tomorrows Child" (by Gregory Page), recorded by Baba Yaga (rock); and "Geneva" (by Steve Saint), recorded by Club of Rome (rock alternative), both on 4th Wave Records.
Tips: "Please have a master quality tape. Balance of Power very rarely accepts low quality demos. No correspondence without SASE. We are very interested in BMI writers."

*BARKING FOE THE MASTER'S BONE, P.O. Box 2790, Cincinnati OH 45201. (513)651-3604. Office Manager: Ann Maire. Music publisher. BMI. Estab. 1989. Publishes 4 songs/year; publishes 2 new songwriters—year. Works with composers and lyricists; teams collaborators. Pays negotiable royalty.
Affiliates: Beat Box Music (ASCAP).
How to Contact: Submit demo tape—unsolicited submissions are OK. Prefers cassette (or VHS videocassette) with 3 songs. SASE. Reports in 2 weeks.
Music: Mostly country, soft rock and pop; also soul and rap. Published "The King of Ragstress Soul" (by Merlin August and Dave Arps) (pop instrumental); "Work it to the Max" and "The Positive Vibe" (by Kevin Curtis) (rap), all recorded by Who's Lipps on Boogie Down Productions Records.
Tips: "First of all, know within your heart where you would like to be several years from now. The begin to seek reasonable ways of getting there. Never allow any musical trends to take away from your own originality."

BARTOW MUSIC, 68 Old Canton Rd N.E., Cartersville GA 30120. (404)382-1442. Publishing Administrator: Jack C. Hill; Producer: Tirus McClendon. Music publisher and record producer (HomeBoy, Ragtime Productions). BMI. Estab. 1988. Publishes 5 songs/year; 5 new songwriters/year. Works with composers and lyricists; teams collaborators. Pays royalty.
How to Contact: Submit a demo tape by mail—unsolicited submissions are O.K. Prefers cassette (or VHS videocassette) with 3 songs and lyric sheets. SASE. Reports in 1 month.
Music: R&B, pop, dance and house. Published"Oh Father" (by Maurice Carroll), recorded by Simply Suave (R&B); "I Need You Tonight" (by Maurice Carroll), recorded by Simply Suave (R&B) dance) and "New Day" (by Tirus McClendon), recorded by Celebrations (R&B dance) all on West View Records.

BEARSONGS, Box 944, Birmingham, B16 8UT **England.** Phone: 44-021-454-7020. Managing Director: Jim Simpson. Music publisher and record company (Big Bear Records). Member PRS, MCPS. Publishes 25 songs/year; publishes 15-20 new songwriters/year.
How to Contact: Prefers reel-to-reel or cassette. SAE and IRC. Reports in 2-3 weeks.
Music: Blues and jazz.

EARL BEECHER PUBLISHING, P.O. Box 2111, Huntington Beach CA 92647. (714)842-8635. Owner: Earl Beecher. Music publisher, record company (Outstanding and Morrhythm Records) and record producer (Earl Beecher). BMI, ASCAP. Estab. 1968. Publishes varying number of songs/year. Works with composers. Pays standard royalty.
How to Contact: Submit a demo tape—unsolicited submissions are OK. Cassettes only. SASE. Reports in 6 weeks.
Music: Pop, ballads, rock, gospel and country. Published "Left in the Cold," "Runnin' from Your Love," "Haunt Me, Taunt Me" all recorded by Shades of Mystery on Morrhythm Records (rock).
Tips: "I am interested mainly in people who want to perform their songs and release albums on one of my labels rather than to submit material to my existing artists."

BEKOOL MUSIC, Box 671008, Dallas TX 75367-8008. (214)750-0720. A&R: Mike Anthony. Music publisher. ASCAP. Estab. 1987. Publishes 12-20 songs/year. Publishes 3 new songwriters/year. Works with composers. Pays standard royalty.
Affiliate(s): Forest Creek Music (BMI).
How to Contact: Write first and obtain permission to submit a tape. Prefers cassette with 1-2 songs and lyric sheet. "We do not return unsolicited material but will contact if interested."
Music: Mostly country and gospel. Published "You Hold My World Together" (by Mitchel, Penny, Grice), recorded by Charlie Pride on 16th Ave./Ritz Records (England) (country); "Lay it Down, Give it Up" (by T. Long, D. Liles and J. Chisum), recorded by Janet Paschal on Canaan Records/Word Records (gospel); and "High School Buddies" (by C. Jones, R. Muir), recorded by the Bama Band on Mercury/Polygram Records.

BENYARD MUSIC CO., Dept. SM, Box 298, Queens NY 11415. (718)657-5363. President: Kevin Benyard. Music publisher and record producer (Stone Cold Productions). BMI NMPA, Harry Fox Agency Estab. 1987. Publishes 5 songs/year; publishes 3 new songwriters/year. Works with composers and lyricists. Pays standard royalty.
How to Contact: Write first and obtain permission to submit. Prefers cassette with 2-5 songs and lyric sheet. SASE (postcard). Reports in 1 month. "No unsolicited material accepted ever."
Music: Mostly R&B, jazz fusion, rock, top 40. Published "Better Wait to Know Her" and "The Time is Right," both written and recorded by K. Benyard and Lorna J. Dance on Jeannae Records (dance). To be released: "Homeless Nation" (by K. Benyard) on A.A.I. Records (R&B single).
Tips: "I'm looking for music and songs that are totally new in approach. I'm interested in releasing the music of the 90's."

BERANDOL MUSIC LTD., Unit 220, 2600 John St., Marham ON L3R 3W3 **Canada**. (416)475-1848. A&R Director: Ralph Cruickshank. Music publisher, record company (Berandol Records), record producer and distributor. BMI. Member CMPA, CIRPA, CRIA. Estab. 1969. Publishes 20-30 songs/year; publishes 5-10 new songwriters/year. Works with composers. Pays standard royalty.
How to Contact: Submit demo tape with 2-5 songs—unsolicited submissions OK. SASE. Reports in 1 week.
Music: Mostly instrumental, children's and top 40.
Tips: "Strong melodic choruses and original sounding music receive top consideration."

HAL BERNARD ENTERPRISES, INC., P.O. Box 8385, 2612 Erie Ave., Cincinnati OH 45208. (513)871-1500. FAX: (513)871-1510. President: Stan Hertzman. Professional Manager: Chuck Fletcher. Music publisher, record company and management firm. Publishes 12-24 songs/year; 1-2 new songwriters/year. Receives 25 submissions/month. Works with composers. Pays standard royalty.
Affiliate(s): Sunnyslope Music (ASCAP), Bumpershoot Music (BMI), Apple Butter Music (ASCAP), Carb Music (ASCAP), Saiko Music (ASCAP), TYI Music (ASCAP) and Smorgaschord Music (AS-CAP).
How to Contact: Submit a demo tape—unsolicited submissions are OK. Prefers cassette with 3 songs and lyric sheet. SASE. Reports in 6 weeks.
Music: Rock, R&B and top 40/pop. Published "Young Lions," "Men in Helicopters," "Phone Call From the Moon," "Standing In the Shadow," "Inner Revolutions" and "This Is What I Believe In" all written and recorded by Adrian Belew on Atlantic Records (progressive pop).
Tips: "Best material should appear first on demo. Cast your demos. If you as the songwriter can't sing it—don't. Get someone who can present your song properly, use a straight rhythm track and keep it as naked as possible. If you think it still needs something else, have a string arranger, etc. help you, but still keep the *voice up* and the *lyrics clear*."

M. BERNSTEIN MUSIC PUBLISHING CO., 2170 S. Parker Rd., Denver CO 80231. (303)755-2613. President: R.J. Bernstein. Music publisher, record company (Finer Arts Records) and record producer (Transworld Records). ASCAP, BMI. Estab. 1960. Publishes 15-25 songs/year; publishes 5-10 new songwriters/year.
How to Contact: Prefers cassette and lyric or lead sheet. Does not return unsolicited material. Reports in 1 month.
Music: Rock, country and jazz. Published "Over and Over" (R&B) and "Dance Baby Dance" (rap) (both by Pamela Dawn), recorded by Penda on Fine Arts Records.
Tips: "No *phone calls* please."

BEST BUDDIES, INC., P.O. Box 121738, Nashville TN 37212-1738. (615)383-7664. Contact: Review Committee. Music publisher, record company (X-cuse Me) and record producer (Best Buddies Productions). BMI. Estab. 1981. Publishes 18 songs/year. Publishes 1-2 new songwriters/year. Works with composers and lyricists. Pays standard royalty.
Affiliate(s): Swing Set Music (ASCAP), Best Buddies Music (BMI).
How to Contact: Write first and obtain permission to submit. Must include SASE with permission letter. Prefers cassette (or VHS videocassette) with maximum 3 songs. SASE. Reports in 8 weeks. Do not call to see if tape received.
Music: Mostly country, rock and roll and pop; also gospel and R&B. Published "Somebody Wrong is Looking Right" (by King/Burkholder), recorded by Bobby Helms; "Give Her Back Her Faith in Me" (by Ray Dean James), recorded by David Speegle on Bitter Creek Records (country); and "I Can't Get Over You Not Loving Me" (by Misty Efron and Bobbie Sallee), recorded by Sandy Garwood on Bitter Creek Records (country).
Tips: "Make a professional presentation. There are no second chances on first impressions."

*BETH-RIDGE MUSIC PUBLISHING CO., Suite 204, 1508 Harlem, Memphis TN 38114. (901)274-2726. Contact: Professional Manager. Music publisher, record company, record producer and recording studio. BMI. Estab. 1978. Publishes 40 songs/year; publishes 10 new songwriters/year. Pays standard royalty.
Affiliate(s): Chartbound Music Ltd. (ASCAP).
How to Contact: "Write to see what our needs are." Prefers 15 or 7½ ips reel-to-reel or cassette (or VHS videocassette) with 3-5 songs and lyric sheet. SASE. Reports in 1 month.
Music: Mostly R&B, top 40, dance and blues; also soul and gospel. Published "Hooked on Love," written and recorded by Eddie Mayberry on Blue Town Records (blues/R&B); "Love Song" (by Steve-A), recorded by First Class Crew on GCS Records; and "Call on Jesus" (by various artists), recorded by Voices of Hope on GCS Records (gospel).

BETTER TIMES PUBLISHING/DORIS LINDSAY PUBLISHING, 1203 Biltmore Ave., High Point NC 27260. (919)882-9990. President: Doris Lindsay. Music publisher, record company (Fountain Records) and record producer (Successful Productions). BMI, ASCAP. Estab. 1979. Publishes 40 songs/year; publishes 6 new songwriters/year. Works with composers and lyricists; teams collaborators. Pays standard royalty.
Affiliate(s): Doris Lindsay Publishing (ASCAP), Better Times Publishing (BMI).
How to Contact: Submit a demo tape by mail — unsolicited submissions are OK. Prefers cassette with 2 songs and lyric sheet. SASE. Reports in 2 months.
Music: Mostly country, pop, contemporary gospel. Also wedding songs, blues, southern gospel and novelty. Published "Share Your Love," written and recorded by Mitch Snow on Fountain Records (country); "What Did You Do With Your Old 45's" (by Hanna/Pickard), recorded by Bobby Vinton on Curb Records (country/pop); "Back In Time," written and recorded by Mitch Snow on Fountain Records (country); and "Another Notch on My Guitar," written and recorded by Larry La Vey on Fountain Records (blues).
Tips: "Have a professional demo made."

BETTY JANE/JOSIE JANE MUSIC PUBLISHERS, 7400 N. Adams Rd., North Adams MI 49262. (517)287-4421. Professional Manager: Claude E. Reed. Music publisher and record company (C.E.R. Records). BMI, ASCAP. Estab. 1980. Publishes 5-10 songs/year; 10 new songwriters/year. Works with composers and lyricists; teams collaborators. Pays standard royalty.
Affiliate(s): Betty Jane Music Publishing Co. (BMI) and Josie Jane Music Publishing Co. (ASCAP).
How to Contact: Submit a demo tape by mail — unsolicited submissions are OK. Prefers cassette or 7½ ips reel-to-reel with up to 5 songs and lyric or lead sheets. "We prefer typewritten and numbered lyric sheets and good professional quality demo tapes." SASE. Reports in 2-3 weeks.
Music: Mostly gospel and country western; also R&B. Published "I Know How the Story Ends" (by C. Cravey); "I Feel Good" (by Ernie Scott); "Open the Windows of Your Soul" (by Corinne Porter), all recorded by Rev. Charles E. Cravey on C.E.R. Records (gospel).
Tips: "Try to be original, present your music in a professional way, with accurate lyric sheets and well made demo tape. Send SASE with a sufficient amount of postage if you wish material returned."

BIG CITY MUSIC, INC., 15 Gloria Lane, Fairfield NJ 07004. (201)808-8280. President: Gary Rottger. Music publisher. BMI. Estab. 1990. Publishes 10 songs/year; publishes 3 new songwriters/year. Teams collaborators. Pays standard royalty.
Affiliate(s): Doozen Music (BMI), Big City Music (BMI).
How to Contact: Submit a demo tape by mail — unsolicited submissions are OK. Prefers cassette and VHS videocassette with 3 songs and lyric sheet. Reports in 3 weeks.
Music: Mostly R&B, rap and rock. Published *I Still Dream About You* (by Byrd, Jett, Rottger), recorded by Joan Jett on CBS Records (rock); *Crushin'* (by Rottger and Fat Boys), recorded by Fat Boys on Polygram Records (rap); and *Rock Rulin'* (by Rottger and Fat Boys), Warner "Disorderlies" soundtrack on Polygram Records (rap).
Tips: "Good clean demo. Songs must compete with current radio."

BIG SNOW MUSIC, P.O. Box 279, Hopkins MN 55343. (612)942-6119. President: Mitch Viegut. Vice President and General Manager: Mark Alan. Music publisher. BMI. Estab. 1989. Publishes 20 new songs/year; publishes 8 new songwriters/year. Works with composers and lyricists; teams collaborators. Pays standard royalty.
How to Contact: Write first and obtain permission to submit. Prefers cassette with 3 songs and lyric sheet. SASE. Reports in 2 months.
Music: Mostly rock, pop and black. Published "Somewhere" (by Mitch Viegut) (pop) and "85 mph" (by Mitch Viegut, Dave Saindon, Roger Prubert) (rock) both on Curb Records and "Thief in the Night" (by Doug Dixon and Mitch Viegut) on Premiére Records (rock) all recorded by Airkraft.

BLACK STALLION COUNTRY PUBLISHING, Box 368, Tujunga CA 91043. (818)352-8142. FAX: (718)352-2122. President: Kenn Kingsbury. Music publisher and book publisher (*Who's Who in Country & Western Music*). BMI. Member CMA, CMF. Publishes 2 songs/year; publishes 1 new songwriter/ year. Pays standard royalty.
How to Contact: Prefers 7½ ips reel-to-reel or cassette with 2-4 songs and lyric sheet. SASE. Reports in 1 month.
Music: Bluegrass, country and R&B.
Tips: "Be professional in attitude and presentation. Submit only the material you think is better than anything being played on the radio."

BLADE TO THE RHYTHM MUSIC, 114-22 116th St., S. Ozone Pk. NY 11420. (718)845-4417. FAX: (718)507-5516. President: Juan Kato Lemus. Music publisher and production company/Producers. ASCAP. Estab. 1990. Publishes 5-10 songs/year; publishes 2-4 new songwriters/year. Hires staff song-writers. "Depending on work." Pays "depending on work to be added or song to be changed."
Affiliate(s): Piedra Productions Music (ASCAP), Davidson Ospina Music (ASCAP), John Wilson Music (ASCAP) and Pavel De Jesus (ASCAP).
How to Contact: Submit a demo tape by mail—unsolicited submissions are OK. Prefers cassette with 2-4 songs and lyric sheet. "Send photo or bio." Does not return unsolicited material. Reports in 4 weeks.
Music: Mostly dance/pop, house and R&B; also freestyle, rap and ballads. Published "No Para" (by Bladerunners), recorded by Sound Factor on Warlock Records (house).

BLUE HILL MUSIC/TUTCH MUSIC, 308 Munger Lane, Bethlehem CT 06751. Contact: Paul Hotchkiss. Music publisher, record company (Target Records, Kastle Records) and record producer (Red Kastle Records). BMI. Estab. 1975. Published 20 songs/year; publishes 1-5 new songwriters/year. Receives 100 submissions/month. Pays standard royalty.
Affiliate(s): Blue Hill Music (BMI) and Tutch Music (BMI).
How to Contact: Write first and obtain permission to submit a tape. Prefers cassette with 2 songs and lyric sheet. "Demos should be clear with vocals out in front." SASE. Reports in 3 weeks.
Music: Mostly country and country/pop; also MOR and blues. Published "Everyday Man" (by M. Terry), recorded by M. Terry on Roto Noto Records (country/pop); "Thinking 'Bout You" (by P. Hotchkiss), recorded by Susan Manning on Target Records (country); and "Stop Look Listen" (by P. Hotchkiss), recorded by Beverly's Hillbilly Band on Trophy Records (country).

BLUE UMBRELLA MUSIC PUBLISHING CO./PARASOL MUSIC PUBLISHING CO., 3011 Beach 40th St., Brooklyn NY 11224. (718)372-6436. Contact: Mr. Kadish Millet. Music publisher. ASCAP, BMI. Publishes 15 songs/year; publishes 7 new songwriters/year. Pays standard royalty.
How to Contact: Submit demo tape—unsolicited submissions are OK. Prefers cassette with 1-10 songs and typed lyric sheet. Prefers studio produced demos. "Wrap cassette well; some cassette boxes have fairly sharp edges and break through envelope. I want a typed lyric sheet and accurate information on who owns the copyright and if it was registered in Washington at the time of submission. Affiliation of writers (ASCAP/BMI) needed to issue proper contract." SASE "*with proper amount of return post-age.*" Reports in 1-3 weeks.
Music: Country and/or anything "truly superior." Published "Through Love" (by Roy Ownbey), re-corded by the Little Big Band on Track Records (sacred/country); "Boomerang" (by Ernie Scott), recorded by the Little Big Band on Track Records (country); and "What's More American Than Soccer?" (by Kadish Millet), recorded by Tony Ansems on Fox Records (novelty).
Tips: "Avoid long letters and don't write saying that the song would be good for Kenny Rogers etc. We know for whom it would be good. Try to reach some of the "stars" of today and you may learn some of the difficulties of what it's all about. Don't send me garbage songs, hoping beyond hope that a fool or a sucker is listening and will take it. This is a highly professional business. If you have a great song . . . make a studio demo."

***BMG ARIOLA BELGIUM N.V. PUBLISHING**, Square Francois Riga, 30, 1030 Brussels **Belgium**. Phone: 02/216-97-80. Publishing Manager: Cesar Boesten. Music publisher. SABAM. Estab. 1987. Publishes 300 songs/year; 20 new songwriters/year. Works with composers and lyricists. Pays standard royalty.
How to Contact: Submit a demo tape by mail—unsolicited submissions are OK. Prefers cassette with 3 songs. Does not return unsolicited material. Reports in 4 weeks.
Music: Mostly pop, rock and R&B; also dance.
Tips: "Do not send typical MOR American style."

***BMG MUSIC PUBLISHING, INC.**, 1133 Avenue of Americas, New York NY 10036. (212)930-4000. FAX: (212)930-4263. Director, East Coast: Jon Bonci. Music publisher. Publishes hundreds of songs/ year as a worldwide company; publishes less than 100 new songwriters/year. Hires staff songwriters.

Works with composers and lyricists; teams collaborators. Pays standard royalty.
Affiliate(s): BMG Songs (ASCAP), Careers—BMG Music (BMI).
How to Contact: Write first and obtain permission to submit. Prefers cassette with 3 songs and lyric sheet. "No overnites or elaborate packages. Let lthe music speak for itself." SASE. Reports in 3 months.
Music: Mostly pop/CHR, R&B/dance/rap, country; also jazz, folk and alternative. Published "Change" written and recorded by Lisa Stansfield and "3 A.M. Eternal" written and recorded by KLF both on Arista Records (single); and "Cry For Help" written and recorded by Rick Astley on RCA Records (single).
Tips: "Study your craft and master it. Submit your best work. In this business your first shot may be your only shot."

*BOB-A-LEW MUSIC, P.O. Box 8649, Universal City CA 91608. (818)506-6331. FAX: (818)506-4735. Director of Creative Activities: Barry Kolsky. Estab. 1985. Hires staff songwriters. Works with composers and lyricists; teams collaborators. Payment negotiable.
Affiliate(s): Bob-a-lew Songs (ASCAP) and Lew-Bob Songs (BMI).
How to Contact: Write or call first and obtain permission to submit. Prefers cassette with 3 songs and lyric sheet. SASE.
Music: Mostly rock, pop and R&B; also dance, college/alternative and country. Published "Slowride" (by Andre Pessis and Bonnie Hayes), recorded by Bonnie Raitt on Capitol Records (single); "Just Take My Heart" (by Andre Pessis), recorded by Mr. Big on Atlantic Records (single); and "Couple Days Off," written and recorded by Huey Lewis on EMI Records (single).

BoDe MUSIC, Suite 228, 18016 S. Western Ave., Gardena CA 90248. President: Tory Gullett. Music publisher. ASCAP, BMI. Estab. 1990. Publishes 12-15 songs/year; publishes 6-10 new songwriters/year. Works with composers and lyricists; teams collaborators. Pays standard royalty.
Affiliate(s): Bo De Music (ASCAP) and Gullett Music (BMI).
How to Contact: Submit demo tape by mail—unsolicited submissions are OK. Prefers cassette with 3 songs and lyric sheet. SASE. Reports in 6 weeks.
Music: Mostly country, R&B, pop. Published "How Many Times" (by Nathan Kory); "The Other Side" (by Kheri Han); and "The Best Heartache a Cheater Ever Had" (by Paul Austin and Sarah Summers).
Tips: "Have the song properly demoed before submitting it. *Know* what your competition is and try to surpass it (or at least match it) in demo quality."

JOHNNY BOND PUBLICATIONS, Dept. SM, 1007 17th Ave., Nashville TN 37212. (615)320-5719. President: Sherry Bond. Music publisher. BMI/ASCAP. Estab. 1955. Publishes 100 songs/year; 1 new songwriter/year. Works with composers. Pays standard royalty.
Affiliate(s): Red River Songs, Inc. (BMI), Crimson Creek Songs (ASCAP).
How to Contact: *Must* call for permission to submit demo cassette. Prefers cassette with 1 song and lyric sheet. SASE. Reports in 1 month.
Music: Country only. Published "Blues Stay Away From Me" (by The Delmore Bros.), recorded by The Judds and Carl Perkins on Universal Records, K.D. Lang on Sire Records and Chris Austin on Warner Bros. Records (country).
Tips: "Because we receive so many requests to submit songs, we are very selective. Big corporations are buying up small publishing companies, making it more difficult to get songs recorded. Songwriters need to know as much as possible about the publishing companies they approach."

BONNFIRE PUBLISHING, P.O. Box 6429, Huntington Beach CA 92615-6429. (714)962-5618. Contact: Eva and Stan Bonn. Music publisher, record company (ESB Records) and record producer. ASCAP, BMI. Estab. 1987. Pays standard royalty.
Affiliate(s): Bonnfire Publishing (ASCAP) and Gather Round Music (BMI).
How to Contact: Submit demo cassette with lyric sheet. Unsolicited submissions OK. SASE. Reports in 1 month.
Music: Country and pop. Published "Toe Tappin' Country Man" and "Three Reasons" (by Jack H. Schroeder), recorded by John P. Swisshelm on ESB Records (country); and "The Gold in This Ring" (by Tice Griffin and Todd Hartman), recorded by Pat Murphy on OL Records (country).

"How to Use Your Songwriter's Market" (at the front of this book) contains comments and suggestions to help you understand and use the information in these listings.

BOOGIETUNES MUSIKPRODUKTION GmbH, Seelingstrasse 33, 1000 Berlin 19, **Germany.** Phone: 030/321 60 47. Managing Director: Timothy E. Green. Music publisher and record company. GEMA. Estab. 1978. Publishes 100 songs/year; publishes 2 new songwriters/year. Teams collaborators. Pays standard GEMA rate.
How to Contact: Submit a demo tape—unsolicited submissions are OK. Prefers cassette. Does not return unsolicited material. "No cassette returns!"
Music: Mostly disco/dance, electronic, rap and house. Published "Sirens," written and recorded by First Chapter on Pool Records (electro); and "Feels Like I'm in Love" (by Ray Dorset), recorded by Kelly Marie on Dance Street Records (dance).

BRANCH GROUP MUSIC, #108-93 Lombard Ave., Winnipeg MB R3B 3B1 **Canada.** (204)957-0085. President: Gilles Paquin. Music publisher, record company (Oak Street Music) and record producer (Oak Street Music). SOCAN. Estab. 1987. Publishes 10 songs/year; publishes 2 new songwriters/year. Works with composers and lyricists; teams collaborators. Pays negotiable royalty.
Affiliate(s): Forest Group Music (SOCAN).
How to Contact: Submit a demo tape by mail—unsolicited submissions are OK. Prefers cassette or VHS videocassette with 2-3 songs and lyric and lead sheet. SASE. Reports in 1-2 months.
Music: Mostly children's and novelty. Published "Sandwiches" (by Bob King), "The Season" (by Fred Penner), and "Christmasy Kind of Day" (by Ken Whiteley); all recorded by Fred Penner on Oak Street Records.

*BRENTWOOD MUSIC, INC., 316 Southgate Ct., Brentwood TN 37027. (615)373-3950. FAX: (615)373-0386. A&R Director: Jack Jezioro. Music publisher, record company. Estab. 1980. Publishes 35-50 songs/year; publishes 1-2 new songwriters/year. Works with lyricists; teams collaborators. Pays standard royalty on publishing; 10% print publishing royalty.
Affiliates: New Spring Publishing (ASCAP), Bridge Building Music (BMI) and Designer Music (SESAC).
How to Contact: Submit demo tape—unsolicited submissions are OK. Prefers cassette with 2-3 songs and lyric or lead sheet. Does not return unsolicited material. Reports in 6-9 months.
Music: Mostly choral anthems, children's and praise/worship; also country, jazz and comedy. Published *When the Time Comes* (by David Kavich), recorded by Sandi Patti on Benson Records (LP); *Seed of Love* (by Daryl Mosley), recorded by The New Tradition; and *Love Knows* (by Mark Baldwin), recorded by the Brentwood Jazz Quartet, both on Brentwood Records (both LP's).
Tips: "Study our product line (available at any Christian bookstore), analyze the type of material we use and submit music in the same overall style."

*BRONX FLASH MUSIC, 3151 Cahuega Blvd. West, Los Angeles CA 90068. (213)882-6127. FAX: (213)882-8414. Professional Manager: Michael Schneider. Music publisher. BMI, ASCAP. Estab. 1982. Publishes 60 songs/per year; publishes 1 new songwriter per year. Hires staff writers. Works with composers; teams collaborators. Pays standard royalty.
Affiliates: Eagles Dare Music (ASCAP) and Kenwon Music (BMI).
How to Contact: Write first for permission to submit.
Music: Mostly pop, R&B and rock. Published "You are My Home" (by F. Wildhorn), recorded by Peabo Bryson (single); "I'll Forget You" and "The Scarlet Pimpernel" (both by F. Wildhorn), both recorded by Linda Eder (both singles), all on EMI.
Tips: "Ideas should be well thought out regarding lyrics, music and especially arrangements."

BROOZBEE MUSIC, INC., Suite 308, 37 East 28th St., New York NY 10016. (212)447-6000. President: Bruce B. Fisher. Music publisher. ASCAP. Estab. 1986. Publishes 8 songs/year; publishes 2 new songwriters/year. Works with composers; teams collaborators. Pays standard royalty.
How to Contact: Submit a demo tape by mail—unsolicited submissions are OK, or call to arrange a personal interview. Prefers cassette or VHS videocassette with 3 songs and lyric sheet. SASE. Reports in 2 months.
Music: Mostly house, dance, hip hop; also rap, R&B and pop. Published "Butt Naked" (by R. Punzone and P. Falcone); "I Love Music" (by G. Sicarp and B.B. Fisher), recorded by Charm on Turnstyle/Atlantic Records (rap/hip hop/pop)
Tips: "The song has to fit in the musical styles we listed and be ready to be recorded for release."

BUG MUSIC, 6777 Hollywood, Los Angeles CA 90028. (213)466-4352. Contact: Fred Bourgoise. Music publisher. BMI, ASCAP. Estab. 1975. Other offices: Nashville and London. We handle administration.
Affiliate(s): Bughouse (ASCAP).
How to Contact: Prefers cassette. Does not return unsolicited material.
Music: All genres. Published "Joey," by Concrete Blonde; "Angel Eyes" (by John Hiatt), recorded by Jeff Healy on Arista Records; "Full Moon Full of Love" (by Leroy Preston), recorded by K.D. Lang; and "Thing Called Love" (by John Hiatt), recorded by Bonnie Raitt.

BURIED TREASURE MUSIC, 524 Doral Country Dr., Nashville TN 37221. Executive Producer: Scott Turner. Music publisher and record producer (Aberdeen Productions). ASCAP. Estab. 1972. Publishes 30-50 songs/year; publishes 3-10 new songwriters/year. Receives 1,500 submissions/year. Works with composers and lyricists. Pays standard royalty.
Affiliate(s): Captain Kidd Music (BMI).
How to Contact: Submit a demo tape—unsolicited submissions are OK. Prefers cassette (or VHS videocassette) with 1-4 songs and lead sheet. Reports in 2 weeks. "Always enclose SASE if answer is expected."
Music: Country and country/pop; also rock, MOR and contemporary. Published "I Will" (by S. Rose), recorded by B. Bare, Mel Tillis, Roy Clark on Hallmark Records; "You Did It All" (by Turner/Baumgartner), recorded by Shelby Lynne on Sony CBS Records; and "The Angels' Song" (by T. Graham), recorded by Lynn Anderson and B. Baker on Polygram Records (all country).
Tips: "*Don't* send songs in envelopes that are 15"x 20", or by registered mail. It doesn't help a bit. Say something that's been said a thousand times before . . . only say it differently. A great song doesn't care who sings it. Songs that paint pictures have a better chance of ending up as videos. With artists only recording 10 songs every 18-24 months, the advice is . . . Patience!"

C.A.B. INDEPENDENT PUBLISHING CO., P.O. Box 26852, Oklahoma City OK 73126. Secretary: Christopher Stanley. Music publisher and record company (Ms'Que Records, Inc.). BMI. Estab. 1988. Publishes 10 songs/year; publishes 5 new songwriters/year. Works with composers. Pays standard royalty.
Affiliate(s): (C.A.B.) Creative Artistic Broadening Industries, Publishing (BMI).
How to Contact: Submit a demo tape by mail—unsolicited submissions are OK. Prefers cassette or VHS videocassette with 3 songs. SASE. Reports in 2 months.
Music: Mostly R&B, rock, pop; also jazz, New Age and gospel. Published "Attack" (R&B); "We Got Funky" (pop) and "Together" (pop), all written by C. Freeman and recorded by Cash & Co. on Ms'Que Records.
Tips: "Make sure you submit your best songs. It's best to get professional advice and demos."

*CACTUS MUSIC AND GIDGET PUBLISHING, 5 Aldom Circle, West Caldwell NJ 07006. Owner: Tar Heel Pete. Music publisher and record company (Dynamite Records). ASCAP, BMI. Estab. 1974. Publishes 5-8 songs/year; publishes 3-5 new songwriters/year. Works with composers. Pays standard royalty.
Affiliate(s): Jimmy Allison Music (BMI).
How to Contact: Write first and obtain permission to submit. Prefers cassette with 3 songs minimum and lyric sheet. Does not return unsolicited material. Reports in 1 month.
Music: Mostly C&W, R&B and blues; also jazz. Published "Give Me Roses" (by Morris Hall Hellman) and "Release You" (by Rose), both recorded by Coleman O'Neal; "Crazy Over You" (by La Flame)(C/W); "Cochabamba" (by Hall) (C/W); and "Days in the Park" (by Bergeron)(rock), all recorded by Tony Ansems on Dynamite Records (rock).

CALIFORNIA COUNTRY MUSIC, 112 Widmar Pl., Clayton CA 94517. (510)672-8201. Owner: Edgar J. Brincat. Music publisher, record company (Roll On Records). BMI. Estab. 1985. Publishes 30 songs/year; publishes 2-4 new songwriters/year. Receives 200 submissions/month. Works with composers and lyricists; teams collaborators. Pays standard royalty.
Affiliate(s): Sweet Inspirations Music (ASCAP).
How to Contact: Submit a demo tape by mail—unsolicited submissions are OK. Prefers cassette with 3 songs and lyric sheet. Any calls will be returned collect to caller. SASE. Reports in 2-4 weeks.
Music: Mostly MOR, contemporary country and pop; also R&B, gospel and light rock. Published "Jack Daniels" (by Barbara Finnicum, Edgar J. Brincat, Patti Leidecker), recorded by Carolyn Rae; "Southern Comfort" and "The Rain" (by Barbara Finnicum, Ed Davie), recorded by Ed Davie (country), all on Roll On Records.
Tips: "Listen to what we have to say about your product. Be as professional as possible."

CALVARY MUSIC GROUP, INC., 142 8th Ave. N., Nashville TN 37203. (615)244-8800. President: Dr. Nelson S. Parkerson. Music publisher and record company ASCAP, BMI, SESAC. Publishes 30-40 songs/year; publishes 2-3 new songwriters/year. Pays standard royalty.
Affiliate(s): Songs of Calvary, Music of Calvary and LifeStream Music, Soldier of the Light, Torchbearer Music.
How to Contact: Accepting material at this time.
Music: Church/religious, contemporary Christian, gospel and wedding music.

CANVIRG MUSIC, Ste. 101, 302 E. Pettigrew St., Durham NC 27701. (919)688-8563. President: Willie Hill. Music publisher and record company (Joy Records). BMI. Estab. 1987. Publishes 10 songs/year; publishes 3 new songwriters/year. Teams collaborators. Pays standard royalty.
How to Contact: Submit a demo tape by mail—unsolicited submissions are OK. Prefers cassette with 4 songs and lyric sheet. Does not return unsolicited material. Reports in 2 weeks.
Music: Mostly R&B, pop and gospel. Published "Step by Step" (by Walter Hill), recorded by Inspire Productions Studio on Joy Records (R&B).

CAPITOL STAR ARTIST ENTS., INC., 386 Clay Ave., Rochester NY 14613. (716)647-1617. Director: Don Redanz. Associate Director: Tony Powlowski. Music publisher, record company and record producer. BMI. Publishes 20 songs/year; publishes 5 new songwriters/year. Pays standard royalty.
How to Contact: Submit a demo tape—unsolicited submissions OK. SASE. Reports in 3 weeks.
Music: Country, gospel, and pop. Published "Dust on Mother's Bible," and "Away from Home" (by Anthony Powlowski), recorded by Tony Starr on Capitol Star (country); and "V-8 Detroit," by A. Powlowski.
Tips: "We like country songs with a heartwarming story."

CARAVELL MAIN SAIL MUSIC, Box 1646, Branson MO 65616. (417)334-7040. President: Keith O'Neil. Music publisher, record producer (Caravell Recording Studio). ASCAP. Estab. 1989. Publishes 5 new songwriters/year. Works with composers and lyricists; teams collaborators. Pays standard royalty of 50%.
How to Contact: Submit demo tape by mail—unsolicited submissions are OK. Prefers cassette with 3 songs and lyric sheet. SASE. Reports in 4 weeks.
Music: Mostly country, pop and gospel. Published "I've Been There Before" by Sue Ann Neal on Caravelle Records; "The Darlin' Boys" and "The Wizard of Song" by Rodney Dillard on Vanguard Records; and "In the Meadow" by Jackie Pope on Caravelle Records.

DON CASALE MUSIC, INC., 377 Plainfield St., Westbury NY 11590. (516)333-7898. President: Don Casale. Record producer, music publisher, artist management; affiliated recording studio. Estab. 1979. Deals with artists, songwriters, managers and agents. Fee derived from sales royalty.
Affiliate(s): Elasac Music (ASCAP), Don Casale Music (BMI).
How to Contact: "I will accept unsolicited cassettes (except during August and September) with one or two songs and a legible, typed lyric sheet (no registered mail). No "lyrics-only" submissions. Please include address and phone number and letter stating exact purpose (publishing deal? record deal? etc.); anything else you'd like to say is welcome too (I frown on 'form' letters). Press kit, bio and photo(s) or VHS videocassette are helpful, if available. For return of your material, always include SASE (envelope *must* be large enough to handle contents). If you don't need your material returned, include a *signed* note stating so and only include SASE for my response letter. Sorry, but I will not listen or correspond without SASE. A call first is very welcome (between 12 noon and 12 midnight EST), but not necessary, or you may inquire first by mail (with SASE). I'll listen to every note of your music and respond to you as soon as possible, usually between two weeks and two months, depending on volume of submissions."
Music: Everything but jazz and classical.
Tips: "Submitted songs should have a 'special' nature about them; a different quality and lyric. Melodies should be particularly 'catchy' and memorable. Songs should be in tune with the current radio market. I want only 'career-starting,' top 10 singles; not B sides or album fillers. Please try to be SELECTIVE and send me that ONE SONG you think is a KILLER; that ONE SONG that JUMPS OFF THE TAPE! Don't include a second song just because there's room on the cassette; if I hear something I like, I'll ask for more. Songwriters seeking a publishing contract need only a simple, in-tune, clear version of the song(s); a big production and recording, although welcome, is not necessary. Artists seeking a recording contract should submit a 'quality' performance (musically and vocally), incorporating their very best effort and their own, preferably unique, style. Your recording needn't be master quality, but your performance should be. I give extra points for following my instructions to the letter."

ERNIE CASH MUSIC, INC., 744 Joppa Farm Rd., Joppa MD 21085. (301)679-2262. President: Ernest W. Cash. Music publisher, record company (Continental Records, Inc.), record producer (Vision Music Group, Inc.) and Vision Video Production, Inc. BMI. Estab. 1987. Publishes 30-60 songs/year; publishes 10-15 new songwriters/year. Works with composers and lyricists; teams collaborators. Pays standard royalty.
Affiliate(s): Big K Music, Inc. (BMI), Guerriero Music (BMI) and Deb Music (BMI).
How to Contact: Submit a demo tape by mail—unsolicited submissions are OK. Write or call to arrange a personal interview. Prefers cassette (VHS videocassette if available) with 3 songs and lyric sheet. SASE. Reports in 2 weeks.

Music: Mostly country, gospel and pop; also R&B and rock. Published "A Man Called Jones" written and recorded by Jimmy Peppers; "If You're Not Here By Closing Time" (by Pam Hanna), recorded by Pam Bailey; and "Kansas Waltz" (by James Hession), recorded by Doug Lester, all on Go-Records, all country.

Tips: "Give me a call, I will review your material."

*CASTLE MUSIC CORP., Suite 201, 50 Music Sq. W., Nashville TN 37203. (615)320-7003. FAX: (615)320-7006. Publishing Director: Ms. Jamey King. Music publisher, record company, record producer. Estab. 1969. Pays standard royalty.

Affiliate(s): Alley Roads Music (BMI), Eddie Ray Music (ASCAP), Cats Alley Music (ASCAP) and Flattop Music (SESAC).

How to Contact: Submit demo tape by mail–unsolicited submissions are OK. Prefers cassette with 3 songs and lyric sheet. SASE. Reports ASAP.

Music: Mostly country, pop and gospel. Published "You Him or Me" written and recorded by Carl Butler (single) and "Think Like a Man, Work Like a Dog" (by Ruthie Steele and Bethany Reynolds), recorded by Tammie Sue (single) and *Women Like You* written and recorded by Doug Cotton (album) all on Castle Records.

CATHARINE COURAGE MUSIC LTD., 48 De Lisle Rd., Bournemouth Dorset BH3 7NG **England**. (202)529755. Director: Mike Shepstone. Music publisher. PRS/MCPS. Estab. 1981. Publishes 7 songs/year. Works with composers. Pays standard royalty of 50%.

How to Contact: Submit a demo tape by mail–unsolicited submissions OK. Prefers cassette with two songs and lyric sheet. SASE. "Don't forget we are answering from the U.K." Reports in 6 weeks.

Music: Mostly pop, rock/pop and R&B.

Tips: "We are urgently looking for Janis Joplin type songs (no sophistication) for new recording project."

CENTER FOR THE QUEEN OF PEACE, P.O. Box 90035, Pasadena CA 91109. Music publisher and record company (Cosmotone Music, Cosmotone Records). ASCAP. Estab. 1984. Publishes 10-12 songs/year; publishes 10 new songwriters/year. Works with composers and lyricists; teams collaborators. Pays standard royalty "and by agreement."

How to Contact: Submit a demo tape by mail–unsolicited submissions are OK. "Will contact only if interested." Prefers cassette or VHS videocassette with lyric sheet.

Music: Mostly gospel and Catholic Marian music; also Christian progressive music. Published "Peace of Heart," "The Sounds of Heaven" written and recorded by Rafael Brom (Christian progressive); and "Padre Pio," written and recorded by Lord Hamilton (Christian pop/rock); all on Cosmotone Records.

*CENTERFIELD PRODUCTIONS, 251 W. 30th St., New York NY 10001. (212)714-1820. General Manager: Daniel Karns. Music publisher, record producer, management company. Estab. 1986. Publishes 30 songs/year; publishes 2-3 new songwriters/year. Works with composers and lyricists; teams collaborators.

Affiliates: Hot Corner Music, Inc. (ASCAP), Golden Mike Music, Inc. (BMI).

How to Contact: Write first and obtain permission to submit a tape. Prefers cassette with 3-4 songs and lyric sheet. SASE. Reports in 1 month.

Music: Mostly interested in R&B/dance, pop and rock; also country, contemporary jazz and house. Published "Alright" (by Roland Clark), recorded by Urban Soul on Chrysalis Records (dance/house); "Say No More" written and recorded by Bendik, recorded on CBS Records (A/C); and "Nothin Could Save Ya" (by Hollywood Impact), recorded by Twin Hype on Profile Records (rap/dance).

Tips: "Listen to every style of music you can get your hands on, and let your own style come forth naturally from that fuel."

CHAPIE MUSIC (BMI), 228 West 5th, Kansas City MO 64105. (816)842-6854. Owner: Chuck Chapman. Music publisher, record company (Fifth Street Records), record producer (Chapman Recording Studios). BMI. Estab. 1977. Publishes 6 songs/year. Receives 4 submissions/month. Works with composers; teams collaborators. Pays standard 50% royalty.

How to Contact: Call to get permission to submit tape. Prefers cassette with 1-3 songs and lyric sheet. SASE. Reports in weeks.

Music: Mostly country, pop, gospel; also jazz, R&B and New Age. Published "Lonely Country Road" and "Talkin 'Bout," both written and recorded by Mike Eisel; and "Sometimes Takes A Woman" (by Greg Camp), recorded by Rick Loveall, all recorded on Fifth Street Records (country).

Tips: "Make it commercial–with a twist on the lyrics."

Close-up

Mike Mainieri
Director of A&R
Centerfield Productions
New York, New York

Photo by Scott Singer

Raised in a family of performers and musicians, Mike Mainieri had two things going for him: talent and encouragement. Mainieri enjoyed an early diet of Glenn Miller, Duke Ellington and Count Basie, in addition to live performances in-home and weekend excursions to Broadway shows in New York.

This exposure, coupled with his aptitude on the vibraphone, led him to a professional career when most of his peers were enduring puberty. At 14, Mainieri took his vibraphone on tour with the Paul Whiteman Orchestra. At 17, he had signed on with Buddy Rich. A year later, he won the International Jazz Critics Award as a vibraphone player.

His 40-year career as a jazz musician, arranger, composer and producer has included involvement on more than 100 gold and platinum albums with the likes of Paul Simon, Linda Ronstadt, Aerosmith, Billy Joel, Carly Simon, George Benson, James Taylor, Bonnie Raitt and Dire Straits. He has won more than 25 Obies and has been nominated three times for Grammy awards (once as best arranger and twice for best contemporary jazz LP). Mainieri currently performs with the jazz fusion group Steps Ahead, formed in 1979. He also serves as senior vice president, executive director and director of A&R with Centerfield Productions, the company he helped co-found in 1986.

Mainieri has a long-term perspective on the evolution of the pop music industry in the U.S. Songwriters today, he says, face an industry fundamentally changed from the one he entered. "It seemed to me in the 60s that a lot of people in the record companies had more musical knowledge than they do today," Mainieri says. "There was a tremendous love for music and a lot of the most talented producers were at record companies. Today, if you're a talented producer, you can make much more money on the outside as a freelance producer. I think a lot of young A&R people today are afraid to sign acts because they don't have the commitment to the musical knowledge and background that their peers did years ago.

"The songwriting craft was tremendous [in the 60s]," he says. "It was brilliant. It was what you compare the 30s and 40s stuff to, you know, Gershwin and Rogers and Hart. The Beatles wrote some real songs . . . I really believe that on a certain level if the Beatles walked into a record company right now with a tape they wouldn't get a contract."

So the challenge to songwriters today, Mainieri says, is to maintain their integrity in the face of industry pressure to limit their efforts to hit-making formulas. "Music that is challenging is very difficult to sell, because (record companies) want ear candy, something incredibly hooky," he says. "But it really doesn't work to conform too much to what you think they want, because there really is an art and craft to writing songs. The most important thing is that (your music) is the essence of you. If you try to be somebody else, then you're really competing with everybody else out there who's making the same mistake. And what happens is the music doesn't ever grow. That's one of the reasons the business is in the doldrums right now."

As A&R director for Centerfield Productions, Mainieri says he sees his share of submissions (30-40 per week), and looks for one particular element in each of them. "(I look for) whether or not the music moves me," he says. "To me, it's all about feeling. You can tell when somebody is trying to write a hit. They're purposely thinking 'I'm going to write something that would be good for Mariah Carey.'"

He also stresses sophisticated production is not necessary for submissions to Centerfield. "If (songwriters) present the song and it moves you, that's enough," he says. "Production will come after. Some people have their computers and machines at home and they can put together a pretty good demo that way, but it's not absolutely necessary."

Centerfield Productions features a diverse roster and has had records appear on the jazz, pop, New Age, rap, club and R&B charts. Recently, Mainieri has produced albums for Bendik (Columbia), Andy Summers (Private Music) and French trumpet player Illouz.

Mainieri says his experience as a musician has helped him develop as a producer. "It's a process," he says, "and I think as I get older it gets easier, because there's less of me in it. When you're younger, as a producer, you're trying to make your own statement. I think one of the main objectives I've found in being a producer is staying out of the way, and letting the music shine right through. It's frustrating, too," he adds, "because there are so many songwriters and so few roles for them today. It's heartbreaking sometimes."

Mainieri is confident enough in his assessment of the industry and the public's taste for more challenging music that he's come up with his own remedy. Development of his new label, Spirit Records, is nearing completion, and Mainieri is excited about the possibilities. "We'll introduce some new artists—whether they're musicians, instrumental artists, singer/songwriters—who really have something to say."

Mainieri says he sees the new label as his opportunity to "pursue the dream one step further, to complete the entire cycle—to find an artist, develop an artist or musical idea and actually get to put it out on your own label and have control of the advertising and promotion so it really has a shot. I see too many fantastic artists who never even get to record, just completely go by the wayside, because of deaf A&R ears."

Despite his concerns about the state of the music industry, Mainieri stops short of discouraging songwriters from persisting with their craft and career plans.

"The road is a bumpy one," he says. "But it's all about believing what you're doing, and not necessarily about success in terms of commercial success. Because every time you bend to make something more commercial or palatable, in the long run you're hurting yourself and all the other songwriters out there. You've got to believe in what you're doing as an artist, that you really have something to say. That's the most important thing."

—Anne Bowling

66 The most important thing is that (your music) is the essence of you. If you try to be somebody else, then you're really competing with everybody else out there who's making the same mistake. And what happens is the music doesn't ever grow. That's one of the reasons the business is in the doldrums right now. 99

—Mike Mainieri

*CHEAVORIA MUSIC CO., 1219 Kerlin Ave., Brewton AL 36426. (205)867-2228. President: Roy Edwards. Music publisher, record company and record producer. Estab. 1972. Publishes 20 new songwriters/year. Works with composers and lyricists; teams collaborators. Pays standard royalty.
Affiliate(s): Baitstring Music (ASCAP) and Chevoria Music (BMI).
How to Contact: Write first to get permission to submit. Prefers cassette with 3 songs and lyric sheet. Does not return unsolicited material. Reports in 1 month.
Music: Mostly R&B, pop and country; also good ballads. Published "Forever and Always" written and recorded by James Rootwood on Bolivia Records (country).

*CHINA GROOVE, 404 St. Henri, Montreal Quebec H3C 2P5 **Canada**. (514)871-8481. Publisher: Mario Rubnikowich. Music publisher. SDE, SOCAN. Estab. 1987. Publishes 6-10 songs/year; publishes 3 new songwriters/year. Hires staff songwriters. Works with team collaborators. Pays standard royalty of 50%.
Affiliate(s): Foxtrot (SOCAN).
How to Contact: Submit a demo tape by mail—unsolicited submissions are OK. Prefers cassette or 15 IPS reel-to-reel with 3 songs and lyric sheet and lead sheet. SASE. Reports in 3-5 weeks.

CHIP 'N' DALE MUSIC PUBLISHERS, INC., 3950 N. Mt. Juliet Rd., Mt. Juliet TN 37122. (615)754-0417. Contact: Karen Jeglum Kennedy. Music publisher, record company (Door Knob Records, Society Records), record producer (Gene Kennedy Enterprises, Inc.). ASCAP. Estab. 1975. Publishes 20-25 songs/year; publishes 10-15 new songwriters/year. Works with composers and lyricists. Pays standard royalty.
Affiliate(s): Door Knob Music Publishing, Inc. (BMI) and Lodestar Music, A Division of Gene Kennedy Enterprises, Inc. (SESAC).
How to Contact: Submit a demo tape by mail—unsolicited submissions are OK. Prefers cassette with 1-3 songs and lyric sheet. Include SASE for tape return and/or response. Send regular mail. SASE. Reports in 1 week.
Music: Mostly country, gospel. Published "Dancin' with an Angel" (by Robert and Lona Preston), recorded by Bo Harrison; "Give Me Just a Little More Time (by S. Ellwanger and R. Porter), recorded by Sandy Elwanger (country); and "Meet My Friend" (by J. Burton and L. Smith), recorded by David Reed (gospel), all on Door Knob Records.
Tips: "Respect our submission policy and keep trying."

CHRIS MUSIC PUBLISHING, 133 Arbutus Ave., P.O. Box 396, Manistique MI 49854-0396. President: Reg B. Christensen. Chief Executive Officer: Ken Mathena. Music publisher and record company (Global Records and Bakersfield Records). Estab. 1956. Publishes 15-35 songs/year; publishes at least 20 new songwriters/year. Pays standard royalty with some exceptions.
Affiliate(s): Sara Lee Music Publishing (BMI).
How to Contact: Submit cassette *only* with 2-5 songs and lyric sheet. Unsolicited submissions OK. "No fancy, big band demo necessary; just one instrument with a clean, clear voice. Copyrighted material only. Send xerox copy of copyright. If not registered with Copyright office, let us know what you've done to protect your material." SASE. Reports in 5-8 weeks.
Music: Mostly teen type novelty, gospel, MOR and novelty rock; also bluegrass, contemporary gospel and soul. Published "TV Cop" written and recorded by Pursuit on Global Records (rock); "Ask Me No Questions" (by Bill Woods), recorded by Helen De Baker; and "I, I, I" written and recorded by Helen DeBaker both recorded on Bakersfield Records (c/w).
Tips: "Give us a good novelty type. Smooth, slow songs only put us to sleep and won't sell anyway."

CHRYSALIS MUSIC GROUP, 810 7th Ave., New York NY 10019. (212)603-8769. Talent Acquisitions: Evon Handras. Music publisher. ASCAP, BMI. Estab. 1972. Publishes 50-100 songs/year; publishes 1-2 new songwriters/year. Receives 40 submissions/month. Hires staff songwriters "in small quantities." Pays royalty—"standard in most cases, but negotiable."
Affiliate(s): Chrysalis Music (ASCAP) and Chrysalis Songs (BMI).
How to Contact: Submit demo tape—unsolicited submissions are OK. Prefers cassette with 3-5 songs and lyric sheet. "Quality is stressed instead of quantity." Returns unsolicited material with SASE. Reports in 1 month.
Music: Mostly pop/R&B and rock. Published "Little Things" (by Troy Taylor), recorded by Boyz II Men on Motown Records (R&B); "The One and Only" (by Nik Kershaw), recorded by Chesney Hawkes on Chrysalis Records (pop); and "I'll Get By" (by Armato/Hill); recorded by Eddie Money on Columbia Records (pop/rock).
Tips: "Write a melody that grabs the listener's ears and doesn't let go. Think of a new way to express a common sentiment. Make the listener feel some kind of emotion. Make sure song has as beginning, middle and an end."

CISUM, Box 192, Pittsburg KS 66762. (316)231-6443. Partner: Kevin Shawn. Music publisher, record company (Cisum), record producer (Cisum). BMI, SESAC and ASCAP. Estab. 1985. Publishes 100 songs/year. Works with composers and lyricists; teams collaborators. Pays standard royalty.
How to Contact: Write first and obtain permission to submit a tape. Prefers cassette (or VHS videocassette if available) and lyric sheet. "Unpublished, copyrighted, cassette with lyrics. Submit as many as you wish. We listen to everything, allow 3 months. When over 3 weeks please call."
Music: Mostly novelty, country and rock; also pop, gospel and R&B. Published "Angry Gun" (by R. Durst), recorded by Gene Straser on Antique Records (country); "Smooth Talk" (by Rhuems), recorded by Rich Rhuems on Antique Records (country); "Mailman Mailman" (by Strasser), recorded by Willie & Shawn on Cisum Records (novelty).
Tips: "Good demo, great song; always put your best effort on the tape first."

R.D. CLEVÈRE MUSIKVERLAG, Postfach 2145, D-6078 Neu-Isenburg, **Germany.** Phone: (6102)52696. Professional Manager: Tony Hermonez. GEMA. Music publisher. Estab. 1967. Publishes 700-900 songs/year; publishes 40 new songwriters/year. Works with composers and lyricists; teams collaborators. Pays standard royalty.
Affiliate(s): Big Sound Music, Hot Night Music, Lizzy's Blues Music, Max Banana Music, R.D. Clevère-Cocabana-Music, R.D. Clevère-Far East & Orient-Music, and R.D. Clevère-America-Today-Music.
How to Contact: "Do not send advance letter(s) asking for permission to submit your song material, just send it." Prefers cassette with "no limit" on songs and lyric sheet. SAE and a minimum of two IRCs. Reports in 3 weeks.
Music: Mostly pop, disco, rock, R&B, country and folk; also musicals and classic/opera.
Tips: "If the song submitted is already produced/recorded professionally on 16/24-multitrack-tape and available, we can use this for synchronization with artists of the various record companies/record producers."

*CLIENTELE MUSIC, 252 Bayshore Dr., Hendersonville TN 37075. (615)822-2364. FAX: (615)264-1256. Director: Thornton Cline. Music publisher. Estab. 1989. Publishes 15 songs/year; publishes 10 new songwriters/year. Works with composers and lyricists. Pays standard 50% royalty.
Affiliate(s): Clientele Music (ASCAP) and Incline Music (BMI).
How to Contact: Submit demo tape by mail—unsolicited submissions are OK. Prefers cassette with 1 song and lyric sheet. "Send only radio ready demos—your No. 1 songs." SASE. Reports in 3 weeks.
Music: Mostly R&B/dance, pop/dance and pop/ballads; also soul, country and contemporary Christian. Published "Shortest Distance Between 2 Hearts" (by Ryan/Cline), recorded by Dagmar on Nickel/Capitol Records; "She Doesn't Know What She's Missing" (by Swiegoda/Cline), recorded by The Manhattans on Cardiac Records; and "Love Saved The Best for Last" (by Wilson/Cline), recorded by Billy and Sarah Craines on ABC Productions Movie of the Week-TV movie "Notorious."
Tips: Send only radio ready demos with only one song and your No. 1 song. Need killer, conversational lyrics (not trite) and killer, catchy strong melodies. Keep current."

COFFEE AND CREAM PUBLISHING COMPANY, 1138 E. Price St., Philadelphia PA 19138. (215)842-3450. President: Bolden Abrams, Jr. Music publisher and record producer (Bolden Productions). ASCAP. Publishes 20 songs/year; publishes 4 new songwriters/year. Works with composers and lyricists; teams collaborators. Pays standard royalty.
How to Contact: Prefers cassette (or VHS videocassette) with 1-4 songs and lyric or lead sheets. Does not return unsolicited material. Reports in 2 weeks "if we're interested."
Music: Mostly dance, pop, R&B, gospel and country. Published "No Time for Tears" (by Bolden Abrams/Keith Batts), recorded by Gabrielle (R&B ballad); "Sly Like a Fox," (by Regine Urbach), recorded by Joy Duncan on Ultimate Records (pop/dance); "If I Let Myself Go" (by Jose Gomez/Sheree Sano), recorded by Evelyn "Champagne" King on RCA Records (pop/ballad).

CONTINENTAL COMMUNICATIONS CORP., 450 Livingston St., Norwood NJ 07648. (201)767-5551. President: Robert Schwartz. ASCAP, BMI. Estab. 1952. Music publisher and record company (Laurie Records and 3C Records). Publishes 50 songs/year; publishes 5-10 new songwriters/year. Works with composers and lyricists; teams collaborators. Pays standard royalty.
Affiliate(s): 3 Seas Music (ASCAP) and Northvale Music (BMI).
How to Contact: Submit demo tape—unsolicited submissions OK. Prefers cassette. SASE. "Submit only a few of the most commercial songs with lead sheets and demo." Reports in 3 weeks.
Music: Mostly rock. Published "Because of You," written and recorded by B. Sunkel on Laurie Records (pop); "Complicated," written and recorded by Allen Bros. on 3C Records (urban); and "Lament 62" (by D. Groom and P. Renari), recorded by D. Groom on Laurie Records (pop).

THE CORNELIUS COMPANIES, 803 18th Ave. South, Nashville TN 37203. (615)321-5333. Owner/ Manager: Ron Cornelius. Music publisher and record producer (The Cornelius Companies, Ron Cornelius). BMI, ASCAP. Estab. 1987. Publishes 60-80 songs/year; publishes 2-3 new songwriters/ year. Occasionally hires staff writers. Receives 250 submissions/month. Works with composers and lyricists; teams collaborators. Pays standard royalty.
Affiliate(s): RobinSparrow Music (BMI).
How to Contact: Write or call first and obtain permission to submit a tape. Prefers cassette with 2-3 songs. SASE. Reports in 2 months.
Music: Mostly country and pop. Published "Time Off for Bad Behavior" (by Lorry Latimer), recorded by Confederate Railroad on Atlantic Records; and "You're Slowly Going Out of My Mind" (by Gordon Dee), recorded by Southern Tracks; both on CBS Records; "These Colors Never Run" (by Gordon Dee).

*COSGROOVE MUSIC INC., P.O. Box 2234, Amagansett NY 11930. (516)329-0753. President: Lance Cosgrove. Estab. 1989. Publishes 15 songs/year; publishes 4-8 new songwriters/year. Works with composers and lyricists. Pays standard royalty.
How to Contact: Submit demo tape—unsolicited submissions are OK. Prefers cassette with 1-2 songs and lyric sheet. "Send only the amount of songs requested." SASE. Reports in 1 month.
Music: Mostly pop/rock, R&B and contemporary country; also heavy metal. Published *Everything You Do (You're Sexing Me)* (by Beau Hill, Fiona and Lance Cosgrove), recorded by Fiona on Atlantic Records (LP).
Tips: "Try and be totally objective about your finished product. Be very aware of song structure, melody and commercial appeal."

COSMOTONE MUSIC, P.O. Box 71988, Los Angeles CA 90071-0988. Music publisher, record company (Cosmotone Records, Cosmotone Studios) and record producer. ASCAP. Estab. 1984. Publishes 10 songs/year; publishes 2 new songwriters/year. Works with lyricists; teams collaborators. Pays standard royalty.
How to Contact: Write first and obtain permission to submit a tape. Prefers cassette (VHS videocassette if available) with all songs and lyric sheet. "Will respond only if interested."
Music: All types. Published "Padre Pio," "Sonnet XVIII" and "O Let Me Be," all written and recorded by Lord Hamilton on Cosmotone Records (Christian/rock pop); and "The Sounds of Heaven" and "Peace of Heart" by Rafael Brom (Christian progressive).

COTTAGE BLUE MUSIC, P.O. Box 121626, Nashville TN 37212. (615)726-3556. Contact: Neal James. Music publisher, record company (Kottage Records) and record producer (Neal James Productions). BMI. Estab. 1971. Publishes 30 songs/year; publishes 3 new songwriters/year. Receives 75 submissions/ month. Works with composers and lyricists. Pays standard royalty of 50%.
Affiliate(s): James & Lee (BMI), Neal James Music (BMI) and Hidden Cove Music (ASCAP).
How to Contact: Submit demo tape—unsolicited submissions OK. Prefers cassette with 2 songs and lyric sheet. SASE. Reports in 4 weeks.
Music: Mostly country, gospel and rock/pop; also R&B. Published "Share This Night" (by Neal James), recorded by Terry Barbay on Kottage Records (contemporary country); "Room by Room" (by Hank Cochran/Neal James), recorded by Billy Don Burns on PJ Hawk Records (country); and "Angel" (by Shirley Jones/Neal James), recorded by Terry Barbay on Kottage Records (country).
Tips: "Screen material carefully before submitting."

COUNTRY BREEZE MUSIC, 1715 Marty, Kansas City KS 66103. (913)384-4454 or 384-1020. President: Ed Morgan. Music publisher and record company (Country Breeze Records and Walkin' Hat Records). BMI, ASCAP. Estab. 1984. Publishes 100 songs/year; publishes 25-30 new songwriters/year. Receives 130 submissions/month. Teams collaborators. Pays standard royalty.
Affiliate(s): Walkin' Hat Music (ASCAP).
How to Contact: Submit a demo tape—unsolicited submissions are OK. Prefers cassette (or VHS videocassette) with 4-5 songs and lyric sheet. SASE. "The songwriter/artist should perform on the video as though on stage giving a sold-out performance. In other words put heart and soul into the project. Submit in strong mailing envelopes." Reports in 2 weeks.
Music: Mostly country (rock/pop/traditional), gospel (southern/bluegrass and black) and rock. Published "He Did It All" (by R. Davis), recorded by Park Bench Quartet on Angel Star Records (southern gospel); "Memories" written and recorded by Johnny Amburgey; and "Hearts of the Night" (by R. Velvin), recorded by Ian Coltair, both on Country Breeze Records (country).
Tips: "Make sure your voice is clear and out front."

COUNTRY STAR MUSIC, 439 Wiley Ave., Franklin PA 16323. (814)432-4633. President: Norman Kelly. Music publisher, record company (Country Star, Process, Mersey and CSI) and record producer (Country Star Productions). ASCAP. Estab. 1970. Publishes 20-30 songs/year; publishes 2-3 new songwriters/year. Receives 400 submissions/year. Works with composers and lyricists; teams collaborators. Pays standard royalty.

Affiliate(s): Kelly Music Publications (BMI) and Process Music Publications (BMI).

How to Contact: Submit demo tape—unsolicited submissions are OK. Prefers cassette with 1-4 songs and lyric or lead sheet. SASE. Reports in 2 weeks.

Music: Mostly country (80%); also rock, gospel, MOR and R&B (5% each). Published "Son of a Cowboy" written and recorded by Jeff Connors; "Love or Pity," written and recorded by Sissy Padilla; and "The Holiday Waltz" (by Stelzer & Wrightman), recorded by Debbie Sue, all on Country Star Records (country).

Tips: "Send only your best songs—ones you feel are equal to or better than current hits."

COWABONGA MUSIC, INC., P.O. Box 630755, Miami FL 33163. (305)935-4880. A&R Director: Jack Gale. Music publisher, record company (Playback Records, Gallery 11 Records, Inc., Ridgewood Records and Caramba! Records) and record producer (Jack Gale). ASCAP. Estab. 1983. Publishes 70 songs/year; publishes 12 new songwriters/year. Receives 100 submissions/month. Pays standard royalty.

Affiliate(s): Lovey Music Inc. (BMI).

How to Contact: Submit a demo tape—unsolicited submissions are O.K. Prefers cassette (or VHS vidoecassette) with maximum of 2 songs and lyric sheet. SASE. Reports in 2 weeks.

Music: Mostly contemporary country and pop. Published "Hard Times Come" (by Court/Leisten), recorded by Terry Smith on Ridgewood Records; "I Just Pretend" (by H. Lindsey), recorded by Cheryl K. Warner; and "Two Steps at a Time" (by L. Rubkoff), recorded by Sylvie, both on Playback Records (country).

COWBOY JUNCTION FLEA MARKET AND PUBLISHING CO., Highway 44 West, Junction 490, Lecanto FL 32661. (904)746-4754. President: Elizabeth Thompson. Music publisher (Cowboy Junction Publishing Co.), record company (Cowboy Junction Records) and record producer. BMI. Estab. 1957. Receives 100 submissions/year. Publishes 5 songs/year. Pays standard royalty or other amount.

How to Contact: Submit demo tape (or VHS videocassette) by mail—unsolicited submissions are OK. SASE. Reports as soon as possible.

Music: Country, western, bluegrass and gospel. Published "I'm A Happy Modern Cowboy," "I'm Like A Turtle in A Turtle Shell" and "It Really Doesn't Matter Now," all written by Boris Max Pastuch and recorded by Buddy Max on Cowboy Junction Records (country).

CREEKSIDE MUSIC, 100 Labon St., Tabor City NC 28463. (919)653-2546. Owner: Elson H. Stevens. Music publisher, record company (Seaside Records) and record producer (Southern Sound Productions). BMI. Estab. 1978. Publishes 30 songs/year; publishes 5 new songwriters/year. Works with composers, lyricists; teams collaborators. Pays 25-50% royalty from record sales.

How to Contact: Submit demo tape—unsolicited submissions OK. Prefers cassette with 3 songs and lead sheets. SASE. Reports in 1 month.

Music: Mostly country, rock and gospel; also "beach music." Published "I'll Never Say Never Again" (by G. Todd and S. Hart) and "Long Country Road" (by G. Taylor) both recorded by Sherry Collins (country); and "Heaven's Ready" (by E. Watson), recorded by The Watson Family (gospel), all on Seaside Records.

Tips: "Be original—search for 'the hook'."

CREOLE MUSIC LTD., The Chilterns, France Hill Dr., Camberley, Surrey GU15 3QA **England.** Director: Bruce White. Music publisher. PRS/MCPS. Estab. 1966. Publishes 20-30 songs/year; publishes 2-3 new songwriters/year. Teams collaborators. Pays standard royalty of 50% ("sometimes higher, 60-40%").

How to Contact: Submit a demo tape by mail—unsolicited submissions OK. Prefers cassette with 3-4 songs. SASE. Reports in 6 weeks.

Music: Mostly pop, dance and rock. Published "Sweet Cherrie," recorded by UB40 on Dep/Virgin Records (reggae); and "Up Town Sharon" (by E. Auld), recorded by In Crowd on Silver Edge Records (pop).

Tips: "We are seeking to acquire or sub publish 'active' pubilshing catalogs or single titles."

CSB KAMINSKY GMBH, Wilhelmstrasse 10, 2407 Bad Schwartau, **Germany.** Phone: (0451)21530. General Manager: Pia Kaminsky. GEMA, PRS. Music publisher and collecting agency. Estab. 1978. Publishes 2-4 songs/year; 1 new songwriter/year. Teams collaborators. Pays 50% if releasing a record; 85% if only collecting royalties.

Affiliate(s): Leosong Copyright Management, Ltd. (London, United Kingdom and Sydney, Australia).

How to Contact: Write and submit material. Prefers cassette or VHS videocassette. Does not return unsolicited material. Reports in 4 weeks.

Music: Mostly pop; also rock, country and reggae.

CUMBERLAND MUSIC GROUP, INC., Suite 4, 30 Music Square West, Nashville TN 37203. (615)256-6822. C.E.O.: Michael E. Lawson. Music publisher and record company (Psychotronic). Works with musicians/artists and songwriters on contract. Royalty varies per contract; statutory rate to publishers per song on records.
Affiliate(s): Obsidian Music (BMI), Obfuscated Music (ASCAP), Cucumberland Music (SESAC), Perspicacious Music (BMI), Psychotronic Publishing (BMI), S.U.Y.T. Publishing (BMI), zzi music (ASCAP).
How to Contact: Submit demo tape—unsolicited submissions OK. Prefers cassette, DAT or VHS videocassette (if available) with 3-5 songs and lyric sheet. SASE. Reports in 2 months.
Music: All types. Published "Throwing Stones" (by Tommy Thompson); "Maria" (by John Keane) and "Rose on Fire" (by J. Thomas Griffith) all recorded by The Dillards on Vanguard Records (folk rock).
Tips: "Have patience, we will contact you if we can use material."

CUNNINGHAM MUSIC, 23494 Lahser, Southfield MI 48034. (313)948-9787. President: Jerome Cunningham. Music publisher. BMI. Estab. 1988. Publishes 3-8 songs/year; publishes 2 new songwriters/year. Receives 4-6 submissions/month. Teams collaborators. Pays standard royalty.
How to Contact: Submit a demo tape by mail—unsolicited submissions are OK. Prefers cassette (or VHS videocassette if available) with 3 songs and lyric sheet. SASE. Reports in 3 weeks.
Music: Mostly R&B, gospel and jazz; also pop and rock. Published "Can't Teach Old Dog Tricks" written and recorded by Vernon B. on 2-Hot Records (R&B).
Tips: Main reason for rejection of submitted material includes: "Incomplete songs, no melody involved. Overall, just poorly prepared presentations."

CUPIT MUSIC, P.O. Box 121904, Nashville TN 37212. (615)731-0100. President: Jerry Cupit. Music publisher and record producer (Jerry Cupit Productions). BMI and ASCAP. Publishes 30 songs/year; publishes 6 new songwriters/year. Receives 20-40 submissions/month. Hires staff songwriters. Works with composers and lyricists/ teams collaborators. Pays standard 50% royalty.
Affiliate(s): Cupit Music (BMI), Cupit Memories (ASCAP).
How to Contact: Submit a demo tape by mail—unsolicited submissions are OK. Prefers cassette with 5 songs and lyric sheet. "Submit tapes with SASE to Eric Marcus. We do not return tapes." Reports in 8 weeks.
Music: Mostly country, southern rock and gospel; also R&B. Published "I Know What You Got Up Your Sleeve," recorded by Hank Williams Jr. on Warner Bros. Records; "The Biggest Thing Around Here," recorded by The Roys on MCA Records; and "For Crying Out Loud," recorded by Clinton Gregory on Step One Records.
Tips: "Keep vocals up front on demos."

D.S.M. PRODUCERS INC., 161 W. 54th, New York NY 10019. (212)245-0006. Producer: Suzan Bader. Music publisher, record producer and management firm (American Steel Management Co.). ASCAP. Estab. 1979. Publishes 25 songs/year; publishes 10 new songwriters/year. Receives 1,000 submissions/year. Works with composers and lyricists. Pays standard royalty.
Affiliate(s): Decidedly Superior Music (BMI).
How to Contact: Write or call first and obtain permission to submit. Prefers cassette (or VHS videocassette) and lyric or lead sheet. SASE. "Include SASE or we do not review nor respond to material." Reports in 3 months.
Music: Mostly top 40, R&B/dance, CHR and rock; also jazz, country and instrumental tracks for background music. Published "I've Been Hurt," written and recorded by H. Lacy (R&B, rock); "Little Thing in Life," written and recorded by Peter Halperin (R&B, jazz); and "Saloon Goonies," written and recorded by Ron Mendelsohn, both on AACL Records (comedy).
Tips: "Get your demo to sound like a master."

DAGENE MUSIC, P.O. Box 410851, San Francisco CA 94141. (415)822-1530. President: David Alston. Music publisher, record company (Cabletown Corp.) and record producer (Classic Disc Production). ASCAP. Estab. 1986. Hires staff songwriters. Works with composers; teams collaborators. Pays standard royalty.
Affiliate(s): Dagene Music, 1956 Music.
How to Contact: Write or call first and obtain permission to submit a tape. Prefers cassette with 2 songs and lyric sheet. "Be sure to obtain permission before sending any material." Does not return unsolicited material. Reports in 1 month.
Music: Mostly R&B/rap, dance and pop. Published "Mind Ya Own" (by Bernard Henderson/Marcus Justice), recorded by 2wo-Dominatorz on Dagene Records; "Started Life" (by David/M. Campbell), recorded by Star Child on Dagene Records; and "Lies," written and recorded by David on Cabletown Records (all rap).

Tips: "It's what's in the groove that makes people move."

DAN THE MAN MUSIC, P.O. Box 81422, Cleveland OH 44181-0422. President: Daniel L. Bischoff. Music publisher, record company (Dan The Man Records) and management firm (Daniel Bischoff Management). ASCAP, BMI. "We have some major label connections. Always looking for top country hit material. Also interested in strong pop-rock material."
Affiliate(s): Bischoff Music Publishing Co. (BMI).
How to Contact: Submit a demo tape—unsolicited submissions OK. Please send cassette or VHS tape and lyrics. "When sending material to us please send a SASE with proper postage for return." Reports in 1 month.
Music: Country, pop/rock. Published "Gently Break A Heart," (by C. Brumfield), recorded by Tommy Becker (country); and "High Priced Gasoline" (by D. Bischoff and S. Bischoff), recorded by Dan The Man on Dan The Man Records (country).

DARBONNE PUBLISHING CO., Route 3, Box 172, Haynesville LA 71038. (318)927-5253. President: Edward N. Dettenheim. Music publisher and record company (Wings Record Co.). BMI. Estab. 1987. Publishes 50 songs/year; publishes 8-10 new songwriters/year. Works with composers and lyricists; teams collaborators. Pays standard royalty.
How to Contact: Submit a demo tape—unsolicited submissions are OK. Prefers cassette or 7½ ips reel-to-reel with up to 12 songs and lyric sheet. SASE. Reports in 6 weeks.
Music: Mostly country and gospel. Published "Bitter Taste of Leaving," written and recorded by T.J. Lynn on Wings Records (country); "Mama" (by E. Dettenheim), recorded by Donna Ray on Wings Records (country); and "Turner Hotel" (by E. Dettenheim), recorded by T.J. Lynn on Wings Records (country).
Tips: "The better the demo—the better your chances of interesting your listener."

JEFF DAYTON MUSIC, P.O. Box 9296, Scottsdale AZ 85252. (602)837-8650. President: Jeff Dayton. Music publisher and record company (Winners Circle). BMI. Estab. 1983. Publishes 10 songs/year; publishes 2 new songwriters/year. Pays standard royalty.
Affiliate(s): Not Yet Music (BMI).
How to Contact: Write first and obtain permission to submit a tape. Prefers cassette with 2 songs and lyric sheet. Does not return unsolicited material. Reports in 2-3 weeks.
Music: Mostly country; also bluegrass and pop. Published "So Blue" (by J. Dayton), recorded by J. Dayton Band (country); "It Ain't Over" (by J. Dayton), recorded by Blaine Brown (country); and "15 Minutes" (by Dayton/Rutowski), recorded by J. Dayton Band (swing), all on Winners Circle Records.

DE DAN MUSIC, 200 Regent Dr., Winston-Salem NC 27103. (919)768-1298. Contact: Dave Passerallo. Music publisher, record company (Boom/Power Play Records) and record producer (Boom Productions Inc.). BMI. Estab. 1989. Publishes 24 songs/year; publishes 2 new songwriters/year. Teams collaborators. Pays standard royalty.
How to Contact: Write first and obtain permission to submit a tape. Prefers cassette or VHS videocassette with 2 songs and lead sheet. SASE. Reports in 3 weeks.
Music: Mostly pop and rock; also rap. Published "I Wanna Know," by Rodney Ballad and John Cody; "Ripped Jeans" and "The Good Ones," both written by John Cody; all produced by D. Passerallo for Boom Productions on Boom/Powerplay Records.
Tips: "Submissions must be worthy of national release and have mass appeal."

THE EDWARD DE MILES MUSIC COMPANY, 8th Fl., 4475 Allisonville Rd., Indianapolis IN 46205. (317)546-2912 or 549-9006. Attn: Professional Manager. Music publisher, record company (Sahara Records), management, bookings and promotions. BMI. Estab. 1984. Publishes 50-75 songs/year; publishes 5 new songwriters/year. Receives 250 submissions/year. Hires staff songwriters. Works with composers and lyricists; teams collaborators. Pays standard royalty of 50%.
How to Contact: Submit demo tape—unsolicited submissions OK. Prefers cassette with 1-3 songs and a lyric sheet. SASE. Does not return unsolicited material. Reports in 1 month.
Music: Mostly top 40 pop/rock, R&B/dance and C&W; also musical scores for TV, radio, films and jingles. Published "Hooked on U" and "Moments," written and recorded by Steve Lynn (R&B); and "No Mercy" (by D. Evans and A. Mitchell), recorded by Multiple Choice (rap), all on Sahara Records.
Tips: "Copyright all songs before submitting to us."

DEAN ENTERPRISES MUSIC PUBLISHING, P.O. Box 620, Redwood Estates CA 95044-0620. (408)353-1006. Attn: Executive Director. Music publisher, record producer, record company (Centaur Records); Member: NAS, TSA, CMRRA, NARAS, Harry Fox Agency. Estab. 1989. Publishes 4-6 songs/year; publishes 3-5 new songwriters/year. Receives 80 submissions/month. Pays standard royalty to writers.

Affiliate(s): Whispering Echoes Music (ASCAP), Mikezel Music Co. (ASCAP) and Teenie Deanie Music Co. (BMI).
How to Contact: "Unsolicited submissions are OK. Prefers maximum of 6 songs with typed lyric sheets and brief letter of introduction. Material must be copyrighted and unassigned. Prefers to keep tapes on file, but will return if fully paid SASE is included. A free evaluation is given with first class SASE, even if tape not returned. Reports in 2-6 weeks. PLEASE, no phone calls. Show name, address, phone number and (c) sign on tape and lyric sheets."
Music: Mostly country, pop, novelty, MOR/easy listening, soft/easy rock, dance (Hi NRG, house, pop), folk, top 40, R&B and some instrumental music which could qualify as movie/TV themes or background music. No rap music, jazz, heavy metal, punk/acid rock. Published "If I Turn Off The Red Light," written and recorded by Jackie Lee Carlyle, "That's Not Me" (by Don Castle) , recorded by Tom Horner and "Like We Used To Do," written and recorded by Bobby Petersen all on Centaur Records (country singles).
Tips: "Learn to handle rejection. Listen to the feedback you get. Learn your craft. Join songwriting organizations, read songwriting books and network as much as possible. Opportunity, talent and connections are the name of the game in the music industry. Watch out for the sharks. NEVER pay to have your song published or recorded if you're a songwriter."

DELEV MUSIC COMPANY, 7231 Mansfield Ave., Philadelphia PA 19138-1620. (215)276-8861. President: W. Lloyd Lucas. Music publisher, record company (Surprize Records, Inc.), record producer and management. BMI, ASCAP, SESAC, SGA, and CMRRA. Publishes 6-10 songs/year; publishes 6-10 new songwriters/year. Pays standard royalty.
Affiliate(s): Sign of the Ram Music (ASCAP) and Gemini Lady Music (SESAC).
How to Contact: Submit demo tape—unsolicited submissions OK. Prefers cassette (or VHS videocassette) with 1-3 songs and lyric sheet. "Video must be in VHS format and as professionally done as possible. It does not necessarily have to be done at a professional video studio, but should be a very good quality production showcasing artist's performance." SASE. "We will not accept certified mail." Reports in 1 month.
Music: R&B ballad and dance-oriented, contemporary Christian/gospel, pop ballads, crossover and country/western. Published "Fat Girls" (by Heston, Webb, Walker/Hudson); recorded by KeeWee on Surprize Records (R&B Rap); "As Far As I Know" (by McInnis/Van/Kermeen); recorded by Marjorie-Jean on Carmel Records (A/C) and "Too Weak to Wait For Your Love" (by Hoch/Saputo); recorded by Alease Medley on Surpize Records (R&B jazz).
Tips: "Songs submitted must be lyrically and melodically strong with good strong hook lines, and tell a story that will appeal to and be related to by the radio-listening and record-buying public. Most important is that the demo be a clear quality product with understandable vocal and lyrics out front."

*FRANK DELL MUSIC, Box 7171, Duluth MN 55807. (218)628-3003. President: Frank Dell. Music publisher, record company, record producer and management. Estab. 1980. Publishes 2 songs/year. Works with composers and lyricists; teams collaborators. Pays standard royalty.
Affiliate(s): Albindell Music (BMI).
How to Contact: Submit demo tape by mail. Unsolicited submissions are OK. Prefers cassette. SASE. Reports in 3 weeks.
Music: Mostly country, gospel and pop. Published "Memories" written and recorded by Frank Dell; "She'll Be There" (by F. Dell and D. Yargling) and *Where Rose Never Fades* (by various), both recorded by Frank Dell all on MSM Records (country).

DEMI MONDE RECORDS & PUBLISHING LTD., Foel Studio, Llanfair Caereinion, POWYS, **Wales.** Phone: (0938)810758 and (0952)883962. Managing Director: Dave Anderson. Music publisher, record company (Demi Monde Records & Publishing Ltd.), record producer (Dave Anderson). Member MCPS. Estab. 1983. Publishes 50-70 songs/year; publishes 10-15 new songwriters/year. Receives 20 submissions/month. Works with composers and lyricists; teams collaborators. Pays standard royalty.
How to Contact: Submit a demo tape—unsolicited submissions are OK. Prefers cassette (or VHS videocassette) with 3-4 songs. SAE and IRC. Reports in 1 month.
Music: Mostly rock, R&B and pop. Published "I Feel So Lazy" (by D. Allen), recorded by Gong on Demi Monde Records (rock); "Phalarn Dawn" (by E. Wynne), recorded by Ozric Tentacles on Demi Monde Records (rock); and "Pioneer" (by D. Anderson), recorded by Amon Dual on Demi Monde Records (rock).

DENNY MUSIC GROUP, 3325 Fairmont Dr., Nashville TN 37203-1004. (615)269-4847. Contact: Pandora Denny. ASCAP, BMI, SESAC. Estab. 1983. Music publisher, record company (Dollie Record Co., Jed Record Production) and record producer. "Also owns Denny's Den, a 24-track recording studio designed for songwriters, which won a Grammy in 1990." Publishes 100 songs/year; 20 new songwriters/year. Works with composer and lyricists; teams collaborators. Pays standard royalty.

How to Contact: Write or call first and obtain permission to submit. Prefers cassette with 3 songs and lyric sheet. Reports in 6 weeks.
Music: Mostly country, gospel and MOR. Published "Cashmere Cowboy" (by F. Hannaway, country); "Inside Information" (by J. Martin, R&B); and "Closer to You" (by T. Rooney, pop).

*DIAMOND WIND MUSIC, P.O. Box 311, Estero FL 33928. (813)267-6578. FAX: (813)267-6000. President: Reenie Diamond. Music publisher, record company (Diamond Wind Records) and record producer (Diamond Wind Productions). BMI. Estab. 1991. Publishes 25-50 songs/year; publishes 10 new songwriters/year. Works with composers and lyricists; teams collaborators. Pays standard royalty.
How to Contact: Write or call first and obtain permission to submit. Prefers cassette (or VHS videocassette) with 3 songs and lyric sheet. "Photo and bio extremely helpful." Does not return unsolicited material. Reports in 2 weeks.
Music: Mostly country, country blues and country pop/rock; also pop and crossover. Published "Forget Him" (by Reenie Diamond), recorded by Bronze Bonneville on Continental Records; "Just For Today," written and recorded by Robert Gomes on A.M.I. Records; and "There's a Woman" (by Janie Eiben and Reenie Diamond), recorded by Janie Eiben on Diamond Wind Records.
Tips: "Prepare your demo thoughtfully with a clean, upfront demo."

DINGO MUSIC, 4, Galleria Del Corso, Milan **Italy** 20122. Phone: (02)76021141. FAX: 0039/2/76021141. Managing Director: Guido Palma. Music publisher and record company (Top Records). SIAE. Estab. 1977. Publishes 30-35 songs/year; publishes 5 new songwriters/year. Hires staff writers. Works with composers and lyricists. Pays standard royalty of 50% and 10% on printed copies.
Affiliate(s): U.C.P. (Ging).
How to Contact: Submit demo tape by mail—unsolicited submissions are OK. Prefers cassette with 2 songs. SAE and IRC. Reports in 2 weeks.
Music: Mostly interested in rock, pop and R&B (pop); also New Age and gospel. Published "Lambada" (by Do Berman) on Top Records; "Per Un Po" (by Palma) on Dingo Records (pop); and "La Vita di un Uomo" (by Caminiti) on Kiwi Records (pop).

DIRECT MANAGEMENT GROUP, #G, 947 N. La Cienega Bl., Los Angeles CA 90069. (310)854-3535. Partners: Martin Kirkup and Steve Jensen. ASCAP, BMI. Estab. 1989. Publishes 10 songs/year; publishes 2-5 new songwriters/year. Works with composers and lyricists; teams collaborators. Pays variable royalty.
Affiliate(s): Direct World Music (ASCAP), Direct Planet Music (BMI).
How to Contact: Write first and obtain permission to submit a tape. Prefers cassette with 3 songs and lyric and lead sheet. SASE. Reports in 2 months.
Music: Mostly rock, pop and alternative. Published "Something New" and "So Much for Love" (by Hanes/Sheldon), recorded by S. Hoffs on Columbia (rock/pop).

DOC PUBLISHING, #4 Lilac Court, Newport News VA 23601. (804)591-2717. A&R: Judith Guthro. Music publisher. SESAC, BMI, ASCAP, SOCAN. Estab. 1975. Publishes 30-40 songs/year; 20 new songwriters/year. Works with composers and lyricists; teams collaborators. Pays standard royalty.
Affiliate(s): Dream Machine (SESAC), Doc Holiday Music (ASCAP).
How to Contact: Submit a demo tape—unsolicited submissions are OK. Does not return submissions. Reports in 2 weeks.
Music: Mostly country and cajun. Published "Call of The Dove," written and recorded by John Lockhart; and "Honky Tonk Herd," written and recorded by Doc Holiday, both on Tug Boat Records (country).

*DON'T CALL ME (D.C.M.) MUSIC, Agmerhurst House, Kitchenham Rd., Ashburnham, Nr. Battle, Sussex TN33 9NB **England.** M. Director: Mr. Bickersteth. Music publisher. PRS. Estab. 1986. Publishes 50 songs/year; 2 new songwriters/year. Sometimes hires staff writers. Teams collaborators. Pays 50-70% depending upon establishment.
How to Contact: Obtain permission before submitting demo tape. Prefers cassette (or VHS videocassette) with 3-5 songs and lyric or lead sheets. "Submissions should be clearly marked with name, address and telephone number." SASE. Reports in 4 weeks.
Music: Mostly rock; also inspirational, folk and blends/fusions. Published "Brian" (by Silas Crawley), recorded by Fat and Frantic (rock skiffle); "Wake Up!" (by V. Strachan), recorded by Mind the Gap (gospel); and "Mystery of Universe" recorded by Clarinet Connection; all on I'll Call You Records.
Tips: "Will consider most styles of music especially acoustic songs at this time."

Listings of companies in countries other than the U.S. have the name of the country in boldface type.

DOOR KNOB MUSIC PUBLISHING, INC., 3950 N. Mt. Juliet Rd., Mt. Juliet TN 37122. (615)754-0417. Contact: Karen Jeglum Kennedy. Music publisher, record company (Door Knob Records, Society Records), record producer (Gene Kennedy Enterprises, Inc.). BMI. Estab. 1975. Publishes 20-25 songs/year; publishes 10-15 new songwriters/year. Works with composers and lyricists. Pays standard royalty.
Affiliate(s): Chip 'n' Dale Music Publishers, Inc. (ASCAP), Lodestar Music, A Division of Gene Kennedy Enterprises, Inc. (SESAC).
How to Contact: Submit a demo tape by mail—unsolicited submissions are OK. Prefers cassette with 1-3 songs and lyric sheet. Include SASE for tape return and/or response. Send regular mail. SASE. Reports in 1 week.
Music: Mostly country and gospel. Published "Beyond Tonight" (by Tommy Willoughby), recorded by Bill Young on Polygram Records; "Mr. Jones, Final Chapter" (by Al Downing), recorded by Big Al Downing on Tug Boat Records; "Forever" (by Tommy Carini), recorded by Brandywine on Door Knob Records (all country).
Tips: "Respect our submission policy and keep trying."

BUSTER DOSS MUSIC, Box 13, Estill Springs TN 37330. (615)649-2577. President: Buster Doss. Music publisher and record company (Stardust). BMI. Estab. 1959. Publishes 500 songs/year; publishes 50 new songwriters/year. Teams collaborators. Pays standard royalty.
How to Contact: Write or call first and obtain permission to submit a tape. Prefers cassette with 2 songs and lyric sheets. SASE. Reports in 1 week.
Music: Mostly country; also rock. Published "You're Gonna Be Mine Tonight" (by Buster Doss), recorded by J.C. Hatfield; and "A Little While," written and recorded by Rooster Quantrell, both on Stardust Records.

*DREZDON BLACQUE MUSIC, 414 N. Quaker Lane, Hyde Park NY 12538. (914)229-7580. Contact: Lisa Fairbanks. Music publisher. ASCAP. Estab. 1986. Publishes 20 songs/year; publishes 1 or 2 new songwriters/year. Pays standard royalty.
How to Contact: Write first and obtain permission to submit a tape. Prefers cassette (or VHS videocassette if available) with up to 4 songs and lyric sheet. Please enclose SASE if to be returned. Does not return unsolicited material. Reports in 1 month.
Music: Mostly rock, pop and R&B; also country. Published "Angeline" (by George Fletcher); "Heart to Heart" (by Lisa Fairbanks); "Can't You See" (by Fairbanks/Fletcher); all recorded by Drezdon Blacque on FLG Records (rock).
Tips: "Don't be content on 'the same old, same old.' We want hooky pop songs a la Heart, Alannah Myles and Fleetwood Mac."

DUANE MUSIC, INC., 382 Clarence Ave., Sunnyvale CA 94086. (408)739-6133. President: Garrie Thompson. Music publisher. BMI. Publishes 10-20 songs/year; publishes 1 new songwriter/year. Pays standard royalty.
Affiliate(s): Morhits Publishing (BMI).
How to Contact: Prefers cassette with 1-2 songs. SASE. Reports in 1 month.
Music: Blues, country, disco, easy listening, rock, soul and top 40/pop. Published "Little Girl," recorded by The Syndicate of Sound & Ban (rock); "Warm Tender Love," recorded by Percy Sledge (soul); and "My Adorable One," recorded by Joe Simon (blues).

DUPUY RECORDS/PRODUCTIONS/PUBLISHING, INC., 2505 North Verdugo Rd., Glendale CA 91208. (818)241-6732. President: Pedro Dupuy. Music publisher, record company and record producer. ASCAP. Songwriters Guild. Estab. 1980. Publishes 50 songs/year; publishes 4 new songwriters/year. Works with composers and lyricists; teams collaborators. Hires staff writers. Pays standard royalty.
How to Contact: Write or call first about your interest or arrange a personal interview. Prefers cassette with 2-4 songs and lyric sheet. SASE. Reports in 1 month.
Music: Mostly R&B and pop; also easy listening, jazz, MOR, soul and top 40. Published "Find a Way," "I Don't Wanna Know," "Precious Love," "Livin for Your Love" and "Show Me The Way," all written and recorded by Gordon Gilman. Other artists include Robert Feeney, John Anthony, Joe Warner, Jon Rider and Kimo Kane.
Tips: "Songs should have very definitive lyrics with hook."

EARTHSCREAM MUSIC PUBLISHING CO., Suite A, 2036 Pasket, Houston TX 77092. (713)688-8067. Contact: Jeff Johnson. Music publisher, record company and record producer. Estab. 1975. BMI. Publishes 12 songs/year; publishes 4 new songwriters/year. Pays standard royalty.

How to Contact: Prefers cassette (or videocassette) with 2-5 songs and lyric sheet. SASE. Reports in 6 weeks.
Music: New rock and top 40/pop. Published "Break Away," written and recorded by Pauline Knox (pop rock); "Goodbye Sexy Carol" written and recorded by Terry Mitchell (new age) and "Do You Remember" (by Pennington/Wells); recorded by Perfect Strangers (pop rock), all on Weeny Dog Records.

ECCENTRAX MUSIC CO., Rt. 1 Box 1675-C, Grayling MI 49738. (517)348-1136. President: Al Bondar. Music publisher (Multi-Music Management). ASCAP. Estab. 1990. Publishes 3 songs/year; publishes 2 new songwriters/year. Works with composers and lyricists; teams collaborators. Pays standard royalty.
How to Contact: Submit a demo tape by mail—unsolicited submissions are OK. Prefers cassette with 3 songs and lyric sheet. "Please make sure lyrics are understandable." SASE. Reports in 1 month.
Music: Mostly pop, country and rock; also children's, R&B. Published "Until That Day" and "It Happens" (by A. Bondar) and "Absolutely Blue" (by G. Dove), all recorded by Allan Paul on Eccentrax Records (country).

EDUCATIONAL CIRCUS COMPANY, P.O. Box 3566, Kansas City KS 66103. President: Tony Osborne. ASCAP. 1989. Publishes 5 songs/year; publishes 2 new songwriters/year. Receives 50 submissions/year. Works with composers and lyricists; teams collaborators. Pays standard royalty of 50%. "Sometimes we will pay an advance to writer/artists."
How to Contact: Submit a demo tape by mail—unsolicited submissions are OK. Prefers cassette (Beta videocassette if available) with no more than 3 songs and lyric sheet. "Include SASE and photo, if possible." SASE. Reports in 1 month.
Music: Mostly rock, soul/R&B and children's; also gospel and Spanish. Published "Where Would I Be? (Davene's Song)," recorded by Lace (love song); "Heros," recorded by Langston (patriotic); "Counting," recorded by Blood in the Saddle (metal); and "Try to Be Like Kids" featured on an award-winning ABC-TV special, all written by Tony Osborne on ECC Records.

ELECT MUSIC PUBLISHING, P.O. Box 22, Underhill VT 05489. (802)899-3787. Founder: Bobby Hackney. Music publisher and record company (LBI Records). BMI. Estab. 1980. Publishes 24 songs/year; publishes 3 new songwriters/year. Works with composers and/or lyricists; teams collaborators. Pays standard royalty.
How to Contact: Submit a demo tape by mail—unsolicited submissions are OK. Prefers cassette and VHS videocassette with 3-4 songs and lyric sheet. SASE.
Music: Mostly reggae, R&B and rap; also New Age, rock and some country. Published "A Little Closer," recorded by The Hackneys (R&B); "Be My Love," recorded by Lambsbread (reggae-rap); and "No Ticket Required," recorded by Lambsbread (reggae); all written by Bobby Hackney and recorded on LBI Records.
Tips: "Send your best works for consideration. Produce your demos as best you can for clarity. Don't send instrumentals."

EMANDELL TUNES, 10220 Glade Ave., Chatsworth CA 91311. (818)341-2264. President/Administrator: Leroy C. Lovett, Jr. Estab. 1979. Publishes 6-12 songs/year; 3-4 new songwriters. Receives 10-15 submissions/month. Pays standard royalty.
Affiliate(s): Ben-Lee Music (BMI), Birthright Music (ASCAP), Northworth Songs (SESAC), Chinwah Songs, Gertrude Music (SESAC), LMS Print/Publishing Co. and Nadine Music International in Zurich, Switzerland.
How to Contact: Write first to get permission to submit tape. Prefers cassette (or videocassette) with 4-5 songs and lead or lyric sheet. Include bio of writer, singer or group. SASE. Reports in 4-6 weeks.
Music: Inspirational, contemporary gospel and chorals. Published "High Places," (by Kevin Gaston); and "Surely Goodness and Mercy" (by Kevin Allen and Peppy Smith), both recorded by the Elect on WFL Records (urban contemporary); "Joy Great Joy" (by Dorinda Clark-Cole), recorded by UNAC 90-Mass Choir on WFL Records (gospel); "Renew Me" (by Eddie Howard), recorded by UNAC 90-Mass Choir on WFL Records (gospel); "The Center of Hope" (by Albert Hartdige), recorded by Voices of Rhema on WFL Records (gospel). All above are SESAC selections. Licensed "How I Got Over" w/m Clara Ward Composition (Gertrude Music-SESAC) in the TV Mini Series "Call To Glory" and "Come On Children, Let's Sing," by Edwin Hawkins (Birthright Music-ASCAP) in a *LaVerne & Shirley* TV episode.
Tips: "Submit high quality demos but keep it simple—no production extras."

EMPTY SKY MUSIC COMPANY, 14th St., P.O. Box 626, Verplanck NY 10596. Promotional Manager: Lisa Lancaster. Music publisher, record company (Empty Sky, Yankee, Verplanck) and record producer (Rick Carbone for Empty Sky). ASCAP, BMI. Estab. 1982. Publishes 15-20 songs/year; publishes

10 new songwriters/year. Works with composer and lyricists; teams collaborators. Pays standard royalty.
Affiliate(s): Empty Sky Music (ASCAP) and Rick Carbone Music (BMI).
How to Contact: Submit a demo tape by mail—unsolicited submissions are OK. Prefers cassette with 3-5 songs and lyric sheet. SASE. Reports in 3 months.
Music: Mostly country, gospel and pop; also rap, rock and rap/gospel. Published "In the Name of Love," written and recorded by Steve Mercer; "Jennifer," written and recorded by Lloyd Candle; and "She's My Girl" (by Keith Alexander and Keith Nelson), recorded by Bosco, all on Empty Sky Records (all pop).

*EMZEE MUSIC, Box 3213, S. Farmingdale NY 11735. (516)420-9169. President: Maryann Zalesak. Music publisher, record company. Estab. 1970. Publishes 30 songs/year; publishes 10 new songwriters/year. Hires staff songwriters. Works with composers and lyricists; teams collaborators. Pays standard royalty.
How to Contact: Submit demo tape by mail. Unsolicited submissions are OK. Prefers cassette with 3 songs and lyric sheet. SASE. Reports in 7-8 weeks.
Music: Mostly rock, pop and country; also R&B and rap. Published "Voyeur," written and recorded by John Jace (single) and *Please Tell Me* (by Tony Novarro), recorded by Emma Zale (rock/pop LP) both on Ivory Tower Records; and "Richest Man" (by John Schachtel), recorded by Emma Zale on Emzee Records (pop/Latin single).

ENTERTAINMENT SERVICES MUSIC GROUP, 42 Music Square West, Nashville TN 37203. (615)252-8282. Executive Administrator: Curt Conroy. Music publisher. BMI. Estab. 1990. Publishes 50-60 songs/year. Pays standard royalty.
How to Contact: Submit a demo tape by mail—unsolicited submissions are OK. Prefers "good quality 3-4 song demo" and lyric sheet. "Guitar or piano-vocal OK." Does not return submitted materials. Reports within 2-6 weeks.
Music: Mostly country (traditional), country rock and country pop; also country blues. Published "I've Been Branded" (by Onassis/Madewell), recorded by Hannah Onassis on Badger Records (country pop); "Wine Over Matter," written and recorded by Pinto Bennett on P.T. Records (country); and "In the Wings," written and recorded by David Stewart on ESI Records (country).
Tips: "Write songs tailor made for certain artists and specify which songs are for which artists. *Listen closely* to current country records. Looking for well-crafted country to country/pop songs that are radio friendly. Company sponsors The Nashville Songwriters Continuing Series. Company periodically selects 12 new original songs by 12 new or unsigned writers, produces a professionally packaged cassette and distributes this cassette to industry decision makers. Selected writers contribute to production costs but enjoy having their material presented in a unique and elite fashion. Request special submission packets by mail."

ERTIS MUSIC COMPANY, P.O. Box 80691, Baton Rouge LA 70898. (504)924-3327. Publisher: Johnny Palazzotto. ASCAP. Estab. 1977. Publishes 10-15 songs/year. Pays standard royalty.
Affiliate(s): Blue Rouge Music (ASCAP).
How to Contact: Submit a demo tape by mail—unsolicited submissions are OK. Prefers cassette with 3-5 songs. SASE. Reports in 2-4 weeks.
Music: Mostly country and zydeco. Published "Come on Home" (by Major Handy), recorded by Nathan & Cha-Chas on Rounder Records (zydeco); "Come on Home," written and recorded by Major Handy on Bedrock Records (zydeco); and "Laissez Les Bon" (by Kelly, J. Didier), recorded by Queen Ida on Sonet Records (zydeco).

EVER-OPEN-EYE MUSIC, Wern Fawr Farm, Pencoed, MID, Glam CF356NB **United Kingdom.** Phone: (0656)860041. Managing Director: M.R. Blanche. Music publisher and record company (Red-Eye Records). PRS. Member PPL and MCPS. Estab. 1980. Publishes 6 songs/year. Works with composers and lyricists; teams collaborators. Pays negotiable amount.
How to Contact: Submit a demo tape —unsolicited submissions are OK. Prefers cassette (or VHS videocassette). SAE and IRC.
Music: Mostly R&B, gospel and pop; also swing. Published "Waiting for Summer" and "Silver Sea," written and recorded by Finn/Healan Universe on Red Eye Records.

Market conditions are constantly changing! If you're still using this book and it is 1994 or later, buy the newest edition of Songwriter's Market at your favorite bookstore or order directly from Writer's Digest Books.

EVOPOETICS PUBLISHING, (formerly Lion Publishing), P.O. Box 71231, Milwaukee WI 53211-7331. (414)332-7474. President: Dr. Martin Jack Rosenblum. Music publisher and record company (Roar Records). ASCAP. Estab. 1969. Receives 20 submissions/month. Works with composers.
Affiliate(s): Roar Recording, American Ranger Incorporated and Lion Publishing.
How to Contact: Write or call first and obtain permission to submit a tape. Prefers cassette and lyric sheet. "No unsolicited submissions with inquiry." SASE. Reports in 1 week.
Music: Mostly country, blues and country rock.

EXCURSION MUSIC GROUP, P.O. Box 9248, San Jose CA 95157. (408)252-3392. President: Frank T. Prins. Music publisher, record company (Excursion Records) and record producer. BMI, ASCAP. Estab. 1976. Publishes 25 songs/year; publishes 5 new songwriters/year. Hires staff writers. Works with composers and lyricists; teams collaborators. Pays standard royalty.
Affiliate(s): Echappee Music (BMI), Excursion Music (ASCAP).
How to Contact: Submit demo tape—unsolicited submissions OK. Prefers cassette or VHS videocassette with 3 songs and lyric sheet. SASE. Reports in 2 weeks.
Music: Mostly pop, country and gospel; also rock & roll and R&B. Published "Rose" (by R. Hepfner), recorded by Bobby C. on Excursion Records (country).
Tips: "Keep writing and honing your craft!"

EYE KILL MUSIC, P.O. Box 242, Woodland PA 16881. A&R: John Wesley. Music publisher. ASCAP. Estab. 1987. Publishes 10 songs/year; publishes 6 new songwriters/year. Works with composers and lyricists. Pays standard royalty.
How to Contact: Submit a demo tape by mail—unsolicited submissions are OK. Prefers cassette with 3 songs and lyric sheet. SASE. Reports in 1 month.
Music: Mostly country and rock. Published "All Over For You" (by Cindy Stone) and "Here Again" (by Guy Stone), both recorded by Paul White; "Two Lonely Hearts," written and recorded by John Maine, Jr., all on Eye Kill Records (all country).

DOUG FAIELLA PUBLISHING, 16591 County Home Rd., Marysville OH 43040. (513)644-8295. President: Doug Faiella. Music publisher, record company (Studio 7 Records) and recording studio. BMI. Estab. 1984. Publishes 25 songs/year; publishes 5 new songwriters/year. Works with composers and teams collaborators. Pays standard royalty.
How to Contact: Write to obtain permission to submit a tape. SASE. Prefers cassette with 3 songs and lyric sheets. Does not return unsolicited material. Reports in 4 weeks.
Music: Mostly country, gospel and rock.

*FAIRWOOD MUSIC LIMITED, 72 Marylebone Lane, London W1M 5FF **United Kingdom**. Phone: (01)487-5044. FAX: (071)935-2270. General Manager: Ms. Verrah Fenton. Music publisher.
Affiliate(s): Joes Songs Inc.
How to Contact: Submit a demo tape by mail—unsolicited submissions are OK. Prefers cassette with lyric sheet. Does not return unsolicited material.
Music: "Songs with good melodic structure. All categories considered." Published "Together" and "Inner City Madness and "Party Party," all written by Hamish Stuart and recorded by Paul McCartney on EMI Records.
Tips: "Regardless of the type/style of song, a basic good melody together with the best presentation affordable by the individual is an advantage."

*FAMOUS MUSIC PUBLISHING COMPANIES, Suite 1000, 3500 W. Olive Ave., Burbank CA 91505. (818)566-7000, FAX (818)566-6680. Creative Dept. Ellie Schwimmer, Jim Vellutato, Roanna Gillespie. Estab. 1929. Publishes 500+ songs/year; 5+ new songwriters/year. Hires staff songwriters. Works with composers and lyricists; teams collaborators. Pays standard royalty.
Affiliate(s): Famous Music (ASCAP) and Ensign Music (BMI).
How to Contact: Write or call first and obtain permission to submit. Prefers cassette with 3 songs and lyric sheet. Does not return unsolicited material. Reports in 1 month.
Music: Mostly rock, R&B and pop. Published "Love . . . Thy Will Be Done" (by Martika/Prince), recorded by Martika on Columbia Records; "So Intense" (by Job/Harrindeer, etc.), recorded by Lisa Fischer on Elektra Records; and "Ballad of Youth" (by Ritchie Sambora/Tom Manolda), recorded by Ritchie Sambora on Mercury Records.

F&J MUSIC. 23, Thrayle House, Stockwell Road, London SW9 0XU **United Kingdom**. (071)274-9533 and (818)962-6547. FAX: (071)737-7881 and FAX: (818)778-0225. Managing Director: Errol Jones. Music publisher and record company (Leopard Music/Jet Set International Records). PRS, BMI. Estab. 1978. Publishes 75 songs/year. Publishes 35 new songwriters/year. Works with composers and lyricists; teams collaborators. Pays standard royalty.

Affiliate(s): EURUSA Worldwide Publishing Affiliate (BMI) and F&J Music Publishing (PRS).
How to Contact: Write first and obtain permission to submit. Prefers cassette (or VHS PAL videocassette) with 3 songs, lyric sheet and lead sheet. Include biography, resume and picture. SASE. Reports in 2 weeks.
Music: Mostly dance, soul and pop; also ballads, reggae and gospel. Published "Time After Time," (by Guy Spell), recorded by Rico J. on Leopard Music/Jet Set International Records (disco/soul); "I Need You" (by F. Campbell/E. North Jr.), recorded by Big Africa (soul/reggae); and "God is Beauty," written and recorded by Evelyn Ladimeji (gospel); both on Leopard Music.

FEZSONGS, 429 S. Lewis Rd., Royersford PA 19468. (215)948-8228. FAX: (215)948-4175. President: Jim Femino. Music publisher, record company (Road Records) and record producer (independent). ASCAP. Estab. 1970. Publishes 12-15 songs/year; publishes 1-2 new songwriters/year. Receives 12-20 submissions/month. Works with composers and lyricists; teams collaborators. Pays standard royalty. "Charges in advance for demo recording services, only if needed."
How to Contact: Submit a demo tape by mail – unsolicited submissions are OK. Prefers cassette (or VHS videocassette) with 3-4 songs and lyric sheet. SASE. Reports in 4-6 weeks.
Music: Mostly rock, country and cross-over. Published "Where Do You Go" (by J. Femino and J. Douglas) and "Maybe" (by J. Femino) both country; and "Next Stop Ecstasy" (by J. Femino and H. Linsley), all recorded by Jim Femino on Road Records (rock).
Tips: Write, write, re-write then write some more."

FIRST MILLION MUSIC, INC., Dept. SM, #207, 50 Music Square West, Nashville TN 37203. (615)329-2591. Vice President: Peggy Bradley. Music publisher. ASCAP. Estab. 1983. Publishes 4 songs/year; 2 new songwriters/year. Pays standard royalty.
Affiliate(s): Old Guide Music (BMI).
How to Contact: Submit a demo tape by mail – unsolicited submissions are OK. Prefers cassette with 3 songs and lyric sheet. SASE. Reports in 2 weeks.
Music: Mostly country, pop and R&B. Published "Love (by Ruddy), recorded by Jill Jordan on Maxx Records (country/uptempo); and "Jewel of the Mississippi" (by Lips Prat), recorded by Don Juan on Maxx Records (country/ballad).

FIRST RELEASE MUSIC PUBLISHING, 6124 Selma Ave., Hollywood CA 90028. (213)469-2296. Creative Director: Danny Howell. Music publisher. BMI, ASCAP, SACEM, GEMA, PRS, MCPS. Publishes 30-50 songs/year. Hires staff songwriters. Pays standard royalty; co-publishing negotiable.
Affiliate(s): Fully Conscious Music, Criterion Music, Cadillac Pink, Atlantic Music, Illegeal Songs, I.R.S. Songs, Reggatta Music, Magnetic Publishing Ltd., Animal Logic Publishing and Blue Turtle Music.
How to Contact: "We *never* accept unsolicited tapes or phone calls – you must have referral or be requested." Returns all unsolicited material. Reports only if interested, but "retain personally written critique for every song I agree to accept."
Music: "We are interested in great songs and great writers. We are currently successful in all areas." Published "Maybe It Was Memphis" (by Mike Anderson), recorded by Pam Tillis on Arista Records (country); and "This Girl" (by C. Converse and M. Mahan), recorded by Tina Bellison on Impact Records (R&B).
Tips: "Show up at one of my guest workshops and play me the last song you would ever play for a publisher; not the worst, the last! Educate yourself as to what writers we represent before pitching me (i.e., Sting, Lyle Lovett, Concrete Blonde)."

FIRST TIME MUSIC (PUBLISHING) U.K. LTD., Sovereign House, 12 Trewartha Road, Praa Sands, Penzance, Cornwall TR20 9ST **United Kingdom**. Phone: (0736)762826. FAX: (0736)763328. Managing Director: Roderick G. Jones. Music publisher, record company (First Time Records, licensed and subsidiary labels), record producer and management firm (First Time Management and Production Co.). PRS. Member of MCPS. Estab. 1986. Publishes 500-750 songs/year; 20-50 new songwriters/year. Hires staff writers. Works with composers and lyricists; teams collaborators. Pays standard royalty; "50-60% to established and up-and-coming writers with the right attitude."
Affiliate(s): Subsidiary and administered catalogues. Sub-publishing worldwide (new associations welcome).
How to Contact: Submit a demo tape – unsolicited submissions are OK. Prefers cassette, 1⅞ ips cassette (or VHS videocassette "of professional quality") with unlimited number of songs and lyric or lead sheets, but not necessary. Reports in 4-10 weeks. SASE in U.K. – SAE and IRC if outside U.K. "Postal costs in the U.K. are much higher than the U.S. – one IRC doesn't even cover the cost of a letter to the U.S., let alone the return of cassettes. Enclose the correct amount for return and contact as stated." Reports in 4-10 weeks.

Music: Mostly country and folk, pop/soul/top 20/rock, country with an Irish/Scottish crossover; also gospel/Christian. Published "The Robinsons Ball" (by Pete Arnold), recorded by Brendan Shine on Play Records (MOR/country); "Sentimental Over You" (by Rod Jones/Colin Eade), recorded by PJ Proby on J'ace Records (pop); "I Wouldn't Have It Any Other Way" (by Bill Allen), recorded by Kenny Paul on Luvinikind Records (country).

Tips: "Have a professional approach—present well produced demos. First impressions are important and may be the only chance you get. Remember that you as a writer/artist are in a competitive market. As an active independent -international publisher we require good writers/artists and product. As a company we seek to work with writers. If the product is good then we generally come up with something in the way of covers. Writers are advised to join the Guild of International Songwriters and Composers in the United Kingdom."

FIVE ROSES PUBLISHING COMPANY, P.O. Box 417, White Sulpher Springs NY 12787. (914)292-4042. President: Sammie Lee Marler. Music publisher. Consultant, management. BMI. Estab. 1989. Publishes 50-75 songs/year. Works with composers and lyricists; teams collaborators. Pays standard royalty.

How to Contact: Submit a demo tape by mail—unsolicited submissions are OK. Prefers cassette with 3 songs. SASE. Reports in 2 weeks.

Music: Mostly country and western, bluegrass, country rock, country gospel, light. Published "If the Good Lord Willin' " (by Marler/Royce), recorded by Jerry Hanlon on Universal Athena (country gospel); "A Love Like You" (by Marler/Smyly), recorded by Lamar Smyly; and "When the Going Gets Tough" (by John Custodie), recorded by John Custodie both on Five Roses (country).

Tips: "We care about the songwriter and keep in personal contact with them. We are one happy family at Five Roses. Always include a SASE for material return. If you are new at songwriting and are looking for a publisher to further your career you should contact us first. We have opened doors for many new songwriters. We also have a Nashville Branch office."

FLAMING STAR WEST, Box 2400, Gardnerville NY 89410. (702)265-6825. Owner: Ted Snyder. Music publisher, record company (Flaming Star Records) and record producer (Flaming Star Records). BMI. Estab. 1988. Works with composers and lyricists; and teams collaborators. Pays standard royalty.

How to Contact: Submit a demo tape by mail—unsolicited submissions are OK. Prefers cassette or VHS videocassette with up to 5 songs and lyric sheets. "If you are sure of your music, you may send more than 5 songs. No heavy metal. All other types." SASE. Reports in 3 weeks.

Music: Mostly country, pop and rock and country rock; also gospel, R&B, New Age and calypso. Published "Jezabel" (country) and "For the Sake of My Children" (ballad), both written and recorded by Ted Snyder on Flaming Star Records.

Tips: "Listen to what is on the radio, but be original. Put feeling into your songs. We're looking for songs and artists to promote overseas. Flaming Star Records is a launching pad for the new recording artist. We try to help where we can."

FOCAL POINT MUSIC PUBLISHERS (BMI), 920 McArthur Blvd., Warner Robins GA 31093. (912)923-6533. Manager: Ray Melton. Music publisher and record company. BMI. Estab. 1964. Publishes 4 songs/year; publishes 1 new songwriter/year. Receives 50 submissions/year. Works with composers. Pays standard royalty. "Songwriters must have BMI affiliation."

How to Contact: Write first to get permission to send a tape. Prefers cassette with 2-4 songs and lead sheet. Prefers studio produced demos. SASE. Reports in 3 months.

Music: Mostly country and gospel; also "old-style pop and humor." Published "Everything Turned Out Good" (by Helen Thomas), recorded by Barbara Richardson on Club 45 Records (country).

Tips: "Try it out on your friends. Go to workshops. Belong to a songwriters group."

FOUR NEWTON PUBLISHING, Rt. 1, Box 187-A, Whitney TX 76692. (817)694-4047. President: Allen Newton. Music publisher, record company (Pristine Records, Pleasure Records, Cactus Flats, MFN). BMI, ASCAP. Estab. 1980. Publishes 20 songs/year; publishes about 10 new songwriters/year. Receives hundreds of submissions/year. Works with composers and lyricists; teams collaborators. Pays standard royalty.

Affiliate(s): Four Newton Publishing (BMI), Stephash Publishing (ASCAP).

How to Contact: Submit a demo tape by mail—unsolicited submissions are OK. Prefers cassette with 3-6 songs and lyric sheets. SASE. Reports in 3-4 weeks.

Music: Mostly country, rock and R&B; also pop, gospel and New Age. Published "Traffic Jam" (by D. Zewalk), recorded by Darryn Zewalk (urban); "In Denver" (by A. Angelini), recorded by Andy Anderson (pop); and "The Cage Inside" (by Alon Decor), recorded by Hidden Shadows (rock) all on Pristine Records.

Tips: "Study the material charting. Learn from the pros."

FOX FARM RECORDING, 2731 Saundersville Ferry Rd., Mt. Juliet TN 37122. (615)754-2444. President: Kent Fox. Music publisher, record producer and demo production recording studio. BMI, ASCAP. Publishes 20 songs/year; publishes 5 new songwriters/year. Works with composers and lyricists; teams collaborators. Pays standard royalty.
Affiliate(s): Blueford Music (ASCAP) and Mercantile Music (BMI).
How to Contact: SASE. Prefers cassette with 4 songs and lyric sheet. Reports in 1 month.
Music: Country, bluegrass and contemporary Christian.
Tips: "If your song is good enough to become a hit, it's worth investing money for a good demo: drums, bass, guitar, keyboard, fiddle, sax, vocals etc."

FOXWORTHY MUSIC INC., 4002 Liggett Dr., San Diego CA 92106. (619)226-4152. President: Douglas Foxworthy. Music publisher, record company (Foxworthy Records) and record producer (Foxworthy Productions). BMI. Estab. 1982. Publishes 5 songs/year; publishes 1 new songwriter/year. Teams collaborators. Pays standard royalty.
Affiliate(s): Foxworthy Music (BMI), Expanding Universe Music (BMI).
How to Contact: Submit a demo tape by mail—unsolicited submissions are O.K. Prefers cassette with 3 songs and lyric sheets. Does not return unsolicited material. Reports in 6 weeks.
Music: Mostly pop, rock and R&B; also rap and new age. Published "Time Out" (by Gary Hyde), recorded by CinCinT (R&B); "Warp Drive" (by Mike Redmond), recorded by Rag Band (rap); and "Avatar" written and recorded by Foxworthy (New Age) all on Foxworthy Records.

FRADALE SONGS, P.O. Box 121015, Nashville TN 37212. President: David Leone. BMI, ASCAP. Estab. 1981. Publishes 50 songs/year; publishes 1 new songwriter/year. Receives 10 submissions/month. Works with composers and lyricists; teams collaborators. Pays standard royalty.
Affilate(s): Fradale Songs (BMI) and Fradale Tunes (ASCAP).
How to Contact: Unsolicited submissions are OK. Does not return unsolicited material. "We strongly suggest that developing writers contact us about critiquing their material—much of successful writing can be learned and Fradale offers workshops and correspondence courses for talented writers." Reports in 3 weeks.
Music: Country and gospel. Published "My Heartache is Here To Stay" (by R. Alscomb), recorded by Pending (country); "Open to Your Love" (by R. Field), recorded by Cheri Lynn on Classic Records (country/pop); and "Red Beans and Rice," written and recorded by B. Slater on Classic Records (country).

FREKO RECORDS, 417 E. Cross Timbers, Houston TX 77022. (713)694-2971. Engineers: Warren Jackson III and Freddie Kober. Music publisher, record company (Freko Records, Honeybee Records) and record producer (Freddie Kober Productions). BMI. Estab. 1976. Publishes 11 songs/year; publishes 3 new songwriters/year. Works with composers and lyricists. Pays standard royalty.
Affiliate(s): Anode Music (BMI).
How to Contact: Submit a demo tape by mail—unsolicited submissions are OK. Prefers cassette with 4-8 songs and lyric sheet. Does not return unsolicited material.
Music: Mostly R&B, rap and gospel; also country, rock and pop. Published "Going Against the Zulu" and "Hampton Inn," recorded by The Takeover (rap); "Living in the Hood," recorded by Insane Criminal; and *A Black Perspective* and "Definition of H-Town," recorded by H-Town Mastermind (rap), all on Freko Records.

FRETBOARD PUBLISHING, Box 40013, Nashville TN 37204. (615)292-2047. Contact: A&R Department. Music publisher, record company (Mosrite Records), record producer (Mark Moseley). BMI. Estab. 1963. Publishes 25 songs/year; publishes 3 new songwriters/year. Works with composers and lyricists. Pays standard royalty.
Affiliate(s): Woodgrain Publishing Co. (ASCAP).
How to Contact: Submit a demo tape by mail. Prefers cassette with 2 songs and lyric sheets. Does not return unsolicited material. Reports in 6 weeks "only if we want to hear more."
Music: Mostly country, rock (not heavy), southern gospel. Published "Even Now" (by Mark Moseley), recorded by Marie Lester (country); "Mommy's Playing Santa Claus" (by Maurice Brandon), recorded by Marie Lester (Christmas); and "Queen For a Day" (by Billy Mize), recorded by Barbara Mandrell (country); all on Mosrite Records.
Tips: "Give us time to get to your songs before you make another contact."

FRICK MUSIC PUBLISHING CO., 404 Bluegrass Ave., Madison TN 37115. (615)865-6380. Contact: Bob Frick. Music publisher, record company and record producer. BMI. Publishes 50 songs/year; publishes 2 new songwriters/year. Works with lyricists. Pays standard royalty.

How to Contact: Call first to get permission to submit. Prefers 7½ ips reel-to-reel or cassette (or videocassette) with 2-10 songs and lyric sheet. SASE. Reports in 1 month.
Music: Mostly gospel; also country, rock and top 40/pop. Published "Follow Where He Leads" by Christine Starling; "I Found Jesus in Nashville" by Lin Butler; and "I Held Up My Hands" by Frank Conrad; all recorded by Bob Scott Frick on R.E.F. Records (gospel); also "My Little Girl" by Scott Frick, and "Time, Tricks and Politics" by Eddie Isaacs.

*FROZEN INCA MUSIC, Suite 333, 1800 Peachtree St., Atlanta GA 30309. (404)355-5580. FAX: (404)351-2786. President: Michael Rothschild. Music publisher, record company and record producer. Estab. 1981. Publishes 12 songs/year; publishes 3 new songwriters/year. Works with composers and lyricists; teams collaborators. Pays negotiated percentage.
Affiliate(s): Landslide Records.
How to Contact: Submit demo tape by mail. Unsolicited submissions are OK. Prefers cassette with 6-12 songs and lyric sheet. SASE. Reports in 1 month.
Music: Mostly R&B, blues and rap; also gospel, country and rock. Published "Highway Man" (by T. Ellis and Eddie Cleaveland); "Sign of the Blues" (by T. Ellis and K. Simmons); and "My Restless Heart" (by T. Ellis) all recorded by Landslide on Alligator Records (LP).
Tips: "We look for strong rhythmic hooks."

FULLTILT MUSIC, 300 Linfield Dr., Vallejo CA 94590. (707)645-1615. President: Jack Walker. Music publisher. BMI. Estab. 1982. Publishes 1 song/year. Receives 3 submissions/year. Works with composers and lyricists; teams collaborators. Pays standard royalty
How to Contact: Submit demo tape, unsolicited submissions are OK. Prefers cassette (or VHS videocassette if available) with 3 songs and lyric sheet. SASE. Reports in 1 month.
Music: We are interested in all types of music. Published "Making Up Lies" (by Wally Jennings) on Americana Records (country single).

GALAXIA MUSICAL S.A. De C.V., Leibnitz 130, D.F. 11590 **Mexico.** (905)511-6684. Managing Director: Arq. Jose G. Cruz. Music publisher. SACM. Publishes 50 songs/year. Receives 150-200 submissions/year. Works with composers and lyricists; teams collaborators. Pays standard royalty.
How to Contact: Write first and obtain permission to submit. "Will only accept submissions from writers who are very familiar with type of music currently being produced in Mexico and Spanish speaking territories." Prefers cassette (or VHS videocassette) with 1-5 songs. SAE and IRC. Reports in 2 weeks.
Music: Pop ballads and rock.
Tips: "A well-prepared demo signals good craftsmanship. Please do not contact us if you are not very familiar with the Latin market."

*GALLO MUSIC PUBLISHERS, A Division of Gallo Africa (PTY) Ltd., P.O. Box 6216, Johannesburg 2000 **South Africa.** Phone: (011)788-0400. Managing Director: Geoff Paynter. Music publisher and record company (Gallo Record Co., Teal Trutone Records and RPM Records.) SAMRO. Estab. 1920. Publishes 500-1,000 songs/year; publishes 10-20 new songwriters/year. Works with composers and lyricists; teams collaborators. Pays negotiable percentage.
Affiliate(s): Music Publishing Co. of Africa (SAMRO), Laetrec Music (SAMRO) and Clan Music (SAMRO).
How to Contact: Submit a demo tape by mail—unsolicited submissions are OK. Prefers cassette (PAL 625 videocassette) with 4-6 songs and lyric sheet. "We do not return unsolicited material, but will contact if interested." Reports in 1 month.
Music: Mostly pop, R&B and rock; also country and gospel. Published "Shoo-Roop!" (by Monaheng Duru), recorded by Mango Grove on Atco Records (pop); "I'm in Love with a Rastaman" (Mbadui Nkosi), recorded by Mahlathini and the Mahotella Queens on Polygram Records (Mbaqanga); "Now or Never" (by Makonotela), recorded by Hugh Masakela on Novus Records (rock).
Tips: "Get the song played live in front of the type of audience you're aiming at, and see what the reaction is, before adjudging it the next smash."

*ALAN GARY MUSIC, P.O. Box 179, Palisades Park NJ 07650. President: Alan Gary. Music publisher. ASCAP. Estab. 1987. Publishes a varying number of songs/year. Works with composers and lyricists. Pays standard royalty.
How to Contact: Submit demo tape—unsolicited submissions are OK. Prefers cassette (or VHS videocassette) with lyric sheet. Does not return unsolicited material.
Music: Mostly pop, R&B and dance; also rock, A/C and country. Published "Liberation" (by Gary/Julian), recorded by Les Julian on Music Tree Records (A/C); "Love Your Way Out of This One" (by Gary/Rosen), recorded by Deborah Steel on Badcatre (contemporary country); and "Dueling Rappers" (by Gary/Free), recorded by Prophets of Boom on You Dirty Rap! Records (rap/R&B).

*GENERAL JONES MUSIC, 3252 Grenoble Lane, Memphis TN 38115. (901)365-1429. Owner: Danny Jones. Music publisher, record producer and recording engineer. Estab. 1980. BMI. Publishes 3-4 songs/year; publishes 1-2 new songwriters/year. Works with composers and lyricists; teams collaborators. Pays standard royalty.
Affiliate(s): General Jones Music (BMI) and Danny Jones Productions.
How to Contact: Write or call first and obtain permission to submit. Prefers cassette (or VHS videocassette) with 3 songs and lyric or lead sheet. SASE. Reports in 4 weeks.
Music: Rock, country and R&B. Published "King of the Cowboys" (by Larry Carney/Roy Rogers, Jr.), recorded by Roy Rogers, Jr. on RCA Records (country); "I Eat Roadkill" (by Dan Hyer), recorded by 50 FT (rock); and "Don't Cheat on Me" written and recorded by Keith Swinton and Steve Rarick (rock) all on RCA Records.

GENETIC MUSIC PUBLISHING, 10 Church Rd., Merchantville NJ 08109. (609)662-4428. Contact: Whey Cooler or Jade Starling. Music publisher, record company (Svengali) and record producer (Whey Cooler Production). ASCAP. Estab. 1982. Publishes 1-5 songs/year. Works with composers and lyricists; teams collaborators. Pays standard royalty.
How to Contact: Write or call first and obtain permission to submit a tape. Prefers cassette or VHS videocassette. SASE. Reports in 3 weeks.
Music: Mostly dance, R&B and pop; also rock and jazz. Published "2 Cool Thing," written and recorded by 2 Cool on Svengali Records (R&B/dance).
Tips: "Just submit it. If we think we can place it we'll hold it on file and submit it to projects as they arise. Should a song be chosen for a given project, we'll then publish the song."

*GFI WEST MUSIC PUBLISHING, 6201 W. Sunset Blvd., Hollywood CA 90028. (310)281-7454. A&R: Janet Jeffrey. Music publisher. Estab. 1991. Publishes 15 songs/year; publishes 9 new songwriters/year. Works with composers and lyricists; teams collaborators. Pays standard royalty.
How to Contact: Submit demo tape by mail—unsolicited submissions are OK. Prefers cassette with 1-5 songs and lyric sheet. "Submissions must be copywritten." Does not return unsolicited submissions. Reports in 3 months.
Music: Mostly pop, rock and R&B; also children's and instrumentals. Published "I Know" (by Janet Jeffrey); "Images of You" (by Janet Jeffrey/John Osher/Andy Grasso); and "Once In Awhile" (by Ramin Sakurai and Janet Jeffrey) all recorded by Janet Jeffrey on Teddy Bear Records (single).
Tips: "Strong melodies attract my attention. Also, I look for cross-over appeal as well as songs that leave you humming the words in your head."

GIFTNESS ENTERPRISE, Suite #5, 1315 Simpson Rd. NW, Atlanta GA 30314. (404)642-2645. Contact: New Song Department. Music publisher. BMI, ASCAP. Publishes 30 songs/year; publishes 15 new songwriters/year. Employs songwriters on a salary basis. Works with composers and lyricsts; teams collaborators. Pays standard royalty.
Affiliate(s): Blair Vizzion Music (BMI) and Fresh Entertainment (ASCAP).
How to Contact: Submit demo tape—unsolicited submissions are OK. Prefers cassette with 4 songs and lyric or lead sheet. SASE. Reports in 1 month.
Music: Mostly R&B, pop and rock; also country, gospel and jazz. Published "This Time" (dance) and "Always Girl" (ballad) (by Cirocco), recorded by Georgio on RCA Records; "Broken Promises" (by J. Calhoun), recorded by S.O.S. Band on Tabu/A&M Records (dance).

GIL-GAD MUSIC, 6015 Troost, Kansas City MO 64110. (816)361-8455. General Manager/Publisher: Eugene Gold. ASCAP, BMI. Estab. 1969. Music publisher and record producer. Publishes 30 or more songs/year; publishes 10 or more new songwriters/year. Teams collaborators. Pays standard royalty.
Affiliate(s): 3G's Music Co., Eugene Gold Music.
How to Contact: Prefers cassette (or videocassette) with 4-6 songs and lyric sheet. SASE. Reports in 2 months.
Music: Mostly R&B, rock and top 40/pop; also disco/dance, gospel and jazz. Published "Magic" (by Cal-Green, Ronnie & Vicky), recorded by Suspension on 3G's (R&B/top pop); "Bootie Cutie," written and recorded by Robert Newsome on 3G's (R&B); and "Diamond Feather," (by M. Murf), recorded by Bad News Band on NMI (R&B).

GLOBEART PUBLISHING, A Division of GlobeArt Inc., Suite 21F, 1755 York Ave., New York NY 10128. (212)860-3023. President: Jane Peterer. Music publisher. BMI, ASCAP. Estab. 1989. Publishes 20 songs/year; publishes 2 new songwriters/year. Works with composers and lyricists. Pays standard royalty.

Affiliate(s): GlobeSound Publishing (ASCAP).
How to Contact: Submit a demo tape by mail—unsolicited submissions are OK. Prefers cassette (or videocassette) with 3-5 songs and lyric or lead sheet. SASE. Reports in 4 weeks.
Music: Mostly pop/R&B, jazz and gospel; also New Age and country. Published "WBF" and "Tired Angel" (by Roebuch), recorded by Burning Core on Ainprep Records (rap).

GMG MUSIC, 1226 17th Ave. South, Nashville TN 37212. (615)327-1632. Vice President: Maurice Godwin. Music publisher, management firm. BMI, SESAC. Estab. 1986. Publishes 15-20 songs/year; publishes 5 new songwriters/year. Receives 400 submissions/month. Works with composers; teams collaborators. Pays standard 50% royalty.
Affiliate(s): Old Empress Music (BMI), Un-Der 16 Songs (SESAC) and Girls on Film Music (BMI).
How to Contact: Submit demo tape—unsolicited submissions OK. Prefers cassette with 4 songs. "Chrome tape (high bias). Include SASE." Reports in 1 month.
Music: Mostly rock-a-billy, pop and R&B; also reggae and country. Published "Real" (by Roy Cathey Jr.), recorded by Mickey Dee on Rock City Records (rock); "Sheila Likes Hollywood" (by Bruce McMaster), recorded by Black Gold Red's (rock); and "Last Refrain," written and recorded by Bruce McMaster on Bullet Records (rock ballad).

GO STAR MUSIC, Suite #20, 4700 Belle Grove Rd., Baltimore MD 21225. (301)789-1005. FAX: (301)789-1006. Owner: William E. Baker. Music publisher, record company (Go Records) and record producer (International Music). Estab. 1988. Publishes 50-100 songs/year; 50 new songwriters/year. Receives 1,200 submissions/year. Pays standard royalty.
Affiliate(s): Billy Baker and Associates, Go Records, Infinity Productions and Independent International Music Associates.
How to Contact: Submit a demo tape. Unsolicited submissions are OK. "Limit 4 songs with lyric sheets, bio and photo. SASE with phone number. List what you would like to achieve." Prefers cassette and lyric or lead sheet. SASE. Reports in 3 weeks.
Music: Mostly rock, pop, country, R&B, New Age and gospel. Published "If You're Not Here" (by Paula Anderson/Pam Bailey), recorded by Closin' Time On Go Records (country); "Numbered Door" (by Roger Ware), recorded by Doug Beacham on Go Records (country); and "Carolina Blue (by Jim Hession), recorded by John Anthony on Go/Silver Dollar Records (country).

JAY GOLD MUSIC PUBLISHING,, (formerly American Songwriter's Group), P.O. Box 409, East Meadow NY 11554-0409. (516)486-8699. President: Jay Gold. Music publisher. BMI. Estab. 1981. Publishes 25 songs/year; 1-2 new songwriters/year. Works with composers and lyricists; teams collaborators. Pays standard royalty.
How to Contact: Submit a demo tape by mail—unsolicited submissions are OK. Prefers cassette with 3 songs and lyric sheets. Reports in 6 weeks.
Music: Mostly pop, rock and country. Published "Tough Guy" (by Jay Gold), recorded by Jail Bait on *Star Search* TV show (pop); "All the Wrong Reasons," written and recorded by Jay Gold on Turbo Records (pop); and "Radio Riot" (by R. Freeman/J. Gold), recorded by Queen City Kids (rock).
Tips: "Make the best demo you can afford. It's better to have a small publisher pushing your songs than a large one keeping them on the shelf."

S.M. GOLD MUSIC, % Compositions, Inc., 36 E. 22nd St., 2nd Floor, New York NY 10010. President: Steven M. Gold. Music publisher and jingle/TV/film score producer. ASCAP. Publishes 5 songs/year. Receives 10 submissions/month. "We employ freelance and staff songwriters/composers who are well-versed in all styles of popular music." Pays standard royalty or cash advance (buy-out).
How to Contact: Submit a demo tape—unsolicited submissions are OK. Prefers cassette with 2 songs. Does not return unsolicited material. No calls please.
Music: Mainstream pop, R&B and dance/pop.
Tips: "We're not looking for 'album tracks' or 'B sides.' Hits only!"

GOLD SOUND MUSIC INC., 3826 Commanche Ave., Las Vegas NV 89121. (702)458-3957. Producer and Publisher: Tom Devito. Music publisher, record company (Moontide Records) and record producer. BMI, ASCAP, SESAC. Estab. 1978. Publishes 30 songs/year; publishes 3 new songwriters/year. Pays standard royalty.
Affiliate(s): Moondance Music (SESAC), MoonDown Music (BMI) and Moontide Music (ASCAP).
How to Contact: Write or call to arrange a personal interview. Prefers cassette or VHS videocassette with 3 songs and lyric and lead sheets. "Phone number on all cassettes." SASE. Reports in 2 weeks.
Music: Mostly easy rock, country and R&B; also pop and MOR.
Tips: "We are looking for strong lyrics and a good melody."

GORDON MUSIC CO., INC., P.O. Box 2250, Canoga Park CA 91306. (818)883-8224. Owner: Jeff Gordon. Music publisher, record company (Paris Records). ASCAP, BMI. Estab. 1950. Publishes 10-20 songs/year. Works with composers and lyricists; teams collaborators. Pays standard royalty or arrangements of many kinds can be made between author and publisher.
Affiliate(s): Marlen Music (ASCAP), Sunshine Music (BMI) and Gordon Music (ASCAP).
How to Contact: Submit demo tape—unsolicited submissions are OK. Prefers cassette (or VHS videocassette) with 3-4 songs and lyric or lead sheets. Does not return unsolicited material. Reports in 1 month.
Music: Mostly pop, children's and rock; also jazz. Published "Izzy, Post of West" and "The Corsican Cat," both written and recorded by Champie (childrens); and "Alfred Hitchcock" (by D. Kahn and M. Lenard), recorded by Failsafe (TV theme); all on Paris Records.

*GOTOWN PUBLISHING COMPANY, P.O. Box H, Leesville LA 71446-3446. (318)239-2850. President: Mr. John E. Kilgore. Music publisher, record company and record producer. BMI. Publishes varying number of songs/year. Pays standard royalty.
How to Contact: Prefers cassette with 2 songs and lead sheet. Include 4×6 photos. Reports within 2 months.
Music: Mostly soul, R&B and urban contemporary gospel. Member (G.M.A.)

RICHARD E. GOWELL MUSIC, 45 7th St., Auburn ME 04210. (207)784-7975. Professional Manager: Rich Gowell. Music publisher and record company (Allagash Country Records, Allagash R&B Records, Gowell Records). BMI. Estab. 1978. Publishes 10-30 songs/year; 5-10 new songwriters/year. Works with composers and lyricists. Pays standard royalty.
Affiliate(s): Global Allagash Music Co. (ASCAP).
How to Contact: Submit a demo tape by mail—unsolicited submissions are OK. Prefers cassette with 2-4 songs and lyric sheets. SASE. Reports in 2-6 weeks.
Music: Mostly country, pop and R&B. Published "Back Home" (by J. Main), recorded by Larry Main (pop/country); "Straight Country Songs" (by J. Gillespie), recorded by Larry Beaird (country); and "Is It My Body You Want," written and recorded by Rich Gowell (50s rock) all on Allagash Country Records.
Tips: "Have a great song with a professional demo and keep plugging to the right people."

GREEN DOLPHIN MUSIC, Suite 2, 27 Fermanagh Ave., Toronto ON M6R1M1 **Canada**. Creative Director: Don Breithaupt. Music publisher. SOCAN. Estab. 1987. Publishes 20-30 songs/year; publishes 2 new songwriters/year. Works with composers and lyricists. Pays standard royalty.
How to Contact: Write first and obtain permission to submit a tape. No calls. Prefers cassette with 3 songs and lyric sheet. SASE. Reports in 2 months.
Music: Mostly pop and A/C; also dance and R&B. Published "Just Like Me" and "Love's Last Stand" (by Don Breithaupt), recorded by Blue Monday (pop); and "Don't Know What You're Missing" (by D. Breithaupt and R. Romball), recorded by Rikki Romball (A/C) all on Marigold Records.
Tips: "We're looking for hits, not album cuts!"

*GREEN MEADOWS PUBLISHING, Rt #4 Box 92, Charlotte Dr., Beaver Dam KY 42320. (502)274-3169. Executive Director: Robert Bailey. Music publisher, record company. Estab. 1991. Publishes 25-30 songs/year; publishes 5 new songwriters/year. Works with composers and lyricists. Pays standard royalty.
How to Contact: Write or call first to obtain permission to submit. Prefers cassette with 5 songs and lyric sheet. Does not return unsolicited material. Reports in 6 weeks.
Music: Mostly rock, folk, country; also gospel, blues and R&B. Published "Land up High," "Black Gold" and "Family Ties" all written and recorded by Robert Bailey on Beatle Records (single).

*GREENAWAY, 38 Evelyn St., Boston MA 02126. (617)296-3327. Artist Relation: Janice Tritto. Music publisher. ASCAP, BMI. Estab. 1985. Publishes 5-7 songs/year; 3-4 new songwriters/year. Works with composers and lyricists; teams collaborators. Pays standard royalty.
Affiliate(s): Stargard Publishing (BMI) and Zatco Music (ASCAP).
How to Contact: Submit a demo tape by mail—unsolicited submissions are O.K. Prefers cassette or VHS videocassette with 5 or less songs and lyric or lead sheets. SASE. Reports in 6 weeks.
Music: Mostly R&B, dance and pop; also rap and reggae. Published "I'll Take A Chance" (dance/pop) and "Your The One For Me" both (by Floyd Wilcox), recorded by Jilly B. on Stargard Records; and "You Are My Everything" (by Floyd Wilcox), recorded by En-Control on Stargard Records (R&B ballad).

MITCH GREENE MUSIC, 1126 S. Federal Hwy., Ft. Lauderdale FL 33316. (305)764-6921. Owner: Mitch Greene. Music publisher. BMI. Estab. 1990. Publishes 10 songs/year; publishes 4 new songwriters/year. Works with composers and lyricists; teams collaborators. Pays standard royalty.
Affiliate(s): Mitch Green Music (BMI).
How to Contact: Submit a demo tape by mail—unsolicited submissions are OK. Prefers cassette with 5 songs and lyric sheet. Submit typed cover letter with brief bio. SASE. Reports in 1 month.
Music: Mostly R&B, rock, blues and jazz. Published "Crazy for You," by Mitch Greene and Bill Streilein.

*GUERILLA MUSIC, Unit 32, Pall Mall Deposit, 124/128 Barlby Rd., London W10 6BL **United Kingdom**. Director: Dick O'Dell. Music publisher. Estab. 1990. Publishes 20 songs/year; publishes 7-8 new songwriters/year. Teams collaborators. Negotiated royalty.
How to Contact: Submit demo tape by mail. Unsolicited submissions are OK. Prefers cassette. SASE. Reports in 1 month.
Music: Mostly dance, singer/songwriter, pop.

HALO INTERNATIONAL (formerly Mount Scott Music), P.O. Box 108, South Newfane VT 05351. Professional Manager: John Gagne. Music publisher, record company (MSM Records, Hālo Records, Bronco Records), record producer; artists signed to labels only. BMI. Estab. 1979. Publishes 1-4 songs/year. Receives up to 200 submissions/year. Works with composers and lyricists; teams collaborators. Pays standard royalty.
Affiliate(s): Pick the Hits Music (ASCAP).
How to Contact: Write first and obtain permission to submit a tape. Prefers cassette with 2 songs and lyric sheets. SASE. Reports in 2-6 weeks.
Music: Mostly contemporary country, traditional country and pop-rock. Published "Here Comes the Rain Again" (by M. Lewis/M. Brush), recorded by Gwen Newton on Halo Records (country).
Tips: "Write first, describing what you have. Send only your BEST 1-2 songs when submitting. Don't send anything NOT in line with what we need at that time. Expect a rejection if it is not a professional song."

HAMMER MUSIK GMBH, Christophstr. 38, 7000 Stuttgart 1, **Germany**. Phone: (0711)6487620-27; FAX: (0711)6487629. Manager: Ingo Kleinhammer. GEMA. Estab. 1982. Music publisher and record company (Avenue and Boulevard). Publishes 100 songs/year; publishes 5 new songwriters/year. Works with composers and lyricists; teams collaborators. Pays standard royalty.
Affiliate(s): Belmont, Sound of the Future and Music Avenue, Westside.
How to Contact: Submit a demo tape—unsolicited submissions are OK. Prefers cassette or VHS videocassette. SAE and IRC.
Music: Mostly dance and disco; also jazz, rock and pop. Published "Perfect," written and recorded by Boys from Brazil on Ariola Records (disco); and "Passion and Pain" (by A. Henningo), recorded by Deborah Sasson on Eighty Eight Records (pop).

HAMSTEIN PUBLISHING COMPANY, INC., P.O. Box 163870, Austin TX 78716. Contact: Director, Creative Services. Music publisher and record producer (Lone Wolf Productions). ASCAP, BMI, SESAC. Estab. 1968. Publishes 600 songs/year. Works with composers and lyricists; teams collaborators. Pays standard royalty.
Affiliate(s): Hamstein Music Company (ASCAP), Howlin' Hits Music, Inc. (ASCAP), Red Brazos Music, Inc. (BMI), Great Cumberland Music (BMI), Edge O'Woods Music (ASCAP), Risin' River Music (SESAC), Upala Music, Inc. (BMI).
How to Contact: Write first and obtain permission to submit a tape. Prefers cassette or VHS videocassette with 3 songs and lyric sheet. SASE. Reports in 1 month.
Music: Mostly pop/dance, rock and country; also R&B, gospel and instrumental. Published *Recycler* (by Gibbons, Hill, Beard), recorded by ZZ Top on Warner Bros. Records (rock); and *Killin' Time*, written and recorded by Clint Black on RCA/BMG Records (country).

Remember: Don't "shotgun" your demo tapes. Submit only to companies interested in the type of music you write. For more submission hints, refer to The Business of Songwriting on page 19.

MARK HANNAH MUSIC GROUP, Suite 250, 1075 NW Murray Road, Portland OR 97229. (503)642-4201. Owner: Mark Hannah. Music publisher, record company (Radioactive Records), record producer (Mark Hannah Productions) and Mark Hannah Management/Personal Management. BMI. Estab. 1988. Publishes 5-10 songs/year; publishes 1-3 new songwriters/year. Receives 30 submissions/month. Works with composers and lyricists; teams collaborators. Pays standard royalty.
How to Contact: Write first and obtain permission to submit a tape. Prefers cassette or 15 ips reel-to-reel (or VHS videocassette) with 1-3 songs and lyric or lead sheets. "The more professional the package and presentation, the better." SASE. Reports in 1 month.
Music: Mostly rock, pop and country; also fusion, New Age and jazz. Published *Modern Day Man*, written and recorded by M. Hannah (hard rock LP); "Crazy Fool," written and recorded by M. Harrop (pop ballad single); and "Billy," written and recorded by Syndi Helms (country single); all on Radioactive Records.
Tips: "Listen to the radio and try to emulate the styles and productions of hit records without infringing on copyrights. First impressions are very important. Be as professional as possible."

HAPPY DAY MUSIC CO., Box 602, Kennett MO 63857. President: Joe Keene. BMI. Publishes 12-20 songs/year; publishes 3-4 new songwriters/year. Pays standard royalty.
Affiliate(s): Lincoln Road Music (BMI).
How to Contact: Submit demo tape—unsolicited submissions OK. Prefers cassette and lead sheet. SASE. Reports in 2 weeks.
Music: Gospel and religious. Published "Merry Christmas" (by Ruth Sellers), recorded by Narvel Felts on Renegade Records (Christmas).

HAPPY HOUR MUSIC, 5206 Benito St., Montclair CA 91763. (714)621-9903. FAX: (714)621-2412. President: Judith M. Wahnon. Music publisher and record company (Happy Hour Music). BMI. Estab. 1985. Publishes 5 songs/year; publishes 3 new songwriters/year. Works with composers.
How to Contact: Write first and obtain permission to submit a tape. Prefers cassette. SASE. Reports in 3 weeks.
Music: Mostly jazz and Brazilian contemporary. Published "The New Lambadas" (by Loão Parahyba); "Alemão Bem Brasileiro" (by Olmir Stocker); "Hermeto Pascoal Egrupo" (by Hermeto Pascoal); and Antonio Adolfo all on Happy Hour Records (Brazilian).

HARMONY STREET MUSIC, Box 4107, Kansas City KS 66104. (913)299-2881. President: Charlie Beth. ASCAP. Estab. 1985. Music publisher, record company (Harmony Street Records), and record producer (Harmony Street Productions). Publishes 30-50 songs/year; publishes 15 new songwriters/year. Receives 100-150 submissions/month. Pays standard royalty.
Affiliate(s): Harmony Lane Music (BMI).
How to Contact: Prefers cassette (or VHS videocassette) with 1-3 songs and lyric sheet or lead sheet. SASE. "Due to the large amount of submissions that we receive we are no longer able to return unsolicited material. We will report within 6 weeks if we are interested."
Music: Country, gospel, rockabilly, pop, R&B, bluegrass and rock. Published "Count Me Present" (by Paulette Howard and Bob Warren), recorded by Cindi Crowley on T&M Records; "I Keep Comin' Back To You" (by Terry Allen and Sue Mahurin), recorded by Terry Allen on Harmony Street Records (country); "So Many Women, So Little Time" (by Edna Mae Foy and Virgil Hooks), recorded by Don Malena on Starquest Records; and "Don't Tell My Heart" (by Scott Hansgen), recorded by Tony Mantor on Harmony Street Records (country).
Tips: "Start with a good strong hook and build your song around it. A song is only as good as the hook or idea. Make each line and verse say something. Keep your lyrics and melody fairly simple but interesting. Your chorus should stand out musically (usually up-lifting). Demos should be clear and clean with voice out front. Try to keep your songs three minutes or less. Songs must be original both musically and lyrically. Send only your best."

HEAVEN SONGS, C-300, 16776 Lakeshore Dr., Lake Elsinore CA 92330. Contact: Dave Paton. Music publisher, record company and record producer. BMI. Publishes 30-50 songs/year; publishes 10 new songwriters/year. Pays standard royalty.
How to Contact: Prefers 7½ ips reel-to-reel or cassette with 3-6 songs and lyric sheet. SASE. Reports in 2 weeks.
Music: Country, dance-oriented, easy listening, folk, jazz, MOR, progressive, R&B, rock, soul and top 40/pop. Published "Daddy's Blue Eyes" and "Hurry Home Soldier," both by Linda Rae and Breakheart Pass.
Tips: Looking for "better quality demos."

HEAVY JAMIN' MUSIC, P.O. Box 1622, Hendersonville TN 37077. (615)822-1044. Manager: S.D. Neal. Music publisher. BMI, ASCAP. Estab. 1970. Publishes 10 songs/year; publishes 4-10 new songwriters/year. Works with composers. Pays standard royalty.

Affiliate(s): Sus-Den (ASCAP), Valynn (BMI) and Dr. Canada (ASCAP).
How to Contact: Submit a demo tape—unsolicited submissions are OK. Prefers 7½ ips reel-to-reel or cassette (or VHS videocassette) with 2-6 songs and lyric sheet. SASE. Reports in 3 weeks.
Music: Mostly rock and country; also bluegrass, blues, easy listening, folk, gospel, jazz, MOR, progressive, Spanish, R&B, soul, top 40/pop and rock-a-billy. Published "Changes" (by R. Derwald), recorded by Richie Derwald on Terock Records (country); "Sex To Be Had" (by M. Finn), recorded by Mickey Finn Band on Terock Records (hard rock) and "Canada (by W. Curtiss), recorded by Rhythm Rockers on Toronto Records (instrumental rock).

HELLO TOMORROW MUSIC GROUP, 4222 Inverness Drive, Pittsburg CA 94565. (510)439-2125. CEO: Don F. Scalercio. ASCAP, BMI, SESAC. Publishes 20-30 songs/year; 2-4 new songwriters/year. Collaborates with composers, A&R and producers. Pays standard royalty.
Affiliate(s): Person to Person Music Publishers (BMI) and Music is Life Publishing (BMI, ASCAP).
How to Contact: Submit demo tape—unsolicited submissions OK. Send 3 songs per cassette with lyric sheet attached. All selected tapes will be submitted to major record companies. If tapes are to be returned, mail SASE. Reports in 6 weeks.
Music: Pop rock, R&B, MOR, C&W (all types), gospel. Published "Hal Blaine, world-renown percussionist with 8 Grammys, over 200 gold and platinum records"—"Strangers in the Night," recorded by Frank Sinatra; "California Dreamin," recorded by The Mamas and the Papas; "Up Up and Away" (written by Jimmy Webb), recorded by The Fifth Dimension.
Tips: "Submit only top quality material. Be aware of artists' current style and direction."

HENLY MUSIC ASSOCIATES, 45 Perham St., W. Roxbury MA 02132. (617)325-4594. President: Bill Nelson. Music publisher, record company (Woodpecker Records) and record producer. ASCAP. Estab. 1987. Publishes 5 songs/year; publishes 5 new songwriters/year. Works with composers and lyricists; teams collaborators. Pays standard royalty.
How to Contact: Submit a demo tape by mail—unsolicited submissions are OK. Prefers cassette with 4 songs and lyric sheet. SASE. Reports in 1 month.
Music: Mostly country, pop and gospel. Published "Big Bad Bruce" (by J. Dean), recorded by B.N.O. (pop); "Do You Believe in Miracles" (by B. Nelson), recorded by Parttime Singers (country); and "Don't Hurry with Love" (by B. Nelson and B. Bergeron), recorded by Bill Nelson (country); all on Woodpecker Records.

HEUPFERD MUSIK VERLAG GmbH, Box 30 11 28, Ringwaldstr. 18, Dreieich D-6072 **Germany.** Phone: (06103)86970. General Manager: Christian Winkelmann. Music publisher. GEMA. Publishes 60-100 songs/year; publishes 2-3 new songwriters/year. Works with composers and lyricists. Pays "royalties after GEMA distribution plan."
Affiliate(s): Edition Payador (GEMA) and Song Bücherei (book series).
How to Contact: Write first and obtain permission to submit. Prefers cassette and lead sheet. SAE and IRC. Reports in 1 month.
Music: Mostly folk, jazz, fusion; also New Age, rock and ethnic music. Published "Valse Mélancolique," written and recorded by Rüdiger Oppermann on Wuntertüte Records (new age); and "A Different Kind of Lovesong" (by Dick Gaughan), recorded by Dick Gaughan and others on Folk Freak Records (folk song).

HICKORY VALLEY MUSIC, 10303 Hickory Valley, Ft. Wayne IN 46835. President: Allan Straten. Music publisher, record company (Yellow-Jacket Records) and record producer (Al Straten Productions). ASCAP, BMI. Estab. 1988. Publishes 10 songs/year; publishes 5 new songwriters/year. Receives 20-25 submissions/month. Works with composers and lyricists; teams collaborators. Pays standard royalty.
Affiliate(s): Hickory Valley Music (ASCAP), Straten's Song (BMI).
How to Contact: Submit a demo tape by mail—unsolicited submissions are OK. Prefers cassette with 3-4 songs and lyric sheets. SASE. Reports in 3-4 weeks.
Music: Mostly country and MOR. "A Rose & A Kiss," written and recorded by April; and "Thank You Note" (by Sylvia Grogg), recorded by April; both on Yellow-Jacket Records (country).
Tips: "Keep it simple—write about one single moment in time and be prepared to re-write."

HICKY'S MUSIC BMI, 2540 Woodburn Ave., Cincinnati OH 45206. (513)681-5436. A&R Director: Smiley Hicks. Music publisher. BMI. Estab. 1985. Publishes 8 songs/year; publishes 4 new songwriters/year. Works with composers and lyricists; teams collaborators. Pays royalty.
How to Contact: Write first to get permission to submit a tape. Prefers cassette with 4 songs and lyric sheets. No porno or dirty lyrics, please. SASE. Reports in 4 weeks.
Music: Mostly R&B, gospel and danceable pop; also rap. Published "Stingy" (by Wavier, Hickland), recorded on Vibe Records (dance); and "Heartbeat" (by Barber, Hickland), recorded on Vibe Records (dance).

HIGH DESERT MUSIC CO., 29526 Peoria Rd., Halsey OR 97348-9742. (503)491-3524. A/R: Karl V. Black. Music publisher, record company. BMI. Estab. 1976. Publishes 30 songs/year. Receives 50 submissions/month. Works with composers and lyricists; teams collaborators. Pays standard royalty.
Affiliate(s): High Desert Music Co. (BMI).
How to Contact: Submit a demo tape by mail—unsolicited submissions are OK. Cassette only. "Be sure name is on everything submitted." Does not return material. No SASE required.
Music: Holiday music; also gospel. Recording artists include Higginbothem, Larry LaVey and Don McHar.
Tips: Main problems with submissions include: "Verses don't time in with chorus or each other. A short story should have a beginning, middle and end. The chorus should blend them together. Somewhere out there there are other words besides I love you/blue/true."

HIGH POCKETS PUBLISHING, 527 Meadow Dr., West Seneca NY 14224. (716)675-3974. President: Nicholas Gugliuzza. Music publisher and record company. BMI and ASCAP. Estab. 1979. Publishes 3 songs/year; publishes 2 new songwriters/year. Receives 44 submissions/month. Works with composers. Pays standard royalty.
How to Contact: Submit a demo tape—unsolicited submissions are OK. Prefers cassette (or VHS videocassette) with 1-3 songs and lyric sheet. SASE. Reports in 1 month.
Music: Mostly rock; also bluegrass and blues. Published "Undeniable," "Don't Shoot My Dog" and "Down in the Valley," written and recorded by Paul Benhatzel on High Pockets Records (rock); "Dreamer," written and recorded by Don Trouble on High Pockets Records (rock); and "Empire," written and recorded by Dale Seawel on High Pockets Records (rock).

HIGH-MINDED MOMA PUBLISHING & PRODUCTIONS, 10330 Cape Arago, Coos Bay OR 97420. (503)888-2320. Contact: Kai Moore Snyder. Music publisher and production company. BMI. Pays standard royalty.
How to Contact: Prefers 7½ ips reel-to-reel or cassette with 4-8 songs and lyric sheet. SASE. Reports in 1 month.
Music: Country, MOR, rock (country) and top 40/pop.
Tips: "We have just started to accept outside material."

HISTORY PUBLISHING CO., Box 7-11, Macks Creek MO 65786. (314)363-5432. President: B.J. Carnahan. Music publisher, record company (BOC, History) and record producer (AudioLoft Recording Studios). BMI. Estab. 1977. Publishes 10-15 songs/year; 2 new songwriters/year. Works with composer and lyricists. Pays standard royalty.
How to Contact: Write first and obtain permission to submit a tape. Prefers cassette with 2 songs and lyric sheets. "We prefer not to keep songs on file. Send a good, clean demo with vocal up front." SASE. Reports in 1 month.
Music: Mostly country and gospel. Published "Big Texas Waltz" (by G. Terry), recorded by Merle Haggard on Curb Records (country); "Remember the Alimony" (by J.B. Haynes), recorded by Bill and Roy on Gallery II Records (country); and "Grovespring Swing" (by F. Stowe), recorded by F. Stowe on History Records (country).

HIT & RUN MUSIC PUBLISHING INC., 1841 Broadway, Suite 411, New York NY 10023. Creative Director: Joey Gmerek. Assistant: Jennifer Chin. Music publisher. ASCAP. Publishes 20-30 songs/ year; publishes 2 new songwriters/year. Hires staff writers. Works with composers and lyricists; teams collaborators. Pays standard royalty.
Affiliate(s): Charisma Music Publishing USA Inc. (ASCAP), Hidden Pun Music Publishing Inc. (BMI).
How to Contact: Write or call first and obtain permission to submit a tape. Prefers cassette (or VHS videocassette) with lyric sheet. Does not return unsolicited material.
Music: Mostly pop, rock and R&B; also dance. Published "The Living Years" (by Mike Rutherford & B.A. Robertson), recorded by Mike & The Mechanics on Atlantic (pop); "Saltwater" written and recorded by Julian Lennon on Atlantic Records (pop); "I Can't Dance" (by Phil Collins/Mike Rutherford/Tony Banks) recorded by Genesis on Atlantic Records (pop) and "It's not a Love Thing," written and recorded by Geoffrey Williams on Gian Records (pop/R&B).

HITSBURGH MUSIC CO., P.O. Box 1431, 233 N. Electra, Gallatin TN 37066. (615)452-0324. President/ General Manager: Harold Gilbert. Music publisher. BMI. Estab. 1964. Publishes 12 songs/year. Receives 30 submissions/month. Pays standard royalty.

Affiliate(s): 7th Day Music (BMI).
How to Contact: Prefers cassette (or quality videocassette) with 2-4 songs and lead sheet. Prefers studio produced demos. SASE. Reports in 6 weeks.
Music: Country and MOR. Published "Make Me Yours" (by K'leetha Gilbert), recorded by Kim Gilbert; and "The Last Kiss" (by Hal Gilbert), recorded by Jean, both on Southern City Records (pop).

HITSOURCE PUBLISHING, INC., 1324 Oakton, Evanston IL 60202. (708)328-4203. President: Alan J. Goldberg. Music publisher. BMI. Estab. 1986. Publishes 12 songs/year; publishes 3-6 new songwriters/year. Receives 150 submissions/year. Works with composers. Pays standard royalty.
Affiliate(s): Grooveland Music (ASCAP).
How to Contact: Write or call first and obtain permission to submit. Prefers cassette with 2 songs and lyric sheet. SASE. Reports in 10 weeks.
Music: Country, pop, rock 'n' roll, R&B and dance. Published "Come on Home" (by Dallas Wayne and Rob Folks), recorded by Dallas Wayne on Morgan Music Records; "Daddy Smoked His Life Away," written and recorded by Brian Gill; and "Water Under a Bridge," written and recorded by Howard Berkman on Hit Source Records.
Tips: "Come up with an original ideal and develop that idea with original and memorable melody and lyrics."

HOLY GRAIL PUBLISHING, 13313 Perthshire St., Austin TX 78729. (512)219-1355. Vice President/A&R: Gary A. Coll. Music publisher and record company (Pendragon Records). BMI. Estab. 1987. Publishes 50 songs/year; 5-10 new songwriters/year. Works with composers. Pays standard royalty.
How to Contact: Write or call first and obtain permission to submit a tape. Prefers cassette with 3 songs and lyric sheet. "Include a self-addressed stamped envelope." Does not return unsolicited material. Reports in 8 weeks. "We now (freelance) produce for artists in the Texas area. Please write for terms and prices."
Music: Mostly jazz, rock and pop; also gospel. Published "Leather Lord" (by Tom Kross), recorded by Young Thunder on Pendragon Records (metal); "Wish A Day" (by J. Cook), recorded by Go Dog Go on Pendragon (pop-rock); and "Lion's Creed" (by Tom Kross and S. Wilcox), recorded by Young Thunder on Pendragon Records (metal).

***HOLY SPIRIT MUSIC,** Box 31, Edmonton KY 42129. (502)432-3183. President: W. Junior Lawson. Music publisher and record company. BMI. Member GMA, International Association of Gospel Music Publishers. Estab. 1973. Publishes 4 songs/year; publishes 2 new songwriters/year. Pays standard royalty. Works with composers.
How to Contact: Submit demo tape—unsolicited submissions OK. Prefers cassette with any number of songs and lyric sheet. SASE. Reports in 3 weeks.
Music: Mostly Southern gospel; also MOR, progressive and top 40/pop. Published "I Went to Jesus," recorded by The Servants; "Excuses," recorded by The Kingsmen; and "Canaanland Is Just in Sight" (by Jeff Gibson), recorded by The Florida Boys (Southern gospel).
Tips: Send "good clear cut tape with typed or printed copy of lyrics."

***HOW THE WEST WAS SUNG,** Suite 114, 10603 N. Hayden Rd., Scottsdale AZ 85260. (602)951-3115. FAX: (602)951-3074. President: Frank Fara. Music publisher, record producer. Estab. 1991. Publishes 15-20 songs/year; publishes 8-10 new songwriters/year. Pays standard royalty.
Affiliate(s): Crystal Canyon Music (ASCAP).
How to Contact: Submit demo tape by mail. Unsolicited submissions are OK.
Prefers cassette (or VHS videocassette if available) with 2-3 songs and lyric sheet. SASE. Reports in 2 weeks.
Music: Mostly western, cowboy songs, country and western; also Southwestern music. Published *Thunder Across the Desert* (by Tom Chambers), (Southwestern CD); *She Rode A Horse Called Buttermilk* (by Frank Fara and Patty Parker) (Western CD), both recorded by Tom and Becki Chambers; and *Sedona Serenade* (by Frank Fara), recorded by Jess Owen (Southwestern CD) all on Comstock Records.
Tips: "Voice out front so you can hear the lyric. Doesn't need to be fully produced demo—voice and guitar or keyboard OK. Don't add long instrumental intros or breaks. Western music is experiencing a resurgence and gaining new popularity because of the interest in the Great American West—everything from cowboys to the environment. Europe and the world are very open to traditional sounds and lyric that Western music offers."

HUMANFORM PUBLISHING COMPANY, Box 158486, Nashville TN 37215. (615)373-9312. Publisher: Kevin Nairon. BMI. Music publisher. Pays standard royalty.
How to Contact: Prefers cassette with 4 songs and lyric and lead sheets. SASE. Reports in 4 weeks.
Music: Mostly pop-oriented country.
Tips: "Please strive for maximum quality when making your demo."

HYBNER MUSIC, P.O. Box 184, Sutherland Springs TX 78161. (512)947-3176. President: Mark Hybner. Music publisher. BMI. Estab. 1981. Publishes 30 songs/year; publishes 5 new songwriters/year. Hires staff writers. Works with composers and lyricists; teams collaborators. Pays standard royalty.
How to Contact: Submit a demo tape by mail—unsolicited submissions are OK. Prefers cassette with 3 songs and lyric sheet. SASE. Reports in 4 weeks.
Music: Pop, country, rock and R&B.

*I.B.D. CONCEPTS INC., P.O. Box 62, New Britain CT 06051. (203)225-6329. Executive Producer: Steven Alimons. Music publisher, record company (In Big Demand Records; I.B.D.; FLESH Beat), record producer (I.B.D. Concepts). BMI. Estab. 1987. Publishes 8 songs/year; publishes 6 new songwriters/year. Teams collaborators. Pays standard royalty.
Affiliates: Illusion in the Wind Productions (BMI).
How to Contact: Submit a demo tape by mail—unsolicited submissions OK. Write to arrange a personal interview. Prefers cassette (or VHS videocassette if available) with 3 songs and lyric sheet. Length of each song not to exceed three minutes. Does not return unsolicited material. Reports in 1 month.
Music: Mostly Latin freestyle, hip-pop and club/dance; also R&B. Published "R U 4 Real Baby" recorded by Mimi on IBD Records (dance pop); "Hourglass Figure" recorded by Roomservice on IBD Records (hip pop); "Here I Am" on Jade on IBD Records (acid house) all written by Antony Solomon.
Tips: "Be very professional in your approach to marketing your material. Remember, no company wants to invest into an entity that didn't invest into themselves."

IN THE STUDIO PUBLISHING, 5209 Indian Head Hwy., Oxon Hill MD 20745. (301)839-6567. President: Steven Franco. Music publisher. BMI, ASCAP. Estab. 1983. Publishes 12 songs/year; 4-10 new songwriters/year. Hires staff writers. Works with composers and lyricists; teams collaborators.
How to Contact: Submit a demo tape by mail—unsolicited submissions are OK. Prefers cassette with 3 songs. Does not return unsolicited material. Reports in 1 month.
Music: Mostly dance, pop, R&B. Published "A Man Is What I Need" (by J. Copeland), recorded by Imaginary Criticism (dance); "Still Gets High" (J. Copeland and D.J. Kool), recorded by D.J. Kool; and "Killing for Fun," recorded by Chanitz (rap), all on Studio Records.

*IN-HOUSE PUBLISHING, INC., 146-05 130th Ave., South Ozone Pk. NY 11436. (718)322-8258. FAX: (718)322-3925. President: Barry Jones. Music publisher. Estab. 1992. Publishes 2 songs/year; publishes 1 new songwriter/year. Hires staff songwriters. Works with composers and lyricists; teams collaborators. Pays negotiated royalty.
How to Contact: Submit demo tape by mail—unsolicited submissions are OK. Prefers cassette with 4 songs and lyric sheet. "Include a music career resume." Does not return unsolicited material. Reports in 1 month.
Music: Mostly popular and dance.
Tips: "Submit quality recording that's easy to listen to."

*INTERMEDIA MUSIK SERVICE GMBH (formerly Intermedia KG), Albrechtstrasse 10, 1000 Berlin 40, Germany. Phone: (030)791 1041. Music publisher, record company and record producer. GEMA, GVL, DMV, IFPI. Estab. 1974. Publishes 50 songs/year; publishes 20 new songwriters/year. Works with composers and lyricists; teams collaborators. Pays standard royalty.
Affiliate(s): Funkturm-Verlage Musikproduktion/Funky Records Produktion.
How to Contact: Submit a demo tape—unsolicited submissions O.K. Prefers cassette or reel-to-reel (or VHS videocassette). SAE and IRC. Reports in 1 month.
Music: Mostly folk and pop; also big band songs, film music and musicals/TV music. Published "Pinoccio" (by Berg), recorded by Mythos Studio on Funky Records (children); "Jugglers" (by Zed Matic), recorded by Tritonus on Roof Records (trash); "Loosers" (by Mentz) recorded by Mythos on Hits & Fun Records (pop-rock).

IT'S REALLY ROB MUSIC, 14016 Evers Ave., Compton CA 90222. Publisher: Robert E. Miles. Music publisher. BMI. Estab. 1988. Publishes 8 songs/year; publishes 8 new songwriters/year. Hires staff writers. Works with composers and lyricists; teams collaborators. Pays standard royalty.
Affiliate(s): Janet Marie Recording.
How to Contact: Submit a demo tape by mail—unsolicited submissions are OK. Prefers cassette (or VHS videocassette if available) with lyric sheet. SASE. Reports in 1 month.

IVORY PALACES MUSIC, 3141 Spottswood Ave., Memphis TN 38111. (901)323-3509. President: Jack Abell. Music publisher, record producer and sheet music publisher. ASCAP. Estab. 1978. Publishes 5 songs/year; publishes 1 new songwriter/year. Works with composers and lyricists; teams collaborators.

Pays standard royalty; sheet music: 10% of retail. "Computerized music typesetting services require a 50% deposit."
How to Contact: Write first and obtain permission to submit. Prefers cassette with 2-5 songs and lyric sheet. "Submit simple demo with clear vocal." SASE. Reports in 2 months.
Music: Mostly religious, educational and classical; also children's and folk. Published "Little One," written and recorded by T. Starr on Ivory Palaces (Christian); "Larkin's Dulcimer Book," written and recorded by Larkin Bryant on Ivory Palaces (folk); and "Sonatina Concertata" (by J.M. Spadden), recorded by L. Jackson on Ivory Palaces (classical).

JACLYN MUSIC, 306 Millwood Dr., Nashville TN 37217-1609. (615)366-9999. President: Jack Lynch. Music publisher, producer, recording company (Jalyn, Nashville Bluegrass and Nashville Country, Recording Companies) and distributor (Nashville Music Sales). BMI, ASCAP. Estab. 1967. Publishes 50-100 songs/year; 25-50 new songwriters/year. Works with composers and lyricists. Pays standard royalties.
Affiliate(s): Jaclyn Music (BMI), Jondil (ASCAP), Jack Lynch Music Group (parent company) and Nashville Country Productions.
How to Contact: Submit a demo tape—unsolicited submissions are OK. Send good quality cassette recording, neat lyric sheets and SASE. Prefers 1-4 selections per tape. Reports in 2 weeks.
Music: Country, bluegrass, gospel and MOR. Published ""Where the Fire Used to Be," written and recorded by Lonnie Pierce, on NCP-C303 Records (country); "It's Hard to Be a Lady" (by Phil Osborne), recorded by Jake Douglas; and "Do You Ever Think of Me" (by Jan Weaver), recorded by Don Hendrix, both on NCP Records (country).
Tips: "Submit strong lyrics, good performance and good sound quality."

JANA JAE MUSIC, P.O. Box 35726, Tulsa OK 74153. (918)749-1647. Secretary: Sue Teaff. Music publisher, record company (Lark Records) and record producer. BMI. Estab. 1977. Publishes 5-10 songs/year; publishes 1-2 new songwriters/year. Pays standard royalty.
How to Contact : Submit demo tape by mail—unsolicted submissions OK. Prefers cassette (or VHS videocassette) with 4-5 songs and lyric and lead sheet if possible. Does not return unsolicited material.
Music : Country, pop and instrumentals (classical or country). Published "Fiddlesticks," "Mayonnaise," "Bus 'n' Ditty" (by Steven Upfold), and "Let the Bible be Your Roadmap" (by Irene Elliot), all recorded by Jana Jae on Lark Records.

*JAELIUS ENTERPRISES, INC., Box 2874, Van Nuys CA 91401. (818)899-4446. President: James Cornelius. Music publisher. ASCAP, BMI. Publishes 3-5 songs/year; publishes 3 new songwriers/year. Pays standard royalty.
Affiliate(s): Jaelius Music (ASCAP), Hitzgalore Music (BMI), Air Rifle Music (ASCAP), Bee Bee Gun Music (BMI).
How to Contact: Write first and obtain permission to submit. Prefers cassette. SASE. Reports in 3 weeks.
Music: Mostly pop, country and gospel; also R&B. Published "New Orleans" written and recorded by J.J. Cale on Silvertone Records (blues/rock); "Slow Motion" and "Live Like A King" (by Johnson/Johnson), recorded by Brojos on Warner Bros. Records (pop).
Tips: "Today's market requires good demos. Strong lyrics are a must."

JA/NEIN MUSIKVERLAG GMBH, Hallerstr. 72, D-2000 Hamburg 13 **Germany**. Phone: (40)4102161. FAX: (040)448850. General Manager: Mary Dostal. Music publisher, record company and record producer. GEMA. Publishes 100 songs/year; publishes 50 new songwriters/year. Receives 30 submissions/month. Works with composers and lyricists; teams collaborators. Pays 50-60% royalty.
Affiliate(s): Pinorrekk Mv., Star-Club Mv., and Wunderbar Mv. (GEMA).
How to Contact: Submit a demo tape—unsolicited submissions are OK. Prefers cassette (or VHS videocassette) and lyric sheet. SAE and IRC. Reports in 6 weeks.
Music: Mostly rock, pop, MOR and blues. Published "Sperma" (by Lisa Politt), recorded by Herrchens Frauchen on Lux Records (cabaret); "Porsche Blues" written and recorded by Hannes Bauer on Ahorn Records (rock); "Rollin' and Squeezin'" (by Axel Zwingenberger), recorded by Mojo Blues Band on EMI Records (boogie woogie).
Tips: "Send single-A-side material only, plus photos (if artist). Leave 2-3 seconds space between the songs. Enclose lyrics. We only give negative reply if SAE and IRC is enclosed. And good isn't good enough!"

JANELL MUSIC, 195 S. 26th St., San Jose CA 95116. (408)286-9840. Owner: Gradie O'Neal. Music publisher. BMI. Estab 1960. Publishes 30-50 songs/year; 20-40 new songwriters/year. Works with composers; teams collaborators. Pays standard royalty.

Affiliate(s): O'Neal and Friend (ASCAP), Tooter Scooter (BMI).
How to Contact: Submit a demo tape by mail—unsolicited submissions are OK. Prefers cassette with 4 songs and lyric sheets. SASE. Reports in 3 weeks.
Music: Mostly top 40 pop, country and rock; also R&B, gospel and New Age. Published "Me & Granpa" (by Joe Richie), recorded by Jaque Lynn on Rowena Records (country); "Viva Mexico" (by Zapateado), recorded by Expression on G.Y.C. Records (Mexican); and "Lady's Choice," written and recorded by Jeannine O'Neal on Rowena Records (country dance music).

JASPER STONE MUSIC (ASCAP)/JSM SONGS (BMI), P.O. Box 24, Armonk NY 10504. President: Chris Jasper. Vice President/General Counsel: Margie Jasper. Music publisher. ASCAP, BMI. Estab. 1986. Publishes 20-25 songs/year. Works with composers; teams collaborators. "Each contract is worked out individually and negotiated depending on terms."
How to Contact: Submit a demo tape by mail—unsolicited submissions are OK. Prefers cassette with maximum of 3 songs and lyric sheets. SASE. Reports in 6 months.
Music: Mostly R&B/pop, rap and rock. Published "Make It Last," recorded by Chaka Khan on Warner Bros. Records; "The First Time," recorded by Chris Jasper on Gold City/CBS Records; and "Dream Lover," recorded by Liz Hogue on Gold City/CBS Records; all written by C. and M. Jasper (R&B).
Tips: "Keep writing. Keep submitting tapes. Be persistent. Don't give it up."

JAY JAY PUBLISHING, 35 NE 62nd St., Miami FL 33138. (305)758-0000. Contact: Walter Jagiello. Music publisher, record company (Jay Jay Publishing) and record producer. BMI. Estab. 1958. One of the founders of NARAS. Publishes 30 songs/year. Pays standard royalty.
How to Contact: Submit a demo tape—unsolicited submissions are OK. Prefers reel-to-reel or cassette (or VHS videocassette) with 2-6 songs and lyric sheet. SASE. Reports in 2 months.
Music: Mostly popular, country, polkas, waltzes and comedy. "The type of songs that were made in the 50's and 60's. No rock and roll." Published "Lover Come Back to Me" (waltz), "Rosemarie, You're for Me" (polka) and "If I Was the President, We'd Have Polkas in Washington D.C." (polka) all recorded by Li'l Wally on Jay Jay Records.
Tips: "Make songs simple lyrics, simple melody, true to life! Send audio demo, sheet music with lyrics."

*JAYLO-BELLSAR MUSIC CO., Suite 16M, 888 8th Ave., New York NY 10019. (212)765-5157. President: Jules Peimer. Music publisher. BMI. Estab. 1972 (approx.) Publishes 6-8 songs/year. Works with composers and lyricists. Pays standard royalty.
How to Contact: Submit a demo tape—unsolicited submissions are OK. Please don't call first—send without calling. Prefers cassette, record or dub with 3-4 songs and lyric or lead sheet. SASE. Reports in 1-3 weeks.
Music: Mostly pop, dance, country and easy listening. Published "Daddy's Side Of The Bed" (by Ray Daroughe), recorded by Philomena Begley on Ritz (London) Records (country); "Legacy" (by Paula Gay/George Banks), recorded by Richard Hayes on GPF Records (pop); and "My World Is Waiting" (by Bob Brittan/Terrence Green), recorded by Polita on Lewis Records (pop ballad).
Tips: "Send only your best songs that have a strong melody, uncomplicated lyrics, and a commercial sound. Must be new and recent material."

JELLEE WORKS MUSIC, P.O. Box 16572, Kansas City MO 64133. Phone: 1(800)283-SONG. President: Jimmy Lee. Music publisher, record company (Heart Land Records), record producer (Jellee Works Productions) and songwriter recording services. ASCAP, BMI. Estab. 1983. Publishes 24-36 songs/year; publishes 12-15 new songwriters/year. "Will work one on one with select songwriters to help them get started." Works with composers and lyricists; teams collaborators. Pays standard royalty.
Affiliate(s): Jellee Works Music (BMI) and Jellee Music Works (ASCAP).
How to Contact: Submit demo tape—unsolicited submissions are OK. Prefers cassette with no more than 2 songs per tape (or VHS videocassette) and lyric sheet. SASE. Reports in 4-6 weeks.
Music: Mostly country, gospel and MOR; also country crossover, rock-a-billy and pop. Published "He Made It So" (by Robert Roberts), recorded by Max Berry (Christian); "Wandering Heart" (by Jack Lawrence), recorded by Dana Laudermilk (traditional country); and "Catch Me I'm Falling" (by Debbie Mills), recorded by Jackie Cotter, all on Heart Land Records.
Tips: "Learn to be professional. We put out a monthly newsletter dedicated to teaching the grassroots songwriter how to achieve success in this business by not only learning the craft but by opening the right doors."

JENNACO-ALEXAS PUBLISHING CO. (BMI), 3365 W. Millerberg Way, W. Jordan UT 84084. (801)566-9542. A&R: Patrick Carrington. Music publisher and record company (Alexas Records). BMI. Estab. 1976. Publishes 6-10 songs/year; publishes 2-3 new songwriters/year. Hires staff writers. Works with composers and lyricists. Pays standard royalty.

Affiliate(s): Alexas Music Group (ASCAP).
How to Contact: Submit a demo tape by mail—unsolicited submissions are OK. Prefers cassette or VHS videocassette with 1-3 songs and lyric sheet. SASE. Reports in 2 months.
Music: Mostly country and pop; also New Age and gospel. Published "Daddy's Blue Eyes" (by Linda Noble), recorded by Linda Rae on Bermuda Dunes Records (country); "West Texas Woman," written and recorded by Fats Johnson on Wildomar Records (country); "Mama You're an Angel in Disguise," written and recorded by Jeff Elder on Alexas Records (country) "She's On Her Own" (by Melfi/ Masters) on Alexas Records (country), "Between Your Heart & Mine" (by Melfi) recorded by Prophesy on Atlantic Rcords (MOR) and "Child of God" (by Melfi) reocrded by Sheri Sampson on Godley Music (gospel).
Tips: "Write from the heart! Write a good story and compliment it with a strong melody. We look for story songs like "Where Have You Been," recorded by Kathy Mattea or "Change My Mind," recorded by Oak Ridge Boys, written by AJ Masters and Jason Bloome."

JERJOY MUSIC, P.O. Box 1264, Peoria IL 61654-1264. (309)673-5755. Professional Manager: Jerry Hanlon. Music publisher. BMI. Estab. 1978. Publishes 4 songs/year; publishes 2 new songwriters/year. Receives 15 submissions/month. Pays standard royalty.
How to Contact: Submit a demo tape—unsolicited submissions are OK. Prefers cassette with 4-8 songs and lyric sheet. SASE. Reports in 2 weeks.
Music: Country (modern or traditional). Published "E.T. We're Missing You," and "Scarlet Woman" (by Jerry Hanlon), recorded by Jerry Hanlon; "Rainy Nights and Honky Tonks," written and recorded by Jerry Hanlon; and "Fast Women and Expensive Toupes" (by Rodger and Jerry Hanlon), recorded by Jerry Hanlon; all on UAR Records (all country singles).
Tips: "Be 'real' in what you write. Don't submit any song that you don't honestly feel is strong in commercial value."

JOEY BOY PUBLISHING CO., 3081 NW 24th St., Miami FL 33142. (305)633-7469. Director: Allen Johnston. Music publisher. BMI. Estab. 1985. Publishes 100-150 songs/year; publishes 12-15 new songwriters/year. Receives 50 submissions/month. Works with composers and lyricists; teams collaborators. Pays standard royalty.
Affiliate(s): Joey Boy Publishing Co. (BMI) and Rice & Beans Publishing (ASCAP).
How to Contact: Write first to get permission to submit a tape. Prefers cassette with no more than 3 songs and lyric sheets. "Type or print lyric sheet legibly please!" SASE. Reports in 6-8 weeks.
Music: Mostly R&B, rap; also dance, jazz and comedy. Published "Nasty Dance" and "Your Mama's on Crack Road" (by R. Taylor), recorded by The Dogs on J.R. Records (rap); and "Hey Ho" (by I.C.P.), recorded by Ice Cold Prod. on Joey Boy Records (rap).
Tips: "Be true to your trade and write about the things you know."

*JOF-DAVE MUSIC, 1055 Kimball Ave., Kansas City KS 66104. (913)342-8456. Owner: David E. Johnson. Music publisher, record company (Cymbal Records). ASCAP. Estab. 1984. Publishes 60 songs/year; 4 new songwriters/year. Works with composers. Pays standard royalty.
How to Contact: Write or call first and obtain permission to submit a tape. Prefers cassette with 3-4 songs and lyric or lead sheets. SASE. Reports in 1 month.
Music: Mostly rock, pop and rap; also serious music, country, R&B. Published "Frozen Roses," "Sailing Home" and "A Symphony with Words" all by Don Grace.

LITTLE RICHIE JOHNSON MUSIC, 1700 Plunket, Belen NM 87002. (505)864-7441. Manager: Tony Palmer. Music publisher, record company (LRJ Records) and record producer. BMI. Estab. 1959. Publishes 50 songs/year; publishes 10 new songwriters/year. Works with composers. Pays standard royalty.
Affiliate(s): Little Cowboy Music (ASCAP)and Litlle Richie Johnson Music (BMI).
How to Contact: Submit a demo tape—unsolicited submissions are OK. SASE. Reports in 6 weeks.
Music: Country and Spanish. Published "Where Did She Go New Mexico" (by Jerry Jaramillo) and "Jumpin Joe's" (by Bruce Cooper), recorded by Little Richie Johnson on LRJ Records (C&W).

JOSENA MUSIC, P.O. Box 566, Los Altos CA 94022. President: Joe Nardone. Music publisher. SESAC. Estab. 1983. Publishes 30-40 songs/year; publishes 1-2 new songwriters/year. Hires staff songwriters. Works with composers and lyricists. Pays standard royalty.
Affiliate(s): Reigninme Music (SESAC).
How to Contact: Write first and obtain permission to submit a tape. Prefers cassette with 3 songs and lyric sheet. Does not return unsolicited material. Reports in 1 month if interested.
Music: Mostly Christian rock/pop, pop and gospel; also modern rock. Published "Coming Home," (by Dino Veloz/Joe Nardone), recorded by Joe Nardone (modern Christian rock); "Make Us One" (by Lee Kalem/Joe Nardone); recorded by Lillie Knauls (gospel); and "Go God's Way" and "In A

Close-up

Allen Johnston
Vice President
Joey Boy Records
Miami, Florida

"Singing is here. It's not coming, it's here. You have to sing
and sing well," states Allen Johnston, the vice president
of Joey Boy Records, a Miami-based music publishing and
record company. After working in radio and as a representative for Fantasy, Ariola and Arista Records, Johnston and
his partner Jose Armada Jr. started Joey Boy in 1986 and
never looked back. R&B and rap are the mainstay of the
company, but Joey Boy has produced music from jazz to reggae. Joey Boy now consists of
four record labels, two publishing affiliates, and a video production company.

Trends in music

Johnston sees gospel returning as an important music type. "And, believe it or not, this
is not going to be contemporary gospel, which most people would imagine it to be," he
says. "We're really going back to the old, tried-and-true, four- and five-part gospel harmony
music." Johnston hopes that the resurgence of traditional gospel music will also spur the
development of a cappella ensembles like Take 6, who have mixed a cappella singing
with contemporary arrangements to produce a popular sound with the positive message of
gospel.

Johnston would also like to produce rap attractive to today's young audience containing
the same positive message. But, Johnston says, "I'm looking for gospel rap that is true to
it, not a 35-year-old guy trying to make rap lyrics to what he thinks is a hip beat." Many of
the rap tapes Johnston has recently received are from people who are trying to write rap
music about life experiences that don't really fit the genre. "I get rap songs from middle-
class housewives who have no idea about it."

Rap has been struggling with what some see as a major problem. A court decision
declared that uncredited sampling of other artists' music is illegal. Many have stated that
this decision will kill rap music, which relies heavily on the use of samples. Johnston dis-
agrees. "The way kids are making records now; they're sampling. If he (the judge) said
'non-credited,' all I've got to do is credit the guy and I'll get away free . . . boom! his name
will be on the album. It's not going to stop." Popular rap artists like Hammer are arranging
royalty agreements with the artists whose music is being sampled. "That's the way to do
it," Johnston says. "Go ahead, since you're going to sample their music, call them up, get
somebody in one of the companies in New York that they'll assign to get the information
for you, take care of the sampling, and give the people their royalties. If you don't cheat,
you won't get cheated."

The Southeast

Johnston feels that the southeastern United States will be a strong region in the music
industry. "It's going to happen out of the southeastern region," Johnston says. "Not necessarily Miami, but Atlanta's going to be a big jump-off spot, with major acts happening

there." Most of Joey Boy's chief competitors are in the Southeast. Miami is developing not only as an urban music center, but the Hispanic population provides a strong market for a growing Latin music industry. In Orlando, Cheetah Records is developing a reputation for quality children's music. With a well-known alternative music center in Athens, Georgia and the southern rock scene in Muscle Shoals, Alabama, the music industry is working hard and successfully in the southeastern United States.

The indies

The focus for aspiring songwriters should be the indie market. Especially if the songwriter feels he is working in an alternative style. Johnston states, "Every time there's a new style it comes from the indies. We have to come up with something new to stay in business." The diverse range of music produced by the independents assures continuing demand for original material from aspiring songwriters.

If you work with an independent record company as an artist as well as a songwriter, be prepared. The smaller companies are similar to the majors in one aspect: their desire to make money is as great as their larger competitors. Because the number of albums made is smaller for independent releases, it's important to the company to know product will sell through. The number of records made, and the revenue from those records will also control the cost of making the recording. "So that means low overheads, low budgets. We do a lot of pre-production so that by the time we get to the studio it doesn't take that long to get to finished product." Johnston says the limited budgets of indie recordings is good for the artist as well. "They have to find ways of becoming more professional and getting their original sound right before getting into the studio." That means doing the preparation and rehearsal before recording.

Making it

Johnston believes getting that first deal is easily done. "Oh, it's easy to get into the business. It's difficult to *stay* in the business. You've got to have something worth something to stay. You can always hit the first deal. Always, easy." Songwriting conventions are a good source of contacts and markets. Any opportunity to meet industry people and network is vital to establishing contact with potential markets and getting your music heard.

The quality of music is always the bottom line, and Johnston says the source of good songs is life experience. "Write about what's really happened to you! That's where I think the songs come from. I don't see how a person can write a love song if they haven't been in love. How can you write about hunger if you've never been hungry? It's that simple. As a writer, you've got to write from the heart of what you know to be true."

—Michael Oxley

66 Go ahead, since you're going to sample their music, call them up, get somebody in one of the companies in New York that they'll assign to get the information for you, take care of the sampling, and give the people their royalties. If you don't cheat, you won't get cheated. **99**

— Allen Johnston

World" (by Mike Palos/Joe Nardone); recorded by Joe Nardone (jazz).
Tips: "Re-evaluate your material. Get other people's opinions before sending out."

JUMP MUSIC, Langemunt 71, 9420 AAIGEM, **Belgium**. Phone: (053)62-73-77. General Manager: Eddy Van Mouffaert. Music publisher, record company (Jump Records) and record producer. Member of SABAM S.V., Brussels. Publishes 100 songs/year; publishes 8 new songwriters/year. Works with composers and lyricists. Pays royalty via SABAM S.V.
How to Contact: Submit demo tape by mail. Prefers cassette. Does not return unsolicited material. Reports in 2 weeks.
Music: Mostly easy listening, disco and light pop; also instrumentals. Published "Ach Eddy" (by Eddy Govert), recorded by Samantha and Eddy Govert (light pop); "Vanavond" (by Eddy Govert), recorded by Danny Brendo (light pop) both on Scorpion Records and "Wien Bleist Wien" (by Eddy Govert) recorded by Le Grand Julot (light pop) on B.M.P. Records.
Tips: "Music wanted with easy, catchy melodies (very commercial songs)."

JUST A NOTE, 1058 E. Saint Catherine, Louisville KY 40204. (503)637-2877. General Partner: John V. Heath. Music publisher, record companies (Hillview, Estate) and record producer (MVT Productions). ASCAP and BMI. Estab. 1979. Publishes 35 songs/year; publishes 10-15 new songwriters/year. Works with composers and lyricists. Pays standard royalty.
Affiliate(s): Just a Note (BMI) and Two John's Music (ASCAP).
How to Contact: Submit a demo tape by mail—unsolicited submissions are OK. Prefers cassette, 7½ ips reel-to-reel or VHS videocassette with 3 song and lead sheet. SASE. Reports in 2 weeks.
Music: Mostly pop, country, R&B and MOR; also gospel. Published "The Train," written and recorded by Whiskers on Estate Records (country); "Heartbreak," written and recorded by Johnny Vee on Estate Records (country); and "Sunshine," written and recorded by Adonis on Hillview Records (rock).

***KAUPPS & ROBERT PUBLISHING CO.**, P.O. Box 5474, Stockton CA 95205. (209)948-8186. FAX: (209)942-2163. President: Nancy L. Merrihew. Music publisher, record company (Kaupp Records), and manager and booking agent (Merri-Webb Prod. and Most Wanted Bookings). Estab. 1990. Pubilshes 15-20 songs/year; publishes 5+ new songwriters/year. Works with composers and lyricists; teams collaborators. Pays standard royalty.
How to Contact: Write or call first and obtain permission to submit. Prefers cassette (or VHS videocassette if available) with 3 songs maximum and lyric sheet. "If artist send PR package." SASE. Reports in 1 month.
Music: Mostly country, R&B, A/C rock; also pop, rock and gospel. Published "Bet My Bottom Dollar" (by N.L. Merrihew and R. Webb), recorded by Rick Webb (country/single); *Lonestar Cowboy*, written and recorded by Stephen Bruce (country LP); and *She Needs More Than Understanding*, written and recorded by Gary Epps (A/C rock LP), all on Kaupp Records.
Tips: "Know what you want, set a goal, focus in on your goals, be open to constructive criticism, polish tunes and keep polishing."

***KAREN KAYLEE MUSIC GROUP**, R.O. #11 Box 360, Greensburg PA 15601. (412)836-0966. President: Karen Kaylee. Music publisher. BMI. Estab. 1989. Publishes 15-20 songs/year; publishes 3 new songwriters/year. Works with composers and lyricists; teams collaborators. Pays standard royalty.
Affiliates: Den-Hawk Music Group (ASCAP).
How to Contact: Submit a demo tape—unsolicited submissions are OK. Prefers cassette (or VHS videocassette) with 3-5 songs and lyric sheet. "No phone calls please." SASE. Reports in 1 month.
Music: Mostly country, gospel and traditional country. Published "Heart Be Still" (by Carlene Haggerty), recorded by Karen Kaylee; "Whistlin' Joe," written and recorded by Karen Kaylee; and "There's a Reason," written and recorded by Lisa Amadio, all on Ka-De Records (all country).
Tips: "Learn your craft well. Be open-minded to fresh new ideas. Believe in yourself, no matter how discouraged you get. There are hits that haven't been written yet."

JOE KEENE MUSIC CO., P.O. Box 602, Kennett MO 63857. (314)888-2995. President: Joe Keene. Music publisher. BMI. Estab. 1968. Publishes 15-20 songs/year; 3-4 new songwriters/year. Pays standard royalty.
Affiliate(s): Lincoln Road Music Co. (BMI), Happy Day Music Co. (BMI); Cone Music Co. (BMI), Smooth Flight Music Co. (BMI).
How to Contact: Submit demo tape—unsolicited submissions OK. Prefers cassette with 3-4 songs and lyric sheets. SASE. Reports in 2 weeks.
Music: Mostly country, gospel and rock. Published "Jealousy" (by Narvel Felts) (country); and "The Worst Case of Love" (by Joe Keene) (rockabilly) both recorded by Stephen Ackel on Fox-Norway Records; and "That's My Hurt for Today" (by Bob Little, Delbert Dees, Doyle Lawrence), recorded by Bob Little on KSS Records (country).

Tips: "Pay attention to the market: write for it."

*KEENY-YORK PUBLISHING, 29 S. Erie, Toledo OH 43602. Contact: Michael Drew Shaw. Music publisher, record company, record producer and film producer. BMI. Publishes 50 songs/year; publishes 4 new songwriters/year. Pays standard royalty.
Affiliate(s): Park J. Tunes (ASCAP) and Newstar International Records.
How to Contact: Prefers cassette with 3 songs maximum and lyric sheet. SASE. Reports in 2 months.
Music: Mostly top 40/pop; also country, easy listening and MOR. Published "Distant Shores," (tribute to Challenger astronauts), by Mick Payne; and *Moonshine,* by Tanguerey, (LP); both on Newstar Records; *Devil's Lake* LP on Newstar, narrative album performed by Michael DeBrakistar; "Place to Hide," by Rococo on Newstar.

KEL-CRES PUBLISHING (ASCAP), 2525 East 12th St., Cheyenne WY 82001. (307)638-9894. A&R Manager: Gary J. Kelley. Music publisher, record company (Rough Cut Records) and record producer (Rough Cut Records). ASCAP. Estab. 1989. Publishes 2 songs/year. Receives 100 submissions/year. Works with team collaborators. Pays standard royalty.
Affiliate(s): Kelley-Kool Music (BMI).
How to Contact: Submit a demo tape by mail—unsolicited submissions are OK. Prefers cassette (or VHS videocassette) with 3 songs and lyric sheets. Guitar/piano demo with "words up front" is sufficient. SASE. Reports in 2 months.
Music: Mostly pop, soul and light-rock; also country, R&B and jazz-rock. Published "Just Say No" and "We Got Soul" (by G.J. Kelley & R.P. Creswell), on Rough Cut Records (rock).
Tips: "Be original. Don't copy someone else. We are a brand new company looking for new style songs. It's time record companies quit putting out albums and tapes with B songs (fill songs, junk songs) and only one or two hits. Don't be afraid to rewrite your songs."

BUTCH KELLY PRODUCTIONS AND PUBLISHING, 11 Shady Oak Trail, Charlotte NC 28210. (704) 554-1162. Manager: Butch Kelly. Music publisher, record company (KAM Executive Records, Fresh Avenue Records and Executive Records), record producer (Butch Kelly Productions), and songwriter. ASCAP, BMI. Estab. 1982. Publishes 10 songs/year; publishes 3 new songwriters/year. Receives 100 submissions/year. Teams collaborators. Pays standard royalty.
Affiliate(s): Music by Butch Kelly and Fresh Avenue.
How to Contact: Write first and obtain permission to submit. Prefers cassette (or VHS videocassette) with 1-6 songs and lyric or lead sheet."Include bio, and photo if possible." SASE. Reports in 2-8 weeks.
Music: Mostly R&B, pop, rap, gospel and rock; also dance oriented, easy listening, jazz, soul and top 40. Published "Power" (by Butch Kelly), recorded by Sunshine on KAM Records (R&B); "Money," written and recorded by Greg B. on KAM Records (R&B); and "War" (by McCrush), recorded by T.K. on KAM Records (pop).
Tips: "Send songs on Maxell UDS II tapes only."

GENE KENNEDY ENTERPRISES, INC., 3950 N. Mt. Juliet Rd., Mt. Juliet TN 37122. (615)754-0417. President: Gene Kennedy. Vice President: Karen Jeglum Kennedy. Music publisher, record company (Door Knob Records), record producer, distributor and promoter. ASCAP, BMI, SESAC. Estab. 1975. Publishes 30-40 songs/year; publishes 15-20 new songwriters/year. Works with composers and lyricists. Pays standard royalty.
Affiliate(s): Chip 'n Dale Music Publishers (ASCAP), Door Knob Music Publishing (BMI) and Lodestar Music (SESAC).
How to Contact: Prefers cassette or 7½ ips reel-to-reel with 1-3 songs and lyric sheet. "We will not accept anything we have to sign for." SASE. Reports in 3 weeks.
Music: Country and gospel. Published "Praise Ye The Lord" (by Linda Almond), recorded by Dave Jeglum (gospel); "Open For Suggestions" (by Wyndi Harp), recorded by Perry La Pointe (country); and "I've Had Enough of You" (by Johnette Burton), recorded by Debbie Rich (country); all on Door Knob Records.

KENNING PRODUCTIONS, Box 1084, Newark DE 19715. (302)737-4278. President: Kenneth Mullins. Music publisher and record company (Kenning Records). BMI. Publishes 30-40 songs/year.
How to Contact: Prefers cassette. Does not return unsolicited material.
Music: Mostly rock, new wave and country; also blues, jazz and bluegrass. Published "Crazy Mama," written and recorded by K. Mullins; "Work Me Over," (by J. Lehane/K. Mullins), recorded by K. Mullins, both on Kenning Records (both rock); and "This Time," (by K. Mullins).

KENO PUBLISHING, P.O. Box 4429, Austin TX 78765-4429. (512)441-2422. Owner: Keith A. Ayres. Music publisher and record company (Glitch Records). BMI. Estab. 1984. Publishes 12 songs/year; publishes 10 new songwriters/year. Works with composers and lyricists; teams collaborators. Pays standard royalty.
How to Contact: Write first and obtain permission to submit a tape. Prefers cassette (and/or VHS videocassette if available) with 2-3 songs and lyric or lead sheets. Does not return unsolicited material.
Music: Rock, rap, reggae and pop; also metal, R&B alternative (all types). Published "I Wrote the Note" (by George Alistair Sanger), recorded by European Sex Machine (computerized); "Here It Is" (by John Patterson), recorded by Cooly Girls (rap); and "Kick'em in the Ass" (by Los Deflectors/ Keith Ayres), recorded by Ron Rogers (rock); all on Glitch Records.

KERISTENE MUSIC, LTD., P.O. Box 390503, Denver CO 80239-1503. (303)425-8726. President: Kenneth H. Smith. Music publisher. BMI. Estab. 1972. Publishes 6-10 songs/year; publishes 6-10 new songwriters/year. Works with composers and lyricists; teams collaborators. Pays standard royalty.
Affiliate(s): Kenneth H. Smith Music (ASCAP), Coleman, Kestin and Smith (BMI) and Heliotrope Music (BMI).
How to Contact: Submit a demo tape by mail—unsolicited submissions are O.K. Prefers cassette (or ½" VHS/¾" videocassette if available) with 3-6 songs and lyric or lead sheets. SASE. Reports in 2 months. "We report only if we're interested."
Music: Mostly C&W, pop and rock; also New Age, R&B and gospel. Published "You Can Make It" (by K.H. Finton), recorded by The Fintons on HT Records (country rock); "Rochelle" (by T. Atwood), recorded by Rochelle; and "Sweet Gypsy Woman" (by K.H. Smith), recorded by Memory Band, both on D-Town Records (dance).

KINGSPORT CREEK MUSIC PUBLISHING, P.O. Box 6085, Burbank CA 91510. Contact: Vice President. BMI. Music publisher and record company (Cowgirl Records). Estab. 1980. Works with composers, lyricists; teams collaborators. Pays standard royalty.
How to Contact: Submit a demo tape—unsolicited submissions are OK. Prefers cassette (or VHS videocassette) with any number of songs and lyric sheet. Does not return unsolicited material. "Include photos and bio if possible."
Music: Mostly country and gospel; also R&B and MOR. Published "My Dear Savior's Love" (gospel); "Picture on the Shelf" and "This Old Bar" (country) all written and recorded by Melvena Kaye on Cowgirl Records.
Tips: "Videocassettes are advantageous."

KOKE, MOKE & NOKE MUSIC, Box 724677, Atlanta GA 30339. (404)355-0909. General Manager: Bryan Cole. Music publisher, record company (Ichiban). BMI. Estab. 1986. Publishes 30-40 songs/ year. Receives 20 submissions/month. Works with composers and lyricists; teams collaborators. Pays standard royalty.
How to Contact: Submit a demo tape by mail—unsolicited submissions are OK. Prefers cassette with 4-5 songs and lyric sheets. "Put contact name and number on the tape." Does not return unsolicited material. Reports back in 2 weeks.
Music: Mostly blues, old R&B style, urban contemporary (dance, rap) and pop. Published "I'd Rather Be Alone" (by Buzz Amato), recorded by Billy Paul on Ichiban Records (R&B); "Straight From Heaven" (by Mark Ford, Joey Johnson), recorded by Rev. Charles McLean on Miracle Records (gospel); "What's the Name of That Thing?" (by Gary "B.B." Coleman), recorded on Ichiban Records (blues).
Tips: "Write from the heart and soul, not the head. Listen to some of our records for direction."

KOMMUNICATION KONCEPTS, (formerly Future Step Sirkle), Box 2095, Philadelphia PA 19103. (215)848-7475. President: S. Deane Henderson. Music publisher and management firm. Publishes 10-15 songs/year; publishes 6 new songwriters/year. Pays standard royalty.
How to Contact: Prefers cassette (or VHS videocassette) with 4-8 songs and lyric sheets. Does not return unsolicited material. Reports in 2 weeks.
Music: Dance-oriented, easy listening, gospel, MOR, R&B, rock, soul, top 40/pop, funk and heavy metal. Published "Fantasy" and "Monica, Brenda and Lisa," recorded by Helen McCormick; "Hot Number" (by John Fitch), recorded by The Racers (heavy rock); "Save and Cleanse Me Jesus" and "In God's Hand" (by Verdelle C. Bryant), recorded by Verdelle & Off Spring Gospel Singers (gospel); "Free the Godfather" and "Illusion of Love" (by Hall Sound Lab in collaborations with Future Step Sirkle).

KOZKEEOZKO MUSIC, Suite 602, 928 Broadway, New York NY 10010. (212)505-7332. Professional Managers: Ted Lehrman and Libby Bush. Music publisher, record producer and management firm (Landslide Management). ASCAP. Estab. 1978. Publishes 5 songs/year; publishes 3 new songwriters/ year. Receives 50 submissions/month. Pays standard royalty.

How to Contact: Write first and obtain permission to submit. Cassettes (or VHS ½" videocassettes) with 2 songs maximum and typewritten lyric sheet for each song. SASE. Reports in 6 weeks.
Music: Mostly soul/pop, dance, pop/rock (no heavy metal), A/C and country. Published "Ain't No Cure For You" (by Ed Chalfin and Tedd Lanson), recorded by Dan Kramer on Thunder Records (pop).
Tips: "Keep abreast of what's happening in pop music today but don't copy. Be unique."

*KREN MUSIC PUBLISHING, 3108 S. Colima Rd., Hacienda Heights CA 91745. (818)855-1692. Co-owner: Kris Clark. Music publisher, record producer (Kren Music Productions). BMI. Estab. 1985. Publishes 10-20 songs/year; publishes 5-10 new songwriters/year. Works with composers and lyricists; teams collaborators. Pays standard royalty.
How to Contact: Submit a demo tape by mail—unsolicited submissions OK. Prefers cassette with 3 songs and lyric sheet. SASE. Reports in 1 month.
Music: Mostly country, pop and rock; also gospel and New Age. Published "Where Fools are Kings" (by Jeffrey Steele), recorded by Steve Wariner on MCA Records (country).

KRUDE TOONZ MUSIC, P.O. Box 308, Lansdale PA 19446. (215)855-8628. President: G. Malack. Music publisher. ASCAP. Estab. 1988.
Affiliate(s): Teeze Me Pleeze Me Music (ASCAP).
How to Contact: Write first and obtain permission to submit a tape. Prefers cassette (or VHS videocassette if available) with 3 songs. SASE.
Music: Mostly rock and pop. Published "Tonight," "Fantasy" and "Love Or Lust" (by G. Malack), recorded by Roughhouse on CBS Records (rock).

RALF KRUEGER MUSIKVERLAG, Leopold St. 11-13, 4000 Dusseldorf NRW **Germany** 0211 364545. Director: Ralf Krueger. Music publisher and record company (A1A). GEMA. Estab. 1984. Publishes 10 songs/year; publishes 2 new songwriters/year. Works with composers and lyricists; teams collaborators.
How to Contact: Submit a demo tape by mail—unsolicited submissions are OK. Prefers cassette with lyric sheets. SAE and IRC. Reports in 2 months.
Music: Soul, funk, hip hop and house with a pop-crossover appeal. Published "Milky Way Kiss" (by Bop Whopper/Sira Ain), recorded by Frank Ananda on A1A (soul-pop-rap); and "Violins" (by George Rockwood, Victor Lovera, Sira Ain, Ama Donya), recorded by Frank Ananda on A1A (new pop).

L TRAIN PUBLISHERS, P.O. Box 140821, Chicago IL 60614-0821. (312)939-5581. President: Frederick S. Koger. Music publisher and record company. ASCAP. Estab. 1987. Publishes 5 songs/year; publishes 2 new songwriters/year. Hires staff writers. Pays standard royalty.
How to Contact: Submit demo tape—unsolicited submissions are OK. Prefers cassette, 7½ ips reel-to-reel with 3-5 songs and lyric or lead sheets. SASE. Reports in 3 weeks.
Music: Mostly R&B, rap and pop; also rock and gospel. Published "Nurse" and "Face the Music," both written and recorded by Terry O on Nickle Plate Records (R&B).

*LACKEY PUBLISHING CO., Box 269, Caddo OK 74729. (405)367-2798. President: Robert F. Lackey. Music publisher and record producer. BMI. Publishes 6-8 songs/year; publishes 3-4 new songwriters/year. Pays standard royalty.
How to Contact: Submit demo tape—unsolicited submissions are OK. Prefers cassette with 1-10 songs. SASE. Reports in 2 months.
Music: Mostly country and MOR; also bluegrass, blues, church/religious, easy listening, folk, gospel, progressive, R&B and top 40/pop. Published "The Devil In Tight Blue Jeans," written and recorded by Franklin Lackey (country); "Teenager in Love," written and recorded by Sherry Kenae (pop/country); and "The Rose of Goodbye" (by Franklin Lackey), recorded by Sherry Kenae (progressive country), all on Uptown Records.
Tips: "Make every word count on the lyrics."

THE LANGFORD COVE MUSIC GROUP, Suite 5, 1622 16th Ave. S., Nashville TN 37212. (615)383-7209. Creative Director: Ted Barton. Office Manager: Charlie Gore. Music publisher. BMI, ASCAP. Estab. 1986. Publishes 200 songs/year; publishes 3 new songwriters/year. Hires staff writers. Works with composers and lyricists; teams collaborators. Pays standard royalty.
Affiliate(s): Ted Barton Music (BMI), Langford Cove Music (ASCAP).
How to Contact: Submit a demo tape by mail—unsolicited submissions are OK. Prefers cassette with 3 songs and lyric sheet. SASE.
Music: Mostly country, R&B and pop; also gospel. Published "Gonna Be A Long Time" (by Duncan Wayne/Jimmy Tittle), recorded by Jimmy Tittle on Dixie Frog France Records; "Jimmy 55," written and recorded by Joe Sun on Dixie Frog France Records; "Heart Trouble," written and recorded by

Ottar Johansen on Sonet Norway Records; "Hank and Bogart Still Live" (by Ted Barton and Joe Sun), recorded by Joe Sun on Dixie Frog France Records; "You Can't Stop These Trains" (by Ted Barton), recorded by Jimmy Tittle on CBS Records.

Tips: "You're competing with the world. You have to make your songs strong enough to be competitive."

LANSDOWNE AND WINSTON MUSIC PUBLISHERS, #318, 1680 Vine St., Hollywood CA 90028. (213)462-2848. Vice President/President: Lynne Robin Green. Music publisher. ASCAP, BMI. Estab. 1958. Publishes 20 songs/year; publishes 10 new songwriters/year. Receives 300 submissions/month. Works with composers and lyricists. Pays standard royalty.

Affiliate(s): Bloor Music Publishers (BMI); Ben Ross Music (ASCAP); Hoffman House Music Publisher (BMI); For Love Forever Music (ASCAP); Clemitco Publishers (BMI).

How to Contact: Submit a demo tape by mail—unsolicited submissions are OK. Prefers cassette with 1-3 songs and lyric sheets. SASE. Reports back in 3 weeks. "No calls."

Music: Mostly R&B (ballads), hip-hop, pop-rock; also alternative. Published "Streetdance," written and recorded by King Errisson on Ichiban Records (R&B worldbeat); "Old Home Place" (by R. Dillard and Mitchell F. Jayne), recorded by The Dillards on Vanguard Records (bluegrass); and "Small Potatoes" (by Lisa Aschmann), recorded by Suzanne Shepard on Epic Records (jazz).

Tips: "You must strive for great story in lyric, memorable melody and great chorus hooks with an original approach to each song's creative aspect."

LANTANA, #308, 9430 Live Oak Pl., Ft. Lauderdale FL 33324. (305)472-7757. President: Jack Bluestein. Music publisher, record company (Twister Records, Quadraphonic Records) and record producer (Quadraphonic Talent/Records). BMI. Estab. 1974. Publishes 50-100 songs/year. Publishes 25-30 new songwriters/year. Works with composers and lyricists; teams collaborators. Pays standard royalty.

Affiliate(s): Pine Island Music (BMI) and Twister Music (ASCAP).

How to Contact: Write first and obtain permission to submit. Prefers cassette or 7½ ips. reel to reel with 3-6 songs and lyric sheet and/or lead sheet. SASE. Reports in 4 weeks.

Music: Country, country pop, R&B and gospel.

LARI-JON PUBLISHING, 325 West Walnut, Rising City NE 68658. (402)542-2336. Owner: Larry Good. Music publisher, record company (Lari-Jon Records) and record producer (Lari Jon Productions). BMI. Estab. 1967. Publishes 20 songs/year; publishes 2-3 new songwriters/year. Receives 100-150 submissions/year. Teams collaborators. Pays standard royalty.

How to Contact: Submit a demo tape by mail—unsolicited submissions are O.K. Prefers cassette with 5 songs and lyric sheet. "Be professional." SASE. Reports in 2 months.

Music: Mostly country, gospel—Southern and '50's rock. Published "Her Favorite Song," written and recorded by Johnny Nace (country); "The Greatest Star" (by Gerald and June Campbell), recorded by Tom Campbell (country gospel); and "Nebraska Land," written and recorded by Larry Good (country), all on Lari-Jon Records.

*LARRIKIN MUSIC, P.O. Box 78, Queen Victoria Building, Sydney NSW 2000 **Australia.** Phone: (02)267-7433. Professional Manager: John Boughtwood. Music publisher. APRA. Works with composers and lyricists.

Affiliate(s): Happy Valley Music (USA), Sleeping Giant (UK), Campbell Connelly (UK) and G. Schirmer (USA).

How to Contact: Submit demo tape—unsolicited submissions are OK. Prefers cassette with 3-4 songs and lyric sheet. SAE and IRC. Reports in 3-4 weeks.

Music: All types.

*LATIN AMERICAN MUSIC CO., INC., P.O. Box 1844, Cathedral Station, New York NY 10025. (212)993-5557. FAX: (212)993-5551. Contact: Mary Huertas. Music Publisher. Estab. 1970. Publishes 20 songs/year; publishes 5 new songwriters/year. Works with composers and lyricists; team collaborators. Pays standard royalty.

Affiliates: The International Music Co.

How to Contact: Write first and obtain permission to submit. Prefers cassette. Does not return unsolicited material.

Music: Mostly Latin American; also reggae. Published "La Finquita" (G. Rosario), recorded by the Believers; "Se Me Van" (by T. Sanchez), recorded by Pupy on CBS Records (LP); and "Te Siento," written and recorded by Lan Franco on Audio Records (LP).

LAYMOND PUBLISHING CO., INC., Box 25371, Charlotte NC 28229. (704)537-0133. A&R Director: Dwight Moody. Music publisher, record company (Panhandle Records, Lamon Records) and record producer (David and Carlton Moody). BMI, ASCAP. Publishes 60-70 songs/year; publishes 20 new songwriters/year. Receives 1200 submissions/year. Works with composers. Pays standard royalty.
Affiliate(s): CDT Productions and Laymond Publishing Co.
How to Contact: Write first and obtain permission to submit. Prefers cassette. SASE. Reports in 10 weeks.
Music: Mostly country, R&B and rock; also gospel. Published "Welcome Home Soldier" (by Lynn Payne), recorded by Moody Brothers (pop-country); "Loving You's the Best Thing I Do" (by Ernie Scotte), recorded by Debbie Dickens (country); and "Hang a Stocking for Me, Mom" (by Charles Hayes), recorded by Moody Brothers (country) all on Lamon Records.

LCS MUSIC GROUP, INC., P.O. Box 815129, Dallas TX 75381. (214)247-7703. Contact: Publishing Assistant. Music publisher. BMI, ASCAP, SESAC. Works with composers. Pays standard royalty.
Affiliate(s): Bug and Bear Music (ASCAP), Chris Christian Music (BMI), Court and Case Music (ASCAP), Home Sweet Home Music (ASCAP) and Monk and Tid Music (SESAC), Preston Christian Music (BMI).
How to Contact: Submit a demo tape by mail—unsolicited submissions are OK. Prefers cassette with lyric sheet (only necessary if the words are difficult to understand). "Put all pertinent information on the tape itself, such as how to contact the writer. Do not send Express!" Does not return unsolicited material.
Music: Mostly contemporary Christian and inspirational. Published "The Me Nobody Knows" (by Vincent Grimes), recorded by Marilyn McCoo on Warner Alliance (contemporary Christian); "Peaceful," written and recorded by Eric Champion on Myrrh Records (contemporary Christian); "Warrior for the Lord" (by Brent Tallent), recorded by Marilyn McCoo on Warner Alliance Records (inspirational).
Tips: Listen to the cutting edge of whatever style you write—don't get caught in a rut stylistically."

LE MATT MUSIC, LTD., %Stewart House, Hillbottom Rd., Highwycombe, Buckinghamshire **United Kingdom** HP124HJ. Phone: (0630)647374. FAX: (0630)647612. Art Director: Xavier Lee. Music publisher, record company and record producer. MCPS, PRS. Member MPA, PPL. Estab. 1971. Publishes 30 songs/year; publishes 10 new songwriters/year. Receives 60 submissions/month. Works with composers, lyricists; teams collaborators. Pays standard royalty.
Affiliate(s): Lee Music, Ltd., Swoop Records, Grenoville Records, Check Records, Zarg Records, Pogo Records, Ltd., R.T.F.M., R.T.L. Music.
How to Contact: Submit demo tape—unsolicited submissions OK. Prefers 7½ or 15 ips reel-to-reel or cassette (or VHS/Beta 625/PAL system videocassette) with 1-3 songs and lyric and lead sheets. "Make sure name and address are on reel or cassette." SAE and IRC. Reports in 6 weeks.
Music: All types. Published "Suburban Stud" (by E. Hunt), recorded by Studs on Zarg Records (punk); "Motorbikin" (by M.J. Lawson), recorded by Emmit Till on Swoop Records (rock); and "Answer Me" (by Ron Lee), recorded by Groucho on Swoop Records (pop/ballad).

LEMON SQUARE MUSIC, Box 671008, Dallas TX 75367-8008. (214)750-0720. A&R: Mike Anthony. Music publisher. ASCAP. Estab. 1979. Publishes 10 songs/year. Teams collaborators. Pays standard royalty.
Affiliate(s): Friends of the General Music (BMI).
How to Contact: Submit a demo tape—unsolicited submissions OK. Prefers cassette with 1-2 songs and lyric sheets. SASE. Reports in 4-6 weeks.
Music: Mostly country and gospel. Published "He's My Gentleman" (by Stan Ratlift), recorded by Audie Henry on RCA Records (country); "Like Goin' Home" (by Allison Gilliam), recorded by Susie Calvin on Canyon Creek Records (pop-country).
Tips: "Fine tune the song. Do a demo that you can hear the melody and lyrics."

LEO-VINCENT MUSIC/OMNI-PRAISE MUSIC, 5934 Blairstone Dr., Culver City CA 90230. (213)558-8168. Owner: Leonardo Wilborn. Music publisher and record producer (LVW Entertainment). ASCAP, BMI. Estab. 1987. Publishes 9-12 songs/year; publishes 2 new songwriters/year. Works with composers and lyricists; teams collaborators. Pays standard royalty.
Affiliate(s): Leo-Vincent Music (ASCAP), Omni-Praise Music (BMI).
How to Contact: Write first and obtain permission to submit a tape, or to arrange a personal interview. Prefers cassette or VHS videocassette with 3 songs and lyric or lead sheet. "Doesn't need to be overproduced. Just a good clean demo. We'll let you know if more is needed." SASE. Reports in 6-8 weeks.

Music: Mostly nu-inspirational, R&B/dance, gospel; also concert pieces (for large ensembles), choral music and pop/country. Published "Lift Every Voice & Sing" (by J. Weldon Johnson, Arr: L. Wilborn), recorded by Federation of Love (gospel); "Free Again" (by Terence Thomas, Tameron Walker), recorded by Federation of Love (inspirational); and "Victory Is Won" (by Esau Joyner, Jr.), recorded by Daily Bread (Christian); all on IHS Records.
Tips: "Write strong material. Keep in touch every 6 months or so. Be patient, production schedules vary. Write lyrics that inspire with good story lines."

LEXINGTON ALABAMA MUSIC PUBLISHING CO., Rt. 1, Box 40, Lexington AL 35648. President: Darrell Glover. Music publisher, record company (Lamp Records), and record producer (Lamp Production Co.). BMI. Estab. 1981. Publishes 30 songs/year; publishes 3-5 new songwriters/year. Receives 20 submissions/month. Works with composers and lyricists; team collaborators. Pays standard royalty.
How to Contact: Submit demo tape—unsolicited submissions OK. Prefers cassette with 3 songs and lyric sheet. SASE. Reports in 1 month "only if material can be used by company."
Music: Mostly country, pop and R&B; also rock and gospel. Published "Big Shuffle" (by Danny Dobbs), recorded by Whiskey Straight (rock); "Pocket Full of 50s," written and recorded by Mark Nanmare (country); and "Thank You Jesus," written and recorded by Kim Weems (gospel); all on Lamp Records.
Tips: "We want strong hooks, unusual ideas, and a new way of expressing old ideas."

LIGHT FORCE MUSIC, P.O. Box 858, Sonoma CA 95476. (707)762-4858. Director of A&R: Shelly Trumbo. Music publisher (Victory, Bay City) and record producer (Victory Media Group). ASCAP. Estab. 1987. Publishes 5 songs/year. Receives 2 submissions/month. Works with composers; teams collaborators. Pays standard royalty.
Affiliate(s): Bay City Music (ASCAP).
How to Contact: Write first and obtain permission to submit a tape. Prefers cassette with 3 songs. Does not return unsolicited material. Reports in 3 months.
Music: Mostly rock, pop and Christian rock; also dance and folk/rock. Published "2 Empty Hearts" (by S. Trumbo), recorded by Shelly T. on Victory Records (rock); "New One" (by R. Prifer), recorded by Justin Sayne on Bay City Records (rock); and "Edge of the Storm" (by M. Allan/S. Trumbo), recorded by Shelly T. on Victory Records (rock).

***DORIS LINDSAY PUBLISHING (ASCAP)**, 1203 Biltmore Ave., High Point NC 27260. (919)882-9990. President: Doris Lindsay. Music publisher and record company (Fountain Records). BMI, ASCAP. Estab. 1979. Publishes 20 songs/year; publishes 4 songwriters/year. Works with composers and lyricists; teams collaborators. Pays standard royalty.
Affiliate(s): Better Times Publishing (BMI) and Doris Lindsay Publishing (ASCAP).
How to Contact: Write first and obtain permission to submit a tape. Prefers cassette with 2 songs. "Submit good quality demos." SASE. Reports in 2 months.
Music: Mostly country, pop and contemporary gospel. Published "Mama Tell Him" (by P.A. Hanna), recorded by Kelli Crafton (country); "Mississippi River Rat" (by Ed Dickey), recorded by Tom Powers (Cajun country); and "Kentucky Plates" (by Pam Hanna), recorded by Pat Repose (country); all on Fountain Records.
Tips: "Present a good quality demo (recorded in a studio). Positive clean lyrics and up-tempo music are easiest to place."

LINEAGE PUBLISHING CO., Box 211, East Prairie MO 63845. (314)649-2211. (Nashville branch: 38 Music Sq. E., Nashville TN 37203. (615)255-8005.) Professional Manager: Tommy Loomas. Staff: Alan Carter and Joe Silver. Music publisher, record producer and record company. BMI. Pays standard royalty.
How to Contact: Query first. Prefers cassette with 2-4 songs and lyric sheet; include bio and photo if possible. SASE. Reports in 1 month.
Music: Country, easy listening, MOR, country rock, and top 40/pop. Published "Yesterday's Teardrops," and "Round & Round," (by Phil and Larry Burchett), recorded by The Burchetts on Capstan Records (country).

LIN'S LINES, #434, 156 Fifth Ave., New York NY 10010. (212)691-5631. President: Linda K. Jacobson. Music publisher. ASCAP. Estab. 1978. Publishes 4 songs/year; publishes 4 new songwriters/year. Works with composers and lyricists; teams collaborators. Pays standard royalty.
How to Contact: Submit a demo tape by mail—unsolicited submissions are OK. Prefers cassette or VHS or ¾" videocassette with 3-5 songs and lyric or lead sheet.; SASE. Reports in 6 weeks.
Music: Mostly rock, pop and rap; also world music, R&B and gospel.

LINWOOD MAXWELL MUSIC, P.O. Box 374, Fairview NJ 07022. (201)941-3987. Vice President Song Review: Denise Allen. Music publisher and record producer (Cliffside Music, Inc.). Publishes 2-4 new songwriters/year. Teams collaborators. Pays standard royalty.
Affiliate(s): Linwood Maxwell Music (BMI), G.G. Music (ASCAP), Wazuri Music (BMI).
How to Contact: Submit a demo tape by mail—unsolicited submissions are OK. Prefers cassette with 2 songs. SASE. Reports in 1 week.
Music: Mostly pop, R&B pop and gospel; also jazz and dance. Published "Mama San," written and recorded by Linwood Simon on Welcome Records (reggae); "Reason for the Season," written and recorded by Gloria Gaynor on New Music Records (pop); and "Strive," written and recorded by Linwood Simon on New Music Records (pop).
Tips: "All songs are not written overnight."

LION HILL MUSIC PUBLISHING CO. (BMI), P.O. Box 110983, Nashville TN 37222-0983. (615)731-6640. Publisher: Wayne G. Leinsz. Music publisher, record company (Richway Records). BMI, ASCAP. Estab. 1988. Publishes 40-50 songs/year; publishes a few new songwriters/year. Receives 100 submissions/year. Works with composers and lyricists; teams collaborators. Pays standard royalty.
Affiliate(s): Mollies Pride Music Publishing Co. (ASCAP).
How to Contact: Submit a demo tape by mail—unsolicited submissions are OK. Prefers cassette with 3 songs and lead sheets. SASE. Reports back in 4 weeks.
Music: Mostly country, pop, humorous; also easy rock, gospel and bluegrass. Published "1956 Cadillac" and "Tell Me, Who Are You" (by Luthi/Bonham), recorded by Clay Bonham; and "The Hard-times" (by Irene Elliott), recorded by Larry Elliott, all on Richway Records (country).

THE LITHICS GROUP, (formerly Terra Lithic Music), P.O. Box 272, Garden City AL 35070. (205)352-4873. President: Dennis N. Kahler. "Growing publisher, always on the lookout for new material. Presently expanding contacts within the Nashville area, pitching to various artists. Critique/work with new writers whose material appeals to us." Publishes 12 songs/year. Pays standard royalty.
Affiliate(s): Terra Lithic (ASCAP), Pyra Lithic (BMI).
How to Contact: Submit demo tape—unsolicited submissions welcomed. "Send cassette tape with no more than 4 songs, including lyric sheets, along with SASE mailer if you wish your tape returned (or $1.50 money order to cover cost of mailer and postage) to our letterhead address. We will reply as soon as possible, with comments on your material."
Music: "Primarily Terra Lithic is interested in country/western and gospel music. We look for songs emotionally charged, unique and with good word pictures." Published "Ride The Spirit Wind" (by D. Nyle), recorded by A. Whitley on Cullman Records (American Indian spiritual chant); and "The Best of His Love" (by Smith, Baker, Nyle), recorded by W.P. Smith on Lithics Records (gospel).
Tips: "Send your *best* material. First, take advantage of the many 'How-To' books offered by Writer's Digest to maximize your skills, and *become competitive!*"

LIVE NOTE PUBLISHING (BMI), Box 16, Hampton VA 23669. (804)838-6930. A&R: Tom or Fonda Breeden. Music publisher. BMI. Estab. 1981. Publishes 20 songs/year; publishes 10 new songwriters/year. Works with composers and lyricists; teams collaborators. Pays standard royalty.
How to Contact: Submit a demo tape by mail—unsolicited submissions are OK. Prefers cassette with 2-3 songs and lyric sheets. SASE. Reports back in 1 month when possible.
Music: Mostly country, rock and pop; also reviewing all types. Published "You Never Told Me" (by Doc Holiday and Tom Breeden), recorded by Savannah Ashley on Tug Boat Records (country); "It's The Music" (by Judith Guthro and Tom Breeden), recorded by Ronn Craddock on Door Knob Records (country); "Juke Box King" (by E. Wohanka, J. Guthro and T. Breeden), recorded by Kevin Irwin on Door Knob Records (country); and "But I Lie," written and recorded by Richie Balin on Door Knob Records (country).
Tips: "Send good quality tapes and typed lyric sheets, and always be sure to include address and phone numbers to contact."

LODESTAR MUSIC, A DIVISION OF GENE KENNEDY ENTERPRISES, INC., 3950 N. Mt. Juliet Rd., Mt. Juliet TN 37122. (615)754-0417. Contact: Karen Jeglum Kennedy. Music publisher, record company (Door Knob Records, Society Records), record producer (Gene Kennedy Enterprises, Inc.). SESAC. Estab. 1978. Publishes 5-10 songs/year; publishes 1-3 new songwriters/year. Works with composers and lyricists. Pays standard royalty.
Affiliate(s): Chip 'n' Dale Music Publishers, Inc. (ASCAP), Door Knob Music Publishing, Inc. (BMI).
How to Contact: Submit a demo tape by mail—unsolicited submissions are OK. Prefers cassette with 1-3 songs and lyric sheet. Include SASE for tape return and/or response. Send regular mail. SASE. Reports in 1 week.

Music: Mostly country and gospel. Published "Me Without You" (by Lance Middlebrook), recorded by Debbie Rich on Door Knob Records (country).
Tips: "Respect our submission policy and keep trying."

LOMAN CRAIG MUSIC, P.O. Box 2955, Nashville TN 37219. (615)331-1219. President: Loman Craig. Engineer/Producer: Tommy Hendrick. Music publisher, record company (Bandit Records), record producer (Loman Craig Productions). BMI, ASCAP, SESAC. Estab. 1979. Publishes 15 songs/year; publishes 5 new songwriters/year. Works with composers and lyricists. Pays standard royalty.
Affiliate(s): Outlaw Music of Memphis (BMI), We Can Make It Music (BMI), Doulikit Music (SESAC), and HIS Records.
How to Contact: Submit a demo tape by mail—unsolicited submissions are OK. Prefers cassette with 2-3 songs and lyric sheet. "Does not have to be a full production demo." SASE. Reports in 3-4 weeks.
Music: Mostly country and pop; also bluegrass and gospel. Published "Memphis Queen" (by Gray-Craig-Craig), recorded by Allan Gray; and "Makin' Up Lies" (by Billy Gambler), recorded by Wally Jemmings; both on Bandit Records; and "Daddy (Can You Hear Me On The Radio)," written and recorded by Patty Pentell.

LOOKING GOOD MUSIC, P.O. Box 6553, Malibu CA 90264. (813)287-5057. C.E.O.: Michael D'Anna. Music publisher, record company (Rock City Records), record producer. Estab. 1984. Publishes 1-20 songs/year; publishes 1-10 new songwriters/year. Works with composers and lyricists. Pays standard royalty.
How to Contact: Write and obtain permission to submit. Prefers cassette with 2-3 songs and lyric sheet. SASE. Reports in 2 weeks.
Music: Mostly pop ballads, rock and New Age; also A/C. Published "I'll Carry On" (single) and *Reaching Out* (album), both written and recorded by Mickey Dee on Rock City Records.

THE LORENZ CORPORATION, 501 E. Third St., Dayton OH 45401-0802. (513)228-6118. Contact: Editorial Department. Music Publisher. ASCAP, BMI. Estab. 1890. Publishes 500 songs/year; 10 new songwriters/year. Hires staff writers. Works with composers and lyricists; teams collaborators. Pays standard royalty.
How to Contact: Submit manuscript (completely arranged); tape not necessary. SASE. Reports in 4 months.
Music: Interested in religious/Christian, high school choral and organ/piano music; also band music.

LOVEY MUSIC, INC., P.O. Box 630755, Miami FL 33163. (305)935-4880. President: Jack Gale. Music publisher. BMI, ASCAP. Estab. 1981. Publishes 25 songs/year; publishes 10 new songwriters/year. Receives 200 submissions/year. Pays standard royalty.
Affiliate(s): Cowabonga Music, Inc. (ASCAP) and Lovey Music, Inc. (BMI).
How to Contact: Submit a demo tape by mail—unsolicited submissions are OK. Prefers cassette or VHS videocassette with 1-2 songs and lyric sheets. SASE. Reports in 2 weeks."
Music: Mostly country crossover and country. Published "When They Ring Those Golden Bells" (by C. Louvin), recorded John Conlee and Charlie Louvin; "Feel Like Traveling On" (by C. Louvin), recorded by Jim and Jessie and Charlie Louvin; and "Silver Eagle Breakdown" (by A. Fouts), recorded by Jeannie C. Riley, all on Playback Records (country).

THE LOWERY GROUP of Music Publishing Companies, 3051 Clairmont Rd. NE, Atlanta GA 30329. (404)325-0832. General Professional Manager: Cotton Carrier. Music publisher. ASCAP, BMI. Estab. 1953. Publishes 100 songs/year; publishes varying number of new songwriters/year. Works with composers and lyricists. Pays standard royalty.
Affiliate(s): Lowery Music Co., Inc. (BMI); Low-Sal, Inc. (BMI); Low-Twi, Inc. (BMI); Low-Ab Music (BMI); Low-Bam Music (BMI); Low-Ja Music (BMI); Low-Rico Music (BMI); Low-Thom Music (BMI); Eufaula Music (BMI); Steel City Music (BMI); Wonder Music (BMI); Eternal Gold Music (BMI); New Testament Music (BMI); Songs of Faith (BMI); Brother Bill's Music (ASCAP); Miss Delta Music (ASCAP); Terri Music (ASCAP); and Holy Ground Music (ASCAP).
How to Contact: Prefers cassette with 3 songs and lyric sheet. Does not return unsolicited material. "No response unless we wish to publish the song."
Music: Mostly country, MOR and pop; also gospel, rock and New Age. Published "Dancin' & Glancin' " (by Sammy Johns) and "Deal With It" (by Scooter Lee), both on Southern Traks Records; "Homesick" (by Travis Tritt) on Warner Brothers Records; and "We Always Agree On Love" (by Doug Stone) on Epic Records.

HAROLD LUICK & ASSOCIATES MUSIC PUBLISHER (BMI), P.O. Box B, Carlisle IA 50047. (515)989-3748. President: Harold L. Luick. Music publisher, record company, record producer and music industry consultant. BMI. Publishes 25-30 songs/year; publishes 5-10 new songwriters/year. Receives 800 submissions/year. Pays standard royalty or will negotiate with established writer.

How to Contact: Write or call first about your interest or arrange a personal interview. Prefers cassette with 3-5 songs and lyric sheet. SASE. Reports in 3 weeks.

Music: Traditional country and hard core country. Published "Mrs. Used To Be" (by Joe E. Harris), recorded by River City Music, Inc. on River City Music Records (country); "Ballad of Deadwood S.P.," written and recorded by Don Laughlin on Kajac Records (historical country).

Tips: "Ask yourself these questions: Does my song have simplicity of lyric and melody? Good flow and feeling? A strong story line? Natural dialogue? Hook chorus, lyric hooks, melody hooks? If it doesn't, then why should a publisher or A&R person take the time to listen to it? Most material that is sent to us is also sent simultaneously to several other publishers. If we are going to publish a song, the writer must assure us that the same music submission isn't floating around out there somewhere."

LYNCLAY PUBLICATIONS INC., Dept. SM, 19938 Patton, Detroit MI 48219. (313)533-4506. Music publisher. ASCAP. Estab. 1989. Publishes 15 songs/year; publishes 1 new songwriter/year. Hires staff writers. Works with composers and lyricists; teams collaborators. Pays standard royalty.

How to Contact: Submit a demo tape by mail—unsolicited submissions are OK. Prefers cassette or VHS videocassette with minimum 3 songs and lyric and lead sheet. SASE. Reports in 1 month to 6 weeks.

Music: All types. Published "Loose Lips" (by A. Taylor), recorded by Twan (pop); "Sally" (by A. Taylor), recorded by Twan (pop); "Saucy Tip" (by L. Clay), recorded by Mr. Mill (rap); *Been Here All the Time* and "The Wolf," by Charles Beverly; all on Torrid Records.

MAC-ATTACK PUBLISHING, Suite 6J, 14699 NE 18th Ave., N. Miami FL 33181. (305)947-8315. President: Michael J. McNamee. Music publisher and record producer (Mac-Attack Prod., Inc.). ASCAP. Estab. 1988. Publishes 3-10 songs/year; publishes 1-5 new songwriters/year. Receives 20-30 submissions/month. Works with composers and lyricists. Pays standard royalty.

How to Contact: Write or call first to get permission to submit a tape. Prefers cassette and VHS videocassette with a maximum of 3 songs and lyric sheet. SASE. Reports in 1-2 months.

Music: Mostly pop, rock, alternative; also R&B, New Age and new contemporary. Published "Give Me A Sign" and "The Face of Fear," written and recorded by Razor on Kinetic Records; and "What Time Is It" (by R. Rodrigeuz), recorded by D.K.Y. on Epic Records (dance/alternative).

Tips: "Less is more and simple is better. Great songs can usually be accompanied by just a guitar or a piano—think about it."

JIM McCOY MUSIC, Rt. 2, Box 114 H, Berkeley Springs WV 25411. Owners: Bertha and Jim McCoy. Music publisher, record company (Winchester Records) and record producer (Jim McCoy Productions). BMI. Estab. 1973. Publishes 20 songs/year; publishes 3-5 new songwriters/year. Receives 400 submissions/year. Pays standard royalty.

Affiliate(s): Alear Music and New Edition Music (BMI).

How to Contact: Write or call first and obtain permission to submit. Prefers cassette, 7½ or 15 ips reel-to-reel (or VHS or Beta videocassette) with 6 songs. SASE. Reports in 1 month.

Music: Mostly country, country/rock and rock; also bluegrass and gospel. Published "Dyin' Pain," written and recorded by J.B. Miller on Hilton Records; "Letter," written and recorded by R. Lee Gray; and "Leavin'," written and recorded by Red Steed, both on Winchester Records (all country).

DANNY MACK MUSIC, 3484 Nicolette Dr., Crete IL 60417. (708)672-6457. General Manager: Daniel H. Mackiewicz. Music publisher and independent record producer. Estab. 1984. Publishes 1-8 songs/year. Pays standard royalty.

Affiliate(s): Syntony Publishing (BMI).

How to Contact: Submit demo tape—unsolicited submissions OK. Prefers cassette or phono records with no more than 4 songs and typed lyric sheets. SASE. Reports in 1-2 weeks.

Music: Mostly country, gospel, (southern/country) and polka. Published "The New Anniversary Waltz" (MOR) and "Accordions and Girls"(MOR polka), written and recorded by Danny Mack; and "In The Doghouse with Daisy" (by G. Skupien), recorded by Danny Mack (novelty polka), all on Briarhill Records.

Tips: "Send me your best, don't explain to me why you think your song is commercial. This business is speculation. Most of all, get to the point, be honest and send me songs not egos. I can tell which is which."

MACMAN MUSIC, INC./FRESH FORCE MUSIC, INC., Suite 201, 3903 SW Kelly, Portland OR 97201. (503)224-7511. Secretary: David Leiken. Music publisher, record company (NuVisions/Lucky) and record producer (Macman Music, Inc., Dark Horse Entertainment). ASCAP, BMI. Estab. 1980. Publishes 20-30 songs/year; publishes 8-10 new songwriters/year. Works with compsers and lyricists; teams collaborators. Pays "deal by deal."

How to Contact: Submit a demo tape by mail—unsolicited submissions are OK. Prefers cassette with lyric sheet.
Music: Mostly R&B/pop, rock and rap; also jazz. Published "If You Were Mine" (by Larry Bell, Hakins, J-Mac), recorded by U-Krew on Enigma/Capitol Records (rap/funk); "Talk About Love" (by Roger Sause), recorded by Shock on Atlantic Records (dance/R&B); and "Be My Girl" (by Marlon McClain), recorded by Dennis Springer on Nasty Mix Jazz Records (jazz).

MAGNEMAR, #C-8, 900 Westgate Ln., Bossier City LA 71112. (318)742-5777. President: Lillian Mills. Music publisher, record company (Bunjak Records) and record producer (Bunjar Records). BMI, ASCAP, SESAC. Estab. 1980. Works with composers and lyricists; teams collaborators. pays standard royalty. "We pay acording to market."
How to Contact: Submit a demo tape by mail—unsolicited submissions are OK. Prefers cassette with unlimited songs. SASE. Reports in 4 weeks.
Music: Mostly country and gospel; also country ballads. Published "If This Ain't Love," "Crazy in Love" and "Country From the Heart" (all by Myrna Freeman and Bunnie Mills), recorded by Bunnie Mills on Bunjak Records (country).
Tips: "Make demo clear. Voice clear. Does not have to be any more than guitar or piano. Send lyric if you want to—lead sheet is not necessary."

MAJESTIC CONTROL MUSIC, Box 330-568, Brooklyn NY 11233. (718)919-2013 and (718)486-6419. A&R Department: Alemo and Hank Love. Music publisher, record company (Majestic Control Records) and record producer (Alemo and Hank Love). BMI. Estab. 1983. Hires staff writers. Works with lyricists. Pays standard royalty.
How to Contact: Submit a demo tape by mail—unsolicited submissions are OK. Prefers cassette with 3 songs. SASE. Reports in 4 weeks.
Music: Mostly rap, R&B and reggae; also house. Published "Cold Sweat" (by Curtis, Moye, Davis), recorded by Majestic Productions (rap 12"); *Lovely, Lovely* (by M. Lowe), recorded by M.C. Lovely (rap LP); and "Front Line" (by Curtis, Moye, Davis), recorded by Majestic Productions (rap 12"); all on Majestic Control Records.

MAJOR BOB/RIO BRAVO MUSIC, 1109 17th Ave. S., Nashville TN 37212. (615)329-4150. Professional Manager: Dan Ekback. Music publisher. ASCAP, BMI. Estab. 1986. Works with composers; teams collaborators.
Affiliate(s): Major Bob Music Co., Inc. (ASCAP) and Rio Bravo Music Co., Inc. (BMI).
How to Contact: Submit demo tape—unsolicited submissions OK. SASE. Reports in 2 weeks.
Music: Mostly country. Published "If Tomorrow Never Comes," "Unanswered Prayers" and "Not Counting You" recorded by G. Brooks; all on Capitol Records and "Like We Never Had A Broken Heart" recorded by Trisha Yearwood.

MAKIN TRACKS MUSIC, 17 Water St., Dracut MA 01826. (508)957-5781. Publisher: Henry Rowe. Music publisher, record company (Hazardous Records) and record producer (Henry Rowe). ASCAP. Estab. 1986. Publishes 4 songs/year; publishes 2 new songwriters/year. Works with composers and lyricists; teams collaborators. Pays standard royalty.
How to Contact: Submit a demo tape by mail—unsolicited submissions are OK. Prefers cassette (VHS videocassette if available) with 4-6 songs and lyric sheet. Does not return unsolicited material. Reports in 2 months.
Music: Mostly metal, rock and pop; also fusion, fazz and New Age. Published "Half Life" and "Danger Zone," by Hazardous Waste (metal); and "Candle to the Magic," by Johann Smith (rock), all recorded by Makin Tracks on Hazardous Records.
Tips: "Have a solid sound and good production."

*MANAPRO (MANAGEMENT ARTIST PRODUCTIONS), 82 Sherman St., Passaic NJ 07055. (201)777-6109. Executive Producer: Tomasito Bobadilla. Music publisher and production company. ASCAP, BMI. Estab. 1987. Publishes 2 songs/year; publishes 3-4 songwriters/year. Hires staff songwriters. Works with lyricists; teams collaborators. Pays standard royalty.
Affiliate(s): No Mas (BMI), In Che (ASCAP), Step on My Head (BMI).
How to Contact: Submit a demo tape by mail—unsolicited submissions are OK. Prefers cassette with 2 songs and lyric sheet. SASE. Reports in 2 months.
Music: Mostly pop, dance and rock; also R&B and new age. Published "Fascination" (by Andy Pemen), by Karizma on Metropolitan Records (dance/pop); "One Way" (by Chene Garcia), by Mellow Dee on Halogram (hip house); "2 Hearts" (by Pacheso), recorded by Time Chambers on Requeslime Records (dance/pop).
Tips: "Songs should have very catchy hooks, must also be very instrumental."

THE MARCO MUSIC GROUP INC., P.O. Box 24454, Nashville TN 37202. (615)269-7074; FAX: (615)269-0131. Professional Manager: Clayton Cooper. Music publisher. Estab. 1988. Publishes approximately 50-75 songs/year; 25-40 new songwriters/year. Receives 1,000 submissions/year. Pays standard royalty.
Affiliate(s): Goodland Publishing Company (ASCAP), Marc Isle Music (BMI) and Gulf Bay Publishing (SESAC).
How to Contact: Submit demo tape—unsolicited submissions OK. Prefers cassette (or VHS videocassette) with 1-3 songs and lyric sheet. SASE. Reports in 2-3 weeks.
Music: Country, MOR and contemporary. Published "I . . . the Injured Party" (by Dennis Scott); "The Night's Still Young" (by Danny Palmer), both recorded by Debra Dudley on Concorde Records; and "Let's Be Lonely Together " (by Scott Summer), recorded by Dale McBride on Con Brio Records.
Tips: "Only send your best 2 or 3 songs with lyrics accompanying. Expect a reply within 4 weeks."

MARULLO MUSIC PUBLISHERS, Suite 201, 5245 Cleveland St., Galveston TX 77550. (409)762-4590. President: A.W. Marullo Sr. Music publisher, record company (Red Dot) and record producer (A.W. Marullo Productions). BMI, SESAC. Estab. 1952. Publishes 27-37 songs/year; publishes 7-14 songwriters/year. Sometimes hires staff writers. Pays standard royalty.
Affiliate(s): Marullo Music (BMI), Don & Willie Music (SESAC).
How to Contact: Submit a demo tape by mail—unsolicited submissions are O.K. Cassette with only 4 songs. SASE. Reports in 7 weeks.
Music: Mostly country, pop and R&B; also rock, top 40 rock, country and dance songs. Published "Do You Feel Sexy" (by T. Pindrock), recorded by Flach Point on Puzzle Red Dot Records (top 40 rock); "Love Machine" (by T. Pindrock), recorded by Susan Moninger on Puzzle Red Dot Records (top 40 rock); and "You Put the Merry in My Christmas" (by E. Dunn), recorded by Mary Craig on Puzzle Red Dot Records (country and top 40 rock).
Tips: "Send only your best songs. The songwriter with a *new* idea is a crank, until the idea succeeds."

MEDIA PRODUCTIONS/RESISTOR MUSIC, 1001½ Elizabeth St., Oak Hill WV 25901. (304)465-1298. Producer: Doug Gent. Music publisher, record company (Resistor Records) and record producer (Media Productions). ASCAP. Estab. 1985. Publishes 20 songs/year; publishes 3 new songwriters/year. Receives 100-120 submissions/year. Works with composers and lyricists; teams collaborators. Pays standard royalty.
Affiliate(s): Resistor Music (ASCAP).
How to Contact: Submit a demo tape by mail—unsolicited submissions are OK. Prefers cassette with 3 songs and lyric sheet. Does not return unsolicited material. Reports in 1 month.
Music: Mostly country, gospel and R&B; also top 40 and rock. Published "Let Me Down Easy" (by R. Rollins), recorded by Scott Ryan on Resistor Records (country).
Tips: "I see an increasing role for the independent publisher/record label/studio in the music business. It is my sincere hope that the opportunities are not taken advantage of."

MEGA-STAR MUSIC, 248 W. 5th St., Deer Park NY 11729. (212)713-5229. General Manager: Barry Yearwood. Music publisher, record producer (Barry Yearwood) and management firm (Power Brokerage Management). Estab. 1984. Publishes 4 songs/year; publishes 4 new songwriters/year. Pays standard royalty.
How to Contact: Submit demo tape—unsolicited submissions OK. Prefers cassette with 4 songs. SASE. Reports in 1 month.
Music: Mostly dance and R&B; also pop. Published "Dancing to the Beat," written and recorded by Henderson and Whitfield on Park Place Records; "Solar Flight," written and recorded by Richard Bush on Island Records; and "Mind Your Own Business," written and recorded by R. Bush on Laser-7 Records.

MERRY MARILYN MUSIC PUBLISHING, 33717 View Crest Dr., Lake Elsinore CA 92532. (714)245-2763. General Manager: Marilyn Hendricks. Music publisher. BMI. Estab. 1980. Publishes 10-15 songs/year; publishes 3-4 new songwriters/year. Receives 25 submissions/month. Pays standard royalty.
How to Contact: Submit a demo tape—unsolicited submissions are OK. No more than 3 songs per submission, one song per cassette. "Submit complete songs only. No lyrics without music." SASE. Reports in 3 weeks.
Music: Mostly country and MOR. Published "Can I Spend the Night With You?" and "He Doesn't Love You" (by Jim Hendricks) ; and "The Wolf" (by M. Sullivan) (all country).
Tips: "Be professional in your presentation. Make sure the tape is cued correctly. Make sure the lyric can be heard over the music."

MICROSTAR MUSIC, #201, 5245 Cleveland St., Virginia Beach VA 23462. (804)499-4434. President: Mark Spencer. Music publisher, record company (MicroStar, MSM) and record producer (MicroStar Music). ASCAP. Estab. 1990. Publishes 60 songs/year; publishes 10 new songwriters/year. Hires staff

writers. Works with composers and lyricists; teams collaborators. Pays standard royalty.
How to Contact: Write first and obtain permission to submit a tape. Prefers cassette with 4 songs and lyric sheets. Does not return unsolicited material. Reports in 4 weeks.
Music: Mostly pop, gospel and country; also R&B. Published "Heart's Desire" (by T. Beiderman), recorded by TK LLegs (pop); "Workin' Man's Dream," written and recorded by Buck Fisher (country); and "Little Miracle," written and recorded by Paul Van Valin (gospel); all on MicroStar Records.
Tips: "Don't send a poor quality demo. If you or someone you know doesn't believe in your material enough to invest your time and money than why should we?"

MIGHTY TWINNS MUSIC, 9134 S. Indiana Ave., Chicago IL 60619. (312)737-4348. General Manager: Ron Scott. Music publisher and record producer. BMI. Member NMPA, Midwest Inspirational Writers Association. Estab. 1977. Publishes 4-10 songs/year; publishes 5 new songwriters/year. Receives 50 submissions/month. Works with composers and lyricists; teams collaborators. Pays standard royalty.
How to Contact: Submit a demo tape—unsolicited submissions are OK. Prefers cassette with 2-4 songs and lyric sheet. SASE "only if you want material returned." Reports in 2-3 months.
Music: Mostly top 40, R&B, "hot" inspirational and gospel; also children's. Published "Steady" and "Reality" (by Chuck Chu), recorded by MTM (reggae).
Tips: Looking for "good hot songs with hot hooks. Please have tapes cued up. *Do not write for permission!* Submit a cued up cassette and wait for our response. No materials returned without proper postage. Take the time to write and re-write to get the song in its best form; then make a good clear/audible demo."

MIMIC MUSIC, Box 201, Smyrna GA 30081. (404)432-2454. Manager: Tom Hodges. Music publisher, record producer, record company (Trend Records, Stepping Stones, BOAM, Trend/Side Records, Trendsetter Records and Atlanta Records) and management company. BMI, ASCAP. Estab. 1965. Publishes 25 songs/year; publishes 7 new songwriters/year. Works with composers and lyricists; teams collaborators. Pays standard royalty.
Affiliate(s): Skipjack Music (BMI), Stepping Stone (BMI) and British Overseas Airways Music/BOAM (ASCAP).
How to Contact: Submit a demo tape—unsolicited submissions are OK. Prefers cassette (or VHS videocassette) with 3-10 songs and lyric sheet. "Open to VHS and also for distribution on accepted videos." SASE. Reports in 4 weeks.
Music: Mostly country; also bluegrass, blues, church/religious, easy listening, gospel, MOR, R&B, rock, soul and top 40/pop. Published "Train of Pain," written and recorded by Shawn Spencer on Trend Records (country); "Sands of Time" (by Shawn Spencer); "Barefoot Lady" (by Tom Cook), both recorded by Charlie and Nancy Cole on Trendsetter Records (country). "I also have Keith Bradford, Bill Price, Dell Wood, Lin Butler, Tara Bailey, Deb Watson and Frank Brannon on a mixed artists cassette album."
Tips: "Do a professional demo."

MINI MAX PUBLISHING, Dept. SM, 932 Nord Ave., Chico CA 95926. (916)345-3027. Publisher: Rich Carper. Music publisher and record company (Casaro Records). BMI. Estab. 1987. Publishes 50-60 songs/year; publishes 10-12 new songwriters/year. Works with composers and lyricists; teams collaborators. Pays standard royalties.
Affiliate(s): Starshine Audio Ent., RSA Productions.
How to Contact: Write first and obtain permission to submit a tape. Prefers cassette with 3 songs and lyric sheet. Does not return unsolicited material. SASE. Reports in 4 weeks.
Music: Mostly country, jazz and R&B; also gospel. Published "Back to Zero," written and recorded by John Peters (jazz/rock); "Sound of Christmas" (by Charlie Robinson), recorded by Lory Dobbs (big band); and "Another Side," written and recorded by Pam Dacus (new age); all on Casaro Records.

MIRAMARE MUSIC UK LTD., (formerly Risson Music), 127 Aldersgate St., London EC1A 4JQ **United Kingdom**. Phone: (44)71-2501910. Contact: A&R Department. Music publisher, record company (Presidential; XXI St. Century, High Density, Renegade), record producer. PRS. Estab. 1987. Publishes 20-30 songs/year; 4-5 new songwriters/year. Receives 8 submissions/month. Works with composers and lyricists; team collaborators. Pays 60% to writers and 40% to publisher.
How to Contact: Submit demo tape—unsolicited submissions are OK. Prefers cassette with 2-5 songs and lyric sheet. Does not return unsolicited material. Reports in 1 month.
Music: Mostly techno-dance and dance; some heavy metal. Published "Hypnotyk," written and recorded by Techno-Logik; "Unreal," written and recorded by Future Tense; and "Relentless," written and recorded by Dark Avenger, all on High Density Records (techno-dance).
Tips: "If substituting dance material it should be a finished product (i.e. not a demo) for licensing. If it is a pop song then a good demo will do."

MOFO MUSIC, 117 W. Rockland, Libertyville IL 60048. (708)362-4060. President: Perry Johnson. Music publisher and record company (Dharma, Future). ASCAP. Estab. 1980. Publishes 3 songs/year. Works with composers. Pays standard royalty.
How to Contact: Submit a demo tape by mail—unsolicited submissions are OK. Prefers cassette with 6 songs and lyric sheets. SASE. Reports in 6 months.
Music: Mostly top 40, pop and R&B; also blues, house and contemporary.

MONEYTIME PUBLISHING CO. (BMI), 742 Rowley St., Owosso MI 48867. (517)723-1796. Director: Jon Harris. Music publisher and record company (Moneytime Records). BMI. Estab. 1990. Publishes 15 songs/year; publishes 3-5 new songwriters/year. Works with lyricists. Pays standard royalty.
Affiliate(s): Moneytime Publishing Co. (BMI).
How to Contact: Submit a demo tape by mail—unsolicited submissions are OK. Prefers cassette with 4-6 songs. SASE. Reports in 1 month.
Music: Mostly rap, R&B and dance; also house, funk and soul. Published "I'll Trip" and "No Parole" (by Jon H. Harris), recorded by The Mad Rapper; and "Bright Lights" (by Brian Hammock), recorded by Children Of A Lesser God, all on Moneytime Records (rap).

*DOUG MOODY MUSIC, Box 1596, San Marcos CA 92069. (619)945-2412. Professional Manager: Eva Watts. Music publisher, record company (Mystic Records—hardcore rock, teen rock; Atmosphear—experimental art label; Clock Records; and Bootleg Records), record and video producer. BMI. Publishes over 100 songs/year; publishes 100+ new songwriter-artists/year. Pays standard royalty.
Affiliate(s): DM Music (BMI), Emit Music, Clock Music, Accumulated Copyrights (BMI), VIM Music Corp., and Variety In Music/New York.
How to Contact: Write first and obtain permission to submit. "Only new songs performed by new groups or local performing groups." Does not return unsolicited material.
Music: "All kinds of rock: hardcore, teen, horror, death and 'thrash'." Published *Dehumanizers in Hollywood*, recorded by Dehumanizers; *From S-I to John*, recorded by Stabb; and *No FX*, recorded by The Original, all hardcore CDs on Mystic Records.
Tips: "We specialize in teen-age entertainment: records, radio shows, videos. We target 11-year-old to 27-year-old market."

MOON JUNE MUSIC, 4233 SW. Marigold, Portland OR 97219. President: Bob Stoutenburg. Music publisher. BMI. Estab. 1971. Pays standard royalty.
How to Contact: Submit demo tape—unsolicited submissions OK. Prefers cassette (or VHS videocassette) with 2-10 songs. SASE. Reports in 2 months.
Music: Country.

THE FRED MORRIS MUSIC GROUP, Dept. SM, Suite 207, 50 Music Sq. West, Nashville TN 37203. (615)329-2591. Publishing Manager: Karen Morris. Music publisher and record company (Maxx Records). Publishes 10-15 songs/year; publishes 2-3 new songwriters/year. Receives 200 submissions/month. Pays standard royalty.
Affiliate(s): Karefree Music (BMI), Karlamor Music (ASCAP), Old Guide Music (BMI), First Million Music (ASCAP).
How to Contact: Submit a demo tape—unsolicited submissions are OK. Prefers cassette (or VHS videocassette) with 3 songs and lyric sheet. SASE. Reports in 1 month.
Music: Country, country/rock. No gospel. Published "Rocks, Rivers & Trees" (by Rod Wimmer), recorded by James Tiller on Maxx Records (country); "Feet of Clay" (by Mark Parsons), recorded by Jeff Davis on Maxx REcords (coungry); and "Strings of My Heart" (by Kevin Tuck Field), recorded by Don Stacy (country/crossover).

MOUNTAIN HERITAGE MUSIC CO., Rt. 3, Box 290, Galax VA 24333. (703)236-9249. Owner: Bobby Patterson. Music publisher and record company (Heritage Records, Frontier Productions and Mountain Records). BMI. Publishes 14 songs/year; publishes 2 new songwriters/year. Works with composers and lyricists. Pays standard royalty.

The asterisk before a listing indicates that the listing is new in this edition. New markets are often the most receptive to unsolicited submissions.

How to Contact: Submit demo tape—unsolicited submissions OK. Prefers cassette with 3 songs and lyric sheet. SASE. Reports in 1 year.
Music: Mostly bluegrass, gospel and Christmas. Published "Basically "B" " (by Tim Smith); "Missy Lynn's Waltz" (by Tim Smith) and Sunday Night" (by Steve Kilby), all instrumental singles on Heritage Records.
Tips: "Words must tell a complete story within 2½-3 minutes."

*MSM MUSIKVERLAG WIEN, Zollergasse 13, Vienna A-1070 **Austria.** Music publisher. AKM, AUME. Estab. 1985. Works with composers and lyricists; teams collaborators. Publishes 40 songs/year; publishes 10 new songwriters/year. Pays standard royalty.
How to Contact: Submit a demo tape by mail—unsolicited submissions are OK. Prefers cassette with lyric sheet. Does not return submitted material. Reports in 8 weeks.
Music: Mostly pop, dance and instrumental music and folk.

MUSIC CITY MUSIC (AUSTRALIA), P.O. Box 1200, Tamworth NSW 2340 **Australia.** Phone: (067)66-3566. Managing Director: Ed Matzenik. Music publisher. APRA. Estab. 1988. Publishes 50 songs/year; publishes 4-5 new songwriters/year. Receives 200 submissions/year. Works with composers and lyricists; teams collaborators. "Pays 50% royalty or as negotiated."
How to Contact: Submit a demo tape by mail—unsolicited submissions are OK. Prefers cassette with lyric or lead sheet. "Mark address of writer clearly on cassette." Does not return unsolicited material. Reports in 1 month.
Music: Mostly country, rock and pop; also blues. Published "Best Performance of the Year" (by Chamber-Jenkins-Cain), recorded by Arthur Blanch (country); and "Fast Lane Livin" (by Rachell), recorded by Twisters (R&B); both on Enrec Records; and "They're Saying No" (by Tranby-Lanyon-Newton), recorded by Enrec studio band on EXTRA Records (political).
Tips: The type of song most frequently asked for by artists who do not write their own material is the "big ballad."

MUSIC FACTORY ENTERPRISES, INC., Suite 300, Ford & Washington, Norristown PA 19401. (215)277-9550. President: Jeffrey Calhoon. Music publisher, record company (MFE Records). BMI. Estab. 1984. Publishes 8 songs/year. Receives 4 submissions/month. Works with composers and lyricists; teams collaborators. Pays "royalty based on length of contract/quantity of records produced, and production expenses."
Affiliate(s): Robin Nicole Music (BMI).
How to Contact: Write or call first and obtain permission to submit a tape. Prefers cassette with 3-4 songs, lyric sheet and lead sheet. "Make sure notations are clear and legible." SASE. Reports in 2-3 weeks.
Music: Mostly 20th Century Minimalism, world beat, alternative rock/pop and new age. Published "Stillwater," "River Run" and "Shamont," all written and recorded by Gregory Darvis on MFE Records (new age).
Tips: "Develop every song fully, be different, submit best quality product you can."

MUSIC IN THE RIGHT KEYS PUBLISHING COMPANY, 3716 West 87th St., Chicago IL 60652. (312)735-3297. President: Bert Swanson. Music publisher. Estab. 1985. Publishes 150 songs/year; publishes 5 new songwriters/year. Works with composers; teams collaborators. Pays standard royalty.
Affiliate(s): Music In The Right Keys (BMI), High 'n Low Notes (ASCAP).
How to Contact: Submit a demo tape by mail—unsolicited submissions are OK. Prefers cassette with 3-5 songs and lyric and lead sheets. "Good demos only." SASE. Reports in 4 weeks.
Music: Mostly country, gospel and pop; also children's songs. Published "Someday" (by Jay Levey) on Music Keys Records (pop); "Forever" written and recorded by Lee Benson (country); and "Tyler-Land" (by Ray Rueck), recorded by Bob Carmon (pop).

MUSICA ARROZ PUBLISHING, 5626 Brock St., Houston TX 77023. (713)926-4432. Administrator of Publishing: Art Gottschalk. Music publisher. ASCAP, BMI. Estab. 1986. Publishes 50 songs/year; publishes 10 new songwriters/year. Works with composers; teams collaborators. Pays standard 50% royalty.
Affiliate(s): Musica Arroz (ASCAP), Defiance Music (ASCAP), Musica Elena (BMI).
How to Contact: Write or call first and obtain permission to submit a tape. Prefers cassette with 5-6 songs and lyric sheet. SASE. Reports in 12 weeks.
Music: Mostly Latin (in Spanish), rap (in Spanish), jazz; also country and rock (in Spanish). Published "Rebelde" (by Alex Gallimore), recorded by Mercedez on Polygram Records (Latin); "Como Yo," recorded by the Basics on Discos MM; "Dime Si Tu Me Quieres" (by Mary G. Henson), recorded by Laura Canales on Capitol/EMI Records (Latin).
Tips: "Do *not* send music other than that in which we are most interested."

MYKO MUSIC, #D203, 1324 S. Avenida, Tucson AZ 85710. (602)885-5931. President: James M. Gasper. Music publisher, record company (Ariana Records) and record producer (Future 1 Productions). BMI. Estab. 1980. Publishes 4 songs/year; publishes 2 new songwriters/year. Receives 5 submissions/month. Works with composers. Pays standard royalty.

How to Contact: Submit a demo tape—unsolicited submissions are OK. Prefers cassette (or ½" VHS videocassette) with 3 songs and lyric sheet. SASE Reports in 1-2 months.

Music: Top 40, dance rock, AOR, R&B, country rock or Tex-Mex. Published "Rip It Up" (by Ruben Ruiz), recorded by The Free Holy Men (Tex-Mex); "Heart Break Underground," written and recorded by Jim Gasper (country crossover); and "Your Simply The Best" (by Scott Smith), recorded by Meat Corral (pop), all on Ariana Records.

Tips: "You've got about 20 seconds up front to catch the listener, do it!"

CHUCK MYMIT MUSIC PRODUCTIONS, 9840 64th Ave., Flushing NY 11324. A&R: Chuck Mymit. Music publisher and record producer (Chuck Mymit Music Productions). BMI. Estab. 1978. Publishes 3-5 songs/year; publishes 2-4 new songwriters/year. Works with composers and lyricists; teams collaborators. Pays standard royalty.

Affiliate(s): Viz Music (BMI) and Tore Music (BMI).

How to Contact: Submit a demo tape by mail—unsolicited submissions are OK. Prefers cassette or VHS videocassette with 3-5 songs and lyric and lead sheets. "Bio and picture would be helpful." SASE. Reports in 1 month.

Music: Mostly pop, rock and R&B. Published "Giving You My Love" (by Nata and Schal), recorded by Laura Dees on VIN Records (pop/ballad); "To Love's a Mortal Sin" (by Chuck Mymit), recorded by The Dellmonts on Poly Records (pop/ballad); and "Tu Eras Mi Corazon" (by C. Mymit), recorded by Maria Calbrera on Amigo Records (latin rock).

Tips: "Have strong confideence in your work but please follow our policy."

NADINE MUSIC, P.O. Box 2, Fronhof 100, CH-8260 Stein am Rhein **Switzerland.** Phone: (054)415415. FAX: (054)415420. Professional Manager: Freddy J. Angstmann. Music publisher, record producer, management firm and booking agency. SUISA, SESAC, BMI, ASCAP. Publishes 50-100 songs/year. Works with composers. Pays standard royalty.

Affiliate(s): Nadine Music (SESAC), Joecliff Music (BMI) and Lauren Music (ASCAP).

How to Contact: Submit demo tape—unsolicited submissions are OK. Prefers cassette (or VHS videocassette [PAL]) with lyric and lead sheets. "Clearly label each item you send; include photo and bio if possible." Include SAE and IRC, or does not return unsolicited material. Reports in 6 weeks.

Music: Gospel, blues and jazz; also R&B and classical. Published "How Long Will My Journey Be," written and recorded by Rev. Thompson on Koch Records (gospel); "Goin' Home," written and recorded by Jerry Ricks on Bayer Records (blues); and "Medley" (by Gershwin/Baker), recorded by Baker on K Records (jazz).

NAMAX MUSIC PUBLISHING, P.O. Box 24162, Richmond VA 23224. President: Nanette Brown. Music publisher. BMI. Estab. 1989. Publishes 2-4 songs/year; publishes 2 new songwriters/year. Works with composers; teams collaborators. Pays standard royalty.

How to Contact: Submit demo tape—unsolicited submissions are OK. Prefers cassette with 2 songs and lyric sheet. "No phone calls please." SASE. Reports in 6 weeks.

Music: Mostly R&B, urban contemporary and pop/top 40; also contemporary gospel. Published "Cynthia" (by Richard Williams), recorded by SoRich on Peak Records (R&B dance).

Tips: "Namax is looking for well constructed songs that deliver a positive message. Material should be as polished as possible."

*NASETAN PUBLISHING, Box 1485, Lake Charles LA 70602. (318)439-8839. Contact: Eddie Shuler. Music publisher. BMI. Estab. 1964. Publishes 35 songs/year; 9 new songwriters/year. Pays standard royalty.

Affiliate(s): Tek Publishing.

How to Contact: Submit demo tape—unsolicited submissions are OK. Prefers cassette with 4 songs maximum and lyric or lead sheet. Reports in 8 weeks.

Music: Novelty songs and story songs. Published "Doctor Oh Doctor," "Call The Cops Have a Family Reunion," and "Slow Horse Trail Ride," all recorded by Bob Brown the Barnyard Troubadour on Goldband Records.

Tips: "Song must have strong storyline with broad appeal for us to be interested."

NASHVILLE SOUND MUSIC PUBLISHING CO., P.O. Box 728, Peterborough, Ontario K9J 6Z8 **Canada.** (705)742-2381. President: Andrew Wilson Jr. Music publisher. SOCAN. Estab. 1985. Publishes 10 songs/year; publishes 5 new songwriters/year. Receives 50 submissions/month. Pays standard royalty.

Affiliate(s): Northern Sound Music Publishing Co. (SOCAN).

How to Contact: Submit demo tape—unsolicited submissions are OK. Prefers cassette or 7½ ips reel-to-reel with 2-4 songs and lyric sheet. "Please send only material you do not want returned. We have an open door policy." Reports in 2 weeks.

Music: Mostly country, country/pop and crossover country; also MOR, top 40, pop/rock and gospel. Published "A Hard Bridge to Cross" (by Stanton, Johnson, Young and Wilson), recorded by Faron Young on Step One Records (country); "Just Beyond the Pain" (by Ron Simons), recorded by Charlie Louvin and Crystal Gayle; and "Feelin' in My Bones" (by Carol Wakeford), recorded by Michele Bishop, both on Playback Records (country).

Tips: "Write the best song you've ever written with a strong hook, tear apart any weak lines, etc. and rewrite it. Then send it to me. We are only looking for the very best songs."

NAUTICAL MUSIC CO., Box 120675, Nashville TN 37212. (615)255-1068. Owner: Ray McGinnis. Music publisher and record company (Orbit Records, Ray McGinnis). BMI. Estab. 1965. Publishes 25 songs/year; 10 new songwriters/year. Receives 10-15 submissions/month. Works with composers. Pays standard royalty.

How to Contact: Submit demo tape—unsolicited submissions are OK. Prefers cassette with 4 songs and lyric sheets. SASE. Reports in 6-8 weeks.

Music: Mostly country ballads and country rock. Published "I Need The Real Thing" (by D. Acuff), recorded by Kim Tsoy (country); "Blame It On the Moonlight" (by T. Harrison), recorded by Da-Kota; and "Top of the Line" (by Stephen Heffker), recorded by Steve Wyles; all on Orbit Records.

Tips: "The trend is back to traditional country music with songs that tell a story."

NEBO RIDGE PUBLISHING COMPANY, P.O. Box 194 or 457, New Hope AL 35760. President: Walker Ikard. Manager: Jim Lewis. Music publisher, promotions firm, record producer, record company (Nebo Record Company), management firm (Nebo Management) and booking agency (Nebo Booking Agency). ASCAP. Estab. 1985. Works with composers and lyricists; teams collaborators. Pays standard royalty.

How to Contact: Submit demo tape—unsolicited submissions are OK. Prefers cassette demo tape (or VHS videocassette) with 1 song and lyric sheet. "A VHS video of a song would be helpful but not absolutely necessary." SASE always. Reports as soon as possible.

Music: Mostly modern and traditional country, modern and traditional gospel, country/rock, rock and roll, pop, MOR and bluegrass. Published "Never Fool Me" (by Flint), recorded by Flint Paint Rock; "Goin' Home" (by Osie), recorded by Osie Whitaker; and "For Your Love" (by Ed), recorded by Ed Walker, all on Nebo Records (country).

Tips: "We're mainly looking for female singers for our Nebo Record label now. Female singers should send a few full-length photos, a personal bio, a professional bio and a cassette demo tape of their songs. A VHS "talk tape" video would also be helpful."

NEON NOTES, 2729 Westwood Dr., Nashville TN 37204. (615)297-2329. President: Roy Yeager. Music publisher and record producer (Rumble Productions). ASCAP, BMI. Estab. 1987. Works with composers; teams collaborators. Pays standard royalty.

Affiliate(s): Yeager Master (BMI).

How to Contact: Submit a demo tape by mail—unsolicited submissions are OK. Prefers cassette with 3-4 songs and lyric sheets. SASE. Reports in 1 month.

Music: Mostly rock, pop and country; also new age.

*NETTWERK PRODUCTIONS, 1250 West 6th Ave., Vancouver, British Columbia V6H 1A5 **Canada**. (604)654-2929. FAX: (604)654-1993. A&R Assistant: Simon Hussey. Music publisher, record company, management company. Estab. 1984. Publishes 100+ songs/year; 4-5 new songwriters/year. Pays standard royalty.

How to Contact: Submit demo tape by mail—unsolicited submissions are OK. Prefers cassette with 4 songs. "Any biographical material would be helpful." Does not return unsolicited material. Reports in 2-3 months.

Music: Mostly rock, punk-funk and dance; also rap, dance-urban and folk-rock. Published "Path of Thorns" (by Sarah McLachlan), recorded by Pierre Marchand; "Killer Inside Me" (by MC900 Ft. Jesus); and "From A Million Miles" (by Single Gun Theory), recorded by Anthony Valcic, all on Nettwerk Records (single).

NETWORK SOUND MUSIC PUBLISHING INC., 119 Peachwood Dr., Swedesboro NJ 08085. (609)467-1682. President, A&R: Vito Fera. Office Manager: Rhonda Fera. Music publisher, record company (S.P.I.N. Records), record producer (Network Sound Productions) and songwriting organization. ASCAP. Estab. 1980. Publishes 10 songs/year; publishes 3 new songwriters/year. Receives 15 submissions/month. Hires staff writers "on agreement terms." Pays standard royalty.

Affiliate(s): Fera Music Publishing (BMI).
How to Contact: Submit a demo tape by mail or UPS with 3 songs maximum and lyric sheet. "Package song material carefully. Always label (name, address and phone) both cassette and lyric sheet. Copyright songs." SASE. Reports in 4 weeks. Unsolicited submissions are OK. Prefers cassette (or VHS videocassette).
Music: Mostly dance/pop, R&B, rock/medium and children's music. Published "You Know How" (by J. Giple), recorded by Steve Clarke (R&B); "Boy It's You" (by J. Giple), recorded by Meeta Gajjar (dance); and "Real Man," written and recorded by Kathy Layfield (ballad), all on S.P.I.N. Records.
Tips: "The 1990s are on their way to exhibiting the highest standards in music technology ever. Consequently, submitting music, especially in dance/pop, in 'raw or unpolished' form makes it somewhat more difficult to recognize the song's potential. The competition is stiff in the music industry and it's time to listen to the songs getting airplay, sharpen your writing skills, feel the 'hook line' and pay more attention to production. Record the best commercial demo you can afford with the lyrics clear and upfront. Best of luck!"

*A NEW RAP JAM PUBLISHING, P.O. Box 683, Lima OH 45802. (419)226-3509. President: James Milligan. Music publisher, record company. New Experience Records/Party House Publishing (BMI), Grand Slam Records/A New Rap Jam Publishing (ASCAP). Estab. 1989. Publishes 30 songs/year; publishes 2-3 new songwriters/year. Hires staff songwriters. Works with composers and lyricists; teams collaborators. Pays standard royalty.
How to Contact: Submit demo tape by mail. Unsolicited submissions are OK. Prefers cassette with 3-5 songs and lyric sheet or lead sheet. SASE. Reports in 1 month.
Music: Mostly R&B, pop, rock/rap; also contemporary, gospel, country, soul. Published "Can't Sleep at Night" (by James Milligan), recorded by James Junior on Grand Slam Records (R&B ballad); "Pure Heart" (by Carl Milligan), recorded by Carl Milligan on New Experience Records (gospel single); "On the Loose" (by Roger Woods), recorded by Just Smooth on Grand Slam Records (rap single).
Tips: "Believe in yourself. Work hard. Keep submitting songs and updates on new songs you have written. Most of all be somewhat patient. If there is interest you will be contacted."

NEWCREATURE MUSIC, Box 148296, Nashville TN 37214-8296. President: Bill Anderson, Jr. Music publisher, record company, record producer and radio and TV syndicator. BMI. Publishes 25 songs/year; publishes 2 new songwriters/year. Pays standard royalty.
How to Contact: Prefers 7½ ips reel-to-reel or cassette (or videocassette) with 4-10 songs and lyric sheet. SASE. Reports in 1 month.
Music: Country, gospel, jazz, R&B, rock and top 40/pop. Published "Cotton, Popcorn, Peanuts and Jesus" (by H. Yates), recorded by Joanne Cash on Jana Records (gospel); "His Love Is the Reason," written and recorded by Danny Vance on Livingsong Records (gospel); "Ragged Ole Memory" (by J. Jerigan), recorded by Jim Chute on Cootico Records (country); and "Barroom Preacher," recorded by Joanne Cash Yates.

*NISE PRODUCTIONS INC., 413 Cooper St., Camden NJ 08102. (609)963-NISE. President: Michael Nise. Music publisher, record company (Power Up-Sutra), recording studio (Power House) and production company. BMI. Publishes 10 songs/year; publishes 5 new songwriters/year. Pays standard royalty.
Affiliate(s): Logo III Records, Power Up Records and Wordan Records.
How to Contact: Prefers cassette (or videocassette) with 3 songs. Send Attention: Dan McKeown. SASE. Reports in 1 month.
Music: Mostly dance-oriented, R&B, country and pop, all with pop crossover potential; also children's, church/religious, easy listening, folk, gospel, jazz, rock, soul and top 40.
Tips: "Submit only well-produced demos."

NOW & THEN MUSIC, Suite 3, 501 78th St., North Bergen NJ 07047. (201)854-6266. Owner: Shane Faber. Music publisher, record company (Now & Then Records) and record producer. BMI. Estab. 1980. Pays standard royalty.
How to Contact: Submit a demo tape by mail—unsolicited submissions are OK. Prefers cassette with 4 songs and lyric sheet. SASE. Reports in 2 months.
Music: Mostly pop, dance and R&B; also rap and New Age.

NRP MUSIC GROUP, 10 Pebblewood, Irvine CA 92714. (714)552-5231. Vice-President: Fred Bailin. Music publisher. BMI, ASCAP. Estab. 1975. Publishes 10-20 songs/year; 2 new songwriters/year. Receives 80-100 submissions/year. Works with composers; teams collaborators. Pays standard royalty.

Affiliate(s): New Ideas Music Co. (BMI), Simma Music Co. Division (ASCAP), Perspective Music Co. (BMI).
How to Contact: Submit a demo tape by mail—unsolicited submissions are OK. Prefers cassette with lead sheets. SASE. Reports in 2 weeks.
Music: Mostly R&B, pop and rock; also rap.
Tips: "Use simple guitar/piano demos for showing songs at their best or worst!"

OBH MUSIKVERLAG OTTO B. HARTMANN, Box 2691, Ch-6901 Lugano **Switzerland.** FAX and Phone: 0041(91)685586. President: Otto B. Hartmann. Music publisher, record company (OKAY/ EXPO, Kick/OBH) and record producer. Estab. 1968. Publishes 100 songs/year; publishes 2 new songwriters/year. Hires staff writers. Works with composers and lyricists. Pays standard royalty.
Affiliate(s): Edition Plural (classical).
Music: Mostly rock, jazz, folk, pop and R&B; also classical.

OKISHER MUSIC, P.O. Box 20814, Oklahoma City OK 73156. (405)755-0315. President: Mickey Sherman. Music publisher, record company (Seeds Records, Okart Records, Homa Records and Okie Dokie Records), record producer and management firm (Mickey Sherman's Talent Management). BMI. Estab. 1973. Member OCMA. Publishes 10-15 songs/year; publishes 2-3 new songwriters/year. Receives 100 submissions/year. Works with composers and lyricists. Pays standard royalty.
How to Contact: Submit demo tape—unsolicited submissions OK. Prefers 7½ ips reel-to-reel or cassette (or VHS videocassette) with 1-3 songs and lyric sheet. "Don't let the song get buried in the videocassette productions; a bio in front of performance helps. Enclose press kit or other background information." Does not return unsolicited material. Reports in 1 month.
Music: Mostly blues, country and ballads; also easy listening, jazz, MOR, R&B and soul. Published "A Brighter Day," written and recorded by Dale Langley (gospel); and "Don't Do the Crime," written and recorded by JanJo (rock), both on Seeds Records.
Tips: "Send 3 songs *only* on good tape with lyric sheet."

OLD EMPRESS MUSIC/DOGHOUSE PRODUCTIONS, Suite 3, 1226 17th Ave. S., Nashville TN 37212. Professional Manager: Maurice Godwin/Hal Godwin. Music publisher. BMI, ASCAP, SESAC. Estab. 1987. Publishes 25-30 songs/year; publishes 5 new songwriters/year. Works with composers and lyricists; teams collaborators. Pays standard royalty.
Affiliate(s): UN-DER 16 Songs (SESAC), Old Empress Music (BMI), Girls on Film Music (BMI).
How to Contact: Submit demo tape—unsolicited submissions are OK. Prefers cassette with 4 songs and lyric sheets. "Use chrome tape only." SASE. Reports in 1 month.
Music: Mostly dance, rock and pop; also country and R&B. Published "Real" (by Roy Cathey Jr.), recorded by Mickey Dee on Rock City Records (rock); "Sheila Likes Hollywood," written and recorded by Bruce McMaster on Black Gold Records (rock); and "Last Refrain," written and recorded by Bruce McMaster on Bullet Records (rock ballad).

*****OLD SLOWPOKE MUSIC,** P.O. Box 52681, Tulsa OK 74152. (918)742-8087. President: Rodney Young. Music publisher, record producer. BMI. Estab. 1977. Publishes 24-36 songs/year; publishes 2-3 new songwriters/year. Works with composers and lyricists; teams collaborators. Pays standard royalty.
How to Contact: Write or call first and obtain permission to submit. Prefers cassette with 4 songs and lyric sheet. SASE. Reports in 4-6 weeks.
Music: Mostly Rock, country and R&B; also jazz. Published *Blue Dancer* written and recorded by Chris Blevins on CSR Records (CD and cassette); *She Can't Do Anything Wrong* (by Davis/Richmond), recorded by Bob Seger on Capitol Records (LP,CD, cassette).

O'LYRIC MUSIC, Suite 1, 1837 Eleventh St., Santa Monica CA 90404. (213)452-0815. President: J. O'Loughlin. Creative Director: Kathryn Haddock. Music publisher, manager (O'Lyric Music Management) and production company. BMI, ASCAP. Member California Copyright Conference. Estab. 1980. Publishes 50-75 songs/year; publishes 10-15 new songwriters/year. Hires staff writers; pays $20,000/year—"only duty expected is songwriting. Writers paid by royalties earned and by advances." Pays standard royalty to outside writers.
Affiliate(s): O'Lyrical Music (ASCAP).
How to Contact: Submit demo tape—unsolicited submissions OK. Prefers cassette with 1-3 songs and lyric sheet. Does not return materials. "Contact on acceptance only." Please no phone calls.
Music: Mostly R&B, rock, top 40, dance and country; also contemporary jazz and soul. Published "I Live for Your Love" (by P. Reswick/S. Werfil/A. Rich), recorded by Natalie Cole on Manhattan Records (R&B/crossover); "Mr. Right" (by T. Shapiro/M. Garvin), recorded by Smokey Robinson on Motown Records (R&B/crossover); and "I've Still Got the Love We Made" (by Shapiro/Garvin/ Waters), recorded by Reba McEntire (country/crossover). Production company works with Double T (Next Plateau Records), Cactus Choir (Atlantic Records), and The Biggs.

Tips: "Please follow our policy without exception."

ONE FOR THE MONEY MUSIC PUBLISHING CO. (BMI), P.O. Box 18751, Milwaukee WI 53218. (414)527-4477. President: Michael W. White. Music publisher, record company (World Class Record Co.) and record producer (MW Communications). BMI. Estab. 1989. Publishes 4-6 songs/year. Works with composers and lyricists; teams collaborators. Pays standard royalty.
How to Contact: Submit demo tape—unsolicited submissions are OK. Prefers cassette or VHS videocassette with 6-8 songs and lyric sheet (if possible). SASE. Reports in 1 month.
Music: Mostly country-rock, country-pop and country; also rock and R&B. Published "Whoops I'm in Love Again" (by White, Kowalski, Barker, Goetzke); "Twenty Three Days" (by M.W. White); and "Just Remember I'm Still Lovin' You" (by Kowalski, White, Barker); all recorded by Sky Harbor Band on World Class Records (country rock).

*ONE HUNDRED GRAND MUSIC, 11 Norton St., Newburgh NY 12550. (914)561-4483. President: Gregg Bauer. Music publisher, record company (100 Grand Records) and record producer. Estab. 1983. Publishes 10 songs/year; publishes 2 new songwriters/year. Teams collaborators. Pays standard royalty.
How to Contact: Write or call first and obtain permission to submit. Prefers cassette (or VHS videocassette) with 3-5 songs and lyric sheet. Submit videocassette "if it has a good story line and good audio." SASE. Reports in 1 month.
Music: Mostly rock, dance and R&B; also dance-oriented, MOR, progressive and soul. Published "Feeling Blue" (by P. Otero and G. Bauer) (rock); "Heart in Distress" by P. Otero; all on 100 Grand Records.

OPERATION PERFECTION, Suite 206, 6245 Bristol Pkwy., Culver City CA 90230. Contact: Larry McGee. Vice-President: Darryl McCorkle. Music publisher. BMI. Estab. 1976. Publishes 15 songs/year; publishes 1-2 new songwriters/year. Receives 200 submissions/year. Works with composers and lyricists. Pays standard royalty.
How to Contact: Submit a demo tape—unsolicited submissions OK. Prefers cassette (or VHS videocassette) with 1-4 songs and lyric sheet. "Please only send professional quality material!" SASE. Reports in 8 weeks.
Music: Rock, rap, pop, MOR/adult contemporary and R&B. Published "We're Number One" (by Liz Davis), recorded by The Saxon Sisters on Boogie Band (rock); "Captain Freedom" and "Voices" (by Kenny Sims), recorded by Sheena Kriss on Mega Star Records (R&B).
Tips: "Study past, present and future trends in the music industry."

ORCHID PUBLISHING, Bouquet-Orchid Enterprises, Box 11686, Atlanta GA 30355. (404)355-7635. President: Bill Bohannon. Music publisher, record company, record producer (Bouquet-orchid Enterprises) and artist management. BMI. Member CMA, AFM. Publishes 10-12 songs/year; publishes 3 new songwriters/year. Works with composers and lyricists; teams collaborators. Pays standard royalty.
How to Contact: Submit demo tape—unsolicited submissions OK. Prefers cassette with 3-5 songs and lyric sheet. "Send biographical information if possible—even a photo helps." SASE. Reports in 1 month.
Music: Religious ("Amy Grant, etc., contemporary gospel"); country ("Garth Brooks, The Trisha Yearwood type material"); and top 100/pop ("Bryan Adams, Whitney Houston type material"). Published "Where Do I Stand" (by Ralph Cherry), recorded by Adam Day; "Cross My Broken Heart" (by Clayton Russ), recorded by Susan Spencer (country); and "I Feel It" (by Tom Latham), recorded by Bandoleers (top 40), all on Bouquet Records.

ORDERLOTTSA MUSIC, (formerly Order Publishing), 6503 York Rd., Baltimore MD 21212. (410)377-2270. President: Jeff Order. Music publisher and record producer (Jeff Order/Order Productions). BMI. Estab. 1986. Publishes 20 songs/year; publishes 3-4 new songwriters/year. Receives 20 submissions/month. Works with composers and lyricists. Pays standard royalty.
How to Contact: Write first to submit a tape. Prefers cassette with 3 songs. SASE. Reports in 1 month.
Music: All types. Published "Won't You Dance With Me," recorded by Tiny Tim (dance); "Sea of Tranquility," "Isis Unveiled," and "Keepers of the Light," written and recorded by Jeff Order on Order Records (instrumental new age).

"How to Use Your Songwriter's Market" (at the front of this book) contains comments and suggestions to help you understand and use the information in these listings.

Tips: "Submit high-quality, well-recorded and produced material. Original styles and sounds. Don't waste our time or yours on copying the music of mainstream artists."

*OSPREY ENTERTAINMENT GROUP INC., P.O. Box 46465, Pass-A-Grille FL 33741. Vice President: Paul Davis. Music publisher, record company. Estab. 1989. Publishes 10 songs/year; 3-4 new songwriters/year. Works with composers and lyricists. Pays standard royalty.
Affiliate(s): OEG Music (BMI) and OEG Records.
How to Contact: Submit demo tape by mail—unsolicited submissions are OK. Prefers cassette with 3 songs and lyric sheet. SASE. Reports in 6-8 weeks.
Music: Mostly rock and pop; also R&B. Published *Pretend*, *Cinema's Crying* and *So With It*, all written and recorded by Michael English on OEG Records (LP).
Tips: "If you think a song would be perfect for a certain artist, mention it. Don't give up; plugging a song takes time."

OTTO PUBLISHING CO., P.O. Box 16540, Plantation FL 33318. (305)741-7766. President: Frank X. Loconto. Music publisher, record company (FXL Records) and record producer (Loconto Productions). ASCAP. Estab. 1978. Publishes 25 songs/year; publishes 1-5 new songwriters/year. Pays standard royalty.
Affiliate(s): Betty Brown Music Co. (BMI), and Clara Church Music Co. (SESAC), True Friends Music (BMI).
How to Contact: Prefers cassette with 1-4 songs and lyric sheet. SASE. Reports in 1 month.
Music: Mostly country, MOR, religious and gospel. Published "Sewing Without Pins" (TV theme) and "Safety Sam" (novelty), both by Frank X. Loconto, recorded by Loconto Productions. Theme Song for "Nightly Business Reports," nationally syndicated TV show, written and recorded by Frank X. Loconto. Also published "Seminole Man" (by Loconto), recorded by James Billie on FXL Records (country).

PADY MUSIC PUBLISHING CO., Box 3500, Pawtucket RI 02861. (401)728-1689. President: Karen Pady. Music publisher, record company (Pady Music Publishing Co.; Big K Records) and record producer (KA Productions, Karen Pady). ASCAP. Estab. 1986. Publishes 6 songs/year; publishes 1 new songwriter/year. Works with composers and lyricists; teams collaborators.
How to Contact: Write first and obtain permission to submit a tape. Prefers cassette or VHS videocassette with any number of songs and lyric sheet. SASE. Reports in 3 weeks.
Music: Mostly pop, rock and light rock; also country rock. Published "(You Were) My Best Friend," recorded by Karyn Krystal (country rock); "I Don't Need You," recorded by Karyn Krystal (rock); and "That's What I'm Living For," recorded by Midnight Fantasy (A/C); all by Karen Padykula on Big K Records.

R.A. PAINTER MUSIC PUBLISHING, P.O. Box 738, Ridgetop TN 37152-0738. (615)851-6860. FAX: (615)851-6857. President: Richard Allan Painter. Music publisher. BMI, ASCAP. Publishes 5-20 songs/year. Publishes 2-5 new songwriters/year. Pays standard royalty.
How to Contact: Send SASE for information.
Music: Suited for audiences that appreciate pop, rock, and R&B; such that translates into broad commercial appeal and staying power in the target market.
Tips: "Pursue excellence and tell the truth as your only artistic moral imperative."

J. S. PALUCH COMPANY, INC./WORLD LIBRARY PUBLICATIONS, INC., 3825 N. Willow Rd., P.O. Box 2703, Schiller Park IL 60176-0703. Music Editors: Mark G. Rachelski, Nicholas T. Freund, Betty Z. Reiber, John S. Paluch. Music publisher. SESAC. Estab. 1913. Publishes 50 or more songs/year; publishes varying number of new songwriters/year; recordings. Receives more than 500 submissions/year. Works with composers and lyricists; teams collaborators.
How to Contact: Submit demo tape by mail—unsolicited submissions are OK. Prefers cassette with any number of songs, lyric sheet and lead sheet. SASE. Reports in 3 months.
Music: Sacred music, songs, hymns, choral settings, descants, psalm settings, masses; also children's sacred music. Published "Alleluia" (by Noel Goemanne); "Glory to God" (by Steven Janco); and "Gather Your Children" (by James Chepponis) (all sacred).
Tips: "Make your manuscript as legible as possible, with clear ideas regarding tempo, etc. Base the text upon scripture."

PANDISC RECORDS, 38 NE 167 St., Miami FL 33162. (305)948-6466. President: Bo Crane. Music publisher and record company (Pandisc, Jamarc). ASCAP, BMI. Estab. 1979. Publishes 50 songs/year; publishes 3-6 new songwriters/year. Receives 200 submissions/month. Works with composers and lyricists; teams collaborators. Pays standard royalty.

Affiliate(s): Whooping Crane Music (BMI) and Hombre Del Mundo (ASCAP).
How to Contact: Submit a demo tape by mail—unsolicited submissions are OK. Prefers cassette with 3 songs and lyric sheet. Does not return unsolicited material.
Music: Mostly rap and R&B. Published "B Girls" (by C. Trahan/L. Johnson), recorded by Young & Restless (rap); and "I Can't Let Go" (by Y. Israel), recorded by Joey Gilmore (blues), both on Pandisc Records; and "I Seen Your Boyfriend," (by Baily/Daniels), recorded by Get Fresh Girls on Breakaway Records (rap).

PARCHMENT HARBOR MUSIC, P.O. Box 10895, Pleasanton CA 94588. (415)846-6194. CEO: Pam Hanna. Music publisher, record company (Wingate Records), record producer (Wingate) and artist management and talent agency (Wingate). BMI. Estab. 1989. Publishes 12 songs/year; publishes 2 new songwriters/year. Receives 50 submissions/month. Works with composers and lyricists; team collaborators. Pays standard royalty.
Affiliate(s): Hugo First Publishing (ASCAP).
How to Contact: Write and obtain permission to submit a tape. Prefers cassette with 2 songs and lyric sheet. "Include SASE and brief writer bio/discography." SASE. Reports in 4 weeks.
Music: Mostly pop, country and R&B; also rock, contemporary Christian and A/C. Published "The Most I Can Do" (by P. Hanna/G. Pickard), recorded by Kayla Moore on Wingate Records (contemporary country); "Lying Next to My Dream" (by R. LeBeau), recorded by Sylvia Winters on Stargem Records (country); and "Last American Hero" (by Dave May and Rusty Colt), recorded by Robyn Banx on Wingate Records (country).

*PARK J. TUNES, 29 S. Erie, Toledo OH 43602. Contact: Michael Drew Shaw. Music publisher, record company and record producer. ASCAP, BMI. Publishes 25 songs/year; publishes 5 new songwriters/year. Pays standard royalty.
Affiliate(s): Keeny/York (BMI), Newstar International Records.
How to Contact: Prefers cassette with 3 songs maximum and lyric sheet. SASE. Reports in 2 months.
Music: Country and top 40/pop. Published "Wherever You Are," recorded by MDS Studio Band; "We Are the Future," recorded by Kerry Clark; "Take a Ride," recorded by Mick Payne; and Michael Drew Shaw's *Devil Lake,* recorded by Michael Drew Shaw, on Newstar International Records (LP).

*PASSING PARADE MUSIC, P.O. Box 872, West Covina CA 91790. Owner: Kelly D. Lammers. Music publisher. ASCAP. Estab. 1972. Publishes 10-30 songs/year; publishes 3-6 new songwriters/year. Works with composers and lyricists; teams collaborators. Pays standard royalty.
How to Contact: Submit demo tape—unsolicited submissions are OK. Prefers cassette with 1-3 songs and lyric sheet. SASE. Reports in 6 weeks.
Music: Mostly country/pop, children's and A/C; also MOR, New Age and soundtrack material. Published "Punkline," recorded by The Surfaris on Koinkidink Records; "The Getaway," recorded by K. Lammers; and "No Turning Back," recorded by Kavaliers, both on Corby Records (all written by K. Lammers).
Tips: "Hone your writing skills, and learn how to get from here to there as quickly and craftily as possible. If it's a ballad, tell a good story. Also, keep our seasoned performers in mind. They need good material too! Everything old is new again, as was proven by Natalie Cole and Harry Connick, Jr. Don't be afraid to write for that big band sound. It may be coming back to a brand new audience, loud and strong."

PDS MUSIC PUBLISHING, P.O. Box 412477, Kansas City MO 64141-2477. Contact: Submissions Department. Music publisher and record company (PDS Records, Universal Jazz, PDS Associated labels). ASCAP, BMI. Estab. 1988. Publishes 30 songs/year; publishes 3-4 new songwriters/year. Receives 4 submissions/month. Works with composers and lyricists. Pays standard royalty.
Affiliate(s): PDS Universal (ASCAP), PDS Worldwide (BMI).
How to Contact: Write first and obtain permission to submit a tape. Prefers cassette with 5-10 songs and lyric sheet. Does not return unsolicited material. Reports in 2 months.
Music: Mostly rap and R&B. Published "I Like the Things You Do" (by Derrick Peters/Kevin Griffin), recorded by Kevin Griffin on PDS Records (R&B); "The Way You Make Me Feel" (by D. Peters), recorded by Legacy on PDS Records (R&B).
Tips: "Follow directions and be patient."

PECOS VALLEY MUSIC, 2709 West Pine Lodge, Roswell NM 88201. (505)622-0244. President: Ray Willmon. Music publisher. BMI. Estab. 1989. Publishes 15-20 songs/year; publishes 3-4 new songwriters/year. Receives 40-50 submissions/month. Works with composers and lyricists; teams collaborators. Pays standard royalty.

How to Contact: Submit a demo tape by mail—unsolicited submissions are OK. Prefers cassette (or VHS cassette if available) with 2-4 songs and lyric sheet. SASE. Reports in 3 weeks.
Music: Mostly country, pop and rock. Published "Week-end Daddy," written and recorded by Ron Shaeder; "Jesus Is My Hero" and "You Can Use My Shoulder," written and recorded by Ray Willmon, all on Sun Country Records (country).
Tips: "Write original lyrics with an understandable story line with correct song form (i.e., AAAA, AABA, ABAB)."

PEERMUSIC, 8159 Hollywood Blvd., Los Angeles CA 90069. (213)656-0364. Director, Creative Services: Nanci M. Walker. Music publisher and artist development promotional label. ASCAP, BMI. Estab. 1928. Publishes 40 songs/year; publishes 2-5 new songwriters/year. Hires staff songwriters. Works with self-contained artists.
Affiliate(s): P.S.O. LTD (ASCAP), Peermusic (BMI).
How to Contact: "Submit material through an established music attorney or manager." Prefer CD or cassette with 3 songs and lyric sheet. Does not return unsolicited material. Reports in 3 months.
Music: Mostly pop, rock, R&B, alternative and all types.

PEGASUS MUSIC, 27 Bayside Ave., Te Atatu, Auckland 8, **New Zealand.** Professional Manager: Errol Peters. Music publisher and record company. APRA. Estab. 1981. Publishes 20-30 songs/year; publishes 5 new songwriters/year. Receives 20-30 submissions/year. Works with composers and lyricists; teams collaborators. Pays 3-5% to artists on contract and standard royalty to songwriters; royalties paid directly to US songwriters.
How to Contact: Submit a demo tape—unsolicited submissions are OK. Prefers cassette with 3-5 songs and lyric sheet. SAE and IRC. Reports in 1 month.
Music: Mostly country; also bluegrass, easy listening and top 40/pop. Published "Hobo In A Silk Shirt" (by Ginny Peters), recorded by Dennis Marsh on Ode Records (country); "I Only See You" (by Ginny Peters), recorded by Cliffie Stone on Capitol Records (country); and "Grand Dad" (by Bill Whall), recorded by Tina Whall on Ode Records (country).
Tips: "Be very direct and do not use too many words. Less is better."

PENNY THOUGHTS MUSIC, 484 Lexington St., Waltham MA 02154. (617)891-7800. President: John Penny. Music publisher, record company (Belmont Records and Waverly Records) and record producer. BMI. Publishes 12-15 songs/year. Receives 10-12 submissions/months. Pays standard royalty.
How to Contact: Write first to get permission to submit a tape. SASE. Reports in 2 weeks.
Music: Mostly country; also contemporary and rock (country). Published "Give It Away," written and recorded by Stan Anderson Jr. on Belmont Records (country); and "The Hurt That Hurts Me" and "You're the Right Love," by Mike Cummings (country).

PERFECTION MUSIC PUBLICATION (BMI), P.O. Box 4094, Pittsburgh PA 15201. (412)782-4477. President: Edward J. Moschetti. Music publisher and record company (Century Records). Estab. 1953. Works with composers.
Affiliate(s): Regal Music Publications (ASCAP).
How to Contact: Write first and obtain permission to submit. Prefers cassette. SASE. Reports in 1 month.
Music: Ballads, country and pop.

PHILIPPOPOLIS MUSIC, 12027 Califa St., North Hollywood CA 91607. President: Milcho Leviev. Music publisher. BMI. Member GEMA, NARAS. Estab. 1975. Publishes 3-5 songs/year; publishes 1-2 new songwriters/year. Works with lyricists. Pays standard royalty.
How to Contact: Submit demo tape—unsolicited submissions are OK. Prefers cassette with 1-3 songs. Prefers studio produced demos. SASE. Reports in 1 month.
Music: Jazz and classical fusion. Published "Minor's Boogie," "Mody Moods" and "B Minor," all written and recorded by Leviev on MA (Japan) Records (jazz).

PIN PUBLISHING, 18 Harvest Ln., Charlotte NC 28210. (704)554-1162. Director: Butch Kelly. Music publisher, record company (Kam Executive, Fresh Aire, New Town Records) and record producer (Butch Kelly Productions). ASCAP, BMI. Estab. 1981. Publishes 10 songs/year; publishes 3 new songwriters/year. Teams collaborators. Pays standard royalty.
Affiliate(s): Pin Publishing (ASCAP), Music by Butch Kelly (BMI).
How to Contact: Write first and obtain permission to submit a tape. Prefers cassette (VHS videocassette) with 3 songs and lyric sheets. SASE. Reports in 2 months.
Music: Mostly pop, R&B and rock; also rap. Published "Power" (by Butch Kelly), recorded by Sunshine on KAM Records (R&B); "Money" (by Greg B.), recorded by Greg B. on KAM Records (R&B); and "War" (by McCrush), recorded by T.K. on KAM Records (pop).

PINE ISLAND MUSIC, #308, 9430 Live Oak Place, Ft. Lauderdale FL 33324. (305)472-7757. President: Jack P. Bluestein. Music publisher, record company and record producer. BMI, ASCAP. Estab. 1973-1974. Publishes 50-100 songs/year; publishes 25-30 new songwriters/year. Receives 100 submissions/month. Works with composers, lyricists; teams collaborators. Pays standard royalty.
Affiliate(s): Lantana Music (BMI) and Twister Music (ASCAP).
How to Contact: Submit a demo tape — unsolicited submissions OK. Prefers cassette or 7½ ips reel-to-reel (or VHS videocassette) with 3 songs and lyric sheet. SASE. Reports in 2-4 months.
Music: Mostly country and pop; also gospel, soft rock and contemporary. Published "Golden Penny" written and recorded by Walt Sambor on Quadrant Records (children's country); "Lucky Is A Man" (by Larry Coen), recorded by Al Williams on Quadrant Records (country/pop); "Kathy, Dear" (by Al Williams), recorded by Kathy Ratzburg on Quadrant Records (pop/C&W) and "Love Was Talking to Us," (by T. Majeski and J. Wagner), recorded by Sherry Victoria Vencill on Quadrant Records (contemporary rock).

PLACER PUBLISHING, Box 11301, Kansas City KS 66111. (913)287-3495 (night). Owner: Steve Vail. Music publisher, record company (System Records) and record producer. ASCAP. Estab. 1980. Publishes 2 songs/year; publishes 1 new songwriter/year. Receives 10 submissions/month. Works with composers and lyricists. Pays standard royalty.
How to Contact: Submit a demo tape — unsolicited submissions are OK. Prefers cassette (or VHS or Beta ½" videocassette) with 10-12 songs. Does not return unsolicited material. Reports in 6 months.
Music: Mostly classical rock, New Age and jazz. Published "Echo Lake," "Mother Earth, Father Sky" and "The Path" (all by Vail and Studna), recorded by Realm on System Records (progressive rock).

PLANET DALLAS RECORDING STUDIOS, P.O. Box 191447, Dallas TX 75219. (214)521-2216. Producer, Music publisher, record producer (Rick Rooney) and recording studio (Planet Dallas). BMI, ASCAP. Estab. 1985. Publishes 50 songs/year; 2-3 new songwriters/year. Receives 20 submissions/month. Works with composers and lyricists; teams collaborators. Pays standard royalty; also depends on deal/studio involvement.
Affiliate(s): Stoli Music (BMI) and Planet Motherslip Music (ASCAP).
How to Contact: Submit demo tape — unsolicited submissions OK. Prefers cassette with 1-3 songs and lyric sheet. SASE for reply. Reports in 8 weeks.
Music: Mostly modern rock. Published "This Property is Condemned" (by P. Sugg), recorded by Maria McKee on Geffen Records (pop); "Tickle" (by U Know Who), recorded by U Know Who on WE—Mix Records (rap); and "Hydrogen City" (by Hydrogen City), recorded by Hydrogen City on H1 Records (rock).

PLATINUM BOULEVARD PUBLISHING, 523 East Prater Ave., Reno NV 89431. (702)358-7484. President: Lawrence Davis. Music publisher. BMI. Estab. 1984. Publishes 12 songs/year; 1 new songwriter/year. Receives 30 submissions/month. Works with composers and lyricists. Pays standard royalty, but will negotiate.
How to Contact: Submit a demo tape by mail — unsolicited submissions are OK. Prefers cassette (or VHS videocassette), with unlimited songs and lyric or lead sheets. "Songs must be in English." Does not return unsolicited material. "We report only if interested."
Music: Mostly rock, country and R&B; also country, jazz and New Age. Published "Long Haul," "Crazy Thing" and "Don't Shut Me Out," all written and recorded by Lawrence Davis on Platinum Boulevard Records (AOR).
Tips: "We own a 24-track studio and are willing to provide inexpensive recording time to qualified artists wishing to improve their demo sound."

*PLATINUM PRODUCTIONS PUBLISHING, 406 Centre St., Boston MA 02130. (617)983-9999. A&R Rep.: Akhil Garland. Music publisher, record company. Estab. 1989. Publishes 2 new songs/year; 2 new songwriters/year. Works with composers and lyricists; teams collaborators. Pays standard royalty.
How to Contact: Submit demo tape — unsolicited submissions are OK. Prefers cassette with 4 songs and lyric sheet. SASE. Reports in 1 month.
Music: Mostly reggae, folk and world beat; also rap/R&B and rock.

POLLYBYRD PUBLICATIONS LIMITED, P.O. Box 8442, Universal CA 91608. (818)506-8533. Professional Manager: Maxx Diamond. Music publisher (Kelli Jai, Pollyann, Ja Nikki, Lonnvaness Branmar and PPL Music). ASCAP, BMI, SESAC. Estab. 1979. Publishes 100 songs/year; publishes 25-40 new songwriters/year. Hires staff writers. Works with composers and lyricists; teams collaborators. Pays standard royalty.

Affiliate(s): Kellijai Music (ASCAP), Pollyann Music (ASCAP), Ja'Nikki Songs (BMI), Branmar (BMI), Lonnvanness (SESAC) and PPL Music (ASCAP).
How to Contact: Submit demo tape—unsolicited submissions are OK. Prefers cassette or VHS videocassette with 4 songs and lyric and lead sheet. SASE. Reports in 6 weeks.
Music: Published "Hero" (by J. Jarrett), recorded by The Band AKA (dance-R&B); "Anything" (by D. Mitchell), recorded by D.M. Groove (dance-R&B); and "Cool Fire" (by J. Jarrett), recorded by Katrina Gibson, all on Bouvier/Sony Records (dance/pop).

*PORTAGE MUSIC, 16634 Gannon W., Rosemont MN 55068. (612)432-5737. President: Larry LaPole. Music publisher. BMI. Publishes 5-20 songs/year. Pays standard royalty.
How to Contact: Prefers cassette with 3 songs and lyric sheet.
Music: Mostly country and country rock.
Tips: "Keep songs short, simple and upbeat with positive theme."

PPI/PETER PAN INDUSTRIES, 88 St. Francis St., Newark NJ 07105. (201)344-4214. Product Manager: Marianne Eggleston. Music publisher, record company (Compose Records, Current Records, Parade Video, Ironbound Publishing, record producer (Dunn Pearson, Jr.); also outside producers. ASCAP, BMI. Estab. 1928. Publishes over 100 songs/year. Hires staff songwriters. Works with composers and lyricists; teams collaborators. Pays standard royalty "based on agreements."
Affiliate(s): Ironbound Publishing (ASCAP), Triloka Records, DA Music.
How to Contact: Submit a demo tape by mail—unsolicited submissions are OK. Prefers cassette (or VHS videocassette if available) with 3-5 songs. "Please include name, address and phone numbers on all materials, along with picture, bio and contact information." SASE. Reports in 3 weeks to 3 months.
Music: Mostly children's—audio, R&B and jazzy; also exercise—video, rock and classical. Published "Beautiful Lullabyes" (by Dunn Pearson, Jr.), recorded by Tawatha Agee and Bill Rippone on Compose Records (children's CD/cass.); "Frankie Paul," written and recorded by Frankie Paul on Tassa/Compose Records (reggae); and "Manhattan Jazz Reunion," written and recorded by Manhattan Jazz Reunion on Compose/Sweet Basil Records (jazz).

PRATT AND MCCLAIN MUSIC (ASCAP), Box 852, Beverly Hills CA 90213. (818)769-2842. President: Jeremy McClain. Music publisher and record producer. Deals with artists and songwriters. Voting member of NARAS. Gold record and Grammy winner on "Happy Days" (theme from TV show). Pays standard royalty.
Affiliate(s): Rock Revival Music Co. (ASCAP).
How to Contact: Submit a demo tape—unsolicited submissions are OK.
Music Mostly pop, rock and some progressive gospel.
Tips: "Direct access to Donna Summer, Christopher Cross, Debbie Boone, Amy Grant and Michael Omartian."

PREJIPPIE MUSIC GROUP, Box 2849, Trolley Station, Detroit MI 48231. (313)581-1267. Partner: Bruce Henderson. Music publisher, record company (PMG Records) and record producer (PMG Productions). BMI. Estab. 1990. Publishes 50-75 songs/year; publishes 2-3 new songwriters/year. Hires staff writers. Teams collaborators. Pays standard royalty.
How to Contact: Submit a demo tape by mail—unsolicited submissions are OK. Prefers cassette with 3-4 songs and lyric sheet. "No phone calls please." SASE. Reports in 6 weeks.
Music: Mostly techno/house, funk/rock, dance; also alternative rock, experimental and jingle-oriented music. Published "Redd Hott" and "Love Me" (by Bruce and Victoria Henderson), recorded by The Prejippies on PMG Records (funky-house); and "Atmosphere 1" (by Bruce and Victoria Henderson), used for several video productions (a jingle).
Tips: "Think your arrangements through carefully. Always have a strong hook (whether vocal-oriented or instrumental)."

PRESCRIPTION COMPANY, 70 Murray Ave., Port Washington NY 11050. (516)767-1929. President: David F. Gasman. Music publisher and record producer. BMI. Pays standard royalty.
How to Contact: Call or write first about your interest. Prefers cassette with any number of songs and lyric sheet. "Send all submissions with SASE (or no returns)." Reports in 1 month.
Music: Bluegrass, blues, children's, country, dance-oriented, easy listening, folk, jazz, MOR, progressive, R&B, rock, soul and top 40/pop. Published "You Came In," "Rock 'n' Roll Blues" and "Seasons" (by D.F. Gasman), all recorded by Medicine Mike on Prescription Records.
Tips: "Songs should be good and written to last. Forget fads—we want songs that'll sound as good in 10 years as they do today. Organization, communication and exploration of form are as essential as message (and sincerity matters, too)."

JIMMY PRICE MUSIC PUBLISHER, Sun-Ray Production Company, 1662 Wyatt Parkway, Lexington KY 40505. (606)254-7474. Owner: Jimmy Price. Music publisher, record company (Sun-Ray, Sky-Vue) and record producer (Jimmy Price Music Publisher). BMI. Estab. 1950. Works with composers and lyricists. Pays standard royalty.
Affiliate(s): Jimmy Price Productions (BMI).
How to Contact: Submit a demo tape by mail—unsolicited submissions are OK. Prefers cassette or track ½ or Full 7½ ips reel-to-reel with 3-7 songs and lyric sheet. SASE. Reports in 5-6 weeks.
Music: Mostly country, gospel and bluegrass. Published "Close to You" (by S. Drouin); "Texas Little Cutie" (by J.T. Price), both recorded by Carry Vice on Sun-Ray Records (country); and "That's OK I Love You" (by R.E. Johnson), recorded by R.E. Johnson on Sky-Vue Records (country).
Tips: "I must have the lyrics to meter. If a person does not know what I mean about bringing lyrics to meter, please check a gospel hymn song book. You will see in each and every staff there is a music note for each and every word or syllable. This way, should I want to add a composition in print I can do so."

PRINCE/SF PUBLICATIONS, 1135 Francisco St., San Francisco CA 94109. (415)775-9627. Artists Representative: Ken Malucelli. Music publisher (Auriga, Christmas) and record producer (Prince/SF Productions). ASCAP. Estab. 1975. Publishes 2 songs/year; publishes 2 new songwriters/year. Works with composers and lyricists "under personal management"; teams collaborators. Pays statutory rate.
How to Contact: Write first and obtain permission to submit a tape. "Unsolicited material not accepted. Work accepted from San Francisco Bay area artists only." Prefers cassette with VHS videocassette with 3 songs and lyric or lead sheet. "Primarily interested in a cappella, novelty, theatrical material." SASE. Reports ASAP.
Music: Mostly original pop, Christmas and satire; also unusual, humorous. Published "Oh What a Heavenly Morn!" (by Ken Malucelli), recorded by Merrie Olde Christmas Carolers on Christmas Records (holiday); "Freedomsong" (by Eric Morris), recorded by The Edlos on Auriga Records (pop); and "Package" (by Eric Morris), recorded by The Edlos on Auriga Records (pop).
Tips: "Work should be unique, high quality, not derivative."

PRITCHETT PUBLICATION (Branch), P.O. Box 725, Daytona Beach FL 32114-0725. (904)252-4848. Vice President: Charles Vickers. Music publisher and record company. (Main office in California.) BMI. Estab. 1975. Publishes 21 songs/year; publishes 12 new songwriters/year. Works with composers and lyricists. Pays standard royalty.
Affiliate(s): Alison Music (ASCAP).
How to Contact: Write first and obtain permission to submit. Prefers cassette with 6 songs and lyric or lead sheet. SASE.
Music: Gospel, rock-disco and country. Published *Walkin On The Water* (by Charles Vickers), recorded by Charles Vickers on King of Kings Records (gospel); and "It'll Be A Cold Day" (by Leroy Pritchett), recorded by Ray Sanders on Allagash Country Records (country).

PROPHECY PUBLISHING, INC., P.O. Box 4945, Austin TX 78765. (512)459-6036. President: T. White. Music publisher. ASCAP. Pays standard royalty, less expenses; "expenses such as tape duplicating, photocopying and long distance phone calls are recouped from the writer's earnings."
Affiliate(s): Black Coffee Music (BMI).
How to Contact: "We now only accept songs which are currently on the charts or have a very good chance of entering them next week."
Music: Published "The Sun and Moon and Stars" and"Woman of the Phoenix," (by Vince Bell), performed by Nancy Griffith on MCA Records.
Tips: "Only songs with immediate projected income would entice us to add to our roster."

PUBLISHING CENTRAL, 7251 Lowell Dr., Overland Park KS 66204. (913)384-6688. Director of Publishing: David Jackson. Music publisher. "We are also a theatrical agency." SAG, ITAA. Estab. 1961. Publishes 5 songs/year; publishes 3 new songwriter/year. Teams collaborators. Pays standard royalty.
Affiliate(s): Jac-Zang (ASCAP), Bunion (BMI).
How to Contact: Submit a demo tape—unsolicited submissions are OK. Prefers cassette with 1-3 songs and lead sheets. SASE. Reports in 2 months.
Music: Mostly country rock, pop and rock; also gospel reggae, alternative, cutting edge and soul (southern). Published "Gospel Classical" and "The Water Is Wide," both written and recorded by Dutton Family on Independent Records (gospel).
Tips: "There is a trend toward more professionalism. More songwriters can actually write music. They provide lead sheets and not just lyrics and tapes. Take advantage of the advances in music technology and put a part of your soul in your composition."

*PUDDLETOWN MUSIC PUBLISHING, 8855 SW Holly, Suite 110, Wilsonville OR 97070. Director A&R: Ray Woods. Music publisher. Estab. 1991. Publishes 30 songs/year; 3 new songwriters/year. Works with composers. Pays standard royalty.
Affiliate(s): Bygum Publishing, Med Sun Music, Affirm Action and Unsingable Songs (all BMI).
How to Contact: Write first and obtain permission to submit. Prefers cassette with 2-3 songs and lyric sheet. SASE. Reports in 2 months.
Music: Mostly alternative rock and hard rock; also music for film, surf tunes and industrial. Published *Meet Mr. Starfish* (by Ted Hibsman), recorded by The Refreshments (CD); *Rugburn*, (by Wammo), recorded by WORM (CD); and "Devil's Child" (by Billy Snow), recorded by Young Turks (single) all on Rainforest Records.
Tips: "Do not submit material in the blind. Do research and contact companies for permission first. Needs are very specific.

PURPLE HAZE MUSIC, P.O. Box 1243, Beckley WV 25802. President: Richard L. Petry. (304)252-4836. A & R: Carol Lee. Music publisher. BMI. Estab. 1968. Publishes 3-5 songs/year; publishes 3-4 new songwriters/year. Receives 150 submissions/year. Works with composers and lyricists; teams collaborators. Pays standard royalty.
How to Contact: Submit demo tape—unsolicited submissions are OK. Prefers cassette with 3-5 songs and lyric sheet. SASE. Reports in 4 weeks.
Music: Country, pop/top 40 and R&B/crossover. Published "Keep Movin' " (by Chuck Paul), recorded by Chuck Paul on Rising Sun Records; "A Little Night Lovin' " (by Carol Lee), recorded by Victor Jackson on Rising Sun Records (R&B); and "Dixieman" (by Don MacLean and Ron Miller), recorded by Cypress Creek on Country Road Records (country).
Tips: "Make sure your song is well written. Submit professional demo by professionals. You are competing with Nashville's best. We have to do what's best by Nashville."

PUSTAKA MUZIK EMI (Malaysia) SDN. BHD., Suite 10.01, 10th Floor, Exchange Square, off Jalan Semantan, Damansara Heights, 50490 Kuala Lumpur, Malaysia. Phone: 03-6277511. Contact: Publishing Manager. Music publisher and record company. Publishes 50 songs/year; publishes 15 new songwriters/year. Receives 200-300 submissions/month. Works with composers and lyricists; teams collaborators. Pays standard royalty
How to Contact: Submit demo tape—unsolicited submissions are OK. Prefers cassette and lyric or lead sheet. Does not return unsolicited material. Reports in 1 month.
Music: Mostly MOR, country and commercial jazz; also blues and rock. Published "Kitalah Bintang" (by Aris Ariwatan), recorded by Ella; "Intan Dan Keca" (by Razman), recorded by Rahmat, both on EMI Records; and "Pada Sywrga" (by Fzuai Marzuki), recorded by Nash on WEA Records (all rock).
Tips: "Please send us properly recorded demo tape containing commercial pop, rock musical material."

QMARK MUSIC, 1201 Carlisle Ave., York PA 17404. (717)843-4228. President: Lewis Quintin. Music publisher. BMI. Estab. 1985. Publishes 12 songs/year; publishes 3 new songwriters/year. Pays standard royalty.
Affiliate(s): Barquin Music (ASCAP).
How to Contact: Write first and obtain permission to submit a tape. Prefers cassette with 2 songs and lyric sheet. Does not return unsolicited material. Reports in 6 weeks.
Music: Mostly country and r&b. Published "José" (by B. Belton), "Subway Casanova" (by Barken), and "Walking Down the Avenue" (by Belton); all recorded by Spyke on Qmark Records (pop/rock).

*QUAN-YAA RECORDS, P.O. Box 16606, Philadelphia PA 19139-0606. (215)747-2256. FAX: (215)471-0415. Vice President of Marketing/Sales: Jackie Campbell. Music publisher, record company. Estab. 1990. Publishes 15 songs/year; publishes 5 new songwriters/year. Works with composers and lyricists; teams collaborators. Pays standard royalty.
How to Contact: Write or call first and obtain permission to submit. Prefers cassette (or VHS videocassette) with 3 songs. "Put name, address and phone number on cassette." SASE. Reports in 1 month.
Music: Mostly R&B, rap and reggae; also pop, country and salsa. Published *Foreigner* (by Bramwell/Russell/Shaw), recorded by Nagasa (reggae LP); "The Master's Here" (by Bryant/Gerring), recorded by Ultrafunk (rap single); and "Count on Me" (by Curry/Virtue), recorded by Lambchops (R&B single), all on Quan-yaa Records.
Tips: "Keep up with the trends. Love songs are in."

R. J. MUSIC, 10A Margaret Rd., Barnet, Herts. EN4 9NP **United Kingdom.** Phone: (01)440-9788. Managing Directors: Roger James and Laura Skuce. Music publisher and management firm (Roger James Management). PRS. Pays negotiable royalty (up to 75%).

How to Contact: Prefers cassette with 1 song and lyric or lead sheet. Does not return material.
Music: Mostly MOR, blues, country and rock; also chart material. "No disco or rap!"

R.T.L. MUSIC, LEE MUSIC, LE MATTE MUSIC, POGO RECORDS, Stewart House, Hill Bottom Road, Sands-Ind. Est., Highwycome, Buckinghamshire HP12 4HJ **United Kingdom**. Telephone (0630)647374. FAX: (0630)647612. A&R: Xavier Lee. Music publisher. PRS (UK). Estab. 1971. Works with composers and lyricists; teams collaborators. Pays standard royalty. Publishes 120 songs/year; publishes 50 new songwriters/year. Receives 10-15 submissions/month.
How to Contact: Submit a demo tape—unsolicited submissions are OK. Prefers cassette, VHS videocassette with 3 songs and lyric or lead sheets. SASE. Reports in 6 weeks.
Music: All types. Published "Time" and "Go Now," written and recorded by Row Lee on Swoop Records (pop); "My Boy," written and recorded by Xavier Lee on Check Records (pop).
Tips: "Be original and don't follow existing trends."

*RAGLAND PUBLICATIONS, Box 43659, Las Vegas NV 89116. (702)794-4588. President: Lou Ragland. Music publisher, record company (Casino Records Inc., Spirit Records of Nevada) record producer (Ragland Enterprises). BMI. Estab. 1962. Publishes 10 songs/year; 2 new songwriters/year. Hires staff writers. Works with composers and lyricists; teams collaborators. Pays standard royalty.
How to Contact: Submit a demo tape—unsolicited submissions are OK. Prefers cassette with 4 songs and lyric sheets. SASE. Reports in 2½ months.
Music: Mostly pop, R&B and all gospel; also rock. Published "Real Love," written and recorded by William Ferguson (pop); "Joey Wish," written and recorded by Ed Tate (country) and ""Put the Merry Back in Xmas" (by GiGi Copeland and Wilma Fickland), recorded by Chocolate Williams (blues), all on Casino Records.
Tips: "Produce the best demo that you can, and use a very very good vocalist!.."

RECORD COMPANY OF THE SOUTH (RCS) & VETTER MUSIC PUB., P.O. Box 14685, Baton Rouge LA 70898. (504)766-3233. FAX: (504)766-4112. General Manager: Johnny Palazzotto. Music publisher. ASCAP, BMI. Estab. 1978. Pays standard royalty.
How to Contact: Submit a demo tape—unsolicited submissions are OK. Prefers cassette with 3-5 songs. SASE. Reports in 2-4 weeks.
Music: Mostly rock, R&B and country. Published "Knockin' Around" (by B. Hornsby), recorded by Joe Doe on Geffen Records (rock); and "Groovin' Out" (by C. Vetter), recorded by Joe Stampley on Paula Records (rock).

RED BOOTS TUNES, (formerly Northwest International Entertainment), 5503 Roosevelt Way NE, Seattle WA 98105. (206)524-1020. FAX: (206)524-1102. Music publisher. ASCAP. Estab. 1991. Publishes 25 songs/year; publishes 2-3 new songwriters/year. Receives 300 submissions/year. Works with teams collaborators. Pays standard royalty.
How to Contact: Submit a demo tape by mail. Prefers cassette with 2-3 songs and lyric sheet. SASE. Reports in 6-8 weeks.
Music: Mostly country; also R&B/rock.
Tips: "Have professional looking lyric sheets and good quality tapes."

*RED BUS MUSIC INTERNATIONAL, LTD., 48 Broadley Terrace, London NW1, **United Kingdom**. 44-(071)-258-0324. FAX: (071)724-2163 . Managing Director: Ellis Elias. Music publisher and record company. PRS, ASCAP, BMI. Member MPA. Publishes 120 songs/year; publishes 6 new songwriters/year. Pays standard royalty; royalties paid to songwriter through US publishing affiliate.
Affiliate(s): Our Music Ltd., Chibell Music Ltd., Grade One Music Ltd. and Mother Goose Music Ltd.
How to Contact: Prefers cassette and lyric sheet. SAE and IRC. Reports in 1 month.
Music: Dance-oriented, MOR, rock and top 40/pop. Published "Cruel Summer" (by Jolley/Swain), recorded by Bananarana on London Records (pop); "Thank You My Love," and "Found My Love" (by John/Ingram), recorded by Imagination on Elektra Records (R&B); and "Soul Street," (by Jolley/Swain), written and recorded by Jolley and Swain on London Records (R&B); "The Flame" (by B. Mitchel/N. Graham), recorded by Cheaptrick on Epic Records.

*JACK REDICK MUSIC, Rt. 1, Box 85, Georgetown SC 29440. Manager: Jack Redick. Works with composers and lyricists. Pays standard royalty.
Affiliate: Wagon Wheel Records.
How to Contact: Prefers cassette (or VHS videocassette) with 1-6 songs, plus typed lyrics; also photo, bio, and credits if possible. SASE. "Never send your original master tape of anything, make copies to mail out. We're mostly interested in unpublished material; indicate if it's copyrighted. Also willing to co-write with lyricists or composers with 50-50, collaboration contract. On lyrics for co-write, send

only material that's clear (not tied up with anyone) and that you're the sole writer on. When submitting a demo, identify the singer."

Music: Mostly traditional country and country gospel, some crossover, rockabilly, humorous and tribute styles. Published "Please Mr. D.J.," "This Man Named Jesus," "My Head Is Spinning" and "Show Me The Stairway".

Tips: "Lyrics should be over music. Tell a new story, or an old story with a new twist. Hooks (attention grabbers) should be in title, and in 'MEAT' of song. DON'T BE A DREAMER, CAUSE WHEN A DREAMER AWAKES THE DREAM IS GONE. BE A WORKER, AND MAKE YOUR DREAMS HAPPEN."

REN MAUR MUSIC CORP., 521 5th Ave., New York NY 10175. (212)757-3638. President: Rena L. Feeney. Music publisher and record company. BMI. Member AGAC and NARAS. Publishes 6-8 songs/year. Pays 4-8% royalty.
Affiliate: R.R. Music (ASCAP).
How to Contact: Prefers cassette with 2-4 songs and lead sheet. SASE. Reports in 1 month.
Music: R&B, rock, soul and top 40/pop. Published "Same Language," "Do It to Me and I'll Do It to You," and "Once You Fall in Love" (by Billy Nichols), recorded by Rena; and "Lead Me to Love" (by Brad Smiley), recorded by Carmen John (ballad/dance), all on Factory Beat Records.
Tips: "Send lead sheets and a good, almost finished cassette ready for producing or remixing."

RHYTHMS PRODUCTIONS, Whitney Bldg., P.O. Box 34485, Los Angeles CA 90034. President: Ruth White. Music publisher and record company (Tom Thumb Records). ASCAP. Member NARAS. Publishes 4-6 cassettes/year. Receives 10-12 submissions/month. Pays negotiable royalty.
Affiliate: Tom Thumb Music.
How to Contact: Submit tape with letter outlining background in educational children's music. SASE. Reports in 2 months.
Music: "We're only interested in children's songs that have educational value. Our materials are sold in schools and homes, so artists/writers with a teaching background would be most likely to understand our requirements." Published "Professor Whatzit®," series including "Adventures of Professor Whatzit & Carmine Cat,"(cassette series for children) and "First Reader's Kit. We buy completed master tapes."

G. RICORDI & C. SPA, Via Berchet 2, Milano 20121 **Italy**. Phone (02)8881234. General Manager Pop Music Publishing Division: Federico Monti Arduini. Music publisher and record producer (Ricordi). S.I.A.E. Estab. 1808. Publishes 100 songs/year; publishes 4-5 new songwriters/year. Hires staff writers. Works with composers and lyricists; teams collaborators.
Affiliate(s): Radio Record RRR, Fama, Ritmi e Canzoni, Pegaso, Fono Film, Iller, Jubal, Edir, Mondia Music, Metron, Editori Associati, Fado, SO.E.DI. Musica, Settebello, Life.
How to Contact: Submit a demo tape by mail—unsolicited submissions are O.K. Prefers cassette (or videocassette if available) with 3/5 songs and lyric or lead sheets. Does not return unsolicited material. Reports in 1 month.
Music: Mostly pop and rock; also New Age. Published "Disperato" (by Masini Bigazzi/Dati), recorded by Marco Masini on Dischi Ricordi Records (pop); "Quattro Amici" (by Paoli/Penzo), recorded by Gino Paoli on WEA Records (pop); "Spunta La Luna Dal Monte (by Marielli Bertoli), recorded by Tazenda on Visa/Dischi Ricordi Records (pop).

RIDGE MUSIC CORP., 38 Laurel Ledge Ct., Stamford CT 06903. President/General Manager: Paul Tannen. Music publisher and manager. Estab. 1961. BMI, ASCAP. Member CMA. Publishes 12 songs/year. Pays standard royalty.
Affiliate(s): Tannen Music Inc. and Deshufflin, Inc.
How to Contact: Submit demo tape—unsolicited submissions OK. Prefers cassette with 3 songs and lyric sheet. SASE. Reports in 2 months.
Music: Country, rock, top 40/pop and jazz.

*__RLB MUSIC PUBLISHING,__ P.O. Box 12174, Toledo OH 43612. Owner: Robert L. Bogart Sr. Music publisher. ASCAP. Estab. 1970. Works with composers and lyricists; teams collaborators.
How to Contact: Submit a demo tape—unsolicited submissions OK. Prefers cassette with 4 songs and lyric sheet. SASE. Reports in 4 weeks.
Music: Mostly country, R&B and rock; also pop, New Age and gospel. Published "I'd Be Lyin," written and recorded by James Beckwith on Bogart Records (country).

FREDDIE ROBERTS MUSIC, P.O. Box 203, Rougemont NC 27572. (919)477-4077. Manager: Freddie Roberts. Music publisher, record company, record producer (Carolina Pride Productions), and management firm and booking agency. Estab. 1967. BMI. Publishes 45 songs/year; publishes 15 new songwriters/year. Works with composers, lyricists; teams collaborators. Pays standard royalty.

How to Contact: Write first about your interest or arrange personal interview. Prefers 7½ ips reel-to-reel or cassette with 1-5 songs and lyric sheet. SASE. Reports in 5 weeks.

Music: Mostly country, MOR and top 40/pop; also bluegrass, church/religious, gospel and southern rock (country). Published "Any Way You Want It" (by B. Fann), recorded by Sleepy Creek (southern rock) on Bull City Records; "Just A Little" (by C. Justis), recorded by Dean Phillips (country) on Ardon Records; and "He Knows What I Need" (by J. Dobbs), recorded by the Roberts Family (gospel) on Bull City Records.

Tips: "Write songs, whatever type, to fit today's market. Send good, clear demos, no matter how simple."

ROB-LEE MUSIC, P.O. Box 37612, Sarasota FL 34237. Vice Presidents: Rodney Russen, Eric Russen, Bob Francis. Music publisher, record company (Castle Records, Rock Island Records and Jade Records), record producer, and manager. ASCAP. Estab. 1965. Publishes 18-36 songs/year; publishes 6 new songwriters/year. Teams collaborators. Pays standard royalty.

Affiliate(s): Heavy Weather Music (ASCAP).

How to Contact: Submit a demo tape—unsolicited submissions OK. Prefers cassette (or VHS videocassette) with 4-8 songs and lyric sheet. Does not return unsolicited material. Reports in 2 weeks.

Music: Dance-oriented, easy listening, MOR, R&B, rock, soul, top 40/pop and funk. Published "The Smoke Is No Joke" (by R. Russet), recorded by Smokin' Bent Cooper on R&B Records (R&B); "Thunder and Lightning" (by Denver Duffey), recorded by Thunder & Lightning on Castle Records (rock); and "Fantasia" (by Lynn Schuette), recorded by Nuelle on Jade Records (ballad-rock).

ROCKER MUSIC/HAPPY MAN MUSIC, P.O. Box 73, 4501 Spring Creek Rd., Bonita Springs, FL 33923-6637. (813)947-6978. Executive Producer: Dick O'Bitts. BMI, ASCAP. Estab. 1960. Music publisher, record company (Happy Man Records, Condor Records and Air Corp Records), record producer (Rainbow Collections Ltd.) and management firm (Gemini Complex). Publishes 25-30 songs/year; publishes 8-10 new songwriters/year. Works with composers; teams collaborators. Pays standard royalty.

Affiliate: Happy Man Music.

How to Contact: Submit a demo tape—unsolicited submissions are OK. Prefers cassette (or VHS videocassette if possible) with 4 songs and lyric sheet or lead sheet. SASE. Do not call. "You don't need consent to send material." Reports in 1 month.

Music: Country, rock, pop and off-the-wall. Published "Hang Tough" and "Girls of Yesterday" (by Lou Cate), recorded by Holly Ronick; and "When You Get Your Woman" (by Ri Hamilton), recorded by Colt Cipson, all on Happy Man Records (country).

Tips: "For speedier response send material to be reviewed to Bonita Springs address."

ROCKFORD MUSIC CO., Suite 6-D, 150 West End Ave., New York NY 10023. Manager: Danny Darrow. Music publisher, record company (Mighty Records), record and video tape producer. BMI, ASCAP. Publishes 1-3 songs/year; publishes 1-3 new songwriters/year. Teams collaborators. Pays standard royalty.

Affiliate(s): Corporate Music Publishing Company (ASCAP) and Stateside Music Company (BMI).

How to Contact: Submit a demo tape—unsolicited submissions are OK. Prefers cassette with 3 songs and lyric sheet. "SASE a must!" Reports in 1 week. *"Positively no phone calls."*

Music: Mostly MOR and top 40/pop; also adult pop, country, adult rock, dance-oriented, easy listening, folk and jazz. Published "Look To The Wind" (by P.S. Stewart/ D. Darrow) (MOR); "Telephones," (by Bert Lee Howery and Danny Darrow) (rock); and Better Than You Know" (by Michael Greer), all recorded by Danny Darrow on Mighty Records.

Tips: "Listen to top 40 and write current lyrics and music."

ROCKLAND MUSIC, INC., 117 W. Rockland, Libertyville IL 60048. (708)362-4060. Contact: Perry or Rick Johnson. Music publisher, record company and record producer. BMI. Estab. 1980. Publishes 5 songs/year. Publishes 2 new songwriters/year. Pays standard royalty.

How to Contact: Submit a demo tape—unsolicited submissions are OK. Prefers cassette with 5 songs and lyric sheet. SASE. Reports in 6 months.

Music: Mostly rock/pop, dance/R&B and country; also blues. Published "This Feels Like Love to Me" (by C. Sermay), recorded by S. Distel (pop).

ROOTS MUSIC, Box 111, Sea Bright NJ 07760. President: Robert Bowden. Music publisher, record company (Nucleus Records) and record producer (Robert Bowden). BMI. Estab. 1979. Publishes 2 songs/year; publishes 1 new songwriter/year. Receives 10 submissions/year. Works with composers and lyricists; teams collaborators. Pays standard royalty.

How to Contact: Submit a demo tape—unsolicited submissions are OK. Prefers cassette (or VHS videocassette) with 3 songs and lyric sheet; include photo and bio. "I only want inspired songs written by talented writers." SASE. Reports in 1 month.
Music: Mostly country and pop; also church/religious, classical, folk, MOR, progressive, rock (soft, mellow) and top 40. Published "Henrey C," "Oh How Miss You Tonight" and "Hurting," all written and recorded by Robert Bowden on Nucleus Records (country).

ROSE HILL GROUP, 1326 Midland Ave., Syracuse NY 13205. (315)475-2936. A&R Director: V. Taft. Music publisher. Estab. 1979. Publishes 1-15 songs/year; publishes 1-5 new songwriters/year. Works with composers and lyricists; teams collaborators. Pays standard royalty.
Affiliate(s): Katch Nazar Music (ASCAP) and Bleecker Street Music (BMI).
How to Contact: Submit demo tape—unsolicited submissions are OK. Prefers cassette. SASE. Reports in 2-4 weeks.
Music: Mostly pop/rock, pop/dance and contemporary country. Published "True Love Never Dies" (by D. Jacobson), recorded by Z Team; and "Win Some, Lose Some" (by Jr. Carlsen), recorded by Fox, both on Sunday Records (pop ballad); and "Noah Jones" (by G. Davidian), recorded by IO on Cherry Records (pop/dance).
Tips: "Write simple, memorable melody lines; strong, real story lines."

STEVE ROSE MUSIC, 790 Boylston St., Boston MA 02199. (617)267-0886. Manager: Steve Rose. Uses two Nashville songpluggers and other contacts to pitch to majors and maintains active relationships with charting indie record labels. Uses Songwriter's Guild contract with two year reversion when a song is held by a producer or label.
Affiliate(s): Has ASCAP and BMI companies.
How to Contact: "Unfortunately we can now accept new submissions ONLY from serious Nashville-oriented writers who have had at least one independent cut. Call first, but only if this is the case. Send up to three of your best with a 29¢ SASE for return of lyrics and comments only. Publishing must be open. Put your phone number on everything." Reports ASAP.
Music: "Country exclusively. And then only well-demoed competitive, pitchable songs. They must be positive and mid- to uptempo."
Tips: "We'll help you revise a good song and we'll team complimentary talents. We are building a national network to show that Music Row is wherever country hits are written. Our best advice is to pitch songs direct to indie labels 'til you get a country cut, then contact us. And don't ever pay upfront for anything except demos when you're starting. Half the demos we take, we redemo at our expense or via a co-writer. Don't send a title that's listed in Phono-Log."

ROYAL FLAIR PUBLISHING, Box 438, Walnut IA 51577. (712)366-1136. President: Bob Everhart. Music publisher and record producer. BMI. Estab. 1967. Publishes 5-10 songs/year; publishes 1-2 new songwriters/year. Works with composers and lyricists. Pays standard royalty.
How to Contact: Submit a demo tape—unsolicited submissions are OK. Prefers cassette with 2-6 songs. SASE. Reports in 9 weeks.
Music: Traditional country, bluegrass and folk. Published "Hero of Gringo Trail," "Time After Time" and "None Come Near," written and recorded by R. Everhart on Folkways Records; and "Smoky Mountain Heartbreak," written and recorded by Bonnie Sanford (all country).
Tips: "Song definitely has to have old-time country flavor with all the traditional values of country music. No sex, outlandish swearing, or drugs-booze type songs accepted. We have an annual Hank Williams Songwriting Contest over Labor Day weekend and winners are granted publishing."

RUSTRON MUSIC PUBLISHERS, 1156 Park Lane, West Palm Beach FL 33417. (407)-686-1354. Professional Managers: Rusty Gordon, Ron Caruso and Davilyn Whims. Music publisher and record producer (Rustron Music Productions). ASCAP, BMI. Estab. 1974. Publishes 100-150 songs/year; publishes 10-20 new songwriters/year. Works with composers and lyricists; teams collaborators. Pays standard royalty.
Affiliates: Ruston Music Publishers (BMI) and Whimsong (ASCAP).
How to Contact: Submit a demo tape (cassette)—unsolicited submissions are OK, or write or call first to get permission to submit a tape. Prefers cassette with 1-3 songs and lyric or lead sheet. "Clearly label your tape and container. Include cover letter." SASE required for all correspondence. Reports in 2-3 months.
Music: Mostly pop (ballads, blues, theatrical, cabaret), progressive country, folk/rock; also R&B and New Age instrumentals. Published "Spirit Dancer" (by Jayne Reby), recorded by Circle & Star on C&S Records (New Age folk fusion); "Midnight Messenger" (by Marianne Flemming), recorded by the Marianne Flemming Band on Mermaid Records (R&B); and "Call of the Dove," written and recorded by Deb Criss on Catalyst Records (New Age folk fusion).

Close-up

Steve Rose
President
Steve Rose Music
Boston, Massachusetts

For Steve Rose, two factors work both for and against him as a music publisher. That these two factors happen to be the same should come as no surprise to songwriters with experience in the often confusing music industry. Factor one: Steve Rose Music's country publishing firms, Just Hits and Keep On Comin', are located in Boston, quite a distance from country music's capitol, Nashville. Factor two: Rose's firm is an indie in fierce competition with the major publishers. But, despite (or because of) the constant competition from the major labels and distance from Nashville, Rose has developed a system of working with songs that has led to success in writing and publishing country music, culminated by a single by Roy Clark, Mel Tillis and Bobby Bare that garnered a review in *Billboard*.

The current trend in country, especially getting back to the basics and the "new traditionalists," pleases Rose. "I hope trends will continue to be cyclical in country music—getting us back to harder-edge songs and story songs." Rose knows that country music has gradually developed a larger audience in the past several years.

Even within the trends, quality material is important. But even more important is the amount of patience required by the songwriter trying to get his material heard. Rose's experience emphasizes this: "I have moved from assuming that it all begins with a song to understanding that it also begins with getting songs heard, overcoming the outsider stigma, and keeping your cool in the face of politics." Rose is overcoming the "outsider stigma" by developing a network of songwriters working outside Nashville. The members of this network act as songpluggers pitching not only their songs, but the entire catalog of the firm.

Rose advises songwriters to take a somewhat different path than the traditional one of going directly to a music publisher. "Publishing is something of a myth in the music industry," he says. "Naturally an unpublished writer needs some access to labels and artists. Usually publishers are this avenue. But most publishers do not get major cuts, so the degree of difficulty is compounded and not necessarily diminished by being 'published'."

Where should aspiring songwriters go to establish themselves? Rose advises, "I encourage beginners to go straight to indie labels because if they can get indie cuts, they can establish the grounds of their professional future. No writer who has not written a few hundred songs and had five to fifteen indie cuts is going to produce a hit." It's only at this point that a songwriter should approach a publisher about pitching material to majors, whom Rose expects will continue the trend of going to the independents for fresh material.

This realistic view of the music industry may seem pessimistic to some, but Rose believes his attitude has only helped. "I believe the strength of my operation is based on people knowing we have professional writers who are dead serious." Rose wraps up his attitude towards the music business in one line: "Pro writers are in it for a living—and for the pleasures of succeeding."

—Michael Oxley

Tips: "Write strong hooks. Keep song length 3½ minutes or less. Avoid predictability—create original lyric themes. Tell a story. Compose definitive melody."

SABTECA MUSIC CO., Box 10286, Oakland CA 94610. (415)465-2805. A&R: Sean Herring. Music publisher and record company (Sabteca Record Co.). ASCAP, BMI. Estab. 1980. Publishes 8-10 songs/year; 1-2 new songwriters/year. Works with composers and lyricists; teams collaborators. Pays standard royalty.
Affiliate(s): Sabteca Publishing (ASCAP), Toylabe Publishing (BMI).
How to Contact: Write or call first and obtain permission to submit a tape. Prefers cassette with 2 songs and lyric sheet. SASE. Reports in 2-3 weeks.
Music: Mostly R&B, pop and country. Published "Only One" (by Bill Charles and Walt Coleman), recorded by Lois Shayne and Charles Brown (R&B); "Bond We Share" (by Lois Johnson), recorded by Lois Shayne (R&B); and "I Know" (by Duane Herring), recorded by Johnny B and Rhythm Method (pop) all on Andre-Romare Records.

*SADDLESTONE PUBLISHING, 264 "H" St., Box 8110-21, Blaine WA 98230. Canada Address: 8821 Delwood Dr., Delta B.C., V4C 4A1 **Canada**. (604)582-7117. FAX: (604)582-8610. President: Rex Howard. Music publisher, record company (Saddlestone) and record producer (Silver Bow Productions). SOCAN, BMI. Estab. 1988. Publishes 100 songs/year; publishes 12-30 new songwriters/year. Receives 70 submissions/month. Hires staff writers. Works with composers and lyricists; teams collaborators. Pays standard royalty.
Affiliate(s): Silver Bow Publishing (SOCAN, ASCAP).
How to Contact: Submit a demo tape by mail—unsolicited submissions are OK. Prefers cassette with 5-7 songs and lyric sheet. "Make sure vocal is clear." SASE. Reports in 3 months.
Music: Mostly country, rock and pop; also gospel and R&B. Published "Fragile" (by James/Bloemhard), recorded by Randy Bailey on Saddlestone Records (R&B); "Serves You Right" (by M. Gardner), recorded by Jim Pilant on E.S.U. Records (crossover ballad); and "All Because of You" (by T. Broderson), recorded by Bill Lowden on E.S.U. Records (country rock).
Tips: "Submit clear demos, good hooks and avoid long intros or instrumentals."

SARISER MUSIC, Box 211, Westfield MA 01086. (413)783-8386. Operations Manager: Alexis Steele. Music publisher and record company (Sweet Talk Records). BMI. Publishes 6-12 songs/year; publishes 1-2 new songwriters/year. Works with composers and lyricists; teams collaborators. Pays standard royalty.
How to Contact: Write first and obtain permission to submit. No calls. Prefers cassette or 7½ IPS reel-to-reel with 3-4 songs and lyric or lead sheet. "Lyrics should be typed; clear vocal on demo." SASE. Reports in 6 weeks.
Music: Mostly country/pop, country/rock and educational material; also soft rock and rockabilly. "We're interested in 50s/60s style 4-part harmony." Published "One Last Kiss" (by Sparkie Allison), recorded by Moore Twinz on MMT Records (country); "Sweet Talk" and "Ride a Rainbow," written and recorded by Sparkie Allison and Ginny Cooper on Sweet Talk Records (country/pop).
Tips: "Lyrics must have positive message. No cheatin' songs. Be unique. Try something different."

*WILLIAM A. SAULSBY MUSIC COMPANY, 311 W. Monroe St. #4872, Jacksonville FL 32202. Producer: Aubrey Saulsby. Estab. 1985. Publishes 8-10 songs/year. Pays standard royalty.
How to Contact: Write first and obtain permission to submit. Prefers cassette or 7½" reel and lyric sheet. Does not return unsolicited material.
Music: Mostly R&B, rap and jazz; also blues, pop and top 40. Published "Because You're Mine" and "Free" (by Willie A. Saulsby), recorded by William Icey; and "The Way That I Am" (by Willie A. Saulsby), recorded by Willie Bones, all on Hibi Dei Hipp Records.

*SAWMILLS MUSIC, South Down, Sandwell, Totnes, South Devon TQ9 7LN **United Kingdom**. (0803)867850. FAX: (0726)832015. Contact: Dennis Smith. Music publisher, record company, record producer. Estab. 1989. Publishes 30 songs/year; publishes 3 new songwriters/year. Works with composers and lyricists. Pays standard royalty.

Remember: Don't "shotgun" your demo tapes. Submit only to companies interested in the type of music you write. For more submission hints, refer to The Business of Songwriting on page 19.

How to Contact: Submit demo tape—unsolicited submissions are OK. Prefers cassette with 4 songs and lyric sheet. SASE. Reports in 2 months.
Music: Mostly pop, rock, background for TV and radio. Published "Diceman" and "Storm" (by A. Gilbert), recorded by Higher Ground on Dangerous Records (12 and 7" single); *No 10 or Bust* (by Hodge/Quinn), recorded by Screaming Lord Sutch and the Monster Raving Loonies on EMI Records (LP).

SCHMERDLEY MUSIC, #G3, 7560 Woodman Pl., Van Nuys CA 91405. (818)994-4862. Owner: Tom Willett. Music publisher, record company (Tomark Records) and record producer (Tomark Records). BMI. Estab. 1969. Publishes 10 songs/year; 2-4 new songwriters/year. Receives 125 submissions/year. Pays standard royalty.
How to Contact: Submit a demo tape—unsolicited submissions are OK. Prefers cassette (or VHS videocassette). SASE. Reports in 4 weeks.
Music: Mostly country and novelty; also rock. Published "I'd Rather Rock & Roll Than Be President" (by Tom Willett), recorded by Herman Schmerdley on Tomark Records (novelty country).
Tips: "Don't get obsessed with the idea of one company publishing your song. Send it to many publishers. Someone may need a song like yours."

*SCI-FI MUSIC, P.O. Box 941, N.D.G., Montreal Quebec H4A 3S3 **Canada.** (514)487-4551. President: Gary Moffet. Music publisher. SOCAN. Estab. 1984. Publishes 10 songs/year; publishes 2 new songwriters/year. Works with composers; teams collaborators. Pays standard royalty of 50%.
How to Contact: Submit demo tape—unsolicited submissions OK. Submit cassette with 3-10 songs and lyric sheet. Does not return material. Reports in 1 month.
Music: Mostly rock and pop. Published "Lonely Child," "The Letter" and "Beyond Time," all written and recorded by Korea on Rammit Records (rock).

SCOTTI BROTHERS MUSIC PUBLISHING, 2114 Pico Blvd., Santa Monica CA 90405. (310)450-3193. Professional Manager: Richie Wise. Music publisher and record company. BMI, ASCAP. Member NMPA, AIMP, RIAA and CMA. Publishes 40 songs/year; publishes 2 new songwriters/year. Pays standard royalty.
Affiliate(s): Flowering Stone and Holy Moley.
How to Contact: Prefers cassette with 1-2 songs and lyric sheet. Does not accept unsolicited material; "we report only if we're interested."
Music: Mostly top 40/pop and country; also easy listening, MOR and rock. Published "Eye of the Tiger" (by J. Peterick/F. Sullivan), recorded by Survivor on Scotti Bros.-CBS Records (rock); "How Do You Fall Out of Love," recorded by Janie Fricke on CBS Records (country-pop); and "Them Good Ol' Boys Are Bad" (J. Harrington/J. Pennig), recorded by John Schneider on Scotti Bros.-CBS Records (country).

SCRUTCHINGS MUSIC, 429 Homestead St., Akron OH 44306. (216)773-8529. Owner/President: Walter E.L. Scrutchings. Music publisher. BMI. Estab. 1980. Publishes 35 songs/year; publishes 10-20 new songwriters/year. Receives 125 submissions/year. Hires staff songwriters. Works with composers and lyricists; teams collaborators. Pays standard royalty of 50%. "Songwriters pay production costs of songs."
How to Contact: Submit a demo tape—unsolicited submissions are OK. Prefers cassette (or videocassette if available) with 2 songs, lyric and lead sheet. Does not return unsolicited material. Reports in 6-12 weeks.
Music: Mostly gospel, contemporary and traditional. Published "The Joy He Brings" (by R. Hinton), recorded by Akron City Mass; "God Has the Power" (by W. Scrutchings), recorded by Gospel Music Workshop Mass on Savoy Records (gospel); and "My Testimony" (by A. Cobb), recorded by Akron City Family Mass Choir on Scrutchings Music (gospel).
Tips: "Music must be clear and uplifting in message and music."

SEA DREAM MUSIC, 236 Sebert Rd., Forest Gate, London E7 0NP **United Kingdom.** Phone: (081)534-8500. Senior Partner: Simon Law. PRS. Music publisher and record company (Plankton Records, Embryo Arts (Belgium), Gutta (Sweden), Wildtracks and Radio Records). Estab. 1976. Publishes 50 songs/year; publishes 2 new songwriters/year. Works with composers and lyricists; teams collaborators. Pays 66⅔% royalty.
Affiliate(s): Scarf Music Publishing, Really Free Music, Ernvik Musik (Sweden).
How to Contact: Submit a demo tape—unsolicited submissions are OK. Prefers cassette with 3 songs and lyric sheet. "Technical information about the recording is useful, as are the songwriter's expectations of the company—i.e., what they want us to do for them." SAE and IRC. Reports in 6 weeks.

Music: Mostly funk/rock, rock and blues. Published "In Times of Rain" (by Simon Law), recorded by Fresh Claim (rock); "If You Climb" (by D. Llewellyn), recorded by Light Factory (children's pop); and "Squeaky Clean" (by Ward/Johnston), recorded by Trevor Speaks (folk/rock), all on Plankton Records.

Tips: "We are specifically interested in material with a Christian bias to the lyrics."

SEGAL'S PUBLICATIONS, Box 507, Newton MA 02159. (617)969-6196. Contact: Charles Segal. Music publisher and record producer (Segal's Productions). BMI, SAMRO. Estab. 1963. Publishes 80 songs/year; publishes 6 new songwriters/year. Works with composers and lyricists. Pays standard royalty.

Affilates: Charles Segals Publications (BMI).

How to Contact: Submit demo tape—unsolicited submissions OK. Prefers cassette (or VHS videocassette) with 3 songs and lyric or lead sheet. SASE. Reports in 6-8 weeks.

Music: Mostly rock, pop and country; also R&B, MOR and children's songs. Published "Give the World a Chance" (by Brilliant), recorded by Rosemary on Spin Records (soft rock); "You're Not Alone" (by Segal), recorded by Troupers on Spin Records (gospel/rock); and "Put Your Faith in Jesus" (by Whewell), recorded by Will Hock on Spin Records (gospel).

Tips: "Listen to what is going on in the music business via TV and radio. Write for a specific artist. Do a simple demo cassette, voice/keyboard; write a clean lead sheet."

SELLWOOD PUBLISHING, 170 N. Maple, Fresno CA 93702. (209)255-1717. Owner: Stan Anderson. Music publisher, record company (Trac Record Co.) and record producer. BMI. Estab. 1972. Publishes 10 songs/year; publishes 3 new songwriters/year. Receives 30-35 submissions/month. Pays standard royalty.

How to Contact: Submit a demo tape—unsolicited submissions are OK. Prefers cassette (or VHS videocassette) with 2 songs and lyric sheet. SASE. Reports in 2 weeks.

Music: Mostly country, gospel, pop, contemporary Christian and rock. Published "Nevada State of Mind" (by Barry Best) and "Don't Walk Away" (by B.G. White), recorded by Trac on Trac Records (country); and "Mighty Rushing Wind" (by Lauren Rackley), recorded by Trac on Psalms Records (gospel).

*SEYCHELLES MUSIC, Box 13 01 44, Cologne 1 D-5000 **Germany.** (0221)72 01 79. FAX: (0221)73 93 476. Managing Director: Walther Kahl. Music publisher. GEMA. Estab. 1977. Publishes 40-50 songs/year; publishes 2-3 new songwriters/year. Pays standard royalty. Works with composers; teams collaborators.

How to Contact: Write or call to obtain permission to submit. Prefers cassette and lyric sheet. SAE and IRC. Reports in 3 weeks.

Music: MOR, rock and country. Published "Seas of Emotions" (by Prezman), recorded by Prezman and Tomas Zelosyi (classic pop); "Danson le Sega," written and recorded by Jocelyn Perreac (sega), both on Seychelles Records; and "Im Stau" (by Tomas Zelosyi), recorded by Dave Dudley on Hoch Records (country).

*SHA-LA MUSIC, INC., 137 Legion Place, Hillsdale NJ 07642. (201)664-1995. FAX: (201)664-1349. President: Robert Allen. Music publisher. Estab. 1987. Publishes 20-30 songs/year; publishes 1-4 new songwriters/year. Works with composers and lyricists. Pays standard royalty.

Affiliate(s): Sha-La Music (BMI) and By The Numbers Music (ASCAP).

How to Contact: Submit demo tape by mail—unsolicited submissions are OK. Prefers cassette with 3 songs and lyric sheet. "Keep package neat to make a good impression." SASE. Reports in 2-4 weeks.

Music: Mostly R&B, pop, dance; also rock and a/c. Published *Good Karma* written and recorded by Monte Farber on Scoresville Music (LP); "S.O.S." (by G. Rottger and R. Allen), recorded by Benny King, Jr. on Big City Music (single).

Tips: "Provide a tape of good quality and make sure the songs come through. Don't overproduce."

*SHANKMAN DE BLASIO MELINA, INC., #202, 2434 Main St., Santa Monica CA 90405. (310)399-7744. FAX: (310)399-2027. Contact: Laurent Besencon. Music publisher, personal management. Playhard Music (ASCAP), Playfull Music (BMI). Estab. 1979. Hires staff songwriters. Works with composers and lyricists; teams collaborators.

How to Contact: Write and call first and obtain permission to submit. Prefers cassette (or VHS or Beta videocassette if available) with 3 songs and lyric sheet. Does not return unsolicited material. Reports in 2 months.

Music: Mostly contemporary hit songs: pop, R&B, dance, rock, ballads. Published *Roll the Dice* (by Gina Gomez), recorded by Color Me Badd on Giant Records (LP); *Safe in the Arms of Love* (by Michael Cruz), recorded by Martika on Columbia Records (LP); "The Sweetest Taboo" (by Sade Adu), recorded by Sade on Epic Records (single).

*SHELLEY MUSIC, 177 Balmoral Dr., Bolingbrook IL 60440. (708)739-0488. President: Guy Shelley. Music publisher. Guy Smilo Music (BMI). Estab. 1992. Publishes 20-50 songs/year; publishes 4 new songwriters/year. Works with composers and lyricists. Pays standard royalty.
How to Contact: Submit demo tape—unsolicited submissions are OK. Prefers cassette with 1-3 songs and lyric sheet. SASE. Reports in 2 months.
Music: Mostly classical (educational), pop-rock, country; also R&B, novelty, MOR. Published *Piano Pieces* (by Donna Shelley) (educational); "Exposition" (by Donna Shelley-Guy Shelley) (classical); "Come And Get It" (by Carson-Shelley).
Tips: "Have a clear clean sounding demo that have your vocals upfront."

SHU'BABY MONTEZ MUSIC, 1447 North 55th St., Philadelphia PA 19131. (215)473-5527. President: Leroy Schuler. Music publisher. BMI. Estab. 1986. Publishes 25 songs/year; publishes 15 new songwriters/year. Pays standard royalty.
How to Contact: Submit a demo tape by mail—unsolicited submissions are OK. Prefers cassette with 4 songs and lyric sheet. SASE. Reports in 1 month.
Music: Mostly R&B, pop and jazz; also rock. Published "Got It Going On," written and recorded by C. Wash; and "You Make Me Happy," written and recorded by Ken Chaney on Logic Records (R&B); and "I'll Do Better," written and recorded by Mac Atkinson on Bang-Bang Records (R&B-pop).
Tips: Write a song with strong drum beats and lyrics."

SIEBENPUNKT VERLAGS GMBH, Habsburgerplatz 1 Rückgebäude, D-8000 München 40 **Germany**. Phone: 089-331808. General Manager: Mr. Schmidt. Music publisher. GEMA. Estab. 1978. Publishes 250 songs/year; publishes 7 new songwriters/year. Works with composers and lyricists; and teams collaborators. Pays standard royalty or by contract.
How to Contact: Submit a demo tape—unsolicited submissions OK with SAEs and IRCs. Prefers cassette (or VHS videocassette) with 2-3 songs. Reports in 3 weeks.
Music: Rock, dance and pop; also fusion-jazz and New Age. Published "Arrivederci" (by Fabiani), recorded by Angelo Fabianai on Polydor Records (pop); "Come on Darling" (by Petit), recorded by Stephen Petit on ICY (BTIG Records) (pop/rock); and "A Higher Ground," written and recorded by Pete Bardens on Miramar Records (space/rock).

SIEGEL MUSIC COMPANIES, 2 Hochlstr, 80 Munich 8000 **Germany**. Phone: 089-984926. Managing Director: Joachim Neubauer. Music publisher, record company, (Jupiter Records and 69-Records) and record producer. Estab. 1948. GEMA. Publishes 1,500 songs/year; publishes 50 new songwriters/year. Hires staff songwriters. Works with composers and lyricists. Pays standard royalty according to individual society.
Affiliate(s): Ed. Meridian, Sound of Jupiter Ltd. (England), Sounds of Jupiter, Inc. (USA), Step Two (Austria), Step One (Holland), Step Four (France), Step Five (Brazil), Step Six (Scandinavia), Step Seven (Australia), Step Eight (Belgium) and Yellowbird (Switzerland).
How to Contact: Submit demo tape—unsolicited submissions are OK. Prefers cassette (or VHS videocassette, but not necessary). SAE and IRC. Reports in 8 weeks.
Music: Mostly pop, disco and MOR; also country and soul. Published "Neon Cowboy" (by Siegel/Kermit/Bellamy), recorded by the Bellamy Brothers on Jupiter Records (country); "Sadeness-Part 1" (by Carly MC/Gregorian/Fairstein), recorded by Enigma on Virgin Records (dance pop); and "Tower of Love" (by Thompson/Whittode/Fallenmeyer), recorded by Chris Thompson on BMG-Ariola (pop).

SILICON MUSIC PUBLISHING CO., Ridgewood Park Estates, 222 Tulane St., Garland TX 75043. President: Gene Summers. Vice President: Deanna L. Summers. Public Relations: Steve Summers. Music publisher and record company (Domino Records, Ltd. and Front Row Records). BMI. Estab. 1965. Publishes 10-20 songs/year; publishes 2-3 new songwriters/year. Pays standard royalty.
How to Contact: Prefers cassette with 1-2 songs. Does not return unsolicited material. "We are usually slow in answering due to overseas tours."
Music: Mostly rockabilly and 50s material; also old-time blues country and MOR. Published "Ready to Ride/Ode to a Stuntman" (from the HBO presentation "Backlot"), written and recorded by Pat Minter on Domino Records; "Loco Cat" (by Eddie Hill/Tom Toms), recorded by Gene Summers on White Label; "Love Me Til I Do," written and recorded by Joe Hardin Brown on Domino Records; "Rockaboogie Shake" (by James McClung), recorded by Gene Summers on Jan Records (Sweden); and "Stevie Ray Vaughn" (by Joe Hardin Brown) and "My Yearbook" (by Deanna Summers), both recorded by Gene Summers on Teardrop Records.

Listings of companies in countries other than the U.S. have the name of the country in boldface type.

Tips: "We are very interested in 50s rock and rockabilly *original masters* for release through overseas affiliates. If you are the owner of any 50s masters, contact us first! We have releases in Holland, Switzerland, England, Belgium, France, Sweden, Norway and Australia. We have the market if you have the tapes! Sample recordings available! Send SASE for catalogue."

*SILVER CHORD MUSIC, 3700 S. Hawthorne, Sioux Falls SD 57105. (605)334-6832. Owners: William Prines III or Vesta Wells-Prines. Music publisher. BMI. Estab. 1990. Publishes 6 songs/year; 2-3 new songwriters/year. Works with composers and lyricists; teams collaborators. Pays standard royalty.
How to Contact: Write to obtain permission to submit a tape. Prefers cassette with 3 songs and lyric sheet. SASE.
Music: Mostly country, pop and gospel; also rock and R&B. Published "Curious Heart (by William Prines III, Wayne Skoblik, Denise Reiner), recorded by Savanna on Savanna Records (country); "Don't Call Me Mamma" (by William Prines III and Vicki Lynn), recorded by Vicki Lynn King on Epic Records (country); "Where Did All My Money Go" written and recorded by Johnny Goings on Omni-Gram Records (pop).

SILVERFOOT PUBLISHING, 4225 Palm St., Baton Rouge LA 70808. (504)383-7885. President: Barrie Edgar. BMI. Music publisher, record company (Gulfstream Records) and record producer (Hogar Musical Productions). Estab. 1977. Publishes 20-30 songs/year; publishes 8-20 new songwriters/year. Receives 200 submissions/year. Pays standard royalty.
How to Contact: Submit a demo tape—unsolicited submissions are OK. Prefers cassette with maximum 4 songs and lyric sheet. "Patience required on reporting time." SASE. Reports in 1-5 months.
Music: Mostly rock, pop, blues ("not soul") and country. Recently published "Blowin Home" (by Paul Delgato); "Dawn's Delight" (by John Clark) and "Have Mercy (by Cynthia Macgregor) (country).

SIMPLY GRAND MUSIC, INC., P.O. Box 41981, Memphis TN 38174-1981. (901)272-7039. President: Linda Lucchesi. Music publisher. ASCAP, BMI. Estab. 1965. Works with composers and lyricists; teams collaborators. Pays standard royalty.
Affiliate(s): Memphis Town Music, Inc. (ASCAP) and Beckie Publishing Co. (BMI).
How to Contact: Write or call first to get permission to submit a tape. Prefers cassette with 1-3 songs and lyric sheet. SASE. Reports in 3 months.
Music: Mostly pop and soul; also country and soft rock.
Tips: "We are the publishing home of "Wooly Bully".

SINUS MUSIK PRODUKTION, ULLI WEIGEL, Teplitzer Str. 28/30, 1 Berlin 33 West Berlin **Germany.** (030)825-5056. FAX: (030)825-4082. Owner: Ulli Weigel. Music publisher, record producer and producer of radio advertising spots. GEMA, GVL. Estab. 1976. Publishes 20 songs/year; publishes 6 new songwriters/year. Works with composers and lyricists; teams collaborators. Pays according to GEMA conditions.
Affiliate(s): Sinus Musikverlag H.U. Weigel GmbH.
How to Contact: Submit a demo tape by mail—unsolicited submissions are O.K. Prefer cassette (or VHS videocassette) with up to 10 songs and lyric sheets. SASE. Reports in 1 month.
Music: Mostly rock, pop and new age; also background music for movies/advertising. Published "Simple Story" recorded by MAANAM on RCA (Polish rock Group); and "Terra-X-Melody" (by Franz Baitzsch), on Hansa (TV background music); *Dic Musik Maschine* (by Klaus Lage), recorded by CWN Productions on Hansa Records (pop/German); and "Maanam" (by Jakowskyl/Jakowska), recorded by CWN Productions on RCA Records (pop/English).
Tips: "Take more time working on the melody than on the instrumentation."

*SISKATUNE MUSIC PUBLISHING CO., 285 Chestnut St., West Hempstead NY 11552. (516)489-0738. FAX: (516)565-9425. President: Mike Siskind. Vice President Creative Affairs: Rick Olarsch. Music publisher. Estab. 1981. Publishes 50 songs/year; 5 new songwriters/year. Works with composers and lyricists; teams collaborators. Pays standard royalty.
How to Contact: Submit demo tape—unsolicited submissions are OK. Prefers cassette with 5-10 songs and lyric sheet. "Send any and all pertinent information." SASE. Reports in 6-8 weeks.
Music: Mostly rock, blues, country; also folk, dance and ballads. Published "Boardwalk," written and recorded by Michael Ellis (LP); and *Guardian Angel* (by Larry Andrews), recorded by Off the Wall both on Storehouse Records (EP).
Tips: "I'm more concerned with the song. As long as the vocals are clear and there is a strong melody, state-of-the-art production isn't essential."

*SIZEMORE MUSIC, P.O. Box 130441, Birmingham AL 35213. (205)951-3717. Contact: Gary Sizemore. Music publisher, record company (The Gas Co.) and record producer (Gary Sizemore). BMI. Estab. 1960. Publishes 5 songs/year; 1 new songwriter/year. Works with composers and lyricists; teams collaborators. Pays standard royalty.

How to Contact: Submit a demo tape by mail—unsolicited submissions are OK. Prefers cassette (or VHS videocassette) with lyric sheets. SASE.
Music: Mostly soul and R&B; also blues, pop and country. Published "Liquor and Wine" and "The Wind," written and recorded by K. Shackleford on Heart Records (country); and "She's Tuff" (by Jerry McCain), recorded by The Fabulous Thunderbirds on Chrysalis Records (blues).

SONG FARM MUSIC, P.O. Box 24561, Nashville TN 37202. (615)321-4875. President: Tom Pallardy. Music publisher and record producer (T.P. Productions). BMI. Member NSAI. Estab. 1980. Publishes 2-5 songs/year; publishes 1-2 new songwriters/year. Works with team collaborators. Receives 3,000 songs/year. Pays standard royalty.
How to Contact: Submit a demo tape—unsolicited submissions are OK. Prefers cassette with maximum 2 songs and lyric or lead sheet. SASE required with enough postage for return of all materials. Reports in 4-6 weeks.
Music: Mostly country, R&B and pop; also crossover and top 40. Published "Mississippi River Rat" (by J. Hall, R. Hall, E. Dickey), recorded by Tom Powers on Fountain Records (Cajun country); "Today's Just Not the Day" (by J. Bell, E. Bobbitt), recorded by Liz Draper (country); and "In Mama's Time" (by T. Crone), recorded by Pat Tucker on Radioactive Records (country/pop).
Tips: "Material should be submitted neatly and professionally with as good quality demo as possible. Songs need not be elaborately produced (voice and guitar/piano are fine) but they should be clear. Songs must be well constructed, lyrically tight, good strong hook, interesting melody, easily remembered; i.e., commercial!"

SONGWRITERS' NETWORK MUSIC PUBLISHING, P.O. Box 190446, Dallas TX 75219. (214)824-2739. President: Phil Ayliffe. Music publisher and record company (Songwriters' Network Records). ASCAP. Estab. 1983. Publishes 3 songs/year. Receives 5-8 submissions/year. Works with composers and lyricists; teams collaborators. Pays standard royalty.
How to Contact: Submit demo tape—unsolicited submissions OK. Prefers cassette with 3 songs and lyric sheets. SASE. Reports in 3 months.
Music: Mostly pop, MOR and adult contemporary country. Published "Crazy About You," written and recorded by Phil Ayliffe on Songwriters' Network Records (jazz/pop).

*SOPRANO MUSIC CO., P.O. Box 7731, Beverly Hills CA 90212. (310)338-9976. Vice President A&R: Joseph Chryar. Music publisher, record company. ASCAP. Estab. 1968. Publishes 15 songs/year; publishes 2 new songwriters/year. Hires staff writers. Works with composers and lyricists; teams collaborators. Pays standard royalty.
Affiliates: Cling Publishing (ASCAP).
How to Contact: Write first and obtain permission to submit. Prefers cassette with 2-3 songs and lyric sheet. Does not return unsolicited submissions. Reports in 6 weeks.
Music: Mostly country, R&B and pop; also jazz and blues. Published "Movin' and Groovin'," written and recorded by J.D. Nichelson; "Peek-a-boo" (by C. Harris), recorded by R. Martin; and "Love Must Go On" (by Tina Lewis), recorded by King Miller, all on Roach Records (all R&B singles).

SOTEX MUSIC, P.O. Box 27, Converse TX 78109-0027. (512)658-6748; 653-3898. Partners: Delbert Richerson and Frank Willson. Music publisher. BMI. Estab. 1989. Publishes 30 songs/year; publishes 5-10 new songwriters/year. Receives 10-15 submissions/month. Pays standard royalty.
How to Contact: Submit a demo tape by mail—unsolicited submissions are OK. Prefers cassette (or ½" VHS videocassette) with 3 songs and lyric sheets. Include name, address, phone number and social security number with submissions. SASE. Reports in 2 months.
Music: Mostly country, country/rock, country/gospel and rock. Published "The Writers" (by Weyman McBride), recorded by Clif McBride on Texas Brand Records (country); "100 Proof" (by Art Sharinger) (country); and "Lovin' You," written and recorded by Candace Howard on BSW Records (country).
Tips: Be original. We prefer 'love' songs."

SOUL STREET MUSIC PUBLISHING INC., 265 Main St., East Rutherford NJ 07073. (201)933-2297. President: Glenn La Russo. Music publisher. ASCAP. Estab. 1988. Publishes 20 songs/year; publishes 5 new songwriters/year. Works with composers. Pays standard royalty.
How to Contact: Submit a demo tape—unsolicited submissions are OK. Prefers cassette with 3 songs and lyric sheet. SASE. Reports in 1 month.
Music: Mostly R&B, dance and rap. Published "Touch Me" (by Carmichael), recorded by Cathy Dennis on Polydor Records (dance); "Symptoms of True Love" (by Harman/Weber), recorded by Tracey Spencer on Capitol Records (R&B); and "Thinking About Your Love," written and recorded by Skipworth and Turner on Island Records (R&B).

SOUND ACHIEVEMENT GROUP, P.O. Box 24625, Nashville TN 37202. (615)883-2600. President: Royce B. Gray. Music publisher. BMI, ASCAP. Estab. 1985. Publishes 120 songs/year; publishes 4 new songwriters/year. Works with composers and lyricists; teams collaborators. Pays standard royalty.
Affiliate(s): Song Palace Music (ASCAP) and Emerald Stream Music (BMI).
How to Contact: Submit a demo tape—unsolicited submissions are OK. Prefers cassette (or VHS videocassette if available) with 3 songs and lyric sheet. SASE. Reports in 2 months.
Music: Gospel. Published "You Are" (by Penny Strandberg Miller), recorded by Revelations on Newind Records (gospel); "I Want My Life To Count" (by Sammy Lee Johnson), recorded by Sammy Lee Johnson on Image Records (gospel); and "The Wonder of Christmas" (by Giorgio Longno/John Ganes), recorded by Giorgio Longno on Candle Records (gospel).

SOUND COLUMN COMPANIES, P.O. Box 70784, Salt Lake City UT 84170. (801)355-5327. President/General Manager: Ron Simpson. Music publisher, record company (SCP Records) and record producer (Sound Column Productions). BMI, ASCAP, SESAC. Member CMA, AFM. Estab. 1968. Publishes 50 songs/year; publishes 2 new songwriters/year. Receives 30 submissions/month. Hires staff writers. Works with composers and lyricists. Pays standard royalty.
Affiliate(s): Ronarte Publications (ASCAP), Mountain Green Music (BMI), Macanudo Music (SESAC).
How to Contact: Submit demo tape—unsolicited submissions OK. Prefers cassette with 1-3 songs and lyric sheet. "We can't listen to outside submissions unless they are complete songs." SASE. Reports as time permits.
Music: Mostly pop, country and A/C; "lean toward power ballads." Published "What I Need" (by Ron Simpson and Anthony Mortimer), recorded by Lita & Kevin on Shadow Mountain Records (pop rap).
Tips: "We very rarely accept outside submissions so be careful about song form and quality of demo. No correspondence or return of materials without SASE. We would like to hear from more SESAC writers. No phone calls, please."

SOUND IMAGE PUBLISHING, 6556 Wilkinson, North Hollywood CA 91606. (818)762-8881. President: Marty Eberhardt. Vice President and General Manager: David Chatfield. Music publisher, record company, record producer and video company. BMI. Member NARAS. Publishes 160 songs/year; publishes 10 new songwriters/year. Pays standard royalty.
How to Contact: Prefers cassette (or VHS videocassette) with 3 songs and lyric sheet. Does not return unsolicited material. Reports in 2 months.
Music: Mostly rock; also dance, R&B.
Tips: "Demos should be professionally recorded. We suggest 16-24 track recording on cassette submissions."

SOUND SPECTRA MUSIC, P.O. Box 2474, Auburn AL 36831-2474. (205)821-4876. President: Larry L. Barker. Music publisher, record company (Rainbow River Records) and record producer (Spectra Productions). BMI. Estab. 1978. Publishes 20 songs/year; 3-5 new songwriters/year. Receives 20 submissions/month. Works with composers and lyricists. Pays standard royalty.
How to Contact: Write first and obtain permission to submit a tape. Prefers cassette with 3-4 songs and lyric sheets. Include SASE for reply. Reports in 8 weeks.
Music: Mostly rock, R&B and New Age; also jazz, gospel and country. Published "Don't Hold Back" (by Ronald La Pread and Larry Barker), recorded by Ronald La Pread on Little Records (R&B); "It's Not Easy" (by Larry Barker), recorded by Lennie Hartzog on Rainbow River Records (pop); and "The Trash Bag's Been Ripped" (by Bruce Yandle), recorded by Mr. Resistor on Rainbow River Records (rock).
Tips: "Write first to determine current needs—then send only your tightest material."

*SOUTHERN MOST PUBLISHING COMPANY, P.O. Box 97, Climax Springs MO 65324. (314)345-1077. President/Owner: Dann E. Haworth. Music publisher, record producer (Haworth Productions), engineer. BMI. Estab. 1985. Publishes 10 songs/year; 3 new songwriters/year. Hires staff songwriters. Works with composers and lyricists; teams collaborators. Pays standard royalty.
Affiliates: Boca Chi Key Publishing (ASCAP).
How to Contact: Submit demo tape—unsolicited submissions are OK. Prefers cassette with 3 songs and lyric sheet. SASE. Reports in 6-8 weeks.
Music: Mostly rock, R&B and country; also gospel and New Age.
Tips: "Keep it simple and from the heart."

SPEEDSTER MUSIC, P.O. Box 96, Glendale AZ 85311. (602)435-0314. Owner: Frank E. Koehl. Music publisher, record company (Auburn Records and Tapes). BMI. Estab. 1988. Publishes 2-8 songs/year; 2 new songwriters/year. Receives 25 submissions/month. Works with composers. Pays standard royalty.

How to Contact: Submit a demo tape—unsolicited submissions are OK. Prefers cassette with 2-4 songs and lyric sheets. "Send only traditional, acoustic country music." SASE. Reports 3 weeks.
Music: Mostly country, traditional and bluegrass. Published "Mr. Woolworth" and "Burglar Man" (by Frank Koehl), recorded by Al Ferguson (folk country); and "Shack Tree," written and recorded by Troy McCourt, all on Auburn Records (country).
Tips: "Keep it country and acoustic. Tell a story simply."

SPRADLIN/GLEICH PUBLISHING, P.O. Box 80083, Phoenix AZ 85060. (602)840-8466. Manager: Lee Gleich. Music publisher. BMI. Estab. 1988. Publishes 4-10 songs/year; 2-4 new songwriters. Works with composers and lyricists; teams collatorators. Pays standard 50% royalty.
Affiliate(s): Spradlin/Gleich Publishing (BMI), Paul Lee Publishing (ASCAP).
How to Contact: Write first for permission to submit. Prefers cassette with 3 songs and lyric sheet or lead sheet. "It must be very good material, as I only have time for promoting songwriters who really care." SASE. Reports in 3 weeks.
Music: Mostly country geared to the US and European country markets; also gospel and theme music. Published "Stranger in Your Heart," written and recorded by Travis Allen on Courage Records; "Sounds of Home" (by Smith, Waymen), recorded by Parrish Wayne Horshburgh on CCEUSA Records and "Dancin Shoes," written and recorded by Kurt McFarland on Comstock Records (country).
Tips: "Send me a request letter, then send me your best song. If it is a quality song that will create interest by us for more material. We are now publishing mostly all country, gospel (country) and rock-a-billy!"

STANG MUSIC INC., 753 Capitol Ave., Hartford CT 06106. (203)951-8175. Producer: Jack Stang. Music publisher, record company (Nickel Records) and record producer (Jack Stang). BMI. Estab. 1970. Publishes 20 songs/year; publishes 2 new songwriters/year. Receives 100 submissions/month. Hires staff writers. Works with composers; teams collaborators. Pays standard royalty.
How to Contact: Submit a demo tape—unsolicited submissions are OK. Prefers cassette with 3 songs and lyric sheets. SASE. Reports in 3 weeks.
Music: Mostly rock, pop, top 40 and R&B; also country. Published "One Heart" (by Finns Field), recorded by Ray Alaire on Nickel Records (pop rock).

STAR INTERNATIONAL, INC., P.O. Box 470346, Tulsa OK 74147. President: MaryNell Jetton. Music publisher. ASCAP. Estab. 1989. Publishes 1-20 songs/year. Pays standard 50% royalty.
How to Contact: Submit a demo tape—unsolicited submissions are OK. Prefers cassette (or VHS videocassette if available) with 1-2 songs and lyric sheet. "If we are interested in your first two songs, we will request more of your material." SASE. Reports in 2 months.
Music: "We accept any type of music material, if it's professional."

*STAR SONG COMMUNICATIONS, 2325 Crestmoor Rd., Nashville TN 37215. Manager/Music Publisher: Jonathan Watkins. Music publisher, record company. Estab. 1974. Publishes 50 songs/year; 2 new songwriters/year. Hires staff songwriters. Works with composers and lyricists; teams collaborators. Pays standard royalty of 50%.
Affiliate(s): Ariose Music (ASCAP), Shepherd's Fold Music (BMI) and Dawn Treader Music (SESAC).
How to Contact: Submit demo tape—unsolicited submissions OK. Prefers cassette with 1-3 songs and lyric sheet. "Do not call or write to see if we liked the tape. If we do—we will call. Make sure we have a phone number." Does not return unsolicited material. "We call back if interested."
Music: Mostly Christian pop, Christian rock and Christian metal and rap; also pop, country and Christian inspirational. Published "Jesus Answers' (by Wagner/Liles), recorded by Michele Wagner on Benson Records (AC); "Nothing But Love," written and recorded by Twila Paris (AC); and "Everybody Knows My Name" (by Thompson/Thompson), recorded by Bride (metal), both on Star Song Records.
Tips: "Wow us in the first 30 seconds. Don't put your best song last."

STARBOUND PUBLISHING CO., 207 Winding Rd., Friendswood TX 77546. (713)482-2346. President: Buz Hart. Music publisher, record company (Juke Box Records, Quasar Records and Eden Records) and record producer (Lonnie Wright and Buz Hart). BMI. Estab. 1970. Publishes 35-100 songs/year; publishes 5-10 new songwriters/year. Works with composers and lyricists; teams collaborators. Pays standard royalty.
How to Contact: Obtain permission before submitting a demo tape. Prefers cassette with 3 songs and lyric sheet. SASE. Reports in 5-6 weeks.
Music: Mostly country, R&B and gospel. Published ""Maybe I Won't Love You Anymore" (by Barbara Hart, Buz Hart), recorded by Johnny Lee on Curb Records; "Let it Slide" (by James Watson/ Buz Hart), recorded by Stan Steel on Gallary II Records; and "Country Boy's Dream," recorded by

Charlie Louvin, Waylon Jennings, and George Jones on Playback Records.

*STONEBESS MUSIC CO., 163 Orizaba Ave., San Francisco CA 94132. (415)334-2247. Director: W.C. Stone. Music publisher. Estab. 1963. Number of songs published/year varies. New songwriters published/year varies. Pays standard royalty.
How to Contact: Submit a demo tape—unsolicited submissions are OK. Prefers cassette with 2 or more songs and lead sheet. SASE. Reports in 3-5 weeks.
Music: Mostly R&B, hard rock, rap. Published "Jet Set," "U Need to be My Girl" and "Syn Copation," written and recorded by the Original Hot Ice Band on Lodestone Records.
Tips: "Only copyrighted songs will be considered. Send proof of copyright."

STONEHAND PUBLISHING, P.O. Box 8178, Victoria BC V8W 3R8 **Canada**. (604)386-0507. Project Director: Linda Ehlers. Music publisher, record companies (Stonehand Records). SOCAN, CMRRA. Estab. 1984. Publishes 6 songs/year; publishes 2-3 new songwriters/year. Receives 20 submissions/month. Pays standard royalty.
How to Contact: Submit a demo tape—unsolicited submissions are OK. Prefers cassette or VHS videocassette with 3 songs and lyric sheets. SASE with IRC. Reports in 4-6 weeks.
Music: Mostly pop/rock, AOR/MOR and country; also folk. Released the album *Leave Me Standing*, by Kin Cain (independent). Published "When I Was a Young Boy," (pop) and "Someone Told Me" (rock), both written and recorded by Kin Cain on Stonehand Records.
Tips: "A song should have a strong hook. Don't use the "formula"; establish your own musical identity."

STRAWBERRY SODA PUBLISHING, 15 Exeter Rd., Kingston NH 03848. (603)642-8493. Coordinator: Harry Mann. Music publisher. ASCAP. Estab. 1988. Publishes 15 songs/year. Publishes 2-4 new songwriters/year. Works with composers and lyricists. Pays standard royalty.
How to Contact: Submit a demo tape—unsolicited submissions are OK. Prefers cassette, 15 IPS reel-to-reel, or VCR videocassette with 3 songs and lyric sheets. SASE. Reports in 6-8 weeks.
Music: Mostly rock, country and pop; "no heavy metal." Published "2 Lane Highway," and "Flight 17" (by Doug Mitchell), both recorded by Doug Mitchell Band (A/C singles); on Kingston Records.
Tips: "Simple, understandable lyrics with a flow. Sequenced, electronic music is going too far. I think the acoustic sound might be ready for a comeback."

STREET SINGER MUSIC, 117 W. 8th, Hays KS 67601. (913)625-9634. President: Mark Meckel. Also Sunset Productions, Suite 200, 1922 Broadway, Nashville TN 37203. (615)327-4425. President: Mark Meckel. BMI. Music publisher, record company (MDM Records) and record producer (Sunset Productions). Estab. 1980. Publishes 60 songs/year; publishes 4 new songwriters/year. Receives 600 submissions/year. Works with composers and lyricists. Pays standard royalty.
How to Contact: Submit a demo tape—unsolicited submissions are OK. Prefers cassette with 2-4 songs and lyric sheet.
Music: Mostly pop/rock; also country swing, country rock, 50s rock, Christmas, R&B, country, gospel and country R&B. Published "Bandito," written and recorded by C. Conley; "Full Moon Crazy" (by Val Stecklein), recorded by Brent Ronen; and "Showdown" (by M. Benish, Jack Routh, Brent Ronen), recorded by Brent Ronen; all on MDM Records (country).
Tips: "Be willing to make changes and work with a producer."

JEB STUART MUSIC CO., Box 6032, Station B, Miami FL 33123. (305)547-1424. President: Jeb Stuart. Music publisher, record producer and management firm. BMI. Estab. 1975. Publishes 4-6 songs/year. Teams collaborators. Pays standard royalty.
How to Contact: Submit a demo tape—unsolicited submissions are OK. Prefers cassette or disc with 2-4 songs and lead sheet. SASE. Reports in 1 month.
Music: Mostly gospel, jazz/rock, pop, R&B and rap; also blues, church/religious, country, disco and soul. Published "I Want to Make Love To You on Christmas Baby," written and recorded by Jeb Stuart on Esquire Int'l Records (blues/ballad); "Showdown" (by Chuck Jones), recorded by Priorty Impact on Esquire Int'l Records (R&B); and "Got Me Burnin' Up" (by Cafidia), recorded by Jeboria Stuart on Great American Records (pop rock).

STYLECRAFT MUSIC CO., P.O. Box 802, 953 Highway 51, Madison MS 39110. (601)856-7468. Professional Manager: Style Wooten. Music publisher, record company (Style Records, Styleway Records and Good News Records), record producer and booking agency. BMI. Estab. 1964. Publishes 20-65 songs/year; publishes 20 new songwriters/year. Receives 50 submissions/month. Pays standard royalty.

How to Contact: Submit demo tape—unsolicited submissions OK. Prefers cassette with 2-4 songs and "typewritten lyric sheet." SASE. Reports in 6-8 weeks.
Music: Country, R&B and black gospel. Published "Let's Take a Vacation to Heaven" parts 1-4 (by Douglas Bell), all recorded by Douglas Bell on Four Winds Records (gospel).
Tips: "Do it right. Don't be one of those 'I can write a song about anything' writers."

SUGAR MAMA MUSIC, #805, 4545 Connecticut Ave. NW, Washington DC 20008. (202)362-2286. President: Jonathan Strong. Music publisher, record company (Ripsaw Records) and record producer (Ripsaw Productions). BMI. Estab. 1983. Publishes 3-5 songs/year; publishes 2 new songwriters/year. Works with composers and lyricists. Pays standard royalty.
Affiliate(s): Neck Bone Music (BMI) and Southern Crescent Publishing (BMI).
How to Contact: Submit demo tape—unsolicited submissions OK. Prefers cassette and lyric sheet. SASE. Reports in 1 month.
Music: Mostly country, blues, rockabilly and traditional rock. Published "It's Not the Presents Under My Tree" (by Billy Poore and Tex Rubinowitz), recorded by Narvel Felts on Renegade Records (country).
Tips: "Send no more then 3-4 songs on cassette with lyric sheet and SASE with sufficient postage. Only authentic country, blues, rockabilly or roots rock and roll."

SUGARBAKERS MUSIC, 404 Bluegrass Ave., Madison TN 37115. (615)865-6380. President: Bob Frick. Music publisher. ASCAP. Estab. 1988. Publishes 20 songs/year; publishes 5 new songwriters/year. Works with composers and lyricists. Pays standard royalty.
How to Contact: Submit a demo tape—unsolicited submissions are OK. Prefers cassette with 2 songs and lyric sheets. Does not return unsolicited material. Reports in 2 weeks.
Music: Mostly gospel, country and pop. Published "Follow Where He Leads" (by Christine Starling); "Jesus is the Answer" (by Esther Stewart); and "Peace Within My Heart" (by Katz/Hopwood); all recorded by Bob Scott Frick on R.E.F. (gospel).

***SUGARFOOT PRODUCTIONS,** P.O. Box 1065, Joshua Tree CA 92252. A&R Director: Sheila Dobson. Music publisher, record company (Sugarfoot, Babydoll, Durban), record producer (Sugarfoot Records). ASCAP. Estab. 1987. Publishes 10-15 songs/year; publishes 4 new songwriters/year. Works with composers and lyricists; teams collaborators. Pays negotiable royalty; statutory rate per song on records.
How to Contact: Submit a demo tape—unsolicited submissions are OK. Prefers cassette with 3 songs and lyric sheet. "Make sure tape and vocal are clear." Does not return material. Reports in 1-2 months.
Music: Mostly jazz, blues, swing, country (Tex) and (GA), R&B, salsa, dance; also bassas, conga; Cuban, easy listening. Published "Not for Love" (by Elijah), recorded by Sugarfoot on Westways Records (R&B); "You're Blue" (by Deke), recorded by Jam'n Jo on Durban Records (jazz); and "2 Me An Yu" (by Dobby), recorded by Aleets on Breton Records (jazz).
Tips: "Listen to Irving Berlin, Cole Porter, Gershwin, Carmichael for professional music and lyrics."

SULTAN MUSIC PUBLISHING, P.O. Box 461892, Garland TX 75046. (214)271-8098. President: Don Ferguson. Music publisher, record company (Puzzle Records), record producer and booking agency (Don Ferguson Agency). BMI. Publishes 15 songs/year, including some new songwriters. Receives 50 submissions/month. Works with composers and lyricists; teams collaborators. Pays standard royalty.
Affiliate: Illustrions Sultan (ASCAP).
How to Contact: Prefers cassette with 3 songs and lyric sheet. SASE. Reports in 3 weeks.
Music: Mostly country; also MOR. Published "What Does It Take," written and recorded by Derek Hartis on Puzzle Records (C&W); "After Burn," written and recorded by Phil Rodgers (jazz); and "Ain't No Way" (by G. Duke), recorded by Flash Point (rock), all on Puzzle Records.
Tips: "The best quality demo makes the listener more receptive."

SULTRY LADY MUSIC, Suite 205, 380 Lafayette Rd., St. Paul MN 55107. (612)228-0719. Professional Manager: Thomas A. Del Vecchio. Music publisher. Publishes 1-2 songs/year; publishes 1 new songwriter/year. Pays standard royalty.
How to Contact: Prefers cassette with 3-5 songs "and a lyric sheet for each song. No submissions will be returned without SASE." Reports in 8 weeks.
Music: Mostly rock, MOR and jazz; also pop, top 40 and blues.

***SUNFLARE SONGS/RECORDS,** 31 W. Church St., Fairport NY 14450. (716)223-2310. President: Garry Manuel. Music publisher, record company, record producer. Estab. 1982. Publishes 20-80 songs/year; publishes 2-4 new songwriters/year. Pays standard royalty.

How to Contact: Submit demo tape—unsolicited submissions are OK. Prefers cassette with 2-3 songs and lyric sheet. "Lyric sheets should be neat, with name, address and phone number." SASE. Reports in 3 months.
Music: Mostly contemporary folk, jazz, adult contemporary; also rock, New Age, country. Published *Woody* (by Garry Manuel), recorded by Sunup; and *Man the Life Boats*, written and recorded by Brian Soule, both on Sunflare Records (LP).
Tips: "Have song professionally recorded. Packaging should be neat and orderly."

SUNSONGS MUSIC/HOLLYWOOD EAST ENTERTAINMENT, 52 N. Evarts Ave., Elmsford NY 10523. (914)592-2563. Professional Manager: Michael Berman. Music publisher, record producer and talent agency. Estab. 1981. BMI, ASCAP, SESAC. Publishes 20 songs/year; publishes 10 new songwriters/year. Pays standard royalty; co-publishing deals available for established writers.
Affiliate(s): Media Concepts Music and Dark Sun Music (SESAC).
How to Contact: Submit demo tape—unsolicited submissions OK. Prefers cassette with 3-4 songs and lyric sheet. SASE. Reports in 5 weeks.
Music: Dance-oriented, techno-pop, R&B, rock (all styles) and top 40/pop. Published "Paradise (Take Me Home)" (by Henderson/Riccitelli), recorded by Lisa Jarrett on Ro-Hit Records (dance); "Come Back to Me (by Henderson/Riccitelli), recorded by The Joneses on Karousell Records (R&B).
Tips: "Submit material with strong hook, good demo, and know the market being targeted by your song."

SUPER RAPP PUBLISHING, Suite 128, 3260 Keith Bridge Rd., Cumming GA 30130-0128. (706)889-8624. President: Ron Dennis Wheeler. Music publisher. BMI. Estab. 1964. Publishes 100 songs/year; 20-25 new songwriters/year. "Sometimes hires staff writers for special projects." Pays standard royalty.
How to Contact: "Send a demo tape/professionally recorded—if not, response time may be delayed. If you need a tape produced or song developed, contact R R & R Productions Inc. first before submitting a badly produced tape. Unsolicited submissions are OK. Send music trax with and without lead vocals. Lyric sheet and chords. Also send music score if possible. Prefers 15 ips and a cassette copy. Clarity is most important. SASE is a must if you want submission returned. Will try to respond within 3 months."
Music: Gospel, rock and pop; also country and R&B. "No new age." Published "No Exception To The Rule" (pop), "Ordinary Hero" (country pop), and "Echoes" (ballad/pop), all written and recorded by T. Prichard on Rapp/RRR Records.
Tips: "I need to understand the words. I'm concerned with the song, not the musicianship."

SWEET INSPIRATION MUSIC, 112 Widmar Pl., Clayton CA 94517. (510)672-8201. Owner: Edgar J. Brincat. Music publisher and record company (Roll On Records). ASCAP, BMI. Estab. 1986. Deals with artists and songwriters. Produces 2-4 singles/year. Pays standard royalty.
Affiliates: California Country Music (BMI).
How to Contact: Submit demo tape—unsolicited submissions are OK. Prefers cassette with 3 songs and lyric sheets. SASE. Reports in 6 weeks.
Music: Mostly MOR, contemporary country or pop; also R&B, gospel and light rock. Published "One Heart At A Time" (A. Leisten/J. Covert), recorded by Steve Jordan on Roll On Records; "Thank God" (A. Leisten/ J. Powell/ W. Horban), recorded by Steve Jordan on Roll On Records; "The Earth Could Move in California" (T. Del Vecchio), recorded by Steve Jordan on Roll On Records; and "Memories of Allison" (Cheitkovich/Bryant), copublished with Sweet Inspirations Music-ASCAP/ Paul Scott Music-ASCAP/Delta R&E-ASCAP, recorded by the world renowned "The Spinners" on Volt Records.

*SWEET TOOTH MUSIC PUB. CO., 2716 Springlake Ct., Irving TX 75060. (214)790-5172. General Manager: Kenny Wayne. Music publisher, record company, record producer, manager and booking agent. BMI. Estab. 1969. Publishes 10-15 songs/year; publishes 6-10 new songwriters/year. Works with composers and lyricists; teams collaborators. Pays standard royalty.
How to Contact: Write or call first and obtain permission to submit. Prefers cassette (or VHS videocassette if available) with 4 songs maximum and lyric sheet. "Do not send meter mail or coupon SASE! Use proper SASE. No tapes will be sent back in #10 envelopes! SASE." Reports in 1-2 months.
Music: Mostly commercial rock, blues, country; also soft rock, soul and gospel. Published "Paradise" (by Larry Shultz and Kenny Wayne), recorded by J.L. Fox and Tuesday Ryann; and "The You In Me" (by Larry Shulz), recorded by J.L. Fox on Candy Records (country single); and *Judgement Day* (by Burton Stinson), recorded by Burton Stinson Band on Candy Records (rock CD and cassette).
Tips: "Don't waste your time re-using old, overused cliches 'I miss you, wanna' kiss you, dream of you, can't drink you off my mind' etc. with old, worn out melodies! Compare your work to the hits of today. Use great hooks and danceable melodies with easy to remember lyrics."

SYNCHRO SOUND MUSIC AB, P.O. Box 1049, Sundbyberg 172 21 **Sweden**. Phone: (46)8-28 13 46. Publishing Manager: Douglas E. Lawton. Music publisher, record company (Synchro Sound Records) and record producer (Synchro Sound Records). STIM (Sweden). Estab. 1986. Publishes 50-75 songs/year; publishes 10-15 new songwriters/year. Hires staff writers. Works with composers and lyricists; teams collaborators. Pays standard royalty.
Affiliate(s): Desert Music AB, Midnight Sun Music AB, and Coste Apetrea Music AB.
How to Contact: Submit a demo tape—unsolicited submissions are OK. Prefers cassette or 15" ips reel to reel (or videocassette) with 4 songs and lyric sheet. Does not return unsolicited material. Reports in 6 weeks.
Music: Mostly pop, rock, classical and New Age; also R&B, country and gospel. Published "Aqua Regia" (by H. Henriksson), recorded by Mother Earth on Compose Records (new instrumental); "Sylvan God" (by C. Apeirea), recorded by Silva on Compose Records (new instrumental); and "Al Ut-Al Ut" (by Barkettes), recorded by Barkettes on Back-1 Records (pop).

TABITHA MUSIC, LTD., 39 Cordery Rd., St. Thomas, Exeter, Devon EX2 9DJ, **United Kingdom**. Phone: 44-0392-79914. Managing Director: Graham Sclater. Music publisher, record company (Tabitha and Willow Records) and record producer. MCPS, PRS. Member MPA. Estab. 1975. Publishes 25 songs/year; publishes 6 new songwriters/year. Works with composers. Pays standard royalty; royalties paid directly to US songwriters.
Affiliate(s): Domino Music and Dice Music.
How to Contact: Submit a demo tape—unsolicited submissions are OK. Prefers cassette with 1-4 songs and lyric sheet. SAE and IRC. Reports in 2 weeks.
Music: Mostly MOR and pop; also country, dance-oriented, Spanish, rock, soul and top 40. Published "Aliens" (by Mark Fojo), recorded by Sovereign on Tabitha Records; "Not A Chance," written and recorded by Simon Galt on Tabitha Records; "Video Boys" (by Goode/Partimeton), recorded by Circuit on Micro Records (electro pop); and "Teenage Love," written and recorded by A. Ford on Tabitha Records (pop).

TANGER-MUSIC PUBLISHING CO., INC., % British Record Corp., 1015 Gayley Ave,. Los Angeles CA 90024. Contact: A&R Department. Music publisher. ASCAP, BMI. Estab. 1981. Publishes 20 songs/year. Receives 150 submissions/month. Works with composers and lyricists; teams collaborators. Pays standard royalty 50%.
Affiliate(s): AKA Music (ASCAP).
How to Contact: Submit a demo tape—unsolicited submissions are OK. Prefers cassette with 3-4 songs and lyric and lead sheet. Does not return unsolicited material. Reports in 2-3 weeks.
Music: Mostly rock, heavy metal and pop; also blues, folk and R&B. Published "Follow Your Heart" and "Suddenly" (by Geoff Gibbs), recorded by Kim DeMarco on British Records (rock ballad); and "Next to Me" (by Mitch Cantor), recorded by Candice Kane on British Records (pop).

DALE TEDESCO MUSIC CO., 16020 Lahey St., Granada Hills CA 91344. (818)360-7329. FAX: (818)886-1338. President: Dale T. Tedesco. General Manager: Betty Lou Tedesco. Music publisher. BMI, ASCAP. Estab. 1981. Publishes 20-40 songs/year; publishes 20-30 new songwriters/year. Receives 80-100 submissions/month. Works with composers and lyricists; teams collaborators. Pays standard royalty.
Affiliate(s): Dale Tedesco Music (BMI) and Tedesco Tunes (ASCAP).
How to Contact: Submit a demo tape—unsolicited submissions are OK. Prefers cassette with 1-2 songs and lyric sheet. SASE or postcard for critique. "Dale Tedesco Music hand-critiques all material submitted. Free evaluation." Reports in 2 weeks.
Music: Mostly pop, R&B and A/C; also dance-oriented, R&B, instrumentals (for television & film), jazz, MOR, rock and soul.
Tips: "Listen to current trends and touch base with the publisher."

TEK PUBLISHING, P.O. Box 1485, Lake Charles LA 70602. (318)439-8839. Administrator: Eddie Shuler. Music publisher, freelance producer. ASCAP, BMI. Estab. 1956. Publishes 50 songs/year; publishes 35 new songwriters/year. Teams collaborators. Pays standard royalty of 50%.

Market conditions are constantly changing! If you're still using this book and it is 1994 or later, buy the newest edition of Songwriter's Market at your favorite bookstore or order directly from Writer's Digest Books.

Affiliate(s): TEK Publishing (BMI), Nassetan (BMI) and EMFS Music (ASCAP).
How to Contact: Submit a demo tape—unsolicited submissions are OK. Prefers cassette with 3 songs and lyric sheet. "Return postage is required for return of material." SASE. Reports in 2 months.
Music: Mostly country and R&B; also cajun, humorist and zydeco. Published "Yesterday's News," recorded by Cari Gregory (contemporary pop); "No Lowdown Boogie" (blues) and "Breaking Down the Door" (Cajun), recorded by Mickey Newman.
Tips: "KEEP WRITING. If you write a thousand songs, and even one is a hit it was all worthwhile. Concentrate on what's going on by listening to broadcasts and see what others are doing. Then try to determine where your story fits."

THEMA-VERLAG, Lacknergasse 6-8/3, Vienna 1170 **Austria.** Phone: (0222)454746. FAX: (0222)459503. Contact: Dr. Georg Strzyzowski. Music publisher, record company (Thema Records) and record producer. AKM, AUME, IFPI, LSG. Estab. 1985. Publishes approximately 100 songs/year; 5 new songwriters/year. Works with composers and lyricists; teams collaborators. Pays standard royalty.
Affiliate(s): Merco, Bronco, Recon, Novale, Jump, Enterprises, Continent, Panorama, Bang, Bang, Young Star Music, Herkules, Mozart Records, Raphaele Records, Present, Vigiesse and Wildfire.
How to Contact: Submit a demo tape—unsolicited submissions are OK. Prefers cassette or 38 ips reel-to-reel (or VHS videocassette) with lyric or lead sheets. SASE. Reports in 1 month.
Music: Mostly MOR, pop and jazz; also classic, rock and folk. Published "Video" (by P. Meissner); "The Way Home" (by Rooner Meye, folk); "Disco Nt" (by Voyage, MOR); "True or False" (by Ines Reiger); and "Nocturne" (by ORF-Symphony Orchestra), all recorded by Strzyzowski on Thema Records.

TIKI ENTERPRISES, INC., 195 S. 26th St., San Jose CA 95116. (408)286-9840. President: Gradie O'Neal. Music publisher, record company (Rowena Records) and record producer (Jeannine O'Neal and Gradie O'Neal). BMI, ASCAP. Estab. 1967. Publishes 40 songs/year; publishes 12 new songwriters/year. Receives 1,200 submissions/year. Works with composers; teams collaborators. Pays standard royalty.
Affiliate(s): Tooter Scooter Music (BMI), Rememberance Music (ASCAP), and Janell Music (BMI).
How to Contact: Submit a demo tape—unsolicited submissions are OK. Prefers cassette with 3 songs and lyric or lead sheets. SASE. Reports in 3 weeks.
Music: Mostly rock/pop, country and gospel; also international, jazz/fusion, rock, R&B, New Age and Spanish. Published ""Solo tu" (by M. Tejeda), recorded by Grupo Expression on G.Y.C. Records (Mexican); "Catfish on a Stick," written and recorded by Jeannine O'Neal on Rowena Records (country dance music); and "Still in Love" (by Yvonne Maxwell), recorded by Janice Edwards on Respond Records (black music).

TIME MINSTREL MUSIC, 502 West 5th St., Cameron MO 64429. (816)632-6039. Director: E.K. Bruhn. BMI. Music publisher, record company (Crusader and Songwriter Showcase), record producer (Crusader Records & Tapes). Estab. 1979. Publishes 10-15 songs/year; publishes 2-5 new songwriters/year. Works with composers and lyricists; teams collaborators. Pays standard royalty.
How to Contact: Write for immediate styles needed. Prefers cassette or 7½ ips reel-to-reel with 1-3 songs and "optional" lyric sheet or lead sheet. "Include short write-up about your interests." SASE. Reports in 10 weeks.
Music: Novelty/show songs, pop, country, soft rock and some gospel; also "clean" comedy show material.
Tips: "We like upbeat songs that are unique in subject matter."

TOMPAUL MUSIC CO., 628 South St., Mount Airy NC 27030. (919)786-2865. Owner: Paul E. Johnson. Music publisher, record company, record producer and record and tape distributor. BMI. Estab. 1960. Publishes 25 songs/year. Receives 250 submissions/year. Works with composers. Pays standard royalty.
How to Contact: Submit a demo tape—unsolicited submissions are OK. Prefers cassette tapes with 4-6 songs and lyric or lead sheet. SASE. Reports in 2 months.
Music: Mostly country, bluegrass and gospel; also church/religious, easy listening, folk, MOR, rock, soul and top 40. Published "My Last Christmas," written and recorded by Carl Tolbert (country); "It Won't Be Long" and "He Owns Everything," written and recorded by Early UpChurch on Stark Records (country gospel).
Tips: "Try to write good commercial type songs, use new ideas, listen to the songs that are played on radio stations today; you could get some ideas. Don't try to make alterations in a song already established."

TOOTER SCOOTER MUSIC (BMI), 195 S. 26th St., San Jose CA 95116. (408)286-9840. Owner: Gradie J. O'Neal. Music publisher. BMI. Estab. 1985. Publishes 15 songs/year; 6 new songwriters/year. Works with composers and lyricists. Pays standard 50% royalty.

Affiliate(s): Janell Music (BMI), O'Neal & Friend (ASCAP) and Remembrance Music (ASCAP).
How to Contact: Submit a demo tape—unsolicited submissions are OK. Prefers cassette with 2-4 songs and lyric sheet. SASE. Reports in 3 weeks.
Music: Country, gospel, pop/rock, Mexican. Published "Hard Times" (by C. Patton) (black); "Love is a Risk" (by R. Lee) (MOR); and "Still in Love" (by Y. Maxwell) (black), all recorded by Janice Edwards on Respond Records.
Tips: "Keep writing and listen to your radio. Never give up."

TOPOMIC MUSIC, 105 Rue de Normandie, Courbevoie 92400 **France.** (1)4333 6515. President: Pierre Jaubert. Music publisher and record producer. SACEM, ASCAP. Estab. 1974. Publishes 60 songs/year; publishes 10 new songwriters/year. works with composers and lyricists; teams collaborators. Pays SACEM royalty which is usually 50/50.
How to Contact: Submit demo tape by mail.
Music: "Looks for new songs for movie soundtracks. Also needs top 40 style singers for movie soundtracks and dance records productions. Topomic Music is looking for new lyricists in English, to write words on compositions already published by Topomic. Writer will receive writer shares only, no publisher share, and lyrics will be published by Topomic for the world." Published "You Call It Love" movie soundtrack), performed by Norwegian singer Karoline Kruger. Also publishes composer Jean Coignoux.

*TORO'NA MUSIC, Box 88022, Indianapolis IN 46208. Contact: A&R Director. Music publisher (Toro'na Music) and record producer (I. McDaniel). BMI. Estab. 1987. Publishes 3 songs/year; publishes 1 new songwriter/year. Hires independent staff writers. Pays standard royalty.
How to Contact: Write first and obtain permission to submit a tape. Direct all correspondence to A&R department. Prefers cassette with 3 songs and lyric sheets. Does not return unsolicited material. Reports in 8 weeks.
Music: Mostly top 40, R&B and gospel; also rap. Published "Second Chance" (ballad-LP) and "Freestyle" (jazz) (by I. McDaniel), recorded by I. McDaniel on Toro'na Records; and "Don't Say No" (by I. McDaniel), recorded by Payage on Brendo Kent Pub (ballad LP).
Tips: "Write first about your interests. No phone calls please."

TRANSITION MUSIC CORP., (formerly Creative Entertainment Music), Suite 700, 6290 Sunset Blvd., Los Angeles CA 90028. Professional Manager: Kim Frascarelli. Music publisher and management firm. BMI, ASCAP. Member NMPA. Estab. 1982. Publishes 35 songs/year; publishes 10 new songwriters/year. Receives 100 submissions/month. Teams collaborators.
Affiliate(s): Creative Entertainment Music (BMI), Pushy Publishing (ASCAP).
How to Contact: Submit a demo tape—unsolicited submissions are OK. Prefers cassette with 1-3 songs and lyric sheet. SASE. Reports in 1 month. "No telephone calls please!"
Music: R&B and dance. Published "Lead Me Into Love" (by Lane/Prentiss), recorded by Anita Baker on Elektra Records (R&B); "Ground Zero" (by Lauren Wood), recorded by Animotion on Polygram Records (rock); "So Happy" (by David Jones), recorded by Eddie Murphy on CBS Records (R&B); and "More Love" (by Steve Lane, Rodney Saulsberry, Peter Brown), recorded by Jasmine Guy on WB Records (R&B).
Tips: "Smart, crafty lyrics and the most up-to-date grooves and record quality demos aren't enough. You also need surprises."

TREASURE TROVE MUSIC, P.O. Box 48864, Los Angeles CA 90048. (213)739-4824. Contact: Professional Manager. Music publisher and record company (L.S. Disc). BMI. Estab. 1987. Publishes 3-15 songs/year; publishes 1-5 new songwriters/year. Receives 20-75 submissions/month. Works with composers and lyricists; teams collaborators. Pays standard royalty.
How to Contact: Submit a demo tape—unsolicited submissions are OK. Prefers cassette (or VHS videocassette) with 1-10 songs and lyric sheet. SASE. Reports in 3 months.
Music: Mostly rock, pop and folk rock; also unique crossover, blues and psychedelic rock. Published "Nobody for President" (by Larry Rosenblum and Peri Traynor); "2002" (by Larry Rosenblum); and "Clouds of Gas" (by Sky and the Bird), all recorded by 92 Bandwagon on L.S. Disc Records.
Tips: "Be real. Believe in yourself. Don't let rejection slow you down."

TRI-SHE KIETA PUBLISHERS, INC., #825, 122 W. Monroe, Chicago IL 60603. President: John Bellamy. Music publisher, record company (Source Records), record producer (Anthony Stephens). BMI. Estab. 1974. Publishes 12 new songs/year; 1-2 new songwriters/year. Works with composers and lyricists; teams collaborators. Pays standard royalty of 50%.

Affiliate(s): Light & Sound Music, Inc. (ASCAP), Source Records, Inc. and Tri-She Kieta Publications, Inc.

How to Contact: Submit demo tape—unsolicited submissions are OK. Prefers cassette (or VHS videocassette if available) with 3 songs and lyric sheet. Does not return unsolicited material. Reports in 3 weeks.

Music: Mostly R&B, pop and gospel. Published "Deeper in Debt" (by Spright Simpson), recorded by The Source (rap); "Crazy for You" (by Kennedy Green), recorded by The Source (R&B); and "Greater By and By" (by Sean Williams), recorded by Sean Williams (gospel), all on Source Records.

TROPICAL BEAT RECORDS/POLYGRAM, (formerly Omni Records, Inc.), P.O. Box 917, Bala Cynwyd PA 19004. (215)828-7030. President: Steven Bernstein. Music publisher and record company. Estab. 1973. BMI. Publishes 50 songs/year; publishes 3-4 new songwriters/year. Employs songwriters on a salary basis. Teams collaborators.

How to Contact: Prefers cassette. Does not return unsolicited material.

Music: R&B and dance ONLY. Published "Closer than Close" (by Terri Price), recorded by Jean Carne; and "Lonely Road" (by Bryan Williams), recorded by Rose Royce, both on Omni Records (both R&B); and "Love Won't Let Me Wait" by Luther Vandross.

TRUSTY PUBLICATIONS, 8771 Rose Creek Rd., Nebo KY 42441. (502)249-3194. President: Elsie Childers. Music publisher, record company (Trusty Records) and record producer. BMI. Member CMA, NAS. Estab. 1960. Publishes 2-3 songs/year; publishes 2 new songwriters/year. Receives 8-10 submissions/month. Works with composers. Pays standard royalty.

Affiliate(s): Sub-publishers: Sunset Music (Italy) and White Label (Holland).

How to Contact: Submit a demo tape—unsolicited submissions are OK. Prefers cassette (or VHS videocassette) with 2-4 songs and lead sheet. SASE. Reports in 1 month.

Music: Mostly country/blues, contemporary Christian, Southern gospel and dance tunes; some rap. Published "Yes It Do" (country/rock), "Pick It Up Easy" (country/pop), and "Southern Belle of Tennessee" (straight country) all by Childers and Williams, recorded by Noah Williams on Trusty Records.

Tips: "Make it different but pattern it after current trends."

TWIN TOWERS PUBLISHING CO., 8833 Sunset Blvd., Penthouse, Los Angeles CA 90069. (213)659-9644. President: Michael Dixon. Director of Publishing: Dave Powell. Music publisher and booking agency (Harmony Artists, Inc.). Works with composers and lyricists. Publishes 24 songs/year. Receives 200 submissions/month. Pays standard royalty.

How to Contact: Call first to get permission to submit a tape. Prefers cassette with 3 songs and lyric sheet. SASE. Will respond only if interested.

Music: Mostly pop, rock and R&B. Published "Magic," from *Ghostbusters* soundtrack on Arista Records; and "Kiss Me Deadly" (by Lita Ford), on RCA Records.

TWL PUBLISHING GROUP, P.O. Box 11227, Detroit MI 48211-0227. Attention: A&R Department. ASCAP, BMI, SESAC. Music publisher and management firm (L2 Management). Estab. 1982. Publishes 10-15 songs/year; publishes 1-2 new songwriters/year. Works with composers; teams collaborators. Pays standard royalty; negotiates foreign subpublishing.

Affiliate(s): Lady Marion, Isle Cay Music, Sunscape Publishing and The Clearwind Publishing Group.

How to Contact: "Solicited submissions only." Write and obtain permission to submit. SASE. Prefers cassette with 2 songs and typed lyric sheet. Reports in 12 weeks.

Music: "Highly commercial" pop/dance, pop/rock and R&B. Published "Don't Stop" (by M. Grabowski), recorded by Cerberus on Starstream (rock); *Champion*, and "What a Friend," written and recorded by Ron Moore on Morada (pop); and "Crazy in Your Ways," written and recorded by R.R. Jackson on Windguest Records (pop).

Tips: "The writer must be flexible and have the (obvious) potential to write not just one commercial success but many. The writer must also have a great amount of persistence, patience and perseverance. The goal of the writer should be close to that of his or her publisher."

*UBM, Mommsenst. 61, 5000 Koln 41 **Germany.** Phone: 43 13 13. President: Uwe Buschkotter. Music publisher, record company and record producer. GEMA (Germany), BMI (USA). Estab. 1968. Publishes 100 songs/year; publishes 10 new songwriters/year. Works with composers. Pays standard royalty.

How to Contact: Submit a demo tape—unsolicited submissions are OK. Prefers cassette (or VHS videocassette) and lead sheets. Does not return unsolicited material. Reports in 4 weeks.

Music: Mostly jazz, pop, MOR, funk and easy listening; also classical.

UDDER PUBLISHING/GOLDEN GELT PUBLISHING, P.O. Box 93457, Hollywood CA 90093. (213)960-9447. President: Adam Rodell. Music publisher, record company (Rodell Records) and record producer (Rodell Records). BMI, ASCAP. Estab. 1984. Publishes 200-300 songs/year; publishes 25-50 new songwriters/year. Works with composers and lyricists; teams collaborators. Pays negotiable royalty. **Affiliate(s):** Expose Music Publishing.
How to Contact: Submit a demo tape—unsolicited submissions are OK. Prefers cassette (or VHS videocassette if available) with 1-3 songs and lyric sheet. Does not return unsolicited material. "We will report back only if we are interested."
Music: Mostly rock, country, alternative, metal and pop; also fusion-progressive, R&B and rap. Published "Birdie Dance" (by Clyde Brewer), recorded by River Road Boys (country); "Pine Tar Bat" (by Dave McEmery), recorded by Red Rover Dave (novelty); and "Rodell Rhapsody," written and recorded by Andrew Rodell (rock); all on Longhorn Records.
Tips: "Send studio or studio quality cassettes only with bio. We openly welcome all types of music. We run periodic nationwide talent searches. Aggressively seeking new material. The artist's devotion and ambition to succeed must be as aggressive as ours!"

UNITED ENTERTAINMENT MUSIC, 3947 State Line, Kansas City MO 64111. (913)262-3555. Director of Publishing: Dave Maygers. Music publisher, record company (Stress Records) and record producer. BMI. Estab. 1972. Publishes 30-40 songs/year; publishes 30-40 new songwriters/year. Pays negotiable royalty.
How to Contact: Submit demo tape—unsolicited submissions OK. Prefers cassette or 15 or 30 ips reel-to-reel and lyric sheet. Does not return unsolicited material. Reports in 1 month.
Music: Mostly rock, R&B/blues and jazz; also country and pop. Published "Steal Away" and "So Lucky" (by R. Lucente), recorded by Bon Ton Band on Stress Records; "Mr. Misery" (by D. Blake), recorded by Tic Toc Boom; and "Weak Heart, Strong Memory," written and recorded by Spike Blake on Stress Records.
Tips: "We are looking for music that suits our artists and has a message that is positive and current. Music should have commercial value."

UNIVERSAL STARS MUSIC, INC., HC-80, Box 5B, Leesville LA 71446. National Representative: Sherree Stephens. Music publisher and record company (Robbins Records). BMI. Publishes 12-24 songs/year; publishes 1 new songwriter/year. Pays standard royalty.
Affiliate: Headliner Stars Music Inc.
How to Contact: Prefers cassette with 1-6 songs and lyric or lead sheets. Does not return unsolicited material. Reports in 1 month, if interested.
Music: Mostly religious; also bluegrass, church, country, folk, gospel and top 40/pop. Published "Jesus, You're Everywhere," "I Can Depend On You," and "I Just Came to Thank You Lord," (all by Sherree Stephens), all recorded by J.J. and S. Stephens on Robbins Records (religious).

UTTER NONSENSE PUBLISHERS, Box 1583, Brantford Ontario N3T 5V6 **Canada.** Phone: (519)442-7368. President: John Mars. Music publisher, record company (Ugly Dog Records) and record producer. SOCAN. Estab. 1979. Publishes 2-5 songs/year; publishes 1 new songwriter/year. Receives 10 submissions/month. Works with composers and lyricists; teams collaborators. Pays standard royalty.
How to Contact: Submit a demo tape—unsolicited submissions are OK. Prefers cassette (or videocassette if available) with lyric or lead sheet. "Send picture of artist(s). We regret that due to the large number of submissions we receive we now can only reply to those artists that we wish to express interest in."
Music: Mostly rock & roll; also new jazz and R&B. Published "Gone Today" (by Mars), recorded by Red Shrimps (rock'n'roll); "Kiss Rap" (by Goulding), recorded by Dr. Chub Master (heavy rock satire); and "I Can Find My Way" (by Mars, Shuetz), recorded by John Mars (rock'n'roll), all on Ugly Dog Records.
Tips: "We are mainly interested in basic, rootsy R&R, and very little of that is sent to us. Also, 9 out of 10 demos are of quality that is virtually undecipherable. Do not waste time with poor quality demos."

VAAM MUSIC GROUP, P.O. Box 29688, Hollywood CA 90029-0688. (213)664-7765. President: Pete Martin. Music publisher and record producer. ASCAP, BMI. Estab. 1967. Publishes 9-24 new songs/year; varying number of new songwriters per year. Receives 50-200 submissions/month. Pays standard royalty.
Affiliate: Pete Martin Music.
How to Contact: Prefers cassette with 2 songs maximum and lyric sheet. SASE. Reports in 1 month. "Small packages only."
Music: Top 40/pop, country and R&B. "Submitted material must have potential of reaching top 5 on charts." Published "Good Girls" (by Kevin Bird), recorded by Valerie Canon on Carrere/CBS Records (R&B dance); "The Greener Years," recorded by Frank Loren on Blue Gem Records (country/

MOR); "Bar Stool Rider" (by Peggy Hackworth); and "I Love a Cowboy," written and performed by Sherry Weston in the feature film "Far Out Man," with Tommy Chong (of Cheech & Chong comedy team) and also co-starring Martin Mull.

Tips: "Study the top 10 in charts in the style that you write. Stay current and up to date to today's market."

VALENTINE MUSIKVERLAG, Box 203312, D-2000 Hamburg 20 **Germany.** Phone: (040) 4300339. FAX: (040)4396587.General Manager: Arno H. van Vught. GEMA. Music publisher, record company (Bandleader Records, Range Records) and record producer. Estab. 1973. Publishes 350 songs/year; publishes 50 new songwriters/year. Pays standard royalty.

Affiliate(s): Mento Music Group KG, Edition RCP Music and Auteursunie.

How to Contact: Submit a demo tape—unsolicited submissions are OK. Prefers cassette and lyric sheet and lead sheet. SAE and IRC. Reports in 2 weeks.

Music: Mostly country, jazz, big band, background music and MOR; also film music. Published *Jazz* (by E. Stanb), recorded by E. Kammler on Playbones Records (MOR); *Born Again*, written and recorded by Reifegerste on DA Music Records (MOR); and *Loose One* (by Brun Kuhles), recorded by Daniel and Claudia on Playbones Records (soft rock).

Tips: "Send full lead sheet and information about the writer(s)."

VALET PUBLISHING CO., #273, 2442 N.W. Market, Seattle WA 98107. (206)524-1020; FAX: (206)524-1102. Publishing Director: Buck Ormsby. Music publisher and record company (Etiquette/ Suspicious Records). BMI. Estab. 1961. Publishes 5-10 songs/year. Receives 300-350 submissions/year. Hires staff songwriters. Pays standard royalty.

How to Contact: Submit a demo tape—unsolicited submissions OK. Prefers cassette with 3-4 songs and lyric sheets. SASE. Reports in 6-8 weeks.

Music: Mostly R&B, rock, pop; also dance and country. Published "Black Lace" (by Roger Rogers), recorded by Kinetics on Etiquette Records (rock); "Hunger and Emotion" (by Rogers/Caldwell), recorded by Kinetics on Etiquette Records (pop); and "One More Time" (by Morrill/French), recorded by Kent Morrill on Suspicious Records (R&B).

Tips: "Production of tape must be top quality; or lyric sheets professional."

*VICTORY MUSIC, P.O. Box 147, Elberton GA 30635. Professional Manager: Dianna Kirk. Music publisher. Estab. 1991. Works with composers and lyricists. Pays standard royalty.

Affiliate(s): Wild Katt Music.

How to Contact: Write first and obtain permission to submit. Prefers cassette with 3 songs and lyric sheet. Does not return unsolicited material. Reports in 2-3 weeks.

Music: Mostly heavy metal, rock, dance. Published "Big Fat Women," "You Dropped a Bomb," "Living in Sin" (by Greg Timms).

VIN-JOY MUSIC, 872 Morris Park Ave., Bronx NY 10462. (212)792-2198. Contact: Vice President. Music publisher, record company (Dragon Records) and record producer. BMI, ASCAP. Estab. 1960. Publishes 14-16 new songs/year; publishes 3-4 new songwriters/year. Works with composers, lyricists; teams collaborators. Pays negotiable amount.

How to Contact: "We accept material by recommendation only." Write or call first to get permission to submit a tape. SASE. Reports in 3 weeks.

Music: Easy listening, MOR, top 40/pop and country. Published "Bunny Tale" (by Heath), recorded by The Bunny Tails (country rock); "A Letter to A D.J. (by Gagliano), recorded by The Caroloms (soft rock); and "Lonely Child" (by Heath), recorded by Smokey Heath (MOR ballad).

Tips: "Material has to be exceptional—not amateurish."

VIRGIN BOY PUBLISHING, 2613 Castle, Irving TX 75038. (214)257-1510. President: James Yarborough. Music publisher, record company (Virgin Boy Records) and record producer. ASCAP. Estab. 1988. Publishes 25 songs/year; publishes 10 new songwriters/year. Works with composers and lyricists; teams collaborators. Pays standard royalty.

Affiliate(s): Virgin Boy Publishing (ASCAP).

How to Contact: Submit a demo tape—unsolicited submissions are OK. Prefers cassette with 3 songs and lyric sheet. Does not return unsolicited material. Reports in 2 months.

Music: Mostly pop, rock and country. Published "A Woman Of Mystery," "Angel In White Satin" and "Looking All Over," all written and recorded by James Yarborough on Virgin Boy Records (pop singles).

VOKES MUSIC PUBLISHING, Box 12, New Kensington PA 15068-0012. (412)335-2775. President: Howard Vokes. Music publisher, record company, booking agency and promotion company. BMI.
How to Contact: Submit cassette (3 songs only), lyric or lead sheet. SASE. Reports within a week.
Music: Traditional country-bluegrass and gospel. Published "Thank You Grand Ole Op'ry," "I'm Falling in Love Again," "Counting Up To Ten" and "Tangled Memories."

M & T WALDOCH PUBLISHING, INC., 4803 S. 7th St., Milwaukee WI 53221. (414)482-2194. VP, Creative Management: Timothy J. Waldoch. Music publisher. Estab. 1990. Publishes 2-3 songs/year; publishes 2-3 new songwriters/year. Works with composers and lyricists; teams collaborators. Pays standard royalty.
How to Contact: Submit demo tape—unsolicited submissions are OK. Prefers cassete with 3-6 songs and lyric sheet or lead sheet. "We prefer a studio produced demo tape." SASE. Reports in 2-3 months.
Music: Mostly country/pop, rock, top 40 pop; also melodic metal, dance, R&B. Published "It's Only Me" and "Let Peace Rule the World" (by Kenny LePrix), recorded by Brigade on SBD Records (rock LP).
Tips: "We want songs with strong melodies and well crafted lyrics. Read *The Craft of Lyric Writing* by Sheila Davis and other books on songwriting to help you develop your craft."

WARNER/CHAPPELL MUSIKVERLAG GESELLSCHAFT m.b.H., Diefenbachgasse 35, Vienna A 1150 Austria. Phone: (0222) 894 19 20; FAX: (0222) 894 16 15. Contact: Florian Czeitschner. Music publisher. AKM. Works with composers and lyricists; teams collaborators.
Affiliate(s): Schneider Musikverlag, Gloria Musikverlag, and Aberbach Musikverlag.
How to Contact: Prefers cassette (or VHS videocassette). SAE and IRC. Reports in 3 months.
Music: Mostly pop, rock and country; also musicals.

WARNER/CHAPPELL MUSIC, INC., 1290 6th Ave., New York NY 10019. (212)399-6910. V.P. Creative Services: Kenny McPhearson. Music publisher. ASCAP, BMI, SESAC. Estab. 1811. Publishes hundreds of songs/year; publishes hundreds of new songwriters/year. Hires staff songwriters. Works with composers and lyricists; teams collaborators.
Affiliate(s): WB Music Corp. (ASCAP), Warner Tamerlane Publishing Corp. (BMI), W.B.M. Music Corp. (SESAC), Warner/Elektra/Asylum Music Inc. (BMI), Warner/Refuge Music Inc. (ASCAP), Warner/Noreale Music Inc. (SESAC), Chappell & Co. (ASCAP), Intersong U.S.A. Inc. (ASCAP), Rightsong Music Inc. (BMI), Unichappell Music Inc. (BMI), Tri-Chappell Music, Inc. (SESAC), Lorimar Music A Corp (ASCAP), Lorimar Music B Corp (BMI), Roliram Lorimar Music (BMI), Marilor Music (ASCAP), Goldline Music (ASCAP) Silverline Music (BMI) and Oakline Music (SESAC).
How to Contact: "Must be solicited by an attorney or management firm." Company policy prohibits unsolicited submissions.
Music: Mostly pop, rock, R&B and country; also rap, jazz and new music.
Tips: "Submit your best song because sometimes you only get to make a first impression. Submit a song you feel most comfortable writing regardless of style."

WATCHESGRO MUSIC, P.O. Box 1794, Big Bear City CA 92314. (714)585-4645. President: Eddie Carr. Music publisher. BMI. Estab. 1987. Publishes 100 songs/year; publishes 5 new songwriters/year. Receives 200 submissions/year. Teams collaborators. Pays standard royalty.
Affiliate(s): Watch Us Climb Music (ASCAP).
How to Contact: Submit a demo tape by mail—unsolicited submissions are OK. Prefers cassette. Does not return unsolicited material. Reports in 1 week.
Music Published "7th & Sundance" (by Aileen/Dempsey), recorded by Rita Aileen (country); "Eatin' My Words" (by M. Jones), recorded by Michael Jones; and "Precious Memories" (by D. Horn), recorded by Cindy Jane, all on Interstate 40 Records (country singles).

WAYNE AND LACEY, 4305 So. 70th St., Tampa FL 33619. (813)621-7055. Publisher: Wayne Lacey. Music publisher, record company (Music City Records) and record producer (Music City Records). BMI. Estab. 1982. Publishes 50 songs/year; publishes 10-15 new songwriters/year. year. Works with composers. Pays standard royalty.
How to Contact: Prefers cassette with 4 songs. Does not return unsolicited material. Reports in 1 month.
Music: Mostly gospel. Published "Only the Blood," "What A Wonderful Day," and "Land Of Promise," (all written by Wayne Lacey), recorded by The Laceys on Music City Records.
Tips: "Submit gospel, southern, bluegrass and traditional."

Close-up

Susan Longacre
Songwriter
Nashville, Tennessee

© 1990 Alan L. Mayer

"There's a formula and I try not to write it," Susan Longacre smiles, explaining her award-winning songwriting technique. "(But) I've always believed you have to know the
rules in order to break them, so you have to study the
basics."

Longacre has the distinction of being one of the few
songwriters who hasn't sold out to music industry politics.
She refuses to write contrived, emotionally devoid lyrics and in this day of self-contained
artists, won't bend her belief system to write with recording artists she doesn't respect as
songwriters.

How has this affected her career? Although it took her five years and over 50 album
cuts before one of her songs was released as a single, she was named SESAC's 1990 Songwriter of the Year and in 1991, received a SESAC National Performance Activity Award
for Kathy Mattea's "Time Passes By," and accepted her second for T.G. Shepherd's "Born
in a High Wind." She's penned "The Truth is Lyin' Next to You," which Randy Travis
included on his Grammy Award-winning LP, *Always and Forever*.

"I feel very proud that I've been able to make my mark without doing anything political,"
she says. "It's very, very hard right now," she continues, alluding to the intensely political
state songwriting is in right now. "But I still believe the universe rewards you for being who
you are. If you stray from that, you're going to be unhappy."

But Longacre isn't naive—she knows that philosophy is a lot easier to say than to live.
"It's hard. I'm at a big publishing company (Warner Chappell) with a lot of great writers
(who are) having No. 1's all the time. If I look on either side of me to what they're doing
and they're writing those clever commercial songs—if I look at that for one minute and get
off my path, I'm lost. I have to focus ahead."

Longacre has spent most of her life focused "ahead" on writing and music, although she
didn't combine the two until she was in her early twenties, when she'd tired of Northeastern
winters, of "moving (musical) equipment through four feet of snow," and moved to Los
Angeles, "where it was warmer."

She got her first break at the Banjo Cafe. Bing Crosby's daughter, Mary, and her hus-
band, Ed Lottimer, came in, liked her original material and invited her to their house to
discuss a publishing contract. She accepted their offer, and while there, listened to another
songwriter's demo tape. "They played me a tape of a turkey farmer from Arkansas," she
recalls. "I thought, 'this guy's music is incredible but his words are not so great.' " The
obvious solution? "We started writing long distance, me and this turkey farmer; I'd send
him the lyric, he'd write the music and send it back, (then) I'd make changes in the music
and send it back." After the two had co-written eight songs together, "I had one of the
great loves of my life fall apart and I knew I wanted to leave LA."

Since she'd always been a country fan anyway, and had even stopped in Nashville to
play a songwriter's showcase on her way to LA, Longacre decided to move to Music City.
The turkey farmer, aka Pal Owen, agreed to meet her there, demos in hand. Once there,

he introduced her to Dianne Petty, SESAC's chief. Longacre admits she was so impressed with Petty, she "signed up with SESAC without even talking to ASCAP or BMI." And in true "dreams-can-come-true-it-can-happen-to-you" fashion, by the end of the first week, she was signed as a staff writer to Window Music, Pete Drake's company.

What advice would she give someone trying to break into the wonderful world of song-writing today? "You've got to be in Nashville, first of all," she says adamantly. "It's a business of people knowing people. You've got to be here.

"You've (also) got to know what is happening on radio, be totally aware and then don't necessarily write what's on radio. Try to find your own voice, your own style. All the great writers in this town—Mike Reid, Don Schlitz, Paul Overstreet, Dave Loggins—have their own style. Those people are being who they are. My biggest advice is to try to be true to yourself, despite how long it's going to take—ten times longer than you think it's going to take; be prepared to dig in and stay with it for the long haul. But when it happens, when you are true to yourself and you start getting the cuts, people know that you're a quality writer, that you're not just a flavor of the month."

And how do you move beyond clever word plays and write songs up to Longacre standards? "My philosophy about a clever title is if you do write it, you've got to write it with feeling, with emotion—not just the craft. It has to have some heart in it; if it doesn't, there's no point in writing it. Emotion is the thing I want in my songs more than any other quality—that's the No. 1 quality that I reach for. Try to write from your feelings about feelings; tell stories about your life and try to get feeling into it. Look to yourself. Watch and learn from everything else but don't try to *be* anything but yourself."

—Marjie McGraw

❝Try to find your own voice, your own style. All the great writers in this town—Mike Reid, Don Schlitz, Paul Over-street, Dave Loggins—have their own style. Those people are being who they are. My biggest advice is to try to be true to yourself, despite how long it's going to take—ten times longer than you think it's going to take; be prepared to dig in and stay with it for the long haul.❞

—Susan Longacre

*WEAVER WORDS OF MUSIC, P.O. Box 803, Tazewell VA 24651. (703)988-6267. President: H. R. Cook. Music publisher and record company (Fireball Records). BMI. Estab. 1978. Publishes 12 songs/year; varying number of new songwriters/year. Works with composers and lyricists; teams collaborators. Pays standard royalty.
How to Contact: Submit a demo tape—unsolicited submissions are OK. Prefers cassette with 3 songs and lyric or lead sheets. SASE. Reports in 1 month.
Music: Mostly country. Published "Winds of Change," written and recorded by Cecil Surrett; "Texas Saturday Night" and "Old Flame Burning," written and recorded by H.R. Cook; all on Fireball Records (country).

WEEDHOPPER MUSIC, 1916 28th Ave. S., Birmingham AL 35209-2605. (205)942-3222. President: Michael Panepento. BMI. Estab. 1985. Music publisher and record company (Pandem Records, Inc.), management firm (Airwave Production Group, Ltd.). Publishes 4-6 songs/year; publishes 3 new songwriters/year. Receives 10 submissions/month. Works with composers and lyricists. Pays standard royalty.
Affiliate: Panepentunes (ASCAP).
How to Contact: Submit demo tape—Unsolicited submissions are OK. Prefers cassette or 15 ips reel-to-reel with 3 songs. SASE. Reports in 10 weeks.
Music: Mostly pop/rock, AOR, R&B/jazz and rock; also all others. Published "Home" and "Land of Kings" (by Kieth Hammrick), recorded by The Skeptics on Pandem Records (modern rock).
Tips: "Send us the best possible demo/example of your work."

BERTHOLD WENGERT (MUSIKVERLAG), Hauptstrasse 100, D-7507 Pfinztal-Soellingen, **Germany.** Contact: Berthold Wengert. Music publisher. Teams collaborators. Pays standard GEMA royalty.
How to Contact: Prefers cassette and complete score for piano. SAE and IRC. Reports in 4 weeks.
Music: Mostly light music and pop.

BOBE WES MUSIC, P.O. Box 28609, Dallas TX 75228. (214)681-0345. President: Bobe Wes. Music publisher. BMI. Publishes 20 songs/year. Receives 4 submissions/month. Pays standard royalty.
How to Contact: Submit a demo tape—unsolicited submissions are OK. Prefers cassette. "State if songs have been copyrighted and if you have previously assigned songs to someone else. Include titles, readable lyrics and your full name and address. Give the same information for your co-writer(s) if you have one. State if you are a member of BMI, ASCAP or SESAC. Lead sheets are not required. Comments will follow only if interested." SASE. No certified mail accepted.
Music: Blues, country, disco, gospel, MOR, progressive, rock (hard or soft), soul, top 40/pop, polka, Latin dance and instrumentals. "Special interest in Christmas songs."

WEST BROADWAY MUSIC, 418-810 W. Broadway., Vancouver, BC V52 4C9 **Canada.** (604)731-3535. Professional Manager: Michael Goodin. Music publisher and management company. SOCAN. Estab. 1989. Publishes 12-15 songs/year; publishes 1-3 new songwriters/year. Works with composers; teams collaborators. Pays standard royalty.
How to Contact: Write or call first and obtain permission to submit a tape. Prefers cassette with 3-5 songs and lyric sheet. SASE. Reports in 4-6 weeks.
Music: Mostly pop, dance and rock; also R&B. Published "Might as Well Party," written and recorded by Al Rodger on Criminal Records (pop); and "Your Place or Mine" (by Al Rodger), recorded by Sharon Lee Williams on Virgin Records (R&B/dance).

WESTUNES MUSIC PUBLISHING CO., Suite 330, 1115 Inman Ave., Edison NJ 08820-1132. (908)548-6700. FAX: (908)548−6748. A&R Director: Brian Dayton. Music publisher and management firm (Westwood Entertainment Group). ASCAP. Publishes 15 songs/year; publishes 2 new songwriters/year. Receives 300-400 submissions/year. Works with composers and lyricists. Pays standard royalty.
How to Contact: Write first and obtain permission to submit. Prefers cassette with 3 songs and lyric sheet. SASE. Reports in 6 weeks.
Music: Mostly rock; also pop. Published "Inside Out," "We Love the Radio," "Heaven on Earth," "Just Three Words," "A Little Bit of Magic" and "Little Soldier" all rock singles written by K. McCabe and recorded by The Numbers on Westwood Records.
Tips: Submit a "neat promotional package; attach biography of the songwriter."

WHIMSONG PUBLISHING ASCAP, 1156 Park Lane, West Palm Beach FL 33417. (407)686-1354. Professional Managers: Rusty Gordon, Ron Caruso and Davilyn Whims. Music publisher and record producer (Rustron Music Productions). Estab. 1990. Works with composers and lyricists; teams collaborators. Pays standard royalty. Publishes 100-150 songs/year; publishes 10-20 new songwriters/year.

How to Contact: Submit a demo tape—unsolicited submissions are OK. Prefers cassette with 1-3 songs and lyric or lead sheet. "Clearly label your tape and container. Include cover letter." SASE required for all correspondence. Reports in 2-3 months.

Music: Mostly pop (ballads, blues, theatrical, cabaret), progressive country, folk/rock; also New Age instrumentals and R&B. Published "Shadow Dancing" (by Gary Barth), recorded by Gary Jess on GJB Records (New Age Fusion); "Home" (by Pricilla Smith), recorded by Cilla Smith on Whimsong Records (A/C); "What Are You Doing" (by Gary Gonzalex and Rick Groom), recorded by Relative Viewpoint on RVP Records (contemporary topical/folk).

Tips: "Write for the market as it really exists, create songs for the recording artists who accept original material, read label credits. Stay tuned to the trends and fusions indicative of the '90s."

WHITE CAR MUSIC (BMI), 11724 Industriplex, Baton Rouge LA 70809. (504)755-1400. Contact: Nelson Blanchard. Music publisher, record company (White Car Records/Techno Sound Records), record producer. BMI, ASCAP. Estab. 1988. Publishes 15 songs/year; publishes 2 new songwriters/ year. Receives 6 submissions/month. Works with composers and lyricists; teams collaborators. Pays standard royalty.

Affiliate(s): Char Blanche Music (ASCAP).

How to Contact: Submit a demo tape by mail—unsolicited submissions are OK. Prefers cassette with 4 songs. Does not return unsolicited material. Reports in 2 weeks.

Music: Mostly country, rock and pop; also R&B. Published "Leading Man" (by Butch Reine), recorded by Atchafalaya on White Car Records (country); "Sail On" (by Blanchard, Watts, Bullion), recorded by Johnsteve on Stebu Records (rock); and "Crazy Bound" (by Blanchard), recorded by Tareva on White Car Records (country).

WHITE CAT MUSIC, Suite 114, 10603 N. Hayden Rd., Scottsdale AZ 85260. (602)951-3115. FAX: (602)951-3074. Professional Manager: Frank Fara. Producer: Patty Parker. Music publisher. Member CMA, CARAS, CCMA, BCCMA and BBB. Estab. 1978. Publishes 30 songs/year; publishes 20 new songwriters/year. Receives 60 submissions/month. "50% of our published songs are from non-charted and developing writers." Pays standard royalty.

Affiliate: Rocky Bell Music (BMI) and How The West Was Sung Music (BMI).

How to Contact: Submit a demo tape—unsolicited submissions are OK. Cassettes only with 2 songs and lyric or lead sheet. SASE. Reports in 2 weeks.

Music: Mostly A/C, traditional country and contemporary country. Published "Sad Time of the Night" (by Eric Bach and Andrew Wolf), recorded by Will Stevens on Corduroy Records in Holland (contemporary country); "Does She Love Me" written and recorded by Paul Gibson on Comstock (traditional country); and "Your Lovin' Arms" (by Roy Ownbey and Dan Conner) (modern C&W).

Tips: "Send only 2 songs—they will be heard faster and listened to more intently! Send up-tempo songs—this will increase your chances. Don't use long instrumental intros and breaks, it detracts from listening to the song itself."

WHITEWING MUSIC, 413 N Parkerson Ave., Crowley LA 70526. (318)783-1601. Owner: Jay Miller. Music publisher, record company (Master-Trak, Showtime, Par T, MTE, Blues Unlimited, Kajun, Cajun Classics) and record producer (Master-Trak Productions). BMI. Estab. 1969. Publishes 25 songs/year. Works with composers and lyricists. Pays standard royalty.

Affiliate(s): Jamil Music (BMI), Whitewing Music (BMI).

How to Contact: Submit a demo tape—unsolicited submissions are OK. Prefers cassette with 3-4 songs and lyric sheets. Does not return unsolicited material.

Music: Mostly country, rock & roll and novelty; also blues, party and cajun. Published "Johnny Can't Dance" (by Mike Doucet, Wayne Toups), recorded by Wayne Toups on Master-Trak (rock) and "Fish Out of Water" (by Wayne Toups) recorded by Zydecajun.

WILCOM PUBLISHING, Box 4456, West Hills CA 91308. (818)348-0940. Owner: William Clark. Music publisher. ASCAP. Estab. 1989. Publishes 10-15 songs/year; publishes 1-2 new songwriters/year. Works with composers and lyricists. Pays standard royalty.

How to Contact: Write first and obtain permission to submit a tape. Prefers cassette with 1-2 songs and lyric sheet. SASE. Reports in 3 weeks.

Music: Mostly R&B, pop and rock; also country. Published "Girl Can't Help It" (by W. Clark, D. Walsh and P. Oland), recorded by Stage 1 on Rockit Records (top 40).

WILD ANGEL, 3500 Llan Beris Ave., Bristol PA 19007. (215)788-2723. President: Johnny Kline. Music publisher, record company (Silver Jet) and record producer (Silver Jet Production). BMI. Estab. 1989. Pays standard royalty.

How to Contact: Submit a demo tape by mail—unsolicited submissions are OK. Prefers cassette with 3 songs and lyric sheet. "No phone calls please." SASE. Reports in 2 weeks.
Music: Mostly rockabilly, country and rock; also gospel. Published "Rockabilly Baby" and "Dean of Rock n Roll," written and recorded by Johnny Kline, on Silver Jet Records (rockabilly).

SHANE WILDER MUSIC, P.O. Box 3503, Hollywood CA 90078. (818)508-1433. President: Shane Wilder. Music publisher (BMI), record producer (Shane Wilder Productions) and management firm (Shane Wilder Artists Management). Estab. 1960. Publishes 25-50 songs/year; publishes 15-20 new songwriters/year. Receives 400 submissions/month. Works with composers. Pays standard royalty.
How to Contact: Submit demo tape—unsolicited submissions OK. Prefers cassette (or VHS videocassette) with 3 songs and lyric sheet. "Include SASE if you wish tape returned. Photo and resume should be sent if you're looking for a producer." Reports in 1 month.
Music: Mostly traditional country and crossover. Published "Fool of the Year" (by Inez Polizzi), recorded by Allen Kart on Century 2 Records (country); "Loose Fittin' Long Johns" (by Inez Polizzi), recorded by Joe Terry on Century 2 Records (country); and "Bring Back Your Love" (by Melanie Kay), recorded by Anne Murray on Capitol Records (country).
Tips: "We no longer accept songs with a reversion clause."

MAURICE WILSON'S MUSIC CO., 6061 W. 83rd Pl., Los Angeles CA 90045. (213)216-0210. President: Morris Lee Wilson. Music publisher, record company (Wilson Records) and record producer (Wilson Music Co.). BMI. Estab. 1978. Publishes 20 new songs/year; publishes 1-20 new songwriters/year. Hires staff writers. Works with composers and lyricists; teams collaborators. Pays standard royalty.
Affiliate(s): Wilson's Music Co., Kat and Morris Wilson Publications, Jack of Diamond Publishing, Country Creations.
How to Contact: Submit a demo tape—unsolicited submissions are OK. Prefers cassette (or VHS videocassette) with any number of songs and lyric and lead sheet. SASE, "but we prefer to keep it on file." Reports in 3 weeks.
Music: Mostly easy listening, country and MOR; also R&B, jazz and children's. Published "Soft Touch" (by Vivian Rummes), recorded by Morris Lee Wilson; "Lady Love" (by Rummes and Wilson), recorded by Rummes and Wilson; and "Vivian Jean" (by Morris Wison), recorded by Morris Lee Wilson, all on C.B.S. Records (R&B).
Tips: "We look for songs that have a good hook line, have something to say and are different from the norm. Publishers are looking for songs that will sound as good in 20 years as they do today."

*WIL-TOO/WIL-SO MUSIC, P.O. Box 120694, Nashville TN 37212. President: Tom Wilkerson. Music publisher, record producer. ASCAP, BMI. Estab. 1969. Publishes 10 songs/year; 2-3 new songwriters/year. Works with composers and lyricists; teams collaborators. Pays standard royalty.
How to Contact: Submit a demo tape—unsolicited submissions OK. Prefers cassette with 3 songs. SASE. Reports in 3-4 weeks.
Music: Mostly country, gospel and contemporary Christian and pop. Published *Lady of Light*; "If There's a Miracle" and "Bridge of Peace" (by Wilkerson-Fielder), recorded by Joyful Pilgrim on Lightstone Records (Christian).

*WIND HAVEN PUBLISHING, 6477 Emerson Ave. S., St. Petersburg FL 33707. (813)343-5456. Contact: Joe Terry. Music publisher, record company, record producer. Estab. 1982. Publishes around 50 songs/year. Works with composers and lyricists; teams collabortors. Standard contract.
How to Contact: Submit demo tape—unsolicited submissions are OK. Prefers cassette 6 songs and lyric sheet. SASE. Reports in 6-8 weeks.
Music: Mostly country, gospel, easy listening; also pop-country, blue grass, rock-a-billy. Published "I'm Stepping Out" (by R.T. Smith and Ray Sanders), recorded by Joe Terry; "Florida Sunshine," written and recorded by Ricky Ward; and "City Life" (by Donna McComb and Joe Terry), by Rick Ward and Joe Terry, all on Wind Haven Records.

WONDERWAX PUBLISHING, P.O. Box 4641, Estes Park CO 80517. (303)586-9005. President: James Haber. Music publisher, record company (DG Records; ? Records). BMI. Estab. 1983. Publishes 5 songs/year; publishes 5 new songwriters/year. Works with composer and lyricists; teams collaborators. Pays standard royalty.
How to Contact: Submit a demo tape—unsolicited submissions are OK. Prefers cassette with 4 songs and lyric sheets. "Listen to your submitted cassette beforehand—check for clarity." SASE. Reports in 2 months.
Music: Mostly rock, pop and R&B; also British 60s rock, novelty and folk. Published "Problems" (by Slash N.F.), recorded by Jimmy Kinks on Bare Records (R&B); "Under a Waterfall (by J. Haber), recorded by Degenerates on Wonderwax Records (folk/trash); and "T-Shirts" (by J. McRoberts), recorded by Big Country on Jerzees Records (rock/pop).

Tips: "If it doesn't seem to slot in with what's considered normal—send it in."

WOODRICH PUBLISHING CO., P.O. Box 38, Lexington AL 35648. (205)247-3983. President: Woody Richardson. Music publisher and record company (Woodrich Records) and record producer. BMI. Estab. 1959. Publishes 25 songs/year; publishes 12 new songwriters/year. Receives 3,000 submissions/year. Works with composers; teams collaborators. Pays 50% royalty less expenses.
Affiliate(s): Mernee Music (ASCAP), Melstep Music (BMI) and Tennesse Valley Music (SESAC).
How to Contact: Submit a demo tape—unsolicited submissions are OK. Prefers cassette with 2-4 songs. Prefers studio produced demos. SASE. Reports in 2 weeks.
Music: Mostly country and gospel; also bluegrass, blues, choral, church/religious, easy listening, folk, jazz, MOR, progressive, rock, soul and top 40/pop. Published "Playing in the Dark" (by T. Rathban), recorded by Thom Rathban on Woodrich Records (jazz); "Welcome Back to Me" (by S. Celia), recorded by Sandra Celia on Woodrich Records (country); and "Little Bird" (by S. Founds), recorded by Susanna Founds on Woodrich Records (pop).
Tips: "Use a studio demo if possible. If not, be sure the lyrics are extremely clear. Be sure to include a SASE with *sufficient* return postage."

WORD MUSIC, Division of Word, Inc., Suite 1000, 5221 N.O'Connor Blvd., Irving TX 75039. (214)556-1900. Creative Director: Debbie Atkins, Word Records: Suite 200, 3319 West End Ave., Nashville TN 37203. (615)385-9673. Music publisher and record company. ASCAP. Member GMA. Publishes 200 songs/year; publishes 1-2 new songwriters/year. Teams collaborators. Pays standard royalty.
Affiliate(s): Rodeheaver (ASCAP), Dayspring (BMI), The Norman Clayton Publishing Co. (SESAC), Word Music (ASCAP), and 1st Monday (ASCAP).
How to Contact: Write or call first to get permission to submit a tape. Prefers cassette (or VHS videocassette) with 1-3 songs and lead sheet. SASE. "Please send a demonstration tape of a choir singing your anthem to Ken Barker, Print Director." Reports in 10 weeks.
Music: Mostly contemporary Christian, Southern gospel, Black gospel, inspiration. Published "Make His Praise Glorious," recorded by Sandi Patti on Word Records (inspirational) and "Watercoloured Ponies," written and recorded by Wayne Watson on Dayspring Records.
Tips: "Lead sheets, or final form—anything submitted—should be legible and understandable. The care that a writer extends in the works he submits reflects the work he'll submit if a working relationship is started. First impressions are important."

WORLD FAMOUS MUSIC CO., 1830 Spruce Ave., Highland Park IL 60035. (708)831-4162. President: Chip Altholz. Music publisher, record producer. ASCAP. Estab. 1986. Publishes 25 songs/year; 3-4 new songwriters/year. Works with composers and lyricists. Pays standard royalty of 50%.
How to Contact: Submit a demo tape—unsolicited submissions are OK. Prefers cassette with 3 songs and lyric sheet. SASE. Reports in 1 month.
Music: Mostly pop, R&B and rock. Published "Jungleman," "Automatic" and "All the Stars" (by N. Bak) recorded by Ten-28 on Pink Street Records (pop/dance).
Tips: "Have a great melody, a lyric that is visual and tells a story and a commercial arrangement."

*YORGO MUSIC, 615 Valley Rd., Up. Montclair NJ 07043. (201)746-2359. President: George Louvis. Music publisher. BMI. Estab. 1987. Publishes 5-10 songs/year; publishes 3-5 new songwriters/year. Works with composers and lyricists; teams collaborators. Pays standard royalty.
How to Contact: Submit demo tape—unsolicited submissions OK. Prefers cassette with 1-3 songs and lyric or lead sheets. "Specify if you are a writer/artist or just a writer." Does not return unsolicited material. Reports in 4-6 weeks.
Music: Mostly R&B, dance and pop; also ballads and pop metal. Published "To the Maximum" (by S. Stone, S. McGhee, G. Louvis), recorded by Steve D the Destroyer on Q-Rap Records (rap); "Love Me True" (by G. Louvis), recorded by Kimiesha Holmes on Quark Records (dance).
Tips: "We also own two production companies and have access to quite a few artists and labels. Be honest about your material; if you wouldn't buy it, don't send it. We are looking for songs and artists."

YOUNG GRAHAM MUSIC (BMI), 19 Music Square W., Nashville TN 27203. (615)255-5740. Vice President: Valerie Graham. Music publisher, record company (Bear Records) and record producer (Bear Records). BMI. Estab. 1989. Publishes 10 songs/year; publishes 4-5 new songwriters/year. Works with composers and lyricists; teams collaborators. Pays standard royalty.
How to Contact: Submit a demo tape—unsolicited submissions are OK. Prefers cassette with 3 songs and lyric sheet. SASE. Reports in 2 weeks.
Music: Mostly country and traditional. "Red Neck" (by Sanger Shafer), recorded by J. Wright; "Eyes As Big As Dallas" (by Gary McCray), recorded by Autumn Day; and "Girls Like Her" (by Wimberly-Hart), recorded by J. Wright; on Bear Records (all country).

Geographic Index
Music Publishers

The U.S. section of this handy geographic index will quickly give you the names of music publishers located in or near the music centers of Los Angeles, New York and Nashville. Of course, there are many valuable contacts to be made in other cities, but you will probably want to plan a trip to one of these established music centers at some point in your career and try to visit as many of these companies as you think appropriate. The International section lists, geographically, markets for your songs in countries other than the U.S.

Find the names of companies in this index, and then check listings within the Music Publishers section for addresses, phone numbers and submission details.

Los Angeles
Audio Music Publishers
AVC Music
Bob-A-Lew Music
Bronx Flash Music
Bug Music
Center for the Queen of Peace
Cosmotone Music
Direct Management Group
Dupuy Records/Productions/
  Publishing, Inc.
Famous Music Publishing
  Companies
First Release Music Publishing
GFI West Music Publishing
Jaelius Enterprises, Inc.
Kingsport Creek Music Pub-
  lishing
Lansdowne and Winston Music
  Publishers
Leo-Vincent Music/Omni-
  Praise Music
O'Lyric Music
Operation Perfection
Peermusic
Philippopolis Music
Pollybyrd Publications Ltd.
Pratt and McClain Music
Rhythms Productions
Schmerdley Music
Scotti Brothers Music Publish-
  ing
Shankman De Blasio Melina,
  Inc.
Soprano Music Co.
Sound Image Publishing
Tanger-Music Publishing Co.,
  Inc.
Transition Music Corp.
Treasure Trove Music
Twin Towers Publishing Co.
Udder Publishing/Golden Gelt
  Publishing
Vaam Music Group

Shane Wilder Music
Maurice Wilson's Music Co.

Nashville
Abingdon Press
Aim High Music Company
Allisongs Inc.
Angelsong Publishing
Another Ear Music
Baby Huey Music
Best Buddies, Inc.
Johnny Bond Publications
Brentwood Music, Inc.
Buried Treasure Music
Calvary Music Group
Castle Music Group
Chip 'N' Dale Music Publish-
  ers, Inc.
Clientele Music
The Cornelius Companies
Cottage Blue Music
Cumberland Music Group
Cupit Music
Denny Music Group
Door Knob Music Publishing,
  Inc.
Entertainment Services Music
  Group
First Million Music, Inc.
Fox Farm Recording
Fradale Songs
General Jones Music
GMG Music
Heavy Jamin' Music
Humanform Publishing Com-
  pany
Jaclyn Music
Gene Kennedy Enterprises,
  Inc.
The Langford Cove Music
  Group
Lion Hill Music Publishing Co.
Lodestar Music, a Division of

Gene Kennedy Enterprises,
  Inc.
Loman Craig Music/Major
  Bob/Rio Bravo Music
The Marco Music Group Inc.
The Fred Morris Music Group
Nautical Music Co.
Neon Notes
Newcreature Music
Old Empress Music/Doghouse
  Productions
Rainbarrel Music Company
Song Farm Music
Sound Achievement Group
Star Song Communications
Wil-Too/Wil-So Music
Young Graham Music

New York
A Street Music
Benyard Music Co.
Big City Music, Inc.
Blade to the Rhythm Music
Blue Umbrella Music Publish-
  ing Co./Parasol Music Pub-
  lishing Co.
BMG Music Publishing, Inc.
Broozbee Music, Inc.
Cactus Music and Gidget Pub-
  lishing
Don Casale Music, Inc.
Centerfield Productions
Chrysalis Music Group
Continental Communications
  Corp.
Cosgroove Music Inc.
D.S.M. Producers Inc.
Emzee Music
Alan Gary Music
Globeart Publishing
S.M. Gold Music
Hit & Run Music Publishing
  Inc.
In-house Publishing, Inc.

Jasper Stone Music/JSM Songs
Jaylo-Bellasar Music Co.
Latin American Music Co., Inc.
Lin's Lines
Linwood Maxwell Music
Majestic Control Music
Manapro (Management Artist
Productions)
Mega-star Music
Chuck Mymit Music Productions
Now & Then Music
PPI/Peter Pan Industries
Prescription Company
Ren Maur Music Corp.
Rockford Music Co.
Sha-la Music. Inc.
Siskatune Music Publishing Co.
Soul Street Music Publishing
Inc.
Sunsongs Music/Hollywood
East Entertainment
Vin-joy Music
Warner/Chappell Music, Inc.
Yorgo Music

International

Australia
Larrikin Music
Music City Music

Austria
MSM Musikverlag Wien
Thema-verlag
Warner/Chappell Musikverlag
Gesellschaft m.b.h.

Belgium
B. Sharp Music
BMG Ariola Belgium N.V.
Publishing
Jump Music

Canada
Alleged Iguana Music
Alternative Directions Music
Publishers
Berandol Music Ltd.
Branch Music Group
China Groove
Green Dolphin Music
Nashville Sound Music Publishing Co.
Nettwerk Productions
Sci-fi Music
Stonehand Publishing
Utter Nonsense Publishers
West Broadway Music

France
Topomic Music

Germany
Boogietunes Musikproduktion
GmbH
R.D. Clevere Musikverlag
CSB Kaminsky GmbH
Hammer Musik GmbH
Heupferd Musik Verlag GmbH
Intermedia Musik Service
GmbH
Ja/Nein Musikverlag GmbH
Ralf Krueger Musikverlag
Seychelles Music
Siebenpunkt Verlags GmbH
Siegel Music Companies
Sinus Musik Produktion, Ulli
Weigel
UBM
Valentine Musikverlag
Berthold Wengert (Musikverlag)

Holland
All Rock Music
Associated Artists Music International (AAMI)

Italy
Dingo Music
G. Ricordi & C. Spa

Malaysia
Pustaka Muzik EMI (Malysia)
SDN. BHD.

Mexico
Galaxia Musical S.A. De C.V.

New Zealand
Pegasus Music

South Africa
Gallo Music Publishers

Sweden
Synchro Sound Music AB

Switzerland
Nadine Music
OBH Musikverlag Otto B. Hartmann

United Kingdom
Bearsongs
Catherine Courage Music Ltd.
Creole Music Ltd.
Don't Call Me (D.C.M.) Music
Ever-Open-Eye Music
Fairwood Music Ltd.
F&J Music
First Time Music (Publishing)
U.K. Ltd.
Guerilla Music
Le Matt Music, Ltd.
Miramare Music UK Ltd.
R.J. Music
R.T.L. Music, Lee Music, Pogo
Records
Red Bus Music International,
Ltd.
Sawmills Music
Sea Dream Music Tabitha Music, Ltd.

Wales
Demi Monde Records & Publishing Ltd.

Music Publishers/'92-'93 Changes

The following markets appeared in the 1992 edition of *Songwriter's Market* but are absent from the 1993 edition. Most of these companies failed to respond to our request for an update of their listing for a variety of reasons. For example, they may have gone out of business, or they may have requested deletion from the 1993 edition because they are backlogged with material. If we know the specific reason, it appears within parentheses.

A.M. Percussion Publications
(requested deletion)
Abiding Love Music Publishing
Aim High Music Company

(ASCAP)
ALA/Bianca SRL
Ambra Music
ARS Nova Publishing

Attid Music Co.
Author's Agency Ltd.
Avilo Music
Baby Raquel Music

Bannerleague, Ltd. T/A Bolts Music
K. Bee Productions Inc/Buzz Records
Beverly Hills Music Publishing
Big Wedge Music
Blenheim Music
Boot Songs
Bucks Music Ltd.
Glen Campbell Music Group (requested deletion)
Capaquarius Publishing and Artist Mgt. Inc.
Century City Music Publishing
Chasann Music (unable to contact)
Chip 'N' Dale Music Publishers
Citko-Slott Publishing Co.
Clotille Publishing
Coppelia
Country Classics Music Publishing Co. (requested deletion)
Country Showcase (unable to contact)
CPA Records & Publishing Co. (out of business)
Crown Music Group (unable to contact)
Crusoe Music Limited
Current Musical Enterprises Inc.
Dark Heart Music (unable to contact)
Jason Dee Music (unable to contact)
Demerie Music (unable to contact)
Diamond State Publishing Co., Inc. (unable to contact)
Directions
E. Minor Music (unable to contact)
Earth and Sky Music Publishing Inc. (requested deletion)
Ediciones Musicales Phonogram S.A.
EKG Music (unable to contact)
Element Movie and Music
Eursong
FAS-ENT Music
Flanary Publishing Co.
Bob Gaffney Music
Larry Gene Music (unable to contact)
Golden Apple Productions (not accepting submissions)
Graduate Music Ltd.
Great Pyramid Music (requested deletion)
Chris Gulian Music (not accepting submissions)
Happy Note Music (unable to contact)
Johann Hartel Musikverlag
Holyrood Productions
Hopsack and Silk Productions
House of Reeds Publishing Co. (no longer in business)
Imaginary Music (requested deletion)
Insurance Music Publishing (unable to contact)
Inter-American Musical Editions (requested deletion)
Interplanetary Music
ISBA Music Publishing Inc.
Jambox Music (unable to contact)
Jammy Music Publishers
Keep Calm Music Limited
King Creole Inc.
Kitty Group Inc.
Lita Music
Lonny Tunes (unable to contact)
Loud & Proud Music
Loux Music Publishing Co.
Loveforce International
Lucky's Kum-Ba-Ya Publishing Co. (not accepting submissions)
Magic Message Music (not accepting submissions)
Marielle Music Publishing Corp. (unable to contact)
Andy Marvel Music (not accepting submissions)
Massmedia
Master Audio Inc./Master Sound, Inc./Lyresong, Inc.
Mia Mind Music
Micah Music
Mighty Soul-Sonic Records (unable to contact)
Millhouse Music
Montina Music (unable to contact)
Mother Bertha Music Publishing Co., Inc.
Mr. Mort Music (unable to contact)
Mystikos Music
National Talent
Nervous Publishing
Ocean Walk Music (unable to contact)
Oh My Gosh Music
Palmetto Productions (requested deletion)
Pamsco International Inc.
Pape Publishing
Prestation Music
Primal Visions Music
Primavera Sound Productions
Quark, Inc.
The Rainbow Collection Inc. (requested deletion)
Ric Rac Music (unable to contact)
Rosemark Publishing
Rough Trade Music Ltd.
Rowilco
Rushwin Publishing
S&R Music Publishing Co.
S.M.C.L. Productions, Inc.
Sabre Music
Tracy Sands Music
Scramrock Music Co. (out of business)
Shaolin Music (unable to contact)
Sho-Doe Music (unable to contact)
Singing Roadie Music
Single Phase Music
Sisipa
Sneak Tip Music
Societe D'Editions Musicales Et Artistiques "Esperance"
Songfinder Music
Sound Advisors Ltd.
Sound Ceremony Records
Sphemusations
SRSF Recordings/Entertainments Enterprises Publishing
Terry Stafford Music
Starquest Music (unable to contact)
Subar Music Publishing Co. Ltd.
Sulzer Music (unable to contact)
Sunset Productions
TAS Enterprises (unable to contact)
Ten of Diamonds Music Publishing (BMI)
Third Millenium Music
Tone Records
21st Century Spirituals (unable to contact)
Two & Two Publishing (unable to contact)
Two Fold Music (unable to contact)
Tommy Valando Publishing Group
Volition Music
Walk on Water Music (requested deletion)
Wilcox Music Organization
Wooden Iron Music (requested deletion)
World Artist
WW Music

Music Print Publishers

The sheet music publisher's function is much more specific than that of the music publisher. Music publishers try to exploit a song in many different ways: on records, videos, movies and radio/TV commercials, to name a few. But, as the name implies, sheet music publishers deal in only one publishing medium: print.

Although the role of the music print publisher has virtually stayed the same over the years, demand for sheet music has declined substantially. Today there are only a few major sheet music publishers in operation, along with many minor ones.

Most songs and compositions fall into one of two general categories: popular or educational music. Popular songs are pop, rock, adult contemporary, country and other hits heard on the radio. They are printed as sheet music (for single songs) and folios (collections of songs). Educational material includes pieces for chorus, band, orchestra, instrumental solos and instructional books. In addition to publishing original compositions, print publishers will sometimes print arrangements of popular songs.

Most major publishers of pop music won't print sheet music for a song until a popular recording of the song has become a hit single, or at least is on the *Billboard* Hot 100 chart. Most of the companies listed here indicate the lowest chart position of a song they've published, to give you a better idea of the market.

Chart action is obviously not a factor for original educational material. What the print publishers look for is quality work that fits into their publishing program and is appropriate for the people who use their music, such as school and church choirs, school bands or orchestras.

When dealing with sheet music publishers, it is generally unacceptable to send out simultaneous submissions; that is, sending identical material to different publishers at the same time. Since most of the submissions they receive involve written music, whether single lead sheets or entire orchestrations, the time they invest in evaluating each submission is considerable—much greater than the few minutes it takes to listen to a tape. It would be discourteous and unprofessional to ask a music print publisher to invest a lot of time in evaluating your work and then possibly pull the deal out from under him before he has given you an answer.

Writers' royalties range from 10-15% of the retail selling price of music in print. For educational material that would be a percentage of the price of the whole set (score and parts). For a book of songs (called a folio), the 10-15% royalty would be pro-rated by the number of songs by that writer in the book. Royalties for sheet music are paid on a flat rate per sheet, which is usually about one-fifth of the retail price. If a music publisher licenses print publishing to a music print publisher, print royalties are usually split evenly between the music publisher and songwriter, but it may vary. You should read any publishing contract carefully to see how print deals fit in, and consult your attorney if you have any questions.

A & C BLACK (PUBLISHERS) LTD., 35 Bedford Row, London WC1R 4JH **England**. Phone: (071)242-0946. Commissioning Editor: Sheena Roberts. Publishes educational material. Prints 6 items/year. Pays a fee per 1,000 copies printed. Query with complete score and tape of piece. Prefers cassette. SASE. Reports in 4-8 weeks.
How to Contact: Query or write first and obtain permission to submit.
Music: Methods books and children's songs/musicals. Published "Green Umbrella," by Jill Bond (assembly stories, songs and poems); "Abracadabra Clarinet," (graded pieces for clarinet); and "Okki-Tokki-Unga," (children's song compilation).

Tips: "We keep a list of good children's songwriters whom we commission to write songs that fit the needs of our compilations. A compilation may consist of around 30-50% commissioned songs. Look at our children's catalogue (available on request) to see what sort of books we publish."

BOSTON MUSIC CO., 172 Tremont St., Boston MA 02111. (617)426-5100. Contact: Editorial Department. Prints 100 pieces/year, both individual pieces and music books. Pays standard royalty.
How to Contact: Submit "legible manuscript." Do not send tapes. SASE. Reports in 5-9 months.
Music: Choral pieces, educational material, instrumental solo pieces, methods books and "piano instructional materials that piano teachers would be interested in."
Tips: "We are *not* interested in today's "pop" music or in vocal music. We are essentially an educational publishing house specializing in keyboard teaching material."

BOURNE COMPANY, 5 W. 37th St., New York NY 10018. (212)391-4300. Contact: Editorial Department. Estab. 1917. Publishes education material and popular music.
Affiliates: ABC Music, Ben Bloom, Better Half, Bogat, Burke & Van Heusen, Goldmine, Harborn, Lady Mac, Murbo Music.
How to Contact: Submit unsolicited demo tape, lead sheet and complete score. SASE. Reports in 3 months.
Music: Band pieces, choral pieces and handbell pieces. Published "You Can Count on Me" (by S. Cahn/N. Monath) (2 part choral) and "Unforgettable" (by Gordon) recorded by Natalie Cole on Electra Records (vocal duet).

DAVIKE MUSIC CO., P.O. Box 8842, Los Angeles CA 90008. (310)318-5289. Owner: Isaiah Jones, Jr. Estab. 1965. Prints 4 songs/year, mostly individual songs. Publishes 3 new songwriters/year. Pays 50% royalty. Works with composers and lyricists; teams collaborators.
How to Contact: Submit demo tape—unsolicited submsisions are OK. Prefers cassette and lead and lyric sheets or complete score. SASE. Reports in 2 months.
Music: Mostly gospel, pop, R&B and inspirational; also folk and country. Published "The Miracle God" by I. Jones and G. Cowart (contemporary gospel) and "God Never Fails" (by Isaiah Jones and J. Hailey), recorded by Inez Andrews on Word Records (gospel).

EMANDELL TUNES, 10220 Glade Ave., Chatsworth CA 91311. (818)341-2264. SESAC affiliate. Administrator: Leroy C. Lovett Jr. Prints 15-20 songs/year, both individual songs and folios. Lowest chart position held by song published in sheet form is 36. Pays statutory royalty or 15¢/song to songwriter for each sheet sold or parts thereof for folios.
Affiliates: Birthright Music (ASCAP), Northworth Songs (SESAC), Ben-Lee Music (BMI) and Adarom Music (ASCAP).
How to Contact: Write and obtain permission to submit. Prefers cassette (or videocassette showing performance—will return) and lyric and lead sheets. SASE. Reports in 4-6 weeks.
Music: Inspirational, contemporary and traditional gospel, and chorals. Published "The Center of Hope" (by Al Hartidge), recorded by Voices of Rhema; "Re-new Me" (by Eddie Howard), recorded by Mattie Moss Clark; "No Greater Love" (by Robert Montgomery), recorded by The Montgomerys, all on WFL Records.

*GENEVOX MUSIC GROUP, 127 9th Ave. N., Nashville TN 37234. (615)251-3770. SESAC, ASCAP and BMI affiliate. Estab. 1986. Music Production Manager: Mark Blankenship. Prints 75-100 songs/year; publishes 10 new songwriters/year. Pays 10% royalty.
How to Contact: Submit demo tape and choral arrangement, lead sheet or complete score. Unsolicited submissions are OK. Prefers cassette with 1-5 songs. SASE. Reports in 2 months.
Music: Choral, orchestral, instrumental solo and instrumental ensemble pieces. "We publish all forms of sacred music including solo/choral for all ages, and instrumental for handbell, organ, piano and orchestra." Published "Little People" (by Mark Lanier), recorded by Jake Hess (southern gospel); "Celebrate Today," by Dennis and Nan Allen (children's music); and "Arise, Your Light Has Come," by David Danner (traditional anthem).
Tips: "Most of what we publish is designed for use by church choirs and instrumentalists. Middle-of-the-road, traditional anthems or hymn arrangements in an SATB/keyboard choral format stand the best chance for serious consideration."

 The asterisk before a listing indicates that the listing is new in this edition. New markets are often the most receptive to unsolicited submissions.

HAMMER MUSIK GMBH, Christophstr. 38, 7000 Stuttgart 1, **West Germany**. Phone: (0711)648-7620-7. FAX: (0711)648-7625. Contact: Ingo Kleinhammer. Prints mostly individual songs. Interested in receiving band pieces, choral pieces and orchestral pieces. Pays 10% royalty/song to songwriter for each sheet sold. Publishes 100 original songs/year.
How to Contact: Prefers cassette. SAE and IRC. Reports in 2 weeks.
Music: Mostly dance, disco and pop; also rock and jazz. Published "Hit You" (by Volker Barber), "Stop The World" (by Jerome Des Arts and Deborah Sasson), and "I'll Be Forever Your Man" (by Jerome Des Arts and Maria Monrose), all recorded by Oh Well, all dance music.

*HINSHAW MUSIC, INC., Box 470, Chapel Hill NC 27514-0470. (919)933-1691. ASCAP affiliate. Editors: Don Hinshaw, Richard Thorne. Estab. 1975. Prints 100 pieces/year, both individual pieces and music books. Publishes educational material. Pays 10% royalty.
Affiliates: Hindon Publications (BMI) and Chapel Hill Music (SESAC).
How to Contact: "Send the complete score. Lyric sheets and/or tapes alone are not acceptable. We do not review lyrics alone. Cassette tapes may be sent in addition to the written ms. Send clear, legible photocopies, *not* the original. Submit only 2 or 3 mss at a time that are representative of your work. An arrangement of a copyrighted work will not be considered unless copy of written permission from copyright owner(s) is attached. Accepts unsolicited submissions. Once an ms has been submitted, do not telephone or write for a 'progress report.' Be patient." Returns unsolicited material. Reports in 3 months.
Music: Choral pieces and piano, organ and instrumental music. Published "Music to Hear" (by G. Shearing); and *Magnificat* (by J. Rutter), recorded by Collegium.
Tips: "Submit your ms to only one publisher at a time. It requires considerable time and expense for us to thoroughly review a work, so we want the assurance that if accepted, the ms is available for publication. We are unable to 'critique' rejected works. A pamphlet, 'Submitting Music for Publication' is available with SASE."

IVORY PALACES MUSIC, 3141 Spottswood Ave., Memphis TN 38111. (901)323-3509. Estab. 1978. President: Jack Abell. Publishes educational material. Prints 5 songs/year, mostly book/tape combinations. Pays 10% retail price or 50% license income.
How to Contact: Write first and obtain permission to submit. Prefers cassette and lyric sheet. Does not return material. Reports in 6-8 months.
Music: Orchestral pieces, instrumental solo pieces, instrumental ensemble pieces, methods books and religious songs. Published "Sonatina Concertata" (by Joe McSpadden), recorded by Linda Jackson and Strings by Archive (classical); "Chamber Music Primer" (by Taylor), recorded by Abell/Jackson/Long (classical); and "Sonatina Concertata 2" (by McSpadden), recorded by Jackson (classical).
Tips: "There should be a demand for the music to be published through established performances."

JUMP MUSIC, Langemunt 71, 9420 Aaigem, **Belgium**. Phone: (053)62-73-77. Estab. 1976. General Manager: Eddy Van Mouffaert. Publishes educational material and popular music. Prints 150 songs/year, mostly individual songs. Pays 5% royalty.
How to Contact: Prefers cassette and lead sheet or complete score. Does not return unsolicited material. Reports in 2 weeks.
Music: Pop, ballads, band pieces and instrumentals. Published "In Jouw Armen," written and recorded by Eddy Govert (ballad); "Niet Met Jij" (by Henry Spider), recorded by Samantha (Flemish); and "Do the Twist" (by Eddy Govert), recorded by Rudy Silvester (Flemish popular).

LANTANA MUSIC, #308, 9430 Live Oak Place, Ft. Lauderdale FL 33324. (305)472-7757. President: Jack P. Bluestein. Pays standard royalty.
How to Contact: Submit demo tape—unsolicited submissions are OK. Prefers cassette or 7½ ips reel-to-reel. SASE. Reports in 1-2 months.
Music: Pop, country, musical comedy, gospel and instrumentals. Published "Buckshot Romance" and "Living It Up" (by E. Miller), recorded by Mark Campbell on Quadrant Records (country); and "Going Down With You" (by F. Mayeski/J. Wagner), recorded by Sherry Victoria Vencik on Quadrant Records (contemporary rock).

*LILLENAS PUBLISHING CO., P.O. Box 419527, Kansas City MO 64141. (816)931-1900. FAX: (816)753-4071. Contact: Music Editor. Music print publisher. ASCAP, BMI, SESAC. Estab. 1930. Publishes 30-40 songs/year; publishes 3-5 new songwriters/year. Works with composers and lyricists; teams collaborators. Pays standard royalty.

Affiliates: Pilot Point Music (ASCAP), PsalmSinger Music (BMI) and Lillenas Publishing Co. (SESAC).
How to Contact: Submit demo tape and/or sheet music—unsolicited submissions are OK. Prefers cassette with 1-3 songs and lead sheet. Does not return unsolicited submissions. Reports in 2-3 months.
Music: Mostly contemporary Christian, traditional gospel and sacred anthems; also patriotic and sacred instrumental. Published "We Shall All Be Changed" (by Tom Fettke); "He is the Amen" (by David Ritter); and "It's Alright Now" (by Mosie Lister) (all choral).
Tips: "We're looking for music that fits the needs of the evangelical church market. Choral music is our forte, but artist-oriented songs are acceptable."

HAROLD LUICK & ASSOCIATES, Box B, Carlisle IA 50047. (515)989-3748 and 989-3676. BMI affiliate. President: Harold Luick. Prints 4-5 songs/year, mostly individual songs. Lowest chart position held by a song published in sheet form is 98. Pays 4% royalty.
How to Contact: Write and obtain permission to submit or submit through publisher or attorney. Prefers cassette or reel-to-reel and lyric sheet. SASE. Reports in 3 weeks.
Music: Mostly traditional country; also novelty songs. Published "Mrs. Used To Be," written and recorded by Joe Harris on River City Records (country).
Tips: "Send us song material that is conducive to type of market today. Good commercial songs."

PHOEBUS APOLLO MUSIC PUBLISHERS, 1126 Huston Dr., Pittsburgh PA 15122-3104. (412)469-1713. FAX: (412)469-3579. Member MPA. Estab. 1989. President: Keith V.A. Bajura. Prints 30-50 works/year. Pays 10% royalty.
Affiliate(s): KVAB Music Publishers (BMI).
How to Contact: Unsolicited submissions are OK. Submit a maximum of 2-3 unsolicited clear and legible mss. Cassette tapes may be sent in addition to the written scores. Lyrics and/or tapes alone are not acceptable. Enclose SASE for the return of your works. Unsolicited works without return postage cannot be returned. Reports sent in 2-4 months.
Music: Sacred and secular choral music. Serious and educational works. The majority of our music is sacred church music. "We do not publish pop, country, R&B or rap music. Solo piano, piano/vocal and other small ensemble works are occasionally considered." Published "The Serenity Prayer" (by Joseph Roff) (religious); "In Lollypop Land" (by Daniel Orinch) (children's); and "Ah, Dearest Jesus" (by David C. Huff) (religious).
Tips: "Submit things that you are proud of. Present them in a neat and professional looking manner."

THEODORE PRESSER CO., Presser Place, Bryn Mawr PA 19010. (215)525-3636. ASCAP, BMI and SESAC affiliate. Contact: Editorial Committee. Member MPA. Publishes 90 works/year. Works with composers. Pays varying royalty.
Affiliate(s): Merion Music (BMI); Elkan Vogel, Inc. (ASCAP); and Mercury Music Corp. (SESAC).
How to Contact: Unsolicited submissions are OK. Prefers cassette with 1-2 works and score. "Include return label and postage." Reports in 2 weeks.
Music: Serious, educational and choral music. "We primarily publish serious music be emerging and established composers, and vocal/choral music which is likely to be accepted in the church and educational markets, as well as gospel chorals of high musical quality. We are *not* primarily a publisher of song sheets or pop songs."

R.T.F.M., % Stewart House, Hillbottom Rd., Highwycombe, Buckinghamshire HP124HJ **United Kingdom.** Phone: (0630)647374. FAX: (0630)647612. A&R: Xavier Lee. Publishes educational material and popular music. Prints 40 songs/year, mostly individual songs. Lowest chart position held by a song published in sheet form is 140. Royalty varies.
Affiliate(s): Lee Music Ltd., Pogo Records Ltd. and R.T.L. Music.
How to Contact: Submit demo tape—unsolicited submissions are OK. Prefers cassette or 7½ or 15 ips reel-to-reel and lyric and lead sheets or complete score. SAE and IRC. Reports in 6 weeks.
Music: All types: band, orchestral, instrumental solo and instrumental ensemble pieces; also radio, TV and film music (specializes in jingles/background music). Published "Knife Edge" (rock); "Missing You" (ballad) both written and recorded by Daniel Boone; and "Motorbiking (by M.J. Lawson), recorded by Emmit Till (rock) all on Swoop Records.

E.C. SCHIRMER ● BOSTON, 138 Ipswich St., Boston MA 02215. (617)236-1935. President: Robert Schuneman. Prints 200 pieces/year, mostly individual pieces and music books. Pays 10% royalty on sales and 50% on performance/license.

Affiliates: Galaxy Music Corporation (ASCAP), E.C. Schirmer Music Co. Inc. (ASCAP), Ione Press, Inc. (BMI), Highgate Press (BMI).
How to Contact: Query with complete score and tape of piece. Prefers cassette. "Submit a clean, readable score." SASE. Reports in 6-8 months.
Music: Choral pieces, orchestral pieces, instrumental solo pieces, instrumental ensemble pieces, methods books, books on music, keyboard pieces.

SEA DREAM MUSIC, 236 Sebert Rd., London E7 0NP **England**. Phone: (081)534-8500. Senior Partner: Simon Law. Publishes educational material and popular music. Estab. 1976. Prints 20 songs/year, mostly individual songs. Has printed sheet music for uncharted songs. Pays 10% royalty per sheet sold.
How to Contact: Submit demo tape—unsolicited submissions OK. Prefers cassette and lyric sheet. SAE and IRC. Reports in 6 weeks.
Music: Band and choral pieces. Mostly funk/rock, rock, blues and gospel. Published "Light Factory" (by Morgan/Paine/Radford), recorded by Fresh Claim on Plankton Records (rock); "Sing Praise" and "Send Me the Helper" (by D. Llewellyn) recorded by Derek Llewellyn on ICC Records (children's pop).

WILLIAM GRANT STILL MUSIC, Suite 422, 22 S. San Francisco St., Flagstaff AZ 86001-5737. (602)526-9355. ASCAP affiliate. Estab. 1983. Manager: Judith Anne Still. Publishes educational material and popular music. Prints 2-3 arrangements/year; 2-3 new arrangers/year. Works with arrangers only. Pays 10% royalty for arrangements sold. "We publish arrangements of works by William Grant Still. This year we are especially interested in developing a catalog of guitar arrangements, though other sorts of arrangements may be considered."
How to Contact: Query. Does not return unsolicited material. Reports in 1 month.
Music: Mostly instrumental solo pieces. Published "Mother and Child" by Timothy Holley; "Memphis Man" by Bert Coleman, for organ (classical); and "Coquette," by Anthony Griggs (classical).
Tips: "We suggest that the prospective arranger familiarize himself with the music of William Grant Still, prepare a sample arrangement and submit it after having been given permission to do so."

3 SEAS MUSIC/NORTHVALE MUSIC, 450 Livingston St., Norwood NJ 07648. (201)767-5551. Vice President: Gene Schwartz. Prints mostly individual songs. Lowest chart position held by a song published in sheet form is 20. Pays 14¢/song to songwriter for each sheet sold.
How to Contact: Unsolicited submissions are OK. Prefers cassette and lyric sheet or complete score. SASE. Reports in 1 month.
Music: Rock and Top 40. Published "Stay With Me" (by James Denton) and "Take Me" (by Peter Mechtinal) recorded by Maurice Williams; "Someday Again," written and recorded by Bill Senkel, all on Laurie Records (pop).
Tips: "Write something fresh and different."

TRANSCONTINENTAL MUSIC PUBLICATIONS, 838 Fifth Ave., New York NY 10021. (212)249-0100. Senior Editor: Dr. Judith B. Tischler. Music publisher. ASCAP. Estab. 1941/1977. Publishes 2 new songwriters/year. Works with composers. Pays 10% royalty. "We publish serious solo and choral music. The standard royalty is 10% except for rentals—there is no cost to the songwriter."
How to Contact: Call first and obtain permission to submit a tape. Prefers cassette. "We usually do not accept lead sheets. Most all of our music is accompanied. Full and complete arrangements should accompany the melody." SASE. Reports in 10-12 months.
Music: Mostly Jewish vocal and Jewish choral. Published "Numi Numi" by Stern (classical); "Biti" (by Isaacson) (Bat Mitzvah Solo) and "Shalom Aleidliean" (by Kaluraweff), recorded by Milnes on Ross Records (choral).
Tips: "Submit clean manuscript or computer typographer with accompaniment. Suitable material of sacred or secular Jewish relevance."

***VIVACE PRESS**, NW 310 Wawawai Rd., Pullman WA 99163. (509)334-4660. FAX: (509)334-3551. Contact: Jonathan Yordy. Publishes mostly classical pieces. Estab. 1990. Publishes 25 pieces of music/year; publishes several new composers/year. Works with composers. Pays 10% royalty for sheet music sales.
How to Contact: Submit demo tape and sheet music—unsolicited submissions OK. Prefers cassette. SASE. Reports in 1 month.
Music: Mostly specialty historical classical, contemporary classical keyboard and sacred choral; also youth musicals. Published *18th Century Women Composers*, by Mary Hester Park; *Quantum Quirks of a Quick Quaint Quark*, by Marga Richter; and *Sonatine d'Amour*, by Arnold Rosner.
Tips: "Know our catalog to determine our intended market. If you haven't heard any compositions we carry, don't submit."

THE WILLIS MUSIC COMPANY, 7380 Industrial Rd., Florence KY 41042. (606)283-2050. SESAC affiliate. Estab. 1899. Editor: David B. Engle. Publishes educational material. Prints 100 publications/year; "no charted songs in our catalog." Pays 5-10% of retail price or outright purchase.
How to Contact: Prefers fully notated score. SASE. Reports in 3 months.
Music: Mostly early level piano teaching material; also instrumental solo pieces, methods books and "supplementary materials-educational material only."

Music Print Publishers/'92-'93 Changes

The following markets appeared in the 1992 edition of *Songwriter's Market* but are absent from the 1993 edition. These companies failed to respond to our request for an update of their listing or requested deletion.

The Lorenz Corporation
Plymouth Music Co., Inc.
    (requested deletion)

Record Companies

Record companies are responsible for recording and releasing records, cassettes and CDs – the mechanical products of the music industry. They sign artists to recording contracts, decide what songs those artists will record, and finally determine which songs to release. They are also responsible for providing recording facilities, securing producers and musicians, and overseeing the manufacture, distribution and promotion of new releases.

Costs for a record company, especially the huge conglomerates, are substantially larger than those of other segments of the music industry. The music publisher, for instance, considers only items such as salaries and the costs of making quality demos. Record companies, at great financial risk, pay for all those services discussed above. It's estimated that 8% of acts on the major labels are paying for the losses incurred by the remaining 92%.

This profit/loss ratio and the continuing economic crunch have caused changes in the record industry. The major labels are signing fewer new acts and are dropping unprofitable ones. This means a shrinking market among the majors for new songs for their acts. Also, the continuing fear of copyright infringement suits has closed avenues to getting new material heard by the majors. They don't listen to unsolicited submissions . . . period. Only songs recommended by attorneys, managers and producers major label employees trust and respect are being heard by A&R people, who have much of the input on what songs should be performed and recorded by a particular act.

So how do you get these valuable recommendations? It's logical that a good way to gain notice from industry people is by networking. Songwriters must take into consideration that talent alone does not guarantee success in the music industry. You must be recognized through contacts (networking). Networking is the process of building an interconnecting web of acquaintances within the music business. The more industry people you meet, the broader your contact base becomes, and your chances of meeting someone who has the clout to get your demo heard increase. If you want to get ahead, and you want to get your music on the desk of an important A&R representative, networking is imperative.

There are also networking opportunities at regional and national music conferences and workshops. If you can afford to attend one or two of these events each year, you will benefit from an immediate increase in the number and quality of your music industry contacts.

Because of the continuing change and ever-smaller market the majors represent, the independent labels take on a new significance for your work. Since they aren't necessarily located in or near the music hubs, the indies can help you develop a very important local base of support for your music. Each independent label usually releases a specific type of music, which also helps you target those companies your submissions should be sent to. And because the number of personnel working for an indie is smaller, chances are good that not only will your submission be listened to, it may be listened to by upper management personnel of the company, who make or approve most recording contracts and influence what songs will be recorded.

The indies may be seen by many to be a stepping stone to a major recording contract. And it's true that the majors view the independents as "workshops"; they watch the indies closely for new styles in music and up and coming bands. But many of the independents are now looking for acts that want to pursue long-term relationships with them. The independents continue to define a new role for themselves as they pick up the slack caused by the cutbacks of the majors.

Many of the following listings are independent labels. They are the most receptive to new material. Just because the companies are small doesn't mean you should forget professionalism. When submitting material to a record company, be very specific about what you are submitting and what your goals are. If you are strictly a songwriter and the label carries a band who you believe would properly present your song, state that in your cover letter. If you are an artist looking for a contract, make sure you showcase your strong points as a performer in the demo package. Whatever your goals are, follow submission guidelines closely, be as neat as possible and include a top-notch demo. If you need more information concerning a company's requirements, write or call for more details.

At the end of this section, you will find a Geographic Index listing alphabetically the record companies in the major music centers — New York, Los Angeles and Nashville — in order to help you plan a trip in the future to one or more of these cities. There is also an alphabetical list of international listings appearing in this section.

ABACUS, Box 111, Newburg WI 53060. (414)675-2839. Producer: Bob Wiegert. Record company, record producer and music publisher (RobJen Music). Works with musicians/artists on contract and musicians on salary for in-house studio work. Pays negotiable royalty to artists on contract; statutory rate to publishers for each record sold.
How to Contact: Write first about your interest. Submit cassette only with 1-3 songs and lyric sheet. Does not return unsolicited material. Reports in 1 month.
Music: New Age, soundtrack productions and fine arts.
Tips: "We are always on the lookout for a talented composer, but write first. Unsolicited material will not be sent back."

ADOBE RECORDS, Dept. SM, Box W, Shallowater TX 79363. (806)873-3537. President: Tom Woodruff. Record company. Estab. 1989. Releases 5 LPs/year. Works with musicians/artists, storytellers and poets on contract. Pays statutory rate.
How to Contact: Write (attn: Sue Swinson) or call first and obtain permission to submit. Prefers cassette or VHS videocassette with 3 songs and lyric or lead sheet. Does not return unsolicited material. Reports in 3 months.
Music: Mostly interested in western, bluegrass and cowboy. Released *Texas When Texas Was Free*, written and recorded by A. Wilkinson; and *Moon Light on the Colorado* (by A. Wilkinson), recorded by J. Stephenson; both on Adobe Records (LPs).

*AIR CENTRAL RECORDINGS, 3700 S. Hawthorne, Sioux Falls SD 57105. Owners: William Prines III or Vesta Wells-Prines. Labels include Omnigram Records. Record company. Estab. 1983. Releases 2 singles, 4-6 LPs and 2-3 CDs/year. Works with musicians/artists on contract. Pays statutory rate to publisher per song on record.
How to Contact: Write to obtain permission to submit. Prefers cassette with 3 songs. SASE. Reports in 3 months.
Music: Mostly country, pop and gospel; also rock and R&B. Released "I Am A Star" written and recorded by Carol Kiefer on Air Central Records (pop single); "Where Did All My Money Go" written and recorded by Johnny Goings on Omnigram Records (pop single); and "Love Made Manifest" written and recorded by Tom Bierer on Air Central Records (gospel LP).

AIRWAVE PRODUCTION GROUP, INC., 1916 28th Ave. South, Birmingham AL 35209. (205)870-3239. President: Michael Panepento. Labels include T.B.B. Records. Record company. Estab. 1985. Releases 4 LPs, 2 EPs and 1 CD/year. Works with musicians/artists on contract and hires musicians for in-house studio work; artist development. Pays 50% royalty to artists on contract; varying rate to publishers per song on record.

The asterisk before a listing indicates that the listing is new in this edition. New markets are often the most receptive to unsolicited submissions.

How to Contact: Submit demo tape—unsolicited submissions are OK. Prefers cassette with 3 songs and lyric sheets. SASE. Reports in 10 weeks.
Music: Mostly pop/top 40, rock and R&B; also country and jazz. Released *Pass the Buck*, written and recorded by F. Fatts on Pandem Records (jazz LP), *The RAW Sessions*, by the Vallejo Bros. on Pandem Records (rock); "This Time" (by J. Bradley), recorded by Dee Bradley on Smoke Stack Records (R&B 45); "Money Talks" (by A.J. Vallejo), recorded by Vallejo Brothers on Pandem Records (rock); "Elvis' Grave" (by Phillips/Panepento) (soundtrack); and "I Wish" (by S. Morris), recorded by The Diptones on Pandem Records (vocal/AC).
Tips: "Make it a complete, neat package!"

AKO RECORDS, 20531 Plummer, Chatsworth CA 91311. (818)998-0443. President: A.E. Sullivan. Labels include Dorn Records and Aztec Records. Record company, music publisher (Amiron Music) and record producer (AKO Productions). Estab. 1980. Releases 2 singles/year. Works with musicians/artists and songwriters on contract. Pays negotiable royalty to artists on contract. Pays statutory rate.
How to Contact: Write first and obtain permission to submit. Prefers cassette (or Beta or VHS videocassette) and lyric sheet. SASE. Reports in 2 months.
Music: Top 40/pop, rock and pop/country. Released *Touch of Fire*, by Touch of Fire; *Gang Back*, by F. Cruz; "Sana Christian," by Sana Christian, and "Helpless" (by R. Black), recorded by Les Staunton, all on AKO Records. Other artists include Rozzi and Cemas.

AKRANA COUNTRY, 120 Mountain View Dr. 5, College Place WA 99324. (509)529-4649. Founder/CEO: Loren Fenton. Labels include Akrana Visions. Record company and music publisher (Akrana Music/ASCAP). Estab. 1990. Releases 1-2 singles and 1 LP/year. Works with musicians/artists and songwriters on contract. Pays statutory rate.
How to Contact: Submit demo tape by mail. Unsolicited submissions are OK. Prefers cassette or VHS videocassette with 1-4 songs and lyric sheet. SASE. Reports in 2-3 weeks.
Music: Mostly contemporary Christian country, gospel and children's music. Released "Throw Wide the Windows," by Benjamin Fenton/Kelly Santee (single); and *Forever Free!*, (LP); both recorded by Loren Fenton on Akrana Music Records.
Tips: "We are looking for contemporary Christian country. Listen for recent songs by Paul Overstreet, Garth Brooks, etc. We want music that can be played on today's country radio stations. Songs must have lyrics with Christian values but not be preachy."

ALCAZAR RECORDS, Box 429, Waterbury VT 05676. (802)244-7845. Manager: Ann Tangney. Labels include Alcazar, Cole Harbor, Fogarty's Cove, Fretless, Alacazam!, Record Rak Records and TOAD. Estab. 1977. Releases 12 LPs and 12 CDs/year. Works with musicians/artists on record contract, songwriters on royalty contract and musicians on salary for in-house studio work. Pays 5-15% royalty to artists on contract. Pays statutory rate to publishers per song on records.
How to Contact: Write or call first and obtain permission to submit. Prefers cassette or VHS videocassette if available with 3 songs and lyric sheet. Does not return unsolicited materials. Reports in 4 weeks.
Music: Children's, folk and blues: also pop/soft rock and avant-garde. Released *Where . . . Fast Lane*, written and recorded by Fred Koller on Alcazar Records (folk LP); Amy and Leslie, written and recorded by *Amy and Leslie* on Alcazar Records (folk LP); and *Peter and the Wolf*, written and recorded by Dave Van Ronk on Alcazam! Records (children's LP). Other artists include Doc Watson, Odetta, George Gritzbach, Priscilla Herdman and Rory Block.
Tips: "Study our releases; are you/your songs appropriate for us? If someone knows everything we've put out and insists they're right for the label, that person/artist will get a serious listen."

ALEAR RECORDS, % McCoy, Route 2, Box 114, Berkeley Springs WV 25411. (304)258-2175. Labels include Master Records, Winchester Records and Real McCoy Records. Record company, music publisher (Jim McCoy Music, Clear Music, New Edition Music/BMI), record producer and recording studio. Releases 20 singles and 10 LPs/year. Works with artists and songwriters on contract; musicians on salary. Pays 2% minimum royalty to artists; statutory rate to publishers for each record sold.
How to Contact: Submit demo tape—unsolicited submissions are OK. Prefers 7½ ips reel-to-reel or cassette with 5-10 songs and lead sheet. SASE. Reports in 1 month.
Music: Bluegrass, church/religious, country, folk, gospel, progressive and rock. Released "Memories of Marty" (by Red Steed); "Dyin' Pain (by J.B. Miller) on Hilton Records and "Let Her" (by R. Lee Gray) on Winchester Records (all country). Also released *Mr. Bluegrass Here's to You*, by Carroll County Ramblers (bluegrass LP). Other artists include Alvin Kesner, Jubilee Travelers, Jim McCoy, and Middleburg Harmonizers.

*ALISO CREEK PRODUCTIONS INCORPORATED, Box 8174, Van Nuys CA 91409. (818)787-3203. President: William Williams. Labels include Aliso Creek Records. Record company. Estab. 1987. Releases 4 LPs and 4 CDs/year. Works with musicians/artists and songwriters on contract. Pays nego-

tiable royalty to artists on contract. Pays statutory rate to publisher per song on record.
How to Contact: Write and obtain permission to submit. Prefers cassette with 3 songs and lyric sheet. SASE. Reports in 3-4 weeks.
Music: Mostly New Age, new acoustic, children's music; also rock, pop and country. Released *Change* written and recorded by Steve Kenyata (new world LP) and *Take a Trip* (by Bob Menn), recorded by various artists (children's LP), both on Aliso Creek Records.
Tips: "We are looking for career singer/songwriters with well-developed material and performance skills and the desire to tour."

ALLAGASH COUNTRY RECORDS, 45 7th St., Auburn ME 04210. (207)784-7975. President/A&R Director: Richard E. Gowell. Labels include Allagash Country Records, Gowell Records and Allagash R&B Records. Record company, music publisher (Richard E. Gowell Music/BMI) and record producer. Estab. 1986. Releases 3-5 singles and 1-3 LPs/year. Receives 50 submissions/month. Works with musicians/artists and songwriters on contract. Pays 3-25% royalty to artists on contract; statutory rate to publisher per song on record.
How to Contact: Submit demo tape—unsolicited submissions OK. Prefers cassette with 2-12 songs and lyric or lead sheet. Returns unsolicited material, with SASE, 1-2 months. Reports in 2-6 weeks.
Music: Mostly country, pop/country and country rock; also R&B/pop. Released "Don't Wake Me" and "I Want to See Her Again" written and recorded by Kevin Cronin (country); "Back Home" (by J. Main) recorded by Larry Main (pop/country) and "Is It My Body You Want?" (by R.E. Gowell) recorded by Rich Gowell (50's rock), all on Allagash Records.
Tips: "We release compact discs worldwide and lease out album projects on singer/songwriters that have original unpublished masters available. 10-12 songs/masters in above styles that we accept, are contracted for this promotion. We work with many new acts with commercial material."

ALPHABEAT, Box 12 01, D-6980 Wertheim/Main, **Germany**. Phone: (09342)841 55. Owner/A&R Manager: Stephan Dehn. A&R National Manager: Marga Zimmermann. Press & Promotion: Alexander Burger. Disco Promotion: Matthias Marth. Music Service: Wolfgang Weinmann. Creative Services: Heiko Köferl. Labels include Alphabeat. Record company and record producer. Releases vary "depending on material available." Works with musicians/artists on contract; hires musicians for in-house studio work. Also works through "license contract with foreign labels." Payment to artists on contract "depends on product." Payment: conditional on German market.
How to Contact: Submit demo tape—unsolicited submissions are OK. Prefers cassette (or PAL videocassette) with maximum of 3 songs and lyric sheet. "When sending us your demo tapes, please advise us of your ideas and conditions." SAE and IRC. Reports in 2 weeks.
Music: Mostly dance/disco/pop, synth/pop and electronic; also R&B, hip hop/rap and ballads. Artists include Martin King, Red Sky, Fabian Harloff, Silent Degree, Mode Control, Mike M.C. & Master J., Skyline, Lost in the Dessert, Oriental Bazar, Voice In Your Head, Love Game, Alpha W. Synthoxx and Interface (ZYX Records).
Tips: "We are a distributor of foreign labels. If foreign labels have interest in distribution of their productions in Germany (also Switzerland and Austria) they can contact us. We distribute all styles of music of foreign labels. Please contact our department "Distribution Service."

*ALTERNATIVE RECORDS, 1610 Riverview St., Eugene OR 97403. A&R: KC Layton. Labels include Alternative Records, Alternative Archive. Record company. Estab. 1979. Releases 3-4 singles, 5 LPs, 1 EP and 5 CDs/year. Works with musicians/artists on record contract. Pays 17% royalty to artists on contract; statutory rate to publisher per song on record.
How to Contact: Write first and obtain permission to submit. Prefers cassette (or VHS videocassette if available) with 5 songs and lyric sheet. SASE. Reports in 4 weeks.
Music: Mostly rock (alternative), pop (again, alternative in nature), country/rock; also experimental and industrial. Released *Songs from the Riverhouse*, written and recorded by Robert Vaughn; *Lost Horizon*, written and recorded by Steve Scott; and *More Miserable Than You'll Ever Be*, written and recorded by 77; all CD/cassettes on Alternative Records.
Tips: "Our label appeals to the thoughtful/creative type of consumers. Artists that approach their work like a Bruce Cockburn or Mark Knopfler are most likely to be signed by us."

AMALGAMATED TULIP CORP., 117 W. Rockland Rd., Libertyville IL 60048. (708)362-4060. Director of Publishing and Administration: P. Johnson. Labels include Dharma Records. Record company and music publisher. Works with musicians on salary; artists and songwriters on contract. Pays royalty to artists and songwriters on contract.
How to Contact: Prefers cassette with 2-5 songs. SASE. Reports in 1-3 months.
Music: Rock (progressive and easy listening), dance/R&B and top 40/pop. Released *Songs by the Group Milwaukee*, by Milwaukee; "Sunday Meetin' In the Morning," by Ken Little and the Band; and "This Feels Like Love to Me," by Mirrors.

AMERICANA RECORDS, INC., 300 Linfield Dr., Vallejo CA 94590. (707)645-1615. President: Jack Walker. Labels include SUS Americana. Record company, music publisher (Americana/BMI) and record producer (Fulltilt Music). Estab. 1982. Releases 2 singles/year. Receives 40-50 submissions/month. Works with musicians/artists on contract. Pays 1-5% royalty to artists on contract; statutory rate to publisher per song on record.
How to Contact: Submit demo tape by mail. Unsolicited submissions are OK. Prefers cassette (or VHS videocassette if available) with 3 songs and lyric sheet. SASE. Reports in 1 month.
Music: Mostly country and bluegrass. Released "Minimum Wage" and "Goodbye Heartache" (by Tommy Johnson), recorded by Wally Jammings on SUS Americana Records (country single).
Tips: "Have a complete package and identify your wants. Our company helps get artists started in the business. The artist should also be aware that our company as well as other small companies don't have big budgets like the majors, so be prepared to spend money on production."

AMERICATONE RECORDS INTERNATIONAL USA, 1817 Loch Lomond Way, Las Vegas NV 89102-4437. (702)384-0030. FAX: (702)382-1926. Estab. 1975. Record company, producer and music publisher. Publishes 50 songs/year. Releases 5 12" singles, 5 EPs and 5 CDs/year. Receives 50 submissions/month. Pays standard royalty.
Affiliates: Americatone Music International (BMI), The Rambolt Music International (ASCAP).
How to Contact: Prefers cassettes and studio production with top sound recordings and lyric sheets. SASE. Reports in 4 weeks.
Music: Mostly country, jazz, R&R, Spanish, classic ballads. Published "You're The Other Part Of Me" (by Anita Johnson), "Memories Search For You" (by Patrick McElhoes); "Good Time Charlies" (by Patrick McElhoes); "Willie" (by Patrick McElhocs) and "I Love Your Waltz" (by Patrick McElhoes), all recorded on Americatone International Records.

THE AMETHYST GROUP LTD./ANTITHESIS RECORDS, 273 Chippewa Dr., Columbia SC 29210-6508. No phone calls please. Contact: A&R. Labels include Amethyst Records and Antithesis Records. Record company, music publisher (Another Amethyst Song/BMI) and management firm. Estab. 1979. Releases 10 singles and 3 LPs/year. Works with musicians/artists on contract. Pays 5-15% royalty to artists on contract. Pays statutory rate to publishers per song on record. International distribution, management, marketing firm. "Our forte is management, with overseas marketing."
How to Contact: Submit demo tape—unsolicited submissions are OK. Prefers cassette (or VHS videocassette) with 3-7 songs and lyric sheet. SASE. Reports within 3-5 weeks only if interested. "Always include return postage for any reply."
Music: Mostly mainstream, pop and R&B; also rock, new music, jazz/rap and heavy metal. Released "Surrender to the Order" recorded by US Steel; "Deadbeat" recorded by Meterpool (dance); and "Media" recorded by Political Asylum all on Amethyst Records (rock). Other artists include J. Blues, Knightmare, Jeromeo, Carnage, True Identity, Toniland, Danny D/X and I-Rock.
Tips: "Try to be realistic about someone investing in your material."

*AMHERST RECORDS, 1800 Main St., Buffalo NY 14208. (716)883-9520. President: Leonard Silver. Contact: Rose Rupert. Record company, music publisher (Harlem Music/BMI and Halwill Music/ASCAP) and management firm (Carefree Management, Inc.). Releases 20 singles and 15 LPs/year. Works with musicians/artists and songwriters on contract.
How to Contact: Submit demo tape—unsolicited submissions OK. Prefers cassette (or VHS videocassette) with 3-10 songs and lyric sheet. Does not return unsolicited material. Reports in 1 month.
Music: Mostly jazz, rock and R&B. Artists include Paul Butterfield, Anthony Watson, Jeff Tyzik, Val Young, Glenn Medeiros, Doc Severensen Gamalon and Jeremy Wall.

AMIRON MUSIC/AZTEC PRODUCTIONS, 20531 Plummer St., Chatsworth CA 91311. (213)998-0443. General Manager: A. Sullivan. Labels include Dorn Records and Aztec Records. Record company, booking agency and music publisher (Amiron Music). Releases 2 singles/year. Works with artists and songwriters on contract. Pays 10% maximum royalty to artists on contract; standard royalty to songwriters on contract. Pays statutory rate to publishers.
How to Contact: Prefers 7½ ips reel-to-reel or cassette and lead sheet. SASE. Reports in 3 weeks.
Music: Dance, easy listening, folk, jazz, MOR, rock ("no heavy metal") and top 40/pop. Released "Look In Your Eyes," by Newstreet; and "Midnight Flight," recorded by Papillon.
Tips: "Be sure the material has a hook; it should make people want to make love or fight. Write something that will give a talented new artist that edge on current competition."

ANGEL STAR RECORDS, 1715 Marty, Kansas City KS 66103. (913)384-4454. President: Ed Morgan. Record company, music publisher (Country Breeze Music/BMI, and Walkin' Hat Music/ASCAP). Releases 15 singles, 12 EPs and 15 cassette albums/year. Receives 130 submissions/month. Works with

musicians/artists and songwriters on contract. Pays 25% royalty to artists on contract, statutory rate to publisher per song on record.
How to Contact: Submit demo tape—unsolicited submissions are OK. Prefers cassette with 3 songs and lyric sheet. SASE. Reports in 2 weeks.
Music: Gospel, southern, country and bluegrass. Released "He Did It All" (by Ray Davis), recorded by Park Bench Qt. on Angel Star Records (gospel); "Baby from Bethlehem" (by J. Watters), recorded by Blest on Angel Star Records (gospel); and "Shadow of the Cross" written and recorded by Wilma Bell on Angel Star Records (gospel).
Tips: "Send no more than 4 songs per cassette with lyric sheets and return postage. Make sure your demo is clear with your voice out front."

A1A RECORDS, Leopold Str. 11-13, 4000 Dusseldorf NRW **Germany.** Phone: (0211)364545. Director: Ralf Krueger. Record company, music publisher (Ralf Krueger Musikverlag) and record producer (Sira Ain/Trance Palace Productions). Estab. 1984. Releases 2 12″ singles, 1 LP and 1 CD/year. Works with musicians/artists and songwriters on contract and hires musicians for in-house studio work. Pays 7-11% to artists on contract.
How to Contact: Submit demo tape—unsolicited submissions are OK. Prefers cassette with lyric sheet. SAE and IRC. Reports in 2 months.
Music: Soul, funk, hip hop and house with a pop-crossover appeal. Released "Milky Way Kiss" (by Bop Whopper/Sira Ain), recorded by Frank Ananda on A1A (soul-pop-rap); and "Violins" (by Georgie Rockwood, Victor Lovera, Sira Ain, Ama Donya), recorded by Frank Ananda on AIA (new pop). Other artists include S.A., Hip Crew and Heaven's Key.

ARIANA RECORDS, 1324 S. Avenida Polae, #0203, Tucson, AZ 85710. (602)577-8669. President: James M. Gasper. Vice President: Thomas M. Dukes. Record company, record producer (Future 1 Productions) and music publisher (Myko Music). Estab. 1980. Releases 1 single and 2 LPs/year. Works with musicians/artists on contract; hires musicians for in-house studio work.
How to Contact: Submit demo tape—unsolicited submissions OK. Prefers cassette with 3-5 songs and lyric sheet. SASE. Reports in 2 months.
Music: Mostly top 40; also R&B, rock, dance rock, pop and AOR. Released "Heartbreak Underground" (by J. Gasper) recorded by the Free Holy Men (country crossover); "Don't Take My Life" (by J. Gasper/T. Privett) recorded by Guys Seeking Paul (G.S.P.) (funk rock); and "Do the Dog" (by J.Gasper/S. Smith) recorded by Meat Corral (funk rock), all on Ariana Records. Other artists include 4 Walls, The El Caminos, Ronnie G, Scott Smith and Damn Shame.
Tips: "Be professional; first impressions are very important."

ASSOCIATED ARTISTS RECORDS INTERNATIONAL, Maarschalklaan 47, 3417 SE Montfoort, **The Netherlands.** Phone: (0)3484-2860. FAX: 31-3484-2860. Release Manager: Joop Gerrits. Labels include Associated Artists, Disco-Dance Records and Italo. Record company, music publisher (Associated Artists International/BUMA-STEMRA, Hilversum Happy Music/BUMA-STEMRA, Intermedlodie/BUMA-STEMRA and Hollands Glorie Productions), record producer (Associated Artists Productions) and TV promotions. Estab. 1975. Releases 10 singles, 25 12″ singles, 6 LPs and 6 CDs/year. Works with musicians/artists and songwriters on contract. Pays 12-18% royalty per record sold; statutory rate to publisher per song on record.
How to Contact: Submit demo tape—unsolicited submissions OK. Prefers compact cassette or 19 cm/sec reel-to-reel (or VHS videocassette) with any number of songs and lyric or lead sheets. Records also accepted. SAE and IRC. Reports in 6 weeks.
Music: Mostly dance, pop, house, hip hop, and rock. Released "Bailar Pegados" (by Anjurez), recorded by Sergio Dalma on Armada Records (ballad); "2V231" (by Picotto) recorded by Anticappella on Jive Records (house/techno); and "Extrasyn" (by Bortolotti), recorded by RFTR on Media Records (house/techno).
Tips: "We invite producers and independent record labels to send us their material for their entry on the European market. Mark all parcels as 'no commercial value—for demonstration only.' We license productions to record companies in all countries of Europe and South Africa."

ATLANTIC RECORDING CORP., 9229 Sunset Blvd., Los Angeles CA 90069. (213)205-7460. A&R Director: Kevin Williamson. Contact: Paul Cooper. Labels include Atco, Cotillion, East-West and Atlantic. "We distribute Island and Virgin." Record company, music publisher. Estab. 1948. Works with artists on contract, songwriters on royalty contract and musicians on salary for in-house studio work.
How to Contact: Prefers cassette with 3 songs (or VHS videocassette). SASE. Reports in 2 weeks. Does not return unsolicited material.
Music: Blues, disco, easy listening, folk, jazz, MOR, progressive, R&B, rock, soul and top 40/pop. Artists included Debbie Gibson, Mike & the Mechanics, INXS, Yes, AC/DC, Pete Townsend, Bette Midler, Ratt, Skid Row and Crosby, Stills, Nash & Young.

*ATTACK RECORDS, Box 3161, Atlanta GA 30302. Producer: C.E. Scott. Labels include Ambush Records. Record company and music publisher (BMI). Estab. 1965. Releases 12 singles, 4 12″ singles, 3 LPs, 4 EPs and 3 CDs/year. Works with musicians/artists and songwriters on contract. Pays 3% royalty to artists on contract; statutory rate to publisher per song on record.
How to Contact: Submit demo tape—unsolicited submissions are OK. Prefers cassette or VHS videocassette with 3 songs and lead sheets. SASE. Reports in 6 weeks.
Music: Mostly pop and R&B. Released "I Wanna Dance With You," "Wild Flower" and "Slow Dance" (all recorded by Sybyo) on Attack Records (pop). Other artists include Sheila Davis, Barbara Rush, The CD's and Cy Boy.
Tips: "Please be patient and write according to the current music trends. We will contact you if we like your material. We're most open to female-oriented, and pop hard-hitting R&B roster."

AUBURN RECORDS AND TAPES, Box 96, Glendale AZ 85311. (602)435-0314. Owner: Frank E. Koehl. Record company and music publisher (Speedster Music/BMI). Estab. 1962. Releases 1-4 singles/year. Receives 15 submissions/month. Works with musicians/artists and songwriters on contract. Pays statutory rate.
How to Contact: Submit a demo tape—unsolicited submissions are OK. SASE. Reports in 3 weeks.
Music: Mostly country, folk and bluegrass. Released "Mr. Woolworth" recorded by Al Ferguson; "Lottery Fever" recorded by Troy McCourt; and "Burglar Man" recorded by Al Ferguson, all on Auburn Records (country/comical).
Tips: "I am looking for songs that are country and comical or the traditional country sound."

AUDEM RECORDS, Box 32A, Albany Post Road, Wallkill NY 12589. (914)895-8397. President: Tom Destry. Record company and record producer (Destry Music). Estab. 1986. Releases 2 singles, 2 LPs/year. Works with musicians/artists and songwriters on contract. Pays 4-9% royalty to artists on contract; statutory rate to publisher per song on record.
How to Contact: Submit demo tape—unsolicited submissions are OK. Prefers cassette, 7½ ips reel-to-reel (or VHS videocassette) with 3 songs and lyric sheet. SASE. Reports in 6 weeks.
Music: Mostly pop, rock and country; also contemporary gospel, R&B and dance. Released "I Hear You Knocking" (by Barthomomeu, King & Domino), recorded by Dave Kennedy and the U.S.A. Band (rock); "I'm Looking for a Miracle" and "Light of My Life" written and recorded by Tom Destry (pop), all on Audem Records (all singles). Other artists include Susan Stanley (country), Helen Angelo (gospel) and Michele Lee (pop).
Tips: "The radio will give you your best key to creativity. Listen to the hits of today, then mold your talents around them. In turn, the combination makes you new."

AUTOGRAM RECORDS, Burgstr. 9, 4405 Nottuln 1, Germany. (02502) 6151. FAX: 1825. Contact: A&R Department. Labels include Autonom, Folk-Record, costbar, Basilikum, Autophon and Roots. Record company. Releases 20-25 CDs and 10 LPs/year. Works with musicians/artists and songwriters on contract. Pays 5% of retail price to artists on contract.
How to Contact: Submit demo tape—unsolicited submissions are OK. Prefers cassette with minimum 3 songs and lyric sheet. SAE and IRC. Reports in 1-2 months. "No stylistic imitations, (no cover versions)."
Music: New-country, country/folk-rock, singer-songwriter (languages mainly German, English, Dutch), ethnic folk music, blues and contemporary guitar music; also classical, contemporary, bluegrass and historical (reissues). Released "All Around the Country" (by T. Kahrs), recorded by Till Kahrs and "1,000 Stukke" (by J. Ottink), recorded by Jon Offink both on Autogram Records (CD); and "Altes Hans" (by W. Schwenleen), recorded by Helmut Bollien on Basilikum Records (CD).

AVANT-GARDE RECORDS CORP., 12224 Avila Dr., Kansas City MO 64145. (816)942-8861. Director A&R/President: Scott Smith. Record company, music publisher and record producer. Estab. 1983. Releases 3 LPs and 3 CDs/year. Receives 4 submissions/month. Pays statutory rate.
How to Contact: Write or call first and obtain permission to submit. Prefers cassette (or VHS videocassette if available) with 4 songs. SASE. Reports in 8 weeks.
Music: Mostly themes, new standards and pop classical, on piano only. Released *30th Anniversary on Stage*, *Dos Amigos*, *American Fantasy*, and *Favorites-On Stage* recorded by Ferrante & Teicher on Avant-Garde Records (LPs).
Tips: "Only send instrumentals—no lyrics. Piano recordings get top priority."

AVC ENTERTAINMENT INC., Suite 200, 6201 Sunset Blvd., Hollywood CA 90028. (213)461-9001. President: James Warsinske. Labels include AVC Records. Record company and music publisher (AVC Music/ASCAP, Harmonious Music/BMI). Estab. 1988. Releases 6-12 singles, 6-12 12″ singles, 3-6 LPs and 3-6 CDs/year. Works with musicians/artists and songwriters on contract. Pays rate of 75% to publishers.

How to Contact: Submit demo tape—unsolicited submissions OK. Prefers cassette and VHS video-cassette with 2-4 songs and lyric sheet. SASE. Reports in 1 month.
Music: Mostly R&B/rap, pop and rock; also funk/soul, dance and metal. Released "In Service" (by Michael Williams) recorded by Madrok on AVC Records (rap); "There's a New Today" written and recorded by Duncan Faure on AVC Records (pop/rock) and "Melissa Mainframe" (by Couts/Hohl/Rocca) recorded by Rocca on Life Records (pop/rock). Other artists include N-Demand, James Richard and 7th Stranger.
Tips: "Be original and contemporary, we take our time selecting our artists, but stay committed to them."

AZRA INTERNATIONAL, Box 459, Maywood CA 90270. (213)560-4223. A&R: Jeff Simins. Labels include Azra, Iron Works, Not So Famous David's Records and Masque Records. Record company. Estab. 1978. Releases 10 singles, 5 LPs, 5 EPs and 5 CDs/year. Receives 20 submissions/month. Works with artists on contract. "Artists usually carry their own publishing." Pays 10% royalty to artists on contract; statutory rate to publishers for each record sold.
How to Contact: Submit demo tape—unsolicited submissions are OK. Prefers cassette (or VHS videocassette) with 3-5 songs and lyric sheet. Include bio and photo. SASE. Reports in 1 month.
Music: Mostly rock, heavy metal, Christian and New Age; also novelty. Released *Winds of Fire*, written and recorded by Pabro Dadivas on Condor Classix Records (new age CD); *Industrial Strength*, (by Al Martinez) recorded by Industrial Strength on Azra Records (electronic CD) and *Super Himalayen*, (by Chris Sanderlain) recorded by Laughing House on World Metal Records (metal LP).
Tips: "We prefer groups that have been together a minimum of 6 months and solo artists who can write for specific projects."

*AZTLAN RECORDS, P.O. Box 5672, Buena Park CA 90622. (714)522-5203. Manager: Carmen Ortiz. Record company, music publisher. Estab. 1986. Releases 1 LP and 1 CD/year. Works with musicians/artists on record contract. Royalty paid to artist on contract varies.
How to Contact: Submit demo tape—unsolicited submissions are OK. Prefers cassette. SASE.
Music: Mostly alternative, industrial, experimental; also gothic, performance poetry and ethnic. Released *Nirvana* written and recorded by 12 artists (compilation LP); *Awaken*, written and recorded by 7 artists (compilation LP); and *Hiding from Fears*, written and recorded by Angel of the Odd (alternative LP), all on Aztlan Records. Other artists include Cecilia, Stereotaxic Device, BlackTape for A Blue Girl and Spiderbaby.
Tips: "Die rather than compromise what you are doing. Music is your life."

*B.P.M. PRODUCTIONS, 4 Norside, Oldmixon Cres, Weston-S-Mare, Avon BS24 9AX **England**. Phone: 0934617373. Production Manager: B.J. Monk. Labels include Shoc Wave, B.P.M. Records. Record company. Estab. 1989. Releases 6 singles, 6 12" singles, 4 LPs and 4 CDs/year. Works with musicians/artists on contract and hires musicians for in-house studio work. Pays 12% royalty to artists on contract; statutory rate to publisher per song on record.
How to Contact: Submit demo tape—unsolicited submissions are OK. Prefers cassette with 3 songs and lyric sheet. SASE. Reports in 3-4 weeks.
Music: Mostly dance, pop, easy listening. Released "Prissy Miss Maybe" (by Haswell andHurrell), recorded by Haswell (single); *Robbie Gill* (by various), recorded by Robbie Gill (LP); and *Give Me a Try* (by various), recorded by Blak Flamez (LP); all on Shoc Wave Records. Other artists include Dr. Barnstorm, Sue Jones, Eddy Gray, Paul Ramos and B.J. Martin.
Tips: "Take care over your recordings. We receive many poor demos and this always puts you off the artist."

BAGATELLE RECORD COMPANY, 400 San Jacinto St., Houston TX 77002. (713)225-6654. President: Byron Benton. Record company, record producer and music publisher (Floyd Tillman Music Co.). Releases 20 singles and 10 LPs/year. Works with songwriters on contract; musicians on salary for in-house studio work. Pays negotiable royalty to artists on contract.
How to Contact: Prefers cassette and lyric sheet. SASE. Reports in 2 weeks.
Music: Mostly country; also gospel. Released "This is Real," by Floyd Tillman (country single); "Lucille," by Sherri Jerrico (country single); and "Everything You Touch," by Johnny Nelms (country single). Other artists include Jerry Irby, Bobby Beason, Bobby Burton, Donna Hazard, Danny Brown, Sonny Hall, Ben Gabus, Jimmy Copeland and Johnny B. Goode.

BAL RECORDS, Box 369, La Canada CA 91012-0369. (818)548-1116. President: Adrian Bal. Record company, record producer and music publisher (Bal & Bal Music Publishing Co./ASCAP, Bal West Music Publishing Company/BMI). Estab. 1965. Releases 2-6 singles/year. Receives 50 submissions/month. Works with artists and songwriters on contract; musicians on salary for in-house studio work.

Works with composers and lyricists; teams collaborators. Pays standard royalty to artists on contract; statutory rate to publishers for each record sold.

How to Contact: Prefers cassette (or videocassette) with 1-3 songs and lyric or lead sheet. SASE. Reports in 15-20 weeks.

Music: Rock, MOR, country/western, gospel and jazz. Released "Fragile" (by James Jackson), recorded by Kathy Simmons (med. rock); "Right to Know" (by James Jackson), recorded by Kathy Simmons (med. rock); "Dance to the Beat of My Heart" (by Dan Gertz), recorded by Ace Baker (med. rock) and "You're A Part of Me," "Can't We Hame Some Time Together," "You and Me" and "Circles of Time" by Paul Richards (A/C).

Tips: "Consider: Will young people who receive an allowance go out and purchase the record?"

BCM-USA, Box 351176, Los Angeles CA 90035. (213)278-9540. Manager: S. Kleinman. Labels include Romance Records. Record company, music publisher BCM-USA Publishing (BMI, GEMA), record producer. Estab. 1987. Works with musicians/artists on contract. Royalty paid to artists on contract varies.

How to Contact: Submit demo tape—unsolicited submissions are OK. Prefers cassette. Does not return unsolicited material. Reports in 1 week.

Music: Mostly dance and rock. Other artists include Technotronics, Steve B., 24! 7, Latoya Jackson.

Tips: "Persist, Be professional! Clearly label cassette with telephone number."

BELMONT RECORDS, 484 Lexington St., Waltham MA 02154. (617)891-7800. President: John Penny. Labels include Belmont Records and Waverly Records. Record company and record producer. Works with musicians on salary for in-house studio work. Pays standard royalty to artists on contract; statutory rate to publisher per song on record.

How to Contact: Write first and obtain permission to submit. Prefers cassette with 3 songs and lyric sheet. SASE. Reports in 3 weeks.

Music: Mostly country. Released *One Step At a Time*, recorded by Cheri Ann on Belmont Records (C&W LP); and *Tudo Bens Sabe*, recorded by Familia Penha (gospel LP). Other artists include Stan Jr., Tim Barrett, Jackie Lee Williams, Robin Right, Mike Walker and Dwain Hathaway.

*BEST WEST PRODUCTIONS, 1301 Morrison, Redlands CA 92374. (714)798-6449/370-1980. Contact: Deborah Harmon. Labels include Best West Records. Record company, music publisher (BMI) and record producer (Best West Records). Estab. 1988. Works with songwriters on royalty contract.

How to Contact: Submit demo tape—unsolicited submissions are OK. Prefers cassette (or any videocassette if available) with 3 songs and lyric sheet. SASE. Reports in 2 weeks to 2 months.

Music: Mostly country and pop.

Tips: "Send your best material only. Simple guitar/vocal or piano/vocal demo preferred. Send bio."

BGM RECORDS, Dept. SM, 4265 Gate Crest, San Antonio TX 78217-3824. (512)654-8773. Contact: Bill Green. Labels include Zone 7, BGM and Rainforest Records. Record company, music publisher (Bill Green Music) and record producer. Estab. 1979. Releases 10 singles and 2-3 LPs/year. Works with songwriters on contract.

How to Contact: Prefers cassette. SASE. Reports in 2 months.

Music: Mostly contemporary country and traditional country. Released "Cajun Baby" (by H. Williams, H. Williams Jr.), recorded by Doug Kershaw (country cajun); "Photographic Memory" (by B. Boyd), recorded by Billy Mata (country); and "Boogie Queen" (by Jenkins, Green), recorded by Doug Karrhau (country cajun); all on BGM Records. Other artists include David Price.

BIG BEAR RECORDS, Box 944, Birmingham, B16 8UT, **United Kingdom**. Phone: 44-021-454-7020. FAX: 44-021-454-9996. A&R Director: Jim Simpson. Labels include Big Bear, Truckers Delight and Grandstand Records. Record company, record producer and music publisher (Bearsongs). Releases 6 LPs/year. Works with artists and songwriters on contract; teams collaborators. Pays 8-10% royalty to artists on contract; 8¼% to publishers for each record sold. Royalties paid directly to the songwriters and artists or through US publishing or recording affiliate.

How to Contact: Prefers 7½ or 15 ips reel-to-reel, DAT, or cassette (or videocassette) and lyric sheet. SAE and IRC. Reports in 2 weeks.

Music: Blues, jazz. Released *This Is It* recorded by King Pleasure on Big Bear Records (R&B LP/CD/MC). Other artists include King Pleasure & the Biscuit Boys, Lady Sings the Blues, Bill Allred, Poorboys and jazz and blues artists.

BIG K RECORDS, Box 3500, Pawtucket RI 02861. (401)728-1689. President: Karen Pady. Record company, music publisher (Big K Records, Pady Music Publishing Co./ASCAP) and record producer (KA Productions, Karen Pady). Estab. 1980. Releases 2 LPs/year. Works with musicians/artists and songwriters on contract and hires musicians.

How to Contact: Write first and obtain permission to submit. Prefers cassette or VHS videocassette with any number of songs and lyric sheet. SASE. Reports in 3 weeks.
Music: Mostly pop, rock and light rock; also A/C, country rock. Released "Cause I Love You" (adult contemporary); "My Friend" (adult contemporary); and "Will I Ever Make It Thru" (rock); all by Karen Pady Kula, recorded by Karyn and Steph on Big K Records. Other artists include Image w/ Camy and Gina, Midnight Fantasy, Pauline Silvia, Ronnie Woods, Together Again and Karyn Krystal.
Tips: "Work to please yourself. Write, sing, or play the type of music that you enjoy. I enjoy many types of music. If I like your demo material or ideas, I will work with you."

BIG PRODUCTIONS RECORDS, Suite 308, 37 East 28th St., New York NY 10016. (212)447-6000. President: Paul Punzone. Record company, music publisher (Humongous Music/ASCAP) and record producer (Big Productions and Publishing Co., Inc.). Estab. 1989. Releases 10 12″ singles/year. Works with musicians/artists and songwriters on contract and hires musicians for in-house studio work. Pays 10% royalty to artists on contract; ¾ of statutory rate to publisher per song on record.
How to Contact: Submit demo tape—unsolicited submissions are OK. Prefers cassette or VHS videocassette with 3 songs and lyric sheet. SASE. Reports in 2 months.
Music: Mostly 12″ house tracks, vocal house and hip hop; also rap, R&B and pop. Released "Mission Accomplished," recorded by Big Baby; "Loose Flutes," recorded by Picture Perfect; and "Get Up," recorded by Big Baby; all written by P. Punzone, G. Sicard and B.B. Fisher on Big Productions Records (house track 12″). Other artists include Charm.
Tips: "We are seeking completed house/sample for immediate release. Send best representation of your work for song or artist submissions."

*BLACK & BLUE, Suite 152, 400D Putnam Pike, Smithfield RI 02917. (401)949-4887. New Talent Manager: Larry Evilelf. Record company. Releases 5-20 LPs, 3-8 EPs, 5-20 CDs/year. Works with musicians/artists on record contract. Pays statutory rate to publisher per song on record.
How to Contact: Submit demo tape—unsolicited submissions are OK. Prefers cassette (or VHS videocassette) with 3 songs and lyric sheet or lead sheet. Does not return unsolicited material. Reports in 6 weeks.
Music: Mostly eclectic, alternative rock, hardcore; also speed metal, C&W and grind core. Released *Darkness in Me* (by Celia Hemken), recorded by Blue Nouveaux (alternative LP); *6th Grade Field Trip* (by Don McCloud), recorded by Bloody Mess and the Skabs (hardcore LP); and *Death Mission* (by Lyndon Cox), recorded by Boorish Book (rock EP), all on Black & Blue Records. Other artists include The Cedar Street Sluts, Algae After Birth & Playpen, Northwinds, Jesse Braintree with Neil & Robert T. Hogg, The Grave Robbers, Holly Would.
Tips: "Be truly original. Sound alikes and trend followers are really not given serious consideration regardless of how good they are."

BLACK DOG RECORDS, Rt. 2 Box 38, Summerland Key FL 33042. (305)745-3164. Executive Director: Marian Joy Ring. A&R Contact: Rusty Gordon, (Rustron Music Productions), 1156 Park Lane, West Palm Beach, FL 33417. (407)686-1354. Record company. Estab. 1989. Releases 2-6 singles and 3 LPs/ year. Pays standard royalty to artists on contract; statutory rate to publishers per song on record.
How to Contact: Submit demo tape by mail to W. Palm Beach address or write or call first and obtain permission to submit. Prefers cassette with 3-6 songs and lyric or lead sheet. SASE required for all correspondence. Reports in 4-6 weeks.
Music: Mostly pop, R&B and folk-rock; also New Age and cabaret. Released *Rising Cost of Love*, "Song for Pedro," "Reflections" and "Same Moon," all written and recorded by Marian Joy Ring on Black Dog Records.

BLUE GEM RECORDS, Box 29688, Hollywood CA 90029. (213)664-7765. Contact: Pete Martin. Record company and record producer (Pete Martin Productions). Estab. 1981. Receives 50-200 submissions/ month. Works with musicians/artists on contract. Pays 6-15% royalty to artists on contract; statutory rate to publisher per song on record.
How to Contact: Submit demo tape—unsolicited submissions are OK. Prefers cassette with 2 songs. SASE. Reports in 3 weeks.
Music: Mostly country and R&B; also pop/top 40 and rock. Released "The Greener Years," written and recorded by Frank Loren (country); "It's a Matter of Loving You" (by Brian Smith), recorded by Brian Smith and Renegades (country); and "Two Different Women" (by Frank Loren and Greg Connor), recorded by Frank Loren (country); all on Blue Gem Records. Other artists include Sherry Weston and Brian Smith & The Renegades (all country).
Tips: "Study top 10 on charts in your style of writing and be current!"

BLUE WAVE, 3221 Perryville Rd., Baldwinsville NY 13027. (315)638-4286. President/Producer: Greg Spencer. Labels include Blue Wave and Blue Wave/Horizon. Record company, music publisher (G.W. Spencer Music/ASCAP) and record producer (Blue Wave Productions). Estab. 1985. Releases 3 LPs and 3 CDs/year. Receives 300 submissions/year. Works with musicians/artists on contract. Royalty varies; statutory rate to publishers per song on records.

How to Contact: Submit demo tape—unsolicited submissions are OK. Prefers cassette (or VHS or Beta videocassette—live performance only) if available and as many songs as you like. SASE. "We contact only if we are interested." Allow 6 weeks.

Music: Mostly blues/blues rock, roots rock and roots R&B/soul; also some roots country/rockabilly or anything with "soul." Released "Cadillac Woman" (by Pete McMahon), recorded by Kingsnakes on Bluewave Records (blues); "Bit Talk" (by Joe Whiting/Mark Doyle), recorded by Backbone Slip on Bluewave Records (blues/rock) and "Snake Eyes" (by Joe Whiting), recorded by Jumpin Joe Whiting on Bluewave Records (blues/rock).

Tips: "Send it only if it's great, what you send must come from the soul. Not interested in top 40, so-called "hits" or commercial music. I'm looking for real, original artists or those who can make someone else's music their own. The singer must be convincing and be able to deliver the message. Please don't call, I listen to everything sent and I will call if you're what I'm looking for. Please, no lyric sheets or photos, I like to listen without any preconceived notions."

*BOGART RECORDS, Box 63302, Phoenix AZ 85082. Owner: Robert L. Bogart Sr. Record Company. Estab. 1991. Works with musicians/artists and songwriters on contract and hires musicians for in-house studio work. Pays royalty to artists on contract; statutory rate to publisher per song on record.

How to Contact: Submit demo tape—unsolicited submissions are OK. Prefers cassette with 4 songs and lyric sheet. SASE. Reports in 1 month.

Music: Mostly country, R&B and rock; also pop, New Age and gospel. Released "I'd Be Ly, In" written and recorded by James Beckwith on Bogart Records (country single). Other artists include Tim Tesch and Earl Eric Brown.

*BOLIVIA RECORDS, 1219 Kerlin Ave., Brewton AL 36426. (205)867-2228. President: Roy Edwards. Labels include Known Artist Records. Record company, record producer and music publisher (Cheavoria Music Co.). Estab. 1972. Releases 10 singles and 3 LPs/year. Works with artists and songwriters on contract; musicians on salary for in-house studio work. Pays 4-5% royalty to artists on contract; statutory rate to publishers for each record sold.

How to Contact: Write first. Prefers cassette with 3 songs and lyric sheet. All tapes will be kept on file. Reports in 1 month.

Music: Mostly R&B, country and pop; also easy listening, MOR and soul. Released "You Are My Sunshine" and "If You Only Knew" written and recorded by Roy Edwards on Bolivia Records (R&B). Other artists include Bobbie Roberson and Jim Portwood.

BOOGIE BAND RECORDS, Suite 206, 6245 Bristol Pkwy., Culver City CA 90230. Contact: Larry McGee. Labels include Dollar Bill Records and Mega Star Records. Record company, music publisher (Operation Perfection Publishing), record producer (Intrigue Productions) and management firm (LMP Management). Estab. 1976. Releases 6 singles, 3 12" singles, 1 LP, 4 EPs and 2 CDs/year. Receives 200-300 submissions/year. Works with musicians/artists and songwriters on contract; musicians on salary for in-house studio work. Pays 10% royalty to artists on contract; statutory rate to publishers per song on record.

How to Contact: Prefers cassette with 1-4 songs and lyric sheet. Does not return unsolicited material. Reports in 2 months. "Please only send professional quality material."

Music: Urban contemporary, dance, rock, MOR/A/C, pop, rap and R&B. Released "Captain Freedom," "Voices" and "Snake," all written and recorded by Captain Freedom on Boogie Band Records. Other artists include the S-Quires, Jim Sapienza, The Allen Brothers, Terri Parondi, Roz Smith, Gary Walker and Cindi Tulk.

BOOM/POWER PLAY RECORDS, Dept. SM, 200 Regent Dr., Winston-Salem NC 27103. (919)768-1298. President: David D. Passerallo. Record company, music publisher (DeDan Music/BMI) and record producer (Boom Productions Inc.). Estab. 1989. Releases 2 singles, 2 LPs and 2 CDs/year. Works with musicians/artists and songwriters on contract and "musicians and artists on production contracts." Pays 8-10% royalty to artists on contract; statutory rate to publisher per song on record.

How to Contact: Write first and obtain permission to submit. Prefers cassette or VHS videocassette with 2 songs and lead sheet. SASE. Reports in 2-3 weeks.

Music: Mostly pop and rock; also rap. Released "Ripped Jeans" (pop/rock); "I Wanna Know" (ballad) and "Lay It Back" (rock/rap); all written and recorded by John Cody on Boom Records. Other artists include China Blue.

Tips: "Have a good positive attitude and be very flexible."

BOUQUET RECORDS, Bouquet-Orchid Enterprises, Box 11686, Atlanta GA 30355. (404)355-7635. President: Bill Bohannon. Record company, music publisher (Orchid Publishing/BMI), record producer (Bouquet-Orchid Enterprises) and management firm. Releases 3-4 singles and 2 LPs/year.

Works with artists and songwriters on contract. Pays 5-8% maximum royalty to artists on contract; pays statutory rate to publishers for each record sold.

How to Contact: Submit demo tape—unsolicited submissions are OK. Prefers cassette with 3-5 songs and lyric sheet. SASE. Reports in 1 month.

Music: Mostly religious (contemporary or country-gospel, Amy Grant, etc.), country ("the type suitable for Clint Black, George Strait, Patty Loveless, etc.") and top 100 ("the type suitable for Billy Joel, Whitney Houston, R.E.M., etc."); also rock and MOR. Released "A Brighter Day" (by Bill Bohannon), recorded by Adam Day (country); "Tear Talk" (by John Harris), recorded by Susan Spencer (country); and "Justify My Love" (by Bob Freeman), recorded by Bandoleers (top 40) all on Bouquet Records.

Tips: "Submit 3-5 songs on a cassette tape with lyric sheets. Include a short biography and perhaps a photo. Enclose SASE."

BOVINE INTERNATIONAL RECORD COMPANY, 593 Kildare Rd., London, Ontario N6H 3H8 **Canada.** A&R Director: J.A. Moorhouse. Labels include Bovine and Solid Ivory Records. Record company. Estab. 1977. Releases 1-10 singles and 1-5 LPs/year. Receives 60 submissions/month. Works with musicians/artists on contract and musicians on salary for in-house studio work. Pays 30-40% royalty to artists on contract; statutory rate to publisher per song on record.

How to Contact: Cassette only with 2-3 songs and lyric and lead sheets. SAE and IRC. Reports in 1 month.

Music: Mostly country, pop and R&B; also children's records, blues and jazz. Released "San Antonio Truckers' Christmas" and "Keep It In Mind," written and recorded by J. Moorhouse; and "Reconsider Me" (by J. Moorhouse), recorded by Keynotes, all country singles on Bovine International Records. Other artists include Merle Morgan and The Rockin Renegades.

BRIER PATCH MUSIC, 3825 Meadowood, Grandville MI 49418. (616)534-6571. Promotion Associate: David Vander Molen. Record company. Estab. 1985. Releases 1 or 2 LPs and 1 CD/year. Works with "our own artists." Pays negotiable royalty to artists on contract.

How to Contact: Write or call first and obtain permission to submit. Prefers VHS videocassette with 3 songs and lyric or lead sheet. SASE. Reports in 3-6 weeks.

Music: Mostly light rock, pop and gospel; also New Age instrumental, children's and peace/justice/folk. Released "Time & Time Again" and "Shine" both written and recorded by Ken Medema on Brier Patch Records (A/C).

Tips: "Original music, with proficient musical background."

BROKEN RECORDS INTERNATIONAL, 305 S. Westmore Ave., Lombard IL 60148. (708)916-6874. International A&R: Roy Bocchieri. Labels include Broken Records International. Record company. Estab. 1984. Works with musicians/artists on contract. Payment negotiable.

How to Contact: Submit demo tape—unsolicited submissions are OK. Prefers cassette or VHS videocassette with at least 2 songs and lyric sheet. Does not return unsolicited material. Reports in 8 weeks.

Music: Mostly rock, pop and dance; also acoustic and industrial. Released *Electric*, written and recorded by LeRoy on Broken Records (pop LP-CD-MC).

BULL CITY RECORDS, Box 6, Rougemont NC 27572. (919)477-4077. Manager: Freddie Roberts. Record company, record producer and music publisher (Freddie Roberts Music). Releases 20 singles and 6 LPs/year. Works with songwriters on contract. Pays standard royalty to artists on contract; statutory rate to publishers for each record sold.

How to Contact: Write or call first about your interest or to arrange personal interview. Prefers 7½ ips reel-to-reel or cassette (or videocassette) with 1-5 songs and lyric sheet. "Submit a clear, up-to-date demo." SASE. Reports in 3 weeks.

Music: Mostly country, MOR, southern rock and top 40/pop; also bluegrass, church/religious, gospel and rock/country. Released "Redeemed" (by Jane Durham), recorded by Roberts Family on Bull City Records (southern gospel); "Almost" (by Rodney Hutchins), recorded by Billy McKellar on Bull City Records (country) and "Not This Time" (by D. Tyler), recorded by Sleepy Creek on Bull City Records (southern rock).

THE CALVARY MUSIC GROUP, Dept. SM, 142 8th Ave. N., Nashville TN 37203. (615)244-8800. Contact: Artist Development Department. Labels include Calvary, Lifestream, Heart Song and Wedding Song. Record company, record producer, music publisher and distribution company. Member GMA. Releases 8 singles and 8 LPs/year. Works with artists and songwriters on contract. Pays statutory rate or negotiates rate to publishers for each record sold.

How to Contact: Not accepting unsolicited material at this time.
Music: Mostly gospel; also wedding music. Released "Going Back" (by Shifflet), recorded by the Freemans on Calvary Records (southern gospel); "I Prayed Through Today," written and recorded by Ronny Hinson on Calvary Records (southern-inspirational); and "Lonely Tonight" (by Wilson), recorded by Karen Wheaton on Life Stream Records (inspirational).

CAMBRIA RECORDS & PUBLISHING, Box 374, Lomita CA 90717. (213)831-1322. Director of Recording Operations: Lance Bowling. Labels include Charade Records. Record company and music publisher. Estab. 1979. Releases 5 cassettes and 6 CDs/year. Works with artists on contract; musicians on salary for in-house studio work. Pays 5-8% royalty to artists on contract; statutory rate to publisher for each record sold.
How to Contact: Write first. Prefers cassette. SASE. Reports in 2 months.
Music: Mostly classical. Released *Songs of Elinor Remick Warren* on Cambria Records (CD). Other artists include Marie Gibson (soprano), Mischa Leftkowitz (violin), Leigh Kaplan (piano), North Wind Quintet, Sierra Wind Quintet and many others.

CANYON CREEK RECORDS, Box 31351, Dallas TX 75231. (214)750-0720. Chief Executive Officer: Bart Barton. A&R: Mike Anthony. Record company, record producer. Estab. 1983. Works with musicians/artists and songwriters on contract. Pays standard royalty to writers on contract. Releases 12 singles/year, 4 LPs/year.
How to Contact: Write first and obtain permission to submit. Prefers cassette (or VHS videocassette) with 2 songs and lyric sheet. Reports in 10 weeks.
Music: Country and gospel. Artists include Audie Henry, Billy Parker and Susie Calvin. Released "She's Sittin' Pretty" (by Bart Barton), recorded by Billy Parker on CCR/RCA Records (country); "I Didn't Know You" (by D. Kirkpatrick/M. McClain), recorded by Audie Henry on CCR/RCA Records (country) and "Alive and Lovin' It" (by D. Kirkpatrick/M. McClain) recorded by Bev Marie on Canyon Creek Records (country).

CAPSTAN RECORD PRODUCTION, Box 211, East Prairie MO 63845. (314)649-2211. Nashville Branch: 38 Music Sq. E., Nashville TN 37203. (615)255-8005. Contact: Joe Silver or Tommy Loomas. Labels include Octagon and Capstan Records. Record company, music publisher (Lineage Publishing Co.) and record producer (Silver-Loomas Productions). Works with artists on contract. Pays 3-5% royalty to artists on contract.
How to Contact: Write first about your interest. Prefers cassette (or VHS videocassette) with 2-4 songs and lyric sheet. "Send photo and bio." SASE. Reports in 1 month.
Music: Country, easy listening, MOR, country rock and top 40/pop. Released "Dry Away the Pain," by Julia Brown (easy listening single); "Country Boy," by Alden Lambert (country single); "Yesterday's Teardrops," by The Burchetts (country single); and "Round & Round," by The Burchetts. Other artists include Bobby Lee Morgan, Skidrow Joe and Fleming.

CAROLINE RECORDS, INC., 114 W. 26th St., 11th Fl., New York NY 10001. (212)989-2929. Director Creative Operations: Janet Billig. Labels include Caroline Records, exclusive manufacturing and distribution of Plan 9 Records, exclusive distribution in the U.S. of EG, Editions EG and Sub-Pop. Record company, music publisher (26th St. Songs, 26th St. Music) and independent record distributor (Caroline Records Inc.). Estab. 1985. Releases 3-4 12″ singles, 10 LPs, 1-2 EPs and 10 CDs/year. Works with musicians/artists on record contract. Pays varying royalty to artists on contract; statutory rate to publisher per song.
How to Contact: Submit demo tape—unsolicited submissions are OK. Prefers cassette with lead sheets and press clippings. SASE. Reports in 3 weeks.
Music: Mostly metal, "hardcore," and alternative/indie rock. Released *Quickness*, written and recorded by Bad Brains on Caroline Records (rock LP); *Bridge* (by Neil Young), recorded by V/A on NO.6 Records/Caroline Records (rock LP); and *God of Thunder* (by Kiss), recorded by White Zombie on Caroline Records (metal EP). Other artists include Naked Raygun, War Zone, Excel, Snake Nation, Unrest, Reverend, Mind Over 4, Pussy Galore, Primus.
Tips: "When submitting a demo keep in mind that we have never signed an artist who does not have a strong underground buzz and live track record. We listen to all types of 'alternative' rock, metal, funk and rap but do not sign mainstream hard rock or dance. We send out rejection letters so do not call to find out what's happening with your demo."

*CAROUSEL RECORDS, INC., 1273½ N. Crescent Hts. Blvd., Los Angeles CA 90046. (213)650-6500. A&R: Stuart Lanis. Record company, music publisher and record producer. Estab. 1963. Releases 3-6 12″ singles and 1-3 LPs/year. Works with musicians and songwriters on contract. Pays statutory rate.
How to Contact: Prefers cassette with 3-6 songs and lyric sheet. SASE. Reports in 3-4 weeks.
Music: Top 40, MOR, country, gospel and children's.

CASARO RECORDS, 932 Nord Ave., Chico CA 95926. (916)345-3027. Contact: Hugh Santos. Record company, music publisher (Mini Max Publishing/BMI), record producer (RSA Productions). Estab. 1988. Releases 5-8 LPs/year. Works with musicians/artists and songwriters on contract; session players. Pays 7% royalty to artists on contract; statutory rate to publisher per song on record.
How to Contact: Submit demo tape—unsolicited sumbissions are OK. Prefers cassette with full project demo and lyric sheet. Does not return unsolicited material. Reports in 4 weeks.
Music: Jazz and country; also R&B and pop. Released "If It Wasn't For Time" written and recorded by Borthwick (country); "Take One" written and recorded by Robinson (jazz) and *Sound of Christmas* (by various), recorded by Lory Dobbs on Casaro Records (big band/LP), all on Casaro Records. Other artists include Marcia Dekorte, Pam Dacus, John Peters and Charlie Robinson.
Tips: "Produce your song well (in tune—good singer). It doesn't need to be highly produced—just clear vocals. Include lyric sheet."

*THE CCC GROUP, INC., Box 853, Ridgeland MS 39158. Professional Manager: King Corbett. Labels include Pleasure Records. Record company. Estab. 1987. Releases 12 singles and 12 LPs/year. Works with musicians/artists and songwriters on contract. Pays 10-20% royalty to artists on contract; statutory rate to publisher per song on record.
How to Contact: Prefers cassette with 2 to 4 songs and lyric or lead sheet. SASE. Reports in 6 weeks.
Music: Mostly traditional country; also spoken word, folk and jazz.
Tips: "Send clean lyric sheets, labels on cassettes."

CDE RECORDS AND TAPES, Box 310551, Atlanta GA 30331. (404)344-7621. President: Charles Edwards. Labels include TBS Records, Tapes Inc. and Nationwide Black Radio. Record Company. Estab. 1978. Releases 4-8 singles, 2-3 12″ singles, 2-5 LPs and 2-5 CDs/year. Receives 3-5 submissions/ month. Works with musicians/artists on contract. Pays negotiable royalty to artists on contract.
How To Contact: Submit demo tape by mail. Prefers cassette (or VHS videocassette) with "several" songs. Does not return unsolicited material. Reports ASAP.
Music: Mostly interested in urban and rap; also gospel, R&B, jazz and pop. Released "Come Inside the Radio" (written and recorded by Chago) on CDE (urban single).
Tips: "Be strong; keep the faith and don't give up. The music business needs new and creative people."

CENTURY CITY RECORDS AND TAPES OF CANADA, 2207 Halifax Cres. N.W., Calgary Alberta T2M 4E1 **Canada.** (403)282-2555. Vice President: Deborah Anderson. Labels include Century City Records. Record company, music publisher (SOCAN) and record producer (Century City). Estab. 1983. Releases 1-2 singles, 1-2 12″ singles, 1-2 Lps, 1-2 EPs and 1-2 CDs/year. Works with musicians/ artists and songwriters on contract and hires musicians for in-house studio work. Pays 5-10% royalty to artists on contract; statutory rate to publishers per song on record.
How to Contact: Write or call first and obtain permission to submit. Prefers cassette or VHS videocassette with 4 songs, lyric sheets and lead sheets ("if available"). SASE. Reports in 1-4 weeks.
Music: Mostly country rock, rock and folk rock; also alternative, New Age and blues. Released "Hand Me Down Clown" (by W. R. Hutchinson), recorded by Warren Anderson (folk rock single); "1,000 Miles Away," written and recorded by Damian Follett (folk rock single); and *Hot From the Streets*, written and recorded by Warren Anderson (rock LP); all on Century City Records. Other artists include Thieves of Silence, Johnny 7, and Rattle Snake Kane.
Tips: "We are very interested in working with artists who have a proven background demonstrated by previous record sales statistics, cult following, media attention, etc. We are also interested in Alberta bands with a western flavour such as K.D. Lang, George Fox, Steve Earle-type music."

CENTURY RECORDS, INC., Box 4094, Pittsburgh PA 15201. (412)781-4557. President: Edward J. Moschetti. Labels include Star Records. Record company. Works with songwriters on contract.
How to Contact: Prefers cassette. SASE. Reports in 2 weeks.
Music: Country; all types of music.

CHA-CHA RECORDS, 902 North Webster St., Port Washington WI 53074. (414)284-3279. President: Joseph C. De Lucia. Labels include Cha-Cha, Cap and Debby. Record company, record producer, and music publisher (Don-Del Music/BMI). Estab. 1955. Releases 1 single and 1 LP/year. Receives 3 submissions/month. Works with artists/musicians and songwriters on contract. Pays negotiable royalty to artists on contract and pubilshers per song on record.

Listings of companies in countries other than the U.S. have the name of the country in boldface type.

How to Contact: Prefers cassette with 4-6 songs and lyric sheet. SASE. Reports in 3 months.
Music: Country, folk, acoustic jazz, rock, and religious. Released *99 Chicks*, by Ron Haydock and the Boppers (rock LP); and "The Jogging Song" by J. DeLucia. Other artists include Don Glasser and Lois Costello.

*CHATTAHOOCHEE RECORDS, 15230 Weddington St., Van Nuys CA 91411. (818)788-6863. Contact: Chris Yardum. Record company and music publisher (Etnoc/Conte). Member NARAS. Releases 4 singles/year. Works with artists and songwriters on contract. Pays negotiable royalty to artists on contract.
How to Contact: Submit demo tape—unsolicited submissions are OK. Prefers cassette with 2-6 songs and lyric sheet. SASE. Reports in 6 weeks "if interested."
Music: Rock.

CHERRY RECORDS, 9717 Jensen Dr., Houston TX 77093. (713)695-3648. Vice President: A.V. Mittelstedt. Labels include AV Records, Music Creek. Record company, music publisher (Pen House Music/BMI) and record producer (AV Mittelstedt Productions). Estab. 1970. Releases 10 singles and 5 LPs/year. Works with musicians/artists and songwriters on contract and hires musicians for in-house studio work. Pays varying royalty to artists on contract; statutory rate to publishers per song on record.
How to Contact: Submit demo tape—unsolicited submissions are OK. Prefers cassette with 2 songs. SASE. Reports in 3 weeks.
Music: Mostly country and pop. Released "Too Cold at Home" (by B. Hardin), recorded by Mark Chestnutt on Cherry Records (country); "Girls Like Her" (by Wimberly-Hart), recorded by Mark Chestnutt on Cherry Records (country); and "Half of Me" (by Wimberly/Trevino), recorded by Geronimo Trevino on AV Records (country crossover). Other artists include Randy Cornor, Roy Hilad, Georgie Dearborne, Kenny Dale, Karla Taylor and Borderline.

*CHERRY STREET RECORDS, Box 52681, Tulsa OK 74152. (918)742-8087. President: Rodney Young. Record company, music publisher. Estab. 1990. Releases 2 CD/year. Works with musicians/artists and songwriters on contract. Pays 5-15% royalty to artists on contract; statutory rate to publisher per song on record.
How to Contact: Write or call first and obtain permission to submit. Prefers cassette (or Beta or VHS videocassette) with 4 songs and lyric sheet. SASE. Reports in 4-6 months.
Music: Mostly rock, country, R&B; also instrumental jazz. Released *Blue Dancer* (by Chris Blevins) on CSR Records (country rock). Other artists include Larry Robkoff, Jackie Fishell, Brad Absher.
Tips: "We are a songwriter label—the song is more important to us than the artist. Send only your best 4 songs."

CIMIRRON/RAINBIRD RECORDS, 607 Piney Point Rd., Yorktown VA 23692. (804)898-8155. President: Lana Puckett. Vice President: Kim Person. Record company. Releases 2-3 singles, 3 LPs, 1 EP and 1 CD/year. Works with musicians/artists on contract. Pays variable royalty to artists on contract. Pays statutory rate.
How to Contact: Write. Prefers cassette with 1-3 songs and lyric sheet. SASE. Reports in 3 months.
Music: Mostly country-bluegrass, New Age and pop. Released "Nutcracker Suite," written and recorded by Steve Bennett (guitar) and "Forever and Always" (by Lana Puckett and Kim Person), recorded by Lana & Kim (country LP); all on Cimirron/Rainbow Records.

CITA COMMUNICATIONS INC., Dept. SM, 676 Pittsburgh Rd., Butler PA 16001. (412)586-6552. A&R/Producer: Mickii Taimuty. Labels include Phunn! Records and Tropē Records. Record company. Estab. 1989. Releases 6 singles, 3 12" singles, 3 LPs, 2 EPs and 5 CDs/year. Works with musicians/artists on record contract. Pays artists 10% royalty on contract. Pays statutory rate to publishers per song on records.
How to Contact: Call first and obtain permission to submit. Prefers cassette (or VHS, Beta or ¾" videocassette if available) with a maximum of 6 songs and lyric sheets. SASE. Reports in 8 weeks.
Music: Interested in rock/dance music and contemporary gospel; also rap, jazz and progressive country. Released "Forged by Fire", written and recorded by Sanxtion on Tropē Records; "I Cross My Heart" (by Taimuty/Nelson), recorded by Melissa Anne on Phunn! Records; and "Fight the Fight," written and recorded by M.J. Nelson on Tropē Records. Other artists include Most High, Sister Golden Hair and Countdown.

CITY PIGEON RECORDS, Box 43135, Upper Montclair NJ 07043. (201)857-2935. President: Richard Reiter. Record company. Estab. 1983. Releases 3 LPs and 3 CDs/year. Receives 25-30 submissions/year. Works with musicians/artists on contract. Pays 10-13% royalty to artists on contract; statutory rate to publishers per song on record.

How to Contact: Write first and obtain permission to submit. Prefers cassette with 3 songs and lyric or lead sheet. SASE. Reports back in 2 weeks.
Music: Mostly jazz; also pop. Released "My Man Mike" and "Color Blind" (by Richard Reiter; "Mel's BBQ" (by James West), all recorded by Crossing Point on City Pigeon/Optimism Records (contemporary jazz). Other artists include Lou Caimano.

CLAY & CLAY, INC., 19938 Patton, Detroit MI 48219. (313)533-4506. Labels include Torrid, Scorcher, Claycastle, 2 Hot. Record company, Music publisher (Lynclay Publications/ASCAP) and record producer. Estab. 1988. Releases 12 singles and 4 LPs/year. Works with musicians/artists and songwriters on contract and hires musicians for in-house studio work. Payment negotiable.
How to Contact: Submit demo tape by mail. Unsolicited submissions are OK. Prefers cassette or VHS videocassette with minimum of 3 songs and lyric or lead sheets. SASE. Reports in 1 month "if interested."
Music: Released "I Want to Be Ready" (by D. Arnold), recorded by Mighty Wings on Claycastle Records (gospel single); "Gettin' 'Em On" (by L. Clay), recorded by Mr. Mill on Torrid Records (rap 12″); and "I Ain't Buyin' It" (by D. Davis/D. Fielderl, M. Field), recorded by D.O.P. on Scorcher Records (rap 12″). Other artists include Jesse Douglas, Relana Harris, Total Darkness, Jamal Morson, Brenda Wilson-Johnson, TCs Tempo, Twan.
Tips: "Submit your best work and understand it doesn't happen overnight."

*CLOUDBURST RECORDS, Box 31, Edmonton KY 42129. (502)432-3183. President: Rev. Junior Lawson. Record company and music publisher (Holy Spirit Music). Releases 3 singles and 4 LPs/year. Works with songwriters on contract. Pays 4% royalty to artists on contract.
How to Contact: Call first. Prefers 7½ ips reel-to-reel or cassette and lyric sheet. SASE. Reports in 3 weeks.
Music: Mostly southern gospel; also country, gospel, MOR and progressive. Released *Introducing the Cornerstones* and *Extra! Extra!*, by The Cornerstones (southern gospel LPs); and *Old-Fashioned Ways*, by the Sounds of Joy (southern gospel LP). Other artists include The Southern-Aires.

CLOWN RECORDS, Box 357, Ridgefield NJ 07660. (201)641-5749. President: C.A. Pruitt. Record company (BMI). Estab. 1987. Works with musicians/artists and songwriters on contract and hires musicians for in-house studio work. Pays negotiable royalty to artists on contract; statutory rate to publisher per song on record. Charges for services in advance "depending on the contract."
How to Contact: Submit demo tape—unsolicited submissions are OK. Prefers cassette and lyric or lead sheet. SASE.

COLLECTOR RECORDS, Box 2296, Rotterdam 3000 CG **Holland**. Phone: (1862)4266. FAX: 1862-4366. Research: Cees Klop. Labels include All Rock, Downsouth, Unknown, Pro Forma and White Label Records. Record company, music publisher (All Rock Music Pub.) and record producer (Cees Klop). Estab. 1967. Releases 10 singles and 30 LPs/year. Works with musicians/artists and songwriters on contract. Pays standard royalty to artist on contract.
How to Contact: Prefers cassette. SAE and IRC. Reports in 1 month.
Music: Mostly 50's rock, rockabilly, hillbilly boogie and country/rock; also piano boogie woogie. Released "Spring in April" (by Pepping/Jellema), recorded by Henk Pepping on Down South Records (50's rock); "Go Cat Go" (by Myers), recorded by Jimmy Myers on White Label Records (50's rock) and "Knocking On the Backside" (by T. Redell), recorded by T. Redell on White Label Records (50's rock).

COMMA RECORDS & TAPES, Postbox 2148, 6078 Neu-Isenburg, **Germany**. Phone: (6102)52696. General Manager: Roland Bauer. Labels include Big Sound, Comma International and Max-Banana-Tunes. Record company. Estab. 1969. Releases 50-70 singles and 20 LPs/year. Works with musicians/artists and songwriters on contract. Pays 7-10% royalty to artists on contract.
How to Contact: Prefers cassette and lyric sheet. Reports in 3 weeks. "Do not send advanced letter asking permission to submit, just send your material, SAE and minimum two IRCs."
Music: Mostly pop, disco, rock, R&B and country; also musicals.

COMSTOCK RECORDS LTD., Suite 114, 10603 N. Hayden Rd., Scottsdale AZ 85260. (602)951-3115. FAX: (602)951-3074. Canadian, United States and European distribution on Paylode & Comstock Records. Production Manager/Producer: Patty Parker. President: Frank Fara. Record company, music publisher (White Cat Music/ASCAP, Rocky Bell Music/BMI, How the West Was Sung Music/BMI), Nashville Record Production, and International Record Promotions. Member CMA, BBB, CCMA, BCCMA, British & French C&W Associations, and CARAS. "Comstock Records, Ltd. has three primary divisions: Production, Promotion and Publishing. We distribute and promote both our self-produced recordings and outside master product." Releases 24-30 singles and 5-6 CDs/year. Receives

30-40 submissions/month. Works with artists and songwriters on contract; musicians on salary. Pays 10% royalty to artists on contract; statutory rate to publishers for each record sold. "Artists pay distribution and promotion fee to press and release their masters."

How to Contact: Submit demo tape—unsolicited submissions OK. Prefers cassette (or VHS videocassette) with 1-4 songs "plus word sheet. Enclose stamped return envelope if cassette is to be returned." Reports in 2 weeks.

Music: Western music, A/C and country. Released "I Saw You Look At Her" by Inger and Her Rhinestone Band; "Big Boys Don't Cry" by Jess Owen; and "Thunder Across the Desert" by Tom and Becki Chambers. Other artists include The Roberts Sisters, Eldon Fault, Jodie Sinclair, Colin Clark, Carl Freberg, Tianna Lefebre and Ray Dean James.

Tips: "We have an immediate need for country material for our European division. Our international division consists of master distribution and promotion to the following nations: England, France, Germany, Belgium, Ireland, Luxembourg, The Netherlands, Scotland, Switzerland, Norway and Canada. Also Denmark and Austria. We do video promotion with air play promotions to C&W networks across North America."

CONCORDE INTERNATIONAL RECORDS, Box 24454, Nashville TN 37202. (615)269-7074. FAX: (615)269-0131. A&R: Clayton Cooper. Record company. Estab. 1990. Releases 3-4 singles and 1-2 LPS/year. Pays statutory rate.

How to Contact: Submit demo tape—unsolicited submissions are OK. "No more than 2 at a time." Prefers cassette. SASE. Reports in 2-3 weeks.

Music: Mostly country, A/C and Christian; also MOR and Christmas. Released "Can't You Just Stay Gone" (by S. Ewing/D. Sampson); "Nothin That A Little Love" (by P. Tillis/P. Brown-Hayes) and "I, The Injured Party" (by D. Scott) all recorded by Debra Dudley on Concorde International (country).

Tips: "Make sure that the hook is fresh, not overdone, be careful to be professional in the sound of submissions. Submit newer material (not more than a few years old if it has shown no previous success)."

COSMOTONE RECORDS, Box 71988, Los Angeles CA 90071-0988. Labels include Cosmotone Music and Center for the Queen of Peace. Record company and music publisher. Estab. 1984. Releases 1 single, 1 12″ single and 1 LP/year. Works with songwriters on contract and hires musicians on salary for in-house studio work. Pays statutory rate to publishers per song on record.

How to Contact: Write first and obtain permission to submit. Prefers cassette (or VHS videocassette). "Will contact only if interested."

Music: All types. Released "Padre Pio," written and recorded by Lord Hamilton on Cosmotone Records (Christian/pop/rock); and "The Sounds of Heaven" and "Peace of Heart," by Rafael Brom (Christian progressive).

COUNTRY BREEZE RECORDS, 1715 Marty, Kansas City KS 66103. (913)384-4454. President: Ed Morgan. Labels include Country Breeze Records, Angel Star Records and Midnight Shadow Records. Record company, music publisher (Country Breeze Music/BMI and Walkin' Hat Music/ASCAP). Releases 15 7″ singles and 20 cassettes/year. Receives 130 submissions/month. Works with musicians/artists and songwriters on contract. Pays 25% royalty to artists on contract; statutory rate to publisher per song on record.

How to Contact: Submit demo tape—unsolicited submissions are OK. Prefers studio-produced demo with 3 songs and lyric sheet. SASE. Reports in 2 weeks.

Music: All types country. Released "Hearts in the Night" and "Born in the Badlands" (by R. Velvin) recorded by Ian Coltaire and "Ain't No Boogie Bears Out Tonight" (T. Arthur/F. Arthur) recorded by Travis Arthur all on Country Breeze Records (country). Other artists include Chill Factor, Edging West.

Tips: "When submitting an artist package we require 3 of your best songs, a short bio and recent photo. Make sure your voice is out front and the songs are strong, both in lyrics and melody."

COUNTRY SHOWCASE AMERICA, 14134 Brighton Dam Rd., Clarksville MD 21029-1327. (301)854-2917. President: Francis Gosman. Record company. Estab. 1971. Releases 5 singles/year. Receives 6 submissions/month. Works with musicians/artists and songwriters on contract. Pays 3% royalty to artists on contract; statutory rate to publishers for each record sold.

How to Contact: Submit demo tape—unsolicited submissions are OK. Prefers cassette and lyric sheet. SASE. Replies in 1 month.

Music: Country. Released "More Than Once In A While" and "Almost In Love" (by Fisher/Weller); and "Tent Meeting Blues" (by Gosman/Vague) all recorded by Johnny Anthony on CSA Records (country).

Tips: "Keep it simple, with words understandable."

COUNTRY STAR INTERNATIONAL, 439 Wiley Ave., Franklin PA 16323. (814)432-4633. President: Norman Kelly. Labels include CSI, Country Star, Process and Mersey Records. Record company, music publisher (Country Star/ASCAP, Process and Kelly/BMI) and record producer (Country Star Productions). Member AFM and AFTRA. Estab. 1970. Releases 10-15 singles and 8-10 LPs/year. Receives 400 submissions/year. Works with musician/artists and songwriters on contract. Works with lyricists and composers. Pays 8% royalty to artists on contract; statutory rate to publishers for each record sold. "Charges artists in advance only when they buy records to sell on personal appearances and show dates."
How to Contact: Prefers cassette with 2-4 songs and lyric or lead sheet. Unsolicited submission OK. SASE. Reports in 2 weeks.
Music: Mostly C&W and bluegrass. Released "Son of a Cowboy" (by J.A. Connors), recorded by Jeffrey Alan Connors (country); "Forever and a Day" (by E. and A. Jackson), recorded by Evelyn and Arlis Jackson; and "A Cowboy's Hope & Prayer" (by W. Inbelli), recorded by Bob Stamper; all on Country Star Records (country). Other artists include Tara Bailey, Bob Stamper and Ron Lauer.
Tips: "Send only your best efforts."

COWBOY JUNCTION FLEA MARKET AND PUBLISHING CO., Highway 44 W., Lecanto FL 32661. (904)746-4754. Contact: Elizabeth Thompson. Record company, record producer (Cowboy Junction Publishing Co.) and music publisher (Cowboy Junction Flea Market and Publishing Co.). Estab. 1957. Releases 3 or more singles, 1-2 12″ singles and 1-2 LPs/year. Receives 100 submissions/year. Works with musicians/artists and songwriters on contract. Pays 50% royalty.
How to Contact: Submit demo tape—unsolicited submissions are OK. Prefers cassette with 1-4 songs and lyric sheet. SASE. Reports ASAP.
Music: Country, gospel, bluegrass and C&W. Released "Desert Storm," "You Are the One" and "It Really Doesn't Matter Now" all by Boris Max Pastuch and recorded by Buddy Max on Cowboy Junction Records (C&W). Other artists include Izzy Miller, Wally Jones, Leo Vargason, Johnny Pastuck, Troy Holliday and Pappy Dunham.
Tips: "Come to one of our shows and present your song (Flea Market on Tuesdays and Fridays, country/bluegrass show every Saturday) or send a tape in."

COWGIRL RECORDS, Box 6085, Burbank CA 91510. Contact: Vice President. Record company and music publisher (Kingsport Creek). Estab. 1980. Works with musicians/artists and songwriters on contract. Pays statutory rate to publishers for each record sold.
How to Contact: Submit demo tape—unsolicited submissions OK. Prefers cassette (or VHS videocassette) with any number of songs and lyric sheet or lead sheet. Does not return unsolicited material. "Include a photo and bio if possible." Pays statutory rate.
Music: Mostly country, R&B, MOR and gospel. Released "My Dear Savior's Love" (gospel), "Picture on the Shelf" and "This Old Bar" (country) all by Melvena Kaye on Cowgirl Records.

CREOLE RECORDS, LTD., The Chilterns, France Hill Dr., Camberley Surrey GU153QA **United Kingdom.** 0276-686077. Managing Director: Bruce White. Labels include Creole, Dynamic, Revue, Cactus, Big, Past Replay. Record company and music publisher (PRS/MCPS—Creole Music Ltd.). Estab. 1966. Releases 15 singles, 15 12″ singles; 20-30 LPs and 20-30 CDs/year. Receives 30-40 submissions/month. Works with musicians/artists and songwriters. Pays artists 8-16% royalty; publishers standard MCPS.
How to Contact: Submit demo tape—unsolicited submissions are OK. Prefers cassette with 3 songs. SAE and IRC. Reports in 6-8 weeks.
Music: Mostly dance, pop and reggae; also oldies. Released *Worst of* (by various artists), recorded by Judge Dread (pop); *Reggae Hits* written and recorded by various artists (reggae); and *English Language* written and recorded by David Donaldson (spoken), all on Creole Records. Artists include Boris Gardiner, Peter Green, In Crowd, Desmond Dekker, Byron Lee, and 2 Dragonaires.

CRYSTAL RAM/APRIL RECORDS, 827 Brazil Pl., El Paso TX 79903. (915)772-7858. Owner: Harvey Marcus. Labels include Crystal Ram, April, T.S.B., and M.C.R. Records. Record company, music publisher and record producer (April Productions). Releases 1-3 singles, 1-3 12″ singles, 1-5 LPs, 1-5 EPs, and 1-3 CDs/year. Works with musicians/artists and songwriters on contract; hires musicians for in-house studio work. Pays 25% royalty to artists on contract; statutory rate to publisher per song on record.
How to Contact: Prefers cassette or 7½ ips reel-to-reel (or VHS videocssette) with one song and lyric or lead sheet. SASE. Reports in 6 weeks.
Music: Mostly jazz/pop, top 40 (ballads) and tex-mex; also country, New Age and Christian/rock. Released *Are We In This for Love* (EP) and "Baby Blue Baby" (single), written and recorded by The Street Boys on T.S.B. Records; and *Endless Dreams*, written and recorded by Ruben Castillo on Crystal Ram Records (LP). Other artists include Ray Justin Vega.

*CURRENT RECORDS, 418 Ontario St., Toronto ON M5A 2W1 **Canada**. (416)921-6535. A&R, New Projects: Trevor G. Shelton. Labels include Rammit Records. Record company, music publisher (Brand New Sounds, Today's Tunes Music, Current Sounds, Rammit Noise) affiliated with SOCAN performing rights organization. Record producer (Trevor G. Shelton). Estab. 1983. Releases 5-10 singles, 5-10 12" singles, 5 LPs, 5 cassettes and 5 CDs/year. Works with musicians/artists on contract. Pays statutory rate to publisher per song.
How to Contact: Submit demo tape by mail. Unsolicited submissions are OK. Prefers cassette with 4 songs. SAE and IRC. Reports in 3-4 weeks.
Music: Mostly rock, pop and dance; also hip hop and rap. Released *The Distance Between* (by Kromm/Arnott), recorded by Strange Advance (rock LP); *Alta Moda* (by Johnson/Orenstein), recorded by Alta Moda (dance/rock LP); and *Small Victories* (by Oates/Segato/Conger), recorded by The Parachute Club (dance LP); all on Current Records. Other artists include Martha and the Muffins, Machinations, Mystery Romance, Andy McLean.
Tips: "Realize you may be turned down, but work hard—don't be discouraged by "thank you—but no thanks" form letters. Keep writing and if A&R departments suggest ideas of improving your material—listen to them, if you think comments are valid, use them."

CURTISS RECORDS, Box 1622, Hendersonville TN 37077. (615)822-1044. President: Wade Curtiss. Record company and producer. Works with artists and songwriters on contract. Pays 15¢/record royalty to artists on contract; 5¢/record royalty to songwriters on contract.
How to Contact: Submit demo tape—unsolicited submissions OK. Prefers cassette with 2-8 songs and lead sheet. SASE. Reports in 3 weeks.
Music: Bluegrass, blues, country, disco, folk, gospel, jazz, rock, soul and top 40/pop. Released "Sex to be Had" by Mickey Finn on Terock Records (hard rock); "Brang" (by E. Bentley) recorded by Rhythm Rockers on Curtiss Records (instr. rock) and "Changes" written and recorded by R. Derwald on Terock Records (country).

D.J. INTERNATIONAL, INC., Dept. SM, 727 W. Randolph St., Chicago IL 60661. (312)559-1845. A&R Director: Martin Luna. Labels include Underground, Fierce, Gangster, Rythm, Mutant. Record company and record producer. Estab. 1985. Releases 75 12" singles and 35 LPs/year. Works with musicians/artists and songwriters on contract and hires musicians for in-house studio work. Payment varies.
How to Contact: Submit demo tape—unsolicited submissions are OK. Prefers cassette with 3 songs and lyric sheets. Does not return unsolicited material.
Music: Mostly dance, house, alternative; also tracks.

DAGENE RECORDS, Box 410851, San Francisco CA 94141. (415)822-1530. President: David Alston. Labels include Dagene Records and Cabletown Corp. Record company, music publisher (Dagene Music) and record producer (David-Classic Disc Productions). Estab. 1987. Works with musicians/artists and songwriters on contract and hires musicians on salary for in-house studio work. Pays statutory rate to publishers per song on record.
How to Contact: Write or call first and obtain permission to submit. Prefers cassette (or VHS videocassette) with 2 songs and lyric sheet. Does not return unsolicited material.
Music: Mostly R&B/rap, dance and pop; also gospel. Released "Mind Ya Own" (by Bernard Henderson/Marcus Justice) recorded by 2WO Dominatorz on Dagene Records; "Started Life" (by David/M. Campbell) recorded by Star Child on Dagene Records and "Lies" written and recorded by David on Cabletown Records (all rap 12"). Other artists include "The D."

DARK HORSE PRODUCTIONS, 1729 N. Third Ave., Upland CA 91786. (714)946-1398. A&R Director: Bill Huff. Record company, music publisher (see Lizard Licks Music, BMI), record producer (Dark Horse Productions). Estab. 1988. Releases 2 LPs and 2 CDs/year. Works with musicians/artists on contract. Pays 6-9% royalty on retail price; statutory rate to publishers per song on records.
How to Contact: Submit demo tape by mail. Prefers cassette with 3-5 songs. SASE. Reports in 4 weeks.
Music: Mostly contemporary jazz, New Age, and traditional jazz. Released *Iridescence* (by Brad Kaenel), recorded by Polyhedra on Dark Horse Records (contemporary jazz) and *Simply Simon* (by D.J. Alverson), recorded by Polyhedra on Dark Horse (contemporary jazz).

*DAT BEAT RECORDS, INC., Suite 4303, 333 E. Ontario, Chicago IL 60611. (312)751-0906. Contact: Robert Shelist. Labels include UBAD Records. Record company. Estab. 1989. Works with musicians/artists and songwriters on contract and hires musicians for in-house studio work. Pays 5-15% royalty to artists on contract; rate to publisher per song on record varies.

How to Contact: Submit demo tape—unsolicited submissions are OK. Prefers cassette with 4 songs and lyric sheet or lead sheet. Does not return unsolicited material. Reports in 2-3 weeks.
Music: Mostly rap, pop, dance; also R&B, rock and New Age. Released *Fever for the Flavor* written and recorded by O.Z. on UBAD Records (LP); *Strictly Soul* recorded by 2 Damn on Dat Beat Records (LP).

DEMI MONDE RECORDS AND PUBLISHING, LTD., Foel Studio, Llanfair Caereinion, Powys, Wales, **United Kingdom**. Phone: (0938)810758. Managing Director: Dave Anderson. Record company and music publisher (Demi Monde Records & Publishing, Lts.) and record producer (Dave Anderson). Estab. 1983. Releases 5 12" singles, 10 LPs and 6 CDs/year. Works with musicians/artists and songwriters on contract; hires musicians for in-house studio work. Pays 10-12% royalty to artists on contract; statutory rate to publisher per song on record.
How to Contact: Prefers cassette with 3-4 songs. SAE and IRC. Reports in 1 month.
Music: Rock, R&B and pop. Released *Hawkwind* and *Amon Duul II & Gong* (by Band), and *Ground-hogs* (by T.S. McPhee), all on Demi Monde Records (LPs).

DHARMA RECORDS, Box 615, 117 W. Rockland Rd., Libertyville IL 60048. (708)362-4060. Vice President: Rick Johnson. Labels include Future and Homexercise. Record company, record producer and music publisher (Amalgamated Tulip Corp.). Releases 3 singles and 2 LPs/year. Works with artists and songwriters on contract. Pays negotiable royalty to artists on contract; negotiable rate to publishers for each record sold.
How to Contact: Prefers cassette with 3-5 songs and lyric sheet. Prefers studio produced demos. SASE. Reports in 6 months.
Music: Rock, top 40/pop, country, dance/R&B, MOR and progressive rock. Released *Active Music for Children*, by Bill Hooper (education LP); "Oh Boy," by Oh Boy (pop rock single); and *Not Marmosets Yet*, by Conrad Black (rock LP).

DISQUES NOSFERATU RECORDS, C.P. 304 Succ. S, Montreal Quebec H4E 4J8 **Canada**. (514)769-9096. Promotion Director: Ginette Provost. Record company. Estab. 1986. Releases 1 12" single and 1 cassette/year. Receives 100 submissions per year. Works with musicians/artists on contract and hires musicians for in-house studio work. Pays statutory rate to publishers per song on records.
How to Contact: Submit demo tape—unsolicited submissions OK. Prefers cassette or VHS videocassette with 3 songs and lyric sheet. Does not return unsolicited submissions. Reports in 3 to 6 months.
Music: Mostly rock and blues; also instrumental and heavy metal. Released "Brulée Parle Blues" (by Fee Ross), recorded by Nosferatu (blues/rock); "Hollywood" (by Fee Ross), recorded by Nosferatu (rock); and "Barracuda Blues" (by J.J. LaBlonde), recorded by Nosferatu (blues/rock).
Tips: "Any artist who signs with us must have stage experience."

DOMINO RECORDS, LTD., Ridgewood Park Estates, 222 Tulane St., Garland TX 75043. Contact: Gene or Dea Summers. Public Relations/Artist and Fan Club Coordinator: Steve Summers. Labels include Front Row Records. Record company and music publisher (Silicon Music/BMI). Estab. 1968. Releases 5-6 singles and 2-3 LPs/year. Works with artists and songwriters on contract. Pays negotiable royalties to artists on contract; standard royalty to songwriters on contract.
How to Contact: Prefers cassette (or VHS videocassette) with 1-3 songs. Does not return unsolicited material. SASE. Reports ASAP.
Music: Mostly 50's rock/rockabilly; also country, bluegrass, old-time blues and R&B. Released "The Music of Jerry Lee," by Joe Hardin Brown (country single); "Ready to Ride," (from the HBO Presentation *Backlot*), by Pat Minter (country single); and *Les Rois Du Rockabilly* and *Juke Box Rock and Roll*, by Gene Summers (50s LPs) and "School of Rock 'N Roll" by Gene Summers (50s EP).
Tips: "If you own masters of 1950s rock and rock-a-billy, contact us first! We will work with you on a percentage basis for overseas release. We have active releases in Holland, Switzerland, Belgium, Australia, England, France, Sweden, Norway and the US at the present. We need original masters. You must be able to prove ownership of tapes before we can accept a deal. We're looking for little-known, obscure recordings. We have the market if you have the tapes! Sample records available. Send SASE for catalogue."

DUPUY RECORDS/PRODUCTIONS/PUBLISHING, INC., 2505 North Verdugo Rd., Glendale CA 91208. (818)241-6732. President: Pedro Dupuy. Record company, record producer and music publisher (Dupuy Publishing, Inc./ASCAP). Releases 5 singles and 3 LPs/year. Works with artists and songwriters on contract; musicians on salary for in-house studio work. Pays negotiable rate to publishers for each record sold.

How to Contact: Write or call first or arrange personal interview. Prefers cassette with 2-4 songs and lyric sheet. SASE. Reports in 1 month.
Music: Easy listening, jazz, MOR, R&B, soul and top 40/pop. Artists include Joe Warner, John Anthony, Robert Feeney, Jon Rider and Kimo Kane.
Tips: Needs "very definite lyrics with hook."

*DYNAMITE, 5 Aldom Circle, West Caldwell NJ 07006. Owner: Tar Heel Pete. Labels include Dynamite, Deadwood and Tar Heel. Record company, record producer and music publisher (Cactus Music and Gidget Publishing/ASCAP). Estab. 1974. Releases 3 singles, 2 cassettes and 1 EP/year. Works with musicians/artists and songwriters on contract.
How to Contact: Write first about your interest. Does not return unsolicited material. Reports in 1 month.
Music: Jazz, R&B, country western, gospel and rock. Released "Have Faith in Jesus" (by Bob Rose) recorded by Tony Ansems on Tar Heel Records (bluegrass, gospel); "What Used to Be" written and recorded by Jimmy Glass on Dynamite Records (country) and "I Just Can't Let You" (by Clevenger Hall) recorded by Audrey Squires on Dynamite Records (country).

E.S.R. RECORDS, 61 Burnthouse Lane, Exeter Devon EX2 6AZ U.K.. Phone: (0392)57880. M.D: John Greenslade. Labels include E.S.R. Label. Record company (P.R.S.) and record producer (E.S.R. Productions). Estab. 1965. Releases 4 singles and 10 LPs/year. Works with musicians on salary for in-house studio work. Pays standard royalty; statutory rate to publisher per song on records.
How to Contact: Submit demo tape by mail—unsolicited submissions are OK. Prefers cassette with 4 songs and lyric sheet. SASE. Reports in 1 month.
Music: Mostly country and MOR. Released "The Best Is Yet To Come" (by John Greenslade), recorded by Marty Henry (country single); "Tomorrow" (by John Greenslade), recorded by Mascarade (MOR); and "A Kind Of Loving" (by T. Jennings), recorded by Mike Scott (MOR), all on E.S.R. Records.

EAST COAST RECORDS INC., 604 Glover Dr., Runnemede NJ 08078. (609)931-8389. President: Anthony J. Messina. Record company and music publisher. Releases 10 singles and 3 LPs/year. Works with artists and songwriters on contract. Pays 4-7% royalty to artists on contract; standard royalty to songwriters on contract.
How to Contact: Prefers 7½ ips reel-to-reel or cassette with 3-12 songs and lyric sheet. SASE. Reports in 3 weeks.
Music: Classical, MOR, rock, and top 40/pop. Released "Remembering," by Lana Cantrell (MOR single); "Drifting Away," by Uproar (rock single); and *England Made Me* (soundtrack from the motion picture), by London Philharmonic (classical LP). Other artists include Lynn Redgrave, Harold Melvin & The Bluenotes, Dakota and Aviator.

*EMZEE RECORDS, Box 3213, S. Farmingdale NY 11735. (212)724-2800, (516)420-9169. President: Dawn Kendall. Labels include Ivory Tower Records. Record company, music publisher (Emzee Music/BMI). Estab. 1970. Releases 35 singles, 20 12″ singles, 15 LPs, 15 EPs, 20 CDs/year. Works with musicians/artists and songwriters on contract and hires musicians for in-house studio work. Royalty to artists on contract varies; statutory rate to publisher per song on record.
How to Contact: Submit demo tape—unsolicited submissions are OK. Prefers cassette with 3 songs and lyric sheet. SASE.
Music: Mostly pop, rock, country; also R&B and gospel. Released *Sleepwalk Talking* written and recorded by Emma Zale (rock LP) and *Please Tell Me* (by Tony Novarro), recorded by Emma Zale (rock/pop LP) both on Ivory Tower Records; "Richest Man" (by John Schactel), recorded by John Sanders on Emzee Records (pop/Latin single). Other artists include Ray Bennett and The Breed, John Jace, Mark Regula.
Tips: "Be persistent and patient."

ESB RECORDS, Box 6429, Huntington Beach CA 92615-6429. (714)962-5618. Executive Producers: Eva and Stan Bonn. Record company, music publisher (Bonnfire Publishing/ASCAP, Gather' Round/BMI), record producer (ESB Records). Estab. 1987. Releases one 1 single, 1 LP and 1 CD/year. Works with musicians/artists and songwriters on contract. Pays negotiable royalty to artists; pays statutory rate to publisher per song on record.
How to Contact: Call first. SASE. Reports in one month.
Music: Mostly country, country/pop, MOR/country; also gospel. Released "You're Workin On Leaving Me" (by Bonn/Cyril Philpott) recorded by Bobby Lee Caldwell; "Toe Tappin Country Man" and "Three Reasons" (by Schroeder) recorded by John P. Swisshelm, all on ESB Records (country).

ETIQUETTE/SUSPICIOUS RECORDS, 2442 N.W. Market #273, Seattle WA 98107. (206)524-1020; FAX: (206)524-1102. President: Buck Ormsby. Labels include Etiquette Records and Suspicious Records. Record company and music publisher (see Valet Publishing). Estab. 1962. Releases 2-3 CDs/year. Receives 300-900 submissions/year. Works with musicians/artists and songwriters on contract. Pays varying royalty to artists on contract. Pays statutory or negotiated rate to publisher per song on record.
How to Contact: Submit demo tape—unsolicited submissions are OK. Prefers cassette with 3-4 songs and lyric sheets. SASE. Reports in 6-8 weeks.
Music: Mostly R&B, rock and pop; also country. Released "Witch," "Psycho" "Don't Believe In Christmas" all (by J. Roslie), recorded by Sonics on Etiquette Records (rock).
Tips: "Tapes submitted should be top quality—lyric sheets professional."

EXCURSION RECORDS, Box 9248, San Jose CA 95157. President: Frank T. Prins. Labels include Echappee Records. Record company, music publisher. ASCAP, BMI. Record producer (Frank T. Prins). Estab. 1982. Releases 2-5 singles, 1 LP and 1 EP/year. Works with musicians/artists and songwriters on contract. Pays 5-6% royalty to artists on contract; statutory rate to publisher per song on record.
How to Contact: Submit demo tape—unsolicited submissions OK. Prefers cassette (or VHS videocassette if available) with 3 songs and lyric sheet and lead sheet. SASE. Reports in 2 weeks.
Music: Mostly pop, rock and country; also gospel and R&B. Released "Rose" (country) and "Brotherly Love" (R&B) (by Robert Hepfner) recorded by Bobby C on Excursion Records. Other artists include Tim Patrick and Destiny.
Tips: "Keep writing and develop craft!"

EXECUTIVE RECORDS, 18 Harvest Lane, Charlotte NC 28210. (704)554-1162. Executive Producer: Butch Kelly Montgomery. Labels include KAM, Executive and Fresh Avenue Records. Record company, record producer (Butch Kelly Productions), music publisher (Butch Kelly Publishing/BMI and Music by Butch Kelly/BMI) and songwriter. Member AGAC. Estab. 1982. Releases 10 singles, 7 12" singles, 3 LPs and 1 CD/year. Receives 100 submissions/year. Works with musicians/artists songwriters on contract; hires musicians for in-house studio work. Pays 50% to artists on contract; statutory rate to publishers for each record sold. "$10 consulting fee."
How to Contact: Submit demo tape—unsolicited submissions are OK. Prefers cassette "on Maxell UDS-II tapes only" (or videocassette) with 3 songs and lyric sheet, pictures and bio. SASE. Submit pictures with demo. Reports in 5 weeks to 2 months.
Music: Mostly R&B, pop dance, rock, top 40, rap and country. Released "Power" (by Butch Kelly), recorded by M.C. Crush on KAM Records (pop); and "Heat It Up" (pop) and "Want to Love You" (R&B) written and recorded by Linda Strate on KAM Records.
Tips: "Keep up with what's playing on radio's top 10."

EYE KILL RECORDS, Box 242, Woodland PA 16881. A&R: John Wesley. Record company and music publisher (Eye Kill/ASCAP). Estab. 1987. Releases 4 singles, 6 12" singles, 10 LPs, 10 EPs and 10 CDs/year. Works with songwriters on contract. Pays statutory rate to publisher per song on record.
How to Contact: Submit demo tape—unsolicited submissions are OK. Prefers cassette with 3 songs and lyric sheets. SASE. Reports in 3 weeks.
Music: Mostly country and rock; also southern rock. Released "JC Carr," written and recorded by Lori Gator (country); "So Far Away," written and recorded by Lori Gator (country); and "Helpless," written and recorded by RJ Walli (country); all on Eyekill Records.
Tips: "Send good clean cassettes of your best 3 songs."

FACTORY BEAT RECORDS, INC., 521 5th Ave., New York NY 10175. (212)757-3638. A&R Director: Rena L. Romano. Labels include R&R, Ren Rom and Can Scor Productions, Inc. Record company, record producer and music publisher (Ren-Maur Music Corp.). Member NARAS, BMI and Songwriters Guild. Releases 4 12" singles and 2 LPs/year. Works with musicians/artists and songwriters on contract; hires musicians for in-house studio work. Pays 4-12% royalty to artists on contract; statutory rate to publishers for each record sold.
How to Contact: Submit cassette with 4 songs and lead sheet. SASE. Reports in 1 month. "Do not phone—we will return material."
Music: Mostly R&B, pop rock and country; also gospel. Released "That's Hot" (by B. Nichols) and "Rise Up" (by B. Nichols/R. Feeney), both recorded by Rena on Factory Beat Records (12" singles).

FAME AND FORTUNE ENTERPRISES, P.O. Box 121679, Nashville TN 37212. (615)244-4898. Producer: Jim Cartwright or Scott Turner. Labels include National Foundation Records and Fame and Fortune Records. Record company, music publisher (Boff Board Music/BMI) and record producer. Estab. 1976. Releases 6 singles, 6 LPs and 6 CDs/year. Receives 200-400 submissions/month. Works with musicians/artists and songwriters on contract. Pays statutory rate to publishers per song on records. Charges for "production services on recordings sessions."

How to Contact: Submit demo tape—unsolicited submissions are OK. Prefers cassette or VHS videocassette with 4 songs and lyric sheet. SASE. Reports in 3-6 weeks.

Music: Mostly country, MOR, med. rock, and pop. Released "The Last Parade," written and recorded by Scott Stallard on Independent Records; "Waltz Across Texas," written and recorded by Yodelin' Lolita; and "Room for Two" written and recorded by Marty James, both on Fame and Fortune Records (all country). Other artists include Angel Connell, Teresa Dalton, Paulette Tyler, Robert Wood and Marty James.

FAMOUS DOOR RECORDS, 1A-1 Estate St. Peter, St. Thomas USVI 00802. (809)775-7428. Contact: Harry Lim. Record company. Member NARAS. Releases 6 LPs/year. Works with artists on contract. Pays 5% in royalty to artists on contract; statutory rate to publishers for each record sold.

How to Contact: Write first. Prefers cassette with minimum 3 songs. Prefers studio produced demos. SASE. Reports in 1 month.

Music: Jazz. Released *L.A. After Dark*, by Ross Tomkins Quartet; *More Miles and More Standards*, by the Butch Miles Sextet; and *Buenos Aires New York Swing Connections*, by George Anders Sextet.

Tips: Looking for "good instrumentals."

FINER ARTS RECORDS/TRANSWORLD RECORDS, 2170 S. Parker Rd., Denver CO 80231. President: R.J. Bernstein. Record company, music publisher (M. Bernstein Music Publishing Co.) and record producer. Estab. 1960. Releases 6 singles, 3 LPs and 2 CDs/year. Receives 100 submissions/month. Works with musicians/artists and songwriters on contract; musicians on salary for in-house studio work. Pays artists on contract 5-7% per record sold.

How to Contact: Write first and obtain permission to submit. Prefers cassette (or VHS videocassette) and lyric sheet or lead sheet. Reports in 3 weeks. "Please no telephone calls."

Music: Mostly interested in R&B, pop and rap. Also interested in jazz and country.

FIRST TIME RECORDS, Sovereign House, 12 Trewartha Rd., Praa Sands, Penzance, Cornwall TR20 9ST **England.** Phone (0736)762826. FAX: (0736)763328. Managing Director A&R: Roderick G. Jones. Labels include Pure Gold Records, Rainy Day Records, Mohock Records and First Time Records. Registered members of Phonographic Performance Ltd. (PPL). Record company and music publisher (First Time Music Publishing U.K. Ltd./MCPS/PRS), and record producer (First Time Management & Production Co.). Estab. 1986. Works with musicians/artists and songwriters on contract; hires musicians for in-house studio work and as commissioned. Royalty to artists on contract varies; pays statutory rate to publishers per song on record subject to deal.

How to Contact: Prefers cassette with unlimited number of songs and lyric or lead sheets, but not necessary. SAE and IRC. Reports in 1-3 months.

Music: Mostly country/folk, pop/soul/top 20, country with an Irish/Scottish crossover; also gospel/ Christian and HI NRG/dance. Released "Songwriters and Artistes Compilation Volume III," on Rainy Day Records; "The Drums of Childhood Dreams," (by Pete Arnold), recorded by Pete Arnold on Mohock Records (folk) and *The Light and Shade of Eddie Blackstone* (by Eddie Blackstone), recorded by Eddie Blackstone on T.W. Records (country).

Tips: "Writers should learn patience, tolerance and understanding of how the music industry works, and should present themselves and their product in a professional manner and always be polite. Listen always to constructive criticism and learn from the advice of people who have a track record in the music business. Your first impression may be the only chance you get, so it is advisable to get it right from the start."

FLAMING STAR WEST, Dept. SM, Box 2400, Gardnerville NV 89410. (702)265-6825. Owner: Ted Snyder. Record company (Flaming Star Records) and record producer. BMI. Estab. 1988. Works with composers and lyricists; teams collaborators. Pays standard royalty.

How to Contact: Submit a demo tape—unsolicited submissions are O.K. Prefers cassette or VHS videocassette with up to 5 songs and lyric sheets. "If you are sure of your music, you may send more than 5 songs. No heavy metal. All other types." SASE. Reports in 3-4 weeks.

Music: Mostly country, pop and rock and country rock; also gospel, R&B, and calypso. Published "Scene of the Crime" and "Little Things" (by Bobby Goldsboro) and "One More Night" (by Jay Lacy), all recorded by Ted Snyder on Flaming Star Records (country).

Tips: "Listen to what is on the radio, but be original. Put feeling into your songs. We're looking for LPs and artists to promote overseas. If you have LP masters we may be interested. We have a juke box program where we can sell your 45s. If you need your record produced we may be able to help. Flaming Star Records is a launching pad for the new recording artist. We try to help where we can. We are submitting songs to artists such as Glen Campbell, Kenny Rogers, and Bill "Crash" Craddock among many others."

FLYING HEART RECORDS, Dept. SM, 4026 NE 12th Ave., Portland OR 97212. (503)287-8045. Owner: Jan Celt. Labels include Flying Heart Records. Record company. Estab. 1982. Releases 2 LPs and 1 EP/year. Works with musicians/artists and songwriters on contract and hires musicians for in-house studio work. Pays 2-10% royalty to artists on contract; negotiable rate to publisher per song on record.
How to Contact: Submit a demo tape by mail. Unsolicited submissions are okay. Prefers cassette with 1-10 songs and lyric sheets. Does not return unsolicited material. "SASE required for *any* response." Reports in 3 months.
Music: Mostly R&B, blues and jazz; also rock. Released "Get Movin" (by Chris Newman), recorded by Napalm Beach (rock); "Down Mexico Way" (by Chris Newman), recorded by Napalm Beach (rock); and "Which One Of You People" (by Jan Celt), recorded by The Esquires (R&B); all on Flying Heart Records. Other artists include Janice Scroggins, Tom McFarland and Obo Addy.
Tips: "Express your true feelings with creative originality and show some imagination. Use high quality cassette for best sound."

FOUNTAINHEAD RECORDS, Box 40128, San Francisco CA 94140. (415)641-6235. General Manager: Trevor Levine. Record company, music publisher (Art of Concept Music, BMI). Estab. 1989. Releases 1 single and 1 cassette/year. Works with musicians/artists and songwriters on contract. Pays 10% royalty to artists on contract; statutory royalty to publisher for each record sold.
How to Contact: Submit demo tape—unsolicited submissions are OK. Prefers cassette with 3-6 songs, lyric and lead sheet. Does not return unsolicited material. Reports in 1 month.
Music: Mostly pop/rock ballads, "moderate-paced meaningful rock (not 'good time rock and roll' or dance music)"; also rock operas, New Age and synthesizer oriented music. Released "Don't Say You Love Me;" "Spare Me Now" and "Winds of Change" written and recorded by Trevor Levine on Fountainhead Records. Other artists include Troubled Souls and Eddy Garcia.
Tips: "We are interested in songs with powerful melodic and lyrical hooks—songs that are beautiful, expressive and meaningful, with uniquely dissonant or dramatic qualities that really *move* the listener. Our songs deal with serious topics, from inner conflicts and troubled relationships to anthems, story songs and "message songs" which address social and political issues—government corruption, women's and minority issues, human and animal rights.

FRESH ENTERTAINMENT, Ste. 5, 1315 Simpson Rd. NW, Atlanta GA 30314. (404)642-2645. Vice President, Marketing/A&R: Willie Hunter. Record company and music publisher (Hserf Music/AS-CAP, Blair Vizzion Music/BMI). Releases 5 singles and 2 LPs/year. Works with musicians/artists and songwriters on contract. Pays 7-10% royalty to artists on contract.
How to Contact: Prefers cassette (or VHS videocassette) with at least 3 songs and lyric sheet. Unsolicited submissions accepted. SASE. Reports in 2 months.
Music: Mostly R&B, rock and pop; also jazz, gospel and rap. Released "This Time (by Cirocco) recorded by Georgio on RCA (R&B/dance); "Broken Promises" (by J. Calhoun) recorded by SOS Band on A&M Records (R&B/dance) and "Sticking to You" (by Cirocco) recorded by Andrew Logan on Motown Records (dance/R&B). Other artists include Sir Anthony with Rare Quality, and Larion.
Tips: "Be creative in packaging material."

*FRESH START MUSIC MINISTRIES, Box 121616, Nashville TN 37212. (615)269-9984. President: Mark Stephen Hughes. Record company, record producer (Mark Stephen Hughes). Estab. 1989. Releases 4 LPs/year. Works with musicians/artists and songwriters on contract. Pays 3-10% royalty to artists on contract; pays statutory rate to publishers per song on record.
How to Contact: Submit demo tape—unsolicited submissions are OK. Prefers cassette (or VHS videocassette) with 3 songs and lyric sheet. SASE.
Music: Mostly Christian; also praise/worship, pop/rock and R&B. Released *Hallowed Be Thy Name*, written and recorded by Lanier Ferguson; *Lost Without Your Love* (by Mark Stephen Hughes), recorded by Kathy Davis; and *Miracles* (by Joe David Smith), recorded by Andy Ward, all on Fresh Start Records.

*FRONTLINE MUSIC GROUP, Box 28450, Santa CA 92799-8450. Contact: Kenny Hicks. Labels include Alarma Records, Frontline Records, MYX Records, Frontline Kid's, Intense Records, Joyful Heart Music, Alarma Intl, Cantio and Graceland. Record company, music publisher (Broken Songs Publishing/ASCAP, Carlotta Music BMI). Estab. 1985. Releases 100 singles, 75 LPs, and 70 CDs/year. Works with musicians/artists and songwriters on contract; musicians on salary for in-house studio work. Pays 75-100% statutory rate to publishers per song on record.
How to Contact: Prefers cassette (or VHS videocassette) with any number of songs and typed lyric sheet. Does not return unsolicited material. Must include SASE for return of product. "We only reply on those of interest—but if you've not heard from us within 4 weeks we're not interested."

Music: Mostly gospel/contemporary/Christian, rock/pop and R&B; also worship and praise, children's product and instrumental/jazz. Released *Change of Heart*, written and recorded by Jon Gibson (R&B LP); *Just Another Injustice*, written and recorded by Mark Farner (rock LP); and *Perfect*, written and recorded by Benny Hester on Frontline Records.
Tips: "Put your best songs at the top of the tape. Submit a *brief* background/history. Listen to product on the label and try writing for a specific artist. Be professional; please don't hound the label with calls."

G FINE RECORDS/PRODUCTIONS, Box 180 Cooper Station, New York NY 10276. (212)995-1608. President: P. Fine. Record company, music publisher (Rap Alliance) and record producer (Lyvio G.). Estab. 1986. Works with musicians/artists on contract. Pays 7-12% royalty to artists on contract; statutory rate to publisher per song on record.
How to Contact: Submit demo tape—unsolicited submissions are OK. Prefers cassette. Include SASE for return of tape. Reports in 2 months.
Music: Mostly "Undercore," college/alternative rock, rap, dance, R&B. Released "Ring the Alarm" (by Lyfid G/Fu-Schnickens) recorded by Fu-Schnickens on Jive Records (rap).

GALLERY II RECORDS, INC., Box 630755, Miami FL 33163. (305)935-4880. President: Jack Gale. Labels include Playback, Ridgewood and Caramba Records. Record company, music publisher (Lovey Music/BMI, Cowabonga Music/ASCAP) and record producer. Estab. 1983. Releases 25 singles, 6 LPs and 12 CDs/year. Receives 200 submissions/year. Works with musicians/artists and songwriters on contract and hires musicians for in-house studio work. Pays statutory rate to publishers per song on record.
How to Contact: Submit demo tape—unsolicited submissions are OK. Prefers cassette (or VHS videocassette) with 2 songs and lyric sheet. SASE. Reports in 2 weeks "if interested."
Music: Mostly contemporary country and traditional country. Released "You Got the Best of Me" (by J. Fuller), recorded by Sandi Thompson; "Don't Light My Fire" (by Eve Shapiro), recorded by Whiskey Creek; and "I Kept It on the Road" recorded by R. Lee Davis; all on Gallery II Records (country). Other artists include Sammi Smith, Del Reeves, Margo Smith, Kitty Wells, Mickey Rooney, Dennis Yost and the Classics IV, Sandi Thompson and R. Lee Davis.

GATEWAY, 4960 Timbercrest, Canfield OH 44406. (216)533-9024. President: A. Conti. Labels include Endive. Record company, music publisher (Ashleycon, BMI), and record producer. Estab. 1987. Releases 6 cassettes and 1 video/year. Receives 6-8 submissions/month. Works with musicians/artists and songwriters on contract. Pays 1-7% royalty to artists on contract.
How to Contact: Submit demo tape—unsolicited submissions are OK. SASE. Reports in 6 weeks.
Music: Mostly new algorithmic, computer generated. Released "Vacillation," (by A. Conti), on Endive Records (algol); "Channel 1" (by A. Conti), on Endive Video (percussion) and "Child Porn" (by M. Eckert), recorded by Artboyz on Endive Records (amerothrust). Other artists include Tootsweet.
Tips: "Include explanation of algorithm used."

***GCS RECORDS**, Suite 206, 1508 Harlem, Memphis TN 38114. (901)274-2726. A&R Director: Loretta Malveau. Labels include Del-A-Ron Records, Great-Day Records and Blue-Town Records. Record company and music publisher. Releases 40 singles and 7 LPs/year. Works with artists on record contract and musicians on salary for in-house studio work. Also works with composers; teams collaborators. Pays 3-7% royalty to artists on contract; statutory rate to publishers for each record sold.
How to Contact: Write or call about your interest or arrange personal interview. Prefers 7½ or 15 ips reel-to-reel or cassette (or VHS videocassette) with 3-5 songs and lyric sheet. "Does not return unsolicited material." Reports in 1 month.
Music: Mostly R&B; also gospel, blues and dance. Released "The Beat is Fresh," by First Class Crew (rap); "He's Coming Back," by Brown Singers (gospel); and "Love Song," by Music Man (R&B).

***GENESEE RECORDS, INC.**, 7931 Genesee, Litchfield MI 49252. (517)542-3051. President: Junior A. Cole. Record company, music publisher (J.A. Cole Publishing) and record producer. Releases 3 singles/year. Works with musicians/artists on contract.

Remember: Don't "shotgun" your demo tapes. Submit only to companies interested in the type of music you write. For more submission hints, refer to The Business of Songwriting on page 19.

How to Contact: Submit demo tape—unsolicited submissions OK. Prefers cassette. SASE. Reports in 6 weeks.
Music: Country. Released "I Won't Go Way Down Deep" and "Good Looking Woman" (by Junior A. Cole), recorded by Country Express on Genesse Records.

GLOBAL PACIFIC RECORDS, 180 E. Napa St., Sonoma CA 95476. (707)996-2748. A&R Director: Howard Morris. Record company and music publisher (Global Pacific Publishing). Releases 10 singles, 12 LPs and 12 CDs/year. Works with musicians/artists and songwriters on contract; hires musicians for in-house studio work. Pays 9% royalty to artists on contract; statutory rate to publishers per song on records.
How to Contact: Call first and obtain permission to submit. Prefers cassette with 3 songs. "Note style of music on envelope." Does not return unsolicited material. Reports in 3 months.
Music: Mostly new age, pop, jazz, "pop/quiet storm"; also rock, blues and classical. Released "Mystic Fire," written and recorded by S. Kindler (jazz); "Seasons," written and recorded by M. Johnathon and "Mango Cooler," written and recorded by C.M. Brothman, all on Global Pacific Records. Other artists include Bob Kindler, David Friesen, Georgia Kelly, Ben Tavera King and Paul Greaver.
Tips: "Write us a hit! Know your label and market you are targeting."

GLOBAL RECORD CO., Box 396, 133 Arbutus Ave., Manistique MI 49854-0396. President: Reg B. Christensen. Labels include Bakersfield Record Company. Record company and music publisher (Chris Music/BMI and Sara Lee Music/BMI). Estab. 1956. Releases 20-40 singles and 5 CDs/year. Works with artists and songwriters on contract. Pays 10-20% royalty to artists on contract; statutory rate to publishers for each record sold.
How to Contact: Submit demo tape—unsolicited submissions are OK. Prefers cassette with 3 songs and lyric sheet. SASE. Reports in 5-8 weeks.
Music: Mostly top 40, R&B, country, MOR, rock, and novelty types. Released "TV Cop" written and recorded by Pursuit on Global Records (rock); "I, I, I" and "Ask Me No Questions," both written and recorded by Helen DeBaker on Bakersfield Records (C&W).
Tips: "We do favor novelty type in rock, pop, or country western format. Be sure voice is clear, above music. Don't turn your song into an instrumental—we want ot hear the story."

GOLD CITY RECORDS, INC., Box 24, Armonk NY 10504. (914)273-6457. President: Chris Jasper. Vice President/General Counsel: Margie Jasper. Labels include Gold City Label (independent distribution and distribution through majors, including CBS). Record company. Estab. 1986. Releases 5-10 singles, 5-10 12″ singles, 3-5 LPs and 3-5 CDs/year. Works with musicians/artists and songwriters on contract and hires musicians for in-house studio work. Pays negotiable rate to publisher per song on record.
How to Contact: Submit demo tape—unsolicited submissions are OK. Prefers cassette with 3 songs and lyric sheets. SASE. Reports in 6 weeks.
Music: Mostly R&B/rap, pop and rock. Released *New Horizons*, written and recorded by Chris Jasper on Gold City/CBS Records (R&B/pop LP).

GOLDBAND RECORDS, Box 1485, Lake Charles LA 70602. (318)439-8839. President: Eddie Shuler. Labels include Folk-Star, Tek, Tic-Toc, Anla, Jador and Luffcin Records. Record company and record producer. Works with artists and songwriters on contract; musicians on salary for in-house studio work. Pays 3-5% royalty to artists on contract; standard royalty to songwriters on contract.
How to Contact: Prefers cassette with 2-6 songs and lyric sheet. SASE. Reports in 2 months.
Music: Blues, country, easy listening, folk, R&B, rock and top 40/pop. Released *Katie Webster Has the Blues* (blues LP) and "Things I Used to Do" (blues single), by Katie Webster; "Waiting For My Child," by Milford Scott (spiritual single); "Gabriel and Madaline," by Johnny Jano (cajun country single); and "Cajun Disco," by the La Salle Sisters (disco single). Other artists incude Jimmy House, John Henry III, Gary Paul Jackson, Junior Booth, Rockin Sidney, Ralph Young, Tedd Dupin, R. Sims, Mike Young and Everett Brady.

GOLDEN BOY RECORDS, 16311 Askin Dr., Pine Mountain Club CA 93222. (805)242-0125. A&R Director: Eddie Gurren. Labels include Golden Boy and Alva. Record company. Releases 6 singles and 2 LPs/year. Works with artists on contract.
How to Contact: Prefers cassette (or videocassette) with maximum 3 songs and lyric sheet. Reports in 3 weeks.
Music: Mostly R&B, urban, dance and soul; also jazz.

GOLDEN TRIANGLE RECORDS, 1051 Saxonburg Blvd., Glenshaw PA 15116. Producer: Sunny James. Labels include Rocken Robin and Shell-B. Music publisher (Golden Triangle/BMI) and record producer (Sunny James). Estab. 1987. Releases 8 singles, 6 12″ singles, 10 LPs and 19 CDs/year. Receives 5 submissions/year. Works with musicians/artists and songwriters on contract and hires musicians for

in-house studio work. Pays 10% royalty to artists on contract; statutory rate to publishers per song on record.
How to Contact: Submit demo tape—unsolicited submissions are OK. Prefers cassette, 15 IPS reel-to-reel (or ½" VHS videocassette) with 3 songs and lyric or lead sheets. SASE. Reports in 1 month.
Music: Mostly progressive R&B, rock and A/C; also jazz and country. Released "Astor" (by S. Bittner) recorded by P. Bittner on Shell-B Records (rock); "Those No's" (by R. Cvetnick) recorded by J. Morello on Rocken Robin Records (R&B) and "Most of All" (by F. Johnson) recorded by The Marcels on Golden Triangle Records (C/A). Other artists include The original Mr. Bassman Fred Johnson of the Marcels (Blue Moon).

GO-ROC-CO-POP RECORDS, % The Voice Notes Publishing Co., 1225 Shallowford Rd., Chattanooga TN 37421. (615)899-9685. President: B.J. Keener. Labels include WAR Records. Record company. Estab. 1984. Works with musicians/artists and songwriters on contract and hires musicians for in-house studio work. Pays standard royalty to artists on contract.
How to Contact: Submit demo tape—unsolicited submissions are OK. Prefers cassette with 1-2 songs and lyric and lead sheets. SASE. Reports in 3 months.
Music: Mostly gospel, rock, country and pop. Other artists include LaWanda, Topaz, Joe Cleve, Johnny Sue, Scotty Duran and Billy Joe.
Tips: "Be sincere, hard working and flexible, with a desire to succeed."

GRASS ROOTS RECORD & TAPE/LMI RECORDS, Box 532, Malibu CA 90265. (213)463-5998. President: Lee Magid. Labels include Grass Roots and LMI Records. Record company, record producer, music publisher (Alexis/ASCAP, Marvelle/BMI, Lou-Lee/BMI) and management firm (Lee Magid Management Co.). Also SESAC. Member AIMP, NARAC. Estab. 1967. Releases 4 LPs and 4 CDs/year. Works with musicians/artists and songwriters on contract. Pays 2-5% royalty to artists on contract; pays statutory rate to publishers per song on record.
How to Contact: Submit demo tape—unsolicited submissions are OK. Prefers cassette with 3 songs and lyric sheet. "Please, no 45s." SASE. Reports in 1 month minimum.
Music: Mostly pop/rock, R&B, country, gospel, jazz/rock and blues; also bluegrass, children's and Latin. Released "What Shall I Do?" (by Quincy Fielding Jr.), "Whenever You Call" (by Calvin Rhone), and "I Got Joy" (by Quincy Fielding Jr.), all recorded by Tremaine Hawkins on Sparrow Records (gospel/R&B). Other artists include Gloria Lynne, Co Co, Becky Barksdale and Texas Blues Society.

GREEN LINNET RECORDS, 43 Beaver Brook Rd., Danbury CT 06810. (203)730-0333. Managing Director: Steve Katz. Record company. Estab. 1978. Releases 16 CDs/year. Works with musicians/artists on contract. Pays artists 8-10%, publishers ½-¾ of statutory rate.
How to Contact: Submit demo tape—unsolicited submissions are OK. Prefers cassette or VHS videocassette with 3 songs and lyric or lead sheet. Does not return unsolicited material. Reports in 2 months.
Music: Mostly folk. Released "Grace in Gravity" (by Jonathan Kimball) recorded by The Story; "Treebranch" (by C. Frappier) recorded by Rare Air and "Reuben's Train" recorded by The Deighton Family, all CDs on Green Linnet Records.
Tips: "You must have a very special talent as a musician or writer (or preferably, both)."

*GUERRILLA RECORDS , Unit 32, Pall Mall Deposit, 124/128 Barlby Rd., London W1O 6Bl UK. (081)964-1199. FAX: (081)964-4876. Directors: Dick O'Dell, William Orbit and Karen Haworth. Record company. Estab. 1990. Releases 10 12" singles, 2-3 LPs, 2-3 CDs/year. Works with musicians/artists on record contract. Pays "50/50 profit split" to artists on contract. Pays statutory rate to publisher per song on record.
How to Contact: Submit demo tape—unsolicited submissions are OK. Prefers cassette with 3-4 songs and lyric sheet. SASE.
Music: Mostly dance and pop. Other artists include Bass-O-Matic, React 2 Rhythm, Supereal, William Orbit and D.O.P.

HACIENDA RECORDS, 1236 S. Staples, Corpus Christi TX 78404. (512)882-7066. Owner: Roland Garcia. Producer: Rick Garcia. Labels include Las Brisas. Record company, music publisher (Alpenglow Music, Dark Heart Music, El Palacio Music, Roland Garcia Music) and record producer. Releases 20-100 singles and 5-20 LPs/year. Works with artists and songwriters on contract; musicians on salary for in-house studio work. Pays royalties or per LP to artists on contract.
How to Contact: Prefers cassette. Does not return unsolicited material. Reporting time varies.
Music: Rock, Spanish and country, pop, MOR, international and gospel. Released "Ready as Hell," (by Jim D./Ricky R./Johnny C.), recorded by Jim Dandy's Black Oak Arkansas (rock single & LP), "It's Majic," (by Pio Trevino), recorded by Majic (English single from Spanish LP); and "Ran Kan

Kan," (by Tito Puente), recorded by Steve Jordan (Spanish single), all on Hacienda Records. Other artists include Freddy Fender, Romance, Gary Hobbs, Fuego, Janie C., Steve Borth and Rowdy Friends.

*H&S RECORDS, Box 515, Waterloo, Ontario N2J 4A9 **Canada**. (519)741-1252. President: William Seip. Record company and music publisher (William Seip Music, Inc.). Estab. 1978. Releases 1-2 LPs and 1-2 CDs/year. Works with musicians/artists on contract. Pays negotiable royalty to artists on contract.
How to Contact: Submit demo tape—unsolicited submissions are OK. Prefers cassette with 3 songs and lyric sheet. Does not return unsolicited material. Reports in 1 month.
Music: Mostly commercial rock, top 40 and hard rock. Released *Breaking Loose*, written and recorded by Helix on H&S Records (all hard rock LPs); and *Ray Lyell*, written and recorded by Ray Lyell on A&M Records.

HAPPY MAN RECORDS, Box 73, 4501 Spring Creek Dr., Bonita Springs FL 33923. (813)947-6978. Executive Producer: Dick O'Bitts. Labels include Happy Man, Condor, Con Air. Record company, music publisher (Rocker Music/BMI, Happy Man Music/ASCAP) and record producer (Rainbow Collection Ltd.). Estab. 1972. Releases 4-6 singles, 4-6 12" singles, 4-6 LPs and 4 EPs/year. Works with musicians/artists and songwriters on contract. Pays statutory rate to publishers per song on records.
How to Contact: Submit demo tape—unsolicited submissions are OK. Prefers cassette (or VHS videocassette if available) with 3-4 songs and lyric sheet. SASE. Reports in 4 weeks.
Music: Mostly country. Released "Old Kentucky Home" (by Roger Wade) recorded by Colt Gipson; "Diamonds & Chills" (by Don Goodwin) recorded by Mary Ann Kennedy and "Junction" written and recorded by Overdue Band, all on Happy Man Records (country). Other artists include Ray Pack and Chris and Lenny.

HARD HAT RECORDS AND CASSETTES, 519 N. Halifax Ave., Daytona Beach FL 32118. (904)252-0381. President: Bobby Lee Cude. Labels include Hard Hat, Maricao, Blue Bandana and Indian Head. Record company, record producer and music publisher (Cude & Pickens Publishing/BMI). Estab. 1978. Releases 12 singles and 12 LPs/year.
How to Contact: Write first. Does not use outside material.
Music: Mostly country; also easy listening, gospel, MOR, top 40/pop and Broadway show. Released "V-A-C-A-T-I-O-N," (by Cude & Pickens) recorded by the Hard Hatters; "Just a Piece of Paper," and "Worried Worried Man," (both by Cude & Pickens) recorded by Blue Bandana Country Band; "Who's Lovin' You" and "Shot In the Dark" by Caz Allen (pop); "Tennessee's On My Mind" and "Texas Red, White and Blue Step" by Caz Allen (country); all singles on Hard Hat Label. Other artists include "Pic" Pickens, Hula Kings, Caribbean Knights and Cityfolks Country Band.

HARMONY STREET RECORDS, Box 4107, Kansas City, KS 66104. (913)299-2881. President: Charlie Beth. Record company, music publisher (Harmony Street Music/ASCAP and Harmony Lane Music/BMI), and record producer (Harmony Street Productions). Estab. 1985. Releases 15-30 singles, 4-6 LPs and 3-5CDs/year. Works with musicians/artists and songwriters on contract; musicians on salary for in-house studio work. Pays 10% royalty (retail) to artists on contract; pays statutory rate to publishers per song on record.
How to Contact: Prefers cassette (or VHS videocassette) with no more than 3 songs and lyric or lead sheet. OK for artists to submit album projects, etc., on cassette. Also photo and bio if possible. "Due to the large amount of submissions that we receive we are no longer able to return unsolicited material. We will report within 6 weeks if interested. Please include a full address and telephone number in all submitted packages."
Music: Mostly country, gospel, rockabilly, pop, R&B, bluegrass and rock. Released "Smooth Talkin' Man" (by Terry Allen & Sue Mahurin) recorded by Terry Allen (country), "If She Leaves My Heart When She Goes" (by Edna Mae Foy and Val Zudell) recorded by Tony Mantor (country); "Like the Flip of a Coin" (by Woody Waldroup) recorded by Woody Wills (country), all on Harmony Street Records. Other artists include Scott Hansgen, The Dusters, Terry Diebold and Georgia Carr.
Tips: "Songs submitted to us must be original, commercial and have a good strong hook. Submit only your best songs. Demos should be clear and clean with voice out front. We are interested in working with commercial artists with a commercial style and sound, professional attitude and career goals. Our records are released world wide and also available for sales world wide. Our standards are high and so are our goals."

*HAZARDOUS RECORDS, 17 Water St., Dracut MA 01826. (508)957-5781. A&R: Henry Rowe. Labels include Moonview Records. Record company. Estab. 1986. Releases 2 singles and 2 LPs/year. Works with musicians/artists and songwriters on contract and hires musicians for in-house studio work. Pays statutory rate to publishers per song on records.

How to Contact: Submit demo tape—unsolicited submissions are OK. Prefers cassette, 15 IPS reel-to-reel (or VHS videocassette) with 4-6 songs and lyric sheet.
Music: Mostly metal, rock and pop; also fusion, jazz and New Age. Released "Half Life" and "Danger Zone," by Hazardous Waste (metal); and "Candle to the Magic," by Johann Smith (rock), all recorded by Makin Tracks on Hazardous Records.

*HEART BEAT RECORDS, 1 Camp St., Cambridge MA 02140. (617)354-0700. Label Coordinator: Chris Wilson. Record company. Estab. 1981. Releases 30 LPs, 30 CDs/year. Works with musicians/artists on record contract. Pays .998% royalty to artists on contract; statutory rate to publisher per song on record.
How to Contact: Submit demo tape—unsolicited submissions are OK. Prefers cassette with 5-10 songs and lyric sheet. Does not return unsolicited material. Reports in 1 week.
Music: Mostly reggae; also Afro-Caribe. Released *He Who Knows It Feels It*, written and recorded by Yami Bold; *Happy Together*, written and recorded by Sugar Minott; and *Solid Foundation*, written and recorded by Winston Jarett all on Heart Beat Records (reggae CD). Other artists include Roots Radics, Chris Wayne, Albert Griffiths, Gregory Isaacs, Little John and Leonard Dillon.
Tips: "Strictly reggae!"

HEART LAND RECORDS, Box 16572, Kansas City MO 64133. (816)358-2542. Executive Producer: Jimmy Lee. Record company, music publisher (Jellee Works Music/BMI, Jellee Music Works/ASCAP), record producer (Jimmy Lee/Heart Land Records) and Jellee Works Productions—"We do own and operate our own recording studios. We produce demos for songwriters that ask for and need our help." Estab. 1982. Releases 6-8 singles and 4-6 LPs/year. Works with musicians/artists and songwriters on contract and hires musicians for in-house studio work. Pays 8-12% royalty to artists on contract; statutory rate to publisher per song on record.
How to Contact: Submit demo tape—unsolicited submissions are OK. Prefers cassette (or VHS videocassette) with no more than 2 songs and lyric sheets. SASE. Reports in 4-6 weeks.
Music: Mostly country, gospel & pop; some R&B and light rock. Released "Attic Full of Love" (by Priscilla McCann), recorded by Jackie Cotter (contemporary country); "Touch You Again" (by Lawrence/Lee), recorded by Dana Loudermilk (country); "Don't Never Say We Through" (by Wayne Brandon), recorded by Max Berry, all on Heart Land Records. Other artists include Joe Donovan, Kevin Eason, Geoff Clark and Stephanie Sieggen.
Tips: "Be professional and follow guidelines for submitting material. We put out a newsletter dedicated to teaching and helping songwriters."

HEATH & ASSOCIATES, #1058, E. Saint Catherine, Louisville KY 40204. (502)637-2877. General Partner: John V. Heath. Labels include Hillview Records and Estate Records. Record company, music publisher (Two John's Music/ASCAP), record producer (MTV Productions and Just a Note/BMI). Estab. 1979. Releases 8-10 singles, 3 12″ singles, 4-5 LPs, 3 EPs and 3 CDs/year. Receives 8-12 submissions/month. Works with musicians/artists and songwriters on contract. Pays 5-10% royalty to artists on contract; statutory rate to publisher per song on record.
How to Contact: Submit demo tape—unsolicited submissions are OK. Prefers cassette, 7½ ips reel-to-reel or VHS videocassette with 3 songs and lead sheets. SASE. Reports in 2 weeks.
Music: Mostly pop, country, R&B and MOR; also gospel. Released "Dry Those Tears," written and recorded by Donald Dodd on Hillview Records (MOR); "Hot," written and recorded by The Word on Estate Records (gospel); and "Crazy Trucker," written and recorded by Michael Palko on Hillview Records (country).
Tips: "Be professional in submissions."

*HEAVY METAL RECORDS, 152 Goldthorn Hill, Penn, Wolverhampton, WV2 3VA **England**. Phone: 44-(0902)-345345. Labels include Heavy Metal Records, Revolver Records, Heavy Metal America, Heavy Metal Worldwide and FM Records. Record company, record producer (FM-Revolver Records Ltd.) and music publisher (Rocksong Music Publishing Ltd./PRS). Releases 10 singles, 10 12″ singles, 20 LPs and 30 EPs/year. Works with musicians/artists and songwriters on contract. Pays negotiable royalty to artists on contract; statutory rate to publishers per song on record.
How to Contact: Submit demo tape—unsolicited submissions are OK. Prefers cassette with 1-3 songs. "Send photos and bios." Does not return unsolicited material. Reports in 1 month.
Music: Mostly heavy metal/hard rock, AOR/FM rock and "alternative" guitar-based rock; also dance and pop. Released recordings by Val Grant, Marky-Mark and the FM Pit Crew and All Rights Reserved (all dance). Other artists include The Vibrators, Wrathchild, Lisa Dominique, White Sister, Tobruk and John Sloman.
Tips: "We are selecting dance floor and R&B radio hits."

HELION RECORDS, Suite 216, 8306 Wilshire Blvd., Beverly Hills CA 90211. (818)352-9174. Vice President, Record Division: Nick Schepperle. Record company and record producer (Greg Knowles). Estab. 1984. Releases 4 CDs/year. Works with musicians/artists on contract; hires musicians for in-house studio work. Pays 5-9% royalty to artists on contract; statutory rate to publisher for each record sold.
How to Contact: Prefers cassette with 3-4 songs and lyric or lead sheet. Does not return unsolicited material. "SASE for reply." Reports in 3 weeks.
Music: Mostly R&B and pop; also country and comedy. Released *Angel* and "Telephone Blues," by Diana Blair; "Keys To The World" by Darleen Koldenhoven; and "The Beer Dawgs" by the Beer Dawgs.
Tips: "Treat your work as a business first and an art form second. You need the business head to get you into the door—then we can see how good your music is."

*HIBI DEI HIPP RECORDS, #4872, 311 W. Monroe St., Jacksonville FL 32202. (904)448-3534. Pro-ducer: Aubrey Saulsby. Record company, music publisher (WASMC/BMI). Estab. 1986. Releases 4-6 singles, 2 12" singles, 1 LP, 1 EP, 1 CD/year. Works with musicians/artists and songwriters on contract and hires musicians for in-house studio work. Pays standard royalty.
How to Contact: Write and obtain permission to submit. Prefers cassette 9 or 7½" reel with 3 songs and lyric sheets. Does not return unsolicited material.
Music: Mostly R&B, rap, jazz; also blues, pop and top/40. Released "Because You're Mine" and "Free" both recorded by William Icey and "The Way That I Am" recorded by Willie Bones, all written by Willie A. Saulsby (R&B). Other artists include Hob Slob, King William.

HOLLYROCK RECORDS, Suite C-300, 16776 Lakeshore Dr., Lake Elisnore CA 92330. A&R Director: Dave Paton. Record company, record producer and music publisher (Heaven Songs/BMI). Releases 4 singles and 6 LPs/year. Works with artists and songwriters on contract; musicians on salary for in-house studio work. Pays negotiable royalty to artists on contract; statutory rate to publishers for each record sold.
How to Contact: Prefers 7½ ips reel-to-reel or cassette with 3-6 songs and lyric sheet. SASE. Reports in 2 weeks.
Music: Progressive, top 40/pop, country, easy listening, folk, jazz, MOR and rock. Released *Everything* (movie soundtrack). Presently working on Linda Rae and Breakheart Pass Album (country), and Gene Mitchener comedy album (sit down comic).

*HOMESTEAD RECORDS, Box 800, Rockville Centre NY 11570. (516)764-6200. A&R Director: Ken Katkin. Labels include Rockville Records. Record company. Estab. 1983. Releases 12 singles, 12 LPs, 2 EPs and 12 CDs/year. Works with musicians/artists on contract. Pays 10-13% royalty to artists on contract; ¾ of statutory rate to publisher per song on record.
How to Contact: Submit demo tape—unsolicited submissions are OK. Prefers cassette with 4 songs. Does not return unsolicited material. Reports in 2-3 months.
Music: Mostly punk rock and rock. Other artists include Styrenes, Love Child, Sebadoh, Seam, Tall Dwarfs, Cake Kitchen.

HOTTRAX RECORDS, 1957 Kilburn Dr., Atlanta GA 30324. (404)662-6661. Vice President, A&R: Oliver Cooper. Labels include Dance-A-Thon, Hardkor. Record company and music publisher (Star-fox Publishing). Releases 12 singles and 3-4 LPs/year. Receives 3000-4000 submissions/year. Works with musicians/artists and songwriters on contract. Pays 5-7% royalty to artists on contract.
How to Contact: Prefers cassette with 3 songs and lyric sheet. SASE. "We will not return tapes without adequate postage." Reports in 3 months. "When submissions get extremely heavy, we do not have the time to respond/return material we pass on. We do notify those sending the most promising work we review, however."
Music: Mostly top 40/pop, rock and country; also hard core punk and jazz-fusion. Released *P Is For Pig*, written and recorded by The Pigs (top 40/pop LP); "The World May Not Like Me" (by Mike Fitzgerald), recorded by Mike Angelo (rock single); and *Introducing The Feel*, written and recorded by The Feel (new rock LP) all on Hottrax Records; also "The Condom Man," recorded by Big Al Jano, and "Ms. Perfection," by Larry Yates (urban contemporary). Other artists include Burl Compton (country), Michael Rozakis & Yorgos (pop), Starfoxx (rock), The Night Shadows (rock), The Bop (new wave), and Secret Lover.

IHS RECORDS, 5934 Blairstone Dr., Culver City CA 90230. (213)558-8168. Vice President, General Manager: Leonardo V. Wilborn. Record company. ASCAP/BMI. Estab. 1990. Releases 2 12" singles and 2 LPs/year. Works with musicians/artists and songwriters on contract. Pays statutory rate to pub-lisher per song on record.

How to Contact: Write first and obtain permission to submit. Prefers cassette or VHS videocassette with 3 songs and lyric sheet. SASE. Reports in 6-8 weeks.
Music: Mostly nu-inspirational, dance/rap and concert; also R&B, gospel and pop. Released "Second Coming" on IHS Records (nu-inspirational); "Righteous" on IHS Records (dance/inspirational); and "Positive Force" on LVW Records (nu-inspirational); all recorded by Federation of Love. Other artists include Daily Bread, Nasa and M.C. Smiley.
Tips: "Be sincere. Stay on top of industry trends. Monitor production schedules."

IMAGINARY RECORDS, 332 N. Dean Rd., Auburn AL 36830. (205)821-JASS. Proprietor: Lloyd Townsend, Jr. Record company, music publisher (Imaginary Music), record producer (Mood Swing Productions) and distribution firm (Imaginary Distribution). Estab. 1982. Releases 1-2 singles, 1-2 12″ singles, 1 LP, 1-2 EPs and 2-3 CDs/year. Receives 15-20 submissions/month. Works with musicians/ artists and songwriters on contract; "will manufacture custom cassettes for a set price." Pays 10-12% royalty to artists on contract; statutory rate to publisher per song on record.
How to Contact: Submit demo tape—unsolicited submissions OK. Prefers cassette or 7½ ips reel-to-reel with 4 songs and lyric or lead sheet. Submissions not returned unless accompanied by SASE. Tapes may be retained for future reference unless return is specifically requested. Reports in 4-6 months.
Music: Mostly jazz, blues and rock; also classical, folk and spoken word. Released "Weirdo" and "No Tomorrow," written and recorded by Engine House on Imaginary Records (hardcore/thrash punk) and "Maple Leaf Rag" (by Scott Joplin) recorded by Patrick Mahony on Imaginary Records (Ragtime). Other artists include Slow Natives, The Moderns, Paul and The Quest, Bone Dali, Nothing Personal, Bob Richardson, Patrick Mahoney, Auburn Knights Orchestra, Yardbird Orchestra and Spraytruck.
Tips: "Be patient! I'm slow . . ."

INTERSTATE 40 RECORDS, Box 1794, Big Bear City CA 92314. (714)585-4645. President: Eddie Lee Carr. Labels include Tracker Records. Record company and music publisher (Watchesgro Music/BMI and Watch Us Climb/ASCAP). Estab. 1979. Releases 12 singles, 1 LP and 2 CDs/year. Works with musicians/artists on contract. Pays 20% royalty to artists on contract; statutory rate to publisher per song on record.
How to Contact: Submit demo tape—unsolicited submissions are OK. Prefers cassette with 3 songs. SASE. Reports in 2 weeks.
Music: Mostly country. Movie and TV credits include "Young Guns of Texas," "Story of Evil Knievel," "Alias Smith & Jones" and "The Christopher Columbus Story."

JALYN RECORDING CO., 306 Millwood Dr., Nashville TN 37217. (615)366-9999. President: Jack Lynch. Labels include Nashville Bluegrass and Nashville Country Recording Company. Record company, music publisher (Jaclyn Music/BMI), record producer, film company (Nashville Country Productions) and distributor (Nashville Music Sales). Estab. 1963. Releases 1-12 LPs/year. Works with musicians/artists and songwriters on contract; hires musicians for in-house studio work; also produces custom sessions. Pays 5-10% royalty to artists on contract; statutory rate to publisher per song on record.
How to Contact: Submit demo tape—unsolicited submissions are OK. Prefers cassette with 1-4 songs and lyric sheets. SASE. Reports in 2 weeks.
Music: Country, bluegrass, gospel and MOR. Released "The Nashville Blues" (by Jack Lynch) recorded by Paul Woods; "Papa" written and recorded by Lonnie Pierce; and "I Dreamed You Back Into My Life" (by Sara Hull) recorded by Glenda Rider, all on NCP Records (country). Other artists include Ralph Stanley, Dave Evans, Country Gentlemen and Larry Sparks.
Tips: "We prefer songs with good lyrics that tell a story with a certain amount of rhyming, a good melody sung by a good singer, and as good a production as is feasible. Our biggest need is good, commercial country songs. Send a good quality cassette recording and a neat lyrics sheet, picture and resume, if available. We make demos at reasonable rates for accepted material."

JAMAKA RECORD CO., 3621 Heath Ln., Mesquite TX 75150. (214)279-5858. Contact: Jimmy Fields. Labels include Felco, and Kick Records. Record producer and music publisher (Cherie Music/BMI). Estab. 1955. Releases 2 singles/year. Works with artists and songwriters on contract; hires musicians for in-house studio work. Works with in-house studio musicians on salary. Pays .05% royalty to artists on contract; statutory rate to publishers for each record sold.
How to Contact: Prefers cassette with songs and lyric sheet. "A new singer should send a good tape with at least 4 strong songs, presumably recorded in a professional studio." Does not return without return postage and proper mailing package. "The post office has written me about returning cassettes in envelopes; they crush, and damage their equipment. I am holding over 5,000 tapes that came without return postage." Reports ASAP.

Music: Country and progressive country. Released "Stand Up For Your Country (And the Color of Your Flag)" (by J. Fields/D. Fields/Kern/Ray), recorded by Ronnie Ray; "Jessie James" and "Let's Save the Memories" (by Curk Ryles), recorded by Ronnie Ray; "Big Iron House" (by George McCoy), recorded by Cliff Price; all on Jamaka Records (modern country). Other artists include Bobby Belev, The Blue Lady, Jim Kern, George McCoy, Lucky LaRue, Bobby Crown, Billy Taylor and Susan Stutts.
Tips: "Songs should have strong lyrics with a good story, whether country or pop."

*J&J MUSICAL ENTERPRISES LTD., Box 575, Kings Park NY 11754. (516)265-5584. Contact: Jeneane Claps. Labels include JAJ Records. Record company and record production. Estab. 1983. Releases 2-3 singles, 1-2 12″ singles, 1-2 LPs, 1-2 EPs and 1-2 CDs/year. Works with musicians/artists on contract and hires musicians for in-house studio work. Pays variable royalty to artists on contract; variable rate to publisher per song on record.
How to Contact: Write first and obtain permission to submit. Prefers cassette with 4 songs and lyric sheet. SASE. Reports in 2 months. "Typed letters preferred."
Music: Mostly progressive and jazz. Released "Touch & Go," "Hold Tight" and "There Will Be Another Day," all written and recorded by J. Claps on JAJ Records (jazz/pop).
Tips: "Be neat, short and present 2-4 songs."

JANET MARIE RECORDING, 14016 Evers Ave., Compton CA 90272. President: Robert E. Miles. Labels include Milon Entertainment. Record company, music publisher (BMI) and record producer. Estab. 1988. Works with musicians/artists and songwriters on contract. Pays statutory rate to publishers per song on record.
How to Contact: Submit demo tape—unsolicited submissions are OK. Prefers cassette (or VHS videocassette if available) with lyric sheet. SASE. Reports in 1 month.

JOEY BOY RECORDS INC., 3081 N.W. 24th St., Miami FL 33142. (305)635-5588. Contact: Cheryl Randal. Labels include J.R. Records, On Top Records. Record company. Estab. 1985. Releases 50 singles, 50 12″ singles, 15-20 EPs and 15-20 CDs/year. Receives 50-75 submissions/month. Works with musicians/artists on contract. Pays 6% royalty to artists on contract; statutory rate to publisher per song on record.
How to Contact: Write or call first and obtain permission to submit. Prefers cassette with 3 songs and lyric sheets. SASE. Reports in 6 weeks.
Music: Mostly rap and dance; also jazz and comedy. Released "The Dogs," "Disco Rick," and "Success-N-Effect," by A.N.M. Other artists include Eric G. and Bettina.
Tips: "Be creative in your writing and exercise patience in your business dealings."

JOYFUL SOUND RECORDS, 130 87th Ave. N., St. Petersburg FL 33702. A&R: Mike Douglas. Record company and music publisher (Nite Lite Music/BMI). Releases various number of singles and LPs/year. Receives 6-8 submissions/month. Pays negotiated royalty to artists and publishers, never less than statutory rate.
How to Contact: "When submitting, send a cassette with 4 songs and lyric or lead sheets. Clearly label each item you send with your name and address." Does not return material. Reports in 1 month.
Music: Children's music and contemporary Christian (no heavy metal gospel).
Tips: "I'm looking for unpublished works—also am not really interested in promoting someone else's finished LP or single. Don't send me material because you like it. Send me songs that others will like."

JUMP RECORDS & MUSIC, Langemunt 71, 9420 Aaigem **Belgium.** Phone: (053)62-73-77. General Manager: Eddy Van Mouffaert. Labels include Jump, Yeah Songs and Flower. Record company, music publisher (Jump Music) and record producer. Estab. 1976. Releases 40 singles, 3 LPs and 1 CD/year. Works with musicians/artists and songwriters on contract. Pays 5% royalty to artists on contract; statutory rate to publisher per song on record.
How to Contact: Submit demo tape—unsolicited submissions are OK. Prefers cassette. Does not return unsolicited material. Reports in 2 weeks.
Music: Mostly easy listening, disco and light pop; also instrumentals. Released "Ach Eddy," recorded by Eddy & Samantha on Style Records; "Wien Bleibt Wien," recorded by Le Grand Julot on BMP Records; and "Vanavond," recorded by Danny Brendo on Scorpion Records all by Eddy Govert (popular). Other artists include Rocky, Eigentijdse Jeugd, Marijn Van Diun, Connie-Linda, Guy Lovely, Tom Davys, Laurie, Cindy, Patrik, Allan David, Peggy Christy, Aswin, Little Cindy, Sandra More, Dolly, Danny Brendo, Christle Love, Sandra Tempsy, Dick Benson, Angie Halloway and Ricky Morgan.

JUSTIN TIME RECORDS INC., Suite 101, 5455 Pare, Montreal Quebec H4P 1P7 **Canada.** (514)738-9533. A&R Director: Jean-Pierre Leduc. Labels include Justin Time Records and Just a Memory Records. Record company, music publisher (Justin Time Publishing and Janijam Music/SOCAN) and record producer (Jim West). Estab. 1982. Releases 12 LPs and 12 CDs/year. Works with musicians/artists and songwriters on contract. Pays statutory rate to publisher per song on record.

How to Contact: Submit demo tape by mail—unsolicited submissions are OK. Prefers cassette (or VHS videocassette if available) with at least 5 songs and lyric sheet. Does not return unsolicited material. Reports in 3 months.

Music: Mostly jazz, blues and gospel; also French pop, comedy and cajun. Released *Northern Summit*, written and recorded by Oliver Jones (jazz CD/MC); *Blues Under A Full Moon* (by Stephen Barry), recorded by Stephen Barry Band (blues CD/MC); and *Montreal Jubilation Gospel Choir* (by various), recorded by M.J.G.C. (gospel CD/MC), all on Justin Time Records.

Tips: "Include a good representation of your work, for example several different styles if applicable. Also, be prepared to *tour* and *promote*."

KAM EXECUTIVE RECORDS, 11 Shady Oak Trail, Charlotte NC 28910. (704)554-1162. Director: Butch Kelly. Labels include Fresh Ave Records, KAM Records, Newtown. Record company (KAM/BMI) and record producer (Butch Kelly Production). Estab. 1981. Releases 5 singles, 5 12″ singles and 10 CDs/year. Works with musicians/artists on contract. Pays 6% royalty to artists on contract. Pays statutory rate to publisher.

How to Contact: Submit demo tape—unsolicited submissions are OK. Prefers cassette (or VHS videocassette) with 3-6 songs and lyric or lead sheets. SASE. Reports in 2 months.

Music: Mostly R&B, pop and rock; also rap and gospel. Released "Waiting" (by Butch Kelly), recorded by A. Brown on KAM Records (R&B); "Miss You" (by Greg Johnston), recorded by Fresh Air on KAM Records (R&B); and "Stumping Blues" (by Kelly Montgomery), on KAM Records (pop). Other artists include The Prep of Rap, Sharon Jordan (R&B), Richard Kirkpatrick (R&B) and Caro (R&B).

*KAUPP RECORDS, Box 5474, Stockton CA 95205. (209)948-8186. President: Nancy L. Merrihew. Record company, music publisher (Kaupp's and Robert Publishing Co./BMI), record producer (Merri-Webb Productions). Estab. 1990. Releases 1 single and 4 LPs/year. Works with musicians/artists and songwriters on contract and hires musicians for in-house studio work. Pays standard royalty; statutory rate to publisher per song on record.

How to Contact: Write or call first and obtain permission to submit. Prefers cassette (or VHS videocassette if available) with 3 songs. SASE. Reports in 1 month.

Music: Mostly country, R&B and A/C rock; also pop, rock and gospel. Released "Bet My Bottom Dollar" (by N.L. Merrihew and R. Webb), recorded by Rick Webb (country single); *Lonestar Cowboy*, written and recorded by Stephen Bruce (country LP); and *More Than Understanding*, written and recorded by Gary Epps (A/C rock LP), all on Kaupp Records. Other artists include David "Dude" Westmoreland, California Gold, Mike Glover, Steve Boutte, Shane "Rockin' Round Boy" Burnett and Nanci Lynn.

Tips: "Know what you want, set a goal, focus in on your goals, be open to constructive criticism, polish tunes and keep polishing."

KICKING MULE RECORDS, INC., Box 158, Alderpoint CA 95411. (707)926-5312. Head of A&R: Ed Denson. Record company and music publisher (Kicking Mule Publishing/BMI and Desk Drawer Publishing/ASCAP). Member NAIRD. Releases 12 LPs/year. Works with artists on contract. Pays 10-16% royalty to artists on contract; standard royalty to songwriters on contract.

How to Contact: Submit demo tape—unsolicited submissions are OK. Prefers reel-to-reel or cassette with 3-5 songs. SASE. Reports in 1 month.

Music: Bluegrass, blues and folk. Released *Solo Guitar* by Tom Ball (folk); *Christmas Come Anew* by Maddie MacNeil (folk); and *Cats Like Angels* by Bob Griffin (piano folk). Other artists include Michael Rugg, Neal Hellman, Bert Jansch, John Renbourn, Stefan Grossman, John James, Happy Traum, Fred Sokolow, Bob Stanton, Bob Hadley, Leo Wijnkamp, Jr., Mark Nelson, Lea Nicholson and Hank Sapoznik.

Tips: "We are a label mostly for instrumentalists. The songs are brought to us by the artists but we contract the artists because of their playing, not their songs. First, listen to what we have released and don't send material that is outside our interests. Secondly, learn to play your instrument well. We have little interest in songs or songwriters, but we are quite interested in people who play guitar, banjo, or dulcimer well."

KILGORE RECORDS, INC., 706 West Mechanic St., Leesville LA 71446-3446. (318)239-2850. President: Mr. John E. Kilgore. Labels include Gotown Records and Kilgore Records. Record company, record producer and music publisher (Gotown Publishing Company/BMI). Releases 6 singles/year. Works with artists and songwriters on contract. Pays statutory rate to publishers for each record sold.

How to Contact: Prefers cassette with 2 songs and lead sheets. SASE. Include 5×7 photo. Reports in 3 months.
Music: Mostly soul and R&B; also urban, contemporary gospel. Released "Just Look," recorded by Ronald Kennedy and Chosen Voices of God Singers.
Tips: "I don't listen to poor quality demos that I can't understand. Submit good material with potential in today's market. Use good quality cassettes."

KING OF KINGS RECORD CO., 38603 Sage Tree St., Palmdale CA 93551-4311. (Branch office: P.O. Box 725, Daytona Beach FL 32015-0725. (904)252-4849.) President: Leroy Pritchett. A&R Director: Charles Vickers. Labels include King of Kings, L.A. International. Record company and music publisher (Pritchett Publications/BMI). Estab. 1978. Releases 1 single and 1 LP/year. Works with musicians/artists and songwriters on contract. Pays 5-10% royalty to artists on contract; statutory rate to publishers per song on record.
How to Contact: Write first for permission to submit. Prefers cassette and lyric sheet. SASE. Reports in 1 month.
Music: Mostly gospel; also country. Released "Walkin' On the Water," "If God Be For You" and "Let Your Light Shine," all written and recorded by Charles Vickers on King of Kings Records (gospel).

KINGSTON RECORDS, 15 Exeter Rd., Kingston NH 03848. (603)642-8493. Coordinator: Harry Mann. Labels include Kingston Records. Record company, music publisher (Strawberry Soda Publishing/ASCAP). Estab. 1988. Releases 3-4 singles, 2-3 12" singles, 3 LPs and 2 CDs/year. Receives 50 submissions/year. Works with musicians/artists and songwriters on contract. Pays 3-5% royalty to artists on contract; statutory rate to publisher per song.
How to Contact: Submit demo tape—unsolicited submissions are OK. Prefers cassette, 15 ips reel-to-reel or VCR videocassette with 3 songs and lyric sheet. SASE. Reports in 6-8 weeks.
Music: Mostly rock, country and pop; "no heavy metal." Released *Two Lane Highway*, written and recorded by Doug Mitchell Band on Kingston Records (folk/rock).

KOTTAGE RECORDS, Box 121626, Nashville TN 37212. (615)726-3556. President: Neal James. Record company, music publisher (Cottage Blue Music/BMI) and record producer (Neal James). Estab. 1979. Releases 4 singles, 2 LPs and 3 CDs/year. Receives 75 submissions/month. Works with musicians/artists on contract. Pays 5% royalty to artists on contract; statutory rate to publisher per song on record.
How to Contact: Write or call first and obtain permission to submit. Prefers cassette with 2 songs and lyric sheet. SASE. Reports in 4 weeks.
Music: Mostly country, rock/pop and gospel; also R&B. Released "Dancin" (by Neal James/Lany Lee), recorded by P.J. Hawk (country); "Share This Night" (by Neal James), recorded by Terry Barbay (contemporary); and "Shiloh" (by Reed Wilcox/Neal James), recorded by Reed Wilcox (contemporary); all on Kottage Records.

KRYSDAHLARK MUSIC, Box 26160, Cincinnati OH 45226. President: Jeff Krys. Artist Management/production company and publisher designed to produce and shop music to record labels and producers. Estab 1986.
How to Contact: Not accepting unsolicited submissions at this time.
Music: Released *The Next Noel* (by Larkin/Dahlgren), recorded by EKIMI on Music West Records (NAC/jazz); *Voice of the Song* by The Village Waytes (vocal-classical/pop); and *Can't Wear the Mask* by Sleep Theatre (modern rock) on KDL Records. Artists include Bill Larkin and Chris Dahlgren of EKIMI; Terri Cantz of Blanche and Deux Boys; Sylvain Acher; Chris Philpotts; Sleep Theatre (Robert Hamrick, Chris Sherman, Johnny Miracle); The Village Waytes: Arranger J. David Moore with Jolynda Bowers, Vera Mariner, Thom Mariner, Michael Oxley and Mark Dietrich; Mr. Lucky: Charles Grund, Rick Lisak and Phil Amalong.

LAMAR MUSIC GROUP, Box 412, New York NY 10462. (914)668-3119. Associate Director: Darlene Barkley. Labels include Lamar, MelVern, Wilson, We-Us and Co. Pub. Record company, music publisher (BMI), and workshop organization. Estab. 1984. Releases 10-12 12" singles and 2-4 LPs/year. Works with musicians/artists and songwriters on contract and hires musicians for in-house studio work.

"How to Use Your Songwriter's Market" (at the front of this book) contains comments and suggestions to help you understand and use the information in these listings.

Pays standard royalty to artists on contract; statutory rate to publisher per song. "We charge only if we are hired to do 'work-for-hire' projects.

How to Contact: Write first and obtain permission to submit. Prefers cassette with 2 songs. Does not return unsolicited material. Reports in 1 month.

Music: Mostly R&B, rap and pop. Released "So In Love" (by R. Robinson), recorded by L. Williams on Macola Records (R&B/dance); "Lose You Love" (by R. Robinson), recorded by Vern Wilson on Lamar Records (R&B/dance); and "Feel Like a Woman" (by Wilson/Johnson), recorded by S. Taylor on MelVern Records (R&B/ballad). Other artists include Barry Manderson and Co/Vern.

Tips: "Members of our company function as singers, songwriters, musicians, producers, executive producers. We basically have all graduated from college in areas related to music or the music business. We either teach about music and the music business or we perform in the business. If you sincerely want to be in this industry this is the type of work you will need to do in order to succeed. It is not as easy as you think."

LANA RECORDS/NUGGET RECORDS, Box 202227, Austin TX 78720. (512)258-0962. Executive Producer: Robby Roberson. Labels include Lana Records, Nugget Country Roots Records, GGT Records and El Country Records. Record company, music publisher (Happy Note Music) and record producer. Releases 3 singles and 2 LPs/year. Works with musicians/artists and songwriters on contract; musicians on salary for in-house studio work. Pays 7-10% royalty to artists on contract; statutory rate to publisher per song on record.

How to Contact: Submit demo tape—unsolicited submissions OK. Prefers cassette with 3 songs and lyric sheet. SASE. Reports in 5 weeks.

Music: Mostly country, gospel, pop, Tex-Mex and soft rock. Released "You Belong to My Heart" by Maria Ellena on Nugget (Tex-Mex); and "Ride This Train" (by Mikal Masters) recorded by Robby Roberson on Nugget Records (country). Other artists include Rosemarie Reedy and Jimmy Walker.

LANDMARK COMMUNICATIONS GROUP, Box 148296, Nashville TN 37214. Producer: Bill Anderson, Jr. Labels include Jana and Landmark Records. Record company, record producer and music publisher (Newcreature Music/BMI and Mary Megan Music/ASCAP) and management firm (Landmark Entertainment). Releases 10 singles, 8 LPs, and 8 CDs/year. Receives 40 submissions/month. Works with musicians/artists and songwriters on contract; hires musicians for in-house studio work. Teams collaborators. Pays 5-7% royalty to artists on contract; statutory rate to publishers for each record sold.

How to Contact: Prefers 7½ ips reel-to-reel or cassette with 4-10 songs and lyric sheet. SASE. Reports in 1 month.

Music: Country/crossover, gospel, jazz, R&B, rock and top 40/pop. Released *Joanne Cash Yates Live . . . w/Johnny Cash*, on Jana Records (gospel LP); *Play It Again Sam*, recorded by Michael L. Pickern on Landmark Records (country LP); *Millions of Miles*, recorded by Teddy Nelson/Skeeter Davis (Norway release) (country LP); *Always*, recorded by Debi Chasteen on Landmark Records (country LP); "You Were Made For Me" by Skeeter Davis and Teddy Nelson on Elli Records/Norway; and *Someday Soon*, recorded by Pam Fenelon on Bil-Mar Records (country LP).

*LANDSLIDE RECORDS, Suite 333, 1800 Peachtree St., Atlanta GA 30309. (404)355-5580. President: Michael Rothschild. Record company, music publisher Frozen Inca Music (BMI) and record producer. Estab. 1981. Releases 2 12" singles, 6 LPs, 6 CDs/year. Works with musicians/artists and songwriters on contract. Pays negotiable rate to artists on contract and publishers per song on record.

How to Contact: Submit demo tape—unsolicited submissions are OK. Prefers cassette with 6-12 songs and lyric sheet. SASE. Reports in 1 month.

Music: Mostly R&B, blues, rap; also gospel, country and techno-pop. Released *Cool On It* and *Fanning The Flames*, both written and recorded by Tinsley Ellis; and *Tore Up*, written and recorded by Nappy Brown, all on Alligator Records (blues LPs). Other artists include Alvin Antonio Youngblood and Gerald Jackson.

LANOR RECORDS, 329 N. Main St., Box 233, Church Point LA 70525. (318)684-2176. Contact: Lee Lavergne. Labels include Lanor Records. Record company and music publisher (Jon Music/BMI). Releases 8-10 cassettes a year. Works with artists and songwriters on contract. Pays 3-5% royalty to artists on contract; statutory rate to writers for each record sold.

How to Contact: Prefers cassette with 2-6 songs. SASE. Reports in 2 weeks.

Music: Mostly country; also rock, soul, zydeco, cajun and blues. Released "*Cajun Pickin'*, recorded by L.A. Band (cajun LP); *Rockin' with Roy*, recorded by Roy Currier (LP) and *Zydeco All Night*, recorded by Joe Walker (zydeco LP), all on Lanor Records.

Tips: Submit "good material with potential in today's market. Use good quality cassettes—I don't listen to poor quality demos that I can't understand."

LARI-JON RECORDS, 325 West Walnut, Rising City NE 68658. (402)542-2336. Owner: Larry Good. Record company, music publisher (LariJon Publishing/BMI) and record producer (Lari-Jon Productions). Estab. 1967. Releases 15 singles and 5 LPs/year. Receives 100-150 submissions/year. Works with songwriters on royalty contract.
How to Contact: Submit demo tape—unsolicited submissions are OK. Prefers cassette with 5 songs and lyric sheet. SASE. Reports in 2 months.
Music: Mostly country, gospel-Southern and '50s rock. Released "Nebraska Land," written and recorded by Larry Good; "The Greatest Star" (by Gerald & June Campbell), recorded by Tom Campbell; and "Her Favorite Song," written and recorded by Johnny Nace, all on Lari-Jon Records (country).

LARK RECORD PRODUCTIONS, INC., Suite 520, 4815 S. Harvard, Tulsa OK 74135. (918)749-1648. Vice-President: Sue Teaff. Record company, music publisher (Jana Jae Music/BMI) and record producer (Lark Talent and Advertising). Estab. 1980. Works with musicians/artists on contract. Payment to artists on contract negotiable; statutory rate to publishers per song on record.
How to Contact: Submit demo tape—unsolicited submissions are OK. Prefers cassette or VHS videocassette with 3 songs and lead sheets. Does not return unsolicited material.
Music: Mostly country, bluegrass and classical; also instrumentals. Released "Fiddlestix" (by Jana Jae); "Mayonnaise" (by Steve Upfold); and "Flyin' South" (by Cindy Walker); all country singles recorded by Jana Jae on Lark Records. Other artists include Syndi, Hotwire and Matt Greif.

LE MATT MUSIC LTD., % Stewart House, Hill Bottom Rd., Highwycombe, Buckinghamshire, HP12 4HJ **England.** Phone: (0630)647374. FAX: (0630)647612. Contact: Ron or Cathrine Lee. Labels include Swoop, Zarg Records, Genouille, Pogo and Check Records. Record company, record producer and music publisher (Le Matt Music, Ltd., Lee Music, Ltd., R.T.F.M. and Pogo Records, Ltd.). Member MPA, PPL, PRS, MCPS. Estab. 1972. Releases 30 12″ singles, 20 LPs and 20 CDs/year. Receives 10-15 submissions/month. Pays negotiable royalty to artists on contract; statutory rate to publishers for each record sold. Royalties paid to US songwriters and artists through US publishing or recording affiliate.
How to Contact: Submit demo tape—unsolicited submissions are OK. Prefers 7½ or 15 ips reel-to-reel or cassette (or VHS videocassette) with 1-3 songs and lyric sheet. Include bio and photo. SAE and IRC. Reports in 6 weeks.
Music: Mostly interested in pop/Top 40; also interested in bluegrass, blues, country, dance-oriented, easy listening, MOR, progressive, R&B, 50s rock, disco, new wave, rock and soul. Released "Annabel," written and recorded by D. Boone (pop); "Witch Woman," written and recorded by R. Dickson on Zarg Records (rock); and "Its a Very Nice," written and recorded by Groucho on Swoop Records (pop). Other artists include Emmitt Till, Touche, Orphan, Jonny Moon, Ian "Sludge" Lees and Kyro.

*LEGS RECORDS, 825 5th St., Menasha WI 54952. (414)725-4467. Executive President: Lori Lee Woods. Labels include Sand Dollar Records. Record company, music publisher (Lori Lee Woods Music/BMI) and record producer. Works with musicians/artists and songwriters on contract.
How to Contact: Write first and obtain permission to submit. Prefers cassette (or VHS videocassette) with 3 songs and lyric or lead sheet. SASE. Reports in 1 month.
Music: Mostly country, rock and gospel.

*JOHN LENNON RECORDS, Box 597, Station "P", Toronto, ON M5S 2T1 **Canada.** (416)658-3726. Contact: Oliver Moore. Record company, music publisher (SOCAN) and record producer (John Lennon Records). Estab. 1979. Releases 3 singles, 2 12″ singles, 1 LP and 2 CDs/year. Works with musicians/artists and songwriters on contract. Pays 12% royalty to artists on contract. Charges advance production fee.
How to Contact: Submit demo tape by mail. No unsolicited submissions. Prefers cassette (or VHS videocassette) with 4 songs and lyric sheets. SAE and IRC required. Reports in 1 month.
Music: Mostly top 40 pop, R&B dance and gospel/country. "You Are Changing" (by O. Hasful and R. Butler), recorded by Carl Ellison; "Summer Nights" (by R. Butler and C. Ellison), recorded by Carl Ellison; and "Get Rich Quick" (by R. Butler), recorded by Yvonne Moore; all on J.L.R.D. Records (all singles). Artists include Alex Jordan and Milton Price.
Tips: "Good quality demo and self addressed, stamped envelope are essential."

LEOPARD MUSIC, 23 Thrayle House, Stockwell Rd., London, SW9 0XU **England.** Phone: (071)738-9577. FAX: (071)737-7881. Executive Producer: Errol Jones. Vice President: Terry Schiavo. Phone: (818)962-6547. FAX: (818)960-8737. Labels include Jet Set Records International (USA). Record company (PRS, BMI) and record producer. Releases 15 singles and 2 LPs/year. Works with musicians/artists and songwriters on contract and hires musicians for in-house studio work. Pays 4-12% royalty to artists on contract, statutory rate to publishers per song on record.

How to Contact: Write first and obtain permission to submit. Prefers cassette (or VHS/PAL videocassette) with 3 songs. SASE. Reports in 2 weeks.

Music: Mostly dance music, soul and pop; also ballad, reggae and gospel. Released "Time After Time" (by Guy Spell), recorded by Rico J (single); "I Need You" (by E. Campbell and E. North Jr.), recorded by Big Africa (single); and *God is Beauty*, written and recorded by Evelyn Ladimeji (LP); all on Leopard Music Records. Other artists include Zoil Foundations and Michael Eytle.

Tips: "Create strong original songs, and artists must have good image."

LION HUNTER MUSIC, Box 110678, Anchorage AK 99511. Vice President: Clive Lock. Record company (BMI). Estab. 1989. Releases 1 single and 1 CD/year. Works with musicians/artists on contract. Pays negotiable royalty to artists on contract; statutory rate to publisher per song on record.

How to Contact: Write first and obtain permission to submit. Prefers cassette with 3 songs and lyric sheet. Does not return unsolicited material.

Music: Mostly rock, pop and R&B. Released "Good-Bye Baby," "That Ain't All (It'll Do)" and "Give Love a Chance" (all by Connett/Lock), recorded by Abandon on Lion Hunter Music (pop/rock). Other artists include The Undertakers (rock).

LIPHONE RECORDS, Box 51, S-451 15 Uddevalla **Sweden.** Phone: 4652262081. FAX Int.: +4652262222. Owner: Borge Lindquist. Record company and music publisher (LiTUNE Music). Estab. 1970. Releases 3-5 singles and 15-20 CDs/year. Works with musicians/artists and songwriters on contract. Pays 3-8% royalty to artists on contract; pays statutory rate to publisher per song on record.

How to Contact: Prefers cassette and lyric sheet; disc to ATARI ST is also OK. Does not return unsolicited material. Reports in 5 weeks.

Music: Mostly country, pop and rock; also folk, R&B, jazz, fusion and gospel. Released "Soft Landing" (by Rolf Jardemark), recorded by Michael Ruff (LA) (CD and LP); "Jon Nagourney," recorded by Jon Nagourney (LA) (CD); and "It's Still Time," written and recorded by Bjorn Vickhoff (LP); all on Liphone Records. Other artists include "about 40 artists from the Scandinavian countries."

LOADING BAY RECORDS, 586, Bristol Road, Selly Oak, Birmingham B29 6BQ **England.** Phone (21)472-2463. FAX: (21)414-1540. M.D.: Duncan Finlayson. Labels include Loading Bay Records, Two Bears Music and Made Up Records. Record company and record producer (Loading Bay Productions). Estab. 1988. Releases 20 12" singles, 3 LPs and 3 CDs/year. Works with musicians/artists on contract and "negotiates one-off licensing deals." Pays 10% royalty; statutory rate to publishers per son on record.

How to Contact: Submit demo tape—unsolicited submissions are OK. Prefers cassette (or D.A.T.) with several songs. SAE and IRC. Reports in 5-6 weeks.

Music: Mostly Hi-NRG-dance and disco dance. Released "Bring on the Boys," written and recorded by Vicki Shepard; "Thank You for Being a Friend" (by A. Gold), recorded by The Golden Girls; and "Angel " (by Parrish), recorded by Beth L'Kem, all on Loading Bay Records (Hi-NRG 12"). Other artists include Rofo, Samantha Gilles, Sheila Steward, Claudia T. and Kelly Marie.

LRJ, Box 3, Belen NM 87002. (505)864-7441. Manager: Tony Palmer. Labels include LRJ, Little Richie, Chuckie. Record company. Estab. 1959. Releases 5 singles and 2 LPs/year. Works with musicians/artists on contract.

How to Contact: Submit demo tape—unsolicited submissions are OK. Prefers cassette. SASE. Reports in 1 month.

Music: Mostly country. Released "If Teardrops Were Pennies" (by Carl Bultes), recorded by Myrna Lorrie; "Sing Me a Love Song" written and recorded by Myrna Lorrie; and "Auction of My Life" written and recorded by Joe King; all on LRJ Records.

LUCIFER RECORDS, INC., Box 263, Brigantine NJ 08203-0263. (609)266-2623. President: Ron Luciano. Labels include TVA Records. Record company, music publishers (Ciano Publishing and Legz Music), record producers (Pete Fragale and Tony Vallo) and management firm and booking agency (Ron Luciano Music Co. and TVA Productions). Works with artists and songwriters on salary and contract. "Lucifer Records has offices in South Jersey, Palm Beach, Florida, Sherman Oaks, California and Las Vegas, Nevada."

How to Contact: Arrange personal interview. Prefers cassette with 4-8 songs. SASE. Reports in 3 weeks.

Music: Dance, easy listening, MOR, rock, soul and top 40/pop. Released "I Who Have Nothing," by Spit-N-Image (rock single); "Lucky," and "Smoke Ya," by Legz (rock singles); and "Loves a Crazy Game," by Voyage (disco/ballad single). Other artists include Bobby Fisher and Jerry Denton.

MAIN TRIPP RECORDS INC., 2804 Beechtree Dr., Sanford NC 27330. (919)774-8926. President: Bill Tripp. Record company and music publisher (BMI). Estab. 1982. Releases 12 singles, and 12 LPs/ year. Works with musicians/artsts and songwriters on contract. Pays statutory rate to publisher per song on record. Write first and obtain permission to submit or to arrange personal interview. Prefers cassette with 3 songs and lyric sheet. Does not return unsolicited material. Reports in 3 months.
Music: Mostly country, gospel and bluegrass. Released *Forever*, written and recorded by Raymond Barns (R&B); *Empty Places*, written and recorded by Don Keatley/Jim Watters (country gospel) both on MTR Records; and *Empty Places*, (by Jim Watters), recorded by The Helmsmen (gospel) on Morning Star Records. Other artists include Pioneers (gospel), Don Keatley, Shine On, Clyde Frazier, Raymond Barnes, Jim Watters.

MAJESTIC CONTROL RECORDS, Box 330-568, Brooklyn NY 11233. (718)919-2013. A&R Department: Alemo. Record company, music publisher (Majestic Control Music/BMI) and record producer (Alemo and Hank Love). Estab. 1983. Works with musicians/artists on contract.
How to Contact: Submit demo tape—unsolicited submissions are OK. Prefers cassette with 3 songs. SASE. Reports in 4 weeks.
Music: Mostly rap, dance and reggae; also house. Released "Cold Sweat" (by Curtis, Moye, Davis), recorded by Majestic Productions (rap, single); *Lovely, Lovely* (by M. Lowe), recorded by M.C. Lovely (rap LP); and "Front Line" (by Curtis, Moye, Davis), recorded by Majestic Productions (rap single), all on Majestic Control Records. Other artists include M.C. Cuba.

MARIAH RECORDS, Box 310, Carmichael CA 95609-310. President: Mari Minice. Record company (Mariah Records). Estab. 1986. Releases 1 single/year. Receives 50 submissions/year. Works with musicians/artists on contract. Pays varying royalty to artists on contract; statutory rate to publishers per song on record.
How to Contact: Submit demo tape—unsolicited submissions are OK. Prefers cassette with any number of songs and lyric sheets. Does not return unsolicited material. Reports in 2 months.
Music: Mostly country/contemporary, pop and rock. Released "Closer to Heaven" (by Jill Wood), recorded by Rachel Minke on Mariah Records (country single).
Tips: "Keep it country—female, contemporary or traditional."

MARZ RECORDS, Dept. SM, 2602 NW 5th Ave., Miami FL 33127. (305)573-5400. Label Manager: Karen Dyer. Labels include Marz Records, Kinetic Records (manufacture and distribute only). Record company and music publisher (Marz Need Music/BMI). Estab. 1990. Releases 6-8 12" singles, 3-5 LPS and 3-5 CDs/year. Works with musicians/artists on record contract. Pays statutory rate to publisher per song on record.
How to Contact: Submit demo tape—unsolicited submissions are OK. Prefers cassette with 3-5 songs and lyric sheet. SASE. Reports in 1 month.
Music: Mostly industrial/progressive and dance; also progressive rock. Released "Algorythm," written and recorded by Force Dimension on Marz Records (industrial, 12"); "Move Out," written and recorded by Another Nation on Kinetic Records (industrial 12"); and "Give Me a Sign," written and recorded by Razor on Kinetic Records (industrial, 12").

MASTER-TRAK ENTERPRISES, Dept. SM, 413 N. Parkerson, Crowley LA 70526. (318)788-0773. General Manager and Chief Engineer: Bobby Terry. Labels include Master-Trak, Showtime, Kajun, Blues Unlimited, Par T and MTE Records. Recording studio and record companies. Releases 20 singles and 6-8 LPs/year. Works with musicians/artists on contract. Pays 6% artist royalty. (No studio charges to contract artists.) Studio available on an hourly basis to the public. Charges for some services: "We charge for making audition tapes of any material that we do not publish."
How to Contact: Prefers cassette and lead sheet. SASE. Reports in 1 month.
Music: Mostly country, rock, R&B, cajun, blues and Zydeco. Released "Johnny Can't Dance" by Wayne Toups (Zydeco), "Tell Me What I Want to Hear Tonight" by Tammy Lynn, and "Only Passing Through" by Freddie Pate on MTE Records (country). Other artists include Al Ferrier, and Fernest & The Thunders.
Tips: "The song is the key. If we judge it to be a good song, we record it and it sells, we are happy. If we mis-judge the song and/or the artist and it does not sell, we must go back to the drawing board."

MAXX RECORDS, Dept. SM, Suite 207, 50 Music Square W., Nashville TN 37203. (615)329-2591. FAX: (615)329-2592. Publishing Manager: Karen Morris. Record company, music publisher (Maxx) and record producer (Fred Morris Music Group). Estab. 1987. Releases varying number of singles/ year. Works with musicians/artists and songwriters on contract. Pays varying royalty to artists on contract; pays statutory rate to publisher per song on record.

How to Contact: Prefers cassette (or VHS videocassette, if artists) with 3-5 songs and lyric sheet. SASE. Reports in 1 month.
Music: Mostly country, pop and rock; "no gospel." Released *Calendar Blues* (by Karren Pell/Dan E. James), recorded by Jill Jordan; and *We're Gonna Love Tonight* (by Eddy Rager/Vernis Pratt), recorded by Don Juan (both singles, LPs and CDs); *Panic* (by Fran Weber), recorded by Don Juan (country rock LP); and "Ease My Mind" (by Sing Me Publishing), recorded by Jill Jordan (country LP); all on Maxx Records.
Tips: "Remember that the music business is that, a business. Talent is not enough anymore. You need an awareness of marketing and what is involved in making commercial decisions of where you are headed."

MCA RECORDS, 8th Fl., 1755 Broadway, New York NY 10019. (212)841-8000. East Coast A&R Director: Susan Dodes. East Coast Vice President: Bruce Dickinson. Labels include Costellation, Cranberry, Curb, IRS, Motown, London, Zebra and Philly World. Record company and music publisher (MCA Music). Works with musicians/artists on contract.
How to Contact: Call first and obtain permission to submit. Prefers cassete (or VHS videocassette) and lyric or lead sheet. SASE.

MCI ENTERTAINMENT GROUP, Suite 830, Universal City Plaza, Universal City CA 91608. (818)506-8533. Vice President A&R: Jaeson Effantic. Labels include Bouvier, Credence, PPL. Record company. Estab. 1979. Releases 50-60 singles, 12 12" singles, 6 LPs and 6 CDs/year. Works with musicians/artists and songwriters on contract and hires musicians for in-house studio work. Pays 8-15% royalty to artists on contract; statutory rate to publisher per song on record.
How to Contact: Write first and obtain permission to submit. Prefers cassette or videocassette with 2 songs. SASE. Reports in 4-6 weeks.
Music: Released *Night Song* (by Gip Noble), recorded by Phuntaine on Bouvier Records (jazz LP); *Fynne as I can B* (by Santiono), recorded by I.B. Fynne on Credence Records (pop LP); and *Love Song* (by DM Groove), recorded by Dale Mitchell on Bouvier Records (R&B LP). Other artists include Big Daddy and Blazers, Lejenz and Condottiere.
Tips: "Don't limit yourself to just one style of music. Diversify and write other styles of songs."

*MDS ENTERTAINMENT, 29 S. Erie, Toledo OH 43602. Manager, A&R: J.P. Jimy. Labels include Toledo Records, Park J. Tunes, Jamestune Records and Newstar International Records. Record company, music publisher (Keeny/York Publishing) and record producer (MDS Productions). Releases 10 singles and 3 LPs/year. Works with musicians/artists and songwriters on contract. Pays standard royalty to artists on contract.
How to Contact: Submit demo tape—unsolicited submissions are OK. Prefers cassette with 3 songs and lyric sheet. Does not return unsolicited material. Reports in 6 weeks.
Music: Country, jazz, rock and MOR. Released "Mr. Sun," written and recorded by MDS (AC); "Pigskin Widow" (by Ellie Morris) and "Bird Feeder Blues" (by Sparrow) all on Newstar Records (rock/dance). Other artists include Suzy Rice, Mark Kieswetter, Lori Lefevre, Dan Faehnle, Kerry Clark, Woody Brubaker, Polyphony, Mick Payne, Patti Whack, Tanguerey, Rococo and Michael Brackistar.
Tips: "Currently seeking new artists for Newstar International Records."

*MERCURY RECORDS, 10th Floor, 11150 Santa Monica Blvd, Los Angeles CA 90025. (818)955-5205. Manager A&R: Bobby Carlton. Director A&R: Mike Sikkus. Labels include Wing Records. Record company. Estab. 1940s. Releases 100-150 singles; 40-60 12" singles, 100-120 LPs, 10 EPs and 100-120 CDs/year. Works with musicians/artists on contract. Pays 9-16% royalty to artists on contract; statutory rate or ¾ of statutory rate "if we do not own publisher."
How to Contact: Write first and obtain permission to submit. Prefers cassette with 4-6 songs. Does not return unsolicited submissions. Reports in 4-6 weeks.
Music: Mostly rock, R&B/dance, pop; also country. Released "Get a Leg Up," written and recorded by J. Mellencamp; "Save the Best" (by Waldman/Lind), recorded by V. Williams; "Winds of Change," written and recorded by the Scorpions, all on Mercury Records. Other artists include The Triplets, Tony! Toni! Tone!, Tears For Fears, Ugly Kid Joe, Material Issue and James.
Tips: "Learn song structure and establish yourself with a reputable publisher."

MICROSTAR RECORDS, Suite 201, 5245 Cleveland St., Dept. SM, Virginia Beach VA 23462. (804)499-4434. President: Mark Spencer. Labels include MicroStar, MSM. Record company, music publisher (ASCAP) and record producer (MicroStar). Estab. 1990. Releases 6 LPs and 6 CDs/year. Works with musicians/artists and songwriters on contract; and musicians on salary for in-house studio work. Pays for in-house studio work 15-20% wholesale. Pays statutory rate to publisher per song on record.

How to Contact: Write first and obtain permission to submit. Prefers cassette with 4 songs and lyric sheet. Does not return unsolicited material. Reports in 4 weeks.
Music: Mostly pop, gospel and country; also R&B. Released *Do You Think We Have a Chance* (by K. Cleveland), recorded by TK Lleggs; *Wearing White With No Shame* (by P. Van Valin), recorded by P. Van Valin; and *Workin' Man's Dream*, written and recorded by B. Fisher; all on MicroStar Records (LPs). Other artists include Don Burford, Tony Hawkins, Charity Jackson, David Givens, Matt Vollmer, and Pam Osborn.
Tips: "Work hard and don't cut corners on your demo. However, don't overproduce it either. If you can't raise enough support on your own to pay for a well-produced demo, then we don't have confidence in your ability to be successful."

MIGHTY RECORDS, Suite 6-D, 150 West End, New York NY 10023. (212)873-5968. Manager: Danny Darrow. Labels include Mighty Sounds & Filmworks. Record company, music publisher, record producer (Danny Darrow). Estab. 1958. Releases 1-2 singles, 1-2 12″ singles and 1-2 LPs/year. Works with songwriters on royalty contract and hires musicians for in-house studio work. Pays standard royalty to artists on contract; statutory rate to publishers per song on record.
How to Contact: Submit demo tape—unsolicited submissions are OK. "No phone calls." Prefers cassette with 3 songs and lyric sheet. SASE. Reports in 1 week.
Music: Mostly pop, country and dance; also jazz. Released *Carnival Nights* (by Vincent C. DeLucia and Raymond Squillacote), recorded by Danny Darrow (country LP); *Impulse*, written and recorded by Danny Darrow (dance LP); and *Corporate Lady* (by Michael Greer), recorded by Danny Darrow (pop) all on Mighty Records.
Tips: "Listen to the hits of Richie, Manilow, Houston and Rogers and write better songs."

MINDFIELD RECORDS, 4B, 500 ½ E. 84th St., New York NY 10028. (212)861-8745. A&R: Guy Torio. Record company, music publisher (Mia Mind Music/ASCAP) and record producer (I.Y.F. Productions). Estab. 1985. Releases 10 singles, 6 12″ singles, 4 LPs and 4 CDs/year. Works with musicians/artists and songwriters on contract. Payment to artists on contract varies; statutory rate to publisher per song on record.
How to Contact: Submit demo tape by mail—unsolicited submissions are OK. Prefers cassette or VHS videocassette with 3 songs. SASE. Reports in 6 weeks.
Music: Mostly rap, house and hip hop; also dance, top 40 and AOR. Released "Cosmic Climb" (by Werner/Sargent), recorded by Madonna (dance); "Gods" (by Werner/Sargent), recorded by Madonna (dance); and "I've Fallen," written and recorded by Baby Oil (house); all on Mindfield Records. Other artists include P.O.A., Electric Sun, Clark After Dark and Papa HaHa.
Tips: "Submit demos on DAT cassettes for best sound quality."

*MIRROR RECORDS, INC., 645 Titus Ave., Rochester NY 14617. (716)544-3500. Vice President: Armand Schaubroeck. Labels include Mirror and House of Guitars Records. Record company and music publisher. Works with artists and songwriters on contract and hires musicians for in-house studio work. Royalty paid to artists varies; negotiable royalty to songwriters on contract.
How to Contact: Prefers cassette or record (or videocassette). Include photo with submission. SASE. Reports in 2 months.
Music: Folk, progressive, rock, punk and heavy metal. Released "Don't Open Til Doomsday" by Chesterfield Kings; "Through The Eyes of Youth" by Immaculate Mary; and "Drunk on Muddy Water" by Chesterfield Kings.

MISSILE RECORDS, Box 5537 Kreole Station, Moss Point MS 39563. (601)475-2098. "No collect calls." President/Owner: Joe F. Mitchell. Record company, music publisher (Bay Ridge Publishing/BMI) and record producer (Missile Records; have also produced for Happy Hollow Records, Myra Records, JB Records, RCI and Wake Up Records). Estab. 1974. Releases 20 singles and 6 LPs/year. Works with artists on contract. Pays 8-10% royalty to artists on contract; statutory rate to publishers for each record sold.
How to Contact: Write first and obtain permission to submit. Include #10 SASE. "All songs sent for review must include sufficient return postage." Prefers cassette with 3-6 songs and lyric sheets. Does not return unsolicited material. Reports in 6 weeks.

Market conditions are constantly changing! If you're still using this book and it is 1994 or later, buy the newest edition of Songwriter's Market at your favorite bookstore or order directly from Writer's Digest Books.

Close-up

Tony Brown
Vice President, A&R
MCA Records
Nashville, Tennessee

Tony Brown is a producer who's never forgotten what it's like to be a musician—years spent as a keyboardist for the Oak Ridge Boys, Elvis Presley and Emmylou Harris' Hot Band. Despite the fact that his current position gives him a lot of control over the production of his artists' recording projects, he has gained tremendous respect for paying attention to the artist's vision. And while Brown is receiving accolades for his production skills, his artists—Vince Gill, Patty Loveless, Lyle Lovett, Steve Earle, Nanci Griffith and Kelly Willis—are racking up awards and airplay.

"When I got to Nashville," he says "the majority of producers I encountered were producing records with *their* vision foremost and the artist's vision secondary. I thought, 'I'm going to keep in mind that I'm working *for* the artists, not *with* the artists.' My job is to help them achieve their vision. If they need my help, I'm there to help them."

Brown has learned to trust his gut instinct on whom to recruit for MCA's country roster. "Every A&R person has his own style. When somebody asks, 'How do you get to be an A&R person?' I say, 'When you get someone at a record company to trust your taste—your taste represents money. If your taste is only mainstream and safe, you're going to run dry. On the other hand, you can be so left and so indulgent that pretty soon everybody who thought you were cool realizes you're not. I like to look to the left and to the right and to the middle.

"When I look for an act, I look for a complete package—how I feel when I first hear the voice, when I meet the act and I like what I see. Then, I want to see if they have some sort of presence onstage. It's a gamble. My job is to sign acts that sell records, but at the same time, I've got to look down the road to where I think country music is going. You affect the music by who you sign to the roster. When I sign acts, I try to think of what is happening on radio right now. But I've always got my eye out for an act that is doing something just a little bit different, because I think it adds spice to your roster. I'm always looking for the next big thing."

One of his most memorable "big things" was the day Lyle Lovett walked into his office. Brown remembers, "He was a totally complete package. His hair, his clothes—the guy was completely developed all the way around. His first albums were his demos that I just mixed. That's the ultimate example of how an artist can come out of nowhere."

Brown also cites Grammy winner Vince Gill as one of his production triumphs. The title cut from the duo's collaboration landed the star his first No. 1 single, a Grammy and a Country Music Association Award for Single of the Year; his two Brown-produced MCA albums went platinum and he was honored as CMA's Male Vocalist of the Year in 1991.

Along with talent and a good gut instinct, Brown feels that in order to be a success in the record industry you have to be willing to meet new people. "The whole deal about this industry is always making new friendships—expanding and meeting new people, especially people who are more talented than you are because otherwise you can't grow."

—Marjie McGraw

Music: Mostly country, gospel, rap and R&B; also soul, MOR, blues, rock, pop, and bluegrass. Released "You Owe Some Back to Me" and "Hello Heartbreak" by Ann Black; "I'll Always Miss You" and "Another Lonely Christmas" by T.C. Bullock; all on Missile Records (country). Other artists include Herbert Lacey, Ann Black, Lori Mark, Jerry Wright, Danny Keebler and Jerry Ann. "Also considering songs on master tape for release in the US and abroad."
Tips: "If a recording artist has exceptional talent and some backing then Missile Records will give you our immediate attention. A bio and cassette tape and picture of the artist should be submitted along with sufficient return postage."

*MODERN BLUES RECORDINGS, Box 248, Pearl River NY 10965. (914)735-3944. Owner: Daniel Jacoubovitch. Record company. Estab. 1985. Releases 1-2 LPs and 1-2 CDs/year. Works with musicians/artists and songwriters on contract. Pays statutory rate to artists on contract and publishers per song on record.
How to Contact: Write or call first and obtain permission to submit. SASE. Reports in 2-4 weeks.
Music: Blues, R&B and soul; also rock 'n roll. Released "Poison Kisses" written and recorded by Jerry Portnoy; "Ida's Song" written and recorded by J. Vaugh and "Frances" written and recorded by Johnson/Maloney, all on Modern Blues Records (blues). Other artists include Clayton Love.

MODERN MUSIC VENTURES, INC., 5626 Brock St., Houston TX 77023. (713)926-4436. Chief Operations Officer: Art Gottschalk. Labels include Discos MM, Double M Records and Foundation. Record company. Estab. 1986. Releases 12 singles, 2 12″ singles, 6 LPs, 2 EPs and 6 CDs/year. Works with musicians/artists on record contract. Pays statutory rate to publisher per song on record.
How to Contact: Write first and obtain permission to submit. Prefers cassette with 5 songs and lyric sheets. SASE. Reports in 12 weeks.
Music: Mostly Latin (in Spanish), country and jazz; also rap and rap (in Spanish). Released *Simplemente*, recorded by Elsa Garcia; *Rebelde*, recorded by Mercedez; and *La Primera Vez*, recorded by The Choice; all on PolyGram Records (LPs). Other artists include Mary Maria, Dallazz, and Michael Flores.

MONEYTIME RECORDS, 742 Rowley St., Owosso MI 48867. (517)723-1796. Director: Jon Harris. Record company and music publisher (Moneytime Publishing Co./BMI). Estab. 1990. Releases 6 singles, 2 12″ singles, 3 LPs, 2 EPs and 3 CDs/year. Works with musicians/artists on record contract. Pays 10% royalty to artists on contract; statutory rate to publisher per song on record.
How to Contact: Submit demo tape—unsolicited submissions are OK. Prefers cassette with 4-6 songs and lyric sheets (picture and bio if possible). SASE. Reports in 4 weeks.
Music: Mostly rap, R&B and dance; also house, funk and soul. Released *I'll Trip* and *No Parole* (by Jon Harris), recorded by The Mad Rapper; and *Brighter Lights* (by Brian Hammock), recorded by Children of A Lesser God, all on Moneytime Records (LP).
Tips: "Put the best you have on the front of the tape, and have copyrights secured."

MOR RECORDS, 17596 Corbel Court, San Diego CA 92128. (619)485-1550. President: Stuart L. Glassman. Record company and record producer. Estab. 1980. Releases 3 singles/year. Receives 250 submissions/year. Works with musicians on salary for in-house studio work. Pays 4% royalty to artists.
How to Contact: Submit demo tape—unsolicited submissions are OK. Prefers cassette (or VHS videocassette). SASE. Reports in 2 months.
Music: Mostly pop instrumental/vocal MOR; also novelty songs. Released "The Maltese Falcon . . . A Simple Solution" by Wally Flaherty (comedy); "Symphony" (public domain) by Piano Man (instrumental pop) and "Fall Softly Snow" (by Jean Surrey) recorded by Al Rosa (Christmas re-issue); all on MOR Records.
Tips: "Send original work. Do not send 'copy' work."

*MSM RECORDS, Box 101, South Newfane, VT 05351. Operating Manager: John Scott. Labels include Hãlo Records and Bronco Records. Record company and music publisher (Mount Scott Music/BMI and Pick The Hits Music/ASCAP). Estab. 1979. Releases 3-4 singles/year. Receives up to 200 submissions/year. Works with songwriters on contract and hires musicians for in-house studio work. Pays 4-8% royalty to artists on contract; statutory rate (or as negotiated) to publisher per song on record.
How to Contact: Write first and obtain permission to submit. Prefers cassette with 2 songs and lyric sheets. Does not return unsolicited material. Reports in 4 weeks.
Music: Mostly folk, traditional country, contemporary country and pop-rock. Released "Here Comes the Rain Again" (by M. Lewis and M. Brush), recorded by Gwen Newton on Halo Records (single cassette). Other artists include Robin Sorensen and Roger Young.
Tips: "Pay careful attention to what you want to say with your music and then present it simply and as well recorded as possible. Vocals upfront and typed lyric sheet."

MS'QUE RECORDS INC., Box 26852, Oklahoma OK 73126. A&R Representative: Christopher Stanley. Record company and music publisher (CAB Industries, Inc./BMI). Estab. 1988. Releases 20 singles, 20 12" singles, 6 LPs and 2 CDs/year. Works with musicians/artists and songwriters on contract and hires musicians for in-house studio work. Pays statutory rate to publisher per song on record.
How to Contact: Submit demo tape by mail—unsolicited submissions are OK. Prefers cassette or VHS videocassette with 3 songs and lead sheet. SASE. Reports in 4-8 weeks.
Music: Mostly R&B, pop and rock; also gospel and jazz. Released "Together" (by C. Freeman), recorded by Cash & Co.; "We've Just Begun" (by C. Freeman), recorded by Cash & Co.; and "Everybody Sing" (by S. DeBrown), recorded by Emotions, all on Ms'Que Records.

MULE KICK RECORDS, 5341 Silvewode Dr., Placerville CA 95667. (916)626-4536. Owner: Doug McGinnis, Sr. Record company and music publisher (Freewheeler Publishing/BMI). Estab. 1949. Works with musicians/artists and songwriters on contract and hires musicians for in-house studio work. Pays artists 6¢ per album; statutory rate to publishers.
How to Contact: Submit demo tape—unsolicited submissions are OK. Prefers cassette with 6-10 songs and lyric and lead sheet. SASE. Reports in 1 month.
Music: Mostly C&W, jazz-AB, and c-rock; also pop. Released "One Man Job" and "Please Play Me A Song" (by Mary Voigt), recorded by Coye Wilcox; and "Mighty Big Man" (by Helen Faye), recorded by Ray Jones all on Lu-Tex Records (country). Other artists include Don McGinnis, Tiny Moore, Dub Taylor, Rome Johnson and Roy Lanham.
Tips: "Keep country country."

MUSCLE SHOALS SOUND GOSPEL, Box 915, Sheffield AL 35660. (205)381-2060. Executive Director: Frank Williams. Record company and record producer (Butch McGhee). Estab. 1986. Releases 6 LPs/year. Receives 50-60 submissions/year. Works with musicians/artists and songwriters on contract and hires musicians for in-house studio work. Pays 8% royalty to artists on contract; statutory rate to publisher per song.
How to Contact: Write first and obtain permission to submit. Prefers cassette or VHS videocassette with 4 songs. Does not return unsolicited material. Reports in 8 weeks.
Music: Mostly gospel, inspirational. Released "Bow Down and Praise Him" (by Butch McGhee, Shawn Lee Sr. and Harvey Thompson Jr.), recorded by Loretta Handy (gospel); "Caught in Your Own Mess" (by Butch McGhee, Shawn Lee Sr. and Harvey Thompson Jr.), recorded by Denise LaSalle (blues); and "Stop That Zero" (by Butch McGhee and Harvey Thompson Jr.), recorded by Denise LaSalle (blues); all on Maleco Records.

MUSIC OF THE WORLD, Box 3620, Chapel Hill NC 27515-3620. President: Bob Haddad. Record company and music publisher (Owl's Head Music/BMI). Estab. 1982. Releases 10 CDs/year. Works with musicians/artists on contract and hires musicians for in-house studio work. Royalty paid to artists on contract varies; statutory rate to publisher per song on record.
How to Contact: Submit demo tape—unsolicited submissions OK. Prefers cassette. SASE. Reports in 1 month.
Music: Only world music. Released "I Remember" and "Fieso Jaiye," written and recorded by I.K. Dairo (Afro pop); and "Grodlaten," written and recorded by Anders Rosén (jazz), all on M.O.W. Records.
Tips: "Submit only traditional world music, or ethnic-influenced modern music."

MUSICLAND PRODUCTIONS, 911 N.E. 17th Ave., Ocala FL 32670. (904)622-5599. Contact: A&R. Music publisher, recording studio and printing shop. BMI. Estab. 1987. Releases 12 songs/year; 4 new songwriters/year. Works with composers. Pays 6% royalty; statutory rate to publishers.
Affiliate: Big Sun Music (BMI).
How to Contact: Submit a demo tape—unsolicited submissions are OK. Prefers cassette with 4 songs and lyric sheet. If possible come in person. "We do not return tapes." Reports in 2 weeks.
Music: Mostly rock, pop and gospel; also country. Produced "It's Christ" (by Grey Wolcott); "Raised on Country Love" (by Paul Parrott); and "Next Payday" (by B. Land), all recorded by Ben Poole on Musicland Productions Records (CHSS.)
Tips: "Spend money to record it the best you can. If you don't believe in it enough no one else will."

NADINE MUSIC, Box 2, Fronhof 100, CH-8260 Stein am Rhein Switzerland. Phone: 054-415-415. FAX: 054-415-420. President: Freddy J. Angstmann. Music publisher and record producer. Releases 12 LPs/year. Works with musicians/artists and songwriters on contract.
How to Contact: Prefers cassette (or VHS/PAL videocassette). SAE and IRC.
Music: Mostly gospel, blues and jazz; also classical. Released *Christmas Album* and *Who Shall Abide* (by Johnny Thompson), and *Gospel at the Opera* (by Radio Zürich) both on Capricorn Records (all LPs). Other artists include Mickey Baker, Erich Lauer, Errol Dixon, Anne Morrëe, Philadelphia Jerry Ricks and Champion Jack Dupree.

NARADA PRODUCTIONS, 1845 North Farwell Ave., Milwaukee WI 53202. (414)272-6700. Contact: Dan Chase. Labels include Narada Equinox, Narada Lotus, Narada Mystique, Sona Gaia. Record company. Estab. 1979. Releases 25 LPs/year. Works with musicians/artists on contract.
How to Contact: Submit demo tape by mail. Unsolicited submissions are OK. Prefers cassette (or VHS videocassette if available). Does not return unsolicited material. Reports in 2 months. .
Music: Mostly instrumental. Released *Mil Amones* written and recorded by Doug Cameron, on Euinox Records; *Dr. D* written and recorded by Spencer Brewer, on Equinox Records; and *Citizen of Time* written and recorded by David Arkenstone, on Mystique Records (instrumental).

NEON RECORDS, 88 Lenox Ave., Paterson NJ 07502. (201)790-7668. A&R Department: Scott Lea. Record company, music publisher (BMI, ASCAP), record producer (Scott Lea Productions) and Scott Lea Publishing. Estab. 1988. Releases 3-6 singles, 2-4 12″ singles, 1-2 LPs, 1-2 EPs and 1-2 CDs/year. Works with musicians/artists and songwriters on contract and hires musicians for in-house studio work. Pays varying royalty to artists on contract; negotiated rate to publisher per song on record.
How to Contact: Call first and obtain permission to submit. Prefers cassette with 3-5 songs and lyric sheet. SASE. Reports in 6 weeks.
Music: Mostly R&B, club, dance, A/C and rock; also pop and jazz. Released "World Without Love" (by Claude S.), recorded by Anything Box on Neon Records (club/ballad); "Stop" (by R. Bonagura and D. Cintron), recorded by Myth on Neon Records (rock) and "How Does Your Heart Feel?" (by P. Castgilin and S. Lea), recorded by Paul Cast on Neon Records (adult contemporary/rock ballad).

*NEPHELIM RECORD (STUDIO WORKS), 404 ST-Henri, Montreal Quebec H3C 2P5 **Canada**. (514)871-8481. Producer: Mario Rubnikowich. Music publisher (SDE, CAPAC) and record producer. Estab. 1986. Releases 10 singles, 2 12″ singles, 6 LPs and 2 CDs/year. Works with musicians/artists and songwriters on contract and hires musicians for in-house studio work.
How to Contact: Submit demo tape—unsolicited submissions are OK. Prefers cassette with 3 songs and lyric or lead sheets. SASE. Reports in 5 weeks.
Music: Mostly new age, pop and R&B; also rock, metal and relaxation. Released "Young/Donato" (by Young/Donato), on Just In Times Records (jazz, LP/CD); "Paul Lauzon" (by Paul Lauzon) on Blue Wing Records (therapy, LP, cassettes); and "Just for Laughs" (by Serge Fiori), on Radio Quebec (radio comedy). Other artists include Michel Laverdiere, Robert LaFond, Oréalis, John Oakley, Marc Chapleau and John Bodine.

NERVOUS RECORDS, Unit 6, 7-11 Minerva Rd., London NW10 6HJ, **England**. Phone: 4481-963-0352. Managing Director: R. Williams. Record company, record producer and music publisher (Nervous Publishing and Zorch Music). Member MCPS, PRS, PPL. Releases 10 CDs/year. Receives 100 submissions/year. Works with songwriters on royalty contract. Pays 5-12% royalty to artists on contract; statutory rate to publishers per song on records. Royalties paid directly to US songwriters and artists or through US publishing or recording affiliate.
How to Contact: Submit demo tape—unsolicited submissions OK. Prefers cassette with 4-15 songs and lyric sheet. SAE and IRC. Reports in 1 month.
Music: Psychobilly and rockabilly. "No heavy rock, AOR, stadium rock, disco, soul, pop—only wild rockabilly and psychobilly." Released *Curse of the Coffin* (by Gararde), recorded by Nerromantix on Nervous Records (psychobilly); *Line Up Linda* (by Bracrenridge), recorded by The Rednecks on Fury Records (punk); and *Crazy Song* (by Verheij), recorded by Catmen on Nervous Records (rockabilly). Other artists include The Griswalds, Rusti Steel, The Tintax Torment and The Nitros.
Tips: "Want wild and fast music—really demented rockabilly, not punk."

*NETTWERK PRODUCTIONS, 1250 W. 6th Ave., Vancouver, British Columbia V6H 1A5 **Canada**. (604)654-2929. A&R Assistant: Simon Hussey. Record company, music publisher (Nettwerk Productions/SOCAN). Estab. 1984. Releases 12-15 singles, 6 LPs, 2 EPs, 6 CDs/year. Works with musicians/artists and songwriters on contract.
How to Contact: Submit demo tape—unsolicited submissions are OK. Prefers cassette. Does not return unsolicited material. Reports in 2-3 months.
Music: Mostly rock, punk-funk, dance; also rap and urban-dance, folk-rock. Released *Solace* (by Sarah McLachlan); *Welcome To My Dream* (by MC900 Ft. Jesus); and *Like Stars in My Hands* (by Single Gun Theory). Other artists include Brothers & Systems, Consolidated, Skinny Puppy, Hilt, Itch and Lava Hay.
Tips: "The music should stand out; try not to copy what you have heard five other bands do before. Try to make it sound interesting to the listeners."

*NEW BEGINNING RECORD PRODUCTIONS, (formerly Four Winds Record Productions Inc.), Box 4773, Fondren Station, Jackson MS 39216-0773. A&R Manager: S. Wooten. Record company. Works with musicians/artists on contract, songwriters on royalty contracts and hires musicians for in-house studio work. "We will work with composers, lyric writers and collaborators on unusual songs. Also new unusual talent is welcome." Pays 10-20% royalty to artists on contract; statutory rate to publishers for each record sold.

How to Contact: Write. Prefers cassette with 2-4 songs. SASE. Reports in 1 month.

Music: Mostly country; also bluegrass and black gospel. Released "Little David," "I'm The One," and "Going Home Look," all written and recorded by Sojourners on New Beginning Records (Southern gospel).

*NEW EXPERIENCE REC/GRAND SLAM RECORDS, Box 683, Lima Ohio 45802. (419)674-4170 or (419)675-2990. Contact: Tanya Milligan. Grand Slam Records. Record company, music publisher (A New Rap Jam Publishing/ASCAP and Party House Publishing/BMI) and record producer (James Milligan). Estab. 1989. Releases 5-10 singles, 5 12″ singles, 3 LPs, 2 EPs, 2 CDs/year. Works with musicians/artists and songwriters on contract and hire musicians for in-house studio work. Pays standard royalty; statutory rate to publisher per song on record.

How to Contact: Submit demo tape—unsolicited submissions are OK. Prefers cassette (or VHS videocassette if available) with 3-5 songs and lyric sheet. SASE. Reports in 1 month.

Music: Mostly R&B, pop and rock/rap; also country, contemporary gospel and soul/top 40. Released "Can't Sleep At Night" (by James Milligan), recorded by James Junior on Grand Slam Records (R&B single); "Lawman" (by Ray Smith), recorded by M.C.Y.T. on New Experience Records (rap 12″ single); and *Still In Touch* written and recorded by Tammy Oats on New Experience Records (gospel LP). Other artists include Anthony Milligan (soul gospel singer), UK Fresh Crew (rap group), Carl Milligan (gospel singer) and Terry Sechrest Band.

*NICKEL RECORDS, 753 Capitol Ave., Hartford CT 06106. (203)524-5656. Producer: Jack Stang. Record company, record producer and music publisher (Stang Music Publishing). Estab. 1971. Releases 2 singles, 2 12″ singles and 2 LPs/year. Works with musicians/artists and songwriters on contract. Pays statutory rate to publishers for each record sold.

How to Contact: Prefers cassette with 1-3 songs and lyric sheet. SASE. Reports in 3 weeks.

Music: Mostly dance and top 40/pop; also easy listening, MOR, R&B and rock. Released *Girls Like You*, written and recorded by Bill Chapin; *Smokin*, by Joe Frazier, "It's So Easy to Fall in Love," by Ray Alaire and Sky, all LPs on Nickel Records. Other artists include Kenny Hamber, Michael Kelly, Perfect Tommy, Alpha Sonas, Damon Sky and Dagmar.

NICKLE PLATE RECORDS, Box 140821, Chicago IL 60614-0821. President: Frederick S. Koger. Record company and music publisher ("L" Train Publishers/ASCAP). Estab. 1987. Releases 3 singles and 3 12″ singles/year. Works with musicians/artists and songwriters on contract. Pays 10% royalty to artist on contract; statutory rate to publisher per song on record.

How to Contact: Submit demo tape—unsolicited submissions are OK. Prefers cassette or 7½ ips reel-to-reel with 3-5 songs and lyric or lead sheets. SASE. Reports in 3 weeks.

Music: Mostly R&B, rap and pop; also rock and gospel. Released "Nurse" and "Face the Music" both written and recorded by Terry Olyan on Nickle Plate Records (R&B). Other artists include Steven Lee and Orlando Sifney.

Tips: Stay with one format. Be serious. Make sure tape is clear, not muffled.

NORTH STAR RECORDS, 95 Hathaway St., Providence RI 02907. (401)785-8400. Executive Vice President: Bruce R. Foulke. Record company and music publisher (Publishing Name: Blue Gate Music/ASCAP). Estab. 1985. Releases 4-5 LPs/year. Works with musicians/artists and songwriters on contract. Pays statutory royalty to artists on contract; statutory rate to publisher per song on record.

How to Contact: Write first and obtain permission to submit. Prefers cassette with 4-5 songs and lyric sheets. Does not return unsolicited material. Reports in 1 month.

Music: Mostly country, R&B and rock/folk; also acoustic traditional, classical and children's music. Released *Cheryl Wheeler* on North Star Records and *Half-A-Book* on Cypress Records, written and recorded by Cheryl Wheeler (rock/country LPs); and *Time Can Be So Magic*, written and recorded by Bill Thomas on North Star Records (children's LP). Other artists include Chili Brothers, Arturo Delmoni, New England Music Collection, Mair-Davis Duo and Hubbards.

Tips: "A professional, well thought-out presentation of your best material is necessary to attract the attention of record label personnel."

NOW & THEN RECORDS, #3, 501 78th St., Dept. SM, North Bergen NJ 07047. (201)854-6266. Contact: Shane Faber. Record company, music publisher (Now & Then Music/BMI) and record producer (Shane "the Dr." Faber). Estab. 1980. Works with musicians/artists and songwriters on contract. Pays 10% royalty to artists on contract; statutory rate to publisher per song on record.

How to Contact: Submit demo tape—unsolicited submissions are OK. Prefers cassette with 4 songs and lyric sheet. SASE.
Music: Mostly pop, dance and R&B; also rap and New Age. Released *Sneak Attack, Beat the Meter* and *Big Ducks*, all LPs recorded by Bad Sneakers. Other artists include Tenita Jordon (R&B), T.T. (dance), Blackhearts (rap), Shane Faber (pop) and Audrey Smith-Bey (pop).

*OCEAN RECORDS INC., 134 Warren St., Roxbury MA 02119. Producer: Jackie Whitehead. Record company, music publisher (Mighty Fine Music/ASCAP) and record producer (O.R. Productions). Estab. 1977. Releases 5 singles, 5 12" singles and 4 LPs/year. Works with musicians/artists, songwriters and producers on contract. Pays statutory rate to publisher per song on record.
How to Contact: Submit demo tape—unsolicited submissions are OK. Prefers cassette. Does not return unsolicited material. Reports in 3 weeks.
Music: Mostly R&B, pop and funk; also rap.
Tips: "Make good quality demo tapes with good highs & lows. Do not use a cassette that has been used 20 times or more. Use a new cassette at all times."

ONE-EYED DUCK RECORDING AND PUBLISHING, 22 Rainsford Rd., Toronto, ON M4L3N4 **Canada.** (416)694-6900. General Manager: Patricia Erlendson. Record company, music publisher (PROCAN) and record producer. Estab. 1983. Releases 1 LP/year. Works with musicians/artists and songwriters on contract. Pays negotiable rate to artists on contract; statutory rate to publisher per song on record. Charges up-front for production.
How to Contact: Write first and obtain permission to submit. Prefers cassette.
Music: Mostly children's. Released "I Can Do Anything," "Sharing" and "Kickoff," recorded by Sphere Clown Band on One-Eyed Duck Records (children's).

ORBIT RECORDS, P.O. Box 120675, Nashville TN 37212. (615)255-1068. Owner: Ray McGinnis. Record company, music publisher (Nautical Music Co.) and record producer (Ray Mack Productions). Estab. 1965. Releases 6-10 singles, 6 12" singles and 4 LPs/year. Receives 15-20 submissions/month. Works with musicians/artists on contract. Pays 8-12% royalty to artists on contract; statutory rate to publisher per song on record.
How to Contact: Prefers cassette with 4 songs and lead sheet. Does not return unsolicited material. Reports in 6-8 weeks.
Music: Country (ballads), country rock and R&B. Released "Burning Love," written and recorded by Alan Warren (hard rock); "I Need the Real Thing," written and recorded by Don Acuff (country); and "She's a Heartbreaker" (by L. Oldham), recorded by LeRoy Steele (country rock); all on Orbit Records. Other artists include LeRoy Steele, and Da-Kota, "a supercharged country rock group."
Tips: "We like artists with individual styles, not 'copy cats'; be original and unique."

*OSPREY ENTERTAINMENT GROUP, INC., Box 46465, Pass-A-Grill FL 33741. President: David Roberts. Labels include OEG Records. Record company, music publisher (OEG Music/BMI). Estab. 1989. Works with musicians/artists and songwriters on contract. Pays 7-10% royalty to artists on contract; statutory rate to publisher per song on record.
How to Contact: Submit demo tape—unsolicited submissions are OK. Prefers cassette (VHS videocassette if available) with 3 songs and lyric sheet. SASE. Reports in 6-8 weeks.
Music: Mostly rock and pop; also R&B. Released *Basic English*, written and recorded by Michael English on OEG Records (LP). Other artists include Cindy Syzer.
Tips: "Send clear, clean, quality demo with photo and bio. A performance video is nice but not required. Don't give up."

PARADE, 88 St. Francis St., Newark NJ 07105. (201)344-4214. Senior Vice President, Product Development/A&R Director: Joey Porello. Labels include Peter Pan, Power, Compose Records, Tronbound, Third Ear, Connection and Jammo. Record company. Estab. 1928. Releases 10-20 singles and 5-10 12" singles, 10-20 LPs, and 10-20 CDs/year. Works with artists and songwriters on contract. Pays varying royalty to artists on contract; statutory rate to publishers for each record sold.
How to Contact: Prefers cassette with 1-3 songs and lyric sheet. SASE. Reports in 2 months.
Music: Mostly dance, children's and MOR; also country, R&B, New Age rock, novelty and classical. Released *Aerobics*, by Joanie Greggains (exercise LP). Other artists include Morton Downey, Jr. (country) and Gilead Limor (New Age).

PARAGOLD RECORDS & TAPES, Box 292101, Nashville TN 37229-2101. (615)859-4890. Director: Teresa Bernard. Record company, music publisher (Rainbarrel Music Co./BMI) and record producer. Estab. 1972. Releases 5 singles, 5 LPs and 1 EP/year. Works with musicians/artists and songwriters on contract. Pays statutory rate to publishers.

How to Contact: Write first and obtain permission to submit. Prefers cassette (or VHS videocassette) with 2 songs and lyric or lead sheets. SASE. "Unpublished songs are welcome. Send only outstanding material." Reports in 6 weeks.

Music: Country and top 40. Released "Rose & Bittercreek" and "Bottle of Happiness" written and recorded by Johnny Bernard; and "Daddy's Last Letter" (by J. Bernard) recorded by J. Lyne all on Paragold Records (country). Other artists include Sunset Cowboy.

Tips: "Must have high quality demo."

PARC RECORDS INC., Suite 205, 5104 N. Orange Blossom Trail, Orlando FL 32810. (407)292-0021. Executive Assistant: Leslie A. Schipper. Record company (Mister Sunshine Music/BMI). Estab. 1985. Releases 4+ singles, 2 12″ singles, 2 LPs and 2 CDs/year. Works with musicians/artists and songwriters on contract.

How to Contact: Prefers cassette (or VHS videocassette) with 3-5 songs and lyric sheet. SASE. Reports in 6-8 weeks.

Music: Mostly rock/metal, dance and jazz/new wave; also A/C and R&B. Released *Lighting Strikes*, recorded by Molly Hatchet on Parc/Capitol Records (rock LP); *China Sky*, recorded by China Sky on Parc/CBS Records (rock LP); and *Ana*, recorded by Ana on Parc/CBS Records (dance LP), (all by various). Other artists include Glen Kelly and Deryle Hughes.

Tips: "Quality songs with good hooks are more important than great production. If it's good, we can hear it."

PAULA RECORDS/JEWEL RECORDS/RONN RECORDS, Box 1125, Shreveport LA 71163-1125. (318)227-2228. Owner: Stanley J. Lewis. Labels include Jewel Records and Ronn Records. Record company and music publisher. Works with musicians/artists and songwriters on contract.

How to Contact: Submit demo tape by mail. Unsolicited submissions are OK. Prefers cassette with 3 songs and lyric sheet. SASE.

Music: Mostly R&B, gospel and country.

PDS RECORDS, Box 412477, Kansas City MO 64141. (816)523-5100. Contact: A&R, Dept. 100. Labels include Universal Jazz, PDS Associated labels. Record company, music publisher (PDS Music Publishing/ASCAP/BMI) and record producer (PDS Productions). Estab. 1988. Releases 8-10 singles, 8-10 12″ singles, 3-5 LPs, 8-10 EPs and 3-5 CDs/year. Works with musicians/artists on contract.

How to Contact: Write first and obtain permission to submit. Prefers cassette (or VHS videocassette) with 4-5 songs and lyric sheet. Does not return unsolicited material. Reports in 2 months.

PENGUIN RECORDS, INC., Box 1274, Miami FL 33261. Product Manager: Michael J. McNamee. Operation Manager: Gregory J. Winters. Labels include Straitgate Records, Penguin Records and Kinetic Records. Record company, music publisher. Estab. 1990. Releases 6 singles, 6 12″ singles, 3 LPs and 3 CDs/year. Works with musicians/artists and songwriters/year. Pays varying royalty.

How to Contact: Obtain permission to submit before sending submissions. Prefers cassette (or VHS videocassette if available) with 3 songs and lyric sheets. SASE. Reports in 2 months.

Music: Mostly dance, pop, rock R&B/rap and alternative/dance; also industrial and Christian. Released "Give Me a Sign" and "The Face of Fear" recorded on Kinetic Records.

Tips: "Be patient! There's a lot of music out there. Everyone will get a chance."

PHOENIX RECORDS, INC., Dept. SM, Box 121076, Nashville TN 27212-1076. (615)244-5357. President: Reggie M. Churchwell. Labels include Nashville International Records. Record company and music publisher (affiliated with both BMI and ASCAP). Estab. 1971. Releases 5-6 singles, 2-3 12″ singles, 2-3 LPs and 1-2 CDs/year. Works with musicians/artists and songwriters on contract. Pays standard royalty to artists on contract; statutory rate to publisher per song on record.

How to Contact: Write first and obtain permission to submit. "You must have permission before submitting any material." Prefers cassette with lyric sheets. Does not return unsolicited material. Reports in 2-3 weeks.

Music: Mostly country, rock and pop; also gospel. Released "Left of Center Line" (by Howard Lips), recorded by Catfish on Phoenix Records (country/rock); and "Littlest Cowboy" written and recorded by Sonny Shroyer on Hazzard Records (children's). Other artists include Conrad Pierce and Clay Jerrolds.

Tips: "We are looking for songs with strong hooks and strong words. We are not simply looking for songs, we are looking for hits."

PILOT RECORDS AND TAPE COMPANY, 628 S. South St., Mount Airy NC 27030. (919)786-2865. President and Owner: Paul E. Johnson. Labels include Stork, Stark, Pilot, Hello, Kay, Sugarbear, Southcoast, Songcraft and Blue Jay. Record company, music publisher (Tompaul Music Company/BMI) and record producer. Estab. 1960. Releases 12 singles and 75 LPs/year. Works with songwriters on contract; musicians on salary for in-house studio work. Pays 30% royalty to artists on contract; statutory rate to publishers per song on record.

How to Contact: Prefers cassette with 6 songs and lyric sheet. SASE. Reports in 2 months. "The songwriters should give their date of birth with submissions. This information will be used when copyrighting a songwriter's song."

Music: Mostly country, gospel and bluegrass; also rock, folk and blues. Released "My Last Christmas," "You and Me Alone Tonight" and "Something Inside Tells Me No," all written and recorded by Carl Tolbert on Pilot Records (country). Other artists include Bobby Atkins, Carl Tolbert, Sam Bray, Ralph Hill, Early Upchurch, Sanford Teague and Don Sawyers.

PLANKTON RECORDS, 236 Sebert Rd., Forest Gate, London E7 0NP **England.** Phone: (081)534-8500. Senior Partner: Simon Law. Labels include Plankton, Sea Dream, Embryo Arts (licensed, Belgium), Gutta (licensed, Sweden), Wildtracks (licensed United Kingdom) and Radio (licensed, United Kingdom). Record company and music publisher (Sea Dream Music, Scarf Music Publishing and Really Free Music). Estab. 1977. Releases 1 CD, 4 LPs, and 1 EP/year. Works with musicians/artists and songwriters on contract. Pays 10% royalty to artists on contract; 7% to publishers per song on record.

How to Contact: Submit demo tape—unsolicited submissions OK. Prefers cassette with 3 songs and lyric sheet. SAE and IRC. Reports in 6 weeks.

Music: Mostly funk/rock, R&B and gospel; also blues. Released "Hard as Nails" (by Simon Lan), recorded by Fresh Claim (rock); "Oxford Town" (by Ward/Johnston) recorded by Trevor Speaks (folk/rock) and "The River" (by Mann/Catley), recorded by Marc Catley/Geoff Mann (progressive), all on Plankton Records. Other artists include Catch 22, Really Free, Ruth Turner, Cheryl Mead and Medals.

Tips: "We specialize in bands with a Christian bias, regardless of their musical style."

PLATINUM BOULEVARD RECORDS, 1558 Linda Way, Reno NV 89431. (702)358-7484. President: Lawrence Davis. Record company. Estab. 1986. Releases 2 singles and 1 LP/year. Works with musicians/artists on contract. Pays negotiable royalty to artists on contract; statutory rate to publisher per song on record.

How to Contact: Submit demo tape by mail—unsolicited submissions are OK. Prefers cassette (or VHS videocassette) with songs and lyric or lead sheets. Does not return unsolicited material. "We report back only if interested."

Music: Mostly rock, pop and R&B; also country, jazz and New Age. Released *Davis*, written and recorded by L.R. Davis on Platinum Blvd. Records (rock LP).

Tips: "When presenting material indicate which artists you have in mind to record it. If you desire to be the recording artist please indicate."

*PLATINUM PRODUCTIONS, 406 Centre St., Boston MA 02130. (617)983-9999. A&R Rep: Akhil Garland. Record company. Estab. 1989. Releases 4 singles, 2 LPs, 6 EPs, 2 CDs/year. Works with musicians/artists and songwriters on contract and hires musicians for in-house studio work. Pays 7% royalty to artists on contract; statutory rate to publisher per song on record.

How to Contact: Submit demo tape by mail—unsolicited submissions are OK. Prefers cassette with lyric sheet. SASE. Reports in 1 month.

Music: Mostly reggae, folk and world beat; also rap/R&B and rock.

PLAY RECORDS, Box 6541, Cleveland OH 44101. (216)467-0300. President: John Latimer. Record company. Estab. 1985. Releases 3 LPs/year. Works with musicians/artists and songwriters on contract.

How to Contact: Submit demo tape by mail—unsolicited submissions are OK. Prefers cassette (or VHS or ¾" videocassettes) with 5 songs and lyric or lead sheets. SASE. Reports in 6 weeks.

Music: Mostly rock, pop and alternative; also blues, jazz and R&B. Released "There Was a Time," written and recorded by The Bellows; "Bombs Away," written and recorded by Serious Nature; and "Mr. Sensible," written and recorded by Mr. Sensible; all on Play Records (rock). Other artists include The French Lenards, 15 60 75, The Adults, Cool Down Daddy, The Bomb, Earl Rays, Zero One, Holy Cows and Ronald Koal.

Tips: "Be patient but persistent. Please correspond by mail only."

"How to Use Your Songwriter's Market" (at the front of this book) contains comments and suggestions to help you understand and use the information in these listings.

***PLAYBACK RECORDS,** Box 630755, Miami FL 33163. (305)935-4880. Producer: Jack Gale. Labels include Gallery II Records, Ridgewood Records. Record company, music publisher (Lovely Music/ BMI and Cowabonga Music/ASCAP), and record producer. Estab. 1983. Releases 48 singles, 2 EPs, 10 CDs/year. Works with musicians/artists and songwriters on contract. Pays statutory rate to publisher per song on record.

How to Contact: Submit demo tape by mail—unsolicited submissions are OK. Prefers cassette (VHS videocassette if available) with 2 songs and lyric sheet. SASE. Reports in 2 weeks.

Music: Mostly country. Released "Here's To The Cowboys" (by David Bracken), recorded by Jennie C. Riley; "Makin' Music" (by J. Clinger), recorded by Charley Louvin, Willie Nelson and Waylon Jennings; and "Hank & Lefty, George & Me" (by Jim Owen), recorded by Tommy Cash with George Jones, all on Playback Records (country singles). Other artists include Ernie Ashworth, Michele Bishop, Whiskey Creek, Jimmy C. Newman, Sammy Smith and Del Reeves.

Tips: "Send only your best. Be open to suggestion. Remember . . . this is a business, not an ego trip."

PLAYBONES RECORDS, Box 203312, D-2000 Hamburg 20, **Germany.** Phone: (040) 4300339. FAX: (040)439.65.87. Producer: Arno v. Vught. Labels include Rondo Records. Record company, music publisher (Mento Music Group KG.) and record producer (Arteg Productions). Estab. 1975. Releases 30 CDs/year. Works with musicians/artists and songwriters on contract. Pays 8-16% royalty to artists on contract.

How to Contact: Submit demo tape—unsolicited submissions are OK. Prefers cassette and lyric or lead sheet. Does not return submitted material. Reports in 2 weeks.

Music: Mostly instrumentals, country and jazz; also background music, rock and gospel. Released *Jazz* (by E. Stanbert), recorded by E. Kammler; and *Loose One* (by Brun/Kuhles), recorded by Daniel & Claudia on Playbones (CD); and *Born Again* written and recorded by Reifegerste on DA Music (CD). Other artists include H.J. Knipphals, Gaby Knies, Jack Hals, H. Hausmann, Crabmeat and M. Frommhold.

PLEASURE RECORDS, Rt. 1, Box 187-A, Whitney TX 76692. (817)694-4047. President: Allen Newton. Labels include Cactus Flats, Pristine, MFN. Record company and music publisher (Four Newton Publishing/BMI). Estab. 1986. Releases 12 singles, 3 12″ singles and 1 LP/year. Works with musicians/ artists and songwriters on contract. Pays 10-20% royalty to artists on contract; statutory rate to publisher per song on record.

How to Contact: Submit demo tape by mail—unsolicited submissions are OK. Prefers cassette with 3 songs and lyric or lead sheets. SASE. Reports in 4-6 weeks.

Music: Mostly country, gospel and rock; also rock-a-billy, R&B and Spanish. Released "I Need A Friend and a Lover" (by M. Hart), recorded by Martha Hart on Pleasure Records (C/W); "Red Hot Mama" (by J. Sipes), recorded by James Sipes on MFN Records (rock-a-billy); and "Woman of the 90s" (by J.A. Blecha), recorded by Judy Welden on Pleasure Records (C/W). Other artists include Denny Glenn, Sherry Fontaine, Blessed Carrion, Felix Van Slyke, Stylle and J. Sam, Angela Long and R.J. Gold.

Tips: "Don't give up the dream."

PMG RECORDS, Box 2849, Trolley Station, Detroit MI 48231. President: Bruce Henderson. Record company, music publisher (Prejippie Music Group/BMI) and record producer (PMG Productions). Estab. 1990. Releases 6-12 12″ singles, 1 LP and 1 EP/year. Works with musicians/artists on contract. Pays statutory rate.

How to Contact: Submit demo tape by mail—unsolicited submissions are OK. Prefers cassette or VHS videocassette with 3-4 songs and lyric sheet. Include photo if possible. No calls please. SASE. Reports in 6 weeks.

Music: Mostly funk/rock, techno/house and dance; also alternative, rock and New Age. Released "Redd Hott," recorded by The Prejippies (funky-house) and "I Just Want Your Love" by Jezebel (house). Other artists include Sacred Places (alternative rock) and Sonic Holocaust (underground/ techno).

Tips: 'A strong hook and melody line are your best weapons! We also look for originality."

POP RECORD RESEARCH, 17 Piping Rock Dr., Ossining NY 10502. (914)762-8499. Director: Gary Theroux. Labels include Surf City, GTP and Rock's Greatest Hits. Record company, music publisher (Surf City Music/ASCAP), record producer and archive of entertainment-related research materials (files on hits and hitmakers since 1877). Estab. 1962. Works with musicians/artists and songwriters on contract and writers/historians/biographers/radio, TV and film producers requiring research help or materials. Pays statutory rate to publisher per song on record.

How to Contact: Submit demo tape, press kits or review material by mail. Unsolicited submissions are OK. Prefers cassette (or VHS videocassette). Does not return unsolicited material.

Music: Mostly pop, country and R&B. Released "The Declaration" (by Theroux-Gilbert), recorded by An American on Bob Records; "Thoughts From a Summer Rain," written and recorded by Bob Gilbert on Bob Records; and "Tiger Paws," written and recorded by Bob Gilbert on BAL Records; all pop singles. Other artists include Gary and Joan, The Nightflight Singers and Ruth Zimmerman.

Tips: "Help us keep our biographical file on you and your career current by sending us updated bios/press kits, etc. They are most helpful to writers/researchers in search of accurate information on your success."

POSITIVE FEEDBACK STUDIOS, (formerly Counterpart Creative Studios), 4010 North Bend Rd., P.O. Box 11333, Cincinnati OH 45211. (513)661-8810. President: Shad O'Shea. Record company, music publisher (Hurdy Gurdy Music Co., Counterpart Music/BMI) and jingle company. Member RIAA. Releases 24 singles and 6 LPs/year. Works with musicians on salary.

How to Contact: Write first. Prefers 7½ ips reel-to-reel with 1-2 songs. Does not return unsolicited material. Reports in 1 week.

Music: Bluegrass, blues, children's, choral, church/religious, classical, country, dance, easy listening, folk, gospel, jazz, MOR, progressive, rock, funk, soul and top 40/pop. Released "McLove Story," by Shad O'Shea on Plantation Records; "Hot Fun in the Summertime," by Dayton on Capitol Records; "Freakazoid" and "Wet My Whistle," by Midnight Star on Warner Bros. Records.

PPI/PETER PAN INDUSTRIES, 88 St. Francis St., Newark NJ 07105. (201)344-4214. Product Manager: Marianne Eggleston. Labels include Compose Records, Current Records, Parade Video, Iron Bound Publishing/Guess Star Records. Record company, music publisher, record producer (Dunn Pearson, Jr.) and outside producers are used also. Estab. 1928. Releases 12 singles, 6 12″ singles, over 28 LPs and 28 CDs/year. Works with musicians/artists and songwriters on contract. Pays royalty per contract; statutory rater per contract to publisher per song on records. "All services are negotiable!"

How to Contact: Write or call first to obtain permission to submit. Prefers cassette (or VHS videocassette if available) with 3-5 songs and lyric sheet. SASE. Reports in 3 months. Does not return unsolicited submissions.

Music: Pop, R&B; also jazz and New Age. Released "Go For The Gusto" (R&B); "Programmed For Love" (jazz); and "Color Tapestry" (jazz) all written and recorded by Dunn Pearson, Jr. on Compose Records.

PRAIRIE MUSIC RECORDS LTD., Box 438, Walnut IA 51577. (712)366-1136. President: Robert Everhart. Record company (BMI) and record producer (Prairie Music Ltd.). Estab. 1964. Releases 2 singles and 2 LPs/year. Works with musicians/artists and songwriters on contract. Pays 5% royalty to artists on contract; statutory rate to publisher per song on record.

How to Contact: Submit demo tape by mail. Unsolicited submissions are OK. Prefers cassette. SASE. Reports in 4 months.

Music: Mostly traditional country, bluegrass and folk. Released "Time After Time," "Street Sleepers" and "Rock of Hollywood," all written and recorded by Bob Everhart on Folkways Records (traditional country). Other artists include Gospel Pilgrims.

PREMIÉRE RECORDS, Box 279, Hopkins MN 55343. (612)942-6119. President: Mitch Viegut. V/P and General Manager: Mark Alan. Record company. Estab. 1988. Releases 6 singles, 2-3 LPs, 2-3 cassettes and 2-3 CDs/year. Receives 200 submissions/year. Works with musicians/artists and songwriters on contract. Pays 10-12% royalty to artists on contract; statutory rate to publisher per song on record.

How to Contact: Submit demo tape by mail. Submissions must be solicited. Prefers cassette (or VHS videocassette) with 3-4 songs. SASE. Reports in 2 months.

Music: Mostly rock, pop and black contemporary. Released "Someday You'll Come Running" (by Judith Randall, Robin Randall, Tony Sciuto) (rock); "Somewhere" (by Mitch Viegut) (pop); and *85 MPH* (Mitch Viegut, David Sainden, Roger Probert) (rock), all recorded by Airkraft on Premiére Records. Other artists include Crash Alley.

*PRESENCE RECORDS, Box 1101, Cromwell CT 06416. (203)721-1049. President: Paul Payton. Record company, music publisher (Paytoons/BMI), record producer (Presence Productions). Estab. 1985. Pays 1-2% royalty to artists on contract; statutory rate to publisher per song on record.

How to Contact: Write and obtain permission to submit. Prefers cassette with 2-3 songs and lyric sheet. Does not return unsolicited material. Reports in 1 month.

Music: Mostly Doo-wop (50s) rock & roll, new wave rock, New Age. Released "Davilee/Go On" (by Paul Payton/Peter Skolnik), recorded by Fabulous Dudes (doo-wop single); and "Boys Like Girls/Relate 2U," written and recorded by Paul Payton (rock single), both on Presence Records.

PRESIDENTIAL ENTERPRISES LTD., 127 Aldergate St., London **England** EC1A 4JQ. Phone: (44)71-2501910. Contact: Roland A. Radelli. Labels include XXIst Century, High Density Records, Renegade Records, Record company and record producer (The Club Studios). Estab. 1986. Releases 12-15 12″ singles and 3-5 LPs/year. Receives 8-10 submissions/month. Works with musicians/artists and songwriters on contract; also Disc-jockeys and remixers. Pays 6-15% royalty to artists on contract; statutory rate to publisher per song on record.

How to Contact: Submit demo tape—unsolicited submissions are OK. Prefers cassette with 2-5 songs and lyric sheet. Does not return unsolicited material. Reports in 1 month.

Music: Mostly house, pop/dance; also soul, rock and reggae. Released *9/0/9 BD*, recorded by "909 BD"; *Dark Avenger*, recorded by Dark Avenger; and *Future Tense*, recorded by Future Tense, all on High Density Records (techno/house 12″ EP).

Tips: "If dance tracks, then must be finished product (no demos). For pop songs/heavy metal, a demo may do."

*PRESTATION MUSIC, 24 Gachard Street, Brussels 1050 **Belgium**. Phone (02)649-2847. General Manager: Pierre Plentinckx. Labels include Selection Records, Multisound Music, B-Sharp. Record company and music publisher (Sabam). Releases 5 CDs/year. Works with musicians/artists and songwriters on contract; hires musicians for in-house studio work.

How to Contact: Submit demo tape—unsolicited submissions are OK. Prefers cassette. SASE. Reports in 1 month.

Music: Mostly instrumental music, jazz and New Age. Released "Aftertouch," recorded by Ivon Poduset on B-Sharp 079 (jazz/fusion); "Picture A View," recorded by Frank Vogance on B-Sharp 080 Records (jazz); and music from 12th Jazz International and Europ' Jazz Contest 90 (jazz).

PRESTO RECORDS, Box 1081, Lowell MA 01853. (617)893-2144. President: Christopher Porter. Record company. Affiliated with Chris Porter Productions Inc. (a booking and management company). Estab. 1989. Releases 2-4 LPs and 2-4 CDs/year. Receives 90 submissions/year. Work with musicians/artists on contract. Pays statutory rate to publisher per song on record.

How to Contact: Submit demo tape by mail—unsolicited submissions are OK. Prefers cassette with 3-4 songs. SASE or SAE and IRC. Reports in 1-2 months.

Music: Mostly guitar-oriented alternative rock. Released "Missed Opportunities" (by Adam Boc), recorded by Miranada Warning; "Say Goodbye," written and recorded by Evol Twin; and "Ed McMahon Says" (by Alan Grandy), recorded by The Terrible Parade all on Presto Records (alternative rock). Other artists include Miles Dethmuffen.

Tips: "We mainly deal with guitar-oriented rock—accessible but not overly commercial. If a songwriter has a band together and they are playing out live regularly, we would be happy to hear their material if it fits in our guidelines."

*PRIME CUT RECORDS, Box 1387, Lyndonville VT 05851. (802)626-3317. President A&R: Bruce James. Record company and record producer. Releases 4-12 singles and 4 LPs/year. Works with musicians/artists and songwriters on contract. Pays statutory rate to publisher for each record sold.

How to Contact: Submit demo tape by mail—unsolicited submissions are OK. Prefers cassette (or VHS videocassette) with 1-5 songs and lyric sheet. "Songs should be hit material telling compelling story." SASE. Reports in 3 weeks only if interested.

Music: Country and top 40/pop. Released *Old Nights*, written and recorded by Jackie O; *In Throughout*, written and recorded by Champlain; and *Dance Dance*, recorded by Dance Dance, all LPs on Prime Cut Records. Other artists include Contagious and Littlewing.

Tips: "Write the song like a book."

PRINCE/SF PRODUCTIONS, 1135 Francisco St., San Francisco CA 94109. (415)775-9627. Artists Representative: Ken Malucelli. Labels include Auriga and Christmas. Music publisher (Prince/SF Publications/ASCAP) and record producer (Prince/SF Productions). Estab. 1975. Releases 1 LP and 1 CD/year. Works with artists under personal management. Pays standard royalty to artists on contract; statutory rate to publishers per song on record.

How to Contact: Works with San Francisco Bay area artists only. Write first and obtain permission to submit. Prefers cassette or VHS videocassette with 3 songs and lyric and lead sheet. SASE. Reports "ASAP."

Music: Mostly pop and Christmas; also satirical and humorous. Released *The Merrie Olde Christmas Carolers* (by Ken Malucelli, arranger), recorded by MOC Carolers on Christmas Records (holiday cassette); *Loud is Good*, written and recorded by The EDLOS on Auriga Records (pop, cassette); and "Freedomsong" (by Eric Morris, composer), recorded by The EDLOS on Auriga Records (pop single).

Tips: "Work should be unique, high quality, not derivative."

PRISTINE RECORDS, Route 1, Box 187-A, Whitney TX 76692. (817)694-4047. President: Allen Newton. Labels include Cactus Flats, MFN, Pleasure Records. Record company and mailing/distributor/promotion. Estab. 1981. Releases 10-12 singles; 3 12″ singles and 10-12 LPs/year. Works with musicians/artists on contract. Pays 10-20% royalty to artists on contract; statutory rate to publisher per song on record.
How to Contact: Submit demo tape by mail—unsolicited submissions are OK. Prefers cassette or 7½ ips reel-to-reel (or VHS videocassette) with 2 songs and lyric or lead sheets. SASE. Reports in 4-6 weeks.
Music: Mostly country, R&B and rock; also gospel. Released "Do Me Good" (by Kristin Kuhlman), recorded by Kuhlmann Sisters (pop); "Masks" (by band), recorded by Requiem (rock); and "Resentless" (by A. Ruven), recorded by Hidden Shadows (rock); all on Pristine Records. Other artists include Linda Roper, Samuel Green, Mickey Drum, Thin Ice, Sherry Fontaine and Stylle.
Tips: "Please allow all publishers and labels adequate time to review submissions before sending additional inquiries. Read, study, listen, and prepare."

*PRODISC (PRODISC LIMITADA), Tomás Andrews 085, Santiago **Chile**. Phone: (562)34-1733. FAX: (562)34-40-64. A&R Director: Oscar Sayavedra. Labels include Cabal (Argentina), Leader Music (Argentina), American Recording (Argentina), Tico (USA), Fania (USA), Cotique (USA), Inca (USA), Barbaro (USA), Vaya (USA); Radio Tripoli (Argentina); SonoMusic (Columbia); Del Cielito (Argentina). Record company, Prodin Chile: Promoter & Production Company—same address. Distributed by Sony Music. Estab. 1989 (Prodin was in 1969). Releases 20 singles, 120 LPs/year. Works with musicians/artists on contract. Pays 4-18% royalty to artists on contract; statutory rate to publisher per song.
How to Contact: Submit demo tape by mail—unsolicited submissions are OK. Prefers cassette or VHS videocassette with 2 or more songs. Does not return unsolicited submissions. Reports in 1 month.
Music: Mostly rock/pop, Latin/salsa/tex mex and R&B; also folk/country, jazz/new age and classic. Released "Sacame Esa Espada" (by E. Franco), recorded by Los Iracundos (ballad); "Come Back to Me" written and recorded by Waldo Fabian (dance); and "El Riff" written and recorded by Pappo (heavy metal); all on Prodisc/Sony Records. Other artists include Luis Alberto Spinetta, Eduardo Falu, Facundo Cabral and Ruben Blades.
Tips: "We're working with a new record company but we're the biggest promotion and production agency in this country. We work to make records hits and big concerts, too."

PUZZLE RECORDS, Box 461892, Garland TX 75046. (214)271-8098. A&R Director: Don Ferguson. Record company, music publisher (Sultan Music Publishing/BMI and Illustrious Sultan/ASCAP), record producer and booking agency (Don Ferguson Agency). Estab. 1972. Releases 7-8 singles and 1-2 LPs/year. Works with artists and songwriters on contract.
How to Contact: Accepts unsolicited material.
Music: Mostly country; also MOR, jazz and light rock. Released "Leave Me Right Now," written and recorded by Bobby Teesdale (MOR); "Ain't No Way," (by Duke/Osborn/Fox), recorded by Flash Point (rock); and "I'm Hurtin," (by Roy Orbison/Joe Melson), recorded by Mary Craig (country); all on Puzzle Records.

R.E.F. RECORDS, 404 Bluegrass Ave., Madison TN 37115. (615)865-6380. Contact: Bob Frick. Record company, record producer and music publisher (Frick Music Publishing Co./BMI). Releases 10 LPs/year. Works with artists and songwriters on contract. Pays 3-5¢ royalty to artists on contract; statutory rate to publishers for each record sold.
How to Contact: Call first. Prefers 7½ ips reel-to-reel or cassette with 2 songs and lyric sheet. SASE. Reports in 1 month.
Music: Country, gospel, rock and top 40/pop. Released "I Love You In Jesus," "Warm Family Feeling," and "Our Favorites," all by Bob Scott Frick. Other artists include Larry Ahlborn, Francisco Morales, Candy Coleman, Peggy Beard, Bob Myers, The Backwoods Quartet, Jim Mattingly, David Barton, Jim Pommert, The Vision Heirs, Eddie Issacs and Craig Steele.

RABADASH RECORDS INC., 4805 Baudin St., New Orleans LA 70119. (504)486-7646. President: John G. Autin. Record company, music publisher (Rabadash Music/ASCAP) and record producer. Estab. 1982. Releases 1 LP and 1 CD/year. Works with musicians/artists and songwriters on contract.
How to Contact: Submit demo tape by mail. Unsolicited submissions are OK. Prefers cassette or VHS videocassette and lyric sheet. SASE. Reports in 3 months.
Music: Mostly R&B, pop and country; also jazz, gospel and rock. Other artists include Anders Osbourne, Lori Frazier.

RADIOACTIVE RECORDS, Suite 250, 1075 N.W. Murray Rd., Portland OR 97229. (503)642-4201. Contact: A&R Dept. Record company, music publisher (Mark Hannah Music Group/BMI), record producer (Mark Hannah Productions) and Mark Hannah Management/Personal Management. Estab.

1985. Releases 5-10 singles, 3-5 12″ singles, 1-3 LPs, 1-3 EPs and 1-3 CDs/year. Receives 30 submissions/month. Works with musicians/artists and songwriters on record contract. Pays 5-10% royalty to artists on contract; statutory rate to publisher per song on record.

How to Contact: Submit demo tape by mail—unsolicited submissions are OK. Prefers cassette or 15 ips reel-to-reel with 1-3 songs and lyric or lead sheets. SASE. Reports in 1-4 weeks.

Music: Mostly rock, pop and country; also fusion, New Age and jazz. Released "Bingo" written and recorded by M. Harrop (pop); "Union Man" (by P. Witt/D. Narlock), recorded by P. Witt (rock) and *Indian Memories*, written and recorded by M. Hannah (rock), all on Radioactive Records. Other artists include Rex E. Plew and Messenger (rock band).

Tips: "Be as professional as possible in your presentation and follow submission requirements as per our listing."

*RAINFOREST RECORDS, Suite 110, 8855 S.W. Holly, Wilsonville OR 97070. Director, A&R: Ray Woods. Record company. Estab. 1990. Releases 3-4 singles, 1 LP and 2-4 CDs/year. Works with musicians/artists on contract. Pays 5-12% royalty to artists on contract; ¾ statutory rate to publisher per song on record.

How to Contact: Write and obtain permission to submit. Prefers cassette with 2-3 songs and lyric sheet. SASE. Reports in 2 months.

Music: Mostly alternative rock; also hip hop and industrial musique. Released *WORM* (by Wammo), recorded by the WORM Band; *The Refreshments* (by various), recorded by The Refreshments; and *Medicine Sunday* (by various), recorded by Medicine Sunday, all on Rainforest Records (CD album). Other artists include Young Turks, Caustic Soda, Scott Appleman and Affirmative Action.

Tips: "We are looking for original music with focus. Your music should complement the label's exisitng roster. It's best to develop your music in front of live audiences first."

RAZOR & TIE MUSIC, #5A, 214 Sullivan St., New York NY 10012. (212)473-9173. President: Cliff Chenfeld. Labels include Razor Edge Records. Record company. Estab. 1990. Releases 15-20 CDs/year. Works with musicians/artists on contract.

How to Contact: Write first and obtain permission to submit. Prefers cassette with 3 songs and lyric sheet. SASE. Reports in 3 weeks.

Music: Mostly rock, pop/R&B and country. Released "You Move Me," "Bad Intent" and "I.C.U.," all written and recorded by Scott Kempner on Razor and Tie Records (rock).

RAZOR RECORDS, 2623 Bosworth, Chicago IL 60614. (312)549-3227. Owner: Mark Lefens. Record company. Estab. 1979. Releases 1 single and 1 LP/year. Works with musicians/artists on contract. Pays statutory rate to publisher per song on record.

How to Contact: Submit demo tape by mail. Unsolicited submissions are OK. Prefers cassette. SASE. "Will report only if interested."

Music: Mostly blues and R&B. Released *After Work* (by various writers), recorded by John Embry; *Set Me Free* (by various writers), recorded by Gloria Hardiman; and *Housefire* (written and recorded by Byther Smith), all on Razor Records (blues LPs) reissued on Rounder's "Bullseye" label.

Tips: "Come up with some good new blues."

RECORD COMPANY OF THE SOUTH, Box 14685, Baton Rouge LA 70809. (504)766-3233. General Manager: Johnny Palazzotto. Record company. Estab. 1978. Works with musicians/artists on contract. Pays 8% royalty to artists on contract; statutory rate to publisher per song on record.

How to Contact: Submit demo tape by mail—unsolicited submissions are OK. Prefers cassette with 3-5 songs. SASE. Reports in 2-4 weeks.

Music: Mostly rock, R&B and country. *Safe With Me*, recorded by Irma Thomas on RCS Records (R&B LP, CD). Other artists include Luther Kent.

*RED BUS RECORDS (INT.) LTD., Red Bus House, 48 Broadley Terrace, London NW1, **England**. (071) 258-0324. FAX: (071) 724-2163. Director: Ellis Elias. Record company and music publisher. Estab. 1969. Releases 7 singles, 3 CDs and 3 LPs/year. Works with musicians/artists on contract. Pays 6-10% royalty to artists on contract.

How to Contact: Submit demo tape—unsolicited submissions are OK. Prefers cassette. SAE and IRC. Reports in 5 weeks.

Music: Mostly dance. Artists include Room 101.

RED DOT/PUZZLE RECORDS, 1121 Market, Galveston TX 77550. (409)762-4590. President: A.W. Marullo Sr. Record company, record producer and music publisher (A.W. Marullo Music/BMI). Estab. 1952. "We also lease masters from artists." Releases 14 12″ singles/year. Works with artists and songwriters on contract; musicians on salary for in-house studio work. Pays 8-10% royalty to artists on contract; statutory rate to publishers for each record sold.

How to Contact: Prefers cassette with 4-7 songs and lyric sheet. SASE. Reports in 2 months.
Music: Rock/top 40 dance songs. Released "Do You Feel Sexy," (by T. Pindrock), recorded by Flash Point (Top 40/rock); "You Put the Merry in My Christmas," (by E.Dunn), recorded by Mary Craig (rock/pop country) and "Love Machine," (by T. Pindrock), recorded by Susan Moninger; all on Puzzle/Red Dot Records.

RED SKY RECORDS, Box 7, Stonehouse, Glos. GL10 3PQ **United Kingdom**. Phone: 0453-826200. Producer: Johnny Coppin. Record company (PRS) and record producer (Red Sky Records). Estab. 1985. Releases 2 singles, 3 LPs and 3 CDs/year. Works with musicians/artists and songwriters on contract and hires musicians for in-house studio work. Pays 8-10% to artists on contract; statutory rate to publisher per song on record.
How to Contact: Submit demo tape by mail—unsolicited submissions are OK. Prefers cassette with 3 songs and lyric sheet. SASE. Reports in 3 months.
Music: Mostly rock/singer-songwriters, modern folk and roots music. Released *Edge of Day*, written and recorded by Laurie Lee & Johnny Coppin; *West Country Christmas*, and *Forest & Vale & High Blue Hill*, written and recorded by Johnny Coppin; all on Red Sky Records (LPs). Other artists include Desperate Men and Phil Beer.

RED-EYE RECORDS, Wern Fawr Farm, Pencoed, Mid-Glam CF35 6NB **United Kingdom**. Phone: (0656)86 00 41. Managing Director: M.R. Blanche. Record company, music publisher (Ever-Open-Eye Music/PRS). Estab. 1979. Releases 4 singles and 2-3 LPs/year. Works with musicians/artists on contract.
How to Contact: Prefers cassette (or VHS videocassette) or 7½ or 15 ips reel-to-reel with 4 songs. SAE and IRC.
Music: Mostly R&B, rock and gospel; also swing. Released "River River" (by D. John), recorded by The Boys; "Billy" (by G. Williams), recorded by The Cadillacs; and "Cadillac Walk" (by Moon Martin), recorded by the Cadillacs, all on Red-Eye Records. Other artists include Cartoon and Tiger Bay.

RHINO RECORDS LTD., The Chilterns, France Hill Dr., Chamberley Surrey GU153QA **England**. Phone: 0276-686077. Director: Bruce White. Record company. Estab. 1970. Releases 12 singles, 12 12″ singles, 10-15 LPs and 10-15 CDs/year. Receives 20 submissions/month. Works with musicians/artists on record contract. Pays 8-16% royalty to artists on contract. Pays 60-75% royalty to publisher per song on record.
How to Contact: Submit demo tape by mail—unsolicited submissions are OK. Prefers cassette with 3-4 songs. SASE. Reports in 6 weeks.
Music: Interested in "most types of music." Released "Take Care," written and recorded by Boris Gardiner (reggae); and "This Is" (by D. Dacres), recorded by Desmond Dekker (reggae), both on Rhino Records; and "Carnival 90," written and recorded by Byron Lee on Dynamic Records (reggae).

RIDGEWOOD RECORDS, Box 630755, Miami FL 33163. (305)935-4880. President: Jack Gale. Labels include Playback, Gallery II, Caramba! Record company, music publisher (Lovey Music/BMI, Cowabonga Music/ASCAP) and record producer (Jack Gale). Estab. 1983. Releases 48 singles and 8 CDs/year. Works with musicians/artists and songwriters on contract. Pays statutory rate to publisher per song on record. "Ridgewood Records is primarily for 'new' artists."
How to Contact: Submit demo tape by mail—unsolicited submissions are OK. Prefers cassette (or VHS videocassette) with 2 songs and lyric sheet. SASE. Reports in 2 weeks.
Music: Mostly country and contemporary country. Released "A Fallen Star" (by J.C. Newman), recorded by Jimmy C. Newman; "Jambalaya" (by H. Wms) recorded by Jimmy C. Newman; and "Nothin' But the Walls" (by H. Wms), recorded by Mark Crigler, all on Ridgewood Records (country). Other artists include Donnie Bowser and Tim Young.
Tips: "Send only the best. Include typewritten lyrics."

RIPSAW RECORD CO., Suite 805, 4545 Connecticut Ave. NW, Washington DC 20008. (202)362-2286. President: Jonathan Strong. Record company, record producer and music publisher (Southern Crescent Publishing/BMI and Sugar Mama Music/BMI). Estab. 1976. Releases 1-2 LPs/year. Works with musicians/artists and songwriters on contract. Payment negotiable with artists on contract. Pays standard royalty to songwriters on contract; statutory rate to publishers for each record sold.
How to Contact: Submit demo tape by mail—unsolicited submissions are OK. Prefers cassette and lyric sheet. SASE. "Invite us to a club date to listen." Reports as soon as possible, generally in a month.
Music: Country, blues, rockabilly and "traditional" rock 'n' roll. Released *Oooh-Wow!*, by the Uptown Rhythm Kings (jump blues). Other artists include Bobby Smith, Billy Hancock, Kid Tater, Cheaters and Tex Rubinowitz.
Tips: "Keep it true roots rock 'n' roll."

*ROACH RECORDS CO., P.O. Box 7731, Beverly Hills CA 90121. (310)338-9976. President: Joseph Chryar. Labels include Asset Records Corporation. Record company. Estab. 1969. Releases 3 singles/year and 2 LP's/year. Works with musicians/artists on contract. Pays 10-15% royalty to artists on contract; pays statutory rate to publishers per song on record.
How to Contact: Write first and obtain permission to submit. Prefers cassette with 3 songs and lyric sheet. Does not return unsolicited material. Reports in 6 weeks.
Music: Mostly Country, R&B and pop; also rock, jazz and blues. Released "Movin'-Groovin'," written and recorded by J.D. Nichelson; "Only a Fool" (by Kent Harris), recorded by Ty Karim; and "Peek-a-Boo" (by Charlie Harris), recorded by R. Martin, all on Roach Records (all R&B singles).

ROAD RECORDS, 429 S. Lewis Rd., Royersford PA 19468. (215)948-8228. Fax: (215)948-4175. President: Jim Femino. Labels include Road Records. Record company and music publisher (Fezsongs/ASCAP). Estab. 1980. Releases 2-5 singles, 1 LP and 1 CD/year. Receives 20 submissions/month. Works with musicians/artists and songwriters on contract. Pays varying royalty to artists on contract; statutory rate to publisher per song on record.
How to Contact: Submit demo tape by mail—unsolicited submissions are OK. Prefers cassette (or VHS videocassette) with 1-3 songs and lyric sheets. SASE. Reports in 4 weeks.
Music: Mostly rock, country and crossover. Released *All Night Party* (by Jim Femino), "Party Tonight" (by Jim Femino), *Just The Good Stuff* (album/CD) and "Nancy's Song" (by Jim Femino); all recorded by Jim Femino on Road Records (rock). Other artists include Paul Waltz Band.

ROBBINS RECORDS, INC., HC80, Box 5B, Leesville LA 71446. National Representative: Sherree Scott. Labels include Headliner Stars Records. Record company and music publisher (Headliner Stars Music and Universal Stars Music/BMI). Estab. 1973. Releases 12-14 singles and 1-3 LPs/year. Works with artists and songwriters on contract. Pays standard royalty to artists on contract; statutory rate to publishers for each record sold.
How to Contact: Submit demo tape by mail—unsolicited submissions are OK. Prefers cassette with 1-6 songs and lyric sheet. Does not return unsolicited material. Reports only if interested.
Music: Mostly church/religious, also bluegrass, country, folk, gospel, and top 40/pop. Released "Jesus, You're Everywhere," "I Can Depend on You," and "I Just Came to Thank You Lord," by J.J. and Sherree Stephens (religious singles). Other artists include Renee Wills and Melodee McCanless.

ROCK CITY RECORDS, (A Division of Rock City Entertainment Co.) Box 6553, Malibu CA 90264. (813)287-5057 (FLA). CEO: Mike Danna. Rock City Entertainment Co. (Rock City Records) and record producer (Mike Danna). Estab. 1984. Releases 3-6 singles, 3-6 cassette singles and 1-3 CDs/year. Works with musicians/artists on contract. Pays 12% royalty to artists on contract; statutory rate to publishers per song on records.
How to Contact: Submit demo tape by mail—unsolicited submissions are OK. Prefers cassette (or VHS videocassette) with 2-3 songs and lyric sheet. SASE. Reports in 4 weeks.
Music: Mostly pop and rock; also soundtracks. Released *Reaching Out*, written and recorded by Mickey Dee on Rock City Records (pop/rock).
Tips: "Sacrifice, patience, persistence, and knowing your abilities will ultimately get you where you're looking to go."

ROCKIT RECORDS, INC., Suite 306 35918 Union Lake Rd., Mt. Clemens MI 48043. (313)792-8452. Music Director: Joseph Trupiano. Receives 70 submissions/month. Record company and music publisher (Bad Grammar Music, Inc. BMI). Estab. 1985. Releases 200 cassette LPs/year. Works with musicians/artists and songwriters on contract. Pays artists 10% royalty; statutory rate to publisher per song on records.
How to Contact: Submit demo by mail—unsolicited submissions are OK. Prefers cassette (or VHS videocassette if available) with 3 songs and lyric sheet. SASE. Reports in 3 weeks.
Music: Mostly pop/dance, pop rock and rock; also alternative rock, new age and urban and R&B. Released "Is Love Enough" (by J. Dudick), recorded by Hot Rod Hearts (country/pop); "She Don't Know" (by Tom Free), recorded by True Destiny (rock); and "Main Emotion" (by Russ Mitchell), recorded by Oscar Charles (dance); all on Rockit Records. Other artists include The Mix, Bob's Night Off, David Hansen, Atlas, Michael Duhnzigger and Oscar Charles.

 The asterisk before a listing indicates that the listing is new in this edition. New markets are often the most receptive to unsolicited submissions.

Tips: "Presently we are most responsive to reviewing material for our compilation CD project. Our artists receive national exposure to major labels (USA), college radio nationally, trade publications, commercial European radio, and European independent labels. Through this project we have generated much exposure nationally for artists as well as have gotten several acts signed to major labels. Artists who are their own writers should refer to what trends and writing styles are being used in today's radio market."

*ROCK'N'ROLL RECORDS, 16 Grove Place, Penarth, S. Glam. CF6 2LD South Wales UK. Phone: (0222) 704279. Director: Paul Barrett. Record company, record producer (Paul Barrett, Robert Llewellyn). Estab. 1991. Releases 3 CDs/year. Works with musicians/artists on contract and hires musicians for in-house studio work. Pays 10% retail royalty to artists on contract; statutory rate to publisher per song on record.
How to Contact: Submit demo tape by mail—unsolicited submissions are OK. Prefers cassette with lyric sheet. SASE. Reports in 3 weeks.
Music: Only fifties rock'n'roll. Released *The Party's Not Over*, written and recorded by various artists on Rock'n'Roll Records (fifties rock'n'roll LP). Other artists include Ray Thompson, Duke and the Dukes, The Class of '58 and Jack Scott.

RODELL RECORDS, Box 93457, Hollywood CA 90093. (213)960-9447. President: Adam Rodell. Record company, music publisher (Udder Publishing/BMI) and record producer (Golden Gelt/ASCAP). Recently established company. Works with musicians/artists and songwriters on contract and hires musicians for in-house studio work. Pays statutory rate to publisher per song on record.
How to Contact: Submit demo tape by mail. Unsolicited submissions are OK. Prefers cassette or VHS videocassette with 1-3 songs and lyric sheet. Does not return unsolicited material. "We will report back only if we are interested."
Music: Mostly rock, country and pop; also R&B, progressive fusion and rap.
Tips: "Send studio or studio quality cassettes only with bio and pictures. Actively seeking new acts and material. The artist's devotion and ambition to succeed must be as aggresive as ours!"

ROLL ON RECORDS®, 112 Widmar Pl., Clayton CA 94517. (510)672-8201. Owner: Edgar J. Brincat. Record company. Estab. 1985. Releases 2-3 LPs/cassettes/year. Receives 200+ submissions/month. Works with musicians/artists and songwriters on contract and hires musicians for in-house studio work. Pays 10% royalty to artists on contract; statutory rate to publisher per song on record.
How to Contact: Submit demo tape by mail—unsolicited submissions are OK. Prefers cassette with 3 songs and lyric sheet. SASE. Reports in 2-4 weeks.
Music: Mostly contemporary/country, MOR and R&B; also pop, light rock and modern gospel. Released "Jack Daniels" (by Barbara Finnicum/Edgar J. Brincat/Pattie Leidecker) and "Southern Comfort" (by Barbara Finnicum), both recorded by Carolyn Rae; "The Rain" (by Barbara Finnicum/Ed Davie) and "I Only Put it On" (by Barbara Finnicum/Ed Davie), both recorded by Ed Davie; and "The Saddest Goodbye" (by Barbara Finnicum/Ed Davie) and "Back In Time" (by Barbara Finnicum/Ed Davie), both recorded by Ed Davie.
Tips: "Be professional, write clearly and always enclose an SASE (many people don't)."

ROSEWOOD RECORDS, Box 364, New Castle PA 16103. (412)654-3023. Owner: Wes Homner. Production Manager: Jay Ed Moore. Record company, music publisher (Mountain Therapy Music/BMI) and record producer (Rosewood Productions). Estab. 1975. Releases 2 singles, 5 cassettes, 2 LPs and 2 CDs/year. Works with musicians/artists and songwriters on contract. Pays according to contract signed with artist; statutory rate to publisher per song on record.
How to Contact: Submit demo tape by mail—unsolicited submissions are OK. Prefers cassette with 3 songs and lyric sheets. Does not return unsolicited material. Reports in 3 weeks.
Music: Mostly southern gospel and bluegrass; also country. Produced "Grave Digger," written and recorded by Ron Mesing for Heritage Records (bluegrass); "Just Like You" (by Pete Wernick), recorded by Full House; and "Sing A Song of Seasons" (by Judy Minouge), recorded by Millcreek Ramblers; "Rock Me Gently" (by Wes Homner), recorded by Jay Moore on Rosewood Records (bluegrass gospel); "Rainbow's End" (by Jim Fiest), recorded by Full House on Rosewood Records (bluegrass); and "Just Can't Win" (by Jim Metz), recorded by Tim Berline on Rosewood Records (bluegrass). Other artists include Rainbow Valley Boys, Mac Martin, Bill Wright, Buzz Matheson, Wildwood Express, Judy Minouge, Timberline, The Ascensions, The Meadors Family and Leather Britches.
Tips: "Please submit only, clean positive love songs and bluegrass/gospel."

ROTO-NOTO MUSIC, 148 Erin Ave., Hamilton Ontario L8K 4W3 **Canada.** (416)796-8236. President: R. Cousins. Labels include Roto-Noto, Marmot, Chandler. Record company, music publisher and record producer. Estab. 1979. Releases 20 singles, 2 12″ singles, 5 LPs and 6 CDs/year. Works with

musicians/artists and songwriters on contract and hires musicians for in-house studio work.
How to Contact: Write first and obtain permission to submit. Prefers cassette with 2 songs and lyric sheets. SASE. Reports in 4 weeks.
Music: Mostly country, pop and rock; also R&B and jazz. Released "Crazy Infatuation" (by E. Domsy/ R. Cousins), recorded by Diane Raeside (country-rock); "Holdin' On" (by R. Peterson), recorded by Jack Diamond (country-A/C); "Makin' It Easy" (by R. Cousins), recorded by Mark LaForme (country); all recorded on Roto Noto Records. Other artists include Bobby McGee, Jack Diamond Band, Eleven Degrees, Harrison Kennedy and Frequency.

ROUND SOUND MUSIC, RR 2, Box 111-C, Cresco PA 18326. (717)595-3149. Owner: Tommy Lewis, Jr. Labels include Round Sound Music, Geodesic Records; Positive Alternative. Record company and record producer. Estab. 1983. Releases 3-5 singles, 5 LPs and 5 CDs/year. Receives 5-10 submissions/ month. Works with musicians/artists and songwriters on contract and hires musicians on salary for in-house studio work. Pays statutory rate to publishers per song on record.
How to Contact: Write or call first and obtain permission to submit. Prefers cassette, 15 ips reel-to-reel or VHS videocassette with 3 songs and lyric and lead sheet. SASE. Reports in 3 months.
Music: Mostly pop and jazz; also New Age, country, R&B, and gospel. Released *You're the Only One* (by T. Lewis), recorded by Joey Price on Geodesic Records (pop); *Some Jazz*, written and recorded by T. Lewis on Positive Alternative Records (jazz); and *Still Thinking of You* (by T. Lewis), recorded by Charade on Geodesic Records (pop).
Tips: "Be honest with yourself, and professional with your presentation."

ROWENA RECORDS, 195 S. 26th St., San Jose CA 95116. (408)286-9840. A&R Director: G.J. O'Neal. Labels include Rowena Records, Chance Records and Jan-Ell Records. Record company. Releases 4 singles, 4 12" singles and 4 CDs/year. Works with musicians/artists and songwriters on contract; hires musicians for in-house studio work. Pays 10% royalty to artists on contract; pays statutory rate to publishers per song on record.
How to Contact: Submit demo tape by mail—unsolicited submissions are OK. Prefers cassette with 4 or more songs and lyric sheet. SASE. Reports in 3 weeks.
Music: Mostly gospel, country and R&B; also pop, rock and New Age. Released "Back On Your Love" (by C. Kamer), recorded by Pat LaRocca (cross over country); "Smoke Smoke That Cig" (by J. O'Neal), recorded by Jeannine O'Neal (country); and "God Made Mamas That Way" (by D. Conway), recorded by Jaque Lynn (country), all on Rowena Records.

RR&R RECORDS, Suite 128, 3260 Keith Bridge Rd., Cumming, GA 30130-0128. (404)889-8624. Contact: Ron Dennis. Labels include Rapture Records, Ready Records, Rapp Records, Y'Shua Records and RR&R Records. Record company, music publisher (Super Rapp Publishing/BMI and Do It Now Publishing/ASCAP), record producer (Ron Dennis Wheeler). Estab. 1966. Releases 5 singles, 5 12" singles, 5 LPs, 5 EPs and 5 CDs/year. Works with musicians/artists and songwriters on contract; hires musicians for in-house studio work. Pays artists 5-15%; statutory rate to publishers per song on record.
How to Contact: Submit demo tape by mail—unsolicited submissions are OK. Prefers cassette (or VHS videocassette) or 15 ips reel-to-reel with lyric or lead sheet. SASE. Reports in 3 months. "Master track demos."
Music: Mostly gospel, rock, pop, country and R&B. Released "Legends Never Die" by Bill Scarbrough on RR&R Records (country); "Lord Paint My Mind" (by Mike Murdock), recorded by Ron Dennis Wheeler on Rapture Records; and "Almost Home Again" (by Louis Brown), recorded by Dennis Wheeler (country). Other artists include Rita Van and Rob McInnis, Dan Carroll, Taylor Prichard and Peter Burwin.
Tips: "Do not try to copy another artist or style of music. Better production masters (if possible) get more attention quicker."

***RTP INTERNATIONAL,** Box 311, 180 Pond St., Cohasset MA 02025. (617)383-9494. President: Rik Tinory. Artist Relations: Claire Babcock. Labels include Sequel and Old Boston. Record company, record producer and music publisher (Old Boston Publishing). Releases 10 singles and 8-12 LPs/year. Works with musicians/artists and songwriters on contract; musicians on salary for in-house studio work.
How to Contact: Call first. Prefers cassette with 1-3 songs and lead sheet. Does not return unsolicited material. "All material submitted must be copyrighted."

***RUFFCUT RECORDS,** 6472 Seven Mile, South Lyon MI 48178. (313)486-0505. Producer: J.D. Dudick. Record company, music publisher (AL-KY Music, ASCAP; Bubba Music, BMI). Estab. 1991. Releases 5 singles and 4 CDs/year. Pays up to 10% royalty to artists on contract; statutory rate to publisher per song on record.

How to Contact: Submit demo tape by mail—unsolicited submissions are OK. Prefers cassette with 2 songs and lyric sheet. SASE. Reports in 1 month.

Music: Mostly rock, pop, country; also alternative. Released *Don't Say Goodbye*, written and recorded by Nothing Big (LP); "Runaway Man" (by Garbo), recorded by The Hubcaps (single); and "Wish You Would" (by Zach Anderson), recorded by Pit Vipers (single), all on Ruffcut Records. Other artists include Laya Phelps, Michael Lachapelle, Point in Time and Kuda.

Tips: "Write songs that mean something, and if other people like it (sincerely) let's hear it. Records sell on musical expression, not marketing hype. Remember to keep the vocals above the music."

SABTECA RECORD CO., Box 10286, Oakland CA 94610. (510)465-2805. President: Duane Herring. Creative Manager: Sean Herring. Record company and music publisher (Sabteca Music Co./ASCAP, Toyiabe Music Co./BMI). Estab. 1980. Releases 3 singles and 1 12″ single/year. Works with songwriters on contract and hires musicians for in-house studio work. Pays statutory rate to publisher per song on record.

How to Contact: Write first and obtain permission to submit. Prefers cassette with lyric sheet. Reports in 3 weeks.

Music: Mostly R&B, pop and country. Released "Come Into My Arms" and "I Dare You," (by Duane Herring), recorded by Johnny B and The Rhythm Method; both on Sabteca Records.

Tips: "Improve your writing skills. Keep up with music trends."

SADDLESTONE RECORDS, 264 "H" Street Box 8110-21, Blaine WA 98230. Canada address: 8821 Delwood Drive N. Delta BC **Canada** V4C 4A1. (604)582-7117. President: Candice James. Labels include Silver Bow Records. Record company, music publisher (Procan, Socan, Saddlestone/BMI) and record producer (Silver Bow Productions). Estab. 1988. Releases 15 singles, 4-6 LPs and 6 CDs/year. Works with musicians/artists on contract. Pays 10-20% royalty to artists on contract; statutory rate to publishers per song on record.

How to Contact: Submit demo tape—unsolicited submissions are OK. Prefers cassette with 3-5 songs and lyric sheet. SASE. Reports in 3 months.

Music: Mostly country, pop and rock; also R&B and gospel. Released "Fragile" (by James/Bloemhard), recorded by Razzy Bailey (R&B/country); "Boots & Jeans" (by Loranger), recorded by Gerry King (country/swing); and "Rock Ya Never Stop Ya" (by Esau), recorded by Black Pearl (rock), all on Saddlestone Records. Other artists include Elmer Fudpucker, Gerry King, Hank Sasaki, Matt Audette, Ray St Gerhain, Rex Howard, Dorrie Alexander, Patty Mayo and Hulio Heart.

Tips: "Send original material, studio produced, with great hooks."

SAHARA RECORDS AND FILMWORKS ENTERTAINMENT, 8th Flr., 4475 Allisonville Rd., Indianapolis IN 46205. (317)549-9006. President: Edward De Miles. Record company, music publisher (EDM Music/BMI) and record producer. Estab. 1981. Releases 15-20 12″ singles and 5-10 LPs/year. Works with musicians/artists and songwriters on contract and hires musicians for in-house studio work. Pays varying royalty to artists on contract; pays statutory rate to publishers per song on record.

How to Contact: Submit demo tape—unsolicited submissions are OK. Prefers cassette with 3-5 songs and lyric sheet. SASE. Reports in 1 month.

Music: Mostly R&B/dance, top 40 pop/rock and contemporary jazz; also TV-film themes, musical scores and jingles. Released "Hooked on U" and "Moments," written and recorded by Steve Lynn (R&B); and "No Mercy" (by D. Evans/A. Mitchell), recorded by Multiple Choice (rap), all on Sahara Records. Other artists include "Lost in Wonder" and "Dvon Edwards".

Tips: "We're looking for strong mainstream material. Lyrics and melodies with good hooks that grab people's attention."

SAN-SUE RECORDING STUDIO, Box 773, Mt. Juliet TN 37122-3336. (615)754-5412. Labels include Basic Records. Owner: Buddy Powell. Record company, music publisher (Hoosier Hills/BMI) and recording studio (16-track). Estab. 1975. Works with artists and songwriters on contract. Releases 7 singles and 3 LPs/year. Pays 8% royalty to artists on contract; statutory rate to publishers for each record sold.

How to Contact: Submit demo tape—unsolicited submissions are OK. Prefers 7½ ips reel-to-reel or cassette with 2-4 songs. "Strong vocal with piano or guitar is suitable for demo, along with lyrics." SASE. Reports in 2 weeks.

Music: Church/religious, country, and MOR. Released "Which Way You Going Billy" (by Sandy Powell); "Don't Cry Daddy" (by Sue Powell) and "My Way" (by Jerry Baird), all on Basic Records (MOR). Other artists include Camillo Phelps.

Tips: "Do not give up on your writing because we or some other publisher reject your material."

SATURN RECORDS, (formerly Siren Records), 802 Walnut, Dept. SM, Houston TX 77002. (713)328-6752. (713)420-3189. Executive Producer: Richard E. Cagle. Labels include Saturn Records. Record company (Siren Records). Estab. 1989. Releases 3 LPs and 1 EP/year. Works with musicians/artists

and songwriters on contract; hires musicians on salary for in-house studio work. Pays 7-10% royalty to artists on contract; statutory rate to publishers per song on records.
How to Contact: Submit demo tape by mail. Unsolicited submissions are OK. Prefers cassette with 4-6 songs and lyric sheet. SASE. Reports in 6 weeks.
Music: Mostly rock, metal and pop; also blues, reggae and country. Released *Dream Come True* (by Kevin Blessington), recorded by Elevator Up (LP); *Premonition* (by Todd Good), recorded by Premonition (LP); and *Experiment* (by Spike Jacobs), recorded by Earth Army (EP), all on Siren Records. Other artists include MXD Emotions, Third Person, Joe "King" Carrasco, Reality, Mickey Jones Project and Academy Black.
Tips: "Send good demo without too many effects. Just keep it simple!"

SCENE PRODUCTIONS, Box 1243, Beckley WV 25802. (304)252-4836. President/Producer: Richard L. Petry. A&R: Carol Lee. Labels include Rising Sun and Country Road Records. Record company, record producer and music publisher (Purple Haze Music/BMI). Member of AFM. Releases 1-2 singles and 1-2 LPs/year. Receives 150-200 submissions/year. Works with musicians/artists and songwriters on contract. Pays 4-5% minimum royalty to artists on contract; standard royalty to songwriters on contract; statutory rate to publishers for each record sold. Charges "initial costs, which are conditionally paid back to artist."
How to Contact: Submit demo tape—unsolicited submissions are OK. Prefers cassette with 2-5 songs and lyric sheet. Prefers studio produced demos. SASE. Reports in 1 month.
Music: Mostly country, top 40, R&B/crossover and pop/rock; also MOR, light and commercial rock. Released "Keep Moving," written and recorded by Chuck Paul (pop); "A Little Night Lovin' " (by Carol Lee), recorded by Victor Jackson (R&B) both on Rising Sun Records; and "Dixieman" (by Don MacLean and Ron Miller), recorded by Cypress Creek on Country Road Records (country). Other artists includes Dave Runion.
Tips: "Make sure it's professionally presented. Don't tell us it's a hit in a long letter; let us decide that!"

SCORE PRODUCTIONS, 3414 Peachtree Rd. NE 640, Atlanta GA 30326-1113. (404)266-8990. A&R Director: Amy Davis. Record company, music publisher and record producer (Score Productions, Inc.). Releases 10 singles, 1000 LPs and 5 CDs/year. Works with musicians/artists and songwriters on contract. Pays negotiable royalty to artists on contract.
How to Contact: Call first and obtain permission to submit. Prefers cassette with 1 song and lyric sheet. SASE. Reports in 1 month.
Music: Rock, country, MOR and pop. Released "Tone Up," "In Concert," and "Silver Anniversary Tribute to the Beatles," all on Perfect Pitch Records.

SCP RECORDS, Division of the Sound Column Companies, Box 70784, Salt Lake City UT 84170. (801)355-5327. A&R Professional Manager: Ron Simpson. Record company with affiliated record producer and music publisher (Ronarte Publications/ASCAP, Mountain Green Music/BMI and Macanudo Music/SESAC). Member CMA, AFM. Estab. 1970. Releases 3 singles and 4 cass/CDs/year. Works with artists and songwriters on contract; hires musicians for in-house studio work. Pays negotiable royalty to artists on contract; statutory rate to publishers for each record sold.
How to Contact: "Unsolicited submissions OK this year (pop ballads, pop uptempo, dance, country, R&B ballad and uptempo). Three songs max on demo tape, please include lyric sheets. No return or correspondence without SASE and sufficient postage. We'll eventually listen to everything. No calls, please."
Music: Pop (dance and A/C), country and contemporary religious. Released *"His Love"* (by various), recorded by Janine Lindsay (contemporary religious); "So Excited" (by Grant), recorded by Shawn K. (pop dance); and "Goodbye I Love You" (by K. Simpson and E. Pearson), recorded by Emily Pearson (contemporary folk), all on SCP Records.

SEASIDE RECORDS, 100 Labon St., Tabor City NC 28463. (919)653-2546. Owner: Elson H. Stevens. Labels include SeaSide and JCB. Record company, music publisher and record producer. Estab. 1978. Releases 10 singles and 15 LPs/year. Works with musicians/artists and songwriters on contract; musicians on salary for in-house studio work, and producers. Receives 15 submissions/month. Pays 3-10% royalty to artists on contract; statutory rate to publisher per song on record.
How to Contact: Submit demo tape—unsolicited submissions are OK. Prefers cassette with 3 songs and lyric or lead sheet. SASE. Reports in 1 month.
Music: Mostly country, gospel and rock; also "beach music." Released "I'll Never Say Never Again" (by G. Todd/T. Everson), recorded by Sherry Collins (country); "Faith of a Tiny Seed" (by R. Lynn), recorded by Randa Lynn (contemporary gospel); "Long Lonesome Road" (by G. Taylor), recorded by Sherry Collins (country); all on SeaSide Records.
Tips: "Send only unpublished material. Songs must have strong hook."

*SEEDS RECORDS, Box 20814, Oklahoma City OK 73156. (405)755-0315. Labels include Homa, Seeds and Okart Records. Record company, record producer, music publisher (Okisher Publishing/BMI), and Mickey Sherman Talent Management. Estab. 1973. Releases 6-12 12" singles, 3 LPs and 3 CDs/ year. Works with songwriters on contract and hires in-house studio musicians. Pays 10% royalty to artists on contract; statutory rate to publishers for each record sold.
How to Contact: Submit demo tape – unsolicited submissions OK. Prefers cassette (or videocassette) with 1-3 songs and lyric sheet. Does not return unsolicited material. Reports in 1 month.
Music: Mostly blues, country and ballads; also easy listening, jazz, MOR, R&B and soul. Released "A Brighter Day," written and recorded by Dale Langley (gospel); and "Don't Do the Crime," written and recorded by Jan Jo (rock), all on Seeds Records. Other artists include Charley Shaw, Ronnie McClendon, Jana Jarvis and The Langley Family.

*SHANACHIE RECORDS, 37 East Clinton St., Newton NJ 07860. (201)579-7763. A&R Director: Randall Grass. Labels include Greensleeves – USA, Message, Ogham and Yazoo Records. Releases 5 singles and 25 CDs/cassettes/year. Works with musicians/artists on contract. Pays statutory rate to publisher per song on record.
How to Contact: Prefers cassette. SASE required for response. Reports in 1 month.
Music: Reggae, Irish and world beat; also folk, African and ethnic. Released *Music for Silences to Come*, written and recorded by Dan Ar Bras on Shanachie (LP); *We've Come a Long Way*, written and recorded by Makem and Clancy on Shanachie Records (LP); and *Until* (by Willie Lindo), recorded by Nadine Sutherland on Meadowlark Records (LP). Other artists incude Rita Marley, Judy Mowatt, Steeleye Span, Yellowan, Augusons Pablo and The Chieftains.

SHAOLIN FILM & RECORDS, Box 387, Hollywood CA 90078. (818)506-8660. President: Richard O'Connor. A&R: Michelle McCarty. Record company, music publisher (Shaolin Music/ASCAP) and record producer (The Coyote). Estab. 1984. Releases 2 singles, 1 LP, 1CD and 1EP/year. Receives 30 submissions/month. Works with musicians/artists on record contract.
How to Contact: Submit demo tape – unsolicited submissions are OK. Prefers cassette with 3-4 songs and lyric sheet. Include bio and press kit. SASE. Reports in 1 month.
Music: Mostly rock, hard rock and pop; also soundtracks. Released "Save the Coyote," "Game of Lies" and "All Screwed Up," all written and recorded by Coyote on Shaolin Film and Records (rock).

*SIGNATURE RECORDS, 500 Newbold St., London Ontario N6E 1K6 **Canada.** (519)686-5060. A&R Director: Geoff Keymer. Record company. Estab. 1982. Releases 5 LPs/year. Works with musicians/ artists on contract and hires musicians for in-house studio work. Pays statutory rate to publisher per song on record.
How to Contact: No unsolicited submissions. "Call or write and we will tell you when to submit." SASE. Responds in 2-3 months.
Music: Mostly MOR/rock, rock and country ballads. Released "Statue," written and recorded by R. Piché; "Cassandra," written and recorded by Cassandra; and "Mike McKenna," written and recorded by Mike McKenna; all on Signature Records (all rock singles).

SILENT RECORDS, Suite 315, 540 Alabama, San Francisco CA 94110. (415)252-5764. FAX: (415)864-7815. President: Kim Cascone. Record company and record producer (Kim Cascone). Estab. 1986. Releases 10 CDs/year. Works with musicians/artists on contract. Accepts LPs and CDs for consideration and distribution. Pays 10-15% of wholesale as royalty to artists on contract; negotiable rate to publishers per song on record.
How to Contact: Write first and obtain permission to submit. Prefers cassette (or VHS videocassette) with press kit (press clips, bio, etc.). Does not return unsolicited material. Reports in 6 months.
Music: Mostly experimental and industrial. Released "Exodus," written and recorded by Pelican Daughters (ambient/pop); and "Hymns from the Furnace" (by Kim Cascone), recorded by PGR (industrial), both on Silent Records. Other artists include Organum, The Haters and Pelican Daughters.
Tips: "Formulate a career strategy and learn your market."

SILVER JET RECORDS, 3500 Llanberis Ave., Bristol PA 19007. (215)788-2723. President: Johnny Kline. Record company, music publisher (BMI) and record producer (Silver Jet). Estab. 1984. Releases 1-2 singles/year. Receives 1-2 submissions/month. Works with musicians on salary for in-house studio work. Pays 10% royalty to artists on contract; statutory rate to publishers per song on record.
How to Contact: Submit demo tape – unsolicited submissions are OK. "No phone calls please." Prefers cassette with 3 songs and lyric sheet. SASE. Reports in 2-3 weeks.
Music: Rockabilly. Released "Good Rockin Tonight" (by Roy Brown); and "It's Late" (by D. Burnette), recorded by Johnny Kline on Siver Jet Records (rockabilly).
Tips: "Submit professional quality tapes."

SIRR RODD RECORD & PUBLISHING CO., Box 58116, Philadelphia PA 19102-8116. President: Rodney J. Keitt. Record company, music publisher, record producer and management and booking firm. Releases 5 singles, 5 12″ singles and 2 LPs/year. Works with musicians/artists and songwriters on contract. Pays 5-10% royalty to artists on contract; statutory rate to publishers for each record sold.
How to Contact: Prefers cassette (or videocassette) with 3-5 songs and lyric sheet. SASE. Reports in 1 month.
Music: Top 40, pop, gospel, jazz, dance and rap. Released "God's Light Is Love" (by Betalove) and "Please Come Home For Christmas" (by Rodney Jerome Keitt).

SKYLYNE RECORDS, (formerly Street Music Records), #17, 61 Canal St., San Rafael CA 94901. (415)453-6270. President/Executive Producer: Jeff Britto. Record company. Estab. 1987. Releases 7 singles and 7 LPs/year.
How to Contact: Prefers cassette or VHS videocassette with 2 songs and lyric sheet. SASE. Reports in 2 weeks.
Music: Mostly rap, R&B and dance; also house and pop. Released "Talking That Bad Talk," recorded by CIA (rap); "Pop Music IZ" (by Corey A. Powell and Mike Pantaleone), recorded by Corey Andre (dance); and "Just Another Sucka" (by Russell L. Montiero and Suzanne Amadeo), recorded by Nite-n-Day (rap); all on Skylyne Records. Other artists include Dávida and Rudy C.

SLAK RECORDS, 9 Hector Ave., Toronto, ON M6G3G2 **Canada**. (416)533-3707. President: Al Kussin. Record company, music publisher (Clotille Publishing/PROCAN) and record producer (Slak Productions). Estab. 1986. Releases 2 singles, 2 12″ singles and 1 LP/year. Receives 10 submissions/month. Works with musicians/artists on contract. Pays 8-12% per record sold. Pays statutory rate to publisher per song on record.
How to Contact: Submit demo tape by mail. Unsolicited submissions are OK. Prefers cassette with 3 songs and lyric sheets. SASE.
Music: Mostly pop, R&B and dance. Released "Go Baby" (by F. Fudge and A. Kussin), recorded by Frankie Fudge; "All Talk" and "In Love" (by Lorraine Scott and A. Kussin), recorded by Lorrain Scott; all on Slak Records (R&B).
Tips: "Most of the material on Slak has been written by me. However, I wish to expand. A small label needs commercial, solid songwriting with good hooks and interesting lyrics."

SONY MUSIC, 34 Music Square E., Nashville TN 37203. (615)742-4321. Labels include Columbia and Epic. Record company.
How to Contact: Write and ask for submission policy.

SOUNDS OF WINCHESTER, Rt. 2, Box 116-H, Berkeley Springs, WV 25411. Contact: Jim or Bertha McCoy. Labels include Alear, Winchester and Real McCoy Records. Record company, music publisher (Jim McCoy Music, Alear Music and New Edition Music/BMI) and recording studio. Estab. 1973. Releases 20 singles and 20 LPs/year. Works with artists and songwriters on contract; musicians on salary for in-house studio work. Pays 2% royalty to artists and songwriters on contract; statutory rate to publishers for each record sold.
How to Contact: Submit demo tape—unsolicited submissions are OK. Prefers 7½ ips reel-to-reel or cassette with 4-12 songs. SASE. Reports in 1 month.
Music: Bluegrass, country, country rock, gospel and top 40/pop. Released "Dyin' Pain" and "I'm Getting No Where At Getting Over You" (by J.B. Miller); and "My Heart Won't Wander," by R. Lee Gray; all on Winchester Records (country). Other artists include Carroll County Ramblers, Alvin Kesner, Bob Myers, George Dove, Bud Armel and Terry McCumbee.

SOURCE RECORDS, INC., #825, 39 S. LaSalle St., Chicago IL. (312)287-2227. President: John Bellamy. Record company. Estab. 1974. Releases 2 singles, 3 12″ singles and 2 LPs/year. Works with musicians/artists and songwriters on contract. Pays statutory rate to publisher per song on record.
How to Contact: Submit demo tape by mail—unsolicited submissions are OK. Prefers cassette (or VHS or ¾″ videocassette if available) with 2 songs and lyric sheet. SASE. Reports in 3 weeks.
Music: Mostly R&B, pop and gospel. Released "Deeper in Debt" (by Spright Simpson) (rap); "Crazy for You" (by Kennedy Green) (R&B); and "Greater By & By" (by Sean Williams) (gospel), all recorded by The Source on Source Records.

SOURCE UNLIMITED RECORDS, 331 E. 9th St., New York NY 10003. (212)473-7833. Contact: Santo. Record company. Estab. 1982. Releases 4 CDs/year. Receives 30 submissions/month. Works with songwriters on contract. Pays 20% royalty to artists on contract; statutory rate to publisher per song on record.

How to Contact: Submit demo tape—unsolicited submissions are OK. Prefers cassette and lyric sheet. SASE. Reports in 1-2 months.

Music: Mostly modern folk, blues and gospel. Released "Help Us to Survive"; "Street Blues Theme" and "Livin' Day to Day," all written and recorded by Santo on Source Unlimited Records (street blues).

Tips: "Write about what you know! Be original."

SOUTHERN TRACKS RECORDS, 3051 Clairmont Rd. NE, Atlanta GA 30329. (404)325-0832. Contact: Mr. Carrier. Record company and record producer. Releases 10 singles and 3 LPs/year. Works with musicians/artists and songwriters on contract. Pays average of 5% royalty to artists on contract.

How to Contact: Prefers cassette with 3 unpublished songs and lyric sheet. Does not return unsolicited material.

Music: Interested in all types of music. Released "Burns Like a Rocket," recorded by Billy Joe Royal; and "We Always Agree on Love," recorded by Atlanta on Southern Tracks Records. Other artists include Bertie Higgins, Sammy Johns, Scooter Lee, Milton Crabapple and Lewis Grizzard.

*STAR RECORD CO., Suite 1700, 521 Fifth Ave., New York NY 10017. (212)682-5844. Record company, record producer and music publisher (McRon Music Co. and The Main Floor). Releases 2-6 LPs/year. Works with songwriters on royalty contract. Pays statutory rate to publishers for each record sold.

STARCREST PRODUCTIONS, INC., 209 Circle Hills Dr., Grand Forks ND 58201. (701)772-6831. President: George J. Hastings. Labels include Meadowlark and Minn-Dak Records. Record company, management firm and booking agency. Estab. 1970. Releases 2-6 singles and 1-2 LPs/year. Works with artists and songwriters on contract. Payment negotiable to artists on contract; statutory rate to publishers for each record sold.

How to Contact: Submit demo tape—unsolicited submissions are OK. Prefers cassette with 1-6 songs and lead sheet. SASE. Reports in 3 months.

Music: Country and top 40/pop. Released "You and North Dakota Nights" (by Stewart & Hastings) recorded by Mary Joyce on Meadowlark Records (country).

STARDUST, Box 13, Estill Springs TN 37330. (615)649-2577. President: Buster Doss. Labels include Stardust, Wizard, Doss, Kimbolon, Flaming Star. Record company, music publisher (Buster Doss Music/BMI) and record producer (Colonel Buster Doss). Estab. 1959. Releases 50 singles and 25 LPs/year. Works with musicians/artists and songwriters on contract and hires musicians for in-house studio work. Pays 8% royalty to artists on contract; statutory rate to publisher per song on record.

How to Contact: Submit demo tape—unsolicited submissions are OK. Prefers cassette with 2 songs and lyric sheets. SASE. Reports in 1 week.

Music: Mostly country; also rock. Released "Resque Me" (by P. Hotchkiss), recorded by Tommy D. on Doss Records; "King Bee" (by B. Doss), recorded by Rooster Q. on Stardust Records; and "Would You" (by B. Doss), recorded by R.B. Stone on Stardust Records; all country. Other artists include Johnny Buck, Hobson Smith, Cliff Archer, Linda Wunder, Buck Cody and Tony Andrews.

STARGARD RECORDS, Box 138, Boston MA 02101. (617)296-3327. Artist Relations: Janice Tritto. Labels include Oak Groove Records. Record company, music publisher (Zatco Music/ASCAP and Stargard Publishing/BMI) and record producer. Estab. 1985. Releases 9 singles and 1 LP/year. Receives 15-20 submissions/month. Works with musicians/artists on contract; hires musicians for in-house studio work. Pays 5-6% royalty to artists on contract; statutory rate to publishers per song on record.

How to Contact: Submit demo tape—unsolicited submissions are OK. Write first to arrange personal interview. Prefers cassette and lyric sheet. SASE. Reports in 6 weeks. "Sending bio along with picture or glossies is appreciated but not necessary."

Music: Mostly R&B, dance/hip hop. Released "I'll Take a Chance" (dance/pop) and "Your the One For Me" (by Floyd Wilcox) recorded by Jilly B. (R&B/dance); and "You Are My Everything" (by Floyd Wilcox), recorded by Andred Dubois (ballad R&B), all on Stargard Records. Other artists include Down Time and En-Control.

STARK RECORDS AND TAPE COMPANY, 628 S. South St., Mount Airy NC 27030. (919)786-2865. President and Owner: Paul E. Johnson. Labels include Stark, Pilot, Hello, Sugarbear, Kay and Red Bird. Record company, music publisher (Tompaul Music Company/BMI) and record producer (Stark Records and Tape Company). Estab. 1960. Releases 8 singles and 3 LPs/year. Works with songwriters on contract. Pays artists 30% royalty per record sold; statutory rate to publishers per song on record.

How to Contact: Submit demo tape—unsolicited submissions are OK. Prefers cassette with 3-5 songs and lyric or lead sheets. SASE. Reports in 2 months.
Music: Mostly pop, country and country gospel; also bluegrass, bluegrass gospel and C&W. Released "It Won't Be Long"; "Won't That Be A Time" and "He Owns Everything," written and recorded by Early UpChurch, all on Stark Records (country gospel). Other artists include Carl Tolbert, Sam Bray, Ralph Hill, Early Upchurch, Sanford Teague and Don Sawyers.
Tips: "Try to write commercial type songs, and use the best backup musicians possible."

STARMAN RECORDS, Box 245569, Sacramento CA 95824. (916)441-1080. A&R: Virgal Covington. Record company, record producer (Starman Records), (SAA, independent label) and in-house studio. Estab. 1976. Deals with artists and songwriters. Produces 3-4 singles and 2-3 LPs/year. Fee derived from outright fee from recording artist or record company. Sometimes charges artists in advance for services; "depends on their input and willingness to be produced on a professional level."
How to Contact: Call first and obtain permission to submit. Prefers cassette or VHS videocassette with 6 songs and lyric and lead sheet. SASE.
Music: Mostly popular MOR, AOR and R&B, New Age and soundtrack; also spoken word, sound effects and novelty or specialties. Produced *Starbreak Vol.1* (compilation), recorded by A.V. Covington (country LP); *Starbreak Vol.2* (by Gospel Choirs), recorded by John Irving (rock Gospel); and "The War Song" (by A.V. Covington), recorded by The Virg (AOR/pop); all on Starman Records. Other artists include Mary Murphy.

STATUE RECORDS, 2810 McBain St., Redondo Beach CA 90278. President: Jim Monroe. A&R Director: Lisa Raven. Record company. Releases 5-10 singles and 10-20 LPs/year. Works with musicians/artists and songwriters on contract. Pays 5-10% or negotiable royalty to artists on contract.
How to Contact: Submit demo tape by mail—unsolicited submissions are OK. Prefers "high quality" cassette with 3-5 songs and lyric sheet. Reports in 1 month. "Please include glossy photo(s) if you are a group looking for a recording deal."
Music: Mostly "up-tempo rock, with *strong* hooks and new wave." Released *Ring Leader* (rock LP), *Chosin Few* (rock LP), *England 402* (rock LP), *Voyager* (rock LP), *Bob Dato* (rock LP), *Hollywood Bears* (rock LP) and *New Dynasty* (rock LP).

STOP HUNGER RECORDS INTERNATIONAL, 1300 Division St., Nashville TN 37203. (615)242-4722. FAX: (615)242-1177. Producer: Robert Metzgar. Record company and music publisher (Aim High Music/ASCAP, Bobby and Billy Music/BMI). Estab. 1971. Releases 16-17 singles, 25 LPs and 25 CDs/year. Works with musicians/artists and songwriters on contract and hires musicians for in-house studio work. Pays statutory rate to publisher per song on record.
How to Contact: Submit demo tape by mail. Unsolicited submissions are OK. Prefers cassette or VHS videocassette with 5-10 songs and lyric sheet. Does not return unsolicited material. Reports in 2 weeks.
Music: Mostly country, traditional country and pop country; also gospel, southern gospel and contemporary Christian. Released *George and Merle* (by H. Cornelius), recorded by Alan Jackson on Arista Records (CD/cassette); *Return of the Ghost Riders* (by Jack Patton), recorded by J. Cash on Polygram Records (CD/cassette); and *Just the Two Of Us* (by Metzgar/Patterson), recorded by C. Twitty on MCA Records (CD/cassette). Other artists include Tommy Cash/Mark Allen Cash (CBS-Sony), Carl Butler (CBS-Sony), Tommy Overstreet (CBS-Sony), Mickey Jones (Capitol), Glen Campbell Band and others.

STRESS RECORDS, 3947 State Line, Kansas City MO 64111. (913)262-3555. Director of A&R: Dave McQuitty. Labels include Graphic Records. Record company and music publisher (United Entertainment Music/BMI). Estab. 1982. Releases 1-2 12" singles, 2-4 LPs, 1-2 EPs and 2-4 CDs/year. Receives 4-6 submissions/month. Works with musicians/artists and songwriters on contract. Pays 10% royalty to artists on contract; negotiable rate to publisher per song on record.
How to Contact: Write first and obtain permission to submit. Prefers cassette (or VHS videocassette) or 15 or 30 ips reel-to-reel with 3-5 songs and lyric sheet. Does not return unsolicited material. Reports in 1 month.
Music: Mostly rock and country; also jazz, R&B and pop. Released *We Only In It For the Monkey* (by R. Lucente), recorded by the Bon Ton Band on Stress Records (LP zydeco); *American Tradition*, written and recorded by The Verandas on Stress Records (LP rock); *The Clique*, written and recorded by The Clique on Graphic Records (LP rock); *Rodeo Rocks Vol 1* (heavy metal LP compilation) on Stress Records and *Weak Heart, Strong Memory* by Spike Blake on Stress Records (country LP). Other artists include The Hollowmen, That Statue Moved, Groovehead and Denov Theives.

STUDIO RECORDS INC., 5209 Indian Head Hwy., Oxon Hill MD 20745. (301)839-6567. President: Steven Franco. Vice President: Michael Pipitone. Record company (BMI). Estab. 1983. Releases 4-10 12" singles, 4 CDs, 4 EPs and 4 LPs/year. Works with musicians/artists and songwriters on contract and hires musicians for in-house studio work and commercial production. Pays 6-10% royalty to artists on contract; statutory rate to publisher per song on record.

How to Contact: Submit demo tape by mail—unsolicited submissions are OK. Prefers cassette with 3 songs. Does not return unsolicited material. Reports in 2 weeks.

Music: Mostly pop, dance and R&B. Released "Girl You Know Its True" (by Anedo, Lyles, Dehewy, Spencer, Hollang), recorded by Numarx on Studio Records (pop). Other artists include Tommi Gee, Patrick Adams and Lisa Bellamy.

STUDIOEAST RECORDING, INC., 5457 Monroe Rd., Charlotte NC 28212. (704)536-0424. Owner: Tim Eaton. Labels include Pyramid Records, Metro Records, Sandblast Records, Sandman, East Coast Records and Peach. Record company, music publisher (Eastwood Publishing) and record producer. Releases 50 singles and 20 LPs/year. Works with musicians/artists and songwriters on contract; hires musicians for in-house studio work. Pays standard royalty to artists on contract.

How to Contact: Prefers cassette or 15 ips reel-to-reel (or VHS videocassette) with any number of songs. Does not return unsolicited material. Reports in 2 months. "If we feel material is unusable we will not contact artist. We will, however, keep material on file for possible future use."

Music: Mostly R&B, country and jazz; also rhythm and black gospel. Released "One More Step," by the Band of Oz on Metro Records; "Lovers' Holiday," by Dink Perry and the Breeze Band on Metro Records; "They Call Me Mr. Bassman" and "Whadja Do That Fo'" by the Catalinas on Metro Records (singles). Presently recording: General Johnson & The Chairman Of The Board for Surfside Records, The Fantastic Shakers for Metro Records, The Catalinas for Metro Records and Part Time Party Time Band for Metro Records.

*SUN DANCE RECORDS, 907 Baltimore St., Mobile AL 36605. Record company. Estab. 1987. Releases 12-15 singles, 8-10 12" singles, 10 LPs and 10 CDs/year. Works with musicians/artists/songwriters on contract and in-house studio musicians on salary. Pays negotiated royalty to artists on contract.

How to Contact: Submit demo tape by mail—unsolicited submissions are OK. Prefers cassette (or VHS videocassette if available) with 2 songs and lyric sheets. SASE. Reports in 8-10 weeks.

Music: Mostly R&B, pop and rap; also rock, gospel and jazz. Released "Mission" (by James Young), recorded by LaShone Glover (pop rock) and "Real World," written and recorded by Ricky Warren (R&B) both on Sun Dance Records. Other artists include Kyle Bush and Magnetics.

Tips: "He that can have patience can have what he will."

SUNDOWN RECORDS, Dept. SM, Box 241, Newbury Park CA 91320. (805)499-9912. Owners: Gilbert Yslas and Richard Searles. Record company, distributor. Estab. 1985. Releases 2 CDs/year. Works with musicians/artists on contract.

How to Contact: Submit demo tape/CD by mail. Prefers cassette. SASE. Reports in weeks.

Music: Contemporary classical/New Age. Released "A Christmas Gift" written and recorded by Yslas/Searles on Sundown Records (New Age); "Dance of the Renaissance" (acoustic); and "Dream of the Troubadour" (acoustic).

*SUNSET RECORDS INC., 1577 Redwood Dr., Harvey LA 70058. (504)367-8501. President: George Leger. Labels include Sunburst Records. Record company, record producer, and music publisher (Country Legs Music/ASCAP and Golden Sunburst Music/BMI). Member CMA. Releases 5 singles/year. Works with artists and songwriters on contract. Works with lyricists and teams collaborators. Pays 7% royalty to artists on contract; statutory rate to publisher per song on record.

How to Contact: "Write first and request permission to submit; then when granted, submit clean, good quality cassette with 3-5 songs and lyric sheet. Identify vocalist on demo tape. Artists send tape showing vocal abilities and explain objectives. SASE with enough postage to return material if requested." Reports in 2 months.

Music: Mostly country; also gospel, progressive country, R&B, and seasonal (Christmas, Mother's Day, etc.). Released "Broken Homes," by Sonny Tears (country single); and "I Don't Care," by Larry Maynard (country single).

Tips: "It's better to have one good, smooth flowing song than having one dozen not flowing smoothly, so take your time to go over your song until it flows right."

SURESHOT RECORDS, Box 1345, Kings Beach CA 96143. (916)546-5381. Contact: Alan Redstone. Record company and music publisher (Magic Message Music/ASCAP). Estab. 1979. Releases 1 single and 1 LP/year. Works with songwriters on contract.

How to Contact: Submit demo tape—unsolicited submissions OK. SASE. Reports in 2 weeks.

Music: Mostly country, A/C and rock; also ballads. Released "This Time Around," written and recorded by Alan Redstone on Sureshot Records (country/rock).

SURPRIZE RECORDS, INC., 7231 Mansfield Ave., Philadelphia PA 19138-1620. (215)276-8861. President: W. Lloyd Lucas. Director of A&R: Darryl L. Lucas. Labels include Surprize and SRI. Record company and record producer (Surprize Records, Inc.). Estab. 1981. Releases 4-6 singles, 1-3 12" singles and 2 LPs/year. Works with musicians/artists and songwriters on contract. Pays 6-10% royalty to artists on contract; statutory rate to publisher per song on record.
How to Contact: Write first and obtain permission to submit. Prefers cassette or VHS videocassette with 4 songs and lyric or lead sheet. SASE. Reports in 3 weeks.
Music: Mostly R&B ballads, R&B dance oriented; also crossover country, gospel and contemporary Christian. Released "Pledging My Love" (by Cobb/McCoy), recorded by Bill Lucas on Surprize Records (R&B single); "Shadow People" (by August/Trantham), recorded by Trilogy on Surprize Records (R&B single); and "Fat Girls" (by Heston/Webb/Walker/Hudson), recorded by KeeWee and produced by Time-Nu Productions Of Detroit Michigan and released on Surprize Records.
Tips: "Be dedicated and steadfast in your chosen field whether it be songwriting and/or performing. Be aware of the changing trends. Watch other great performers and try to be as good, if not better. 'Be the best that you can be.' And as Quincy Jones says, 'Leave your egos at the door' and take all criticisms as being positive, not negative. There is always something to learn. Artists with upcoming R&B ballad and dance oriented recording projects are Lamar, and Lease Medley and a male gospel group looking for material ala the Williams brothers, BeBe and CeCe Winans."

SUSAN RECORDS, Box 1622, Hendersonville TN 37077. (615)822-1044. A&R Director: D. Daniels. Labels include Denco Records. Record company and music publisher. Releases 2-20 singles and 1-5 LPs/year. Works with artists and songwriters on contract. Pays 20¢/record to artists on contract; statutory rate to publishers per song on record. Buys some material outright; payment varies.
How to Contact: Submit demo tape—unsolicited submissions OK. Prefers cassette with 1-6 songs and lead sheet. SASE. Reports in 3 weeks.
Music: Blues, country, dance, easy listening, folk, gospel, jazz, MOR, rock, soul and top 40/pop.

SWEET TALK RECORDS, Box 211, Westfield MA 01086. (413)783-8386. Operations Manager: Alexis Steele. Labels include Sweet Talk Records. Record company and music publisher (Sariser Music/BMI). Estab. 1987. Releases 2 LPs/year. Receives 10-15 submissions/year. Works with musicians/artists and songwriters on contract. Pays statutory rate to publisher per song on record.
How to Contact: Write first and obtain permission to submit. No phone calls. Prefers cassette or 7½ ips reel-to-reel (or VHS #¼" videocassette) with 3-4 songs and lyric or lead sheet. SASE. Reports in 6 weeks.
Music: Mostly country/pop, country/rock and educational material; also soft rock and rockabilly. Released "Magic & Music," written and recorded by Sparkie Allison on Sweet Talk Records (jazz); and "One Last Kiss" (by Sparkie Allison) recorded by The Moore Twins on MMT Records (country).
Tips: "Be unique. Try something different. Avoid the typical love songs. We look for material with a universal positive message. No cheatin' songs, no drinkin' songs."

SWOOP RECORDS, Stewart House, Hillbottom Rd., Highwycombe, Bucks, HP124HJ **England.** Phone: (0630)647374. A&R Director: Xavier Lee. Labels include Grenoullie, Zarg, Pogo and Check. Record company, music publisher (R.T.L. Music) and record producer (Ron Lee). Estab. 1976. Releases 50 singles, 50 12" singles, 60 LPs and 60 CDs/year. Receives 10-15 submissions/month. Works with musicians/artists and songwriters on contract. Royalty paid to artists varies; statutory rate to publishers per song on record.
How to Contact: Submit demo tape—unsolicited submissions OK. Prefers cassette, (or VHS videocassette) with 3 songs and lyric or lead sheet. SAE and IRC. Reports in 6 weeks.
Music: Interested in all types. Released "Gotta Do It All Again" (ballad) and "Sily Dived" (pop), written and recorded by D. Boone; and "Not this Time" (by Dewie Boone) recorded by Lelly Boone (rock), all on Swoop Records. Other artists include Orphan, Groucho, Sight-n-Sound, Mike Sheridan, The Night Riders and Studs.
Tips: "Be original."

TABITHA RECORDS, Sandpiper Court, Harrington Lane, Exeter HX6 8N5 **England.** Phone: (0392)79914. Managing Director: Graham Sclater. Labels include Willow and Domino. Record company (PRS/MCPC/PPL) and record producer (Graham Sclater). Estab. 1975. Releases 6 singles, 2 12" singles, 4 LPs and 2 CDs/year. Works with musicians/artists on contract. Pays 4-8% royalty to artists on contract; statutory rate to publisher per song on record.
How to Contact: Submit demo tape by mail. Unsolicited submissions are OK. Prefers cassette (or VHS videocassette if available) with 4 songs. SASE. Reports in 1 month.
Music: Mostly pop, rock and country; also R&B and folk. Released "Aliens," written and recorded by Mark Fojo; "Fuzzin' The Tracks" (by Sting), recorded by Flic; and "Not A Chance," written and recorded by Simon Galt; all on Tabitha Records (all pop singles). Other artists include Andy Ford, Deparate Measures and 'Ot Nuts.

Close-up

John Keany
Songwriter, The Spelvins
New York, New York

"It's very difficult for the A&R people to sign a band. I know their jobs are on the line. It's a very powerful business, and it's easier to make decisions about a band that sounds like another band that's already got a potential marketplace." This may sound like an apology for the current attitude of the music industry toward new talent, but it's actually a statement made by John Keany, guitarist and songwriter of The Spelvins, a New York-based band which had not one, but two major label recording contracts evaporate before the group entered the studio.

The Spelvins formed after playing in different cover bands during college. The group's "nucleus," consisting of guitarist/songwriter Keany, lead singer Bird (so called because his last name is Canary) and keyboard player Dave Bondi moved to New York four years ago in search of a drummer and a recording contract. After a procession of drummers were auditioned, hired and replaced, the group finalized their lineup with percussionist Drew Overlin. The last piece of the puzzle in place, the group developed original material, solidified their sound, and went in search of their second goal: a major label recording contract.

The Spelvins' music did attract attention. One company approached the group, and an oral agreement was made. But mysteriously, the company didn't follow through with a contract. Unruffled, the band turned to a second interested company waiting for the result of the first negotiation. Demos made as part of the previous agreement were sent to the second company. The label's A&R corps came to performances. Another deal was struck and approved; all seemed to be going well. But this contract also was to prove fruitless; the executive who approved the deal left the label soon after approval to head another company, and the A&R representative who had recruited The Spelvins for the label was fired. The Spelvins were left "twisting in the wind," as Keany says. After recovering from the frustration of New York's seeming rejection of the group, the band went to Los Angeles to showcase. Representatives of Zoo/Praxis Entertainment heard and liked the group and later signed them to a recording contract.

Keany is philosophical about the long road The Spelvins have gone down in their pursuit of a career. "I think it's been a good learning experience for all of us," he says. "It's really past the point of playing head games in the band. We've been through hell and back; we've been together for years. So, we've got a thick skin about a lot of stuff. We support each other."

The focus for The Spelvins changed from career success to quality of music as the group struggled with business issues. "I think what we really value are the songs," Keany says. "We want to make music that means something to us. We realize there's a musical climate out there; one can make that kind of record." Keany feels the current climate in the music industry is conducive to music like The Spelvins'. "We feel that we're a rock band, an American rock band. We play guitars with amps and we're loud. I see a return to that [kind of band]. We've been doing similar things for about four years. Now it seems there's more interest in the type of thing we do. Things are coming around again."

Have the members of the group learned any important lessons? "I know it sounds really basic," says Keany, "but if there's a problem, there's a problem. If someone doesn't come out and say they're behind you, then they're not quite there yet. The biggest lesson of all is there are people out there who do like your music. It's all a matter of timing; more than that it's all a matter of really knowing what you're about and being able to deal with the fact that certain people can't hear it [your songs]."

Keany speaks often about the importance of the band working together to make decisions and define roles. "I think that roles get more defined. Somebody has to talk to the record company; it can't be all four of us. Who is good at business, who is good at whatever? And everybody, with a little pushing and shoving, screaming and yelling, comes to a decision. I think we worked the bugs out before the record deal, and that works to our advantage in our career. When we do have success with this record, it will be because we took care of our personal business before hand."

Starting that career was a struggle for the members of The Spelvins. Keany believes that the situation is the same for all aspiring artists and songwriters: "I think it's very difficult [to begin]. I think it all depends on knowing yourself, what you do. Know your limitations and strengths, and then really push them. It takes a frankness about your ability to get ahead. You have to take criticism well, because you're going to get pounded on. Usually people want an excuse not to sign you because of blah blah blah. You have to figure out what is actual criticism that you can use, as opposed to that stuff that you can't."

Knowing what criticism is constructive and using it has helped The Spelvins to identify their style, to hone their songwriting craft and musical skills and learn to work with the often confusing music industry. The goal for the group isn't to be successful, but to continue to produce the music that is uniquely theirs, regardless of fashion. "We're happy to let other people call us whatever they want to call us," Keany says. "We're all broke anyway, so what's the point? A year from now, if we're still broke, that's fine, as long as we take our album home and like it."

—Michael Oxley

The Spelvins (from left to right): John Keany, guitar; Michael Canary, vocals; David Bondy, bass and keyboards; and Drew Vogelman, percussion.

TARGET RECORDS, Box 163, West Redding CT 06896. President: Paul Hotchkiss. Labels include Kastle Records. Record company, music publisher (Tutch Music/Blue Hill Music) and record producer (Red Kastle Prod.). Estab. 1975. Releases 6 singles and 4 compilation CDs/year. Works with songwriters on contract. Pays statutory rate to publisher per song on record.

How to Contact: Write first and obtain permission to submit. Prefers cassette with 2 songs and lyric sheet. SASE. Reports in 2-3 weeks.

Music: Country and crossover. Released "Thinking Bout You" written and recorded by Susan Rose Manning on Target Records (country pop); "Homegrown" (by P. Hotchkiss) recorded by Michael Brey on Roto Noto Records (country) and "Can't Win for Losin" (by P. Hotchkiss) recorded by Susan Rose Manning on Target Records (country). Other artists include Beverly's Hillbilly Band, Randy Burns, Rodeo and Al & Kathy Bain.

TEROCK RECORDS, Box 1622, Hendersonville TN 37077. (615)822-1044. Manager: S.D. Neal. Labels include Terock, Susan, Denco, Rock-A-Nash-A-Billy. Record company, record producer, and music publisher (Heavy Jamin' Music/ASCAP). Estab. 1959. "We also lease masters." Member ASCAP, BMI. Releases 8-12 singles and 3-6 12" singles/year. Receives 300 submissions/month. Works with musicians/artists and songwriters on contract and hires musicians for in-house studio work. Pays artists on contract 25¢ per record sold; standard royalty to publishers per song on record.

How to Contact: Submit demo tape—unsolicited submissions are OK. Prefers cassette with 3-6 songs and lyric sheet. SASE. Reports in 3 weeks.

Music: Mostly rock'n'roll, country and rockabilly; also bluegrass, blues, easy listening, folk, gospel, jazz, MOR, progressive, Spanish, R&B, soul and top 40/pop. Released "That's Why I Love You," by Dixie Dee (country); "Born to Bum Around," by Curt Flemons (country); and "Big Heavy," by the Rhythm Rockers (rock).

Tips: "Send your best."

3 G'S INDUSTRIES, 6015 Troost, Kansas City MO 64110. (816)361-8455. General Manager: Eugene Gold. Labels include NMI, Cory, 3 G's and Chris C's Records. Record company, record producer and music publisher (Eugene Gold Music and Gid-Gad Music). Releases 8 singles and 6 LPs/year. Works with musicians/artists and songwriters on contract; hires musicians for in-house studio work. Pays 4-6% royalty to artists on contract; statutory rate to publishers for each record sold.

How to Contact: Prefers cassette (or videocassette) with 4-8 songs and lyric sheet. SASE. Reports in 1 month.

Music: Mostly R&B and jazz; also church/religious, gospel and soul. Released "Solitude," written and recorded by Jeff Lucas; "Young Tender" (by M. Gilmore/J. Spradlin), recorded by Mark Gilmore; and "Remember" recorded by Wings of Graces, all on 3G's Records (singles). Other artists include Suspension, L. Washington, Thrust's, James "Fuzzy" West, Cal Green and L.S. Movement Band.

TIMELESS ENTERTAINMENT CORP., 10 Pebblewood, Irvine CA 92714-4530. (714)552-5231. Vice President: Fred Bailin. Labels include Perfect, Goldisc. Record company. Estab. 1978. Releases 3-6 cassette singles, 3 12" singles, and 4 CDs/year. Receives 100-150 submissions/year. Works with musicians/artists and songwriters on contract. Pays 8% royalty to artists on contract; statutory or negotiated rate to publisher per song on record.

How to Contact: Submit demo tape—unsolicited submissions are OK. Prefers cassette with 3 songs and lead sheets. SASE. Reports in 2 weeks.

Music: Mostly R&B, pop and rock; also rap. Released "Changed Man" (by Kower/Wilson), recorded by Indestructable MC on Perfect Records (urban contemporary). Artists include Ecstacy, Passion and Pain, Indestructible MC.

TOMARK RECORDS, #G3, 7560 Woodman Pl., Dept. SM, Van Nuys CA 91405. (818)994-4862. Owners: Tom Willett and Mark Thornton. Labels include Tomark Records. Record company, music publisher (Schmerdley Music and Ocean Walk Music/BMI) and record producer. Estab. 1988. Releases 1 single and 1 LP/year. Receives 125 submissions/year. Works with musicians/artists and songwriters on contract.

How to Contact: Submit demo tape by mail. Unsolicited submissions are OK. Prefers cassette or 7½ ips reel-to-reel (or VHS videocassette) with songs. SASE. Reports in 4 weeks.

Music: Mostly country and novelty; also rock. Released "My Ex-Ex Wife" (by Tom Willett), recorded by Tomark (country novelty); "Christmas Will Be Blue in California," by Mark Thornton (Christmas country); and "Christopher Columbus," by Mark Thornton and Tom Willett (country).

TOMMY BOY MUSIC, INC., 1747 First Ave., New York NY 10128. (212)722-2211. A&R Director/ R&B, Dance/Rap: Kevin Maxwell. Record company, music publisher (T-Boy/T-Girl). Releases 15-20 singles and 5-10 LPs/year. Works with musicians/artists on contract; pays varying royalty to artists on contract.
How to Contact: Call first and obtain permission to submit. Prefers cassette with 1-3 songs and lyric sheet, clearly marked with submitter name and phone number. Materials not returnable. "When submitting a demo, please do not call to see if we are going to use it. If we are, you will be the first to know."
Music: Mostly rap, R&B and dance/pop. No rock or New Age. 1989 releases included "Me Myself and I," "Say No Go" and "Buddy" by De La Soul; "Doowutchyalike" and "The Humpty Dance" by Digital Underground; "You Are the One" by TKA; "Dance for Me" and "Ladies First" by Queen Latifah.

TOP RECORDS, Gall. del Corso, 4 Milano 20122 **Italy**. Phone: (02)76021141. FAX: (0039)276021141. Manager/Director: Guido Palma. Labels include United Colors Productions, Dingo Music, Telex Music and Record, KIWI Record, Smoking Record and Tapes. Estab. 1979. Record company and music publisher. Releases 20 singles, 20 12″ singles, 30 LPs, 15 EPs and 40 CDs/year. Receives 200 submissions/year. Works with musicians/artists and songwriters on contract and hires in-house studio musicians. Pays 10% royalty to artists on contract.
How to Contact: Prefers cassette (or videocassette) with 5 songs and lyric sheet. Does not return unsolicited material.
Music: Mostly pop and dance; also soundtracks. Released "Manbo Jumbo" (by Prado), recorded by Mirella Banti (dance); "Unastoria" (by Politano), recorded by Giannini (pop); and "Capricci di Donna" written and recorded by Daiano (Italian style), all on Top Records. Other artists include Tina Charles, Gisa, Marisa Sacchetto, Gil Ventura, Antonio Gallo, Santarosa, Petula Clark, Georgio Chiosso, Diego D'Aponte, Ella Williams, Double B and Renato DiBi.

TOP TRAX, Box 738, Ridgetop TN 37152-0738. (615)851-6860. FAX (615)851-6857. President: Richard Allan Painter. Record company, music publisher (R.A. Painter Music/ASCAP, Richard Painter Music/ BMI), Painter Music TelePro-Motions. Member NARAS, GMA, NAPE. Top Trax has three primary divisions: Song Production, Promotion and Publishing. Manufactures and markets self-produced recordings and outside master product. Releases quarterly compilation CD sampler with up to 20 singles/ year. Works with artists and songwriters on contract; musicians on salary. Pays 7% royalty to artists on contract; statutory rate to publishers for each record sold. Artists pay manufacturing and marketing fee to press and release their masters.
How to Contact: Send SASE for information. Reports in 2-6 weeks.
Music: Suited for radio formats CHR, AOR, A/C, and UC; such that translates into broad commercial appeal and staying power in the target market.
Tips: "Be yourself. Offer a unique style, versatility and musical diversity to your audience. Pursue excellence and tell the truth as your only artistic moral imperative. Replicate your studio sound on stage. Be prepared to embark on an ambitious promotional appearance schedule in support of your released recording(s)."

TOUCHE RECORDS, Box 96, El Cerrito CA 94530. Executive Vice President: James Bronson, Jr. Record company, record producer (Mom and Pop Productions, Inc.) and music publisher (Toulouse Music Co./BMI). Member AIMP. Releases 2 LPs/year. Works with artists and songwriters on contract; musicians on salary for in-house studio work. Pays statutory rate to publishers per song on record.
How to Contact: Prefers cassette with 2-4 songs and lyric sheet. SASE. Reports in 1 month.
Music: Mostly jazz; also bluegrass, gospel, jazz, R&B and soul. Released *Bronson Blues* (by James Bronson), *Nigger Music* and *Touché Smiles* (by Smiley Winters), all recorded by Les Oublies du Jazz Ensemble on Touché Records (all LPs). Other artists include Hi Tide Harris.

TRAC RECORD CO., 170 N. Maple, Fresno CA 93702. (209)255-1717. Owner: Stan Anderson. Record company and music publisher (Sellwood Publishing/BMI). Estab. 1972. Releases 10-20 singles and 5 LPs and 2 CDs/year. Receives 30-35 submissions/month. Works with musicians/artists on contract, songwriters on royalty contract and in-house musicians on contract. Pays 13% royalty to artists on contract. Pays statutory rate to publisher per song on record.

Listings of companies in countries other than the U.S. have the name of the country in boldface type.

How to Contact: Submit demo tape—unsolicited submissions are OK. Prefers cassette (or VHS videocassette) with 2-4 songs and lyric sheet. SASE. Reports in 2 weeks.
Music: Country, top 40 gospel, contemporary Christian and rock. Released "Bare Your Soul" (by Denise Benson), recorded by Jessica James and "West Coast Girls," written and recorded by Barry Best, both on Trac Records (country); and "Mighty Rusing Wind" (by Lauren Rackley), recorded by The Rackleys on Psalms Records. Other artists include Gil Thomas, Ron Arlen and Ric Blake.

TREND RECORDS, Box 201, Smyrna GA 30081. (404)432-2454. President: Tom Hodges. Labels include Trendsetter, Trend/Side Atlanta, British Overseas Airways Music and Stepping Stone Records. Record company, music publisher (Mimic Music/BMI, Skipjack Music/BMI and British Overseas Airways Music/ASCAP), record producer and management firm. Estab. 1965. Releases 12 singles, 3 12″ singles, 15 LPs and 5 CDs/year. Works with musicians/artists and songwriters on contract. Pays 15% royalty to artists on contract; standard royalty to songwriters on contract; statutory rate to publisher per song on records.
How to Contact: Submit demo tape—unsolicited submissions are OK. Prefers cassette with 3-6 songs and lead sheet. SASE. Reports in 3 weeks.
Music: Country, bluegrass, gospel, MOR, rock and soul. Released "Not Enough Country" (by A. Beasley), recorded by Joey Welz; "Train of Pain" written and recorded by Shawn Spencer (country); and "Sands of Time" (by Shawn Spencer), recorded by Charlie and Nancy (country/MOR); all on Trend Records. Other artists include Jimmy Moore, Ray Macdonald, Jimmy Williams, Bobby Martin, Soul-jers and Dennis & The Times, Ginny Peters, Deb Watson, Charlotte Bradford, Fred Eubanks, Keith Bradford, Charlie and Nancy Cone, Shawn Spencer and Joey Welz.

TRUSTY RECORDS, 8771 Rose Creek Rd., Nebo KY 42441. (502)249-3194. President: Elsie Childers. Record company and music publisher (Trusty Publications/BMI). Member NSAI, CMA. Estab. 1950. Releases 2 singles and 2 LPs/year. Receives 8-10 submissions/month. Works with musicians/artists and songwriters on contract. Pays 3% royalty to artists on contract; statutory rate to publishers for each record sold.
How to Contact: Prefers cassette with 2-4 songs and lead sheet. SASE. Reports in 1 month.
Music: Mostly country; also blues, church/religious, dance, easy listening, folk, gospel, MOR, soul and top 40/pop. Released "I Melt Into Your Eyes" (by E. Childers), recorded by Noah Williams; "Sassy Little Country Girl" and "I Don't Have a Lot of Money" written and recorded by E. Childers/N. Williams, both on Trusty Records (country/pop).

TUG BOAT RECORDS, #4 Lilac Court, Newport News VA 23601. (804)591-2717. A&R: Judith Guthro. Record company, music publisher (Doc Publishing/BMI, Dream Machine/SESAC) and record producer (Doc Holiday Productions). Estab. 1967. Releases 12 singles, 15 12″ singles, 15 LPs, 15 EPs, and 4 CDs/year. Works with musicians/artists and songwriters on contract and hires musicians for in-house studio work. Pays varying royalty to artists on contract; statutory rate to publisher per song on record.
How to Contact: Submit demo tape by mail—unsolicited submissions are OK. Prefers cassette with 1 song and lyric sheets. Does not return unsolicited submissions.
Music: Mostly country, top 40 and rock. Released "Mr. Jones" (by Al Downing) recorded by Big Al Downing; "Cajun Baby" (by Hank Williams Jr & Sr) recorded by Doug Kershaw & Hank Jr. and "Don't Mess with My Toot Toot" (by Fats Domino) recorded by Fats Domino and Doug Kershaw, all on Tug Boat Records (country). Other artists include Ronn Craddock, Tracy Wilson, Doc Holiday, Big Al Downing Jolene, Eagle Feather, John Lockhart M.D.

UGLY DOG RECORDS, Box 1583, Brantford ON N3T 5V6 **Canada.** (519)442-7368. President: John Mars or A&R: Angela Richardson. Labels include Ugly Dog Records. Record company, music publisher (Utter Nonsense Publishing/SOCAN) and record producer (John Mars). Estab. 1979. Releases 1 single and 1 LP/year. Works with musicians/artists and songwriters on contract. Royalty to artists on contract varies as negotiated; statutory rate to publisher per song on record.
How to Contact: Submit demo tape—unsolicited submissions are OK. Prefers cassette (or videocassette if available). "We regret that (due to the large number of submissions we receive) we now can only reply to those artists that we wish to express interest in."
Music: Mostly rock, new jazz and R&B. Released "I Want A Girl Like You" (by Mars/ Hepburns/ Arazquel/Tremblay and Albon), recorded by John Mars on Ugly Dog Records (rock); and "I'm Feeling A Lil' Bit under the Table" (by Mars), recorded by John Mars on Ugly Dog Records (rock). Other artists include The Recognitions, The Martians, The Popp Tarts, Red Shrimps, Eddie Haskell's Jacket, and Dr. Chub Master.
Tips: "Send high quality demo with lots of songs. Send pictures or video."

UNIVERSAL-ATHENA RECORDS, Box 1264, Peoria IL 61654-1264. (309)673-5755. A&R Director: Jerry Hanlon. Record company and music publisher (Jerjoy Music/BMI). Estab. 1978. Releases 1-2 singles and 1 LP/year. Receives 15 submissions/month. Works with musicians/artists on contract; hires musicians on salary for in-house studio work. Pays statutory rate to publishers for each record sold.
How to Contact: Submit demo tape—unsolicited submissions are OK. Prefers cassette with 4-8 songs and lyric sheet. SASE. Reports in 2-3 weeks.
Music: Country. Released "Cotton to Satin" (by Jim Vest); "Ring Around the Rose" (by J. Hanlon/J. Schneder); and "Thank You Lord" (by L. Lester), all recorded by Jerry Hanlon on Universal Athena Records (country).
Tips: Be extremely critical and make realistic comparisons of your work before submission."

VIBE RECORDS, Dept. SM, 2540 Woodburn Ave., Cincinnati OH 45206. (513)961-0602. A&R Director: Smiley Hickland. Record company. Estab. 1985. Releases 2 singles and 3 12″ singles/year. Works with musicians/artists on contract. Pays varying royalty to artists on contract; statutory rate to publisher per song.
How to Contact: Write first and obtain permission to submit. Prefers cassette with 4 songs and lyric sheet. SASE. Reports in 4 weeks.
Music: Mostly R&B, gospel and pop; also rap and dance. Released "Heartbeat" (by Hicks) (R&B dance); "All About Town" (by Barber) (pop); and "Stingy" (by Waiver) (R&B dance); all on Vibe Records. Other artists include Kenny Hill, Greg Jackson, Trina Best, Sandy Childress, Tim Napier and Kim Seay.

VICOR MUSIC CORP., 782 Aurora Blvd., Cubao, Quezon City, **Philippines.** Phone: 721-3331 to 34. President: Florendo Garcia, Jr. Labels include Blackgold Records, Sunshine Records and Vicor International. Record company, music publisher (Bayanihan Music Phils., Inc.), record producer (Vicor Music and Blackgold Records), and booking firm (Vicor Entertainment Corporation). Releases 60 singles, 30 CDs and 50 LPs/year. Receives 12 submissions/month. Works with musicians/artists and songwriters on contract; musicians on salary for in-house studio work. Pays 4-10% royalty to artists on contract.
How to Contact: Write or call first and obtain permission to submit. Prefers cassette with 2 songs and lyric or lead sheet. Does not return unsolicited material.
Music: Mostly ballads, country, rock and disco. Released "Buhay Ng Buhay Ko" (by Nonong Pedero), recorded by Regine Velasquez (ballad); "Angel" (by Eric Antonio), recorded by TUX (ballad); and "Hold On" (by Dingdong Eduque) recorded by SIDE A (pop), all on on Sunshine Records. Other artists include Pops Fernandez, Tots Tolentino, Janno Gibbs, Racel Tuazon and Panjee Gonazlez.

VIRGIN BOY RECORDS, 2613 Castle, Irving TX 75038. (214)257-1510. President: James Yarbrough. Labels include Virgin Boy Records. Record company, music publisher (Virgin Boy Records & Publishing/ASCAP) and record producer (James Yarbrough). Estab. 1988. Releases 4 singles and 2 LPs/year. Receives 15 submissions/year. Works with songwriters on contract; hires musicians on salary for in-house studio work. Pays statutory rate to publishers per song on records.
How to Contact: Submit demo tape—unsolicited submissions are OK. Prefers cassette with 3 songs and lyric sheet. Does not return unsolicited material. Reports in 6 weeks.
Music: Mostly pop, rock and country. Released "Something's Got Me," "Make a New Start" and "Playlike Lover," all written and recorded by James Yarbrough on Virgin Boy Records (pop singles).

VOKES MUSIC PUBLISHING & RECORD CO., Box 12, New Kensington PA 15068. (412)335-2775. President: Howard Vokes. Labels include Vokes and Country Boy Records. Record company, booking agency and music publisher. Releases 8 singles and 5 LPs/year. Works with artists and songwriters on contract. Pays 2½-4½¢/song royalty to artists and songwriters on contract.
How to Contact: Submit cassette only and lead sheet. SASE. Reports in 2 weeks.
Music: Country, bluegrass, gospel-old time. Released "From Dusk Til Dawn" by Lenny Gee and "For The Sake of The Children" by Laura Lee Reddig, both on Vokes Records; and "Tribute To Riley Puckett" by Uncle Rufus Brewster on Country Boy Records.

WATCHESGRO MUSIC, Box 1794, Big Bear City CA 92314. (714)585-4645. Watch Us Climb Music President: Eddie Carr. Interstate 40 Records and videos by Watchesgro Productions. Estab. 1987. Releases 12 singles/year. Works with songwriters on contract. Pays 100% royalty to artists on contract; statutory rate to publisher per song on record.
How to Contact: Submit demo tape—unsolicited submissions are OK. Prefers cassette with minimum of 2 songs. Does not return unsolicited material. Reports in 1 week.
Music: Mostly country and country rock. Movie & TV credits include "Young Guns of Texas," "The Story of Evil Knievel" and "Alias Smith & Jones."

WEDGE RECORDS, Box 290186, Nashville TN 37229-0186. (615)754-2950. President: Ralph D. Johnson. Labels include Wedge Records, Dome Records and Fleet Records. Record company, music publisher (Big Wedge Music/BMI and Pro-Rite Music/ASCAP), record producer (Ralph D. Johnson) and Pro-Star Talent Agency. Estab. 1960. Releases 10 singles, 2 LPs and 2 CDs/year. Works with musicians/artists and songwriters on contract. Pays 10% royalty to artists on contract; statutory rate to publisher per song on record.
How to Contact: Submit demo tape—unsolicited submissions OK. Write or call first to arrange personal interview. Prefers cassette and lyric or lead sheet. SASE. Reports in 2 weeks.
Music: Mostly country and country crossover; also rock, gospel, pop and R&B. Released "I Ain't Gonna Leave You Now" (by Roy August), recorded by Cindy Jackson (R&B); and "The Want to Went Too Far" (by Roy August), recorded by LeAnn Ginotti on Wedge Records (country).

WESTPARK MUSIC - RECORDS, PRODUCTION & PUBLISHING, Box 260227, Rathenauplatz 4 D-5000 Cologne 1 **West Germany**. Phone: (49)221 247644. FAX: (49)221 231819. Contact: Ulli Hetscher. Labels distributed by BMG Ariola. Estab. 1986. Releases 3-4 singles, 10-12 LPs and 10-12 CDs/year. Receives 50-60 submissions/month. Works with musicians/artists on contract; tape lease. Pays 8-14% royalty to artists on contract.
How to Contact: Submit demo tape by mail. Unsolicited submissions are OK. Prefers cassette with 5-6 songs and lyric sheets. Does not return unsolicited material. Reports in 2-3 months.
Music: Everything apart from mainstream-pop, jazz, classical. "The only other criterion is: we simply should love it." Released "Lovers in a Dangerous Time" (by B. Cockburn), recorded by Barenaked Ladies (folk) and "Wonderin' Where Lions Are" recorded by B-Funn (pop/dance) on Westpark Records; and "Man Overboard" written and recorded by P. Millins on SM/Ariola Records (rock ballad).
Tips: "Mark cassette clearly. No high quality cassettes expected. We only send letters back!!"

WHITESTOCKING RECORDS, Box 250013, Atlanta GA 30325. (404)352-2263. A&R Department: Steve Hill. Labels include Tigersteeth and Garwize. Estab. 1990. Releases 4 12″ singles and 4 CDs/year. Works with musicians/artists and songwriters on contract. Pays 5-7% royalty to artists on contract; statutory rate to publisher per song on record.
How to Contact: Submit demo tape—unsolicited submissions are OK. Prefers cassette with 3 songs and lyric sheets. SASE required. Reports in 3 months.
Music: Mostly dance and R&B or rock, and danceable Christian music. Quality metal will be listened to also.
Tips: "We listen for danceability, musicality and lyrical content."

WILD PITCH RECORDS LTD., 231 West 29th St., New York NY 10001. (212)594-5050. President: Stu Fine. Record company and music publisher (Frozen Soap Songs/ASCAP). Estab. 1989. Releases 1 single, 8-10 12″ singles and 5 LPs/year. Works with musicians/artists and songwriters on contract. Pays ¾ rate to publishers per song on records.
How To Contact: Submit demo tape—unsolicited submissions are OK. Prefers cassette (or ½″ video-cassette if available) with 1-3 songs and lyric sheet. Does not return unsolicited material. Reports in 2 weeks.
Music: Mostly rap, dance and R&B. Released *Manifest* (by Elam Martin), recorded by Gary Starr and *Let Me Show You* (by R. Frazier), recorded by Chill Rob G, all on Wild Pitch Records (LP; 12″). Other artists include Gary Starr, Lord Finesse and Chill Rob G.
Tips: "Work hard; write about something real!"

WILSON'S MUSIC CO.; MAURICE/NE PRODUCTIONS, 6061 W. 83rd Place, Los Angeles CA 90045. (213)216-0210. President: Morris Lee Wilson. Labels include Wilson Records, Time West Records and Imma Banks Records. Record company, music publisher (BMI) and record producer (Wilson Music Co.). Estab. 1978. Releases 10 singles, 5 LPs and 2 CDs/year. Receives 12 submissions/month. Works with musicians/artists and songwriters on contract and hires musicians on salary for in-house studio work. Pays statutory rate.
How to Contact: Submit demo tape—unsolicited submissions are OK. Prefers cassette (VHS video-cassette) with any number of songs and lyric and lead sheet. SASE for return "but we prefer to keep it on file." Reports in 2-3 weeks.
Music: Mostly easy listening, country and MOR; also R&B, jazz and children's. Released "Soft Touch" (by Vivian Rummer) recorded by Morris Lee Wilson; "Lady Love" (by Rummer/Wilson), recorded by Rummer/Wilson and "Vivian Jean" (by Morris Wilson), recorded by Morris Lee Wison, all on CBS Records (R&B). Other artists include Bonnie Lou Young, Linda Moore, Duane Crone, Bonnie Skinner, Greg Coleman and Wayne St. John.
Tips: "Songs must have a good hook line, have something to say, and be different from the norm."

WINCHESTER RECORDS, Rt. 2, Box 114H, Berkeley Springs WV 25411. Owners: Bertha or Jim McCoy. Labels include Master, Mountain Top and Winchester. Record company, music publisher and record producer (Jim McCoy Productions). Estab. 1973. Releases 12 singles, 6 CDs and 6 LPs/year. Works with musicians/artists and songwriters on contract; musicians on salary for in-house studio work. Pays standard royalty to artists on contract.
How to Contact: Submit demo tape—unsolicited submissions are OK. Prefers cassette, or 7½ or 15 ips reel-to-reel (or VHS or Beta videocassette) with 6 songs and lyric or lead sheet. SASE. Reports in 1 month.
Music: Mostly country, rock and gospel; also country/rock and bluegrass. Released "Dyin Pain" (by J.B. Miller), recorded by Hilton; "I'll Bet You're the Best I'll Ever Do" (by Jim McCoy); and "Let Her" (by R. Lee Gray), all on Winchester Records (country). Other artists include Bud Armel, Terry McCumbee, George Dove, J.B. Mitler and R. Lee Gray.

WINDHAM HILL PRODUCTIONS, Box 9388, Palo Alto CA 94305. Contact: A&R Department. Labels include Windham Hill and Windham Hill Jazz. Record company. Estab. 1976. Works with musicians/artists on contract.
How to Contact: Write first and obtain permission to submit. "We are not accepting unsolicited material. Detailed queries are welcome. Do not send recordings until requested. We prefer a referral from a reputable industry person." Prefers cassette with 3 songs. SASE. Reports in 2 months.
Music: Mostly pop, jazz and original instrumental. Released *Metropolis*, recorded by Turtle Island String Quartet (new acoustic jazz LP); *Sampler '89*, written and recorded by various artists on Windham Hill Records (instrumental LP); and *Switchback* (by S. Cossu, Van Manakas), recorded by Scott Cossu on Windham Hill Records (jazz, ensemble LP). Other artists include William Ackerman, George Winston, Philip Aaberg, Michael Hedges, The Nylons and Montreux.

WINGATE RECORDS, Box 10895, Pleasanton CA 94588. (415)846-6194. CEO: P. Hanna. Record company, music publisher (Parchment Harbor Music/BMI and Hugo First Publishing/ASCAP), record producer (Wingate Productions) and Artist Management and Talent Agency. Estab. 1989. Releases 12 singles, 2 LPs and 2 EPs/year. Works with musicians/artists and songwriters on contract. Pays statutory rate to publishers per song on record.
How to Contact: Write and obtain permission to submit. Prefers cassette (or VHS videocassette if available) with 2 songs and lyric sheet. SASE. Reports in 4 weeks.
Music: Mostly pop, country and rock; also contemporary Christian and A/C. Released "Heart Let Him Go" (by Pam Hanna), recorded by Kelli Crofton; "More Bullets Ramone," written and recorded by Billy Truitt; and "The Most I Can Do" (by P. Hannan & G. Pickord), recorded by Kayla Moore, all on Wingate Records (country). Other artists include Debbie Eden, Marty Ross, Kelli Crofton and Kayla Moore.
Tips: "Make your music stand out in a crowd!"

WINGS RECORD COMPANY, Dept. SM, Route 3, Box 172, Haynesville LA 71038. (318)927-5253. President: E. Dettenheim. Record company and music publisher (Darbonne Publishing Co./BMI). Estab. 1987. Releases 4 singles and 4-8 LPs/year. Works with musicians/artists on record contract. Pays 5-10% royalty to artists on contract; statutory rate to publishers per song on record.
How to Contact: Prefers cassette, 7½ ips reel-to-reel with at least 3 songs and lyric sheeet. Does not return unsolicited material. Reports in 3 months.
Music: Mostly country, rock and gospel; also pop and R&B. Released "Man in the Mirror" written and recorded by Leon Martin on Wings Records (country); "Still Haven't Let You Go" written and recorded by Kate Chandler on Wings Records (contemporary country); and "Turner Hotel" written by E. Dettenheim performed by Skidrow Joe on Wings Records (country).

WOODRICH RECORDS, Box 38, Lexington AL 35648. (205)247-3983. President: Woody Richardson. Record company and music publisher (Woodrich Publishing Co./BMI, Mernee Music/ASCAP and Tennessee Valley Music/SESAC) and record producer (Woody Richardson). Estab. 1959. Releases 12 singles and 12 LPs/year. Works with songwriters on contract. Pays 10% royalty to writers on contract; statutory rate to publisher per song on records.
How to Contact: Prefers cassette with 4 songs and lyric sheet. "Be sure to send a SASE (not a card) with sufficient return postage." Reports in 2 weeks. "We prefer a good studio demo."
Music: Mostly country; also gospel, comedy, bluegrass, rock and jazz. Released "Playing in the Dark," written and recorded by Thom Ralhbun (jazz); "Welcome Back to Me," written and recorded by Sandra Celia (country); and "Rachel" (by Jos. M. Procopid), recorded by The Attitude (rock), all on Woodrich Records.
Tips: "Use a good studio with professional musicians. Don't send a huge package. A business envelope will do. It's better to send a cassette box."

YELLOW JACKET RECORDS, 10303 Hickory Valley, Ft. Wayne IN 46835. President: Allan Straten. Record company. Estab. 1985. Releases 8-10 singles, 1 LP and 1 CD/year. Receives 20-25 submissions/year. Works with musicians/artists and songwriters on contract; hires musicians for in-house studio work. Pays 7-10% royalty to artists on contract; statutory rate to publisher per song on records.
How to Contact: Submit demo tape by mail—unsolicited submissions are OK. Prefers cassette with 3-4 songs and typed lyric sheet. SASE. Reports in 3-4 weeks.
Music: Country and MOR. Released singles "A Rose and a Kiss" (by April) and "Love Is" (by S. Grogg and A. Straten); and *April In Love* (LP), all on Yellow Jacket Records.

YOUNGHEART MUSIC, Box 6017, Cypress CA 90630. (714)995-7888. President: James Connelly. Record company. Estab. 1975. Releases 1-2 LPs/year. Works with musicians/artists and songwriters on contract. Pays statutory rate.
How to Contact: Submit demo tape—unsolicited submissions are OK. SASE. Reports in 4 weeks.
Music: Mostly children's and educational. Released "Three Little Pig Blues" and "A Man Named King," written and recorded by Greg Scelsa and Steve Millang all on Youngheart Records.
Tips: "We are looking for original, contemporary, motivating music for kids. Songs should be fun, educational, build self-esteem and/or multicultural awareness. New original arrangements of classic songs or nursery rhymes will be considered."

ZANZIBAR RECORDS, 2019 Noble St., Pittsburgh PA 15218. (412)351-6672. A&R Manager: John C. Antimary. Labels include A.W.O.L. Records. Record company and music publisher (RTD Music/BMI). Estab. 1980. Releases 6-12 singles, 4-8 12" singles and 6 LPs/year. Receives 22 submissions/month.Works with musicians/artists and songwriters on contract and hires musicians for in-house studio work. Pays 6-8% royalty to artists on contract; statutory rate to publisher per song on record.
How to Contact: Submit demo tape by mail. Unsolicited submissions are OK. Or call first to arrange personal interview. Prefers cassette (or VHS videocassette) with 4 songs and lyric sheet. SASE. Reports in 1 month.
Music: Mostly rock, progressive and R&B; also pop, rap and metal. Released "Long Winter" (by T. J. Wilkins) recorded by Affordable Floor (new music); "Going Home" and "Reunion," written and recorded by Lenny Collini (rock) all on Zanzibar Records. Other artists include Bunky Gooch, Necropolis, Post Mortem, Good Earth and Corky Zapple.
Tips: "When sending demos of your songs, please make sure that they are recorded on good cassette tapes."

Geographic Index
Record Companies

The U.S. section of this handy geographic index will quickly give you the names of record companies located in or near the music centers of Los Angeles, New York and Nashville. Of course, there are many valuable contacts to be made in other cities, but you will probably want to plan a trip to one of these established music centers at some point in your career and try to visit as many of these companies as you think appropriate. The International section lists, geographically, markets for your songs in countries other than the U.S.

Find the names of companies in this index, and then check listings within the Record Companies section for addresses, phone numbers and submission details.

Los Angeles
Aliso Creek Productions Inc.
Atlantic Recording Corp.
AVC Entertainment Inc.
BCM-USA
Blue Gem Records
Carousel Records, Inc.
Chattahoochee Records
Cosmotone Records
Cowgirl Records
Dupuy Records/Productions/
  Publishing, Inc.
Helion Records
IHS Records
MCI Entertainment Group
Mercury Records
Roach Records Co.
Rodell Records
Shaolin Film & Records
Tomark Records
Wilson's Music Co.; Maurice/
  NE Productions

Nashville
The Calvary Music Group
Concorde International Records
Curtiss Records
Fame and Fortune Enterprises
Fresh Start Music Ministries
Jalyn Recording Co.
Kottage Records
Landmark Communications
  Group
Maxx Records
Orbit Records
Paragold Records & Tapes
Phoenix Records, Inc.
San-Sue Recording Studio
Sony Music
Stop Hunger Records International
Susan Records
Terock Records

Wedge Records

New York
Big Productions Records
Caroline Records, Inc.
City Pigeon Records
Clown Records
Dynamite
Emzee Records
Factory Beat Records, Inc.
G Fine Records/Productions
Gold City Records, Inc.
Homestead Records
J&J Musical Enterprises Ltd.
Lamar Music Group
Majestic Control Records
MCA Records
Mighty Records
Mindfield Records
Modern Blues Recordings
Neon Records
Now & Then Records
Parade PPI/Peter Pan Industries
Razor & Tie Music
Source Unlimited Records
Star Record Co.
Tommy Boy Music, Inc.
Wild Pitch Records Ltd.

International

Belgium
Jump Records & Music
Prestation Music

Canada
Bovine International Record
  Company
Century City Records and
  Tapes of Canada
Current Records

Disques Nosferatu Records
H&S Records
Justin Time Records Inc.
John Lennon Records
Nephelim Record (Studio
  Works)
Nettwerk Productions
One-Eyed Duck Recording and
  Publishing
Roto-Noto Music
Saddlestone Records
Signature Records
Slak Records
Ugly Dog Records

Chile
Prodisc (Prodisc Limitada)

Germany
Alphabeat
A1A Records
Autogram Records
Playbones Records
Westpark Music—Records,
  Production & Publishing

Holland
Associated Artists Records International

Italy
Top Records

The Philippines
Vicor Music Corp.

Sweden
Liphone Records

Switzerland
Nadine Music

United Kingdom
B.P.M. Productions
Big Bear Records

Collector Records
Comma Records and Tapes
Creole Records, Ltd.
Demi Monde Records and Publishing
E.S.R. Records
First Time Records
Guerrila Records

Heavy Metal Records
IRS Records Ltd.
Le Matt Music Ltd.
Leopard Music
Loading Bay Records
Nervous Records
Plankton Records
Presidential Enterprises Ltd.

Red Bus Records (Int.) Ltd.
Red Sky Records
Red-Eye Records
Rhino Records
Rock'n'Roll Records
Swoop Records
Tabitha Records

Record Companies/'92-'93 Changes

The following markets appeared in the 1992 edition of *Songwriter's Market* but are absent from the 1993 edition. Most of these companies failed to respond to our request for an update of their listing for a variety of reasons. For example, they may have gone out of business or they may have requested deletion from the 1993 edition because they are backlogged with material. If we know the specific reason, it appears within parentheses.

Aarson Records
Alyssa Records
Amazing Records (not accepting submissions)
American Music Company/CUCA Record and Cassette Manufacturing Co.
Avalantic Records
Barnett Productions Inc.
Bassment Records (out of business)
Beau-Jim Records Inc. (unable to contact)
BGS Productions Ltd.
Big L Productions Ltd., Inc.
Black Moon Records, Inc.
Bolts Records
British Records
C.P.I. Records
Cactus Records
Challedon Records
Charta Records
Chrysalis Records (requested deletion)
The Chu Yeko Musical Foundation
Compo Record and Publishing Co. (requested deletion)
Da-Mon Records
Digital Music Products Inc. (backlogged with material)
Directions
Discos CBS Saicf
Emotive Records (requested deletion)
Empty Sky Records
Fascination Entertainment (unable to contact)
John Fischer & Associates
Flying Fish Records, Inc. (not accepting submissions)
Fountain Records
Freko Records (requested deletion)
Glenlyd Grammofon ApS (out of business)
Get Wit It Production Records (unable to contact)

The Ghetto Recording Company
Gold Castle Records (unable to contact)
Hysteria Records
I'll Call You (I.C.Y.) Records
Intrepid Record
IRS Records Ltd.
ISBA Records (requested deletion)
J.L.I Records
J/L Entertainment Group
King Klassic Records
Sid Kleiner Music Enterprises Inc. (not accepting submissions)
L.S. Records
La Louisianne Records (backlogged with material)
Lambda Records
Le Disque Holland B.V./B&B Records
Massmedia
Maxima Records
Maximus Records
Meda Records Inc. (requested deletion)
Mega Records APS
Metal Blade Records (requested deletion)
Mighty Soul-Sonic Records (unable to contact)
Monticana Records
MSB, Ltd.
Music for Little People (not accepting submissions)
Next Step Records (requested deletion)
NFS Records Inc. (unable to contact)
Northeastern Records (requested deletion)
Nucleus Records
Nude Records
The Orange Record Company
Orinda Records (unable to contact)
Orleans Records

Palmetto Productions (unable to contact)
Parham Sound Studio
Pendragon Records
Penthouse Music
PSP Records (unable to contact)
Railroad Records
Rambo Star Records (unable to contact)
Reality Records Productions
Reca Music Production
Relativity Records Inc.
Rex Music Inc.
Ric Rac Records (unable to contact)
Ricochet Records
Rock In Records
Rosie Records
Roxtown Records (out of business)
Royal Records
S.O.C.
Sam Records Inc.
Scrapbook Records
Sealed with a Kiss, Inc. (unable to contact)
Sisipa Record Co., Inc. (unable to contact)
Sneak Tip Records, Inc.
Sound Development Releasing Group Ltd.
Sound Image Records (requested deletion)
Sphemusations
Survivor Records/H.I.T. Records
Texas Crude (unable to contact)
Timeless Productions (backlogged with material)
Tom Thumb Music (requested deletion)
Velvet Productions
Walk on Water Records (temporarily out of business)
White Car Records
World Artist

Record Producers

The independent producer can best be described as a creative coordinator. He's usually the one with the most creative control over the recording project and is ultimately responsible for the finished product. Although some larger record companies have their own in-house producers, it's more common for a record company today to contract out-of-house, independent producers for recording projects.

Producers can be valuable contacts for songwriters because they work so closely with the artists whose records they produce. They are usually creative and artistic people, typically with a lot more freedom than others in executive positions, and they are known for having a good ear for hit song potential. Many producers are songwriters, musicians and artists themselves. Since they have the most influence on a particular project, a good song in the hands of the producer at the right time stands a good chance of being cut. And even if the producer is not working on a specific project, they are well-acquainted with record company executives and artists, and they can often get material through doors not open to you.

Even so, it can be difficult to get your tapes to the right producer at the right time. Many producers write their own songs and even if they don't write, they might be involved in their own publishing companies so they have instant access to all the songs in their catalogs. It's important to understand the intricacies of the producer/publisher situation. If you pitch your song directly to a producer first, before another publishing company publishes the song, the producer may ask you for the publishing rights (or a percentage thereof) to your song. You must decide whether the producer is really an active publisher who will try to get the song recorded again and again, or whether he merely wants the publishing because it means extra income for him from the current recording project. You may be able to work out a co-publishing deal, where you and the producer split the publishing of the song. That means that he will still receive his percentage of the publishing income, even if you secure a cover recording of the song by other artists in the future. But, even though you would be giving up a little bit initially, you may benefit in the future.

The listings that follow outline which aspects of the music industry each producer is involved in, what type of music he is looking for, what records and artists he's recently produced and what artists he produces on a regular basis. Study the listings carefully, noting the artists he works with, and consider if any of your songs might fit a particular artist's or producer's style.

A & R RECORDING SERVICES, 71906 Highway 111, Rancho Mirage CA 92270. (619)346-0075. Producer-Engineer: Wade Perluss. Record producer. Estab. 1978. Deals with artists. Fee derived from sales royalty when song or artist is recorded, outright fee from recording artist and outright fee from record company.
How to Contact: Submit demo tape by mail—unsolicited submissions are OK. Prefers cassette (or VHS videocassette if available) with 4 songs and lyric or lead sheets. SASE. Reports in 2 months.
Music: Mostly pop, country and gospel; also rock. Produced "What Will You Say" (by Richard Carl), recorded by Positive Influence (single); *By Request*, written and recorded by Brent Streeper (LP); and *One Fine Touch*, recorded by Scott Beaty (LP), all on Accent Records. Other artists include Paul Gerkin, Mike Babbitt, David Powell and Diann Torrey.

*"A" MAJOR SOUND CORPORATION, 7808 Yonge St., Thornhill Ontario L4J 1W3 **Canada**. (416)889-7264. FAX: (416)889-7264. Record Producer: Paul C. Milner. Record producer and recording engineer. Estab. 1985. Deals with artists and songwriters. Fee derived from sales royalty when song or artist is recorded, or outright fee from recording artist or record company.

How to Contact: Submit demo tape by mail—unsolicited submissions are OK. Prefers cassette (or DAT) with 3-4 songs and lyric sheet. Reports in 3-6 weeks.

Music: Mostly rock, pop and metal; also R&B and gospel. Produced *Two Answers/Until The Time* (by H.P.M.) on Word/Sony Records (rock/LP); *Blood River* (by Morris/Abbott) on INDI Records (rock/LP); and *No Sign Of Rain* (by K. Jordan/T. McCauley on Columbia/Sony Records (pop/rock/LP), all recorded by Paul Milner. Other artists include Freewill, Trains Of Winter and Scream Freedom.

Tips: "Submit strong material, know your market. The bottom line is a good song."

*A STREET MUSIC, 445 W. 45th. St., New York NY 10036. (212)903-4773. A&R Director: K. Hall. Record producer, music publisher (A Street Music/ASCAP). Estab. 1986. Produces 6 LPs, 1 EP and 5 CDs/year. Deals with artists and songwriters. Fee derived from sales royalty or outright fee from recording artist or record company.

How to Contact: Submit demo tape—unsolicited submissions are OK. Prefers cassette or DAT with 3 songs. Lyric sheets optional. Reports in 1-2 months. Artists send pictures. *SASE only* will receive reply; include adequate postage for tape return if desired. Reports in 1-2 months.

Music: Mostly rock, heavy metal, alternative rock and pop/rock; will listen to R&B, R&B/pop and dance. Produced "Feeding Time At The Zoo" (by Nicarry/Strauss), recorded by Ripper Jack on A Street Records (heavy rock); "Zeudus" (by Weikle), recorded by Zeudus on A Street Records (heavy inst. rock); and "Return To You" (by Brad Mason), recorded by Debbie O. on A Street Records (pop/blues). Other artists include The Mercuries, Parrish Blue, Rockamatic Street Kid and Donatello.

Tips: "Don't over-produce your demo; we want to hear the song. A good vocalist will help. Enclose an SASE."

ABERDEEN PRODUCTIONS, (A.K.A. Scott Turner Productions), 524 Doral Country Dr., Nashville TN 37221. (615)646-9750. President: Scott Turner. Record producer and music publisher (Buried Treasure/ASCAP, Captain Kidd/BMI). Estab. 1971. Deals with artists and songwriters. Works with 30 new songwriters/year. Produces 10 singles, 15-20 12" singles, 8 LPs and 8 CDs/year. Fee derived from sales royalty and production fee.

How to Contact: Submit demo tape—unsolicited submissions OK. Prefers cassette with maximum 4 songs and lead sheet. SASE. Reports in 2 weeks.

Music: Mostly country, MOR and rock; also top 40/pop. Produced "We Are All Americans" (by S.C. Rose), recorded by Roy Clark (country); "Appalachian Blue" (by S.C. Rose), recorded by Roy Clark (country); and "Coming to My Senses" (by Audie Murphy, S. Turner, M. Jaden), recorded by Jim Cartwright (country). Other artists include Slim Whitman, Jonathan Edwards, Don Malena, Hal Goodson, Jimmy Clanton, Bobby Lewis and Del Reeves.

Tips: "Be unique. A great song doesn't care who sings it . . . but there is a vast difference between a good song and a great song."

*ACCENT RECORDS, 71906 Highway 111, Rancho Mirage CA 92270. (619)346-0075. CEO: Scott Seely. Record producer and music publisher (S&R Music). Deals with artists. Produces 10 singles and 5 LPs/year. Fee derived from sales royalty.

How to Contact: Submit demo tape—unsolicited submissions OK. Prefers cassette with any number of songs and lyric sheet. SASE. Reports in 6 weeks.

Music: Mostly A/C, country and MOR; also all other types. Produced "Run for Your Innocence" written and recorded by Zaxas (rock); "What Will You Say" (by Rick Carl), recorded by Positive Influence (gospel/rock); and "One Fine Touch," written and recorded by S. Scott Beaty (piano), all on Accent Records. Other artists include Chante, Kirby Hamilton, Eddie Rose, Don Malena, The Last Live Band, Jeri Sullivan, Jeffer, Ray Dean and Buddy Merrill.

ACTIVE SOUND PRODUCTIONS, 314 C St., So. Boston MA 02127. (617)269-0104. Owner: Larry Lessard. Record producer and recording studio. Estab. 1981. Deals with artists and songwriters. Produces 5 singles, 2 12" singles, 3 LPs, 2 EPs and 2 CDs/year. Fee derived from sales royalty when song or artist is recorded. Charges for studio time.

How to Contact: Submit demo tape by mail—unsolicited submissions are OK. Prefers cassette (or 15 IPS reel-to-reel or DAT videocassette if available) with 3-5 songs and lyric sheet. SASE. Reports in 1 month.

 The asterisk before a listing indicates that the listing is new in this edition. New markets are often the most receptive to unsolicited submissions.

Music: Mostly pop (A/C), dance and rock; also R&B. Produced *FTS* (by Nick Gerboth), recorded by FTS on Major Label Records (alternative). Other artists include Candy Machine.
Tips: "Concentrate on melody. Make the song honest. Know what market you're trying to go for. But most of all have fun and do music that satisfies you."

*AFFINITY PRIVATE MUSIC-Division of Omega Organization International, Box 33623 Song, Seattle WA 98133. Communications Director: Cameron Powers. Record producer, record company and complete touring productions. Estab. 1971. Deals with artists and songwriters. Produces 12 LPs and 12 CDs/year. Fee derived from outright fee from recording artist or record company.
How to Contact: Write first and obtain permission to submit. SASE. Prefers cassette with 3 songs. "We don't accept already fully produced works." Does not return unsolicited material. "We only acknowledge if we are interested."
Music: Mostly electronic, new age and folk; also mature female vocalists, world and esoteric new genres. Produced "Window In The Storm" (by Chatelaine/Werth) on Omega Records (fusion); "Seraphim Suite" (by Affinity) on Omega Records (neo-classical electronic); and "Outward Band" (by Aldridge) on St. Elmo's Records (folk), all recorded by Affinity Private Music. Other artists include Saint Elmo's Choir, Pan Genre and Affinity.
Tips: "You may be disappointed if you fail, but you are doomed if you don't try. We produce collaboratively with selected artists at all appropriate levels of involvement and guidance. Preference given to artists recording in our studios."

AKO PRODUCTION, 20531 Plummer, Chatsworth CA 91311. (818)998-0443. President: A. Sullivan. Record producer and music publisher (Amiron). Deals with artists and songwriters. Produces 2-6 singles and 2-3 LPs/year. Fee derived from sales royalty.
How to Contact: Write first and obtain permission to submit. Prefers cassette (or Beta or VHS videocassette if available) and lyric sheet. SASE.
Music: Pop/rock and modern country. Produced *Lies in Disguise*, by Gang Back (pop LP); and *Touch of Fire* (LP) and "Try Me" (pop single) by Sana Christian; all on AKO Records.

ALLEN-MARTIN PRODUCTIONS INC., 9701 Taylorville Rd., Louisville KY 40299. (502)267-9658. Audio Engineer: Nick Stevens. Record producer and music publisher (Always Alive Music, Bridges Music/ASCAP, BMI). Estab. 1965. Deals with artists. Produces 10 singles, 5 12″ singles, 20 LPs, 5 EPs and 20 CDs/year. Fee derived from sales royalty when song or artist is recorded, outright fee from recording artist or outright fee from record company.
How to Contact: Submit demo tape by mail. Unsolicited submissions are OK. Prefers cassette (or ¾″ or ½″ videocassette if available) with several songs and lyric sheet. Artist photo is desirable. Does not return unsolicited material. Reports in 2 months.
Music: Mostly country, gospel and pop; also rock, R&B and rap. Produced *Delta*, written and recorded by Duke Robillaro on Rovrene Records (R&B LP); *Exquisite Fashion*, written and recorded by Duke Robillaro on X Mode Records (rock LP); and *More Praise* (by Harold Moore), recorded by Duke Robillaro on X Mode Records (gospel LP). Other artists include J.P. Pennington, Larnelle Harris, Turley Richards, Shaking Family and Michael Jonathon.

*ALPHA MUSIC PRODUCTIONS, Box 14701, Lenexa KS 66285. (913)441-8618. President: Glenn Major. Record producer, music publisher (Alpha House Publishing/BMI) and record company (AMP Records). Estab. 1982. Deals with artists and songwriters. Produces 5 singles, 2 LPs and 1 CD/year. Receives 8-10 submissions/month. Fee derived from sales royalty when song or artist is recorded.
How to Contact: Submit demo tape by mail—unsolicited submissions are OK. Prefers cassette (or VHS videocassette if available) with 3-5 songs and lyric sheet. Include cover letter, bio and pictures. SASE. Reports in 2 months.
Music: Mostly country, rock and folk. Produced "Rottgutt" (Bill Colbyrn), recorded by Rottgutt (rockabilly); *Bloods Hot Eyes* (by Jerry Dowell) recorded by T-Thunders Band on Thunderhorse Records (Christian R&B/ folk LP); *With Love* (traditional), recorded by Maid in the Myddle on Maiden Records (Irish folk-CD); and "On the Diagonal," written and recorded by Beth Scalet on AMP Records (pop, folk). Other artists include Ken Zans and Big Toe.
Tips: "Be realistic in your expectations. Get lots of opinions from your peers."

*ALSTATT ENTERPRISES, Suite 273, 4255 E. Charleston, Las Vegas NV 89104. (702)431-9424. FAX: (702)641-5124. President: Albert J. Statti. Record producer, music publisher. Estab. 1989. Deals with artists and songwriters. Produces 3-4 singles, 1-2 LPs and 1-2 CDs/year. Fee derived from sales royalty or outright fee from recording record company.
How to Contact: Submit demo tape by mail—unsolicited submissions are OK. Prefers cassette with 3 songs and lyric or lead sheets. SASE. Reports in 2-3 months.
Music: Mostly R&B, popular and MOR/rock.

BUZZ AMATO, 2310-D Marietta Blvd., Atlanta GA 30318. (404)355-0909. Producer: Buzz Amato. Record producer and record company (Ichiban, Gold Key, Curton, J&S). Estab. 1987. Deals with artists. Produces 8 singles, 4 12″ singles, 10 LPs and 10 CDs/year. Fee derived from sales royalty when song or artist is recorded.
How to Contact: Submit demo tape by mail—unsolicited submissions are OK. Prefers cassette with 3 songs and lyric or lead sheets. "List how material was cut—instruments, outboard, tape format, etc." SASE. Reports in 6-8 weeks.
Music: Mostly R&B (urban), blues and pop; also jazz. Produced "So Important," written and recorded by Ben E. King on Ichiban Records (R&B); "The Woman In Me," recorded by Trudy Lynn on Ichiban Records (R&B) and "Deuce," recorded by Deuce on Wrap Records (rap). Other artists include Three Degrees, Chi-lite and Bob Thompson.
Tips: "Pay attention to the artist and styles when sending demos. Too many times a writer will send material that has nothing to do with what that artist is about."

AMETHYST RECORDS, INC., Box 82158, Oklahoma City OK 73148. (405)632-2000. General Manager: Russell Canaday. Record company (Amethyst Records, Inc.). Estab. 1988. Deals with artists and songwriters. Produces 10 singles, 25 LPs, 3 EPs and 3 CDs/year. Recording cost derived from recording artist or Amethyst record company. "If artist is unknown, we sometimes charge an outright fee. It depends on exposure and work."
How to Contact: Submit demo tape by mail—unsolicited submissions are OK. Prefers cassette with 3 songs and lyric or lead sheets. SASE. Reports in 3 months.
Music: Mostly country, gospel, easy listening; also R&B. Produced "Going on With My Jesus" recorded by Wanda Jackson; *Blues Man* (by Hank Williams, Jr.), recorded by Henson Cargi (country); and "Higher" (by Mark Bryan) recorded by Sherman Andrus (gospel), all on Amethyst Records. Other artists include Cissie Lynn, Wanda Jackson, Rita King and several Oklahoma Opry artists.
Tips: "Have one or two of your best songs professionally recorded so the prospective listener will understand more about the song and its production style."

BILL ANDERSON JR., Box 148296, Nashville TN 37214. (615)889-4977. Record producer. Estab. 1976. Deals with artists only. Produces 4 singles and 5 LPs/year. Fee derived from outright fee from recording artist and record company.
How to Contact: Submit demo tape by mail—unsolicited submissions are OK. Prefers cassette with 4 songs and lyric sheets. SASE.
Music: Mostly country, gospel and pop/crossover. Produced "Jesus Is Lord" (by Randy Weiss), recorded by Joanne Cash Yates with Johnny Cash on Crosstalkin' Records (gospel); and *Debi Chasteen*, recorded by Debi Chasteen on Lan Records (country LP). Other artists include Vernon Oxford (country), Skeeter Davis and Teddy Nelson (country).

WARREN ANDERSON, 2207 Halifax Cres NW, Calgary Alta. T2M 4E1 **Canada**. (403)282-2555. Producer/Manager: Warren Anderson. Record producer (Century City Music-SOCAN) and record company (Century City Records). Estab. 1983. Deals with artists and songwriters. Produces 1-6 singles, 1-2 LPs, 1-2 EPs and 1-2 CDs/year. Fee derived from sales royalty (typically 2%) and/or outright fee from record company.
How to Contact: Write first and obtain permission to submit. Prefers cassette or VHS videocassette with 4 songs and lyric or lead sheet. SASE. Reports in 4 weeks.
Music: Mostly country rock, rock and folk rock; also alternative, jazz and C&W. Produced "Angel" (by Warren Anderson), recorded by Fran Thieven on Bros. Records; "Hot from the Streets" (by Warren Anderson) recorded by Robert Bartlett on Century City Records; "1000 Miles Away" (by Damian Follett), recorded by Warren Anderson on Century City Records; all rock singles.
Tips: "Rockers moved over to C&W and took it places that the cowboy wouldn't recognize. I'm into Chris Isaak, Steve Earl, Blue Rodeo, K.D. Lang, Roger McGuinn, John Couger Mellencamp. I'm into pushing the envelope of country rock into the 21st century."

ANDREW & FRANCIS, Box 64-1008, Chicago IL 60664-1008. (312)326-5580. Talent Representative: Katie Major. Record producer and management agency. Estab. 1984. Deals with artists and songwriters. Produces 4 LPs, 5 EPs and 1 CD/year. Fee derived from sales royalty when song or artist is recorded.
How to Contact: Submit demo tape by mail—unsolicited submissions are OK. Prefers cassette (or VHS videocassette if available) with 1-7 songs and lyric sheet. "Don't be afraid to submit! We are here to help you by reviewing your material for possible representation or production." Does not return unsolicited material. Reports in 2 months.
Music: Mostly rock (commercial), hard rock and dance rock; also classical guitar, instrumental rock and solo guitar. Produced "Passion in Disguise," written and recorded by Blake Clifford (commercial rock); "Gettin Picked Up," written and recorded by Brian Kalan (black rap); and "Yuppie Fever"

written and recorded by Jim Glomak (funk rock), all on Demo Records. Other artists include Mike Martis, Pat O'Donnell & Squish, G.N. & Jeff, Black Monkeys, UR3XMY Size and Jughead.

Tips: "If you're not sure of yourself, send it anyway. You don't have anything to lose. We aren't a huge corporation and we aren't trying to be, but we are professionals who may be able to help you and you may be able to help us."

*ANGEL FILMS COMPANY, 967 Hwy 40, New Franklin MO 65247-9998. (314)698-3900. VP Production: Matthew Eastman. Record producer and record company (Angel One). Estab. 1980. Deals with artists and songwriters. Produces 5 LPs, 5 EPs and 5 CDs/year. Receives 20 submissions/month. Fee derived from sales royalty when song or artist is recorded.

How to Contact: Submit demo tape by mail—unsolicited submissions are OK. Prefers cassette (or VHS videocassette if available) with 3 songs. "Send only original material, not previously recorded, and include a bio sheet on artist." SASE. Reports in 1 month.

Music: Mostly pop, rock and rockabilly; also jazz, R&B and country. Produced *Fairy Bride*, written and recorded by Bill Hoehne; *G-String* (by Pat Donovon), recorded by Avanti; and *Hawiki*, written and recorded by Hawiki, all on Angel One Records (rock LPs). Other artists include Chi Kim Le, Darla Russell and Young Love.

Tips: "Don't try to copy other people. Just be yourself. Send your best material only. Don't overwork what you submit, keep it simple."

APON RECORD COMPANY, INC., P.O. Box 3082, Steinway Station, Long Island City NY 11103. (718)721-5599. Manager: Don Zemann. Record producer and music publisher (Apon Publishing). Estab. 1957. Deals with artists and songwriters. Produces 100 singles, 50 LPs and 50 CDs/year. Fee derived from sales royalty and outright fee from recording artist or record company.

How to Contact: Prefers cassette with 2-6 songs and lyric sheet. SASE. Reports in 1 month.

Music: Classical, folk, Spanish, Slavic, polka and Hungarian gypsy (international folk music). Produced *Czech Polkas* (by Slavko Kunst), recorded by Prague Singers on Apon Records; "Hungarian Gypsy" (by Deki Lakatos), recorded by Budapest on Apon Records; and "Polka - Dance With Me" (by Slavko Kunst), recorded by Prague on Apon Records.

APRIL RECORDING STUDIOS/PRODUCTIONS, 827 Brazil Pl., El Paso TX 79903. (915)772-7858. Owner: Harvey Marcus. Record producer, music publisher (Crystal Ram Records Publishing/BMI), record company (April and Crystal Ram Records) and recording studio. Deals with artists and songwriters. Produces 1-3 singles/year 1-3 12″ singles, 1-5 LPs, 1-5 EPs and 1-3 CDS/year. Receives 35 submissions/month. Fee derived from sales royalty and/or outright fee from record company.

How to Contact: Prefers cassette or 7½ ips reel-to-reel (or VHS videocassette) with 1-3 songs and lyric or lead sheets. "Include current updated listing of all available past recordings, publishing and performances of your material." SASE. Reports in 2 months.

Music: Mostly jazz, R&B and new wave/rock; also "all ballads and material with crossover possibilities, such as Mex/Tex, country and instrumental." Produced *Topaz* (compilation), recorded by Topaz (Christian/pop); *Foot Prints*, written and recorded by Jaime Gallindo (Christian/easy listening); and *Sinai* (compilation), recorded by Sinai (Christian/Spanish pop); all on Xavier Records. Other artists include Patricia and Pamela Thoreson, Ruben Cruz and Robert Cast.

Tips: "Please be patient! We answer and listen to all material. Also, leave out all the flashy solos unless the song is an instrumental."

ARCADIA PRODUCTIONS, INC., 425 Windsor Pkwy. NE, Atlanta GA 30342. (404)255-3284. FAX: (404)255-8723. Owner: Sammy Knox. Record producer, music publisher (Axl's Gruv Music-ASCAP) and record company (Arista). Estab. 1986. Deals with artists and songwriters. Produces 20 singles, 6 12″ singles and 2 LPs/year. Fee derived from sales royalty or outright fee from record company.

How to Contact: Submit demo tape by mail. Unsolicited submissions are OK. Prefers cassette (or VHS videocassette if available) with 3 songs. SASE. Reports in 2 weeks.

Music: Mostly R&B, rock and pop; also gospel. Produced "Good Old Days" (by K. Kendrick/S. Knox); "Do You Still Remember Love" (by Tommy Dean, Marty Kearns, S. Knox); and "I Just Laugh" (by K. Kendrick, S. Knox, Ken Cummings); all recorded by Geoff McBride on Arista Records. Other artists include Shiela Jackson and Michael Meredith.

aUDIOFILE TAPES, 209-25 18th Ave., Bayside NY 11360. Sherriff, aT County: Carl Howard. Cassette-only label of alternative music. Estab. 1984. Deals with artists and songwriters. Produces about 25 cassettes/year. Receives 15-20 submissions/year. "Money is solely from sales. Some artists ask $1 per tape sold."

How to Contact: Submit demo tape by mail—unsolicited submissions are OK. Prefers cassette. "Relevant artist information is nice. Master copies accepted on metal cassette. We trade submissions for cassettes on the label." SASE. Reports in 2 weeks.

Music: Mostly psych/electronic rock, non-rock electronic music, progressive rock; also free jazz and world music. Produced "Guilt Trip" recorded by Ron Anderson; "Magnavido" recorded by Screamin' Popeyes and "Live Bootleg from Switzerland" recorded by Ulterior Lux, all on aT Records. Other artists include Through Black holes Band, Nomuzic, Alien Planetscapes, Doug Michael & The Outer Darkness, and Mental Anguish.
Tips: "Please, no industrial music, no deliberately shocking images of racism and sexual brutality. And no New Age sleeping pills. Outside of that, go go go."

*AURORA PRODUCTIONS, 7415 Herrington N.E., Belmont MI 49306. Producer: Jack Conners. Record producer and engineer/technician. Big Rock Records and Ocean Records. Estab. 1984. Deals with artists and songwriters. Produces 2 singles, 2 LPs and 1 CD/year. Fee derived from outright fee from recording artist.
How to Contact: Write first and obtain permission to submit. Prefers cassette with 1 song. Does not return unsolicited material. Reports in 3 weeks.
Music: Mostly classical, folk and jazz; also pop/rock and New Age. Produced "Peace On Earth" (by John & Danny Murphy), recorded by The Murphy Brothers on Ocean Records (single); "Swimmer's Song," written and recorded by Steve Turner on Ocean Records (single); and *The Burdons*, written and recorded by The Burdons on Big Rock (LP).

BAL RECORDS, Box 369, LaCanada CA 91012-0369. (818)548-1116. President: Adrian Bal. Record producer and music publisher (Bal & Bal Music). Estab. 1965. Bal West estab. 1988. Deals with artists and songwriters. Produces 3-6 singles/year. Fee derived from sales royalty.
How to Contact: Submit demo tape by mail—unsolicited submission are OK. Prefers cassette with 3 songs and lyric sheet. SASE. Reports in 1-3 months.
Music: Mostly MOR, country, jazz, R&B, rock and top 40/pop; also blues, church/religious, easy listening and soul. Produced "Right To Know" and "Fragile" (by James Jackson), recorded by Kathy Simmons on BAL Records (rock); "Dance To The Beat of My Heart" (by Dan Gertz), recorded by Ace Baker on BAL Records (rock); and "You're A Part of Me," "Can't We Have Some Time Together," "You and Me," and "Circles of Time," written and recorded by Paul Richards on BAL Records (A/C).
Tips: "Write and compose what you believe to be commercial."

TED BARTON, Suite S, 1622 16th Ave. S., Nashville TN 37212. (615)383-7209. Producer: Ted Barton. Record producer and music publisher (Ted Barton Music/BMI, Langford Cove Music/ASCAP). Estab. 1986. Deals with artists and songwriters. Produces 3-4 singles, 2-3 LPs and 2-3 CDs/year. Fee derived from sales royalty when song or artist is recorded and outright fee from record company.
How to Contact: Submit demo tape by mail—unsolicited submissions are OK. Prefers cassette with maximum of 3 songs and lyric sheet. "Send only your best material." Does not return unsolicited material.
Music: Mostly country, R&B and pop; also gospel. Produced "Hank & Bogart Still Live" (by Joe Sun/Ted Barton), recorded by Joe Sun on Dixie Frog France Records (country single); "Blue Norweigian Moon" (by Don Goodman/Richie Rector), recorded by Ottar Johanson on Sonet Norway (country single); and "Have Heartache Will Travel" (by M & J. Harrison/Ted Barton), recorded by Julie Harrison on S&H UKA (country single). Other artists include Smith/Harrison, Jimmy Tittle, Steve Crunk and Duncan Wayne.
Tips: "Be dedicated to your craft and art."

BAY FARM PRODUCTIONS, Box 2821, Duxbury MA 02364. (617)585-9470. Producer: Paul Caruso. Record producer and in-house 24-track recording facility. Estab. 1985. Deals with artists and songwriters. Produces 6 singles, 4 LPs, 2 EPs and 6 CDs/year. Fee derived from sales royalty when song or artist is recorded, outright fee from recording artist, or outright fee from record company.
How to Contact: Submit demo tape by mail—unsolicited submissions are OK. Prefers cassette or VHS videocassette with 3 songs and lyric and lead sheet (if available). "Please use a high quality cassette." SASE. Reports in 1-2 months.
Music: Mostly A/C, dance and R&B; also folk, pop and rock. Produced *Dancing in the Mystery*, written and recorded by Becky Williams (folk/pop/AC); *The McQueens*, (by various artists), recorded by The McQueens (rock); and *Ali London*, (by Caruso), recorded by Ali London (dance/pop/R&B). Other artists include Ashbury Queen and Dioney Figus.
Tips: "We accept all submissions, but it is easier for us to work with artists from the New England area."

BELL RECORDS INTERNATIONAL, Box 725, Daytona Beach FL 32115-0725. (904)252-4849. President: LeRoy Pritchett. Record producer, music publisher and record company (Bell Records International). Estab. 1985. Deals with artists and songwriters. Produces 12 singles, 12 LPs and 12 CDs/year. Fee derived from sales royalty when song or artist is recorded.

How to Contact: Write first and obtain permission to submit. Prefers cassette.
Music: Mostly R&B, gospel and rock; also country and pop. Produced *Hot In The Gulf* (R&B LP by Billy Brown) and *Hold To God's Hand* (gospel LP by James Martin), both recorded by Charles Vickers on Bell Records. Other artists include Bobby Blue Blane and Little Anthony.

HAL BERNARD ENTERPRISES, INC., P.O. Box 8385, Cincinnati OH 45208. (513)871-1500. President: Stan Hertzmann. Record producer and music publisher (Sunnyslope Music Inc. and Bumpershoot Music Inc.). Deals with artists and songwriters. Produces 5 singles and 3-4 LPs/year. Fee derived from sales royalty.
How to Contact: Prefers cassette with 1-3 songs and lyric sheet. SASE. Reports in 1 month.
Music: Produced *Inner Revolution* by Adrian Belew on Atlantic Records; *Psychodots*; recorded by Psychodots on Strugglebaby Records; and *Young and Rejected*, recorded by Prizoner on Strugglebaby Records.

RICHARD BERNSTEIN, 2170 S. Parker Rd., Denver CO 80231. (303)755-2613. Contact: Richard Bernstein. Record producer, music publisher (M. Bernstein Music Publishing Co.) and record label. Deals with artists and songwriters. Produces 6 singles, 2 12″ singles, 6 LPs and 6 CDs/year. Receives 200 submissions/month. Fee derived from sales royalty, outright fee from songwriter/artist and/or outright fee from record company.
How to Contact: Prefers cassette and lyric or lead sheets. Does not return unsolicited material. Reports in 6-8 weeks.
Music: Rock, jazz and country.
Tips: "No telephone calls *please*."

BIG BEAR, Box 944, Birmingham, B16 8UT, **United Kingdom**. Phone: 44-21-454-7020. Managing Director: Jim Simpson. Record producer, music publisher (Bearsongs) and record company (Big Bear Records). Works with lyricists and composers and teams collaborators. Produces 10 LPs/year. Fee derived from sales royalty.
How to Contact: Write first about your interest, then submit demo tape and lyric sheet. Reports in 2 weeks.
Music: Blues and jazz.

BIG CITY MUSIC, INC., 15 Gloria Lane, Fairfield NJ 07004. (201)808-8280. President: Gary Rottger. Estab. 1990. Deals with artists and songwriters. Produces 6 singles, 6 12″ singles and 2 LPs/year. Fee derived from sales royalty or outright fee from record company.
How to Contact: Submit demo tape by mail—unsolicited submissions are OK. Prefers cassette (or VHS videocassette if available) with 3 songs and lyric sheet. Does not return unsolicited material. Reports in 3 weeks.
Music: Mostly dance, rap and rock. Produced "Ring My Bell" (by Knight), recorded by Karen King on Power Records (dance single); *Crushin* and *Comin' Back Hard Again* (by Rottger and Fat Boys), recorded by Fat Boys on Polygram Records.
Tips: "Have a good clean demo which competes with current radio."

BIG PICTURE RECORD CO., #7A, 101 E. 9th Ave., Anchorage AK 99501. (907)279-6900. Producer/Owner: Patric D'Eimon. Record producer and record company (Big Picture Records). Estab. 1983. Deals with artists and songwriters. Produces 5 LPs/year. Fee derived from outright fee from recording artist.
How to Contact: Submit demo tape by mail. Unsolicited submissions are OK. Prefers cassette or VHS videocassette with 4 songs and lyric sheet. SASE. Reports in 6 weeks.
Music: Mostly country, pop/rock, R&B; also folk, New Age, "in between styles." Produced "The Journey," written and recorded by Patric D'Eimon on (contemporary folk); *PBL*, written and recorded by PBL (rap) and "Marge Ford (by various), recorded by Marge Ford-Two Sisters. Other artists include Jim Shepard, Jeni Davis, Steve Cook and Tim Rogons.
Tips: "Educate yourselves in the recording/production process."

BIG PRODUCTIONS AND PUBLISHING CO. INC., Suite 308, 37 E. 28th St., New York NY 10016. (212)447-6000. FAX: (212)447-6003. President: "Big" Paul Punzone. Record producer, music publisher (Humongous Music Publishing/ASCAP) and record company (Big Productions). Estab. 1989. Deals with artists and songwriters. Produces 12 12″ singles/year. Fee derived from sales royalty when song or artist is recorded, and outright fee from recording artist or record company. Charges upfront "only when hired for independent projects."
How to Contact: Write or call first to arrange personal interview. Prefers cassette with 3 songs and lyric sheet. "We are looking for artists and independent productions for release on Big Productions Records. Artists will be signed as a production deal to shop to other labels. We mainly release 12″

house tracks on Big Productions Records." SASE. Reports in 6 weeks.
Music: Mostly house, hip-hop and pop dance. Produced "Big House" (by P. Punzone/H. Romero) and "Mission Accomplished" (by P. Punzone/B. Fisher/G. Sicard), both recorded by Big Baby; and "Loose Flutes" (by P.Punzone/B. Fisher/G. Sicard), recorded by Picture Perfect, all on Big Productions Records (all house 12″ singles).
Tips: "Please submit only musical styles listed. We want finished masters of 12″ house material."

BLADE TO THE RHYTHM MUSIC PRODUCTIONS, 114-22 116th St., Ozone Park NY 11420. (718)641-9335 or FAX: (718)845-4417. President: Juan-Kato Lemus. Record producer, music publisher (Blade to the Rhythm/ASCAP) and production company. Estab. 1987. Deals with artists and songwriters. Produces 4 12″ singles, 2 LPs and 6 EPs/year. Fee derived from sales royalty or outright fee from record company. "May charge in advance for services, depending on deal made with artist or songwriter."
How to Contact: Submit demo tape by mail. Unsolicited submissions are OK. Prefers cassette with 2-4 songs and lyric sheet. "Send photograph and brief bio and tell us what type of music you do." Does not return unsolicited material. Reports in 1 month.
Music: Mostly dance/pop, house and R&B; also rap, freestyle and ballads. Produced "What Was I Thinking Of" (by Vince DeMar and Rob Caputo), on 2nd Self Records (freestyle); "The Afterworld" (by J. Lemus and R. Checo), recorded by Orchestra Three on Blade to the Rhythm Records (house); and "Leave Me This Way" (by D. Ospina), recorded by Margie Martineé on Metropolitan Records (freestyle). Other artists include Aviance, Mari, Max, Hugo Fernandez, Magic Juan and Davidson.
Tips: "Be patient and the time and effort will pay off. The good songs sell because of the proper steps taken at the appropriate time."

BLAZE PRODUCTIONS, 103 Pleasant Ave., Upper Saddle River NJ 07458. (201)825-1060. Record producer, music publisher (Botown Music) and management firm. Estab. 1978. Deals with artists and songwriters. Fee derived from sales royalty, outright fee from recording artist or record company.
How to Contact: Prefers cassette (or VHS videocassette) with 1 or more songs and lyric sheet. Does not return unsolicited material. Reports in 1 week.
Music: Pop, rock and dance. Produced "Circus Trash" (by Karl DeKisa), recorded by Melissa K. on Local Records; "Point of A Hulk" (by Peace/Stevens) recorded by AK Peace; and "For Now," written and recorded by Blaze, both on Botown Records.

*BLUE BAKER MUSIC, 103 Lincoln Dr., West Union IA 52175. Owner: Doug Koempel. Record producer, record company (Bird-On-Fire Records) and music publisher (Blue Baker Music/BMI). Estab. 1979-80. Deals with artists and songwriters. Produces 2-3 singles, 5 LPs and 2-3 CDs/year.
How to Contact: Write or call first and obtain permission to submit. Prefers cassette (or VHS videocassette if available) with 2-3 songs and lyric sheet. Does not return unsolicited material. Reports in 2-3 months.
Music: Mostly country, easy listening and pop/rock. Produced "My Baby Came Back" by D. Koempel (country single); and *Tightrope!* and *Waiting For Your Love*, both by Koempel-Conner (country LPs), all recorded by Memory Brothers on Bird-On-Fire Records. Other artists include Cheri Kothenbeutel, Dennis Van Hove, John Rees, Mike Williams and Dale Sorenson.

PETER L. BONTA, 2200 Airport Ave., Fredericksburg VA 22401. (703)373-6511. Studio Manager: Buffalo Bob. Record producer. Estab. 1980. Deals with artists and songwriters. Produces 8-12 singles, 5-8 LPs and 4-6 CDs/year. Fee derived from sales royalty, outright fee from recording artist or record company.
How to Contact: Write or call first and obtain permission to submit. Prefers cassette with 3-4 songs and lyric sheet. SASE. Reports in 6 weeks.
Music: Mostly roots rock, country rock and blues; also country and Bluegrass. Produced *Like Cowboys Do* (by Michael Davis), recorded by The Bullets on Like Cowboys Do Music Records; *The Big DC Jamboree*, written and recorded by various artists on Run Wild Records; and *So Far . . . So What* (by Al & Jimmy Pheromone), recorded by The Pheromones on E.C. Records. Other artists include Tom Principato, Billy Hancock, Buffalo Bob & The Heard, Escape and Mark Mansfield.

BOOM PRODUCTIONS, INC., Dept. SM, 200 Regent Dr., Winston-Salem NC 27102. (919)768-1881. President: Dave Passerallo. Record producer, music publisher (DeDan Music/BMI) and record company (Boom/Power Play Records). Estab. 1989. Deals with artists and songwriters. Produces 2 singles, 2 LPs and 2 CDs/year. Fee derived from sales royalty.
How to Contact: Write first and obtain permission to submit. Prefers cassette (or VHS videocassette if available) with 2 songs and lead sheet. SASE. Reports in 2-3 weeks.
Music: Mostly pop, rap and rock. Produced "Ripped Jeans," by John Cody (pop); and "Guilty," by Paul Krege (rock/pop); both produced by Dave Passerallo on Boom Powerplay Records.
Tips: "Artist must be able to sign a production agreement."

*ROBERT BOWDEN, Box 111, Sea Bright NJ 07760. President: Robert Bowden. Record producer, music publisher (Roots Music/BMI) and record company (Nucleus Records). Estab. 1979. Deals with artists and songwriters. Produces 3 singles and 1 LP/year. Fees derived from sales royalty.
How to Contact: Submit demo tape or write to arrange personal interview. Prefers cassette (or VHS videocassette if available) with 3 songs and lyric sheet. SASE. Reports in 1 month.
Music: Mostly country; also pop. Produced "Henrey C" and "Selfish Heart," written and recorded by Bowden; and "Always" (by Sisison), recorded by Marco Sisison, all on Nucleus Records.

BRIEFCASE OF TALENT PRODUCTIONS, Suite 52, 1124 Rutland, Austin TX 78758. (512)832-1254. Owner: Kevin Howell. Record producer and live/recording engineer. Deals with artists. Produces 1 LP, 2 EPs and 1 CD/year. Fee derived from outright fee from recording artist or outright fee from record company.
How to Contact: Submit demo tape — unsolicited submissions OK. Prefers cassette (or VHS videocassette if available) with 4 songs and lyric sheet. Does not return unsolicited material. Reports in 3 weeks.
Music: Mostly alternative progressive rock (classic) and heavy metal; also R&B. Produced *Big Tim* and *Hell's Jazz*, written and recorded by Cold Six on Indus Records (jazz); and *Thin Line* (by Chris Smith) recorded by Blacksmith on Smith Records (heavy metal). Other artists include Jigsaw and Hide the China.
Tips: "Eighty percent of the people listening to your submission are engineers of some sort, so a poor quality demo will not get past the first 30 seconds. Make it sound professional and as good as budget allows!"

RAFAEL BROM, Box 71988, Los Angeles CA 90071-0988. Producer: Rafael Brom. Record producer, music publisher (ASCAP), record company (Cosmotone Records). Estab. 1984. Deals with artists and songwriters. Produces 1 LP/year.
How to Contact: Write first to obtain permission to submit. Prefers cassette (or VHS videocassette if available) with several songs and lyric sheet. Does not return unsolicited material. "Will contact only if interested."
Music: All types. Produced "Padre Pio," "Sonnet XVIII," "The Sounds of Heaven" and "Peace of Heart," all written and recorded by Lord Hamilton on Cosmotone Records (Christian/rock pop). Other artists include Adrian Romero and Thomas Emmett Dufficy.

*BROOKE PRODUCTIONS, INC., 1721 Ferrari Dr., Beverly Hills CA 90210. President: Skip Drinkwater. Record producer. Estab. 1971. Deals with artists and songwriters. Produces 4-5 singles, 2-3 12″ singles and 2-4 LPs/year. Fee derived from sales royalty or outright fee from recording artist or record company.
How to Contact: Submit demo tape by mail — unsolicited submissions are OK. Prefers cassette or ½″ VHS videocassette with 1-3 songs. SASE.
Music: Mostly R&B, pop and dance. Produced "Heartbeats Accelerating" (by McGarigles), recorded by Waiting Souls on Columbia Records (pop/Reggae dance); "Da Me La Fama," recorded by Latin Science on Columbia Records (Latin rap/dance); and "Don't Call Us" (by Mahal/Feldman), recorded by Taj Mahal on Private Music/BMG (urban/pop). Other artists include The Hooters, Tommy Conwell & The Young Rumblers and Hall & Oates.
Tips: "Work hard, study structure, stay true."

BROOZBEE MUSIC, INC., Suite 308, 37 East 28th St., New York NY 10016. (212)447-6000. President: Bruce B. Fisher. Record producer and music publisher (Broozbee Music, Inc./ASCAP). Estab. 1986. Deals with artists and songwriters. Produces 8 12″ singles/year. Fee derived from sales royalty or outright fee from recording artist (if hired for independent project) or record company.
How to Contact: Submit demo tape by mail — unsolicited submissions are OK. Prefers cassette (or VHS videocassette if available) with 3 songs and lyric sheet. "Send what you consider to be the best representation of your talent." SASE. Reports in 2 months.
Music: Mostly house, hip hop and dance; also rap, R&B and pop. Produced *Butt Naked* (by P. Falcone, P. Punzone, B.B. Fisher and G. Sicarp) recorded by Charm on Big Beat/Atlantic Records (rap).
Tips: "Quality, not quantity, is the most important."

*C.S.B. MIX INC., 50 Donna Court #11, Staten Island NY 10314. (718)698-4641. Contact: Carlton Batts. Record producer (The Bat Cave Recording Studio, Frankford/Wayne Mastering and Slam City Studios). Estab. 1989. Deals with artists and songwriters. Produces 15 singles, 4 12″ singles, 2 LPs and 1 EP/year. Fee derived from sales royalty when song or artist is recorded and outright fee from record company.

How to Contact: Submit demo tape by mail—unsolicited submissions are OK. Prefers cassette with 3 songs. "A picture and/or bio are a must!" Does not return unsolicited material. Reports in 2 weeks.
Music: Mostly R&B, dance and hip-hop; also rap, jazz and pop. Produced "Let It Flow" (by C. Batts), recorded by Troy Taylor on Motown Records (R&B/single); "Primetime" (by C. Batts), recorded by Jocelyn Brown on RCA Records (dance single); and "Thrills & Chills" (by C. Batts), recorded by Whitney Houston on Arista Records (R&B single). Other artists include Leslie Fine, The Boys Club One on One and Alan Rules.
Tips: "Be ready to work your butt off."

PETER CARDINALI, 12 Ecclesfield Dr., Scarborough ON M1W 3J6 **Canada**. (416)494-2000. Record producer/Arranger (Peter Cardinali Productions Inc./SOCAN) and Cardster Music (publishing), BMI, SOCAN. Estab. 1975. Deals with artists and songwriters. Produces 6-8 singles, 4-5 12″ singles, 8-10 LPs and 8-10 CDs/year.
How to Contact: Write or call first and obtain permission to submit. Prefers cassette with 4-6 songs and lyric sheets. SASE. Reports within weeks.
Music: Mostly pop, R&B, dance and funk/jazz. Produced *Big Fat Soul*, written and recorded by John James on Attic/A&M Records (dance LP); "The Bear Walks" (by P. Cardinali/H. Marsh), recorded by Hugh Marsh on Duke St./WEA Records (R&B/jazz LP); and "Moments" (by J. Nessle), recorded by See on A&M Records (pop single). Other artists include Rick James and Teena Marie.

CARLYLE PRODUCTIONS, 1217 16th Ave. South, Nashville TN 37212. (615)327-8129. President: Laura Fraser. Record producer, record company (Carlyle Records) and production company. Estab. 1986. Deals with artists and songwriters. Produces 6 singles and 6 LPs/CDs per year.
How to Contact: Submit demo tape by mail—unsolicited submissions are OK. Prefers cassette with 3 songs and lyric sheet. Does not return unsolicited material. Reports in 1 month.
Music: Mostly rock, pop and country. Produced *The Grinning Plowman* (by Michael Ake), recorded by The Grinning Plowman (pop/rock); *Dessau* (by Donn Ellis) recorded by Dessau (dance); and *Dorcha* (by The Simnoz Brothers) recorded by Dorcha (rock), all on Carlyle Records, Inc.

CAROLINA PRIDE PRODUCTIONS, Box 6, Rougemont NC 27572. (919)477-4077. Manager: Freddie Roberts. Record producer, music publisher (Freddie Roberts Music/BMI), record company, management firm and booking agency. Estab. 1967. Deals with artists, songwriters and session musicians. Produces 12 singles, 7 LPs, 2 EPs and 3 CDs/year. Fee derived from sales royalty.
How to Contact: Call or write first. Prefers 7½ ips reel-to-reel or cassette with 1-5 songs and lyric sheet. SASE. Reports in 5 weeks.
Music: Mostly country, MOR and top 40/pop; also bluegrass, church/religious, gospel and country rock. Produced "Restless Feeling," written and recorded by Rodney Hutchins (country/rock) on Catalina Records; "Empty" (by David Laws), recorded by Jerry Harrison (country) on Celebrity Circle Records; and "Redeemed" (by Jane Durham), recorded by The Roberts Family (Southern gospel) on Bull City Records. Other artists include Sleepy Creek, Lady Luck, Billy McKellar and C.J. Jackson.

*EDDIE CARR, Box 1794, Big Bear City CA 92314. (714)585-4645. President: Eddie Carr. Record producer, music publisher (Watchesgro Music) and record company (Interstate 40 Records). Estab. 1987. Deals with artists and songwriters. Produces 12 singles/year. Fee derived from sales royalty or outright fee from recording artist.
How to Contact: Submit demo tape by mail—unsolicited submissions are OK. Prefers cassette with 2 songs and lyric sheets. Does not return unsolicited submissions. Reports in 1 week.
Music: Mostly country. Produced "Bottom of a Mountain" (Soundwaves Records), "Fairy Tales" (Master Records), and "Cripple Cowboy" (Tracker #1 Records); all written and recorded by Don McKinnon (all singles). Movie and TV credits include "Young Guns of Texas," "The Story of Evil Knievel," "Alias Smith & Jones" and "Christopher Columbus Story." Other artists include Ripplin' Waters, Rosemary, Michael Angel, Chris Riley, Pete Tavarez, Sharon Hauge, Michael Jones and Chuck Carter.
Tips: "I want publishing on songs. Will try to place artist. It's costing more to break in new artists, so songs must be strong."

STEVE CARR, % Hit & Run Studios, 18704 Muncaster Rd., Rockville MD 20855. (301)948-6715. Owner/Producer: Steve Carr. Record producer (Hit & Run Studios). Estab. 1979. Deals with artists and songwriters. Produces 10 singles, 2 12″ singles, 8 LPs, 4 EPs and 10 CDs/year. Fee derived from outright fee from recording artist.
How to Contact: Write or call first and obtain permission to submit. Prefers cassette with 3 songs. "Do NOT send unsolicited material! Write name and phone number on cassette shell. Will call back if I can do anything with your material."

Music: Mostly pop, rock and R&B; also country. Produced/recorded *Billy Kemp* (by Billy Kemp), on Essential Records (LP); *Classic Rock*, written and recorded by various artists (oldies digital remaster) on Warner Bros. Records; "Frontier" (by R. Kelley), recorded by Frontier Theory on TOP Records (rock CD); *The Wolves* (by Band), on Top Records (LP); and "Bomb Squad" (by Lorenzo), on Their Own Records (single); all recorded by Hit & Run. Other artists include Beyond Words, Steve Nally/Deep End, Oho, Voodoo, Love Gods, Necrosis, Debra Brown and Universe. Produces and digitally remasters Time-Life Music's Rock n' Roll, Country Classics and R&B Series.

*DON CASALE MUSIC, INC., 377 Plainfield St., Westbury NY 11590. (516)333-7898. President: Don Casale. Record production, music publishing, artist management; affiliated recording studio. Estab. 1979. Deals with artists, songwriters, managers and agents. Fee derived from sales royalty.
Affiliates: ELASAC MUSIC (ASCAP), Don Casale Music (BMI).
How to Contact: "I will accept unsolicited cassettes (except during August and September) with one or two songs and legible, typed lyric sheets (no registered mail). No "lyrics-only" submissions. Please include address and phone number and letter stating exact purpose (publishing deal?; record deal?; etc.); anything else you'd like to say is welcome, too (I frown on 'form' letters). Press kit, bio and photo(s) or VHS videocassette are helpful, if available. For return of your material, always include SASE (envelope *must* be large enough to handle contents). If you don't need your material returned, include a *signed* note saying so and only include SASE for my response letter. Sorry, but I will not listen or correspond without SASE. A call first is very welcome (between 12 noon and 12 midnight EST), but not necessary, or you may inquire first by mail (with SASE). I'll listen to every note of your music and respond to you as soon as possible, usually between two weeks and two months, depending on volume of submissions."
Music: Everything but jazz and classical.
Tips: "Submitted songs should have a 'special' nature about them; a different quality and lyric. Melodies should be paritularly 'catchy' and memorable. Songs should be in tune with the current radio market. I want only 'career-starting', top 10 singles; not B sides or album fillers. Please try to be SELECTIVE and send me that ONE SONG you think is a KILLER; that ONE SONG that JUMPS OFF THE TAPE! Don't include a second song just because there's room on the cassette. Songwriters seeking a publishing contract need only a simple, in-tune, clear version of the song(s); a big production and recording, although welcome, is not necessary. Artists seeking a recording contract should submit a 'quality' performance (musically & vocally), incorporating their very best effort and their own, preferably unique, style. Your recording needn't be master quality, but your performance should be. I give extra points for following my instructions to the letter."

JAN CELT, 4026 NE 12th Ave., Portland OR 97212. (503)287-8045. Owner: Jan Celt. Record producer, music publisher (Wiosna Nasza Music/BMI) and record company (Flying Heart Records). Estab. 1982. Deals with artists and songwriters. Produces 2 LPs, 1 EP and 2 CDs/year. Receives 300 submissions/month.
How to Contact: Submit demo tape by mail—unsolicited submissions are OK. Prefers cassette with 1-10 songs and lyric sheets. SASE. Reports in 4 months.
Music: Mostly R&B, rock and blues; also jazz. Produced "Voodoo Garden," written and recorded by Tom McFarland (blues); "Bong Hit" (by Chris Newman), recorded by Snow Bud & the Flower People (rock); and "She Moved Away" (by Chris Newman), recorded by Napalm Beach, all on Flying Heart Records. Other artists include The Esquires and Janice Scroggins.
Tips: "Be sure your lyrics are heartfelt; they are what makes a song your own. Abandon rigid stylistic concepts and go for total honesty of expression."

CHALLEDON PRODUCTIONS, 5th Floor, Pembroke One Bldg., Virginia Beach VA 23462. General Counsel: Richard Shapiro. Record producer and record company (Challedon Records). Estab. 1990. Deals with artists and songwriters. Produces 1-2 singles, 1-2 albums/year. Fee derived from sales royalty.
How to Contact: Write first and obtain permission to submit. Prefers cassette (or VHS videocasette if available) with up to 3 songs and lyric sheet. Reports in 4 weeks.
Music: Mostly rock, pop and alternative/college rock; also some R&B. Produced *Hired Gun* (by J. Sullivan), recorded by Challedon Productions at Master Sound on Challedon Records (LP). Other artists include The Martians.

CHUCK CHAPMAN, 228 W. 5th St., Kansas City MO 64105. (816)842-6854. Office Manager: Gary Sutton. Record producer and music publisher (Fifth Street Records/BMI). Estab. 1973. Deals with artists and songwriters. Fee derived from sales royalty when song or artist is recorded, outright fee from recording artist or outright fee from record company. "Charges upfront for recording only."

How to Contact: Write or call first and obtain permission to submit. Prefers cassette (or ½" or ¾" videocassette if available) with 3 songs and lyric sheet. Include SASE. Does not return unsolicited material. Reports back in 1 month.
Music: Mostly country, gospel and rock; also rap, jazz and spoken word. Produced "Rumor Has It" (by Sheli), recorded by Freddie Hunt on Fifth Street Records (country single); and "Cold As Ashes" (by Lee Bruce), recorded by Montgomery Lee on Opal Records (country single). Other artists include Conrad Morris and Eisel & The Haymakers.

CHROME DREAMS PRODUCTIONS, 5852 Sentinel St., San Jose CA 95120. (408)268-6066. Owner: Leonard Giacinto. Record producer. Estab. 1982. Deals with artists and songwriters. Produces 15 singles and 8 12" singles/year. Fee derived from outright fee from recording artist.
How to Contact: Submit demo tape by mail—unsolicited submissions are OK. Write or call first to arrange personal interview. Prefers cassette (or ½" VHS videocassette if available). SASE. Reports in 1 month.
Music: Mostly rock, New Age, avant-garde and college radio. Produced "Dogface Blues" (by S. Jacobs) recorded by Sara Nicole Jacobs (blues); "Yer Country Club" (by 'Guitar Slingerz') recorded by Uzi's (metal); and "White Dress" (by K. Hildebrandt), recorded by Paruque (AOR); all on independent record labels. Other artists include Hurricanes, Jump Street, The Krells and Pat Lydon Memorial Irish Jug Band. Also produced soundtrack for V. Volkoff's film *The Garage Door*.
Tips: "Try to get emotion across in your work."

THE CLUB STUDIOS, 127 Aldersgate St., London EC1A 4JQ **England**. (44)71-2501910. Contact: Roland A. Radaelli. Record producer, music publisher (Miramare Music UK LTD/PRS) and record company (Presidential Enterprises, Ltd.). Estab. 1986. Deals with artists and songwriters. Produces 20-30 12" singles and 3-5 LPs/year. Receives 8 submissions/month. Fee derived from sales royalty or outright fee from recording artist or record company. Charges for services in advance "only when productions are for other labels or publishers."
How to Contact: Submit demo tape—unsolicited submissions are OK. Prefers cassette with 2-5 songs and lyric sheet. Does not return unsolicited material. Reports in 1 month.
Music: Mostly techno/house, pop. Produced *Recycler*, written and recorded by N/A/M on Warrior Records (12" Techno); *Future Tense*, written and recorded by Future Tense on High Density Records (12" Techno); and *Krono-Log 1*, written and recorded by various artists on High Density Records (12" Album/Techno). Other artists include Dark Avenger; Dreamdance/ Techno Logik; O/S/T; 909 BD.
Tips: "Be up to date with the trends in your chosen style of music; be original but not too ahead of the current fashions!"

*****COFFEE AND CREAM PRODUCTIONS**, (formerly Bolden Productions), 1138 E. Price St., Philadelphia PA 19138. Producer: Bolden Abrams, Jr.. Record producer, music publisher (Coffee and Cream Publishing Company/ASCAP) and record company (Coffee and Cream Records). Produces 12 singles, 12 12" singles and 6 LPs/year. Fee derived from sales royalty or outright fee from recording artist or record company.
How to Contact: Prefers cassette with 1-4 songs and lyric sheet. Does not return unsolicited material. Reports in 2 weeks.
Music: Mostly R&B, pop and country; also gospel, and dance. Produced "No Time for Tears," (by Beau Winters and Keith Batts), recorded by Gabrielle on Saphire Records; and "Starting All Over Again," (by Oscar Patterson and Jim Avery) and 'Ooh I Can't Get Over You," (by Oscar Patterson, Ross Barnes and Jim Avery), both recorded by Wayne Hunter on Spiketown Records.

COLLECTOR RECORDS, Box 2296, Rotterdam Holland 3000 CG **The Netherlands**. Phone: 1862-4266. FAX: 1862-4366. Research: Cees Klop. Record producer and music publisher (All Rock Music). Deals with artists and songwriters. Produces 8-10 singles and up to 30 LPs/year. Fee derived from sales royalty.
How to Contact: Submit demo tape—unsolicited submissions OK. Prefers cassette. SAE and IRC. Reports in 1 month.
Music: Mostly 50s rock, rockabilly and country rock; also piano boogie woogie. Produced *Eager Boy* (by T. Johnson), recorded by Lonesome Orifier; *Tehm Saturday*, written and recorded by Malcolm Yelvington, both on Collector Records; and *All Night Rock*, written and recorded by Bobby Hicks on White Label Records (all 50s rock). Other artists include Teddy Redell, Gene Summers, Benny Joy and the Hank Pepping Band.

COM'TECH PRODUCTIONS, INC., P.O. Box 28816, Philadelpha PA 19151. (215)473-5527. General Manager: Leroy Schuler. Record producer. Estab. 1990. Deals with artists and songwriters. Fee derived from outright fee from record company. Produces 6 singles, 25 12" singles and 3 LPs/year.

How to Contact: Submit demo tape by mail. Unsolicited submissions are OK. Prefers cassette with 4 songs and lyric sheet. SASE. Reports in 3 weeks.
Music: Mostly R&B, pop and jazz. Artists include Lavelle, Clint Washington and Felice. Produced "Here We Go Again," "I'll Do Better" (by SBmm), recorded by Mack Atkinson on Bend-Bang Records (single 7"); and "Do Me Right" (by SBmm), recorded by Debra Scott on Big Bang Records (LTD cassette).

CONTINENTAL COMMUNICATIONS CORP., Suite 212, 450 Livingston St., Norwood NJ 07648. (201)767-5551. Vice President: Gene Schwartz. Record producer and music publisher (3 Seas Music/ASCAP and Northvale Music/BMI) and record company (3C Records and Laurie Records). Estab. 1985. Deals with artists and songwriters. Produces 25 singles, 12 12" singles, 20 LPs and 10 CDs/year. Fee derived from sales royalty.
How to Contact: Prefers cassette and lyric sheet. "Send only a few of your most commercial songs." SASE. Reports in 2 weeks.
Music: Mostly rock and pop, urban; also dance-oriented and top 40/pop. Artists include Human Beings, Barbara M and Bill Sunkel.

COPPELIA, 21 rue de Pondichery, Paris 75015 **France**. Phone: (1)45673066. FAX: (1)43063026. Manager: Jean-Philippe Olivi. Record producer, music publisher (Coppelia/SACEM), record company (Olivi Records) and music print publisher. Deals with artists and songwriters. Produces 8 singles and 4 LPs/year. Fee derived from sales royalty or outright fee from recording artist or record company.
How to Contact: Prefers cassette. SAE and IRC. Reports in 1 month.
Music: Mostly pop, rock and New Age; also background music and film/series music. Produced "No'mad" written and recorded by Alain Mion (jazz); and "Corsica," recorded by Petru Guelfucci, both on Olivi Records. Other artists include Pino Lattuca, Christian Chevallier and Robert Quibel.

JOHNNY COPPIN/RED SKY RECORDS, Box 7, Stonehouse, Glos. GL10 3PQ U.K. Phone: 0453-826200. Record producer, music publisher (PRS) and record company (Red Sky Records). Estab. 1985. Deals with artists and songwriters. Produces 2 singles, 3 LPs and 3 CDs/year. Fee derived from sales royalty when song or artist is recorded.
How to Contact: Submit demo tape by mail—unsolicited submissions are OK. Prefers cassette with 3 songs and lyric sheet. SASE. Reports in 3 months.
Music: Mostly rock, modern folk and roots music. Produced *Edge of Day*, written and recorded by Laurie Lee and Johnny Coppin (LP); *Songs on Lonely Roads*, recorded by Johnny Coppin and David Goodland (musical drama LP); and *West Country Christmas*, written and recorded by Johnny Coppin (LP); all on Red Sky Records. Other artists include Desperate Men and Phil Beer.

DANO CORWIN, 5839 Silver Creek, Azle Rd., Azle TX 76020. (817)281-8888. Record producer, music video and sound production company. Estab. 1986. Works with artists and songwriters. Produces 6 singles, 3 12" singles, 5 EPs and 2 CDs/year. Receives 200 submissions/year. Fee usually derived from sales royalty, but negotiated on case-by-case basis.
How to Contact: Submit demo tape—unsolicited submissions are OK. Prefers cassette (or VHS videocassette if available) with 3 songs and lyric sheet. "Keep songs under 4 minutes. Only copyrighted material will be reviewed. Please do not send material without copyright notices." SASE, "but prefers to keep material on file." Reports in 6 weeks.
Music: Mostly rock; also pop, New Age and dance. Produced "Be Mine Tonight" (by Craig Cole/Keny McClurg), recorded by Sound Dog on MLM Records (rock single); *Shine* (by W. Thomas), recorded by W. Thomas Band on TBO Records (rock EP); and *Meticulus* (by Mary Beringer), recorded by Aria on MR Records (New Age EP). Other artists include Demur Cull, The Kindreds, The W-4's, Twice Four and Maxamum.
Tips: "Keep songs simple and melodic. Write as many songs as possible. Out of a large quantity, a few quality songs may emerge."

DAVE COTTRELL, 1602 8th Ave. South, Fort Dodge IA 50501. Producer: Dave Cottrell. Record producer. Estab. 1969. Deals with artists and songwriters. Producers 25 singles, 10 LPs, 10 EPs and 25 CDs/year. Receives 15 submissions/month. Fee derived from outright fee from recording artist or outright fee from record company.

Remember: Don't "shotgun" your demo tapes. Submit only to companies interested in the type of music you write. For more submission hints, refer to The Business of Songwriting on page 19.

How to Contact: Submit demo tape by mail—nsolicited submissions are OK. Prefers cassette with 4 songs and lyric sheet. SASE. Reports in 1 week.
Music: Mostly rock, pop and gospel; also country, R&B and disco. Produced "Change Of Address," written and recorded by Donna Rogers (country single); *Verne Fibiker* (by various songwriters), recorded by Verne Fibiker (accordian LP); and *Battalian*, written and recorded by Battalian (metal LP), all on Independent Records. Also, "For the Sheer Fun of It!" written, recorded, produced and performed by Dave Cottrell, currently in label negotiation. Credits include work with Ray Manzerak of The Doors, Jan & Dean, Bobby Vee, The Beach Boys and more.
Tips: "Avoid clutter and multi-track overkill. Too many sounds and tracks ruin the sound. Write music that you enjoy. Be honest and creative. There is no room for the weak and insane in the music business."

COUNTRY STAR PRODUCTIONS, Box 569, Franklin PA 16323. (814)432-4633. President: Norman Kelly. Record producer, music publisher (Country Star Music/ASCAP, Kelly Music/BMI and Process Music/BMI) and record company (Country Star, Process, Mersey and CSI Records). Estab. 1970. Deals with artists and songwriters. Produces 5-8 singles and 5-8 LPs/year. Receives 100 submissions/year. Works with 3-4 new songwriters/year. Works with composers and lyricists; teams collaborators. Fee derived from sales royalty or outright fee from recording artist or record company.
How to Contact: Submit demo tape—unsolicited submissions OK. Prefers cassette with 2-4 songs and lyric or lead sheet. SASE. Reports in 2 weeks.
Music: Mostly country (80%); also rock (5%), MOR (5%), gospel (5%) and R&B (5%). Produced "Dealing with the Devil," written and recorded by Ron Lauer; "The Holiday Waltz" (by Wrightman-Stelezer), recorded by Debbie Sue; and "Little Falling Star" (by K. Casteel), recorded by Virge Brown; all country singles on Country Star Records. Other artists include Bob Stamper and Jeffrey Allan Connors.
Tips: "Submit only your best efforts."

*COWBOY JUNCTION FLEA MARKET AND PUBLISHING CO., Hwy. 44 and Jct. 490, Lecanto FL 32661. (904)746-4754. Contact: Elizabeth Thompson. Record producer and music publisher (Cowboy Junction/BMI). Deals with artists and songwriters. Produces 3-4 singles and 2 12″ singles/year. Works with 6 new songwriters/year. Works with lyricists and composers; teams collaborators. Fee derived from sales royalty.
How to Contact: Submit demo tape—unsolicited submissions OK. Prefers 7½ ips reel-to-reel or cassette with 3 songs and lyric sheet. SASE. Reports ASAP.
Music: C&W, country gospel and bluegrass. Produced "Desert Storm," "You Are the One" and "Will You Please Get Up My Love" (by Boris Max Pastuch), recorded by Buddy Max on Cowboy Junction Records (C&W). Other artists include Leo Vargason, Charlie Floyd, Lloyd Stevens, Troy Holliday and Wally Jones.
Tips: "Come to our Flea Market on Tuesday or Friday and show to the public, and who knows? Also, if possible, come to our Music Show at Cowboy Junction on Saturday at 2 p.m. and ask to be placed on stage to present your material to the public. (We are closed and on tour July and August of each year.)"

*CREATIVE MUSIC SERVICES, 838 Fountain St., Woodbridge CT 06525. Owner: Craig Calistro. Record producer (Ace Record Company). Estab. 1989. Deals with artists and songwriters. Produces 50 singles, 20 12″ singles, 15 LPs and 15 CDs/year. Fee derived from sales royalty when song or artist is recorded, outright fee from recording artist or record company.
How to Contact: Submit demo tape by mail—unsolicited submissions are OK. Prefers cassette (or VHS videocassette if available) and 1-3 songs and lyric and lead sheets. "Send photo if available." SASE. Reports in 2-3 weeks.
Music: Mostly pop/top 40 and dance; also jazz. Produced "Tell Me" (by Craig Calistro), recorded by J. Lord (single); *Don't Throw This Love Away* (by Brenda Lee), recorded by Brenda Lee (LP); and *Pillow Talk* (by H.L. Reeves), recorded by Tanya (LP), all on Ace Records. Other artists include Sharon Dominguez and Ken Aldrich.

JERRY CUPIT PRODUCTIONS, Box 121904, Nashville TN 37212. (615)731-0100. Producer: Jerry Cupit. Record producer and music publisher. Estab. 1984. Develops artists and songwriters. Fee derived from sales royalty, outright fee from record company or artist.
How to Contact: Write or call to arrange an interview. Does not return material.
Music: Mostly country, rock and gospel; also R&B. Produced *Never in a Million Tears*, (by Janice Honeycutt, Ken Mellons, Tim McGraw and Gene Simmons), recorded by Tim McGraw of Curb Records (country LP); "Your Coffee's On the Table" (by Scotty Robinson and David and Faye Brewer), recorded by San Antonio Rose on RCA-Canada and "Gone But Not Forgotten" (by Jerry

Cupit), recorded by Orion on K-TEL Records. Other artists include Freddie Hart, Ken Mellons, James Payne, Tracy Lea Reynolds and Jack Robertson.

WADE CURTISS, Box 1622, Hendersonville, TN 37077. A&R Director: Wade Curtiss. Record producer and record company (Terock Records). Estab. 1959. Deals with artists and songwriters. Produces 12-20 singles, 6 12″ singles, 12-20 LPs, 4 EPs and 6 CDs/year. Fee derived from outright fee from recording artist. Charges "artists for sessions."
How to Contact: Submit demo tape by mail—unsolicited submissions are OK. Prefers IPS reel-to-reel or "all kinds" of videocassettes (if available) with 4-10 songs and lyric sheets. SASE. Reports in 3 weeks.
Music: Interested in "all kinds." Produced "Changes," written and recorded by R. Derwald; and *Rock*, written and recorded by Mickey Finn (rock LP), both on Terock Records. Other artists include Dixie Dee, Greg Paul and Rhythm Rockers.

S. KWAKU DADDY, Box 424794, San Francisco CA 94142-4794. (415)239-3640. President: S. Kwaku Daddy. Record producer and record company (African Heritage Records Co.). Deals with artists and songwriters. Produces 6 LPs/year.
How to Contact: Submit demo tape—unsolicited submissions OK. Prefers cassette. Sometimes returns unsolicited material. Reports in 2 weeks.
Music: Mostly African pop, R&B and gospel. Produced *Times of Change, Life's Rhythms* and *Heritage IV*, all by S. Kwaku Daddy, all on African Heritage Records (LPs).

DANNY DARROW, Suite 6-D, 150 West End Ave., New York NY 10023. (212)873-5968. Manager: Danny Darrow. Record producer, music publisher (BMI, ASCAP), record company (Mighty Records) and Colley Phonographics—Europe. Estab. 1958. Deals with songwriters only. Produces 1-2 singles, 1-2 12″ singles and 1-2 LPs/year. Fee derived from royalty.
How to Contact: Submit demo tape by mail—unsolicited submissions are OK. "No phone calls." Prefers cassette with 3 songs and lyric sheet. SASE. Reports in 1 week.
Music: Mostly pop, country and dance; also jazz. Produced "Look to the Wind," (by P. Stewart/D. Darrow) (MOR); "Telethones,' (by R.L. Lowery/D. Darrow) (rock); and "Better Than You Know," (by M. Greer/R.L. Lowery/D. Darrow) (MOR), all recorded by Danny Darrow on Mighty Records.
Tips: "Listen to the hits of Richie, Manilow, Houston and Rogers and write better songs."

*DATURA PRODUCTIONS, 4400 Sarah St. #12, Burbank CA 91505. (818)558-1329. Producer/Owner: Richardo Broadus. Record producer. Estab. 1990. Deals with artists and songwriters. Fee derived from sales royalty when song or artists is recorded.
How to Contact: Write or call first and obtain permission to submit. Prefers cassette (or VHS videocassette if available) and lead sheet. SASE. Reports in 6 weeks.
Music: Mostly rock, R&B and alternative; also New Age, dance and rap.

MIKE DE LEON PRODUCTIONS, 14146 Woodstream, San Antonio TX 78231. (512)492-0613. Owner: Mike De Leon. Record producer, music publisher (BMI) and record company (Antonio Records). Estab. 1983. Deals with artists and songwriters. Produces 15 singles and 5 LPs/year. Receives 10 submissions/month. Fee derived from sales royalty when song or artist is recorded and outright fee from record company.
How to Contact: Submit demo tape by mail—unsolicited submissions are OK. Prefers cassette (or VHS videocassette if available) with any number of songs and lyric or lead sheets. "Include contact number and any promo materials." SASE. Reports in 2 months.
Music: Mostly pop/rock, R&B and Latin. Produced *Marina's Momento*, recorded by Marina Chapa; *Elegante*, written and recorded by DeLeon Bros.; and *Debut*, written and recorded by Claudia (all LPs).
Tips: "Feel free to submit material, but be patient. Need good pop and Latin material for existing artist clientele. All *good* material consistently suceeds. Se habla español."

EDWARD DE MILES, 8th Floor, 4475 Allisonville Rd., Indianapolis IN 46205. (317)549-9006. President: Edward De Miles. Record producer, music publisher (Edward De Miles Music Co./BMI), record company (Sahara Records). Estab. 1981. Deals with artists and songwriters. Produces 15-20 singles, 15-20 12″ singles, 5-10 LPs and 5-10 CDs/year. Receives 100 submissions/year. Fee derived from sales royalty.
How to Contact: Submit demo tape—unsolicited submissions OK. Prefers cassette (or VHS or Beta ½″ videocassette if available) with 1-3 songs and lyric sheet. SASE. Reports in 1 week.
Music: Mostly R&B/dance, top 40 pop/rock and contemporary jazz; also country, TV and film themes—songs and jingles. Produced "Hooked on U" and "Moments," written and recorded by Steve Lynn (R&B); "No Mercy" (by D. Evans, A. Mitchell), recorded by Multiple Choice (rap), all on

Sahara Records. Other artists include Lost in Wonder, D'von Edwards and Ultimate Force.
Tips: "Copyright all material before submitting. Equipment and showmanship a must."

DEMI MONDE RECORDS & PUBLISHING LTD., Foel Studio, Llanfair Caereinion, Powys, SY21 0RZ
Wales. Phone: 0938-810758. Managing Director: Dave Anderson. Record producer, music publisher
(PRS & MCPS) and record company (Demi Monde Records). Estab. 1982. Deals with artists and
songwriters. Produces 5 singles, 15 12" singles, 15 LPs and 10 CDs/year. Fee derived from combination
of sales royalty, outright fee from recording artist, outright fee from record company and studio
production time.
How to Contact: Submit demo tape by mail—unsolicited submissions are OK. Prefers cassette with
3 or 4 songs and lyric sheet. SASE. Reports in 2 months.
Music: Mostly rock, pop and blues. Produced *Average Man*, written and recorded by D. Carter (LP);
She, written and recorded by D. Allen (LP/CD); and *Full Moon*, recorded by Full Moon (LP/CD), all
on Demi Monde Records. Other artists include Gong, Amon Duul and Groonies.

WARREN DENNIS, (formerly Warren Dennis Kahn), 540 B. E. Todd Rd., Santa Rosa CA 95407.
(707)585-1325. President/Owner: Warren Dennis Kahn. Record producer and independent producer.
Estab. 1976. Deals with artists and songwriters. Produces 10 LPs and 10 CDs/year. Fee derived from
sales royalty when song or artist is recorded, outright fee from recording artist, or outright fee from
record company. Does not return unsolicited submissions.
How to Contact: Write or call first and obtain permission to submit. Prefers cassette with 2-3 songs
and lyric sheet. Reports in 1 month. Does not return unsolicited submissions.
Music: Mostly New Age, pop and gospel; also country, rock and R&B. Produced *Music to Disappear
in 2* (by Rafael), recorded by WDK on Hearts of Space Records (New Age LP); *Tokewki* (by Tokewki)
on TKM Records (world LP); and *Stone by Stone* (by M. Pomer) on Peartree Records (Christian LP);
all recorded by WDK. Other artists include Michael Pomer, Buddy Comfort and Constance Demby.
Tips: "Have a clear understanding of who you wish to reach and what you're trying to accomplish."

DETROIT PRODUCTIONS, Box 265, N. Hollywood CA 91603-0265. (818)569-5653. President/Executive
Producer: Randy De Troit. Vice President: Ciara Dortch. Co-Producer: Jade Young. Independent
Television Producer of network TV shows, cable-TV series. Works with freelance producers/promot-
ers for local and national broadcast on assignment basis only; gives unlimited assignments per year.
Buys all rights outright or pays percentage if applicable.
How to Contact: "Send edited version of work on VHS or broadcast quality tape. All categories of
music plus surrealism, new concept, idealistic or abstract material by mail for consideration; provide
resume/bio with photos (if available) for filing for possible future assignments." SASE. Reports within
one month.
Music: Produces weekly Cable-TV series—"Inner-Tube Presents." Features actors, actresses, singers,
bands, models, dancers, rappers and whole independent production companies for Chicago Access
Network channels 19 and 21. Produces documentaries, industrials, commercials, musicals, talent showcases (new performers), news, plays, lectures, concerts, talk-show format with host, music-videos,
contests. Uses all types of programming; formats are color Super-VHS, broadcast quality ¾" and 1"
videotape, or film to video.
Tips: "An imaginative freelance producer is an invaluable asset to any production house, not only as
a constant source of new and fresh ideas, but also for pre- and post-production supportive elements,
contributing just as much as any staffer. Because of the nature of the business, we tend to be more
open to outside sources, especially when it is to our benefit to keep new blood flowing. Indies tend to
lean towards seeking unknowns, because their styles are usually, in our opinion, more unique."

JOEL DIAMOND ENTERTAINMENT, (formerly Silver Blue Productions), 5370 Vanalden Ave., Tar-
zana CA 91356. (818)345-2558. Executive Vice President: Scott Gootman. Contact: Joel Diamond.
Record producer and music publisher and manager. Deals with artists and songwriters. Receives 40
submissions/month. Fee derived from sales royalty.
How to Contact: Prefers cassette with 1-3 songs and lyric sheet. SASE.
Music: Dance, easy listening, country, R&B, rock, soul and top 40/pop. Produced "Love is the Rea-
son," by Engelbert Humperdinck on BMG Records; "Do You Love Me," by David Hasselhoff on
BMG Records; "Heaven In The Afternoon," by Lew Kyrton on Timeless; "I Am What I Am," by
Gloria Gaynor (single); "Where the Boys Are," by Lorna; "One Night In Bangkok," by Robey; and
"Love is the Reason" (by Cline/Wilson), recorded by E. Humperdinck and G. Gaynor on Critique
Records (A/C).

*COL. BUSTER DOSS PRESENTS, Box 13, Estill Springs TN 37330. (615)649-2577. Producer: Col.
Buster Doss. Record producer, record company (Stardust, Wizard) and music publisher (Buster Doss
Music/BMI). Estab. 1959. Deals with artists and songwriters. Produces 100 singles, 10 12" singles, 20
LPs and 10 CDs/year.

How to Contact: Submit demo tape by mail—unsolicited submissions are OK. Prefers cassette with 2 songs and lyric sheet. SASE. Reports in 2 weeks.
Music: Pop, country and gospel. Produced "Hard Times" (by Bennie Ray), "Where Were You" (by B. Doss) and "Shoebox of Memories" (by Hobson Smith), all on Stardust Records. Other artists include Johnny Buck, Tony Andrews, Cliff Archer, Linda Wunder and Sonny Carson.

DRAGON RECORDS, INC., 872 Morris Park Ave., Bronx NY 10462. (212)792-2198. Vice President: Mr. "G". Record producer and music publisher (Vin-Joy Publishing). Estab. 1954. Deals with artists and songwriters. Produces 16 singles, 20 LPs and 10 CDs/year. Receives 100 submissions/month. Fee derived from sales royalty.
How to Contact: "We accept material by recommendation only." SASE. Reports in 3 months.
Music: Easy listening, country, MOR and top 40/pop. Produced "Promise Me" (by J. Heath), recorded by Smokey Heath; "A Letter to D.J." (by V. Gagliano) and "One Prayer," (by Gagliano and Heath), both recorded by Joyce Heath (both singles). Other artists include Dickie Do and The Don'ts, The Go-Go's and Prometheus.

DUANE MUSIC, INC., 382 Clarence Ave., Sunnyvale CA 94086. (408)739-6133. President: Garrie Thompson. Record producer and music publisher. Deals with artists and songwriters. Fee derived from sales royalty.
How to Contact: Prefers cassette with 1-2 songs. SASE. Reports in 1 month.
Music: Blues, country, rock, soul and top 40/pop. Produced "Wichita," on Hush Records (country single); and "Syndicate of Sound," on Buddah Records (rock single).

E P PRODUCTIONS, 7455 Lorge Cr., Huntington Beach CA 92647. (714)842-5524. Business Manager: Billy Purnell. Record producer and record company (Venue Records, Branden Records). Estab. 1987. Deals with artists and songwriters. Produces 5-10 singles, 1-2 12″ singles, 2-5 LPs, 1-5 EPs and 1 CD/year. Receives 15-20 submissions/year. Fee derived from sales royalty when song or artist is recorded, outright fee from recording artist and outright fee from record company. (All terms are negotiable.) "Some artists come to us for production work only—not on our label. For this we charge a flat fee. We *never* charge songwriters unless for demos only."
How to Contact: Submit demo tape by mail—unsolicited submissions are OK. Prefers cassette with 1-3 songs and lyric sheet. SASE. Reports in 3-4 weeks.
Music: Mostly pop, R&B and contemporary Christian; also country and rock. Produced "Get Around" (by Paul Belsito), recorded by London Issue on Venue Records (alternative rock); "Who Are We," written and recorded by Erica Tingle on Brendon Records (contemporary Christian); and "Warrior," written and recorded by Reiko Takahashi on Victor Records (pop rock). Other artists include The Book, Bob Curren, Contempt, Nazarene Mohammed and Ledda Orece.
Tips: "Be professional—typed lyric sheets and cover letter are so much easier to work with along with a well-produced demo. Don't compromise on the quality of your songs or your package."

LEO J. EIFFERT, JR., Box 5412, Buena Park CA 90620. (213)721-7260. Owner: Leo J. Eiffert, Jr. Record producer, music publisher (Eb-Tide Music/BMI, Young Country Music/BMI) and record company (Plain Country). Estab. 1967. Deals with artists and songwriters. Produces 15-20 singles and 5 LPs/year. Fee derived from sales royalty.
How to Contact: Submit demo tape by mail—unsolicited submissions are OK. Prefers cassette with 2-3 songs, lyric and lead sheet. SASE. Reports in 3-4 weeks.
Music: Mostly country and gospel. Produced "Ride 'Em Wild" (by Bobby Lynn Compton and Joe Eiffert), recorded by Joe Eiffert and "You Want What?" (by Leo J. Eiffert, Jr.), recorded by Tecci Clarke; both on Plain Country Records. Other artists include Crawfish Band, Brandi Holland and David Busson.
Tips: "Just keep it real country."

*8TH STREET MUSIC, 204 E. 8th St., Dixon IL 61021. Producer: Rob McInnis. Record producer. Estab. 1988. Deals with artists and songwriters. Fee derived from sales royalty when song or artist is recorded.
How to Contact: Submit demo tape by mail. Unsolicited submissions are OK. Prefers cassette with 3-6 songs and lyric sheet. "No phone calls please. Just submit material and we will contact if interested." SASE. Reports is 2 months.
Music: Mostly interested in top 40/pop, dance and new rock; also R&B, country and teen pop. Produced "Black Roses," written and recorded by Michelle Goeking (alternative); "Legend of Leo Mongorin," written and recorded by Jim Henkel (folk); and "What's the Matter Elsie," (by Van/McInnis) recorded by Bob's Night Off (soundtrack/alternative, all on 8th St. Records. Other artists include Rita Van (top 40/dance), Jason Kermeen (country), Jeff Widdicombe (country), J&J (teen pop), Michelle Goeking (alternative) and Jim Henkel (folk).

Tips: "Just because we pass on the first tape, doesn't mean we will on the second or third. Keep at it!"

*ERIC ELWELL, Sync or Swim Productions, Box 7682, Overland Park KS 66207-0682. President: Eric Elwell. Record producer and production company. Estab. 1989. Deals with artists and songwriters. Produces 10 singles, 5 LPs, 10 EPs and 5 CDs/year. Fee derived from sales royalty when song or artist is recorded, outright fee from recording artist or outright fee from record company.
How to Contact: Submit demo tape by mail—unsolicited submissions are OK. Prefers cassette with lyric sheet. Reports in 1 month.
Music: Mostly rock, country and contemporary Christian; also jazz and acoustic. Produced "It's Not Over" (by McLain), recorded by Shooting Star on JRS Records (LP/CD); and "Moon Behind The Clouds" (by Clark), recorded by Paul Clark on Seed Records (CD). Other artists include The Front, The Rainmakers, Mitchell's Ritual, Foxy Foxy, Kill Whitey, Full Circle, University of Kansas and U&R Records..

GEOFFREY ENGLAND, 2810 McBain, Redondo Beach CA 90278. (213)371-5793. Contact: Geoffrey England. Record producer. Deals with artists and songwriters. Produces 10 singles/year. Fee derived from sales royalty and/or outright fee from record company.
How to Contact: Prefers cassette and lyric sheet. SASE. Reports in 2 weeks.
Music: Mainstream melodic rock. Produced "Steppenwolf Live" on Dunhill Records; and "If Licks Could Kill," by Virgin on Statue Records.

*ENGLISH VALLEY MUSIC, Suite 454, 101 Northcreek Blvd., Goodlettsville TN 37072. Owner/Producer: Jan Pulsford. Record producer (ASCAP) and record company (English Valley Music). Estab. 1988. Deals with artists and songwriters. Produces 6 LPs and 2 CDs/year. Fee derived from sales royalty when song or artist is recorded; outright fee from recording artist; or outright fee from record company.
How to Contact: Submit demo tape by mail—unsolicited submissions are OK. Prefers cassette with 3 songs. "Emphasize good quality songs, not good quality demos." SASE. Reports in 4 weeks.
Music: Mostly pop, dance and R&B; also rock, alternative and underground. Produced *Better Than Nothing* (by Craig Wiseman/J. Pulpeto), recorded by Tentu on EVM Records (LP); *Waiting for the Right Time*, written and recorded by Gilly Elkin on Mantabridge Records (LP); and *Identity*, written and recorded by Jan Pulsford on Atmosphere Records (CD). Other artists include The Few, Felicia Collins and Garth Hewitt.
Tips: "Work hard and leave your ego at the door. Be professional . . . our aim is to record music for music's sake but we all have to make a living. Drugs and booze went out in the 60s."

ESQUIRE INTERNATIONAL, Box 6032, Station B, Miami FL 33123. (305)547-1424. President: Jeb Stuart. Record producer, music publisher and management firm. Deals with artists and songwriters. Produces 6 singles and 2 LPs/year. Fee derived from sales royalty or independent leasing of masters and placing songs.
How to Contact: Submit demo tape—unsolicited submissions OK. Prefers cassette or disc with 2-4 songs and lead sheet. SASE. Reports in 1 month.
Music: Blues, church/religious, country, dance, gospel, jazz, rock, soul and top 40/pop. Produced "Hey Foxy Lady" (by J. Stuart), recorded by Shaka Zula A.R. (R&B); "All the Love I've Got" (by C. Jones), recorded by Jeb Stuart (jazz); and "Got To Be Crazy, Baby" (by J. Stuart), recorded by Jeb Stuart (R&B); all on Esquire Int'l Records. Other artists include Moments Notice, Cafidia and Night Live.
Tips: "When sending out material make sure it is well organized, put together as neatly as possible and it is of good sound quality."

*EXECUTIVE SOUND PRODUCTIONS, #220, 6922 Hollywood Blvd., Hollywood CA 90028. Professional Manager: Fredrick Irams. Record producer, music publisher (Kelins Craft Music Co./ASCAP), recording studio. Estab. 1984. Deals with artists and songwriters. Produces 6 singles, 6 12″ singles, 3 LPs and 3 CDs/year. Fee derived from sales royalty when song or artist is recorded.
How to Contact: Write first and obtain permission to submit. Prefers cassette with 2 songs and lyric sheet. Does not return unsolicited material. Reports in 1 month.
Music: Mostly R&B and pop; also rap. Produced "Just Call Him," recorded by Nicholas on A&M Records (gospel single); "Wake Up," recorded by Shelumer on Epic Records (R&B single); and "So Much Better With You" recorded by Philip Bailey on Columbia Records (R&B single), all written by Demetric Collins.
Tips: "Keep package simple and focused. Show clear understanding of your concepts."

SHANE FABER, 501 78th St., #3, Dept. SM, North Bergen NJ 07047. (201)854-6266. Contact: Shane Faber. Record producer, music publisher (Now & Then Music/BMI) and record company (Now & Then Records). Estab. 1980. Deals with artists and songwriters. Produced 6 singles and 2 LPs/year.

Fee derived from sales royalty or outright fee from recording artist or record company.
How to Contact: Submit demo tape by mail. Unsolicited submissions are OK. Prefers cassette with 4 songs and lyric sheet. SASE. Reports in 2 months.
Music: Mostly pop, dance and R&B; also rap and New Age. Produced "Partyline," recorded by 5th Platoon on SBK Records; "Turtle Power," recorded by Partners In Krime on SBK Records; and "U Shouldn't Wonder" (by Audrey Smith Bly). Other artists include Tenita Jordon (R&B), Blackhearts (rap) and T.T. (dance).

*FACTORY BEAT RECORDS, INC., 521 5th Ave., New York NY 10175. (212)757-3638. Producer/President: Rena L. Feeney. Record producer, music publisher (Ren-Maur Music/BMI) and record company (R&R and Rer-Rom Records). Produces 4-6 singles, 4 12″ singles and 2 LPs/year. Fee derived from sales royalty.
How to Contact: Prefers cassette with 2-4 songs and lyric sheet only. SASE. Reports in 3 weeks.
Music: R&B, rock, soul and top 40/pop. Produced *That's Hot* and *Same Language* (by B. Nichols), and *Rise Up* (by R. Feeney/B. Nichols), all recorded by "Rena" on F.B.R. Inc. Records (all LPs).
Tips: "Have a finished product, ready to master and press for commercial use."

R. L. FEENEY, 17th Fl., 521 5th Ave., New York NY 10175. (212)757-3638. Producer: R.L. Feeney. Record producer and record company (Factory Beat Records, Inc.). Estab. 1979. Deals with artists and songwriters. Produces 1-2 LPs/year. Fee derived from sales royalty when song or artist is recorded.
How to Contact: Submit demo tape by mail — unsolicited submissions are OK. Prefers cassette with 4 songs. SASE. Reports in 1 month.
Music: Mostly R&B, pop and contemporary. Produced "Once You Fall In Love" (R&B ballad single) and "Same Language," by Billy Nichols (R&B dance single), recorded by Rena on FBR, Inc. Records.

*VITO FERA PRODUCTIONS, 119 Peachwood Dr., Swedesboro NJ 08085. (609)467-1682. Producer: Vito Fera. Office Manager: Rhonda Fera. Record producer, music publisher (Network Sound Music Publishing/ASCAP and Fera Music Publishing/BMI). Estab. 1980. Produces 5 singles, 1 LP and 4 EPs/year. Fee derived from outright fee from artist or record company.
How to Contact: Submit demo tape — unsolicited submissions OK. Prefers cassette (or VHS cassette if available) with 3 songs maximum, lyric sheet and cover letter. "Carefully label cassette with name, address and phone number. Photo and bio helpful if seeking artist contract." SASE. Reports in 4 weeks.
Music: Mostly pop/dance, R&B/funk and medium rock; also ad/jingles and A/C. Produced "Heartbroken" (by Hilley/Barrett), recorded by Keith Hilley (rock ballad); "Real Man" (by K. Layfield), recorded by Lisa Damiani (pop ballad); and "Separate Lives" (by M. Lichtenfeld), recorded by Lichtenfeld/Stokking (country), all on S.P.I.N. Records. Other artists include Chill, Meeta Gajjar and Carmen Tomassetti.
Tips: "The look, the song, the desire are the attributes of a music career. You have got to love this business; eat, drink and sleep music. Be professional."

DON FERGUSON PRODUCTIONS, Box 461892, Garland TX 75046. (214)271-8098. Producer: Don Ferguson. Record producer (Sultan Music/BMI and Illustrious Sultan/ASCAP), record company (Puzzle Records). Estab. 1972. Deals with artists and songwriters. Produces 10-15 singles, 4-5 cassettes and 2-3 CDs/year. Receives 15-75 submissions/year. "Fees are negotiated."
How to Contact: Submit demo tape by mail — unsolicited submissions are OK. Prefers cassette with 3 songs and lyric sheet. "Include bio." SASE. Reports in 2 weeks.
Music: C&W, pop and MOR. Produced "Knock on Wood" (by S. Cropper, E. Floyd), recorded by Diane Elliott (C&W); "The Woman on Your Mind" (by L. Schonfeld), recorded by Lonny Jay (pop); and "Eight Days a Week" (by Lennon, McCartney), recorded by Mary Craig (C&W); all on Puzzle Records. Other artists include Heartland (band), Flashpoint (band), Charlie Shearer, Derek Hartis, Phil Rodgers and Jimmy Massey.

FESTIVAL STUDIOS, 2112 17th St., Kenner LA 70062. (504)469-4403. Engineer/Producer: Rick Naiser/Michael Borrello. Record producer, music publisher (Homefront Music/BMI), record company (Homefront Records) and recording studio (Festival Studios). Estab. 1988. Deals with artists and songwriters. Produces 12 singles, 6 12″ singles, 15 LPs, 10 EPs and 5 CDs/year. Fee derived from sales royalty or outright fee from reocrding artist or record company.
How to Contact: Submit demo tape by mail. Unsolicited submissions are OK. Prefers cassette, DAT or ½″ VHS or Beta videocassette with 4 songs. "Send any pictures, press clips, reviews and any promo material available." Reports in 1 month.
Music: Mostly rock, pop and New Age; also rap, R&B and other. Produced *In It To Win It* (by Def Boyz), on Big T Records (rap LP); *EHG* (by EHG), on Intellectual Convulsion Records (sludge metal LP); and *Red Headed Step Children of Rock* (by Force of Habit), on Riffish Records (pop LP); all

Close-up

Aaron Tippin
Singer/Songwriter
Nashville, Tennessee

Country singer/songwriter Aaron Tippin says successful songwriters should be like submarines, with their sonar turned on and periscopes up, listening to people's conversations for song ideas.

"I'm sitting here right now just thinking that you're going to say something that's going to make a great song," he tells this writer, "and I'm going to have to get out of here to write it down.

"I'm never totally into a conversation," he continues. "Most of the time, I can't remember people's names, because once they say 'Hi, I'm so-and-so,' I start listening to what they say, because they are going to say something. People always talk in cliches. So many times that makes a great country song."

Tippin, an artist on the RCA label, says his interest in country music dates back to a Christmas in the early 70s when he still lived near Travelers Rest, South Carolina. "One of my buddies got a portable 8-track tape player," he recalls, "but we didn't have any tapes to play in it, except his daddy's tape of Hank Williams Sr.'s greatest hits. At first, we were making sport of it—whooping and hollering. But later, I took that tape home and couldn't stop playing it. I wore it out."

The influence of Hank Williams Sr. still shows in Tippin's bluesy—sometimes howling—singing style. His drawl is as Southern as the tattoo on his right arm of a palmetto, South Carolina's state tree. He's been criticized for sounding "too country," but his unique sound has helped him carve his niche in Nashville.

Tippin has also relied on his songwriting ability to make it in the business. He started making connections in music publishing after he and a co-writer had a Christmas song, "Happy Birthday, Jesus," published by Nashville's Charlie Monk. Tippin wrote the song while driving a front-end loader.

Monk encouraged Tippin to leave South Carolina and move to Nashville about five years ago to try his hand at songwriting. Tippin says he had dabbled in songwriting and performing with small country and bluegrass bands before the move, but with little success.

"I had put out records on an independent label," he says. "Five or six times a year, we would pile into a car and we'd all go to Nashville, and we would try to get people to listen to our songs. I had written songs and boy, I thought they were great. They weren't. But it was a learning process."

With Monk's help, Tippin eventually landed a job as a staff writer at Acuff-Rose Publishers. He sang on his own demos, which enabled him to get his unique sound in front of record executives. RCA liked his music and released his first LP, *You've Got to Stand for Something*, in 1991.

While at Acuff-Rose, Tippin learned that the best country songs deal with emotion. As he explains, "Emotions are the most powerful part of country songs. No matter what that emotion is; sadness, happiness. In the case of 'You've Got to Stand for Something,' patriotism or just being proud of yourself. Anything that can touch your emotions; that's the perfect country song."

On his debut album, Tippin wrote or co-wrote every song. He likes to collaborate, he says, because he's found two minds are better than one. What's more, a writing partner can bring a song to its full potential.

While in Nashville, Tippin also learned that a truly great song can be heard on a demo without spending too much money on studio time. As he advises, "The best thing is to go into the studio with a decent microphone so that the words can be heard. Have someone play guitar, or play guitar yourself, and just get the vocal and the rhythm of the song out. The biggest mistake that's ever made is people try to go in and mix a record. When you're doing a demo, the vocal should be the most outstanding thing, clear of anything, because when you're trying to pitch a song, you've got to get that song heard first. All the hoopla and great playing in the world won't make a great song."

Tippin keeps a journal which contains a list of ideas for future songs. "Of course, there's some (ideas) that have been in there five or six years," he says, "and I keep going over them, saying 'What made me write this down?' But one day the thought that said 'Whew, that's good!' will come back to me."

Although Tippin is only in his early 30s, he has lived through some rough times. For example, he knows what driving a truck, being a "starving" musician and working the "graveyard shift" feel like. And he knows too well how divorce feels and the pain of the death of a teenage brother. These experiences, he admits, give him ideas for writing songs. "Everything that has happened makes me what I am on paper, in the songs I write," he says. "Usually, putting my life down in there illustrates the majority of country fans' (lives)."

Before he signed a record deal, Tippin says he definitely paid his dues as an aspiring Nashville songwriter. Says Tippin: "I lived in a low-rent apartment complex, drove my beat-up old car. I could afford to eat dried beans that I'd cook in a crock pot. And when macaroni was on sale I could have that. And I learned to love the life of being in the music business in those days. So anything above that is gravy.

"And if it all falls to pieces tomorrow and I go back to writing songs, so what? I had fun and I'm thankful for the days I've had. I want to keep writing, I want to keep singing. I want to keep working as hard as I can to do better. But you've got to realize that you're in love with the music business. And I've said it before, and I'll say it again; if I have to sleep under a bridge in Nashville, I'm going to be downtown writing songs when the sun shines because it's what I love to do. And the rest of it . . . it isn't that important."

— Tyler Cox

❝When you're doing a demo, the vocal should be the most outstanding thing, clear of anything, because when you're trying to pitch a song, you've got to get that song heard first. All the hoopla and great playing in the world won't make a great song.❞

—Aaron Tippin

recorded by Festival. Other artists include Ice Mike, Ice Nine, RSBR, Common Knowledge and Mooncrikits.

Tips: "Concentrate on songwriting as a craft—don't spend time or money on embellishing demos. Raw demos leave room for the producer's creative input. Record demos quickly and move on to the next project."

FIRST TIME MANAGEMENT & PRODUCTION CO., Sovereign House, 12 Trewartha Rd., Praa Sands, Penzance, Cornwall TR20 9ST **England**. Phone: (0736)762826. FAX: (0736)763328. Managing Director: Roderick G. Jones. Record producer, music publisher (First Time Music Publishing U.K. Ltd. MCPS/PRS), record company (First Time, Mohock Records, Rainy Day Records and Pure Gold Records), licensed and subsidiary labels and management firm (First Time Management & Production Co.), commercial music library. Estab. 1986. Deals with artists and songwriters. Produces 5-10 singles and 5 LPs/year. EPs and CDs subject to requirements. Fee derived from sales royalty.
How to Contact: Prefers cassette with unlimited number of songs and lyric or lead sheets. SAE and IRC. Reports in 10 weeks.
Music: Mostly country/folk, pop/top 40, country with an Irish/Scottish crossover, rock, soul, jazz funk, fusion, dance and reggae. Produced "Yours Forever" (by Rod Jones/Colin Eade), recorded by Colin Eade on Panama Music Productions (instrumental); "Shades of Blue" (by Laurie Thompson), recorded by Laurie Thompson on Panama Music Productions (instrumental theme music); and "Baristoned" (by Simon Hipps), recorded by Simon Hipps on Panama Music Productions (jazz instrumental). Other artists include Rod Jones and Willow.

FOX FARM RECORDING, 2731 Saundersville Ferry Rd., Mt. Juliet TN 37122. (615)754-2444. President: Kent Fox. Record producer (Mercantile Productions) and music publisher (Mercantile Music/BMI and Blueford Music/ASCAP). Estab. 1970. Deals with artists and songwriters. Produces 20 singles/year. Fee derived from outright fee from recording artists. Charges in advance for studio time.
How to Contact: Submit demo tape by mail—unsolicited submissions are OK. Prefers cassette (or VHS videocassette if available). SASE. Reports in 3 months.
Music: Country, bluegrass, gospel and contemporary Christian.

BOB SCOTT FRICK, 404 Bluegrass Ave., Madison TN 37115. (615)865-6380. Contact: Bob Scott Frick. Record producer and music publisher (R.E.F.). Estab. 1958. Deals with artists and songwriters only. Produces 12 singles, 30 12″ singles and 30 LPs.
How to Contact: Submit demo tape by mail—unsolicited submissions are OK. Write first and obtain permission to submit.
Music: Produced "I Found Jesus in Nashville," recorded by Bob Scott Frick; "Love Divine," recorded by Backwoods; and "A Tribute," recorded by Visionheirs on R.E.F. (gospel). Other artists include Larry Ahlborn, Bob Myers Family, David Barton, The Mattingleys and Jim Pommert.

THE FRICON ENTERTAINMENT CO., INC., 1048 S. Ogden Dr., Los Angeles CA 90019. (213)931-7323. Attention: Publishing Department. Music publisher (Fricon Music Co./BMI, Fricon Music Co./ASCAP) and library material. Estab. 1981. Deals with songwriters only. Fee derived from sales royalty.
How to Contact: Write first and obtain permission to submit. Prefers cassette with 1 song and lyric and lead sheet. SASE. Reports in 8 weeks.
Music: Mostly TV/film, R&B and rock; also pop, country and gospel.
Tips: "Ask for permission, submit one song with typed lyrics and be patient."

G FINE, Box 180, Cooper Station, New York NY 10276. (212)995-1608. Vice President: Lyvio G. Record producer, music publisher (Rap Alliance, Inc.) and record company (G Fine). Estab. 1986. Fee derived from sales royalty or outright fee from recording artist or record company.
How to Contact: Submit demo tape by mail. Unsolicited submissions are OK. Prefers cassette with 3 or more songs. "Send photo, if possible." SASE. Reports in 2 months.
Music: "Undercore" alternative rock, dance, rap, R&B. Produced "Ring the Alarm" (by Fu-Schnikens/Lyviog), recorded by Fu-Schnikens on Jive Records (rap/dance).

JACK GALE, Box 630755, Miami FL 33163. (305)935-4880. Contact: Jack Gale. Record producer, music publisher (Cowabonga Music/ASCAP) and record company (Playback Records). Estab. 1983. Deals with artists and songwriters. Produces 48 singles, 10 LPs and 10 CDs/year. Fee derived from sales royalty.
How to Contact: Submit demo tape by mail. Unsolicited submissions are OK. Prefers cassette (or VHS videocassette if available) with 2 songs and lyric sheets. SASE. Reports in 2 weeks.
Music: Mostly contemporary country and country crossover. Produced "Somewhere Beyond the Pain" (by Ron Simmons), recorded by Crystal Gayle and Charlie Louvin; "Guess Things Happen That Way" (by Jack Clements), recorded by Johnny Cash and Tommy Cash; and "Here's To The Cowboys" (by

David Brackin), recorded by Jeannie C. Riley; all on Playback Records (country). Other artists include Melba Montgomery, Jimmy C. Newman, Michele Bishop, Sammi Smith, Ernie Ashworth, Hank Sasaki, Sylvie, Whiskey Creek and Angele Christie.
Tips: "Submit only your best—be honest—understand that this is a business, not a hobby."

GEORGE D. PRODUCTIONS, INC., #3, 19300 SW 106 Ave., Miami FL 33157. (305)573-5767. Director/Producer: George D. Record producer, music publisher (BMI) and demo label (Custom Sounds). Estab. 1990. Deals with artists and songwriters. Fee derived from sales royalty when song or artist is recorded, outright fee from recording artist or outright fee from record company.
How to Contact: Submit demo tape by mail—unsolicited submissions are OK. Prefers cassette with 2 songs and lyric sheet. SASE. Reports in 3 weeks.
Music: Mostly R&B, rap and dance; also jazz, reggae and pop. Produced "It's About Time," (by George D.), recorded by Mellow J (rap); "The Other Lover Boy," (by Angela Bostic), recorded by Angie B. (dance/pop); and "D's Theme," written and recorded by George D. (instrumental/jazz), all on Amran Records. Other artists include Angel and US1.
Tips: "Be honest and professional within yourself before you seek honesty in any other company."

*GO JO PRODUCTION, 195 S. 26th St., San Jose CA 95116. (408)286-9840. Owner: G.J. O'Neal. Estab. 1980. Deals with artists and songwriters. Fee derived from outright fee from recording artist or record company. Charges for arranging.
How to Contact: Submit demo tape by mail—unsolicited submissions are OK. Prefers cassette. SASE. Reports in 2-3 weeks.
Music: Mostly country, gospel, Mexican; also rock, pop and urban contemporary. Produced "When You Have The Time For Me" (by R. Lee/C. Patton/Y. Maxwell), recorded by Janice Edwards on Respond International Records (urban contemporary); *Helen Reyes* (by Helen Reyes and others), recorded by Helen Reyes (traditional Mexican and country); and *New American Music* (by Jeannine O'Neal and others), recorded by Jeannine O'Neal (country). Other artists include Jaque Lynn and Sister Suffragette.

*JAY GOLD-TURBO RECORDS, Box 409, East Meadow NY 11554. (516)486-8699. President: Jay Gold. Record producer, music publisher (Jay Gold Music/BMI) and record company (Turbo). Estab. 1981. Deals with artists and songwriters. Produces 5 singles and 2 12″ singles/year. Fee derived from sales royalty or outright fee from recording artist or record company.
How to Contact: Submit demo tape by mail—unsolicited submissions are OK. Prefers cassette with 3 songs and lyric sheet. Reports in 5 weeks.
Music: Mostly pop and rock. Produced "All the Wrong Reasons" (pop 12″); "Better Love" (pop 12″); and "Radio Riot" (rock single); all written and recorded by Jay Gold on Turbo Records.
Tips: "Review your lyrics and be open to changes."

GRAPEVINE STUDIOS, Box 8324, Gadsden AL 35902. (205)442-3330. Owner: Chris Mahy. Recording studio. Estab. 1988. Deals with artists and songwriters. Produces 20 LPs and 10 CDs/year. Fee derived from outright fee from recording artists or outright fee from record company. "Charges artists 10% in advance to book studio time."
How to Contact: Write or call first and obtain permission to submit. Prefers cassette with several songs and lead sheet. SASE. Reports in 2 months.
Music: Mostly gospel, pop and jazz; also country and rock. Produced *Get Ready* (by Penny Halloway) and *Welcome To The Human Race* (by Bob McLeod), recorded by Glory Bound Trio on Independent Records (LP).

GRASS RECORDING AND SOUND, 800 Arbor Place, Del Rey Oaks CA 93940. (408)394-1065. Owner: Michael Grass. Record producer, record company (Blackend Earth, Rabid Records) and recording studio (Live Sound Service). Estab. 1989. Deals with artists and songwriters. Produces 2 singles, 1 LP and 4 EPs/year. Fee derived from sales royalty when song or artists is recorded and outright fee from recording artist. "We sometimes require 50% cash deposit for recording only."
How to Contact: Submit demo tape by mail—unsolicited submissions are OK. Prefers cassette (or VHS videocassette if available) with 1-5 songs and lyric sheet. "Don't be overly persistent. I will listen to *all* tapes, and if I like you, I'll call you." SASE. Reports in 6 weeks.
Music: Mostly thrash metal, mainstream metal and hard rock; also punk, rap and fusion. Produced "Resurrection" (by D. Guyot), recorded by Speed Demon (metal); "What You're Worth" (by S. Patterson), recorded by Battle Cry (hard rock); and "Murder Sex Racism Be" (by M. Bilac), recorded by Cremation (metal), all on Blackened Earth. Other artists include Hydra, Morbadeth and Deus Ex Machine.
Tips: "Too many posers! No Milli Vanilli! Have your material well rehearsed, don't waste time and energy rehearsing in the studio."

*GREEN DREAM PRODUCTIONS, P.O. Box 872, West Covina CA 91790. Owner: Kelly D. Lammers. Record producer and music publisher (Passing Parade Music/ASCAP). Estab. 1989. Deals with artists and songwriters. Produces 3-6 singles and 24 LP's/year. Fee derived from sales royalty when song or artist is recorded or outright fee from record company.

How to Contact: Submit demo tape—unsolicited submissions are OK. Prefers cassette with 1-3 songs and lyric sheet. SASE. Reports in 6 weeks.

Music: Mostly children's, country and pop; also holiday, and New Age. Produced "Let Me Be a Kid" (by K.D. Lammers), recorded by Neighborhood Kids; and "Punkline" (by K.D. Lammers), recorded by The Surfaris, both on Koinkidink Records.

Tips: When writing for children, keep the message positive and uplifting. When writing for adults, keep the lyrics either fun or sophisticated, but please not corny, especially in country. The children's market has shifted from a subsidiary market to a strong market of its own and needs to be fed. When writing, keep our children in mind."

*GUESS WHO?? PRODUCTIONS, 140-23 Einstein Loop North, Bronx NY 10475-4973. (212)379-1831. Director: David Pellot. Record producer. Estab. 1988. Deals with artists and songwriters. Produces 10-15 singles/year. Fee derived from sales royalty or outright fee from recording artist or record company.

How to Contact: Submit demo tape by mail—unsolicited submissions are OK. Prefers cassette and lyric sheet. SASE. Reports in 1 week.

Music: Mostly dance, rap and top 40; also R&B, house/underground and Latin/jazz.

MARK HANNAH PRODUCTIONS, Suite 250, 1075 N.W. Murray Rd., Portland OR 97229. (503)642-4201. Owner: Mark Hannah. Record producer, music publisher (Mark Hannah Music Group/BMI), record company (Radioactive Records) and Mark Hannah Management/personal manager. Estab. 1985. Deals with artists and songwriters. Produces 5-10 singles, 1-3 LPs and 1-3 EPs/year. Fee derived from sales royalty.

How to Contact: Write first and obtain permission to submit. Prefers cassette or 15 ips reel-to-reel with 1-3 songs and lyric or lead sheets. SASE. Reports in 1 month.

Music: Mostly rock, pop and country; also fusion, New Age and jazz. Produced *Modern Day Man*, written and recorded by M. Hannah (hard rock LP); "Crazy Fool," written and recorded by M. Harrop (pop ballad single); "Billy," written and recorded by Syndi Helms (country single); "You Stole My Heart Away," written and recorded by P. Witt (pop-rock single); "Forced to Have Sex with an Alien," written and recorded by M. Harrop (comedy single); and *Desert Moon*, written and recorded by M. Hannah (New Age LP); all on Radioactive Records. Other artists include Ray Overton, Rex E. Plew and Messenger (rock band).

*HAPPY DAYS MUSIC/JEREMY MCCLAIN, Box 852, Beverly Hills CA 90213. (818)769-2842. President: Jeremy McClain. Record producer and music publisher. Voting member of NARAS. Deals with artists and songwriters. Produces 12 singles, 1-2 12" singles and 3 LPs/year. Fee derived from sales royalty or outright fee from record company.

How to Contact: Submit demo tape—unsolicited submissions are OK. Prefers cassette (or VHS videocassette) and lyric or lead sheet. SASE. Reports in 4-6 weeks.

Music: Mostly rock, top 40, and country; also contemporary gospel. Produced "Devil With The Blue Dress," by Pratt & McClain/Warner Brothers Records (rock single); and "The Way Things Used To Be," by Tom Gillan/Brother Love Records (country single). "Worked with Michael Bolton. In addition, we have direct publishing access to Christopher Cross, Donna Summer, Debbie Boone, Amy Grant and Michael Omartian."

HARD HAT PRODUCTIONS, 519 N. Halifax Ave., Daytona Beach FL 32118-4017. (904)252-0381. President/Producer: Bobby Lee Cude. Record producer, music publisher (Cude & Pickens Publishing) and record company (Hard Hat). Estab. 1978. Works with artists only. Fee derived from contract. Produces 12 singles and 4 LPs/year.

How to Contact: Produces "only in-house material." Write first and obtain permission to submit. Prefers cassette with 4 songs and lyric sheet "from performing artists only."

Music: Mostly pop, country and easy listening; also MOR, top 40/pop and Broadway show music. Produced "V-A-C-A-T-I-O-N" (by Cude/Pickens), recorded by The Hard Hatters (pop single); "Just a Piece of Paper" and "Worried Worried Men" (by Cude/Pickens), recorded by the Blue Bandana Country Band (country singles); all on Hard Hat Records. Also, "Blow Blow Stereo," "Don't Stop,"

"Hootchie Cootch Girl" and "There Ain't No Beer in Heaven That's Why I Drink It Here," all by Caz Allen on Hard Hat Records.

STEPHEN A. HART/HART PRODUCTIONS, 1690 Creekview Cir., Petaluma CA 94954. (707)762-2521. Executive Producer: Stephen A. Hart. Record producer. Estab. 1975. Deals with artists and songwriters. Produces 8 LPs and 8 CDs/year. Fee derived from outright fee from recording artist or record company.
How to Contact: Submit demo by mail—unsolicited submissions are OK. Prefers cassette with 3 songs and lyric sheet. SASE. Reports in 3 months.
Music: Mostly pop, rock and instrumental. Produced "10-9-91," written and recorded by Vasco Rossi (rock); and *Guernica* (by Vasco), recorded by Guernica (rock), both on FMI Records.
Tips: "Demo tape should have three songs maximum—big production not necessary."

*HAWORTH PRODUCTIONS, Box 97, Climax Springs MO 65324. (314)345-1077. President/Producer: Dann E. Haworth. Record producer and music publisher (Southern Most Publishing/BMI). Estab. 1985. Deals with artists and songwriters. Produces 5 singles, 3 12″ singles, 10 LPs, 5 EPs and 10 CDs/year. Fee derived from sales royalty or outright fee from recording artist or record company.
How to Contact: Submit demo tape by mail—unsolicited submissions are OK. Prefers cassette or 7½ ips reel-to-reel with 3 songs and lyric or lead sheets. SASE. Reports in 6-8 weeks.
Music: Mostly rock, country and gospel; also jazz, R&B and New Age. Produced *Christmas Joy* (by Esther Kreak) on Serene Sounds Records (CD). Other artists include The Hollowmen, Jordan Border, Jim Wilson, Tracy Creech and Tony Glise.
Tips: "Keep it simple and from the heart."

HEARING EAR, 730 S. Harvey, Oak Park IL 60304. (708)386-7355. Owner: Mal Davis. Record engineer and producer. Estab. 1970. Deals with artists and songwriters. Engineers and/or produces 6 LPs and 4 CDs/year. Receives 6 submissions/month. Fee derived from sales royalty when song or artist is recorded, outright fee from recording artist or outright fee from record company.
How to Contact: Write first and obtain permission to submit. Prefers cassette (or VHS videocassette if available) with up to 6 songs and lyric or lead sheets. Does not return unsolicited material.
Music: Mostly pop, gospel and rock; also R&B, rap and metal. Engineered *Master & the Musician*, by Phil Keaggy; *Awaiting Your Reply*, by Resurrection Band; and *House of Peace*, recorded by Jim Croegaert (MOR/worship).

*HEART CONSORT MUSIC, 410 1st St. W., Mt. Vernon IA 52314. (319)895-8557. Manager: Catherine Lawson. Record producer, record company, music publisher. "We are a single in-house operation." Estab. 1980. Deals with artists and songwriters. Produces 2-3 CDs/year. Fee derived from sales royalty or outright fee from recording artist or record company.
How to Contact: Submit demo tape by mail—unsolicited submissions are OK. Prefers cassette (or VHS videocassette if available) with 3 songs and 3 lyric sheets. We do not return unsolicited material. Reports in 3 weeks.
Music: Mostly jazz, New Age and contemporary. Produced "Across the Borders," "Panama," "Persio" (by James Kennedy), all recorded by John Reasoner on Heart Consort Music (jazz CDs).
Tips: "We are interested in original jazz/New Age artists with quality demos and original ideas."

*NEIL HENDERSON PRODUCTIONS, Suite 49, 4740 N. Mesa, El Paso TX 79912. (915)544-4618. Owner/Producer: Neil Henderson. Record producer and music publisher (Multibravo Music-ASCAP). Estab. 1990. Deals with artists and songwriters. Produces 3-4 singles, 10-12 LPs, 4-5 EPs and 10-12 CDs/year. Fee derived from sales royalty when song or artist is recorded or outright fee from recording artist or record company.
How to Contact: Call first and obtain permission to submit. Prefers cassette (or VHS videocassette if available) with 3-5 songs and lyric sheet or lead sheet. "Photos are helpful, if available. 8×10s preferred, but anything is OK." Does not return unsolicited material. Reports in 3-4 weeks.
Music: Mostly rock or metal, jazz and top 40; also country, Hispanic and contemporary Christian. Produced *Loco* (by Ritchie Carmona), recorded by Amanecer on Quality Records (Hispanic LP); *Purgatory*, written and recorded by Mark Moore on Voyager (new age LP); and *Little Champs* (by

Jimmy Leeah), recorded by 2-B on Independent Records (jazz LP). Other artists include Billy Townes (jazz), Elise (top 40-dance), Tangent (jazz) and Selah (contemporary Christian).
Tips: "Have a concept of where you want your band to go. Be open to suggestions that may help your band or song to reach its full potential. Even though the marriage of technology and music is on the rise, there seems to be an increasing focus on the quality of the performance—keep this in mind while in the studio."

HERITAGE MUSIC, #311, 41 Antrim Cr., Scarborough ON M1P4T1 **Canada.** (416)292-4724. President: Jack Boswell. Record producer and record company (Condor-Oak). Estab. 1967. Deals with artists and songwriters. Produces 10-15 LPs/year. Fee derived from sales royalty.
How to Contact: Submit demo tape by mail—unsolicited submissions are OK. Prefers cassette with 3-4 songs and lyric sheet. SASE. Reports in 4-5 weeks.
Music: Mostly country, country gospel and instrumental. Produced "Bent River Boogie," written and recorded by Smiley Bates; "Lotta Livin," written and recorded by Ed Forrest; and "Last of Reasons" (by Roy Payne and Ed Keough), recorded by Roy Payne, all on Condor Records.

*HIT AND RUN STUDIOS INC., 18704 Muncaster Rd., Rockville MD 20855. (301)948-6715. Owner/ Producer: Steve Carr. Record producer and recording studio. Deals with artists and songwriters. Produces 12 singles, 2 12" singles, 8 LPs, 4 EPs and 10 CDs/year. Receives 75 submissions/year. Fee derived from outright fee from songwriter/artist and/or record company.
How to Contact: Call or write first and obtain permission to submit. Prefers cassette. Does not return unsolicited material. "Write your name and phone number on the cassette shell. I'll call you back if I can do anything with your material."
Music: Mostly rock, rockabilly and funk; also reggae, country and blues. Produced *Classic Rock*, *R&B* and *Country*, all written and recorded by various artists on Time Warner Records. Other artists include Billy Kemp and The Paradise Rocker, Cashmere and Internal Void.

HOBAR PRODUCTION, 27 Newton Pl., Irvinston NJ 07111. (201)375-6633. President: Randall Burney. Record producer, record company (Independent). Estab. 1987. Deals with artists and songwriters. Produces 4 singles, 6 12" singles and 2 LPs/year. Fee derived from outright fee from record company.
How to Contact: Submit demo tape by mail—unsolicited submissions are OK. Prefers cassette (or VHS videocassette if available) with 4 songs and lyric or lead sheets. SASE. Reports in 2 weeks.
Music: Mostly R&B, pop and gospel; also country and rap. Produced "Hold Me Tight" (by Bill Irving), recorded by Pam Robertson (R&B); "Watching You" (R&B) and "Get up Everybody" (by Robert Moss) (Hiphouse), both recorded by Inseperable all on Atlantic East/West.

HOGAR MUSICAL PRODUCTIONS, 4225 Palm St., Baton Rouge LA 70808. (504)383-7885. President: Barrie Edgar. Record producer and music publisher (Silverfoot). Deals with artists and songwriters. Produces 0-5 singles and 0-2 LPs/year. Receives 75 submissions/year. Fee derived from outright fee from record company.
How to Contact: Submit demo tape—unsolicited submissions are OK. Prefers cassette with maximum 4 songs and lyric sheet. SASE. Reports in 1-5 months.
Music: Mostly rock, blues ("not soul"), country and pop. Produced "Louisiana's Basin Child," by Top Secret (rock single, Gulfstream Records).
Tips: "Don't give up—we've listened to five submissions over a four year period before we found something we liked by that writer."

HORIZON RECORDING STUDIO, Rte. 1, Box 306, Seguin TX 78155. (512)372-2923. Owner/Producer: H.M. Byron. Record producer, music publisher (Route One Music/BMI) and record company (Route One Records, Starmaker Records). Estab. 1988. Deals with artists and songwriters. Produces 25-30 singles and 5-7 LPs/year. Fee derived from sales royalty when song or artist is recorded or outright fee from recording artist.
How to Contact: Submit demo tape—unsolicited submissions are OK. Prefers cassette (or VHS videocassette if available) with a maximum of 5 songs and lyric sheet. SASE. Reports in 3 weeks.
Music: Mostly country, gospel and pop. Produced "The Last Song" (by B. Dees, R. Orbison), recorded by Mike Lord; "When We See Old Glory Fly," written and recorded by Stan Crawford (patriotic); and "Untitled," written and recorded by Brett Marshall (gospel), all on BSW Records. Other artists include Stan Crawford and Bobby O'Neal.
Tips: "Before spending megabucks to demo a song, submit it for appraisal. Piano or guitar and voice are all that is necessary."

HORRIGAN PRODUCTIONS, Box 41243, Los Angeles CA 90041. (213)256-0215. President/Owner: Tim Horrigan. Record producer and music publisher (Buck Young Music/BMI). Estab. 1982. Deals with artists and songwriters. Produces 5-10 singles, 3-5 LPs, 3-5 EPs and 3-5 CDs/year. Receives 100

submissions/year. Fee derived from sales royalty or outright fee from recording artist or record company. "We do some work on spec but the majority of the time we work on a work-for-hire basis."
How to Contact: Submit demo tape by mail. Unsolicited submissions are OK. Prefers cassette (or VHS videocassette if available) with 1-5 songs and lyric sheets. "Please do not call first; just let your music do the talking." "No tapes returned. Will reply if interested."
Music: Mostly R&B, pop and rock; also country. Produced "Rubber Room" (by Porter Wagoner), recorded by Johnny Legend on Dionysus Records (rock); "Just For Awhile," recorded by Jimmy Roland on SGP Records (R&B); and "Golden Lady" (by Stevie Wonder), recorded by Mike Quick on SGP Records (R&B). Other artists include Keo (world beat/pop).
Tips: "Write from the heart with eyes on the charts."

I.Y.F. PRODUCTIONS, 4B, 500½ E. 84th St., New York NY 10028. (212)861-8745. A&R: Steven Bentzel. Record producer, music publisher (Mia Mind Music/ASCAP) and record company (Mixedfield Records). Estab. 1990. Deals with artists and songwriters. Produced 30 singles, 8 12" singles, 6 LPs and 8 CDs/year. Fee derived from sales royalty.
How to Contact: Submit demo tape by mail. Unsolicited submissions are OK. Prefers cassette (or VHS videocassette if available) with 3 songs. SASE. Reports in 6 weeks.
Music: Mostly rap, house, hip hop; also dance, top 40 and AOR. Produced "Boyfriend," written and recorded by Baby Oil on Profile/CBS Records (rap, single); "I've Fallen," written and recorded by Baby Oil on Profile/CBS Records (house); and "Get Down" (by Bentzel/Torio), recorded by Madonna on Replay Records (hip house). Other artists include P.O.A., Electric Sun, Clark After Dark, Papa Haha, Q.O.S. and Datman.
Tips: "Submit demos on DAT cassettes for best sound quality."

*INDEPENDENT AUDIO SERVICES, 4131-M Conway Ave., Charlotte NC 28209-2641. (704)523-4071. Producer-Engineer: Stephen Fitzstephens. Record producer and production and engineering service. Estab. 1977. Deals with artists and songwriters. Fee derived from hourly rate.
How to Contact: Write or call first to arrange personal interview. Prefers cassette, 15 or 7.5 ips reel-to-reel (or VHS or U-matic videocassette if available) with 3 songs and lyric sheets. "Save your money and write or call first. I don't need much material to start off project." SASE. Reports in 3 weeks.
Music: Produced *In the Key of Z* (by Lance Tait), on Tait Records (LP demo folk/rock); and "Traditional Tunes" (by Bill Mulligan), on Prime Records (folk rock single); all recorded by Fitz. Other artists include Steven Sacher, Steven Farzan and Memphis Pilgrims.
Tips: "Write or call to book a presentation (performance or listening interview) at a studio of mutual choice. No snyths, drum synths or sequencers."

*INNERSOUNDS PRODUCTIONS, 193 LaMartine St., Boston MA 02130. (617)524-3597. Writer/Producer: Jerry Smith, Jr. Record producer and commercial music firm. Estab. 1986. Deals with artists and songwriters. Produces 10-15 singles, 10 LP's and 1-2 CD's/year. Paid by outright fee from recording artist.
How to Contact: Write Or call first and obtain permission to submit. Prefers cassette with 1-4 songs and lyric sheet. "Make sure tape is cued and labeled." SASE. Reports in 4-5 weeks.
Music: Mostly pop, R&B and rock; also rap, country and New Age. Produced "Hello Paradise" (by Cheryl Mason), recorded by Judy Collins for ABC's *One Life to Live*; *With Every Beat* (by Smith/McManus), recorded by Oslo on Viking Records (CD); and "Different Tongues," written and recorded by Amy Beeton on Flammy Pie Records. Other artists include Fred Curry and Greg French.
Tips: "Be creative . . . I hear too many 'sound-alikes' today. MIDI is a very big market of the future. A computer is necessary tool for today's writers."

INSPIRE PRODUCTIONS, INC., Suite 101, 302 E. Pettigrew St., Durham NC 27701. (919)688-8563. President: Willie Hill. Record producer (BMI) and record company (Joy Records). Estab. 1988. Deals with artists and songwriters. Produces 10 singles, 1 12" single, 1 LP and 1 CD/year. Fee derived from sales royalty when song or artist is recorded.
How to Contact: Submit demo tape by mail—unsolicited submissions are OK. Prefers cassette with 4 songs and lyric sheet. Include bio and picture. Reports in 2 weeks.
Music: R&B, gospel and pop. Produced "Step By Step" (by Walter Hill), recorded by Inspire on Joy Records (R&B LP/CD).
Tips: "Do your homework."

INTRIGUE PRODUCTION, Suite 206, 6245 Bristol Parkway, Culver CA 90230. (213)417-3084, ext. 206. Producer: Larry McGee. Record producer and record company (Intrigue Productions). Estab. 1986. Deals with artists and songwriters. Produces 6 singles, 3 12" singles, 1 LP, 4 EPs and 2 CDs/year. Fee derived from sales royalty.

How to Contact: Submit demo tape by mail—unsolicited submissions are OK. Prefers cassette or reel-to-reel (or VHS videocassette if available) with 1-4 songs and lyric sheets. "Please put your strongest performance upfront. Select material based on other person's opinions." SASE. Reports in 2 months.

Music: Mostly R&B, pop, rap and rock; also dance and A/C. Produced "We're No. 1" (by Liz Davis), recorded by Saxon Sisters on Boogie Band Records (pop 12″); "Captain Freedom" and "Voices" (by Kenny Simms), recorded by Shena Kriss on Mega Star Records (R&B single and EP); and "Space Lady," written and recorded by Bill Sawyer on Dollar Bill Records (soul). Other artists include Star Flower and En-Tux.

Tips: "Decide which marketplace you would be most competitive in. Then create a commercial concept for you or your group."

*DAVID IVORY PRODUCTIONS, 212 N. 12th St., Philadelphia PA 19107. (215)948-3448. Manager: Vince Kershner. Record producer. Estab. 1986. Deals with artists only. Produces 3 singles, 2 12″ singles, 5 LPs and 4 CDs/year. Fee derived from "varying proportions of outright fee and royalties."

How to Contact: Submit demo tape—unsolicited submissions are OK. Prefers cassette with 3 songs. Does not return unsolicited material. Reports in 6 weeks.

Music: Mostly rock, pop and jazz. Produced *Its a Tough Town*, written and recorded by the Cutaways!; and *Tear Down the Walls*, written and recorded by Vince Rollins on Rage-N-Records (AOR); and *AKA Dancor* (by Norman Weharm), recorded by Dancor on Shoreline Records (AOR). Other bands include Zooboys, X-it, Bo Diddley, Frank Davenport, Dave Cullen and Blue Counterpoint.

*J.L. PRODUCTIONS, 4303 Teesdale Ave., Studio City CA 91604. (818)760-7651. Owner: Jeff Lorensen. Record producer and engineer. Estab. 1988. Deals with artists only. Produces 10 singles, 15 12″ singles, 4 LPs and 4 CDs/year.

How to Contact: Call or write first for permission to submit. Prefers cassette (or VHS videocassette if available) with 3 songs and lyric sheet. SASE. Reports in 1 month.

Music: Mostly pop, rock and R&B; also alternative and New Age. Produced "Too Young to Love You," written and recorded by Timmy T. on Quality Records (pop). Mixed "Fallen Angel" (by Sami McKinney), recorded by Lisa Taylor on Giant Records (pop/R&B); and "I Want To Fall In Love" (by K.C. Porter), recorded by Lisa Taylor on Giant Records (pop/R&B). Other artists include Paul Young, Fine Young Cannibals, Kim Bassinger, Isley Bros., Troy Johnson and Earth Wind and Fire.

Tips: "Make it simple, meaningful. Write from your soul, not your mind."

JAG STUDIO, LTD., 3801-C Western Blvd., Raleigh NC 27606. (919)821-2059. Record producer, music publisher (Electric Juice Tunes/BMI), record company (JAG Records) and recording studio. Estab. 1981. Deals with artists and songwriters. Produces 10 singles, 12 LPs and 6 CDs/year. Receives 6 submissions/month. Fee derived from outright fee from recording artist or record company.

How to Contact: Write or call first and obtain permission to submit. SASE. Reports in 1-2 months.

Music: Mostly pop/dance, rap and rock; also country and gospel. Produced *Dream Train* (by the Accelerators), produced by Dick Hodgin for Profile Records (CD) and *Rockin with the Blues* (by Skeeter Brandon and Hwy. 61), recorded by Byron McCay for Bug You Records (CD). Other artists include Johnny Quest, Bad Checks, Hootie & the Blowfish, Annabel Lee, Ellen Harlow, Stacy Jackson, Doug Jervey, Katherine Kennedy, and Cry of Love.

Tips: "Be prepared. Learn something about the *BUSINESS* end of music first."

NEAL JAMES PRODUCTIONS, Box 121626, Nashville TN 37212. (615)726-3556. President: Neal James. Record producer, music publisher (Cottage Blue Music/CBMI, Neal James Music/BMI) and record company (Hidden Cove Music/ASCAP), Estab. 1971. Produces 16 singles and 4 CDs and LPs/year. Receives 75-100 submissions/year. Deals with artists and songwriters. Fee derived from sales royalty when song or artist is recorded, outright fee from recording artist and outright fee from record company.

How to Contact: Submit demo tape—unsolicited submissions are OK. Prefers cassette (or VHS videocassette if available) with 2 songs and lyric sheet. SASE. Reports in 1 month.

Music: Mostly country, pop/rock and R&B; also gospel. Produced "Angel" (by Shirley Jones/Neal James), recorded by Terry Barbay (country); "Shiloh" (by Reed Wilcox/ Neal James), recorded by Reed Wilcox (pop); "The Lips That Say I Love You" (by Ted Yost, Kenny Shingava, Neal James), recorded by Ted Yost (pop); all on Kottage Records. Other artists include P.F. Hawk, Reggie Whitaker, Scott Stallard, Willie T. Burkett and Teri LaFaye. "We also produce television specials and music videos. Currently we are producing projects featuring Merle Haggard, Johnny Paycheck, Hank Cochran, George Jones, Willie Nelson and Dottie West."

SUNNY JAMES, 1051 Saxonburg Blvd., Glenshaw PA 15116. Producer: Sunny James. Record producer, music publisher, record company (Golden Triangle). Estab. 1987. Deals with artists only. Produces 2 singles, 8 12" singles, 18 LPs and 9 CDs/year. Receives 100 submissions/month. Fee derived from sales royalty or outright fee from record company.
How to Contact: Submit demo tape by mail—unsolicited submissions are OK. Prefers cassette, 15 ips reel-to-reel (or ½" VHS videocassette if available) with 3 songs and lyric or lead sheet. SASE. Reports in 2 months.
Music: Mostly R&B, country, rock; also A/C and jazz. Produced "Baby Blue," written and recorded by F. Johnson (12"); "Dear Don't Wait For Me" (by F. Johnson), recorded by The Marcels (7"); and "After You," written and recorded by F. Johnson (single); and "Blue Moon," "Most of All" and "10 Commandments," all written by F. Johnson and recorded by The Marcels on Golden Trianble Records. Other artists include Joe DeSimone, Steve Grice (The Boxtops), The Original Marcels, Bingo Mundy, Cornelius Harp, Fred Johnson, Richard Harris, Brian (Badfinger) McClain and City Heat.

ALEXANDER JANOULIS PRODUCTIONS, 1957 Kilburn Dr., Atlanta GA 30324. (404)662-6661. President: Alex Janoulis. Record producer. Deals with artists and songwriters. Produces 6 singles and 2 LPs/year. Fee derived from sales royalty or outright fee from recording artist or record company.
How to Contact: Write first and obtain permission to submit. "Letters should be short, requesting submission permission." Prefers cassette with 1-3 songs. "Tapes will not be returned without SASE." Reports in 2 months.
Music: Mostly top 40, rock, pop; also black and disco. Produced "He's A Rebel," (by Gene Pitney), recorded by Secret Lover on HotTrax Records (pop single); *Stop!*, written and recorded by the Chesterfield Kings on Mirror Records (rock LP); and *P is For Pig*, written and recorded by The Pigs on HotTrax Records (pop LP). Other artists include Night Shadows, Starfoxx, Splatter and Big Al Jano. "Album produced for Chesterfield Kings was reviewed in *Rolling Stone*."

PIERRE JAUBERT, 105 Rue De Normandie, Courbevoie 92 400 **France**. Phone: (1)4333-6515. Contact: President. Casting agent for singers to perform songs in movie soundtracks. Estab. 1959. Deals with singers and songwriters. Produces 3 singles, 2 12" singles and 5 LPs/year. Fee derived from sales royalty.
How to Contact: Submit demo tape by mail. Prefers cassette with one song only.
Music: Dance and pop/top 40. Produced "You Call It Love" (by Karoline Kruger), by Virugen on Carrere Records (pop); "Si Je Te Mens" (by Xenia), recorded by Cariaire on Carrere Records (disco/pop); "Mirabelle" (by E. Dooh), recorded by Farid Feajer on Marshall Records (ballad) and "I Know It's a Lie" by Karoline Kruger on Carrere Records. Other artists include Richard Sanderson, Cook da Books and Katla Blas.

JAY JAY PUBLISHING & RECORD CO., 35 NE 62nd St., Miami FL 33138. (305)758-0000. Owner: Walter Jagiello. Record producer, music publisher (BMI) and record company (Jay Jay Record, Tape and Video Co.). Estab. 1951. Deals with artists and songwriters. Produces 12 singles, 12 LPs and 12 CDs/year. Fee derived from sales royalty.
How to Contact: Submit demo tape—unsolicited submissions are OK. Prefers cassette (or VHS videocassette if available) with 6 songs and lyric and lead sheet. "Quality cassette or reel-to-reel, sheet music and lyrics." SASE. Reports in 3 months.
Music: Mostly ballads, love songs, country music and comedy; also polkas and waltzes. Produced *No Beer in Heaven* and *All Night with Li'l Wally* (by Walter E. Jagiello), recorded by Li'L Wally; and *Animal Dittie For Kiddie* (by Al Trace), recorded by Li'L Wally and Capt. Stubby, all on Jay Jay Records. Other artists include Casey Siewierski, Eddie and the Slovenes, Polka Sizzlers, Americas Greatest Polka Band and the Lucky Harmony Boys.
Tips: "We need songs with meaning and feeling—true to life. Submit simple ballads which are melodic with nice rhyming lyrics such as happy polkas, 40s, 50s and 60s and country music. Also big band with violins, saxes and muted trumpets."

JAZZAND, 12 Micieli Pl., Brooklyn NY 11218. (718)972-1220. President: Rick Stone. Record producer, music publisher (BMI) and record company. Estab. 1984. Deals with artists only. Produces 1 LP/year. Fee derived from outright fee from recording artist or record company.
How to Contact: Write or call first and obtain permission to submit. Prefers cassette. Does not return unsolicited material. Reports in 2 weeks.
Music: Mostly jazz (straight ahead), bebop and hard bop. Produced *Blues for Nobody* and *Far East* (CDs), both written and recorded by Rick Stone on Jazzand Records (jazz).
Tips: "We are a small artist-owned label. We may in the future consider doing collaborative projects with other artists and labels. Our main concern is good music; we don't expect to get rich doing this."

JERICHO SOUND LAB, Box 407, Jericho VT 05465. (802)899-3787. Owner: Bobby Hackney. Record producer, music publisher (Elect Music/BMI) and record company (LBI Records). Estab. 1988. Deals with artists and songwriters. Produces 5 singles, 2 12" singles and 3 LPs/year. Fee derived from sales royalty.
How to Contact: Submit demo tape—unsolicited submissions are OK. Prefers cassette or VHS videocassette with 3-4 songs and lyric sheet. SASE.
Music: Mostly reggae, R&B and pop; also New Age and rock. Produced "Do the Reggae" (reggae) and "Be My Love" (both by B. Hackney), recorded by Lambsbread (reggae and rap); and "A Little Closer" (by B. Hackney), recorded by Hackneys, all on LBI Records.
Tips: "Make it clear what you want. We look for labels to distribute our songs, so we like finished product to present. We record it, or you record it, as long as it's a professional presentation."

JOHNNY JET RECORDS, 101-1431 Howe St., Vancouver B.C. V6Z 1R9 **Canada.** (604)685-2002. A&R: Dale Penner or John Livingston. Record producer, music publisher (Johnny Jet Music/BMI, PRO-CAN) and record company (Johnny Jet Records). Estab. 1990. Deals with artists and songwriters. Produces 12 singles and 6 LPs/year. Receives 45 submissions/month. Fee derived from sales royalty. Distribution in Canada by A&M Records.
How to Contact: Submit demo tape by mail. Unsolicited submissions are OK. Prefers cassette with a maximum of 3 songs and lyric sheet. "Artists should include photo." Reports in 2 months.
Music: Mostly pop, dance and R&B. Produced *Dream A Little Dream* and *Tima B!* (by John Dexter & others), recorded by various artists on A&M Records (pop LP).

*LITTLE RICHIE JOHNSON, Box 3, Belen NM 87002. (505)864-7441. Contact: Tony Palmer. Record producer, music publisher (BMI) and record company (LRJ). Estab. 1959. Deals with artists only. Produces 6 singles, 3 12" singles, 6 CDs and 6 LPs/year. Fee derived from outright fee from recording artist.
How to Contact: Submit demo tape by mail—unsolicited submissions are OK. Prefers cassette with 4 songs. SASE. Reports in 1 month.
Music: Mostly country. Produced "Keeper of the Keys," (by Wayne Steward), recorded by Jerry Jaramillo (country) and "Mario & the General" written and recorded by Joe King, both on LRJ Records. Other artists include Sam West IV, Elmer Fudpucker, Tommy Thompson, Rowe Bros., Bonnie Lou Bishop and Lacy Salazas.

RALPH D. JOHNSON, 114 Catalpa Dr., Mt. Juliet TN 37122. (615)754-2950. President: Ralph D. Johnson. Record producer, music publisher (Big Wedge Music) and record company. Estab. 1960. Deals with artists and songwriters. Produces 10 singles/year. Fee derived from sales royalty and outright fee from record company.
How to Contact: Submit demo tape—unsolicited submissions are OK. Prefers cassette with maximum of 4 songs. SASE. Reports in 2 weeks.
Music: Mostly country and novelty. Recorded "Little Green Worm" (by Cal Veale), recorded by Dave Martin (novelty); "In the Middle of the Nighttime" (by Ralph D. Johnson), recorded by Joey Weltz (country); and "They Finally Got Around to You" (by T. J. Christian), recorded by T. J. Christian (country), all on Wedge Records.
Tips: "Be critical of your own material before submitting."

*DANNY JONES PRODUCTIONS, 3752 Grendole Ln., Memphis TN 38115. (901)365-1429. Producer: Danny Jones. Record producer, music publisher (General Jones Music/BMI) and recording engineer. Deals with artists and songwriters. Produces 4 singles and 2 LPs/year. Fee derived from sales royalty, outright fee from artist and/or outright fee from record company.
How to Contact: Write or call first and obtain permission to submit. Prefers cassette (or VHS videocassette) with 3-6 songs and lyric sheet. "Please enclose name, address and phone number. Cassettes will not be returned." Reports in 1 month.
Music: Mostly R&B. Produced "Jump Back/Death Chick" (by Justin Short), recorded by Hyper Cadaver (alternative funk); "I Care/The Door Is Open," written and recorded by Arletta Nightingale (R&B); "Women Soldier/Lonely Days Lonely Nights" (by Vince Ellison/ Jackie Reddick), recorded by Brothers 'n' Arms (R&B), all on Gilliam Records.
Tips: "Send potential hit songs in a neat, professional manner."

*TYRONE JONES PRODUCTIONS, Tremont Ave., Orange NJ 07050. (201)676-9310. Owner: Tyrone Jones. Record producer. Estab. 1986. Deals with artists and songwriters. Produces 50 singles, 30 12" singles, 40 LPs/year. Fee derived from outright fee from recording artist.
How to Contact: Submit demo tape—unsolicited submissions are OK. Prefers cassette (or VHS videocassette if available) and lyric sheet. "Include name, address, copyright notice." SASE.
Music: Mostly R&B, jazz and rap.

JUMP PRODUCTIONS, 71 Langemunt, 9420 Aaigem **Belgium**. Phone: (053)62-73-77. General Manager: Eddy Van Mouffaert. Record producer and music publisher (Jump Music). Estab. 1976. Deals with artists and songwriters. Produces 25 singles, 2 LPs/year. Fee derived from sales royalty.
How to Contact: Prefers cassette. Does not return unsolicited material. Reports in 2 weeks.
Music: Mostly ballads, up-tempo, easy listening, disco and light pop; also instrumentals. Produced "Ach Eddy" (by Eddy Govert), recorded by Samantha and Eddy Govert on Carrere Records (light pop); "Al Wat Je Wilt" (by Eddy Viaene) recorded by Fransis on Scorpion Records (light pop); and "International" (by Eddy Govert), recorded by Le Grand Julot on B.M.P. (ambiance). Other artists include Angie Halloway, Debby Jackson, Ricky Morgan and Sandra Tempsy.

JUNE PRODUCTIONS LTD., "Toftrees," Church Rd., Woldingham, Surrey CR3 7JH **England**. Managing Director: David Mackay. Record producer, music producer (Sabre Music) and record company (Tamarin, PRT Records). Estab. 1970. Produces 6 singles, 3 LPs and 3 CDs/year. Deals with artists and songwriters. Fee derived from sales royalty.
How to Contact: Prefers cassette with 1-2 songs and lyric sheet. SAE and IRC. Reports in 2 weeks.
Music: MOR, rock and top 40/pop. Produced "Paris," the rock opera, soon to be released. Currently producing: Up With People, Jon English, Peter Hewitt and Smith-Wade Band. Past hits include "It's a Heartache" (by Bonnie Tyler); "I'd Like to Teach the World to Sing," and "Look What They've Done To My Song," by the New Seven; and hits for Cliff Richard, Cilla Black, Frankie Miller, Blue Mink, Gene Pitney and Joe Fagin.

BUTCH KELLY PRODUCTION, 11 Shady Oak Trail, Charlotte NC 28210. (704)554-1162. Executive Director: Butch Kelly. Record producer, music publisher (Butch Kelly Publishing/ASCAP and Music by Butch Kelly/BMI) and record company (KAM Executive and Fresh Avenue Records). Estab. 1985. Deals with artists and songwriters. Produces 4 singles, 4 12″ singles 4 EPs/year. Receives 500 submissions/month. Fee derived from sales royalty or outright fee from recording artist or record company.
How to Contact: Submit demo tape—unsolicited submissions are OK. Prefers cassette (or VHS videocassette if available) with 1-6 songs and lyric or lead sheet. "Send your best song on Maxell UDS II tape, along with picture and bio." SASE. Reports in 2 weeks-2 months.
Music: Mostly pop and R&B; also rock and jazz. Produced "Waiting" (by B. Kelly), recorded by Caro; "Love You" (by B. Kelly), recorded by Sunshine; and "Where Have You Been" (by A. Brown); all R&B singles on KAM Records. Other artists include Melissa Kelly.

GENE KENNEDY ENTERPRISES, INC., 3950 N. Mt. Juliet Rd., Mt. Juliet TN 37122. (615)754-0417. President: Gene Kennedy. Vice President: Karen Jeglum Kennedy. Record producer, independent distribution and promotion firm and music publisher (Chip 'N' Dale Music Publishing, Inc./ASCAP, Door Knob Music Publishing, Inc./BMI and Lodestar Music/SESAC). Estab. 1975. Deals with artists and songwriters. Produces 40-50 singles and 3-5 LPs/year. Fee derived from sales royalty or outright fee from recording artist or record company.
How to Contact: Submit demo tape—unsolicited submissions are OK. Prefers 7½ ips reel-to-reel or cassette with up to 3 songs and lyric sheet. "Do not send in a way that has to be signed for." SASE. Reports in 1 week.
Music: Country and gospel. Produced "Beyond Tonight" (by T. Willoughby), recorded by Bill Young on Polygram Records (country); "Meet My Friend" (by J. Burton & L. Smith), recorded by David Reed on Door Knob Records (gospel); and "Give Me Just A Little More Time" (by S. Ellwanger & R. Porter), recorded by Sandy Ellwanger on Door Knob Records (country). Other artists include Fleatwater Sound Shop, Rick Lee Jackson, Sonya Smith, Bo Harrison, Lee Gander, Brandywine, Wade Everett and Hope Cooper.

***EDDIE KILROY,** Box 1441, Franklin TN 37065. (615)794-4424. Contact: Eddie Kilroy. Record producer and music publisher. Estab. 1970. Deals with artists and songwriters. Produces 3-4 singles/year. Fee derived from sales royalty when song or artist is recorded.
How to Contact: Submit demo tape—unsolicited submissions are OK. Prefers cassette with 2 songs and lyric sheet. "No calls." Reports in 2 months.
Music: Country only.

Listings of companies in countries other than the U.S. have the name of the country in boldface type.

KINGSPORT CREEK MUSIC, Box 6085, Burbank CA 91510. Contact: Vice President. Record producer and music publisher. Deals with artists and songwriters.
How to Contact: Submit demo tape—unsolicited submissions are OK. Prefers cassette (or VHS videocassette). Does not return unsolicited material. "Include photo and bio if possible."
Music: Mostly country, MOR, R&B, pop and gospel. Produced "My Dear Savior's Love" (gospel), "Picture on the Shelf," and "This Old Bar" (country), all written and recorded by Melvena Kaye on Cowgirl Records.

*KINGSTON RECORDS AND TALENT, 15 Exeter Rd., Kingston NH 03848. (603)642-8493. Coordinator: Harry Mann. Record producer, music publisher (Strawberry Soda Publishing/ASCAP) and record company (Kingston Records). Estab. 1988. Deals with artists and songwriters. Produces 3-4 singles, 2-3 12″ singles; 2-3 LPs and 1-2 CDs/year. Fee derived from sales royalty.
How to Contact: Submit demo tape—unsolicited submissions are OK. Prefers cassette with 1-2 songs and lyric sheet. SASE. Reports in 6-8 weeks.
Music: Mostly rock, country and pop; "no heavy metal." Produced *5¢ Strawberry Soda* (country rock LP) and "Message To You" (ballad rock single), written and recorded by Doug Mitchell; and *Songs Piped from the Moon,* written and recorded by S. Pappas (rock ballads, avante guard LP); all on Kingston Records. Other artists include Bob Moore, Candy Striper Death Orgy, Pocket Band, Jeff Walker, J. Evans, NTM and Miss Bliss.
Tips: "I believe electronic music is going a bit too far and there is an opportunity for a comeback of real as opposed to sequenced music."

KMA, #1204, 1650 Broadway, New York NY 10019. (212)265-1570. A&R Director: Morris Levy. Record producer, music publisher (Block party Music/ASCAP). Estab. 1987. Deals with artists and songwriters. Produces 2 12″ singles, 3 LPs and 3 CDs/year. Fee derived from sales royalty or outright fee from recording artist or record company.
How to Contact: Submit demo tape by mail. Prefers cassette. SASE. Reports in 1 month.
Music: Mostly R&B, dance and rap; also movie music. Produced *In The Blood* (by Kissel/Halbreich), recorded by various artists on Ryko Records (African LP); *Arnold Schwarzenegger's Total Body Workout* (by various), recorded by Arnold Schwarzenegger on CBS Records (exercise LP); *Surrender* (by Kissell), recorded by Robin Clark and the David Bowie Band on HME/CBS Records (R&B/pop LP).
Tips: *Original* lyrics a huge plus.

*GREG KNOWLES, Suite 216, 8306 Wilshire Blvd., Beverly Hills CA 91502. (818)845-2849. Vice President/Record Division: Nick Schepperle. Record producer and record company (Helion Records). Estab. 1984. Deals with artists and songwriters. Produces 4 CDs/cassettes per year. Fee derived from outright fee from recording artist or record company. Charges for "production services for artists not signed to our company."
How to Contact: Submit demo tape—unsolicited submissions are OK. Prefers cassette with 3-4 songs and lyric or lead sheet. "Mention in your cover letter if your demo is a production submission rather than for label consideration." SASE. Reports in 3 weeks.
Music: Produced *Angel,* written and recorded by Diana Blair (country LP); *Swingstreet* (by Miriam Cutler), recorded by Swingstreet (jazz LP); "Keys To The World" by Darleen Koldenhoven; and "The Beer Dawgs" by the Beer Dawgs; all on Helion Records. Other artists include Dave Wagner, Jan Marie Cheatum and Johnny Rey.
Tips: "The quality of demos has risen dramatically over the last couple years. Send in a high quality tape with a nice (promo) package. This way we hear and see you at your best."

*KNOWN ARTIST PRODUCTIONS, 1219 Kerlin Ave., Brewton AL 36426. (205)867-2228. President: Roy Edwards. Record producer, music publisher (Cheavoria Music Co./BMI and Baitstring Music/ASCAP) and record company (Bolivia Records and Known Artist Records). Estab. 1972. Deals with artists and songwriters. Produces 10 singles and 3 LPs/year. Fee derived from sales royalty.
How to Contact: "Write first about your interest." Prefers cassette with 3 songs and lyric sheet. Reports in 1 month. "All tapes will be kept on file."
Music: Mostly country, R&B and pop; also easy listening, MOR and soul. Produced "Got To Let You Know," "You Are My Sunshine" and "You Make My Life So Wonderful," all written and recorded by Roy Edwards on Bolivia Records (R&B). Other artists include Jim Portwood, Bobbie Roberson and Brad Smiley.
Tips: "Write a good song that tells a good story."

FRANK E. KOEHL, P.O. Box 96, Glendale AZ 85311. (602)435-0314. Owner: Frank E. Koehl. Record producer and music publisher (Auburn Records & Tapes, estab. 1962. Speedstar Music/BMI, estab. 1989). Deals with artists and songwriters. Produces 3-5 singles and 7 LPs/year. Receives 25 submissions/month. Fee derived from sales royalty.

How to Contact: Submit demo tape by mail. Unsolicited submissions are OK. Prefers cassette with 2-4 songs and lyric sheet. SASE. Reports in 3 weeks.
Music: Mostly country, bluegrass and traditional music. Produced "Mr. Woolworth" and "Burglar Man" (by Frank Koehl) recorded by Al Ferguson on Auburn Records (folk country); also "Shack Tree" written and recorded by Troy McCourt on Auburn Records (country). Other artists include Cherry River Boys.
Tips: "Keep it country. No rock. Looking for traditional country and bluegrass, mostly acoustic. Country is going back to the older traditional songs."

ROBERT R. KOVACH, Box 7018, Warner Robins GA 31095-7018. (912)953-2800. Producer: Robert R. Kovach. Record producer. Estab. 1976. Deals with artists and songwriters. Produces 6 singles, 2 cassettes and 1 CD/year. Receives 200 submissions/year. Works with composers. Fee derived from sales royalty.
How to Contact: Submit demo tape – unsolicited submissions are OK. Prefers cassette with 4 songs and lyric sheet. SASE. Reports in 3 months.
Music: Mostly country and pop; also easy listening, R&B, rock and gospel.
Tips: "Be simple and sincere with your songs. Write in the form of normal conversation with a twist."

*KREN MUSIC PRODUCTIONS, 3108 S. Colima Rd., Hacienda Heights CA 91745. (818)855-1692. Co-owner: Kris Clark. Record producer, music publisher (BMI). Estab. 1985. Deals with artists and songwriters. Produces 10 singles and 4 LPs/year. Fee derived from sales royalty when song or artist is recorded.
How to Contact: Submit demo tape – unsolicited submissions are OK. Prefers cassette with 3 songs and lyric sheet. SASE.
Music: Mostly country, pop and rock; also gospel, R&B and New Age. Produced *Twinkle, Twinkle Lucky Star* (country) and *Chill Factor* (country LP) both written and recorded by Merle Haggard on Epic/CBS Records. Other artists include Jamie K.Watson.

*L.A. ENTERTAINMENT, 29836 W. Rainbow Crest Dr., Agoura Hills CA 91301. (818)889-8578. FAX: (818)889-8578 Ext. 222. VP West Coast A&R: Glen D. Ducan. Record Producer (Jim Ervin Productions), record company (Blue Monkey Records) and music publisher (T&S Music Publishing/ASCAP). Estab. 1988. Deals with artists and songwriters. Fee derived from sales royalty when song or artist is recorded, outright fee from recording artist or record company.
How to Contact: Submit demo tape – unsolicited submissions are OK. Prefers cassette (or videocassette if available) with 3 songs, lyric and lead sheets if available. "All written submitted materials (i.e. lyric sheets, letter, etc.) should be typed." SASE. Reports in 3 weeks.
Music: Mostly pop/rock, New Age and alternative; also R&B, jazz and country.
Tips: "A hit song is a hit song, whether it is recorded in a professional environment or at your home. Concentrate first on the writing of your material and then record it to the best of your ability. A professional sounding recording may help the presentation of a song, but it will not make or break a true hit."

LAMON RECORDS/PANHANDEL RECORDS, Box 25371, Charlotte NC 28229. (704)537-0133. President: Dwight Moody. A&R: Carlton Moody. Record producer and music publisher (Laymond Publishing Co. and CDT Productions). Estab. 1962. Deals with artists, songwriters and publishers. Produces 35 singles, 4 12" singles, 20 LPs and 5 CDs/year. Receives 300-750 submissions/year. Fee derived from outright fee from recording artist.
How to Contact: Write first and obtain permission to submit. Prefers cassette (or VHS videocassette if available) with minimum 2 songs. SASE. Reports in 1 month.
Music: Mostly country, beach, gospel, rock and R&B. Produced "Hang A Stocking" (by Charles Hayes) and Dreaming (by D.C. Moody), recorded by Moody Bros. (country), and "Long Way to Go" (by S. Turner); recorded by Turner Family (gospel), all on Lamon Records. Other artists include George Hamilton, Chip, Gray Roy, Moody Bros, Billy Scott, Amanda Page and Vanessa Parker.

*LANDMARK AUDIO OF NASHVILLE, Box 148296, Nashville TN 37214-8296. Producers: Bill Anderson, Jr. and D.D. Morris. Record producer, music publisher (Newcreature Music/BMI) and TV/radio syndication. Deals with artists and songwriters. Produces 12 singles and 12 LPs/year. Works with 9 new songwriters/year. Works with composers and lyricists; teams collaborators. Fee derived from sales royalty.
How to Contact: Prefers 7½ ips reel-to-reel or cassette (or videocassette) with 4-10 songs and lyric sheet. SASE. Reports in 1 month.
Music: Mostly country crossover; also blues, country, gospel, jazz, rock and top 40/pop. Produced *Sincerely, Rhonda*, by Rhonda Ingle on Phonorama Records (MOR LP); and *The Traditional Continues*, by Vernon Oxford on Audiograph Records (country LP). Other artists include Pam Fenelon, Skeeter

Davis, Teddy Nelson, JoAnne Cash Yates, Eveline, De Fox and Wayne Oldham.

*LARI-JON PRODUCTIONS, 325 W. Walnut, Rising City NE 68658. (402)542-2336. Owner: Larry Good. Record producer, music publisher (Lari-Jon Publishing/BMI) and record company (Lari-Jon Records). Estab. 1967. Deals with artists and songwriters. Produces 10 singles and 5 LPs/year. Receives 150 submissions/year. "Producer's fees are added into session costs."
How to Contact: Submit demo tape by mail—unsolicited submissions are OK. "Must be a professional demo." SASE. Reports in 2 months.
Music: Country, gospel-Southern and 50's rock. Produced *Oldies With A New Swing*, recorded by Kent Thompson (country swing); *The Greatest Star* (by Gerald and June Campbell), recorded by Tom Campbell (country gospel); and "Nebraskaland," written and recorded by Larry Good, all on Lari-Jon Records. Other artists include Brenda Allen and Johnny Nace.
Tips: "Be professional in all aspects of the music business."

LARK TALENT & ADVERTISING, Box 35726, Tulsa OK 74153. (918)749-1648. Owner: Jana Jae. Record producer, music publisher (Jana Jae Music/BMI) and record company (Lark Record Productions, Inc.). Estab. 1980. Deals with artists and songwriters. Fee derived from sales royalty when song or artist is recorded.
How to Contact: Submit demo tape—unsolicited submissions are OK. Prefers cassette or VHS videocassette with 3 songs and lead sheet. Does not return unsolicited material.
Music: Mostly country, bluegrass and classical; also instrumentals. Produced "Fiddlestix" (by Jana Jae); "Mayonnaise" (by Steve Upfold); and "Flyin' South" (by Cindy Walker); all country singles recorded by Jana Jae on Lark Records. Other artists include Sydni, Hotwire and Matt Greif.

JOHN LATIMER, Box 6541, Cleveland OH 44101. (216)467-0300. Producer: John Latimer. Record producer, record company (Play Records) and independent. Estab. 1985. Deals with artists and songwriters. Produces 1-2 LPs/year. Fee derived from sales royalty or outright fee from recording artist or record company.
How to Contact: Submit demo tape—unsolicited submissions are OK. Prefers cassette (or ¾" or VHS videocassette if available) with 5 songs and lyric or lead sheets. SASE. Reports in 6 weeks.
Music: Mostly rock and alternative. Produced *Exhibit A*, *Exhibit B* and *Exhibit C* (compilations) on Play Records. Other artists include The Bellows, I-TAL U.S.A., Serious Nature, Hipshot and Mike O'Brien.

SCOTT LEA PRODUCTIONS, 88 Lenox Ave., Paterson NJ 07502. (201)790-7668. President: Scott Lea. Record producer, music publisher (Scott Lea Publishing/BMI) and record company (Neon Records). Estab. 1988. Deals with artists and songwriters. Produces 5 singles, 20 12" singles, 2 LPs, 1 EP and 2 CDs/year. Fee derived from outright fee from recording artist or record company.
How to Contact: Submit demo tape by mail. Unsolicited submissions are OK. Prefers cassette or VHS videocassette with 2-4 songs. SASE. Reports in 2-4 weeks.
Music: Mostly club, R&B and rap; also house, jazz and rock. Produced *What Exit?*, written and recorded by various artists on Neon Records (various rock LP); *Pursuit of Peace*, written and recorded by Scott Lea on Neon Records (contemporary jazz LP); and *Ebony* (by various artists), recorded by Ebony on World One Records (club/dance LP). Other artists include Bugle Boyz, Dana Way, Latin Lover, Maja Hall, Ari Goodman and The Fiendz.

JOHN LEAVELL, 2045 Anderson Snow, Spring Hill FL 34609. (904)799-6102. Producer: John Leavell. Record producer and recording studio. Estab. 1980. Deals with artists and songwriters. Produces 10-12 singles/year. Fee derived from outright fee from recording artist. Charges artist upfront for demo production.
How to Contact: Submit demo tape—unsolicited submissions are OK. Prefers cassette (or VHS videocassette if available) with 4-5 songs and lyric sheet. SASE. Reports in 4 weeks.
Music: Mostly Christian rock, Christian contemporary and gospel; also rock and country. Produced "Sons of Thunder" (by Tom Jim Dave Butler), recorded by Sons of Thunder; "Final Stand" (by Joch St. Chvel), recorded by Final Stand; and "Arsenal" (by M.S.S.C), recorded by Arsenal, all on Leavell Records (Christian metal). Other artists include Johnny Grubbs, Greg Eadler, Tom Butler, Tom Martin, Patricia Tassie, John Leavell and Morning Star.
Tips: "Make the best first impression you can! Always keep writing new material."

LEE SOUND PRODUCTIONS, RON LEE, VALUE FOR MONEY, HOPPY PRODUCTIONS, Stewart House, Hill Bottom Road, Sands-Ind. Est., Highwycombe, Buckinghamshire HP12-4HJ **England**. Phone: (0630)647374. FAX: (0630)647612. Contact: Catherine Lee. Record producer. Estab. 1971. Deals with artists and songwriters. Fee derived from sales royalty or outright fee from recording artist and record company.

Affiliates: Value For Money and Hoppy Productions.
How to Contact: Submit demo tape by mail—unsolicited submissions are OK. Prefers cassette (or VHS/PAL videocassette if available) with 3 songs and lyric sheet or lead sheets. SAE and IRC. Reports in 6 weeks.
Music: All types. Produced "I Hate School," "Razor Blades" and "Panda Patrol," (all by E. Hunt), recorded by Studs on Zarg Records (punk). Other artists include Emmit Till and Touché.

LEMON SQUARE PRODUCTIONS, P.O. Box 671008, Dallas TX 75367. (214)750-0720. A&R: Mike Anthony. Producer: Bart Barton. Record producer, music publisher and record label. Deals with artists and songwriters. Produces 2 singles and 3 LPs/year. Fee derived from sales royalty.
How to Contact: Write first and obtain permission to submit. Prefers cassette and lyric sheet or lead sheet. Does not return unsolicited material. Reports in 2 months.
Music: Mostly country and gospel. Produced "Like Goin' Home" (by Allison Gilliam), recorded by Susie Calvin on Canyon Creek Records (country); "Still Fallin' " (by Dave Garner), recorded by Audie Henry on RCA/Canada Records (country); and "Lord If I Make It To Heaven" (by Dale Vest/T. Overstreet), recorded by Billy Parker on RCA/Canada Records (country). Other artists include Glen Baily, Susie Calvin and Bev Marie.

*LEOPARD MUSIC, 23, Thrayle House, Stockwell Road, London, SW9 0XU **England.** Phone: (071)738-9577 and (818)962-6547. Executive Producer: Errol Jones. Record producer (F&J Music/PRS, BMI) and record company (Leopard Music, Jet Set International). Estab. 1978. Deals with artists and/or songwriters. Produces 6 singles, 6 12″ singles and 2 LPs/year. Fee derived from sales royalty.
How to Contact: Write first and obtain permission to submit. Prefers cassette (or VHS PAL videocassette) with 3 songs and lyric or lead sheets. "Include biography, resume and picture." SASE. Reports in 2 weeks.
Music: Mostly dance music, soul and pop; also ballad, reggae and gospel. Produced "Time After Time" (by Guy Spells), recorded by Rico J (single); "I Need You" (by E. Campbell and E. North Jr.), recorded by Big Africa (single); and *God is Beauty*, written and recorded by Evelyn Ladimeji (LP); all on Leopard Music. Other artists include Samantha Simone and The Sea.

TOMMY LEWIS, JR., RR 2, Box 111-C, Cresco PA 18326. (717)595-3149. Owner/Producer: Tommy Lewis, Jr. Record producer and record company (Round Sound Music). Estab. 1983. Deals with artists and songwriters. Produces 3-5 singles, 2-3 LPs and 2-3 CDs/year. Receives 50 submissions/month.
How to Contact: Write or call first and obtain permission to submit. Prefers cassette or DAT (and VHS videocassette if available) with 3 songs and lyric and lead sheet. "Be professional in your presentation." SASE. Reports in 2-3 months.
Music: Mostly pop and jazz; also New Age, country, R&B and gospel. Produced "I'm All Alone," written and recorded by J. Schick (pop/single); *He Died For You*, recorded by Ransomed on W.C. Productions Records (Christian rock/album); "No Easy Way" (by T. Lewis, Jr.), recorded by Gloria Kay (country/single); "Chasing The Dream" (by T. Lewis and J. Price) recorded by Charade on Round Sound Records (pop/jazz); and "One Way Ticket" (by T.L./J. Yaz) recorded by Joe Yaz on Geodesic Records (A/C). Other artists include John Schick and Jim Henderschedt.
Tips: Don't quit . . . Keep trying . . .after 50 rejections the 51st try could mean "YES!"

*LIGOSA ENTERTAINMENT CORP., Suite 1101, 200 Park Ave., New York 10003. Office Manager: Pete Tufel. Record producer, recording company and music publisher. Estab. 1985. Deals with artists and songwriters. Produces 10 singles, 10 12″ singles, 2 LPs and 2 CDs/year. Fee derived from sales royalty when song or artist is recorded, outright fee from recording artist or record company.
How to Contact: Submit demo tape—unsolicited submissions are OK. Prefers cassette with 3 songs and lyric sheet. Reports in 2 weeks.
Music: Mostly dance/club, ballads, R&B and pop. Produced *No More Games* (by various writers), recorded by New Kids On Block on CBS Records; *Bad Of The Heart* (by various writers), recorded by George LaMond on CBS Records; and *Made Up My Mind* (by Gold), recorded by Safire on Polygram Records, all LPs.
Tips: "Don't get discouraged. Keep trying and sending. We are picky."

LINEAR CYCLE PRODUCTIONS, Box 2608, Sepulveda CA 91393-2608. Producer: R. Borowy. Record producer. Estab. 1980. Deals with artists and songwriters. Produces 15-25 singles, 6-10 12″ singles, 15-20 LPs and 10 CDs/year. Fee derived from sales royalty or outright fee from recording artist.
How to Contact: Submit demo tape—unsolicited submissions are OK. Prefers cassette or 7⅛ ips reel-to-reel (or ½″ VHS or ¾″ videocassette if available). SASE. Reports in 1 month.
Music: Mostly rock/pop, R&B/blues and country; also gospel and comedy. Produced "Lowin' Low" (by S. Smoothe) recorded by Lyle Slink on Flote Records (A/C); "9th Sim-o-tee" (by B. Tovhan-EL) recorded by Broken Sproket Holes on Digit Records (dance); and "Afraka Sheee" (by PPL-Tyrone

Jones), recorded by PPX3A-Melvin on Yo! Records (rap). Other artists Joe Gizpeeskii, The Eat 'N Yells, Too Black For The Public, The Lasso Boys, Tommy Sqish and Eugene Cornblatt and his Orchestra.
Tips: "The better the song AND the demo reel, the better the chances that we would not only consider it, but the chances are greater that we'll listen to it!"

LISTEN PRODUCTIONS, Box 1155, Hollywood CA 90078. (310)473-7480. President: Daniel Keller. Record producer. Estab. 1986. Deals with artists and songwriters. Fee derived from sales royalty or outright fee from recording artist or record company.
How to Contact: Write first to get permission to submit. "No phone calls please." Prefers cassette or DAT (or VHS videocassette if available) with maximum 4 songs and lyric sheet. "If artist, submit photos if available." SASE. Reports in approximately 6 weeks.
Music: Alternative rock, alternative acoustic, world-beat, techno-industrial-hip-hop.
Tips: "We are interested in artists/writers with something to say, and a style of saying it. There are more than enough generic songs and sounds to go around . . . We're looking for people who place artistic integrity above marketability."

LIVE PRODUCTIONS INC., Box 448, Hanover VA 23069. (804)730-1765. FAX: (804)730-1838. President: Patrick D. Kelley. Record producer, music publisher (Studley Publishing), record company (Live Productions) and recording studio (The Fishing Hole). Estab. 1988. Deals with artists and songwriters. Produces 8 LPs/year. Fee derived from sales royalty. "We charge clients not on our label for studio time."
How to Contact: Submit demo tape—unsolicited submissions are OK. Prefers cassette (or VHS videocassette if available) with any number of songs and lyric sheet. "Be specific on what you are seeking (publishing, recording contract, etc.)." SASE. Reports in 1 month.
Music: Country, gospel, and pop; also rock, folk and children's. Produced *The Girl I Left Behind* (by Public Domain), recorded by Southern Horizon (Civil war period music); "It's Probably Magic" (by Original/cover), recorded by George Turman (children's), both on Live Productions Records; and *1991 Christmas Concert* (by Public Domain), recorded by Church of the Redeemer on CRI Records (religious). Other artists include Andy & Cindy & Thensome; Highways & Heartaches, Allen Watkins and Grey Granger.

LOCONTO PRODUCTIONS, Box 16540, Plantation FL 33318. (305)741-7766. President: Frank X. Loconto. Record producer and music publisher. Estab. 1978. Deals with artists and songwriters. Produces 20 singles and 20 LPs/year. Fee derived from sales royalty, outright fee from songwriter/artist and/or outright fee from record company.
How to Contact: Write first and obtain permission to submit. Prefers cassette. SASE.
Music: Produced "Calypso Alive and Well," written and recorded by Obediah Colebrock (island music); "Standing on the Top" (by various artists), recorded by Mark Rone (C&W); and "Walking On Air" (by Ken Hatch), recorded by Frank Loconto (motivational); all on FXL Records. Other artists include Bruce Mullin, Bill Dillon and James Billie (folk music).

HAROLD LUICK & ASSOCIATES, Box B, Carlisle IA 50047. (515)989-3748. Record producer, music industry consultant and music publisher. Deals with artists and songwriters. Produces 20 singles and 6 LPs/year. Fee derived from sales royalty, outright fee from artist/songwriter or record company, and from consulting fees for information or services.
How to Contact: Call or write first. Prefers cassette with 3-5 songs and lyric sheet. SASE. Reports in 3 weeks.
Music: Traditional country, gospel, contemporary country and MOR. Produced Bob Everhart's LP *Everhart*; Don Laughlin's *Ballads of Deadwood S.D.* LP; Lee Mace's Ozark Opry albums; and Darrell Thomas' singles and LPs. "Over a 12-year period, Harold Luick has produced and recorded 412 singles and 478 albums, 7 of which charted and some of which have enjoyed independent sales in excess of 30,000 units."
Tips: "We are interested in helping the new artist/songwriter make it 'the independent way.' This is the wave of the future. As music industry consultants, our company sells ideas, information and results. Songwriters can increase their chances by understanding that recording and songwriting is a business. 80% of the people who travel to large recording/publishing areas of our nation arrive there totally unprepared as to what the industry wants or needs from them. Do yourself a favor. Prepare, investigate and only listen to people who are qualified to give you advice. Do not implement anything until you understand the rules and pitfalls."

JACK LYNCH/NASHVILLE COUNTRY PRODUCTIONS, 306 Millwood Dr., Nashville TN 37217. (615)366-9999. Producer: Col. Jack Lynch. Record producer, music publisher (BMI), record company and distributor (Nashville Music Sales). Estab. 1963. Deals with artists and songwriters. Produces 12

LPs/year. Fee derived from sales royalty or outright fee form recording artist.

How to Contact: Submit demo tape by mail. Unsolicited submissions are OK. Prefers cassette with 1-4 songs and lyric sheet. "Send picture and resume, if available. Send good quality demo cassette recording, neat lyric shccts." SASE. Reports in 2 weeks.

Music: Mostly country, bluegrass and religious; also MOR, folk and comedy/novelty. Produced "I Can't Afford to Buy You Diamonds" (by Bob Jenkins), recorded by Charlie Sizemore on NCP Records (country); "Pretty Sparkling Wine," written and recorded by Lonnie Pierce on NCP-C303 Records (country); and "The Nashville Blues" (by Jack Lynch), recorded by Paul Woods on NCP-302 Records (country). Other artists include Jack Lynch and The Nashville Travellers.

Tips: "Submit strong lyrics, good performance and good sound quality."

*M.R. PRODUCTIONS, 404 St-Henri, Montreal Quebec H3C 2P5 **Canada**. (514)871-8481. Producer: Mario Rubnikowich. Record producer, record company (Nephelim Records, MGR). Estab. 1987. Deals with artists and songwriters. Produces 3 singles, 3 LPs and 4 CDs/year. Fee derived from outright fee from record company and sales.

How to Contact: Submit demo tape by mail—unsolicited submissions are OK. Prefers cassette, 15 ips reel-to-reel with 3 songs and lyric or lead sheets. SASE. Reports in 5 weeks.

Music: Mostly New Age, pop and rock.

MAC-ATTACK PRODUCTIONS, INC., Suite 6J, 14699 N.E. 18th Ave., N. Miami FL 33181. (305)947-8315. President: Michael J. McNamee. Record producer and music publisher (Mac-Attack Publishing/ASCAP). Estab. 1987. Deals with artists and songwriters. Produces 10-12 singles, 3-10 LPs and 3-10 CDs/year. Fee derived from sales royalty or outright fee from recording artist or record company. "Depending upon the contract, a percentage to cover expenses that *will* be made."

How to Contact: Write or call first and obtain permission to submit. Prefers cassette (or VHS videocassette if available) with a maximum of 3 songs and lyric sheet. "I can't stand formalities. Be yourself when writing your letter. Communication is the key to a great relationship." SASE. Reports in 1-2 months.

Music: Mostly progressive rock and alternative; also progressive dance, R&B and "anything different." Produced "Set Your Body in Motion" (by McNamee, Avanzini & MK), recorded by Split Decision on UNR Records (house/R&B); and "Let Me Show You Something" (by McNamee), recorded by Ricochet on UNR Recrods (techno/house).

Tips: "There's no need to rush anything. Let it come naturally—don't try to force it. Remember, you and I will be gonc one day, but our songs will never die."

JIM McCOY PRODUCTIONS, Rt. 2, Box 114, Berkeley Springs WV 25411. President: Jim McCoy. Record producer and music publisher (Jim McCoy Music/BMI). Estab. 1964. Deals with artists and songwriters. Produces 12-15 singles and 6 LPs/year. Fee derived from sales royalty.

How to Contact: Submit demo tape—unsolicited submissions are OK. Prefers cassette or 7½ or 15 ips reel-to-reel (or Beta or VHS videocassette if available) with 6 songs and lyric or lead sheets. SASE. Reports in 1 month.

Music: Mostly country, rock and gospel; also country/rock and bluegrass. Produced "Dyin' Rain" and "I'm Gettin Nowhere," both written and recorded by J.B. Miller on Hilton Records (country). Other artists include Mel McQuain, Red Steed, R. Lee Gray, John Aikens and Jim McCoy.

BUTCH MCGHEE, TYRA MANAGEMENT GROUP, Box 915, Sheffield AL 35660. (205)381-2060. President: Frank Williams. Record producer and record company (Muscle Shoals Sound Gospel Records, Ameika Records). Estab. 1985. Deals with artists and songwriters. Produces 4 12″ singles, 10 LPs and 10 CDs/year. Fee derived from sales royalty. "Before project a production fee is charged."

How to Contact: Write first and obtain permission to submit. Prefers cassette (or VHS videocassette if available) with 3 songs and lyric sheets. "Send biography and photo if possible." Does not return unsolicited material. Reports in 8 weeks.

Music: Mostly gospel, R&B and country. Produced *2nd Chance*, recorded by Loretta Handy on Ameika Records (LP); *Anybody Can, God Can*, recorded by Voices of Cosmo on MSSG Records (LP); and *Pamela Davies and True Spirit*, recorded on MSSG Records (LP). Other artists include Keith Pringle, Stefania Stone Fierson, Vanessa Bell Armstrong, Charles Fold and Fold Singers.

Tips: "Supply gospel and inspirational material with a strong message. Clean demos and lyric sheets."

MADISON STATION PRODUCTIONS, 953 Highway 51, Box 1951, Madison MS 39130-1951. (601)856-7468. Producer: Style Wooten. Record producer and record company (Madison Station Records). Estab. 1988. Works with artists and songwriters. Produces 15 singles and 12 LPs/year. Fee derived from sales royalty or outright fee from record company.

How to Contact: Write or call first and obtain permission to submit. Prefers cassette with 1-3 songs and lyric sheet. SASE.
Music: Modern country and R&B.

*MAGIC APPLE RECORDS, Box 530547, Miami FL 33153-0547. (305)758-1903. Producer and A&R: David Lopez. Record producer, record company and music publisher. Estab. 1990. Deals with artists and songwriters. Produces 3-5 singles and 3-5 12″ singles/year. Fee derived from sales royalty when song or artist is recorded or advances from recording company.
How to Contact: Submit demo tape—unsolicited submissions are OK. Prefers cassette (or VHS videocassette if available) with 1-3 songs. "Include pictures and bios if available." SASE. Reports in 2-3 weeks.
Music: Mostly dance, pop and rock; also rap. Produced "Without Your Love" and "Don't Let Me Go" (by Nardy), recorded by Nardy (dance-single); and "Hard Core Rebel" written and recorded by Rio & Cap (rap-single); all on Magic Apple Records.
Tips: "Follow up on all demos sent."

*LEE MAGID PRODUCTIONS, Box 532, Malibu CA 90265. (213)463-5998. President: Lee Magid. Record producer and music publisher (Alexis Music, Inc./ASCAP, Marvelle Music Co./BMI, Gabal Music Co./SESAC), record company (Grass Roots Records and LMI Records) and management firm (Lee Magid Management). Estab. 1950. Deals with artists, songwriters and producers. Produces 4 singles, 4 12″ singles, 8 LPs and 8 CDs/year. Publishes 10-15 new songwriters/year. Works with artists and songwriters; teams collaborators. Fee derived from sales royalty and outright fee from recording artist.
How to Contact: "Send cassette giving address and phone number; include SASE." Prefers cassette (or VHS videocassette) with 3-6 songs and lyric sheet. "Please only one cassette, and photos if you are an artist/writer." Does not return unsolicited material. Reports only if interested, "as soon as we can after listening."
Music: Mostly R&B, rock, jazz and gospel; also pop, bluegrass, church/religious, easy listening, folk, blues, MOR, progressive, soul, instrumental and top 40. Produced "What Shall I Do?" (by Quincy Fielding, Jr.); "I Got Joy" (by Quincy Fielding, Jr.) and "Whenever You Call" (by Calvin Rhone); all recorded by Tramaine Hawkins on Sparrow Records (gospel rock). Other artists include Perry "The Prince" Wacker.
Tips: "The visual effect is just as important as the audio. An act should have theatrical as well as musical ability."

MAJA MUSIC, (formerly Michael Aharon Music), 335 Lyceum Ave., Philadelphia PA 19128. (215)487-1359. Owners: Michael Aharon and John Anthony. Record producer. Estab. 1984. Deals with artists. Produces 3 LPs, 4 EPs and 3 CDs/year. Receives 20 submissions/month. Fee derived from outright fee from recording artist or record company. "Fee covers arrangement, production, pre-production and programming. For demos, fee also covers all recording costs."
How to Contact: Submit demo tape—unsolicited submissions are OK. Prefers cassette with 3-6 songs. Reports in 3 weeks.
Music: Mostly folk-rock and pop/urban contemporary; also New Age, world-beat and experimental. Produced *I Will Stand Fast*, written and recorded by Fred Small on Flying Fish Records (folk/rock LP); *Out of the Darkness*, written and recorded by Tom Juravitch on Flying Fish Records (folk/rock LP); and *Jaguar*, written and recorded by Fred Small on Flying Fish Records (folk/rock LP). Other artists include Heather Mullen, Charlie Cooper Project and Julia Haines.
Tips: "Send material which exhibits your personal style and creativity, even if it is not 'commercial' material. Individuality is starting to matter again. Lyrics are starting to matter again. Singer-songwriters are on the radio again."

*MAKERS MARK MUSIC PRODUCTIONS, 3033 W. Redner St., Philadelphia PA 19121. (215)236-4817. Record Producer: Caprice-Paul E. Hopkins. Record producer. Estab. 1991. Deals with artists and songwriters. Produces 15 singles, 5 12″ singles and 4 LPs/year. Fee derived from sales royalty or outright fee from recording artist or record company (depending on situation).
How to Contact: Write or call first to arrange personal interview. Prefers cassette with 2-4 songs and lyric sheet. "Explain concept of your music and/or style, and your future direction as an artist or songwriter."
Music: Mostly R&B, dance/hip house and rap. Produced "Move Somethin'," written and recorded by Caprice (dance); "The Feelins," written and recorded by Caprice (R&B); and "Get Funky" (by P. Hopkins/C. Caruth/G. Reed), recorded by Larry Larr on Ruff House/Columbia Records (hip house). Other artists include Above All, Angelica, E.T.S., Creative Habit, Children of Tomorrow, Troy G and G.Q. Connection.
Tips: "Be creative with your music and keep a commercial awareness on targeted market."

LITO MANLUCU (Magic Music Production), 4121 N. Laramie, Chicago IL 60641. Producer: Lito Manlucu. Record producer. Estab. 1991. Deals with artists and songwriters. Produces 1 single, 1 LP and 1 CD/year. Fee derived from outright fee from recording artist.
How to Contact: Submit demo tape—unsolicited submissions OK. Prefers cassette with 3 songs and lyric sheet. SASE. Reports in 2 weeks.
Music: Mostly pop, R&B and rock; also foreign music, dance. Produced "Blue Jean" (by Lito Manlucu) recorded by Jane Park on Independent Records (dance/pop).

*COOKIE MARENCO, Box 874, Belmont CA 94002. . Record producer/engineer. Estab. 1981. Deals with artists and songwriters. Produces 10 CDs/year. Fee derived form sales royalty or outright fee from recording artist or record company.
How to Contact: Write first and obtain permission to submit. Prefers cassette with 8 songs and lyric sheet. Does not return unsolicited material. Reports in 8 months.
Music: Mostly R&B dance, alternative modern rock, instrumental, ethnic and avante-garde; also classical, pop and jazz. Producer on *Winter Solstice II*, written and recorded by various artists; *Heresay* (by Paul McCandless); and *Turtle Island String Quartet* (by Turtle Island), all on Windham Hill Records (instrumental LP/CD). Other artists include Modern Mandolin Quartet, Ladysmith Black Mambazo, Alex DeGrassi and Art Lande.

*JOHN MARS, Box 1583, Brantford ON N3T 5V6 **Canada**. Phone: (519)442-7368. Contact: John Mars. Record producer, music publisher (Utter Nonsense Publishing/SOCAN) and record company (Ugly Dog Records). Estab. 1979. Deals with artists and songwriters. Produces 1 single and 1 LP/year. Fee derived from outright fee from recording artist.
How to Contact: Submit demo tape—unsolicited submissions are OK. Prefers cassette or CD (or videocassette if available) with 4 songs. "Submit black and white photo of artist or group."
Music: Mostly rock. Produced "Oh Yeah" (by Mars/Templeton), recorded Children and Daniel Lanois; *Annihilated Surprise* (by Broomer/Mars), recorded by J. Mars and Mark Wright; and *Electric Playground* (by Mars/Lanzalone/Sinkowski/Tremblay), recorded by J. Mars and Bob Doidge; all on Ugly Dog Records. Other artists include The Recognitions, The Martians, The Popp Tarts, Red Shrimps, Eddie Haskell's Jacket and Dr. Chub Master.
Tips: "Make sure your demo is recorded by a pro studio—the majority of the tapes we get are virtually undecipherable. Why waste your money mailing out poor quality demos?"

*PETE MARTIN/VAAM MUSIC PRODUCTIONS, Box 29688, Hollywood CA 90029-0688, (213)664-7765. President: Pete Martin. Record producer, music publisher (Vaam Music/BMI, Pete Martin Music/ASCAP) and record company (Blue Gem Records). Estab. 1982. Deals with artists and songwriters. Produces 12 singles and 5 LPs/year. Fee derived from sales royalty. (Send small packages only.)
How to Contact: Prefers cassette with 2 songs and lyric sheet. SASE. Reports in 1 month.
Music: Mostly top 40/pop, country and R&B. Producer of country acts: Sherry Weston, Frank Loren, Brian Smith & The Renegades. Pop acts: Victoria Limon, Cory Canyon.
Tips: "Study the market in the style that you write. Songs must be capable of reaching top five on charts."

PATRICK MELFI, 3365 W. Millerberg Way, W., Jordan VT 84084. (801)566-9542. Contact: Patrick Melfi. Record producer, music publisher (BMI) and record company (Alexas Records). Estab. 1984. Deals with artists and songwriters. Produces 6 singles, 2 LPs, 1 EP and 2 CDs/year. Fee derived from outright fee from recording artist or record company.
How to Contact: Submit demo tape—unsolicited submissions are OK. Prefers cassette (or VHS videocassette if available) with 1-6 songs and lyric or lead sheet. SASE. Reports in 2 months.
Music: Mostly country and pop; also oldies and gospel. Produced "She's On Her Own" (by P. Melfi/AJ Masters), recorded by AJ Masters; "Between Your Heart & Mine" (by Melfi) recorded by Prophesy on Atlantic Records (MOR); and "Child of God" (by Melfi/Kone), recorded by Sheri Sampson on Godley Music Records (gospel). Other artists include Crossfire and Hard Riders.
Tips: "Write from the heart! Write a good story and compliment it with a strong melody. Good production is a must. Always start with a great hook!"

METROMEDIA PRODUCTIONS, Suite 306, 822 11th Ave. SW, Calgary AB T2R 0E5 **Canada**. President: Lanny Williamson. Record producer, music publisher (Zimmy Music/SOCAN) and recording studio. Estab. 1988. Deals with artists and songwriters. Produces 20 singles, 3 LPs and 3 CDs/year. Fee derived from outright fee from recording artist.

How to Contact: Submit demo tape—unsolicited submissions are OK. Prefers cassette with 4 songs and lyric sheet. "Please enclose picture and bio." SASE. Reports in 2 weeks.
Music: Mostly pop, R&B and rock; also funk, country and alternative. Produced *Between Friends* (by Rio/Leitl), recorded by Leitl on Freedom Records (LP); "This Love So Real" (by Samuels), recorded by Richard Samuels on Bimini Records (A/C) and "Our Love" (by McDonald), recorded by Boys San Go on Bimini Records. Other artists include Rio-Grace Under Pressure, Richard Sarvecs and Eddy & The Earthtones.
Tips: "Keep an open mind and expect rejection. Staying power=success!"

*LENA MICHALS ENTERTAINMENT, (formerly Laurel Canyon Productions), 1802 Laurel Canyon Boulevard, Los Angeles CA 90046. (213)656-1277. Artist Acquisitions/Manager: Lena Michals. AS-CAP and BMI. Estab. 1980. Deals with artists and songwriters. Fee derived from sales royalties or outright fee from record company. Charges for studio time and materials.
How to Contact: Submit demo tape—unsolicited submissions are OK. Prefers cassette with 3-4 songs and lyric sheet. Reports in 3-4 weeks.
Music: Mostly R&B, dance/pop, rock; also instrumental and country. Produced all 6 *Fame* albums (by Barry Fasman), recorded by Fame cast on RCA Records (pop LPs); *Champaign* (by Dana Walden), recorded by Champaign on CBS Records (R&B LP); and *Pauli Carman* (by Barry Fasman), recorded by Pauli Carman on CBS Records (R&B LP). Other artists include Debbie Allen, Johnny Mathis and Michelle Forrester.
Tips: "Be persistant and believe in yourself."

MICROSTAR PRODUCTIONS, Dept. SM, Suite 201, 52451 Cleveland St., Virginia Beach VA 23462. (804)499-4434. President: Mark Spencer. Record producer, music publisher and record company (MircoStar, MSM). Estab. 1990. Deals with artists and songwriters. Produces 6 LPs and 6 CDs/year. Fee derived from sales royalty.
How to Contact: Write first and obtain permission to submit. Prefers cassette with 4 songs and lyric sheet. Does not return unsolicited material. Reports in 4 weeks.
Music: Mostly pop, gospel and country; also R&B. Produced *Do You Think We Have a Chance?* (by K. Cleveland), recorded by TK Llegs; *Wearing White With No Shame*, written and recorded by P. VanValin; and *Workin' Man's Dream*, written and recorded by B. Fisher; all on MicroStar Records (LP). Other artists include Don Burford, Tony Hawkins, Charity Jackson, David Givens, Matt Vollmer and Pam Osborn.
Tips: "Work hard and don't cut corners on your demo. If you won't spend your time and money on it than why should we?"

MIGHTY SOUNDS AND FILMWORKS, Suite 6-D, 150 West End Ave., New York NY 10023. (212)873-5968. Manager: Danny Darrow. Record producer, music publisher (Rockford Music Co./BMI) and record company (Mighty Sounds and Filmworks). Works with artists and songwriters. Produces 1-2 singles, 1-2 12" singles, 1-2 LPs and 1-2 EPs/year. Receives 200 submissions/month. Fee derived from sales royalty.
How to Contact: Submit demo tape—unsolicited submissions OK. Prefers cassette with 2-3 songs. SASE. No phone calls. Reports in 1 week.
Music: Mostly A/C, country and adult rock. Produced "Look To The Wind" (by P. Stewart/D. Darrow) (MOR); "Telephones" (by R.L. Lowery/D. Darrow) (rock) and "Better Than You Know" (by Michael Green) (MOR), all recorded by Danny Darrow on Mighty Records.
Tips: "Listen to the top 40 hits and write better songs."

ROBERT E. MILES/King Eugene Productions, 14016 Evers Ave., Compton CA 90222. A&R: Robert E. Miles. Record producer, music publisher (King Eugene Productions/BMI). Estab. 1988. Deals with artists and songwriters. Fee derived from sales royalty when song or artist is recorded or outright fee from record company.
How to Contact: Submit demo—unsolicited submissions are OK. Prefers cassette (or VHS videocassette if available) with several songs and lyric sheet. SASE. Reports in 1 month.
Music: Mostly rap, R&B and pop/dance. Produced "Kickin' It," written and recorded by King Eugene Revue on Janet Marie Records (R&B single); "Home Girl," recorded by Cassie 'D' on Janet Marie Records (rap single); and "Blow My Thang," written and recorded by Mig-X on Micon Records (rap single). Other artists include Ordinary People (R&B/gospel group).
Tips: "We are looking for some hot R&B/gospel acts to work with A.S.A.P."

JAY MILLER PRODUCTIONS, 413 N. Parkerson Ave., Crowley LA 70526. (318)783-1601 or 788-0773. Contact: Jay Miller. Record producer and music publisher. Deals with artists and songwriters. Produces 50 singles and 15 LPs/year. Fee derived from sales royalty.

How to Contact: Arrange personal interview. Inquiries are invited. Prefers cassette for audition.
Music: Mostly country; also blues, Cajun, disco, folk, gospel, MOR, rock, top 40/pop and comedy.
Working on video productions. Produced *Zydecajun*, by Wayne Toups on Mercury Records (LP); "I
Wish I Had A Job," by Paul Marx (single); and "The Likes Of Texas," by Sammy Kershaw (single).
Other artists include Wayne Toups, Tammy Lynn, John Fred and Camey Doucet.

MĪMÁC PRODUCTIONS, 1433 Cole Pl., Hollywood CA 90028. (213)856-8729. Artist Services: Robyn
Whitney. Record producer and studio-TRAX recording. Estab. 1979. Deals with artists and songwriters. Fee derived from sales royalty or outright fee from recording artist or record company. "If not a
spec deal, we are for hire for production services."
How to Contact: Submit demo tape by mail. Unsolicited submissions are OK. Prefers cassette (or
VHS videocassette if available) with 4 songs and lyric sheets. "Not interested in rap, pop/dance or
country. We specialize in hard rock, heavy metal, unique R&B and some mature pop." SASE. Reports
in 5 weeks.
Music: Mostly hard rock, heavy metal and funk/rock; also unique R&B, mature pop and mature Latin
pop. Produced *Total Eclipse* (by Total Eclipse), recorded by Total Eclipse on A&M Records (rock);
Juicy Talk, written and recorded by Jerry Riopelle on Warner Bros. Records (country rock); and *Music
Speaks Louder than Words* (by G. Abbot/A. Barykin), recorded by Emmanuel on Sony Records (Latin
pop). Other artists include Charlie Mitchell.
Tips: "Have your act totally developed: exact genre of music, detailed image, perfected songs. We
don't want to teach you your craft."

MR. WONDERFUL PRODUCTIONS, INC., 1730 Kennedy Rd., Lousiville KY 40216. (502)774-1066.
President: Ronald C. Lewis. Record producer, music publisher (Ron "Mister Wonderful" Music/BMI
and 1730 Music/ASCAP) and record company (Wonderful Records and Ham Sem Records). Estab.
1984. Deals with artists and songwriters. Produces 2 singles and 3 12″ singles/year. Fee is derived from
outright fee from recording artist or record company. "We also promote records of clients nationwide
to radio stations for airplay."
How to Contact: Prefers cassette with 4 songs and lyric sheet. SASE. Reports in 2 weeks.
Music: Mostly R&B, black gospel and rap. Produced "Am I Good" (by Ron Lewis) and "Just Another
In My Past" (by Pam Layne), both recorded by Amanda Orch (R&B); and "Just Do It," written and
recorded by Boyz from the Ville (rap), all on Wonderful Records.

MJM PRODUCTIONS, Box 654, Southbury CT 06488. Owner: Michael McCartney. Record producer
and music publisher (On The Button/BMI). Estab. 1988. Deals with artists and songwriters. Produces
5 singles/year. Fee derived from sales royalty or outright fee from recording artist.
How to Contact: Submit demo tape—unsolicited submissions are OK. Prefers cassette with 3-5 songs
and lyric sheet. "Give details as to what your goals are: artist in search of deal or writer wishing to
place songs." SASE. Reports in 3-4 weeks.
Music: Mostly country/rock, pop rock and R&B. Produced "Help Me Find a Way" and "Goin' to
Hollywood," both pop/rock singles on Giant Records.

MOM AND POP PRODUCTIONS, INC., Box 96, El Cerrito CA 94530. Executive Vice President: James
Bronson, Jr. Record producer, record company and music publisher (Toulouse Music/BMI). Deals
with artists, songwriters and music publishers. Fee derived from sales royalty.
How to Contact: Prefers cassette with 2-4 songs and lyric sheet. SASE. Reports in 1 month.
Music: Bluegrass, gospel, jazz, R&B and soul. Artists include Les Oublies du Jazz Ensemble.

MOOD SWING PRODUCTIONS, 332 N. Dean Rd., Auburn AL 36830. (205)821-JASS. Contact: Lloyd
Townsend, Jr. Record producer, music publisher (Imaginary Music), record company (Imaginary
Records) and distribution (Imaginary Distribution). Estab. 1982. Deals with artists. Produces 1-2
singles, 1-2 LPs, 1-2 EPs and 1-2 CDs/year. Receives 10-15 submissions/month. Fee derived from sales
royalty.
How to Contact: Submit demo tape—unsolicited submissions are OK. Prefers cassette or 7½ ips
reel-to-reel with 4 songs and lyric sheet or lead sheet. "Submissions not returned unless accompanied
by SASE; may be retained for future reference unless return specifically requested." Reports in 4-6
months.
Music: Mostly jazz; also classical, blues and rock. Produced "Weirdo/No Tomorrow," written and
recorded by Engine House (hardcore trash funk); *Maple Leaf Rag* (by Scott Joplin), recorded by
Patrick Mahoney (ragtime); and *Bone Dali*, written and recorded by Bone Dali (punk junk), all on
Imaginary Records. Other artists include Spraytruck.
Tips: "Be patient! I'm slow . . ."

*MARK J. MORETTE/MARK MANTON, 10815 Bodine Rd., Clarence NY 14031. (716)759-2600. Owner: Mark J. Morette. Record producer and record company (MarkJazz/Epigram). Estab. 1962. Deals with artists and songwriters. Produces 5-10 singles and 3-5 CDs/year. Fee derived from sales, pre-arranged agreements. "Changes for studio time, production time and personal time."
How to Contact: Write or call first and obtain permission to submit. Prefers cassette with 5-10 songs and lyric or lead sheets. SASE. Reports in 6 months.
Music: Mostly New Age/jazz, heavy metal, heavy pop. Produced *Kryst the Conqueror*, written and recorded by Kryst The Conqueror on Cyclopean Records (Thrash/Heavy metal); *Family Tree* (by Mark Manton), recorded by Men Of Murder on Epigrapm Records (Death Metal); and *Slaughtered Grace* (by Sal Bee), recorded by Slaughtered Grace on Cyclopean Records (Thrash). Other artists include Sitting Duck and Bordello Beat.
Tips: "Please, be a musician as well as a showman. Dollars are at a premium now. Know your music before you enter studio, label, or management."

ERIC MORGESON, 5619 N. Beech Daly, Dearborn Heights MI 48127. President: Eric Morgeson. Record producer. Estab. 1980. Deals with artists and songwriters. Produces more than 15 singles and 5 albums/year. Fee derived from sales royalty or outright fee from recording artist or record company.
How to Contact: Submit demo tape—unsolicited submissions are OK. Prefers cassette with 3 songs and lyric sheet. Include SASE. Reports in 6 weeks.
Music: Mostly R&B, pop and rock. Produced "Something 'Bout Your Touch," recorded by Sharon Bryant on Wing Records (R&B), and "Stay With Me," recorded by Gerry Woo on Polygram Records (R&B). Other artists include Tamika Patton, Billy Always, Fred Hammond, Krystol and Chris Bender.
Tips: "Be willing to rewrite. We just need A-sides."

*MOUNTAIN THERAPY MUSIC, Box 364, New Castle PA 16103. (412)654-3023. Contact: Jay Moore. Record producer and music publisher (Rosewood Records). Deals with artists and songwriters. Produces 5 singles, 2 12" singles, 2 CDs and 6 LPs/year. Fee derived from outright fee from recording artist.
How to Contact: Submit demo tape—unsolicited submissions are OK. Prefers cassette and lyric sheet. SASE. Reports in 3 weeks.
Music: Bluegrass/gospel and country. Produced "The Family Song," written and recorded by Todd Wher (pop/jazz); "Long Way to Go," written and recorded by Steve Schuffert (country crossover); and "Little Church," written and recorded by Terry Rechtenweld (contemporary gospel), all on Rosewood Records. Other artists include Judy Minouge, Full House, Wildwood Express, Mac Martin and Buzz Matheson.
Tips: "Please send only the type of music requested. No more than 3 songs per demo. Strong lyrics and melody."

GARY JOHN MRAZ, 1324 Cambridge Dr., Glendale CA 91205. (818)246-PLAY. Producer: Gary Mraz. Record producer. Estab. 1984. Deals with artists and songwriters. Produces 6-12 12" singles and 2-6 LPs/year. Fee derived from sales royalty or outright fee from record company.
How to Contact: Submit demo tape—unsolicited submissions are OK. Prefers cassette (or VHS videocassette if available) with 3 songs and lyric sheets. "Does not return unsolicited material." Reports in 6 weeks.
Music: Mostly dance, pop and R&B. Produced *Studio Voodoo*, written and recorded by Studio Voodoo on Dr. Dream Records (alternative dance); and *Swing Gang*, written and recorded by Swing Gang on Radio Magic Records (alternative dance). Other artists include Jon Holland, Stacy O, Bunji Jumpers and The Moosters.
Tips: "Get your finished product to the untapped college radio market."

*MULTI SOUND IMAGES, 601 N. Sixth St., Allentown PA 18102. (215)432-4040. Producer/Publisher: Mark Stocker. Record producer, music publisher (Multi Sound Images Music/BMI, Minnow Music/ASCAP) and record company (Little Apple Records). Estab. 1988. Deals with artists and songwriters. Produces 6 singles, 1 LP and 1 EP/year. Fee derived from sales royalty or outright fee from recording artist or record company.

The asterisk before a listing indicates that the listing is new in this edition. New markets are often the most receptive to unsolicited submissions.

How to Contact: Submit demo tape—unsolicited submissions are OK. Prefers cassette with 3 songs and lead sheet. "I want fresh, interesting material that is well-recorded and which directly competes with the top Billboard singles." SASE. Reports in 8 weeks.
Music: Mostly country, pop and gospel; also New Age, R&B and rock. Produced "Don't Love the Magic" (by Mark Stocker/Susan Fredericks/Carole Silvcy), recorded by Valley Voices on MSI Records (pop/top 40). Other artists include Doc Randolph, Marian Himes and Susan Piper.
Tips: "Keep your submissions straightforward, clean, well-recorded, and well written."

ROSS MUNRO/RANDOM ENTERTAINMENT INC., 121 Logan Avenue, Toronto Ontario M4M 2M9 Canada. (416)406-4121. FAX: (416)406-0319. Producer: Ross Munro. Record producer, music publisher (Toon Town Music/CAPAC, ASCAP). Estab. 1980. Deals with artists and songwriters. Produces 4-6 singles and 3-4 albums/year. Fee derived from fees and/or sales royalty.
How to Contact: Write or call first to obtain permission to submit. Prefers cassette (or VHS videocassette if available) with 2-4 songs and lyric sheets. "Does not return unsolicited material." Reports in 1 month.
Music: Mostly rock, pop and country. Produced *Thrill of the Chase*, written and recorded by Simon Chase on Axe Records (rock LP); *Breathless*, written and recorded by Jannetta on Trilogy Records (rock LP); *After The Storm*, written and recorded by Danny Brooks on Trilogy Records (rock LP) and "Mark On My Heart," by Janetta on Trilogy Record (rock/pop album).

MUSIC FACTORY ENTERPRISES, INC., Ste. 300, Ford & Washington Sts., Norristown PA 19401. (215)277-9550. Producer: Jeffrey Calhoun. Record producer, music publisher and record company (MFE Records). Estab. 1984. Deals with artists only. Produces 3-10 singles, 1-5 12" singles, 20 LPs and 1-5 CDs/year. Receives 4-5 submissions/month. Fee derived from sales royalty or outright fee from recording artist or record company. "Charges on project basis for independents; deal contingent upon artists contract with label."
How to Contact: Write first and obtain permission to submit. Prefers cassette (or ½" VHS videocassette if available) with 3-4 songs and lyric sheet. SASE. Reports in 2-3 weeks.
Music: Mostly alternative rock/pop, world beat and 20th century classical. Produced "Alien Babies," written and recorded by Steve Pullara (childrens/novelty); "Bulkhead," written and recorded by Naked Twister (alternative); and "Martin's Law," written and recorded by Bill Martin (rock), all on MFE Records. Other artists include Robert Moran and Gregory Darvis.
Tips: "Send fully developed material. Be different. For distribution deals, submission of finished masters is the easiest way for a band to 'get signed.' "

MUSIPLEX, (formerly George Pappos/Cheshire Sound Studios), 2093 Faulkner Road, N.E., Dept. SM, Atlanta GA 30324. (404)321-2701. Producer/Engineer: Gcorge Pappas. Record producer, engineer. Estab. 1967. Deals with artists and songwriters. Produces 5 singlcs, 5 12" singles, 3 LPs, 4 EPs and 5 CDs/year. Fee derived from outright fee from recording artist or record company.
How to Contact: Call first to arrange personal interview. Prefers cassette with 3-5 songs and lyric or lead sheets. "In order for any material to be returned a SASE must accompany any and all material submitted." SASE. Reports in 2 months.
Music: Alternative rock, rap and R&B; also gospel, rock and pop. Produced *Scarred But Smarter* recorded by Drivin'n'Crying on Island Records; and *Stiff Kitty* on Drastic Measures Records and *Nihilist*, written and recorded by Nihilist on Metal Blade Records. Recently credited work: Bobby Brown/Big Daddy Kane; Lateasha (Motown); Kinetic Dissent (Road Racer); Michelle Shocked (Polygram); Georgia Satellites (Elektra).

CHUCK MYMIT MUSIC PRODUCTIONS, 9840 64th Ave., Flushing NY 11374. Contacts: Chuck and Monte Mymit. Record producer and music publisher (Chuck Mymit Music Productions/BMI). Estab. 1978. Deals with artists and songwriters. Produces 8-10 singles, 2-4 12" singles, 3-5 LPs and 3-5 CDs/year. Fee derived from sales royalty or outright fee from recording artist or record company.
How to Contact: Submit demo tape—unsolicited submissions are OK. Prefers cassette (or VHS videocassette if available) with 3-5 songs and lyric or lead sheet. SASE. Reports in 1 month.
Music: Mostly pop, rock and R&B. Produced *Wanna Love You* (by Monte Mymit), recorded by Laura Cabrera on SMC Records (rap/rock); "Easy Lovin' " (by C. Mymit-Donnell & Cody), recorded by Linda L. on RCA Records (pop); and *The Last Girl in the World*, written and recorded by Pat Hully (rock). Other artists include Rita Rose, Tony Spataro, and The Dellmonts.

NARADA PRODUCTIONS, 1845 North Farwell, Milwaukee WI 53202. (414)272-6700. A&R Coordinator: Dan Chase. Record producer, music publisher and record company (Narada Records). Estab. 1980. Deals with artists only. Produces 30 LPs and 30 CDs/yaer. Fee derived from sales royalty when song or artist is recorded.

How to contact: Submit demo tape by mail. Unsolicited submissions are OK. Prefers cassette (or VHS videocassette if available) with 5 songs. Does not return unsolicited material. Reports in 2 months.

Music: New Age, instrumental and world beat; also film and television sound tracks.

Tips: "We want instrumental music."

NASHVILLE COUNTRY PRODUCTIONS, 306 Millwood Dr., Nashville TN 37217. (615)366-9999. President/Producer: Colonel Jack Lynch. Record producer, music publisher (Jaclyn Music/BMI), record companies (Jalyn and Nashville Country Productions) and distributor (Nashville Music Sales). Estab. 1987. Works with artists and songwriters. Produces 1-12 LPs/year. Fee derived from sales royalty or outright fee from artist or record company; "We do both contract and custom recording."

How to Contact: Submit demo tape, or write or call first and obtain permission to submit or arrange personal interview. Prefers cassette with 1-4 songs and lyric or lead sheet. SASE. Reports in 10 days.

Music: Mostly country, bluegrass, MOR and gospel; also comedy. "We produced Keith Whitley and Ricky Skaggs' first album." Produced "Where the Fire Used to Be," written and recorded by Lonnie Pierce on NCP-C303 Records; "Rosita" (by Art Scharinger), recorded by Jim Miller; and "Mama Paid A Call (by Shirley Hickcox), recorded by Lindsey Pruitt both on NCP Records (country). Other artists include Jack Lynch and The Nashville Travelers.

Tips: "Prepare a good quality cassette demo, send to us along with a neat lyrics sheet for each song and a resume and picture."

*NEBO RECORD COMPANY, Box 194 or 457, New Hope AL 35760. Manager: Jim Lewis. Record producer, music publisher (Nebo Ridge Publishing/ASCAP) and record company (Nebo Record Company). Estab. 1985. Deals with artists and songwriters. Fee negotiable.

How to Contact: Submit demo cassette tape by mail—unsolicited submissions are OK. Prefers cassette tape or VHS videocassette with 1 song and lyric sheet. "It is OK to send a videocassette, but not a must. Send 1 song only. Songwriters should be sure to send a SASE. Send a neat professional package. Send only 1 song." Does not return unsolicited material. Reports "as soon as possible."

Music: Mostly modern country, traditional country and gospel; also rock, R&B and pop. Produced "Memories" (by Flint) recorded by Flint Paint Rock; "Long Gone" written and recorded by Ed Walker and "Blue Again" (by Osie) recorded by Osie Whitaker ; all on Nebo Records (country). Other artists include James W. Hilliard, James Pence and Flint Paint Rock.

Tips: "Send us a professional bio package and your *best* songs for review."

BILL NELSON, 45 Perham St., W. Roxbury MA 02132. Contact: Bill Nelson. Record producer and music publisher (Henly Music/ASCAP). Estab. 1987. Deals with artists and songwriters. Produces 6 singles and 6 LPs/year. Fee derived from outright fee from recording artist.

How to Contact: Submit demo tape by mail—unsolicited submissions are OK. Prefers cassette with 3-4 songs and lyric sheet. SASE. Reports in 3-4 weeks.

Music: Mostly country, pop and gospel. Produced "Big Bad Bruce" (by J. Dean), recorded by B.N.O.; "Do You Believe in Miracles" (by B. Nelson), recorded by Part-Time Singers; and "Don't Hurry With Love" (by B. Bergeron), recorded by B.N.O.; all on Woodpecker Records (all singles).

NEW DAWN PRODUCTIONS/SOUTH BOUND PRODUCTIONS, Box 111, Newbury WI 53060. (414)675-2839. Producer: Robert Wiegert. Record producer and music publisher (RobJen Music, Trinity Music and Great Northern Lights Music). Works with artists and songwriters. Fee derived from sales royalty.

How to Contact: Prefers 7½ ips reel-to-reel or cassette with 3 songs and lyric sheet. Does not return unsolicited material. Reports in 1 month.

Music: New Age and fine arts music.

Tips: "If we feel a song is a hit, we do everything possible to get it cut. But writers must be self critical and write, write, write."

NEW EXPERIENCE RECORDS, Box 683, Lima OH 45802 (419)674-4170 or (419)675-2990. Music Publisher: James L. Milligan Jr. Vice President: Tonya Milligan. Record producer, music publisher and record company (New Experience Records, Grand-Slam Records, Rap Label). Estab. 1989. Deals with artists and songwriters. Produces 5 12" singles, 2 LPs, 1 EP and 2 CDs/year. Fee derived from sales royalty when song or artist is recorded, outright fee from recording artist or outright fee from record company, "depending on services required."

How to Contact: Submit demo tape—unsolicited submissions are OK. Prefers cassette with a minimum of 3 songs and lyric or lead sheets (if available). "If tapes are to be returned, proper postage should be enclosed and all tapes and letters should have SASE for faster reply." Reports in 1 month.

Music: Mostly pop, R&B and rap; also gospel, contemporary gospel and rock. Produced "Blue Haze" (by James Milligan), recorded by James Junior on Amethyst Records (R&B); "Lawman" (by Ray Smith), recorded by M.C.Y.T. on New Experience Records (rap); and *Still In Touch*, written and recorded by Tammy Oaks on New Experience Records (gospel). Other artists include Techno 3, Melvin Milligan, Robert Perry, Anthony Milligan, Just Smooth, Roger Wads and Carl Milligan.

Tips: "Believe in yourself. Work hard. Keep submitting songs and demos. Most of all, be patient; if there's interest you will be contacted."

NEW HORIZON RECORDS, 3398 Nahatan Way, Las Vegas NV 89109. (702)732-2576. President: Mike Corda. Record producer. Deals with singers preferably. Fee derived by sales royalty.

How to Contact: Submit demo tape—unsolicited submissions are OK. Prefers cassette with 1-3 songs and lyric sheet. SASE.

Music: Blues, easy listening, jazz and MOR. Produced "Lover of the Simple Things," "Offa the Sauce" (by Corda & Wilson) and "Go Ahead and Laugh," all recorded by Mickey Rooney on Prestige Records (London). Artists include Bob Anderson, Jan Rooney, Joe Williams, Robert Goulet and Bill Haley and the Comets.

Tips: "Send good musical structures, melodic lines, and powerful lyrics or quality singing if you're a singer."

*NISE PRODUCTIONS, INC., 413 Cooper St., Camden NJ 08102. (609)963-6400. Contact: Dan McKeown. Record producer, music publisher (Nise Productions Inc./BMI) and record company (Power Up, Euro-American Intn'l). Estab. 1981. Deals with artists and songwriters. Produces 1-5 singles and 1-5 LPs/year.

How to Contact: Submit demo tape by mail—unsolicited submissions are OK. Prefers cassette with 3 songs and lyric sheets. SASE. Reports in 2-3 weeks.

DAVID NORMAN PRODUCTIONS, #1632, 639 Garden Walk Blvd., College Park GA 30349. (404)994-1770. Producer/Engineer: David Norman. Record producer. Estab. 1986. Deals with artists and songwriters. Produces 6 singles, 5 LPs, 5 EPs and 4 CDs/year. Receives 200 submissions/year. Fee derived from outright fee from recording artist or outright fee from record company.

How to Contact: Submit demo tape by mail—unsolicited submissions are OK. Prefers cassette with 5 songs. "Please send photo." SASE. Reports in 2 weeks.

Music: Mostly funk and R&B; also techno-music. Produced "So Inclined," recorded by AC Black on Allegro Records (dance/rock); "Derek Coile," recorded by Derek Coile on Macola Records (dance); and "Wages of Syn," recorded by Synical on Kudzu Records (techno). Other artists include Christina.

Tips: "I see the music industry being overkilled by musical programming on computers. Hopefully, in the coming years, music will once again resort to real drummers and musicians actually playing the music themselves."

*NOT RECORDS TAPES, Box 29161, Los Angeles CA 90029. President: Mike Alvarez. Record producer, record company and music publisher. Estab. 1984. Deals with artists and songwriters. Produces 2 singles, 2 12″ singles, 2 LPs, 2 EPs and 2 CDs/year. Fee derived from sale of product.

How to Contact: Submit demo tape by mail—unsolicited submissions are OK. Prefers cassette with lyric sheet. Does not return unsolicited material.

Music: Mostly industrial, film and alternative. Produced "Love" and "On The Beach" (by Alverez), recorded by M. Alverez on Not Records Tapes Records (singles); and *Rave On* (by Jones), recorded by Ken Jones on Mansion On A Hill Records (LP). Other artists include Roky Erickson, Mike Avarez, Woodshock and Ken Jones.

Tips: "We are diverse in our music needs."

*NOT-2-PERFECT PRODUCTIONS, 615 Valley Rd., Upper Montclair NJ 07043-1403. (201)746-2359. Owner: George Louvis. Record producer. Estab. 1989. Deals with artists and songwriters. Produces 8-10 12″ singles and 2-4 LPs/year. "We pay all recording costs then recoup from record companies advance and royalties."

How to Contact: Submit demo tape—unsolicited submissions are OK. Prefers cassette with 1-2 songs and lyric sheet. "If you are submitting as an artist include a picture and bio if available." Does not return unsolicited material. Reports in 4-6 weeks.

Music: Mostly R&B, club dance and rap; also pop rock, pop dance and pop metal. Produced "To the Maximum" (by Steven McGhee, G. Louvis, Sly Stone), recorded by Steve D the Destroyer on Q-Rap (rap 12″ single); "Gotta Have It" (G. Louvis), recorded by Liberation on Republic Records (club 12″ single); "Love Me True" (by G. Louvis), recorded by Kimiesha Holmes on Quark Records (Club 12″ single). Other artists include Tammy Francica, Blaze (co-produce), One & One.

Tips: "Be patient. In the first six months of 1989 we signed 3 artists, produced them, shopped deals for them and got deals for all three. Submit your best material and learn to be objective. Don't believe that just because you wrote it, it's great. If you wouldn't buy it don't send it."

NOW+THEN MUSIC, Dept. SM, 501 78th St., #3, North Berger NJ 07047&. (201)854-6266. President: Shane Faber. Record producer, music publisher (Now+Then Music/BMI) and record company (Now-+Then Records). Estab. 1980. Deals with artists and songwriters. Produces 10 singles and 2 LPs/year. Fee derived from sales royalty when song or artist is recorded, outright fee from recording artist and outright fee from record company. "I'm usually hired to produce and record masters for artists by their management or labels—or to mix their material."
How to Contact: Submit demo tape by mail. Unsolicited submissions are OK. Prefers cassette (or DAT or VHS videocassette if available) with 4 songs and lyric sheet. SASE. Reports in 2 months.
Music: Mostly rap, R&B and rock; also quiet storm, New Age and world beat. Produced "Turtle Power" (written and recorded by Partners In Kryme), on SBK Records (rap single); "Work" (by Faber/King Davis), recorded by BTXpress (R&B single); and "Partyline," recorded by 5th Platoon on SBK Records (rap single).

*NUCLEUS RECORDS, Box 111, Sea Bright NJ 07760. President: Robert Bowden. Record producer, music publisher (Roots Music/BMI) and record company (Nucleus Records). Estab. 1979. Deals with artists and songwriters. Produces 2 singles and 1 LP/year. Fee derived from sales royalty.
How to Contact: Submit demo tape—unsolicited submissions are OK. Prefers cassette with 3 songs and lyric sheets. SASE. Reports in 4 weeks.
Music: Mostly country and gospel; also pop. Produced "Pressure Cooker," written and recorded by Jean Schweitzer (country); "Always," written and recorded by Marco Sision (pop); and "Selfish Heart," written and recorded by Robert Bowden (country); all on Nucleus Records.

OGDENHOUSE MUSIC PRODUCTIONS, Los Angeles CA 90046. (213)851-0458. President: Byron De Lear. Record producer and songwriter (De Lear Music/ASCAP). Estab. 1987. Deals with artists and songwriters. Produces 3-5 singles, and 3-4 LPs/year.
How to Contact: Call first and obtain permission to submit. Prefers cassette with 3 songs and lyric sheets. Reports in 6 weeks.
Music: Mostly pop, rock and R&B; also MOR and country. Produced *Warren Hill*, recorded by Warren Hill on BMG/Novus Records (R&B/jazz LP); "Ready," recorded by Joey Diggs on Capitol Records (pop single); and "Cold Shoulder," written and recorded by Taz on Monster Records (rock EP).

JEANNINE O'NEAL PRODUCTIONS, 195 S. 26th St., San Jose CA 95116. (408)286-9840. FAX: (408)286-9845. Producer: Jeannine O'Neal. Record producer and arranger. Deals with artists and songwriters. Produces 10 singles, 5 12" singles, 6 LPs and 2 CDs/year. Fee derived from sales royalty, outright fee from songwriter/artist and/or outright fee from record company.
How to Contact: Submit demo tape—unsolicited submissions are OK. Prefers cassette with 3 songs and lyric or lead sheets. SASE. Reports in 2-3 weeks.
Music: Mostly rock/pop, country and gospel; also jazz and international. Produced "Before, After" and "Oh Why," recorded by Sister Suffragette (pop/rap); *Up On the Edge*, by Jaque Lynn (country LP); *Can You Feel It* by Charlie (country LP); "Get Me to the Country," by Larry Martinez (country); "One From the Heart," by Practical Jokes (New Age/alternative rock); "Grandpa Lee" by Helen Reyes (country); "Celebramos Tu Victoria" by Diego Moreno, Jr. (contemporary Christian/Mexican); and "New American Music" by Jeannine O'Neal (country).

ORDER PRODUCTIONS, 6503 York Rd., Baltimore MD 21212. (410)377-2270. President: Jeff Order. Record producer and music publisher (Order Publishing/ASCAP and Orderlottsa Music/BMI). Estab. 1986. Deals with artists and songwriters. Fee derived from sales royalty and outright fee from recording artist and record company.
How to Contact: Submit demo tape—unsolicited submissions are OK. "Lyric sheets without recorded music are unacceptable." Prefers cassette with 3 songs and lyric sheet. SASE. Reports in 1 month.
Music: Works with all types of music. Produced "Won't You Dance With Me" (by Jeff Order), recorded by Tiny Tim (dance/single); *Sea of Tranquility, Isis Unveiled,* and *Keepers of the Light,* written and recorded by Jeff Order (New Age LPs). Other artists include Stephen Longfellow Fiske, (Higher Octave) and Rock Group Boulevard.
Tips: "We only work with songwriters and artists who are seriously committed to a career in music. Submissions must be professionally recorded. Learn as much about the business of music as possible. Don't expect someone to invest in your art if you haven't done it first!"

JOHN "BUCK" ORMSBY/ETIQUETTE PRODUCTIONS, Suite 273, 2442 N.W. Market, Seattle WA 98107. (206)524-1020. FAX: (206)524-1102. Publishing Director: John Ormsby. Record producer (Etiquette/Suspicious Records) and music publisher (Valet Publishing). Estab. 1980. Deals with artists

and songwriters. Produces 1-2 singles, 3-5 LPs, and 3-5 CDs/year. Fee derived from sales royalty.
How to Contact: Prefers cassette (or VHS videocassette if available) with lyric or lead sheet. SASE.
Music: R&B, rock, pop and country. Produced *Snake Dance* (by Rogers), recorded by Kinetics on Etiquette Records (LP); and *Hard to Rock Alone*, written and recorded by K. Morrill on Suspicious Records (LP); and *Crazy 'Bout You*, (by R. Rogers), recorded by Kinetics on Etiquette Records. Other artists include Jerry Roslie.
Tips: "Tape production must be top quality; lead or lyric sheet professional."

JOHNNY PALAZZOTTO/PAL PRODUCTIONS, Box 80691, Baton Rouge LA 70898. (504)924-3327.
Owner: Johnny Palazzotto. Record producer and music publisher (Ertis Music Co./ASCAP). Estab.
1980. Deals with artists and songwriters. Produces 1 single, 1 LP and 1 CD/year.
How to Contact: Submit demo tape—unsolicited submissions are OK. Prefers cassette with 3-5 songs. "Please try to be objective regarding your own material, maybe let someone whose opinion you respect choose your submissions." Reports in 2-4 weeks.
Music: Mostly rock n' roll, R&B and country; also zydeco, cajun and gospel. Produced "TeNiNeNi Nu" (by Slim Harpo) and *Keep on Walkin'* (by Major Handy); both recorded by Major Handy on Maison de Soul (zydeco). Other artists include Raful Neal, Rudy Richard and Henry Gray.

MICHAEL PANEPENTO/AIRWAVE PRODUCTION GROUP INC., 1916 28th Ave. South, Birmingham AL 35209. (205)870-3239. Producer: Michael Panepento. Record producer, music publisher (Panelips Music/BMI) and record company (Pandem Records Inc.). Estab. 1985. Deals with artists and songwriters. Produces 5 singles, 2 12" singles, 4 LPs, 5 EPs and 3 CDs/year. Fee derived from sales royalty.
How to Contact: Submit demo tape—unsolicited submissions are OK. Prefers cassette with 3 songs and lyric sheet. SASE. Reports in 10 weeks.
Music: Mostly rock, R&B and pop; also jazz and country. Produced *Home* (by Keith Hammrick), recorded by The Skeptics (modern rock); *Drivin Me Crazy* (by Larry Shaw) recorded by Radio Ranch (country); and *Diptones "Live"* (by various), recorded by The Diptones on Pandem Records (MOR). Other artists include Syntwister, Kelly O'Neal and Elvis' Grave.

PANIO BROTHERS LABEL, Box 99, Montmartre, Saskatchewan S0G 3M0 **Canada.** Executive Director: John Panio, Jr. Record producer. Estab. 1977. Deals with artists and songwriters. Produces 1 single and 1 LP/year. Receives 6 submissions/month. Works with lyricists and composers and teams collaborators. Fee derived from sales royalty or outright fee from artist/songwriter or record company.
How to Contact: Submit demo tape—unsolicited submissions are OK. Prefers cassette with any number of songs and lyric sheet. SASE. Reports in 1 month.
Music: Country, dance, easy listening and Ukrainian. Produced *Ukranian Country*, written and recorded by Vlad Panio on PB Records (LP).

***PARADISE ALLEY PRODUCTIONS,** 201-1505 W. 2nd Ave., Vancouver B.C. V6H 3Y4 **Canada.**
(604)731-3535. FAX: (604)731-2466. Manager: Michael Godin. Record producer. Estab. 1987. Deals with artists and songwriters. Fee derived from fee and sales royalty.
How to Contact: Call first. Prefers cassette (or VHS videocassette if available with 3-5 songs and lyric sheet. SASE. Reports in 6-8 weeks.
Music: Mostly rock, pop and dance. Produced "Not Like Kissing You" (by J. Dexter), recorded by Westend Girls on A&M Records (dance pop single); and *Bob's Your Uncle*, recorded by Bob's Your Uncle on Dr. Dream Records (LP).

PATTY PARKER, Suite 114, 10603 N. Hayden Rd., Scottsdale AZ 85260. (602)951-3115. FAX: (602)951-3074. Producer: Patty Parker. Record producer, record company (Comstock, Paylode), miscellaneous independent releases. Estab. 1978. Deals with artists and songwriters. Produces 18 singles, and 4-5 CDs/year. Receives 60 submissions/month. Fee derived from outright fee from recording artist or recording company. "We *never* charge to songwriters!! Artist's fee for studio production/session costs."
How to Contact: Submit demo tape—unsolicited submissions are OK. Prefers cassette (or VHS videocassette if available) with 4 songs and lyric sheet. Voice up front on demos. SASE. Reports in 2 weeks.
Music: Mostly country—traditional to crossover, western and some A/C. Produced "Sedona Serenade" (by Frank Fara), recorded by Jess Owen on Comstock Records (country); "Santa Fe Night," written and recorded by Carl Freberg on Comstock Records (country); and "Have Love Will Travel" (by Joe Radosevich), recorded by Jodie Sinclair on Comstock Records (country). Other artists include Paul Gibson, Colin Clark, The Roberts Sisters, and Horst Krush (Switzerland).
Tips: "Writers should strive to write medium to uptempo songs—there's an abundance of ballads. New artists should record medium to uptempo material as that can sometimes better catch the ear of radio programmers."

DAVE PATON, The Idea Bank, 16776 Lakeshore Dr., C-300, Lake Elsinore CA 92330. Contact: Dave Paton. Record producer and music publisher (Heaven Songs/BMI). Deals with artists and songwriters. Produces 20 singles and 3-5 LPs/year. Fee negotiable.
How to Contact: Submit demo tape—unsolicited submissions are OK. Prefers 7½ ips reel-to-reel or cassette with 3-6 songs and lyric sheet. SASE. Reports in 4 weeks.
Music: Country, dance, easy listening, jazz, MOR, progressive, R&B, rock, top 40/pop and comedy. Produced "Steal My Heart," "Heartache Highway" and "Love is a State of Mind," all written by A.J. Masters and recorded by Linda Rae on Hollyrock Records (country).

*MARTIN PEARSON MUSIC, Seestrasse 91, Zurich, CH 8002 **Switzerland.** Phone: (01)202-4077. Contact: Martin Pearson. Record producer, music publisher and record company. Works with artists and songwriters. Produces 2 singles, 2 12″ singles, 1 LP and 1 CD/year. Fee derived from sales royalty or outright fee from record company.
How to Contact: Submit demo tape—unsolicited submissions are OK. Prefers cassette (or PAL videocassette) with 6 songs and lyric sheet. SAE and IRC. Reports in 2 months.
Music: Mostly pop, rock and R&B; also disco/rock, disco and techno. Produced "Riot in the Night," written and recorded by the Monsters on West Virginia Records (rock); "Keep Going On," written and recorded by Ashantis on Bantam Records (pop/disco); and "Clock Out," written and recorded by Meanviles on Black Cat Records (rock). Other artists include Sam (guitar band).

*PEGMATITE PRODUCTIONS, (formerly Outlook Productions), c/o The Outlook, Box 180, Star Route, Bethel ME 04217. (207)824-3246. Record producer. Deals with artists and songwriters. Produces 12 singles and 6 LPs/year. Fee derived from sales royalty and/or outright fee from record company.
How to Contact: Prefers cassette or 15 ips reel-to-reel (or VHS videocassette if available) with 1 song and lyric sheet. "Please include your name and phone number on the tape." Does not return unsolicited material. Reports in 3 months.
Music: Mostly rock, pop and country; also new wave, heavy metal and avant-garde. Produced "Out Of The Woods," written and recorded by various artists; "Smell The Probe," written and recorded by Sonny Probe (rock humor); and "Shut Up," written and recorded by Darien Brahms (rock), all on Tourmaline Music Records.

JOHN PENNY, 484 Lexington St., Waltham MA 02154. (617)891-7800. President: John Penny. Record producer, music publisher (Penny Thoughts Music/BMI) and record company (Belmont Records, Waverly Records). Produces 15 singles and 6 LPs/year. Deals with songwriters and artists. Fee derived from fee from recording artist.
How to Contact: Write first and obtain permission to submit. Prefers cassette with 3-4 songs. SASE. Reports in 4 weeks.
Music: Mostly C&W, rock. Produced *Hands of a Dreamer*, written and recorded by Larry Flint (LP and single); "Good Timer," written and recorded by Stan Jr. Anderson (single); and "Nights Out at the Days Inn" (by J. Fox/L. Wilson/R. Ball), recorded by Jimmy Allen; all country/western on Belmont Records. Other artists include Jackie Lee Williams, Tim Barrett, John Hicks, Paul Metcalf, Rick Robinson and The Bayou Boys and Mike Cummings.

*PERSIA STUDIOS, 378 Bement Ave., Staten Island NY 10310. (718)816-6384. Studio Owner: Chris Vollor. Producer/engineer. Estab. 1982. Deals with artists and songwriters. Produces 5-10 singles, 2 LPs and 3 CDs/year. Fee derived from recording artist or record company. Charges for studio time—session players.
How to Contact: Submit demo tape—unsolicited submissions are OK. Prefers cassette/DAT (or VHS videocassette if available) with 3-4 songs. Does not return unsolicited material. Reports in 2 months.
Music: Mostly rock, pop and R&B; also alternative, dance and industrial and jazz/New Age. Produced *Sleeper*, written and recorded by Sleeper on Tragic Life Records (punk/alternative); *Nick DiSla*, written and recorded by Nick DiSla on 101 Records (dance); and *Sal: A Rock Opener*, written and recorded by In Crowd on Tragic Life Records (pop). Other artists include Boom Tech, Sweet Con, Vienna, 2 Am Cupid and DEA.

*PAUL PETERSON CREATIVE MANAGEMENT, 9005 Cynthia, #309, Los Angeles CA 90069. (310)273-7255. Contact: Paul Peterson. Record producer, music publisher and personal management firm. Estab. 1983. Deals with artists and songwriters. Produces 2 LPs and 2 CDs/year. Fee derived from sales royalty or outright fee from songwriter/artist or record company.

How to Contact: Submit demo tape—unsolicited submissions are OK. Prefers cassette and lyric sheet. SASE. Reports in 3 weeks.

Music: Mostly rock, pop and jazz; also country. Produced "Lost Cabin" (by Steve Cash), recorded by Ozark Mountain Daredevils on Legend Records (country/rock); "The Lost Tapes" (by various artists), recorded by National Lampoon on National Lampoon Records (comedy); and *Everything's Alright*, written and recorded by Priscilla Bowman on Legend Records (blues/rock LP). Other artists include Man About Town (modern rock), 3 Norwegians (pop/rock) and Brewer & Shipley.

PHANTOM PRODUCTIONS, INC., Box 90936, Austin TX 78709-0936. (512)288-1044. FAX: (512)288-4748. Director: Chris or Martin Theophilus. Record producer, music publisher (Mystikos Music/BMI) and record company (Phantom Records, US and UK). Estab. 1964. Deals with artists and songwriters. Produces 20 singles, 10 LPs and 5 CDs/year. Fee derived from sales royalty when song or artist is recorded.

How to Contact: Submit demo tape—unsolicited submissions are OK. Prefers cassette (or VHS videocassette if available) with 4-6 songs and lyric sheet. SASE. Reports in 6 weeks.

Music: Mostly pop, New Age, alternative rock and country; also R&B, gospel, jazz and Latin. Produced *Shadow Of A Doubt* (country CD/LP written and recorded by Mark Luke Daniels); *Chambridge Circus* (rock LP written and recorded by John Cambridge); and *Bare Bones and Railroad Tones* (country LP/cassette written and recorded by Mark Luke Daniels), all on Phantom Records. Other artists include Tracy Lyn, The Twins, James Hinkle, John Cambridge (UK) and Black Pearl.

Tips: "Most of the artists we work with are singer/songwriters. We find we react best to artists who know what they want, have spent some amount of time developing their skill and following . . . and who have a well produced demo with professional packaging. We look for artists with international potential."

PHILLY BREAKDOWN, 216 W. Hortter St., Philadelphia PA 19119. (215)848-6725. President: Matthew Childs. Record producer, music publisher (Philly Breakdown/BMI) and record company (Philly Breakdown). Estab. 1974. Deals with artists and songwriters. Produces 3 singles and 2 LPs/year. Fee derived from sales royalty when song or artist is recorded.

How to Contact: Submit demo tape—unsolicited submissions are OK. Prefers cassette with 4 songs and lead sheet. SASE. Reports in 6 weeks.

Music: Mostly R&B, hip hop and pop; also jazz, gospel and ballads. Produced "Love Slave" and "How Would You Feel," both written by Matt Childs and recorded by Gloria Clark on Philly Breakdown Records. Other artists include Leroy Christy, Mark Adam and Herb Colley.

Tips: "Be original and creative and stay current. Be exposed to all types of music."

PINE ISLAND MUSIC, (formerly Quadraphonic Talent, Inc.), #308, 9430 Live Oak Place, Ft. Lauderdale FL 37324. (305)472-7757. President: Jack P. Bluestein. Record producer and music publisher. Estab. 1973. Deals with artists and songwriters. Produces 5-10 singles/year. Fee derived from sales royalty.

How to Contact: Artist: query, submit demo tape. Songwriter: submit demo tape and lead sheet. Prefers cassette or 7½ ips reel-to-reel with 1-4 songs. SASE. Reports in 1-2 months.

Music: Blues, country, easy listening, folk, gospel, jazz, MOR, rock, soul and top 40/pop. Produced "Love Was Talking To Us" (by P. Wayeski & J. Wagner), recorded by Sherry Vencil (rock); "Buckshot Romance" (by E. Miller & F. Lancaster), recorded by Mark Campbell (country); and "I'm Living It Up" (by E. Miller), recorded by Vickie Ray Skipper (country), all on Quadrant Records.

Tips: "Write good saleable material and have an understandable demo made."

PLANET DALLAS, P.O. Box 191447, Dallas TX 75219. (214)521-2216. Manager: Tammy Whitt. Record producer, music publisher (Planet Mothership/BMI, Stoli Music/ASCAP) and recording studio (Hot Dog Productions Co.). Estab. 1985. Deals with artists and songwriters. Produces 30 singles, 30 12" singles, 20 LPs, 30 EPs and 20 CDs/year. Fee derived from sales royalty or outright fee from recording artist or record company.

How to Contact: Submit demo tape by mail or write first and obtain permission to submit. Prefers cassette (or VHS videocassette if available) with 4 songs and lyric sheet. Reports in 4-6 weeks. Send SASE for reply.

Music: Mostly modern rock and top 40. Produced *Princess Tex*, (by Hal West) recorded by Princess Tex (pop/LP) on Horsehead Records; *King*, written and recorded by The Daylights (punk/funk EP) on 109 Records; and *To Hell and Back*, written and recorded by Nemesis (rap LP) on Profile Records. Other artists include Shock Tu, The Trees and The Mystics.

PLAYTOWN SOUND PRODUCTIONS, 625 Connable Ave., Petoskey MI 49770. (616)347-0063. Owner: Bob Bollinger. Record producer and engineer/producer. Estab. 1987. Deals with artists and songwriters. Produces 50 singles and 10 LPs/year. Fee derived from outright fee from recording artist. Charges upfront: "We receive a deposit for orchestrating services."

How to Contact: Submit demo tape—unsolicited submissions are OK. Prefers cassette with 4 songs and lyric or lead sheets. "Telephone us after mailing cassette." SASE. Reports in 1-2 weeks.
Music: Mostly pop, rock and folk/rock; also country, folk and metal. Produced "Sweet Dreams," written and recorded by Kurt Puffpaff (rock); "Balance," written and recorded by Randy Newsted (soft rock) and "Shelter in the Country," written and recorded by Kerry West (folk rock). Other artists include Terry Becks, Sue Pocklinton, Kirby Snively, Bryan Connolly and The Night Rockers.
Tips: "Learn patience. Steady hard work always yields good results."

POKU PRODUCTIONS, (formerly Jon E. Shakka Productions), 176 B Woodridge Cres., Nepean ON K2B 7S9 **Canada.** (613)596-5638. President: Jon E. Shakka. Record producer (SOCAN). Estab. 1988. Deals with artists and songwriters. Produces 1 single and 1 12″ single/year. Fee derived from sales royalty when song or artist is recorded, outright fee from recording artist or outright fee from record company.
How to Contact: Submit demo tape—unsolicited submissions are OK. Prefers cassette (or VHS videocassette if available) with 4 songs and lyric sheet. SASE. Reports in 4 months.
Music: Mostly funk, rap and house music; also pop, ballads and funk-rock. Produced "Shake Your Pants" (by J. Poku/E. Poku), recorded by Jon E. Shakka on Sizzle Records (rap 12″ single); "Time To Make A Change" (soul/rap) and "Tell Them You Won't Leave" (soul/ballad), both by J. Polu/A. Skyy, recorded by August "Hip" Skyy on Poku Records.
Tips: "Don't follow trends—set them. Be professional, and know the business. First, hold on to a piece of that publishing."

*POMGAR PRODUCTIONS, Box 707, Nashville TN 37076-0707. Manager: Don Pomgar. Record producer, music publisher (One Time Music/BMI, Two Time Music/ASCAP). Estab. 1989. Deals with artists and songwriters. Produces 1 12″ single, 4 LPs, 1 EP and 4 CDs/year. Fee derived from sales royalty when song or artist is recorded, outright fee from record company.
How to Contact: Submit demo tape—unsolicited submissions are OK. Prefers cassette with 1 to 10 songs and lyric sheet. "If you're an artist send a picture and your best vocal songs. If you're a writer don't send a picture—just your best songs." SASE. Reports in 1 month.
Music: Mostly country, pop and rock. Produced *Love Me Like You Mean It* (by Tom Rhody & Tony Keeler) recorded by Tom Rhody on CCR (country) and *It'll Fly* written and recorded by Nina Byzantine on Plex Records (pop/dance). Other artists include Danny Leader (country independent artist), Terry Bower (pop/rock) and Turmoil.
Tips: "Here's what we're about. We try to find great songs to use with the artists we produce. Our artists are released on independent labels with the goal of shopping them to a major label for rerelease or distribution. We also pitch songs regularly to major artists through our publishing company. We're growing fast—we need songs."

*POTTEMUS PRODUCTIONS, 29 S. Erie, Toledo OH 43602. President: Loomis T. Shaw. Record producer and music publisher. Deals with artists and songwriters. Produces 5-10 singles and 1-5 LPs/year. Fee derived from sales royalty.
How to Contact: Prefers cassette with 3 songs and lyric sheet. Does not return unsolicited material. Reports in 6 weeks.
Music: Country, MOR, jazz and rock. Produced "Ring-a-Ding," and "Helluva Nite," by Hotlix on MDS Records (MOR singles); and "A Place to Hide," by Mikki Walsh on Jamestune Records (MOR single). Other artists include Lori Le Fevre, Nevada Flatts, Mick Payne, Polyphony, Woody Brubaker, Kerry Clark and Ebenezr.
Tips: "Actively seeking acts for new record label (Newstar International Records) during next two years. Interested in self-contained acts ready to tour. Will review any type act regardless of music style."

PREJIPPIE MUSIC GROUP, Box 2849, Trolley Station, Detroit MI 48231. President: Bruce Henderson. Record producer, music publisher (Prejippie Music Group/BMI) and record company (PMG Records). Estab. 1990. Deals with artists and songwriters. Produces 6-12 12″ singles, 1 LP and 1 EP/year. Negotiates between sales royalty and outright fee from artist or record company.
How to Contact: Submit demo tape—unsolicited submissions are OK. No phone calls please. Prefers cassette with 3-4 songs and lyric sheets. SASE. Reports in 6 weeks.
Music: Mostly funk/rock and techno/house; also alternative rock, experimental music (for possible jingle/scoring projects). Produced "Redd Hott" by The Prejippies, and "I Just Want Your Love" by Jezebel; all by PMG Productions on PMG Records. Other artists include Sacred Places (alternative rock) and Sonic Holocaust (underground/tecno).
Tips: "We're looking for songwriters who have a good sense of arrangement, a fresh approach to a certain sound and a great melody/hook for each song."

THE PRESCRIPTION CO., 70 Murray Ave., Port Washington NY 10050. (516)767-1929. President: David F. Gasman. Vice President A&R: Kirk Nordstrom. Tour Coordinator/Shipping: Bill Fearn. Secretary: Debbie Fearn. Record producer and music publisher (Prescription Co./BMI). Deals with artists and songwriters. Fee derived from sales royalty or outright fee from record company.
How to Contact: Write or call first about your interest then submit demo. Prefers cassette with any number of songs and lyric sheet. Does not return unsolicited material. Reports in 1 month. "Send all submissions with SASE or no returns."
Music: Bluegrass, blues, children's, country, dance, easy listening, jazz, MOR, progressive, R&B, rock, soul and top 40/pop. Produced "You Came In" and "Rock 'n' Roll Blues," by Medicine Mike (pop singles, Prescription Records); and *Just What the Doctor Ordered*, by Medicine Mike (LP).
Tips: "We want quality—fads mean nothing to us. Familiarity with the artist's material helps too."

PRIMAL PRODUCTIONS, INC., Suite 133, 3701 Inglewood Ave., Redondo Beach CA 90278. (213)214-0370. Vice President/Producer: Jeffrey Howard. Record producer, music publisher (Primal Visions Music/BMI) and record company (Primal Records). Estab. 1985. Deals with artists and songwriters. Produces 6 singles, 3 LPs and 3 CDs/year. Production charges vary from artist to writer. Charges in advance for services. "This doesn't always apply, but generally we get 50% production fees in advance on projects we produce, 50% on delivery of finished masters."
How to Contact: Write or call first and obtain permission to submit or to arrange personal interview. Prefers (DAT) cassette (or VHS videocassette if available) with 1-5 songs and lyric sheet. "Send only your best and strongest material. Demos are OK but use of high quality cassettes and packaging does reflect on your level of professionalism." SASE. Reports in 6 weeks.
Music: Mostly rock and hard rock, pop and R&B/dance/rap; also country, New Age and heavy metal. Produced *The Passion*, written and recorded by Jeffrey Howard for Primal Records (rock/hard-rock); and *Keeper of the Flame*, written and recorded by Jeff Laine. Other artists include Christopher Fedrov and Cynne Eslin.
Tips: "Always believe in yourself and your material. Don't write what you think *we* want to hear. We're interested in strong material performed by people with a passion for what they do. I have recently seen a trend toward rap music on the West Coast, and there seems to be no end in sight to that. Commercial hard rock has literally turned radio into the 'Rock 40' and that also will continue to be a strong contender in the commercial music market."

PRINCE/SF PRODUCTIONS, 1135 Francisco St., San Francisco CA 94109. (415)775-9627. Artists Representative: Ken Malucelli. Record producer, music publisher (Prince/SF Publications/ASCAP) record company (Auriga, Christmas). Estab. 1975. Deals with artists only. Produces 1 LP and 1 CD/year. Fee derived from sales royalty when song or artist is recorded.
How to Contact: Write first and obtain permission to submit. Prefers cassette (or VHS videocassette if available) with 3 songs and lyric and lead sheet. "Primarily interested in a cappella, novelty, theatrical material." SASE. Reports in 1 week.
Music: Mostly original pop, Christmas and satire; also unusual and humorous. Produced *The Merrie Olde Christmas Carolers*, (by Ken Malucelli), recorded by MOCCarolers on Christmas Records (Holiday, cassette); *Loud is Good* (by The EDLOS), recorded by The EDLOS on Auriga Tapes and CDs (pop, cassette); "Freedomsong" (by Eric Morris), recorded by The EDLOS on Auriga Tapes (pop single) and A Capellan Christmas (by The EDLOS), recorded by The EDLOS on Auriga Tapes and CDs.
Tips: "Work should be unique, high quality, not derivative."

*WILLIAM PRINES III, 3700 S. Hawthorne, Sioux Falls SD 57105. (605)334-6832. Producer: William Prines III. Record producer. Estab. 1977. Deals with artists and songwriters. Produces 4 singles, 6 LPs and 2 CDs/year.
How to Contact: Write first and obtain permission to submit. Prefers cassette with 3 songs and lyric sheet. SASE. Reports in 3 months.
Music: Mostly country, pop and gospel; also rock, R&B and children's. Produced *Curious Heart* (by William Prines III and Wayne Skoblik), recorded by Savanna on Savanna Records (country); *I Am A Star*, written and recorded by Carol Kiefer; and *This I Know*, recorded by Doug and Beth Snyder (gospel and pop), both on Air Central Records.

*PROUD PORK PRODUCTIONS, 230 Montcalm St., San Francisco CA 94941. (415)648-9099. President: Scott Mathews. Record Producer and music publisher (Hang On to Your Publishing/BMI). Estab. 1975. Deals with artists and songwriters. Produces 6 singles, 6 12″ singles, 3 LPs and 4 CDs/year. Fee derived from sales royalty when song or artist is recorded, outright fee from recording artist or outright fee from record company.

How to Contact: Submit demo tape—unsolicited submissions are OK. Prefers cassette. Does not return unsolicited material. Reports in 2 months.
Music: Mostly rock/pop, country and R&B. Produced *Riding With The King*, written and recorded by John Hiatt on Geffen Records; *Brother Aldo*, written and recorded by Chuck Prophet on Fire Records; and *Planet Earth*, written and recorded by Paul Kantner on RCA Records (all LPs). Have produced Roy Orbison, Rosanne Cash, The Sextants and Jenni Muldaur."

R.E.F. RECORDS, 404 Bluegrass Ave., Madison TN 37115. (615)865-6380. President: Bob Frick. Manager: Shawn Frick. A&R Director: Scott Frick. Record producer and music publisher (Frick Music Publishing Co./BMI). Deals with artists, songwriters and producers. Produces 2 singles and 10 LPs/year. Fee derived from sales royalty.
How to Contact: Submit demo tape—unsolicited submissions are OK. Prefers 7½ ips reel-to-reel or cassette with 2-10 songs and lyric sheet. SASE. Reports in 2 weeks.
Music: Mostly gospel; also country, rock and top 40/pop. Produced "My Little Girl," written and recorded by Scott Frick on R.E.F. Records (Texas swing); and "What Peace" and "Put on Religion" (by Swindell), recorded by Bob Scott Frick on Touch Records (gospel). Other artists include Larry Ahlborn.

RANDALL PRODUCTIONS, Box 265, N. Hollywood CA 91603-0265. (312)509-6397 and (818)569-5653. President: Ashley Brown. Record producer, video producer and musical services to artists/songwriters. Produces 5 singles, 2 LPs and 2 music videos/year. Fee derived from sales royalty.
How to Contact: Prefers cassette (or VHS videocassette if available) with 3-5 songs and lyric sheet. "Clearly label each item you send. Include photo/bio if available." SASE. Does not return material with no return postage. Reports in 1 month, "but be patient."
Music: Mostly R&B, soul, funk, pop, blues, gospel; also accepting finished masters of these and rock (heavy, hard, metal, some acid) for Grandville Rock Sampler album. Produced *Mama Was Right*, recorded by Mack Simmons on Grandville Records (blues/R&B LP); and *Mr. Joy*, recorded by The Jade (LP), with newest singles "Mr Joy/Sweet Love," "Thunderkeeper/The Poetry of You" released overseas and distributed by Timeless Records/London (R&B/pop).

RAY MACK PRODUCTIONS, Box 120675, Nashville TN 37212. (615)255-1068. Owner: Ray McGinnis. Record producer, music publisher (Nautical Music Co./BMI), (Orbit Records). Estab. 1965. Deals with artists and songwriters. Produces 8 singles, 2 12" singles and 4 CDs/year. Fee derived from sales royalty.
How to Contact: Submit demo tape—unsolicited submissions are OK. Prefers cassette with 4 songs and lyric sheet. SASE. Reports in 6 weeks.
Music: Mostly country, rock and country rock. Produced *Super Country*, recorded by Da-Kota (country rock); Pure Country, recorded by Kim Tsoy; and *I've Always Been Country*, recorded by Sonny Martin (LP); all on Orbit Records. Other artists include Duren Taylor and Steve Wyles.
Tips: "Have a good demo tape available with top-notch songs. You will have a better chance of being heard."

RED KASTLE PRODUCTIONS, Box 163, West Redding CT 06896. President: Paul Hotchkiss. Record producer and music publisher. Deals with artists and songwriters. Produces 10 singles, 2 EPs, 2 LPs and 2 CDs/year. Fee derived from sales royalty.
How to Contact: Prefers cassette with 2 songs and lyric sheet. Include bio. SASE. Reports in 3 qweeks.
Music: Mostly country and country/pop. Produced "Honky Tonk Darlin" (by P.Hotchkiss), recorded by Susan Rose Manning on Target Records (country); "Not Enough Time," written and recorded by Michael Terry on Roto Noto Records (country); and "Thinking About You" (by P. Hotchkiss), recorded by Susan Rose Manning on Target Records (country). Other artists include Big John Hartman, Beverly's Hill-Billy Band, Susan Rose and Leigh Henry.

REVOLVER FM RECORDS LTD., (formerly FM-Revolver Records Ltd.), 152 Goldthorn Hill, Penn, Wolverhampton, WV2 3JA, **England.** Also, 28 Talbot Rd., London W2 JLJ **England.** Phone: 071-243-0992, 44-(0)902-345345. A&R: Paul Birch. Record producer, music publisher (Rocksong Music Publishing Co.) and record company (Heavy Metal America, Heavy Metal Records, Heavy Metal Worldwide, FM Records and Black, Revolver Records). Works with artists, songwriters and label producers. Produces 35 LPs/year.
How to Contact: Prefers cassette (or VHS/PAL or NTSC videocassette if available) with 1-3 songs. Does not return unsolicited material. Reports in 1 month.
Music: Pop, rock, AOR, dance and alternative. Artists include Stone Roses, Asia, Bruce Cockburn and Magnum.
Tips: "Send good photographs, short bio (50-100 words maximum); and *relevant* press clippings, i.e., charts, etc."

RIDGE RECORDING STUDIOS, 399 Cahaba Road, Greenville AL 36037. (205)382-7800. Record producer and recording studio. Deals with artists and songwriters. Produces 3-5 singles and 3 LPs/year. Receives 3 submissions/year.
How to Contact: Submit demo tape—unsolicited submissions are OK. Prefers cassette with 3 songs and lyric sheet. "Also will accept standard MIDI files for production purposes." SASE. Reports in 2 months.
Music: Mostly country/rock, country and pop; also rock and jazz. Produces Ralph Sutton (jazz), Danny Black (country/pop) and Fred Hardwicke (A/C).

RIGEL MEDIASOUND, (formerly Randy B. McCoy), Box 678, Baird TX 79504. (915)893-2616. Producer/Engineer: Randy B. McCoy. Record producer. Estab. 1985. Deals with artists and songwriters. Produces 10 singles and 4 LPs/year. Receives 150-200 submissions/year. Fee derived from outright fee from artist. Charges artist up front for "all phases of project from start to finish, including production, arrangements, presentation, etc."
How to Contact: Submit demo tape—unsolicited submissions are OK. Prefers cassette with 3-4 songs and lyric sheet. "Make sure vocals can be clearly heard, and keep the arrangments simple and basic." SASE. Reports in 3-4 weeks.
Music: Produced "The Expression on Their Face," written and recorded by Bob Shipley (country); *Harry Perry Band* (by various artists), recorded by Harry Perry Band (jazz); and *Code Of The West*, written and recorded by various artists (country); all on Code Of The West Records. Other artists include Willy Ray Band and Abilene Christian University.
Tips: "Submit material that is upbeat and pertains to the events and feelings of today. Be basic—originality presents itself in simple form."

*RIPSAW PRODUCTIONS, #805, 4545 Connecticut Ave. NW, Washington DC 20008. (202)362-2286. President: Jonathan Strong. Record producer, music publisher (Sugar Mama Music/BMI) and record company (Ripsaw Records). Deals with artists and songwriters. Produces 0-4 singles and 0-3 LPs/year.
How to Contact: Submit demo tape—unsolicited submissions are OK. Prefers cassette and lyric sheet. SASE. Reports "as quickly as time allows."
Music: Country, blues, rockabilly and roots rock. Helped produce "It's Not the Presents Under My Tree," recorded by Narvel Fetts on Renegade Records (45) and "Oooh-Wow!" recorded by Uptown Rhythm Kings (LP & cassette); produced *Two Sides*, written and recorded by Bobby Smith (EP); and *Wanted: True R&R*, written and recorded by Billy Hancock (EP); last three recorded on Ripsaw Records.

ROCK & TROLL PRODUCTIONS, 19 Chase Park, Batavia NY 14020. (716)343-1722. Vice President: Guy E. Nichols. Record producer, music publisher and record company (Rock & Troll Records). Estab. 1981. Deals with artists and songwriters. Produces 25 singles and 2 LPs/year. Fee derived from sales royalty or outright fee from recording artist.
How to Contact: Submit demo tape—unsolicited submissions are OK. Prefers cassette with 4 songs and lyric sheet. SASE. Reports in 4 weeks.
Music: Mostly rock, pop and R&B. Produced *Heartbreaker*, written and recorded by Lost Angels; and *Little Trolls*, written and recorded by Little Trolls; both on R&T Records (rock LPs).

ROCKIT RECORDS, INC., Suite 306, 35918 Union Lake Rd., Mt. Clemens MI 48043. Production Director: Joe Trupiano. Record Producer: J. D. Dudick. Record producer, music publisher, in-house studio (Ruffcut Recording Studio, Bad Grammar Music/BMI and Broadcast Music, Inc./BMI), record company (Rockit Records) and management company. Estab. 1985. Deals with artists and songwriters. Produces 10-20 singles and 4 CDs/year. Receives 100 submissions/month. Fee derived from outright fee from recording artist.
How to Contact: Prefers cassette (or videocassette if available) with 3-4 songs and lyric sheet. SASE. Reports in 6 weeks.
Music: Mostly pop/rock, R&B/pop, mainstream rock, New Age and heavy metal; also jingles, easy listening, ballads, dance-oriented and MOR. Produced "Choose Life," written and recorded by Laya Phelps (rock); "Main Emotion," written and recorded by Oscar Charles; and "Sin Alley" (by Bob Josey), recorded by Johnny Terry (pop); all on Rockit Records. Other artists include Tuff Kids, Thionne Carpenter, Bamboo Blonde, David Hensen and Hot Rod Hearts.
Tips: "We are presently open for producing outside projects *with self-supporting budgets*. This allows our clients the opportunity to shop their own master or sign it to Rockit Records *if* our A&R approves and also considering whether we have an open door policy at the time. Through this project several acts have been signed to major labels in the U.S., as well as indie labels in Europe. We have charted many of our acts on commercial radio in Europe."

*ROCKLAND MUSIC, INC., 117 W. Rockland Rd., Libertyville IL 60048. (708)362-4060. President: Perry Johnson. Record producer (Destiny Productions, Inc. and Mo Fo Music) and music publisher (Rockland Music and Amalgamated Tulip Corp.). Deals with artists and songwriters. Produces 4-12 singles and 2 LPs/year. Fee derived from sales royalty.
How to Contact: Prefers cassette with 1-5 songs and lyric sheet. SASE. Reports in 6 months.
Music: Mostly dance/R&B, top 40/pop, rock and country; also pop, MOR and blues. Produced *Animation*, by Animation (pop/rock LP); *Taxi*, by Taxi (hard rock LP); and *Nightbeat*, by Oh Boy (pop LP on Rockland Records). Other artists include Madelyn Brown, McCormick Sinclair, Linda Quick, and Slim Huston.
Tips: "Send single commercial songs, not album cuts."

*ROCKSTAR PRODUCTIONS, P.O. Box 131, Southeastern PA 19399. (215)3379556. Executive Vice President: Jeffrey Sacks. Director of Marketing: Roni Sacks. Record producer and record company (Rockstar Records). Estab. 1988. Deals with artists and songwriters. Produces 5 singles/year. Fee derived from sales royalty.
How to Contact: Submit demo tape—unsolicited submissions are OK. Prefers cassette with 2 songs and lyric sheets. Does not return unsolicited material. Reports in 6 weeks.
Music: Mostly rock and pop. Produced "What a Cover Can" and "Me," written and recorded by Scot Sax (rock); and "Another You" (by Seeker), recorded by Lola (pop), all on RKS Records.

ROCKY MOUNTAIN HEARTLAND PRODUCTIONS, Box 6904, Denver CO 80206. (303)841-8208. Executive Producer: Steve Dyer. Record and video producer and advertising firm (full service—brochures, demo kits, promo packs, graphics, photography). Deals with artists and songwriters. Fee derived from sales royalty or outright fee from songwriter/artist or record company.
How to Contact: Submit demo tape—unsolicited submissions are OK. Prefers cassette (or videocassette if available) with 3-5 songs and lyric sheet or lead sheet. Does not return unsolicited material. Reports in 2-3 weeks.
Music: Mostly gospel, top 40 and rock; also jazz and country. "Music open and not limited to these types." Produced *The Best Is Yet to Come*, by Kent Parry (big band and orchestra gospel LP); *From Here to Kingdom Come*, by Heart Song (mild gospel/top 40 LP); and *Going, Going, Gone*, by Heart Song (gospel rock LP); all on Record Harvest Records; and *From My Heart*, by Beth Chase.
Tips: "Contact us for specific suggestions relating to your project."

ADAM RODELL/RODELL RECORDS, P.O. Box 93457, Hollywood CA 90093. (213)960-9447. President: Adam Rodell. Record producer, music publisher (Udder Publishing/BMI, Golden Gelt/ASCAP) and record company (Rodell Records). Estab. 1989. Deals with artists and songwriters. Fee derived from sales royalty or outright fee from recording artist or record company.
How to Contact: Submit demo tape by mail. Unsolicited submissions are OK. Prefers cassette (or VHS videocassette if available) with 3 songs and lyric and lead sheet. Does not return unsolicited material. "We will report back only if we are interested."
Music: Mostly rock, country and pop; also R&B, progressive fusion and rap.
Tips: "We aggressively seek well-produced and professionally recorded demos. The artist's devotion and ambition to succeed must be aggressive as ours!"

MIKE ROSENMAN, 45-14 215 Pl., Bayside NY 11361. (718)229-4864. Producer: Mike Rosenman. Record producer and arranger. Estab. 1984. Deals with artists and songwriters. Produces 4-6 singles, 1-2 LPs and 1 EP/year. Fee derived from sales royalty or outright fee from recording artist.
How to Contact: Submit demo tape—unsolicited submissions are OK. Prefers cassette (or VHS videocassette if available), with 2-4 songs and lyric sheet. Include address and phone number. Put phone number on cassette. Does not return unsolicited material. Will not return solicited tapes without SASE. Reports in 8 weeks.
Music: Mostly pop, R&B, dance/disco and rock. Produced "Don't Do It" (by Clilli) recorded by La Dolce Vita on Warlock/Bellaphone Records (dance 12"); "Fools For Love" (by Clilli) recorded by La Dolce Vita on Warlock/Bellaphon Records (dance 12") and "From Now On" recorded by Wacky Child on Luna Records (rock single). "We also produce jingles and 'sound-alike' song parodies."

Remember: Don't "shotgun" your demo tapes. Submit only to companies interested in the type of music you write. For more submission hints, refer to The Business of Songwriting on page 19.

Tips: "Send simple demos of good songs. Please write, don't phone to ask about sending tapes. Include SASE if you want your tape back."

HENRY ROWE, 17 Water St., Dracut MA 01826. (508)957-5781. Producer: Henry Rowe. Record producer, music publisher and record company (Hazardous Records). Estab. 1986. Deals with artists and songwriters. Produces 50 singles and 5 LPs/year. Fee derived from sales royalty or outright fee from recording artist or record company.
How to Contact: Write or call first to arrange personal interview. Prefers cassette with 4 songs and lyric sheet. Does not return unsolicited material. Reports in 6-8 weeks.
Music: Mostly metal, rock and pop; also fusion, jazz and New Age. Produced "Half Life" and "Danger Zone" by Hazardous Waste (metal); and "Candle to the Magic," by Johann Smith (rock), all recorded by Making Tracks on Hazardous Records.

RR & R PRODUCTIONS, (formerly Rapp Productions, Inc.), Suite 128, 3260 Keith Bridge Rd., Cumming GA 30130-0128. (404)889-8624. Owner/President: Ron Dennis. Record producer, music publisher (Super Rapp Publishing/BMI and Do It Now Publishing/ASCAP) and record company (RR&R, Rapp Records, Rapture, Ready Records and Yshua Records). Estab. 1964. Works with artists and songwriters. Produces 10-20 singles, 10-20 LPs, 10-20 EPs and 10-20 CDs/year.
How to Contact: Prefers cassette (Type II) or 15 or 30 ips reel-to-reel (or VHS videocassette if available) with lyric chords and lead sheet. "Demo should have lead vocal and music and also a recording of music tracks without vocals." SASE. Reports in 3 months.
Music: Mostly R&B gospel and pop rock. Produced *Free At Last*, written and recorded by Mike Bell on Rapture Records (gospel); *Tommow Looks Like Yesterday* (by Louis Brown), recorded by Ron Dennis on RR & R Records (country crossover); and "Tribute to a King," by Chuck Carter on RR&R Records (pop). Other artists include Lynda Marr, Bill Scarbrough, Jez Davidson, Mike Bell, Dan Carroll, Sydney Australia's Stephen Concon, Chuck Carter, Peter Bunwen, Taylor Prichard, and Otis Reding; also Patty Weaver on Warner Brothers and approximately 50 others in the past to reach the charts.

*RUSHWIN PRODUCTIONS, P.O. Box 1150-SM93, Buna TX 77612. (409)423-2521. Owner/Manager: James Gibson. Record producer, music publisher (Rushwin Publishing). Estab. 1985. Deals with artists and songwriters. Receives 500 submissions/year. Fee derived from sales royalty, outright fee from songwriter/artist and/or outright fee from record company, depending on the project.
How to Contact: Submit demo tape—unsolicited submissions are OK. Prefers cassette with 1-4 songs and "typed lyric sheet. Clearly label each item sent. Include photo and bio if available. SASE (6x9 or larger)." Reports ASAP.
Music: Southern/country gospel only. Produced "Reachin' Thru The Thorns" (by James Gibson), recorded by the Gibsons (gospel single); *You're a Saint or You Ain't* (by Randy Lawrence and Bill Fisher), recorded by The Harbringers (gospel LP); and *Jesus I Love You* (by Paul A. Hammock), recorded by The Gibsons (gospel LP); all on Gold Street Records.
Tips: "We consider sincere, hard working artists who are willing to grow with us. We are a small independent operation on the grow. It would be most helpful if the artists would include a press package with their submissions. This would familiarize us with their ministry/music (past, present and future plans). We have an open door policy for songwriters. We utilize material similar to that which appears on the music charts published by *The Gospel Voice* and *The Singing News*."

RUSTRON MUSIC PRODUCTIONS, 1156 Park Lane, West Palm Beach FL 33417. (407)686-1354. A&R Directors: Rusty Gordon, Ron Caruso and Steve Mikes. Record producer, manager and music publisher (Rustron Music Publishers/BMI, Whimsong Publishing/ASCAP). Estab. 1970. Works with artists and songwriters. Produces 6-10 LPs/cassette albums/year. Fee derived from sales royalty or outright fee from record company. "This branch office reviews all material submitted for the home office in Hartsdale NY."
How to Contact: Submit demo tape—unsolicited submissions are OK. Prefers cassette with 1-3 songs and lyric or lead sheet. "Songs should be 3½ minutes long or less and must be commercially viable for today's market. Singer/songwriters and collaborators are preferred." SASE required for all correspondence. Reports in 2-3 months.
Music: Mostly progressive country, pop (ballads, blues, theatrical, cabaret) and folk/rock; also R&B, New Age folk fusion and New Age. Produced "We Know Where to Go" (by Gary Gonzalez/Rick Groom), recorded by Relative Viewpoint on RVP Records (contemporary); "Midnight Messenger," written and recorded by Marianne Flemming on Mermaid Records (blues/rock); and "Now Is The Time" (by J. Reby, D. Tyson, B. Pedicord), recorded by Circle & Star on C&S Records (new age folk fusion). Other artists include Ellen Hines, Deb Criss, Robin Plitt, Steve Mikes and Two of Hearts.
Tips: "Write from the heart. Don't be redundant. Develop lyrical themes, be unpredictable. Compose definitve melodies."

JOJO ST. MITCHELL, 273 Chippewa Dr., Columbia SC 29210-6508. Executive Producer and Manager: Jojo St. Mitchell. Record producer. Deals with artists and songwriters. Produces 10 singles and 4 LPs/year. Fee derived from sales royalty, booking and licensing.
How to Contact: Prefers cassette (or VHS videocassette if available) with 3-7 songs; include any photos, biography. SASE. Reports in 3-6 weeks, if interested. Enclose return postage.
Music: Mostly mainstream, pop and R&B; also rock, new music and jazz/rap. Produced *Wheels of Steel* (by R. Clavon/J. Aiken), recorded by Unique Force (rap LP); *Can't Stop Thinking of You* (by L.S. Skinkle), recorded by Jr. Ellis (pop ballad, LP); "Complicated Love," recorded by True Identity; and *Miracle* (by K. Lyon/T. Lyon), recorded by Kat Lyon (pop LP). Other artists include Carnage, Synthetic Meat, Progress In April, Body Shop, Political Asylum and U.S. Steel.

*SAS CORPORATION/SPECIAL AUDIO SERVICES, Suite 519, 503 Broadway, New York NY 10012. (212)226-6271. FAX: (212)226-6357. Owner: Paul Special. Record producer. Estab. 1988. Deals with artists and songwriters. Produces 3 singles, 1 12" single, 5 LPs, 1 EP and 5 CDs/year. Fee derived from sales royalty when song or artist is recorded, outright fee from recording artist or outright fee from record company.
How to Contact: Submit demo tape—unsolicited submissions are OK. Prefers cassette with 1-10 songs and lyric sheet. Does not return unsolicited material. Reports in 2-3 weeks.
Music: Mostly hard rock, funk rock and metal; also alternative, industrial and rap. Produced "Color Of Darkness," written and recorded by Maria Excommunikata on Megaforce Records (alternative/single); "Love U/Duke," written and recorded by Heads Up! on Emergo Records (funk rock EP); and "Hope/Emelda" (by Van Orden/Hoffman), recorded by The Ordinaires on Bar None Records (alternative/single). Other artists include Central Europe, Band Of Weeds, Peter Moffit and Kablama Chunk.
Tips: "Don't be afraid to bring up new and unusual ideas."

SATURN PRODUCTIONS, 802 Walnut, Dept. SM, Houston TX 77002 (713)328-6752. Executive Producer: Richard E. Cagle. Record producer (Saturn Productions) and record company (Siren Records). Estab. 1989. Deals with artists and songwriters. Produces 3 LPs and 1 EP/year. Fee derived from sales royalty when song or artist is recorded, outright fee from recording artist or outright fee from record company.
How to Contact: Submit demo tape by mail. Unsolicited submissions are OK. Prefers cassette with 4-6 songs and lyric sheet. "Send a complete promo pack (pictures, tapes, and bio). SASE. Reports in 6 weeks.
Music: Mostly funk, heavy rock and top 40; also thrash, reggae and blues. Produced *Royal & Loyal* (written and recorded by Joe "King" Carrasco), on Royal Rio Records; *Voices of Red God* (by compilation of various songwriters and recording artists), on Saturn Redords; and *MXD Emotions* (written and recorded by MXD) on Saturn Records (all LPs). Other artists include Dead Horse, Flesh Mop, Panjam Drum, Elevator Up, Social Deceit and Hunger.
Tips: "Funk will get much bigger in the 90s. New labeling laws are just the beginning, unfortunately."

*SCL PRODUCTIONS INC., Box 49464, Atlanta GA 30359. President: S.C. Lewanowicz. Record producer, record company and television production company. Skull Records and Skull Studios. Estab. 1984. Deals with artists and songwriters. Produces 8 singles/year. Fee derived from sales royalty when song or artist is recorded, outright fee from recording artist or outright fee from record company.
How to Contact: Submit demo tape—unsolicited submissions are OK. Prefers cassette (or VHS videocassette). "High-quality demos preferred." SASE. Reports in 1 month.
Music: Mostly metal, rock and pop; also rap and R&B. Produced "Girls," "Dreams" and "When" (by K.C. Steele), recorded by K.C. Steele on Skull Records (singles).
Tips: "We're looking for groove-oriented instrumental music; no ballads, please."

*SEGAL'S PRODUCTIONS, Box 507, Newton MA 02159. (617)969-6196. Contact: Charles Segal. Record producer, music publisher (Segal's Publications/BMI, Samro South Africa) and record company (Spin Records). Works with artists and songwriters. Produces 6 singles and 6 LPs/year. Fee derived from sales royalty.
How to Contact: Submit demo tape—unsolicited submissions are OK. Prefers cassette (or VCR videocassette) with 3 songs and lyric sheet or lead sheet of melody, words, chords. "Please record keyboard/voice or guitar/voice if you can't get a group." SASE. Reports in 6-8 weeks.
Music: Mostly rock, pop and country; also R&B and comedy. Produced "Give the World a Chance" (by Brilliant), recorded by Rosemary (soft rock); "You're Not Alone" (by Segal), recorded by Troupers (gospel/rock); and "Put Your Faith in Jesus" (by Whewell), recorded by Will Hock (gospel), all on Spin Records. Other artists include Gus Wyburd.
Tips: "I find that lots of artists are not ready for the big time when they've had their first hit record. So do your studying before that and listen to lots of artists/styles."

SHARPE SOUND PRODUCTIONS, Box 140536, Nashville TN 37214. (615)391-0650. Producer/Engineer: Ed Sharpe. Record producer. Estab. 1990. Deals with artists and songwriters. Fee derived from sales royalty or outright fee from recording artist or record company.
How to Contact: Submit demo tape—unsolicited submissions are OK. Prefers cassette (or VHS videocassette if available) with 4 songs and lyric sheet. SASE. Reports in 2 months.
Music: Pop, R&B, rock, folk, country, contemporary Christian and storytelling. Produced *Cherokee Legends*, recorded by Kathi Smith on Cherokee Pub Records (spoken stories LP); "Ladder in Your Head," written and recorded by Totally Square on Moo Records (rock); "There in Your Heart," written and recorded by C.M.S. on Frankincense Records (Christian) and "One God," written and recorded by Susan Van Dyke on SSP Records (A/C). Other artists include Kimberly Johnson, Susan St. Charles and Children at Heart.
Tips: "Put best work first on demos with emphasis on vocal."

SIERRA WEST MUSIC, 13 Winter Creek Ln., Canyon CA 94516. (415)376-6135. Producer: Neil J. Young. Record producer (8- and 24-track studios). Estab. 1969. Deals with artists and songwriters. Produces 15-40 LPs and 3 12″ singles/year.
How to Contact: Call first and obtain permission to submit or to arrange a personal interview. Prefers cassette (or VHS videocassette if available) with 5 songs and lyric sheet. "Authors must have songs copywritten in their name." Does not return unsolicited material. Reports in 3 weeks.
Music: Mostly acoustic or vocal story songs, country rock or folk rock; also ballads. Produced "She Can" (by Steve Sesken), recorded by Alabama (country single); "Wrong" (by Steve Sesken), recorded by Waylon Jennings (country singles); *Feelin' Good*, written and recorded by David Rea on Canadian River (LP); and *One Voice*, by David Maloney (LP).

SILICON CHIP RECORDING COMPANY, 1232 Cedar Rd., Ambler PA 19002. (215)542-0785. President: Christian Barth. Record producer and demo and jingle studio. Estab. 1986. Deals with artists and songwriters. Produces 35-40 singles, 5-6 LPs and 5-6 CDs/year. Fee derived from sales royalty or outright fee from recording artist and record company.
How to Contact: Write or call first and obtain permission to submit. Unsolicited submissions are OK. Prefers cassette with 3 songs and lyric sheet. "We will respond only if interested." SASE. Reports in 4 weeks.
Music: Mostly rock, dance and pop; also gospel, country and New Age. Produced "Shout Away" (by T. Stratton & J. Goodwin), recorded by The Cause (progressive rock); "Real Blood I'm Bleedin" (by G./ Katocs), recorded by Khshe (A/C); and "Heaven Don't Rock" (by K. D'Rourke), recorded by Down & Out (hard rock). Other artists include Militant Minister, AWOL Posse, Kilroy, Q.B. Austin, Green Effect, Poison Ladd, Laura Herbert and Richard Vise.
Tips: "Write lots of songs; don't concentrate on only two or three. You may have to write 10 songs to discover one great one."

SIR GARRETT PRODUCTIONS, 10346 NE Chowning, Kansas MO 64155. (816)734-2159. Contact: Auska Garrett. Record producer (Sir Garrett Productions) and record company. Estab. 1987. Deals with artists and songwriters. Produces 2 singles, 3 12″ singles and 2 LPs. Fee derived from sales royalty.
How to Contact: Submit demo tape by mail. Unsolicited submissions are OK. Prefers cassette (or VHS videocassette if available) with 3 songs and lyric sheets. "Include a short resume of music background along with cassette and picture." Does not return unsolicited submissions. Reports in 3 months.
Music: Mostly R&B, rock, pop and gospel; also jazz, soul and blues. Produced "Let Me Have the Stranger," written and recorded by Auska Garrett (pop) and "Give Me That Feeling," written and recorded by Ricky Dotson (R&B), both on S&G Productions Records. Other artists include Rap Inc., Ralf Dixon, Gavin Johnson, Cal Green, Unidos Band and Mac Lace Band.
Tips: "Keep your songs short and simple. Always have a good beat."

MIKE SISKIND, 285 Chestnut St., W. Hempstead NY 11552. (516)489-0738. Staff Producer: Mike Siskind. Record producer and record company (Storehouse Records). Deals with artists only. Produces 1 singles, 1-3 LPs and 1-3 EPs/year. "Fee varies project to project."
How to Contact: Submit demo tape—unsolicited submissions are OK. Prefers cassette (or VHS videocassette if available) with 5-8 songs and lyric sheet. "If interested in pursuing project, I will contact you." Does not return unsolicited material. Reports in 6 weeks.
Music: Mostly rock, folk and soul; also pop. Produced "No Reason" (by Larry Andrews), recorded by Off the Wall (rock); "The Personals" (by L. Andrews/M. Ellis), recorded by Off the Wall (rock); and "New York City Night" (by M. Siskind), recorded by Michael Ellis (rock); all on Storehouse Records.
Tips: "Let the producer produce. He may hear a diamond in the rough that you don't even realize you have."

SKYLYNE RECORDS, (formerly Street Music), Suite 17, 61 Canal St., San Rafael CA 94901. (415)453-6270. Managing Partner: Jeff Britto. Record producer, music publisher (ASCAP) and record company (Street Music Records). Estab. 1987. Deals with artists and songwriters. Produces 6 singles, 6 12″ singles and 6 LPs/year, "depending on roster." Receives 10-20 submissions/month. Fee derived from sales royalty when song or artist is recorded.
How to Contact: Submit demo tape—unsolicited submissions are OK. Prefers cassette (or VHS videocassette if available) with 4 songs and lyric sheet. Include 8 × 10 glossy photo if available. SASE. Reports in 2 weeks.
Music: Mostly rap, R&B and dance/house; also pop. Produced "Peace To All Mankind" (by Nite-N-Day) (rap); "Wisemen Speak" (by Fokus) (rap); and "Yo Jill!" (by Kenny S.) (dance), all on Skylyne Records. Other artists include Eastro & Romeo, Live & Direct, Kick Something Mello, Dangerous D, Mind Power and Concrete Jungle.
Tips: "Don't short change your lyrics or music production by taking short cuts to meet production schedules. An assembly-line approach to songwriting is not good. Never release substandard material for consideration unless you like rejection. I see a definite trend in CHR formats accepting more ethnically diverse music, thus showcasing artists who until recently were locked out of the top 40 market."

SNEAK TIP RECORDS INC./HIP WRECKIN RECORDS LTD., Suite 3A, 98-05 67th Avenue, Forest Hills NY 11375. (718)271-5149. Record producer, music publisher (Sneak Tip Music/Uncle J Music) and record company. Estab. 1990. Deals with artists and songwriters. Produces 5-10 singles/year. Fee derived from sales royalty.
How to Contact: Write or call first to arrange a personal interview. Prefers cassette. SASE. Reports in 4 weeks.
Music: Mostly house, and club; also pop, R&B and freestyle. Produced "I Wanna Dance With U," written and recorded by J. Swift on Sneak Tip Records (hip-house); "The Asylum" (by The Asylum, Norty Cotto & B.B. Keys), on Hip Wreckin Recs. (techno) and "I Remember" (by Norty Cotto) recorded by Jana on Sneak Tip Records (freestyle). Other artists include Rhingo and Tavier.
Tips: "Dance music or R&B only please! Be patient on response."

SONGWRITERS' NETWORK, Box 190446, Dallas TX 75219. (214)824-2739. President: Phil Ayliffe. Record producer, music publisher (Songwriters' Network Music Publishing/ASCAP), and record company (Songwriters' Network Records). Estab. 1983. Deals with artists and songwriters. Produces 1 LP/year. Receives 5-8 submissions/month. Fee derived from sales royalty.
How to Contact: Submit demo tape—unsolicited submissions are OK. Prefers cassette (or videocassette if available) with 5 songs and lyric sheet. "Five songs should include an uptempo opener; an uptempo, positive song; a ballad; a hand-clapping rouser; and a dramatic, personal philosophy song as a closer. Vocal must be mixed up-front. Any straining to hear the lyric and the tape is immediately rejected. Material is returned only if accompanied by an SASE." Reports in 3 months.
Music: A/C, pop and MOR. Produced "Flying Free," written and recorded by Phil Ayliffe on Songwriters' Network Records (New Age/pop).
Tips: "We are most interested in working with the singer/songwriter/producer entrepreneur, so we would like the best produced material possible, though vocal and instrument demo is OK."

SOUND ARTS RECORDING STUDIO, 2036 Pasket, Houston TX 77092. (713)688-8067. President: Jeff Wells. Record producer and music publisher (Earthscream Music). Deals with artists and songwriters. Estab. 1974. Produces 12 singles and 3 LPs/year. Fee derived from outright fee from recording artist.
How to Contact: Submit demo tape—unsolicited submissions are OK. Prefers cassette with 2-5 songs and lyric sheet. SASE. Reports in 1 month.
Music: Mostly pop/rock and dance. Produced "We Can't Be Stopped," recorded by Geto Boys; "Mr. Scarface is Badd," written and recorded by Scarface (rap); and "Convicts" (by Convicts), all on Rap-A-Lot/Priority Records (rap). Other artists include Perfect Strangers, Third Language and Pauline Knox.

SOUND COLUMN PRODUCTIONS, Division of Sound Column Companies, Box 70784, Salt Lake City UT 84170. (801)355-5327. President/General Manager: Ron Simpson. Record producer, media producer, music publisher (Ronarte Publications/ASCAP, Mountain Green Music/BMI and Macanudo Music/SESAC) and record company (SCP Records, Big Sky Records). Estab. 1970. Looking for songs our artists can record. Produces 3 singles and 5 LPs/year. Fee derived from sales royalty or outright fee on media productions, demos and albums produced for outside labels.
How to Contact: Submit demo tape—unsolicited submissions are OK. Unsolicited submissions of three songs maximum (with pop or R&B, uptempo and ballads, also contemporary Christian. No metal or rap.) "We listen to everything, eventually. Remember, we can't return materials or correspondence unless you include SASE. No phone calls please."

Music: Pop, R&B, country, contemporary Christian. "We produce albums under contract for various labels, and demo packages for client artists." Produced "In Your Loving Hands" (by Clive Romney) (pop/R&B), and "What I Need" (by Ron Simpson/Anthony Mortimer) (pop/rap), recorded by Lita & Kevin on Shadow Mountain Records. Other artists include Gary Voorhees and Shawn.
Tips: "We respond to clean production and must have current-style songs. We accepted several songs by outside writers this past year."

SOUND CONTROL PRODUCTIONS, 2813 Azalea Pl., Nashville TN 37204. (615)269-5638. Producer: Mark. Record producer and record company (Mosrite Records). Estab. 1982. Deals with artists and songwriters. Produces 30 singles, 8 LPs and 2 CDs/year. Fee derived from sales royalty or outright fee from recording artist or record company—"sometimes all or a combination of these." Charges 50% in advance for services. "I don't want to pay studio time and musicians when the client doesn't show."
How to Contact: Submit demo tape by mail. Unsolicited submissions are OK. Prefers cassette with 3 songs and lyric sheet. "Don't submit anything in which you need to explain what the song or you are trying to say—let the performance do that." Does not return unsolicited material. Reports in 8 weeks.
Music: Mostly country, gospel and bluegrass; also Christmas. Produced *Paddy Kelly* (by various artists), recorded by Paddy Kelly (country LP); *The Thorntons* (by various), recorded by Thorntons on Bridge Records (gospel LP); and *The Lewis Family* (by various artists), recorded by The Lewistown on Benson Records (gospel bluegrass LP).

SOUNDS OF WINCHESTER, Rt. 2 Box 114 H, Berkley Springs WV 25411. Contact: Jim McCoy. Record producer, music publisher (New Edition Music, Jim McCoy Music and Sleepy Creek Music) and record company (Winchester, Faith and Master Records). Deals with artists and songwriters. Produces 20 singles and 10 LPs/year. Fee derived from sales royalty.
How to Contact: Submit demo tape—unsolicited submissions are OK. Prefers 7½ ips reel-to-reel or cassette with 4-10 songs and lead sheet. SASE. Reports in 1 month.
Music: Bluegrass, country, gospel and country/rock. Produced "Dyin' Pain" and "I'm Getting Nowhere," written and recorded by J.B. Miller on Hilton Records; and "Let Her," written and recorded by R. Lee Gray on Alear Records (all country). Other artists include Jim McCoy, Red Steed, Kim Segler, Carroll County Ramblers.

SOUNDSTAGE SOUTH, 5183 Darlington Dr., Memphis TN 38118. (901)363-3345. President: Fred B. Montgomery. Rock & "New" country production and artist development. Estab. 1990. Deals with artists and songwriters. Fee derived from sales royalty when song or artist is recorded. "In 1992-93, SoundStage intends to provide a 40,000 square foot Rehearsal/Production Facility to area contemporary musicians and songwriters on a daily and monthly rental basis - to include a demo recording studio, private rehearsal studios and showcase room."
How to Contact: Submit demo tape—unsolicited submissions are OK. Prefers cassette (or VHS videocassette if available) with 3 songs and lyric sheet. Does not return unsolicited material. Reports in 6-8 weeks.
Music: Mostly rock, blues rock and contemporary country; also country/rock.
Tips: "I represent selected songwriters/artists in the Memphis/Mid-South area in development, preproduction, demo production and general support in shopping original material to publishers and labels." Music trends: "I see young rock musicians moving away from metal and back to more melodic, less shock oriented presentation and performance, and I see an enormous crossover occuring in contemporary country, i.e. Highway 101, Restless Heart, Desert Rose Band."

SOUTHERN SOUND PRODUCTIONS, 100 Labon St., Tabor City NC 28463. (919)653-2546. President: Elson H. Stevens. Record producer, music publisher (Creekside Publishing, SeaSide Records/BMI) and record company. Estab. 1978. Deals with artists, songwriters and radio stations. Produces 15 singles, 16 EPs and 16 LPs/year. Fee derived from sales royalty or outright fee from recording artist.
How to Contact: Submit demo tape—unsolicited submissions are OK. Prefers cassette with 1-3 songs and lyric or lead sheets. SASE. Reports in 1 month.
Music: Mostly country; also bluegrass, gospel, rock (country and hard) and beach music. Produced "I'll Never Say Never Again" (by G. Todd/S. Holt), recorded by Sherry Collins on SeaSide Records; "Long Country Road" (by G. Taylor), recorded by Sherry Collins on Country SeaSide Records and "Heaven's Ready" (by E. Watson), recorded by The Watson Family on SeaSide Records (gospel).

"How to Use Your Songwriter's Market" (at the front of this book) *contains comments and suggestions to help you understand and use the information in these listings.*

Other artists include The Austin Brothers, The Halls, Horac Buddy Brumble, OceanSide and Sagebrush.
Tips: "Be original. Be ready to commit to music."

SPHERE PRODUCTIONS, Box 991, Far Hills NJ 07931-0991. (908)781-1650. FAX: (908)781-1693. President: Tony Zarrella. Talent Manager: Louisa Pazienza. Record producer, artist development, management and placement of artists with major/independent labels. Produces 5-6 singles and 3 CDs/ year. Receives 150-300 submissions/quarterly. Estab. 1988. Deals with artists and songwriters. Fee derived from percentage royalty of deal, outright fee from record company.
How to Contact: Submit demo tape—unsolicited submissions are OK. Prefers cassette (or VHS videocassette) with 3-5 songs and lyric sheets. "Include as much information as possible: photos, press, resume (a must), goals and specifics on character of project submitted, etc." SASE. Reports in 8 weeks.
Music: Specialize in pop (mainstream), progressive/rock, New Age and cross-over country/pop. Also film soundtracks. Produced "All Heart" (by T. Zarrella), recorded by 4 of Hearts (pop/rock); and "Speed of Light" recorded by Traveller, both on Sphere Records. Also works with Oona Falcon and Steel Vision in the Future.
Tips: "Be able to take direction and have trust and faith in your producer or manager."

JACK STANG, 753 Capitol Ave., Hartford CT 06106. (203)524-5656. Producer: Jack Stang. Record producer, music publisher (Stang Music/BMI) and record company (Nickel Records). Estab. 1970. Deals with artists and songwriters. Produces 5 singles and 5 12″ singles/year. Fee derived from sales royalty.
How to Contact: Submit demo tape—unsolicited submissions are OK. Prefers cassette with 3 songs and lyric sheets. SASE. Reports in 3 weeks.
Music: Mostly pop, rock and dance; also country. Produced "For What We've Got," written and recorded by Ray Alaire (top 40); "Shortest Distance" (by Cléntel), recorded by Dagmar (top 40/ dance); and "We Have It All," by Ray Alaire and Sky (A/C), all on Nickel Records (all singles).

*STARK RECORDS AND TAPE CO., 628 S. South St., Mount Airy NC 27030. (919)786-2865. Contact: Paul E. Johnson. Record producer and music publisher (TomPaul Music Company/BMI). Estab. 1960. Deals with artists, songwriters, publishers and recording companies. Produces 8 singles and 3 LPs/ year. Works with 80 new songwriters/year. Fee derived from sales royalty.
How to Contact: Submit demo tape—unsolicited submissions are OK. Prefers cassette with 4-6 songs and lyric sheet. SASE. "Return address should be on the SASE." Reports in 2 months.
Music: Country, bluegrass, pop and gospel. Produced "It Won't Be Long," "Won't That Be a Time" and "He Owns Everything," all written and recorded by Early Upchurch on Stark Records (country/ gospel). Other artists include Carl Tolbert, Sam Bray, Ralph Hill, Bobby Lee Atkins, Sanford Teague and Don Sawyers.

A. STEWART PRODUCTIONS, 22146 Lanark St., Canoga Park CA 91304. (818)704-0629. President: Art Stewart. Record producer and music publisher (Famosonda Music/BMI and Sonada/ASCAP). Estab. 1975. Deals with artists and songwriters. Produces 1 single and 1 LP/year. Receives 8 submissions/year. Fee determined by sales royalty.
How to Contact: Write to obtain permission to submit. Prefers 7½ ips reel-to-reel or cassette with 1-4 songs and lyric sheet. SASE. Reports in 1 month.
Music: All types; mostly soul. Produced "Got To Give It Up" (by M. Gaye), recorded by Sterling (soul); "Come Into These Arms," written and recorded by Dion Pride (pop/rock); and *Second Son*, written and recorded by Dion Pride (pop/rock). Co-produced "You and I" (by R. James) and "Sucker For Your Love" (by Teena Marie).

STUDIO CITY PRODUCTIONS, 2810 McBain, Redondo Beach CA 90278. (213)371-5793. Staff Producer: Geoff England. Record producer. Estab. 1982. Deals with artists and songwriters. Produces 15 singles, 20 12″ singles, 10 LPs, 5 EPs and 35 CDs/year. Fee derived from sales royalty or outright fee from recording artist or record company.
How to Contact: Submit demo tape—unsolicited submissions are OK. Prefers cassette (or VHS videocassette if available) with 1-5 songs and lyric sheet. SASE. Reports in 2 weeks.
Music: Mostly rock and pop. Produced *Steppenwolf Live*, recorded by Steppenwolf on ABC Records (LP); *Ring Leader*, recorded by Ring Leader on Statue Records (LP); and *Rock City*, recorded by John Verla on Statue Records (LP).

SUCCESSFUL PRODUCTIONS, 1203 Biltmore Ave., High Point NC 27260. (919)882-9990. President: Doris Lindsay. Record producer, music publisher (Better Times Publishing/BMI) and record company (Fountain Records). Estab. 1979. Deals with artists and songwriters. Produces 3 singles and 2 LPs/ year. Fee derived from sales royalty.

How to Contact: Submit demo tape—unsolicited submissions are OK. Prefers cassette with 2 songs and lyric sheet. "Send a professional demo." SASE. Reports in 2 months.
Music: Mostly country, pop and contemporary gospel; also blues, children's and southern gospel. Produced "American Song" (by K. Roeder/M. Terry) recorded by Terry Michaels (country); "Back In Time" written and recorded by Mitch Snow (country) and "Crossroads of My Life" (by Larry Lavey/Dave Right) recorded by Larry La Vey (blues), all on Fountain Records. Other artists include Pat Repose.
Tips: "Use a professional demo service."

*PRESTON SULLIVAN ENTERPRISES, 1217 16th Ave. S., Nashville TN 37212. (615)327-8129. President: Preston Sullivan. Record producer. Deals with artists and songwriters. Produces 10 singles and 4 LPs/year.
How to Contact: Submit demo tape—unsolicited submissions are OK. Prefers cassette (or videocassette) and lyric sheet. Does not return unsolicited material. Reports in 3 weeks.
Music: Mostly hard rock, alternative rock, pop and R&B. Produced "The Grinning Plowman" (by Michael Ake), recorded by The Grinning Plowmen (pop/rock); "Dessau" (by John Elliott), recorded by Dessau (dance) and "Dorcha," recorded by Dorcha (rock), all on Carlyle Records.

SURPRIZE RECORDS, INC., P.O. Box 42707, Dept. SM, Philadelphia PA 19101-2707. (215)276-8861. President: W. Lloyd Lucas. Record producer, music publisher (Delev Music Co./BMI, Sign of the Ram Music/ASCAP, Gemini Lady Music/SESAC) and management firm. Estab. 1981. Deals with artists, songwriters and publishers. Produces 3-6 singles, 2-3 12" singles and 3-6 LPs/year. Fee derived from sales royalty.
How to Contact: Prefers cassette with 1-3 songs and lyric or lead sheet. SASE. Reports in 1 month.
Music: R&B, soul, top 40/pop, dance-oriented, MOR and gospel. Recently released "Fat Girls," produced by Tine-Nu Productions, written by B. Heston, E. Webb, L. Walker and J. Hudson, on Surprize Records. Other artists that are scheduled to be produced are Lamar Lucas, who will be performing "Just Dance" (written by Willie McClain, C. Hawthrone and Willie McClain, Jr.).
Tips: "We are impressed with very positive lyrics and great hooklines and near finished demo 'masters'. It does not matter if the artist has had extensive experience working in front of an audience, but it does matter if his or her attitude is in a positive posture. Determination and the ability to take constructive criticism is most important. We have no time for ego trippers."

SWEET INSPIRATION MUSIC, 112 Widmar Pl., Dept., SM, Clayton CA 94517. (510)672-8201. Owner: Edgar J. Brincat. Record producer, music publisher (California Country Music/BMI, Sweet Inspirations Music/ASCAP and record company (Roll On Records). Estab. 1986. Deals with artists and songwriters. Produces 2-4 singles/year. Pays standard royalty.
How to Contact: Submit demo tape—unsolicited submissions are OK. Prefers cassette with 3 songs and lyric sheets. SASE. Reports in 6 weeks.
Music: Mostly MOR, contemporary country or pop; also R&B, gospel and light rock. Published "I'll Take Country Music Anytime" (by John Cover, Ann Leisten, Phil Monton), recorded by John Covert on Roll On Records.

SYNDICATE SOUND, INC., 475 5th St., Struthers OH 44471. (216)755-1331. President: Jeff Wormley. Audio and video production company and record and songpromotion company. Estab. 1987. Deals with artists and songwriters. Produces 3-4 singles, 1-2 12" singles, 15-20 LPs, 10-15 EPs and 4-5 CDs/year. Receives 30 submissions/year. Fee derived from combination of sales royalty when song or artist is recorded, outright fee from recording artist or record company hourly recording or producing fee and third party financing.
How to Contact: Submit demo tape—unsolicited submissions are OK. "Please send a promo package or biography (with pictures) of band, stating past and present concerts and records." SASE. Reports in 2 months.
Music: Mostly rock, pop and Christian rock; also country, R&B and hardcore. Produced *Heart Break Train* (by Wayne Mackey), recorded by Bruised Badly on Syndicate Sound Records (LP); "You're Not My Lover Anymore" (by Frank Pank), recorded by Rambeling Rock on Syndicate Sound Records (cass/single); and "Christmas in Youngstown" (by Chris Hamby), recorded by Christopher Records (cass/single). Other artists include Fingernail Moon, February, John Horvath and George Lang (of Seeking Princess).

SYSTEM, Box 11301, Kansas City KS 66111. (913)287-3495. Executive Producer: Steve Vail. Record producer, management firm, booking agency and film company. Estab. 1978. Deals with artists and songwriters. Produces 1-3 LPs/year. Fee derived from outright fee from songwriter/artist or record company.

How to Contact: Prefers cassette or 7½ ips reel-to-reel (or ½" or ¾" VHS or ½" Beta videocassette if available) with 1-10 songs and lyric sheet. Does not return unsolicited material. Reports in 6 months.
Music: "Classical rock, New Age, jazz fusion and art rock." Produced *The Path*, recorded by Realm (proressive rock LP/CD); *Outlines*, recorded by Navigator (dance rock LP); and "Time Tales," written and recorded by Vail & Studna, all on System Records.

TABITHA PRODUCTIONS, Sandpiper Court, Harrington Lane, Exeter EX4 8N5 **England**. Phone: 44-0392-79914. Producer: Graham Sclater. Record producer, music publisher (Tabitha Music, Ltd.) and record company (Tabitha/Willow Records). Works with artists and songwriters. Produces 6 singles and 2 LPs/year. Works with 6 new composers and songwriters/year. Fee derived from sales royalty.
How to Contact: Prefers cassette with 2-6 songs and lyric sheet. SAE and IRC. Reports in 3 weeks.
Music: Mostly AOR, MOR and pop; also country, dance, soul and rock. Produced "I'm Your Man," written and recorded by Tony Carey on Tabitha Records (pop); "Groovy Kind of Love" (by Bayer-Sager), recorded by Andy Ford (pop/reggae); and "Summer Love Affair" (by Bradbury/Artes), recorded by Beat the Heat (pop). Other artists include Shoot to Kill, Colin Wilson, FLIC, Simon Galt and Mark Fojo.

GARY TANIN, 2139 N. 47th St., Milwaukee WI 53208. (414)444-2404. Producer: G. Tanin. Record producer. Estab. 1970. Deals with artists and songwriters. Produces 4 singles and 2 LPs/year. Fee derived from outright fee from recording artist or record company.
How to Contact: Submit demo tape – unsolicited submissions are OK. Prefers cassette with 3 songs and lyric sheet. "On demos, piano line and vocals are OK. Prefer as complete a submission as possible." SASE. Reports in 2 months.
Music: Mostly rock, pop and New Age. Produced *Softworks Vol. 1*, written and recorded by Junior Brantley on Softworkds Records (R&B); *Otto and The Elevators*, written and recorded by G. Tanin on Vera Records (rock LP); *Coming Home*; (by Billy Wallace), recorded by Billy Wallace (jazz LP); and "Cheap Love, Easy Money," written and recorded by White Lie on White Lie Records (pop rock single).

TCC PRODUCTIONS, (Division of Tech-Coh Communications), 6331 Bahama Shores Drive S., St. Petersburg FL 33705-5437. (813)867-8546. FAX: (813)867-8330. President/Producer: Paul Hayes. Record producer, music publisher (Hayes Publishing Group/BMI) and record company (TCC Records, Seyah Records, Nivik Records). Estab. 1959. Deals with artists and songwriters. Fee derived from sales royalty when song or artist is recorded and outright fee from record company.
How to Contact: Submit demo tape – unsolicited submissions are OK. Prefers cassette with no more than 3 songs and lyric sheet. "If an artist, do not submit photos or video. Submit a *brief* bio if available, but it's not required." SASE. Reports in 2 weeks. "All unsolicited material must have a notification of copyright on the package in addition to a copyright notice on each enclosed submission. Material not bearing a copyright notice will be returned unopened."
Music: Mostly R&B, country and pop. Produced "I'm Serious," written and recorded by JJ Johnson on Capitol Records (R&B 12" single); "Fantasy" (by Rufus Spencer), recorded by Alma Davis on Macola Records (R&B 12" single); and "Taking Care Of Business" (by Randy Bachman), recorded by Alma Davis on TCC/Macola Records (R&B 12" single). Other artists include Laurie Kittle, Hal O'Neil and Michael Battle.
Tips: "Songwriter: Write material that listeners can relate to with a strong hook. Artist: Believe in yourself and be willing to give 200% to a project. Be *unwilling* to do material that you don't believe in. Provide assigned producer with your input. You are the frosting on the cake so share your thoughts."

TEROCK RECORDS, Box 1622, Hendersonville TN 37077. President: Wade Curtiss. Record producer and music publisher. Deals with artists and songwriters. Fee derived from sales royalty.
How to Contact: Submit demo tape – unsolicited submissions are OK. Prefers cassette tape with 2-6 songs and lyric sheet. SASE. Reports in 3 weeks.
Music: Bluegrass, blues, country, dance, easy listening, folk, gospel, progressive, R&B, hard rock, soul, top 40/pop, rockabilly and rap. Artists include Rhythm Rockers.

*TEXAS MUSIC MASTERS/WRIGHT PRODUCTIONS, (formerly Lonnie Wright), Rt. 14 Box 1039, Hwy 64 E., Tyler TX 75707. (214)566-5653. Vice President: Lonnie Wright. Record producer. Estab. 1987. Deals with artists and songwriters. Produces 30 singles and 6-7 LPs/year. Fee derived from outright fee from recording artist or label.
How to Contact: Submit demo tape – unsolicited submissions are OK. Prefers cassette with 3 songs and lyric sheet. SASE. Reports in 3 weeks.
Music: Mostly country, gospel and rock. Produced "Smokin," recorded by Woody Wills on OL Records (country); "Cowboy Sings The Blues" (by Chad Sheldon), recorded by Chad Sheldon on Shanny Records (country); and "Could You Love A Heart Like Mine?" (by Rob Baze), recorded by Touch

Close-up

Christine Lavin
Songwriter
New York, New York

Photo by E. Lieberman

Christine Lavin has been a busy woman. The "cheerleader" of acoustic music's recent past included two album releases, executive production of a third and organization and performance in a tour, "Buy Me, Bring Me, Take Me, Don't Mess My Hair: Life According to Four Bitchin' Babes," featuring some of acoustic music's finest songwriters. 1992 didn't slow down a bit either. She continued touring with the "Babes," hosted a radio show on American Public Radio, and prepared and published a songbook of her most popular songs. A busy woman.

A network for opportunity

When speaking about the music business, Lavin rarely mentions only herself. She firmly believes that the community of songwriters and performers provides a base for creating opportunities. The musical community also is a support mechanism for songwriters. Lavin emphasizes connecting with other writers "to realize that you're not alone. Songwriting is a very solitary kind of thing, and a great thing is to get together with other people who are trying to do the same thing. See if collaborations come out of it, or just friendships, so that you can have a network or community."

The network of traveling performers is also important. Lavin makes a point of recommending acts to performance venues: "As soon as I started traveling and performing, I immediately saw that I could fill a place and maybe play there twice a year. But I'm very aware of the fact that they're open 340 to 364 days a year, and that they all need good performers. So as soon as I found a new place, I would pass the word. And lots of musicians are passing that kind of information [about other artists] all the time."

Organizing songwriters for performance benefits the whole group. Lavin's advice: "It shows there's strength in numbers. If you're out there, slugging away by yourself, find other people who are doing this. Think about putting a show together, or doing co-bills, but it's always best when you share the stage. People who are not likely to come out to hear one folksinger will come out and hear three or four." Artists and songwriters have the opportunity to expand their audience through these multi-artist shows.

Lavin used this same idea when she decided to produce the compilation album *When October Goes*. "For years, I'd been talking myself blue in the face about how great this person is and that person. And finally I thought 'I'll just make a tape.' I put a very strong song of mine I know people want and let them buy this tape so they can hear this stuff." The album is sold by Lavin and the 12 artists on the album at their own solo performances. This has an added benefit for the group, Lavin says. "Everybody who's on the record is helping to support and promote the career of everybody else who's on the record." This kind of promotion and support can only take place when cooperation has been successful. Lavin continues, "These things can only come about when there's enough people working that they stop feeling they're competing for the same job."

Learning the hard way

Have all these collective efforts taught Lavin anything? "Yeah," she laughs. "every time I do it I swear I'll never do it again." Although her manager handles most of Lavin's business affairs, Lavin has learned about the intricacies of the music business herself the hard way: by doing it herself. She's learned about being flexible when performances don't make as much money as she would have liked, about mailing lists and their importance, recording, promoting and even shipping her own recordings.

Lavin has also made musical discoveries as a result of being involved with more than one facet of the business. Her evaluation of material has improved, especially related to programming full albums. "I have to deal with rejecting songs. And who am I? I'm just another songwriter. But when you're putting these (albums) together, many times it's just a matter of what goes with what. You're trying to get a balanced variety of things that are always in the same dynamic range." Making and producing albums teach the sort of lessons important for all aspiring songwriters. How to program selections on demos and timing your pitch sessions are steps on the path to success.

Writing the music

Lavin is probably best known for her humorous material; "Sensitive New Age Guys" and "Good Thing He Can't Read My Mind" are two of her best-known songs. These songs tend to be related to contemporary issues with what Lavin calls "a limited shelf life." The more serious ballads deal with universal topics or feelings and stand the test of time. Lavin's songs, whether humorous or not, come to her first as ideas. Some ideas appear complete, while others need to be worked on. "Then," Lavin says, "I walk around with it. A lot of my songs are to a walking tempo, because that's how I write them. And I'm trying to teach myself to walk in ¾ time or in reggae time!"

Lavin also has several techniques for dealing with writer's block. If she is struggling to write, she will learn a song by another writer. "Chances are very good that the song will contain a chord change or a melodic line or a lyric rhythm different from how I normally write. It's like adding a new vocabulary. One new chord can get you going in a whole new direction."

And if that doesn't work, there's a piece of advice she was given by Tom Paxton, another well-known songwriter: "Tom Paxton told me those are the times you are 'filling up the tanks.' To be a good writer you need experiences to draw from. Don't panic if you're not writing; just take care of the business of living, and the ideas will come along."

—Michael Oxley

❝If you're out there, slugging away by yourself, find other people who are doing this. Think about putting a show together, or doing co-bills, but it's always best when you share the stage.❞

—Christine Lavin

of Country on OL Records (country). Presently working with artists Glenda Sue Foster, Pat Murphy, Craig Robbins, Ty Black and Winston Stroup.

TOMSICK BROTHERS PRODUCTIONS, 21271 Chardon Rd., Dept. SM, Euclid OH 44117. (216)481-8380. President: Ken Tomsick. Record producer and record company (Recording Studio). Estab. 1982. Deals with artists and songwriters. Produces 2-5 LPs/year. Also produces original music for TV, radio, video and ad jingles. Fee derived from outright fee from recording artist. Charges in advance for studio time.
How to Contact: Write first and obtain permission to submit. Prefers cassette. "We have arrangers to help produce your sound." Does not return unsolicited material. Reports in 2 months.
Music: Mostly ethnic, polka and New Age/experimental. Produced "Joey Now" (by Joey Tomsick), recorded by Joey Tomsick Orchestra on TBP Records (polka/waltzes); and "Polkaerobics" (by Lynn Marie Rink), recorded by Lynn-Marie Hrouat-Rink on Rink Entertainment (polka/exercise). Other artists include Laurence Nozik.

TOUGH GUYS PRODUCTIONS, INC., Box 381463, Miami FL 33238. (305)757-7038. Chairmen: David and Chancy. Estab. 1986. Deals with artists and songwriters. Fee derived from sales royalty when song or artist is recorded.
How to Contact: Submit demo tape—unsolicited submissions are OK. Prefers cassette (or VHS videocassette if available) with 2-3 songs and lyric sheet. "Pictures and/or bios are recommended, but not necessary." SASE. Reports in 2-3 weeks.
Music: Mostly pop/dance, R&B/dance and rap; also pop/rock. Produced "Without Your Love" and "Don't Let Me Go," written and recorded by Nardy (dance); and "Hardcore Rebel," written and recorded by Riotcap (rap), all on Magic Apple Records.
Tips: "Know your field, and also your business."

TRAC RECORD CO., 170 N. Maple, Fresno CA 93702. (209)255-1717. Owner: Stan Anderson. Record producer, music publisher (Sellwood Publishing/BMI) and record company (Trac Records). Estab. 1972. Works with artists and songwriters. Produces 10-20 12" singles, 5 LPs and 1 CD/year. Fee derived from sales royalty or outside investors.
How to Contact: Submit demo tape—unsolicited submissions are OK. Prefers cassette with 3 songs and lyric sheet. "Studio quality." SASE. Reports in 2 weeks.
Music: Mostly country, gospel, pop and rock. Produced "Bare Your Soul" (by Denise Benson), recorded by Jessica James on Trac Records (country); "Mighty Rushin Wind" (by The Rackleys), recorded by The Rackleys on Psalm Records (gospel); and "West Coast Girls" (by Barry Best), recorded by Barry Best on Trac Records (country). Other artists include Jessica James, Robin Sharkey, Ron Arlen, B.G. White and Rick Blake.

TREND PRODUCTIONS, Dept. SM, Box 201, Smyrna GA 30081. (404)432-2454. Manager: Tom Hodges. Record producer, music publisher (Mimic Music, Stepping Stone Music, Skip Jack Music/BOAM, ASCAP), record company (Trend, Atlanta, Stepping Stone and Trendsetter Records and British Overseas Airways Music) and artist management. Estab. 1965. Deals with artists, songwriters and musicians. Produces 7 singles, 3 12" singles, 8 LPs and 3 CDs/year. Fee derived from sales royalty or outright fee from record company or music publisher.
How to Contact: Prefers cassette with 3-10 songs and lyric sheet. SASE. Reports in 3 weeks.
Music: Mostly country, gospel and MOR; also bluegrass, blues, R&B, rock, soul and top 40/pop. Produced "Jessica," written and recorded by G. Peters on BOAM #1 Records; "Don't Mess with the IRS" (by Dan/Rita/Al Rita), recorded by Marion Frizzell on Trend Records (country novelty); and "Another Footprint," recorded by Joann Johnson on Trend Records (country). Other artists include Rick Sumner, Terry Brand, Keith Bradford and Bobby Martin.

TRIPLANE PRODUCTION, 325 Winter Cress Dr., Henderson NV 89015. (702)564-3794. Producer: Vales Crossley. Record producer and music publisher. Estab. 1978. Deals with artists and songwriters. Produces 6 singles, 2 12" singles, 3 LPs, 3 EPs and 2 CDs/year. Fee derived from sales royalty when song or artist is recorded, outright fee from recording artist or outright fee from record company.
How to Contact: Write or call first and obtain permission to submit. Prefers cassette (or VAC videocassette if available) with 3-6 songs and lyric sheet. Does not return unsolicited material. Reports in 4-6 weeks.
Music: Mostly top 40 R&B, soul and rap; also New Age and rock. Produced *Check Mates Live* (by various), recorded by Vales Crossley on Checkmate Records (dance/LP); and *Street Wise* (by L. Thomas), recorded by Vales Crossley on Street Records (rap/single). Other artists include Plattels, Chrissie Zastzow and Mipori Powels.
Tips: "Be as ready to take care of business as you are to record."

TURNER PRODUCTIONS, Box 64895, Baton Rouge LA 70896. (504)925-0988. Indie Producer: Henry Turner. Record producer (BMI) and record companies (Hit City Records and Genesis Gospel Records). Estab. 1984. Deals with artists and songwriters. Produces 2-5 singles and 2-5 LPs/year. Fee derived from sales royalty or outright fee from recording artist or record company. "We charge a production fee."
How to Contact: Write or call first and obtain permission to submit. Prefers cassette with 3 songs and lyric sheet. "Stay basic in your ideas." Does not return unsolicited material. Reports in 1 month.
Music: All types. Produced "Hey Bartender" (by Eldon Ray), recorded by Eldon Ray and Kross Kountry (country); "I'll Be There For You" (by Frank Longo/Johnny Capplan), recorded by Johnny Capplan (country/rock); and "Say You Love It" (by Johnny Capplan), recorded by Johnny Capplan (country/rock), all on Hit City Records. Other artists include Henry Turner Jr. and Flavor (R&B/reggae/soul/funk), Radical Rhadd Hunt (dance funk/reggae), Sister Pepper James (gospel) and Billy Averett (country).
Tips: "Be sure you can afford the business of music and you can win big if you are willing to stop reading about it and start living it."

27TH DIMENSION INC., Box 1149, Okeechobee FL 34973-1149. (800)634-6091. President: John St. John. Record producer, music publisher (ASCAP, BMI) and music library. Estab. 1986. Deals with composers and songwriters. Produces 10 CDs/year. Fee derived from outright fee from record company and "performances."
How to Contact: Write or call first and obtain permission to submit. Prefers cassette. Does not return unsolicited submissions. Reports in 1 month.
Music: Mostly industrial, pop jazz and industrial fusion; also pop, impressionalism and descriptive. "Instrumentals only!"

***UP ALL NIGHT ENTERPRISES**, P.O. Box 1403, Maplewood NJ 07040. (201)763-4616. General Manager: Mark Partis. Record producer, music publisher, artist management. Estab. 1992. Deals with artists and songwriters. Fee derived from sales royalty when song or artist is recorded and outright fees from recording artist or record company.
How to Contact: Submit demo tape—unsolicited submissions are OK. Prefers cassette (or VHS videocassette) with 3 songs and lyric sheet. "Send photo and bio if available." Does not return unsolicited material.
Music: Mostly pop/rock, jazz fusion and R&B; also hard rock.
Tips: "Our emphasis is on the artist/songwriter as the key element in the recording, production and presentation of the music."

LUCIEN VECTOR, #3, 4747 N. Kenneth, Chicago IL 60630. Producer: Lucien Vector. Composer/arranger. Estab. 1985. Produces 5-10 singles, 0-3 12" singles, 2-4 LPs and 2-4 CDs/year. Receives 5-10 submissions/month. Fee derived from sales royalty when song or artist is recorded, outright fee from recording artist or outright fee from record company.
How to Contact: Submit demo tape—unsolicited submissions are OK. Prefers cassette with 1-4 songs and lyric sheet. Does not return unsolicited material. Reports in 1 month.
Music: Mostly pop-rock, world beat, ethno-pop and dance/rap; also electronic, soundtracks and theatrical. Produced *Healthy System* (by Johny K), recorded by TIC Productions on TIC Productions Records (pop LP); *Recitations of Norwid* (by Stan Borys), recorded by Chicago Trax on Nike Records (ethno-pop LP); and *The Mark* (by Dr Pepper and the X Factor), recorded by Fast Forward Sound Design on St. Christopher Records (pop-rock LP). Other artists include Nancy Davis, Tony Brajer and Miroslaw Rogala. Also produced soundtracks for "Ditka On Motivation" with Mike Ditka; "Great Crimes of the Century," "Nature Is Leaving Us" and many others.
Tips: "Work on the details only after the foundation is sound."

CHARLES VICKERS MUSIC ASSOCIATION, Box 725, Daytona Beach FL 32015-0725. (904)252-4849. President/Producer: Dr. Charles H. Vickers D.M. Record producer, music publisher (Pritchett Publication/BMI, Alison Music/ASCAP) and record company (King of Kings Records and L.A. International Records). Deals with artists and songwriters. Produces 3 singles and 6 LPs/year. Works with 1 new songwriter/year. Teams collaborators. Fee derived from sales royalty.
How to Contact: Write first and obtain permission to submit. Prefers 7½ ips reel-to-reel or cassette with 1-6 songs. SASE. Reports in 1 week.
Music: Mostly church/religious, gospel and hymns; also bluegrass, blues, classical, country, easy listening, jazz, MOR, progressive, reggae (pop), R&B, rock, soul and top 40/pop. Produced "Walking on the Water," "Let Us Pray," "Always Depend on Jesus," "The Lord is My Proctor" and "Everyday is a Holy Day," all written and recorded by C. Vickers on King of King Records.

*THE VICTORY LABEL, 1054 Conifer Lane, Petaluma CA 94954. Director of A&R: Shelly Trumbo. Record company, music publisher. ASCAP affiliate. Estab. 1985. Deals with artists and songwriters. Produces 5 singles, 2 12″ singles, 7 LPs, 10 EPs and 10 CDs/year. Fee is derived from sales royalty.
How to Contact: Write first and obtain permission to submit. Prefers cassette (or VHS videocassette if available) with 3 songs and lyric sheet. Does not return unsolicited material. Reports in 3 months.
Music: Mostly rock, pop and Christian rock; also dance. Produced "Out of Control" and "Shelly T," both recorded by Shelly T. on Victory Records (rock).

*VISUAL MUSIC, Box 86967, San Diego CA 92138-6967. (619)427-4290. Director of Production: Jay Henry. Record producer, record company and music publisher. Estab. 1977. Deals with artists and songwriters. Produces 6 singles, 2 12″ singles and 4 LPs/year. Fee derived from sales royalty, outright fee from recording artist, record company or investor.
How to Contact: Submit demo tape—unsolicited submissions are OK. Prefers cassette (or VHS videocassette if available) with 3-4 songs and lyric sheet. Does not return unsolicited material. Reports in 2-3 months.
Music: Mostly R&B, rap and dance/pop; also progressive country, hip hop and disco (70s style). Produced "Work Your Body" (by R. Michaels) and "Reality" (by F. Grimmet), recorded by Immage; and "Message To The Black Man" (by D. Colman), recorded by Different Shade of Black (all singles). Other artists include Lori Rose, Heavy-D, and Kimona 117.
Tips: "Have everything together before you contact a producer. If additional material or info is needed you can respond quickly."

WILLIAM F. WAGNER, Suite 218, 14343 Addison St., Sherman Oaks CA 91423. (818)905-1033. Contact: Bill Wagner. Record producer. Estab. 1957. Deals with artists and songwriters. Produces 4-6 singles, 2-4 LPs and 2-4 CDs/year. Works with 25 new songwriters/year. Fee derived from sales royalty or outright fee from recording artist record company.
How to Contact: Prefers cassette with 1-5 songs. "No lyric sheets. Material should be copyrighted." SASE. Reports in 1 month.
Music: Mostly top 40, pop, country and jazz; also blues, choral, gospel, easy listening, MOR, progressive, rock, soul and pop. Produced "Sings Mercer," recorded by Dewey Erney on Legend Records (MOR jazz); "Digital Page," recorded by Page Cavanaugh on Legend Records (jazz); "Sandy Graham," recorded by Sandy Graham on Muse Records. Other artists include Frank Sinatra, Jr., Mike Randall and Rick Whitehead.
Tips: "Send a competitive demo—a kitchen production with amateur musicians/and/or singers wastes all of our time."

THE WEISMAN PRODUCTION GROUP, 449 N. Vista St., Los Angeles CA 90036. (213)653-0693. Contact: Ben Weisman. Record producer and music publisher (Audio Music Publishers). Estab. 1965. Deals with artists and songwriters. Produces 10 singles/year. Receives 50-100 submissions/month. Fee derived from sales royalty.
How to Contact: Prefers cassette with 3-10 songs and lyric sheet. SASE. "Mention *Songwriter's Market*. Please make return envelope the same size as the envelopes you send material in, otherwise we cannot send everything back. Just send tape." Reports in 1 month.
Music: Mostly R&B, soul, dance, rap and top 40/pop; also all types of rock.
Tips: "Work on hooks and chorus, not just verses. Too many songs are only verses."

SHANE WILDER PRODUCTIONS, Box 3503, Hollywood CA 90078. President: Shane Wilder. Record producer and music publisher. Deals with artists and songwriters. Produces 10-15 singles and 5 LPs/year. Receives 100-150 submissions/month. Fee derived from sales royalty and production fees.
How to Contact: Accepts unsolicited submissions. Prefers cassette with 6-8 songs and lyric sheet. SASE. Reports in 4 weeks.
Music: Country. Produced "Fool Of The Year" (by Inez Pouzzi), recorded by Allen Karl on Century 2 (country) and "Album Project" (by various), recorded by Beryl Bittner (country). Other artists include Priscilla Emerson and Laurie Loman (MCA recording artist).
Tips: "Be highly commercial with your own style."

TOM WILLETT, TOMMARK RECORDS, #G3, 7560 Woodman Pl., Van Nuys CA 91405. (818)994-4862. Owners: Tom Willett and Mark Thornton. Record producer, music publisher (Schmerdley Music/BMI) and record company (Tomark Records). Estab. 1988. Deals with artists and songwriters. Produces 1 single and 1 CD/year. Receives 150 submissions/year.
How to Contact: Submit demo tape—unsolicited submissions are OK. Prefers cassette (or VHS videocassette if available) with any number of songs and lyric sheets. SASE. Reports in 4 weeks.
Music: Mostly country and novelty; also folk. Produced "Joe's Blues," written and recorded by Joe Wolverton (country instrumental); "Please Don't Play My Record On The Radio" (by Tom Willett), recorded by Herman Schmerdley (novelty country); and "So Many Men So Little Time" (by Nat

Wyner/Sharon Lynne), recorded by American Made Band (C&W swing), all on Tommark Records.
Tips: "Submit bio, resume, cassette. Send a good quality recording. Music is becoming even more lucrative than before. A good song can generate a good album or even a TV program or movie."

FRANK WILLSON, Box 2297, Universal City TX 78148. (512)653-3989. Producer: Frank Willson. Record producer (BMI) and record company (BSW Records). Deals with artists and songwriters. Estab. 1987. Produces 4 singles, 12-15 12″ singles, 10-12 LPs, 3 EPs and 5 CDs/year. Receives 20 submissions/month. Fee derived from sales royalty.
How to Contact: Submit demo tape—unsolicited submissions are OK. Prefers cassette with 3-4 songs and lyric sheets. SASE. Reports in 4 weeks.
Music: Mostly country and rock. Produced "Cowboys Do Not Gamble With Love" (by Howard), recorded by Candee Land on BSW Records (country). Other artists include Mike Lord and Bobby Lloyd.

WIZARDS & CECIL B, 1111 Second St., San Rafael CA 94901. (415)459-6714. Producers: David Lewark and Pete Slauson. Record producer and music publisher. Estab. 1978. Deals with artists and songwriters. Produces 10 singles, 10 12″ singles, 15 LPs and 15 CDs/year. Fee derived from sales royalty when song or artist is recorded, outright fee from recording artist, outright fee from record company and/or 24-track studio income.
How to Contact: Submit demo tape—unsolicited submissions are OK. Prefers cassette with several songs. SASE. Reports in 2 months.
Music: All kinds of music. Produced "New Rider of Purple Sage," recorded by W&CB on MU Records; "Nick Gravenities," recorded by In Mix on MU Records; and "Sarah Campbell," recorded by W&CB on Kalidascope Records, all written by J. Dawson (C&W). Other artists include Caribbean All Stars with Carlos Santana, released 1992.

*WLM MUSIC/RECORDING, 2808 Cammie St., Durham NC 27705-2020. (919)471-3086. Owner: Watts Lee Mangum. Recording studio (small). Estab. 1980. Deals with artists and songwriters. Produces 6-8 singles/year. Receives 8-10 submissions/month. Fee derived from outright fee from recording artist. "In some cases—an advance payment requested for demo production."
How to Contact: Submit demo tape—unsolicited submissions are OK. Prefers cassette with.2-4 songs and lyric or lead sheets (if possible). SASE. Reports in 3 months.
Music: Mostly country, country/rock and blues/rock; also pop, rock and R&B. Produced "High Time" (by Clayton Wrenn), recorded by Clayton/Mangum on WLM Records (country); "Blue Windows" (by Wrenn/Hill), recorded by Clayton/Mangum on WLM Records (country rock/blues); and "After All" (by Clayton Wrenn), recorded by Clayton/Mangum on WLM Records (country/blues). Other artists include Barry Hayes.
Tips: "Submit good demo tapes with artist's ideas, words, and music charted if possible."

RAY WOODBURY/WOODBURY/LYMAN MANAGEMENT, Suite 244, 112 N. Harvard Ave., Claremont CA 91711. (714)626-4245. Record producer and record company. Deals with artists and songwriters. Produces 4 singles, 2 12″ singles, 3 LPs and 3 CDs/year.
How to Contact: Call first and obtain permission to submit. Prefers cassette (or VHS videocassette if available) with 5 songs and lyric sheet. SASE.
Music: Interested in all types of music. Produced "Pretty Wiped Out" (by Jerry Joseph), recorded by Little Women on OuterSpace Records (rock single); "Hot Diggitty Dogs" (by Mr. P), recorded by Desperation Squad on OuterSpacc Records (alternative rock single); and "Alternate Roots," written and recorded by Cardiff Reefers on Grow Records (reggae single).

*GEOFF WORKMAN/ORIGINAL PROJECTS UNLIMITED, 36 West 3rd Ave., Denver CO 80223. (303)722-9653 or (213)519-3215. President: Lauri Day-Workman. Record producer. Estab. 1986. Deals with artists and songwriters. Produces 3 LPs, 3 EPs and 3 CDs/year. Fee derived from sales royalty or outright fee from recording artist or record company. "Requires deposit for time block of a project."
How to Contact: Submit demo tape by mail. Unsolicited submissions are okay. Prefers cassette with 3-4 songs and lyric sheet. Include promotional kit and picture. SASE. Reports in 6 weeks.
Music: Mostly rock, heavy metal and pop; also alternative. Engineered *Every Dog Has It's Day* (by Salty Dog), recorded by Salty Dog and *Last Decade, Dead Century* (by Warrior Soul), recorded by Warrior Soul, both on Geffen Records (rock LP). Other artists include Drivin'-n-Cryin'.

*STEVE WYTAS PRODUCTIONS, 165 Linden St., New Britain CT 06051. (203)224-1811. Contact: Steven J. Wytas. Record producer. Estab. 1984. Deals with artists only. Produces 4-8 singles, 6 12″ singles, 3 LPs, 3 EPs and 2 CDs/year. Fee derived from outright fee from recording artist or record company. "Expenses, sub-contractor fees, etc."

How to Contact: Submit demo tape — unsolicited submissions are OK. Prefers cassette (or VHS-¾″ videocassette) with several songs and lyric or lead sheet. "Include live material if possible." Does not return unsolicited material. Reports in 2 months.
Music: Mostly rock, metal, pop, top 40, country/acoustic; also R&B, soul and comedy. Produced "Mental Gymnastics" on MGA records, (single) *Free World* on TOTC Records (album disc) and "Indy Records" (single), both written and recorded by Leigh Gregory. Other artists include Flying Nuns, Sons of Bob, MG's, Mud Solo, Stupe, Wayne and Garth, Savage Brothers and Those Melvins.

JAMES YARBROUGH, 2613 Castle, Irving TX 75038. (214)257-1510. President: James Yarbrough. Record producer, music publisher (ASCAP) and record company (Virgin Boy Records). Estab. 1988. Deals with artists and songwriters. Produces 3 singles, 4 12″ singles and 2 LPs/year. Fee derived from sales royalty when song or artist is recorded.
How to Contact: Submit demo tape — unsolicited submissions are OK. Prefers cassette with 3 songs and lyric sheet. Does not return unsolicited material. Reports in 6 weeks.
Music: Mostly pop, rock and country. Produced "Something's Got Me," "Make A New Start" and "Playlike Lover," all written and recorded by James Yarbrough, on Virgin Boy Records (all pop singles).

JOHN YOUNG, Dept. SM, Suite C, 19 Music Square W., Nashville TN 37203. (615)255-5740. Record producer, music publisher, record company (Bear Records) and Young Graham Music. Estab. 1989. Deals with artists and songwriters. Produces 10 singles/year. Fee derived from sales royalty and outright fee from recording artist. Charges artists in advance for services.
How to Contact: Write or call first and obtain permission to submit. Prefers cassette with 3 songs and lyric sheet. SASE.
Music: Mostly country and gospel. Produced "Girls Like Her" (by Gant), recorded by J. Wright; "Red Neck, Blue Monday" (by Shafer), recorded by J. Wright; and "Down Home" (by Shephard), recorded by T. Roberson, all on Bear Records (all country). Other artists include Patton Ray, Autumn Day and Jimmy Peacock.

JOHN ZAPPLE, 2019 Noble St., Pittsburgh PA 15218. (412)351-6672. A&R Department: John Zapple. Record producer. Estab. 1980. Deals with artists and songwriters. Produces 5 LPs and 4 EPs/year. Receives 20 submissions/month. Fee derived from sales royalty.
How to Contact: Submit demo tape — unsolicited submissions are OK. Prefers cassette with 5 songs and lyric sheets. SASE. Reports in 2 weeks.
Music: Mostly rock, R&B/dance and new music; also gospel rock. Produced "Give Me Liberty Or Give Me Death," written and recorded by various artists (metal); and "Fire In Faith," written and recorded by Revelation's Fire (gospel rock). Other artists include Seance and Post Mortem.
Tips: "Send 5 to 8 of your best song's with photos and press kit."

ZAR MUSIK, Dreilindenstr. 42, Saint Gall, CH 9011 **Switzerland**. Phone: (071)255-666. A&R Director: Victor Waldburger. Record producer, music publisher and record company (Masters Records). Deals with artists and songwriters. Estab. 1980. Produces 5 singles, 5 LPs and 5 CDs/year. Fee derived from sales royalty, outright fee from recording artist or record company.
How to Contact: Send cassette (or VHS videocassette if available) and lyric or lead sheet. Reports only if interested.
Music: Mostly commercial pop, dance and rock/heavy metal. Produced "Miracles" (by Tony Sachary) on CBS Records (pop); "Gold for Iron" (by Ex-Yello Carlos Perou) on WEA Records (techno); and "Check and Mate" (by Sultan) on CTE/BMG Germany.

Record Producers/'92-'93 Changes

The following markets appeared in the 1992 edition of *Songwriter's Market* but are absent from the 1993 edition. Most of these companies failed to respond to our request for an update of their listing for a variety of reasons. For example, they may have gone out of business or they may have requested deletion because they are backlogged with material. If we know the specific reason, it appears within parentheses.

Acram Productions
ALA Bianca Publishing Group
All Star Productions (unable to contact)
Jim Allison/Allisongs Inc. (requested deletion)
Barnett Productions Inc.
The Beau-Jim Agency, Inc.
Best Buddies Productions (requested deletion)
Blue Sun Productions (requested deletion)
Burning Tyger Music (requested deletion)
Calliope Productions
Mark Carvel
Clay/Twan
Michael Collins/Refined Records
Ron Cornelius
Counterpoint Productions (unable to contact)
The Coyote (unable to contact)
Creative Artworks Inc./B&W Productions
Remy David's Audio Oasis
Carlo Ditta
Jamie Dyce/Radio Active Records (requested deletion)
E.S.R. Productions
Farallone Productions
Folsom Productions (out of business)
Bob Gaffney Productions
The Gland Puppies Inc.
Jon Gorr/Massmedia
RL Hammel Associates Inc.
Ernie Hatton/Bill Winborne/Sandy Contella

Lawrence Herbst (unable to contact)
Highland Records (unable to contact)
Jazzmark Sound Studio
Johann Kaplan Music Group
Johnny Kline
Jury Krytiuk Productions
LVW Entertainment
Lyx Music Production & Recording Studios
Harvey Marcus
Marketunes Inc.
Midwest Records
Mr. Mort Enterprises (unable to contact)
A.V. Mittlestedt
Modern Music Ventures Inc.
Monkey's Uncle Productions
More Coffee Productions/Wesley Bulla
Munich Productions/Records
Neon Jukebox Production
Nightwork Records
NRB Productions
Keith O'Neill/Caravelle Records (unable to contact)
Orange Productions (unable to contact)
Karen Pady-ka Productions
Mick Parker
Chris Pati Productions
Dave Pell Productions/Digital
Prairie Music Ltd. (unable to contact)
Robby Roberson Productions (unable to contact)
Rob Roberts/Ocean Hills Music Group

Rolling Road Productions, Inc. (requested deletion)
Rooster Productions (out of business)
Sand Hand Records Inc.
Silver J. Sargeant
Jason Schwartz-U.S.A. Entertainment
Scrapbook Music Productions
September Music Productions
Silsar Productions
Singing Cat Music
Gary R. Smith Production
Sound Advisors Ltd.
Jack Stand
Star Sound and Recording
Steppin' Out Music (unable to contact)
Stone Cold Productions
F.B. Swegal
Third Floor Productions
The Thomas Group (unable to contact)
Toro'na Int'l.
Total Trak Productions
Robin Tracy (unable to contact)
United Recording Studio
Walk on Water Productions (temporarily out of business)
Waterfall Productions
WIR (World International Records)
World Artist
World Record Company (unable to contact)
Christoff Wybouw

Managers and Booking Agents

Managers and booking agents are part of the circle of music industry professionals closest to the artists themselves. Working for and with their clients, they are a vital part of an aspiring artist's career.

The artist manager is a valuable contact, both for the songwriter trying to get songs to a particular artist and for the songwriter/performer. Often the manager is the person closest to the artist, and he may have heavy influence in what type of material the performer uses. Remember that managers of nationally-known acts are usually located in the major music hubs. Don't expect these "big time" managers to be the easiest people to approach, because they're not. Many songwriters are trying to get songs to these people, and in most cases they only accept material from music publishers or producers who they know personally or professionally.

You need not go further than your own hometown, however, to find artists hungry for good, fresh material. Managers of local acts often have more to say in the choice of material their clients perform and record than managers in major hubs, where the producer often makes the final decision on what songs are included. Locally, it could be the manager who not only chooses songs for a recording project, but also selects the producer, the studio and the musicians.

If you are an artist or artist/songwriter seeking management, take care in selecting your representation. A manager needs to know of all aspects of the music industry. His handling of publicity, promotion and finances, plus his contacts within the industry will shape your career. Look for a manager or agency who will take an interest in your development; this can be worked into a management agreement to help insure management is working on your behalf. Above all don't be afraid to ask questions about any aspects of the relationship between you and a prospective manager. He should be willing to explain any confusing terminology or discuss plans with you before taking action. Remember: a manager works *for the artist*. His main function is advising and counseling his clients, not dictating to them.

Another function of the manager is to act as liaison between the artist and the booking agent. Some management firms may also handle booking. However, it may be in your interest to look for a separate booking agency. It will give you another member of the team working to get your work heard in live performance, and adds to the network necessary to make valuable contacts in the industry. Since their function is mainly to find performance venues for their clients, booking agents represent many more acts than a management firm, and have less contact with the individual acts. They may review material for the artists they work with, but don't have as much individual contact. A booking agent will charge a commission for their services, as will a management firm. Managers usually ask for a 15-20% commission on an act's earnings for their services; booking agents charge less.

Talent, originality, credits, dedication, self-confidence and professionalism are qualities that will attract a manager to an artist—and a songwriter. Before submitting to a manager or booking agent, be sure he's searching for the type of music you offer. And, just as if you were contacting a music publisher or producer, always be as organized and professional as possible. *Billboard* also publishes a list of managers/booking agents in *Billboard's International Talent and Touring Directory*.

The firms listed in this section have provided information about the types of acts they currently work with and the type of music they're interested in. You'll also find submission requirements and information about items to include in a press kit. Each listing in this section will also specify whether the company is a management firm, a booking agency or both.

A•C•E TALENT MANAGEMENT, Unit 24, 4544 Dufferin St., Downsview Ont. M3H 5X2 **Canada.** President: Raymond A Sare. Management firm. Estab. 1984. Represents local, regional or international individual artists, groups, songwriters, models and actors; currently handles 15 acts. Receives 15% commission. Reviews materials for acts.
How to Contact: Call first to arrange personal interview. Prefers cassette (or VHS videocassette if available) with 5 songs and lyric sheets. Does not return unsolicited material. Reports in 2 weeks.
Music: Mostly rock, pop and dance; also country and R&B. Deals with groups, vocalists and songwriters. Current acts include The Act (progressive rock), Joy Ride (metal-pop) and Riothouse (crossover country rock).
Tips: "Press kit should include the following items; bio, song list, photo, original lyric sheets (typed) and VHS videotape of live performance."

*ABSOLUTE ENTERTAINMENT INC., 273 Richmond St. W, Toronto, Ontario M5V 1X1 **Canada.** Contact: Wayne Thompson. Management firm. Estab. 1973. Represents local, regional or international individual artists and groups; currently handles 3 acts. Receives 20% commission. Reviews material for acts.
How to Contact: Submit demo tape by mail—unsolicited submissions are OK. Prefers cassette (or VHS videocassete if available) with 4 songs and lyric sheet. SASE. Reports in 2-3 weeks.
Music: Mostly pop, rock and R&B. Works primarily with vocalists, singer/songwriters. Current acts include The Nylons (a capella), Infidels (rock) and Watertown (singer/songwriter).
Tips: "Be aggressive, be patient, be polite."

ACADEMY AWARD ENTERTAINMENT, 11 Shady Oak Trail, Charlotte NC 28210. (704)554-1162. Agent: Butch Kelly. Management firm, music publisher (Butch Kelly Productions, Music By Butch Kelly/BMI), record company (KAM Executive and Fresh Avenue Records), record producer and promoter (Sunshine Record Promotions). Estab. 1987. Represents national acts and comedians. Currently handles 10 acts. Receives 20% commission. Reviews material for acts.
How to Contact: Submit demo tape—unsolicited submissions are OK. Prefers cassette or records (or VHS videocassette if available) with 5-10 songs. "Send bio information, 8x10 photo, press kit or news clips if possible." SASE. Reports in 2-8 weeks.
Music: Rock, pop, R&B, rap, beach, soul, gospel, country and comedy. Works primarily with show and dance groups, vocalists, bar bands and concerts. Current acts include Fresh Air (R&B), Lady Crush (rapper), Dean Mancuso (country), Melisa Kelly (R&B/pop), L.A. Star (R&B), Caro (R&B) and Platters (show).

*ACOUSTIWORKS, 3818 Cleghorn Ave., Nashville TN 37215. President: Tom Wilkerson. Management firm. Represents nationally known individual artists only; currently handles 4 acts. Receives 10-20% commission. Reviews material for acts.
How to Contact: Submit demo tape by mail—unsolicited submission are OK. Prefers cassette with 3 songs. SASE. Reports in 3-4 weeks.
Music: Mostly country, gospel and contemporary Christian and pop. Works primarily with vocalists. Current acts include Ed Bruce (singer/songwriter/actor) and George Westermeyer (singer/songwriter).

*ADAMS & GREEN ENTERTAINMENT, #59, 2802 W.T.C. Jester, Houston TX 77018. (713)541-5200. Owner: Robert Messer. Management firm, booking agency, music publisher (Messer Music/ASCAP) and record company (Nuts & Bolts Productions). Estab. 1978. Represents individual artists, groups and songwriters. Deals with regional (SW) individual artists, groups and songwriters; currently handles 58 acts. Receives 20% commission. Reviews material for acts.
How to Contact: Submit demo tape by mail—unsolicited submissions are OK. Prefers cassette (or VHS videocassette if available) with 4 songs and lyric sheets. SASE. Reports in weeks.
Music: Mostly pop, country and rock; also industrial. Works primarily with dance bands. Current acts include In the Jeans (dance), Man & Machine (dance) and Twenty Mondays (dance).

The asterisk before a listing indicates that the listing is new in this edition. New markets are often the most receptive to unsolicited submissions.

*ADELAIDE ROCK EXCHANGE, 186 Glen Osmond Rd., Fullarton SA **Australia** 5063. Phone: (08)338-1844. Managing Editor: Brian Gleeson. Management firm, booking agency. Estab. 1982. Represents national and international individual artists and groups. Receives 5-10% commission. Reviews material for acts.

How to Contact: Submit demo tape by mail—unsolicited submissions are OK. Prefers cassette (or VHS videocassette if available). SASE. Reports in 2 months.

Music: Mostly rock, pop, R&B; also duos, solos and sight artists. Primarily works with recording bands, dance and concept bands. Current acts include Zep Boys (Led Zeppelin concept band), High Voltage (AC/DC concept band), Chunky Custard (70's glam rock show band) and Ian Polites (pianist/vocalist).

Tips: "Please have all demo tapes, bios and photos with a track list and, most importantly, contact numbers and addresses."

AFTERSCHOOL PUBLISHING COMPANY, Box 14157, Detroit MI 48214. (313)571-0363. President: Herman Kelly. Management firm, booking agency, record company (Afterschool Co.) and music publisher (Afterschool Pub. Co.). Estab. 1978. Represents individual artists, songwriters, producers, arrangers and musicians. Currently handles 8 acts. Receives 20% commission. Reviews material for acts.

How to Contact: Submit demo tape by mail—unsolicited submissions are OK. Prefers cassette with 3 songs and lyric or lead sheet. If seeking management, include resume with demo tape and bio in press kit. SASE. Reports in 2 weeks to 1 month.

Music: Mostly pop, jazz, rap, country and folk. "What we are seeking now is comedy on the subjects of food, clothes, sports, cars and love." Works primarily with small bands and solo artists. Current acts include Herman Kelly, Rendell Star (singer/songwriter), James Garland (pop/jazz, folk), Nona Woods (songwriter), Jeff Harris (songwriter) and T. Stevenson.

AKO PRODUCTIONS, 20531 Plummer, Chatsworth CA 91311. (818)998-0443. President: A.E. Sullivan. Management firm, booking agency, music publisher and record company (AKO Records, Dorn Records, Aztec Records). Estab. 1980. Represents local and international artists, groups and songwriters; currently handles 3 acts. Receives 10-25% commission. Reviews material for acts.

How to Contact: Write first and obtain permission to submit. Prefers cassette with maximum of 5 songs and lyric sheet. If seeking management, include cassette, picture and lyrics in press kit. SASE. Reports in 1 month.

Music: Mostly pop, rock and top 40. Works primarily with vocalists, dance bands and original groups. No heavy metal. Current acts include Les Staunton's, Touch of Fire, Rumor Habit, Radio Radio and The Stereo Band.

MARK ALAN AGENCY, Box 279, Hopkins MN 55343. (612)942-6119. President: Mark Alan. Management firm and booking agency. Represents individual artists, groups and songwriters; currently handles 8 acts. Receives 20% commission. Reviews material for acts.

How to Contact: Submit demo tape by mail—unsolicited submissions are OK. Prefers cassette (or VHS videocassette if available). If seeking management, include photo, bio, press clips and reviews in press kit. Does not return material. Reports in 90 days.

Music: Rock, pop, R&B (black) and new wave. Works primarily with groups and solo artists. Current acts include Airkraft (rock band), Zwarté (rock band), Crash Alley (rock band), Mistress (rock band), Milwaukee Iron (rock band), Tamara (rock band), Michael Cuts Forth (pop) and Band of Gypsies.

Tips: "We work with bands that tour nationally and regionally and record their original songs and release them on major or independent labels. We book clubs, colleges and concerts."

ALEXAS MUSIC GROUP, 3365 W. Millerberg Way, West Jordan UT 84084. (801)566-9542. President: Patrick Melfi. Management firm, booking agency (BMI) and record company (Alexas Records/ASCAP). Estab. 1976. Represents local, regional or international individual artists, groups and songwriters; currently handles 10 acts. Receives 15% commission. Reviews material for acts.

How to Contact: Submit demo tape by mail—unsolicited submissions are OK. Submit VHS videocassette only with 1-3 songs and lyric sheets. Does not return unsolicited material. Reports in 2 months.

Music: Mostly country and pop; also New Age and gospel. Represents well-established bands and vocalists. Current acts include A.J. Masters (singer/songwriter), Crossfire, Hardriders and Midnight Country, The Drifters and The Crests (16 Candles).

GREG ALIFERIS MANAGEMENT, 3406 N. Ocean Blvd., Ft. Lauderdale FL 33308. (305)561-4880. President: Greg Aliferis. Management firm, music publisher (Rumrunner Music/BMI) and record company (Rumrunner Records, Inc.). Estab. 1980. Represents local and southeast individual artists, groups and songwriters; currently handles 5 acts. Reviews material for acts.

How to Contact: Submit demo tape by mail—unsolicited submissions are OK. Prefers cassette (or VHS videocassette) with 3 songs and lyric sheet. If seeking management, include 3- or 4-song demo cassette, photo and current address and phone number in press kit. SASE. Reports in 2-3 months.
Music: Mostly dance, rap and pop. Works primarily with rap groups, dance groups and female vocalists. Current acts include Side F-X (rap), Mario (rap), Reggie LaLanne (rap) and Don't Know Yet (dance).

ALL STAR TALENT & PROMOTIONS, Box 37612, Sarasota FL 34237. (813)377-1877. Executive Vice President: Lynn Russen. Management firm, booking agency, music publisher (Rob Lee Music/BMI) and record company (Castle, TCB, Jade, Rock Island). Estab. 1965. Represents local, regional and international individual artists and groups; currently handles 32 acts. Receives 15-25% commission. Reviews material for acts.
How to Contact: Submit demo tape by mail—unsolicited submissions are OK. Prefers cassette (or VHS videocassette if available). If seeking management, include 8×10 glossy, demo tape, video, bio and credits in press kit. Does not return material. Reports in 2 weeks.
Music: Mostly rock, pop and dance. Current acts include Dreta Warriors, Fantastics, Adrienne West (R&B), Thunder & Lightening (rock) and Derrek Dukes.

*ALL STAR TALENT AGENCY, Box 82, Greenbrier TN 37073. (615)643-4208. Agent: Joyce Kirby. Booking agency. Estab. 1966. Represents professional individuals, groups and songwriters; currently handles 6 acts. Receives 15% commission. Reviews material for acts.
How to Contact: Submit demo tape by mail—unsolicited submissions are OK. Prefers cassette with 4 songs and lead sheet (VHS videocassette if available). SASE. Reports ASAP. If seeking management, press kit should include bios and photos.
Music: Mostly country; also bluegrass, gospel, MOR, rock (country) and top 40/pop. Works primarily with dance, show and bar bands, vocalists, club acts and concerts. Current acts include Alex Houston (MOR/country), Ronnie Dove (country/MOR) and Jack Greene (country).

ALOHA ENTERTAINMENT, Box 2204, 14 Sherman St., Auburn NY 13021. (315)252-1863. Publicist/Manager: Art Wenzel. Management and public relations firm. Estab. 1982. Represents local, Central New York, international and national touring acts and groups.
How to Contact: Submit demo tape by mail—unsolicited submissions are OK. Prefers cassette. Reports in 3 weeks.
Music: Mostly rock, metal and blues; also jazz and R&B. Current acts include Sacred Death (speed metal band), The Kingsnakes (real blues), Ruff Haus (R&B), Crucifier (thrash metal), Axiom (hard rock), Paul Quinzi Project (pop) and Flaming Buddhas (thrash).

AMERICAN ARTIST, INC., 604 Glover Dr., Runnemede NJ 08078-1225. (609)931-8389. President: Anthony Messina. Management firm. Represent local, regional or international individual artists, groups and songwriters; currently handles 4 acts. Receives 15% commission. Reviews material for acts.
How to Contact: Submit demo tape by mail—unsolicited submissions are OK. Prefers cassette or 7½ ips reel-to-reel (or VHS videocassette if available) with 3 songs and lyric sheets. Does not return unsolicited material. Reports in 6 weeks.
Music: Mostly MOR, rock and R&B. Works primarily with vocalists and dance bands. Current acts include Harold Melvin and The Bluenotes, Delfonics, Electric City and Jimmy Harnen.

*AMERICAN FAMILY ENTERTAINMENT, Box 605, Harrison AR 72602. (501)741-5250. Contact: Mike Bishop. Management firm. Estab. 1983. Represents regional individual artists and groups; currently handles 3 acts. Receives 10% commission. Reviews material for acts.
How to Contact: Submit demo tape by mail—unsolicited submissions are OK. Prefers cassette with 2-5 songs and lyric or lead sheets. Does not return unsolicited material. Reports in 3 weeks.
Music: Mostly country, pop and gospel; also bluegrass and patriotic. Works primarily with vocalists/show bands. Current acts include Country Time, Mike Bishop and Dale Bishop.
Tips: "Send driving commercial country tunes for males. Send good love songs and gospel for females."

AMERICAN FAMILY TALENT, (formerly Festival Family Enterprises, Ltd.), Box 87, Skidmore MO 64487. (816)928-3631. Personal Manager: Jonnie Kay. Management firm (Max Stout Publishing/BMI) and record company (Max Stout Records). Estab. 1973. Currently handles 2 acts. Receives 10-15% commission. Reviews material for acts.
How to Contact: Submit demo tape by mail—unsolicited submissions are OK. Prefers cassette (or videocassette of performance) with 2 songs with lyric and lead sheets. Reports in 1 year.
Music: Mostly ballads, pop and country; also patriotic. Works primarily with variety showbands and dance bands. Current acts include Britt Small and Festival (brass band/variety) and Matt and Robyn Rolf (country show band).

Tips: "We're looking for ballads written for a bass voice, mass vocals and brass; also looking for comedy tunes and patriotic songs."

*THE AMETHYST GROUP LTD., 273 Chippewa Dr., Columbia SC 29210-6508. (803)750-5391. Management firm. Represents individual artists, groups and songwriters; currently handles 11 acts. Receives 15-25% commission. Reviews material for acts. "Signs original artists."
How to Contact: Prefers cassette (or VHS videocassette if available) with 3-7 songs and lyric sheet. "Be creative, simple and to the point." SASE. Reports in 5 weeks if interested. "No phone calls, please."
Music: Mostly mainstream, rock, metal and pop; also R&B and new music. Current acts include Political Asylum, Bodyshop, Knightmare, Jr. Ellis, Carnage, True Identity, Ted Neiland, Toni Land and Synthetic Meat.
Tips: "Be prepared to sign, if we're interested. We won't spend a lot of time convincing anyone what we can do for them. We are way too busy with current recording artists. We help organize radio and retail promotion for three record labels in the U.S. We develop recording artists and market them for further distribution, promotion. Our resources cover booking agencies, major and independent record companies, distributors, TV and radio stations, newspapers and trade publications, independent talent, record promoters and producers—all on national level. Most artists we represent *are not* in S.C. We are not just another small, local management firm. We also manufacture CDs, records, cassettes, photographs and other items to enhance an artist's career. Recently signed distribution and licensing with many territories in Europe."

*DAVID ANTHONY PROMOTIONS, 649 Knutsford Rd., Latchford, Warrington Cheshire WA4 1JJ England. Phone: (0925)32496. Projects Manager: David Wright. Management firm and booking agency. Represents local individual artists, groups and songwriters; currently represents 6 acts; standard commission of 20%. Reviews material for acts.
How to Contact: Prefers cassette with 3 songs and lyric sheet. SAE and IRC. Reports in 3 weeks.
Music: Mostly country, rock; also pop. Current acts include Rick Astley (vocalist/songwriter), Mark Williamson (MOR pop), The Pleasure Babes (MOR/pop), Kelly Hampson (MOR pop) and Eglin O'Neill (pop duo).

*ARISTOMEDIA, (formerly Aristo Music Group), Box 22765, Nashville TN 37202. (615)269-7071. President: Jeff Walker. Publishing Manager: Terri Walker. Publicity/media management firm. Represents artists, groups and songwriters. "We deal with artists on a national and international level." Currently handles 10 clients. Receives negotiable commission for public relations services "based on estimated time and services involved." Reviews material for acts.
How to Contact: Submit demo tape—unsolicited submissions are OK. "At present we are only interested in artists with national distribution." Prefers cassette with 1-2 songs (or videocassette if available). If seeking management, include cassette tape, video tape, photo (8×10 bw) bio, fact sheet, press clippings and anything else that would add insight into artist in press kit. Prefers a "low-key, patient approach." SASE. Reports in 6-8 weeks.
Music: Country, easy listening, MOR and top 40/pop. Works primarily with country groups and artists. Current acts include Bailey & The Boys (country music duet), Chris Ledoux (recording artist) and Lorrie Morgan (recording artist).
Tips: Songwriters "need to be professional in their approach to the music business. Have established affiliated publishing companies."

*VIC ARKILIC, Box 261, Mt. Vernon VA 22121. (703)780-4726. Manager: Vic Arkilic. Management firm. Estab. 1986. Represents local individual artists and groups; currently handles 1 act. Receives 15% commission. Reviews material for acts.
How to Contact: Submit demo tape by mail—unsolicited submissions are OK. Prefers cassette (or VHS videocassette) with 4 songs and lyric sheet. SASE. Reports in 3 months.
Music: Mostly rock, pop and folk. "We work with self-contained groups who are also songwriters." Current acts include The Tools (rock group).
Tips: "Please submit finished demos only!"

THE ARTIST GROUP, Box 27696, St. Louis MO 63146. (314)576-7625. Manager: Keith Davis. Management firm and booking agency. Estab. 1987. Represents individual artists and groups from anywhere; currently handles 5 acts. Receives 15-25% commission. Reviews material for acts.
How to Contact: Submit demo tape by mail—unsolicited submission are OK. Prefers cassette (or VHS videocassette if available) with 4 songs and lyric sheet. If seeking management, include demo tape, picture and lyric sheet in press kit. Does not return unsolicited material. Reports in 1 month.

Music: Mostly rock, alternative (new music) and funk. Works primarily with rock bands—dance funk bands. Current acts include Aynthem (objectivist-oriented rock), Saturn Cats (pop metal show group) and Tyrant (pop metal group).
Tips: "Submit quality demos, lyric sheets. Wait for a response. We will respond within 4 weeks of receipt."

ARTISTIC DEVELOPMENTS INTERNATIONAL, INC. (A.D.I.), Box 6386, Glendale CA 91225. (818)501-2838. Management Director: Lisa Weinstein. Management firm. Estab. 1988. Represents local, regional and international individual artists, groups and songwriters. Reviews material for acts.
How to Contact: Call or write first and obtain permission to submit. Prefers cassette with unlimited number of songs and lyric sheet. SASE. Reports in 4-6 weeks.
Music: Mostly cross-over artists, AC/pop and alternative/rock; also world beat/pop and R&B/dance. Works primarily with singer/songwriters, bands and performance artists.
Tips: "A song writer should have a professional quality tape that highlights his versatility and artistic vision. Lyric sheets should be included. An artist should submit a recent 8×10 photo that reflects his/her musical vision. Name and phone number should be on everything! Both artist and songwriter should include a cover letter stating intent and artistic vision."

ASA PRODUCTIONS MANAGEMENT, Box 244, Yorba Linda CA 92686. (714)693-7629. President: Craig Seitz. Management firm. Estab. 1986. Represents local, regional and international individual artists and groups; currently handles 3 acts. Receives 20% commission. Reviews material for acts.
How to Contact: Submit demo tape by mail—unsolicited submissions are OK. Prefers cassette (or VHS videocassette if available). SASE. Reports in 1 month.
Music: Mostly country and bluegrass. Works primarily with show/concert groups. Current acts include Barbara Morrison and Sierrah Band, Insight (rock) and Strip (hard rock).

*ATCH RECORDS AND PRODUCTIONS, Suite 300, Fondren, Houston TX 77096-4502. (713)981-6540. President: Charles Atkinson. Management firm, record company. Estab. 1989. Represents local, regional and international individual artists, groups and songwriters; currently handles 2 acts. Receives 15-20% commission. Reviews material for acts.
How to Contact: Submit demo tape—unsolicited submissions are OK. Prefers cassette with 2 songs and lyric sheet. Reports in 1 month.
Music: Mostly R&B, country and gospel; also pop, rap and rock. Works primarily with vocalists and group. Current acts include Ace Duce (rap group) and LaRue (country group).
Tips: "You must be ready for hard work toward a career in the music industry."

BABY SUE, Box 1111, Decatur GA 30031-1111. (404)288-2073. President: Don W. Seven. Management firm, booking agency, record company (Baby Sue); "we also publish a magazine which reviews music." Estab. 1983. Represents local, regional or international individual artists, groups and songwriters; currently handles 3 acts. Receives 10% commission. Reviews material for acts.
How to Contact: Submit demo tape by mail—unsolicited submissions are OK. Prefers cassette (or VHS videocassette if available) with 4 songs and lyric sheets. Does not return unsolicited material. Reports in 2 weeks.
Music: Mostly rock, pop and alternative; also country and religious. Works primarily with multi-talented artists (those who play more than 1 instrument). Current acts include LMNOP (rock), Stephen Fievet (pop) and Bringbring (poetic music).

BACK DOOR MANAGEMENT, #1054, 6237 S. Transit Rd., Lockport, NY 14094. (716)343-6502. President: Richard Anselmo. Management firm and booking agency. Estab. 1990. Represents local, regional and international individual artists, groups, songwriters and comedians; currently handles 6 acts. Receives 15-25% commission. Reviews material for acts.
How to Contact: Write or call first and obtain permission to submit. Prefers cassette or VHS videocassette with 3-6 songs and lyric and lead sheets. Reports in 2 months.
Music: Mostly rock, folk and pop; also R&B, heavy metal and industrial. Works primarily with individual artists, duos/groups and songwriters. Current acts include Lorie McCloud (singer/songwriter), "Outside Lookin' In" (rock group) and Paul Quintlone (singer/songwriter).
Tips: "Hard work coupled with originality produces results."

*BACK PORCH BLUES, Box 14953, Portland OR 97214. (503)233-6827. General Manager: Jeffrey Dawkins. Management firm. Estab. 1988. Represents individual artists and groups from Pacific Northwest; currently handles 3 acts. Receives 17% commission. Reviews material for acts.

How to Contact: Submit demo tape by mail—unsolicited submissions are OK. Prefers cassette (or VHS videocassette if available) with 6 songs and lyric sheet. SASE. Reports in 2 months.
Music: Mostly traditional blues, R&B and country; also blues, gospel and solo piano. Works primarily with blues bands, jazz singers and jazz groups. Current acts include Sheila Wilcoxson, Back Porch (blues group) and Gordon Neal Herman.
Tips: "We want simple songs that tell a story. Good blues or country songs should touch the heart."

BARNARD MANAGEMENT SERVICES (BMS), 2219 Main St., Santa Monica CA 90405. (213)396-1440. Agent: Russell Barnard. Management firm. Estab. 1979. Represents artists, groups and songwriters; currently handles 3 acts. Receives 10-20% commission. Reviews material for acts.
How to Contact: Write first and obtain permission to submit. Prefers cassette with 3-10 songs and lead sheet. Artists may submit VHS videocassette (15-30 minutes) by permission only. SASE. Reports in 1 month.
Music: Mostly country crossover; also blues, country, R&B, rock and soul. Works primarily with country crossover singers/songwriters and show bands. Current acts include Helen Hudson (singer/songwriter), Mark Shipper (songwriter/author), Mel Trotter (singer/songwriter) and Sally Spurs (singer).
Tips: "Semi-produced demos are of little value. Either save the time and money by submitting material 'in the raw,' or do a finished production version."

BDO SEIDMAN, 1200 Statler Towers, Buffalo NY 14202. (716)853-9333. Partner: Richard A. Romer. Management firm. Estab. 1982. Represents individual artists and groups; currently handles 5 acts. Commission is "based on hourly rate of $175/hour." Reviews material for acts.
How to Contact: Submit demo tape by mail—unsolicited submissions are OK. Prefers cassette. "Would like to see live performance videocassette." If seeking management include photo and biographic summary in press kit. Does not return unsolicited material. Reports in 2 weeks.
Music: Mostly R&B and rap. Works primarily with R&B acts and vocalists. Current acts include Rick James (R&B), Erskine Williams (R&B) and Val Young (R&B).
Tips: "Have original material that has a different sound."

*BIG HOUSE MANAGEMENT PTY LTD., Box 10, Broadway, Sydney NSW **Australia** 2007. Phone: (02)360 2550. Directors: Jon Ashcroft and Michael Dibbs. Management firm and booking agency. Estab. 1987. Represents local and international individual artists, groups and songwriters; currently handles 12 acts. Receives 20% commission. Reviews material for acts.
How to Contact: Submit demo tape by mail—unsolicited submissions are OK. Prefers cassette (or VHS/PAL videocassette) with 4 songs and lyric sheet. SAE and IRC. Reports in 6-8 weeks.
Music: Mostly rock, pop and soul/R&B; also country rock, country pop and contemporary jazz. Works primarily with vocalists, original contemporary bands and dance bands. Current acts include Jim Chaney (rock singer/songwriter), Jeff St. John (rock singer/songwriter) and Baby Loves to Cha Cha Dance Band (songwriters).
Tips: "Present submissions with all pertinent details."

*J. BIVINS' PRODUCTIONS, Box 763843, Dallas TX 75376. (214)709-7561. Management firm and record company (Avonna Records, Inc.). Estab. 1991. Represents individual artists, groups and songwriters from anywhere; currently handles 12 acts. Receives 15-25% commission. Reviews material for acts.
How to Contact: Submit demo tape by mail—unsolicited submissions are OK. Prefers cassette (or VHS videocassette if available) with 3 songs. Does not return unsolicited material. Reports in 3 weeks.
Music: Mostly R&B, rock and gospel (top 40). Works primarily with vocalists and dance bands. Current acts include Joe Petty, Sloe Breeze and Curtis Steward III.

*BLACK STALLION COUNTRY PRODUCTIONS, INC., Box 368, Tujunga CA 91043. (818)352-8142. President: Kenn E. Kingsbury, Jr.. Management firm, production company and music publisher (Black Stallion Country Publ./BMI). Estab. 1979. Represents individual artists from anywhere; currently handles 3 acts. Receives 15-25% commission. Reviews material for acts.
How to Contact: Submit demo tape by mail—unsolicited submissions are OK. Prefers cassette with 3 songs and lyric sheet. SASE. Reports in 2 months.
Music: Mostly country, R&B and A/C. Works primarily with country acts, variety acts and film/TV pictures/actresses. Current acts include Lane Brody (singer country), Thom Bresh (musician) and Gene Bear (TV host).
Tips: "Be professional in presentation. Make sure what you present is what we are looking for (i.e., don't send rock when we are looking for country)."

*BLANK & BLANK, Suite 308, 1530 Chestnut St., Philadelphia PA 19102. (215)568-4310. Treasurer, Manager: E. Robert Blank. Management firm. Represents individual artists and groups. Reviews material for acts.
How to Contact: Submit demo tape by mail—unsolicited submissions are OK. Prefers videocassette. Does not return material.

T.J. BOOKER LTD., Box 969, Rossland, B.C. V0G 1Y0 **Canada.** (604)362-7795. Contact: Tom Jones. Management firm, booking agency and music publisher. Estab. 1976. Represents local, regional or international individual artists, groups and songwriters; currently handles 25 acts. Receives 10-15% commission. Reviews material for acts.
How to Contact: Submit demo tape by mail—unsolicited submissions are OK. Prefers cassette (or videocassette if available) with 3 songs. If seeking management, include demo tape, picture and bio in press kit. Does not return unsolicited material.
Music: Mostly MOR, crossover, rock, pop and country. Works primarily with vocalists, show bands, dance bands and bar bands. Current acts include Kirk Orr (comedian), Tommy and T Birds (50s show band), Zunzee (top 40/pop), Mike Hamilton and Eclipse.
Tips: "There is always a market for excellence."

*BOUQUET-ORCHID ENTERPRISES, Box 11686, Atlanta GA 30355. (404)355-7635. President: Bill Bohannon. Management firm, booking agency, music publisher (Orchid Publishing/BMI) and record company (Bouquet Records). Represents individuals and groups; currently handles 4 acts. Receives 10-15% commission. Reviews material for acts.
How to Contact: Submit demo tape by mail—unsolicited submissions are OK. Prefers cassette (or videocassette if available) with 3-5 songs, song list and lyric sheet. Include brief resume. Press kits should include current photograph, 2-3 media clippings, description of act, and background information on act. SASE. Reports in 1 month.
Music: Mostly country, rock and top 40/pop; also gospel and R&B. Works primarily with vocalists and groups. Current acts include Susan Spencer, Jamey Wells, Adam Day and the Bandoleers (top 40/pop group).

DAVID BRODY PRODUCTIONS, 4086 Royal Crest, Memphis TN 38115. (901)362-1719. President: David or Gina Brody. Management firm and music publisher (Brody-Segerson Publishing/BMI). Estab. 1986. Represents international individual artists, groups and songwriters; currently handles 5 acts. Reviews material for acts.
How to Contact: Call first and obtain permission to submit. Prefers cassette (or VHS videocassette if available) with 3 songs and lyric sheet. If seeking management, include audio tape, bio and photos in press kit. SASE.
Music: Interested in all music. Works primarily with comedians, announcers, singers and actors. Current acts include Corinda Carford (country singer), Rick Landers (singer/songwriter) and Jimmy Segerson (R&B singer).

BROTHERS MANAGEMENT ASSOCIATES, 141 Dunbar Ave., Fords NJ 08863. (201)738-0880 or 738-0883. President: Allen A. Faucera. Management firm and booking agency. Estab. 1972. Represents artists, groups and songwriters; currently handles over 100 acts. Receives 15-20% commission. Reviews material for acts.
How to Contact: Query by mail. Prefers cassette (or VHS videocassette if available) with 3-6 songs and lyric sheets. Include photographs and resume. If seeking management, include photo, bio, tape and return envelope in press kit. SASE. Reports in 2 months.
Music: Mostly pop, rock, MOR and R&B. Works primarily with vocalists and established groups. Current acts include Ben E. King, Makana (rock), Waterfront (top 40/show), Chelsea (top 40/rock), Benny Troy and Company (top 40/show), Kitten (dance), James Brown and other track artists.
Tips: "We need very commercial, chart-oriented material."

BSC PRODUCTIONS, INC., Box 368, Tujunga CA 91043. (818)352-8142. President/General Manager: Kenn E. Kingsbury, Jr. Management firm and music publisher (Black Stallion Country Publishing, BMI). Estab. 1979. Represents individual artists and songwriters. Deals with local, national and international artists. Currently handles 2 acts. Reviews material for acts. Producer of "Bear Country" TV show.
How to Contact: Submit demo tape by mail. Unsolicited submissions are OK. Prefers cassette (or 7½ ips reel-to-reel if available) with 3 songs and lyric sheets. SASE. Reports back in 2 months.
Music: Country, blues and A/C. Works primarily with vocalists, comedians, magicians and film/TV actors and actresses. Current acts include Lane Brody (performer/actress), Gene Bear (performer/actor) and Thom Bresh (entertainer, musician and actor).

Tips: "If you are pitching as a songwriter don't sent press kits! If you are pitching as an artist send picture, bio and best possible tape."

*DOTT BURNS TALENT AGENCY, 478 Severn, Tampa FL 33606. (813)251-5882. Owner: Dott Burns. Estab. 1970. Represents individual artists, groups, actors, celebrities from coast to coast; currently handles 10 acts. Reviews material for acts.
How to Contact: Submit demo tape by mail—unsolicited submissions are OK. Prefers cassette with 1-3 songs. SASE. Reports in 2-3 weeks.
Music: Mostly country, jazz and pop. Current acts include Platters, Judy Clayton (blues singer), Peter Palmer and Aniko Ferrell and The Shirelles.

C & M PRODUCTIONS INC., 5114 Albert Dr., Brentwood TN 37027. (615)371-5098. FAX: (615)371-5317. Manager: Ronald W. Cotton. Management firm, booking agency and music publisher. Represents international individual artists; currently handles 2 acts on Polygram Records. Receives 15% commission.
How to Contact: Submit demo tape by mail—unsolicited submissions are OK. Prefers cassette (or VHS videocassette if available) with 3 songs and lead sheets. If seeking management include picture, tape and bio in press kit. Does not return material. Reports in 1 week.
Music: Mostly country, gospel and pop. Current acts include Rowna Reeves (country).

*CAHN-MAN, 5332 College Ave., Oakland CA 94618. (510)652-1615. Contact: Elliot Cahn/Jeff Saltzman/David Hawkins. Management and law firm. Estab. 1986. Represents local, regional and international individual artists, groups and songwriters. Receives 20% commission; $175/hour as attorneys. Reviews material for acts.
How to Contact: Submit demo tape by mail—unsolicited submissions are OK. Prefers cassette (or videocassette). If seeking management, include tape, photo, relevant press and bio in press kit. We do not return unsolicited material. Reports in 4-6 weeks.
Music: Mostly rock, metal and pop; also R&B. Current acts include Testament (metal), Exodus (metal), Primus (alternative), Mulhoney (alternative) and Jesse Colin Young (singer/songwriter).
Tips: "Send simple, straightforward packet including tape, photo, bio and relevant press clippings."

CAM MUSIC, LTD., 6620 Swansdown Dr., Loves Pk IL 61111. (815)877-9678. CEO: Chip Messiner. Management firm, booking agent, producer and publisher. Estab. 1983. Represents local and regional individual artists, groups and songwriters; currently handles 6 acts. Receives 15-25% commission. Reviews material for acts.
How to Contact: Write first and obtain permission to submit. Prefers cassette (or videocassette of performance, if available) with 3 songs, lyric sheets and SASE. If seeking management, include a cover letter, up to date info on writer or artist, photo (if looking to perform), bio, tape or CD. "Do not send full songs. 60-90 seconds is enough." Does not return unsolicited material. Reports in 2 months.
Music: Mostly country, bluegrass and folk; also MOR, jazz and children's. Works primarily with concert tour bands, show bands and festival bands. Current acts include Special Consensus (bluegrass), Cumberland Mountain Band (country) and Sundowners (country).
Tips: "A career in music does not happen overnight. If it did you wouldn't know what to do with your overnight success. You have to work for it. Be professional. Don't send out sloppy promotional kits. Your demo is the first impression that we hear and see. Impress me. One of the things that will make me turn off the tape machine is a demo that does not have the vocal UP front and solos. I want to hear the song."

CAPITOL MANAGEMENT, 1300 Division St., Nashville TN 37203. (615)242-4722. Producer: Robert Metzgar. Management firm, booking agency, music publisher (Aim High Music Co.) and record company (Stop Hunger Records International, Bobby & Billy Music). Estab. 1971. Represents local, regional or international individual artists, groups and songwriters; currently handles 24 acts. Receives 15% commission. Reviews material for acts.
How to Contact: Submit demo tape by mail. Unsolicited submissions are OK. Prefers cassette (or videocassette of live performance, if available). SASE. Reports in 1 week.
Music: Mostly traditional country, contemporary country and southern gospel; also pop rock, rock-a-billy and R&B. Works primarily with major label acts and new acts shopping for major labels. Current acts include Carl Butler (CBS records), Tommy Cash (CBS Records), Tommy Overstreet (CBS Re-

> *"How to Use Your Songwriter's Market"* (at the front of this book) contains comments and suggestions to help you understand and use the Information in these listings.

cords), Mark Allen Cash, Mickey Jones and The Glen Campbell Band.
Tips: "Getting us on your team is the single best thing you could ever do for your career in the city of Nashville."

*ERNIE CASH ENTERPRISES, (formerly Vision Music Group Inc.), 744 Joppa Farm Rd., Joppa Towne MD 21085. (301)679-2262. FAX: (301)687-4102. President: Ernest W. Cash. Management firm, music publisher (Ernie Cash Music/BMI), record company (Confidential Records Inc.). Estab. 1988. Represents local, regional or international individual artists, groups, songwriters. Reviews material for acts.
How to Contact: Write or call first to arrange personal interview. Prefers cassette (or VHS videocassette if available) with 3 songs and lyric and lead sheet. If seeking management, include 3 songs on cassette format with lead sheets or lyric sheets and self addressed envelope in press kit. SASE. Reports in 1 week.
Music: Mostly country, pop and gospel; also contemporary, light rock and blues. Works primarily with individual country artists and groups. Current acts include Ernie Cash, Ernie C. Penn, Johnny Anthony and Jimmy Peppers (country singer).
Tips: "Above all be honest with me and I will work with you. Please give me time to review your material and give it a justifiable chance with our music group."

CAT PRODUCTION AB, Rörstrandsgatan 21, Stockholm 11340 **Sweden.** Phone: (08)317-277. Managing Director: Christina Nilsson. Management firm and booking agency. Estab. 1972. Represents individual artists, groups and songwriters; currently handles 3 acts. Receives 15% commission. Reviews material for acts.
How to Contact: Prefers cassette (or VHS videocassette if available) with 4-6 songs and lyric or lead sheet. SAE and IRC. Reports in 1 month.
Music: Mostly R&B, rock and gospel; also "texts for stand-up comedians." Works primarily with "concert bands like Janne Schaffers' Earmeal. Rock-blues-imitation shows." Current acts include Jan Schaffer (lead guitar, songwriter), Tod Ashton (singer, blues/rock guitar and harmonica player, stand up comedian) and Malou Berg (gospel singer).

*CAVALRY PRODUCTIONS, (formerly Rocken Davie Productions), Box 70, Brackettville TX 78832. (512)563-2759 and (512)563-2236 (studio). Contact: Rocco Fortunato. Management firm and record company. Estab. 1979. Represents regional (Southwest) individual artists and groups; currently handles 4 acts. Reviews material for acts.
How to Contact: Submit demo tape—unsolicited submissions are OK. Prefers cassette with 3 songs and lyric sheet. SASE. Reports in 1 month.
Music: Mostly country, country-pop and country-cross over; also Spanish, gospel and novelty. Works primarily with single vocalists and various vocal groups "2 to 4 voices." Current acts include Bob Macon (country), Penny Ingram (gospel) and Trio Cancioneros del Recuerdo (Spanish trio).
Tips: "Material 'in the raw' is OK if you are willing to work with us to develop it."

*CENTERFIELD PRODUCTIONS, 251 W. 30th St., New York NY 10001. (212)714-1820. General Manager: Daniel Karns. Management firm, music publisher (Golden Mike/BMI, Hot Corner/ASCAP), record production company. Estab. 1986. Represents local, regional or international individual artists, groups, songwriters and producers; currently handles 15 acts. Receives 20% commission. Reviews material for acts.
How to Contact: Write first and obtain permission to submit. Prefers cassette with 3-4 songs and lyric sheet. "Include anything that lends credibility to the act or its potential, but avoid exaggerated, biased biography material in press kit." SASE. Reports in 1 month.
Music: Mostly R&B/dance, pop and rock; also country, contemporary jazz and house. Current acts include Bendik (contemporary pop/rock singer/songwriter), Twin Hype (rap duo), Steps Ahead (contemporary jazz/fusion group).

PAUL CHRISTIE MANAGEMENT, Box 96, Avalon NSW 2107 **Australia.** Phone: (02)415-2722. Managing Director: Paul Christie. Management firm (Paul Christie Management/APRA). Estab. 1982. Represents local, regional and international individual artists, groups and songwriters; currently handles 5 acts. Receives 20% commission. Reviews material for acts.

Market conditions are constantly changing! If you're still using this book and it is 1994 or later, buy the newest edition of Songwriter's Market at your favorite bookstore or order directly from Writer's Digest Books.

How to Contact: Submit demo tape by mail—unsolicited submissions are OK. Prefers cassette or VHS videocassette with 4 songs and lyric or lead sheet. Does not return submitted material. Reports in 1 week.
Music: Mostly rock, pop/rock and pop/R&B. Works primarily with rock acts, singer/writers, all composers. Current acts include Party Boys (2-guitar power rock), Tim Gaze (singer/writer), The Breed (AOR), Zillian and the Zig Zag Men (surf punk/thrash) and Miss Julieanne Henry (jazz/blues).
Tips: "Divorce yourself from all the rock music industry mythology and all the emotional issues, and assess yourself in terms of 'what really is'."

*CIRCUIT RIDER TALENT & MANAGEMENT CO., 123 Walton Ferry Rd., 2nd Floor, Hendersonville TN 37075. (615)824-1947. FAX: (615)264-0462. President: Linda S. Dotson. Management firm, booking agency and music publisher (Channel Music, Cordial Music). Represents individual artists, songwriters and actors; currently handles 5 acts. Receives 15% commission. Reviews material for acts.
How to Contact: Write or call first and obtain permission to submit. Prefers cassette (or videocassette) with 3 songs and lyric sheet. Videocassettes required of artist's submissions. SASE. Reports in 6 weeks. If seeking management, press kit should include bio, photo, and tape with 3 songs.
Music: Mostly pop, country and gospel; also R&B and comedy. Works primarily with vocalists, special concerts, movies and TV. Current acts include Sheb Wooley (country & comedy), Buck Trent (country & comedy) and Alton McClair (gospel).
Tips: "Artists have your act together. Have a full press kit, videos and be professional. Attitudes are a big factor in my agreeing to work with you (no egotists). This is a business and your career we will be building."

*CLASS ACT PRODUCTIONS/MANAGEMENT, Box 55252, Sherman Oaks CA 91413. (818)980-1039. President: Peter Kimmel. Management firm, music publisher, production company. Estab. 1985. Represents local, regional or international individual artists, groups, songwriters, actors and screenwriters. Receives 20% commission. Reviews material for acts.
How to Contact: Submit demo tape by mail—unsolicited submissions are OK. Prefers cassette (VHS videocassette if available) with 3-5 songs and lyric sheet. If seeking management, include pictures (if artist); bio (if relevant); lyric sheets (essential); and cassette tape or CD in press kit. SASE. Reports in 1 month.
Music: Mostly rock, pop and country rock; also dance, R&B and country.

*CLASS ACTS, Box 641, Freeport ME 04032. (207)865-6600. Northeast Marketing Coordinator: C.H. Burr. Management firm and booking agency. Estab. 1979. Represents East Coast/South West individual artists and groups; currently handles 15 acts. Receives 15-20% commission. Reviews material for acts.
How to Contact: Call first and obtain permission to submit. Prefers cassette (or VHS videocassette if available) with 3-4 songs and lyric sheet. Does not return unsolicited material. Reports in 2-6 weeks.
Music: Mostly modern contemporary, rock contemporary and R&B; also comedy. Works primarily with bands. Current acts include The Boyz (rock contemporary), The Sense (modern contemporary) and Bicycle Thieves (modern contemporary).

CLIFFSIDE MUSIC INC., Box 374, Fairview NJ 07022. (201)941-3987. Song Review: Denise Allen. Management firm and music publisher (Wazuri/BMI, G.G./ASCAP). Represents local, regional and international individual artists and songwriters; currently handles 3 acts. Receives 20-25% commission. Reviews material for acts.
How to Contact: Submit demo tape by mail—unsolicited submissions are OK. Prefers cassette with 2 songs. SASE. Reports in 1 week.
Music: Mostly R&B crossover, pop/MOR and gospel; also jazz. Represents recording and touring singers, backup bands and songwriters (known and unknown). Current acts include Gloria Gaynor (R&B/pop/gospel), Moett (rap) and Five O (R&B).
Tips: "Get real! Do not try to write every song overnight."

CLOCKWORK ENTERTAINMENT MANAGEMENT AGENCY, Box 1600, Haverhill MA 01831. (508)373-6010. President: Bill Macek. Management firm and booking agency. Represents groups and songwriters throughout New England; currently handles 2 acts. Receives 15% commission. Reviews material for acts.
How to Contact: Query or submit demo tape. Prefers cassette with 3-12 songs. "Also submit promotion and cover letter with interesting facts about yourself." Does not return unsolicited material unless accompanied by SASE. Reports in 1 month.
Music: Rock (all types) and top 40/pop. Works primarily with bar bands and original acts. Current acts include Head First (4 piece cover/original rock) and Take One (5 piece cover/original rock).

*COCOS ISLAND RECORDS, INC., Box 773 Bondi Junction, NSW **Australia** 2022. (02)3607639. A&R Manager: Sam Nun. Management firm and record company (Cocos Island Records). Estab. 1980. Represents international individual artists, groups and songwriters; currently handles 10 acts. Receives 20% commission. Reviews material for acts.
How to Contact: Submit demo tape—unsolicited submissions are OK. "Suggest one video featuring marketable song on first album. Aim: Worldwide release through major label." Does not return unsolicited material. Reports in 2 months.
Music: Interested in any music. Current acts include No Screaming Kids (pop), Noel Wilson (folk), Peter Liberty (Christian) and Urbane Guerillas (soft/heavy metal).
Tips: "Aim for the top. We'll take you over the top."

RAYMOND COFFER MANAGEMENT, S. The Lake, Bushey Herts WD2 1HS UK. Phone: (44)8195-05489. FAX: (44)8195-07617. Contact: Raymond Coffer. Management firm. Estab. 1984. Represents local, regional and international individual artists and groups; currently handles 5 acts. Receives 20% commission. Reviews material for acts.
How to Contact: Submit demo tape by mail—unsolicited submissions are OK. Prefers cassette (or PAL or VHS videocassette if available) with 4 songs and lyric sheet. Does not return unsolicited material. Reports in 4 weeks.
Music: Mostly rock and pop. Works primarily with bands. Current acts include Love & Rockets, Cocteau Twins, Ian McCulloch, Smashing Punpkins, Curve and Xymox.

COLE CLASSIC MANAGEMENT, Suite 207, 4150 Riverside Dr., Burbank CA 91505. (818)841-6365. A&R Manager: Earl Cole. Management firm. Represents local, regional, international individual artists, groups and producers. Currently handles 8 acts. Receives 10-15% commission. Reviews material for acts.
How to Contact: Submit demo tape by mail—unsolicited submissions are OK. Prefers cassette with 2-3 songs and lyric sheets. If seeking management, include bio, photos, cassette tape with 3 songs and lyric sheets in press kit. SASE. Reports in 3-4 weeks.
Music: Mostly R&B, pop and jazz; also gospel. Works primarily with vocalists and dance bands. Current acts include Surface (R&B group), Paul Jackson Jr. (R&B/jazz guitarist) and Barbara Weathers (R&B vocalist).

*COMMON SENSE MANAGEMENT, LTD., 71-07 67th St., Glendale NY 11385-7069. President: Thomas W. Heid. Management firm. Estab. 1988. Represents local, regional or international individual artists, groups and songwriters. Receives 20% commission. Reviews material for acts.
How to Contact: Submit demo tape by mail—unsolicited submissions are OK. Prefers cassette (VHS videocassette if available) with 3 songs and lyric sheet. If seeking management, include photo, lyrics, short biography and cassette in press kit. SASE. Reports in 1 month.
Music: Mostly rock and pop; also country and R&B. Works with all types of artists/groups/songwriters except gospel and rap. Current acts include Jay T. Baron (singer/songwriter).

*CONCEPT 2000 INC., 2447 W. Mound St., Columbus OH 43204. President: Brian Wallace. Management firm and booking agency (Concept 2000 Music/ASCAP). Estab. 1981. Represents international individual artists, groups and songwriters; currently handles 5 acts. Receives 10-20% commission. Reviews material for acts.
How to Contact: Submit demo tape by mail—unsolicited submissions are OK. Prefers cassette with 4 songs. Does not return unsolicited material. Reports in 2 weeks.
Music: Mostly country, gospel and pop; also jazz, R&B and soul. Current acts include Oasis (gospel group), The Stand (rock), Gene Walker (jazz), Victor Alexeeff (classical pianist), and Jennifer Nicole (pop).

MIKE CONSTANTIA ENTERTAINMENT, 41 Manchester Rd., Warrington, Cheshire WA1 4AE **England.** Phone: (0925)810979. Managing Director: M. Constantinou. Booking agency. Represents local individual artists and groups; currently handles 400 acts. Receives 15% commission. Reviews material for acts.
How to Contact: Submit demo tape—unsolicited submissions are OK. Prefers cassette (or VHS videocassette). SAE and IRC. Reports in 3 months.
Music: Mostly pop, country and R&B. Works primarily with vocalists and bands. Current acts include Billy Brown and Mark Williamson.

*COUNTDOWN ENTERTAINMENT, 109 Earle Ave., Lynbrook NY 11563. (516)599-4157. President: James Citkovic. Management firm, consultants. Estab. 1983. Represents local, regional and international individual artists, groups, songwriters and producers; currently handles 12 acts. Receives 20% commission. Reviews material for acts, and for music publishing.

How to Contact: Submit demo tape by mail—unsolicited submissions are OK. Prefers cassette (or VHS, SP speed videocassette if available) with songs and lyric sheet. If seeking management, include cassette tape of best songs, 8×10 pictures, VHS video, lyrics, press and radio playlists in press kit. SASE. Reports in 6 weeks.

Music: Mostly pop/rock, nu-music and alternative/dance; also R&B, pop/dance and hard rock. Deals with all styles of artists/songwriters/producers. Current acts include: World Bang (euro-dance), The Art-Officials (pop/alternative), Ken Kushner, Drew Miles and Nick Phillips (pop/rock/dance).

Tips: "Send hit songs, only hit songs, nothing but hit songs."

COUNTRY MUSIC SHOWCASE INTERNATIONAL, INC., Box 368, Carlisle IA 50047. (515)989-3676 or (515)989-3748. President: Harold L. Luick. Vice President: Barbara A. Lancaster. Management firm and booking agency "for acts and entertainers that are members of our organization." Estab. 1984. Represents individual artists, groups and songwriters; currently handles 18-20 acts. Receives 5-20% commission.

How to Contact: Prefers cassette with 3 songs and lyric sheet (or VHS videocassette showing artist on the job, 3 different venues). If seeking management, include 8×10 pictures, resume, past performance, audio tape and video tape of act in press kit. SASE. Reports in 3 weeks. "Must be paid member of Country Music Showcase International, Inc., to receive review of work."

Music: Mostly contemporary, hard core country and traditional country; also bluegrass, western swing and comedy. Works primarily with "one person single acts, one person single tape background acts and show bands." Current acts include Mr. Elmer Bird (banjo virtuoso), Country Classics USA (12-piece stage show), The Dena Kaye Show, Britt Small and Allen Karl.

Tips: "We want artists who are willing to work hard to achieve success and songwriters who are skilled in their craft. Through educational and informative seminars and showcases we have helped many artist and songwriter members achieve a degree of success in a very tough business. For information on how to become a member of our organization, send SASE to the above address. Memberships cost $40.00 per year for artist or songwriter memberships."

COUNTRY STAR ATTRACTIONS, 439 Wiley Ave., Franklin PA 16323. (814)432-4633. Contact: Norman Kelly. Management firm, booking agency, music publisher (Country Star Music/ASCAP) and record company (Country Star, Process, Mersey and CSI Records). Estab. 1970. Represents artists and musical groups; currently handles 4-6 acts. Receives 10-15% commission. Reviews material for acts.

How to Contact: Submit demo tape—unsolicited submissions are OK. Prefers cassette with 2-4 songs and lyric or lead sheet; include photo. SASE. Reports in 2 weeks.

Music: Mostly country (80%); rock (5%) and gospel (5%). Works primarily with vocalists. Current acts include Junie Lou, Ron Lauer and Debbie Sue, all country singers.

Tips: "Send only your very best efforts."

COURTRIGHT MANAGEMENT INC., 201 E. 87th St., New York NY 10128. (212)410-9055. Contacts: Hernando or Doreen Courtright. Management firm. Estab. 1984. Represents local, regional and international individual artists, groups, songwriters and producers. Receives 20% commission. Reviews material for acts.

How to Contact: Submit demo tape by mail—unsolicited submissions are OK. Prefers cassette (or VHS videocassette if available) with 4 songs and lyric sheet. If seeking management, include photos in press kit. SASE. Reports in 3 weeks.

Music: Mostly rock and metal; also pop and blues. Current acts include Mass (group), Eddie Kramer (producer), Deena Miller (alternative) and Steve Johnstad (rock).

COVER AGENCY, #103, 300 North 240 West, Salt Lake City UT 84103. (801)364-9706. Booking Agent: William Larned. Management firm and booking agency. Estab. 1984. Represents local, regional and international individual artists and groups. Currently handles 180 acts. Receives 15% commission. Reviews material for acts.

How to Contact: Submit demo tape by mail—unsolicited submissions are OK. Prefers cassette (or VHS videocassette if available) with 4 songs and lead sheets. If seeking management, include photo, good quality tape, song list, bio, equipment list and list of venues played. Does not return unsolicited material. Reports in 2-3 months.

Music: Mostly modern, funk, top 40, reggae and rock. Works primarily with dance bands, show bands, touring acts and bar bands. Current acts include Irie Heights (reggae), Tempo Timers (R&B/blues) and The Gamma Rays (modern).

Tips: "We are not really interested in original material, we are looking for cover bands that can play clubs in the intermountain area."

CRASH PRODUCTIONS, Box 40, Bangor ME 04402-0040. (207)794-6686. Manager: Jim Moreau. Booking agency. Estab. 1967. Represents individuals and groups; currently handles 9 acts. Receives 10-25% commission.
How to Contact: Submit demo tape by mail—unsolicited submissions are OK. Prefers cassette (or VHS videocassette if available) with 4-8 songs. "To all artists who submit a video: We will keep it on file for presentation to prospective buyers of talent in our area—no longer than 15 minutes please. The quality should be the kind you would want to show a prospective buyer of your act." Include resume and photos. "We prefer to hear groups at an actual performance." If seeking management, include 8 × 10 black & white photos, cassette, press clips and a video cassette in press kit. SASE. Reports in 3 weeks.
Music: Mostly 50s-60s and country rock, top 40; also rock and polish. Works primarily with groups who perform at night clubs (with an average of 150-200 patrons) and outdoor events (festivals and fairs). Current acts include Coyote (country rock), Bushwhack (50s and 60s), Air Fare (top 40) and Kaktus (country).
Tips: "We are a small company with no big promises that we cannot fulfill. Our main business is as a booking agency for acts. We do not reject material from songwriters, but very seldom do we get to use their services; we do keep them on file."

CRAWFISH PRODUCTIONS, Box 5412, Buena Park CA 90620. (213)721-7260. Producer: Leo J. Eiffert, Jr. Music publisher (Young Country/BMI) and record company (Plain Country Records). Estab. 1968. Represents local and international individual artists and songwriters; currently handles 4 acts. Commission received is open. Reviews material for acts.
How to Contact: Submit a demo tape by mail—unsolicited submissions are OK. Prefers cassette with 2-3 songs and lyric sheet. SASE. Reports in 3 weeks.
Music: Mostly country and gospel. Works primarily with vocalists. Current acts include Brandi Holland, Teeci Clarke, Joe Eiffert (country/gospel) and Crawfish Band (country).

*CREATIONS, LTD., 308 Hampstead N., Antioch TN 37013. (615)360-2272. Owners: Carmen Robinson and Jewell Frazier. Management firm. Estab. 1991. Represents individual artists, groups, songwriters and dancers from the South; currently handles 2 acts. Receives 25% commission. Reviews material for acts.
How to Contact: Submit demo tape by mail—unsolicited submissions are OK. Prefers cassette with 2 songs and lyric sheet. Does not return unsolicited material. Reports in 4-6 weeks.
Music: Mostly R&B, pop and gospel; also dancers and producers. Works primarily with vocalists and dance bands. Current acts include B.O.M.B. (group).
Tips: "Be precise, professional, disciplined."

*CRISS-CROSS INDUSTRIES, #191, 4708 Park Granada Blvd., Calabasas CA 91302. (818)222-4362. FAX: (818)222-7649. President: Doc Remer. Management firm and music publisher (Menachan's Music/ASCAP, Eyenoma Music/BMI). Estab. 1984. Represents individual artists, groups and songwriters from anywhere; currently handles 1 act. Receives 15-20% commission. Reviews material for acts.
How to Contact: Write or call first and obtain permission to submit. Prefers cassette (or VHS videocassette if available) with 3 songs and lyric sheet. SASE. Reports in 3-6 weeks.
Music: Mostly R&B and pop. Works primarily with vocalists and self contained bands. Current acts include Chill Factor (band).
Tips: "You must currently be a working act. Make the words to the songs so they can be understood. The music should not be as loud as the vocals."

BOBBY LEE CUDE'S GOOD AMERICAN MUSIC/TALENT/CASTING AGENCY, 519 N. Halifax Ave., Daytona Beach FL 32118-4017. FAX: (904)252-0381. CEO: Bobby Lee Cude. Music publisher (BMI) and record company (Hard Hat). Estab. 1978. Represents international individual artists. Receives 15% commission. Reviews material for acts.
How to Contact: Write first and obtain permission to submit. Prefers cassette (or videocassette) with 2 songs, lyrics and lead sheets. "No unsolicited material reviewed."
Music: Mostly pop and country. Current acts include Caz Allen and "Pic" Pickens.
Tips: "Read music books for the trade."

*THE CURRENT ENTERTAINMENT CORPORATION, 418 Ontario St., Toronto, Ontario, M5A 2W1 Canada. (416)921-6535. President: Gerry Young. A&R Special Projects: Trevor G. Shelton. Project Manager: Shelly Pybus. Management firm (Current Management), music publisher (Current Sounds/SOCAN and Brand New Sounds Music/SOCAN) and record company (Rammit Records). Represents individual artists, groups and songwriters; currently handles 6 acts. Reviews material for acts.

How to Contact: Submit demo tape—unsolicited submissions are OK. Prefers cassette (or ½" VHS videocassette) with 3-4 songs and lyric sheet. SAE and IRC. Reports in 1 month.
Music: Mostly intelligent dance/pop; also rock and new music. Works primarily with groups, vocalists. Current acts include S.E. Jam, Born Yesterday and Delee.

*CURRENT RECORDS/MANAGEMENT, 418 Ontario St., Toronto, Ontario, M5A 2W1 **Canada**. (416)921-6535. A&R-New Projects: Trevor G. Shelton. Management firm, music publisher (Current Sounds/CAPAC, PROCAN) and record company (Current Records, Rammit Records). Estab. 1983. Represents local, regional or international individual artists, groups and songwriters; currently handles 10 acts. Reviews material for acts.
How to Contact: Submit demo tape by mail—unsolicited submissions are OK. Prefers cassette (or VHS videocassette if available) with 4-5 songs and lyric sheets. If seeking management, include demo tape with 3-4 songs and "letter explaining what it is you're looking for" in press kit. SASE. Reports in 1-6 weeks.
Music: Mostly dance, pop and rock; also R&B, alternative, rap/hip, house etc. Works primarily with dance, pop and rock bands. Current acts include S.E. Jam., Oscar Chares and Red Eye Express (all dance, R&B).
Tips: "If you have a videocassette of your performance, please send it, but it's not a necessity. Performances can be simple. No need for big-budget videos."

D.A.G. PROMOTIONS LTD., 28 Bolton St., London WI **England**. Phone: (01)876-4433. Director: D. Gordon. Management firm. Estab. 1983. Represents individual artists and groups; currently handles 5 act. Receives 20% commission. Reviews material for acts.
How to Contact: Write or call first and obtain permission to submit. Prefers cassette with 4 songs and lyric sheet. Does not return unsolicited material.
Music: Mostly pop and rock. Works primarily with singer/songwriters, solo artists and rock bands. Current acts include Paul Jackson (singer/songwriter), Shannon Sweeney (singer/songwriter), Hold The Frame (rock) and Eddie Kidd (rock).

D MANAGEMENT COMPANY, Box 121682, Nashville TN 37212. President: Douglas Casmus. Management firm and music publisher (N2D/ASCAP and Breezeway/BMI). Estab. 1987. Represents individual artists and songwriters; currently handles 2 acts. Receives 15-25% commission. Reviews material for acts.
How to Contact: Write first and obtain permission to submit (include SASE for response). Prefers cassette with 2 songs and lyric sheets. Does not return unsolicited material. Reports in 1 month.
Music: Mostly rock, pop and country. Current acts include Dobie Gray and David Murphy.

*D.S.M. PRODUCERS INC., Suite 803, 161 West 54th St., New York NY 10019. (212)245-0006. Director of Publishing: E. T. Toast. Production firm and music publisher (ASCAP) and producers. Estab. 1979. Represents local, regional and international individual artists, groups and songwriters. Currently handles 6 acts. Commission is negotiated. Reviews material for acts.
How to Contact: Submit demo tape by mail—unsolicited submissions are OK. Prefers cassette (or VHS videocassette). "Be sure you and your vocals are up front in sound. Be sure to eye the camera so we can get to know you.") Include 2 songs and lyric or lead sheets. SASE. Reports in 3 months.
Music: Mostly pop, dance, top 40, Latin and rock; also country, R&B and New Age jazz/instrumental. Works primarily with vocalists, instrumentalists—we produce 10 albums a year of instrumental music and vocal groups. Current acts include Hubert Lacy (R&B), Peter Halprin (rock) and Clive Smith (AOR).
Tips: "Be sure the vocal is up in the mix so we can hear the words as well as the music."

D&D TALENT ASSOCIATES, Box 308, Burkeville VA 23922. (804)767-4150. Owner: J.W. Dooley, Jr. Booking agency. Estab. 1976. Currently handles 2 acts. Receives 10% commission. "Reviews songs for individuals in the jazz and 40s-50s field only."
How to Contact: Submit demo tape by mail—unsolicited submissions are OK. Prefers cassette (or videocassette) with 1-6 songs and lead sheet. If seeking management, include tape, lead sheets and any written information pertaining to the request in press kit. SASE. Reports in 2 weeks.

Remember: Don't "shotgun" your demo tapes. Submit only to companies interested in the type of music you write. For more submission hints, refer to The Business of Songwriting on page 19.

Music: Mostly jazz and 40s-50s music. Works primarily with vocalists, comics. Current acts include Johnny Pursley (humorist) and David Allyn (vocalist).
Tips: "Just send the best songs possible—although I am doing no booking now, for practical reasons, I will try to give free advice if possible. Since I am not in a metro area, possible contacts are probably out at this time. Don't contact me to produce miracles. I can be a sounding board for the music only—someone to at least listen and hopefully, make suggestions."

D & R ENTERTAINMENT, 308 N. Park, Broken Bow OK 74728. (405)584-9429. President: Don Walton. Management firm. Estab. 1987. Represents international individual artists and groups; currently handles 3 acts. Receives 15-20% commission. Reviews material for acts.
How to Contact: Submit demo tape by mail—unsolicited submissions are OK. Prefers cassette with any number of songs and lyric or lead sheet. Does not return unsolicited material. "I would like to know publishing company of any material sent." SASE. Reports in 3 months "if interested."
Music: Country and pop country. Current acts include Nanette Garner (country), Rick Thompson (country) and Rachel Garrett (country).
Tips: "Make sure everything submitted is copyrighted! If it isn't I won't consider it."

*DARKHORSE ENTERTAINMENT, 3453 Oak Glen Dr., Los Angeles, CA 90068. (213)969-0117. Contact: Michael Mavrolas or Marlow McClain. Management firm and music production. Estab. 1986. Represents international individual artists, groups and songwriters; currently handles 5 acts. Receives 15% commission.
How to Contact: Submit demo tape by mail—unsolicited submissions are OK. Prefers cassette and lyric sheet. SASE. Reports in 3-4 weeks.
Music: Mostly urban, dance and rap. Current acts include The U-Krew (R&B rap Enigma Records), Nyssa Dickson (R&B dance female vocals black), Rodney-O/Joe Cooley (Nastymix Record rap).
Tips: "Looking to represent great urban-dance-rap songwriters."

*DAS COMMUNICATIONS, LTD., 83 Riverside Dr., New York NY 10024. Management firm. Estab. 1975. Represents individual artists, groups and producers from anywhere. Receives 20% commission. Reviews material for acts.
How to Contact: Call first. Prefers cassette with 3 songs and lyric sheet. SASE.
Music: Mostly rock, pop and dance; also alternative. Current acts include Natural Selection (top 40/pop), BeBe & CeCe Winans (contemporary Christian/gospel/R&B), Spin Doctors (college/alternative rock), Keith Thomas (producer/songwriter/arranger) and Jim Steinmen (producer/songwriter).

*BRIAN DE COURCY MANAGEMENT, Box 96, South Yarro, 242 Toorak Rd., Melbourne, Victoria 3141 **Australia.** Phone: (03)836-9621. C.E.O.: Brian de Courcy. Management firm. Estab. 1974. Represents local, regional or international individual artists, groups, songwriters, DJ's, music journalists and TV performers; currently handles 10 acts. Receives 15-25% commission. Reviews material for acts.
How to Contact: Write or call first and obtain permission to submit. Prefers cassette (any videocassette if available) with lyric and lead sheet. SASE. Reports in 2 weeks.
Music: Mostly rock and pop. Works primarily with rock/pop acts. Current acts include John Justin (rock), Ronnie Charles (rock) and Benjamin Hugg (rock/folk).

THE EDWARD DE MILES COMPANY, Vantage Point Towers, 4475 N. Allisonville Rd., 8th Floor, Indianapolis, IN 46205. (317)549-9006. FAX: (317)549-9007. President & CEO: Edward De Miles. Management firm, booking agency, entertainment/sports promoter and TV/radio broadcast producer. Estab. 1984. Represents film, television, radio and musical artists; currently handles 15 acts. Receives 10-20% commission. Reviews material for acts. Regional operations in Chicago, Dallas, Houston and Nashville through marketing representatives. Licensed A.F. of M. booking agent.
How to Contact: Submit demo tape by mail—unsolicited submissions are OK. Prefers cassette with 3-5 songs, 8x10 black and white photo and lyric sheet. "Copyright all material before submitting." If seeking management, include demo cassette with 3-5 songs, 8×10 black & white photo and lyric sheet in press kit. SASE. Reports in 1 month.
Music: Mostly country, dance, R&B/soul, rock, top 40/pop and urban contemporary; also looking for material for television, radio and film productions. Works primarily with dance bands and vocalists. Current acts include Lost in Wonder (progressive rock/dance band), Steve Lynn (R&B/dance) and De Vell (R&B/dance).
Tips: "Performers need to be well prepared with their presentations (equipment, showmanship a must)."

DEBBIE DEAN AND ASSOC., Box 687, Ashland City TN 37015. (615)746-2758. FAX: (615)746-2758. Contact: Debbie Dean. Overseas booking agency, record promotion and public relations firm. Estab. 1988. Represents local, regional and international individual artists; currently handles 6 acts. Receives 15% commission. Reviews material for acts.

How to Contact: Submit demo tape by mail—unsolicited submissions are OK. Prefers cassette with 3 songs and lyric sheet. If seeking management, include good quality black & white photo, good one page bio and released or soon to be released 45, CD, album or cassette in press kit. SASE. Reports in 2 weeks.
Music: Mostly country traditional and MOR country. Works primarily with artists who can also play a guitar or some instrument. Current acts include David Walsh, Ann Holland, Bobby G. Rice, Lori Johnson, T.C. Bullock and Charlie Fields (songwriter).

BILL DETKO MANAGEMENT, 127 Shamrock Dr., Ventura CA 93003. (805)644-0447. Owner: Bill Detko. Management firm. Estab. 1987. Represents local, regional and international individual artists, groups and songwriters; currently handles 4 acts. Receives 20% commission. Reviews material for acts.
How to Contact: Submit demo tape by mail—unsolicited submissions are OK. Prefers cassette or CD with 3 songs and lyric sheet. If seeking management, include bio, photo and lyrics in press kit. Does not return material.
Music: Mostly rock, metal, alternative; "songwriters with great songs." Current acts include Stuart Hamm (bass player/writer/solo artist), Ian Gillan (in North America only) and Watchtower (metal).
Tips: "Great songs are most important."

*ANDREW DINWOODIE MANAGEMENT, Box 1936, Southport, QLD **Australia** 4215. Phone: (075)376222. Manager: Andrew Dinwoodie. Management firm, booking agency. Estab. 1983. Represents regional (Australian) individual artists, groups and songwriters; currently handles 2 acts. Receives 10-20% commission. Reviews material for acts.
How to Contact: Submit demo tape by mail—unsolicited submission are OK. Prefers cassette (VHS PAL if available) with lyric sheet. SASE. Reports in 6 weeks.
Music: Mostly country, R&B and rock/pop; also bluegrass, swing and folk. Current acts include Bullamakanka, Donna Heke and the Moderation Band.

*MICHAEL DIXON MANAGEMENT, 119 Pebblecreek R., Franklin TN 37064. (615)791-7731. Management firm. Estab. 1982. Represents major label rock artists, individual artists, groups and songwriters; currently handles 4 acts. Receives 20% commission. Reviews material for acts.
How to Contact: Submit demo tape by mail—unsolicited submissions are OK. Prefers cassette (or VHS videocassette if available) with 3-4 songs and lyric sheet. Does not return unsolicited submissions. Reports in 3-4 weeks.
Music: Mostly rock, pop and alternative; also gospel and R&B. Works primarily with rock bands with mostly self written material with an occasional outside song(s). Current acts include Fifteen Strings (rock band), Thurn & Taxis (progressive rock), Fleming & John (pop/rock), and Anthony Crawford (singer/songwriter).
Tips: "All it takes is a unique, one of a kind, said in a new and different way, song that is stunning. One great song will open the door. 2-3 good songs will get you on our list of developing songwriters with potential."

DMR AGENCY, Suite 250, Galleries of Syracuse, Syracuse NY 13202-2416. (315)475-2500. Contact: David M. Rezak. Booking agency. Represents individuals and groups; currently handles 50 acts. Receives 15% commission.
How to Contact: Submit demo tape by mail—unsolicited submissions are OK. Submit cassette (or videocassette) with 1-4 songs and press kit. Does not return material.
Music: Mostly rock (all styles), pop and blues. Works primarily with dance, bar and concert bands; all kinds of rock for schools, clubs, concerts, etc. Current acts include Tryx (rock), Windsong (dance/pop) and Jeff Gordon (rock).
Tips: "We strictly do booking and have no involvement in artist repertoire. We prefer regionally-based bands with a high percentage of cover material."

COL. BUSTER DOSS PRESENTS, Drawer 40, Estill Springs TN 37330. (615)649-2577. Producer: Col. Buster Doss. Management firm, booking agency, record company (Stardust Records) and music publisher (Buster Doss Music/BMI). Estab. 1959. Represents individual artists, groups, songwriters and shows; currently handles 15 acts. Receives 15% commission. Reviews material for acts.
How to Contact: Prefers cassette with 2-4 songs and lyric sheet. SASE. Reports in 2 weeks.
Music: Country, gospel and progressive. Works primarily with show and dance bands, single acts and package shows. Current acts include Rooster Quantrell, Sonny Carson, Hobson Smith, Tony Caldarona, Buck Cody, Cliff Archer, Linda Wunder, Benny Ray, Clayton Michaels, Honey James, Gilbert Gann, The Border Raiders, Tony Andrews and Jess Demaine.
Tips: "Tell the truth! No hype."

DSI THEATRICAL PRODUCTIONS, 660 NE 139th Street, N. Miami FL 33161. (305)891-4449 or (305)891-0158. Artistic Director: Scott Evans. Management firm and booking agency. Estab. 1979. Represents local, regional or international individual artists, groups, songwriters, comedians, novelty acts, dancers and theaters; currently handles more than 200 acts. Receives 10-25% commission. Reviews material for acts.

How to Contact: Submit demo tape by mail—unsolicited submissions are OK. Prefers cassette (or ½" videocassette if available) with 3 songs. If seeking management, include picture, resume, flyers, cassette or video tape. Does not return unsolicited material.

Music: Mostly pop, R&B and Broadway. Deals with "all types of entertainers; no limitations." Current acts include Scott Evans (variety song & dance), Doris Zinger (female vocalist) and Joy Deco (dance act).

Tips: "Submit neat, well put together, organized press kit."

EARTH TRACKS ARTISTS AGENCY, Suite 286, 4712 Avenue N, Brooklyn NY 11234. Managing Director-Artist Relations: David Krinsky. Management firm. Estab. 1990. Represents individual artists, groups and songwriters from anywhere; currently handles 3 acts. Receives 10-25% (depends) commission. Reviews material for acts.

How to Contact: Submit demo tape by mail—unsolicited submissions are OK, accompanied by release form and SASE. "Do not call to submit tapes. Mail in for review. No calls will be returned, unsolicited or accepted, under any conditions." Prefers cassette (or VHS and/or ¾" videocassette) with 3-6 songs and lyric sheet. If seeking management, include 1 group photo, all lyrics with songs, a cassette/CD of 3-6 original songs and the ages of the artists. "We do not return unsolicited material if international." Reports in 1 month.

Music: Mostly commercial rock (all kinds), pop/dance/rap, post modern rock/folk rock; also novelty/comedy songs. Works primarily with commercial, original, solo artists and groups, songwriters in the rock, pop, dance areas (no country, thrash or punk). Current acts include Heavy Connection (rock), Bella (pop/dance artist) and Bi-Coastals (comedy/satire artist). "We're looking for original acts who wish to be signed to record labels in the rock, pop and rap categories. (No 'show bands' 'cover bands', etc.)."

Tips: "Submit a package of completed songs along with lyrics, photo of artist/group, or songwriter credits if any. A video on VHS accepted if available. If no package available send a cassette of what you as an artist consider best represents your style. Strong meaningful songs are preferred, as well as light pop rock for top 40 release. Will submit quality songwriter's material to name artists. All materials must be accompanied by a release form and all songs must be copyrighted."

ECI, INC., 1646 Bonnie Dr., Memphis TN 38116. (901)346-1483. Vice President: Bernice Turner. Management firm, booking agency, music publisher and record company (Star Trek). Estab. 1989. Represents local, regional and international individual artists and groups; currently handles 3 acts. Receives 25% commission. Reviews material for acts.

How to Contact: Submit demo tape by mail—unsolicited submissions are OK. Prefers cassette with 2 songs. If seeking management, include good demo tape, background of recorded materials, and any promo materials on writer in press kit. SASE. Reports in 2 weeks.

Music: Mostly R&B and country. Works primarily with show groups. Current acts include Kool and The Gang, Robby Turner and Something Special.

*STEVE ECK ENTERTAINMENT, 721 Boundary Ave., Hanover PA 17331. (717)632-4075. Owner: Steve Eck. Management firm, booking agency and record company (Aria Records). Represents regional (Mid-Atlantic states) individual artists, groups and songwriters; currently handles 3 acts. Receives 10-15% commission. Reviews material for acts.

How to Contact: Submit demo tape by mail—unsolicited submissions are OK. Prefers cassette with minimum of 2 songs and lyric sheet. If seeking management, include bio, 8 × 10 photo and song list in press kit. SASE. Material is reviewed with artist and then sent on to Nashville to our record label. Reports in 2 months.

Music: Mostly country, pop and rock. Works primarily with country and country rock recording artists and groups. Current acts include Bruce Van Dyke, Longshot Band and Freedom Express.

Tips: "Send a top quality demo with lyric sheet keeping in mind that we will send this to our record company in Nashville for consideration."

*EL GATO AZUL AGENCY, 64 Mill St., Chico CA 95928. (916)345-6615. Owner/Agent: Karen Kindig. Management firm and booking agency. Estab. 1989. Represents local, regional and individual artists, groups and songwriters; currently handles 3 acts. Receives 10-15% commission. Reviews material for acts.

How to Contact: Submit demo tape by mail—unsolicited submissions are OK. Prefers cassette (or VHS videocassette if available) with 3 songs and lyric and lead sheet. If seeking management, include bio, discography, photo, demo tape and press clippings in press kit. SASE. Reports in 2 weeks.
Music: Mostly jazz/pop, "ethno-pop" and pop-rock. Works primarily with jazz artists, pop artists/ groups (especially "rock en español") vocalists, ethnic musicians. Current acts include Alejandro Santos (composer/flutist), Crystal Sullivan (singer/songwriter) and Dino Saluzzi (composer/bandoneonist).
Tips: "Have faith in your abilities and be patient and persistent."

ELLIPSE PERSONAL MANAGMENT, % Boxholder 665, Manhattan Beach CA 90266. (310)546-2224. Contact: Mr. L. Elsman. Management firm. Represents local individual artists, vocalists and vocalist/ songwriters. Receives 15% commission and up (P.M. contract). Reviews material for acts.
How to Contact: Prefers cassette with 3 songs. Does not return unsolicited material. Reports in 5 weeks.
Music: Mostly rock, modern rock, pop rock, AOR and R&B/soul. Works mostly with local male vocalists. Current acts include Eric Tage (teen vocalist).
Tips: "How quickly someone responds to your demo tape is a good indication of how good your material is, but only to a point. We often do reply, however do not assume your songs are hopelessly bad if you do not hear from us, because we do not return audio tapes. Teen vocalists should send a snapshot and a demo, if available. We want to know if you have any problems with tobacco, alcohol or drugs, as well as your goals and ambitions. Feel free to call when phone rates are down. Saturdays 10 a.m. to 12 noon, (Pacific Time), is good. We have to monitor all incoming calls, so let us know who you are, and if we are here, we can pick it up."

*ENCORE TALENT, INC., 2137 Zercher Rd., San Antonio TX 78209. (512)822-2655. President: Ronnie Spillman. Management firm and booking agency. Estab. 1979. Represents regional individual artists and groups from Texas. Receives 15% commission. Reviews material for acts.
How to Contact: Submit demo tape by mail—unsolicited submissions are OK. Prefers cassette with 4 songs. SASE. Reports in 2 weeks.
Music: Mostly country. Works primarily with dance bands. Current acts include Jay Eric (writer/ country singer), The Nashville Sounds (country band) and Damara Smith (country singer).

ENTERTAINMENT MANAGEMENT ENTERPRISES, 454 Alps Rd., Wayne NJ 07470. (201)694-3333. President: Richard Zielinski. Management firm. Estab. 1982. Represents artists and musical groups; currently handles 2 acts. Receives minimum of 20% commission. Reviews material for acts.
How to Contact: Prefers cassette (or VHS videocassette) with 4-6 songs and lyric sheet. Include 8 × 10 glossy and bio. "Let us know, by mail or phone, about any New York area performances so we can attend." SASE. Reports in 2 weeks.
Music: Mostly rock. Works primarily with rock groups with vocals, synthesized rock, contemporary singers and club bands. Current acts include Voyager (progressive rock) and Mirrors' Image (metal).
Tips: "A good press kit is important."

ENTERTAINMENT UNLIMITED ARTIST INC., 64 Division Ave., Levittown NY 11956. (516)735-5550. Senior Agent: George I. Magdaleno. Management firm and booking agency. Estab. 1960. Represents local, regional and international individual artists, groups and songwriters; currently handles 30 acts. Receives 15% commission. Reviews material for acts.
How to Contact: Submit demo tape by mail—unsolicited submissions are OK. Prefers cassette (or VHS videocassette if available) with 4 songs and lyric and lead sheet. If seeking management, include tape, bio and photos in press kit. SASE. Reports in 3-4 weeks.
Music: Mostly rock, pop and R&B; also country and jazz. Current acts include Orleans (rock group), Ben E. King (rock-pop), Tiny Tim, Richie Havens (folk), the Drifters and the Coasters.

ENTERTAINMENT WORKS, 2400 Poplar Dr., Baltimore MD 21207. (301)788-5095. President: Nancy Lewis. Management firm, booking agency and public relations/publicity firm. Estab. 1989. Represents local, regional and international groups; currently handles 5 acts. Receives 10-15% commission. Reviews material for acts.
How to Contact: Call for permission to submit. Prefers cassette with 3 songs "plus biography/publicity clips/photo." If seeking management, include group biography, individual biographies, 8 × 10 black & white glossy, all press clips/articles, PA requirements list and stage plot in press kit. Does not return material. Reports in 1 month.
Music: Mostly reggae and African. Works primarily with vocalists/dance bands. Current acts include Uprising (reggae band), Third Eye (reggae band) and Freedom of Expression (reggae band).
Tips: "Start with a phone call to introduce yourself, followed by a well-recorded 3-song demo, band member biographies, and all publicity clips."

*EVANS-SCHULMAN PRODUCTIONS, INC., Suite 240 Two Professional Dr., Gaithersburg MD 20879. (301)670-0050. President: Michael Evans. Management firm, booking agency and music publisher (Snooliemusic/BMI). Estab. 1989. Represents national individual artists, groups and songwriters; currently handles 9 acts. Receives 15-20% commission. Reviews material for acts.
How to Contact: Submit demo tape by mail—unsolicited submissions are OK. Prefers cassette with 3 songs and lyric sheet. SASE. Reports in 1 month.
Music: Mostly R&B, urban contemporary and Carolinas' beach' music. Works primarily with vocalists, vocal groups. Current acts include The Clovers (vocal group), Phil Flowers (vocalist/songwriter) and Bob McCoy (vocalist/songwriter/producer).
Tips: "We're looking for mainstream hits rather than alternative music."

*EVENTS UNLIMITED, Box 6541, Cleveland OH 44101. (216)467-0300. President: John Latimer. Management firm, booking agency, record company (Play Records) and TV show ("Alternate Beat"). Estab. 1985. Represents local, regional and international individual artists, groups and songwriters. Currently handles 18 acts. Receives 25% commission. Reviews material for acts.
How to Contact: Submit demo tape by mail—unsolicited submissions are OK. Prefers cassette with 5 songs. SASE. Reports in 6 weeks.
Music: Mostly rock and alternative. Current acts include I-Tal (reggae club band), The Bellows (rock concert acts) and Serious Nature (rock concert act).
Tips: "Be professional, persistent, and patient. Correspond by mail only."

*FAR WEST ENTERTAINMENT, INC., #225, 334 N.E. Northgate Way, Seattle WA 98125. (206)362-1850. FAX: (206)362-1831. Booking agency. Estab. 1971. Represents local and regional (Northwest) artists and groups; currently handles 20-30 acts. Receives 10-15% commission.
How to Contact: Submit demo tape by mail—unsolicited submissions are OK. Prefers cassette (or VHS videocassette if available) with 3-4 songs. "On videos, please make the sound quality the best possible. Let us see you on the tape. There is nothing worse than unfocused, poor quality videos." Does not return material. Reports in 2-3 weeks.
Music: Mostly pop-dance, rock and R&B. Works primarily with pop-dance-top 40 club bands. Current acts include Boy Toy (top 40 rock), Zerod' Zero (top 40/dance) and Savannah (rock/dance).
Tips: "Dance bands with a 'show'—steps, energy, dance moves go over well. Please send in professional looking and sounding promo and tape! The better you present yourself the better chance you have of getting bookings."

*FAT CITY ARTISTS, Suite #2, 1226 17th Ave. South, Nashville TN 37212. (615)320-7678. President: Rusty Michael. Management firm, booking agency, lecture bureau and event agency. Estab. 1972. Represents international individual artists, groups, songwriters and authors; currently handles 100 acts. Receives 20% commission. Reviews material for acts.
How to Contact: Submit demo tape by mail—unsolicited submissions are OK. Prefers cassette, CD or video with 4-6 songs. Does not return unsolicited material. Reports in 2 weeks.
Music: Mostly rock, pop and R&B; also jazz, C&W and new wave/heavy metal. "We represent all types of artists." Current acts include Doug Clark and the Hot Nuts (top 40), Little Milton (blues), Neighborhood Texture Jam (alternative), Michael Dillon and The Guns (country rock), Johnny Shines (Delta blues), The Planet Rockers (rockabilly), Harmonica Red & Jimmy Markham and the Jukes and Southern Culture on the Skids.
Tips: "Send all available information including audio, video, photo and print. If you do not have a professional package available, inquire. We also have advertising/promo department to develop effective promo kits."

JIM FEMINO PRODUCTIONS, (formerly Music Services of America), 429 South Lewis Rd., Royersford PA 19468. (215)948-8228. FAX: (215)948-4175. President: Jim Femino. (Fezsongs/ASCAP) publishing branch, record company (Road Records) and independent producer/engineer with own 24-track facility. Estab. 1970. Represents singer/songwriters; currently handles 2 acts.
How to Contact: Submit demo tape—unsolicited submissions are OK. Prefers cassette with two songs only. SASE. Replies in 4-6 weeks.
Music: Country and rock. Works primarily with vocalists and songwriters. Currently working with Jim Femino (writer/artist), Lovesimple (artist) and C.S.R. (rock band).

FRED T. FENCHEL ENTERTAINMENT AGENCY, 2104 S. Jefferson Avenue, Mason City IA 50401. (515)423-4177. General Manager: Fred T. Fenchel. Booking agency. Estab. 1964. Represents local and international individual artists and groups. Receives 15% commission. Reviews material for acts.

How to Contact: Submit demo tape by mail (videocassette if available). Unsolicited submissions are OK. Does not return unsolicited material.
Music: Mostly country, pop and some gospel. Works primarily with dance bands, show groups; "artists we can use on club dates, fairs, etc." Current acts include The Memories, D.C. Drifters, Convertibles and Cadillac. "We deal primarily with established name acts with recording contracts, or those with a label and starting into popularity."
Tips: "Submit good material with universal appeal and be informative on artist's background."

*FIREBALL MANAGEMENT, Box 588, Freeport NY 11520. President: Joel Peskin. Management firm. Estab. 1979. "We advance nationwide tours and coordinate promotion with record companies." Submit demo tape by mail. Unsolicited submissions are OK. Receives 20% commission. Reviews material for acts.
How to Contact: Submit demo tape by mail—unsolicited submission are OK. Prefers cassette (or videocassette of performance if available) with 2-5 songs. "Send professional, well-lit videos." If seeking management, include cassette tape and photo in press kit. Does not return material. Do not call. Reports in 1 month.
Music: Hard rock. Works primarily with hard rock concert groups. "We also do tour and retail merchandising."

FIRST TIME MANAGEMENT, Sovereign House, 12 Trewartha Rd., Praa Sands-Penzance, Cornwall TR20 9ST **England**. Phone: (0736)762826. FAX: (0736)763328. Managing Director: Roderick G. Jones. Management firm. Estab. 1986. Represents local, regional and international individual aritsts, groups and songwriters. Receives 20% commission. Reviews material for acts.
How to Contact: Submit demo tape by mail—unsolicited submissions are OK. Prefers cassette or 15 ips reel-to-reel (or VHS videocassette) with 3 songs and lyric sheets. SASE. Reports in 4-8 weeks.
Music: Mostly dance, top 40, rap, country, gospel and pop; also all styles. Works primarily with songwriters, composers, vocalists, groups and choirs. Current acts include Pete Arnold (folk) and Willow.
Tips: "Become a member of the Guild of International Songwriters and Composers. Keep everything as professional as possible. Be patient and dedicated to your aims and objectives."

FIVE STAR ENTERTAINMENT, 10188 Winter View Dr., Naples FL 33942. (813)566-7701 and (813)566-7702. Assistant Manager: Sid Kleiner. Management firm, booking agency (Five Star Entertainment Service), record company and audiovisual firm (Sid Kleiner Video Enterprises, Inc.) and record producer. Represents individual artists and groups; currently handles over 15 acts. Receives 15-25% commission. Reviews material for acts.
How to Contact: Submit demo tape by mail—unsolicited submissions are OK. Prefers VHS (or super VHS) videocassette only with maximum of 6 songs. If seeking management, include audio and video demo tapes, photos, equipment list, song list, salary range and availability in press kit. SASE. Reports in 1 month.
Music: Mostly swing, MOR and country; also jazz, dixie, ethnic, pop and rock. Works primarily with organized dance bands and self-contained singles. Current acts include Gents of Jazz (light jazz), The Dave Kleiner Show (easy listening) and The Magic Diamond (musical variety show).
Tips: "Furnish as much information as possible: glossies, VHS video demo tapes (1½ choruses), song lists, equipment lists, availability, price per single engagement, price per on-going weekly engagement, costuming, etc."

FLASH ATTRACTIONS AGENCY, 38 Prospect St., Warrensburg NY 12885. (518)623-9313. Agent: Wally Chester. Management firm and booking agency. Estab. 1952. Represents artists and groups; currently handles 106 acts. Receives 15-20% commission. Reviews material for acts. "We are celebrating 40 years in business, and are fully licensed by the American Federation of Musicians and the State of New York."
How to Contact: Submit demo tape by mail—unsolicited submissions are OK. Prefers cassette for singers, VHS videocassette for acts, with 1-6 songs with lead and lyric sheets. Songwriters and artists may submit "professionally done" videocassettes. If seeking management, entertainers should include professionally-done videotape or cassette, 8×10 photo, resume, song list and history of the act in press kit. Songwriters should include professionally-done cassette, lead sheet, lyrics and music. SASE. Reports in 2 months.
Music: Mostly country, calypso, Hawaiian and MOR; also blues, dance, easy listening, jazz, top 40, country rock and Latin, plus American Indian Shows. Works primarily with vocalists, dance bands, lounge acts, floor show groups and ethnic shows. Current acts include Prince Pablo's Caribbean Extravaganza (steel drum band and floor show), Mirinda James (Nashville recording artist and her country cross/over show band), Loi Afo and "Island Call," The Country Belles (all girl variety band), The Ronnie Prophet Country Music Show (Canada's #1 recording and TV star), N.C. Preservation

Dixieland Jazz Band, The Robin Right Country Music Show (voted New England's #1 entertainer and band), Wally Chester's "Spark and a Flame Duo" (lounge act), Eagle Feather (country music band and Canadian Indian dancers) and Kit McClure and her all female 17 piece big band sound.
Tips: "Submit songs that have public appeal, good story line and simplicity. Good cassettes and band-show videos are mandatory for promotion."

THE FLYING DUTCHMAN, Box 9027, Amsterdam HOL 1006AA **Netherlands.** Phone: (020)669-1981. Artist Manager: TJ Lammers. Management firm and music publisher (Rock Rose-BUMA/STEMRA). Estab. 1980. Represents local, regional and international individual artists, groups and songwriters; currently handles 7 acts. Receives 20% commission. Reviews material for acts.
How to Contact: Submit demo tape by mail—unsolicited submissions are OK. Prefers cassette (or VHS videocassette if available) with 2-4 songs. Does not return unsolicited material. Reports in 1 month.
Music: Mostly rock, pop and alternative; also country, folk and blues. Works primarily with hard rock, rock, pop and folk rock bands and singers. Current acts include Gringos Locos (hard rock band), Personnel (roots rock band), A Girl Called Johnny (female rock/R&B singer/songwriter) and Power-play (rock).
Tips: "Put name and number on the cassette."

*FOLSOM MANAGEMENT, 43 McKee Dr., Mahwah NJ 07430. (201)529-3550. President: Edward Feldsott. Management firm. Estab. 1991. Represents local individual artists, groups and songwriters; currently handles 3 acts. Receives 15-20% commission. Reviews material for acts.
How to Contact: Submit demo tape by mail—unsolicited submissions are OK. Prefers cassette with 3-4 songs and lyric sheet. SASE. Reports in 3 months.
Music: Mostly blues rock, progressive and commercial rock; also metal and top 40/pop. Current acts include Mike Taylor (blues rock), Paul Dianno (heavy metal) and Jennifer Ferguson (commercial rock).

WILLIAM FORD PERSONAL MANAGEMENT INC., #5D, 17 E. 7th St., New York NY 10003. (212)477-5586. President: Bill Ford. Estab. 1983. Represents local individual artists and groups; currently handles 2 acts. Receives 20% commission. Reviews material for acts.
How to Contact: Submit demo tape by mail—unsolicited submissions are OK. Prefers cassette (or VHS videocassette if available) with 3 or 4 songs and lyric sheet. SASE. Reports in 4 weeks.
Music: Mostly pop, rock and R&B. Works primarily with pop vocalists, performing rock bands and acts. Current acts include Rev. Conner Tribble (rock performer and band writer) and Loni Singer (vocalist, pop and dance).
Tips: "Have a considerable amount of patience and work very hard on the performance of the right song."

THE FRANKLYN AGENCY, #312, 1010 Hammond St., West Hollywood CA 90069. (213)272-6080. President: Audrey P. Franklyn. Management firm, public relations firm and cable production company plus part owner of A&E Productions. "Producing weekend singer showcases." Represents artists, musical groups and businesses; currently handles 3 acts. Receives 10-15% commission. Reviews material for acts.
How to Contact: Query by mail, arrange personal interview, or submit demo. Prefers cassette (or videocassette if available) with 4 songs and lead sheet. SASE. Reports in 2 weeks.
Music: Mosly rock, country and pop; also blues, easy listening, gospel, jazz, MOR, progressive and R&B. Works primarily with rock bands and single soloist singers. Current acts include Carlena Williams, The Chodes and Merrell Fankhauser.
Tips: "No amateurs—be funded for promotional efforts."

FREADE SOUNDS ENTERTAINMENT & RECORDING STUDIO, North 37311 Valley Rd., Chattaroy WA 99003. (509)292-2201. FAX: (509)292-2205. Agent/Engineer: Tom Lapsansky. Booking agency and recording studio. Estab. 1967. Represents groups; currently handles 10-13 acts. Receives 10% commission. Reviews material for acts.
How to Contact: Query by mail or submit demo. Prefers cassette (or videocassette, "please pick best vocal song, best instrumental and best song performer likes to perform") with 4-6 songs and pictures/song list. SASE. Reports in 2 weeks.
Music: Mostly top 40/rock; also R&B and production rock. Works primarily with dance/concert groups and bar bands. Current acts include Lynx, Nobody Famous, Rockaholics, Black Eagle, Crazy Legs, Fuzzy Logic, Mr. E. and Uncle Nasty.

*FREEFALL TALENT GROUP, 18 Grandview St., Huntington NY 11743. (516)423-9310. President: Mark Puma. Management firm. Estab. 1979. Represents local, regional or international individual artists and groups; currently handles 2 acts. Receives 20% commission. Reviews material for acts.

How to Contact: Call first and obtain permission to submit. Prefers cassette (or VHS videocassette if available). SASE.
Music: Mostly rock and pop. Current acts include Kix (hard rock band) and TNT (hard rock band).

BOB SCOTT FRICK ENTERPRISES, 404 Bluegrass Ave., Madison TN 37115. (615)865-6380. President: Bob Frick. Booking agency, music publisher (Frick Music Publishing Co./BMI and Sugarbaker Music Publishing/ASCAP) and record company (R.E.F. Recording Co). Represents individual artists and songwriters; currently handles 5 acts. Reviews material for acts.
How to Contact: Submit demo tape by mail, or write or call first to arrange personal interview. Prefers cassette with 3 songs and lyric sheet. SASE. Reports in 1 month.
Music: Mostly gospel, country and R&B. Works primarily with vocalists. Current acts include Bob Scott Frick (guitarist, singer), Larry Ahlborn (singer), Bob Myers (singer), Teresa Ford, Eddie Isaacs, Scott Frick, Jim and Ruby Mattingly and David Barton.

*FULL TILT MANAGEMENT, Box 1578, Sioux Falls SD 57106. (605)332-0078. President: Chris Van Buren. Management firm, booking agency and record company (Top Shelf Records). Estab. 1972. Represents regional Mid-West groups; currently handles 12 acts. Receives 15-20% commission. Reviews material for acts.
How to Contact: Submit demo tape by mail—unsolicited submissions are OK. Prefers cassette with 3 songs and lyric sheet. Does not return unsolicited material. Reports in 6-8 weeks.
Music: Mostly rock; also pop and country. Works primarily with rock, dance and country bands. Current acts include Innuendo (rock), Concrete Jungle (rock) and Street Legal (rock/pop).
Tips: "Full tilt looks for artists with the drive to do whatever it takes to succeed in the music industry."

*FUTURE STAR ENTERTAINMENT, 315 South Beverly Dr., Beverly Hills CA 90212. (310)553-0990. President: Paul Shenker. Management firm. Estab. 1982. Represents local, regional or international individual artists and groups; currently handles 6 acts. Receives 20% commission. Reviews material for acts.
How to Contact: Write or call first and obtain permission to submit. Prefers cassette (or VCR optional) with 3-5 songs and lyric sheet. Does not return unsolicited material. Reports in 4-6 weeks.
Music: Mostly rock, pop and R&B. Works primarily with rock bands. Current acts include City of Faith (R&B), The Dickies (punk) and Tom Batoy (solo pop artist).

GLO GEM PRODUCTIONS, INC., Box 427, Port Huron MI 48061. (313)984-4471. Public Affairs Coordinator: James David. Management firm and booking agency. Estab. 1974. Represents local, Midwestern and international individual artists, groups and songwriters; currently handles 35 acts. Receives 15-20% commission. Reviews material for acts.
How to Contact: Write first and obtain permission to submit. Prefers cassette or 7½ ips reel-to-reel (or ½ VHS videocassette of live performance, if available) with 2 songs and lyric or lead sheets. Does not return unsolicited material. Reports in 3 weeks.
Music: Mostly country, MOR and blues; also folk, jazz and pop. Works primarily with vocalists, show groups and dance bands. Current acts include Cliff Erickson (songwriter/entertainer), Jimmy Cox (show person/songwriter) and Burnwood (showband/songwriters).

*GLOBAL ASSAULT MANAGEMENT, Suite 1632, 639 Gardenwalk Blvd., College Park GA 30349. (404)994-1770. Contact: David Norman. Management firm and booking agency. Represents groups and production teams. Currently handles five acts. Receives 15-20% commission. Reviews material for acts or available on consultant basis.
How to Contact: Send photo, bio, 8×10 photos, VHS videocassette, audio cassette, songlist. SASE. Reports in 2 weeks.
Music: Mostly self-contained R&B and alternative groups. Current acts include The Mirthmakers, 20/20 Vision, Faces, The Women, Shyrod and The Project.
Tips: "If you are a group that is highly polished and professional and think internationally about your music, you should definitely contact us. We are presently also booking groups in Asia and Europe."

MICHAEL GODIN MANAGEMENT, INC., #201-1505 West 2nd Ave., Vancouver BC V6H 3Y4 Canada. (604)731-3535. Professional Manager: Carey Fok. Management firm and music publisher (West Broadway Music/SOCAN). Estab. 1986. Represents local, regional and international individual, groups, songwriters and record producers/engineers; currently handles 6 acts. Receives 20% commission.

How to Contact: Submit demo tape by mail—unsolicited submissions are OK. Prefers cassette or VHS videocassette with 3-5 songs and lyric sheet. SASE. Reports in 6-8 weeks.
Music: Mostly pop, rock and dance. Work primarily with pop singers/songwriters. Current acts include Paul Janz (pop singer/songwriter), Young Gun (hard rock), Sonny Boy (alternative rock), Dale Denner (producer/engineer), Luke Koyle and Christopher Dedrick (film and television composers).

*GOLDEN BULL PRODUCTIONS, Box 81153, Chicago IL 60681-0153. (312)731-6549. Manager: Jesse Dearing. Management firm. Estab. 1984. Represents local and regional (Midwest) individual artists, groups and songwriters; currently handles 4 acts. Receives 12-30% commission. Reviews material for acts.
How to Contact: Submit demo tape by mail—unsolicited submissions are OK. Prefers cassette (or VHS videocassette) with 4-5 songs and lyric or lead sheet. If seeking management, include demo tape, bio and 8×10 black and white photo in press kit. SASE. Reports in 2 months.
Music: Mostly R&B, pop and rock; also gospel, jazz and blues. Works primarily with vocalists, bands. Current acts include Lost and Found (R&B band), Keith Stewart (songwriter) and A. Lock (singer).

GOLDEN CITY INTERNATIONAL, Box 410851, San Francisco CA 94141. (415)822-1530. Manager: Mr. Alston. Management firm, booking agency and record company (Dagene Records, Cabletown). Estab. 1987. Represents regional (Bay area) individual artists, groups and songwriters; currently handles 3 acts. Receives 25% commission. Reviews material for acts.
How to Contact: Write or call first and obtain permission to submit. Prefers cassette with 2 songs and lyric sheet. Does not return unsolicited material. Reports in 3 weeks.
Music: Mostly R&B/dance, rap and pop; also gospel. Current clients include Marcus Justice (songwriter), Zwo Dominatorz (artist) and David Alston (producer).

CHRIS GREELEY ENTERTAINMENT, Box 593, Bangor ME 04402-0593. (207)827-4382. General Manager: Christian D. Greeley. Management firm and booking agency. Estab. 1986. Represents local, regional and international individual artists, groups, songwriters and disc-jockeys; currently handles 4 acts. Receives 10-15% commission. Reviews material for acts.
How to Contact: Submit demo tape by mail—unsolicited submissions are OK. Prefers cassette (or VHS videocassette if available) with 1-4 songs. SASE. Reports in 2 weeks.
Music: Mostly rock, country and pop. "I'm open to anything marketable." Wide range of musical styles. Current acts include Rick Finzel (original artist/songwriter) and Soundtrac (regional top 40 dance band).
Tips: "Be positive! Work hard and smart. Treat your music interest as a business. Be open to other ideas. Be willing to spend money on your craft."

GEOFFREY HANSEN ENTERPRISES, LTD., Box 63, Orinda CA 94563. Agent: J. Malcom Baird. Management firm and booking agency. Represents artists, groups and songwriters. Receives 15-25% commission. Also paid on a contract basis. Reviews material for acts.
How to Contact: Submit demo tape—unsolicited submissions are OK. Include photograph, song list and cover letter. Prefers cassette. If seeking management include quality photographs, song list, and a resume of professional experience in press kit. "Also the act should be dressed according to the market, i.e. tuxedo/gown for hotels; casual for fairs; etc." SASE. Reports in 6 weeks.
Music: Top 40/country, R&B, MOR and jazz in English, Spanish, French and Japanese. Works with top 40 and standard jazz recording acts and overseas international stars. Current acts include The Ronettes (oldies), Pilita Corrales (Hispanic), and Connie Francis (oldies).
Tips: "We are always looking for new talent. Anyone who has a demo and is interested in international bookings and career development, contact us. We are ready to listen. We are looking for female vocalists, girl groups, show bands, jazz, western swing, cajun and Tex-Mex musical acts to tour overseas in Europe, the Far East, Hawaii, Japan and various foreign markets as well as in the USA. Send photos, bio, song list, demo tape and SASE. All styles of music wanted."

HEAVYWEIGHT PRODUCTIONS & UP FRONT MANAGEMENT, 2734 East 7th St., Oakland CA 94601. (415)436-5532. Vice President: Charles M. Coke. Management firm, music publisher and record company (Man Records). Estab. 1988. Represents local, regional and international individual artists, groups, songwriters and producers; currently handles 6 acts. Receives 20% commission. Reviews material for acts.

How to Contact: Submit demo tape by mail—unsolicited submissions are OK. Prefers cassette with 4 songs and lyric or lead sheet (optional). If seeking management, include good bio and pictures, good 4-song tape and phone number to reach sender in press kit. Does not return unsolicited material. Reports within 3 weeks.

Music: Mostly R&B, rock and country; also pop, Latin and jazz. Works primarily with vocalists. Current acts include John Payne (R&B), Black Moriah (rock) and Ronnie Kimball (country).

Tips: "Listen to trends in today's market place. If you're writing with someone in mind, research their music. Write strong hooks, and don't forget people will always be dancing no matter the type of music. Don't write over the listeners' heads."

BOB HINKLE MANAGEMENT, 17 Cadman Plaza West, Brooklyn NY 11201. (718)858-2544. President: Bob Hinkle. Management firm. Represents individual artists, groups and songwriters. Currently handles 5 artists. Receives 15-25% commission. Reviews material for acts.

How to Contact: Submit demo tape by mail—unsolicited submissions are OK. Prefers cassette (or ¾" or VHS videocassette if available) with 3-5 songs and lyric sheet. Artist should send a videocassette of his/her performance. Does not return unsolicited material. Reports in 1 month.

Music: Mostly children's. Works primarily with recording bands, soloists and children's performers. Current acts include Peter Combe, Glenn Bennett and Sylvia (all children's performers).

Tips: "Tailor writing to needs of artists without losing what makes your writing unique."

HITCH-A-RIDE MANAGEMENT, Box 1001, Florence KY 41022-1001. (606)371-5469. Manager: J.H. Reno. Management firm, booking agency and publishing company. Represents professional individuals, groups and songwriters; currently handles 4 acts. Receives 15% commission. Reviews material for acts.

How to Contact: Prefers cassette (or videocassette—"be natural") with 1-4 songs and lyric sheet. Does not accept unsolicited submissions. SASE. Reports in 1 month.

Music: Mostly modern country and light cross-over rock. Works primarily with vocalists. Current acts include Sheila Reno, Pam Hanna, Mike Tomlin and Jack Reno (country vocalists).

HOLIDAY PRODUCTIONS, 1786 State Line Road, Lagrange GA 30240. (404)884-5369. President: Phyllis Imhoff. Management firm and music publisher (Silverstreak Music/ASCAP). Estab. 1983. Represents local, regional and international individual artists and songwriters; currently handles 2 acts. Receives 15-20% commission. Reviews material for acts.

How to Contact: Submit demo tape by mail—unsolicited submissions are OK. Prefers cassette or VHS videocassette with an unspecified number of songs and lyric sheet. SASE. Reports in 2 weeks.

Music: Mostly country and pop. Works primarily with dance bands and show bands with strong lead vocalists. Current acts include Scooter Lee (country singer) and Dealer's Choice (country band).

DOC HOLIDAY PRODUCTIONS, 5405 Echo Pines Circle W., Fort Pierce FL 34951. (804)591-2717 or (407)595-1441. Vice President: Judith Guthro. Management firm, booking agent, music publisher (BMI, ASCAP, SESAC) and record company (Tug Boat Records). Estab. 1985. Represents international individual artists, groups and songwriters; currently handles 47 acts. Receives 15-25% commission. Reviews material for acts.

How to Contact: Submit demo tape by mail. Unsolicited submissions are okay. Prefers cassette with 1 song and lyric sheet. If seeking management, include 8 × 10 photo, press clippings, press experiments and demo tape in press kit. Does not return unsolicited material. Reports in 2 weeks.

Music: Mostly country, pop and rock. Works primarily with vocalist dance bands. Current acts include Doug "The Ragin Cajun" Kenshaw (cajun), Big Al Downing (country) and Doc Holiday (country rock).

*HORIZON MANAGEMENT INC., 659 Westview Station, Binghamton NY 13905. (607)772-0857. Contact: New Talent Department. Management firm and booking agency. Estab. 1968. Represents local, regional or international individual artists, groups and songwriters; currently handles 1,500 acts. Receives 20% commission. Reviews material for acts.

How to Contact: Call first and obtain permission to submit. Prefers cassette (or VHS videocassette if available) with 1-4 songs and 1 lyric or lead sheet. Does not return unsolicited material.

Music: Mostly top 40 lounge and show, top 40 country and top 40 rock; also classic rock, oldies and original. Works primarily with bands (all styles). Current acts include Bluesman Willy (blues-recording artist), Joey Dee &Starlighters (50s recording artist) and Drifters (50s recording artist).

*KATHY HOWARD MANAGEMENT, Box 477, Rozelle N5W **Australia** 2106. Estab. 1985. Represents local individual artists and groups; currently handles 1 act. Commission fluctuates. Reviews material for acts.

How to Contact: Submit demo tape by mail—unsolicited submissions are OK. Prefers cassette. SASE. Reports in 2 months.
Music: Rock and rock-pop; also rock pop groups. Current acts include Choirboys (rock), Inspirit (rock) and Say Yes (pop rock).
Tips: Please send only rough demos, produced demos not essential, lyric sheet preferred."

*IMPRESARIO LIMITED, #230, 16535 W. Bluemound, Brookfield WI 53005. (414)786-5600. Vice President: Stephen Knill. Management firm. Estab. 1990. Deals with local, regional or international groups and songwriters; currently handles 1 act. Receives 15-20% commission. Reviews material for acts.
How to Contact: Write or call first and obtain permission to submit. Prefers cassette with 3 songs and lyric sheet. Does not return unsolicited material. Reports in 6 weeks.
Music: Mostly country and rock. Works primarily with country and rock artists/groups. Current acts include Molly & the Heymakers.

INERJÉ PRODUCTIONS, RECORDS, MANAGEMENT, 661 N. 13th St., Philadelphia PA 19123. (215)236-5358. President: Inerjé Barrett. Management firm, music publisher (Inerjé Publishing/AS-CAP) and record company (Inerjé Records). Estab. 1990. Represents local, regional and international individual artists, groups, songwriters and producers; currently handles 5 acts. Receives 20% commission. Reviews material for acts.
How to Contact: Submit demo tape by mail—unsolicited submissions are OK. Prefers cassette (or VHS videocassette if available) with 3-5 songs. SASE. Reports in 6 weeks.
Music: Gospel. Works primarily with vocalists and choirs. Current acts include Tony Gilmore (vocalist), Bryant Pugh (producer, writer, musician) and Damien Core (artist).
Tips: "Please be sure that you are interested in gospel music. Write clearly or type information. Please give ample time for the review of material. Be vocally strong."

INTERMOUNTAIN TALENT, Box 942, Rapid City SD 57709. (605)348-7777. Owner: Ron Kohn. Management firm, booking agency and music publisher (Big BL Music). Estab. 1978. Represents individual artists, groups and songwriters; currently handles 30 acts. Receives 10-20% commission. Reviews material for acts.
How to Contact: Submit demo tape by mail—unsolicited submissions are OK. Prefers cassette with 3 songs and lyric sheet. Artist may submit videocassette. If seeking management, include tape, video and photo in press kit. SASE. Reports in 1 month.
Music: Mostly rock; also top country/rock. Works with solo acts, show bands, dance bands and bar bands. Current acts include Cross Winds (light rock), Partners (variety duo) and Jasen Scholous (rock).

INTERNATIONAL TALENT NETWORK, 17580 Frazho, Roseville MI 48066. Executive Vice President of A&R: Ron Geddish. Booking agency. Estab. 1980. Represents Midwest groups; currently handles 3 acts. Receives 20% commission. Reviews material for acts.
How to Contact: Submit demo tape by mail—unsolicited submissions are OK. Prefers cassette (or VHS videocassette of performance if available) with 3-5 songs and lyric sheet. Does not return unsolicited material. Reports in 1 month.
Music: Works primarily with rock, pop and alternative-college acts. Current acts include His Name Is Alive (group/alternative), Elvis Hitler (rock group) and The Look (A&M/Canada rock group).
Tips: "If we hear a hit tune—rock, pop, alternative college—we are interested."

ISSACHAR MANAGEMENT, Suite 10F, 111 Third Ave., New York NY 10003. (212)477-7063. FAX: (212)477-1469. President: Jack Flanagan. Management firm and booking agency specializing in tour consulting. Estab. 1990. Represents international individual artists and groups and studio engineers and musicians.
How to Contact: Submit demo tape by mail—unsolicited submissions are OK. If seeking management, include tape, lyrics, photo, bio and press clips in press kit. Reports in 3 months.
Music: Mostly rock, R&B and reggae; also pop and funk. Current acts include Chuck Valle, Todd Youth, Murphy's Law (rock), B.A.L. Productions and The Dickies (punk).

*ITS HAPPENING PRESENT ENTERTAINMENT, Box 222, Pittsburg CA 94565. (510)779-4341. President: Charles Barner Jr.. Management firm, booking agency and record company (Black Diamond Record and D. City Record—affiliate). Estab. 1989. Represents local, regional or international individual artists and songwriters; currently handles 5 acts. Receives 15% commission. Reviews material for acts.

How to Contact: Submit demo tape by mail—unsolicited submissions are OK. Prefers cassette with 2 songs and lyric sheet. SASE. Reports in 3 weeks.
Music: Mostly pop, R&B and jazz; also rap, country and classical. Works primarily with vocalist songwriters, rap groups, bands, instrumentalists. Current acts include Jerry "J." (vocalist jazz/R&B), Nick Depaulo (vocalist/pop) and Too Nice (rapper).
Tips: "Please, copyright all your material as soon as possible. Don't let anyone else hear it until that's done first. You have to be swift about hearing, slow about speaking and slow about giving. Be true to the game or your art or craft."

*J & V MANAGEMENT, 143 W. Elmwood, Caro MI 48723. (517)673-2889. Management: John Timko. Management firm, booking agency. Represents local, regional or international individual artists, groups and songwriters; currently handles 4 groups. Receives 20% commission. Reviews material for acts.
How to Contact: Submit demo tape by mail—unsolicited submissions are OK. Prefers cassette with 3 songs maximum and lyric sheet. If seeking management, include cassette tape, lyric sheet and short reference bio in press kit. SASE. Reports in 3 weeks.
Music: Mostly country. Works primarily with vocalists and dance bands. Current acts include John Patrick (country singer/songwriter) and John Patrick Timko (songwriter).

JACKSON ARTISTS CORP., (Publishing Central), Suite 200, 7251 Lowell Dr., Shawnee Mission KS 66204. (913)384-6688. President: Dave Jackson. Management firm, booking agency (Drake/Jackson Productions), music publisher, (All Told Music/BMI, Zang/Jac Publishing/ASCAP and Very Cherry/ ASCAP), record company and record producer. Represents artists, groups and songwriters; currently handles 12 acts. Receives 15-20% commission from individual artists and groups; 10% from songwriters. Reviews material for acts.
How to Contact: Query, arrange personal interview or submit demo. Prefers cassette (or VHS video-cassette of performance if available) with 2-4 songs and lead sheet. "List names of tunes on cassettes. May send up to 4 tapes. Although it's not necessary, we prefer lead sheets with the tapes—send 2 or 3 that you are proud of. Also note what 'name' artist you'd like to see do the song. We do most of our business by phone. We prefer good enough quality to judge a performance, however, we do not require that the video or cassettes be of professional nature." Will return material if requested with SASE. Reports in 2 months.
Music: Mostly gospel, country and rock; also bluegrass, blues, easy listening, disco, MOR, progressive, soul and top 40/pop. Works with acts that work grandstand shows for fairs as well as bar bands that want to record original material. Current acts include Dixie Cadillacs (country/rock), Impressions (50's and 60's), Gary Adams Players (pop), Tracie Spencer, Paul & Paula, Bill Haley's Comets, Max Groove (jazz) and The Dutton Family (classical to pop).
Tips: "Be able to work on the road, either as a player or as a group. Invest your earnings from these efforts in demos of your originals that have been tried out on an audience. And keep submitting to the industry."

JACKSON/JONES MANAGEMENT, 5917 West Blvd., Los Angeles CA 90043. (213)296-8742. Manager: E.J. Jackson. Management firm. Estab. 1984. Represents local, regional and international individual artists and groups; currently handles 4 acts. Receives 25% commission. Reviews material for acts.
How to Contact: Submit demo tape by mail—unsolicited submissions OK. Prefers cassette (or VHS videocassette if available) with 3 songs and lyric sheet. If seeking management, include bio, photo and demo tape in press kit. SASE. Reports in 4 weeks.
Music: Mostly R&B, pop and top 40. Works primarily with vocalists, producers and dance bands. Current acts include Vesta (R&B/pop singer), Glamour (R&B female trio) and Karel (dance/urban).

ROGER JAMES MANAGEMENT, 10A Margaret Rd., Barnet, Herts EN4 9NP **England.** Phone: (01)440-9788. Professional Manager: Laura Skuce. Management firm and music publisher (R.J. Music/ PRS). Estab. 1977. Represents songwriters. Receives 50% commission; reviews material for acts.
How to Contact: Prefers cassette with 3 songs and lyric sheet. Does not return unsolicited material.
Music: Mostly pop, country and "any good song."

*JAVA MANAGEMENT, Box 431, Thiensville WI 53092. (414)355-2467. Manager: Steve Ruth. Management firm and record company (JAVA Records). Estab. 1979. Represents local, regional and international individual artists, groups and songwriters; currently handles 3 acts. Receives 15% commission. Reviews material for acts.
How to Contact: Submit demo tape by mail—unsolicited submissions are OK. Prefers cassette (or VHS videocassette of performance if available) with 3 songs and lyric or lead sheets. If seeking management, include cassette, video, CD and reprints in press kit. SASE. Reports in 1 month.

Music: Mostly Caribbean styles, Latin and African; also instrumental jazz rock and ethnic. Works primarily with touring and recording dance bands and industrial AV composers. Current acts include Java (Caribbean dance band), The Cheddarheads (eclectic rock band), and SR Music.
Tips: "Take chances, we want unique and sometimes eccentric material."

JOHNS & ASSOCIATES, % Ward Johns and Ken Thompson, Suite 101, 550 E. Plumb Lane, Reno NV 89502. (702)827-3648. Management firm and market consultants. Estab. 1981. Represents artists, groups and songwriters; currently handles 6-12 acts. "We represent all types of music to record labels and booking/management firms throughout the world." Reviews material for motion pictures and artists.
How to Contact: Query by mail, arrange personal interview or submit demo tape. Prefers cassette (or VHS or Beta videocassette of live performance, if available) with 4-10 songs and lyric sheet. "It's important to have VHS or Beta tape and a professional 16-24 track demo. Also send pictures and printed resume."
Music: Mostly commercial: top 40 original music; up to date rock; cross-over pop and C/W.
Tips: "Send new material with strong hooks. Although it is not mandatory, a videocassette is a big help for an artist's marketing potential. We have music mortgage brokers helping to find financial opportunities for booking agencies, management firms and record labels as our secondary income resource."

C. JUNQUERA PRODUCTIONS, Box 393, Lomita CA 90717. (213)325-2881. Co-owner: C. Junquera. Management firm and record company (NH Records). Estab. 1987. Represents local, regional and international individual artists and songwriters; currently handles 1 act. Receives a flat fee, depending on project costs. Reviews material for acts.
How to Contact: Write first and obtain permission to submit. Prefers cassette with 1-3 songs and lyric sheet. If seeking management, include 8×10 photo, business card, bio, photocopies of news articles and sample of product. SASE. Reports in 1-2 months.
Music: Mostly traditional country and country pop; also easy listening. Works primarily with vocalists. Current acts include Nikki Hornsby (singer/songwriter) and Mary Ryan (songwriter).

R.J. KALTENBACH PERSONAL MANAGEMENT, Box 510, Dundee IL 60118-0510. (708)428-4777. President: R.J. Kaltenbach. Management firm. Estab. 1980. Represents national touring acts only (individual artists and groups); currently handles 3 acts. Receives 15-20% commission. Reviews material for acts.
How to Contact: Submit demo tape by mail—unsolicited submissions are OK. Prefers cassette (or VHS ½" videocassette) with 3 songs and lyric sheet. Reports in 1 month "if we are interested in material."
Music: Country, rock/pop and contemporary Christian. Works primarily with "national acts with recording contracts or deals pending." Current acts include T.G. Sheppard (national recording artist), Ron David Moore (new Christian artist) and Mike Redmond and Magazine (Chicago-based rock act).
Tips: "We deal only with professionals who are dedicated to their craft and show lots of promise."

*(KAM) EXECUTIVE RECORDS, 11 Shady Oak Trail, Charlotte NC 98210. (704)554-1169. Executive Director: Butch Kelly. Record company (KAM Executive Records/BMI). Estab. 1982. Represents local, regional and international individual artists, groups and songwriters. Currently handles 10 acts. Receives 15% commission. Reviews material for acts.
How to Contact: Submit demo tape—unsolicited submissions are OK. Prefers cassette (or VHS videocassette) with 3-6 songs. "Send professional video of performance if available." SASE. Reports in 6-8 weeks.
Music: Mostly pop, R&B and rock; also rap and dance. Works primarily with vocalists and show or dance bands. Current acts include Lady Krush, Caro and Richard Kirkpatrick.

KAUFMAN HILL MANAGEMENT, Suite 613, 410 S. Michigan Ave., Chicago IL 60605. (708)739-4577. Contact: Don Kaufman or Shawn Hill. Management firm (also Mozart Midnight Productions, Inc.) and record company (Vamp Records). Estab. 1982. Represents individual artists, groups and songwriters; currently handles 6 acts. Receives 20% commission. Reviews material for acts.
How to Contact: Submit demo tape by mail—unsolicited submissions are OK. Prefers cassette (or VHS videocassette if available) with 2-6 songs and lyric sheet. If seeking management, include photo, cassette and note as to why submitting in press kit. Does not return any material. Reports back only if interested.
Music: Mostly R&B, pop, rock and rap. Works primarily with singer/songwriters, bands, groups and vocalists. Current acts include Kevin Irving (lead singer of Club Nouveau, R&B), Jeannie Withrow (pop/rock singer/songwriter), Darcsyde (rap) and Tribal Opera (progressive band).
Tips: "Submit by mail. If you have what we need, we will be in touch."

*KEY ARTIST MANAGEMENT & ENTERTAINMENT CONSULTANTS, 500 Newbold St., London, Ontario N6E 1K6 **Canada**. (519)686-5060. Director: Geoff Keymer. Management firm and record company (Signature Records). Represents individual artists and groups; currently handles 3 acts. Receives 10-25% commission. Reviews material for acts.
How to Contact: "I am not accepting unsolicited material."
Music: Mostly pop, rock, MOR and new music. Works primarily with solo artists and vocalists. Represents Cassandra (rock vocalist) and Mike McKenna (MOR vocalist).

HOWARD KING AGENCY, INC., 7050 Babcock Ave., North Hollywood CA 91605. President: Howard King. Management firm and booking agency. Estab. 1962. Represents artists, groups and songwriters. Receives 10-20% commission. Reviews material for acts.
How to Contact: Write or call first and obtain permission to submit. Prefers cassette or VHS videocassette with maximum 3 songs, photo, publicity material and lyric sheet. If seeking management, include photos, tapes and video (if possible), and well-written resume, song lists and good writers. SASE. Reports in 3 months.
Music: Mostly top 40; also country, dance-oriented, easy listening, jazz, MOR, rock and pop. Works primarily with top 40 artist singles, duos and groups. Current acts include L.S. Acapella Symphony (vocal-comedy).

JEFF KIRK, 7108 Grammar Rd. S.W., Fairview TN 37062. (615)799-8674. Owner/President: Jeff Kirk. Management firm and booking agency. Estab. 1981. Represents regional (mid-South) individual artists; currently handles 3 acts. Commission varies. Reviews material for acts.
How to Contact: Submit demo tape by mail—unsolicited submissions are OK. Prefers cassette (or VHS videocassette if available) with 1-3 songs and lyric or lead sheet. If seeking management, include bio, recent performance, recent recordings and picture (optional). Does not return unsolicited material. Reports in 1 month.
Music: Mostly jazz, pop and rock. Works primarily with jazz groups (4-6 members), instrumental and vocal. Current acts include Jeff Kirk Quartet (mainstream jazz) and New Vintage (jazz fusion).
Tips: "Please submit brief demos with as high audio quality as possible."

*BOB KNIGHT AGENCY, 185 Clinton Ave., Staten Island NY 10301. (718)448-8420. President: Bob Knight. Management firm, booking agency, music publishing and royalty collection firm. Estab. 1971. Represents artists, groups and songwriters; currently handles 7 acts. Receives 10-20% commission. Reviews material for acts and for submission to record companies and producers.
How to Contact: Submit demo tape by mail—unsolicited submissions are OK. Prefers cassette (or videocassette) with 5-10 songs and lead sheet "with bio and references. Send photos of artists and groups." If seeking management, include bios, video cassette and audio cassette in press kit. SASE. Reports in 1 month.
Music: Mostly top 40/pop; also easy listening, MOR, R&B, soul and rock (nostalgia 50s and 60s). Works primarily with lounge groups, high energy dance, 50's acts and show groups. Current acts include The Elegants (oldie show); Gengo & Gregorio (top 40); and The AD-LIBS (oldie show).

*S.V. KYLES & ASSOCIATES, Box 8305, Houston TX 77288. (713)662-4196. Sr. Consultant: Sirron Kyles. Management firm. Represents international individual artists and groups; currently handles 5 acts. Receives 15-20% commission. Reviews material for acts.
How to Contact: Submit demo tape by mail—unsolicited submissions are OK. Prefers cassette (or VHS videocassette) with 3 songs. Does not return unsolicited material. Reports in 1 month.
Music: Mostly rock, country and R&B; also pop and dance. Recent acts include Storm (rock), Aubrey Dunnham (jazz) and Jerry Stanley (country).

LANDMARK DIRECTION COMPANY, INC., Box 132, Amelia OH 45102. (513)752-0611. President: James B. Williams. Management firm, booking agency, music publisher (Landmark Publishing/BMI) and record company (JAB Production Co., Inc.). Estab. 1987. Represents regional (Midwest) individual artists, groups and songwriters; currently handles 6 acts. Receives 10-35% commission. Reviews material for acts.
How to Contact: Submit demo tape by mail—unsolicited submissions are OK. Prefers cassette (or VHS videocassette of performance if available) with best 3 songs and lyric or lead sheets. If seeking management, include photo, demo tape, bio and repertoire in press kit. SASE. Reports in 6 weeks.
Music: Mostly country, pop and R&B. Works primarily with individual and group recording artists/road acts. Current acts include Just Another Band (country group) and Michael Denton (country crossover solo).
Tips: "Only send your best material, and send it only to *one* company at a time. Make your presentations brief and as described above. Have all your material copyrighted before submitting."

LANDSLIDE MANAGEMENT, 928 Broadway, New York NY 10010. (212)505-7300. Principals: Ted Lehrman and Libby Bush. Management firm and music publisher (KozKeeOzko Music). Estab. 1978. Represents singers, singer/songwriters and actor/singers; currently handles 2 singing acts. Reviews material for acts.
How to Contact: Call or write first to obtain permission to submit."Potential hit singles only." SASE. "Include picture, resume and (if available) ½" videocassette if you're submitting yourself as an act." Reports in 6 weeks.
Music: Dance-oriented, MOR, rock (soft pop), soul, top 40/pop and country/pop. Current acts include Deborah Dotson (soul/pop/jazz), Loretta Valdespino (pop) and Tedd Lawson (songwriter).

LARI-JON PROMOTIONS, Box 216, 325 W. Walnut, Rising City NE 68658. (402)542-2336. Owner: Larry Good. Music publisher (Lari-Jon Publishing Co./BMI) and record company (Lari-Jon Records). "We also promote package shows." Represents individual artists, groups and songwriters; currently handles 5 acts. Receives 15% commission. Reviews material for acts.
How to Contact: Submit demo tape by mail—unsolicited submissions are OK. Prefers cassette with 5 songs and lyric sheet. If seeking management, include 8×10 photos, cassette and bio sheet in press kit. SASE. Reports in 2 months.
Music: Mostly country, gospel and 50s rock. Works primarily with dance bands and show bands. Represents Larry Good (singer/writer), Tommy Campbell (singer/songwriter), Kent Thompson (singer), Nebraskaland 'Opry (family type country show) and Brenda Allen (singer/comedienne).

DAVID LEFKOWITZ MANAGEMENT, 3470 Nineteenth St., San Francisco CA 94110. (415)777-1715. Contact: David Lefkowitz. Management firm. Represents individual artists, groups and songwriters from northern California; currently handles 3 acts. Receives 15-20% commission. Reviews material for acts.
How to Contact: Submit demo tape—unsolicited submissions are OK. Prefers cassette with 3-5 songs and lyric sheet. If seeking management, include cassette with 3-5 songs, lyric sheet, bio and photo in press kit. Does not return unsolicited material. Reports in 1-2 months.
Music: Mostly alternative music, rock, pop and R&B. Works with modern rock bands. Represents Limbomaniacs (funk/rock band), Primus (funk/thrash band) and MCM and the Monster (rap/rock band).

LEMON SQUARE MUSIC, Box 671008, Dallas TX 75367-8008. (214)750-0720. Contact: Bart Barton. Production company. Represents artists, groups and songwriters; currently handles 7 acts. Reviews material for acts.
How to Contact: Query by mail, then submit demo tape. Prefers cassette with 2-4 songs. SASE. Reports in 1 month.
Music: Country and gospel. Works primarily with show bands. Current acts include Dania Presley (country), Freed (progressive country artist), Craig Solieau (comedy act), Audie Henry (progressive country singer), Susie Calvin (gospel) and Billy Parker (traditional country and country gospel).

THE LET US ENTERTAIN YOU CO., Suite 204, 900 19th Ave. S., Nashville TN 37212-2125. (615)321-3100. Administrative Assistant: Corrine. Management firm, booking agency and music publisher (AS-CAP/SESAC/BMI). Estab. 1968. Represents groups and songwriters; currently handles 50-60 acts. Receives 15% commission. Reviews material for acts.
How to Contact: Prefers cassette or videocassette and lyric sheet. Does not return unsolicited material. Reports only if interested.
Music: Mostly country, pop, R&B; also rock and new music. Works with all types of artists/groups/songwriters. Current acts include Everyday People, Tom Grant and Hot Roxx.

PAUL LEVESQUE MANAGEMENT INC., 154 Grande Cote, Rosemere QC J7A 1H3 **Canada.** A&R Director: Michael Todd. Management firm, music publisher and record company (Artiste Records). Estab. 1987. Represents local, regional and international individual artists, groups and songwriters; currently handles 6 acts. Reviews material for acts.
How to Contact: Submit demo tape by mail—unsolicited submissions are OK. Prefers cassette (or VHS/Beta videocassette if available) with 3-6 songs and lyric sheet. "Send photos and bio if possible." SASE. Reports in 1 month.
Music: Mostly rock and pop. Current acts include Paradox (rock band), The Tribes of March (rock band) and Sonya Papp (pop singer/songwriter).

LEVINSON ENTERTAINMENT VENTURES INTERNATIONAL, INC., Suite 650, 1440 Veteran Avenue, Los Angeles CA 90024. (213)460-4545. President: Bob Levinson. Management firm. Estab. 1978. Represents national individual artists, groups and songwriters; currently handles 4 acts. Receives 15-20% commission.

How to Contact: Write first and obtain permission to submit or to arrange personal interview. Prefers cassette (or VHS videocassette) with 6 songs and lead sheet. "Inquire first. Don't expect video to be returned unless SASE included with submission and specific request is made." Does not return unsolicited material. Reports in 6 weeks.
Music: Rock, MOR, R&B and country. Works primarily with rock bands and vocalists.
Tips: "Should be a working band, self-contained and, preferably, performing original material."

*RICK LEVY MGT, 1602 Shenandoah Ct., Allentown PA 18104. (215)398-2686. President: Rick Levy. Management firm, booking agency, music publisher (Flying Governor Music/BMI) and record company (Luxury Records). Estab. 1985. Represents local, regional or international individual artists and groups; currently handles 3 acts. Receives 10-20% commission. Reviews material for acts.
How to Contact: Submit demo tape by mail—unsolicited submissions are OK. Prefers cassette (or VHS videocassette if available) with 3 songs and lyric sheet. SASE. Reports in 1 month.
Music: Mostly R&B (no rap), pop and country. Current acts include Jay & Techniques (60s hit group), Rock Roots (variety-classic rock, rockabilly) and Levy/Stocker (songwriters).
Tips: "In this business, seek out people better and more successful than you. Learn, pick their brains, be positive, take criticism and keep pluggin' no matter what."

LINE-UP PROMOTIONS, INC., 9A, Tankerville Place, Newcastle-Upon-Tyne NE2 3AT **United Kingdom.** Phone: (091)2816449. FAX: (091)212-0913. Director: C.A. Murtagh. Management firm, promotion company, record company (On-Line Records), music publisher (On Line Records & Publishing) and record producer. Represents individual artists, groups and songwriters; currently handles 6-8 acts. Receives 15% commission.
How to Contact: Submit demo tape—unsolicited submissions are OK. Prefers audio cassette (and videocassette if available) and lyric sheet. "Send full press kit, commitments and objective." Does not return unsolicited material. Reports in 1 month. "We're looking for professional acts who can entertain in city centers and unusual situations; e.g., tea dances, supermarkets, metro stations and traditional venues."
Music: Mostly acoustic pop, rock, new world, Afro and reggae; also country, Celtic and English. Works primarily with original groups (not MOR). Current acts include Swimming Pool (fine art rock), Royal Family (post punk exploitative), APU (Andean music), Big Life (country/folk/pop), The Tommy Chase Quartet (swing jazz) and Hank Wangford (country).

LMP MANAGEMENT FIRM, Suite 206, 6245 Bristol Pkwy., Culver City CA 90230. Contact: Larry McGee. Management firm, music publisher (Operation Perfection, Inc.) and record company (Boogie Band Records Corp.). Represents individual artists, groups and songwriters; currently handles 40 acts. Receives 15% commission. Reviews material for acts.
How to Contact: Submit demo tape—unsolicited submissions are OK. Prefers cassette (or videocassette of performance) with 1-4 songs and lead sheet. "Try to perform one or more of your songs on a local TV show. Then obtain a copy of your performance. Please only send professional quality material. Keep it simple and basic." If seeking management, include audio cassette, videocassette, photo and any additional promotional materials in press kit. SASE. Reports in 2 months.
Music: Mostly pop-oriented R&B; also rock and MOR/adult contemporary. Works primarily with professionally choreographed show bands. "Current acts include Sheena-Kriss (self-contained band), Bill Sawyer (showband), En-Tux (vocal group) and Starflower (vocal group).
Tips: "Do research on current commercial marketplace. Take the necessary steps, time, talent and money to present a professional product."

LONG DISTANCE ENTERTAINMENT PRODUCTIONS INC., 6801 Hamilton Ave., Cincinnati OH 45224. (513)522-9999. Vice President: Gary R. Kirves. Booking agency. Estab. 1985. Represents groups; currently handles 25 acts. Receives 15-20% commission. Reviews material for acts.
How to Contact: Submit demo tape by mail—unsolicited submissions are OK. Prefers cassette or videocassette with 2 songs and lyric sheet. If seeking management, include demo tape with 3 songs, video of live performance and photos in press kit. Does not return material. Reports in 1 month.
Music: Mostly rock and pop. Deals with metal to mainstream rock bands. Some top 40. Current acts include The Take, Axis Alley and Strutter (tribute to classic KISS).
Tips: "Send photos with tape so we can get visual about project."

*LOOSE LEAF RECORDS, Suite 472, 1442-A Walnut St., Berkeley CA 94709. (415)337-4353. Manager: Robert Finn. Management firm and record company (Loose Leaf Records). Estab. 1980. Represents Western individual artists and groups; currently handles 4 acts. Receives 15-20% commission. Reviews material for acts.

How to Contact: Submit demo tape by mail—unsolicited submissions are OK. Prefers cassette (or VHS videocassette if available) with 3-4 songs. Does not return unsolicited material. Reports in 4-6 weeks.
Music: Mostly rock (alternative) and folk-rock. Works primarily with dance bands. Current acts include Rabbit Choir, Buzz Feed Back and Sam Bay (all alternative rock).
Tips: "Get a quality marketable product. Sell everything, buy a great tour van, tour like hell. Make a name. Don't stop."

LOWELL AGENCY, 4043 Brookside Ct., Norton OH 44203. (216)825-7813. Contact: Leon Seiter. Booking agency. Estab. 1985. Represents regional (Midwest and Southeast) individual artists; currently handles 3 acts. Receives 10% commission. Reviews material for acts.
How to Contact: Submit demo tape by mail—unsolicited submissions are OK. Prefers cassette with 4 songs and lyric sheet. If seeking management, include demo cassette tape in press kit. SASE. Reports in 1 month.
Music: Mostly country. Works primarily with country vocalists. Current acts include Leon Seiter (country singer/entertainer/songwriter), Ford Nix (bluegrass singer and 5 string banjo picker) and Tom Durden (country singer, co-writer of "Heartbreak Hotel").

RON LUCIANO MUSIC CO., Box 263, Brigantine NJ 08203. (609)266-2623. President: Ron Luciano. Management firm, booking agency and record company (Lucifer Records Inc.). Represents local, regional and international individual artists and groups; currently handles 4 acts. Receives 10-20% commission. Reviews material for acts. "There is a $25 fee for reviewing, due to the heavy amount of mail we receive each week. The fee is good for 1 year on all submissions."
Affiliates: Ciano Publishing and Legz Music.
How to Contact: Submit demo tape by mail—unsolicited submissions are OK. Prefers cassette with 4-8 songs. SASE. Reports in 4 weeks to 3 months.
Music: Mostly oldies, rock and top 40; anything commercial. Current acts include Bobby Fisher (singer/songwriter), Tony Vallo (comedian/songwriter) and Jay and The Techniques (oldies group).

LUSTIG TALENT ENTERPRISES, INC., (formerly Hollander-Lustig Entertainment), Suite 103, 321 Northlake Blvd., N. Palm Beach FL 33408. (407)863-5800. President: Richard Lustig. Booking agency. Estab. 1986. Represents local, regional and international individual artists and groups. Receives 10-20% commission. Reviews material for acts.
How to Contact: Submit demo tape by mail—unsolicited submissions are OK. Prefers cassette or VHS videocassette. If seeking management, include pictures, resume, song list, audio cassette demo tape, and video demo tape in press kit. SASE.
Music: All types. Works primarily with dance bands and disc jockeys. Current acts include Nightfall (band), Tony Mitchell (magician) and Richard Lustig (disc jockey).
Tips: "Have good promo kit. Be easy to work with. Do a professional job for the client."

***RICHARD LUTZ ENTERTAINMENT AGENCY,** 5625 0 St., Lincoln NE 68510. (402)483-2241. General Manager: Cherie Worley. Management firm and booking agency. Estab. 1964. Represents individuals and groups; currently handles 200 acts. Receives 15-20% minimum commission.
How to Contact: Submit demo tape by mail—unsolicited submissions are OK. Prefers cassette (or videocassette) with 5-10 songs "to show style and versatility" and lead sheet. "Send photo, resume, tape, partial song list and include references. Add comedy, conversation, etc., to your videocassette. Do not play songs in full—short versions preferred." If seeking management, include audio cassette and photo in press kit. SASE. Reports in 1 week.
Music: Mostly top 40 and country; also dance-oriented and MOR. Works primarily with bar and dance bands for lounge circuit. "Acts must be uniformed." Current acts include The Partners (variety), Jenny Lynn & The Men (country) and Flim Flam & Chicago Jam (blues/jazz).

MĆ LAVENE & ASSOCIATES, Box 26852, Oklahoma OK 73126. Vice President: S. McCurtis. Management firm, booking agency, music publisher (C.A.B. Independent Publishing Company/BMI) and record company (MśQue Records). Estab. 1988. Represents local, regional and international individual artists, groups and songwriters; currently handles 10 acts. Receives 15-20% commission. Reviews material for acts.
How to Contact: Submit demo tape by mail—unsolicited submissions are OK. Prefers cassette (or VHS videocassette if available) with 3 songs and lead sheet. If seeking management, include professional demo with 3 of your best songs, photo if possible and more background information in press kit. SASE. Reports in 2 months.
Music: Mostly pop, R&B and rock; also jazz and gospel. Works primarily with dance bands and vocalists. Current acts include Magnolia (rock group), Season Gospel Choir (gospel) and Liesure (jazz).

Tips: "We are looking for new artists and songwriters, and we are looking forward to being a stepping stone to the majors."

*THE McDONNELL GROUP, 27 Pickwick Lane, Newtown Square PA 19073. (215)353-8554. Contact: Frank McDonnell. Management firm. Estab. 1985. Represents local, regional or international individual artists, groups and songwriters; currently handles 5 acts. Receives 20-25% commission. Reviews material for acts.
How to Contact: Submit demo tape by mail—unsolicited submissions are OK. Prefers cassette (or VHS videocassette if available) with 4 songs and lyric sheet. SASE. Reports in 4-6 weeks.
Music: Mostly rock, pop and R&B; also country. Current acts include Johnny Bronco (rock group), Mike Forte (producer/songwriter) and Jim Salamone (producer/songwriter/arranger).

*MCFADDEN ARTIST CORPORATION, 818 18th Ave. S., Nashville TN 37203. (615)242-1500. Chairman: Jack McFadden. Management firm and music publisher (Music General Corp.). Represents individual artists and groups; currently handles 12 acts. Reviews material for acts.
How to Contact: Prefers cassette with 3-4 songs and lyric sheet. Does not return unsolicited material. Reports as soon as possible.
Music: Mostly country, country rock and pop/black. Current acts include Buck Owens, Gene Watson, Ken Meeker, DeAna Cox, Billy Ray Cyrus, Eddy Raven, Daryl Pillow, Paul Pace and Jim Collins.

*MAGIANˢᵐ (a div. of Universal World Unlimited, Inc.), 6733 Rhode Island Dr., E., Jacksonville FL 32209. (904)764-3685. Founder & President: Morris King, Jr.. Management firm. Estab. 1985. Represents local, regional and international individual artists, groups, songwriters and producers; currently handles 3 acts. Receives negotiable commission. Reviews material for acts.
How to Contact: Submit demo tape by mail—unsolicited submissions are OK. Prefers cassette (or VHS videocassette if available) with 3-5 songs and lyric sheet. SASE. Reports in 2 weeks.
Music: Mostly pop, R&B and jazz; also rock, gospel and country. Works primarily with vocalists, message rappers, top 40 bands. Current acts include Raap Mr. Jhaaeˢᵐ (message rapper/writer), Vedia (vocalist/songwriter) and Just Twoˢᵐ (vocal duo).
Tips: "Do not approach MAGIANˢᵐ if your are not dedicated, patient, and if you are looking for a miracle."

MAGIC MANAGEMENT AND PRODUCTIONS, 178-49 131st Ave., Jamaica NY 11434. (718)949-0349. General Manager: Bryan P. Sanders. Management firm, booking agency and concert productions firm. Estab. 1987. Represents regional (New York tri-state) individual artists, groups and disc-jockeys; currently handles 12 acts. Receives 20% commission. Reviews material for acts.
How to Contact: Write first and obtain permission to submit. Prefers cassette (or VHS videocassette if available) with minimum of 2 songs and lyric sheet. "Be natural and relaxed. Tape of a song should be no longer than 5-6 minutes in length. Performance length (VHS) no longer than 20 minutes and 4 songs." SASE. Reports in 1-2 months.
Music: Mostly R&B, "Crossover Club Music" and rap; also "club DJ mixes," gospel and jazz. Works primarily with dance bands, vocalists and disc-jockeys. Current acts include K-Nice Productions (disc jockey/dancers), The Wonder Ones aka T.W.O. (rappers) and Majique (jazz/R&B band).
Tips: "Keep in mind that it's not necessarily the size of the company but what that company can do for you that makes the difference."

MAGNUM MUSIC CORPORATION LTD., 8607-128 Avenue, Edmonton Alberta **Canada** T5E 0G3. (403)476-8230. FAX: (403)472-2584 Manager: Bill Maxim. Booking agency, music publisher (Ramblin' Man Music Publishing/PRO, High River Music Publishing/ASCAP) and record company (Magnum Records). Estab. 1984. Represents international individual artists, groups and songwriters; currently handles 4 acts. Reviews material for acts.
How to Contact: Write first and obtain permission to submit. Prefers cassette with 3-4 songs. If seeking management, include photo and bio in press kit. SASE. Reports in 1 month.
Music: Mostly country and gospel. Works primarily with "artists or groups who are also songwriters." Current acts include Catheryne Greenly (country), Thea Anderson (country) and Nolan Murray (country).
Tips: "Prefers finished demos."

Listings of companies in countries other than the U.S. have the name of the country in boldface type.

MAJESTIC PRODUCTIONS, Box 330-568, Brooklyn NY 11233-0016. (718)919-2013. A&R: Hank Love or Alemo. Management firm and record company (Majestic Control Records). Estab. 1983. Represents international individual artists and groups; currently handles 3 acts. Reviews material for acts.
How to Contact: Submit demo tape by mail—unsolicited submissions are OK. Prefers cassette (or VHS videocassette) with 2 songs. SASE. Reports in 2 months.
Music: Mostly rap, urban, hip-house, R&B and reggae. Current acts include rap groups, solo artists and urban dance groups.

*MANAGEMENT ASSOCIATES, 1920 Benson Ave., St. Paul MN 55116. (612)699-1155. FAX: (612)699-1536. Managers: David Fish or Dan Hexter. Management firm. Represents international individual artists and groups; currently handles 4 acts. Commission varies. Reviews material for acts.
How to Contact: Submit demo tape by mail—unsolicited submissions are OK. Prefers cassette (or VHS-NTSC videocassette if available) with 1-4 songs and lyric sheet. SASE.
Music: Mostly R&B, country and pop; also contemporary R&B artists/groups and country artists. Current clients include The Commodores, Debra Laws, Charley Pride and Neal McCoy.

RICK MARTIN PRODUCTIONS, 125 Fieldpoint Road, Greenwich CT 06830. (203)661-1615. President: Rick Martin. Personal manager and independent producer. Holds the Office of Secretary of the National Conference of Personal Managers. Represents groups, artists/songwriters, actresses/vocalists. Currently handles 5 acts. Receives 15-25% commission. "Occasionally, we are hired as consultants, production assistants or producers of recording projects." Reviews material for acts.
How to Contact: Submit demo tape by mail—unsolicited submissions are OK. Prefers cassette (or VHS videocassette) with 2-4 songs. "Don't worry about an expensive presentation to personal managers or producers; they'll make it professional if they get involved." Artists should enclose a photo. "We prefer serious individuals who will give it all they have for a music career."
Music: Mostly top 40, rock and dance; also easy listening and pop. Produces rock dance groups, female vocalists, songwriters and actress/vocalists (pop). Current acts include Babe Marisa Mercedes (vocalist/pianist/songwriter), Sabel (actress/vocalist), Robert and Steven Capellan (songwriters/vocalists) and the Rivera Sisters (vocalists).
Tips: "The tape does not have to be professionally produced—it's really not important what you've done—it's what you can do now that counts."

MASTER TALENT, 245 Maple Ave. W., Vienna VA 22180. (703)281-2800. Owner/Agent: Steve Forssell. Booking agency. Estab. 1989. Represents local and regional (mid-Atlantic) individual artists and groups; currently handles 4 acts. Receives 10-20% commission.
How to Contact: Submit demo tape—unsolicited submissions are OK. Prefers cassette (or VHS/ Beta videocassette) with 4+ songs and lyric or lead sheet. SASE. Reports in 1 month.
Music: Mostly hard rock/metal, progressive/alternative and R&B/dance; also variety/covers. Works primarily with hard rock groups. Current acts include The Excentrics (rock), Company of Wolves (rock), Silence (thrash metal), Danny Blitz (power pop), Blues Saraceno (guitar rock) and Randy Coven (bass instrumental rock).
Tips: "Submit only best work when it's *ready*. We're looking for professionally managed groups/artists with good publicist/promotion. Product in market is a plus."

*PHIL MAYO & COMPANY, Box 304, Bomoseen VT 05732. (802)468-5011. President: Phil Mayo. Management firm and record company (Thrust Records). Estab. 1981. Represents international individual artists, groups and songwriters. Receives 20% commission.
How to Contact: Submit demo tape by mail—unsolicited submissions are OK. Prefers cassette (or VHS videocassette) with 3 songs and lyric or lead sheet. If seeking management, include bio, photo and lyric sheet in press kit. SASE. Reports in 3-5 weeks.
Music: Mostly rock, pop and R&B; also gospel. Works primarily with dance bands, vocalists, rock acts. Current acts include The Drive (R&B act).

*MC PROMOTIONS & PUBLIC RELATIONS, 8504 Willis Ave. #6, Panorama City CA 91402. (818)892-1741. Promotes local country artists. Receives 10% commission. Reviews material for acts.
How to Contact: Submit demo tape by mail—unsolicited submissions are OK. Prefers cassette (or videocassette). If seeking management, include videocassette or cassette demo with bio and picture in press kit. Does not return material. Reports in 3 weeks.
Music: Mostly country. Works primarily with vocalists. Current acts include Diana Blair (singer/ songwriter) and Dawna Kay (singer/songwriter).

MCI MUSIC GROUP, Suite 830, 10 Universal Plaza, Universal CA 91608. (818)506-8533. Director: Max Diamond. Management firm, music publisher (Kellijai and Pollyann Music/ASCAP, Janikki Songs, Branmar Songs/BMI and Lonnvaness Music/SESAC) and record company (PPL, Bouvier, Credence

Records). Estab. 1979. Represents local, regional and international individual artists, groups and songwriters; currently handles 15 acts. Receives 25% commission. Reviews material for acts.
How to Contact: Submit demo tape—unsolicited submissions are OK. Prefers cassette (or videocassette of performance) with no more than 4 songs and lyric or lead sheets. SASE. Reports in 6 weeks.
Music: Mostly R&B, pop and dance. Current acts include I.B. Fynne, Lejenz, D.M. Groove, Phuntaine, The Band AKA, Katrina Gibson and Yvette Craddock.

*MEIER TALENT AGENCY, 511 W. 3rd St., Hazleton PA 18201. (717)454-8767. Owner: Harry Meier. Booking agency. Estab. 1972. Represents local, regional or international individual artists and groups; currently handles 12 acts. Receives 15% commission. Reviews material for acts.
How to Contact: Submit demo tape by mail—unsolicited submissions are OK. Prefers cassette (or VHS videocassette if available) with 3-5 songs. Does not return unsolicited material. Reports in 1 week.
Music: Mostly pop-top 40, oldies and country. Works primarily with hi-tech, dance-oriented duos. Current acts include Clique (top 40 duo), Greg Palmer (vocalist); and Fifth Avenue (duo-dance).

*M-80 MANAGEMENT CO., 5214 Western Blvd., Raleigh NC 27606. (919)851-5083. Contact: Dick Hodgin. Management firm. Estab. 1985. Represents local, regional or international individual artists and groups; currently handles 3 acts. Receives 15% commission. Reviews material for acts.
How to Contact: Submit demo tape by mail—unsolicited submissions are OK. Prefers cassette with 3 songs. SASE. Reports in 2 weeks.
Music: Mostly rock. Current acts include The Accelerators, The Flat Duo Jets and Johnny Quest.

ALEX MELLON MANAGEMENT, Box 614, New Kensington PA 15068. (412)335-5152. President: Alex Mellon. Estab. 1978. Represents individual artists, groups and songwriters; currently handles 3 acts. Receives 20% commission. Reviews material for acts.
How to Contact: Submit demo tape by mail—unsolicited submissions are OK. Prefers cassette or videocassette with 3-4 songs. "Video is almost a must. Everyone I deal with wants to 'see' the act." SASE. If seeking management, include all press clippings, a photo, brief bio and a good quality demo in press kit. Reports in 1 month.
Music: Mostly pop, rock and country. Works primarily with pop acts and songwriters. Current acts include Shilly Shally (pop act), Stan Xidas (producer/songwriter) and The Works (pop-rock).

*MERRI-WEBB PRODUCTIONS, Box 5474, Stockton CA 95205. (209)948-8186. President: Nancy L. Merrihew. Management firm, music publisher (Kaupp's & Robert Publishing Co./BMI), record company (Kaupp Records). Represents regional (California) individual artists, groups and songwriters; currently handles 14 acts. Receives 10-15% commission. Reviews material for acts.
How to Contact: Write or call first and obtain permission to submit. Prefers cassette (or VHS videocassette if available) with 3 songs maximum and lyric sheet. SASE. Reports in 1 month.
Music: Mostly country, A/C rock, R&B; also pop, rock and gospel. Works primarily with vocalists, dance bands and songwriters. Current acts include Rick Webb (singer/songwriter), Gary Epps (singer/songwriter) and Stephen Bruce (singer/songwriter).
Tips: "Know what you want, set a goal, focus in on your goals, be open to constructive criticism, polish tunes and keep polishing."

JOSEPH C. MESSINA, CARTOON RECORDS, INC., 424 Mamaroneck Avenue, Mamaroneck NY 10543. (914)381-2565. Attorney/Manager. Represents artists, groups, songwriters, movie directors and screen writers; currently handles 3 acts. Receives negotiable commission.
How To Contact: Prefers cassette with 1-2 songs and lead sheet. Does not return unsolicited material.
Music: Works primarily with male and female vocal/dance. Current acts include Andrea (top 40 dance).

*METROPOLITAN TALENT AUTHORITY, 109 Earle Ave., Lynbrook NY 11563. (516)599-4157. President: J.C. Management firm and consultants. Estab. 1985. Represents local and international individual artists, groups and songwriters; currently handles 1 act. Receives 15-25% commission. Reviews material for acts.
How to Contact: Submit demo tape by mail—unsolicited submissions are OK. Prefers cassette and lyric sheet. If seeking management, include cassette tape of best songs, 8× 10 pictures, bio, press, radio play lists and VHS video in press kit. SASE. Reports in 4-5 weeks.
Music: Mostly rock, nu-music and pop/rock/dance; also R&B, rap and hard rock. Works primarily with bands, songwriters, producers. Current acts include Pleasure Chamber, Fighter Town and Oh Boy.

Tips: "We want quality artists with originality, vision and distinctive lead vocal. Imaginative—intelligent lyrics, memorable hooks and melodies. Also, artists must look great, present themselves well and have a positive image through their music and look."

M-5 MANAGEMENT, INC., 23 SE 4th St., Minneapolis MN 55414. (612)331-3222. President: Micah McFarlane. Management firm. Estab. 1988. Represents Midwest groups; currently handles 2 acts. Receives 15% commission. Reviews material for acts.
How to Contact: Write or call first and obtain permission to submit. Prefers cassette or VHS videocassette with 3 songs and lyric sheet. If seeking management, include lyric sheet, glossy photo and bio in press kit. SASE. Reports in 1 month.
Music: Mostly pop, reggae and rock; also R&B and gospel. Works primarily with pop and reggae groups. Current acts include Ipso Facto (rock/reggae), Julitta McFarlane (R&B/reggae) and Monte Moir.
Tips: "Make sure songs are complete in structure."

*MIDCOAST, INC., 1002 Jones Rd., Hendersonville TN 37075. (615)264-3896. Managing Director: Bruce Andrew Bossert. Management firm and music publisher (MidCoast, Inc./BMI). Estab. 1984. Represents individual artists, groups and songwriters; currently handles 3 acts. Reviews material for acts.
How to Contact: Submit demo tape—unsolicited submissions are OK. Prefers cassette (or VHS videocassette) or 7½ ips reel-to-reel with 2-4 songs and lyric sheet. If seeking management, include "short" bio, tape, photo and announcements of any performances in Nashville area in press kit. SASE. Reports in 6 weeks if interested.
Music: Mostly rock, pop and country. Works primarily with original rock and country bands and artists. Current acts include Ghost Money (rock), Cinema (rock) and Lee Owens (singer/songwriter).
Tips: "We need good songs and good voices."

*MID-EAST ENTERTAINMENT INC., Suite 200, 553 S. Limestone, Lexington KY 40508. (606)254-3327. Agent: Robert Moser. Represents artists and groups; currently handles over 300 acts. Receives 10-20% commission. Reviews material for acts.
How to Contact: Submit demo tape by mail—unsolicited submissions are OK. Prefers cassette with 3-6 songs, photo and songlist. Songs should have 1 verse, 1 bridge and 1 chorus. If seeking management, include tape, photo and play list in press kit. SASE. Reports in 6 months.
Music: Mostly top 40 and R&B; also country, dance-oriented, easy listening, jazz, rock, soul and pop. Works primarily with dance bands. Current acts include Paradox (top 40/rock), The Sensations (top 40/classics), Duos (top 40/oldies), Hawkeye (50's-80's dance), City Heat (top 40/classics) and Nervous Melvin (college rock).

THE GILBERT MILLER AGENCY, INC., Suite 243, 21243 Ventura Blvd., Woodland Hills CA 91364. (818)377-5900. Agent: Jeff Miller. Booking agency. Represents musical and variety/novelty acts; currently handles 4 bands. Receives 15% commission. Reviews material for acts.
How to Contact: Prefers record, CD or cassette on a record label, 8x10 photo. "MTV-quality videos accepted. Will only call if song or group is accepted. Accepted groups will be notified in 1 month. No kits will be returned." If seeking management, include current CD with 100 station airplay list, photo and bio.
Music: Mostly rock. Works primarily with heavy metal hard rock, new wave, nostalgia rock and New Age groups. Current acts include Eric Burdon (classic rock), Greg Wright (hard rock), Midnight Voyeur (hard rock), Terriff (heavy metal), Sick Puppies (jazz/fusion/hard rock), No Mercy (hard rock) and Perfect Stranger (new wave).

MKM MUSIC PRODUCTIONS LTD., Suite 503, 556 Laurier Avenue West, Ottawa, Ontario K1R 7X2 Canada. (613)234-5419. President: Michael Mitchell. Management firm. SOCAN (PROCAN and CAPAC). Estab.1982. Represents individual Canadian artists. Currently handles 3 acts. Receives 20% commission. Review material for acts.
How to Contact: Submit demo tape by mail—unsolicited submissions are OK. Prefers cassette with 3 songs and lyric sheet. If seeking management, include good quality demo tape in press kit. SASE "but only with Canadian postage." Reports in 3 weeks.
Music: Folk and pop. Works with concert folk groups. Current acts include The Michael Mitchell Band (pop/folk), Joan MacIsaac (folk) and Mike Sutton (songwriter).
Tips: "Always interested in new, well written original material."

*MOORE ENTERTAINMENT GROUP, 11 Possum Trail, Saddle River NJ 07458. (201)327-3698. President: Barbara Moore. Estab. 1984. Represents individual artists and groups; currently handles 8 acts. Receives 10% commission. Reviews material for acts.

How to Contact: Submit demo tape by mail—unsolicited submissions are OK. Prefers cassette (or videocassette if available) and lyric sheet. "Include photo and bio." If seeking management, include tape, photo and bio in press kit. SASE. Reports in 3 weeks.
Music: Mostly dance, rock, R&B and pop. Works primarily with vocalists. Current acts include Mike Giorgio (rock/pop), Lou Taylor (dance/rock), Mike Tyler (R&B), Paradise (dance/R&B), Angela Warren (A/C), Andrew Martin (New Age) and Antongne (dance/pop).

MORSE ENTERTAINMENT GROUP, INC., Box 6980, Beverly Hills CA 90212. (213)276-9261. Contacts: Adam Sandler, Mark Adams, Eric Ross, Cathy Gooden. Management firm and record company (Litigous Records). Estab. 1982. Represents local, regional and international individual artists, groups and songwriters; currently handles 6 acts. Receives 15% commission. Reviews material for acts.
How to Contact: Submit demo tape by mail—unsolicited submissions are OK. Prefers cassette with 3-5 songs and lyric sheet. SASE. Reports in 2 weeks.
Music: Mostly rock and pop. Works primarily with solo artists, rock acts, and groups and artists who are hyphenates; i.e. singer-songwriter-producer. Current acts include Aviators (rock band) and Kilowatt (rock band).
Tips: "Send us your best stuff—don't ask us to hear through a lousy mix or unfinished demos—put your best foot forward."

MOZART MIDNIGHT PRODUCTIONS, Suite 613, 410 S. Michigan Ave., Chicago IL 60605. (708)739-4577. President: Don Kaufman. Management firm. Estab. 1982. Represents international individual artists, groups and songwriters; currently handles 6 acts. Receives 20% commission. Reviews material for acts.
How to Contact: Submit demo tape by mail—unsolicited submissions are OK. Prefers cassette with 3-10 songs and photo. Does not return unsolicited material. Reports back only if interested.
Music: Mostly dance-pop, light rock and R&B; also metal, ballads and rap. Works primarily with singer/songwriters. Current acts include Kevin Irving (lead singer of Club Nouveau), Darcsyde (rap group), Tribal Opera (progressive rock group) and Jeannie Withrow (pop rock singer/songwriter).

MUSIC MANAGEMENT ASSOCIATES, A Sound Column Company, Suite 258, 42 Music Square W., Nashville TN 37203. (615)244-4331. President: Ron Simpson. Estab. 1991. Management company, affiliated with Sound Column Productions. Represents individual artists, bands and songwriters. "Our specialty is helping our clients take the "significant next step," i.e. market focus, material selection, demo recordings, image/photos, contacting industry on artist's behalf, etc. Various fee structures include commission, project bid, hourly rate. We can sometimes secure third party financing to develope unique, exciting artists."
How to Contact: Submit demo tape by mail—unsolicited submissions are OK. Should include cassette, VHS video (optional), photos. No returned materials or correspondence without SASE and sufficient postage. "No phone calls, please."
Music: All styles except metal, rap. Current artists include Janine Lindsay and Gary Voorhees (contemporary Christian recording artists), and Shawn Kay (pop recording artist).

MUSIC, MARKETING & PROMOTIONS, INC., Box 22, South Holland IL 60473. (219)365-2516. President: Michael Haines. Management firm. Estab. 1987. Represents international individual artists, groups and songwriters; currently handles 3 acts. Receives 15-20% commission. Reviews material for acts.
How to Contact: Submit demo tape by mail—unsolicited submissions are OK. Prefers cassette (or VHS videocassette if available) with 3-4 songs and lyric sheet. If seeking management, include bio, picture and demo tape or video in press kit. SASE. Reports in 3 weeks.
Music: Mostly rock, country and pop; also R&B. Works primarily with pop/rock bands, solo artists and songwriters. Current acts include Rick Airiab (jazz/pop writer), Rick Anthony (country songwriter) and Face of Luxury (pop/rock band).
Tips: "Send clear demos. We're most interested in the song, not the production, but it must be audible."

*MUSIC MATTERS, Box 3773, San Rafael CA 94912-3773. (415)457-0700. Management firm. Estab. 1990. Represents local, regional or international individual artists, groups and songwriters; currently handles 2 acts. Receives 15% commission. Reviews material for acts.
How to Contact: Submit demo tape by mail—unsolicited submissions are OK. Prefers cassette (or VHS videocassette if available) with lyric sheet. Does not return unsolicited material.
Music: Mostly rock, blues and pop; also jazz and R&B. Works primarily with songwriting performers/bands (rock). Current acts include Canned Heat (rock/blues group) and Olivia Rosestone (singer/songwriter).

*MUSICMATTERS!, 9233 Gloxinia, San Antonio TX 78218. (512)651-6939. Manager: Jean Estes. Management firm. Represents local, regional and international individual artists, groups and songwriters; currently handles 5 acts. Reviews material for acts.
How to Contact: Write or call first and obtain permission to submit. Prefers cassette (or VHS videocassette if available) with 3 songs. Does not return unsolicited material. Reports in 6 weeks.
Music: Mostly jazz. Current acts include Mike Brannon (jazz guitarist/songwriter), True Diversity (jazz group) and Manhattan Latin.

MUSKRAT PRODUCTIONS, INC., 44 N. Central Ave., Elmsford NY 10523. (914)592-3144. Contact: Bruce McNichols. Estab. 1970. Represents individuals and groups; currently represents 15 acts. Deals with artists in the New York City area. Reviews material for acts.
How to Contact: Write first. Prefers cassette (or short videocassette of performance) with 3 songs minimum. SASE. Reports "only if interested."
Music: "We specialize in old-time jazz, dixieland and banjo music and show," also old time, nostalgia, country and jazz. Works primarily with dixieland, banjo/sing-along groups to play parties, Mexican mariachi bands and specialty acts for theme parties, dances, shows and conventions. Current acts include Smith Street Society Jazz Band (dixieland jazz), Your Father's Mustache (banjo sing-along), Roaring 20s Revue (show and dance band) and Harry Hepcat and the Boogie Woogie Band (50s rock revival).

*N&M ENTERTAINMENT AGENCY, Box 19242, Johnston RI 02919. (401)944-6823. President: Raymond A. Dimiccio. Management firm and booking agency. Estab. 1971. Represents local, regional or international individual artists, groups and songwriters; currently handles 38 acts. Receives 15% commission. Reviews material for acts.
How to Contact: Submit demo tape by mail—unsolicited submissions are OK. Prefers cassette with 3 songs and lyric or lead sheets. SASE. Reports in 3-4 weeks.
Music: Mostly R&B, pop and rock; also top 40 dance/punk.

FRANK NANOIA PRODUCTIONS AND MANAGEMENT, 1999 N. Sycamore Ave., Los Angeles CA 90068. (213)874-8725. President: Frank Nanoia. Management and production firm. Represents artists, groups and songwriters. Produces TV specials and concerts. Currently handles 15 acts. Receives 15-25% commission. Reviews material for acts.
How to Contact: Prefers 7½, 15 ips reel-to-reel or cassette (or videocassette of live performance, if available) with 3-5 songs and lyric and lead sheets. "Professional quality please. Check sound quality as well." Does not return unsolicited material. Reports "only if material is above average. No phone calls please."
Music: Mostly R&B and dance, also top 40/pop, jazz fusion, country, easy listening, MOR, gospel and soul. Works primarily with soloists, Latin jazz and R&B groups. Current acts include Marc Allen Trujillo (vocalist/songwriter); Paramour (R&B show group), and Gilberto Duron (recoring artist). Current productions include "The Golden Eagle Awards," The Caribbean Musical Festival and "The Joffrey Ballet/CSU Awards."

*NASH ANGELES INC., Box 363, Hendersonville TN 37077. (615)824-8845. Manager: Wilson Frazier. Management firm and music publisher (BMI). Represents individual artists, groups and songwriters; currently handles 1 act. Receives 25% commission. Reviews material for acts.
How to Contact: Prefers cassette (or videocassette) with lyric sheet. Does not return unsolicited material. Reports in 1 month.
Music: Mostly country-pop, AOR, country and pop; also rock. Works primarily with vocalists. Current act is Eddie Reasoner (singer/songwriter).

NATIONAL ENTERTAINMENT, INC., Suite 6, 5366 N., Northwest Hwy., Chicago IL 60630. (312)545-8222. FAX: (312)545-3714. President/General Manager: Roger Connelly. Management firm and booking agency. Estab. 1989. Represents local, regional and international individual artists, groups and songwriters; currently handles 100 acts. Receives 15% commission. Reviews material for acts.
How to Contact: Write or call first and obtain permission to submit. Prefers cassette (or VHS videocassette if available) with 1 song and lyric sheet. If seeking management, include cassette audio or videotape (VHS) for each song and lyric sheets in press kit. SASE. Reports in 2 weeks.
Music: Mostly pop, rock and R&B. Works primarily with dance bands, singers and singer/songwriters. Current acts include Dave Pisciotto (guitarist/songwriter), Dynasty (8 piece dance band) and Ivory (5 piece dance band).
Tips: "Your promotional package is our only representation of your talent. Be prepared to take the necessary steps to organize your materials into a professional presentation."

*NEKO ENTERTAINMENT & MUSIC MANAGEMENT CO., Suite 2-SW, 14225 Union, Riverdale IL 60627. (708)201-7676. FAX: (708)201-7674. Marketing Agent: A.W. Bolden. Management firm. Estab. 1990. Represents regional artists (Midwest USA) and individual artists and groups from Jamaica, songwriters, seminars, recitals and workshops; currently handles 6 acts. Receives 20% commission. Reviews material for acts.
How to Contact: Write or call first to arrange personal interview. Prefers cassette (or VHS videocassette if available) with at least 3 songs and lyric or lead sheets. Does not return unsolicited material. Reports in 6 weeks.
Music: Mostly classical, jazz, gospel; also R&B, rock and rap. Works primarily with vocalists who also write, bands who perform and read, composers. Current acts include A Classic Act®, Sharon and Karen Lee, Rapresentatives®, TWO Much®, Contrary Motion® and Moor Intelligence®.
Tips: "Understand the function and value of representation. Learn the industry. Do not trust anyone who guarantees 'pie in the sky.' Make a reasonable schedule to reach your goals, and don't give a time limit. Remember, Michael Jackson and Prince were not built in a day!"

*JACK NELSON & ASSOCIATES, 5800 Valley Oak Dr., Los Angeles CA 90068. (213)465-9905. Assistant: Shawn Brogan. Management firm. Estab. 1981. Represents local, regional or international individual artists, groups and songwriters; currently handles 6 acts. Receives 15% commission. Reviews material for acts.
How to Contact: Call first and obtain permission to submit. Prefers cassette (or videocassette if available) with 2-4 songs and lyric sheets. If seeking management, include quality demo, lyric sheet and bio in press kit. SASE. Reports in 1 month.
Music: Currents acts include Jeffrey Osborne, Kathy Sledge, Bryan Ioun, Randy Ran and Joey Diggs.

NELSON MANAGEMENT, Francisco de Rojas, 9, Madrid 28010 **Spain**. Phone: (1)445 12 07. Director: Nelson Hernán Muñoz. Management firm, booking agency and music publisher. Estab. 1980. Represents individual artists, groups and songwriters; currently handles 20 acts. Receives 20% commission. Reviews material for acts.
How to Contact: Write first and obtain permission to submit or to arrange personal interview. Prefers cassette (or VHS/PAL videocassette if available) with 5 songs and lyric or lead sheets. Does not return unsolicited material. Reports in 3 weeks.
Music: Mostly jazz, fusion and ethnic music. Works primarily with show bands, vocalists, musicians and songwriters. Current acts include Javier Mora (jazz fusion), Edardo LaGuillo (new age) and Pedro Ample (songwriter/singer).
Tips: "Send us professional samples of your work with the conditions of the type of deal you are looking for."

*NEXT MILLENNIUM, LTD., Box 507, Lenox Hill Station, New York NY 10021. (212)879-9483. President: Joe Lo Cicero. Management firm. Estab. 1989. Represents local and Northeast individual artists and groups.
How to Contact: Submit demo tape by mail—unsolicited submissions are OK. Prefers cassette (or VHS videocassette) with 3 songs and lyric sheet. Does not return unsolicited material. Reports in 3 months.
Music: Mostly rock and dance. Current acts include The Panic Club (alternative/dance group) and Randi Robics (children's exercise program).

NORTHSTAR MANAGEMENT INC., 33532 Five Mile Rd., Livonia MI 48154. (313)427-6010. President: Angel Gomez. Management firm. Estab. 1979. Represents local and international individual artists, groups and songwriters; currently handles 4 acts. Receives 10-25% commission. Reviews material for acts.
How to Contact: Prefers cassette (or videocassette of performance) with 3-5 songs. SASE. Reports in 4 weeks.
Music: Mostly rock, pop and top 40; also metal. Works primarily with individual artists, groups (bar bands) and songwriters. Current acts include Think Pink (new music), Billy the Kid (rock), Controversy (Top-40), Hunter Brucks (rock), Reckless Youth (rock) and Art Reed (rock).
Tips: "Think about what you're sending. Are you proud? If so, send it!"

CRAIG NOWAG'S NATIONAL ATTRACTIONS, 6037 Haddington Drive, Memphis TN 38119-7423. (901)767-1990. Owner/President: Craig Nowag. Booking agency. Estab. 1958. Represents local, regional and international individual artists and groups; currently handles 37 acts. Receives 15-25% commission.
How to Contact: Submit demo tape by mail—unsolicited submissions are OK. Prefers cassette (or VHS videocassette if available) with 3-5 songs. Does not return unsolicited material. Reports in 5 weeks.

Music: Mostly R&B, pop and blues; also pop/rock, crossover country and re-makes. Works primarily with oldies record acts, dance bands, blues bands, rock groups, R&B dance bands and nostalgia groups. Current acts include Andy Childs (pop), Johnny Tillotson and The Famous Unknowns and The Coasters.

Tips: "If the buying public won't buy your song, live act or record you have no saleability, and no agent or manager can do anything for you."

N2D, Box 121682, Nashville TN 37212-1682. Contact: Douglas Casmus. Management firm and publisher (Breezeway Publishing Companies). Represents artists, groups, songwriters and comedians; currently handles 2 acts. Reviews material for acts.

How to Contact: Prefers cassette with 2 songs and lyric sheet. Does not return material. Reports only if interested.

Music: Country, rock and comedy. Current acts include David Murphy and Johnny Cobb (rock). "We've had songs recorded by Julio Iglesias, Ray Charles, John Denver, John Conlee, Dobie Gray and more."

Tips: "Looking for great songs—any format. Also open to crazy and novelty material."

OAK STREET MUSIC, 108-93 Lombard Ave., Winnipeg, Manitoba R3B 3B1 **Canada.** Phone: (204)957-0085. FAX: (204)943-3588. CEO: Gilles Paquin. Record label and music publisher. Estab. 1987. Roster includes performers, songwriters and musicians; currently handles 12 acts. Sister company, Paquin Entertainment Group, heads up the artist management division.

How to Contact: Submit demo tape by mail—unsolicited submissions are OK. Prefers cassette (or VHS videocassette if available) with maximum 4 songs and lyric or lead sheet. "Something which shows the artist's capabilities—doesn't need to be fancy. Be *factual*." SASE.

Music: Primarily a family entertainment label, with interest also in the pop/rock genres. Current acts include Fred Penner (children's entertainer) and Al Simmons (singer/actor/comic).

OB-1 ENTERTAINMENT, Box 22552, Nashville TN 37202. (615)672-0307. Partner-in-charge: Jim O'Baid. Management firm and artist development. Estab. 1990. Represents local, regional and international individual artists, groups and songwriters; currently handles 2 acts. Receives 10-20% commission. Reviews material for acts.

How to Contact: Submit demo tape by mail—unsolicited submissions are OK. Prefers cassette (or VHS videocassette if available) with 3 songs. If seeking management, include cassette with 3 songs, 8×10 photo, bio and video cassette (if possible) in press kit. Does not return unsolicited material. SASE must accompany all other submissions. Reports in 2 months.

Music: Mostly country, pop and R&B; also rock. Works primarily with singer/songwriters and groups. Current acts include John and Lisa Stroud (country duet), The Tanaro Sisters (country duet) and Casey Rockefeller (singer/songwriter).

Tips: "Keep your ego in place. Be able to accept criticism."

ON THE LEVEL MUSIC!, 807 South Xanthus Pl., Tulsa OK 74104-3620. President: Fred Gage. Management firm and booking agency. Estab. 1971. Represents individual artists, groups and songwriters; currently handles 12 acts. Receives 15-25% commission. Reviews material for acts.

How to Contact: Submit demo tape by mail—unsolicited submissions are OK. Prefers cassette (or VHS videocassette if available) with 4 songs and lyric or lead sheets. For video: "Full length not needed, short clips only." If seeking management, include picture, 4-song demo (video if possible) and short bio in press kit. SASE. Reports in 1 month.

Music: Mostly rock, pop and gospel. Works primarily with rock groups. Current acts include Second Chapter of Acts (Christian rock), Allan Bradley (rock) and Toymakers Dream (Broadway type).

Tips: "Be great not just good and be hungry to make it."

ON TOUR PRODUCTIONS, 4600 Iris St., Rockville MD 20853. (301)946-9093. President A&R: Dana Sharpe. Management firm, booking agency and promotion agency. Estab. 1989. Represents national individual artists and groups; currently handles 25 acts. Receives 15% commission. Reviews material for acts.

How to Contact: Submit demo tape by mail—unsolicited submissions are OK. Prefers cassette or VHS videocassette with 3 songs and lyric sheet. SASE. Reports in 1 month.

Music: Mostly rock, progressive and metal; also any rock styles and punk/hardcore. Current acts include Backseat Driver (hard rock), Monalisa (metal/rock) and Bedlam (metal).

Tips: "Be brief but to the point. Long-winded demo packs and full EP cassettes are a pain. What I need is a tape, photo, history or bio (once again, be brief), song list (include covers) and employment history (in music)."

*ONSTAGE MANAGEMENT GROUP, 143 Kelly Rd., Bastrop TX 78602. (512)321-4777. Owner: Jack Yoder. Management firm and booking agency. Represents local, regional or international individual artists and groups; currently handles 3 acts. Receives 15-25% commission. Reviews material for acts.
How to Contact: Write or call first and obtain permission to submit. Prefers cassette (or VHS videocassette if available) with 3 songs. Does not return unsolicited material. Reports in 3 months.
Music: Mostly country and rock. Works primarily with vocalists and/or groups. Current acts include Peter Tork, K.C. & Sunshine Band and Davy Jones.

*ONTARIO BLUEGRASS INC., 64 Market St., Brockport NY 14420. (716)637-2040. President: Paul Pickard. Booking agency. Estab. 1984. Represents local and regional groups; currently handles 1 group. Receives 20% commission. Reviews material for acts.
How to Contact: Write or call first and obtain permission to submit. Prefers cassette with 6 songs. Does not return unsolicited material. Reports in 2 weeks.
Music: Strictly gospel. Current acts include Pickard Brothers.

OPERATION MUSIC ENTERPRISES, 1400 E. Court St., Ottumwa IA 52501. (515)682-8283. President: Nada C. Jones. Management firm and booking agency. Represents artists, groups and songwriters; currently handles 4 acts. Receives 15% commission. Reviews material for acts.
How to Contact: Submit demo tape—unsolicited submissions are OK. Prefers cassette (or VHS videocassette if available) and lyric sheet. "Keep material simple. Groups—use *only group* members—don't add extras. Artists should include references. SASE. Reports in 6-8 weeks.
Music: Mostly country; also blues. Works primarily with vocalists and show and dance groups. Current acts include Reesa Kay Jones (country vocalist and recording artist), John Richards Show, Country with Class, Prairie Fire and Larry Gillaspie, the Rocky Mountain White Water Band and White River Country (country/bluegrass).

OREGON MUSICAL ARTISTS, Box 122, Yamhill OR 97148. (503)662-3309. Contact: Michael D. LeClair. Management firm and production agency. Estab. 1982. Represents artists, groups and songwriters; currently handles 3 acts. Receives 10-25% commission. Reviews material for acts.
How to Contact: Submit demo tape by mail—unsolicited submissions are OK. Prefers cassette with 3-10 songs and lyric sheet (or videocasette if available). Does not return unsolicited material. Reports in 1 month.
Music: Mostly top 40/pop and R&B; also blues, church/religious, country, dance, easy listening, gospel, jazz, MOR, progressive, hard and mellow rock and soul. Works primarily with writers and bar bands "with excellent vocalists." Current acts include The Hoyt Brothers (easy country ballads), Lee Garrett (songwriter) and Boomer Band (50's bar band).

*DEE O'REILLY MANAGEMENT, LTD., 112 Gunnersbury Ave., London W54HB **England**. Phone: (01)993-7441. Contact: Carol Wilmot. Management firm, booking agency (Central Booking Agency), music publisher (Orestes Music Publishing, Ltd.) and record company (Orestes Recording Company). Represents individual artists, groups and songwriters; currently handles 18 acts. Receives variable commission. Reviews material for acts.
How to Contact: Submit demo tape—unsolicited submissions are OK. Prefers cassette with 2-3 songs and lyric sheet. SAE and IRC. Reports in 1 month.
Music: Mostly pop and rock; also "special music projects for recording and/or television." Works primarily with pop vocalists and bands. Current acts include Gary Wilmot (actor/singer), David Smart (composer), Bobby Pearce (singer/songwriter), Garry Judd (composer), Hannah Jones (singer) and Ria (singer/composer).

ORIGINAL PROJECTS UNLIMITED, INC., 36 West 3rd Ave., Denver CO 80223. Also Suite 439, 8491 Sunset Blvd., West Hollywood CA 90069. (213)519-3215. (303)722-9653. President: Lauri Day-Workman. Management firm (Original Projects Unlimited, Inc.). Estab. 1986. Represents international groups and producers/engineers; currently handles 4 acts and 2 producers. Receives 15-20% commission.

The asterisk before a listing indicates that the listing is new in this edition. New markets are often the most receptive to unsolicited submissions.

How to Contact: Submit demo tape by mail—unsolicited submissions are OK. Prefers cassette with 3-4 songs, lyric sheet and photo/promotional/package. SASE. Reports in 4-6 weeks.
Music: Mostly rock, metal and pop; also alternative. Works primarily with rock and heavy metal bands; producers/engineers. Current acts include Strange Parade (rock/band), Dogs of Pleasure (rock/band), Geoffrey Workman (producer/engineer), Free the Werewolves (rock band), Logan (rock band) and Gary Wagner (engineer/producer).
Tips: "Must be original, hardworking and professional. Mostly interested in bands that promote themselves, believe in themselves and have some knowledge of the music business. Must be marketable."

OVERLAND PRODUCTIONS, 1775 Broadway, New York NY 10019. (212)489-4820. Managing Director: Andrea Starr. Management firm, music publisher (Mucho Loco Music, Loco de Amor Music), record company (Radioactive) and record producer (Overland Productions Co.). Represents local, regional and international individual artists, groups and songwriters; currently handles 10 acts. Reviews material for acts.
How to Contact: Submit demo tape by mail—unsolicited submissions are OK. Prefers cassette (or VHS videocassette if available) with 3-5 songs and lyric sheet. If seeking management, include a clear demo tape consisting of artist's best works, photos, bios, discography and press releases in press kit. Does not return unsolicited submissions. Reports in 6 weeks.
Music: Mostly rock, pop and R&B; also modern music and dance. Interested in "innovative, intelligent, progressive-rockin." Current acts include David Byrne, Dee-Lite, Ramones, Debbie Harry, Talking Heads, The Toll, B.A.D., Tom Tom Club.
Tips: "Submit 3-5 of best songs—neatly labeled with pix, press bio and video (if available). Listing of any upcoming gigs."

*RICHARD A. PAINTER & ASSOCIATES, Box 738, Ridgetop TN 37152-0738. (615)851-6860; FAX: (615)851-6857. President: Richard Allan Painter. Management firm. Estab. 1984. Represents individual artists, groups and songwriters; currently handles 4 acts. Receives 10-30% commission. Also provides professional Career Development Services for serious (but unmanaged) performers for a fee. Reviews material for acts.
How to Contact: Send SASE for information.
Music: Suited for audiences that appreciate pop, rock, and R&B; such that translates into broad commercial appeal and staying power in the target market. Current acts include Trace Balin, Modern Logic, Color Blind and Bash.
Tips: "Pursue excellence and tell the truth as your only artistic moral imperative. Replicate your studio sound on stage. Embark on an ambitious promotional appearance schedule in support of your released recording(s). I prefer self-contained working acts. Must possess appearance/presence/performance conducive to electronic and print media exposure. I help artists that want to concentrate on the art of music while I handle their business of music. They want their art to come out in performances that my business efforts procure. In accordance with a mutually devised Career Plan, I assemble and direct a Support Team for the artist, comprised of all the necessary professional players who endeavor to support and guide the artist through each step on their road to sustained success."

PAQUIN ENTERTAINMENT GROUP, 108-93 Lombard Ave., Winnipeg MB R3B 3B1 **Canada**. (204)947-9200. Artist Relations: Richard Mills. Management firm and booking agency. Estab. 1984. Represents local, regional and international individual artists; currently handles 3 acts. Reviews material for acts.
How to Contact: Write or call first and obtain permission to submit. Prefers cassette or VHS videocassette with 3 songs and lyric sheet. SASE. Reports in 3 weeks.
Music: Mostly children's music, folk music and comedy; also New Age and classical. Works primarily with family performers. Current acts include Fred Penner (family entertainer/songwriter), Norman Foote (entertainer/songwriter) and Al Simmons (entertainer/songwriter).

*DAVE PATON MANAGEMENT, Suite C-300, 16776 Lakeshore Dr., Lake Elsinore CA 92530. (714)699-9339. Contact: Dave Paton. Management firm and record company (Hollyrock Records). Estab. 1973. Represents local, regional or international individual artists; currently handles 2 acts. Receives 20-25% commission. Reviews material for acts. "Associated with 'Artist Viability Research' placing acts with major labels."
How to Contact: Submit demo tape by mail—unsolicited submissions are OK. Prefers cassette (or VHS videocassette if available) with 4 songs and lyric sheet. SASE. Reports in 1 month.
Music: Mostly country, country/rock and rock; also pop. Works primarily with vocalists. Current acts include Linda Rae (country artist) and Breakheart Pass (country group).

JACKIE PAUL MANAGEMENT AND CONSULTANT FIRM, 559 Wanamaker Rd., Jenkintown PA 19046. (215)884-3308. FAX: (215)884-1083. President: Jackie Paul. Management firm (Terrance Moore Music, Inc./BMI). Estab. 1985. Represents local and national artists, groups, producers and

musicians. Currently handles 2 acts. Receives 15-35% commission. Reviews material for acts.
How to Contact: Call first and obtain permission to submit. Prefers cassette (or VHS videocassette
if available) with 1-3 songs and lyric or lead sheets. "It's not mandatory but if possible, I would prefer
a videocassette. A video simply helps get the song across visually. Do the best to help portray the
image you represent, with whatever resources possible." If seeking management, include no more
than 3 copyrighted songs, photo, bio (short and to the point), video (if possible), contact name,
telephone number and address in press kit. SASE. Reports in 2-4 weeks.
Music: Mostly rap, pop and R&B/dance. Works primarily with vocalists (all original acts). Current
acts include Blue Eagle (pop singer/songwriter, producer/musician) and Terrance T'Luv (R&B-dance
singer/songwriter/producer).

*THE PERCEPTION WORKS INC., Suite F-2, 3390 W. 86th St., Indianapolis IN 46268. (317)876-5776.
President: Lawrence Klein. Management firm. Estab. 1986. Deals with local, regional or international
individual artists and groups; currently handles 8 acts. Receives 10% commission. Reviews material
for acts.
How to Contact: Submit demo tape by mail—unsolicited submissions are OK. Prefers cassette (or
VHS videocassette if available) with 4 songs and lyric sheet. Does not return unsolicited material.
Reports in 6 weeks.
Music: Mostly rock, R&B and pop; also country and blues. Works primarily with rock bands, R&B
bands, blues bands, jazz bands, pop bands. Current acts include Under Fire (5 piece classic rock), 1-
800 (pop 4 picce), Michael Brown Group (5 piece jazz), Spellbound (5 piece rock), The Shades (5
piece blues) and The Bitter Ends (4 piece alternative).

PERFORMERS OF THE WORLD, Suite #215, 14011 Ventura Blvd., Sherman Oaks CA 91423. (818)995-
2475. President: Terry Rindal. Artist Development: Nita Scott. Booking agency. Estab. 1989. Repre-
sents local, regional and international individual artists and groups.
How to Contact: Submit demo tape by mail—unsolicited submissions are OK. Prefers cassette (or
VHS videocassette if available) with several songs and lyric sheet. If seeking management, include
photo, bio, press clippings and recorded material in press kit. Does not return unsolicited material.
Reports in 1 month. "Send SASE or portrait for reply."
Music: Mostly world music, jazz and R&B; also folk and pop. Current acts include David Wilcox (folk
singer/songwriter), Jon Hendricks (jazz singer), Eliza Gilkyson (singer/songwriter), Zachary Richard
(cajun rocker) and Hugh Masekela (South African trumpeter).

*PERSONIFIED MANAGEMENT, Suite 51, 8306 Wilshire Blvd., Beverly Hills CA 90211. (213)960-
5771. Owner: Lamont Patterson. Estab. 1989. Represents local, regional or international individual
artists, groups and songwriters; currently handles 3 acts. Receives 20% commission. Reviews material
for acts.
How to Contact: Submit demo tape by mail—unsolicited submissions are OK. Prefers cassette (or
VHS videocassette if available) with 3 songs and lyric sheet. SASE. Reports in 2 weeks.
Music: Mostly pop, R&B and hip-hop. Works primarily with R&B vocalist/groups, rap acts. Currently
acts include Money Man Ice (rap) and De Emprezz.

PAUL PETERSON CREATIVE MANAGEMENT, #309, 9005 Cynthia, Los Angeles CA 90069. (213)273-
7255. Contact: Paul Peterson. Management firm. Represents artists and groups from the Midwest and
West Coast; currently handles 4 acts. Receives 20% commission. Reviews material for acts.
How to Contact: Submit demo tape by mail—unsolicited submissions are OK. Prefers cassette (or
¾" or VHS videocassette if available) with 2-4 songs and lyric sheet. If seeking management, include
photo, brief bio and touring/recording experience in press kit. Submit demo tape by mail. Unsolicited
submissions are OK. SASE. Reports in 1 month.
Music: Mostly pop/rock and rock; also jazz and alternative rock. Works with rock bands doing original
material. Current acts include Man About Town (pop/rock band), Brian Savage (jazz/New Age), 3
Norwegians (pop/rock), Brewer & Shipley (country/rock) and National Lampoon's Lost Tapes (comedy).

*PHIL'S ENTERTAINMENT AGENCY LIMITED, 889 Smyth Rd., Ottawa Ontario K1G 1P4 **Canada**.
(613)731-8983. President: Phyllis Woodstock. Booking agency. Estab. 1979. Represents artists and
groups; currently handles 50 acts. Receives 10% commission. Reviews material for acts "occasionally."
How to Contact: Submit demo tape by mail—unsolicited submissions are OK. Prefers cassette (or
videocassette) with 4-7 songs. "Be sure the name of artist and date of completion are on the video."
Does not return unsolicited material. Reports in 2-3 weeks.
Music: Mostly country; also country/rock, MOR and old rock 'n' roll. "We work with show bands,
male and female vocalists, bar bands and dance bands on a regular basis." Current acts include Ralph
Carlson (country/bluegrass), Neville Wells (country) and Bruce Golden (country-country/rock).

Tips: "Be professional and business-like. Keep agency supplied with up-to-date promo material and develop entertainment ability. Videotape your live performance, then give yourself an honest review."

*GREGORY PITZER ARTIST MANAGEMENT, Box 460527, Houston TX 77056. (713)980-0539. President: Gregory Pitzer. Estab. 1987. Represents local, regional or international individual artists, groups and songwriters; currently handles 5 acts. Receives negotiable commission. Reviews material for acts.
How to Contact: Submit demo tape by mail—unsolicited submissions are OK. Prefers cassette (or VHS videocassette if available) with 3-5 songs and lyric or lead sheets. SASE. Reports in 2-3 weeks.
Music: Mostly rock, pop and alternative; also country. Works primarily with bands/vocalists. Current acts include Twenty Mondays (pop/alternative), Rag Doll (pop/rock) and Hayden Minor (pop singer/songwriter).

*PLACER PUBLISHING, Box 11301, Kansas City KS 66111. (913)287-3495. Owner: Steve Vail. Management firm, booking agency, music publisher (ASCAP) and record company (System Records). Estab. 1980. Represents local, regional and international individual artists, groups and songwriters; currently handles 3 acts. Receives 50% commission. Reviews material for acts.
How to Contact: Write or call first and obtain permission to submit. Prefers cassette or 7½ reel-to-reel (or VHS or Beta videocassette) with lyric sheets. Does not return unsolicited material. Reports in 6 weeks.
Music: Mostly New Age, progressive and jazz or fusion. Works primarily with esoteric or avant-garde groups or individuals. Current acts include Realm (progressive rock group), David Sears, Darrel Studna and Lake Furney.
Tips: "Be creative. Please no mainstream tunes."

PLATINUM EARS LTD., 285 Chestnut St., West Hempstead NY 11552. (516)489-0738. President: Mike Siskind. Management firm, music publisher (Siskatune Music Publishing Co./BMI) and record company (Storehouse Records). Estab. 1988. Represents local, regional and international individual artists, groups and songwriters; currently handles 2 acts. Receives 15-20% commission. Reviews material for acts.
How to Contact: Submit demo tape by mail—unsolicited submissions are OK. Prefers cassette (or VHS videocassette if available) with 5-8 songs and lyric sheet. If seeking management, include tape (cassette or VHS), photo, bio and tearsheets in press kit. "Put time into this. After all, it is your career we're talking about." SASE. Reports in 3 months.
Music: Mostly rock, pop and R&B; also blues, world beat and jazz. Works primarily with bands (primarily rock of some type). Current acts include Van Gogh's Ear (rock) and Michael Ellis (songwriter).
Tips: "Be professional and don't second guess decisions. As students of the business of music, we attempt to place you with reputable people. If a deal seems too good to be true, many times it is."

PLATINUM GOLD MUSIC, Ste. 1200, 9200 Sunset Blvd., Los Angeles CA 90069. Managers: Steve Cohen/David Cook. Management firm, production company and music publisher. ASCAP. Estab. 1978. Represents local or regional (East or West coasts) individual artists, groups and songwriters; currently handles 3-4 acts. Receives 15-20% commission. Reviews material for acts.
How to Contact: Write or call first and obtain permission to submit. Prefers cassette (or VHS videocassette if available) with 3 songs and lyric sheets. If seeking management, include photo, bio and press clip if available in press kit. Does not return unsolicited material. Reports in 2-8 weeks.
Music: Mostly interested in contemporary R&B, dance/pop, hip hop/rap; also pop rock, hard rock and pop. Works most often with vocalists. Current acts include Troop (R&B vocal group), Def Jef (rap/hip hop), Ku De Tah (alternative rock) and Tairrie B. (pop/rap).
Tips: "No ballads. We do not look for potential; be prepared and professional before coming to us—and ready to relocate to West Coast if necessary."

POWER STAR MANAGEMENT, #618, 6981 N. Park Dr., Pennsauken NJ 08109. (609)486-1480. President: Brian Kushner. Management firm. Estab. 1981. Represents international individual artists and groups; currently handles 4 acts. Receives 20% commission. Reviews material for acts.
How to Contact: Submit demo tape by mail—unsolicited submissions are OK. Prefers cassette (or VHS videocassette if available) with 4 songs and lyric sheet. SASE. Reports in 3 weeks.
Music: Mostly pop/dance, rock and R&B. Current acts include Britny Fox, Linear, Alisha, Tuff and Mariah.

PREMIER ARTISTS, 9 Dundas Ln., Albert Park, Victoria 3206 **Australia.** Phone: (03)699-9555. FAX: (03)695-7819. Booking agency. Estab. 1975. Represents groups; currently handles 100 acts. Receives 10% commission. Reviews material for acts.

How to Contact: Submit demo tape—unsolicited submissions are OK. Prefers cassette (or VHS videocassette of live performance, if available) with 2 or 3 songs. Does not return unsolicited material. Reports in 2 weeks.
Music: Mostly rock and pop. Works primarily with bar bands. Current acts include Baby Animals, Jimmy Barnes, Boom Crash Opera, The Angels, Crowded House and Hoodoo Gurus.

*PREMIER ARTISTS SERVICES, INC., 1401 University Dr., Coral Springs FL 33071. (305)755-1700. Contact: Jim Ramos. Management firm and booking agency. Estab. 1978. Represents local, regional or international individual artists, groups and songwriters; currently handles 7 acts. Receives 10-20% commission. Reviews material for acts.
How to Contact: Submit demo tape by mail—unsolicited submissions are OK. Prefers cassette with 4 songs and lyric sheet. Does not return unsolicited material. Reports in 1 month.
Music: Mostly pop, country (progressive) and rock. Works primarily with vocalists, rock and blues bands. Current acts include Frank Sinatra (singer), Elin Michaels (singer) and Joey Bonanassa (blues band).
Tips: "Send us a country/blues/rock hit for Elin Michaels (harder edge Bonnie Raitt)."

*PRO TALENT CONSULTANTS, Box 1192, Clearlake Oak CA 95423. (707)998-3587. Coordinator: John Eckert. Management firm and booking agency. Estab. 1979. Represents individual artists and groups; currently handles 9 acts. Receives 15% commission. Reviews material for acts.
How to Contact: Submit demo tape—unsolicited submissions are OK. Prefers cassette (or VHS videocassette if available) with 4 songs and lyric sheet. "We prefer audio cassette (4 songs). Submit videocassette with live performance only." If seeking management, include an 8×10 photo, a cassette of at least 4-6 songs, a bio on group/artist and business card or a phone number with address to contact in press kit. SASE. Reports in 3 weeks.
Music: Mostly country, country/pop and rock. Works primarily with vocalists, show bands, dance bands and bar bands. Current acts include John Richards (country singer), Glenn Elliott Band (country group) and Just Us (country).
Tips: "Never give up if you're *honestly* interested in working in the show/music business. The music business is the greatest business to be in, but only the strongest performers who believe in themselves survive."

PROCESS TALENT MANAGEMENT, 439 Wiley Ave., Franklin PA 16323. (814)432-4633. Contact: Norman Kelly. Management firm. Estab. 1970. Represents artists and groups; currently handles 4-8 acts. Receives 10-15% commission. Reviews material for acts.
How to Contact: Submit demo tape—unsolicited submissions are OK. Prefers 7½ ips reel-to-reel, cassette or 8-track cartridge with 2-6 songs. "Send your best songs and performances with photo, audiocassette and SASE. Reports in 2 weeks.
Music: Mostly country; also bluegrass, gospel and MOR. Works primarily with vocalists, self-contained country shows and bar bands. Current acts include Junie Lou, Debbie Sue and Bob Stamper.

R.V.O. (ROBERT VERKAIK ORGANIZATION), Singel 402, Amsterdam 1016 AK **Netherlands.** Phone: (20)6254258. FAX: (20)6236930. Manager: Robert Verkaik/Robert van Kleef/Marcél Albers. Management firm, booking agency and music publisher. Estab. 1986. Represents local, regional and international individual artists, groups, songwriters and recording studios in Europe and production companies; currently handles 8 acts. Reviews material for acts.
How to Contact: Submit demo tape by mail only—unsolicited submissions are OK. Prefers cassette (or VHS videocassette if available) with 3 songs and lyric sheet. SASE. Reports in 6 weeks.
Music: Mostly rock, pop and dance. Works primarily with groups and producers. Current acts include The Pilgrims, Tambourine and Easy Money.

THE RAINBOW COLLECTION, LTD., Box 300, Solebury PA 18963. (215)838-2295. President: Herb Gart. Management, record production and publishing firm. Represents artists, groups and songwriters; currently handles 10 acts. Reviews material for acts. Signs songwriters.
How to Contact: Prefers cassette (or VHS videocassette) with 3 songs. "Be true to the intent of the song, and don't hide the performer. Simple and straightforward preferred." Enclose lyrics. Does not return unsolicited material. Reports in 6 weeks.
Music: Mostly rock, pop, heavy metal; also R&B, rap, country and dance-oriented. Works "almost exclusively with strong songwriters whether they are solo artists or bands." Current acts include Rattling Bones, Michael Purington, Marc Berger and The Headcleaners, Jack the Wrapper, Chain of Fools and Sugar Blue.
Tips: "Don't necessarily worry about current trends in music. Just do what you do to the best of your ability. With our company the song is the thing even if production-wise it's in its infant stages. If you feel you have a great and unique talent, contact us."

RAINBOW COLLECTION LTD., 4501 Spring Creek Rd., Bonita Springs FL 33923. (813)947-6978. Executive Producer: Richard (Dick) O'Bitts. Management firm, record company (Happy Man Records) and music publisher (Rocker Music and Happy Man Music). Represents individual artists, groups, songwriters and producers; currently handles 5 acts. Reviews material for acts.
How to Contact: Submit demo tape by mail—unsolicited submissions are OK. Prefers cassette (or VHS videocassette of live performance, if available) with 4 songs and lyric sheet. If seeking management, include photos, bio and tapes in press kit. SASE. Reports in 1 month.
Music: Mostly country, pop and rock. Works primarily with writer/artists and groups of all kinds. Current acts include Holly Ronick, Colt Gipson (traditional country), Overdue (rock), Flo Carter and the Bengter Sisters (gospel).

*RAW LTD, Box 486, Philadelphia PA 19105. (215)232-9023. President: David Reckner. Management firm. Estab. 1987. Represents local, regional or international individual artists, groups and producers; currently handles 3 acts. Receives 15-20% commission. Reviews material for acts.
How to Contact: Submit demo tape by mail—unsolicited submissions are OK. Prefers cassette. Does not return unsolicited material. Reports in 3 months.
Music: Mostly rock. Works primarily with alternative rock bands. Current acts include Dead Milkmen, Baby Flamehead and Low Road.
Tips: "Have your own voice or personality."

*RED GIANT RECORDS AND PUBLISHING, 3155 South., 764 East., Salt Lake City UT 84106. (801)486-4210. President: Anthony Perry. Music publisher (Red Giant Records) and record company (Red Giant). Estab. 1982. Represents local, regional and international individual artists, groups and songwriters. Curently represents 4 artists and groups. Receives 10-15% commission. Reviews material for acts.
How to Contact: Submit demo tape by mail—unsolicited submissions are OK. Prefers cassette (or ½ VHS videocassette if available) with 3-4 songs and lyric or lead sheets. Does not return unsolicited material. Reports in 1-2 months.
Music: Mostly jazz, avant rock, country/R&B and R&B. Works primarily with instrumentalists, vocalists and bands. Current acts include John Herron (songwriter), Spaces (vocal group), Bombs Away (R&B) Armed & Dangerous (R&B), and Alan Roger Nichols (jazz/New Age songwriter).

*REED SOUND RECORDS, INC., 120 Mikel Dr., Summerville SC 29485. (803)873-3324. Contact: Haden Reed. Management firm. Represents artists and groups; currently handles 3 acts. Receives 10% commission. Reviews material for acts.
How to Contact: Submit demo tape by mail—unsolicited submissions are OK. Prefers cassette with 1-4 songs. SASE. Reports in 1 month.
Music: Mostly country; also church/religious, easy listening and gospel. Current acts include Haden Reed (country songwriter), Vocalettes (gospel) and Happy Jack Band (country).
Tips: "We're looking for songs written in A,B,A,B (chorus, verse, chorus, verse) style. Copyright your songs."

RICHARD REITER PRODUCTIONS, Box 43135, Upper Montclair NJ 07043. (201)857-2935. President: Richard Reiter. Management firm, booking agency, music publisher (Marchael Music/ASCAP) and record company (City Pigeon Records). Estab. 1974. Represents local individual artists, groups and songwriters; currently handles 6 acts. Receives 15-20% commission. Reviews material for acts.
How to Contact: Write first and obtain permission to submit. Prefers cassette with 3-6 songs and lyric sheet. If seeking management, "include nice folder with logo, 8 × 10 glossy photos (that print media will find exciting and print), enticing description of music act, reviews (don't pad it) and performing credits in press kit." SASE. Reports in 2 weeks.
Music: Mostly jazz, R&B and pop. Works primarily with instrumental jazz groups/artists, vocalists of jazz/swing. Current acts include Crossing Point (fusion), Lou Caimano (jazz sax) and Tricia Slafta (swing jazz vocalist).

REM MANAGEMENT, 9112 Fireside Dr., Indianapolis IN 46250. President: Bob McCutcheon. Management firm. Estab. 1987. Represents local, regional and international individual artists and groups; currently handles 2 acts. Receives 20% commission. Reviews material for acts.

"How to Use Your Songwriter's Market" (at the front of this book) contains comments and suggestions to help you understand and use the information in these listings.

How to Contact: Submit demo tape—unsolicited submissions are OK. Prefers cassette with 3 songs. SASE. Reports in 1 month.
Music: Mostly hard rock and R&B. Current acts include Sweet Fa (rock group) and Cyclone Temple (hardcore group).

RENERI INTERNATIONAL PRODUCTIONS, Box 32, Emerson NJ 07630. (201)265-1043. Contact: Ray Reneri. Management firm. Estab. 1966. Represents local, regional and international individual artists and groups; currently handles 15-25 acts. Reviews material for acts.
How to Contact: Submit demo tape by mail—unsolicited submissions are OK. Prefers cassette (or VHS videocassette if available) with 3-5 songs. Include photo and bio sheet. If seeking management, include cassette, videocassette, photo and background information in press kit. SASE. Reports in 1 month.
Music: Mostly rock, pop, R&B and C&W. Works primarily with vocalists and bands. Current acts include Baron (rock) and Tyrn Around (pop).

JOEY RICCA, JR.'S ENTERTAINMENT AGENCY, 408 S. Main St., Milltown NJ 08850. (201)287-1230. Owner/President: Joseph Frank Ricca, Jr. Management firm and booking agency. Estab. 1985. Represents individual artists, groups and songwriters; currently handles 75-100 acts. Receives 10-15% commission. Reviews material for acts.
How to Contact: Write or call to arrange personal interview. "We prefer that all material be copyrighted and that a letter be sent right before submitting material, but neither of these is essential." Prefers cassette (or videocassette if available) with 3-4 songs and lyric or lead sheets. SASE. Reports in 8 weeks.
Music: Mostly love songs/ballads, songs for big band vocalists, and soft jazz/Latin; also good commercial material. Works with show bands, dance bands and bar bands. Current acts include Maria Angela, Donny "Z," Anthony Paccone, One Trak Mind and Diamond.
Tips: "Good lyrics and strong musical arrangements are essential if one of our vocalists are to select a song they would like to sing. No matter what others may think of your work submit the songs you like best that you wrote. I look for good love songs, ballads and Broadway play type compositions. No metal please."

*RICH + FAMOUS MANAGEMENT INC., 267 Park Place, Brooklyn NY 11238. (718)638-6950. Owner: Richard Levine. Management firm. Estab. 1986. Represents local and regional (Southeast) individual artists, groups and songwriters. Currently handles 4 acts. Receives 15-20% commission. Reviews material for acts.
How to Contact: Submit demo tape by mail—unsolicited submissions are OK. Prefers cassette with 3 songs and lyric sheets. If seeking management, include brief bio, photo and chrome cassette in press kit. SASE. Reports in 1 month.
Music: Mostly rock, pop and R&B. Works primarily with rock bands, vocalists and songwriters. Current acts include Lava Love (alternative pop), Swimming Pool Q's (rock), Jeff Calder (acoustic) and Gigi (vocalist).
Tips: "Keep sending material. Please give me the time to really listen to it and we'll see if there's a fit."

RIOHCAT MUSIC, Box 764, Hendersonville TN 37077-0764. (615)824-1435. Contact: Robert Kayne. Management firm, booking agency, record company (Avita Records) and music publisher (Riohcat Music/BMI). Estab. 1975. Represents individual artists and groups; currently handles 4 acts. Receives 20% commission. Reviews material for acts.
How to Contact: Submit demo tape by mail—unsolicited submissions are OK. Prefers cassette and lead sheet. If seeking management, include resume, previous experience, tape, photo and press clippings in press kit. SASE. Reports in 2 weeks.
Music: Mostly contemporary jazz and fusion. Works primarily with jazz ensembles. Current acts include Jerry Tachoir Quartet, Marlene Tachoir and Jerry Tachoir/Van Manakas Duo.
Tips: "Be organized, neat and professional."

A.F. RISAVY, INC., 1312 Vandalia, Collinsville IL 62234. (618)345-6700. Divisions include Artco Enterprises, Golden Eagle Records, Swing City Music and Swing City Sound. Contact: Art Risavy. Management firm and booking agency. Estab. 1960. Represents artists, groups and songwriters; currently handles 50 acts. Receives 10% commission. Reviews material for acts.
How to Contact: Submit demo tape by mail—unsolicited submissions are OK. Prefers 7½ ips reel-to-reel or cassette (or VHS videocassette if available) with 2-6 songs and lyric sheet. If seeking management, include pictures, bio and VHS videocassette in press kit. SASE. Reports in 2 weeks.

Music: Mostly rock, country, MOR and top 40. Current acts include Sammy and the Snow Monkeys, The Blast, Bedrock, Billy-Peek, Jules Blatner, Seen, Catch, Inside Out, Cruz'n, Fallback, Lang & McClain, Jim & Dave and the Chapman Brothers.
Tips: Artists should be "well-dressed, polished and ambitious. VHS videotapes are very helpful."

RNJ PRODUCTIONS, INC., 11514 Calvert St., North Hollywood CA 91606. (818)762-6105. President: Rein Neggo, Jr. Management firm. Estab. 1974. Represents individual artists; currently handles 8-10 acts. Receives 10-25% commission. Reviews material for acts.
How to Contact: Prefers cassette with 3 songs and lead sheet. SASE. Reports in 1 month.
Music: Mostly A/C, country, pop and folk. Works primarily with vocalists and concert artists. Current acts include Glenn Yarbrough, Arizona Smoke Review, Limeliters, Bill Zorn, Jon Benns, The Kingston Trio and The New Christy Minstrels.

ROCK-A-BILLY ARTIST AGENCY, Box 1622, Hendersonville TN 37077. (615)822-1044. A&R Director: S.D. Neal. Management firm, booking agency and record company. Estab. 1974. Represents artists and groups; currently handles 20 acts. Receives 15% commission. Reviews material for acts.
How to Contact: Submit demo tape—unsolicited submissions are OK. Prefers cassette (or VHS videocassette if available) with 2-6 songs and lyric sheet. SASE. Reports in 3 weeks.
Music: Mostly R&B, rock and country; also all other types including rockabilly. Works primarily with vocalists. Current acts include Dixie Dee, Rhythm Rockers, Rufus Thomas, Richie Derwald, Mickey Finn Band and Greg Paul.

*SAMUEL ROGGERS & ASSOC., Box 8305, Houston TX 77288. (713)683-2298 and (713)662-4196. Senior Consultant: Sirron Kyles. Management firm and booking agency. Estab. 1971. Represents local and international individual artists and groups. Receives 15% commission. Reviews material for acts.
How to Contact: Submit demo tape by mail—unsolicited submissions are OK. Prefers cassette (or VHS videocassette if available) with 3 songs and lyric sheets. SASE. Reports in 3 weeks—2 months.
Music: Mostly rock, R&B and country; also gospel and comedy. Works primarily with concert acts. Current acts include Sevea South Seas (Polynesian singer/songwriter), Mad Man Justice (rock singer/songwriter) and Mark Allen (singer/songwriter).

*ROGUE MANAGEMENT, 109 Earle Ave., Lynbrook NY 11563. (516)599-4157. President: James Citkovic. Partner: Ralph Beauchamp. Management firm. Estab. 1986. Represents local, regional or international individual artists, groups, songwriters and producers; currently handles 8 acts. Receives 10-25% commission. Reviews material for acts.
How to Contact: Submit demo tape by mail—unsolicited submissions are OK. Prefers cassette (or VHS videocassette if available), 8 × 10 pictures with 4 songs and lyric sheet. Does not return unsolicited materials. Reports in 4-5 weeks.
Music: Mostly alternative, rock and pop/dance; also industrial, rave and techno. Current acts include The Fiction Scene (dance), Jeff Gordon (folk) and Freedom (alternative rock).

JEFFREY ROSS MUSIC, #203, 219 1st Ave. S., Seattle WA 98104. (206)343-5225. Contact: Jeffrey Ross. Management firm and music publisher (High-tech Music/BMI). Estab. 1978. Represents local, regional and international individual artists, groups and songwriters; currently handles 5 acts. Receives 15-20% commission. Reviews material for acts.
How to Contact: Write or call first and obtain permission to submit. Prefers cassette with 5 songs and lyric sheet. SASE. Reports in 2 months.
Music: Mostly pop/R&B; also rock and alternative. Works primarily with vocalists and instrumentalists. Current acts include Skywalk (jazz rock), Laura Love (folk funk alternative), David Ellis (country/rock) and Friesen & Kropinsky (jazz).
Tips: "We are artist development-oriented and appreciate true talent."

RUSTRON MUSIC PRODUCTIONS, Send all artist song submissions to: 1156 Park Lane, West Palm Beach FL 33417. (407)686-1354. Main Office: 33 Whittier, Hartsdale, NY 10530. ("Main office does not review new material—only South Florida Branch office does.") Artists' Consultants: Rusty Gordon and Davilyn Whims. Composition Management: Ron Caruso. Arranger/Producer: Steve Mikes. Management firm, booking agency, music publisher (Rustron Music Publishers/BMI and Whimsong Publishing/ASCAP) and record producer (Rustron Music Productions). Estab. 1970. Represents individuals, groups and songwriters; currently handles 25 acts. Receives 10-25% commission for management and/or booking only. Reviews material for acts.

How to Contact: Submit demo tape — unsolicited submissions are OK. Prefers cassette with 3-6 songs and lyric or lead sheet. "SASE required for all correspondence." Reports in 2-3 months.
Music: Blues (country folk/urban, Southern), country (rock, blues, progressive), easy listening (ballads), R&B, folk/rock New Age instrumentals and New Age folk fusion. Current acts include Relative Viewpoint (socio/environmental folk), Marianne Flemming Band (modern blues fusion) and Deb Criss (New Age folk fusion).
Tips: "Send cover letter, typed lyric sheets for all songs. Carefully mix demo, don't drown the vocals, 3-6 songs in a submission. Send photo if artist is seeking marketing and/or production assistance."

SA'MALL MANAGEMENT, Suite 830, 10 Universal City Plaza, Universal City CA 91608. (818)506-8533. Manager: Nikki Ray. Management firm. Estab. 1990. Represents local, regional and international individual artists, groups and songwriters; currently handles 9 acts. Receives 25% commission. Reviews material for acts.
How to Contact: Submit demo tape — unsolicited submissions are OK. Prefers cassette with 2 songs and lyric and lead sheet. SASE. Reports in 6 weeks.
Music: All types. Current acts include The Band AKA, I.B. Fynne, Phuntaine, Yuehe, Katrina Gibson, I.B. Fynne and Robert Forman.
Tips: "Be professional, say no to drugs and become educated in the business of music."

SANDCASTLE PRODUCTIONS, 236 Sebert Road, Forest Gate, London E7 ONP **United Kingdom**. Phone: (081)534-8500. Senior Partner: Simon Law. Management firm, music publisher (Sea Dream Music/PRS, Scarf Music Publishing and Really Free Music/PRS) and record company (Plankton Records, Embryo Arts/Belgium, Wildtracks and Gutta/Sweden) and record producers. Estab. 1980. Represents individual artists, groups and songwriters; currently handles 10 acts. Receives 10% commission. Reviews material for acts.
How to Contact: Submit demo tape — unsolicited submissions are OK. Prefers cassette with 3 songs and lyric sheet. SAE and IRC. Reports in 6 weeks.
Music: Mostly funk/rock, blues and rock. Works primarily with bands or artists with a Christian bias to their material. Current acts include Fresh Claim (funk rock), Medals (jazz/rock) and Trevor Speaks (folk).
Tips: "Have a commitment to communication of something real and honest in 'live' work."

*LONNY SCHOENFELD AND ASSOCIATES, P.O. Box 460086, Garland TX 75046. (214)497-1616. President: Lonny Schoenfeld. Management firm, booking agency and music publisher (Lonny Tunes/BMI). Estab. 1988. Represents local, regional or international individual artists, groups and songwriters; currently handles 3 acts. Receives 15% commission. Reviews material for acts.
How to Contact: Submit demo tape — unsolicited submissions are OK. Prefers cassette with 3-5 songs and lyric sheet. Does not return unsolicited material. Reports in 2 weeks.
Music: Mostly country, pop, and rock. Works primarily with vocal groups and comedians. Current acts include Heartland (country top 40 group), Tim Roby (Elvis Presley impersonator) and Doug Richardson (comedian).
Tips: "If you and your material are not 'first class' and submitted in a professional package, we won't be interested in working with you."

*SELECT ARTISTS ASSOCIATES, 7300 E. Camelback Rd., Scottsdale AZ 85251. (602)994-0471. FAX: (602)481-0549. President: Charles T. Johnston. Management firm. Estab. 1967. Represents local, regional or international individual artists and groups; currently handles 15 acts. Receives 20% commission. Reviews material for acts.
How to Contact: Submit demo tape by mail — unsolicited submissions are OK. Prefers cassette (or VHS videocassette if available) with 3-5 songs and lyric or lead sheets. Does not return unsolicited material. Reports in 3 weeks.
Music: Mostly pop, R&B and rock. Works primarily with vocalists, bands. Current acts include Ruben Macias (R&B), Jodi Light (R&B/pop) and Mario Mendivil (R&B).
Tips: "Be professional in what you submit."

*770 MUSIC INC., Box 773 Bondi Junction, New South Wales 2022 **Australia**. Phone: (612)360-7639. A&R Representative: Mr. Nun. Management firm, booking agency, music publisher (770 Music), record company (770 Music) and record producer (770 Productions). Estab. 1980. Represents individual artists, groups and songwriters; currently handles 44 acts. Receives 25% commission. Reviews material for acts.
How to Contact: Submit demo tape — unsolicited submissions are OK. Prefers cassette (or VHS or Beta videocassette) with 10 songs and lyric or lead sheets. Does not return unsolicited material. Reports back in 3 months.

Music: Mostly triple crossover—country, rock and pop. Works primarily with dance bands, showbands and individual artists and songwriters. Current acts include Andy and Kouros (soft rock), Little Sharky and the White Pointer Sisters (heavy metal) and Havoc in the Ballroom (jazz/blues).
Tips: "Company Motto: The love you make equals the love you create."

SHAPIRO & COMPANY, C.P.A. (A Professional Corporation), Suite 620, 9255 Sunset Blvd., Los Angeles CA 90069. (213)278-2303. Certified Public Accountant: Charles H. Shapiro. Business management firm. Estab. 1979. Represents individual recording artists, groups and songwriters. Commission varies.
How to Contact: Write or call first to arrange personal interview.
Music: Mostly rock and pop. Works primarily with recording artists as business manager.
Tips: "We assist songwriters with administration of publishing."

MICKEY SHERMAN ARTIST MANAGEMENT & DEVELOPMENT, Box 20814, Oklahoma City OK 73156. (405)755-0315. President: Mickey Sherman. Management firm. Estab. 1974. Represents individual artists and songwriters; currently handles 6 acts. Receives 10-15% commission. Reviews material for acts.
How to Contact: Submit demo tape—unsolicited submissions are OK. Prefers cassette (or VHS videocassette of live performance, if available) with 3 songs and lyric sheet or lead sheet. If seeking management, include thumbnail biography/picture/press clippings and resume in press kit. "Keep videos simple. Use good lighting." Does not return unsolicited material. Reports in 1 month.
Music: Mostly blues, pop and country; also R&B, rock and easy listening. Works primarily with vocalists and showbands. Current acts include Janjo (singer/harmonica), Benny Kubiak (fiddler), Charley Shaw (vocalist), Dale Langley (gospel/country singer) and The Burton Band.

PHILL SHUTE MANAGEMENT PTY. LTD., Box 273, Dulwich Hill NSW 2203 **Australia.** Phone: (02)5692152. Managing Director: Phill Shute. Management firm, booking agency and record company (Big Rock Records). Estab. 1979. Represents local individual artists and groups; currently handles 3 acts. Receives 25% commission. Reviews material for acts. Charges fee for reviewing material.
How to Contact: Submit demo tape by mail—unsolicited submissions are OK. Prefers cassette with 4 songs and lyric sheet. SAE and IRC. Reports in 2 months.
Music: Mostly rock, pop and R&B; also country rock. Works primarily with rock bands, pop vocalists and blues acts (band and vocalists). Current acts include Chris Turner (blues/guitarist/vocalist), Collage (pop/rock band) and Big Rock Band (rock'n'roll).
Tips: "Make all submissions well organized (e.g. bio, photo and experience of the act). List areas in which the act would like to work, complete details for contact."

SIDARTHA ENTERPRISES, LTD., Box 1414, East Lansing MI 48823. (517)655-4618. President: Thomas R. Brunner. Management firm and booking agency. Estab. 1968. Represents artists and groups; currently handles 3 acts. Receives 15-20% commission. Reviews material for acts.
How to Contact: "Always make phone contact first." Prefers cassette (or videocassette) with at least 4 songs and lyric sheet. SASE. Reports in 1 month. If seeking management, press kit should include video tape, 8×10 photo and lyric sheet.
Music: Rock and top 40/pop. Works primarily with bar bands and recording acts. Current acts include Sheer Threat (rock), Rumble (rock) and Wrek Havock.

SIMMONS MANAGEMENT CO., Box 18711, Raleigh NC 27619. (919)851-8321. FAX: (919)851-8441. President: Harry Simmons. Management firm. Represents producers, artists, groups and songwriters; currently handles 10 acts and 4 producers. Receives 15-20% commission. Reviews material for acts.
How to Contact: Submit demo tape by mail—unsolicited submissions are OK. Prefers cassette or DAT (or VHS videocassette of performance) with 3-6 songs and lyric sheet; also submit promotional material, photos and clippings. "Videocassette does not have to be professional. Any information helps." If seeking management, include wide range of photos in press kit. SASE. Reports in 6 weeks.
Music: Mostly modern pop; also modern rock, new wave, rock, metal, R&B and top 40/pop. Works primarily with "original music recording acts or those that aspire to be." Current acts include Don Dixon (producer, songwriter and recording artist), Marti Jones (recording artist), The Woods (recording artists, songwriters), Billy C. Wirtz (recording artist), Jim Brock (recording artist), Steve Haigler (producer) and Table (original music).
Tips: "We are interested in strong songs; style is not so important."

*SINGERMANAGEMENT, INC., Suite 1403, 161 West 54th St., New York NY 10019. (212)757-1217. President: Robert Singerman. Management consulting firm. Estab. 1982. Represents local, regional or international individual artists and groups; currently handles 7 acts. Receives hourly fee, negotiated retainer, plus 5% commission. Consults artists and songwriters.

How to Contact: Submit demo tape by mail—unsolicited submissions are OK. Prefers cassette (or VHS videocassette if available). Does not return unsolicited submissions. If seeking management, include tape, lyric sheet and bio in press kit.
Music: Current acts include Thrillcat (pop rock), Combo Limbo (pop rock) and Caroline Docktorow (folk bluegrass rock).

T. SKORMAN PRODUCTIONS, INC., 4700 L.B. McLeod Rd., Orlando FL 32811. (305)843-4300. FAX: (305)843-7161. President: Ted Skorman. Management firm and booking agency. Estab. 1983. Represents groups; currently handles 40 acts. Receives 10-25% commission. Reviews material for acts.
How to Contact: "Phone for permission to send tape." Prefers cassette with 3 songs (or videocassette of no more than 15 minutes). "Live performance—no trick shots or editing tricks. We want to be able to view act as if we were there for a live show." SASE. Reports in 6 weeks.
Music: Mostly top 40 and dance; also rock, MOR and pop. Works primarily with high-energy dance acts, recording acts, and top 40 bands. Current acts include Ravyn and The End (funk and roll), Virgie and Right on Cue (R&B), Tim Mikus (rock) and Gibralter (R&B).
Tips: "We have many pop recording acts, and are looking for commercial material for their next albums."

SKYLINE MUSIC CORP., Box 31, Lancaster NH 03584. (608)586-7171. FAX: (603)586-7078. President: Bruce Houghton. Management firm (Skyline Management), booking agency (Skyline Music Agency), record company (Adventure Records) and music publisher (Campfire Music and Skyline Music). Estab. 1984. Represents 15 individual artists and groups. Currently handles 15 acts. Receives 10-15% commission. Reviews material for acts.
How to Contact: Submit demo tape by mail—unsolicited submissions are OK. Prefers cassette (or videocassette if available) with 3 songs. "Keep it short and sweet." SASE. Reports in 1 month.
Music: Mostly rock and folk; also pop. Works primarily with concert rock attractions and dance bands. Current acts include Foghat (rock), The Outlaws (rock), Toy Caldwell (rock), Rick Danko, Badfinger, New Riders of the Purple Sage and Leslie West (rock).

*SKYSCRAPER ENTERTAINMENT, 113 S. 21st St., Philadelphia PA 19103. (215)851-0400. Contact: Alan Rubens. Management and consulting firm and music publisher (BMI/ASCAP). Estab. 1989. Represents local, regional or international individual artists, groups and songwriters; currently handles 3 acts. Receives 20% commission. Reviews material for acts.
How to Contact: Submit demo tape by mail—unsolicited submissions are OK. Prefers cassette with 2 or 3 songs and lyric sheet. SASE. Reports in 1 month.
Music: Mostly pop and dance, R&B and hip-hop. Works primarily with vocalists (solor or group). Current acts include Barrio Boyzz (pop group), The Boys (R&B crossover) and Steve Tracy (pop/dance/writer).

DAN SMITH AGENCY, Box 3634, Shawnee Mission KS 66203. (913)648-3906. Contact: Dan Smith. Management firm and booking agency. Estab. 1979. Represents artists, groups and songwriters in the Midwest; currently handles 5 acts. Receives 10% commission. Reviews material for acts.
How to Contact: Submit demo tape by mail—unsolicited submissions are OK. Prefers cassette with 3-5 songs and lyric sheet (or VHS videocassette if available). "Make sound quality clear and mixed well." If seeking management, include photo, bio, song list, press clips, audio tape and video tape (optional) in press kit. SASE. Reports in 1 month.
Music: Mostly country rock, top 40, progressive and R&B; also bluegrass, blues, country, dance-oriented, folk, jazz, MOR and soul. Works primarily with dance, bar and concert bands. Current acts include Riverrock (country rock), Crossroads (country rock), Dixie Cadillacs (country rock), Blackwater (country rock) and La Rose (R&B, MOR, soul).
Tips: "Have complete promo package—bio, photo (glossy), song list, credits, etc."

*SOPRO, INC., Box 227, Chicago Ridge IL 60415. (312)425-0174. Contact: Bud Monaco or Red Rose. Management firm and artist development firm. Represents artists and groups in the local region; currently handles 5 acts. Receives maximum 15-20% commission. Reviews material for acts.
How to Contact: Write first and obtain permission to submit. Prefers cassette with 2-3 songs and lead sheet. SASE. Reports in 1 month.
Music: Mostly rock, blues and top 40; also R&B, MOR and progressive rock. Works primarily with concert rock, blues and dance-oriented bands. Current acts include Don Griffin and The Griff Band (rock/blues), The Midwest Expedition (rock), Jody Noa & The Sho'Nuff Blues Band (blues), Joe Jammer & The Kissing Bandits (rock) and Tommy Biondo (rock).

SOUND '86 TALENT MANAGEMENT, Box 222, Black Hawk SD 57718. (605)343-3941. Management firm. Estab. 1974. Represents 10 artists and groups. Receives 5-10% commission. Reviews material for acts.

How to Contact: Query by mail or submit demo tape. Prefers cassette (or VHS videocassette-professional) with 3-8 songs and lyric sheet. SASE. Reports in 1 month.
Music: Rock (all types); also bluegrass, country, dance, easy listening and top 40/pop. Works primarily with single artists. Current artists include Danny Wayne (songwriter), Road House (blues), Johnny Thunder Band and Black Hills Country Band.

*SOUTHERN CONCERTS, 8665 Oakwood, Olive Branch MS 38654. (601)895-8333. President: Buddy Swords. Management firm, record company (SCR Records), record producer and music publisher (Buddy Swords Music and Swamp Fox Music). Represents artists; currently handles 5 acts. Receives 20% commission. Reviews material for acts.
How to Contact: Submit demo tape by mail. Unsolicited submissions are OK. Prefers cassette (or videocassette) with maximum 4 songs. Reports in 2 weeks.
Music: Mostly country, rock and blues. Works primarily with groups at festivals, concerts and bars. Current acts include Jerry Lee Lewis, Wendel Adkins, Tony Joe White, Dennis James and Don McMinn.

SP TALENT ASSOCIATES, Box 475184, Garland TX 75047. Talent Coordinator: Richard Park. Management firm and booking agency. Represents individual artists and groups; currently handles 7 acts. Receives negotiable commission. Reviews material for acts.
How to Contact: Prefers VHS videocassette with several songs. SASE. Reports back as soon as possible.
Music: Mostly rock, nostalgia rock, country; also specialty acts and folk/blues. Works primarily with vocalists and self-contained groups. Current acts include Joe Hardin Brown (C&W), Rock It! (nostalgia) and Renewal (rock group).
Tips: "Appearance and professionalism are *musts*!"

SPIDER ENTERTAINMENT CO., 5 Portsmouth Towne, Southfield MI 48075. (313)559-8230. President: Arnie Tencer. Vice President: Joel Zuckerman. Management firm. Estab. 1977. Represents artists, groups and songwriters; currently handles 1 act. Receives minimum 20% commission. Reviews material for acts.
Affiliates: Forever Endeavor Music, Inc.
How to Contact: Submit demo tape by mail—unsolicited submissions are OK. Prefers cassette (or videocassette if available) with 3 songs. If seeking management, include picture, songs and bio in press kit. SASE. Reports in 3 weeks.
Music: Mostly rock and roll, contemporary pop; also top/40 pop. Works primarily with "rock bands with good songs and great live shows." Current acts include Legal Tender (high energy "Detroit" rock band).
Tips: Artists "must have commercially viable material."

*SPIRIT SOUND CO., 3415 Clear Acre Ln., Reno NV 89512. (702)673-4680. Owner/Agent: Bob Woerner. Booking agency. Estab. 1977. Represents West Coast & Northwest individual artists and groups; currently handles 20-40 acts. Receives 15% commission. Reviews material for acts.
How to Contact: Submit demo tape by mail—unsolicited submissions are OK. Prefers cassette (or VHS videocassette if available) with 5-8 songs. SASE.
Music: Mostly variety, country and pop; also rock, blues and jazz. Works primarily with show acts/ dance bands. Current acts include Joey Carmon (band leader/singer/songwriter), David Grimes (singer/songwriter) and Ray Ernst (singer/songwriter).
Tips: "Present photos, bio, songlists (original & copy) audio for visual tape, list of places performed."

*SQUAD 16, Box 65, Wilbraham MA 01095. (413)599-1456. President: Tom Najemy. Booking agency. Estab. 1990. Represents Northeast individual artists, groups and songwriters; currently handles 15 acts. Receives 15% commission. Reviews material for acts.
How to Contact: Write or call first and obtain permission to submit. Prefers cassette with 4 songs. Does not return unsolicited material. Reports in 1 month.
Music: Mostly contemporary, funk/hiphop and rock; also reggae, world beat and jazz & blues; also contemporary rock, funk, or dance bands and acoustic performers. Current acts include The Posse NFX (funk, HipHop, Rap band), In The Flesh (progressive rock band) and Floating Boats (rock-a-lypso band).
Tips: "Do as much on your own so as to impress and put a buzz in the ears of those who can help you go further in the business."

STAR ARTIST MANAGEMENT INC., 17580 Frazho, Roseville MI 48066. (313)778-6404. President: Ron Geddish. Chairman: Joe Sgroi. Executive VP: Tony Pasqualone. Director of Canadian Operations: Brian Courtis. Director of West Coast Operations: S.D. Ashley. Director of East Coast Operations: Nat Weiss. Management firm (business and personal). Estab. 1972. Represents solo rock performers and rock groups. Receives 5% (business management), 15-20% (personal management). Reviews material for acts.

How to Contact: Submit demo tape by mail—unsolicited submissions are OK. Prefers cassette (or videocassette if available) with 2 songs. Does not return material. Reports in 1 month.

Music: Rock and alternative/college. Works primarily with alternative music and rock groups. Current acts include Elvis Hitler (Restless Records), His Name is Alive (4AD Records), The Look (A&M/Canada) and League of Nations (track records).

STARCREST PRODUCTIONS, INC., 209 Circle Hills Dr., Grand Forks ND 58201. (701)772-6831. President: George J. Hastings. Management firm and booking agency. Estab. 1970. Represents artists, groups and songwriters; currently handles 8 acts. Receives negotiable commission. Reviews material for acts.

How to Contact: Submit demo tape by mail—unsolicited submissions are OK. Prefers 7½ ips reel-to-reel or cassette with 2-10 songs with lyric and lead sheet. SASE. Reports in 4 months.

Music: Mostly country/gospel. Works primarily with vocalists and dance bands. Current acts include Mary Joyce (country/gospel), Swinging Doors (country/country rock), The Pioneers (country/country rock), The Teddy Bears (dance, show), George Hastings (songwriter), Bob Angel (country songwriter) and Gene Wyles (country).

*THE STARSOUND ENTERTAINMENT GROUP, Box 381078, Germantown TN 38183. (901)756-0944. President: David Paige. Management firm. Estab. 1984. Represents local, regional or international individual artists, groups and songwriters; currently handles 4 acts. Receives 20% commission. Reviews material for acts.

How to Contact: Call first and obtain permission to submit. Prefers cassette with 3-4 songs. Does not return unsolicited material. Reports in 1 month.

Music: Mostly pop, pop/rock and urban; also country. Works primarily with "artist/groups who are also songwriters. We also work with vocalists who do not write. Will work with someone who is strictly a songwriter." Current acts Kevin Paige (artist Chrysalis Records), Barbara Carter (artist, writer) and Jim Robinson (staff writer, Warner Chappell).

Tips: "Be specific regarding your type of music, tell me about what you do best."

STARSTRUCK PRODUCTIONS, 2167 Genesee, Buffalo NY 14211. (716)896-6666. FAX: (716)896-6855. General Manager: Tom McGill. Management firm and booking agency. Represents 24 groups. Receives 15-20% commission.

How to Contact: Write or call first and obtain permission to submit. Prefers cassette (or VHS videocassette if available) with 4-6 songs and lyric sheet. Please send current press kit with photo. SASE. Reports in 2-3 weeks.

Music: Mostly rock, pop, top 40. Works primarily with rock groups. Current acts include Only Humen (top 40 recording group, EMQ America Records), The Tweeds (rock/recording), Big Wheelie and The Hubcaps (nostalgia/touring act), Lady Fire (rock), Sky High (rock) and Wright of Way (rock).

Tips: "Approach your career realistically. Overnight success stories are few and far between. Write solid, commercial material and be persistent."

*STEELE MANAGEMENT, 7002 124th Tcr. N. Largo FL 34643. (813)530-9291. President: Brett R. Steele. Management firm. Estab. 1987. Represents local, regional or international individual artists, groups and songwriters; currently handles 1 act. Receives 20% commission. Reviews material for acts.

How to Contact: Submit demo tape by mail—unsolicited submissions are OK. Prefers cassette (or VHS videocassette if available) with 5 songs and lyric sheet. SASE. Reports in 1 month.

Music: Mostly rock and pop; also dance pop and R&B. Works primarily with rock bands, songwriters. Current acts include Roxx Gang and Kevin Steele (songwriter).

Tips: "Submit the most professional and comprehensive package you can put together."

*STEELE PRODUCTION, 9 Sandy Hollow, Smithtown NY 11787. (516)543-7352. President: Bob Wieser. Management firm and booking agency. Estab. 1982. Represents local, regional or international individual artists, groups and songwriters; currently handles 2 acts. Receives negotiable commission. Reviews material for acts.

How to Contact: Submit demo tape by mail—unsolicited submissions are OK. Prefers cassette (or VHS videocassette if available) with 2-5 songs and lyric sheet. SASE. Reports in 2-3 weeks.

Music: Pop, rock and R&B; also metal and thrash. "Open to all types of music." Current acts include Diane O'Neill (songwriter), Dymyn (pop group) and Vision (metal band).

Tips: "Plan to work really hard and be ready to do what needs to be done."

BILL STEIN ASSOCIATES INC., Box 1516, Champaign IL 61824. Artists Manager: Bill Stein. Management firm and booking agency. Estab. 1983. Represents artists and groups; currently handles 6 acts. Receives 10-15% commission. Reviews material for acts.
How to Contact: Submit demo tape by mail—unsolicited submissions are OK. Prefers cassette (or Beta videocassette of live performance, if available) with 3-6 songs and promotional material. "Send complete promo package including video and audio tapes, pictures, references, song and equipment lists." SASE. Reports in 1 month.
Music: Mostly pop rock, country and nostalgia; also dance, R&B, progressive and soul. Works primarily with bar bands, dance bands and concert groups. Current acts include Gator Alley (country), Kick in the Pants (nostalgia), High Sierra (country rock), Greater Decatur R&B Revue (nostalgia), Pink Flamingoes (nostalgia), Griz England & 95Q Band and Ken Carlyle.

RONALD STEIN PRODUCTIONS, Box 12194, Dallas TX 75225. (214)369-3800. President: Ronald Stein. Management firm, booking agent, music publisher (Westhaven Publishing), record company (Request Records) and talent agency (Star Images). Estab. 1985. Represents local, regional and international groups and individual artists; currently handles over 200 acts. Receives varying commission. Reviews material for acts.
How to Contact: Submit demo tape by mail—unsolicited submissions are accepted only if copyrighted. Prefers cassette (or VHS videocassette if available) with at least 3 songs. If seeking management, include up-to-date resume with complete name, address and phone number, 8 × 10 black/white and 8 × 10 color photographs and professional quality demo tape. SASE. "We report back only if we are interested in their work."
Music: All styles, but mostly pop and MOR. Works with groups and individual artists. Current acts include Fact Four (dance band), Lisa Waggoner (singer) and Paul Lister (pianist).

AL STRATEN ENTERPRISES, 10303 Hickory Valley, Ft. Wayne IN 46835. President: Allan Straten. Management firm, music publisher (Hickory Valley Music/ASCAP and Straten's Songs/BMI) and record company (Yellow Jacket Records). Represents individual artists and songwriters; currently handles 6 acts. Receives 10-20% commission. Reviews material for acts.
How to Contact: Submit demo tape by mail—unsolicited submissions are OK. Prefers cassette with a maximum of 4 songs and lyric sheet. SASE. Reports in 1 month.
Music: Mostly traditional and contemporary country—no rock. Works primarily with vocalists and writers. Current acts include April (country vocalist), Mike Vernaglia (country/MOR/singer/songwriter), Roy Allan (vocalist/writer), Sylvia Grogg (writer) and John Malcrow (songwriter).

STRICTLEY BUSINESS MUSIC MANAGEMENT, 691 ½ N. 13th St., Philadelphia PA 19123. (215)765-1382. President: Le Roy Rowe. Management firm and booking agency. Estab. 1989. Represents local, regional and international individual artists, groups, songwriters and producers; currently handles 15 acts. Receives 20-25% commission. Reviews material for acts.
How to Contact: Call first and obtain permission to submit. Prefers cassette or VHS videocassette with 3-5 songs, lyric sheet and photo. SASE. Reports in 1 month.
Music: Mostly R&B, pop and rock, and rap; also gospel. Current acts include Live & Direct (vocalists/artist), Ron Ali (vocalists) and Damon Cory (vocalist/songwriters).

*SUCCESSFUL PRODUCTIONS, 1203 Biltmore Ave., High Point NC 27260. (919)882-9990. President: Doris Lindsay. Management firm, music publisher and record company (Fountain Records). Estab. 1979. Represents local, regional or international individual artists and songwriters; currently handles 3 acts. Receives 10-20% commission. Reviews material for acts.
How to Contact: Submit demo tape by mail—unsolicited submissions are OK. Prefers cassette with 2 songs and lyric sheet. SASE. Reports in 2 months.
Music: Mostly country, novelty and pop; also gospel. Works primarily with vocalists and bands. Current acts include Mitch Snow (vocalist/songwriter), Pat Repose (vocalist) and Larry Lavey & Blue Monday Band.
Tips: "Present a good quality demo recorded in a studio. Positive, clean lyrics and up tempo music are easiest to place."

Remember: Don't "shotgun" your demo tapes. Submit only to companies interested in the type of music you write. For more submission hints, refer to The Business of Songwriting on page 19.

*SUMMIT PRODUCTIONS/STELLAR PRODUCTIONS, Suite 301, 1115 N. 5th St., Reading PA 19601. (215)376-0577. FAX: (215)929-2436. President: Michael Gryctko. Management firm, booking agency and record company (Arctic Records). Estab. 1982. Represents local, regional and international individual artists and groups; currently handles 3 acts. Receives 15-20% commission. Reviews material for acts.
How to Contact: Submit demo tape by mail—unsolicited submissions are OK. Prefers cassette (or VHS videocassette if available) with 3 songs and lyric sheet. SASE. Reports in 6 weeks.
Music: Mostly rock, pop/top 40 and R&B. Current acts include Bashful (rock), Ripper Jack (rock) and Bast Rachet (modern rock).
Tips: "Be persistent and devoted."

THE T.S.J. PRODUCTIONS INC., 422 Pierce St. NE, Minneapolis MN 55413-2514. (612)331-8580. Vice President/Artist Manager: Katherine J. Lange. Management firm and booking agency. Estab. 1974. Represents artists, groups and songwriters; currently handles 1 international act. Receives 10-15% commission. Reviews material for acts.
How to Contact: Call or write first before sending package. Prefers "cassette tapes only for music audio (inquire before sending video), with 2-6 songs and lyric sheet." SASE. Reports in 2 weeks.
Music: Mostly country rock, symphonic rock, easy listening and MOR; also blues, country, folk, jazz, progressive, R&B and top 40/pop. Currently represents Thomas St. James (songwriter/vocalist).
Tips: "We will view anyone that fits into our areas of music. However, keep in mind we work only with national and international markets. We handle those starting out as well as professionals, but all must be marketed on a professional level, if we work with you."

*TABITHA MUSIC, Sandpiper Ct., Harrington Ln., Exeter, EX4 8NS **United Kingdom**. Phone: (0392)462294. FAX: (0392)462299. Managing Director: Graham Sclater. Management firm, music publisher and record company (Tabitha Records). Estab. 1975. Represents local, regional and international individual artists, groups and songwriters. Reviews material for acts.
How to Contact: Submit demo tape by mail—unsolicited submissions are OK. Prefers cassette (or VHS videocassette if available) with 4 songs. SASE. Reports in 1 month.
Music: Mostly rock, pop and country; also R&B and folk. Works primarily with vocalists/groups. Current acts include Andy Ford (vocalist), Sovereign (R&B group) and Flic (pop group).

*TALENT ASSOCIATES OF WISCONSIN, INC., Box 588, Brookfield WI 53008. (414)786-8500. President: John A. Mangold. Management firm and booking agency. Estab. 1971. Represents local groups; currently handles 20 acts. Receives 15-20% commission. Reviews material for acts.
How to Contact: Submit demo tape by mail—unsolicited submissions are OK. Prefers cassette (or VHS videocassette if available) with 3 songs. Does not return unsolicited material. Reports in 1 month.
Music: Mostly variety shows, rock/pop and dance; also R&B and jazz. Works primarily with variety, rock and dance bands. Current acts include Booze Bros. (revue R&B show band), Mirage (top 40 dance band) and Catch A Wave (Beach Boys show & more).
Tips: "We're always looking for bands with high energy and a good stage presence, who enjoy what they're doing and radiate that through the audience, leaving all parties involved with a good feeling."

TAS MUSIC CO./DAVE TASSE ENTERTAINMENT, Route 2 Knollwood, Lake Geneva WI 53147-9731. Contact: David Tasse. Booking agency, record company and music publisher. Represents artists, groups and songwriters; currently handles 50 acts. Receives 10-20% commission. Reviews material for acts.
How to Contact: Prefers cassette (or videocassette if available) with 2-4 songs and lyric sheet. Include performance videocassette if available. SASE. Reports in 3 weeks.
Music: Mostly pop and jazz; also dance, MOR, rock, soul and top 40. Works primarily with show and dance bands. Current acts include Geneva Band (pop), Highlights (country) and Major Hamberlin (jazz).

TEXAS MUSIC MASTERS, Rt. 14 Box 1039, Tyler TX 75707. (903)566-5653. Vice President: Lonnie Wright. Management firm, music publisher and record company (TMM, Juke Box, Quazar). Estab. 1970. Represents international individual artists, groups and songwriters; currently handles 3 acts. Receives 6% commission. Reviews material for acts.
How to Contact: Write or call first for permission to submit. Prefers cassette with 3 songs. If seeking management, include short bio and photo with press kit. SASE. Reports in 3 weeks.
Music: Mostly country, gospel and blues. Works primarily with vocalists, writers and dance bands. Current acts include Aubrey T. Heird (singer), Ronny Redd (singer), Craig Robbins (singer) and Ty Black (singer).
Tips: "Be professional with demos."

*THEATER ARTS NETWORK/STEPHEN PRODUCTIONS, 15 Pleasant Dr., Lancaster PA 17602. (717)394-0970. Promotions: Stephanie Lynn Brubaker. Management firm and booking agency. Estab. 1977. Represents East Coast individual artists and groups; currently handles 6-10 acts. Receives 10-20% commission. Reviews material for acts.

How to Contact: Write or call first and obtain permission to submit. Prefers cassette (or VHS videocassette if available). Does not return unsolicited material.

Music: Mostly comedy/music, Christian contemporary and rock. Current acts include "Stephen and Other Dummies" (comedy/music/ventriloquism) and Ken Hussar (comedy/folk singer).

3L PRODUCTIONS, 3578 Silverplains Dr., Mississauga, Ontario L4X 2P4 **Canada**. (416)625-2165 or (416)238-2901. Manager: Gino Latini. Management firm and music publisher (Caras ITAA/CIRPA). Estab. 1985. Represents local and regional (Ontario) individual artist and groups; currently handles 5 acts. Receives 10-15% commission. Reviews material for acts.

How to Contact: Call first to arrange personal interview. Prefers cassette (or VHS videocassette) with 3 songs and lyric sheet. SASE and IRC. Reports in 1 month.

Music: Mostly rock, pop and R&B. Works primarily with dance band with good vocals, bar bands and recording bands. Current acts include Ten Seconds Over Tokyo (rock/pop), Tribal Son (new music), Champions (classic rock) and Power Circus (pop/rock).

Tips: "Be willing to work hard and be patient until the right break comes along."

TIMELESS PRODUCTIONS, 401-675 West Hastings, Vancouver BC V6B 1N2 **Canada**. (604)681-3029. FAX: (604)683-5357. President: Larry Gillstrom. Management firm, booking agency and record company (Magestic Records). Estab. 1984. Represents local, North American and international individual artists, groups and songwriters; currently handles over 80 acts. Receives 5-25% commission. Reviews material for acts.

How to Contact: Submit demo tape by mail—unsolicited submissions are OK. "Wait at least 30 days before following up." Prefers cassette or VHS videocassette with 3 songs and lyric sheet. SASE. Reports in 3 months.

Music: Mostly hard rock, mainstream pop and alternative rock; also New Age and hard core/metal. Works primarily with vocalists, self-contained rock bands and writers. Current acts include Young Gun (rock band), Kick Axe (rock band) and Lions Gate (rock band).

A TOTAL ACTING EXPERIENCE, Suite 206, Dept. Rhymes-1, 14621 Titus St., Panorama City CA 91402. Agent: Dan A. Bellacicco. Talent agency. Estab. 1984. Represents vocalists, lyricists, composers and groups; currently handles 27 acts. Uses the services of in-house talent for scoring of motion pictures, television, videos, musicals, jingles, TV commercials and material for major recording artists. Receives 10% commission. Reviews material for acts. Agency License: TA-0698.

How to Contact: Submit demo tape by mail—unsolicited submissions are OK. Prefers cassette (or VHS videocassette if available) with 3-5 songs and lyric or lead sheets. Please include a revealing "self talk" at the end of your tape. "Singers or groups who write their own material must submit a VHS videocassette with photo and resume." If seeking management, include VHS videotape, 5 8×10 photos, "superb" cover letter, professional typeset resume and business card in press kit. SASE. Reports in 6-12 weeks only if interested.

Music: Mostly top 40/pop, jazz, blues, country, R&B, dance and MOR; also "theme songs for new films, TV shows and special projects."

Tips: "No calls please. We will respond via your SASE. Your business skills must be strong. Please use a new tape and keep vocals up front. We welcome young, sincere talent who can give total commitment, and most important, *loyalty*, for a long-term relationship. We are seeking female vocalists (a la Streisand or Whitney Houston) who can write their own material, for a major label recording contract. Your song's story line must be as refreshing as the words you skillfully employ in preparing to build your well-balanced, orchestrated, climactic last note! Try to eliminate old, worn-out, dull, trite rhymes. A new way to write/compose or sing an old song/tune will qualify your originality and professional standing."

TREND RECORDS, Box 201, Smyrna GA 30081. (404)432-2454. President: Tom Hodges. Music publisher (Mimic Music/BMI, Boam/ASCAP) and record company (Trend Recording, Stepping Stone, Trend Setter, Proud Eagle Records, British Overseas Airways Music, Kennesaw Records). Estab. 1965. Represents local, regional and international individual artists, groups and songwriters. Currently handles 20 acts. Receives 15% commission. Reviews material for acts.

How to Contact: Submit demo tape by mail. Unsolicited submissions are OK. Prefers cassette (or videocassette if available) with 10-12 songs and lyric sheets. If seeking management, include press kit picture/professional cassette tape/clippings from news and other publications in press kit. SASE. Reports in 1 month.

Music: Mostly country, gospel and R&B; also jazz, pop and MOR. Works primarily with vocalists. Current acts include Shawn Spencer, Charlie & Nancy Cole and Joey Welz (country).

*TRIANGLE TALENT, INC., 10424 Watterson, Louisville KY 40299. (502)267-5466. President: David II. Snowden. Booking agency. Represents artists and groups; currently handles 85 acts. Receives 10-20% commission. Reviews material for acts.
How to Contact: Submit demo tape by mail—unsolicited submissions are OK. Prefers cassette (or VHS videocassette) with 2-4 songs and lyric sheet. If seeking management, include photo, audio cassette of at least 3 songs, and video if possible in press kit. SASE. Reports in 3 weeks.
Music: Rock/top 40 and country. Current acts include Rizzotto Sisters (contemporary country), Lee Bradley (contemporary country), Karen Kraft (country) and Andy Childs (pop).

*THE TRINITY STUDIO, Box 1417, Corpus Christi TX 78403. (512)880-9268. Owner: Jim Wilken. Management firm, booking agency, record company (TC Records) and recording studio. Estab. 1988. Represents individual artists, songwriters and dancers from Texas; currently handles 4 acts. Receives 5-15% commission. Reviews material for acts.
How to Contact: Submit demo tape by mail—unsolicited submissions are OK. Prefers cassette (or VHS videocassette of available). Does not return unsolicited material. Reports in 2 weeks.
Music: Mostly Christian, country and A/C; also pop, gospel and rock. Works primarily with vocalists, dancers and songwriters. Current acts include Leah (singer), Merrill Lane (singer/songwriter) and Elddy Trevino (singer/songwriter).
Tips: "you must maintain a positive attitude about your career. Have faith in your work and don't get discouraged—keep at it."

*TSMB PRODUCTIONS, Box 1388, Dover DE 19903. (302)734-2511. Chief Executive Officer: Terry Tombosi. Management firm, booking agent, music publisher (BMI) and record company (TSMB Records). Estab. 1983. Represents local, regional or international individual artists, groups and songwriters; currently handles 20 acts. Receives 10-15% commission. Reviews material for acts.
How to Contact: Submit demo tape by mail—unsolicited submissions are OK. Prefers cassette (or VHS videocassette if available) with 3 songs and lyric or lead sheets. SASE. Reports in 6 weeks.
Music: Mostly rock, blues and country; also Xmas songs. Works primarily with show bands and bands with 3 yr. longevity. Current acts include The Hubcaps, The Admirals and The Cutters (all show groups).
Tips: "Follow directions. Be completely prepared. The standard things like demos, pictures, set lists, bios need to be ready but often they aren't."

UMBRELLA ARTISTS MANAGEMENT, INC., Box 8385, 2612 Erie Ave., Cincinnati OH 45208. (513)871-1500. FAX: (513)871-1510. President: Stan Hertzman. Management firm. Represents artists, groups and songwriters; currently handles 5 acts.
How to Contact: Submit demo tape by mail—unsolicited submissions are OK. Prefers cassette with 3 songs and lyric sheet. SASE. If seeking management, press kit should include a short bio, reviews, photo and cassette. Reports in 3 months.
Music: Progressive, rock and top 40/pop. Works with contemporary/progressive pop/rock artists and writers. Current acts include Psychodots (modern band), Prizoner (rock band), America Smith (modern band), Spike (rock band) and Adrian Belew (artist/producer/songwriter/arranger whose credits include Frank Zappa, David Bowie, Talking Heads, Tom Tom Club, King Crimson, Cyndi Lauper, Lauric Anderson, Paul Simon, The Bears and Mike Oldfield).

UNITED ENTERTAINMENT, 3947 State Line, Kansas City MO 64111. Agency Manager: Joel Hornbostel. Operations Manager: Dave Maygers. Management firm, booking agency, music publisher (United Entertainment Music/BMI) and record company (Stress Records). Estab. 1972. Represents local, regional and international individual artists, groups and songwriters; currently handles 25 acts. Receives 15% commission. Reviews material for acts.
How to Contact: Submit demo tape by mail—unsolicited submissions are OK. Prefers cassette (or VHS videocassette if available) with 3-5 songs and lyric sheets. If seeking management, include glossy photo, song list, 3-4 song demo cassette bio and equipment information in press kit. Does not return material. Reports in 1 month.
Music: Mostly rock, pop and country; also gospel, blues and R&B. Works primarily with rock bands. Current acts include The Hollow Men, The Bon Ton (soul accordian band), The Songs of Rex, Spike Blake, That Statue Moved, Sing Sing, Groovehead, Dixie Cadillacs and Riverrock.

VAN DYKE ENTERPRISES, Box 275, Hanover PA 17331. (717)632-4075. Manager: Steve Eck. Management firm, booking agency and record company (Aria Records). Estab. 1983. Represents local, regional and international individual artists; currently handles 4 acts. Receives 10% commission. Reviews material for acts.

How to Contact: Submit demo tape by mail—unsolicited submissions are OK. Prefers cassette (or videocassette of live performance if available) with 4 songs and lyric sheet. SASE. Reports in 2 months.
Music: Mostly country, country rock, pop and rock. Works primarily with dance bands and bar bands. Current act includes Bruce Van Dyke (country), Freedom Express (variety) and Long Shot Band (country).
Tips: "We are looking for clean country ballads and up-tempo country songs."

HANS VAN POL MANAGEMENT, P.O. Box 9010, Amsterdam HOL 1006AA **Netherlands.** Phone: (31)20610-8281. FAX: (31)20610-6941. Managing Director: Hans Van Pol. Management firm and booking agency. Estab. 1984. Represents regional (Holland/Belgium) individual artists and groups; currently handles 5 acts. Receives 20-25% commission. Reviews material for acts.
How to Contact: Call first and obtain permission to submit. Prefers cassette or VHS videocassette with 3 songs and lyric sheets. SASE. Reports in 1 month.
Music: Mostly dance: rap/swing beat/hip house/R&B/soul/c.a.r. Current acts include Tony Scott (dance/rap), Roxy D, Zhype (swingbeat singer), Girlstreet (girlgroup, dance), Roxanna (singer/song-writer) and Stacey Paton (rap/house).

*VICTORY ARTISTS, 1054 Conifer Ln., Petaluma CA 94954. (707)762-4858. Contact: Gary Daniel. Management firm, music publisher (ASCAP) and record company (Victory Label/Bay City). Estab. 1985. Represents Northern California individual artists and groups; currently handles 1 act. Receives 15-20% commission. Reviews material for acts.
How to Contact: Write or call first and obtain permission to submit. Prefers cassette (or VHS videocassette if available) with 3 songs and lyric sheets. Does not return unsolicited material. Reports in 3 months.
Music: Mostly rock, pop and country. Works primarily with female front with band. Current acts include Shelly T (rock singer), Marcus James (pop singer) and Mark Allan (songwriter).
Tips: "Don't hype us. Just give us your best examples."

VOKES BOOKING AGENCY, Box 12, New Kensington PA 15068-0012. (412)335-2775. President: Howard Vokes. Represents individual traditional country and bluegrass artists. Books name acts in on special occasions. For special occasions books nationally known acts from Grand Ole Op'ry, Jamboree U.S.A., Appalachian Jubliee, etc. Receives 10-20% commission.
How to Contact: New artists send 45 rpm record, cassette or LP. Reports back within a week.
Music: Traditional country, bluegrass, old time and gospel; definitely no rock or country rock. Current acts include Howard Vokes & His Country Boys (country) and Mel Anderson.
Tips: "We work mostly with traditional country bands and bluegrass groups that play various bars, hotels, clubs, high schools, malls, fairs, lounges, or fundraising projects. We work at times with other booking agencies in bringing acts in for special occasions. Also we work directly with well-known and newer country, bluegrass and country gospel acts not only to possibly get them bookings in our area, but in other states as well. We also help 'certain artists' get bookings in the overseas market-place."

BEN WAGES AGENCY, 2513 Denny Ave., Pascagoula MS 39567. (601)769-7104. FAX: (601)769-8590. Owner: B. Wages. Management firm and booking agency. Estab. 1978. Represents local, regional and international individual artists, groups and songwriters; currently handles 200 acts. Receives 10-15% commission. Reviews material for acts.
How to Contact: Submit demo tape by mail—unsolicited submissions are OK. Prefers cassette (or VHS videocassette of live performance, if available). Reports in 1 month. If seeking managment, press kit should include photo, tape and any written promo. SASE.
Music: Mostly country/nostalgia and rock. Works primarily with name acts, dance bands and bar bands. Current acts include Jimmy Wages (rock-a-billy), Ace Cannon (country) and Ben Wages & The Uptown Band (variety).

*WALKER MANAGEMENT, 10974 SW 75 Ter, Miami FL 33173. President: Cliff Walker. Management firm and booking agency (ASCAP). Estab. 1983. Represents Southern individual artists and groups; currently handles 5 acts. Receives 20% commission. Reviews material for acts.
How to Contact: Submit demo tape by mail—unsolicited submissions are OK. Prefers cassette with 3 songs. Does not return unsolicited material. Reports in 2 weeks.
Music: Mostly pop; also jazz. Works primarily with vocalists and dance bands. Current acts include Tim Cashion (pop vocalist/songwriter), Pangaea (dance group), Ed Calle (saxophonist/songwriter) and Debbie Spring (vocalist/fiddler).

WESTWOOD ENTERTAINMENT GROUP, Suite 330, 1115 Inman Avenue, Edison NJ 08820-1132. (908)548-6700. FAX: (908)548-6748. President: Victor Kaplij. Director of A&R: Brian Clayton. Artist management agency (Westunes Music/ASCAP). Estab. 1985. Represents regional artists and groups;

currently handles 1 act. Receives 15% commission. Reviews material for acts.
How to Contact: Prefers cassette with 3 songs and lyric sheet. SASE. Reports in 6 weeks.
Music: Mostly rock; also pop. Works primarily with singer/songwriters, show bands and rock groups. Current acts include Kevin McCabe (rock), Ground Zero (rock) and Trooper (rock).
Tips: "Present a professional promotional/press package with 3 song limit."

SHANE WILDER ARTISTS' MANAGEMENT, Box 3503, Hollywood CA 90078. (818)508-1433. President: Shane Wilder. Management firm, music publisher (Shane Wilder Music/BMI) and record producer (Shane Wilder Productions). Represents artists and groups; currently handles 10-12 acts. Receives 15% commission. Reviews material for acts.
How to Contact: Submit demo tape by mail—unsolicited submissions are OK. Prefers cassette (or videocassette of performance if available) with 4-10 songs and lyric sheet. If seeking management, include good 8×10 glossy prints, resume and press releases in press kit. SASE. Reports in 1 month.
Music: Country. Works primarily with single artists and groups. Current acts include Inez Polizzi, Billy O'Hara and Melanie Ray (songwriters).
Tips: "Make sure your work is highly commercial. We are looking for strong female country songs for major artists. Material should be available for publishing with Shane Wilder Music/BMI. We do not accept any songs for publishing with a reversion clause."

*WISE ARTIST MANAGEMENT, 13603 Fawn Ridge Blvd., Tampa FL 33626. (813)920-6959. Contact: Douglas F. Simms. Estab. 1976. Represents local, regional or international individual artists, groups, songwriters and broadcast personalities; currently handles 3 acts. Receives 15-20% commission. Reviews material for acts.
How to Contact: Write or call first and obtain permission to submit. Prefers cassette (or VHS videocassette if available) with 3-5 songs and lyric sheet. SASE. Reports in 1 month.
Music: Mostly rock, blues and country. Works primarily with single artists with group vocals—groups with great harmonies. Current acts include Peter Treiber (rock/blues singer/songwriter), Greg LaSalle (songwriter/producer) and Rick Wise (singer/songwriter).

*WISE ENTERTAINMENT, INC., Box 8656, Columbia SC 29202. (803)957-9090. Contact: Doug Baker. Management firm and booking agency. Estab. 1982. Represents individual artists and groups; currently handles 65 acts. Receives 15% commission. Reviews material for acts.
How to Contact: Submit demo tape by mail—unsolicited submissions are OK. Prefers cassette (or VHS videocassette) with lyric sheet. "Only live performance videos will be reviewed." If seeking management, include 8×10 photo, songlist, bio, equipment list and "live performance" audio/video tape in press kit. SASE. Reports in 2-3 weeks.
Music: Country, top 40/variety, pop/rock, and R&B. Works primarily with country and top 40 show and dance bands. Current acts include Dixiana (country/variety), Almost Nuts (adult show group), Teddy Spencer and Nu-South (country), Still Cruzin' (nostalgia/R&B) and High Tide (R&B dance).

RICHARD WOOD ARTIST MANAGEMENT, 69 North Randall Ave., Staten Island NY 10301. (718)981-0641. Contact: Richard Wood. Management firm. Estab. 1974. Represents musical groups; currently handles 2 acts. Receives 10-15% commission. Reviews material for acts.
How to Contact: Submit demo tape—unsolicited submissions are OK. Prefers cassette and lead sheet. SASE. Reports in 1 month.
Music: Mostly dance, R&B and top 40/pop; also MOR. Works primarily with "high energy" show bands, bar bands and dance bands. Current acts include K-Bass (rap), Brother & Sister and Impulse (both R&B).
Tips: "Please be versatile and able to make changes in material to suit the type of acts I represent. Most of the material I receive only deals with love as a theme. Try to write to other subjects that are contemporary, such as honesty, politics and peace in the world. Pay special attention to lyrics—try to go beyond the basics and paint pictures with the words."

WORLD WIDE MANAGEMENT, Box 599, Yorktown Heights NY 10598. (914)245-1156. Director: Mr. Steve Rosenfeld. Management firm and music publisher (Neighborhood Music/ASCAP). Estab. 1971. Represents artists, groups, songwriters and actors; currently handles 4 acts. Receives 20% commission. Reviews material for acts.
How to Contact: Write or call first and obtain permission to submit or to arrange personal interview. Prefers cassette (or videocassete of performance) with 3-4 songs. SASE. Reports in 2 months.
Music: Mostly contemporary pop, folk, folk/rock and New Age; also A/C, rock, jazz, bluegrass, blues, country and R&B. Works primarily with self-contained bands and vocalists. Current acts include Scarlet Rivera, Bill Popp & The Tapes, Don Himlin and M,M,M&S.

*WYATT MANAGEMENT INC., Suite #289, 5677 Del Prado Dr., Tampa FL 33617. (813)989-9220. FAX: (813)980-2002. President: Warren Wyatt. Management firm. Estab. 1976. Represents regional and international individual artists, groups and songwriters; currently handles 4 acts. Receives 10-20% commission. Reviews material for acts.
How to Contact: Submit demo tape by mail—unsolicited submissions are OK. Prefers cassette (or ½″ VHS videocassette) with 2-10 songs and lyric sheet. If seeking management, include band biography, photos, video, members' history, press and demo reviews in press kit. SASE. Reports in 4 weeks.
Music: Mostly rock, pop and R&B; also heavy metal, hard rock and top 40. Works primarily with pop/ rock groups. Current acts include Crimson Glory (hard rock), Saigon Kick (alternative/hard rock), Venus D'Milo (rap/hard rock) and Zerop (pop rock).
Tips: "Always submit new songs/material, even if you have sent material that was previously rejected; the music biz is always changing."

*Y-NOT PRODUCTIONS, Box 902, Mill Valley CA 94942. (415)898-0027. Administrative Asst.: Lane Lombardo. Management firm and music publisher (Lindy Lane Music/BMI). Estab. 1989. Represents West Coast-USA individual artists, groups and songwriters; currently handles 4 acts. Receives 10-20% commission. Reviews material for acts.
How to Contact: Submit demo tape by mail—unsolicited submissions are OK. Prefers cassette (or VHS videocassette if available) with 3 songs. SASE. Reports in 1 month.
Music: Mostly contemporary jazz, pop and R&B/rock. Works primarily with instrumental groups/ vocalists. Current acts include Tony Saunders (bassist/songwriter), Paradize (contemporary jazz) and Darrayl Curtice (vocalist-rock).

ZANE MANAGEMENT, INC., 6th Fl., The Bellevue, Broad and Walnut Sts., Philadelphia PA 19102. (215)790-1155. FAX: (215)790-0509. President: Lloyd Zane Remick. Entertainment/sports consultants and managers. Represents artists, songwriters, producers and athletes; currently handles 5 acts. Receives variable commission.
How to Contact: Prefers cassette and lyric sheet. SASE. Reports in 1 month.
Music: Dance, easy listening, folk, jazz (fusion), MOR, rock (hard and country), soul and top 40/pop. Current acts include Bunny Sigler (disco/funk), Pieces of a Dream (consultant), Grover Washington, Jr. (management), Phyllis Nelson (management) and Sister Sledge.

ZAR MANAGEMENT, Dreilinden Str. 42, St. Gallen CH 9011 **Switzerland**. Holder: Victor Waldburger. Management firm, music publisher (Zar Musikveriag), record label and record producer. Estab. 1980. Represents individual artists, groups, songwriters and producers; currently handles 5 acts. Reviews material for acts. Receives 20% commission.
How to Contact: Write or call to submit or to arrange a personal interview. Prefers cassette (or European VHS videocassette). Reports only if interested.
Music: Mostly pop, dance, hard rock, heavy metal. Current acts include Taboo, Just Two and Give Give.

ZEE TALENT AGENCY, 3095 Sinclair St., Winnipeg, Manitoba R2P 1Y6 **Canada**. (204)338-7094. FAX: (204)334-5515. President/Agent: Linda Zagozewski. Agent: Duncan Wilson. Booking agency. Estab. 1980. Represents groups; currently handles 22 acts. Receives 10-15% commission. Reviews material for acts.
How to Contact: Submit demo tape—unsolicited submissions are OK. Prefers cassette (or videocassette of performance). "Submit song list of originals and/or covers, picture and equipment list." SAE and IRC. Reports in 2 weeks.
Music: Mostly rock, top 40 and country/rock; also contemporary, variety and show music. Current acts include Musiqa (variety), Maclean & Maclean (comedy team) and Bad Habit (top 40 and R&B).

Managers and Booking Agents/'92-'93 Changes

The following markets appeared in the 1992 edition of *Songwriter's Market* but are absent from the 1993 edition. Most of these companies failed to respond to our request for an update of their listing for a variety of reasons. For example, they may have gone out of business or they may have requested deletion because they are backlogged with material. If we know the specific reason, it appears within parentheses.

Aim High Productions/IMA
Alligator Records and Artist Management
Anjoli Productions
Attractions, Ltd.
Gary Bailey Entertainment Agency
Be-All and End-All
Best Buddies Inc. (requested deletion)
J. Bird Booking—The Entertainment Agency
Bojo Productions Inc.
Bonnie Lou Enterprises
Brier Patch Music
Brusco/Pace Management Co.
BSA Inc.
Joe Buchwald (requested deletion)
Butterfly Promotions
C.I.A.
C.M. Management (not accepting submissions)
Capital Artists Ltd.
Capitol Management
Carman Productions Inc.
Charta Records
Chasimone Enterprises
Cloana Music Group
Burt Compton Agency
Countrywide Producers
Dangerous Management
Brad Davis Inc.
De-El Music Management Inc.
Double Tee Promotions Inc.
Duncan Management Inc.
Jim Dunlop Productions
Tom Elliott Productions
Emarco Management (not accepting submissions)
Entertaining Ventures Management Inc.
Scott Evans Productions
Full Circle Talent Agency
Gangland Artists
Goldberg Talent Management

Gravity Pirates Management
Bill Hall Entertainment & Events
George Harness Associates
Head Office Management
Headquarters Entertainment Corporation
Hot Rock Artist Management
International Talent Services, Inc.
J. Bird Entertainment Agency
Jam Management
Jampop Ltd.
Jana Jae Enterprises
Janc Management
JBK Productions Ltd.
JMar Productions
KA Productions
Kalimba Productions, Inc.
L.D.F. Productions
Leroi and Associates
Loconto Productions (not accepting submissions)
Jeffrey Loseff Management
Lotus Productions (unable to contact)
Loud & Proud Management
M.S. Associates
Kevin Mabry Enterprizes
Andrew McManus Management
Maine-ly Country Music
David Maldono Management
Ed Malhoit Agency (unable to contact)
Media Promotion Enterprises
Momentum Management
Music Star Agency, Inc. (International Headquarters)
Nelson Road Management
New Artist's Productions
New Audience Productions, Inc.
New Stars Entertainment Agency
Noveau Talent

The Office, Inc.
Oldies-But-Goodies Specialty!
Open Door Management
Oracle Entertainment
Orpheus Entertainment
Palmetto Productions
Paradise Productions
Performance Group
Phoenix Talent, Ltd.
Possibilities Unlimited, Inc.
PPK AG
Propas Management Corporation
The Record Company of the South (RCS)
Walt Reeder Productions, Inc.
Revel Management
Rochester Talent Unlimited
Rockville Music Management
Jay B. Ross & Associates P.C.
Charles R. Rothschild Productions Inc.
Salt Works Music, Inc.
Shoe String Booking Agency
Silver Creek Partnership
Sound Advisors Ltd.
Southern Nights Inc.
Stinnette Entertainment Agency
Sunset Productions
The Talent Connection
TBM Entertainment (unable to contact)
Tip Top Attractions/KAM Management
Tryclops Ltd.
Twin City Talent
Richard Varrasso Management
Velvett Recording Company
Louis Walsh Management/ Booking Agency
Windfall Talent
Wingate
Wolftracks Management
Douglas A. Yeager Productions, Inc.

Advertising, AV and Commercial Music Firms

The music for a commercial or audiovisual presentation is secondary to the picture (for TV, film or video) or the message being conveyed. Commercial music must enhance the product; it must get the consumer's attention, move him in some way and, finally, motivate him — all without overpowering the message or product it accompanies. Songwriters in this area are usually strong composers, arrangers and, sometimes, producers.

The commercial music market is somewhat different than the others listed in this book. In a way, the composer is expected to have made an investment before beginning to submit work. (See the Close-up in this section with John Henry.) When dealing with commercial music firms, especially audiovisual firms and music libraries, high quality production is very important. Your demo might be kept on file by these companies and used or sold as you sent it. This assumes that the composer either owns recording equipment or electronic instruments (for MIDI composers), or at least has access to these resources.

The type of demo, then, that might be sent to a music publisher or record company will not be accepted by these companies. Also, your list of credits should be part of your submission to give the company an idea of your experience in this field. In general, it's important to be as professional as you can in your submissions to these markets; fully-produced demo tapes and complete press kits are what will get your product recognized and heard.

Commercial music and jingle writing can be a lucrative field for the composer/songwriter who is energetic, has a gift for strong hook melodies, and is able to write in many different styles. The problem is, there are many writers and few jobs — it's a very competitive field. A writer in this field must be good and must usually write quickly on spec.

Advertising agencies

Ad agencies work on assignment as their clients' needs arise. They work closely with their clients on radio and TV broadcast campaigns. Through consultation and input from the creative staff, ad agencies seek jingles and music to stimulate the consumer to identify with a product or service.

When contacting ad agencies, keep in mind they are searching for music that can capture and then hold an audience's attention. Most jingles are quick, with a strong, memorable hook line that the listener will easily identify with. Remember, though, that when an agency is listening to a demo, they are not necessarily looking for a finished product so much as for an indication of creativity and diversity. Most composers put together a reel of excerpts of work from previous projects, or short pieces of music which show they can write in a variety of styles.

Audiovisual firms

Audiovisual firms create a variety of products. Their services may range from creating film and video shows for sales meetings (and other corporate gatherings) and educational markets, to making motion pictures and TV shows. With the increase of home video use, how-to videos are a big market now for audiovisual firms, as are spoken word educational videos.

Like advertising firms, AV firms usually work on specification, so audiovisual producers looking for new songwriters search for those with versatile, well-rounded approaches. The key to submitting demos to these firms is to demonstrate your versatility in writing specialized background music and themes. Listings for companies will tell what facet(s) of the audiovisual field they are involved in and what types of clients they serve.

Commercial music houses and music libraries

Commercial music houses are companies which are contracted (either by an advertising agency or the advertiser himself) to compose custom jingles. Since they are neither an ad agency or an audiovisual firm, their main concern is music. And they use a lot of it—some composed by inhouse songwriters and some contributed by outside writers.

Music libraries are a bit different in that their music is not custom composed for a specific client. They provide a collection of instrumental music in many different styles that, for an annual fee or on a per use basis, the customer can use however he chooses (most often in audiovisual and multi-media applications).

When searching for a commercial music house or music library, they will be indicated in the listings as such by bold typeface.

The commercial music market is similar to most other businesses in one aspect; experience is important. Keep in mind that until you develop a list of credits, pay for your work may not be high. Also, don't pass up work opportunities if the job is non- or low paying. Remember, these assignments will help make contacts, add to your experience and improve your marketability.

Most of the companies listed in this section pay by the job, but there may be some situations where the company asks you to sign a contract that will specify royalty payments. If this happens, be sure you research the contract thoroughly, and that you know exactly what is expected of you and how much you'll be paid.

Sometimes, depending upon the particular job and the company, a composer/songwriter will be asked to sell one-time rights or all rights. One time rights entail using your material for one presentation only. All rights means that the buyer can use your work any way he chooses for as long as he likes. Again, be sure you know exactly what you're giving up, and how the company may use your music in the future.

For additional names and addresses of advertising agencies who may use jingles and/or commercial music, refer to the *Standard Directory of Advertising Agencies* (National Register Publishing Co.). For a list of audiovisual firms, check out the latest edition of *Audiovisual Marketplace* (published by R.R. Bowker).

THE AD AGENCY, Box 2316, Sausalito CA 94965. Creative Director: Michael Carden. Advertising agency and **jingle/commercial music production house.** Clients include business, industry and retail. Estab. 1971. Uses the services of independent songwriter/composers and lyricists for jingles for public relations/promotions/publicity and commercials for radio and TV. Commissions 20 composers and 15 lyricists/year. Pays by the job.
How to Contact: Query with resume of credits. Prefers cassette with 5-8 songs and lyric sheet. SASE, but prefers to keep materials on file. Reports in 2 weeks. Pays by the job.
Music: Uses variety of musical styles for commercials, promotion, TV, video presentations.
Tips: "Our clients and our needs change frequently."

THE AD TEAM, 15251 NE 18th Ave., N. Miami Beach FL 33162. (305)949-8326. Vice President: Zevin Auerbach. Advertising agency. Clients include automobile dealerships, radio stations, TV stations, retail. Seeking background music for commercials and jingles. Uses the services of independent songwriters for jingles for commercials. Commissions 4-6 songwriters. Pays by the job.
How to Contact: Submit demo tape of previously aired work. Prefers cassette. SASE.
Music: Uses all styles of music for all kinds of assignments. Most assignments include writing jingles for radio and television campaigns.

ADVANCE ADVERTISING AGENCY, 606 E. Belmont, Fresno CA 93701. Manager: Martin Nissen. Advertising agency. Clients include manufacturers, retailers, marketers, financial institutions. Estab. 1950. Uses the services of music houses and lyricists for commercials for radio and TV. Pays "by prior agreement." Buys all rights.

How to Contact: Submit demo tape. Prefers cassette with any number of songs. SASE, but prefers to keep materials on file. Include business card. Reports in 2 weeks.
Music: Uses easy listening, up-tempo, Dixieland and C&W for commercials.
Tips: "Listen carefully to the assignment. Don't be too sophisticated or abstract. Stay simple and translatable. Aim toward individual listener."

ALEXIS MUSIC INC. (ASCAP), MARVELLE MUSIC CO. (BMI), Box 532, Malibu CA 90265. (213)463-5998. President: Lee Magid. Music publishing and production. Clients include all types—record companies and advertising agencies. Estab. 1960. Uses the services of music houses, independent songwriters and producers for scoring of recordings, background music for film or video or theatre, jingles for commercials, commercials for radio and TV and manufacturers, events, conventions, etc. Commissions 5 composers and 5 lyricists/year. Pays by the job or by royalty. Buys all rights, publishing.
How to Contact: Submit demo tape of previous work or tape demonstrating composition skills or query with resume of credits. Prefers cassette (or VHS videocassette) with 3 pieces and lyric sheets. "If interested, we will contact you." SASE; keeps material on file only if needed. Include phone number and address on tape. Reports in 6 weeks.
Music: Uses R&B, gospel, jazz, Latin, Afro-Cuban, country; anything of substance.
Tips: "Send me a good demo that can be understood so that we can judge. Send only one cassette."

AMERICAN MEDIA CONCEPTS, INC., Dept. SM, 31 E. 32nd St., New York NY 10016. Contact: Creative Director. Advertising agency. Clients include regional retail businesses. Estab. 1982. Uses the services of music houses for jingles and commercials for radio and TV. Commissions 1-3 composers and 1-3 lyricists/year. Pays by the job. Buys all rights.
How to Contact: Submit demo tape of previous work. Prefers cassette. "No phone calls." Does not return unsolicited material; prefers to keep on file. Reports "on as-needed basis."
Music: Uses up-tempo for commercials—humorous lyrics preferred.
Tips: "Enclose letter with demo tape."

*ANDERSON COMMUNICATIONS, Dept. SM, 2245 Godbyrd, Atlanta GA 30349. (404)766-8000. President: Al Anderson. Producer: Vanessa Vaughn. Advertising agency and syndication operation. Estab. 1971. Clients include major corporations, institutions and media. Uses the services of music houses for scoring and jingles for TV and radio commercials and background music for TV and radio programs. Commissions 5-6 songwriters or composers and 6-7 lyricists/year. Pays by the job. Buys all rights.
How to Contact: Call first and obtain permission to submit. Prefers cassette. SASE, but prefers to keep material on file. Reports in 2 weeks or "when we have projects requiring their services."
Music: Uses a variety of music for music beds for commercials and jingles for nationally syndicated radio programs and commercials targeted at the black consumer market.
Tips: "Be sure that the composition plays well in a 60 second format."

ANGEL FILMS COMPANY, 967 Hwy. 40, New Franklin MO 65274-9998. Phone/FAX: (314)698-3900. President: Arlene Hulse. Motion picture and record production company (Angel One Records). Estab. 1980. Uses the services of independent songwriters/composers, lyricists and in-house agency for scoring and background music for feature films, music videos, cartoons, television productions and records. Commissions 12-20 composers and 12-20 lyricists/year. Payment depends upon budget; each project has a different pay scale. Buys all rights.
How to Contact: Submit demo tape of previous work or tape demonstrating composition skills; submit manuscript showing music scoring skills; query with resume of credits; or write to arrange personal interview. Prefers cassette (or VHS videocassette) with 3 pieces and lyric and lead sheet. "Do not send originals." SASE, but prefers to keep material on file. Reports in 3 weeks to 1 month.
Music: Uses basically MOR, but will use anything (except C&W and religious) for record production, film, television and cartoon scores.
Tips: "We prefer middle of the road music, but are open to all types. We use a lot of background music in our work, plus we have our own record label, Angel One, that is looking for music to record. Don't copy other work. Just be yourself and do the best that you can. That is all that we can ask."

 The asterisk before a listing indicates that the listing is new in this edition. New markets are often the most receptive to unsolicited submissions.

*ANGLE FILMS, Suite 240, 1341 Ocean Ave., Santa Monica CA 90401. President: John Engel. Motion picture production company and freelance producer. Estab. 1985. Clients include advertising agencies and motion picture production/distribution companies. Uses the services of music houses and independent songwriters/composers for scoring of films and commercials for TV. Pays by the job or other arrangement "entirely dependent on production and company contracting us." Buys one-time rights.
How to Contact: Prefers cassette with 5 pieces and lyric sheet. Does not return unsolicited material; prefers to keep on file. Reports only if interested.
Music: Uses all genres for short drama and feature films.
Tips: "Submit large-orchestra pieces and arrangements and be patient."

APON PUBLISHING COMPANY, INC., Dept. SM, Box 3082 Steinway Station, Long Island City NY 11103. (718)721-5599. Manager: Don Zeemann. Jingle/**commercial music production house, music sound effect library** and background music. Clients include background music companies, motion picture companies and advertising agencies. Estab. 1957. Uses the services of own special suppliers for background music for every use of the industries, jingles for advertising agencies and commercials for radio and TV. Payment is negotiated. Buys all rights.
How to Contact: Send demo cassette with background music, no voices. Prefers cassette with 2-5 pieces. SASE, but prefers to keep material on file. Reports in 2 months. No certified or registered mail accepted.
Music: Uses only background music, no synthesizer life instruments.

ATLANTIC FILM AND VIDEO, Dept. SM, 171 Park Lane, Massapequa NY 11758. (516)798-4106. Sound Designer: Michael Canzoneri. Motion picture production company. Clients include industrial/commercial. Estab. 1986. Uses the services of independent songwriters for background music for movies and commercials for TV. Commissions 1 composer and 1 lyricist/year. Pays $200-250/job. Buys one-time rights.
How to Contact: Submit demo tape of previous work or query with resume of credits. Prefers cassette or 7½ ips reel-to-reel. "Please specify what role you had in creating the music: composer, performer, etc." SASE, but prefers to keep material on file. Reports in 6 weeks.
Music: Uses jazz—modern, classical for films.
Tips: "Have patience and good songs."

AUTHENTIC MARKETING, 25 W. Fairview Ave., Dover NJ 07801. (201)366-9326. Director: Dan Kassell. Advertising agency. Estab. 1986. Uses the services of music houses, independent songwriters/composers, lyricists and arrangers for jazz video scripts. Commissions 5 composers and 5 lyricists/year. Pays 1-50% royalty. Buys one-time rights. Also provides services as a jazz artist's rep, business consultant or promotion consultant in New York City.
How to Contact: Query with resume of credits and cassette (or VHS videocassette). Does not return unsolicited material. Reports in 6 weeks.
Music: Uses jazz for background music for videoscripts.

AVID PRODUCTIONS, 235 E. 3rd Ave., San Mateo CA 94401. (415)347-3417. Producer: Chris Craig. Music sound effect library, scoring service, **jingle/commercial music production house** and video productions. Clients include corporate clients/independent producer. Estab. 1984. Uses the services of independent songwriters/composers for scoring of video production, corporate identity themes and jingles for video production. Commissions 1-2 composers/year. Pays $100-500/job. Rights negotiable.
How to Contact: Write or call first to arrange a personal interview. Prefers cassette (or VHS/¾" videocassette) with 2 songs. Prefers to keep material on file. Reports in 4 weeks.
Music: Uses up-tempo, high-tech sounds for training tapes/corporate ID pieces.

BALL COMMUNICATIONS, INC., 1101 N. Fulton Ave., Evansville IN 47710. (812)428-2300. President/Creative Director: Martin A. Ball. Audiovisual and television production and meeting production firm. Clients include Fortune 500 firms. Estab. 1960. Uses the services of lyricists and independent songwriters/composers for jingles, background music and theme songs. Commissions 4 songwriters and 4 lyricists/year. Pays $1,500-2,500/job. Buys all rights.
How to Contact: Prefers cassette or ½" videocassette. Does not return unsolicited material; prefers to keep on file. Responds by letter or telephone. SASE. Reports in 2 months.
Music: All types. Uses theme songs/jingles.

Listings of companies within this section which are either commercial music production houses or music libraries will have that information printed in boldface type.

TED BARKUS COMPANY, INC., 1512 Spruce St., Philadelphia PA 19102. (215)545-0616. President: Allen E. Barkus. Advertising agency. Uses the services of independent songwriters and music houses for jingles and background music for commercials. Commissions 1-3 songwriters/year. Pays by the job. Buys all rights.

How to Contact: Call to arrange personal interview or write to obtain permission to submit. Prefers cassette (or VHS videocassette) with 3-5 pieces. SASE, but prefers to keep material on file "when the style matches our objectives."

Music: Uses various styles of music depending upon client needs for "positioning concepts with musical beds, doughnut for inserted copy."

Tips: "Learn as much as possible about the product and who the consumer will be before starting a project. Understand that the commercial also has to work with the print and television media in terms of everything else the client is doing."

AUGUSTUS BARNETT ADVERTISING/DESIGN, Dept. SM, 632 St. Helens Ave., Tacoma WA 98402. (206)627-8508. President/Creative Director: Augustus Barnett. Advertising agency/design firm. Clients include food and service, business to business and retail advertisers. Estab. 1981. Uses the services of independent songwriters/composers for scoring of and background music for corporate video work, and commercials for radio. Commissions 1-2 composers and 0-1 lyricist/year. Buys all rights; one-time rights or for multiple use.

How to Contact: Query with resume of credits; write first to arrange personal interview. Prefers cassette. Does not return unsolicited material; prefers to keep on file. Reports in 4 months.

Music: Uses up-tempo, pop and jazz for educational films and slide presentations.

BASSET & BECKER ADVERTISING, Box 2825, Columbus GA 31902. (404)327-0763. Partner: Bill Becker. Advertising agency. Clients include medical/healthcare, banking, auto dealers, industrial, family recreation/sporting goods, business to business advertisers. Estab. 1972. Uses the services of music houses and independent songwriters/composers for scoring of and background music for TV spots and AV presentations, jingles for TV spots, AV presentations and radio, and commercials for radio and TV. Commissions 2 composers/year. "Prefers to work with engineer/producer, not directly with composer." Pays by the job. Buys all rights.

How to Contact: Submit demo tape of previous work. Prefers cassette, 7.5/15 ips reel-to-reel, or ¾ or VHS videocassette. Does not return unsolicited material; prefers to keep on file.

BAXTER, GURIAN & MAZZEI, INC., Dept. SM, 8501 Wilshire Blvd., Beverly Hills CA 90211. (213)657-5050. Contact: Steven C. Sperber. Advertising agency. Clients include healthcare, pharmaceutical and consumer businesses. Estab. 1969. Uses the services of music houses for background music for videos, jingles for radio and television spots and commercial for radio and TV. Commissions 1 composer and 1 lyricist/year. Pays $15-20K/job. Buys all rights.

How to Contact: Prefers cassette. "Be patient." Does not return unsolicited material; prefers to keep on file.

Music: "Open to all" styles of music for radio and TV jingles and soundtracks.

*BELL & ROBERTS, 1275 N. Manassero St., Anaheim Hills CA 92807. (714)777-8600. Contact: Thomas Bell. Advertising agency. Clients include business to business, consumer and retail/electronics, toys, food service and financial firms. Estab. 1980. Uses the services of music houses and independent songwriters/composers for commercials for radio and TV. Commissions 1-2 composers and 1-2 lyricists/year. Pays by the job. Buys all rights.

How to Contact: Submit demo tape of previous work. Prefers cassette (or VHS videocassette) with songs and lead sheets. SASE, but prefers to keep material on file. Reports in 3 weeks.

Music: Uses up-tempo, jazz and pop for commercials and educational films.

RON BERNS & ASSOCIATES, 520 N. Michigan Ave., Chicago IL 60611. (312)527-2800. President: Ron Berns. Advertising agency. Uses services of independent songwriters for jingles. Pays by the job. Buys all rights.

How to Contact: Submit demo tape of previous work. Prefers cassette. Prefers studio produced demo. Does not return unsolicited material; prefers to keep on file. Reports when needed.

THE BLACKWOOD AGENCY, INC., Suite 100, 2187 Jolly Rd., Okemos MI 48864. (517)349-6770. Production Manager: Christine Gaffe. Advertising agency. Estab. 1979. Clients include financial and package goods firms. Uses services of music houses for scoring of commercials and training films, background music for slide productions, jingles for clients and commercials for radio and TV. Commissions 3 composers/year. Pays by the job. Buys all rights.

How to Contact: Submit demo tape of previous work. Prefers cassette (or ¾" videocassette) with 6-10 songs. SASE, but prefers to keep material on file.
Tips: "Give us good demo work."

BLATTNER/BRUNNER INC., 814 Penn Ave., Pittsburgh PA 15222. (412)263-2979. Broadcast Production Coordinator: Traci Trainor. Clients include retail/consumer, service, high-tech/industrial. Estab. 1975. Uses the services of music houses and independent songwriters/composers for scoring of commercials and videos, background music for TV and radio spots, jingles for TV and radio spots and commercials for radio, TV. Commissions 2-3 composers/year. Pays by the job. Buys all rights or one-time rights, depending on the job.
How to Contact: Submit demo tape of previous work demonstrating composition skills or write first to arrange personal interview. Prefers cassette (or VHS or ¾" videocassette) with 5-10 songs. SASE but prefers to keep submitted materials on file. Reports in 1 month.
Music: Uses up-beat, "unique-sounding music that stands out" for commercials and industrial videos.
Tips: "We're always interested in hearing new pieces."

BRADLEY COMMUNICATIONS, Dept. SM, Suite 200, 1840 S. Bragaw, Anchorage AK 99508. (907)276-6353. Copywriter: Katie Hickey. Advertising/public relations agency. Clients include tourism and development. Estab. 1968. Uses the services of music houses for background music for informative videos, telecommunications, and jingles and commercials for radio/TV. Pays by the job. Buys one-time rights.
How to Contact: Submit demo tape of previous work which demonstrates composition skills. Cassette, VHS or ¾" videocassette. SASE, but prefers to keep materials on file. Reports back "when need arises."
Music: Uses up-tempo and emotional music.

BRAUNCO VIDEO, INC., Dept. SM, Box 236, Warren IN 46792. (219)375-3148. Producer: Magley Tocsin. Video production company. Estab. 1988. Clients include industrial manufacturing, service companies, factories, United Way agencies, entertainers, songwriters, etc. Uses the services of independent songwriters/composers and house studio bands for jingles and background music for corporate video presentations. Commissions composers. Pays by the job. Buys all rights.
How to Contact: Submit demo tape of previous work or write to arrange personal interview. Prefers cassette or 15 ips reel-to-reel (or ¾" videocassette) with many pieces. "We have no use for lyric or vocals." Does not return unsolicited material.
Music: Uses up-tempo, heavy metal, R&B with a bit of jazz influence and soft music for promotional corporate demos.
Tips: "Believe in yourself."

BROACH AND CO., Dept. SM, Box 1139, Greensboro NC 27402. (919)373-0752. Creative Director: Allen Broach. Advertising agency. Clients include furniture, banking, and consumer goods firms. Estab. 1982. Uses the services of music houses and independent songwriters/lyricists for scoring, background music for commercials and videos, jingles for commercials and commercials for radio and TV. Commissions 1-5 composers and up to 3 lyricists/year. Buys all rights or one-time rights.
How to Contact: Submit demo tape of previous work or tape demonstrating compositional skills. Prefers cassette with 6-10 songs and lead sheet. Does not return unsolicited submissions; prefers to keep submitted material on file.

BROADCAST VIDEO, INC., Dept. SM, 20377 N.E. 15th Ct., Miami FL 33179. (305)653-7440. Senior Audio Engineer: Scott Pringle. Film/video post production house. Clients include advertising agencies, film/video producers. Audio department established 1988. Uses the services of music houses, independent songwriters/composers and music libraries for scoring and background music for commercials, documentaries and corporate presentations; jingles for commercials; and commercials for radio and TV. Pays by the job. Rights negotiated with client.
How to Contact: Query with resume of credits or write first to arrange personal interview. Prefers cassette or 7.5 or 15 ips reel-to-reel (or any videocassette). SASE, but prefers to keep material on file. Reports in 1 month.
Music: "We use music for commercials the most, but use songwriters most often for lengthier programs—corporate, documentaries, etc."

BUTWIN & ASSOCIATES, INC., 8700 Westmoreland Ln., Minneapolis MN 55426. (612)546-0203. President: Ron Butwin. Clients include corporate and retail. Estab. 1977. Uses the services of music houses, lyricists and independent songwriters/composers for scoring, background music, jingles and commercials for radio, TV. Commissions 3-5 composers and 1-3 lyricists/year. Pays varying amount/job. Buys all rights and one-time rights.

How to Contact: Submit demo tape of previous work. Write first to arrange personal interview. Prefers cassette, ¼" videocassette. "We are only interested in high-quality professional work." SASE, but prefers to keep material on file.
Music: Uses easy listening, up-tempo, pop and jazz for slide presentations and commercials.

CALDWELL VANRIPER, 1314 N. Meridian, Indianapolis IN 46202. (317)632-6501. Vice President/ Executive Producer: Sherry Boyle. Advertising agency and public relations firm. Clients include industrial, financial and consumer/trade firms. Uses jingles and background music for commercials. Commissions 25 pieces/year.
How to Contact: Submit demo tape of previously aired work or submit tape showing jingle/composition skills. Prefers standard audio cassette. SASE, but prefers to keep materials on file. "Sender should follow up on submission. Periodic inquiry or reel update is fine."
Tips: "Show range of work on reel, keep it short."

CALF AUDIO, 157 Gray Rd., Ithaca NY 14850. (607)272-8964. President: Haines B. Cole. Vice President: J. Todd Hutchinson. Producer/Engineer: Alfred B. Grunwell. Assistant Engineer: Margaret T. Baker. Professional audio analysis and design, 24-track recording studio, audiovisual firm and **music/ sound effects library.** Estab. 1977. Uses the services of music houses and independent songwriters/ composers for background music, jingles and radio and TV commercials and audiovisual presentations. Pays $1,000-2,000/job. Buys all rights.
How to Contact: Submit demo tape of previous work; write to arrange personal interview. Prefers cassette or 15 ips reel-to-reel with 3-5 pieces. Send "full documentation." Does not return unsolicited material; prefers to keep on file. Reports in 3 weeks.
Music: Uses contemporary pop for educational films, slide presentations and commercials.
Tips: "Assimilate but don't duplicate works from the past. Take direction well."

*THE CAMPBELL GROUP, 326 N. Charles St., Baltimore MD 21201. (410)547-0600. Associate Creative Director: Randi Abse. Advertising agency. Clients include hotels, restaurants, destinations, automobile dealerships, publications. Estab. 1986. Uses the services of music houses and independent songwriters/composers for scoring of video sales presentations, background music for radio and TV, jingles for radio and TV and commercials for radio and TV. Commissions 10 composers/year. Pays $3,000-6,000/job. Buys all rights or one-time rights.
How to Contact: Submit demo tape of previous work. Prefers cassette (or ½" VHS or ¾" cassette) with 5-10 songs. Does not return unsolicited material; prefers to keep on file. Reports in 2-3 weeks.
Music: Uses up-tempo, pop, jazz and classical for commercials.
Tips: "Send demo of work, rates, brochure if available."

CANARY PRODUCTIONS, Box 202, Bryn Mawr PA 19010. (215)825-1254. President: Andy Mark. **Music library.** Estab. 1984. Uses the services of music houses and independent songwriters for background music for AV use, jingles for all purposes, and commercials for radio. Commissions 10 composers/year. Pays $500-1,000 for 10 cuts of full length music, or on consignment per composition. "No songs, please!"
How to Contact: Prefers cassette with 5-10 pieces. SASE. Reports in 2 weeks.
Music: All styles, but concentrates on industrial. "We pay cash for produced tracks of all styles and lengths. Production value is imperative. No scratch tracks accepted."
Tips: "Send quality, not quantity."

CANTRAX RECORDERS, Dept. SM, 2119 Fidler Ave., Long Beach CA 90815. (213)498-6492. Owner: Richard Cannata. Recording studio. Clients include anyone needing recording services (i.e. industrial, radio, commercial). Estab. 1980. Uses the services of independent songwriters/composers and lyricists for scoring of jingles, soundtracks, background music for slide shows and films, jingles for radio, commercials for radio and music demos and music videos. Commissions 10 composers/year. Pays by the job. Buys all rights.
How to Contact: Submit demo tape of previous work demonstrating composition skills. Prefers cassette or 7½/15 ips reel-to-reel (or VHS videocassette) with lyric sheets. "Indicate noise reduction if used. We prefer reel to reel." SASE, but prefers to keep material on file. Reports in 2 weeks.
Music: Uses jazz, New Age, rock, easy listening and classical for slide shows, jingles and soundtracks, etc.
Tips: "Send a 7½/15 ips reel for us to audition; you must have a serious, professional attitude."

CAPITOL PRODUCTION MUSIC, #718, 6922 Hollywood Blvd., Hollywood CA 90028. (213)461-2701. Managing Director: Ole Georg. Scoring service, **jingle/commercial music production house, music sound effect library.** Clients include broadcast, corporate/industrial, theatrical, production/post-production houses. Uses the services of independent songwriters/composers for 35-70 minutes of music

beds for CD library. Commissions 6 composers/year. Pays by the job. Buys all rights.
How to Contact: Submit resume of credits and compositional styles. No tapes please. All resumes kept on file for future consideration. "No report unless we have interest." No calls please. Reports in 4-6 months.
Music: Uses hot pop, "big acoustic," corporate industrial, atmospheric.
Tips: "Material most likely to be considered is that with heavy dynamics and strong edit-points."

*CARLETON PRODUCTIONS INC., 1500 Merivale Rd., Ottawa K2E 6Z5 Ontario **Canada**. Producer: Bill Graham/Mark Ross/Randi Hansen. Audiovisual firm and TV & video production. Clients include Canadian and American TV networks, government, corporate and producers. Estab. 1973. Uses the services of music houses, independent songwriters/composers and lyricists for scoring of music beds, stings, bridges, openings, background music for corporate and sales plus drama, jingles for sales presentations and commercials for TV. Commissions 25-50 composers and 1-3 lyricists/year. Pays by the job or by royalty. Buys one-time rights "determined by project."
How to Contact: Submit demo tape of previous work. Prefers cassette. "Include past credits." Does not return unsolicited material; prefers to keep on file.
Music: Uses all types for mainly corporate video, sales video and TV beds.

*CASANOVA-PENDRILL PUBLICIDAD, 3333 Michelson, Irvine CA 92715. (714)474-5001. Production: Kevan Wilkinson. Advertising agency. Clients include consumer and corporate advertising—Hispanic markets. Estab. 1985. Uses the services of music houses, independent songwriters/composers and lyricists for radio, TV and promotions. Pays by the job or per hour. Buys all rights or one-time rights.
How to Contact: Submit demo tape of previous work, tape demonstrating composition skills and manuscript showing showing music scoring skills. Prefers cassette (or ¾ videocassette). "Include a log indicating spot(s) titles." Does not return unsolicited material; prefers to keep on file.
Music: All types of Hispanic music (e.g., salsa, mevengue, flamenca, etc.) for television/radio advertising.

*CHANNELL ONE VIDEO, Box 1437, Seabrook NH 03874. (603)474-5046. President: Bill Channell. Audiovisual firm, motion picture production company and TV programmer. Clients include TV stations, broadcast, cable and corporate clients for TV ads, and product videos. Uses music houses, independent songwriters/composers, lyricists and music libraries for scoring of TV programs; background music for TV ads, training, sales, industrial and sports videos; jingles for TV ads; and commercials for TV. Pays by the job. Buys all rights or one-time rights.
How to Contact: Query with resume of credits or submit demo tape of previous work or tape demonstrating composition skills. Prefers cassette (or ¾" or VHS videocassette). Does not return unsolicited material; prefers to keep on file. Reports in 3-6 weeks.
Music: Uses up-tempo music for all kinds of assignments.

CHANNEL ONE VIDEO TAPE INC., Dept. SM, 3301 NW 82nd Ave., Miami FL 33122. (305)592-1764. General Manager: Jay P. Van Dyke. Video production house, **music library**. Estab. 1969. Clients include commercial, industrial, medical and network programs. Uses music library for commercials for TV and industrials, medical, programs. Pays by the job or "yearly fee." Buys all rights.
How to Contact: Submit demo tape of previous work. Prefers 7½ ips reel-to-reel. Does not return unsolicited material; prefers to keep on file. Reports if interested.
Music: Uses all styles of music for all kinds of assignments.

*CHANNEL 3 VIDEO, Box 8781, Warwick RI 02888. (401)461-1616. President: Jeffrey B. Page. Audiovisual firm and video production/post production services. Clients include educational, commercial, industrial, retail firms and others. Uses the services of music houses, independent songwriters/composers and lyricists for scoring of documentary works, background music for industrials, jingles for product presentations, commercials for radio and TV and multimedia events. Commissions 5 composers and 2 lyricists/year. Pays $50-500/job. Buys all rights or one-time rights; depends on the job.
How to Contact: Submit demo tape of previous work, tape demonstrating composition skills or manuscript showing music scoring skills. Prefers cassette or 15 ips reel-to-reel (or ¾" or ½" VHS videocassette) with 3-5 pieces and lyric or lead sheets. "All submissions will be put in permanent file and not returned. At the artist's request they will be destroyed if requested in writing." Reports back in 5 weeks.
Music: Uses all styles of music.

CHAPMAN RECORDING STUDIOS, 228 W. 5th, Kansas City MO 64105. (816)842-6854. Contact: Chuck Chapman. Custom music and production. Clients include video producers, music producers, musicians and corporations. Estab. 1973. Uses the services of independent songwriters/composers and arrangers for background music for video productions; jingles for radio, TV, corporations; and

commercials for radio and TV. Commissions 4 composers and 4 lyricists/year. Buys all rights.
How to Contact: Call to arrange submission of tape demo. Prefers cassette. SASE, but prefers to keep material on file. Reports in 2 months.
Music: Uses all styles, all types for record releases, video productions, and TV and radio productions; and up-tempo and pop for educational films, slide presentations and commercials.

CHASE/EHRENBERG & ROSENE, INC., 211 E. Ontario, Chicago IL 60611. (312)943-3737. Executive Vice President: John Rosene. Advertising agency. Clients include retailers and national manufacturers. Estab. 1942. Uses the services of music houses, independent songwriters/composers and needle drop for scoring of commercials and commercials for radio, TV. Commissions 1 or 2 composers/year. Pays by the job. Buys all rights.
How to Contact: Submit demp tape of previous work demonstrating composition skills. Write or call first to arrange personal interview. Prefers cassette. Does not return unsolicited material but prefers to keep on file.
Music: Uses up tempo, rock, pop for commercials.

*CHECKMARK COMMUNICATIONS MULTI-MEDIA, (formerly Centra Advertising Company), Checkerboard Square, St. Louis MO 63164. (314)982-1000. Broadcast Services Manager: Linda Schumacher. Advertising agency. Clients include packaged goods and public service firms. Estab. 1983. Uses the services of music houses, independent songwriters and lyricists for commercials for radio and TV. Buys all rights.
How to Contact: Submit demo tape of previous work. Prefers cassette. Does not return unsolicited material. Prefers to keep material on file.
Music: Uses up-tempo for TV and radio commercials and "long form for corporate training/industrial use."

CHIAT/DAY/MOJO ADVERTISING, Dept. SM, 320 Hampton Dr., Venice CA 90291. (213)314-5000. President/Executive Director: Lee Clow. Chief Creative Officer: Steve Rabosky. Serves health care, packaged food, home loan, automotive, electronics and motorcycle clients. Uses background music in commercials. Commissions 1 piece/year. Pays by the job.
How to Contact: Submit demo tape of previously aired work. Prefers 7½ ips reel-to-reel. SASE. Reports "as soon as possible."

CINEVUE, Box 428, Bostwick FL 32007. (904)325-5254. Director/Producer: Steve Postal. Motion picture production company. Estab. 1955. Serves all types of film distributors. Use the services of independent songwriters and lyricists for scoring of and background music for movies and commercials. Commissions 10 composers and 5 lyricists/year. Pays by the job. Buys all rights or one-time rights.
How to Contact: Query with resume of credits or write to arrange personal interview. Prefers cassette or reel-to-reel with 10 pieces and lyric or lead sheet. SASE, but prefers to keep material on file. "Send good audio-cassette, then call me in a week." Reports in 1 week.
Music: Uses all styles of music for features (educational films and slide presentations). "Needs horror film music on traditional instruments—no electronic music."
Tips: "Be flexible, fast—do first job free to ingratiate yourself and demonstrate your style."

CLEARVUE/EAV INC., Dept. SM, 6465 N. Avondale, Chicago IL 60631. (312)775-9433. Chairman of the Board: William T. Ryan. President: Mark Ventling. Vice President: Matt Newman. Audiovisual firm. Serves the educational market. Estab. 1969. "We only produce core curriculum and enrichment videos for pre-primary through high school students." Uses the services of independent songwriters. Commissions 3 songwriters or composers/year. Pays by the job.
Music: "We are seeking original video proposal and finished product focusing on the teaching of music skills."
Tips: "Look at our catalog—fill in the missing pieces."

COAKLEY HEAGERTY, 1155 N. 1st St., San Jose CA 95112. (408)275-9400. Creative Director: Susann Rivera. Advertising agency. Clients include consumer, business to business and high tech firms. Estab. 1966. Uses the services of music houses for background music for commercials and jingles. Commissions 15-20 songwriters/year. Pays by the job. Buys all rights.
How to Contact: Submit demo tape of previously aired work. Prefers cassette or 7½ ips reel-to-reel with 8-10 pieces. Does not return unsolicited material; prefers to keep material on file. Reports in 6 months.
Music: All kinds of music for jingles and music beds.
Tips: "Send samples of just commercials, no scores please. Be patient."

COMMUNICATIONS CONCEPTS INC., Box 661, Cape Canaveral FL 32920. (407)783-5320. Manager: Jim Lewis. Audiovisual firm. Clients include resorts, developments medical and high tech industries. Uses the services of music houses, independent songwriters, lyricists and music libraries and services for scoring of TV shows and AV presentations, background music for AV programs and marketing presentations, jingles for commercials and AV programs, and commercials for radio and TV. Commissions 2-3 composers/year and 1-2 lyricists/year. Pays $50-5,000/job. Buys all rights or one-time rights.
How to Contact: Prefers cassette. Does not return unsolicited material; prefers to keep on file.
Music: Corporate, contemporary and commercial.

COMMUNICATIONS FOR LEARNING, 395 Massachusetts Ave., Arlington MA 02174. (617)641-2350. Executive Producer/Director: Jonathan L. Barkan. Audiovisual and design firm. Clients include multinationals, industry, government, institutions, local, national and international nonprofits. Uses services of music houses and independent songwriters/composers for scoring and background music for audiovisual and video soundtracks. Commissions 1-2 composers/year. Pays $2,000-3,000/job. Buys one-time rights.
How to Contact: Submit demo tape of previous work or tape demonstrating composition skills. Prefers cassette or 7½ or 15 ips reel-to-reel (or ½" or ¾" videocassette). Does not return unsolicited material; prefers to keep material on file. "For each job we consider our entire collection." Reports "depending on needs."
Music: Uses all styles of music for all sorts of assignments.
Tips: "Please don't call. Just send good material and when we're interested, we'll be in touch."

CONTINENTAL PRODUCTIONS, Box 1219, Great Falls MT 59405. (406)761-8816. Production Sales/ Marketing: Duke Brekhus. Video production house. Clients include advertising agencies, business, industry and government. Uses the services of independent songwriters/composers for TV commercials and non broadcast programs and jingles for TV commercials. Commissions 1-6 composers/year. Pays $85-500/job. Buys all rights or one-time rights.
How to Contact: Write or call first and obtain permission to submit. Prefers cassette (or ½" VHS videocassette). SASE, but prefers to keep on file. Reports in 2 weeks.
Music: Uses contemporary music beds and custom jingles for TV and non-broadcast video.
Tips: "Songwriters need to build a working relationship by providing quality product in short order at a good price."

T. COOKE PRODUCTIONS, INC., Dept. SM, 955 Gardenview Office Pkwy., St. Louis MO 63141. (314)997-3200. President: Thomas Cooke. Audiovisual firm and motion picture production company. Clients include Fortune 500 industrial/consumer products companies. Uses services of independent songwriters/composers, lyricists and music houses for scoring of industrial video/film, background music for A/V programs. Commissions 4-6 composers/year. Pays $3,000-6,000/job. Buys all rights.
How to Contact: Submit demo tape of previous work or query with resume of credits. Prefers cassette with 6 songs. SASE, but prefers to keep material on file.
Music: Uses music to sell, hype, motivate for slide presentations, corporate image videos, and live industrial stage shows.

CORPORATE COMMUNICATIONS INC., Main St., Box 854, N. Conway NH 03860. (603)356-7011. President: Kimberly Beals. Advertising agency. Estab. 1983. Uses the services of music houses, independent songwriters/composers for background music, jingles and commercials for radio/video. Commissions 2 or more composers/year. Pays by the job. Buys all rights or one-time rights.
How to Contact: Submit demo tape of previous work demonstrating composition skills. Query with resume of credits. Prefers cassette (or ½" videocassette) with 5 songs. Does not return unsolicited material; prefers to keep on file.
Music: Uses varying styles of music for varying assignments.

CREATIVE ASSOCIATES, Dept. SM, 626 Bloomfield Ave., Verona NJ 07044. (201)857-3444. Production Coordinator: Susan Graham. Audiovisual firm. Clients include commercial, industrial firms. Estab. 1975. Uses the services of music houses and independent songwriters/composers for scoring of video programs, background music for press tours and jingles for new products. Pays $300-5,000+/ job. Buys all or one-time rights.
How to Contact: Submit demo tape of previous work demonstrating composition skills or query with resume of credits. Prefers cassette or ½" or ¾" VHS videocassette. Prefers to keep material on file.
Music: Uses all styles for many different assignments.

CREATIVE AUDIO PRODUCTIONS, 326 Santa Isabel Blvd., Laguna Vista, Port Isabel TX 78578. (512)943-6278. Owner: Ben McCampbell. **Jingle/commercial music production house.** Serves ad agencies, broadcast stations (TV and radio), video/film production houses and advertisers. Uses the services

of lyricists for jingles for commercials and commercials for radio and TV. Commissions 1 composer and 2 lyricists/year. Fees negotiable. Buys one-time rights.
How to Contact: Submit demo tape of previous work. Prefers cassette with 3-5 songs. Does not return unsolicited material; prefers to keep on file. Reports in 3 weeks.
Music: Uses pop, up-tempo, country, rock and reggae for commercials.

CREATIVE HOUSE ADVERTISING, INC., Suite 301, 30777 Northwestern Hwy., Farmington Hills MI 48334. (313)737-7077. Senior Vice President/Executive Creative Director: Robert G. Washburn. Advertising agency and graphics studio. Serves commercial, retail, consumer, industrial, medical and financial clients. Uses the services of songwriters and lyricists for jingles, background music for radio and TV commercials and corporate sales meeting films and videos. Commissions 3-4 songwriters/year. Pays $1,500-5,000/job depending on job involvement. Buys all rights.
How to Contact: Query with resume of credits or submit tape demo showing jingle/composition skills. Submit cassette (or ¾″ videocassette) with 6-12 songs. SASE, but would prefer to keep material on file. "When an appropriate job comes up associated with the talents/ability of the songwriters/musicians, then they will be contacted."
Music: "The type of music we need depends on clients. The range is multi: contemporary, disco, rock, MOR and traditional."
Tips: "Be fresh, innovative and creative. Provide good service and costs."

CREATIVE SUPPORT SERVICES, 1950 Riverside Dr., Los Angeles CA 90039. (213)666-7968. Contact: Michael M. Fuller. **Music/sound effects library**. Clients include audiovisual production houses. Estab. 1978. Uses the services of independent songwriters and musicians for background music for audiovisuals and commercials for radio. Commissions 3-5 songwriters and 1-2 lyricists/year. Pays by the job. Buys exclusive distribution rights.
How to Contact: Write or call first. Prefers cassette ("chrome or metal only") or 7½ ips reel-to-reel with 3 or more pieces. Does not return unsolicited material; prefers to keep on file. "Will call if interested."
Music: Uses "industrial music predominantly, but all other kinds or types to a lesser degree."
Tips: "Don't assume the reviewer can extrapolate beyond what is actually on the demo."

CRESWELL, MUNSELL, FULTZ & ZIRBEL, Box 2879, Cedar Rapids IA 52406. (319)395-6500. Vice President/Manager Broadcast Production Services: Mike Murray. Assistant Broadcast Coordinator: Judy Gibson. Advertising agency. Serves agricultural, consumer and industrial clients. Uses songwriters and music houses for jingles and background music in commercials and multi-image soundtracks. Commissions 7-8 songwriters for 15 pieces/year. Pays by the job. Buys rights on talent residuals.
How to Contact: Submit demo tape of previously aired work. Prefers 7 or 15 ips reel-to-reel or cassette with 7-8 songs maximum. Does not return unsolicited material. Reports "when we want figures on a job."
Music: All types. Likes to hear a good range of music material. Will listen to anything from "small groups to full orchestration."
Tips: "Create unique, recognizable melodies."

R.J. DALE ADVERTISING INC., Dept. SM, #2204, 500 N. Michigan Ave., Chicago IL 60611. (312)644-2316. Executive Vice President: William Stewart. Advertising agency. Clients include H&BA Manufacturers, retail bank, lottery, food, distilled spirits manufacturers. Estab. 1979. Uses the services of music houses and independent songwriters/composers for background music for sales meetings and commercials for radio and TV. Commissions 5 composers/year. Pays by the job. Buys all rights or two-year rights.
How to Contact: Submit demo tape of previous work showing range of ability. Prefers cassette (or ¼″ U-matic videocassette). SASE, but prefers to keep material on file.
Music: Uses pop, jazz, fusion and R&B for commercials.

dbF A MEDIA COMPANY, Box 2458, Waldorf MD 20604. (301)843-7110. President: Randy Runyon. Advertising agency, audiovisual firm and audio and video production company. Clients include business and industry. Estab. 1981. Uses the services of music houses, independent songwriters/composers and lyricists for background music for industrial videos, jingles for radio and TV and commercials for radio and TV. Commissions 5-12 composers and 5-12 lyricists/year. Pays by the job. Buys all rights.
How to Contact: Call first for permission to submit or query with resume of credits. Prefers cassette or 7½ IPS reel-to-reel (or VHS videocassette) with 5-8 songs and lead sheet. SASE, but prefers to keep material on file. Reports in 2 weeks.
Music: Uses up-tempo contemporary for industrial videos, slide presentations and commercials.
Tips: "We're looking for commercial music, primarily adult contemporary."

*DELTA DESIGN GROUP, INC., Dept. SM, 409 Washington Ave., Greenville MS 38701. (601)335-6148. President: Noel Workman. Advertising agency. Serves industrial, health care, agricultural and retail commercial clients. Uses the services of songwriters for jingles. Commissions 3-6 pieces/year. Pays $500-2,500/job. Buys "rights which vary geographically according to client. Some are all rights; others are rights for a specified market only. Buy out only. No annual licensing."
How to Contact: Submit demo tape showing jingle/composition skills. Prefers 7½ ips reel-to-reel with 3-6 songs. "Include typed sequence of cuts on tape on the outside of the reel box." SASE. Reports "when services are needed."
Music: Needs "30- and 60-second jingles for agricultural, health care, auto dealers and chambers of commerce."

*THE DENNIS GROUP, INC., (formerly Dennis R. Green And Associates, Inc.), Suite 150, 29425 Northwestern Hwy., Southfield MI 48034. (313)355-3800. President: Dennis R. Green. Advertising agency. Clients include retail and industrial firms. Estab. 1991. Uses the services of music houses for jingles for radio and television and commercials for radio and TV. Commissions 6 composers/year. Pays $1500-2500/job. Buys all rights.
How to Contact: Submit a demo tape of previous work or query with resume of credits. Prefers cassette or 7.5 ips reel to reel (or VHS videocassette) with 6-10 songs. SASE, but prefers to keep submitted material on file. Reports back in two weeks.
Music: All kinds, depending on clients' needs.
Tips: "Send a demo reel and keep in touch."

DISK PRODUCTIONS, 1100 Perkins Rd., Baton Rouge LA 70802. (504)343-5438. Director: Joey Decker. **Jingle/production house.** Clients include advertising agencies, slide production houses and film companies. Estab. 1982. Uses independent songwriters/composers and lyricists for scoring of TV spots and films and jingles for radio and TV. Commissions 7 songwriters/composers and 7 lyricists/year. Pays $1,750/job. Buys all rights.
How to Contact: Prefers cassette or 7½ ips reel-to-reel (or ½" videocassette) and lead sheet. SASE, but prefers to keep material on file. Reports "immediately if material looks promising."
Music: Needs all types of music for jingles, music beds or background music for TV and radio, etc.
Tips: "Advertising techniques change with time. Don't be locked in a certain style of writing. Give me music that I can't get from pay needle-drop."

*DONCHRIST VISUAL COMMUNICATIONS, 267 Hodden Ave., Collingswood NJ 08108. President: Gary Steglor. Audiovisual firm and video production company. Estab. 1952. Uses the services of music houses, independent songwriters/composers and music libraries for videos and AV shows. Pays by the job. Buys one-time rights.
How to Contact: Call first to arrange personal interview. Prefers cassette (or ¾" videocassette). SASE, but prefers to keep material on file. Reports in 3 weeks.
Music: Uses all for video productions/AV shows.
Tips: "Be good, be fast, be cheap."

DRGM, 50 Washington St., Dept. SM, Reno NV 89503. (702)786-4900. Also Suite A, 2275 Renaissance Dr., Bldg. 3, Las Vegas NV 89119. (702)736-0065. Vice President/Creative Services: Randy Snow. Creative Director/Reno: Ron Cooney. Creative Director/Las Vegas: Michael Mayes. Advertising agency. Clients include tourism, hotel-casino, retail, financial and healthcare. Estab. 1970. Uses the services of music houses for scoring of television/radio, background music for television/radio, jingles for TV/radio and commercials for radio and TV. Commissions 4-5 composers/year. Pays by the job. Buys all rights.
How to Contact: Submit demo tape of previous work. Prefers cassette (or ¾" videocassette). SASE, but prefers to keep material on file. Reports in 2 weeks.
Music: Uses contemporary and up-tempo for jingles and commercials.
Tips: "Send me a reel—be aware that clients in Nevada do not understand things like big budgets, royalty payments, etc."

DSM PRODUCERS INC., Suite 803, 161 W. 54th St., New York NY 10019. (212)245-0006. Vice President, National Sales Director: Doris Kaufman. Scoring service, **jingle/commercial music production house** and original stock library called "All American Composers Library" record producers. Clients include networks, corporate, advertising firms, film and video, book publishers (music only). Estab. 1979. Uses the services of independent songwriters/composers and "all signed composers who we represent" for scoring of film, industrial films, major films—all categories; background music for film, audio cassettes, instore video—all catagories; jingles for advertising agencies and commercials for radio and TV. Pays 50% royalty; 50% of licensing fees; 100% of writer royalty from performance affiliation. Publishes 25 new composers annually.

How to Contact: Submit tape demonstrating composition skills. Prefers cassette (or VHS videocassette) with 2 songs and lyric or lead sheet. "Keep the vocals up in the mix—use a large enough return envelope to put in a standard business reply letter." SASE. Reports in 3 months.
Music: Uses dance, New Age, country and rock for adventure films and sports programs.
Tips: "Send the closest to a 'master' tape as you can. If you want production tips, you can call the company. Keep your vocals up. Digital tracks can make a big difference in your presentation."

ROY EATON MUSIC INC., 595 Main St., Roosevelt Island NY 10044. (212)980-9046. President: Roy Eaton. **Jingle/commercial music production house.** Clients include advertising agencies, TV and radio stations and film producers. Estab. 1982. Uses the services of independent songwriters/composers and lyricists for scoring of TV commercials and films; background music for TV programs; jingles for advertising agencies and commercials for radio and TV. Commissions 10 composers and 1 lyricist/year. Pays $50-3,000/job. Buys all rights.
How to Contact: Submit demo tape of previous work. Prefers cassette with 3-5 pieces. Does not return unsolicted material; prefers to keep on file. Reports in 6 months.
Music: Uses jazz fusion, New Age and rock/pop for commercials and films.

ELITE VIDEO PRODUCTIONS, 1612 East 14th St., Brooklyn NY 11229. (718)627-0499. President: Kalman Zeines. Video production company. Clients include educational and industrial. Estab. 1978. Uses the services of music houses, lyricists and independent songwriters/composers for background music for narration and commercials for TV. Commissions 2 lyricists and 5 composers/year. Pays $35-1,800/job. Buys all rights.
How to Contact: Submit demo tape of previous work. Prefers cassette. "Call first." Does not return unsolicited material; prefers to keep materials on file. Reports back in 2 weeks. Assignments include work on educational films.

*EMERY ADVERTISING, 1519 Montana, El Paso TX 79902. (915)532-3636. Producer: Steve Osborn. Advertising agency. Clients include automotive dealerships, banks, hospitals. Estab. 1977. Uses the services of music houses, independent songwriters/composers and lyricists for jingles and commercials for television and radio. Commissions 6 composers and 4 lyricists/year. Pays $250-1,000/job. Buys all rights and one-time rights.
How to Contact: Submit demo tape of previous work. Prefers cassette. Does not return unsolicited material; prefers to keep on file. Reports in 2 weeks.
Music: Uses up-tempo and pop for commercials.

ENSEMBLE PRODUCTIONS, Box 2332, Auburn AL 36831. (205)826-3045. Owner: Barry J. McConatha. Audiovisual firm and video production/post production. Clients include corporate, governmental and educational. Estab. 1984. Uses services of music houses and independent songwriters/composers for scoring of documentary productions, background music for corporate public relations and training videos, jingles for public service announcements, and for montage effects with A/V and video. Commissions 0-5 composers/year. Pays $50-250/job or $25-50/hour, depending upon project. Buys all rights and one-time rights.
How to Contact: Submit demo tape of previous work demonstrating composition skills. Unsolicited submissions are OK. "Needs are sporadic, write first if submission to be returned." Prefers cassette or 7½/15 ips reel-to-reel (or VHS videocassette) with 3-5 songs. "Most needs are upbeat industrial sound but occasional mood setting music also. Inquire for details." Does not return unsolicited material; prefers to keep on file. Reports in 2-3 weeks "if solicited."
Music: Uses up-beat, industrial, New Age, and mood for training film. PR, education and multimedia.
Tips: "Stay away from disco sound!"

ENTERTAINMENT PRODUCTIONS, INC., #744, 2210 Wilshire Blvd., Santa Monica CA 90403. (310)456-3143. President: Edward Coe. Motion picture and television production company. Clients include motion picture and TV distributors. Estab. 1972. Uses the services of music houses and songwriters for scores, production numbers, background and theme music for films and TV and jingles for promotion of films. Commissions/year vary. Pays by the job or by royalty. Buys all rights.
How to Contact: Query with resume of credits. Demo should show flexibility of composition skills. "Demo records/tapes sent at own risk—returned if SASE included." Reports by letter in 1 month, "but only if SASE is included."
Tips: "Have resume on file. Develop self-contained capability."

F.C.B. LEWIS, GILMAN & KYNETTE, INC., (formerly Lewis, Gilman & Kynette, Inc.), Dept. SM, 200 South Broad St., Philadelphia PA 19102. (215)790-4100. Broadcast Business Manager: Valencia Tursi. Advertising agency. Serves industrial and consumer clients. Uses music houses for jingles and back-

ground music in commercials. Pays creative fee asked by music houses.
How to Contact: Submit demo tape of previously aired work. "You must send in previously published work. We do not use original material." Prefers cassette. Will return with SASE if requested, but prefers to keep on file.
Music: All types.

RICHARD R. FALK ASSOC., 1472 Broadway, New York NY 10036. (212)221-0043. President: Richard Falk. Public Relations. Clients include national theatrical, corporate and stars. Estab. 1940. Uses the services of lyricists for promotions. Commissions 2-3 composers and 2-3 lyricists/year. Pays $100/job. Buys one-time rights.
How to Contact: Send a simple flyer on some past credits, nothing too involved. SASE. Reports in 1 week.

FILM AMERICA, INC., Dept. SM, Suite 209, 3177 Peachtree Rd. NE, Atlanta GA 30305. (404)261-3718. President: Avrum Fine. Motion picture editing house. Clients include advertising agencies, corporate audiovisual producers and film/tape producers. Uses the services of music houses and independent songwriters for scoring of industrial films/TV spots; lyricists for jingles for TV spots, commercials for TV and theater trailers. Commissions 3 composers and 3 lyricists/year. Pays by the job. Buys all rights.
How to Contact: Submit demo tape of previous work. Prefers cassette (or VHS videocassette). Does not return unsolicited material; prefers to keep on file. Reports in 4 weeks.
Music: "All contemporary idioms."

FINE ART PRODUCTIONS, 67 Maple St., Newburgh NY 12550. (914)561-5866. Producer/Researcher: Richard Suraci. Advertising agency, audiovisual firm, scoring service, **jingle/commercial music production house**, motion picture production company and **music sound effect library**. Clients include corporate, industrial, motion picture, broadcast firms. Estab. 1987. Uses services of music houses, independent songwriters/composers and lyricists for scoring, background music and jingles for various projects and commercials for radio and TV. Commissions 1-10 songwriters or composers and 1-10 lyricists/year. Pays by the job, by royalty or by the hour. Buys all rights or one-time rights.
How to Contact: Submit demo tape of previous work or tape demonstrating music scoring skills, submit manuscript showing music scoring skills, query with resume of credits or write to arrange personal interview. Prefers cassette (or ½", ¾", or 1" videocassette) with as many songs as possible and lyric or lead sheets. SASE, but prefers to keep material on file. Reports in 3 months.
Music: Uses all types of music for all types of assignments.

GARY FITZGERALD MUSIC PRODUCTIONS, Suite B29, 37-75 63rd St., Woodside NY 11377. (718)446-3857. Producer: Gary Fitzgerald. Scoring service, **commercial music production house and music/sound effects library**. "We service the advertising and record community." Estab. 1987. Uses the services of independent songwriters, vocalists, lyricists and voice-over talent for scoring of TV, radio and industrials; background music for movies; jingles for TV, radio and industrials; and commercials for radio and TV. Commissions 4-5 composers and 2 lyricists/year. Pays per project. Rights purchased depends on project.
How to Contact: Submit demo tape of previous work or tape demonstrating composition skills. Prefers cassette. SASE, but prefers to keep material on file. "A follow-up call must follow submission." Reports in 1 month.
Music: Uses all styles of music.
Tips: "Always submit what you feel is your strongest work. Be persistent."

FOREMOST FILMS AND VIDEO, INC., 7 Regency Dr., Holliston MA 01746. (508)429-8046. President: David Fox. Video production company. Clients include consumer and corporate/industrial firms. Estab. 1983. Uses the services of independent songwriters and music houses for corporate and industrial videos. Commissions 1-2 composers and 1-2 lyricists/year. Buys all rights.
How to Contact: Submit demo tape of previous work. Prefers cassette, CD or 7½ ips reel-to-reel (or ½" or ¾" videocassette) with 2-3 pieces and lyric or lead sheet. SASE. Reports within weeks.
Music: Styles of music used and kinds of assignments depend on specific jobs.

FREDRICK, LEE & LLOYD, 235 Elizabeth St., Landisville PA 17538. (717)898-6092. Vice President: Dusty Rees. **Jingle/commercial music production house**. Clients include advertising agencies. Estab. 1976. Uses the services of independent songwriters/composers and staff writers for jingles. Commissions 2 composers/year. Pays $650/job. Buys all rights.
How to Contact: Submit tape demonstrating composition skills. Prefers cassette or 7½ ips reel-to-reel with 5 jingles. "Submissions may be samples of published work or original material." SASE. Reports in 3 weeks.

Music: Uses pop, rock, country and MOR.
Tips: "The more completely orchestrated the demos are, the better."

FREED & ASSOCIATES, Suite 220, 3600 Clipper Mill Rd., Dept. SM, Baltimore MD 21211. (301)243-1421. Senior Writer/Broadcast Producer: Jeff Grutkowski. Advertising agency. Clients incluse a variety of retail and non-retail businesses. Estab. 1960. Uses the services of music houses and independent songwriters/composers for background music for television commercials, jingles for TV/radio commercials and commercials for radio and TV. Commissions 4-5 composers and 2-4 lyricists/year. Pays $2,000-10,000/job. Buys all rights or one-time rights, depending on the project.
How to Contact: Submit demo tape of previous work. Prefers cassette (or ½" or ¾" videocassette). Does not return unsolicited material; prefers to keep on file. Reports in 1 month.
Music: Uses varying styles for commercials and corporate videos.

PAUL FRENCH AND PARTNERS, 503 Gabbettville Rd., LaGrange GA 30240. (404)882-5581. Contact: Ms. Gene Ballard. Audiovisual firm. Uses the services of music houses and songwriters for musical scores in films and original songs for themes; lyricists for writing lyrics for themes. Commissions 20 composers and 20 lyricists/year. Pays minimum $500/job. Buys all rights.
How to Contact: Submit demo tape of previous work. Prefers reel-to-reel with 3-8 songs. SASE. Reports in 2 weeks.

FRENCH & ROGERS, INC., Suite 115, 5455 Corporate Dr., Troy MI 48098. (313)641-0010. Creative Director: David Morningstar. Advertising agency. Clients include industrial firms. Estab. 1966. Uses the services of independent songwriters/composers for scoring of video tape productions. Commissions 1 composer/year. Pays negotiated rate by the job. Buys all rights.
How to Contact: Submit demo tape of previous work. Prefers cassette with 3 or more songs. Does not return unsolicited material; prefers to keep material on file.
Music: Uses up-tempo, jazz for trade show tapes and product demonstrations.

FRONTLINE VIDEO & FILM, 243 12th St., Del Mar CA 92014. (619)481-5566. Production Manager: Alicia Reed. Television and video production company. Clients include sports programming in jetskiing, surfing, skiing, skateboarding, boardsailing; medical patient education; and various industrial clients. Estab. 1983. Uses the services of independent songwriters/composers for background music for sports programming and industrial clients; intros, extros. Commissions 5 composers/year. Pays by the composition $35-150 per cut.
How to Contact: Submit demo tape of previous work. Prefers cassette. Does not return unsolicited material, but prefers to keep material on file. "We contact artists on an 'as needed' basis when we're ready to use one of their pieces or styles."
Music: Uses up-tempo, jazzy, rock. "We buy works that come to us for national and international TV programming."
Tips: "Background music for surfing, jetskiing and other sports is our biggest area of need. Current-sounding, driving pieces in rock or jazzy styles are appropriate. We don't have time to respond to every submission, but if your tape is here at the right time and we like it, we'll contact you."

FURMAN FILMS, INC., Box 1769, Dept. SM, Venice CA 90294-1769. (213)306-2700. Producers: Will Furman/Norma Doane. Motion picture production company. Clients include business, industry and education. Uses services of music houses and songwriters for "occasional use for original music and lyrics for motion pictures and background/theme music; rarely use lyricists." Payment varies according to budget. Buys all rights.
How to Contact: Query with resume of credits or submit demo tape of previous work. Prefers cassette with 5-10 songs. Does not return unsolicited material; "kept on file for reference."

JAN GARDNER AND ASSOCIATES, Suite 229, 3340 Poplar, Memphis TN 38111. (901)452-7328. Production Director: Greg Hyde. Advertising agency. Serves hospitals, healthcare providers; also automotive, financial and retail businesses. Uses services of songwriters, lyricists and music houses for jingles, commercial and A/V presentations. Commissions 2 songwriters and 2 lyricists/year. Pays by the job, $500-5,000. Buys all rights.
How to Contact: Submit demo tape of previous work. Prefers 7½ ips reel-to-reel or cassette with 3-12 songs. SASE, but prefers to keep material on file.
Music: "We have a wide range of clients and needs."
Tips: "Submit your demo and be willing to spec for bidding."

GEER DUBOIS ADVERTISING INC., Dept. SM, 114 Fifth Ave., New York NY 10011. (212)741-1900 ex. 277. Vice President/Broadcast Business Manager: Celine Hubler. Producer: Paul Muniz. Advertising agency. Clients include national, regional and local advertisers. Estab. 1935. Uses the services of music houses and independent songwriters/composers for scoring of TV and radio commercials, background music, jingles and commercials for radio and TV. Commissions 25 composers/year. Pays $750-3,000/job. Buys all rights.

How to Contact: Submit demo tape of previous work; query with resume of credits; write to arrange personal interview or contact Laura Hatton at the above address. Prefers cassette (or ¾″ videocassette). "Keep it short with brief samples of your work." SASE, but prefers to keep material on file. "Unless there's a specific job, I don't have the time to report back on submissions."

Music: Uses all styles—depending on the commercial—for commercials only.

Tips: "Send a cassette or ¾″ videotape with 8-10 samples of your best work with a short letter telling us who you are."

*BOB GERARDI MUSIC PRODUCTIONS, 160 W. 73rd St., New York NY 10023. (212)874-6436. President: Bob Gerardi. Scoring service and jingle/commercial music production house. Clients include feature film producers, television producers, advertising agencies. Estab. 1975. Uses the services of independent songwriters/composers, lyricists and sound designers for scoring for film and television; background music for industrials, commercials for radio and TV. Commissions 2 composers and 2 lyricists/year. Pays by the job. Buys all rights.

How to Contact: Write or call first to arrange personal interview. Prefers cassette with 3 songs. "Keep demo short." Does not return unsolicited material; prefers to keep on file.

Music: Uses pop, easy listening and jazz for commercials, education film, feature and TV.

GILLESPIE ADVERTISING, INC., International Corporate Center, Dept. SM, Box 3333, Princeton NJ 08543. (609)799-6000. Associate Creative Director: Bill Spink. Advertising agency. Clients include NBA basketball team, national yogurt franchise chain, shopping malls, several banks, a swimwear company, a chain of drug stores plus several industrial and business to business accounts. Estab. 1974. Uses the services of music houses and independent songwriters/composers for scoring of TV spots and sales videos, jingles for radio & TV and commercials for radio and TV. Commissions 4 composers/year. Pay varies by the job.

How to Contact: Submit demo tape of previous work. Write or call first to arrange personal interview. Prefers cassette (or ½″ videocassette) with 5-10 songs. Does not return unsolicited material; prefers to keep on file.

Music: Uses all types for commercials and videos.

Tips: "Never underestimate the power of your demo!"

*GK & A ADVERTISING, INC., Suite 510, 8200 Brookriver Dr., Dallas TX 75247. (214)634-9486. Advertising agency. Clients include retail. Estab. 1982. Uses the services of music houses, independent songwriters/composers and lyricists for jingles for commercials for radio and TV. Commissions 1 composer and 1 lyricist/year. Pays by the job. Buys all rights.

How to Contact: Submit demo tape of previous work. Prefers cassette (or VHS videocassette). Does not return unsolicited material; prefers to keep on file. Reports in 2 weeks.

Music: Uses all types for commercials.

*GLAZEN ADVERTISING, (formerly Traynor, Breehl & Glazen Advertising), Dept. SM, 1250 Old River Rd., Cleveland OH 44113. (216)241-7200. FAX: (216)241-4126. Creative Director: Alan Glazen. Advertising agency. Clients include consumer, retail. Estab. 1972. Uses the services of music houses, independent songwriters/composers and arrangers for jingles for radio/TV spots and commercials for radio and TV. Commissions 6-10 composers/year. Pays $1,500-6,000/job. Buys all rights.

How to Contact: Submit demo tape of previous work. Prefers cassette (or ¾ videocassette) with 5-7 songs. Does not return unsolicited material; prefers to keep on file.

Music: Uses pop, jazz, classical and esoterica for commercials.

Tips: "Put your best foot forward. Lead off with a song you are willing to be judged on."

*GOLD COAST ADVERTISING ASSOCIATION INC., 3625 N.W. 82nd Ave., Miami FL 33166. (305)592-1192. President/Creative Director: Stuart Dornfield. Advertising agency. Clients include retail/beer/financial/automotive/business-to-business/package goods. Estab. 1982. Uses the services of music houses and independent songwriters/composers for commercials for radio and TV. Commissions 5 composers/year. Pays by the job. Buys all rights or 1 year licenses and/or buyouts.

How to Contact: Send cassette of radio and TV jingles and post-scoring. Prefers cassette. "Include approximate cost of music pieces." Does not return unsolicited material; prefers to keep on file. Reports "when the need of a project arises."

Music: Uses all for commercials.

Tips: "Know what sells and what doesn't in advertising!"

GREINKE, EIERS AND ASSOCIATES, Suite 332, 2466 N. Oakland Ave., Milwaukee WI 53211-4345. (414)962-9810. FAX: (414)964-7479. Staff: Arthur Greinke, Patrick Eiers, Lora Nigro. Advertising agency and public relations/music artist management and media relations. Clients include small business, original music groups, special events. Estab. 1984. Uses the services of independent songwriters/ composers, lyricists and music groups, original rock bands and artists for scoring of video news releases, other video projects, jingles for small firms and special events and commercials for radio and TV. Commissions 4-6 composers and 4-6 lyricists/year. Paid by a personal contract.
How to Contact: Query with resume of credits. Prefers compact disc or cassette (or DAT tape or VHS videocassette) with any number of songs and lyric sheet. "We will contact only when job is open — but will keep submissions on file." Does not return material.
Music: Uses original rock, pop, heavy rock for recording groups, commercials, video projects.
Tips: "Try to give as complete a work as possible without allowing us to fill in the holes. High energy, be creative, strong hooks!"

GRS, INC., 13300 Broad St., Pataskala OH 43062. (614)927-9566. Manager: S.S. Andrews. Teleproduction facility. Estab. 1969. Varied clients. Uses the services of music houses and independent songwriters/composers for jingles and background music. Pays by the job. Buys all rights.
How to Contact: Submit demo tape of previous work. Prefers cassette. Does not return unsolicited material; prefers to keep on file.
Music: All styles for commercials.
Tips: "Follow our instructions exactly."

HEPWORTH ADVERTISING CO., 3403 McKinney Ave., Dallas TX 75204. (214)526-7785. President: S.W. Hepworth. Advertising agency. Clients include financial, industrial and food firms. Estab. 1952. Uses services of songwriters for jingles. Pays by the job. Buys all rights.
How to Contact: Call first and obtain permission to submit or submit demo tape of previously aired work. Prefers cassette. SASE. Reports as need arises.

HEYWOOD FORMATICS & SYNDICATION, 1103 Colonial Blvd., Canton OH 44714. (216)456-2592. Owner: Max Heywood. Advertising agency and consultant. Clients include radio, television, restaurants/lounges. Uses the services of music houses and record companies and writers for background music for video presentation and industrial, and commercials for radio and TV. Payment varies per project.
How to Contact: Submit demo tape of previous work. Prefers cassette or 7½ or 15 ips reel-to-reel (or VHS/Beta videocassette). SASE.
Music: Uses pop, easy listening and CHR for educational films, slide presentations and commercials.

HILLMANN & CARR INC., 2121 Wisconsin Ave. NW, Washington DC 20007. (202)342-0001. President: Alfred Hillmann. Vice President/Treasurer: Ms. Michal Carr. Audiovisual firm and motion picture production company. Estab. 1975. Clients include corporate, government, associations and museums. Uses the services of music houses and independent songwriters/composers for scoring of films, video productions, PSA's and commercials for radio and TV. Commissions 2-3 composers/year. Payment negotiable.
How to Contact: Query with resume of credits, or submit demo tape of previous work or tape demonstrating composition skills, or write to arrange personal interview. Prefers cassette (or ¼" VHS or Beta videocassette) with 5-10 pieces. Does not return unsolicited material; prefers to keep on file only when interested. Reports in 1 month. SASE.
Music: Uses contemporary, classical, up-tempo and thematic music for documentary film and video productions, multi-media exposition productions, public service announcements.

THE HITCHINS COMPANY, 22756 Hartland St., Canoga Park CA 91307. (818)715-0510. President: W.E. Hitchins. Advertising agency. Estab. 1985. Uses the services of independent songwriters/composers for jingles and commercial for radio and TV. Commissions 1-2 composers and 1-2 lyricists/year. Will negotiate pay. Buys all rights.
How to Contact: Query with resume of credits. Prefers cassette or VHS videocassette. "Check first to see if we have a job." Does not return unsolicited material; prefers to keep on file.
Music: Uses variety of musical styles for commercials.

HODGES ASSOCIATES, INC., P.O. Box 53805, 912 Hay St., Fayetteville NC 28305. (919)483-8489. President/Production Manager: Chuck Smith. Advertising agency. Clients include industrial, retail and consumer ("We handle a full array of clientel."). Estab. 1974. Uses the services of music houses and independent songwriters/composers for background music for industrial films and slide presentations, and commercials for radio and TV. Commissions 1-2 composers/year. Pays by the job. Buys all rights.

How to Contact: Submit demo tape of previous work. Prefers cassette. Does not return unsolicited material; prefers to keep on file. Reports in 2-3 months.
Music: Uses all styles for industrial videos, slide presentations and TV commercials.

HODGES MEDIA GROUP, Dept. SM, Box 51483, Palo Alto CA 94303. (415)856-7442. Contact: Ed Hodges. Advertising agency and **music sound effect library.** Clients include sportswear, automotive. Estab. 1987. Uses the services of music houses for backgroung music for industrial videos and commercials for radio and TV. Commissions 3 composers/year. Pays $300-500/job. Buys all rights.
How to Contact: Submit demo tape of previous work. Prefers cassette (or VHS, −f8″ videocassette). Does not return unsolicited material; prefers to keep materials on file. Reports in 3 weeks.
Music: Uses metal, drums and bass line.

*HOFFMAN/LEWIS, 1900 Embarcadero, Oakland CA 94606. (510)536-0500. Exec. Producer: Patti Dudgeon. Advertising agency. Clients include automotive/computer/wine/package goods/bank. Estab. 1985. Uses the services of music houses and independent songwriters/composers for scoring of TV and radio commercials and jingles and commercials for TV and radio. Commissions 5 composers, 2-3 lyricists/year. Pays by the job. Buys all rights and cycles.
How to Contact: Submit demo tape of previous work. Prefers cassette (or ¾″ videocassette) with 8-14 songs. "Include log of songs and client or agency." SASE, but prefers to keep material on file. Reports in 1 month.
Tips: "Be complete. Have a point of view. Don't try to be all things to all people. Have high production values and standards."

HOME, INC., 731 Harrison Ave., Boston MA 02118. (617)266-1386. Director: Alan Michel. Audiovisual firm and video production company. Clients include cable television, nonprofit organizations, pilot programs, entertainment companies and industrial. Uses the services of music houses and independent songwriters/composers for background music for videos and TV commercials. Commissions 2-5 songwriters/year. Pays $50-300/job. Buys all rights or one-time rights.
How to Contact: Query with resume of credits, or submit demo tape of previous work. Prefers cassette with 6 pieces. Does not return unsolicited material; prefers to keep on file. Reports as projects require.
Music: Mostly synthesizer. Uses all styles of music for educational videos.
Tips: "Have a variety of products available and be willing to match your skills to the project and the budget."

INTERMEDIA, 2720 Turner St., Victoria B.C. V8T 4V1 **Canada.** (604)389-2800. Fax: (604)389-2801. President: A.W. (Tony) Reynolds. Motion picture production company. Clients include industrial, educational, broadcast and theatrical. Estab. 1980. Uses the services of independent songwriters/composers for scoring of TV shows and films, jingles for commercials and commercials for radio and TV. Commissions 2-3 composers/year. Pays by the job. Buys all, one-time or varying rights.
How to Contact: Submit demo tape of previous work. Prefers cassette. SASE, but prefers to keep material on file. Reports in 2 weeks.
Music: Uses up-tempo, pop, jazz and classical for theatrical films, educational films and commercials.
Tips: "Be professional and competitive—current standards are very high."

INTERNATIONAL MEDIA SERVICES, INC., Dept. SM, 718 Sherman Ave., Plainfield NJ 07060. (908)756-4060. President: Stuart Allen. Audiovisual firm, motion picture and television production company. Clients include schools, businesses, advertising and entertainment industry. Uses the services of music houses, songwriters/composers and lyricists for scoring of corporate and broadcast programs, background music for television and film, jingles for cable TV and broadcast spots, and commercials for radio and TV. Commissions 30 composers and 25 lyricists/year. Pays "per contract or license." Buys all rights or one-time rights.
How to Contact: Query with resume of credits or arrange personal interview. 'We accept no unsolicited material, contact required first." Prefers 7½ ips reel-to-reel, cassette (or ¼″ videocassette) with 4-10 songs. SASE.
Tips: "Stay with professional and high quality material. Be persistent. Have a good broadcast quality demo. Follow-up periodically."

IZEN ENTERPRISES, INC., Dept. SM, 26 Abby Dr., E. Northport NY 11731. (516)368-0615. President: Ray Izen. Video services. Clients are various. Estab. 1980. Uses the services of music houses, independent songwriters/composers and lyricists for scoring of customized songs and background music. Commissions 2 composers and 2 lyricists/year. Pay is open. Buys all rights.
How to Contact: Submit demo tape of previous work. Prefers cassette or VHS videocassette. SASE, but prefers to keep material on file.

THE JAYME ORGANIZATION, 25825 Science Park Dr., Cleveland OH 44122. (216)831-0110. Sr. Art Director: Debbie Klonk. Advertising agency. Uses the services of songwriters and lyricists for jingles and background music. Pays by the job. Buys all rights.
How to Contact: Query first; submit demo tape of previous work. Prefers cassette with 4-8 songs. SASE. Responds by phone as needs arise.
Music: Jingles.

K&R'S RECORDING STUDIOS, 28533 Greenfield, Southfield MI 48076. (313)557-8276. Contact: Ken Glaza. Scoring service and **jingle/commercial music production house.** Clients include commercial, industrial firms. Services include sound for pictures (music, dialogue). Uses the services of independent songwriters/composers for scoring, background music, jingles and commercials for radio and TV, etc. Commissions 1 composer/month. Pays by the job, royalty or hour. Buys all rights.
How to Contact: Write or call first to arrange personal interview. Prefers cassette (or ¾″ or VHS videocassette) with 5-7 pieces minimum. "Show me what you can do in 5 to 7 minutes." SASE. Reports in 2 weeks.
Music: "Be able to compose with the producer present."

***KATSIN/LOEB AND PARTNERS,** 1050 Battery St., San Francisco CA 94111. (415)399-9960. Producer: Andrea Sanchez. Advertising agency. Clients include cellular phone service, TV and radio stations, hotel/resorts, healthcare. Estab. 1989. Uses the services of independent songwriters/composers for commercials for radio and TV. Commissions 2-3 composers/year. Pays $10,000/job. Buys all rights.
How to Contact: Submit demo tape of previous work. Prefers cassette (or ¾″ videocassette). SASE, but prefers to keep material on file. Reports in 6 weeks.
Music: Uses up-tempo, pop and jazz for commercials.
Tips: "Have patience. We don't have large quantity of work, but we like hearing fresh, creative talent."

KAUFMANN ADVERTISING ASSOCIATES, INC., Dept. SM, 1626 Frederica Rd., St. Simons Island GA 31522. (912)638-8678. President: Harry Kaufmann. Advertising agency. Clients include resorts. Estab. 1964. Uses the services of independent songwriters/composers and lyricists for scoring of videos, background music for videos, radio, TV, jingles for radio and commercials for radio and TV. Commissions 0-2 composers and 0-2 lyricists/year. Pays by the job.

***KEATING MAGEE LONG ADVERTISING,** 2223 Magazine, New Orleans LA 70130. (504)523-2121. President: Thomas J. Long. Advertising agency. Clients include retail, consumer products and services, business-to-business. Estab. 1981. Uses the services of independent songwriters/composers for scoring, background music, jingles and commercials for radio and TV. Commissions 4 composers/year. Pays $1,000+/job. Buys all rights.
How to Contact: Submit demo tape of previous work. Prefers cassette (or VHS videocassette). Does not return unsolicited material; prefers to keep on file.
Music: Uses all for commercials, presentations.

KELLIHER/SAMETS, 130 S. Willard St., Dept. SM, Burlington VT 05401. (802)862-8261. Associate: David Worthley. Marketing communications firm. Clients include consumer, business-to-business, trade, public service; local, regional, national. Estab. 1977. Uses the services of music houses and independent songwriters/composers for scoring of commercials, background music for commercials, industrial, jingles for commercial, commercials for radio and TV. Commissions 6 composers/year. Pays $100-2,000/job. Buys all rights.
How to Contact: Submit demo of previous work. Submit tape demonstrating composition skills. "Do not call." Prefers cassette (or VHS videocassette) with lead sheet. Does not return unsolicited material; prefers to keep on file. "Will call if needed."
Music: Uses folk, New Age, jazz, classical, blues, funk, be-bop, swing, gospel, impressionist and expressionist.
Tips: "No interest in 'over produced' sound; looking for creativity and toe-tapping; ability to convey *mood*; *no* show-biz."

KEN-DEL PRODUCTIONS INC., First State Production Center, 1500 First State Blvd., Wilmington DE 19804-3596. (302)999-1164. Estab. 1950. A&R Director: Shirley Kay. General Manager: Edwin Kennedy. Clients include publishers, industrial firms and advertising agencies. Uses services of song-

---

Listings of companies within this section which are either commercial music production houses or music libraries will have that information printed in boldface type.

writers for slides, film scores and title music. Pays by the job. Buys all rights.
How to Contact: Submit demo of previous work. Will accept audio or video tapes. SASE, but prefers to keep material on file. Reports in 2 weeks.

SID KLEINER MUSIC ENTERPRISES, 10188 Winter View Dr., Naples FL 33942. (813)566-7701 and (813)566-7702. Managing Director: Sid Kleiner. Audiovisual firm. Serves the music industry and various small industries. Uses the services of music houses, songwriters and inhouse writers for background music; lyricists for special material. Commissions 5-10 composers and 2-3 lyricists/year. Pays $25 minimum/job. Buys all rights.
How to Contact: Query with resume of credits or submit demo tape of previously aired work. Prefers cassette with 1-4 songs. SASE. Reports in 5 weeks.
Music: "We generally need soft background music, with some special lyrics to fit a particular project. Uses catchy, contemporary, special assignments for commercial/industrial accounts. We also assign country, pop, mystical and metaphysical. Submit samples—give us your very best demos, your best prices and we'll try our best to use your services."

*KTVU RETAIL SERVICES, Box 22222, Oakland CA 94623. (510)874-0228. TV station and retail Marketing Director: Richard Hartwig. Retail TV commercial production firm. Estab. 1974. Clients include local, regional and national retailers. Uses the services of music houses, independent songwriters/composers, lyricists and music libraries for commercials for radio and TV. Commissions 50 composers and 4 lyricists/year. Pays by the job. Buys all rights.
How to Contact: Submit demo tape of previous work. Prefers cassette or 7½ ips reel-to-reel with 6 pieces. SASE, but prefers to keep material on file.
Music: All styles for TV and radio commercials.

LA BOV AND BEYOND MUSIC PRODUCTION, Box 5533, Ft. Wayne IN 46895. (219)420-5533. Creative Director: Cheryl Franks. President: Barry La Bov. Scoring service and **commercial music production house.** Clients include advertising agencies, film production houses and A/V firms. Uses the services of independent songwriters/composers and lyricists for scoring and background music for films, TV and audiovisual projects; jingles and commercials for radio and TV. Commissions 4-10 composers and 2-5 lyricists/year.
How to Contact: Submit demo tape of previous work, tape showing composition skills or manuscript showing music scoring skills. Prefers cassette, 7½ or 15 ips reel-to-reel (or VHS videocassette) with 5-10 pieces. SASE, but prefers to keep material on file. Reports in 3 weeks. "We will call when tape has been received and evaluated."
Music: Uses all styles of music for all kinds of assignments from commercials to songs. "We look for positive, eager writers who strive to create unique, outstanding music."
Tips: "Try new approaches and work to keep a fresh sound. Be innovative, conceptually strong, and positive."

LANE AUDIO PRODUCTIONS, INC., 1507 Wesley, Springdale AR 72764. President: Richard Eby. **Jingle/commercial music production house** and general recording studio. Clients include corporate clients (J.B. Hunt, IBM), local agencies and businesses (jingles). Estab. 1988. Uses the services of independent songwriters/composers, lyricists and voice talent (singing and spoken), musicians for background music for various projects, jingles for local businesses and commercials for radio and TV. Commissions 4-8 composers and 2-4 lyricists/year. Pays $75-400/job or 20-50% royalty. Buys all rights, one-time rights and percentage of rights.
How to Contact: Submit demo tape of previous work demonstrating composition skills. Prefers cassette or 7.5 or 15 IPS reel-to-reel with 3-5 songs and lyric sheet. Does not return unsolicited material; prefers to keep on file. Reports in 2 weeks.
Music: Uses all types for commercials, production music on training tapes, etc. "Most useful to us right now is easy listening instrumental but we will listen to anything."

LANGE PRODUCTIONS, 7661 Curson Terrace, Hollywood CA 90046. (213)874-4730. Production Coordinator: Darlene Hall. Medical video production company. Clients include doctors, hospitals, corporations. Estab. 1987. Uses services of independent songwriters/composers for scoring and background music for medical videos. Commissions 6 composers/year. Pays by the job, $300-700. Buys all rights.
How to Contact: Submit demo tape of previous work. SAE, but prefers cassette. Prefers to keep materials on file. Reports in 3 weeks.

LAPRIORE VIDEOGRAPHY, 86 Allston Ave., Worcester MA 01604. (508)755-9010. Owner: Peter Lapriore. Video production company. Clients include business, educational and sports. Estab. 1985. Uses the services of music houses and independent songwriters/composers and music houses for background music for industrial productions and commercials for TV. "We also own a music library."

Commissions 2 composers/year. Pays $150-1,000/job. Buys all rights, one-time rights and limited use rights.

How to Contact: Submit demo tape of previous work demonstrating composition skills. Prefers cassette or VHS videocassette with 5 songs and lyric sheet. Does not return material, but prefers to keep material on file. Reports in 3 weeks.

Music: Uses medium, up-tempo, jazz and classical for marketing, educational films and commercials.

LEDFORD PRODUCTIONS, INC., Dept. SM, Box 7363, Furnitureland Station, High Point NC 27264-7363. (919)431-1107. President: Hank Ledford. Audiovisual firm and advertising firm. Clients include banks, manufacturers of heavy duty equipment and luxury items and Fortune 500 companies. Uses music houses for background music for video/slide shows and radio commercials. Commissions 25 pieces or songs/year. Pays by the job. Buys all rights or one-time rights.

How to Contact: Submit demo tape of previous work. Prefers cassette (or ¾" VHS videocassette). Does not return unsolicited material; prefers to keep on file.

Music: Uses music for videos, slide presentation-industrial/product introductions.

S.R. LEON COMPANY, INC., Dept. SM, 29 West Main, Oyster Bay NY 11731. (516)922-0031. Creative Director: Max Firetog. Advertising agency. Serves industrial, drug, automotive and dairy product clients. Uses jingles and background music for commercials. Commissions vary. Rights purchased are limited to use of music for commercials.

How to Contact: Submit demo tape of previously aired work. Prefers cassette. No length restrictions on demo.

Music: Uses all types.

LOTT WALKER ADVERTISING, 2648 Ridgewood Rd., Jackson MS 39216. (601)981-9810. Art Director: Dennis Heckler. Advertising agency. Clients include financial, healthcare and telecommunications. Estab. 1976. Uses the services of music houses and independent songwriters/composers for jingles for commercials for radio and TV. Commissions 1-2 composers and 1-2 lyricists/year. Pays by the job. Buys all rights and one-time rights.

How to Contact: Submit demo tape of previous work. Prefers cassette. "Let us know your rates." Does not return unsolicited material; prefers to keep on file.

Music: Uses all types of music for all kinds of assignments.

WALTER P. LUEDKE & ASSOCIATES, INC., Suite One, Eastmoor Bldg., 4223 E. State St., Rockford IL 61108. (815)398-4207. Secretary: Joan Luedke. Advertising agency. Estab. 1959. Uses the services of independent songwriters/composers and lyricists for background music for clients, jingles for clients and commercials for radio and TV. Commissions 1-2 composers and 1-2 lyricists/year. Pays by the job. Buys all rights.

How to Contact: Submit demo tape of previous work demonstrating composition skills, or write first to arrange personal interview. Prefers cassette. "Our need is infrequent, best just let us know who you are." SASE, but prefers to keep material on file. Reports in 1 month.

Music: Uses various styles.

LUNA TECH, INC., Dept. SM, 148 Moon Dr., Owens Cross Roads AL 35763. (205)725-4224. Chief Designer: Ken Coburn. Fireworks company. Clients include theme parks, municipalities and industrial show producers. Estab. 1969. Uses music houses, independent songwriters and client music departments for scoring of music for fireworks displays. Commissions 1-2 composers/year. Pays $500-3,000/job. Buys all rights or one-time rights.

How to Contact: Query with resume of credits or submit demo tape of previous work. Prefers cassette (or VHS videocassette) with 1-5 pieces. Does not return unsolicited material; prefers to keep on file. Reports in 1 month; will call if interested.

Music: "Music for fireworks choreography: dynamic, jubilant, heraldic, bombastic, original."

Tips: "Send us a demo tape showing your composition skills and tailored as much as possible toward our needs."

LYONS PRESENTATIONS, 715 Orange St., Wilmington DE 19899. (302)654-6146. Audio Producer: Gary Hill. Audiovisual firm. Clients include mostly large corporations: Dupont, ICI, Alco Standard. Estab. 1954. Uses the services of independent songwriters/composers and lyricists for scoring of multi-image, film and video. Commissions 8-12 composers/year. Pays by the job. Buys all rights.

How to Contact: Submit demo tape of previous work. Prefers cassette, 15 IPS reel-to-reel, (or VHS or ¾" videocassette) with 3-4 songs. "No phone calls please, unless composers are in local area." SASE, but prefers to keep submitted materials on file.

Music: Usually uses up-tempo motivational pieces for multi-image, video or film for corporate use.
Tips: "Pays close attention to the type of music that is used for TV spots for large companies, like AT&T."

MCCAFFREY AND MCCALL ADVERTISING, 8888 Keystone Crossing, Indianapolis IN 46240. (317)574-3900. V.P./Associate Creative Director: William Mick. Advertising agency. Serves consumer electronics, technical ecucation, retail and commercial developers. Estab. 1984. Uses the services of music houses for scoring, background music and jingles for radio and TV commercials. Commissions 3 composers/year; 1 lyricist/year. Pays $3,000-5,000/job. Buys all rights.
How to Contact: Submit demo tape of previous work and write to arrange personal interview. Prefers cassette (or ¾″ videocassette) with 6 songs. SASE, but prefers to keep submitted materials on file.
Music: High-energy pop, sound-alikes and electronic for commercials.
Tips: "Keep in touch, but don't be a pest about it."

McCANN-ERICKSON WORLDWIDE, Dept. SM, Suite 1900, 1360 Post Oak Blvd., Houston TX 77056. (713)965-0303. Creative Director: Jesse Caesar. Advertising agency. Serves all types of clients. Uses services of songwriters for jingles and background music in commercials. Commissions 10 songwriters/year. Pays production cost and registrated creative fee. Arrangement fee and creative fee depend on size of client and size of market. "If song is for a big market, a big fee is paid; if for a small market, a small fee is paid." Buys all rights.
How to Contact: Submit demo tape of previously aired work. Prefers 7½ ips reel-to-reel. "There is no minimum or maximum length for tapes. Tapes may be of a variety of work or a specialization. We are very open on tape content; agency does own lyrics." SASE, but prefers to keep material on file. Responds by phone when need arises.
Music: All types.

McDONALD DAVIS & ASSOC., Dept. SM, 250 W. Coventry Ct., Milwaukee WI 53217. (414)228-1990. Senior Vice President/Creative Director: Steve Preston. Advertising agency. Uses music houses for background music for commercials. Commissions 15 composers and producers/year. Pays $1,000-3,000/job. Buys all rights.
How to Contact: Write to arrange personal interview or submit demo tape of previously aired work or tape demonstrating composition skills. Prefers cassette (or ¾″ videocassette) with 10 pieces and resume of credits. Does not return unsolicited material; prefers to keep on file. "We report in 1 week on solicited material."
Music: Uses all styles of music for post-scoring television commercials.

LEE MAGID INC., (Alexis Music Inc., Marvelle Music Co., Gabal Music) Box 532, Malibu CA 90265. (213)463-5998. President: Lee Magid. Audiovisual firm, scoring service and motion picture production company. Clients include record labels, producers, networks, video/film companies, television, and commercial sequences. Uses the services of songwriters, lyricists and composer/arrangers for scoring, themes and background music for films and videos, jingles and commercials for radio and TV. Commissions 8-10 lyricists/year. Buys all rights. Pays by the job or by royalty.
How to Contact: Send resume of credits or submit tape demonstrating composition skills. Prefers cassette (or videocassette) with maximum 3 songs (or 3 minutes). "I would make direct contact with songwriter/composer and designate preference and style." Reports in 1 month.
Music: Mostly R&B, jazz and gospel; also country, pop and rock. Vocals and/or instrumental.
Tips: "Use your instincts. Write songs for visual and musical memory effect. Try to become an innovator. Think ahead."

MALLOF, ABRUZINO & NASH MARKETING, 477 E. Butterfield Rd., Lombard IL 60148. (708)964-7722. President: Ed Mallof. Advertising agency. Works primarily with auto dealer jingles. Estab. 1980. Uses music houses for jingles. Commissions 5-6 songwriters/year. Pays $600-2,000/job. Buys all rights.
How to Contact: Submit demo tape of previous work. Prefers cassette with 4-12 songs. SASE; but prefers to keep material on file. Reports "when we feel a need for their style."
Tips: "Send samples that are already produced and can be relyricized."

*MANN ADVERTISING, Dept. SM, 466 Hanover St., Box 3818, Manchester NH 03105. (603)625-5403. Broadcast Producer: Warren Mann. Advertising agency. Clients include retail/industrial/hi-tech. Estab. 1974. Uses the services of independent songwriters and music houses for background music for industrial videos and commercials for radio and TV. Commissions 7-10 songwriters/year. Pays $3,000-7,000/job. Buys all rights and one-time rights.
How to Contact: Submit demo tape of previous work. Prefers cassette (or VHS videocassette) with 3-7 songs. SASE, but prefers to keep material on file. Reports in 2 weeks.
Music: Uses up tempo, easy listening, jazz for commercials, slide shows, industrial videos.
Tips: "Present clean clear work—make it your best work *only*."

*MARK CUSTOM RECORDING SERVICE, INC., 10815 Bodine Rd., Clarence NY 14031-0406. (716)759-2600. Vice President: Mark T. Morette. **Jingle/commercial music production house**. Clients include ad agencies. Estab. 1962. Uses the services of independent songwriters/composers for commercials for radio and TV. Commissions 2 composers/year. Pays $25/hour.
How to Contact: Write. Prefers cassette with 3 songs. Does not return unsolicited material; prefers to keep on file.
Music: Uses pop and jazz for radio commercials.

*THE MARKETING CONNECTION, Dept. SM, 7000 Lake Ellenor, Orlando FL 32809. (407)855-4321. Vice President, Sales: Leon Lebeau. Audiovisual firm. Uses services of music houses, independent songwriters/composers, lyricists and recording studios for scoring of A/V sound tracks and videos, walk-in music for shows, jingles for videos (non-commercial) and sound effects. Commissions 2-3 composers and 1-2 lyricists/year. Pays by the job, $30-50/hour or local studio rates. Buys all rights or one-time rights.
How to Contact: Submit demo tape of previous work; call first to arrange personal interview. Prefers cassette (or ¾" or ½" videocassette) or 7½ ips reel-to-reel. "New material only." SASE, but prefers to keep material on file. Reports in several weeks.
Music: Uses up-tempo, pop and jazz for educational and training films and slide presentations.

MASTER MANAGEMENT MUSIC, #242, 1626 W. Wilcox St., Los Angeles CA 90028. (213)871-8054, ex. 516. President/CEO: George Van Heel. Advertising agency, **jingle/commercial music production house**, promotion/production company and music publishing company (BMI). Estab. 1987. Uses the services of music houses, independent songwriters/composers and lyricists for scoring, background music and jingles for campaigns and commercials for radio/TV. Commissions 1 composer and 1 lyricist/year. Pays per job or by the hour. Buys all rights.
How to Contact: Write first to arrange personal interview. "No personal deliveries; by appointment only!" Prefers cassette or VHS videocassette with 3 songs and lyric and lead sheets. "All songs must be patriotic." Does not return unsolicited submissions; prefers to keep materials on file. Reports in 2 months.
Music: Pop/rock style for campaigns, educational and music videos.
Tips: "Work hard, be patient and follow up by a letter for recommended materials submitted."

MAXWELL ADVERTISING INC., Dept. SM, 444 W. Michigan, Kalamazoo MI 49007. (616)382-4060. Creative Director: Jess Maxwell. Advertising agency. Uses the services of lyricists and music houses for jingles and background music for commercials. Commissions 2-4 lyricists/year. Pays $4,000-20,000/job. Buys all rights or one-time rights.
How to Contact: Submit demo tape of previously aired work or tape demonstrating composition skills. Prefers cassette (or VHS videocassette). No returns; prefers to keep material on file.
Music: Uses various styles of music for jingles and music beds.

MEDIA CONSULTANTS, Box 130, Sikeston MO 63801. (314)472-1116. Owner: Richard Wrather. Advertising agency. Clients are varied. Estab. 1979. Uses the services of music houses, independent songwriters/composers and lyricists for scoring of and background music for jingles, industrial video and commercials for radio and TV. Commissions 10-15 composers and 10-15 lyricists/year. Pays varying amount/job. Buys all rights.
How to Contact: Submit a demo tape of previous work demonstrating composition skills. Accepts unsolicited submissions. Prefers cassette (or ½" or ¾" videocassette). Does not return unsolicited material; prefers to keep on file.
Music: Uses all styles of music for varied assignments.

MEDIA PRODUCTIONS, Dept. SM, 2095 N. Andrews Ext., Pompano Beach FL 33069. (305)979-6467. President: Jim Haney. Motion picture, TV and post-production company. Clients include advertising agency and commercial production company. Uses the services of music houses and independent songwriters/composers for TV commercials. Commissions 2 composers and 2 lyricists/year. Pays $200-2,000/job. Buys all rights.

The asterisk before a listing indicates that the listing is new in this edition. New markets are often the most receptive to unsolicited submissions.

How to Contact: Submit tape demonstrating composition skills or manuscript showing music scoring skills. Prefers 7½ ips reel-to-reel (or ¾" videocassette) with 4-8 songs and lyric sheet. SASE, but prefers to keep material on file. Reports in 2 months.
Music: Uses up-tempo and pop music for commercials.

MID-OCEAN RECORDING STUDIO, 1578 Erin St., Winnepeg Namitoba R3E 2T1 **Canada.** (204)774-3715. Producer/Engineer: Dave Zeglinski. **Jingle/commercial music production house.** Clients include retail/corporate. Estab. 1980. Uses the services of independent songwriters/composers and producers for jingles for commercials for radio and TV. Commissions 3-5 composers/year. Pays $300-500/job. Buys all rights.
How to Contact: Submit demo tape of previous work. Prefers cassette with 1 or 2 songs. Does not return unsolicited material; prefers to keep submitted material on file. Reports in 1 month.
Music: Uses easy listening, up-tempo, pop for commercials.

JON MILLER PRODUCTION STUDIOS, 7249 Airport Rd., Bath PA 18014. (215)837-7550. Executive Producer: Jon Miller. Audiovisual firm, jingle/commercial music production house and video production company. Clients include industrial, commercial, institutional and special interest. Estab. 1970. Uses the services of music houses, independent songwriters/composers and lyricists for scoring of themes and background music for audio and video production and live presentations. Commissions 5-15 composers and 2-5 lyricists/year. Pays by the job. Buys all rights or one-time rights.
How to Contact: Submit demo tape of previous work. Query with resume of credits and references. Prefers cassette with 7 songs and lyric or lead sheets. Does not return unsolicited material; prefers to keep on file. Reports in 2-3 weeks.
Music: Uses up tempo and title music, introduction music for industrial marketing and training videos.
Tips: "Provide professional product on time and within budget. Keep communication open."

MITCHELL & ASSOCIATES, Dept. SM, 7830 Old George Town Rd., Bethesda MD 20814. (301)986-1772. President: Ronald Mitchell. Advertising agency. Serves food, high-tech, transportation, financial, real estate, automotive and retail clients. Uses independent songwriters, lyricists and music houses for background music for commercials, jingles and post-TV scores for commercials. Commissions 3-5 songwriters and 3-5 lyricists/year. Pays $3,000-10,000/job. Buys all rights.
How to Contact: Submit demo tape of previously aired work. Prefers cassette or 7½ ips reel-to-reel. Does not return unsolicited material; prefers to keep on file.
Music: "Depends upon client, audience, etc."

MONTEREY BAY PRODUCTION GROUP, INC., 561 Arthur Rd., Watsonville CA 95076. (408)722-3132. FAX: (408)728-2709. President: Larry W. Eells. Audio/video production services. Clients include industrial business and broadcast. Estab. 1985. Uses the services of independent songwriters/composers for scoring of promotional, educational and commercial videos. Commissions 3-10 composers/year. Pays negotiable royalty.
How to Contact: Submit demo tape of previous work. Query with resume of credits. Prefers cassette (or VHS videocassette) with 5 songs. SASE, but prefers to keep material on file. Reports in 1 month.
Music: Uses all types for promotional, training and commercial.

MORRIS MEDIA, Dept. SM, #105, 2730 Monterey, Torrance CA 90503. (213)533-4800. Acquisitions Manager: Roger Casas. TV/video production company. Estab. 1984. Uses the services of music houses, independent songwriters/composers and lyricists for jingles for radio and TV commercials. Commissions 5 composers and 2 lyricists/year. Pays by the job or by the hour. Buys all rights.
How to Contact: Query with resume of credits "Write first with short sample of work." Does not return unsolicited material; prefers to keep submitted material on file. Reports in 2 weeks.
Music: Uses classical, pop, rock and jazz for music video/TV.
Tips: "Persist with good material, as we are very busy!"

MOTIVATION MEDIA, INC., 1245 Milwaukee Ave., Glenview IL 60025. (708)297-4740. Production Manager: Glen Peterson. Audiovisual firm, video, motion picture production company and business meeting planner. Clients include business and industry. Estab. 1969. Uses the services of songwriters and composers "mostly for business meetings and multi-image production"; lyricists for writing lyrics for business meeting themes, audience motivation songs and promotional music for new product introduction. Commissions 3-5 composers/year. Payment varies. Buys one-time rights.
How to Contact: Query with resume of credits; or submit demo tape of previous work. Prefers cassette with 5-7 songs. SASE. Responds when the need arises.
Music: Uses "up-beat contemporary music that motivates an audience of sales people."
Tips: "Be contemporary."

ERIC MOWER & ASSOCIATES, Dept. SM, 96 College Ave., Rochester NY 14607. (716)473-0440. President/Chief Creative Officer: John R. Brown. Advertising agency. Member of AFTRA, SAG, ASCAP. Serves consumer and business-to-business clients. Uses independent songwriters, lyricists and music houses for jingles. Commissions 12 songwriters and 4 lyricists/year. Pays $5,000-40,000/job.
How to Contact: Query. Prefers cassette with 3-5 songs. SASE.
Music: "We're seriously interested in hearing from good production sources. We have some of the world's best lyricists and songwriters working for us, but we're always ready to listen to fresh, new ideas."

MTC PRODUCTION CENTER, (formerly American Video Factory), 4150 Glencoe Ave., Dept. SM, Marina Del Rey CA 90292. (213)823-8622. Audio: Ron Bryan. Scoring service and jingle/**commercial music production house.** Clients include advertising, corporate, entertainment and other businesses. Uses the services of independent songwriters/composers for background music for commercials, feature films, industrials, jingles and commercials for radio and TV. Commissions 5 composers and 5 lyricists/year. Pays by the job. Buys all rights.
How to Contact: Write or call first to arrange personal interview. Prefers cassette. SASE. Prefers to keep submitted materials on file. Reports in 2 weeks.
Music: Uses jazz, classical, new age, pop and up-tempo.

MULTI IMAGE PRODUCTIONS, Dept. SM, 8849 Complex Dr., San Diego CA 92123. (619)560-8383. Sound Editor/Engineer: Jim Lawrence. Audiovisual firm and motion picture production company. Serves business, corporate, industrial, commercial, military and cultural clients. Uses music houses, independent songwriters/composers/arrangers and lyricists for scoring of industrials, corporate films and videos; background music for AV, film, video and live shows; and jingles and commercials for radio and TV. Commissions 2-10 composers and 2-5 lyricists/year. Pays $500+/job. Buys all rights.
How to Contact: Query with resume of credits or write to obtain permission to submit. Prefers 7½ or 15 ips reel-to-reel with 2-5 pieces. Does not return unsolicited material; prefers to keep on file. Reports in 6 weeks.
Music: Uses "comtemporary, pop, specialty, regional, ethnic, national and international" styles of music for background "scores written against script describing locales, action, etc. We try to stay clear of stereotypical 'canned' music and prefer a more commercial and dramatic (film-like) approach."
Tips: "We have established an ongoing relationship with a local music production/scoring house with whom songwriters would be in competition for every project; but an ability to score clean, full, broad, contemporary commercial and often 'film score' type music, in a variety of styles would be a benefit."

MUSIC LANE PRODUCTIONS, Dept. SM, Box 3829, Austin TX 78764. (512)476-1567. Owner: Wayne Gathright. Music recording, production and jingle/commercial music production house. Estab. 1980. Serves bands, songwriters and commercial clients. Uses the services of music houses and independent songwriters/composers for jingles and commercials for radio and TV. Pays by the job. Buys one-time rights.
How to Contact: Submit demo tape of previous work or tape demonstrating composition skills; or query with resume of credits. Prefers cassette. Does not return unsolicited material; prefers to keep on file. Reports in 6 weeks.
Music: Uses all styles.

MUSIC MASTERS, 2322 Marconi Ave., St. Louis MO 63110. (314)773-1480. Producer: Greg Trampe. **Commercial music production house** and **music/sound effect library.** Clients include multi-image and film producers, advertising agencies and large corporations. Estab. 1976. Uses the services of independent songwriters/composers and lyricists for background music for multi-image and film, jingles and commercials for radio and TV. Commissions 6 composers and 2 lyricists/year. Pays $100-2,000/job. Buys all rights.
How to Contact: Query with resume of credits or write and obtain permission to submit. Prefers cassette or 7½ or 15 ips reel-to-reel (or Beta or VHS videocassette) with 3-6 pieces. SASE, but prefers to keep material on file. Reports in 2 months.
Music: "We use all types of music for slide presentations (sales & motivational)."
Tips: "Resume should have at least 3 or 4 major credits of works completed within the past year. A good quality demo is a must."

MYERS & ASSOCIATES, Dept. SM, Suite 203, 3727 SE Ocean Blvd., Stuart FL 34996. (407)287-1990. Senior Vice President: Doris McLaughlin. Advertising agency. Estab. 1973. Serves financial, real estate, consumer products and hotel clients. Uses music houses for background music for commercials and jingles. Commissions 2-3 songwriters/year and 2-3 lyricists/year. Pays by the job. Buys all rights.

How to Contact: Submit demo tape of previously aired work. Prefers cassette. Does not return unsolicited material; prefers to keep on file.
Music: Uses "various styles of music for jingles, music beds and complete packages depending on clients' needs."

FRANK C. NAHSER, INC., Dept. SM, 18th Floor, 10 S. Riverside Plaza, Chicago IL 60606. (312)845-5000. Contact: Bob Fugate. Advertising agency. Serves insurance, telecommunications, toys, bicycles, hotels, and other clients. Uses the services of independent songwriters/composers, lyricists and music houses for scoring of television commercials, background music for commercials for radio and TV and music for industrial/sales presentations and meetings. Commissions 6-10 songwriters and 4 lyricists/year. Pays $5,000-15,000 for finished production or varying royalty. Buys one-time rights.
How to Contact: Submit demo tape of previous work. Prefers cassette. Does not return unsolicited material; prefers to keep on file. "No phone calls, please. When a cassette is submitted we listen to it for reference when a project comes up. We ignore most cassettes that lack sensitivity toward string and woodwind arrangements unless we know it's from a lyricist."
Music: "We mostly use scores for commercials, not jingles. The age of the full sing jingle in national TV spots is quickly coming to an end. Young songwriters should be aware of the difference and have the expertise to score, not just write songs."
Tips: "The writing speaks for itself. If you know composition, theory and arrangement it quickly becomes evident. Electronic instruments are great tools; however, they are no substitute for total musicianship. Learn to read, write, arrange and produce music and, with this book's help, market your music. Be flexible enough to work along with an agency. We like to write and produce as much as you do."

NEW & UNIQUE VIDEOS, 2336 Sumac Dr., San Diego CA 92105. (619)282-6126. Contact: Pat Mooney. Production and worldwide distribution of special interest videotapes to varied markets. Estab. 1981. Uses the services of independent songwriters for background music in videos. Commissions 2-3 composers/year. Pays by the job, by royalty or by the hour. Buys all rights.
How to Contact: Accepts unsolicited submissions. Prefers cassette. SASE. Reports in 2-4 weeks.
Music: Uses up-tempo, easy listening and jazz for educational film and action/adventure, nature and love stories.
Tips: "We want to hear positive, happy music suitable as background for our special interest titles."

NOBLE ARNOLD & ASSOCIATES, Dept. SM, Suite 202 N, 1501 Woodfield Rd., Schaumburg IL 60173. (708)605-8808. Creative Director: John Perkins. Advertising agency. Clients include communication and health care firms. Estab. 1970. Uses the services of independent songwriters/composers for jingles. Commissions 1 composer and 1 lyricist/year. Pays by the job. Buys all rights.
How to Contact: Submit demo tape of previous work. Prefers cassette. Does not return unsolicited material. Reports in 4 weeks.

NORTHLICH STOLLEY LAWARRE, INC., 200 West Fourth St., Cincinnati OH 45202. (513)421-8840. Broadcast Producer: Judy Merz. Advertising agency. Clients include banks, hospitals, P&G, Cintas, Queen City Metro, Dayton Power and Light, Mead Paper. Estab. 1949. Uses the services of independent songwriters and music houses for jingles and background music for commercials. Commissions 3-5 composers/year. Pays by the job. Rights purchased varies.
How to Contact: Submit demo tape of previous work demonstrating composition skills or query with resume of credits. Prefers cassette. SASE, but prefers to keep materials on file.
Music: Uses all kinds for commercials.

NORTON RUBBLE & MERTZ, INC. ADVERTISING, 2R, 112 N. Green, Chicago IL 60607. (312)942-1405. President: Sue Gehrke. Advertising agency. Clients include consumer products, retail, business to business. Estab. 1987. Uses the services of music houses and independent songwriters/composers for jingles for radio/TV commercials. Commissions 2 composers/year. Pays by the job.
How to Contact: Submit tape demonstrating composition skills; query with resume of credits. Prefers cassette. SASE, but prefers to keep material on file. Reports in 2 weeks.
Music: Uses up-tempo and pop for commercials.

OMNI COMMUNICATIONS, Dept. SM, 655 W. Carmel Dr., Carmel IN 46032-2669. (317)844-6664. President: W. H. Long. Television production and audiovisual firm. Estab. 1978. Serves industrial, commercial and educational clients. Uses the services of music houses and songwriters for scoring of films and television productions; background music for voice overs; lyricists for original music and themes. Commissions varying number of composers and lyricists/year. Pays by the job. Buys all rights.

How to Contact: Query with resume of credits. Prefers reel-to-reel, cassette (or videocassette). Does not return unsolicited material. Reports in 2 weeks.
Music: Varies with each and every project; from classical, contemporary to commercial industrial.
Tips: "Submit good demo tape with examples of your range to command the attention of our producers."

ON-Q PRODUCTIONS, INC., 618 Gutierrez St., Santa Barbara CA 93103. (805)963-1331. President: Vincent Quaranta. Audiovisual firm. Clients include corporate accounts/sales conventions. Uses the services of music houses, independent songwriters/composers and lyricists for scoring of and background music for media productions and TV commercials. Commissions 1-5 composers and 1-5 lyricists/year. Pays $100-1,000/job. Buys all rights or one-time rights.
How to Contact: Call for permission to submit demo tape. Prefers cassette or 15 ips reel-to-reel (or VHS videocassette). SASE, but prefers to keep material on file. Reports in 1 month.
Music: Uses up-tempo music for slide and video presentations.

OVERCASH & MOORE, INC., Dept. SM, Suite 805, 3100 Smoketree Ct., Raleigh NC 27609. (919)872-0050. Creative Director: Jim Moore. Advertising agency. Clients include retail and business-to-business. Uses services of music houses and independent songwriters/composers for background music for videos and training films and commercials for radio and TV. Commissions 4-5 composers/year. Pays by the job. Buys all rights.
How to Contact: Submit demo tape of previous work. Prefers cassette (or VHS videocassette) with 4-5 pieces. Does not return unsolicited material; prefers to keep on file. Reports in 2 months.
Music: Uses popular, jazz and classical for commercials and videos.
Tips: "Send memorable lyrics, hummable tunes. No clichés."

OWENS POLLICK AND ASSOCIATES, Suite 1500, 2800 North Central, Dept. SM, Phoenix AZ 85004. (602)230-7557. Broadcast Producer: Susan Reed. Advertising agency. Clients include health care, automotive aftermarket and newspapers. Estab. 1986. Uses the services of music houses for scoring of commercials for radio/TV. Commissions 4-10 composers/year; 4-10 lyricists/year. Pays $2,000/job. Buys all rights.
How to Contact: Submit demo tape of previous work. Prefers cassette or ¾" videocassette. Does not return unsolicited material; prefers to keep materials on file.
Music: Up-tempo, jazz and classical for commercials.

PAISANO PUBLICATIONS/EASYRIDERS HOME VIDEO, Box 3000, Agoura Hills CA 91364. (818)889-8740. Producer/Director: Rick Schmidlin. Home video and TV productions. Clients include consumer/motorcycle enthusiasts. Estab. 1971. Uses the services of music houses, independent songwriters/composers and pre-recorded bands for scoring of video and TV, background music for video and TV, jingles for radio spots and commercials for radio and TV. Commissions 2-3 composers/year. Pays $100/minute of usage. Buys all rights.
How to Contact: Write first to arrange personal interview. Prefers cassette (or VHS/¾" videocassette). SASE, but prefers to keep material on file. Reports in 1-2 months.
Music: Uses rock/country/contemporary.
Tips: "Harley riders a plus."

PHD VIDEO, 143 Hickory Hill Cir., Osterville MA 02655. (508)428-7198. Acquisitions: Violet Atkins. Motion picture production company. Clients include business and industry, production and post-production video houses and ad agencies. Estab. 1985. Uses the services of music houses, independent songwriters/composers and lyricists for scoring and background music for commercials, home video and motion pictures and jingles for TV commercials. Commissions 10-12 composers and 10-12 lyricists/year. Pay is negotiable. Buys all rights preferably or one-time rights in certain circumstances.
How to Contact: Submit demo tape of previous work. Prefers cassette (or VHS videocassette). SASE but prefers to keep material on file. Reports in 1-2 months.
Music: Uses up-tempo and pop for commercials, motion pictures and TV shows.
Tips: "Be persistent. Constantly send updates of new work. Update files 1-2 times per year if possible. We hire approximately 25% new composers per year. Prefer to use composers/lyricists with 2-3 years track record."

PHILADELPHIA MUSIC WORKS, INC., Box 947, Bryn Mawr PA 19010. (215)825-5656. President: Andy Mark. **Jingle producers/music library producers.** Uses independent songwriters and music houses for background music for commercials and jingles. Commissions 20 songwriters/year. Pays $200/job. Buys all rights.

How to Contact: Submit demo tape—unsolicited submissions are OK. Prefers cassette. "We are looking for quality jingle tracks already produced, as well as instrumental pieces between 2 and 3 minutes in length for use in AV music library." SASE, but prefers to keep material on file. Reports in 4 weeks.
Music: All types.
Tips: Looking for "knowledge of the jingle business and what works as background music for audiovisual presentations, such as slide shows, video training films, etc."

PHOTO COMMUNICATION SERVICES, INC., Box 508, Acme MI 49610. (616)679-1499; (616)938-5694. President: Lynn Jackson. Audiovisual firm and motion picture production company. Serves commercial, industrial and nonprofit clients. Uses services of music houses, independent songwriters, and lyricists for jingles and scoring of and background music for multi-image, film and video. Negotiates pay. Buys all rights or one-time rights.
How to Contact: Submit demo tape of previous work, tape demonstrating composition skills or query with resume of credits. Prefers cassette or 15 ips reel-to-reel (or VHS videocassette). Does not return unsolicited material; prefers to keep on file. Reports in 6 weeks.
Music: Uses mostly industrial/commercial themes.

PHOTO COMMUNICATIONS CORP., 815 Greenwood Ave., Dept. SM, Jenkintown PA 19046. (215)572-5900. Vice President-Sales and Marketing: Raymond E. Baker Jr. Audiovisual production company. Estab. 1970. Serves corporate, industrial, educational, business-to-business and pharmaceutical clients. Uses services of music houses, independent songwriters/composers and lyricists for scoring and background music for videos and multi-image programs. Commissions 1-2 composers and 1-2 lyricists/year. Pays by the job. Buys all rights or one-time rights; other rights sometimes.
How to Contact: Submit demo tape of previous work demonstrating composition skills or query with resume of credits. Prefers cassette with 4-5 pieces and lyric sheet. Sometimes returns unsolicited material with SASE; prefers to keep material on file.
Music: Uses up-tempo, dramatic, pop, classical, MOR, new age and electronic music for educational films, slide presentations, videos, corporate overviews, etc.
Tips: "Be flexible, creative and versatile."

POP INTERNATIONAL CORPORATION, Box 527, Closter NJ 07624. (201)768-2199. Producers: Arnold De Pasquale and Peter DeCaro. Motion picture production company. Estab. 1973. Clients include "political campaigns, commercial spots, business and industry concerns as a production service; feature films and documentaries as producers." Uses services of music houses and songwriters for "mood purposes only on documentary films. However, Pop International Productions does conceptualize major theatrical and/or album musical projects." Commissions commercial and soundtrack pieces for entertainment specials. Commissions 2-3 composers/year. Pays by the job or by royalty. Rights are negotiable.
How to Contact: Submit demo tape of previously aired work. Prefers cassette with 2-4 songs. "We review tapes on file, speak with agents and/or referrals, then interview writer. Once committee approves, we work *very* closely in pre-production." SASE. Reports in 4 weeks.
Music: Uses "mood music for documentaries, occasionally jingles for spots or promotional films or theme music/songs for dramatic projects (the latter by assignment only from producers or agencies). Some material is strictly mood, as in documentary work; some is informative as in promotional; some is motivating as in commercial; some is entertaining as in theatrical/TV."
Tips: "Be persistent and very patient. Try to get an agent, use demos and build a reputation for working very closely with scriptwriters/producers/directors."

PPI (PETER PAN INDUSTRIES), PARADE VIDEO, CURRENT RECORDS, COMPOSE RECORDS, 88 St. Frances St., Newark NJ 07105. (201)344-4214. Product Manager: Marianne Eggleston. Video, record label, publishing. Clients include songwriters, music and video. Estab. 1928. Uses the services of music houses, independent songwriters/composers, lyricists, produces video and music for scoring, background music, jingles and commercials for radio and TV. Commissions 100's of composers and lyricists/year. Pays by the job, royalty and per agreement. Rights negotiable.

Market conditions are constantly changing! If you're still using this book and it is 1994 or later, buy the newest edition of Songwriter's Market at your favorite bookstore or order directly from Writer's Digest Books.

How to Contact: Submit demo tape and manuscript showing previous work, composition and scoring skills. Query with resume of credits. Prefers cassette or ½ or ¾ videocassette with 6 songs and lyric sheet. Also include a picture and bio of the artist. SASE. Prefers to keep material on file "if we like it for possible reference when we're looking for new materials. Completed projects preferred!" Reports in 3 weeks to 3 months.

Music: Uses all musical styles, including children's and health and fitness.

Tips: "Research the market to find out what's hot on the market and what consumers are buying. Material should be totally developed and the ideas concrete."

PREMIER VIDEO, FILM AND RECORDING CORP., Dept. SM, 3033 Locust St., St. Louis MO 63103. (314)531-3555. President: Wilson Dalzell. Secretary/Treasurer: Grace Dalzell. Audiovisual firm, album producer and motion picture production company. Estab. 1931. Uses the services of songwriters for jingles and scoring and original background music and lyrics to reinforce scripts. Commissions 6-10 pieces and 5-10 lyricists/year. Pays by the job or by royalty. Buys all rights and "occasionally one-time rights with composer retaining title."

How to Contact: Query with resume of credits. Prefers 7½ or 15 ips reel-to-reel or cassette with any number of songs. SASE. Reports "as soon as possible with a short note using self-addressed envelope enclosed with submitted work informing talent they are on file for future reference."

Music: "As we serve every area of human development, all musical art forms are occasionally used."

Tips: "A limited need for music makes freelance writers a necessity. Be flexible. Have a simple, precise portfolio. Be sure your resume is direct, to-the-point and includes an honest review of past efforts. Be patient."

*PRESTIGE PRODUCTIONS, 1717 SW 10th Ave., Ft. Lauderdale FL 33315. (305)463-7062. Director of Production: Werner H. Stemer. Audio production firm. Clients include advertising companies and video producers, record and production companies. Estab. 1984. Uses the services of independent songwriters/composers and lyricists for record productions, background music for commercial/industrial/travel video, jingles for TV spots and commercials. Pays by the job.

How to Contact: Query with resume of credits or submit demo tape of previous work or manuscript showing music scoring skills. Prefers cassette (or VHS videocassette) with 2-6 pieces. "Enclose short description and critique of each submission." Does not return unsolicited material; prefers to keep on file. Reports in 6 weeks.

Music: Uses rock, pop, jazz, fusion and classical-pop for various productions.

PRICE WEBER MARKETING COMMUNICATIONS, INC., Dept. SM, Box 99337, Louisville KY 40223. (502)499-9220. Producer/Director: Kelly McKnight. Advertising agency and audiovisual firm. Estab. 1967. Clients include Fortune 500, consumer durables, light/heavy industrials and package goods. Uses services of music houses, and independent songwriters/composer for scoring, background music and jingles for industrial and corporate image films and commercials for radio and TV. Commissions 6-8 composers/year. Pays by the job ($500-2,000). Buys all rights or one-time rights.

How to Contact: Submit demo tape of previous work demonstrating composition skills. Prefers cassette with 10 pieces. "Enclose data sheet on budgets per selection on demo tape." Does not return unsolicited material; prefers to keep on file. "We report back only if we use it."

Music: Uses easy listening, up-tempo, pop, jazz and classical for corporate image industrials and commercials.

Tips: "Keep us updated on new works or special accomplishments. Work with tight budgets of $500-2,000. Show me what you're best at—show me costs."

*PRO VIDEO SALES COMPANY, 1252 E. Hillsborough Ave., Tampa FL 33604. (800)780-8857. Consulting Audio/Video Sales Engineer: Mel Smith. Advertising agency, audiovisual firm, scoring service, **jingle/commercial music production house**, motion picture production company and **music sound effect library**. Clients include film editors and independent producers. Estab. 1983. Uses the services of music houses, independent songwriters/composers, lyricists and music programmers for scoring, background music, and jingles for advertising, audiovisuals, commercials, motion pictures, commercials for radio and TV and slide shows and videos. Commissions 9 composers and 9 lyricists/year. Pays $300/job, by royalty 7% or $40/hour. Buys all rights.

How to Contact: Query with resume of credits. Prefers cassette or IPS reel-to-reel (or videocassette) with 5 songs, lyric and lead sheets. Returns unsolicited material. Reports in 5-6 months.

Music: Uses easy listening, up-tempo, pop, jazz, classical, R&B and MOR for educational films, slide presentations, commercials, slide shows, songs and videos.

Tips: "Make your demo as contemporary as possible. Innovative sounds, strong hooks, tight lyrics."

PROFESSIONAL MEDIA SERVICES, Suite 205, 18530 Beach Blvd., Huntington Beach CA 92648. (714)964-0542. Owner: Roy Moosa. Advertising production firm. Clients include "corporate promos and TV commercials." Estab. 1982. Uses the services of independent songwriters for scoring of com-

mercials, corporate presentations, background music for training tapes, jingles for TV and commercials for radio and TV. Commissions 2 composers/year. Pays by the job. Buys all rights.
How to Contact: Query with resume of credits. Prefers cassette or reel-to-reel (or videocassette). Does not return unsolicited material; prefers to keep on file. Reports "as needed."
Music: "Upbeat background" music.
Tips: "Keep a video resume of your work."

PUBLICIS, INC., Dept. SM, 1675 Broadway, New York NY 10019. (212)956-8550. Creative Director: Nick LaMicela. Group Creative Director: Glen Jacobs. Advertising agency. Clients include retailers of cosmetics, beauty aids and fragrances; also retailers of cellular telephones and FAX machines. Estab. 1931. Uses the services of music houses for background music for test spots and commercials for radio and TV. Commissions 2 composers/year. "Rights purchased depends on job."
How to Contact: Submit demo tape of previous work. Prefers cassette or ¾" videocassette. Does not return unsolicited material; prefers to keep on file.
Music: Uses music for commercials.

PULLIN PRODUCTIONS LTD., 822 5th Ave. SW, Calgary, Alberta T2P 0N3 **Canada**. (403)234-7885. President: Chris Pullin. Clients include business and industry. Uses the services of music houses, songwriters and lyricists for "original songs and themes for multi-image, motion picture and multimedia." Commissions 4 composers and 2 lyricists/year. Pays minimum $500/job. Buys all rights.
How to Contact: Submit demo tape (or vidcocassette) of previous work. Prefers reel-to-reel with 4-10 songs but "any format is OK." Does not return unsolicited material. "Contact is made only if interested."
Music: Looking for "strong themes for any number of instruments/vocals (single instrument to full orchestra). Requirements for each job are very carefully specified."

*PYRAMID PRODUCTIONS, 714 Cabin Dr., Mill Valley CA 94941-3981. (415)381-6282. Producer/ Engineer: Bill Bailey. **Jingle/commercial music production house, music sound effect library** and recording studio. Clients include film, radio and TV (private talent). Uses the services of independent songwriters/composers and lyricists for scoring of jingles and films, background music for voice overs, jingles for radio, film and TV and commercials for radio and TV. Commissions 3-10 composers and 10 lyricists/year. Pays $50-300/job or $30-60/hour, "depending onclient and talent." Buys all or one-time rights.
How to Contact: Submit demo tape of previous work, tape demonstrating composition skills or manuscript showing music scoring skills; query with resume of credits or write to arrange personal interview. Prefers cassette, 7½-30 ips reel-to-reel (or videocassette) with 3 songs and lyric or lead sheets. SASE, but prefers to keep material on file. Reports in 6-8 weeks.
Music: Uses New Age, pop, rock & roll and fusion for film and commercials.

QUALLY & COMPANY INC., #2502, Huron Plaza, 30 East Huron, Chicago IL 60611. (312)944-0237. President/Creative Director: Robert Qually. Advertising agency. Uses the services of music houses, independent songwriters/composers and lyricists for scoring, background music and jingles for radio and TV commercials. Commissions 2-4 composers and 2-4 lyricists/year. Pays by the job, by royalty sometimes. Buys various rights depending on deal.
How to Contact: Submit demo tape of previous work or query with resume of credits. Prefers cassette (or ¾" Beta videocassette). SASE, but prefers to keep material on file. Reports in 2 weeks.
Music: Uses all kinds of music for commercials.

BILL QUINN PRODUCTIONS, 710 Cookman Ave., Asbury Park NJ 07712. (908)775-0500. Production Manager: Bill Newman. Audiovisual firm and motion picture production company. Estab. 1983. Clients include corporate, advertisers on cable and network TV and production companies. Uses the services of independent songwriters/composers and music houses for scoring of original productions and industrial films, background music for client accounts, commercials for radio and TV and video/film production. Commissions 15-20 composers/year. Pays by the job or approximately $25/hour. Buys one-time rights or all rights.
How to Contact: Submit demo tape of previous work or query with resume of credits. Call first to arrange personal interview. Prefers cassette. Will return unsolicited material accompanied by an SASE, but prefers to keep on file. "We respond by phone whenever we find music that fits a particular need."
Music: "We don't use one type of music more than another because our client list is rather lengthy and extremely varied. We use rock, pop, MOR, C&W, etc. Most often we commission music for TV and radio commercials. Interested in doing business with people in the New York and New Jersey area."
Tips: "Be flexible, able to work quickly and possess a working knowledge of all types of music."

RAMPION VISUAL PRODUCTIONS, 316 Stuart St., Boston MA 02116. (617)574-9601. Director/Camera: Steven V. Tringali. Motion picture production company. Clients include educational, independent producers, corporate clients and TV producers. Estab. 1982. Uses the services of independent songwriters/composers for jingles, background music and scoring to longer form programming. Commissions 4-6 composers/year. Pays by the job. Buys all rights.
How to Contact: Submit demo tape of previous work or query with resume of credits. Prefers cassette with variety of pieces. Does not return unsolicited material; prefers to keep material on file.
Music: Uses all styles for corporate, educational and original programming.
Tips: "Submit a varied demo reel showing style and client base."

REED PRODUCTIONS, INC., Box 977, Warsaw IN 46580. (219)267-4199. President: Howard Reed. Audiovisual firm and motion picture production company. Serves medical-industrial clients. Uses the services of music houses, independent songwriters/composers and lyricists for background music for audiovisual and video and commercials for TV. Commissions 1 composer and 1 lyricist/year. Pays $100-500/job. Buys all rights or one-time rights.
How to Contact: Submit demo tape of previous work. Prefers cassette (or VHS videocassette). SASE. Reports in 3 weeks.
Music: Uses traditional music for industrial, medical, audiovisual and video projects.

RESPONSE GRAPHICS, Suite 130, 5620 Old Bullard Rd., Tyler TX 75703. (903)593-2362. President: Bill Bell. Advertising agency, audiovisual firm and **music sound effect library.** Clients include full service, banks, retail, industrial and music industry. Estab. 1954. Uses the services of music houses for background music for commercials, audiovisual presentations and jingles for commercials for radio and TV. Commissions 4-5 composers/year. Pays $250-2,000/job. Buys shared rights.
How to Contact: Submit demo tape of previous work. Prefers cassette or 7½ or 15 ips reel-to-reel with 3-4 songs and lyric sheet. SASE, but prefers to keep material on file. Reports in 3 weeks.
Music: Uses modern contemporary and C&W for films, commercials and audiovisual.
Tips: "Be cost effective."

RIGHT TRACKS PRODUCTIONS LTD., Dept. SM, 226 B. Portage Ave., Saskatoon SK S7H 0Y0 **Canada.** (306)933-4949. Producer/Studio Manager: Lyndon Smith. Scoring service and jingle/commercial music production house. Clients include ad agencies, corporations, film and video producers. Estab. 1986. Uses the services of independent songwriters/composers, lyricists, singers, session players, programmers, and arrangers for scoring of film and broadcast television, jingles for radio and TV, commercials for radion and TV, and AV soundtracks. Commissions 5 composers and 5 lyricists/year. Pays by the job, by royalty, or per hour. Buys all rights.
How to Contact: Submit demo tape of previous work; query with resume of credits. Prefers cassette or 7½/15 ips reel-to-reel. Does not return material; prefers to keep on file.
Music: "Depends on job/target market."

RTG PUBLISHING, INC., 130 E. 6th St., Cincinnati OH 45202. President: John Henry. Music Publisher. Clients include network TV (U.S.), foreign TV, and syndicated television producers. Uses services of MIDI composers to supply background and feature music. Currently seeking produced, unpublished, original songs for placement on one of several TV programs. Writers paid performance royalties through BMI/ASCAP and applicable synchronization fees.
How to Contact: Composers should submit resume and demo cassette of appropriate material (i.e. examples of TV background scoring only). Songwriters should send no more than three songs on one cassette. SASE. Do not call. Reports in 4-6 weeks.
Music: Song should be pop or A/C. No country, heavy metal, or rap.
Tips: "Listen to what the marketplace is using before submitting material."

RUFFCUT RECORDING, 6472 Seven Mile, Dept. SM, South Lyon MI 48178. (313)486-0505. Production Manager: J.D. Dudick. Jingle/commercial production house. Clients include advertising agencies and industrial accounts. Estab. 1990. Uses the services of independent songwriters/composers for background music for industrial films, jingles for local and national accounts and commercials for radio and TV. Commissions 4-5 composers and 1-2 lyricists/year. Pays by the job ($100-2,500) or by royalty (10-20%). Buys one-time rights.
How to Contact: Submit tape demonstrating composition skills. Prefers cassette with 3-5 songs and lyric sheets. Does not return unsolicited material; keeps material on file. Reports in 2-4 weeks.
Music: "All styles that are creative and unique" for commercials/radio, film presentations.
Tips: "Don't worry about the production; keep it catchy with a melody you will hum to."

Close-up

John Henry Kreitler
President, RTG Music
Cincinnati, Ohio

Audiovisual and commercial music markets are different from any other in one very important way. "Unfortunately, today's marketplace expects composers to make the [financial] investment," says John Henry Kreitler, president of Cincinnati's RTG Music. The company works in all aspects of commercial music, but has had its biggest success in writing music for daytime television. RTG currently scores music for daytime TV's "As the World Turns," "Guiding Light" and "Another World." In 1991 their work on "Guiding Light" earned them a daytime Emmy.

"You have to invest in enough equipment to sound like what you're hearing [finished production], because competition has led producers to expect it and because often production budgets are small or non-existent," Kreitler continues. This means composers often get little or no "upfront" money and work from royalties that can sometimes take a year to collect.

Hard work and investment of time and money are key to making it in this segment of the music industry. Kreitler himself entered commercial music after completing a master's degree in composition. His first project: a corporate film for a baby food manufacturer. How did he make the contact? "I got out the Yellow Pages and called all the film companies in town to inquire as to whether or not they would be interested in using me," Kreitler says. "That first film job I did didn't pay anything. I wanted the experience; I wanted to be able to say, 'I've done a film.' "

Kreitler tells two other stories about the importance of investing time in gaining commercial music experience: about the music supervisor of another daytime show working without pay for two years; and another about a writer for another program who began his commercial music career as a runner for the network producing the show. "There's a little bit of a 'Catch-22' in this business," Kreitler says. "Until you do something, how can you prove you can do it? You just have to start with anybody you can find. You have to be prepared to sacrifice."

This may present a somewhat discouraging view of commercial music, but Kreitler is quick to point out that these sacrifices aren't as great as they appear. "You can probably work anywhere if you're talented and aggressive. We've proven that you don't have to go to L.A. or New York in order to do music for national TV," Kreitler says. "I think I would encourage a young writer to start out with a small market and get his chops together."

He advises composers choosing to establish a local base to pick a segment of the market to work in. Then, "find out who's doing what you want to do. Start talking to those people. If you're unwilling to go out and talk, you're going to have a tough time succeeding. The ones who succeed are natural hustlers; they go out and find business for themselves."

Since so much of the music being produced for commercial and audiovisual use (especially in daytime TV) is electronic, aspiring composers gain another advantage. "There are more opportunities than ever before for writers because we've moved so much to electronic," says Kreitler. "Ten years ago there may have been the same number of composers who could write, but to put a piece of music on tape took a lot of production money, a recording studio and musicians. Now, a person with a fairly small investment in some MIDI equipment can sit in his own apartment or garage and do the same thing."

Combine many composers competing for the same jobs and technology that gives most composers an easy way of working, and the next challenge arises. How does the aspiring composer get his music heard, and how does he acquire work? Kreitler gives one concise piece of advice. "Present yourself professionally, do it aggressively and hope your luck is good." Aggressive and professional submission includes high production values for the demo tape and a well-organized, typed resume. The resume should identify the experience you feel is most appropriate for the company you're submitting to. "The last person I took on [for out-of-house work] sent me a reel, and before I listened I read his resume. He had daytime television on it already, and it convinced me to listen to the reel." Kreitler also adds networking to the mix. "So much of it [succeeding] boils down to who you know. Not, 'My uncle knows somebody.' It's 'Who did I meet this week? Who did I spend time visiting with?' "

There are important preparatory steps an aspiring composer can take before beginning the process of marketing his music. "No. 1: Get an education," says Kreitler. "[then] do as much music in as many circumstances as you can to get as much experience as you can. Because the experience is one of the biggest factors that will come into play in your success." Ability to work in many styles is also important. The way to gain that flexibility in style is "listen to what's going on in the marketplace," Kreitler says. "If you want to write for television, sit at home and watch television. If you want to write for films, go to films. Buy soundtracks. Listen to what people are doing, so you can understand what the standards are."

In learning about and listening to the music being used in the commercial and audiovisual marketplace, Kreitler warns not to fall into a dangerous trap. "You can become submerged creatively," he says. "The purpose of becoming aware of what the market is doing isn't to be a copycat. It's to understand and draw from what others are doing and find yourself creatively."

Finding yourself creatively also involves evaluation. Kreitler recommends asking the companies you submit to for an evaluation of your material. If they have time, commercial music firms are usually glad to evaluate submitted material. He also stresses the importance of objective self-evaluation. One of the best self-testing tools involves comparison with other material. "The composer turns on the television and hears what's being played on television," Kreitler says. "Then he sits down and writes a piece of music he imagines would fit into that [program]. One of the best things that he can do is take his composition and play it beside the other one. Then listen to the differences, and assess if production values are adequate and whether or not the music is as interesting."

Talent is the most important factor in the commercial music market. Education and flexibility will help develop and express that talent, and professional presentation along with experience will give you the opportunities to exercise that talent and be successful. Evaluating the talent constantly will provide a measure of the music's quality, says Kreitler. "If the talent is there, then the other factors will come into play." That applies equally to the more established composers in the field. "I'm doing all these things every day," says Kreitler. "We haven't stopped now that we've succeeded. We're going out there and doing the work I'm talking about all the time."

—Michael Oxley

CHUCK RUHR ADVERTISING, Dept. SM, 1221 Nicollett Mall, Minneapolis MN 55403. (612)332-4565. Creative Director: Marilyan Pocius. Advertising agency. Serves consumer and industrial clients; client list available on request. Uses the services of songwriters and music houses for jingles and background music. Commissions 4-5 songwriters and 1-2 lyricists/year. Pays by the job. Initial fee negotiated, after that pays union scales. Pays residuals for subsequent use of material. Rights purchased are negotiable.
How to Contact: Submit demo tape of previous work. Prefers cassette. Reports "when needed."
Music: Uses background music and "originals befitting the message."
Tips: "Be original and be flexible. Study the best examples."

CHARLES RYAN ASSOCIATES, Dept. SM, Box 2464, Charleston WV 25329. (304)342-0161. Vice President/Account Services: Tad Walden. Advertising agency. Clients in a variety of areas. Uses the services of music houses for scoring, background music, jingles and commercials for radio and TV. Commissions 2-3 songwriters/composers/year. Pays by the job. Buys all rights.
How to Contact: Submit demo tape of previous work or tape demonstrating composition skills; query with resume of credits; or write to arrange personal interview. Prefers cassette with 15-20 songs. SASE, but prefers to keep on file.
Music: Uses easy listening, pop, jazz, classical for educational films, slide presentations and commercials.
Tips: "The first 2 songs/samples on demo tape better be good or we'll listen no further."

S.A. PRODUCTIONS, INC., Dept. SM, 330 W. 58th St., New York NY 10019. (212)765-2669. President: Stan Applebaum. Scoring service, **commercial music production house** and **music/sound effect library**. Clients include motion picture production companies and advertising agencies, Broadway, music publishing and industrials. Estab. 1968. Uses the services of independent composers for scoring, background music, and composers/lyricists for jingles for national radio and TV commercials and industrials. Pays by the job. Buys all rights, one-time rights or negotiates rights purchased.
How to Contact: Query with resume of credits, or submit demo tape of previous work or tape demonstrating composition skills or manuscript showing music scoring skills, or write to arrange personal interview. Prefers cassette or 15 or 7½ ips reel-to-reel with 5-10 pieces. SASE, but prefers to keep material on file. Reports in 1 month.
Music: Uses all styles of music for various kinds of assignments.
Tips: "Be original with interesting harmonic and melodic development, and lyrics that are inventive and interesting."

*PATRICK WILLIAM SALVO, Dept. SM, Suite 2, 8686 W. Olympic Blvd., Los Angeles CA 90035. (213)659-1792. Founder: Patrick William Salvo. Advertising agency and public relations, management. Clients include entertainment business, film, television, advertising radio. Estab. 1980. Uses the services of music houses, independent songwriters/composers and lyricists for jingles and background music for radio and TV commercials.
How to Contact: Write or call first to arrange personal interview. Prefers cassette (or VHS videocassette). Does not return unsolicited material; prefers to keep submitted material on file.
Music: Interested in all styles of music.

SCHEMBRI VISION, Dept. SM, 2156 Story Ave., Bronx NY 10473. (212)863-2986. Manager: Sal Schembri, Jr. Jingle/**commercial music production house**. Advertising agency. Serves retail and industrial clients. Uses the services of independent songwriters/composers for background music and jingles for TV commercials. Pays $250/job. Buys one-time rights.
How to Contact: Submit demo tape of previous work. SASE. Reports in 3 weeks.
Music: Uses easy listening and rap music for commercials.

*CARL SCHURTZ MUSIC, 401 E 82nd St., New York NY 10028. (212)737-3069. Contact: Carl Schurtz. **Jingle/commercial music production house**. Clients include AV production companies, corporate clients, TV, cable, radio, recorded books and museum tours. Uses the services of independent songwriters/composers for background music for industrials and jingles for broadcast (radio, TV). Commissions 1 composer/year. Pays $100-1,000/job. Buys all or one-time rights.
How to Contact: Submit tape demonstrating composition skills or query with resume of credits. Prefers cassette. Does not return unsolicited material; prefers to keep material on file. Reports in 2 months.

Listings of companies within this section which are either commercial music production houses or music libraries will have that information printed in boldface type.

Music: Uses pop from hard driving to laid back, copy cats or pop tunes for industrials, multi image, videos (corporate) and jingles.

SEASIDE PRODUCTIONS, Box 93, Sea Isle City NJ 08243. Producer: Gregory C. Guarini. Scoring service and **jingle/commercial music production house**. Clients are mostly businesses and bands in Delaware Valley. Estab. 1987. Uses the services of independent songwriters/composers and lyricists for "management and publishing." Commissions 12 composers and lyricists/year. Pays by the job or by royalty. Rights purchased "depend on situation."
How to Contact: Submit tape demonstrating composition skills—unsolicited submissions are OK. Prefers cassette (or VHS videocassette) with 4 songs and lyric or lead sheet. SASE, but prefers to keep material on file. Reports in 2 weeks.
Music: Uses rock and soul for all types of assignments.

SHAFFER SHAFFER SHAFFER, INC., Dept. SM, 1070 Hanna Bldg., Cleveland OH 44115. (216)566-1188. President: Harry Gard Shaffer, Jr. Advertising agency. Clients include consumer and retail. Uses services of songwriters, lyricists and music houses for jingles and background music. Commissions 6 songwriters/year. Pays $2,000-15,000/job. Buys all rights.
How to Contact: Query with resume of credits. Prefers 7½ ips reel-to-reel with 6-12 songs. Prefers to keep material on file. Responds as needs arise.

*SIGNATURE MUSIC, INC., Box 98, Buchanan MI 49107. (616)695-3068. President: Bill Mullin. **Music sound effect library**. Clients include corporate/institutional/commercial production. Estab. 1984. Uses the services of music houses and independent songwriters/composers for background music for media production. Commissions 5-10 composers/year. Pays 9-14% royalty. Buys all rights.
How to Contact: Submit demo tape of previous work. Prefers cassette with 6 songs. Does not return unsolicited material; prefers to keep on file. Reports in 1 week.
Music: Uses all for syndication.
Tips: "Present professional, creative, high caliber work. Be ASCAP affiliated."

SILVER BURDETT & GINN, Dept. SM, CN 018, 250 James St., Morristown NJ 07960. (201)285-8002. Music Editor: Donald Scafuri. Publisher of textbooks and records for kindergarten through 8th grade. Estab. 1864. "Our books and records are sold directly to schools and are evaluated and chosen for use according to the adoption procedures of a particular school district." Uses the services of music houses, songwriters and lyricists for original songs for children K-8; lyricists for translating foreign lyrics into a singable English version and "writing original lyrics to a folk tune or a melody composed by someone else." Commissions 0-20 lyricists and 0-20 pieces/year. Pays $55-75 for lyrics and arrangements; up to $400 for original compositions (reprint rights plus statutory record royalty). Buys one-time rights for educational use.
How to Contact: Submit lead sheets of previous work. Prefers cassette. SASE. Reports in 1 month. Free catalog available.
Music: "We seek virtually any kind of song that is suitable both in words and music for children to sing. We are particularly interested in songs that are contemporary pop or folk-like in style."
Tips: "Become acquainted with teachers and students in elementary or junior high classrooms. Find out what music they are presently using and what they would like to use."

SINGER ADVERTISING & MARKETING, INC., 1035 Delaware Ave., Buffalo NY 14209. (716)884-8885. Senior Vice President: Marilyn Singer. Advertising agency. Clients include health care, professional football, travel service and industrial. Estab. 1969. Uses the services of music houses for background music for slide presentations, industrial videos, jingles for health care and professional football and commercials for radio and TV. Commissions 1-2 composers and 3-4 lyricists/year. Pay varies.
How to Contact: Submit demo tape of previous work. Prefers cassette or 15 ips reel-to-reel or ½" videocassette. SASE. Reports in weeks.
Music: Uses up-tempo pop and New Age jazz for commercial jingles and slide presentations.
Tips: "Study our client list and their current work and then submit."

ROBERT SOLOMON AND ASSOCIATES ADVERTISING, Dept. SM, Suite 1000, Dept. SM, 505 N. Woodward, Bloomfield Hills MI 48304. (313)540-0660. Attention: Copywriter/Producer. Advertising agency. Clients include "food service accounts, convenience stores, retail accounts and small service businesses." Uses independent songwriters, lyricists and music houses for jingles and special presentations. Commissions 1-10 songwriters and 1-10 lyricists/year. Pays by the job. Buys all rights.
How to Contact: Submit demo tape of previously aired work. Prefers cassette or 7½ ips reel-to-reel with 1-5 pieces and lyric or lead sheets. "Submissions must be up-to-date and up to industry standards." Does not return unsolicited material; prefers to keep on file.

Music: "MOR, pop or rock jingles describing specific products or services."
Tips: "Please make sure all information presented is CURRENT!"

SONIC IMAGES PRODUCTIONS, INC., Dept. SM, 4590 MacArthur Blvd. NW, Washington DC 20007. (202)333-1063. Vice President/Director of Video Services: Jolie Barbiere. Audiovisual firm, scoring services, **commercial music production house,** motion picture production company, **music/sound effect library,** CD-I/interactive multimedia development. Clients include independent producers, government, entertainment, associations, etc. Uses the services of music houses, independent songwriters/composers and lyricists for scoring of video and film productions; background music for art/experimental films and videos; jingles, public service announcements and radio and TV commercials. Commissions 2-4 composers and 1-2 lyricists/year. Pay varies. Buys all rights.
How to Contact: Submit demo tape of previous work or tape demonstrating composition skills. Prefers cassette (or ¾" VHS or Beta videocassette). "Include a resume." Does not return unsolicited material; prefers to keep on file. Reports if interested.
Music: Uses all commercial and classical styles of music for all kinds of assignments.
Tips: "We look for a clean professional product. Our clients demand it!"

*SOPERSOUND MUSIC LIBRARY, Box 498, Palo Alto CA 94302. (800)227-9980. Production Manager: Bruce Hemingway. **Music sound effect library.** Clients include all types. Estab. 1977. Uses the services of independent songwriters for music library product. Commissions 2-3 composers/year. Pays by the job, by royalty, by hour, or "per production." Buys all rights.
How to Contact: Submit demo tape of previous work. Prefers cassette. SASE. Reports in 1 month.
Music: Uses all for music library product.

SORIN PRODUCTIONS, INC., Freehold Executive Center, 4400 Route 9 S., Freehold NJ 07728. President: David Sorin. Audiovisual firm. Serves corporate and industrial clients. Uses services of music houses and independent songwriters/composers for background music for industrials. Commissions 1-3 composers and 1-3 lyricists/year. Pays by the job. Buys all rights.
How to Contact: Query with resume of credits. "No submissions with initial contact." Does not return unsolicited material; prefers to keep solicited materials on file. Reports in 1 month.
Music: Uses up-tempo and pop for audio, video and slides.

SOTER ASSOCIATES INC., 209 North 400 W., Provo UT 84601. (801)375-6200. President: N. Gregory Soter. Advertising agency. Clients include financial, health care, municipal, computer hardware and software. Estab. 1970. Uses services of music houses, independent songwriters/composers and lyricists for background music for audiovisual presentations and jingles for radio and TV commercials. Commissions 1 composer, 1 lyricist/year. Pays by the job. Buys all rights.
How to Contact: Submit tape demonstrating previous work and composition skills. Prefers cassette or VHS videocassette. Does not return unsolicited submissions; prefers to keep materials on file.

*SOUND IDEAS, Suite #4 105 W. Beaver Creek Rd., Richmond Hill ON L4B 1C6 **Canada.** (416)886-5000. FAX: (416)866-6800. President: Brian Nimens. **Music/sound effect library.** Clients include broadcast, post-production and recording studios. Estab. 1978. Uses the services of music houses. Commissions 5-10 composers/year. Pays by the job. Buys all rights.
How to Contact: Submit demo tape of previous work. Prefers cassette with 5-10 songs. Does not return unsolicited material; prefers to keep on file. Reports in 1 month.
Music: Uses full range for all kinds of assignments.

SOUND WRITERS PUBLICATIONS, INC., 223-225 Washington St., Dept. SM, Newark NJ 07102. (201)642-5132. Producer/Engineer: Kevin Ferd. Advertising agency, audiovisual firm and jingle/commercial music production house. Clients include major labels and large corporations. Estab. 1980. Uses the services of independent songwriters/composers and lyricists for scoring of jingles and TV commercials. Most writing, producing and engineering done in-house. Buys all rights and one-time rights.
How to Contact: Submit demo tape of previous work. Prefers cassette or ¾" videocassette. "We have a no return policy on all material." Prefers to keep material on file. Reports back in 4 weeks.
Music: Uses all types of music for commercials, training tapes and music videos.
Tips: "We don't like big egos."

SOUND*LIGHT PRODUCTIONS, 1915 Webster, Birmingham MI 48009. (313)642-3502. Producer: Terry Luke. Audiovisual firm. Estab. 1974. Clients include corporations, industrial, motivational, New Age, churches and educational institutions. Uses the services of music houses and independent songwriters/composers for jingles, background music for TV commercials, slide presentations and training videos. Commissions 3-10 songwriters and 2-3 lyricists/year. Pays $40-3,000/job or $4-65/hour. Buys all rights or one-time rights.

How to Contact: Submit demo tape of previous work—unsolicited submissions are OK. Prefers cassette (or VHS videocassette). SASE, but prefers to keep material on file. Reports in 1 month.

Music: Uses up-tempo, rock, spiritual, easy listening and inspirational for slide presentations, training videos and artistic video-MTV.

Tips: "Be creative and upbeat."

SPECTRUM SOUND STUDIOS, INC., Dept. SM, 1634 SW Alder, Portland OR 97205. (503)248-0248. Director of Music Operations: Karl Rasmussen. **Jingle/commercial music production house, music sound effect library** and broadcast production. Estab. 1973. Clients include advertising agencies, corporations and music businesses. Uses the services of independent songwriters/composers for scoring of in-house corporate video, jingles for commercial production and commercials for radio and TV. Commissions 8 composers and 2 lyricists/year. Pays by the job. Rights are up to client.

How to Contact: Submit demo tape of previous work or query with resume of credits. Prefers cassette or 15 ips reel-to-reel (or ¾" videocassette). SASE. Reports in 1 month.

Music: Uses all styles of music for all kinds of assignments.

SPIVACK ADVERTISING, INC., 7 Church Lane, Baltimore MD 21208. (301)484-9510. President: Irvin Spivack. Advertising agency. Clients include retail, financial, banking, medical and business-to-business. Estab. 1979. Uses the services of music houses for jingles for commercials for radio. Pay is negotiable.

How to Contact: Submit demo tape of previous work. Prefers cassette. SASE, but prefers to keep material on file.

Music: Generally up-tempo, but it really depends on clients.

STARWEST PRODUCTIONS, INC., Dept. SM, Studio A, 4910 Fox St., Denver CO 80216. (303)295-2222. President: Steven Pettit. Audiovisual firm and jingle **commercial music production house.** Clients include Fortune 500 companies to mom and pop shops. Estab. 1979. Uses the services of music houses and independent songwriters/composers for commercials for radio and TV. Commissions 2 composers and 2 lyricists/year. Pays $2,000/job. Buys all rights and rights with royalties.

How to Contact: Submit demo tape of previous work or query with resume of credits. Prefers 7½ ips reel-to-reel with 5-10 songs. SASE, but prefers to keep material on file. Reports in 1 month.

Music: Uses up-tempo music for slide presentations and live performances.

Tips: "Make my foot tap."

STATION BREAK PRODUCTIONS, Dept. SM, Suite 1, 40 Glen St., Glen Cove NY 11542. (516)759-7005. Producer: Stephen Meyers. Advertising agency and jingle/**commercial music production house.** Clients include ad agencies, retail businesses, hotels, restaurants, corporate and special projects. Estab. 1985. Uses the services of independent songwriters/composers and singers, and MIDI composers with performer voice overs for commercials for radio and TV. Commissions 2 composers and 1 lyricist/year. Pays by the job. Buys all rights.

How to Contact: Submit demo tape of previous work or write to arrange personal interview. Prefers cassette with 4 pieces. Does not return unsolicited material; prefers to keep material on file. Reports in 1 month.

Music: Uses pop, classical and dance for industrial and commercials.

Tips: "Send your best work to date. Start with your strongest style."

STRATEGIC PROMOTIONS, INC., Dept. SM, Suite 250, 2602 McKinney, Dallas TX 75204. (214)871-1016. President: Grahame Hopkins. Advertising agency, marketing. Clients include fast food, retail food, food service, beverage, beer. Estab. 1978. Uses the services of music houses and independent songwriters/composers for scoring of music tracks for TV commercials and background music for TV & radio commercials. Commissions 2-3 composers/year. Pays by the job.

How to Contact: Submit demo tape of previous work. Submit tape demonstrating composition skills. Prefers cassette (or ¾" videocassette) with 4-5 songs. "No phone calls please. Does not return unsolicited material; prefers to keep submitted materials on file.

Music: Uses all types of music for industrial videos, slide presentations and commercials.

Tips: "Submit your favorite and personal best work."

STRAUCHEN ASSOCIATES, INC., Dept. SM, 3388 Erie Ave., Cincinnati OH 45208. (513)871-5353. President: Stephen H. Strauchen. Advertising agency. Clients include financial, food, business-to-business and insurance. Estab. 1981. Uses the services of music houses and independent songwriters/composers for scoring of commercial jingles and sales films and background music for radio, TV and

audiovisual presentations. Commissions 3-4 composers/year; 1 lyricist/year. Pays $500-1,000/job or $20-30/hour. Buys all rights.
How to Contact: Submit demo tape of previous work. Prefers cassette, 7½ ips reel-to-reel or VHS videocassette. SASE, but prefers to keep materials on file.
Music: Easy listening, up-tempo, pop and jazz.
Tips: "Be specific regarding rates, use rights, etc."

*STUDIO M PRODUCTIONS UNLTD., 8715 Waikiki Station, Honolulu HI 96830. (808)734-3345. Sr. Producer: Mike Michaels. Audiovisual firm. Clients include ad agencies, TV producers and travel companies. Estab. 1969. Uses the services of music houses and independent songwriters/composers for background music for TV programs, films, industrial and travalogs, jingles for commercials and industrials and commercial for radio and TV. Commissions 1-2 composers and 1-2 lyricists/year. Pays by the job or by the hour. Buys all rights (usually) or one-time rights (occasionally).
How to Contact: Submit demo tape of previous work or write with resume of credits. Prefers cassette (or VHS videocassette) with a few pieces. SASE, but prefers to keep material on file. Reports in 4-6 weeks.
Music: Uses easy, pop, up-tempo and some jazz for commercials, programs and industrials.

SULLIVAN & FINDSEN ADVERTISING, Dept. SM, 2165 Gilbert Ave., Cincinnati OH 45206. (513)281-2700. Director of Broadcast Production: Kirby Sullivan. Advertising agency. Clients include consumer and business-to-business firms. Uses the services of music houses, independent songwriters/composers and lyricists for scoring, background music, jingles and commercials for radio and TV. Commissions 3 composers and 3 lyricists/year. Pays by the job. Buys all rights.
How to Contact: Submit demo tape of previous work. Prefers cassette. Does not return unsolicited material; prefers to keep material on file. "We report back when we need some work."
Music: Uses all styles for commercials.

TALCO PRODUCTIONS, 279 E. 44th St., New York NY 10017, (212)697-4015. President: Al Lawrence. Audiovisual firm, TV and motion picture production company. Clients include corporate, nonprofit and educational organizations. Uses the services of music houses and independent songwriters/composers and lyricists for scoring and background music for film, TV and radio. Commissions 2-3 composers and 0-3 lyricists/year. Pays by the job. Buys all rights.
How to Contact: Query with resume of credits. Do not send unsolicited submissions. SASE for reply. "Do not submit demo unless request is made!" Reports in 3 weeks.
Music: Uses easy listening, up-tempo, pop, jazz, classical, A/C and rock for educational films and documentaries.
Tips: "Send credits only. No tapes, discs, etc."

TEEMAN/SLEPPIN ENTERPRISES INC., Dept. SM, 147 W. 26 St., New York NY 10001. (212)243-7836. President: Bob Teeman. Vice President: Stu Sleppin. Management, motion picture and music video production company. Clients include artists, film companies, TV stations and corporate sponsors. Uses the services of independent songwriters/composers and lyricists for scoring of TV shows and films and original songs. Commissions 3 composers and 3 lyricists/year. Pays by the job. Rights negotiable.
How to Contact: Submit demo tape of previous work or write to arrange personal interview. Prefers cassette (or VHS or ¾" videocassette). SASE, but prefers to keep material on file. Reports in 2 months.
Music: Uses pop and dance for original songs tied into a film or campaign.

TELECINE SERVICES & PRODUCTION LTD., 23 Seapoint Ave., Blackrock, Co. Dublin Ireland. Phone: 353 1 2808744. FAX: 353 1 808679. Director: Anabella Nolan. Audiovisual firm and video production house. Estab. 1977. Clients include advertising and commercial business. Uses the services of songwriters and music houses for original songs for TV commercials and audiovisual and video programs; lyricists for writing lyrics for commercials and conference themes. Commissions 5 songwriters/composers and 3 lyricists for 20 pieces/year. Pays $5,000/job. Buys all rights or rights within one country.
How to Contact: Submit tape demonstrating composition skills. Prefers 15 ips reel-to-reel or cassette with 3-10 songs. SAE and IRC. Reports in 1 month.
Tips: "Understand our marketing needs; know the difference between European and U.S. tastes."

TEXAS AFFILIATED PUBLISHING COMPANY, "STREETPEOPLES WEEKLY NEWS", Box 270942, Dallas TX 75227-0942. (214)941-7796. Contact: Editor. Advertising agency and newspaper publisher. Clients are corporate and retail. Estab. 1977. Uses the services of independent songwriters/composers, lyricists and music houses for commercials for radio and TV. Pays negotiable amount. Buys all rights and one-time rights.

How to Contact: Submit demo tape of previous work or write first to arrange personal interview. "No phone calls please. Send *no* originals, include SASE for returns. Our current project is about the problems of the 'homeless.' Persons writing songs about this may want to send for a copy of 'Street-peoples Weekly News' to get an idea of what's involved. Send $2 to cover handling/postage." SASE, but prefers to keep materials on file. Reports in 3 weeks.
Music: Uses easy listening, up-tempo for commercials. "We're interested in many types/styles according to job need of our clients. Also need music production for intros on radio talk shows."

TOP OF THE MOUNTAIN PUBLISHING/POWELL PRODUCTIONS, Suite 123, 11701 S. Belcher Rd., Largo FL 34643. (813)530-0110. FAX: (813)536-3681. Administrator: Dr. Tag Powell. Publisher of books, audio-cassettes and seminars (producer). Clients include domestic and foreign distributors of books and audiocassettes. Estab. 1980. Uses independent songwriters/composers for background music for subliminal audiocassettes and New Age type music audiocassettes. Pays by the job. Buys all rights.
How to Contact: Submit demo tape of previous work. Prefers cassette with 5-7 songs. Does not return material. Prefers to keep submitted materials on file. Reports in 2 weeks to 6 months.
Music: Uses New Age instrumental.
Tips: "Reduce price to get started."

TRF PRODUCTION MUSIC LIBRARIES, Dept. SM, 1619 Broadway, New York NY 10019. (212)753-3234. President: Michael Nurko. **Music/sound effect libraries.** Estab. 1931. Uses services of independent composers for jingles, background and theme music for all media including films, slide presentations, radio and television commercials. Pays 50% royalty.
How to Contact: Submit demo tape of new compositions. Prefers cassette with 3-7 pieces.
Music: Primarily interested in instrumental music for assignments in all media.

TRI VIDEO TELEPRODUCTION, Box 8822, Incline Village NV 89452-8822. (702)323-6868. Director: Jon Paul Davidson. Documentary and corporate television production firm. Clients include corporate accounts, primarily in health care and telecommunications. Estab. 1978. Uses the services of music houses and independent songwriters/composers for scoring of logo soundbeds and intro/conclusions and background music for transitions and presentations. Commissions 0-1 composers/year. Pays $500-2,000/job. Buys all rights and/or one-time rights.
How to Contact: Query with resume of credits. Prefers cassette with 1-3 pieces. Does not return material; prefers to keep on file. "We do not report back. We will use on-file tapes to demo to clients when making selection. If your work is what client likes and is appropriate, we will contact you."
Music: Uses easy, up-tempo and classical for educational and industrial.
Tips: "The corporate market is quite varied. Needs are of every type. Just keep in touch. We do lots of custom work rather than volume, so number of projects is small each year."

TULLY-MENARD, INC., 2207 S. Dale Mabry, Tampa FL 33629. (813)253-0447. Broadcast Producer: Robert A. Ackroyd. Advertising agency. Estab. 1960. Clients include a fast food restaurant, supermarket, theme park, retailers, manufacturers, car dealer. Uses the services of songwriters and music houses for TV and radio commercials, jingles, background music and film and AV soundtracks. Commissions 1-2 songwriters/composers per year. Payment negotiable, "dependent on project, budget and needs." Buys all rights.
How to Contact: Write or call for permission to submit demo tape of previous work. Prefers cassette or 7½ ips reel-to-reel with 5-8 songs. SASE, but prefers to keep material on file. "We research our file at the onset of need to determine candidates and parameters, then obtain bids and demos."
Music: "Broadcast and off-line; jingles and music tracks. Institutional jingles for a wide variety of clients."
Tips: "Stay current with today's sound, but be different—give it your own personality. Listen carefully to the parameters we give you, and if you don't quite grasp what we're looking for, ask! Provide the same package services as major music houses but with more originality and ingenuity."

TULLYVISION STUDIOS, Dept. SM, 465 Main St., Tullytown PA 19007. (215)946-7444. Producer: Michelle A. Powell. Audiovisual firm. Clients include corporate/industrial. Estab. 1983. Uses the services of music houses and independent songwriters/composers for marketing, training and corporate image videotapes. Commissions 3 composers/year. Pays $500/job. Buys all rights or one-time rights.
How to Contact: Submit demo tape of previous work. Query with resume of credits. Prefers cassette or ¾" VHS videocassette with 3 songs. SASE, but prefers to keep submitted materials on file. Reports in 3 weeks.
Music: Uses up-tempo and pop for educational films and slide presentations.

27TH DIMENSION INC., Box 1149, Okeechobee FL 34973-1149. (800)634-0091. President: John St. John. Scoring service, **jingle/commercial music production house** and **music sound effect library**. Clients include A/V producers, video houses, recording studios and radio and TV stations. Estab. 1986. Uses the services of independent songwriters/composers for scoring of library material and commercials for radio and TV. Commissions 10 composers/year. Pays $100-1,000/job; publishing (performance fees). "We buy the right to use in our library exclusively." Buys all rights except writer's publishing. Writer gets all performance fees (ASCAP or BMI).
How to Contact: Submit tape demonstrating composition skills or call. Prefers cassette. "Call before sending." SASE, but prefers to keep on file. Reports in 1 month.
Music: Uses industrial, pop jazz, sports, contemporary and New Age for music library.
Tips: "Follow style instructions carefully."

UMBRELLA MEDIA, 11314 NE 26th Av., Vancover WA 98686. (206)690-3833. President: Sid Brown. Advertising agency and audiovisual firm. Clients include high tech, educational and human services organizations. Estab. 1975. Uses the services of independent songwriters/composers and lyricists for scoring of TV productions, corporate videos and commercials for TV. Commissions 2 composers and 2 lyricists/year. Pays $50-500/job or 10% royalty.
How to Contact: Submit demo tape of previous work or query with resume of credits. Prefers cassette, 7½ IPS reel-to-reel (or VHS videocassette) with no more than 10 songs and lyric sheet. SASE, but prefers to keep submitted material on file. Reports in 1 month.
Music: Uses classic, New Age, rock, folk, jazz for educational, corporate, documentary, videos and slide shows.

*UNITED ENTERTAINMENT PRODUCTIONS, 3947 State Line, Kansas City MO 64111. (913)262-3555. Operations Manager: Dave Maygers. Recording studio, artist management, publishing company and record company. Serves musical groups, songwriters and ad clients. Estab. 1972. Uses the services of independent songwriters, lyricists and self-contained groups for scoring of album projects, background music for ads and industrial films, jingles and commercials for radio and TV. Pays negotiable royalty. Buys all rights or one-time rights.
How to Contact: Submit demo tape of previous work demonstrating composition skills. "Send cassette of material and lyric sheet when applicable." Does not return unsolicited material; prefers to keep material on file. Reports in 1 month.
Music: "Rock, pop, R&B, jazz, country to be used in music projects."

VIDEO I-D, INC., Dept. SM, 105 Muller Rd., Washington IL 61571. (309)444-4323. Manager, Marketing Services: Gwen Wagner. Post production/teleproductions. Clients include industrial and business. Estab. 1978. Uses the services of professional library music for video production pieces and commercials. Buys all rights.
How to Contact: Submit demo tape of previous work. Prefers cassette or VHS videocassette with 5 songs and lyric sheet. SASE, but prefers to keep submitted materials on file. Reports in 3 weeks.
Music: "Musical styles depend upon client preference."

VINEBERG COMMUNICATIONS, Dept. SM, Suite B-800, 61-20 Grand Central Pkwy., Forest Hills NY 11375. (718)760-0333. President: Neil Vineberg. Jingle/commercial music production house. Clients include TV/film producers. Estab. 1986. Uses the services of independent songwriters/composers and lyricists for background music for TV/film, corporate videos/film and commercials for radio and TV. Commissions 5 composers and 2 lyricists/year. Pays by the job. Buys all rights and one-time rights.
How to Contact: Submit demo tape of previous work. Submit tape demonstrating composition skills. Query with resume of credits. Write first to arrange personal interview. Prefers cassette (or VHS videocassette) with 4 songs and lead sheet (if possible). "No calls. Write only." SASE, but prefers to keep material on file. Reports in 1 month.
Music: Uses all types except classical.

VIP VIDEO, Film House, 143 Hickory Hill Cir., Osterville MA 02655. (508)428-7198. President: Jeffrey H. Aikman. Audiovisual firm. Clients include business, industry and TV stations. Estab. 1983. Uses the services of music houses, independent songwriters/composers and lyricists for scoring of multi-image productions, background music for videotapes and motion pictures and jingles for TV commercials. Commissions 15-20 composers and 15-20 lyricists/year. Pays by the job, amounts vary depending on the length and complexity of each project. Buys all rights, but can handle one-time rights for special projects.
How to Contact: Submit demo tape of previous work. Prefers cassette with 1-2 songs. SASE but prefers to keep material on file unless specifically stated. Reports in 6-8 weeks.
Music: Uses easy listening, pop and up-tempo for feature films, TV series, TV pilots and background for videotapes. Currently working on scoring series of 26 feature length silent films. If project is successful, this series will be added to at the rate of 13 per year.

Tips: "Constantly update your files. We like to hear from songwriters, lyricists and composers at least 3-4 times per year."

VISION FILM GROUP, INC., Dept. SM, 72 Princess St. 2nd Fl., Winnipeg, Manitoba R3B 1K2 **Canada**. (204)942-6215. President: Al Rosenberg. Audiovisual firm, motion picture and music video production company. Estab. 1985. Clients include industrial and entertainment firms. Uses the services of music houses, independent songwriters/composers and lyricists for background music for audiovisual and videos, and TV commercials. Commissions 3-5 composers and 2-4 lyricists/year. Pays $100-500/job. Buys all rights or one-time rights.
How to Contact: Submit demo tape of previous work, or tape demonstrating composition skills. Prefers cassette (or Beta videocassette). Does not return unsolicited material; prefers to keep on file. Reports in 2 weeks.
Music: Uses rock, contemporary, new age, up-tempo, unpublished music for videos, marketing programs, audiovisual presentations and commercials.
Tips: "Currently looking for fresh material for a rock musical for TV and video—as well as touring."

*VOICES/LIVING LIBRARY, Box 153, La Grange IL 60525. (708)579-9578. Owner: Charles Fuller. Music sound effect library. Clients include industrial, advertising, independent producers. Estab. 1966. Uses the services of independent songwriters/composers and small, new buyout libraries for scoring of industrials and background music for industrials. Commissions 3 composers/year. Pays for buyout only. Buys non-exclusive, library rights.
How to Contact: Submit samples of "library" collection. Prefers cassette or 15 IPS reel-to-reel. "Our most urgent need is for small group classic style and modern 'quiet' small group themes, solo instruments with reprise material; moods for scoring purposes." SASE, but prefers to keep material on file. Reports in 2 weeks.
Music: Uses a variety, but only from composer's library for industrial, educational and documentary.
Tips: "We're small and don't use a lot of material, but we'll listen to anyone who is good. We also recommend artists to other firms. Send your best work."

BEN WAGES AGENCY, 2513 Denny Ave., Pascagoula MS 39567. (601)769-7104. FAX: (601)769-8590. Owner/President: Ben Wages. Advertising agency, management firm, booking agency and record company (Sea Coast Recording). Estab. 1978. Uses the services of independent songwriters. Pays by the job, by royalty or per hour. Buys all rights or one-time rights. Depends on particular situation.
How to Contact: Write or call to arrange personal interview or submit demo tape of previously aired work. Prefers cassette (or VHS videocassette). SASE, but prefers to keep material on file. Reports in 4 weeks.
Music: "Country is predominantly used. Assignments are most often commercial jingles."
Tips: "Be as professional as possible when submitting material and be thorough. Neatness is always a plus. Would advise sending copyrighted material only. Include as much info as possible."

WEBER, COHN & RILEY, 444 N. Michigan Ave., Chicago IL 60611. (312)527-4260. Executive Creative Director: C. Welch. Advertising agency. Serves real estate, business, financial and food clients. Estab. 1960. Uses music houses for jingles and background music for commercials. Commissions 2 songwriters and 2 lyricists/year. Pays $500 minimum/job. Buys all rights or one-time rights, "open to negotiation."
How to Contact: Write a letter of introduction to creative director. SASE. "We listen to and keep a file of all submissions, but generally do not reply unless we have a specific job in mind." Songwriters may follow up with a phone call for response.
Music: "We use music for a variety of products and services. We expect highly original, tight arrangements that contribute to the overall concept of the commercial. We do not work with songwriters who have little or no previous experience scoring and recording commercials."
Tips: "Don't aim too high to start. Establish credentials and get experience on small local work, then go after bigger accounts. Don't oversell when making contacts or claim the ability to produce any kind of 'sound.' Producers only believe what they hear on sample reels. Produce a sample reel that's professional and responsive to today's needs. Present a work that is creative and meets our strategies and budget requirements."

*WEST COAST PROJECTIONS, 6349 Naucy Ridge Dr., San Diego CA 92121. (619)452-0041. Producer: David Gibbs. Audiovisual firm and video production. Estab. 1980. Uses the services of music houses and independent songwriters/composers for scoring and background music. Commissions 3 composers/year. Pays by the job. Buys one-time rights.
How to Contact: Submit demo tape of previous work. Prefers cassette or any videocassette. Does not return unsolicited material; prefers to keep on file. Reports only if interested.
Music: Uses up tempo pop for rock videos and corporate image presentations.

WESTERN PUBLISHING COMPANY, INC., Dept. SM, 1220 Mound Ave., Racine WI 53404. (414)633-2431. Golden Entertainment: Virginia Clapper. Children's publisher. Distributes entertainment products through mass market channels. Estab. 1907. Uses the services of music houses, independent songwriters/composers and lyricists for scoring of and background music for songs, short films and storytelling audio cassettes. Commissions 2-3 composers and 4-5 lyricists/year. Pays by the job. Buys all rights. Work for hire arrangement preferred.
How to Contact: Submit demo tape of previous work. Write first to arrange personal interview. Prefers cassette (or VHS videocassette) with 2-6 songs and lead sheets. SASE, but prefers to keep submitted materials on file. Reports in 6 weeks.
Music: Uses children's songs for film scores; book and tape audio productions.
Tips: "Expect to be employed on a work for hire basis, allowing straight buy-out of all rights."

WESTON WOODS STUDIOS, 389 Newtown Turnpike, Weston CT 06883. Production Manager: Paul R. Gagne. Audiovisual firm, motion picture production company. "We produce films and audio visual products based on children's picture books." Clients include educational/institutional market and home market video. Estab. 1955. Uses services of independent composers and copyists for scoring of short films and filmstrip soundtracks. Commissions 3-5 composers/year. Pays $600-3500/job. Buys all rights.
How to Contact: Submit demo tape of previous work, tape demonstrating composition scores or query with resume of credits. Prefers cassette. "Write only; we cannot accept telephone queries." SASE, but prefers to keep material on file. Reports in 6-12 months.
Music: Uses serious non-commercial scoring for acoustic instruments (synth OK) in classical, folk, or ethnic styles for educational films and filmstrips of children's stories; no driving rhythm tracks; no songs, please—especially "kiddie songs."

WHITE PRODUCTION ARCHIVES, INC., Dept. SM, 12233 South Pulaski Rd., Alsip IL 60658. (708)385-8535. President: Matthew White. Motion picture production company. Produces home video entertainment programs. Estab. 1987. Uses the services of independent songwriters/composers for scoring of offbeat documentaries; videogame tapes. Commissions 5 composers/year. Pays by the job. Buys all rights.
How to Contact: Submit demo tape of previous work. Prefers cassette. Does not return unsolicited material. Prefers to keep submitted materials on file.
Music: Uses material for home videos.

WINMILL ENTERTAINMENT, 813 N. Cordova St., Burbank CA 91505-2924. (818)954-0065. Director/Music Videos: Chip Miller. Motion picture and music video production company. Clients include record labels, network/cable TV, MTV and motion picture studios. Estab. 1987. Uses the services of music houses, lyricists and independent songwriters/composers for scoring of motion pictures, background music for motion pictures, commercials for TV and music videos for special accounts (i.e. fashion etc.). Commissions 3-12 composers and 1-3 lyricists/year. Pay commensurate with film budget allocation. Rights bought depends on project.
How to Contact: Query with resume of credits. SASE. Report back depends on project deadline and needs.
Music: Music depends upon the project.

EVANS WYATT ADVERTISING, 346 Mediterranean Dr., Corpus Christi TX 78418. (512)854-1661. Owner: E. Wyatt. Advertising agency. Clients are general/all types. Estab. 1975. Uses the services of music houses and independent songwriters/composers for background music for soundtracks, jingles for advertising and commercials for radio and TV. Commissions 8-10 composers/year. Pays by the job. Buys all rights.
How to Contact: Submit demo tape of previous work demonstrating composition skills; query with resume of credits; or write first to arrange personal interview. Prefers cassette. SASE, but prefers to keep material on file. Reports in 2 months.
Music: Uses all types for commercials plus videos mostly.
Tips: "Make it *easy* to judge your work! Be sure you've got the talent you claim and present it clearly. If we don't like your pitch immediately, chances are we won't like your work."

YARDIS CORPORATION, 9138 West Chester Pike, Upper Darby PA 19082. (215)789-2200. Chairman: Ray Rosenberg. Advertising agency. Clients include travel, financial, car dealers, tour operators. Estab. 1946. Uses the services of music houses and independent songwriters/composers for background music for video presentations, jingles for various spots and commercials for radio and TV. Payment depends on circumstances. Rights purchased depends on circumstances.

How to Contact: "Call; go from there." Prefers cassette (or VHS videocassette). Does not return unsolicited material; prefers to keep material on file.
Music: Uses various styles for various assignments.

GREG YOUNGMAN MUSIC, Box 381, Santa Ynez CA 93460. (805)688-1136. Advertising agency/ audio production. Serves all types of clients. Local, regional and national levels. Uses the services of independent composers/copywriters for commercials, jingles and audiovisual projects. Commissions 12-20 composers/year. Pays $500-10,000/project. Buys all rights.
How to Contact: Submit demo tape of previously aired work. Prefers cassette, R-DAT or reel-to-reel. SASE, but prefers to keep tape on file. Reports in 1 month.
Music: Uses all types for radio commercials, film cues.
Tips: "We're looking for something we've never heard before. A sound that's fresh and innovative."

ZM SQUARED, Dept. SM, 903 Edgewood Lane, Box 2030, Cinnaminson NJ 08077. (609)786-0612. Owner: Pete Zakroff. Estab. 1971. Clients include colleges, schools, businesses and audiovisual producers. Uses the services of songwriters "for themes for our no-needledrop music library, background for audiovisual presentations and jingles. We prefer to work with composer/arranger/performer and use primarily background music." Commissions 2-5 composers/year. Pays 10-35% royalty. Buys all rights.
How to Contact: Submit demo tape of previous work. Prefers cassette with 4-6 songs. SASE. Reports in 3 weeks. Free catalog available.
Music: "We require a variety of background music—educational and industrial for general use with audiovisual programs."
Tips: "Know what we want and be able to produce what you write."

*Z-NOTE MUSIC, Box 2162, Ocean NJ 07712. (908)922-7713. Producer: David Zwisohn. Scoring service and **jingle/commercial music production house** and **music library.** Clients include corporate, industrial, education, public service, commercial (local, regional and national). Estab. 1984. Uses the services of independent songwriters/composers and lyricists for background music for continually expanding music library, audio programs, jingles for commercial, trade show themes and logos and commercials for radio and TV. Commissions 5-20 composers and 5-10 lyricists/year. Pays by the job. Buys all rights and one-time rights.
How to Contact: Submit demo tape of previous work or tape demonstrating composition skills. Prefers cassette (or DAT) or 15 IPS reel-to-reel with 3-10 songs and lyric sheet. "MIDI files (with track documentation) are acceptable as well (Macintosh format)." Does not return unsolicited material; prefers to keep on file. Reports in 3-4 weeks.
Music: Uses contemporary jazz, commercial rock, pop, dance, contemporary, classical for jingle tracks and lyrics, industrial and corporate video, music library.
Tips: "Show us a sound that has character, regardless of the style. Music with emotion is more important than a mere show of virtuosity. Be able to provide a fast turnaround if required."

Advertising, AV and Commercial Music Houses/ '92-'93 Changes

The following markets appeared in the 1992 edition of *Songwriter's Market* but are absent from the 1993 edition. Most of these companies failed to respond to our request for an update of their listing for a variety of reasons. For example, they may have gone out of business or they may have requested deletion because they are backlogged with material. If we know the specific reason, it appears within parentheses.

Norman Beerger Productions
    (requested deletion)
Covenant Productions -- Anderson University
Cross Keys Advertising
Effective Learning Systems Inc.
    (not accepting submissions)
Fancy Free Music
Gardiner—A Marketing Company (not accepting submissions)
Glyn-Net, Inc.

International Motion Pictures
    Ltd.
Key Productions Inc.
Kimbo Educational Sound Arts
    Inc. (requested deletion)
National Teleproductions Inc.
Notch/Bradley (requested deletion)
Michael Pollack Productions
Premium Communications of
    America
Pro/Creatives

Rhythms Productions
Schoenback Advertising Inc.
Tamara Scott Productions
Seattle Motion Picture Service
Souvenirs of Hawaii
Spartronix Video Services
Stan & Lou Inc.
Stone & Adler
TPS Video Svc.
Western Publishing Company
    Inc.
Sandy Wilbur Music, Inc.

Play Producers and Publishers

Writing music for the stage is a considerable challenge in the theater of the 1990s. Conventional wisdom says that if a composer or playwright doesn't have a production to his credit, he will have a difficult time establishing himself. Play producers in the major markets, especially Broadway, won't often take a chance on unproven talent when productions routinely cost millions of dollars and a show must run for several years to break even. It's a classic "Catch-22"; the aspiring playwright needs experience to get his work produced, but can't get that experience without production.

Fortunately, the conventional wisdom about musical theater may not be accurate. Many venues for new musical works exist; this section lists them. Contained within are listings of theater companies, producers, dinner theaters, and publishers of musical theater works. We've separated this section into two subsections: one for publishers and one for producers. All these markets are interested in and actively seeking new musical theater works of all types for their stages or publications.

Many of these listings are small theaters run on a nonprofit basis. Their budgets for production and rehearsal time will of necessity be limited. Keep this in mind when preparing to submit your work. When submitting, ask about other opportunities available for your work. Perhaps a theater or company is celebrating an anniversary, either for itself or the city it operates in. Some companies or theaters may like your work, but may wish to present it in revue form. Others may be looking for incidental music for a spoken word play. Do research and ask questions to help increase your chances of consideration.

Use research and further education to help you enrich your personal experience and therefore your work. As a composer for the stage, you need to know as much as possible about the theater and how it works, its history and the different roles played by the people involved in it. Flexibility is a key to successful productions, and having a knowledge of how the theater works will only aid you in cooperating and collaborating with the work's director, producer, technical people and actors.

Working with others

Because the theater is primarily a collaborative enterprise, working with another person in the writing of musicals can only improve the quality of the work. The great names in musical theater come in pairs, even today. Look for the opportunity to collaborate on works for the stage. Organizations like Dramatists Guild may also be a resource in finding collaborators. Check at local colleges or theater groups. Get involved with local theater groups or take classes; it will further add to your experience and knowledge as well as introduce you to possible collaborators.

Read the following listings carefully for information on each market, the type of work being sought, and their submission procedures. Research further the markets that you believe will be interested in your work. And when you've decided on the best markets for your work, follow submission procedures meticulously.

Play Producers

THE ACTING COMPANY, Dept. SM, Box 898, Times Sq. Station, New York NY 10108. (212)564-3510. Play producer. Estab. 1972. Produces 2-3 plays/year. "Have done musicals in the past. We are a national touring company playing universities and booking houses." Pays by royalty or negotiated fee/commission. Submit through agent only. SASE. Reports in 12 weeks.
Musical Theater: "We would consider a wide variety of styles—although we remain a young, classical ensemble. Most of our classical plays make use of a lot of incidental music. Our company consists of 17 actors. All productions must be able to tour easily. We have no resident musicians. Taped sound is essential. Actors tend to remain active touring members for 2-3 seasons. Turnover is considerable. Musical ability of the company tends to vary widely from season to season. We would avoid shows which require sophisticated musical abilities and/or training."

ALLEGHENY HIGHLANDS REGIONAL THEATRE, 526 West Ogle St., Ebensburg PA 15931. (814)472-4333. Artistic Director: Mark Hirschfield. Play producer. Estab. 1974. Produces 5 plays and 2 musicals (1 new musical every third year). "Rural audience, many elderly, many families; we have 2 spaces—a 200 seat arena (4 shows) and a 600 seat proscenium (3 shows)." Pays $50-125/performance. Query with synopsis, character breakdown and set description. SASE. Reports in 3 months.
Musical Theatre: "Small cast, full-length musicals, preferably orchestrated for no more than 6 musicians. Anything set in Pennsylvania about Pennsylvanians is of particular interest. Also interested in musicals for children, either one-act or full-length. Roles for children are a plus. We have difficulty finding men to audition. Few men's roles are a plus. No more than 19-20 including chorus, no more than 2-3 settings. We had original music scored for scene changes and intermission music for *She Stoops To Conquer*. Perhaps some underscoring for a mystery would be fun."
Productions: *Oklahoma!*, by Rodgers & Hammerstein; *Cabaret*, by Kander & Ebb; *George M*, by George M. Cohan; *Robber Bridegroom*, by Robert Waldman; *Anything Goes*, by Cole Porter; *Oliver!*, by Lionel Bart.

AMAS MUSICAL THEATRE INC., 1 E. 104th St., New York NY 10029. (212)369-8000. Producing Director: William Michael Maher. Founder/Artistic Director: Rosetta Lenoire. Produces 2 or 3 original musicals/year. Presents 2 children's theater productions and one summer tour. "AMAS is a multiracial theater, dedicated to bring all people—regardless of race, creed, color or religion—together through the performing arts." Does not pay for manuscripts but "provides a top quality New York showcase with a good record of commercial pick-ups." Submit script with cassette tape of score (or partial score) with SASE.
Musical Theater: Musicals only. "All works to be performed by multi-racial casts. Musical biographies especially welcome. Cast size should be under 13 if possible, including doubling. Because of physical space, set requirements should be relatively simple. We do not want to see material with explicit sex or violence or very strong language. Prefer themes of love, joy and togetherness."
Productions: *Bubbling Brown Sugar; Bingo*, by Hy Gilbert, George Fischoff and Ossie Davis (Negro baseball leagues); *Dazy*, by Phillip Rose; *Hot Sake; Prime Time*, by Johnny Brandon; and *Step Into My World*, by Miki Grant.
Tips: "A good melody line is important, ideally one that children and adults can hum and sing. Lyrics should tell a story; avoid repetition."

AMELIA MAGAZINE, 329 "E" St., Bakersfield CA 93304. (805)323-4064. Editor: Frederick A. Raborg, Jr. Play publisher. Estab. 1983. Publish 1 play/year. General audience; one-act plays published in *Amelia Magazine*. Best play submitted is the winner of the annual Frank McClure One-Act Play Award. Submit complete manuscript and score per contest rules by postmark deadline of May 15. SASE. Reports in 6-8 weeks. "We would consider publishing musical scores if submitted in clean, camera-ready copy—also single songs. Payment same as for poetry—$25 plus copies."

AMERICAN STAGE FESTIVAL, Dept. SM, Box 225, Milford NH 03055. (603)673-4005. Associate Producing Director: Richard Rose. Regional theater. Estab. 1974. Produces 15 plays and 2 musicals (1 new musical)/year. Receives 50 submissions/year. 500 seat theater, Broadway-sized stage, summertime audience. Pays 4-7% royalty.
How to Contact: Submit query letter with synopsis. Reports immediately.
Musical Theater: "We are interested in musicals that tell a story, in which songs make a dramatic contribution. Particularly interested in a return to popular song formats, used dramatically, not nostalgically." Cast and musicians should not total more than 15. Musicals should use traditional song forms.

Productions: *Peg O' My Heart*, by David Heneker (musical comedy); *The Last of the Souhegans*, by Andrew Howard (musical comedy); and *Feathertop*, by Skip Kennon (musical comedy).

ARIZONA THEATRE COMPANY, P.O. Box 1631, Tucson AZ 85702. (602)884-8210. Artistic Director: David Goldstein. Professional regional theater company. Members are professionsls. Performs 6 productions/year, including 1 new work. Audience is middle and upper-middle class, well-educated, aged 35-64. "We are a two-city operation based in Tucson, where we perform in a 603-seat newly renovated, historic building, which also has a 100-seat flexible seating cabaret space. Our facility in Phoenix, the Herberger Theater Center, is a 712-seat, proscenium stage." Pays 4-10% royalty. Query first. Reports in 5 months.
Music: Musicals or musical theater pieces. 15-16 performers maximum including chorus. Instrumental scores should not involve full orchestra. No classical or operatic.
Performances: Barbara Damashek's *Quilters* (musical theater piece); Sondheim/Bernstein's *Candide* (musical); and Anita Ruth/American composer's *Dreamers of the Day* (musical theater piece).
Tips: "As a regional theater, we cannot afford to produce extravagant works. Plot line and suitability of music to further the plot is an essential consideration."

ARKANSAS REPERTORY THEATRE, 601 Main, P.O. Box 110, Little Rock AR 72203. (501)378-0445. Contact: Brad Mooy. Play producer. Estab. 1976. Produces 9 plays and 2 musicals (1 new musical)/ year. Receives 10 submissions/month. "We perform in a 354-seat house and also have a 99 seat blackbox." Pays 5-10% royalty or $75-150 per performance.
How to Contact: Query with cover letter, 10-page synopsis and cassette. SASE. Reports in 6 months.
Musical Theater: "Small casts are preferred, comedy or drama and prefer shows to run 1:45 to 2 hours maximum. Simple is better; small is better, but we do produce complex shows. We aren't interested in children's pieces, puppet shows or mime. We always like to receive a tape of the music with the book."
Productions: *Into the Woods*, Sondheim/Lapine (Grimm's Fairy Tales Compilation); *Oil City Symphony*, by Hardwick Craver, Monk, Murfitt (American Small Town Spoof); *Nunsense*, by Dan Goggin (Catholicism Revue, nuns tap dancing).
Tips: "Include a *good* cassette of your music, *sung well*, with the script."

ARKANSAS STATE UNIVERSITY-BEEBE CAMPUS, P.O. Box H, Beebe AR 72012. (501)882-6452. Director of Theater: L.R. Chudomelka. Play producer. Produces 5 plays (1 musical)/year. Receives 5 submissions/year. Plays are performed in a "600 seat theater (proscenium) in a city of 4,000, 30 miles from metropolitan area of more than 200,000." Pays by royalty. Submit complete manuscript and score. SASE. Reports in 2 weeks.
Musical Theater: "Material should be within the ability of traditional community college with traditional and non-traditional students: simple dancing, innovative and traditional, not over-sophisticated (somewhat family oriented). Variety of music styles and balanced major role shows—no 'star' shows. Flexible cast size, props, staging, etc. We do not want unnecessary profanity or 'operatic' material."
Productions: *Two By Two*, Rodgers/Charmino/Stone (Noah and the Rain); *High Button Shoes*, by Styne/Cahn/Longstreet (nostalgia).
Tips: "Music should be singable and vary in style. Songs should be an intricate part of the show and not just put in for spectacle. Major roles should be balanced between 4 or 5 characters, rather than one-character shows with chorus."

*ARROW ROCK LYCEUM THEATRE, Main St., Arrow Rock MO 65320. (816)837-3311. Artistic Director: Michael Bollinger. Play producer. Produces 7 plays and 3-4 musicals/year. "Lyceum is a not-for-profit regional theatre, and performs in its own theater space seating 208." Pays negotiable flat fee to each individual author/composer. Query with synopsis, character breakdown and set description (rather than entire script). SASE. Reports in 5 months.
Musical Theater: "We produce a varied and diverse season each year. Each season consists of 3-4 diverse musicals, 1 classic, 1 American drama, 1 comedy or mystery, and 1 wild card. All topics and styles are considered, as long as they are quality material. The theatre is not large, has little fly space, and generally operates in repertory with several other plays. Fifteen or fewer characters is best."
Productions: *Smoke on the Mountain*, *Gypsy*, *Guys and Dolls*, *The Diary of Anne Frank*, *Working*, *From Dust Thou Art* and *The Doctor in Spite of Himself*.

The asterisk before a listing indicates that the listing is new in this edition. New markets are often the most receptive to unsolicited submissions.

*ASHLAWN-HIGHLAND SUMMER FESTIVAL, Route 2 Box 37, Charlottesville VA 22902. (804)296-1188. General Manager: Judith H. Walker. Play producer. Estab. 1977. Produces 1 musical and 2 operas/year. "Our operas and musicals are performed in a casual setting. The audience is composed of people from the Charlottesville area."
How to Contact: Query first. SASE. "We try to return items after review but depending on the time of year response time may vary."
Musical Theater: "We are very open to new ideas and young artists.Included in our season is a summer Saturday program designed for children. We enjoy puppet shows, story tellers and children-related plays. We are a small company with a limited budget. Our cast is usually 12 performers and a volunteer local chorus. Minimal scenery is done. Our audience is composed of families with children and retired adults. Material should suit their tastes." Would consider original music for use in a play being developed.
Performances: W.A. Mozart's *The Marriage of Figaro*; Johann Strauss' *Die Fledermaus*; and Rodgers and Hammerstein's *Oklahoma*.

ASOLO CENTER FOR THE PERFORMING ARTS, (formerly Asolo Theatre Company), Dept. SM, 5555 N. Tamiami Trail, Sarasota FL 34243. (813)351-9010. Contact: Literary Manager. Play producer. Produces 7-8 plays (1 musical)/year. Plays are performed at the Asolo Mainstage (500-seat proscenium house) or by the Asolo Touring Theater (6-member company touring the Southeast). Pays 5% minimum royalty. "We no longer accept unsolicited manuscripts or tapes. Inquiries should be made in the form of a letter, a one-page synopsis, and a self-addressed, stamped postcard." SASE.
Musical Theater: "We want small non-chorus musicals only. They should be full-length, any subject, with not over 10 in the cast. There are no restrictions on production demands; however, musicals with excessive scenic requirements may be difficult to consider."
Productions: *Smoke on the Mountain, Gypsy, Guys and Dolls, The Diary of Anne Frank, Working, From Dust Thou Art* and *The Doctor in Spite of Himself.*

BAILIWICK REPERTORY, Dept. SM, 1225 West Bellmont, Chicago IL 60657. (312)883-1091. Executive Director: David Zak. Play producer. Estab. 1982. Produces 5 mainstage, 5 one-act plays and 1-2 new musicals/year. "We do Chicago productions of new works on adaptations that are politically or thematically intriguing and relevent. We also do an annual director's festival which produces 50-75 new short works each year." Pays 5-8% royalty. "Send SASE (business size) first to receive manuscript submission guidelines. Material returned if appropriate SASE attached."
Musical Theater: "We want innovative, dangerous, exciting and issue-oriented material."
Productions: *Wild Honey*, by Chekha/Frayn; *Animal Farm* (musical), by Orwell/Hall/Peaslee/Mitchell; *Nebraska*, by Logan; *Blues in the Night* (musical); and *Songs of the Season* (musical).
Tips: "Be creative. Be patient. Be persistant. Make me believe in your dream."

BERKSHIRE PUBLIC THEATRE, P.O. Box 860, 30 Union St., Pittsfield MA 01202. (413)445-4631. Artistic Director: Frank Bessell. Play producer. Estab. 1976. Produces 9 plays (2 musicals)/year. "Plays are performed in a 285-seat proscenium thrust theatre for a general audience of all ages with wide-ranging tastes." Pays negotiable royalty or negotiable amount per performance. Unsolicited submissions OK. SASE. Reports in 3 months.
Musical Theater: Seeking musicals with "no more than 3 acts (2½ hours). We look for fresh musicals with something to say. Our company has a flexible vocal range. Cast size must be 2-50, with a small orchestra." Would also consider original music "for a play being developed and possibly for existing works."
Productions: *Jesus Christ Superstar*, by Rice/Lloyd-Webber (gospel/life of Christ); *Rhapsody*, by George Gershwin (revue of Gershwin music); *Company*, by Sondheim/Furth (modern relationships).
Tips: "We are a small company. Patience is a must. Be yourself – open, honest. Experience is not necessary but is helpful. We don't have a lot of money but we are long on nurturing artists! We are developing shows with commercial prospects to go beyond the Berkshires, i.e., a series of rock music revues is now in its fifth year."

BRISTOL RIVERSIDE THEATRE, Dept. SM, Box 1250, Bristol PA 19007. (215)785-6664. Artistic Director: Susan D. Atkinson. Play producer. Estab. 1986. Produce 5 plays, 2 musicals/year (1 new musical every 2 years). "New 302-seat proscenium Equity theater with audience of all ages from small towns and metropolitan area." Pays by royalty 6-8%. Submit complete manuscript, score and tape of songs. SASE. Reports in 6 months.
Musical Theatre: "No strictly children's musicals. All other types with small to medium casts and within reasonable artictic tastes. Prefer one-set; limited funds rectrict. Does not wish to see anything catering to prurient interests."

Productions: *The Robber Bridegroom*, by Alfred Uhry/R. Waldman (E. Welty novella - 1790s Mississippi delta); *A Day in Hollywood/A Night*, by Frank Lazarus/D. Vosburgh (1930s Hollywood); and *Sally Blane, World's Greatest Girl Detective*, by David Levy/Leslie Eberhard (spoof of teen detective genre).
Tips: "He or she should be willing to work with small staff, open to artistic suggestion, and aware of the limitations of newly developing theaters."

CALIFORNIA MUSIC THEATRE, #400M, 2500 E. Colorado, Pasadena CA 91107. (818)792-0776. Artistic Director: Gary Davis. Play producer. Estab. 1986. Produces 4 musicals (1 new musical)/year. "Plays produced at Raymond Theatre, Pasadena. Proscenium-1,900 seats. Base of 13,000 subscribers/average of 25,000 per production." Pays by royalty. Submit complete manuscript, score and tape of songs. SASE. Reports in 3 months.
Musical Theater: "Our audience is rather conservative."
Productions: *Babes in Toyland*, by Toby Bluth (new adaptation); *Strike Up the Band*, by Gershwin/Kaufman; and *Drood*, by Rupert Holmes.
Tips: "Please understand that we place great importance on lyrics. If it doesn't read well, we do not pursue the piece beyond the initial reading."

*CENTER THEATER, 1346 W. Devon, Chicago IL 60660. (312)508-0200. Contact: Literary Manager. Play producer. Estab. 1984. Produces 6 plays and 1 musical (1 new musical)/year. "Our 80 seat modified thrust theater has produced 3 original musicals, based on novels or plays." Pays 3-10% royalty.
How to Contact: Agent submission only. Reports in 3 months.
Musical Theater: 8 person maximum.
Productions: *The Black Tulip*, by Tracy Friedman/Brian Lasser (adaptation of Dumas novel); *Two Many Bosses*, by Dan La Morte/Donald Coates (musical adaptation of "Servant of Two Masters"); *Lysistrata 2411 A.D.*, by Dale Calandra/Donald Coates (futuristic musical adaptation).

CIRCA' 21 DINNER PLAYHOUSE, Dept. SM, Box 3784, Rock Island IL 61204-3784. (309)786-2667. Producer: Dennis Hitchcock. Play producer. Estab. 1977. Produces 1-2 plays, 4-5 musicals (1 new musical)/year. Receives 2 submissions/month. Plays produced for a general audience. Two children's works per year, concurrent with major productions. Pays by royalty. Query with synopsis, character breakdown and set description or submit complete manuscript, score and tape of songs. SASE. Reports in 8 weeks.
Musical Theater: "For children's musicals we prefer 2-act, 1½ hour limit with cast of no more than 10, piano and percussion accompaniment, and limited scenic requirements. Folk or fairy tale themes. Works that do not condescend to a young audience yet are appropriate for entire family. We're also seeking full-length, small cast musicals suitable for a broad audience." Would also consider original music for use in a play being developed.
Productions: *Singin in the Rain*, by Betty Comden and Adolph Green; *7 Brides for 7 Brothers*, by Lawrence Kasha and David Landay; *Pump Boys and Dinettes* and *Snow White Goes West*, by Jim Filer.
Tips: "Small, upbeat, tourable musicals (like *Pump Boys*) and bright musically-sharp children's productions (like those produced by Prince Street Players) work best. Keep an open mind. Stretch to encompass a musical variety—different keys, rhythms, musical ideas and textures."

CIRCLE IN THE SQUARE THEATRE, Dept. SM, 1633 Broadway, New York NY 10019. (212)307-2700. Literary Advisor: Nancy Bosco. Play producer. Estab. 1951. Produces 3 plays/year; occasionally produces a musical. Pays by royalty. Query with a letter, 1-page synopsis and script sample (10 pages). Reports in 6 months.
Musical Theater: "We are looking for original material with small cast and orchestra requirements. We're not interested in traditional musical comedies." Will consider original music for use in a play being developed or in a pre-existing play at the option of the director.
Production: *Pal Joey*.

CITIARTS THEATRE, 1950 Parkside Dr., Concord CA 94519. (510)671-3065. Artistic Director: Richard H. Elliott. Play producer. Estab. 1973. Produces 8 plays and 4 musicals (0-4 new musicals)/year. "CitiArts/Theatre Concord is the resident theater in the 203-seat Willows Theatre, a proscenium stage, in Concord, located in suburban San Francisco." Pays 5-12% royalty, or terms negotiated.
How to Contact: Submit complete manuscript and score. SASE. Reports in 3 months.
Musical Theater: "Full-length musicals addressing contemporary themes or issues, small to mid-size cast (maximum 15 characters) with maximum 15 instruments. Topics which appeal to an educated suburban and liberal urban audience are best. Maximum 15 cast members, 15 musicians, prefer unit set (we have no fly loft or wing space)." "We often commission original scores for straight plays. Composer should send resume and recorded example of work with scores if possible."

Productions: *Smoke On The Mountain*, by Ray/Bailey (white southern gospel); *Nunsense*, by Goggin (religious satire); *Grease*, by Jacobs/Casey (50s rock).
Tips: "Be prepared and believe in your material."

CITY THEATRE COMPANY, INC., 315 S. Bellefield Ave., Pittsburgh PA 15203. (412)431-4400. Resident Dramaturg: Scott Cummings. Play producer. Estab. 1974. Produces 5 plays/year. "Plays are performed in an intimate 117 seat Thrust-Stage Theatre to an adventurous subscriber base." Query with synopsis, character breakdown and set description. Does not return unsolicited material. Reports in 2-3 weeks for query; 3-4 months for script.
Musical Theater: "We want sophisticated plays with music. We prefer a small cast with no more than 10 (including musicians) and single set because we have thrust stage capabilities only. We don't want traditional, large cast musical comedies."
Productions: *Painting It Red*, by Steven Dietz (modern romance); *Lovers and Keeper*, by Irene Fornes (failed romance); and *Maybe I'm Doing It Wrong*, by Randy Newman (musical review).

THE CLEVELAND PLAY HOUSE, P.O. Box 1989, Cleveland OH 44106. (216)795-7010. Literary Manager: Roger T. Danforth. Professional theater. Estab. 1915. Pays by royalty. Agent submission only. Reports in 4 months.
Music: Seeks only musical theater.
Tips: "Find agent to submit."

CLEVELAND PUBLIC THEATRE, 6415 Detroit Ave., Cleveland OH 44102. (216)631-2727. Director of Playwright Development: Linda Eisenstein. Play producer. Estab. 1983. Produces 6 plays plus 12 staged readings; much performance art, 1-2 musicals and 1 new musical/year. "We are a progressive urban loft theater (80-150 seats) with audiences that are adult and sophisticated—mix of yuppies, artists, radicals and punks." Submit complete manuscript, score and tape of songs. Pays $25-50/performance. Unsolicited submissions OK. SASE. Reports in 3-6 months.
Musical Theater: "We seek progressive, political, alternative and outrageous musicals. Also music for our performance art and sound festivals—cutting edge experimental. Don't expect a realistic set—we do mostly 3-quarter and arena, with no fly space. We don't want to see fluff or traditional Broadway fare, would-be Broadway fare or traditional children's plays." "A writer must think weird; don't watch TV. We use several local composers (Cleveland) to write our 'incidental' music."
Production: *Kitchen Table U*, by Yvetta, Andika, Kenyette Adrine-Robinson (choreopoem by black women poets); *Street Sense*, by Migdalia Cruz and Linda Eisenstein (contemporary opera with Latino themes); *Night Night Max*, by Michael Salinger and the Nova Lizard Project (performance art musical about a baby's experience).
Tips: "We work primarily with local artists—showcase your work in one of our Vaudevilles or Festivals of short works."

*COCKPIT IN COURT SUMMER THEATRE, 7201 Rossville Blvd., Baltimore MD 21237. (410)522-1434. Managing Director: F. Scott Black. Play producer. Estab. 1973. Produces 6-8 plays and 5-7 musicals/year. "Audiences range from mature to senior citizens. Plays are produced at 3 locations: Mainstage (proscenium theater), Courtyard (outdoor theater) and Cabaret (theater-in-the-round)."
How to Contact: Query first. SASE. Reports in 2 months.
Musical Theater: "Seeking musical comedy and children's shows. We have the capacity to produce large musicals with up to 76 cast members."
Productions: *Annie Get Your Gun*, by Irving Berlin; *They're Playing Our Song*, by Neil Simon; and *Brigadoon*, by Lerner and Loewe.
Tips: "We look for material that is perhaps different but still appeals to a community theater audience."

THE COTERIE, 2450 Grand Ave., Kansas City MO 64108. (816)474-6785. Artistic Director: Jeff Church. Play producer. Estab. 1979. Produces 7-8 plays/year. Plays produced at Hallmark's Crown Center in downtown Kansas City in The Coterie's resident theater (capacity 240). A typical performance run is one month in length. "We retain some rights on commissioned plays. Writers are paid a royalty for their work per performance or flat fee."
How to Contact: Query with synopsis and character breakdown. Submit complete manuscript and score "if established writer in theater for young audiences. We will consider musicals with smaller orchestration needs (3-5 pieces), or a taped score. SASE. Reports in 2-4 months.
Musical Theater: "Types of plays we produce: pieces which are universal in appeal; plays for all ages. They may be original or adaptations of classic or contemporary literature. Limitations: Typically not more than 12 in a cast—prefer 5-9 in size. No fly space or wing space. Material we want/do not want to see: No couch plays. Prefer plays by seasoned writers who have established reputations.

Groundbreaking, and exciting scripts from the youth theater field welcome. It's perfectly fine if your musical is a little off center."

Productions: *Animal Farm*, by Sir Peter Hall; *The Wind in the Willows*, (adapted), by Doug Post; and *The Ugly Duckling*, by Pamela Sterling, music by Chris Limber.

Tips: "Make certain your submitted musical to us is very theatrical and not cinematic. Writers need to see how far the field of youth and family theater has come—the interesting new areas we're going—before sending us your query or manuscript. We LIKE young protagonists in our plays, but make sure they're not romanticized or stereotyped good-and-bad like the children's theater playwrights of yesterday would have them."

*CREATIVE PRODUCTIONS, INC., 2 Beaver Pl., Aberdeen NJ 07747. (201)566-6985. Director: Walter L. Born. Play producer. Estab. 1970. Produces 3 musicals (1-2 new musicals)/year. "Our audience is the general community with emphasis on elderly and folks with disabilities. We use local public school theater facilities." Pays by royalty or per performance, as required by broadway rental houses. Query with synopsis, character breakdown and set description. SASE. Reports in 1 month.

Musical Theater: "We want family type material (i.e. *Brigadoon*, *Charlie Brown*) with light rock to classical music and a maximum running time of two hours. The subject matter should deal with older folks or folks with disabilities. We have no flying capability in facility; cast size is a maximum 10-12; the sets are mostly on small wagons, props aren't anything exotic; the orchestra is chamber size with standard instruments. We don't want pornographic material or children's shows. We want nothing trite and condescending in either the material or the treatment. We like the unusual treatment well-structured and thought out, with minimal sets and changes. We can't handle unusual vocal requirements. We prefer an integrated piece with music a structural part from the beginning."

Productions: *Gifts of Magi*, by O. Henry (unselfish love); *Wind in Willows*, by Jane Iredale.

Tips: "We are actively seeking a playwright and composer to write a musical for us."

CREATIVE THEATRE, 102 Witherspoon St., Princeton NJ 08540. (609)924-3489. Artistic Director: Eloise Bruce. Play producer. Estab. 1969. Produces 5 plays, all with music (1 new musical)/year. "Plays are performed for young audiences grades K-6. The plays are always audience participation and done in schools (45 minute format)." Pays a fee for writing and production and royalty for two seasons. Then per performance royalty fee. Query with synopsis, character breakdown and set description. SASE. Reports in 1 month.

Musical Theater: "Audience participation plays, 45 minutes in length, 4-6 performers, usually presentational style. Topics can range from original plots to adaptations of folk and fairytales. Staging is usually in the round with audience of no more than 300/seating on the floor. No lighting and usually piano accompaniment. Actor is focus with strong but very lean set and costume design." Does not wish to see plays without audience participation. "We are not doing as many "heavy musicals," but are looking for light plays with less music."

Productions: *The Bremen Town Musicians*, by Joan Prall (origianl fairy tale); *Where Snow Falls Up*, by Mark Schaeffer (original holiday show); and *The Island of Yaki Yim Bamboo*, by Fred Rohan Vargas.

Tips: "Develop child centered work which encourages the imaginations of the audience and is centered in child play."

CREEDE REPERTORY THEATRE, P.O. Box 269, Creede CO 81130. (719)658-2541. Producing/Artistic Director: Richard Baxter. Play producer. Estab. 1966. Produces 6 plays and 1 musical/year. Performs in 187-seat proscenium theatre; audience is primarily tourist base from Texas, Oklahoma, New Mexico and Colorado. Pays 7% royalty. Query first. SASE. Reports in 1 year.

Musical Theater: "We prefer historical western material with cast no larger than 11. Staging must be flexible as space is limited."

Productions: *Baby Doe Tabor*, by Kenton Kersting (Colorado history); *A Frog in His Throat*, by Feydeau, adapted by Eric Conger, (French farce); and *Tommyknockers*, by Eric Engdahl, Mark Houston and Chris Thompson (mining).

Tips: "Songwriter must have the ability to accept criticism and must be flexible."

DEPARTMENT OF THEATRE, MICHIGAN STATE UNIVERSITY, Dept. SM, East Lansing MI 48824-1120. (517)353-5169. Producer/Director: Dr. Jon Baisch. Produces 7-10 plays and 4-6 musicals (1-2 new musicals), 4-6 large scale and small revue musicals/year. Payment negotiable. "Our audiences are students, faculty, and members of the Lansing community. We use 8 theatres, ranging from 100 to 2,500 seats, including proscenium, platform, arena, and cabaret theatre types. We stage everything from large-scale productions with orchestra and large casts to small-cast, intimate shows and cabaret entertainment. We seek both adult and children's shows, all types for a variety of audiences. We often use original music composed by faculty or students in MSU's School of Music. They are available to us for the whole term of rehearsal and production." Performance rights negotiable. Query with synopsis and production specifications. SASE. Reports in 1 month.

Musical Theater: "We are interested in all types of new musicals. However, we are espcially interested in small cast revues and book shows for cabaret and summer theatre productions, and unusual material for our small arena and studio theatres."

Productions: *A Chorus Line* and *Brigadoon*.

*THE DEPOT THEATRE, Box 414, Westport NY 12993. (518)962-4449. Associate Director: Keith Levenson. Play producer. Estab. 1979. Produces 3-5 plays/year; produces 2-3 musicals (1 new musical)/year. "Plays are performed in a renovated 19th century train depot with 136 seats and proscenium stage. Audience is regional/tourist from north of Albany to Montreal." Pays by commission.

How to Contact: Submit manuscript and score through agent. SASE. Reports in 6 weeks.

Musical Theater: "We have no restrictions on the type of musical, though we prefer full-length. We are currently interested in cast sizes that do not exceed 13 people—preferably smaller! Our theater has no fly or wing space to speak of and designs tend to be limited to unit or 'conceptual' sets. Our 'orchestra' is limited to acoustic piano and synthesizers. We do not wish to see previously produced scripts unless there has been radical changes to the material or previous presentation was in workshop form. The purpose of the Depot Theatre's New American Musicals Project is to nurture the development of new musicals by emerging songwriters/composers. Our intent is to give the musical a full production so that the writers can see what they have and so the piece can have a life beyond our stage. We look for a collaborative spirit and writer willing to listen to directors, work with them toward a common goal of the best production possible and be able to maintain a sense of humor and an understanding of our limited resources." Would consider original music for use in a play being developed.

Performances: *Winchell*, by Martin Charnin and Keith Levenson (Walter Winchell); *Willpower*, by Danny Troob and Jamie Donnelly (reverse Pygmalion theme, contemporary); and *Galileo*, by Jeanine Levenson, Alexa Junge and Keith Levenson.

Tips: "We enjoy working with people who view the process as a collaborative adventure, can be flexible, accept constructive criticism and keep smiling."

*STEVE DOBBINS PRODUCTIONS, 650 Geary St., San Francisco CA 94102. Executive Director: Mike Lojkoviz. Play producer. Estab. 1978. Produces 4 plays and 1 new musical/year. Plays performed for San Francisco Bay Area audiences. Pays 5% royalty. Query with synopsis, character breakdown, set description and tape of songs. SASE. Reports in 6 months.

Musical Theater: "We seek all types of material as long as the ideas are new. No formula scripts." Would consider original music for use in a play being developed.

Productions: *Dylan Thomas*, by Kevin Reilly (life of the poet); *Doo Wop*, (Black musical); *Dan White Incident*, by Steve Dobbins (actual recreational of the Dan White case); and *With Relish*, by Morris Bobrow (food).

Tips: "Write to us explaining your idea."

EAST WEST PLAYERS (EWP), Dept. SM, 4424 Santa Monica Blvd., Los Angeles CA 90029. (213)660-0366. Artistic Director: Nobu McCarthy; Dramaturg: Brian Nelsen. Professional Equity company, established 1965, performing under the Equity 99-seat theater plan for all audiences. Presents one (1) mainstage musical per season, 4-6 productions a year. Receives 4-6 submissions/year. Also has play reading series and writer's laboratory for selected projects, including musicals. Submit complete ms (book & lyrics) and tape of songs. If enough interest generated will ask to see complete score. No ms or tape returned without SASE. Submit to ATTN: Dramaturg. Reports in 6 months. Dramatists Guild approved contract offered, percentage of box office gross against set per performance fee.

Musical Theater: "We are interested in musicals dealing with Asian-American themes and experiences and focus, Asian stories and musicals using non-traditional casting; musicals that are melodious, highly theatrical and imaginative theater pieces. Our acting company is 98% Asian-Pacific/Asian-American, so the majority of important roles should by playable by Asian actors. A cast of 15 to 18 is the largest we can handle readily, and we would prefer smaller casts. We are also establishing a youth theater program, and would be interested in well-written, small cast musicals for that as well. Nothing 'cute,' however. We have used original musical scores for plays originated here or for production revivals of established plays, and we are always open to doing so. All of our productions have music and/or sound effects involved. The demands of the production dictate the uses of music and sound."

Productions: *Company*, by Sondheim/Furth (contemporary relationships); *A Chorus Line*, by Kirkwood/Dante/Hamlisch/Kelban (contemporary show business); *Canton Jazz Club*, by Magwili/Dang/Wang/Iwataki (original musical, Chinatown nightspot, 1943 Los Angeles).

Tips: "East West Players was founded by a group of Asian-American actors weary of playing stereotypes in theater and film. Writers should bear this in mind. It would help if the writers would find out the types of productions we do before they submit."

EL TEATRO CAMPESINO, P.O. Box 1240, San Juan Bautista CA 95045. (408)623-2444. Music Director: David Silva. Theater company. Members are professionals and amateurs. Performs 2 concerts/year including 2 new works. Commissions 0-1 composer or new work/year. "Our audiences are varied — non-traditional and multi-cultural. We perform in our own theater as well as area theaters and other performing arts spaces (indoor and outdoor)." Pays $50-750 for outright purchase. Query first. SASE. Reports in 1 month.
Music: "We are interested in cultural and multi-cultural music in all styles and lengths. We are especially interested in blends of cultural/contemporary and indigenous music."
Performances: *La Vizgen Del Tepeyac* (cultural); *The Rose of the Rancho* (Old California); and *Zoot-Suit* (1940s).

THE EMPTY SPACE THEATRE, P.O. Box 1748, Seattle WA 98111-1748. (206)587-3737. Artistic Director: Kurt Beattie. Play producer. Estab. 1974. Produces 5 plays and varying number of new musicals/year. "We have a subscription audience, mainly composed of professionals. We produce in our own theatre." Pays by royalty. Query with synopsis, character breakdown and set description. SASE. Reports in 4 months.
Musical Theater: "We want broadly comic, satirical or political pieces and all musical idioms, from classical to whatever is the current end of the musical spectrum. We have no limitations, though we rarely produce more than one large cast show per year. We don't want old-fashioned show biz yawners, or yuppie angst. We regularly employ composers/sound designers."
Productions: *Smokey Joe's Cafe*, by Burke Walker (song revue).
Tips: "Avoid musical-comedy formulae."

ENSEMBLE THEATRE OF CINCINNATI, Dept. SM, 1127 Vine St., Cincinnati OH 45210. (513)421-3556. Artistic Director: David A. White III. Play producer. Estab. 1986. Produces 6 plays (3 new musicals in 5 years)/year. "We are dedicated to the development of new works. We produce a 6 show season in a beautifully renovated 130-seat 3/4 thrust theater." Pays $600-1,000 outright purchase.
How to Contact: Submit complete manuscript, score and tape of songs. SASE. Reports in 2 months.
Musical Theater: Adult-oriented, risk-taking, simple set, cast of 6-10, with a simple orchestration. Material should be submitted in September or October for consideration for upcoming season.
Productions: *Taming of the Shrew*, by William Shakespeare; *Sleeping Beauty*, and *There's a Ringing in My Ears*, by Kate Dahlgren, Norma Jenks, Mah Wehner and Joe M. McDonough.

THE FIREHOUSE THEATRE, 11 and Jackson, Omaha NE 68102. (402)346-6009. Dinner theater. Estab. 1972. Producer 6 plays and 1-2 musicals/year. Receives 10-20 submissions/year. General audience. Pays royalty. Query with synopsis, character breakdown and set description. Submit complete ms, score and tape of songs. SASE.
Musical Theater: General interest. "We are a small house of 289 seats. Budget is what limits the scale of production."
Productions: *Best Little Whorehouse In Texas*, by Larry King and *Pump Boys & Dinnettes* by Jim Wann.

*FOOLS COMPANY, INC., 358 W. 44th St., New York NY 10036. (212)307-6000. Artistic Director: Martin Russell. Play producer. Estab. 1970. Produces 4-6 plays/year; produces 1-2 musicals (1-2 new musicals)/year. "Audience is comprised of general public and teens, ages 16-20. Plays are performed at the John Houseman Theater Studio."
How to Contact: Submit complete manuscript, score and tape of songs. SASE. Reports in 2 weeks.
Musical Theater: "We seek new and unusual, contemporary and experimental material. We would like small, easy-to tour productions. Nothing classical, or previously produced." Would also consider original music for use in a play being developed.
Productions: *She Closed Her Eyes to the Sun*, by Jill Russell and Lewis Flinn (fantasies and realities of relationships).
Tips: "Be open to suggestions; be able to work within a group."

THE WILL GEER THEATRICUM BOTANICUM, P.O. Box 1222, Topanga CA 90290. (213)455-2322. Artistic Director: Ellen Geer. Play producer. Produces 4 plays, 1-2 new musicals/year. Plays are performed in "large outdoor amphitheater with 60'x 25' wooden stage. Rustic setting." Pays by royalty or per performance. Query with synopsis, tape, character breakdown and set description. SASE. Submit scripts from September through December.
Musical Theater: Seeking social or biographical works, children's works, full length musicals with cast of up to 10 equity actors (the rest non-equity). Requires "low budget set and costumes. We emphasize paying performers." Would also consider original music for use in a play being developed. Does not wish to see "anything promoting avarice, greed, violence or apathy."
Productions: *Worker's U.S.A.*, a compilation work (labor unions).
Tips: "Reach us with idea and show enthusiasm for theater."

GEORGE STREET PLAYHOUSE, 9 Livingston Ave., New Brunswick NJ 08901. (908)846-2895. Associate Artistic Director: Wendy Liscow. Producing Director: Gregory Hurst. Produces 7 plays, including 1 musical and 1-2 new musicals/year. Receives 10 musical submissions/month. "We are a 367-seat thrust theater and 100-seat black box, working under a LORT C-contract with a 5,500 subscriber base." Fees vary. "Each situation is handled individually." "Professional recommendation only." SASE. Reports in 2 months.
Musical Theater: Seeking musical adaptations. "We are interested in a variety of themes and formats. We aren't seeking to limit the things we read."
Productions: *Johnny Pye and the Fool Killer,* by Mark St. Germain and Randy Curtis (Americana); *Jekyll and Hyde,* by Lee Thuna, Herman Sachs and Mel Mandel; and *Tales of Tinseltown,* by Michael Colby and Paul Katz (30s Hollywood musical).

GREAT AMERICAN CHILDREN'S THEATRE COMPANY, Dept. SM, 304 E. Florida, Milwaukee WI 53204. (414)276-4230. Managing Director: Annie Jurczyk. Producer: Teri Mitze. Play producer. Estab. 1976. Produces 1 or 2 plays/musical/year. Has done new musicals in the past. Audience is school age children. Pays a negotiable royalty. Query with synopsis, character breakdown and set description. Does not return unsolicited material. Reports as quickly as possible, "depending on our workload."
Musical Theater: Children's musicals. Average cast size is 13. No adult productions. "We have used original music as background for our plays."
Productions: *Charlie & the Chocolate Factory,* by Roald Dahl (children's story); *Charlotte's Web,* by Joseph Robinette (children's story); and *Cinderella,* by Moses Goldberg (children's story).
Tips: "Persevere! Although we don't use a lot of musicals, we will consider one that is of excellent quality."

HERITAGE ARTISTS AT THE MUSIC HALL, Dept. SM, Box 586, Cohoes NY 12047. (518)235-7909. Executive Director: Joseph McConnell. Artistic Director: David Holdgrivey. Musical and play producer. Estab. 1982. Produces 6 musicals (1-3 new musicals)/year. "We perform a subscription series of small and/or principal musicals in the 250-300 seat Cohoes Music Hall." Pays negotiable royalty per performance. Submit synopsis, character breakdown and tape. SASE. Reports in 8 weeks.
Musical Theater: Seeking "adult themes, plays with music, review/cabaret shows and children's musicals." Requires "smaller casts." "Regular season runs from mid-October to June. This is a *professional* company (Equity, SSDC, AFM)."
Productions: *Romance, Romance,* by Harman and Herrmann; *Jacques Brel,* by Blau and Shuman; *No Way to Treat a Lady,* by Douglas J. Cohen; and *Beehive,* by Larry Gallagher.

HIP POCKET THEATRE, 1627 Fairmount Ave., Ft. Worth TX 76104-4237. (817)927-2833. Producer: Diane Simons. Play producer. Produces 10 plays/year (including new musicals). Estab. 1977. "Our audience is an eclectic mix of Ft. Worth/Dallas area residents with varying levels of incomes and backgrounds. Payment varies according to type of script, reputation of playwright, etc." Query with synopsis, character breakdown and set description; "please include tape if possible." SASE. Reports in 2 months.
Musical Theater: "We are not interested in cabaret revues, but rather in full-length pieces that can be for adults and/or children. We tend to produce more fanciful, whimsical musicals (something not likely to be found anywhere else), but would also consider political pieces. Basically, we're open for anything fresh and well-written. We require no more than 15 in a cast, and a staging would have to adapt to an outdoor environmental thrust stage." Would also consider original music for use in a play being developed.
Productions: *Cowtown!,* Johnny Simons and Douglas Balentine (history of Ft. Worth); *Tom Sawyer-A Banjo Commedia,* adapted by J. Simons and *Pinocchio Commedia,* by Johnny Simons and Michael Pellechia.
Tips: "Think creative, complex thoughts and musical visions that can be transformed into reality by creative, visionary musicians in theaters that rarely have the huge Broadway dollar. Cast size must be kept to a minimum (no more than 15)."

HORIZON THEATRE CO., P.O. Box 5376, Station E, Atlanta GA 30307. (404)584-7450 or (404)523-1477. Co-Artistic Director: Lisa Adler. Play producer. Estab. 1983. Produces 3 plays and 1 musical/year. "Our audience is comprised mostly of young professionals looking for contemporary comedy with a little social commentary. Our theater features a 160-200 seat facility with flexible stage." Pays 6-8% royalty. Query with synopsis, character breakdown, set description and resume. SASE. Reports in 1-2 years.
Musical Theater: "We prefer musicals that have a significant book and a lot of wit (particularly satire). Our casts are restricted to 10 actors. We prefer plays with equal number of male and female roles, or more female than male roles. We have a limited number of musicians available. No musical revues and no dinner theater fluff. One type of play we are currently seeking is a country musical with

women's themes. We generally contract with a musician or sound designer to provide sound for each play we produce. If interested send resume, references, tape with music or sound design samples."
Productions: *Angry Housewives*, by A.M. Collins and Chad Henry.
Tips: "Have patience and use subtle persistence. Work with other theater artists to get a good grasp of the form."

JEWISH REPERTORY THEATRE, Dept. SM, 344 E. 14th St., New York NY 10003. (212)674-7200. Director: Ron Avni. Associate Director: Edward M. Cohen. Play producer. Estab. 1974. Produces 5 plays and 1-2 new musicals/year. Pays 6% royalty. Submit complete manuscript, score and tape of songs. SASE. Reports in 4 weeks.
Musical Theater: Seeking "musicals in English relating to the Jewish experience. No more than 8 characters. We do commission background scores for straight plays."
Productions: *Kumi—Leml* (musical farce); *The Special* (musical comedy); and *The Shop on Main Street* (musical drama).

*LAGUNA PLAYHOUSE, 606 Laguna Canyon Rd., Laguna Beach CA 92651. (714)497-5900 ext. 206. Artistic Director: Andrew Barnicle. Play producer. Estab. 1920. Produces 7-10 plays/year; produces 2-3 musicals/year (3 new musicals in last 3 years). Audience is "middle to upper class suburban mainstream. 9,000 subscribers in resort town. Plays performed in 420 seat luxury theater."
How to Contact: Query with synopsis, character breakdown and set description. SASE. Reports in 2 months "depending on time of year and workload."
Musical Theater: "Seek children's plays (we have an acclaimed youth theater), adult, aesthetic non-'dance' shows with small orchestra ('Tintypes', '1940's Radio Hour'). We have no orchestra pit, limited dance budget. Cast 15-20 maximum on large proscenium stage. Submit homogeneous work, not books that are excuses for songs of line-through."
Productions: *She Loves Me*, by Masterhoff (love); *On the Town*, by Bernstein/Green (New York City); and *Wonderful Life*, by Harnik (the James Stewart Christmas movie).
Tips: "Allow at least one year advance on project."

THE LAMB'S THEATRE CO., Dept. SM, 130 W. 44th St., New York NY 10036. (212)997-0210. Literary Manager: Kathy Cohn. Play producer. Estab. 1984. Produces 2-3 plays, 1 musical (1 new musical)/ year. Receives 5-10 submissions/month. Plays are performed for "the off-Broadway theater audience, also group sales including school programs from New York public high schools and colleges in the area." Pays by royalty. Query with synopsis, character breakdowns and set description. SASE. Reports in 6 months.
Musical Theater: "We are looking for full length musicals that are entertaining, but moving, and deal with serious issues as well as comic situations. No one-act plays. Large-cast epics are out. Both our spaces are intimate theaters, one an 85-seat black box space and one a 345-seat proscenium. Material with explicit sex and nudity and plays which require large amounts of obscene language are not appropriate for this theater. We require a small orchestra in a musical."
Productions: *Johnny Pye & The Foolkiller*, by R. Courts/M. St. Germain (original musical based on Stephen V. Benet short story); *The Gifts of the Magi*, by R. Courts/M. St. Germain (original musical based on O. Henry short stories).

LOS ANGELES DESIGNERS' THEATRE, P.O. Box 1883, Studio City CA 91614-0883. (818)769-9000, (213)650-9600 or (310)247-9800. Artistic Director: Richard Niederberg. Play producer. Estab. 1970. Produces 20-25 plays, 8-10 new musicals/year. Plays are produced at several locations, primarily Studio City, California. Pays by royalty. Submit complete manuscript, score and tape of songs, character breakdown and set descriptions. Video tape submissions are also accepted. SASE. Reports in 3-4 months but faster if cassette of show is included with script.
Musical Theater: "We seek out controversial material. Street language OK, nudity is fine, religious themes, social themes, political themes are encouraged. Our audience is very 'jaded' as it consists of TV, motion picture and music publisher executives who have 'seen it all.' " Does not wish to see bland, "safe" material. We like first productions. "In the cover letter state in great detail the proposed involvement of the songwriter, other than as a writer (i.e. director, actor, singer, publicist, designer, etc.). Also, state if there are any liens on the material or if anything has been promised."
Productions: *Offenbach in the Underworld*, by Frederick Grab (biography with can-can); *Is Nudity Required*, by Stephen Oakley (comedy); and *Wonderful World of Waiver?* (backstage musical). Also *Vine Street*, by H.D. Parkin III (street musical with film/video elements); *All Coked Out* by S. Oakley and M Guestello (musical tragedy on drug use); *Rainbows' End* by Margaret Keifer (songwriters struggle/musical); *Hostages* (political musical) and *Love Song of Ned Wells* (poetry set to music; urban unrequited love story).
Tips: "Make it very 'commercial' and inexpensive to produce. Allow for non-traditional casting. Be prepared with ideas as to how to transform your work to film or videotaped entertainment."

*JOHN B. LYNCH, JR., 1401 Atlantic Ave., Ocean City MD 21842. (410)289-6166. Producer: John B. Lynch, Jr. Play producer. Estab. 1978. Produces 2 musicals/year. "Audience range: 30 years old to senior citizens. Musicals performed in dinner theater format." Pays by $125-150/week royalty or $1000 outright purchase.
How to Contact: Query with synopsis. SASE. Reports in 2-3 weeks.
Musical Theater: "We usually perform musical revues using original and established musical numbers with little dialogue. Show to be based on one theme with two 40-45 minute acts. Must have some comedy and be acceptable for children who attend with parents. we keep cast size to eight (four men, four women) for revues. Do not wish to see overly dramatic, heavy material. It can be naughty (Like *Sugar Babies* but nothing overly suggestive. We require a full list of musical numbers with a brief description of the blocking. If show is purchased, full musical arrangement is required."
Productions: *Putting on the Glitz*, by Dr. Douglas Smith (murder mystery 1930's); *Nunsense*, by Dan Goggins; and *Hollywood*, by John Rampage (silent movies to present).
Tips: "We have done one production of all original music, but find that our audience like things that are familiar for some of the revue. Be flexible enough to change specified musical material as we may not have a performer who vocally suits the number, but may shine in another number that fits the theme."

MAGNIFICENT MOORPARK MELODRAMA AND VAUDEVILLE CO., 45 E. High St., Moorpark CA 93021. (805)529-1212. Producer: Linda Bredemann. Play producer. Estab. 1982. Produces 7 new musicals/year. "Our audience is family and church groups, ages 2 to 90." Pays by royalty, outright purchase or per performance. Submit complete manuscript, score and tape of songs. SASE. Reports in 12 months.
Musical Theater: "We want plays set in any era, but must have a villain to boo—hero to cheer—heroine to ahh. Each act should run no more than 1 hour with a 2 act maximum. We want family-oriented comedies only. Cast should be no more than 20. We have a small stage (30×30). We don't want obscene, vulgar or off-color material. We want up beat music—can be popular songs or old time."
Productions: *Robin Hood*, by Tim Kelly; *Cinderella Meets the Wolfman*, by Tim Kelly (fairy tale); and *Sourdough*, by Dexter Fisch (Western).
Tips: "Have fun. Make the characters memorable, lovable and believable. Make the music tuneful and something to hum later."

MANHATTAN THEATRE CLUB, Dept. SM, 453 W. 16th St., New York NY 10011. (212)645-5590. Director of Script Department: Kate Loewald. Artistic Associate: Michael Bush. Play producer. Estab. 1971. Produces 8 plays and sometimes 1 musical/year. Plays are performed at the Manhattan Theatre Club before varied audiences. Pays negotiated fee. Query with synopsis, "5-10 page libretto and lyric sample." SASE. Reports in 6 months.
Musical Theater: "Small cast, original work. *No* historical drama, verse drama or children's plays." Will consider original music for use in a play being developed or in a pre-existing play.
Productions: *Real Life Funnies*, by Alan Menken and Howard Ashman (topical New York City); *Livin' Dolls*, by Scott Wittman and Marc Shaiman; *Ain't Misbehavin'*, by Fats Waller and Richard Maltby; *On the Swing Shift*, by Michael Dansicker and Sarah Schlesinger; *Urban Blight*, by Richard Maltby, Jr., David Shire and others; and *1-2-3-4-5*, by Maury Yeston and Larry Gelbart.

*MERRY-GO-ROUND PLAYHOUSE, P.O. Box 506, Auburn NY 13021. (315)255-1305. Assistant to the Producer: Maureen Harrington. Play producer and literary manager. Estab. 1958. Produces 10-16 plays/year; produces 5-6 (1-2 new musicals)/year. "We are a touring children's/youth company which performs throughout the U.S. We also are summer company which performs in our existing theater - a refurbished carousel seating 325." Pays by 8-15% royalty or $25-35/performance.
How to Contact: Submit complete manuscript, score and tape of songs. SASE. Reports in 1-3 months.
Musical Theater: "In the past we have done puppet shows, nursery shows, etc. on any and all topics. The required length for children's shows are 35-50 minutes. Because of touring we like to keep casts under six. Set must be 'tourable.' We lean towards educational material and fairy tales with a twist." Would consider original music for a play being developed or use in a pre-existing play.
Performances: *Cinderhood*, by Dennis McCarthy (fractured fairy tale); *I Never Saw Another Butterfly*, by Louis Goldberg (children in World War II Jewish camps); and *Dinosaurs, Dinosaurs, Dinosaurs*, by Rick Balian (body puppet show on 4 fables).
Tips: "Be willing to adapt material. Be willing to work late on long and short notice."

MILWAUKEE REPERTORY THEATER, Dept. SM, 108 E. Wells St., Milwaukee WI 53202. (414)224-1761. Artistic Assistant: Norma Saldivar. Play producer. Estab. 1954. Produces 17 plays and 5 cabaret shows/year. "The space is a 106 seat cabaret with a very small playing area (8x28)." Pays by royalty. Send script and/or cassette. SASE. Reports in 3-4 months.

Musical Theater: "Cast size must be limited to 3 singers/performers with minimum movement. Suitable for cabaret. Must appeal to a broad adult audience and should not run longer than 1 hour. We also seek to explore a multi-cultural diversity of material."
Productions: *A Little Tom Foolery*, by Tom Lehrer (political satire); *Jukejointjammin*, by R. Meiksins & B. Roberts (1930s jazz); and *A Gershwin Serenade*, by Larry Deckel (musical retrospective).

MIXED BLOOD THEATRE CO., 1501 S. 4th St., Minneapolis MN 55454. (612)338-0937. Script Czar: David Kunz. Play producer. Estab. 1976. Produces 4-5 plays a year and perhaps 1 new musical every 2 years. "We have a 200-seat theater in a converted firehouse. The audience spans the socio-economic spectrum." Pays 7-10% royalty. Submit complete manuscript, score and tape of songs. SASE. Reports in 6 weeks.
Musical Theater: "We want full-length, non-children works with a message. Always query first. Never send unsolicited script or tape."
Productions: *Black Belts* in house production (great African-American singers).
Tips: "Always query first. Be professional. Surprise us."

MUSIC THEATRE OF ARIZONA, Suite I, 422 S. Madison Ave., Tempe AZ 85281. (602)829-0008. Artistic Director: Charles Raison. Music theater production company. Members are professionals and amateurs. Performs 3-7 productions/year, including 1-2 new works. "Performs in three venues: 3,000 seat concert hall (Grady Garmage on ASU's campus) a 7,000 seat concert hall (Sundome) and an 800 seat theater (Herberger) where new works are performed." Pays by royalty (varies). Submit complete score and tapes of pieces. SASE. Reports in 3 months.
Music: "New musical theater works, preferably small casts—any style, from country to jazz, pop, etc. Small casts up to 15 preferred due to Lort contract demands. No hard rock or material you would consider inappropriate for general public. Suggestive material is fine, vulgar is another thing. Stick to *musical theater* format."
Performances: Rodgers & Hammerstein's *The King & I* (musical); Maltby & Shine's *Starting Here Starting Now* (musical revue); Charles Strouse's *Annie* (musical); and Nancy Loeds' *Scrooge: A Musical Ghost Story* (premiere musical).
Tips: "Be flexible and willing to share and blend with the creative effort, without giving up your initial intent. Share and compromise instead of becoming stubborn or closed to any new idea or thought."

MUSICAL THEATRE WORKS, INC., Dept. SM, 440 Lafayette St., New York NY 10003. (212)677-0040. Business Manager: Mike Teele. Produces new musicals exclusively. Estab. 1983. 14 productions have transferred to Broadway, off-Broadway and regional theater. Produces 3-4 new musicals and 12-16 readings each season. Productions and readings are held at the Theatre at Saint Peter's Church, Citicorp Center. No payment for productions.Submit complete script, cassette tape of songs and SASE. Reply in 2-4 months.
Musical Theater: "We are seeking full-length book/avant-garde musicals which have never been produced. Fourteen cast maximum. Full, but modest productions in 164-seat modern off-Broadway theater for metropolitan NYC audience. Only completed projects will be considered for development."
Productions: *Whatnot*, by Howard Crabtee and Mark Waldrop (won 1990 Richard Rodgers Award); *Love in Two Countries*, by Sheldon Harnick and Tom Shepard (operetta); *Collette Collage*, by Tom Jones and Harvey Schmidt (on the life of French writer Collette); and *The Next to Last Revue*, by Martin Sharnin (skits about life in NYC).

MUSIC-THEATRE GROUP INC., Dept. SM, 29 Bethune St., New York NY 10014. (212)924-3108. Managing Director: Diane Wondisford. Music-theater production company. Produces 6 music-theater pieces/year. Plays are performed "off-broadway in New York City; for summer audiences in Stockbridge, MA." Pays negotiable royalty or fees. Query with synopsis, character breakdown, set description and tape of music. SASE.
Musical Theater: "We don't actually seek developed properties, but examples of people's work as an indication of their talent in the event that we might want to suggest them for a future collaboration. The music must be a driving element in the work. We generally work with not more than 10-12 in cast and a small band of 4-5."
Productions: *Cinderella/Cendrillon*, based on the opera by Jules Massenet; *The Garden of Earthly Delights*, by Martha Clarke; and *Juan Darien*, by Julie Taymor and Elliot Goldenthal.

NATIONAL MUSIC THEATER CONFERENCE, O'Neill Theater Center, 234 West 44th St., #901, New York NY 10036. (212)382-2790. Artistic Director: Paulette Haupt. "The Conference develops new music theater works." Estab. 1978. Develops 3-4 musicals each summer. 8-10 professional songwriters/ musicians participate in each event. Participants include songwriters, composers, opera/musical theater and lyricists/librettists. "The O'Neill Theater Center is in Waterford, Connecticut. The audiences for the staged readings of works-in-progress are a combination of local residents, New York and regional theater professionals. Participants are selected by artistic director and selection panel of professionals." Pays a stipend, room and board, and all costs of the workshops are covered. Query first. SASE. Response within 3-4 months. Entry Fee $20.

Musical Theater: "The Conference is interested in all forms of music theater. Staged readings are presented with script in hand, minimal props, piano only. There are no cast limitations. We don't accept works which have been previously produced by a professional company."

Productions: *Witch!*, by Mike Champagne and Elliot Weiss; *Till*, by John Clifton; *Hit the Lights!*, by Michele Lowe and Chris Hajian.

NATIONAL MUSIC THEATER NETWORK, INC., Dept. SM, Third Floor, 1460 Broadway, New York NY 10036. President: Timothy Jerome. Service to evaluate new musical works and publish a catalogue of recommended works to play producers. "Our catalogue of recommended works is targeted to approximately 7,000 regional theaters and musical producers interested in presenting new works. Our 'sampler' series concerts feature excerpts from recommended works for the NYC area. In 1991-92 we will present 20 concerts featuring recommended works. Producers contact us for creators' works. We contact creators and creators contact producers." Receives 5 submissions/month. Submit complete manuscript, score and tape of songs. Writers are required to "fill out our submission form plus $30 fee." SASE. Reports in 6 months.

Musical Theater: "We accept all styles. Take the time to present your materials neatly. We accept only *completed* musicals and operas, i.e. script/score/tape."

Tips: "Use us as a resource to help you market your work." "Submit a synopsis which captures the heart of your piece; inject your piece with a strong voice and intent and try to surprise and excite us."

THE NEW CONSERVATORY CHILDREN'S THEATRE COMPANY & SCHOOL, Dept. SM, 25 Van Ness, San Francisco CA 94102. (415)861-4914. Executive Director: Ed Decker. Play producer. Estab. 1981. Produces about 5 plays and 1 or 2 musicals (1 new musical)/year. Audience includes families and community groups; children ages 14-19. "Performance spaces are 50-150 seat theater, but we also tour some shows. Pays $25-35 per performance. If we commission, playwright receives a commission for the initial run and royalties thereafter; otherwise playwright just gets royalties."

How to Contact: Query with synopsis, character breakdown and set description. SASE. Reports in 3 months.

Musical Theater: "We seek innovative and preferably socially relevant musicals for children and families, with relatively small cast (stage is small), in which all roles can be played by children. We have a small stage, thus cannot accommodate plays casting more than 10 or 12 people, and prefer relatively simple set requirements. Children cast are in the 9-19 age range. We do not want mushy, cute material. Fantasy is fine, as is something like Sendak & King's *Really Rosie*, but nothing gooey. We are very interested in using original music for new or existing plays. Songwriters should submit a resume and perhaps a tape to let us know what they do."

Productions: *Consensus*, by Dylan Russell (American family); *Get Real!*, by Doug Holsclaw (AIDS education, age 9-12); *Kegger*, by Megan Terry (teen alcohol use).

Tips: "Be flexible, able to revise and open to suggestions!"

NEW THEATRE, Dept. SM, Box 650696, Miami FL 33265. (305)595-4260. Executive Artistic Director: Rafael de Acha. Play producer. Estab. 1986. Produces 10 plays and 2 musicals (2 new musicals)/year. Audience is mixed urban South Florida, with median age of 35, mostly upper-class white and Hispanic. Pays by royalty. Query with synopsis, character breakdown and set description. SASE. Reports in 3 months.

Musical Theater: "Specifically small, revue-style musicals, such as *Brecht on Brecht*; *Side by Side*; *Oh, Coward*, etc. Also interested in experimental work along the lines of *Three Postcards*, etc. We perform in a 70-seat black box theater, with modest production values." Would consider original music for use in a play being developed, but "that kind of work requires the composer to be involved very heavily. We often use incidental music specially composed for a play and have also commissioned original works."

Productions: *Feiffer's People*, by Jules Feiffer (satire); *Dear Liar*, by Jerome Kilty (biographical play); *Spoon River Anthology*, by Edgar Lee Masters (play with music) and *You are Here*, by Susan Westfall and Bernard Harding.

Tips: "Keep lines of communication open."

*NEW TUNERS THEATRE, Theatre Building, 1225 Belmont, Chicago IL 60657. (312)929-7287. Associate Producer: Allan Chambers. Play producer. Estab. 1968. Produces 3 musicals (3 new musicals)/year. "We play to mixed urban and suburban audiences. We produce in a 148-seat theater in the Theatre Building." Pays 6-12% royalty.

How to Contact: Submit synopsis and a letter of intention. SASE. Reports in 6 months.

Musical Theater: "We look at all types of musical theater, traditional as well as more innovative forms. We have an interest in children's theater. Fifteen is the maximum cast size we can consider and less is decidedly better. We work with a younger (35 and under) company of actors.

Productions: *High Fidelity*, by Philip Seward (operetta loosely based on Shaw and Chekov short plays); *10 Minute Tuners '91*, various (ten-minute musicals); *Charlie's Oasis*, by Jane Boyd and Gregg Opelka (group effort to save a favorite landmark).

Tips: "Attend as many plays with music and musicals as possible. Find out why something works and doesn't work. Find your own musical voice."

NEW VIC SUPPER THEATRE, Dept. SM, 755 S. Saginaw, Flint MI 48502. (313)235-8866. Executive/Artistic Director: Julianne Schmidt. Play producer. Estab. 1981. Produces 8-10 plays and 2-3 musicals/year. Audience is a wide range of dinner theater patrons from old to young. Half of the audience is generated by group sales. Perform on small proscenium with thrust. Query with synopsis, character breakdown and set description. SASE. Reports in six months.

Musical Theater: "We will look at most any style or topic of musical; 20-25 is top end of cast size. Staging is detailed but limited because of smaller stage. We will try and accommodate most shows." Will consider adding original music to an already existing show. Last season added original music to a production of Moliere's *The Miser*.

Productions: *1940s Radio Hour*, by Walton Jones; *Joseph and the Amazing Technicolor Dreamcoat*, by Andrew Lloyd Weber & Tim Rice; and *Olymus On My Mind*, by Barry Harmon & Grant Sturale.

Tips: "We have a pretty strong following that has built up with us in our eight years of existence. They are an older audience primarily, but getting younger all the time. Excessive swearing and strong sexual content should be avoided."

NEW YORK STATE THEATRE INSTITUTE, Dept. SM, PAC 266, 1400 Washington Ave., Albany NY 12222. (518)442-5399. Literary Manager: James Farrell. Play producer. Produces approximately 5 plays (2 new musicals)/year. Plays performed for student audiences grades K-12, family audiences and adult audiences. Two theaters: main theater seats 950 with full stage, studio theater seats 450 with smaller stage. Pay negotiable. Submit complete manuscript and tape of songs. SASE. Response in 3-4 months.

Musical Theater: Looking for "intelligent and well-written book with substance, a score that enhances and supplements the book and is musically well-crafted and theatrical. Length: up to 2 hours. Could be play with music, musical comedy, musical drama. Excellence and substance in material is essential. Cast could be up to 12; orchestra size up to 8."

Productions: *Pied Piper*, by Adrian Mitchell/Dominic Muldowney (musical adaptation of the classic tale); *The Snow Queen*, by Adrian Mitchell/Richard Peaslee (musical adaptation of the Andersen fairy tale).

Tips: "There is a great need for musicals that are well-written with intelligence and substance which are suitable for family audiences."

NEW YORK THEATRE WORKSHOP, 18th Floor, 220 W. 42 St., New York NY 10036. (212)302-7737. Artistic Director: James C. Nicola. Play producer. Produces 4 mainstage plays and approximately 50 readings/year. "Plays are performed in the Perry Street Theatre, Greenwich Village. Audiences include: subscription/single ticket buyers from New York area, theater professionals, and special interest groups. Pays by negotiable royalty." Query with synopsis, character breakdown and set description. SASE. Reports in 4 months.

Musical Theater: "As with our non-musicals, we seek musicals of intelligence and social consciousness that challenge our perceptions of the world and the events which shape our lives. We favor plays that possess a strong voice, distinctive and innovative use of language and visual imagery. Integration of text and music is particularly of interest. Musicals which require full orchestrations would generally be too big for us. We prefer 'musical theater pieces' rather than straightforward 'musicals' per-se. We often use original music for straight plays that we produce. This music may be employed as pre-show, post-show or interlude music. If the existing piece lends itself, music may also be incorporated within the play itself. Large casts (12 or more) are generally prohibitive and require soliciting of additional funds. Design elements for our productions are of the highest quality possible with our limited funds—approximately budgets of $10,000 are allotted for our productions."

Productions: *The Waves*, adopted from Virginia Woolf's novel, music and lyrics by David Bucknam and text and direction by Lisa Peterson; *My Children! My Africa*, by Athol Fugard; and *Mad Forest*, by Caryl Churchill.

Tips: "Submit a synopsis which captures the heart of your piece; inject your piece with a strong voice and intent and try to surprise and excite us."

NEXT ACT THEATRE, (formerly Theatre Tesseract), Dept. SM, Box 394, Milwaukee WI 53201. (414)278-7740. Artistic Director: Jonathan Smoots. Estab. 1984. 4 productions/year, of which 1 is a musical. Playwrights paid by royalty (5-8%). "Performance spaces vary greatly but generally seat 349. We have 1,000 season subscribers and single ticket buyers of every age range and walk of life." Pays $30-50 per performance. Submit complete manuscript, score and tape of songs with at least one professional letter of recommendation. SASE.
Musical Theater: "We produce Broadway and off-Broadway style material, preferring slightly contro-versial or cutting edge material (i.e. *March of the Falsettos*). We have never produced a work that has not been successful in some other theatrical center. We are very limited financially and rarely stage shows with more than 6 in the cast. Props, sets and costumes should be minimal. We have no interest in children's theater, mime shows, puppet shows, etc. We have never yet used original music for our plays. We may consider it, but there would be little if any money available for this purpose."
Productions: *Billy Bishop Goes to War,* by John Gray/Eric Peterson (World War I flying ace); *A . . . My Name is Alice,* by various writers (women's themes); and *Damn Tango,* by Helena Dynerman (European translation of 17 tangos with cast of 17 singer/dancers).

NORTHSIDE THEATRE COMPANY OF SAN JOSE, 848 E. William St., San Jose CA 95116. (408)288-7820. Artistic Director: Richard T. Orlando. Play producer. Estab. 1979. Produces 6 plays and an occasional musical/year. "Family entertainment, plays are performed at the Olinder Theatre." Pays by royalty. Query with synopsis, character breakdown and set description. SASE. Reports in 3 weeks.
Musical Theatre: "Classic family plays (with a twist or different concept)." Cast size: 10-15. Sets: Unit in concept with simple additions. Staging: proscenium with thrust. Small 90 seat theater fully equipped. "We are interested in new ideas and approaches. Production should have social relevancy." Will consider using original music for already existing plays. "Example: the underscoring of a Shakes-peare piece."
Productions: *A Christmas Carol,* by Charles Dickens (seasonal); *After the Rain,* by John Bowen (future civilization); and *Voices from the High School,* by Peter Dee (youth and their lives).
Tips: "Be aggressive, sell your idea and be able to work within the budget and limitations that the artistic director is confined to."

ODYSSEY THEATRE ENSEMBLE, Dept. SM, 2055 S. Sepulveda Blvd., Los Angeles CA 90025. (213)477-2055. Literary Manager: Jan Lewis. Play producer. Estab. 1969. Produces 9 plays, 1 musical and 1-2 new musicals/year. Receives 3-4 submissions/month. "Our audience is predominantly over 35, upper middle-class, audience interested in eclectic brand of theater which is challenging and experimental." Pays by royalty (percentage to be negotiated). Query with synopsis, character break-down and set description. Query should include resume(s) of artist(s) and tape of music. SASE. "Unsolicited material is not read or screened at all." Reports on query in 2 weeks; manuscript in 6 months.
Musical Theater: "We want nontraditional forms and provocative, unusual, challenging subject mat-ter. We are not looking for Broadway-style musicals. Comedies should be highly stylized or highly farcical. Works should be full-length only and not requiring a complete orchestra (small band pre-ferred.) Political material and satire are great for us. We're seeking interesting musical concepts and approaches. The more traditional Broadway-style musicals will generally not be done by the Odyssey. If we have a work in development that needs music, original music will often be used. In such a case, the writer and composer would work together during the development phase. In the case of a pre-existing play, the concept would originate with the director who would select the composer."
Productions: *Symmes' Hole,* by Randolph Dreyfuss (search for the center of the earth); *Spring Awak-ening,* by Frank Wedekind (sexual awakening in youth); *McCarthy,* by Jeff Goldsmith (Senator Joe McCarthy); *Struggling Truths* (the Chinese invasion of Tibet); and *It's A Girl* (a capella musical for 5 pregnant women).
Tips: "Stretch your work beyond the ordinary. Look for compelling themes or the enduring questions of human existence. If it's a comedy, go for broke, go all the way, be as inventive as you can be."

OFF CENTER THEATRE, 1501 Broadway, New York NY 10036. (212)768-3277. Producer: Abigail McGrath. Play producer. Estab. 1968. Produces varying number of plays and new musicals/year. The plays are performed "off-Broadway." Pays percentage of box office receipts after initial expenses have been recouped. Query first. SASE. Reports in 3 months.
Musical Theater: Socially relevant. Not for children/young audiences. Issue oriented, small cast.
Productions: *Just for Fun—The Music of Jerome Kern* (revue); *Biting the Apple,* by Tony McGrath and Stanley Seidman (revue); and *Hello, This Is Barbara, I'm Not in Right Now . . . ,* by Barbara Schotten-feld (singles in New York City).

Tips: "Must be in New York City area for a length of time to work on a piece during readings and/or workshop—without guarantee of production."

OLD GLOBE THEATRE, P.O. Box 2171, San Diego CA 92112. (619)231-1941. Literary Manager: Mark Hofflund. Artistic Director: Jack O'Brien. Produces 12 or 13 plays/year, of which a varying number are musicals. "This is a regional theater with three spaces: 600-seat proscenium, 225-seat arena and large outdoor summer stage. We serve a national audience base of over 260,000." Query with synopsis and letter of introduction, or submit through agent or professional affiliation. No unsolicited material please. SASE. Reports in 4-8 months. Receives 100 submissions/year.
Musical Theater: "We look for skill first, subject matter second. No prescribed limitations, though creators should appreciate the virtues of economy as well as the uses of extravagance. Musicals have been produced on all three of our stages."
Productions: *Pastorela '91*, by Raul Moncada (traditional Latin-American Christmas); *Lady Day at Emerson's Bar and Grill*, by Lanie Robertson (Billie Holiday); *Forever Plaid*, by Stuart Ross ('50/'60s male quartet).
Tips: "Fall in love with a great book and a great writer."

OMAHA MAGIC THEATRE, 1417 Farnam St., Omaha NE 68102. (402)346-1227. Artistic Director: Jo Ann Schmidman. Play producer. Estab. 1968. Produces 8 performance events with music/year. "Plays are produced in our Omaha facility and on tour throughout the midwest. Our audience is a cross-section of the community." Pays standard royalty, outright purchase ($500-1,500), per performance $20-25. Query with synopsis, character breakdown and set description. SASE. Reports in 6 months.
Musical Theater: "We want the most avant of the avant garde—plays that never get written, or if written are buried deep in a chest because the writer feels there are not production possibilities in this nation's theaters. Plays must push form and/or content to new dimensions. The clarity of the playwright's voice must be strong and fresh. We do not produce standard naturalistic or realistic musicals. At the Omaha Magic Theatre original music is considered as sound structure and for lyrics."
Productions: *Body Leaks*, by Megan Terry, Jo Ann Schmidman and Sora Kimberlain (self-censorship); *Sound Fields/Are We Here*, by Megan Terry, Jo Ann Schmidman and Sora Kimberlain (a new multi-dimensional performance event about acute listening); and *Headlights*, by Megan Terry (literacy in America).

THE OPEN EYE: NEW STAGINGS, Dept. SM, 270 W. 89th St., New York NY 10024. (212)769-4143. Artistic Director: Amie Brockway. Play producer. Estab. 1972. Produces 9 one-acts, 5-6 full length or new stagings for youth; varying number of new musicals. "Plays are performed in a well-designed and pleasant theater seating 115 people." Pays on a fee basis or by commission. "We are pleased to accept unsolicited play manuscripts under the following conditions: 1) The script must be clean (no pencil marks, magic markers, paste overs, etc.); 2) It must be bound; 3) A self-addressed stamped envelope must be enclosed for each manuscript's return. Also keep in mind: the best time for submission is from April through July. We receive many scripts, and reading takes time. Please allow 3-6 months for a response. Please do not send synopses of your plays. Instead, please consider carefully whether you think your play is something New Stagings should read, and if it is, send the complete script."
Musical Theater: "New Stagings is committed to innovative collaboration and excellence in performance of both classic and new material, presenting the finest of professional talents—established artists and relative newcomers alike. We produce plays which invite us as artists and audience to take a fresh look at ourselves and the world of which we are a part. We seek to involve the performers and the audience in the live theater experience. And we are making a concerted effort to reach new audiences, young and old, and of all ethnic backgrounds. New Stagings for Youth is a not-for-profit professional theater company whose aim is to develop new theater audiences by producing plays for children and young people. New Stagings Lab offers opportunities to performing artists (directors, playwrights, actors, dancers, musicians) to develop new theater pieces through a program of rehearsed readings and workshops. Our stage is roughly 20' x 25' which limits the size of the set, cast and other related details and also, we do not have the height for a fly system. We seldom do political or propaganda related plays. We frequently use music to enhance a script, as well as performing plays with music in them, and also musicals. We believe in using various forms of art (music, movement) in most of our productions."

"How to Use Your Songwriter's Market" (at the front of this book) contains comments and suggestions to help you understand and use the information in these listings.

Productions: *Eagle or Sun*, by Sabina Berman (The Mexican Conquest); *A Woman Called Truth*, by Sandra Acher (Life of Sojourner Truth); and *A Place Beyond the Clouds*, by Sandra Biano (Myths and Stories of Flying).
Tips: "Come see our work."

OZARK ACTORS THEATRE, Dept. SM, Box K, Rolla MO 65401. (314)364-9523. Artistic Director: F. Reed Brown. Play producer. Estab. 1987. Produces 3 plays and 1 musical/year. South-central Missouri is a rural (primarily agricultural) area. O.A.T. is located in Rolla, which houses the Univesity of Missouri-Rolla. Pays by royalty. Query with snyopsis, character breakdown and set description. SASE. Reports in 2-3 months.
Musical Theatre: "Virtually any subject is desired. We look for shows/musicals that will fit into a summer stock season. Musicaltheatre. No opera." Primarily small casts (not to exceed 15). Relatively small (unit) sets. Without major technical requirements. "O.A.T. does not wish to produce material which might be viewed controversial. Such as strong sexual, racial or political views. No strong language." Will consider original music for work already in progress. "We produced an original work entitled *Voices* with writings by Van Gogh, Thoreau, Emily Dickenson, Ann Frank and Helen Keller. The score composer is Alan Johnson."
Productions: *Voices*, compiled by Fred Brown, music by Alan Johnson (life, death, criticism); *I Do! I Do!*, by Schmidt/Jones (marriage); and *The Boys Next Door* by Tom Griffin (the mentally handicapped).

PAPER MILL PLAYHOUSE, Brookside Dr., Milburn NJ 07041. (201)379-3636. Contact: Angelo Del Rossi. Play producer. Produces 2 plays and 4 musicals (1 new musical)/year. "Audience based on 40,000 subscribers; plays performed in 1,192-seat proscenium theatre." Pays negotiable royalty or will option play under Dramatist Guild. "A synopsis of book plus tape of songs should be submitted first. Scores not necessary. Letter of introduction should accompany each submitted synopsis." SASE. Letter in 2 weeks, response in 6 months.
Musical Theater: Seeking "traditional Broadway sized musicals—either original or adaptations. One act plays are not considered. Developing works can be submitted to our musical workshop series. No cast size limitations—minimum of 5 characters usually to maximum size of 40-45." No nudity, profanity, etc.
Productions: *Me and My Girl*; *Greasepaint*; *Lend Me a Tenner*; *To Kill a Mockingbird* and *A Chorus Line*.
Tips: "New musicals are sought for our Musical Theatre Project development program, which includes a series of staged readings and laboratory (workshop)."

PENNSYLVANIA STAGE COMPANY, 837 Linden St., Allentown PA 18101. (215)434-6110. Artistic Director: Peter Wrenn-Meleck. Play producer. Estab. 1979. Produces 7 plays (1 new musical)/season "when feasible. We are a LORT D theatre with a subscriber base of approximately 6,000 people. Plays are performed at the Pennsylvania Stage Company in the J.I. Rodale Theatre." Playwrights paid by 5% royalty (per Dramatist's Guild contract). Query with synopsis, character breakdown, set description and a tape of the music. "Please do not send script first." SASE. Reports in 2 months.
Musical Theater: "We are interested in full-length musicals which reflect the social, historical and political fabric of America. We have no special requirements for format, structure or musical involvement. We ask that once submission of a musical has been requested, that it be bound, legibly typed and include SASE. Cast limit of 10, but we prefer cast limit of 8. One set or unit set. Ours is a 274 seat house, there is no fly area, and a 23-foot proscenium opening."
Productions: *Just So*, by Mark St. Germain (based on Rudyard Kipling's *Just So Stories*); *Smilin' Through*, by Ivan Menchell (British Music Hall circa WWII); *Song of Myself*, by Gayle Stahlhuth, Gregory Hurst and Arthur Harris.
Tips: "Avoid duplication of someone else's style just because it's been successful in the past. I see far too many composers aping Stephen Sondheim's songwriting, for example, without nearly as much success. Despite all the commercial constraints, stick to your guns and write something original, unique."

PLAYHOUSE ON THE SQUARE, 51 S. Cooper, Memphis TN 38104. (901)725-0776. Executive Producer: Jackie Nichols. Play producer. Produces 12 plays (4 musicals)/year. Plays are produced in a 260-seat proscenium resident theater. Pays $500 for outright purchase. Submit complete manuscript and score. Unsolicited submissions OK. SASE. Reports in 4 months.
Musical Theater: Seeking "any subject matter—adult and children's material. Small cast preferred. Stage is 26' deep by 43' wide with no fly system." Would also consider original music for use in a play being developed.

Productions: *Gypsy*, by Stein and Laurents; *The Spider Web*, by Agatha Christie (mystery); and *A Midsummer Night's Dream*, by William Shakespeare.

PLAYWRIGHTS HORIZONS, 416 W. 42nd St., New York NY 10036. (212)564-1235. Director: Nicholas Martin. Literary Manager/Musical Theater Program Director. Play producer. Estab. 1971. Produces about 6 plays and 2 new musicals/year. "A general New York City audience." Pays by fee/royalty. Send script and tape (not necessarily complete). SASE. Reports in 6 months.
Musical Theater: "No revivals or children's shows; otherwise we're flexible. We can't do a Broadway-size show. We generally develop work from scratch; we're open to proposals for shows, and ideas from bookwriters or songwriters. We have frequently commissioned underscoring and incidental music."
Productions: *Lucky Stiff*, by Lynn Ahrens/Stephen Flaherty (musical comedy); *The Heidi Chronicles*, by Wendy Wasserstein (play); and *Driving Miss Daisy*, by Alferd Uhry (play).

PUERTO RICAN TRAVELING THEATRE, Dept. SM, 141 W. 94th St., New York, NY 10025. (212)354-1293. Producer: Miriam Colon Valle. Play Producer. Estab. 1967. Produces 4 plays and 1 new musical/year. Primarily an Hispanic audience. Playwrights are paid by stipend.
How to Contact: Submit complete manuscript and tape of songs. SASE. Reports in 6 months.
Musical Theater: "Small cast musicals that will appeal to Hispanic audience. Musicals are bilingual; we work in Spanish and English. We need simple sets and props and a cast of about 8, no more. Musicals are generally performed outdoors and last for an hour to an hour and 15 minutes."
Productions: *Chinese Charades*, by Manuel Perralras, Sergio Garcia and Saul Spangenberg (domestic musical); *El Jardin*, by Carlos Morton, Sergio Garcia (Biblical musical); and *Lady With A View*, by Eduardo Ivan Lopez and Fernando Rivas (Statue of Libery musical).
Tips: "Deal with some aspect of the contemporary Hispanic experience in this country."

THE REPERTORY THEATRE OF ST. LOUIS, P.O. Box 191730, St. Louis MO 63119. (314)968-7340. Associate Artistic Director: Susan Gregg. Play producer. Estab. 1966. Produces 9 plays and 1 or 2 musicals/year. "Mainstream regional theater audience. We produce all our work at the Loretto Hilton Theatre." Pays by royalty. Query with synopsis, character breakdown and set description. SASE. Reports in 8 months.
Musical Theater: "We want plays with a small cast and simple setting. No children's shows or foul language. After a letter of inquiry we would prefer script and demo tape."
Productions: *1940's Radio Hour*, by Walt Jones; *Almost September*, by David Schechter; *The Merry Wives of Windsor, Texas*, by John Haber.

RICHARD ROSE—AMERICAN STAGE FESTIVAL, Dept. SM, Box 225, Milford NH 03055. (603)673-4005. Producing Director: Richard Rose. Play producer. Estab. 1975. Produces 5 mainstage plays, 10 children's, and 1-2 musicals/year. Plays are produced in 500 seat proscenium stage for a general audience. Pays 8-10% royalty or outright purchase of $2,000. Submit complete manuscript, score and tape of songs. SASE.
Musical Theater: "We seek stories about interesting people in compelling situations. Besides our adult audience we have an active children's theater. We will not do a large chorus musical if cast size is over 18. We use original music in plays on a regular basis, as incidental music, pre-show and between acts, or as moments in and of themselves."
Productions: *Rhymes with Evil*, by Charles Traeger (psych thriller); *Peg O' My Heart*, by David Heneker (romantic musical); *Sullivan And Gilbert*, by Ken Ludwig (comic musical); *Starmites*, by Barry Keating (rock/comic book fantasy); and *The Last of the Souhegans*, by Andrew Howard.
Tips: "Write about characters. Understand the reasons why characters break into song. Submit legible script and listenable cassette. And please keep writing!"

SEATTLE GROUP THEATRE, Dept. SM, Box 45430, Seattle WA 98145-0430. (206)685-4969. Producing Director: Paul O'Connell. Artistic Director: Tim Bond. Estab. 1978. Produces 6 plays and 1-2 musicals (1 new musical)/year. 200 seat intimate theater; 10' ceiling limit; 35' wide modified thrust; 3 piece band. Pays 6-8% royalty. Query with synopsis, character breakdown and set description. Does not return unsolicited material.
Musical Theater: "Multicultural themes; relevant social issues, (race relations, cultural differences, war, poverty, women's issues, homosexuality, physically challenged, developmentally disabled). Address the issues that our mission focuses on." Past musicals include *A-My Name is Alice*, *Rap Master Ronnie*, *Jacques Brel is Alive*, *Stealing*, *Voices of Christmas*. Cast size of 10 maximum.
Productions: *It's a Girl*, by Tom Burrows; *Fraternity*, by Jeff Stetson and *Latins Anonymous*, by Armando Lomina, Diane Rodriguez, Luisa Leschin and Rick Najera.

SECOND STAGE THEATRE, P.O. Box 1807, Ansonia Station, New York NY 10023. (212)787-8302. Dramaturg/Literary Manager: Erin Sanders. Play producer. Estab. 1979. Produces 4 plays and 1 musical (1 new musical)/year. Receives 30 submissions/year. Plays are performed in a small, 108 seat off-

Close-up

Stephen Flaherty
Theatrical Composer
New York, New York

It's generally assumed that the market for new musical theater is closed to all but a few. Names like Stephen Sondheim
and Andrew Lloyd Webber are considered synonymous
with American musical theater productions. But composer/
playwright Stephen Flaherty has an important point to
make: those names are associated with Broadway, which
represents only a small part of the potential productions of
musical theater. "It's just so difficult to get things produced now [on Broadway], because
of the economics of it," says Flaherty. "I think producers, nine times out of ten, play things
incredibly safe. I think off-Broadway theaters are much more adventuresome."

Adventuresome musical theater has been key in the work of Flaherty and lyricist partner
Lynn Ahrens. They have collaborated since 1983 on several musical theater works, includ-
ing *Once on This Island*, nominated for 8 Tony Awards in 1991, the Richard Rodgers
Award-winning *Lucky Stiff*, and a fall 1992 production of *My Favorite Year* at New York's
Lincoln Center Theater. Projects for the future include another stage musical, *Bedazzled*,
and work on an animated movie musical for Walt Disney Studios.

Despite his current success, Flaherty says that hard work is a necessity for established
as well as aspiring writers for the theater. "You have to know as much [as you can] about
playwriting, dramatic structure, acting styles, musical styles." He continues, "In other
words, if you can know something about all the different areas of the theater, it's only going
to make your material richer." Flaherty's own studies include a degree in composition,
study of playwriting, theater history, conducting, and even painting. "Sure, this yielded
several bad paintings and worse plays," says Flaherty, "but I learned more about the
language of my theater collaborators by painting those bad paintings.

"I believe theater is by nature a collaborative medium," Flaherty continues. "History
has always shown us that." Musical theater pairs such as Ira and George Gershwin, Rodgers
and Hammerstein and Lerner and Loewe are part of that history. The music of Alan
Menkin and Howard Ashman (*Little Mermaid, Beauty and the Beast*) have made their names
known more recently. Although both Flaherty and his partner Ahrens have written both
text and music on their own, within their partnership Flaherty writes music and Ahrens
lyrics. Flaherty comments, "It's really like taking a ball and throwing it back and forth to
each other." This spontaneity is something that begins with the show's plot. Characters are
developed, the dramatic situation is discussed, programming of songs is considered. "And
then at some point, when we've talked enough about the situation and dramatic stuff, at
some point you have to jump in. I try to come up with some kind of rhythm or a snippet of
melody or something that suggests the emotional tone of the scene. Usually from that,
Lynn starts to work with the words. The more you work with a collaborator," Flaherty says,
"the more it's really about improvising in a room. Sometimes I've written complete melodies, sometimes she's written complete lyrics. But usually it comes from improvising together, making sure we're on the same beam."

Collaborating isn't limited to simply the writing of the show. The collaborative process can be continued on a larger scale with development in workshops. Flaherty says, "I find that until I can see the material performed live, with actors on a stage, it is really hard to develop it. It isn't until I see it up on its feet that I can shape it." Flaherty has worked with the BMI, ASCAP, Dramatists Guild and Playwrights Horizons workshops on his material. Although the workshops have very different focuses, workshops provide concentrated knowledge in certain areas. This knowledge aids in the development of the musical material and the playwright. Flaherty still develops his material in an informal workshop made up of friends and colleagues in musical theater. He's also developed strong ties with Playwrights Horizons, a nonprofit workshop and play producer.

The nonprofit theater company provides many things to the playwright, most important, a center of operations. "To align yourself with a theater or creative home base . . . I found that really important in my life," Flaherty says. "It's a question of where you can develop new work. I don't think you can develop anything where you don't have this sense of safety and security. That's what I really found in the not-for-profit theater; that they really nurture the writer. They're interested in the writers developing as artists and developing careers, as opposed to producing this one show."

Nonprofit theater, especially regional nonprofit, could be an alternative for musical playwrights unable to move to or work in New York, which Flaherty sees as the center of American musical theater. "It was difficult for me doing theater work in the Midwest because I wasn't getting a lot of feedback," says Flaherty. "When I moved to New York all of a sudden there was this whole community of people." But when asked if New York is the place for writers for the theater, Flaherty replied, "I shouldn't say that, because the minute you say that, people say, 'Look at all this wonderful work in regional theater.' There are musicals starting in Chicago and other cities. But I think if you're really serious about having a career in the theater, especially musical theater, I think at some point you're going to cross through New York."

More important than where to go and how to write, Flaherty believes that where the music comes from is central to success. "Never limit your imagination or never limit yourself by thinking, 'I can only do this'," Flaherty says, "People keep saying 'Oh, those old-fashioned musicals.' There are so many different kinds of shows and ways music can be used that haven't been tapped into yet. I'd like to believe there will still be audiences for interesting uses of music and drama together."

—Michael Oxley

❝It's a question of where you can develop new work. I don't think you can develop anything where you don't have this sense of safety and security. That's what I really found in the not-for-profit theater; that they really nurture the writer. They're interested in the writers developing as artists and developing careers, as opposed to producing this one show.❞

—Stephen Flaherty

Broadway House." Pays variable royalty. Query with synopsis, character breakdown and set description. No unsolicited manuscripts. SASE. Reports in 4 months.

Musical Theater: "We are looking for innovative, unconventional musicals that deal with sociopolitical themes."

Productions: *In a Pig's Valise,* by Eric Overmyer and Kid Creole (spoof on 40's film noir); *Boho Days,* by Jonathan Larson (New York angst); and *The Good Times Are Killing Me,* by Lynda Barry (a play with music).

Tips: "Query with synopsis character break-down and set description. Invite to concert readings in New York area."

SOUTH WESTERN COLLEGE, 900 Otay Lakes Rd., Chula Vista CA 92010. (619)421-6700. Artistic Director: W. Virchis. Play, mime and performance art work producer. Estab. 1964. Produces 6 plays and 2 musicals (1 new musical)/year. Query with synopsis. SASE. Reports in 6 weeks.

Productions: *Evita* (world college premiere); *Wiz* (black musical); *Jesus Christ Superstar* (rock opera); *Pancho Diablo* (Chicano); *Nine* (musical); *Leader of the Pack* (musical); *Laguna,* by Vic Bemeil; *Plymouth Rock,* by Scott Busath; *Nightshriek* (world premiere, rock musical based on MacBeth); and *Fantasma* (world premiere), by Edward Gallardu and Mark Allen Trujillo.

STAGE ONE, 425 W. Market St., Louisville KY 40202. (502)589-5946. Producing Director: Moses Goldberg. Play producer. Estab. 1946. Produces 8-10 plays and 0-2 musicals (0-2 new musicals)/year. Receives 200 submissions/year. "Young people ages 5-18." Pays 3-6% royalty, $1,500-3,000 outright purchase or $25-75 per performance. Submit complete manuscript and tape of songs. SASE. Reports in 4 months.

Musical Theater: "We seek stageworthy and respectful dramatizations of the classic tales of childhood, both ancient and modern. Ideally, the plays are relevant to young people and their families, as well as related to school curriculum. Cast is rarely more than 12."

Productions: *Bridge to Terabitha,* by Paterson/Toland/Leibman (contemporary novel); *Little Red Riding Hood,* by Goldberg/Cornett (fairytale); and *Tale of Two Cities,* by Kesselmann (French Revolution).

Tips: "Stage One accepts unsolicited manuscripts that meet our artistic objectives. Please do not send plot summaries or reviews. Include author's resume, if desired. In the case of musicals, a cassette tape is preferred. Cast size is not a factor, although, in practice, Stage One rarely employs casts of over 12. Scripts will be returned in approximately 3-4 months, if SASE is included. No materials can be returned without the inclusion of a SASE. Due to the volume of plays received, it is not possible to provide written evaluations."

TADA!, 120 West 28th St., New York NY 10001. (212)627-1732. Artistic Director: Janine Nina Trevens. Play producer. Estab. 1984. Produces 3 staged readings and 3-4 new musicals/year. Receives 50 outside submissions/year. "TADA! is a company producing works performed by children ages 6-17 for family audiences in New York City. Performances run approximately 30-35 performances. Pays 5% royalty. Query with synopsis and character breakdown or submit complete manuscript, score and tape of songs. SASE. Reports in 2-3 months.

Musical Theater: "We do not produce plays as full productions. At this point, we do staged readings of plays. We produce original commissioned musicals written specifically for the company."

Productions: *B.O.T.C.H.,* by Daniel Feigelson and Jon Agee (the action takes place in the subway system where children, finding their way out run into fun); and *Rabbit Sense,* by John Kroner, Gary Gardner, Davidson Lloyd (TADA!'s versions of the Uncle Remus tales, loosely based on the originals and told through stories and songs).

Tips: "When writing for children don't condescend. The subject matter should be appropriate but the music/treatment can still be complex and interesting."

*TENNESSEE REPERTORY THEATRE, 427 Chestnut St., Nashville TN 37203. (615)244-4878. Associate Artistic Director: Don Jones. Play producer. Estab. 1985. Produces 5-6 plays/year; produces 3-4 musicals (1-2 new musicals)/year. "A diverse audience of theater goers including people from Nashville's music business. Performances in a 1000-seat state-of-the-art proscenium stage."

How to Contact: Query with synopsis, character breakdown and set description. SASE. Reports in 6-8 months.

Musical Theater: "We are interested in all types of new musicals, with a leaning toward musicals that are indigenous or related to the Southern experience. We also prefer musicals with social merit. For our workshop productions there is minimal use of most elements because work on the piece is primary. For a mainstage production there are no particular limits. We budget accordingly."

Performances: *Some Sweet Day,* by D. Jones, M. Pirkle and L. Sikelu (overcoming racism to form a union); *Ain't Got Long to Stay Here,* by Barry Scott (Martin Luther King); and *A House Divided,* by M. Pirkle and Mike Reid (Civil War).

Tips: "You should submit your work with an open mind toward developing it to the fullest. Tennessee Rep can be integral to that."

THEATRE FOR YOUNG AMERICA, 7204 W. 80th St., Overland Park KS 66204. (913)648-4604. Artistic Director: Gene Mackey. Play producer. Estab. 1977. Produces 8 plays (1-2 new musicals)/year. For children, preschool to high school. Pays $15-35/performance. Unsolicited submissions OK. SASE. Reports in 2 months.
Musical Theater: 1-1½ hour productions with small cast oriented to children and high-school youths. "A clear, strong, compelling story is important; a well known title is very important."
Productions: *Androcles and the Lion,* by Aurand Harris and Glen Mack; *Little Lulu,* by Chad Henry (musical for young audience); *The Hare and the Tortoise,* by Cheryl Benge and Gene Mackey (adapted from Aesop's fable); *Tom Sawyer,* by Michael Dansicker and Sarah Marie Schlesinger (adapted from Mark Twain's novel); and *Chicken Little,* by Gene Mackey (book) and Chery Benge (music); among many other productions.

THEATRE OFF PARK, 224 Waverly Pl., New York NY 10014. (212)627-2556. Artistic Director: Albert Harris. Play producer. Estab. 1974. Produces 2-3 plays, variable number of musicals (1 new musical)/year. "We reach a broad audience of primarily middle-income, multi-ethnic and -racial patrons. Our audiences include many seniors and other Manhattanites from all walks of life." Pays by fee, approximately $1,500/work. Query with synopsis, character breakdown and set description. SASE. Reports in 2 months.
Musical Theater: "We desire to produce new musicals of many styles and lengths which give light to a diversity of social issues and lifestyles. We also encourage adaptations or revivals of rarely produced or never performed works of recognized authors. Cast limit is 8. We simply require originality and sophistication in style and presentation. Some projects envisioned would require an original incidental score."
Productions: *Stardust,* by Harris/Parish (musical revue 20's-50's); *Mlle. Colombo,* by Dulchin, Harris, Valenti (Paris, 1900); *I Could Go On Lip-synching,* by Epperson/Ross (Hollywood parody).
Tips: "Find a showcase for your work in New York which we may attend or secure the services of a New York agent who is familiar with our work and will submit for you."

THEATRE WEST VIRGINIA, Box 1205, Beckley WV 25802. (800)666-9142. General Manager: Johanna E. Young. Play producer. Estab. 1955. Produces 7-9 plays and 2-3 musicals/year. "Audience varies from main stream summer stock to educational tours to dinner theater." Pays 5% royalty or $25 per performance. Query with synopsis, character breakdown and set description; should include cassette tape. SASE. Reports in 2 months.
Musical Theater: "Theatre West Virginia is a year-round performing arts organization that presents a variety of productions including community performances such as dinner theater, *The Nutcracker* and statewide educational programs on primary, elementary and secondary levels. This is in addition to our summer, outdoor dramas of *Hatfields & McCoys* and *Honey in the Rock,* now in their 29th year." Anything suitable for secondary school tours and/or dinner theater type shows. No more than 7 in cast. Play should be able to be accompanied by piano/synthesizer.
Productions: *Thomas Jefferson Still Survives,* by Nancy Moss (historical); *Frogsong,* by Jean Battlo (literary/historical); *Guys & Dolls,* by Frank Loesser; *Grease* (currently in production), by Jim Jacobs and Warren Casey; and *Murder at the Howard Johnsons,* by Ron Clark/Sam Bobrick (comedy).

THEATREVIRGINIA, 2800 Grove Ave., Richmond VA 23221-2466. (804)367-0840. Artistic Director: William Gregg. Play producer. Estab. 1955. Produces 5-9 plays (2-5 musicals)/year. "Plays are performed in a 500-seat LORT-C house for the Richmond-area community." Payment subject to negotiation. "Please submit synopsis, sample of dialogue and sample of music (on cassette) along with a self-addressed, stamped letter-size envelope. If material seems to be of interest to us, we will reply with a solicitation for a complete manuscript and cassette. Response time for synopses is 4 weeks; response time for scripts once solicited is 5 months."
Musical Theater: "We do not deal in one-acts or in children's material. We would like to see full length, adult musicals. There are no official limitations. We would be unlikely to use original music as incidental/underscoring for existing plays, but there is potential for adapting existing plays into musicals."
Productions: *West Memphis Mojo,* by Martin Jones; *Sweeney Todd,* by Stephen Sondheim; and *South Pacific,* by Rodgers and Hammerstein.
Tips: "Read plays. Study structure. Study character. Learn how to concisely articulate the nature of your work. A beginning musical playwright, wishing to work for our company should begin by writing a wonderful, theatrically viable piece of musical theatre. Then he should send us the material requested in our listing, and wait patiently."

THEATREWORKS, 1305 Middlefield Rd., Palo Alto CA 94301. (415)323-8311. Literary Manager: Jeannie Barroga. Play producer. Estab. 1970. Produces 7 plays and 5 musicals (2 new musicals)/year. Theatrically-educated suburban area bordering Stanford University 30 miles from San Francisco and San Jose — 3 mainstages and 2 second stage performance spaces. Pays per contract. Submit complete manuscript, score or sample songs and tape of songs; synopses and character breakdowns helpful. SASE. Reports in 3-5 months.
Musical Theater: "We use original songs and music in many of our classics productions, for instance specially composed music was used in our production of the *The Tempest* for Ariel's song, the pageant song, the storm and the music of the isles. We are looking both for full-scale large musicals and smaller chamber pieces. We also use original music and songs in non-musical plays. No ancient Roman, ancient Greek or biblical settings please!"
Productions: 1990-1992 musical productions include: *Go Down Garvey* (world premiere musical); *Miami Lights* (writers in residence); *Galileo* (2nd production in writers residence); *Into the Woods, Oliver, Peter Pan, Hi Hat Hattie, O Pioneers*.
Tips: "Write a great musical. We wish there were more specific 'formula,' but that's about it. If it's really terrific, we're interested."

THEATREWORKS/USA, 890 Biway, New York NY 10003. (212)677-5959. Literary Manager: Barbara Pasternack. Play producer. Produces 10-13 plays, all are musicals (3-4 new musicals)/year. Audience consists of children and families. Pays 6% royalty and aggregate of $1500 commission-advance against future royalties. Query with synopsis, character breakdown and sample scene and song. SASE. Reports in 6 months.
Musical Theater: "One hour long, 5-6 adult actors, highly portable, good musical theater structure; adaptations of children's literature, historical or biographical musicals, issues, fairy tales — all must have something to say. We demand a certain level of literary sophistication. No kiddy shows, no camp, no fractured fables, no shows written for school or camp groups to perform. Approach your material, not as a writer writing for kids, but as a writer addressing any universal audience. You have one hour to entertain, say something, make them care — don't preach, condescend. Don't forget an antagonist. Don't waste the audience's time. We always use original music — but most of the time a project team comes complete with a composer in tow."
Productions: *Jekyll and Hyde*, book and lyrics by David Crane and Marta Kaufmann, music by Michael Sklopf; *Columbus*, by Jonathan Bolt, music by Doug Cohen, lyrics by Thomas Toce; *Class Clown*, book by Thomas West, music by Kim Oles, lyrics by Alison Hubbard.
Tips: "Write a good show! Make sure the topic is something we can market! Come see our work to find out our style."

13TH STREET REPERTORY COMPANY, 50 W. 13th St., New York NY 10011. (212)675-6677. Dramaturg: Ken Terrell. Play producer. Estab. 1974. Produces 6 plays/year including 2 new musicals. Receives 16 submissions/month. Audience comes from New York and surrounding area. Children's theater performs at 50 W. 13th in NYC. "We do not pay. The value to the playwright is having a New York production. We are off off-Broadway." Submit complete manuscript, score and tape of songs. SASE. Reports in 2 months.
Musical Theater: Children's musicals and original musical shows. Small cast with limited musicians. Stagings are struck after each performance. Would consider original music for "pre-show music or incidental music."
Productions: *Journeys*, a collaborative effort about actors' work in New York City.

UNIVERSITY OF ALABAMA NEW PLAYWRIGHTS' PROGRAM, P.O. Box 870239, Tuscaloosa AL 35487-0239. (205)348-5283. Director/Dramaturg: Dr. Paul Castagno. Play producer. Estab. 1982. Produces 8-10 plays and 1 musical/year; 1 new musical every other year. Receives 2 musical submissions/month. University audience. Pays by arrangement. Submit complete manuscript, score and tape of songs. SASE. Reports in 2 months.
Musical Theater: Any style or subject (but no children's or puppet plays). No limitations — just solid lyrics and melodic line. Drama with music, musical theater workshops, and chamber musicals. Jazz or "New Age" musicals.
Productions: *Gospel According to Esther*, by John Erlanger.
Tips: "Take your demos seriously — use a recording studio — and get *singers* to showcase your work. Use fresh sounds not derivative of the latest fare. While not ironclad by any means, musicals with Southern themes might stand a better chance."

THE UNUSUAL CABARET, 14½ Mt. Desert St., Bar Harbor ME 04609. (207)288-3306. Artistic Director: Gina Kaufmann. Play producer. Estab. 1990. Produces 4 plays and 4 new musicals/year. Educated adult audiences. 50 seat cabaret. "A casual, festive atmosphere." Pays by royalty (10% of Box). Submit complete manuscript, score and tape of songs. SASE. Reports in 1 month.

Musical Theater: "We produce both musical and non-musical scripts—45 minutes to 1¼ hours in length. Stylistically or topically unique scripts are encouraged. We strive for as diverse a season as possible within our technical limitations. Our maximum cast size is 8, but cast sizes of 4 or fewer are necessary for some of our productions. Our technical capabilities are minimal. Audience participation and non-traditional staging are possible because of the cabaret setting. We encourage musical *plays* as well as more traditional musicals. Piano is usually the only instrument. We consider adaptations if the written material is being used in an original way in conjunciton with the music."
Productions: *Hamlet; the Anti-Musical*, by Mark Milbauer and David Becker; *Dead Poets*, by Jeff Goode and John Gay (Emily Dickinson, Walt Whitman and Edgar Allen Poe); *The Beggar's Opera* (adaptation), by John Gay/adaptation: Gina Kaufmann (economic and social structure of society).
Tips: "We come from the Brecht/Weill tradition of challenging ourselves and our audiences stylistically and intellectually."

WALNUT STREET THEATRE COMPANY, 825 Walnut St., Philadelphia PA 19107. (215)574-3584. Literary Manager: Alexa Kelly. Play producer. Estab. 1982. Produces 8 plays and 2 musicals (1 new musical)/year. Plays produced on a mainstage with seating for 1,052 to a family audience; and in studio theatres with seating for 79-99 to adult audiences. Pays by royalty or outright purchase. Query with synopsis, character breakdown, set description, and ten pages. SASE. Reports in 5-6 months.
Musical Theater: "Adult Musicals. Plays are for a subscription audience that comes to the theatre to be entertained. We seek musicals with lyrical non-operatic scores and a solid book. We are looking for a small musical for springtime and one for a family audience at Christmas time. We would like to remain open on structure and subject matter and would expect a tape with the script. Cast size: around 30 equity members (10 for smaller musical); preferably one set with variations." Would consider original music for incidental music and/or underscore. This would be at each director's discretion.
Productions: *Jesus Christ Superstar*, by Rice/Lloyd-Webber; *How It Ws Done In Odessa*, by Zurbin/Haagensen; *Big River*, by Houptman/Miller.
Tips: "Send a *good quality* tape recorded in a studio with *good* singers. We listen to the tape first and if that doesn't jump out at us we don't go any further with it."

WASHINGTON JEWISH THEATRE, 6125 Montrose Rd., Rockville MD 20852. (301)881-0100. Artistic Director: Laurie Wessely. Play producer. Estab. 1984. Produces 3-5 plays/year; 50% of productions are musicals (1-2 new musicals)/year. "We are looking for new plays that have some type of Jewish theme. These themes may include biographical plays, plays with Jewish characters in leading roles, World War II plays, etc." Pays 4-8% royalty, per performance $50-100.
How to Contact: Submit complete manuscript, score and tape of songs. SASE. Does not return materials. Reports in 6 months.
Musical Theater: "We like musicals with simple sets and few characters. We have no restrictions on style, but topics must in some way conform to the concept of Jewish theater. Our usual running time is 120 minutes including intermission."
Productions: *Esther*, by Swados; *Cabaret*, by Kander and Ebb; *First Nights*, by Randoy and Glossman.

WATERLOO COMMUNITY PLAYHOUSE, Box 433, Waterloo IA 50704. (319)235-0367. Managing Director: Charles Stilwill. Play producer. Estab. 1917. Produces 12 plays (1-2 musicals)/year. "Our audience prefers solid, wholesome entertainment, nothing risque or with strong language. We perform in Hope Martin Theatre, a 368-seat house." Pays $15-150/performance. Submit complete manuscript, score and cassette tape of songs. SASE.
Musical Theater: "Casts may vary from as few as 6 people to 54. We are producing children's theater as well. We're *especially* interested in new adaptations of classic children stories."
Productions: *Music Man*, by Meredith Wilson (traditional); *Nunsense*, by Dan Goggin; *Oklahoma*, by Rogers & Hammerstein (traditional).
Tips: Looking for "new adaptations of classical children's stories or a good Christmas show."

WEST COAST ENSEMBLE, Box 38728, Los Angeles CA 90038. (213)871-8673. Artistic Director: Les Hanson. Play producer. Estab. 1982. Produces 6-9 plays and 1 new musical/year. Receives 75 submissions/year. "Our audience is a wide variety of Southern Californians. Plays will be produced in one of our two theaters on Hollywood Boulevard." Pays $35-50 per performance. Submit complete manuscript, score and tape of songs. SASE. Reports in 6 months.
Musical Theater: "There are no limitations on subject matter or style. Cast size should be no more than 12 and sets should be simple. If music is required we would commission a composer, music would be used as a bridge between scenes or to underscore certain scenes in the play."
Productions: *Gorey Stories*, by Stephen Currens (review based on material of Edward Gorey) and *Dreamers*, by Tony Tanner (musical of "A Midsummer Night's Dream").
Tips: "Submit work in good form and be patient. We look for musicals with a strong book and an engaging score with a variety of styles."

JENNY WILEY THEATRE, Box 22, Prestonsburg KY 41653-0022. (606)886-9274. General Manager: Tedi Vaughan. Play producer (Jenny Wiley Drama Association, Inc./JWDA). Produces 3-4 musicals plus 2 new musicals/year. Plays are performed for "both local and tourist audience, low middle to upper income (20-25,000 average attendance in summer) in Jenny Wiley State Resort Park Amphitheatre." Pays outright purchase of $4,000-6,000, by royalty or per performance. "Additional payment in ensuing years of performance is negotiable." SASE. Reports in 1 month.

Musical Theater: Seeking "family oriented shows and theater for young audiences not exceeding 2 hours performance time. The works should not call for more than 20 in the ensemble. Twentieth century setting works best, but historical works with music are strongly considered. Musicals should deal with Appalachia or Kentucky historical figures. Shows are produced outdoors—beware of flashy spectacle at outset of show (while it's still daylight). It must be, at its basis, family entertainment." Would also consider original music for use in play being developed "either as performance music (score and vocal), as part of a musical theater production, or as background (underscoring)."

Productions: *Big River*, by Roger Miller (Huck Finn and Jim on Mississippi); *Jenny Wiley Story*, by Dan Stein (historic drama); *Grease*.

Tips: "Present a scenario/synopsis for consideration. Call and discuss proposal or show to know if and when we might be interested in material. If we are interested, we will give aid in developing it (and funding it if it falls under our funding resource availabilities). We would like to develop quality works with appropriate music that deal with historical themes, Appalachian tales and young audience pieces. At present we need music for the Jenny Wiley Story. We want exciting original music based on colonial period music or adaptations of music of that period."

WILMA THEATER, 2030 Sansom St., Philadelphia PA 19103. (215)963-0249. Artistic Producing Director: Jiri Zizka; Artistic Producing Director: Blanka Zizka. Play producer. Produces 4-5 plays (1-2 musicals)/year. Plays are performed for a "sophisticated, adventurous, off-beat and demanding audience," in a 100-seat theater. Pays 6-8% of gross income. Submit synopsis, score and tape of songs. SASE. Reports in 2 months.

Musical Theater: Seeks "innovative staging, universal issues, political implications and inventive, witty approach to subject. We emphasize ensemble style, group choreography, actors and musicians overlapping, with new, inventive approach to staging. Do not exceed 4-5 musicians, cast of 12, (ideally under 8), or stage space of 30x20." Also interested in plays with music and songs.

Productions: *Hairy Ape*, by O'Neil (search for self-identity); *The Mystery of Irma Vep* by Charles Ludlum; *Incommunicado*, by Tom Dulak; *Marat/Sade* (basic questions of human existence); and *Three Guys Naked From the Waist Down* (worship of success).

Tips: Don't think what will sell. Find your own voice. Be original, tune to your ideas. characters and yourself."

WISDOM BRIDGE THEATRE, Dept. SM, 1559 W. Howard St., Chicago IL 60626. (312)743-0486. Producing Director: Jeffrey Ortmann. Play producer. Estab. 1974. Produces 4 plays and 1 musical/year. Plays performed in a 200-seat professional, off-loop theater. Pays 5-8% royalty. Submit through agent only. Does not return unsolicited material. Reports in 2 months.

Musical Theater: "Adult audience, not youth or children's theater. Musical should be well-written, average 2 hours in length. This is a smaller theater, so cast size should be limited." Considers original music for use in plays being developed or for use on existing plays.

Productions: *Forever Plaid*, by Stuart Ross (50s and 60s); and *Lady Day*, by Lanie Robertson (Billy Holiday).

WOMEN'S PROJECT AND PRODUCTIONS, JULIA MILES, ART DIRECTOR, 7 W. 63rd St., New York NY 10023. (212)873-3040. Literary Manager: Susan Bougetz. Estab. 1978. Produces 3 plays/year. Pays by outright purchase. Submit through agent only. SASE. Reports in 3 months. "Adult audience. Plays by women only."

Musical Theater: "We usually prefer a small to medium cast of 3-6. We produce few musicals and produce *only* women playwrights."

Productions: *A . . . My Name is Alice*, conceived by Joan Micklin Silver and Julianne Boyd (satire of women's issues); *Ladies*, by Eve Ensler (homelessness); and *O Pioneers!*, by Darrah Cloud (adapted) from Will Cather's novel.

Tips: "Resist sending early drafts of work."

WOOLLY MAMMOTH THEATRE CO., Dept. SM, 1401 Church St. NW, Washington DC 20005. (202)393-3939. Literary Manager: Greg Tillman. Play producer. Estab. 1978. Produces 3-4 plays/year. Submit complete manuscript and score and tape of songs. SASE. Reports in 8 weeks.

Musical Theater: "We do unusual works. We have done one musical, the *Rocky Horror Show* (very successful). 8-10 in cast. We do not wish to see one-acts. Be professional in presentation."
Productions: *The Day Room, Luna Vista, The Sound Man* and *The Rocky Horror Show*.
Tips: "Just keep writing! Too many people expect to make it writing one or two plays. I don't think a writer is up to speed until the fifth or sixth work!"

WORCESTER FOOTHILLS THEATRE CO., Dept. SM, 074 Worcester Center, Worcester MA 01608. (508)754-3314. Literary Manager: Thomas Ovellette. Play producer. Estab. 1974. Produces 7 plays and 1 or 2 musicals (indefinite new musicals)/year. Receives 10 submissions/month. "General audience, multi-generational. Plays are produced at Worcester Foothills Theatre, a 349-seat Proscenium stage. Pays by negotiable royalty. Query with synopsis, character breakdown and set description. SASE. "Reports back in 4 weeks for synopsis, 3-4 months for scripts."
Musical Theater: "Full length preferred, one-acts considered. Any style or topic. No gratuitous sex, violence or language. Generally a cast of 8-10 and a single set but these are not rigid restrictions."
Productions: *Ain't Misbehavin*, by Richard Moltby and Murray Horowitz (Fat's Waller music); *A Day in Hollywood*, by Dick Vosburgh and Frank Lazarus; and *Little Shop of Horrors*, by Howard Ashman/ Alan Menken; and *A Funny Thing Happened on the Way to the Forum*, by Burt Shevelove and Larry Gelbart.

Play Publishers

ARAN PRESS, 1320 S. Third St., Louisville KY 40208. (502)636-0115. Editor/Publisher: Tom Eagan. Play publisher. Estab. 1983. Publishes 40-50 plays, 1-2 musicals and 1-2 new musicals/year. Professional, college/university, community, summer stock and dinner theater audience. Pays 50% production royalty or 10% book royalty. Submit manuscript, score and tape of songs. SASE. Reports in 1-2 weeks.
Musical Theater: "The musical should include a small cast, simple set for professional, community, college, university, summer stock and dinner theater production."
Publications: *Comedy of History*, by Dick W. Zylstra (musical history); *The Big Dollar*, by Herschel Steinhardt (real estate business); and *Caribbean Blue*, by Jonathan Lowe (tropical island revolution).

BAKER'S PLAYS, 100 Chauncy St., Boston MA 02111. (617)482-1280. Editor: John B. Welch. Play publisher. Estab. 1845. Publishes 15-22 plays and 3-5 new musicals/year. Plays are used by children's theaters, junior and senior high schools, colleges and community theaters. Pays 50% royalty or 10% book royalty. Submit complete manuscript, score and cassette tape of songs. Receives 50-75 submissions/year. SASE. Reports in 2-3 months.
Musical Theater: "Seeking musicals for teen production and children's theater production. We prefer large cast, contemporary musicals which are easy to stage and produce. Plot your shows strongly, keep your scenery and staging simple, your musical numbers and choreography easily explained and blocked out. Originality and style are up to the author. We want innovative and tuneful shows but no X-rated material. We are very interested in the new writer and believe that, with revision and editorial help, he can achieve success in writing original musicals for the non-professional market." Would consider original music for use in a play being developed or in a pre-existing play.
Publications: *The High School That Dripped Gooseflesh*, by Tim Kelly, Ole Kittleson and Arne Christianson (rock 'n roll high school horror spoof); *Just Friends*, by Scanlan/Cangzano (high school friendships); and *Silent Bells*, by Jane O'Neill, Charles Apple (Christmas fable).
Tips: "As we publish musicals that can be produced by high school theater departments with high school talent, the writer should know if their play can be done on the high school stage. I recommend that the writer go to performances of original musicals whenever possible."

CONTEMPORARY DRAMA SERVICE, 885 Elkton Dr., Colorado Springs CO 80907. (719)594-4422. Executive Editor: Arthur Zapel. Assistant Editor: Rhonda Wray. Play publisher. Estab. 1979. Publishes 40-50 plays and 4-6 new musicals/year. "We publish for young children and teens in mainstream Christian churches and for teens and college level in the secular market. Our musicals are performed in churches, schools and colleges." Pays 10% royalty (for music books), 50% royalty for performance and "sometimes we pay royalty up to buy-out fee for minor works." Query first with synopsis, character breakdown and set description. SASE. Reports in 4-6 weeks.
Musical Theater: "For churches we publish musical programs for little children and teens to perform at Easter, Christmas or some special occasion. Our school musicals are for teens to perform as class plays or special entertainments. Cast size may vary from 5-25 depending on use. We prefer more parts for girls than boys. Music must be written in the vocal range of teens. Staging should be relatively simple but may vary as needed. We are not interested in elementary school material. Elementary level

is OK for church music but not public school elementary. Music must have full piano accompaniment and be professionally scored for camera-ready publication."
Publications: *The Phantom Of The Op'ry*, by Tim Kelly (a spoof of the famous mystery set in Skunk Creek, Nevada); *Beauty And The Beast*, by Lee Ahlin and Philip Hall (the classic love story set to music) and *The Little Star: A Christmas Musical*, by Michael Vigilant and Gerald Castle (the Christmas story from the star's viewpoint for a children's Sunday school department).
Tips: "Send us a cassette recording of your work."

THE DRAMATIC PUBLISHING COMPANY, 311 Washington St., Woodstock IL 60098. (815)338-7170. Music Editor: Dana Smith. Play publisher. Publishes 35 plays (3-5 musicals)/year. Estab. 1885. Plays used by community theaters, high schools, colleges, stock and professional theaters, churches and camps. Pays standard royalty. Submit complete manuscript, score and tape of songs. SASE. Reports in 3 months.
Musical Theater: Seeking "children's musicals not over 1¼ hours, and adult musicals with 2 act format. No adaptations for which the rights to use the original work have not been cleared. If directed toward high school market, large casts with many female roles are preferred. For professional, stock and community theater small casts are better. Cost of producing a play is always a factor to consider in regard to costumes, scenery and special effects." Would also consider original music for use in a pre-existng play "if we or the composer hold the rights to the non-musical work."
Publications: *The Phantom of the Opera*, book by Joseph Robinette and music by Robert Chauls (new musical based on the original book by Gaston Leroux); *Narnia*, book by Jules Tasca, lyrics by Ted Drachman and music by Thomas Tierney (musical based on C.S. Lewis' *The Lion, The Witch, and The Wardrobe*); *Sail Away*, book and music by Noel Coward; *Shakespeare and the Indians*, book and lyrics by Dale Wasserman, music by Allan Jay Friedman (from the author of Man of La Mancha comes this new musical).
Tips: "We are looking for new innovative works with small ensembles. The knowledge of synthesizers is an asset for today's market. Children's musicals are our main interest."

ELDRIDGE PUBLISHING CO., INC., P.O. Drawer 216, Franklin OH 45005. (513)746-6531. Editor: Nancy S. Vorhis. Play publisher. Estab. 1906. Publishes 20 plays and 2-3 musicals/year. Seeking "large cast musicals which appeal to students. We like variety and originality in the music, easy staging and costuming. We serve the school and church market, 6th grade through 12th; also Christmas and Easter musicals for churches." Would also consider original music for use in a play being developed; "music that could make an ordinary play extraordinary." Pays 35-50% performance royalty, $150-500 for outright purchase or 10% copy sales. Submit tape with manuscript if at all possible. Unsolicited submissions OK. SASE. Reports in 2 months.
Publications: *Don't Rock the Boat*, by Tim Kelly and Larry Nestor (cruise ship capers); *I am A Star!*, by Billie St. John and Wendell Jimerson (high schoolers vying for movie roles); *Triple Play*, by Hal Kesler and Larry Nestor (1920s baseball game).
Tips: "We're always looking for talented composers but not through individual songs. We're only interested in complete school or church musicals. Lead sheets, cassette tape and script are best way to submit. Let us see your work!"

ENCORE PERFORMANCE PUBLISHING, P.O. Box 692, Orem UT 84057. (801)225-0605. Editor: Michael C. Perry. Play publisher. Estab. 1979. Publishes 5-12 plays (including musicals)/year. "We are interested in plays which emphasize strong family values and play to all ages of audience." Pays by royalty; 50% performance, 10% book. Query with synopsis, character breakdown and set description, then submit complete manuscript, score and tape of songs. SASE. Reports in 6 weeks to 3 months.
Musical Theater: Musicals of all types for all audiences. Can be original or adapted. "We tend to favor shows with at least an equal male/female cast." Do not wish to see works that can be termed offensive or vulgar. However, experimental theater forms are also of interest.
Publications: *Puss in Boots*, by Greg Palmer (family); *The Big Bad Wolf and How He Got That Way*, by Greg Palmer (adult); and *The Secret Garden*, by Frumi Cohen (family).
Tips: "Always write with an audience in mind."

THE FREELANCE PRESS, Box 548, Dover MA 02030. (508)785-1260. Managing Editor: Narcissa Campion. Play publisher (but is affiliated with a play producer). Estab. 1979. Publishes 20 plays/year; 19 musicals (3 new musicals/year.) "Pieces are primarily for elementary to high school children; large casts (approximately 30); plays are produced by schools and children's theaters." Pays 10% of purchase price of script or score, 70% of collected royalty. Submit complete manuscript and score. SASE. Reports in 6 months.
Musical Theater: "We publish previously produced musicals and plays for children in the primary grades through high school. Plays are for large casts (approximately 30 actors and speaking parts) and run between 45 minutes to 1 hour and 15 minutes. Subject matter should be contemporary issues

(sibling rivalry, friendship, etc.) or adaptations of classic literature for children (*Alice in Wonderland*, *Treasure Island*, etc.). We do not accept any plays written for adults to perform for children."
Publications: *Monopoly*, by T. Dewey/Megan (3 high school students live out the board game); *No Zone*, by T. Dewey/Campion (environmental fantasy about effects of global warming); *The Pied Piper*, P. Houghton/Hutchins (adaptation of Browning poem).
Tips: "We enjoy receiving material that does not condescend to children. They are capable of understanding many current issues, playing complex characters, acting imaginative and unconventional material, and singing difficult music."

SAMUEL FRENCH, INC., 45 W. 25th St., New York NY 10010. (212)206-8990. Editor: Lawrence Harbison. Play publisher. Estab. 1830. Publishes 90-100 plays and 5-6 new musicals/year. Receives 100 new musical submissions per year. Amateur and professional theaters. Pays 80% of amateur royalties; 90% of professional royalties. Query first, then submit complete manuscript and tape of songs. SASE. Reports in 6 weeks to 8 months.
Musical Theater: "We publish primarily successful musicals from the NYC stage." Don't submit large-cast, big "Broadway" musicals which haven't been done on Broadway.
Publications: *Starmites*, by Keating and Ross; *Me and My Girl*, by various; and *Chess*, by Nelson/Rice/Ulvaeus/Andersson.

HEUER PUBLISHING CO./ART CRAFT PUBLISHING CO., Box 248, Cedar Rapids IA 52406. (319)364-6311. Publisher: C. Emmett McMullen. Play publisher. Estab. 1928. "We sell exclusively to junior and senior high school groups throughout the U.S. and Canada; individually, some church and related groups." Pays by royalty or by outright purchase. Query with synopsis, character breakdown and set description. SASE. Reports in 2 months.
Musical Theater: "We prefer comedies with a large number of characters. All material must be suitable for high school production and be within the scope of high school actors. We do not publish individual music. All music should be within the play material."

LILLENAS DRAMA RESOURCES, P.O. Box 419527, Kansas City MO 64141. (816)931-1900. Editor/Consultant: Paul M. Miller. Play publisher. Estab. 1912. Publishes 10 collections (2 full-length) and 4 program collections, 3 musicals (3 new musicals)/year. "Our plays and musicals are performed by churches, Christian schools, and independent theater organizations that perform 'religious' plays." Pays 10% royalty, by outright purchase ($5 per page for program material only), or $10-25/performance (selected).
How to Contact: Submit complete ms and score or, preferably, submit complete ms, score and tape of songs. SASE. Reports in 3 months.
Publications: *You Can Get There From Here*, by Lawrence & Andrea Enscoe (Youth issues plays); *Journey to the Center of the Stage*, by Martha Bolton (monologues); and *Pew Prompters*, by Lawrence & Andrea Enscoe (short sketches for church use).
Tips: "Remember that religious theater comes in all genres: do not become historically biblical; take truth and couch in terms that are understandable to contemporary audiences in and out of the church. Keep 'simplicity' as a key word in your writing; cast sizes, number of scenes/acts, costume and set requirements will affect the acceptance of your work by the publisher and the market."

C. EMMETT MCMULLEN, Heuer Publishing Co., Box 248, Cedar Rapids IA 52406. (319)364-6311. Editor: C. Emmett McMullen. Play publisher. Estab. 1928. Produces 10-15 plays/year. Plays and musicals are geared toward church groups and junior and senior high schools. Pays by royalty or by outright purchase. Submit complete manuscript and score. SASE. Reports in 2 months.
Musical Theatre: "Seeking material for high school productions. All writing within the scope of high school groups. No works with X-rated material or questionable taboos. Simplified staging and props. Currently seeking material with larger casts, preferably with more women than male roles."
Publications: *Robin Hood*, by Dan Neidermyer; *Invisible Boy*, by Robert Frankel; and *Murder At Coppersmith Inn*, by Dan Neidermyer.
Tips: "We are interested in working with new writers. Writers need to consider that many plays are presented in small—often not well-established stages."

MERIWETHER PUBLISHING, LTD. (CONTEMPORARY DRAMA SERVICE), 885 Elkton Dr., Colorado Springs CO 80907. (303)594-4422. Editor/President: Arthur Zapel. Play publisher. Estab. 1968. Publishes 40 plays and 5-10 musicals (5 new musicals)/year. Receives 40 musical play submissions/year. "We publish musicals for church school, elementary, middle grade and teens. We also publish musicals for high school secular use. Our musicals are performed in churches or high schools." Pays 10% royalty or by negotiated sale from royalties. "Sometimes we pay a royalty to a limited maximum." Query with synopsis, character breakdown and set description or submit script with cassette tape of songs. SASE. Reports in 1 month.

Musical Theater: "We are always looking for good church/school musicals for children. We prefer a length of 15-20 minutes, though occasionally we will publish a 3-act musical adaptation of a classic with large casts and sets. We like informal styles, with a touch of humor, that allow many children and/or adults to participate. We like musicals that imitate Broadway shows or have some name appeal based on the Classics. Box office appeal is more critical than message—at least for teenage and adult level fare. Musical scripts with piano accompaniments only. We especially welcome short, simple musicals for elementary and teenage, church use during the holidays of Christmas and Easter. We would like to know of arrangers and copyists."

Publications: *Beauty and the Beast*, by Lee Ahlin and Philip Hall; *Pinnochio*, by Larry Nestor and Miriam Schuman; and *Steamboat*, by Charles Boyd and Yvonne Boyd.

Tips: "Tell us clearly the intended market for the work and provide as much information as possible about its viability."

PIONEER DRAMA SERVICE, P.O. Box 22555, Denver CO 80222. (303)759-4297. Play publisher. Estab. 1963. "Plays are performed by junior high and high school drama departments, church youth groups, college and university theaters, semi-professional and professional children's theaters, parks and recreation departments." Playwrights paid by royalty (10% sales) $250-500 or by outright purchase and 50% production royalty. Unsolicited submissions OK. Reports in 6 weeks.

Musical Theater: "We seek full length children's musicals, high school musicals and one act children's musicals to be performed by children, secondary school students, and/or adults. As alway, we are seeking musicals easy to perform, simple sets, many female roles and very few solos. Must be appropriate for educational market. Developing a new area, we are actively seeking musicals to be produced by elementary schools—20 to 30 minutes in length, with 2 to 3 songs and large choruses. We are not interested in profanity, themes with exclusively adult interest, sex, drinking, smoking, etc. Several of our full-length plays are being converted to musicals. We edit them, decide where to insert music and then contact with someone to write the music and lyrics."

Publications: Published *Krazy Kamp*, by Kelly/Francoeur (comedy); *Robin Hood*, by Kelly/Christiansen/Kittleson (adaptation); *Hagar the Horrible*, by Eleanor and Ray Harder (comic strip adaptation).

Tips: "Look through our catalog. Write for junior high/high school market."

PLAYERS PRESS, INC., Box 1132, Studio City CA 91614. (818)789-4980. Associate Editor: Marjorie Clapper. Vice President: Robert W. Gordon. Play publisher. Estab. 1965. Publishes 20-30 plays, 8-10 musicals and 1-3 new musicals/year. Plays are used primarily by general audience and children. Pays 10% royalty or negotiable outright purchase. Submit complete manuscript, score and tape of songs. SASE. Reports in 1 year.

Musical Theater: "We will consider all submitted works. Presently musicals for adults and high schools are in demand. When cast size can be flexible (describe how it can be done in your work) it sells better."

Publications: *The Deerstalker*, by Doug Flack (Sherlock Holmes-musical); *Rapunzel N the Witch*, by William-Alan Landes (children's musical); and *Sunnyside Junior High*, by Rick Woyiwoda (teen musical).

Tips: "When submitting, it is best to send a clean, clear sounding tape with music. We do not publish a play or musical which has not been produced."

SALOME: A JOURNAL FOR THE PERFORMING ARTS, 5548 N. Sawyer, Chicago IL 60625. (312)539-5745. Editor: Effie Mihopoulos. Play publisher and magazine publisher. Estab. 1975. Plays and individual songs are published in the magazine. Pays by a copy of the magazine. Query with synopsis, character breakdown and set description, or submit complete manuscript, score and tape of songs. Unsolicited submissions OK. SASE. Reports in 2 weeks.

Musical Theater: Seeks eclectic plays and music. "Good quality is the only criterion."

Publications: *Jean Le Baptiste*, by Kirby Olson (2 characters interacting in a bar).

Play Producers and Publishers/'92-'93 Changes

The following markets appeared in the 1992 edition of *Songwriter's Market* but are absent from the 1993 edition.

The Alpha Theatre Project Inc.
American Living
William Carey College Dinner Theatre
Centenary College, Theatre Department

Eccentric Circles Theatre (out of business)
Geof English, Producer
Florida Studio Theatre
Don and Pat MacPherson Productions

National Music Theater Network Inc.
North Carolina Black Repertory Company
Syracuse Talent Company Inc.
Theatre Three

Fine Arts

For the aspiring composer it is vital to have his work performed for interested listeners. A resume of performances aids in identifying a composer within the concert music community. One excellent, exciting performance may lead to others by different groups or commissions for new works. (For more on this see the Close-up in this section with Libby Larsen.)

All of the groups listed in this section are interested in hearing new music. From chamber groups to symphony orchestras, they are open to new talent and feel their audiences are progressive and interested enough to support new music.

Bear in mind the financial and artistic concerns as you submit material. Fine arts groups have extremely high standards. Don't hurt your chances by sending anything but your best compositions. Always follow their submission instructions diligently. Be professional when you contact the music directors; and keep in mind the typical fine arts audience they are selecting music for. Chamber musicians and their audiences, for instance, are a good source for performance opportunities. Their repertoire is limited and most groups are enthusiastic about finding or commissioning new works. Furthermore, the chamber music audience is smaller and likewise enthusiastic enough to enjoy contemporary music.

Don't be disappointed if the payment offered by these groups seems small. Most fine arts music organizations are struggling economically and can't pay large fees to even the most established composers. Inquire into other opportunities to submit your work; many of these groups also offer periodic competitions for new works. Also, most of these ensembles belong to a blanket organization representing that genre. See the Organizations and Contests and Awards sections for more information and possibilities.

*ADRIAN SYMPHONY ORCHESTRA, 110 S. Madison St., Adrian MI 49221. (517)264-3121. Music Director: David Katz. Symphony orchestra and chamber music ensemble. Estab. 1981. Members are professionals. Performs 14 concerts/year including 2-3 new works. Commissions 1 new composer or new work/year. 1,200 seat hall—"Rural city with remarkably active cultural life." $100-2,500 for outright purchase. Submit complete score and tapes of piece(s). SASE. Reports in 6 months.
Music: Chamber ensemble to full orchestra. "Limited rehearsal time dictates difficulty of pieces selected." Does not wish to see "rock music or country western—not at this time."
Performances: Michael Pratt's *Dancing on the Wall* (orchestral—some aleatoric); Sir Peter Maxwell Davies' *Orkney Wedding* (orchestral); Gwyweth Walker's *Fanfare, Interlude, Finale* (orchestral).

AFTER DINNER OPERA CO., INC., 23 Stuyvesant St., New York NY 10003. (212)477-6212. Executive Director: Dr. Richard Flusser. Opera Company. Estab. 1949. Members are professionals. Performs 30 concerts/year, including 4 new works. Concert hall "varies from 200 to 900 seats." Pays $0-500/performance. "Send SASE with postage, or materials cannot be returned. Do not send your only copy. Mail to: Dr. Richard Flusser (H140), After Dinner Opera Co., Inc., Queensborough Community College, 222-05 56th Ave., Bayside, NY 11364-1497. We report to all submissions in May of every year."
Music: "Seeks piano vocal scores with indications of instruments from 2-17, chamber size operas from 10 minutes long to 2 hours; no more than 10 singers. Especially interested in 3 character operas under one hour in length. Also interested in operas for children. No gospel or heavy metal rock."
Performances: H.H. Beach's *Cabildo* (one act opera), William Grant Still's *Troubled Island* (opera) and Seymour Barab's *Fair Means or Foul* (children's opera).
Tips: "Start with an interesting, singable libretto. Make sure that you have the rights to the libretto."

*THE AKRON CITY FAMILY MASS CHOIR, 429 Homestead St., Akron OH 44306. (216)773-8529. President: Walter E.L. Scrutchings. Vocal ensemble. Estab. 1984. Members are professionals. Performs 2 concerts/year; performs 35 new works/year. Commissions 15 composers or new works/year.

Audience mostly interested in black gospel music. Performs in various venues. Composers paid by 50% royalty. Submit complete score and tapes of piece(s). Does not return unsolicited material. Reports in 2 months.

Music: Seeks "traditional music for SATB black gospel; also light contemporary. No rap or non-spiritual themes."

Performances: R.W. Hinton's "The Joy He Brings"; W. Scrutchings' "God Has the Power to Change Things"; and K. Woolridge's "Love Song."

THE AMERICAN BOYCHOIR, Lambert Dr., Princeton NJ 08540. (609)924-5858. Music Director: James H. Litton. Professional boychoir. Estab. 1937. Members are highly skilled children. Performs 200 concerts/year, including 15-20 new works. Commissions 1-2 composers or new works/year. Performs community concerts and for local concert associations, church concert series and other bookings. Pays by commission. Query first. SASE. Reports in 6 months.

Music: "Dramatic works for boys voices (age 10-14); 15 to 20 minutes short opera to be staged and performed throughout the USA." Choral pieces, either in unison, SSA, SA or SSAA division; unaccompanied and with piano or organ; occasional chamber orchestra accompaniment. Pieces are usually sung by 26 to 50 boys. Composers must know boychoir sonority.

Performances: Ned Rorem's *Who Has Seen The Wind* (song cycle for boys' voices); Daniel Pinkham's *Angels are Everywhere* (song cycle for boys' voices); Milton Babbitt's *Glosses* (motet for boys' voices); David Diamond's *This Sacred Ground*; and Daniel Gawthrop's *Mary Speaks*.

*ARTEA CHAMBER ORCHESTRA, #301, 2261 Market St., San Francisco CA 94114. (415)824-1234. Director: Dusan Bobb. Chamber orchestra. Estab. 1979. Members are professionals. Performs 5 concerts/year including 2 new works. Commissions 1 composer or new work/year. Herbst Theatre (928) and War Memorial Green Room (300). Mostly mature, educated, upper income audience. Pays small honorarium. Query first. Does not return unsolicited material.

Music: Seeks music for string orchestra/chamber orhcestra, 5'-30' length. 15-36 performers. Must be written within the range of the instrument. Must be legible. No pops, electronic or amplified, percussion barrage.

Performances: David Carlson's *Violin Concerto* (symphonic); Manley Romero's *Concertino for Violin* (chamber orchestra); Zeljenka's *Musica Slovaka* (string orchestra).

*ARTS COUNCIL OF GREATER KINGSPORT, 1200 E. Center St., Kingsport TN 37660. (615)392-8420. Interim Director: Donna Mason. Arts council. Estab. 1969. Members are professionals and amateurs. "We perform in a small concert hall of 350. We do produce a chamber concert series."

How to Contact: Query first. Does not return unsolicited material.

ASHEVILLE SYMPHONY ORCHESTRA, P.O. Box 2852, Asheville NC 28802. (704)254-7046. Music Director: Robert Hart Baker. Symphony orchestra, chamber ensemble, and youth orchestra. Performs 20 concerts/year, including 2 new works. Members are professionals. Commissions 1 composer or new work/year. Concerts performed in Thomas Wolfe Auditorium, which seats 2,400. Subscription audience size is approximately 1,900. Pays by outright purchase (up to $1,000 when commissioning) or via ASCAP or BMI. Submit complete score and tape of pieces. SASE. Reports in 10 weeks.

Music: Seeks "classical, pops orchestrations, full modern orchestral works, concertos and chamber music. Winds in triplicate maximum; not too many extreme high ranges or exotic time signatures/notation. Do not send unaccompanied choral works or songs for voice and piano only."

Performances: Douglas Ovens' *Play Us A Tune* (cycle for mezzo and orchestra); Howard Hanger's *For Barbara* (for jazz ensemble and orchestra); and Robert Hart Baker's *Fantasie* (arrangement of Chopin work for orchestra).

AUGSBURG CHOIR (AUGSBURG COLLEGE), 731 21st Ave. S., Minneapolis MN 55454. Director of Choral Activities: Thomas D. Rossin. Vocal ensemble (SATB choir). Members are amateurs. Performs 30 concerts/year, including 5-10 new works. Commissions 1-2 composers or new works/year. Receives 10 submissions/year. Concerts are performed in churches, concert halls, schools. Pays by outright purchase. Submit complete score. SASE. Reports in 1 month.

The asterisk before a listing indicates that the listing is new in this edition. New markets are often the most receptive to unsolicited submissions.

Music: Seeking "sacred choral pieces, no more than 5-7 minutes long, to be sung a capella or with obbligato instrument. Can contain vocal solos. We have 50-60 members in our choir. We do not want secular, jazz or pop songs."

Performances: Donald Busarow's *Hymne*; Leland Sateren's *Laudate* and Stephen Paulus' *Peace*.

AUREUS QUARTET, 22 Lois Ave., Demarest NJ 07627-2220. (201)767-8704. Artistic Director: James J. Seiler. Vocal ensemble (a cappela ensemble). Estab. 1979. Members are professionals. Performs 35-40 concerts/year, including 3 new works. Pays $150-1,500 for outright purchase. Query first. SASE. Reports in 1 month.

Music: "We perform anything from pop to classic—mixed repertoire so anything goes. Some pieces can be scored for orchestras as we do pops concerts. Up to now, we've only worked with a quartet. Could be expanded if the right piece came along. Level of difficulty—no piece has ever been to hard." Does not wish to see electronic or sacred pieces. "Electronic pieces would be hard to program. Sacred pieces not performed much. Classical/jazz arrangements of old standards are great!"

Tips: "We perform for a very diverse audience—luscious, four part writing that can showcase well-trained voices is a must. Also, clever arrangements of old hits from '20s through '50s are sure bets. (Some pieces could take optional accompaniment.)"

BALTIMORE OPERA COMPANY, INC., 101 W. Read St., Baltimore MD 21201. (301)727-0592. Artistic Administrator: James Harp. Opera company. Estab. 1950. Members are professionals. Performs 16 concerts/year. Receives 10 outside submissions/year. "The opera audience is becoming increasingly diverse. Our performances are given in the 3,000-seat Lyric Opera House." Pays by outright purchase. Submit complete score and tapes of piece(s). SASE. Reports in 1-2 months.

Music: "Our General Director, Mr. Michael Harrison, is very much interested in presenting new works. These works would be anything from Grand Opera with a large cast to chamber works suitable for school and concert performances. We would be interested in perusing all music written for an operatic audience."

Performances: Verdi's *Don Carlo*, Donizetti's *La Fille Du Régiment*; and Mozart's *Die Zauberflöte*.

Tips: "Opera is the most expensive art form to produce. Given the current economic outlook, opera companies cannot be too avant garde in their selection of repertoire. The modern operatic composer must give evidence of a fertile and illuminating imagination, while also keeping in mind that opera companies have to sell tickets."

BILLINGS SYMPHONY, 401 N. 31st St. 5th Floor, Billings MT 59101. (406)252-3610. Music Director: Dr. Uri Barnea. Symphony orchestra, orchestra and chorale. Estab. 1950. Members are professionals and amateurs. Performs 10 concerts/year, including 5-8 new works. Audience: mostly adults. Hall: Alberta Bair Theater (capacity 1,418). Pays by royalty or outright purchase. Query first. SASE. Reports in 4 months.

Music: Any style. Traditional notation preferred.

Performances: Ellen Taaffe Zwilich's *Images* (two pianos and orchestra), Allen Vizzutti's *Snow Scenes* (trumpet and orchestra) and Graham Whettam's *An English Suite* (orchestra).

Tips: "Write *good* music. Make sure score and parts are legible and ready for use (rehearsal numbers, other instructions, etc.)."

THE BOSTON MUSICA VIVA, Suite 612, 295 Huntington Ave., Boston MA 02116-5713. Manager: Hilary Field. Chamber music ensemble. Estab. 1969. Members are professionals. Performs 12-20 concerts/year, including 6-10 new works. Commissions 3-5 composers or new works/year. "We perform our subscription series in a hall that seats 300, and our audience comes from Boston, Cambridge and surrounding areas. Frequent tours have taken the ensemble across the U.S. and the world." Pays by commission. Submit complete score and tapes of piece(s). Does not return unsolicited material. Reports in months.

Music: "We are looking for works for: flute, clarinet, percussion, piano, violin, viola and cello plus vocalist (or any combination thereof). Made for no more than 10 performers. We're looking for exciting avant garde music. We don't particularly want to see anything on the pop side."

Performances: HK Gruber's *Cello Concerto in One Movement* (chamber concerto); Paul Earls' *Eliotime* (chamber work); Kathryn Alexander's *Song of Songs* (song cycle); and William Kraft's *Settings from Pierrot Lunaire* (world premiere).

BRECKENRIDGE MUSIC INSTITUTE, P.O. Box 1254, Breckenridge CO 80424. (303)453-9142. Executive Director: Pamela G. Miller. Chamber orchestra with ensembles: brass and woodwind quintets and a vocal quartet. Estab. 1980. Members are professionals. Performs more than 30 concerts/year, including several new works. Commissions 1 composer or new work/year. "We perform our main festival season in a tent—we are in a resort area, so our audiences are a mix of local citizens and visitors." Chamber orchestra concerts: 300-400 people; chamber ensemble recitals: 125-250 people;

choral/orchestra concert: 450 people. "Our concerts include remarks, notes and commissioned work." Query first. Does not return unsolicited material. Usually reports in several months, but depends on the time of year the work is submitted.
Music: "Typically, we try to premiere an orchestral piece each year and highlight the composer's other work during a 4-5 day composer-in-residence program. We need *chamber* orchestra or ensemble music only—nothing for more instrumentation." Doesn't want to see "pops."
Performances: Evan Copley's *Symphony No. 8* (world premiere); Cecil Effinger's *Capriccio for Chamber Orchestra* (world premiere); William Schmidt's *Miniatures for Chamber Orchestra* (world premiere); and Sharon Davis' *Songs for Soprano and Orchestra* (world premiere).

BREMERTON SYMPHONY ASSOCIATION INC., 535B 6th St., P.O. Box 996, Bremerton WA 98310. (206)373-1722. Contact: Music Director. Symphony orchestra. Estab. 1942. Members are amateurs. Performs 8 concerts/year, including a varying number of new works. The audience is half seniors, half adult. 1,200-seat hall in Bremerton High School; excellent acoustics. Submit complete score and tape of piece(s). SASE. Reports in 1 month.
Music: Submit works for full orchestra, chorus and soloists. "Should be good for competent community orchestras." Do not wish to see "pop" music charts.
Performances: Rick Vale's *Symphony #1 "Christmas"* (orchestra/chorus/soloists).

BREVARD SYMPHONY ORCHESTRA, INC., P.O. Box 361965, Melbourne FL 32936-1965. (407)242-2024. Chairman: Darcie Jones-Francey. Symphony orchestra. Estab. 1954. Members are professionals and amateurs. Performs 15-20 concerts/year. "King Center for the Performing Arts, Melbourne, FL: 1,842 seats; Fine Arts Auditorium, Cocoa, FL: 599 seats; Astronaut High School Auditorium, Titusville, FL: 399 seats." Pay negotiable "(VERY limited funding)." Submit complete score and tapes of piece(s). SASE. Reports in 2 months.
Music: "Submit orchestral works with and without soloists, full symphonic orchestration, 5-45 minutes in length, contemporary and popular styles as well as serious compositions." "No non-orchestral materials. Our community is fairly conservative and inexperienced in contemporary music, so a subtle, gradual introduction would be appropriate."
Performances: Brahms' *Academic Festival Overture* (orchestra); Bruch's *Scottish Fantasy for Violin* (orchestra); Shostakovich's *Symphony #5* (orchestra).
Tips: "Remember the audience that we are trying to introduce and educate."

CANADIAN CHILDREN'S OPERA CHORUS, #215, 227 Front St. E., Toronto **Canada** M5A 1E8. (416)366-0467. Manager: Suzanne Bradshaw. Children's vocal ensemble. Estab. 1968. Members are amateurs. Performs 2-3 concerts/year. Performs choral Christmas concert in a church with candlelight; spring opera production often at Harbourfront, Toronto. Pays by outright purchase; "CCOC applies to Ontario Arts Council or the Canada Council for commission fees." Query first. SAE and IRC. Reports in 2 months.
Music: "Operas of approximately 1 hour in length representing quality composers. In addition, the portability of a production is important; minimal sets and accompaniment. CCOC prefers to engage Canadian composers whose standards are known to be high. Being a nonprofit organization with funding difficulties, we prefer piano accompaniments or just a few instruments."
Performances: W.A. Mozart's *Bastien & Bastienne*; Poulenc's *Petites Voix*; and John Rutter's *Dancing Day* (all operas).

*CANTATA ACADEMY, 2441 Pinecrest Dr., Ferndale MI 48220. (313)546-0420. Music Director: Frederick Bellinger. Vocal ensemble. Estab. 1961. Members are professionals. Performs 10-12 concerts/year including 5 works. Commissions 1-2 composers or new works/year. "We perform in churches and small auditoriums throughout the Metro Detroit area for audiences of about 500 people." Pays $100-500 for outright purchase. Submit complete score. SASE. Reports in 1-3 months.
Music: Four-part a cappela and keyboard accompanied works, two and three-part works for men's or women's voices. Some small instrumental ensemble accompaniments also acceptable. Work must be suitable for forty voice choir. No works requiring orchestra or large ensemble accompaniment. No pop.
Performances: Charles S. Brown's *Five Spirituals* (concert spiritual); Bruno Kazenas' *Music When Soft Voices Die* (A capella with soprano solo); and Libby Larsen's *Ringetanze* (Christmas choral with handbells & keyboard).
Tips: "Be patient. Would prefer to look at several different samples of work at one time."

CAPITAL UNIVERSITY CONSERVATORY OF MUSIC OPERA/MUSICAL THEATRE, 2199 E. Main St., Columbus OH 43209-2394. (614)236-6122. Director, Opera/Musical Theatre: William Florescu. College opera/musical theater program. Estab. 1970. Members are students. Performs 2 concerts/year, including 1-2 new works. Commissions 1 composer or new work/year. Receives 3-4 outside submissions/

year. "The audience is basically a community arts audience and family and friends of performers. Mees Hall Auditorium (cap. 1,100) is where we perform big, standard works. The Toledo Room (cap. 255) is where we perform chamber and experimental works. Both of these halls are to be upgraded and renovated in the next year-and-a-half." Pays by royalty or $50-150 per performance. Submit complete score and tapes of piece(s). SASE. Reports in 2 weeks.

Music: "I am seeking music theater pieces, particularly of a 'chamber' nature. I am open to a wide variety of musical styles, although the music should be singable for undergraduates; piano or small ensemble accompaniment. Ideally, pieces should be for 4-6 performers, most of whom will be able to tackle a wide variety of musical styles. Ideal length for works should be 15 minutes to 45 minutes. I am not particularly interested in 'rock' pieces, although if they work theatrically, I would certainly consider them."

Performances: Chris Becker's (a Capital student) *Satie* (music theater piece); Gustav Holst's *The Wandering Scholar* (chamber opera); and Milton Granger's *The Proposal* (chamber opera).

Tips: "If a composer is interested in writing for the situation we have here at Capital, I would suggest he or she either write or call me to *specifically* discuss a project. This will help both sides bring the performance about."

CARSON CITY CHAMBER ORCHESTRA, P.O. Box 2001, Carson City NV 89702-2001 or 191 Heidi Circle, Carson City NV 89701-6532. (702)883-4154. Conductor: David C. Bugli. Amateur community orchestra. Estab. 1984. Members are amateurs. Performs 5 concerts, including 1 new work/year. Receives 3 outside submissions/year. "Most concerts are performed for about 300 listeners in the Carson City Community Center Auditorium, which seats 840. However, the mid-December concerts have audiences as large as 700. We have no provisions for paying composers at this time but may later." Submit complete score. SASE. Reports in 2 months.

Music: "We want classical, pop orchestrations, orchestrations of early music for modern orchestras, concertos for violin or piano, holiday music for chorus and orchestra (children's choirs and handbell ensemble available), music by women, music for brass choir. Most performers are amateurs, but there are a few professionals who perform with us. Available winds and percussion: 2 flutes and flute/piccolo, 2 oboes (E.H. double), 3 clarinets in B flat, 1 bass clarinet, 2 bassoons, 3 or 4 horns, 3 trumpets, 3 trombones, 1 tuba, timpani, and some percussion. Strings: 10-12-3-5-2. Avoid rhythmic complexity (except in pops); no 12-tone music that lacks melodic appeal. Composers should contact us first. Each concert has a different emphasis. Note: Associated choral group, Carson Chamber Singers, performs several times a year with the orchestra and independently."

Performances: Ernest Martinez' *Torbellino*; David Bugli's *State of Metamorphosis* (overture); and *Variations on "My Dancing Day"* (theme and variations on an English Christmas carol). Premieres also include arrangements of Christmas and popular tunes.

Tips: "It is better to write several short movements well than to write long, unimaginative pieces, especially when starting out. Be willing to revise after submitting the work, even if it was premiered elsewhere."

CASCADE SYMPHONY ORCHESTRA, 9630 214th Pl. S.W., Edmonds WA 98020. (206)778-6934. Director/Conductor: Roupan Shakarian. Manager: Ed Aliverti. Symphony orchestra. Estab. 1962. Members are professionals and amateurs. Performs 4-5 concerts/year, including 2-3 new works. "Audience is knowledgeable with a variety of backgrounds and interests—excellent cross-section. Perform in a rather old auditorium seating 950." Submit complete score and tapes of pieces. SASE. Reports in 6 weeks.

Music: "Music should be suitable for symphony orchestra. Nothing over 20 minutes."

Performances: Paul Creston's *Dance Overture* (various dance rhythms); and Daniel Barry's *Sound Scapes* (Premiere based on ostenatos).

*CENTRAL KENTUCKY YOUTH ORCHESTRA, 161 North Mill St., Lexington KY 40507. (606)254-0796. Music Director: Elizabeth Stoyanovich. Youth orchestra. Estab. 1947. Members are amateurs and students. Performs 6 concerts/year including 1 new work. Commissions 1 composer or new works/year. "Singletary Center for the Arts holds 1,500 people; it is a modern auditorium. Our audience is mostly parents and friends of Central Kentucky Youth Orchestra." Pays commission. Submit complete score and tapes of piece(s). SASE. Reports in 2-6 months.

Music: 4,2,3,2, 6,4,3,1 percussion and full strings; youth orchestra level. The musicians are high school students.

CHAMBER MUSIC IN YELLOW SPRINGS, INC., P.O. Box 448, Yellow Springs OH 45387. (513)767-1458. President: Bruce Bradtmiller. Chamber music presenting organization. Estab. 1983. Members are volunteer staff. Performs 5 concerts/year. "Have commissioned a composer once in 1989. The audience is very enthusiastic and quite knowledgeable in chamber music. The hall is a church, seating 280 with excellent acoustics." Pays $5,000 for outright purchase. Query first.

Music: "We are interested in innovative chamber music; however the composer should approach us with an ensemble identified. We are a chamber music presenting organization. We rarely present groups with more than 6 performers." Does not wish to see popular music.
Performances: Rick Sowash's *Anecdotes and Reflections* (instrumental, chamber work, violin, cello, piano, clarinet).
Tips: "We book primarily on the quality of ensemble. A composer should make an arrangement with a top-notch group and approach us through the ensemble's agent."

CHORUS OF WESTERLY, 16 High St., Westerly RI 02891. (401)596-8664. Music Director: George Kent. Community chorus. Estab. 1959. Members are professionals and amateurs. Performs 12 concerts/year including 1-2 new works. "4 'major works' concerts/year and 2 'pops' concerts/year. Summer pops reaches audiences of 28,000." Pays by outright purchase. Submit complete score and tapes of pieces. Reports in 3 weeks.
Music: "We normally employ a full orchestra from Boston. Major works desired — although 'good' pops charts considered."
Performances: Brahms' *Requiem* and Holst's *Choral Symphony*.

CINNABAR OPERA THEATER, 3333 Petaluma Blvd. N., Petaluoma CA 94952. (707)763-8920. Artistic Director: Marvin Klebe. Opera company. Estab. 1974. Members are professionals. Performs 35 concerts/year, including 2 new works. "Audience is ⅓ local, ⅓ Sonoma county, ⅓ greater San Francisco Bay area; theater is converted mission revival schoolhouse seating 99-150; no orchestra pit." Pays by arrangement with composer. Query first. SASE.
Music: "Our musical taste can best be described as eclectic. We produce full-length and one-act works; small orchestrations are preferred. Small casts are preferred. We are interested in works appropriate for opera singers who are also actors."

COLORADO CHILDREN'S CHORALE, Suite 1020, 910 15th St., Denver CO 80202. (303)892-5600. Artistic Director: Duain Wolfe. Vocal ensemble and highly trained children's chorus. Estab. 1974. Members are professionals and amateurs. Performs 100-110 concerts/year, including 3-5 new works. Commissions 1-3 composers or new works/year. Receives 3-4 outside submissions/month. "Our audiences' ages range from 5-80. We give school performances and tour (national, international). We give subscription concerts and sing with orchestras (symphonic and chamber). Halls: schools to symphony halls to arenas to outdoor theaters." Pays $100-500 outright purchase (more for extended works). Submit complete score and tapes of piece(s). Does not return unsolicited material. Reports in 2 months.
Music: "We want short pieces (3-5 minutes): novelty, folk arrangement, serious; longer works 5-20: serious; staged operas/musicals 30-45 minutes: piano accompaniment or small ensemble; or possible full orchestration if work is suitable for symphony concert. We are most interested in SA, SSA, SSAA. We look for a variety of difficulty ranges and encourage very challenging music for SSA-SSAA choruses (32 singer, unchanged voices). We don't want rock, charts without written accompaniments or texts that are inappropriate for children. We are accessible to all audiences. We like some of our repertoire to reflect a sense of humor, others to have a message. We're very interested in well crafted music that has a special mark of distinction."
Performances: Henry Milliconi's *The Midnight Ride of Paul Revere* (contemporary); Randall Thompson's *The Place of the Blest* (sacred, medieval text); Sherman and Sherman's *Tom Sawyer*; and Lee Hoiby's *The Nations Echo 'Round*.
Tips: "Submit score and tape with good cover letter, resume and record of performance. Wait at least 3 weeks before a follow-up call or letter."

*COMMONWEALTH OPERA INC., 160 Main St., Northampton MA 01060. (413)586-5026. Artistic Director: Richard R. Rescia. Opera company. Estab. 1977. Members are professionals and amateurs. Performs 4 concerts/year. "We perform at the Academy of Music at Northampton in an 800 seat opera house. Depending on opera, audience could be family oriented or adult." Pays by royalty. Query first. Does not return materials. Reports in months.
Music: "We are open to all styles of opera. We have the limitations of a regional opera company with local chorus. Principals come from a wide area. We look only at opera scores."
Performances: Leoncavallo's *I Pagliacci* (opera); Mozart's *Don Giovanni* (opera); and Menotti's *Amahl and the Night Visitors* (opera).
Tips: "We're looking for opera that is accessible to general public and performable by standard opera orchestra."

*COMMUNITY MUSIC PROJECT, P.O. Box 68, Jamestown NY 14702-0068. (716)664-2227. General Manager/Artistic Director: Elaine Hammond/Lee Spear. Vocal ensemble and community chorus. Estab. 1978. Members are both professionals and amateurs. Performs 12-15 concerts/year including

4-6 new works. "Performs in various venues: Civic center (1300 seat) and local churches (200-500 seat). Jamestown is a small city in Western NY state with a moderately sophisticated audience." Query first. SASE. Reports in 6 months.
Music: 3-10 minute choral work, SATB, in English, with or without accompaniment. "Emphasis on sensitive English language prosody."
Performances: Sang Wook Jo's *I Wandered Lonely as a Cloud* (SATB chorus with pf.); Aaron Copland's *In the Beginning* (M-S, SATB chorus unaccompanied); and Ann Kearns' *The Angle of a Landscape* (SATB chorus unaccompanied).

CONCORDIA: A CHAMBER SYMPHONY, 21st Floor, 330 Seventh Ave., New York NY 10001. (212)967-1290. Executive Director: Leslie Stifelman. Symphony orchestra. Estab. 1984. Members are professionals. Performs 5 concerts/year, including 5-6 new works. Commissions 2-3 composers or new works/year. Receives 35-40 outside submissions/year. "Lincoln Center, Alice Tully Hall. Audiences between 28 and 50 years, mostly." Pays contest winner's prize and copying. Query first. SASE. Reports in 4 months.
Music: 11 minutes, 2,2,2,2/2,2,1,0/strings percussion; piano.
Performances: Jon Deak's *The Legend of Spuyten Duyvil*; Laura Karpman's *Switching Stations* (jazz fusion); Michael Daugherty's *Snap*; and Jeffrey Hass's *City Life* (jazz scored for chamber orchestra).
Tips: In 1992 Concordia introduced The Concordia American Composer's Award sponsored by American Express Company. Call for information.

CONNECTICUT CHORAL ARTISTS, 90 Main St., New Britain CT 06051. (203)224-7500. Artistic Director: Richard Coffey. Professional concert choir. Estab. 1974. Members are professionals. Performs 10-15 concerts/year, including 2-3 new works. "Mixed audience in terms of age and background; performs in various halls and churches in the region." Payment "depends upon underwriting we can obtain for the project." Call and obtain permission to submit. "No unsolicited submissions accepted." SASE. Reports in 6 months.
Music: Seeking "works for mixed chorus of 36 singers; unaccompanied or with keyboard and/or small instrumental ensemble; text sacred or secular/any langauge; prefers suites or cyclical works, total time not exceeding 15 minutes. Performance spaces and budgets prohibit large instrumental ensembles. Works suited for 750-seat halls are preferable. Substantial organ or piano parts acceptable. Scores should be very legible in every way. Though not a requirement, we find that works with sacred texts get wider coverge."
Performances: Bernstein's *Missa Brevis (1988* regional premiere; based upon his *The Lark*); Frank Martin's *Mass for Double Chorus* (regional premiere); Villa-Lobos' *Magdalena* (performed 1987 revival at Lincoln Center and recorded for CBS).
Tips: "Use conventional notation and be sure manuscript is legible in every way. Recognize and respect the vocal range of each vocal part. Work should have an identifiable *rhythmic* structure."

*CYPRESS "POPS" ORCHESTRA, P.O. Box 2623, Cypress CA 90630-1323. (714)527-0964. Music Director: John E. Hall III. Symphony orchestra. Estab. 1989. Members are professionals. Performs 10 concerts/year including 25 new works. Commissions 2 composers or new works/year. Average family size 4—popular entertainment for all age levels. Pays by outright purchase $200-500. Submit complete score and tapes of piece(s). SASE. Reports in 1 month.
Music: Strictly popular light classical selections 5-12 minute duration for full orchestra. #1 level of proficiency—very high. Contemporary films, TV themes/songs of 70s to present.
Performances: Friedman's "Millinenum" (John Williams Style orchestral) and "New York, New York" (vocal arrangement); J. Bradley's "On a Wonderful Day" (vocal); and "God Bless the USA" (vocal).
Tips: "1990s composers need to be conscious of audiences listening capabilities. Should compose or arrange material in popular styled selections."

*DALLAS CHAMBER ORCHESTRA, #302, 3630 Harry Hines, Dallas TX 75219. (214)520-3121. Executive Director: Jack Bunning. Chamber orchestra. Estab. 1979. Members are professionals. Performs 30 concerts/year including 3-4 new works. Pays by royalty, outright purchase or performance. Query first. SASE. Reports in 6-8 months.

DENVER CHAMBER ORCHESTRA, #1360, 1616 Glenarm Pl., Denver CO 80202. (303)825-4911. Executive Director: Barbara Kelly. 35 piece chamber orchestra. Estab. 1968. Members are professionals. Performs 25 concerts/year, including 1 new work. Commissions 1 composer or new work/year. "Perform in a 500-seat auditorium in an arts complex and at Historic Trinity Church in Denver which seats 1,100. Usually pay the composer's air fare and room and board for the performance; sometimes an additional small stipend." Query first. SASE. Reports in 2 months.

Music: Seeks "10-12 minute pieces orchestrated for 35-40 instruments. No pop, symphonic."
Performances: Edward Smaldone and Otto Luening's *Dialogue*; and Steven Heitzig's *Flower of the Earth: Homage to Georgia O'Keefe*.
Tips: "Submit a query, which we will submit to our music director."

*DESERT CHORALE, P.O. Box 2813, Santa Fe NM 87504-2813. (505)988-2282. FAX: (505)988-7522. Music Director: Lawrence Bandfield. Vocal ensemble. Members are professionals. Performs 50 concerts/year including 2 new works. Commissions 1 new composer or new work/year. "Highly sophisticated, musically literate audiences. We sing most concerts in a 220-year-old adobe church which seats 250." Pays by royalty and/or additional commission. Query first. Phone interview with Music Director preferred." Does not return unsolicited material. Reports in 8 months.
Music: "Challenging chamber choir works 6 to 20 minutes in length. Accompanied works are limited by space—normally no more than 5 or 6 players. No more than 24 singers, but they are all highly skilled musicians. No short church anthem-type pieces."
Performances: Dominick Argento's *al Toccata of Galuppi's* (mixed choir, strigrtet, harpsichord); Lawrence Cave's *The Seasons of Meng-Hao-Jan* (unaccompanied mixed choir); and Steven Sametz's *O Llama de amor Viva* (unaccompanied mixed choir).

DIABLO VALLEY PHILAHARMONIC, 321 Golf Club Rd., Pleasant Hill CA 94523. (510)685-1230, Ext. 454. Conductor: Fredric Johnson. Symphony orchestra. Estab. 1974. Members are both professionals and amateurs. Performs 5 concerts/year, including 2 new works. Sometimes commissions 1 composer or new work/year. "We perform in a 400-seat hall to a California audience. They'll go for anything new or unique if we don't overload them (i.e. quantity)." Pays through ASCAP. Submit complete score or complete score and tapes of piece(s). SASE.
Music: "Music must be for full romantic orchestra, without extra parts (harp, piano, English horn, Kazoo)—it's too expensive. Pieces should be of reasonable difficulty for about 65 musicians."
Performances: Marilyn Shufro's *Ciudades: Toledo y Seville* (orchestra); Earle Browne's *Modules* (orchestra); and Aaveneinen's *Rain* (suite for accordian/strings).
Tips: "Our orchestra is formed at the beginning of the season; it's tough to get the good musician in mid-season, so please avoid extra or exotic instruments."

EASTERN NEW MEXICO UNIVERSITY, Station 16, Portales NM 88130. (505)562-2736. Director of Orchestral Activities: Robert Radmer. Symphony orchestra, small college-level orchestra with possible choral collaboration. Estab. 1934. Members are students (with some faculty). Performs 6 concerts/year, including up to 2 new works. Receives 10 submissions/year. "Our audiences are members of a college community and small town. We perform in a beautiful, acoustically fine 240-seat hall with a pipe organ." Query first, submit complete score and tapes of piece(s), submit complete score or submit through agent only. SASE. Reports in 2 months.
Music: "Pieces should be 12-15 minutes; winds by 2, full brass. Work shouldn't be technically difficult. Organ, harpsicord, piano(s) are available. We are a small college orchestra; normal instrumentation is represented but technical level uneven throughout orchestra. We have faculty available to do special solo work. We like to see choral-orchestral combinations and writing at different technical levels within each family, i.e., 1st clarinet might be significantly more difficult than 2nd clarinet."
Performances: Poulenc's *Gloria* (choral/orchestra); Mozart's *Requiem* (choral/orchestra); John Dankworth's *Tom Sawyer's Saturday Night* (narrator/orchestra).
Tips: "I would like to see a choral/orchestral score in modern idiom for vocal solo(s), a chamber choir and large chorus used in concertino/ripeno fashion, with full brass and percussion, featuring first chair players."

EUROPEAN COMMUNITY CHAMBER ORCHESTRA, Fermain Howe, Dolphin St., Colyton EX136LM **United Kingdom**. Phone: (44)297 52272. General Manager: Ambrose Miller. Chamber orchestra. Members are professionals. Performs 70 concerts/year, including 5-10 new works. Commissions 2 composers or new works/year. Performs regular tours of Europe, Americas and Asia, including major venues. Pays $500/performance. Query first. SAE and IRC. Reports in 3 months.
Music: Seeking compositions for strings, 2 oboes and 2 horns with a duration of about 10 minutes.
Performances: John McCabe's *Red Leaves* (strings, 2 oboes, 2 horns); Giovanni Sollima's *The Columbus Egg* (strings); Javier Darias' *Terra Mutante* (strings).
Tips: "European Community Chamber Orchestra works without conductor, so simplicity is paramount."

Listings of companies in countries other than the U.S. have the name of the country in boldface type.

FAIRFAX SYMPHONY ORCHESTRA, Box 1300, Annandale VA 22003. (703)642-7200. Composer-in-Residence: Daniel E. Gawthrop. Symphony orchestra. Estab. 1957. Members are professionals. Performs 50 concerts/year, including 2 new works. Receives 12 submissions/year. "We perform at two halls: George Mason University's Concert Hall which seats 1939; and The Kennedy Center Concert Hall which seats 2759." Pays by commission. Submit complete score and tape of pieces. SASE. Reports in 2-3 months.
Music: "All styles appropriate to symphony orchestra (106 players) or chamber orchestra (50 players). Do not want pop or New Age music."
Performances: Ellen Taafe Zwilich's *Cello Symphony*; David Stock's *Symphony in One Movement*; Michael Colgrass's *As Quiet As . . .*; Daniel E. Gawthrop's *Merlin's Vision*; and Nicholas Maw's *Spring Music*.

THE FLORIDA ORCHESTRA, Suite 512, 1211 N. Westshore Blvd., Tampa FL 33607. (813)286-1170. General Manager: Alan Hopper. Symphony orchestra. Estab. 1968. Members are professionals. Performs 150 concerts/year, including 2 new works. Audiences are "young professionals to established community business people. We perform in three halls of high artistic quality." Average seating is 2,000 per hall. Submit complete score and tapes of piece(s). SASE. Reports in months.
Music: "We want high quality popular programming for pops, park and youth concerts; 5-15 minutes in length utilizing full orchestra. We don't want electric instruments. We like nostalgia, pops or light classical arrangement."
Performances: Joan Tower's *Island Rhythms* (contemporary symphonic); John Harbison's *Remembering Gatsby* (contemporary symphonic); and St. Saens' *Carnival of the Animals* (light classical).
Tips: "Make it marketable within the context of a symphony orchestra that is trying to appeal to a wide audience."

FLORIDA SPACE COAST PHILHARMONIC, INC., P.O. Box 3344, Cocoa FL 32924 or 2150 Lake Dr., Cocoa FL 32926. (407)632-7445. General Manager: Alyce Christ. Artistic Director and Conductor: Maria Tunicka. Philharmonic orchestra and chamber music ensemble. Estab. 1986. Members are professionals. Performs 7-14 concerts/year. Concerts are performed for "average audience – they like familiar works and pops. Concert halls range from 600 to 2,000 seats." Pays 10% royalty (rental); outright purchase of $2,000; $50-600/performance; or by private arrangement. Query first; submit complete score and tape of piece(s). SASE. Reports 1-3 months; "our conductor tours frequently thus we have to keep material until she has a chance to see and hear it."
Music: Seeks "pops and serious music for full symphony orchestra, but not an overly large orchestra with unusual instrumentation. We use about 60 musicians because of hall limitations. Works should be medium difficulty – not too easy and not too difficult – and not more than 10 minutes long." Does not wish to see avante-garde music.
Performances: Marta Ptaszynska's *Marimba Concerto* (marimba solo); Prof. Charles Gabrielle's *Christopher Columbus Suite for Symphony Orchestra* (world premiere); Dr. Elaine Stone's *Christopher Columbus Suite for Symphony Orchestra* (world premiere).
Tips: "If we would commission a work it would be to feature the space theme in our area."

*FONTANA CONCERT SOCIETY, 821 W. South St., Kalamazoo MI 49007. (616)382-0826. Artistic Director: Neill Sanders. Chamber music ensemble presenter. Estab. 1980. Members are professionals. Performs 20 concerts/year including 1-2 new works. commissions 1 composers or new works/year. Summer – 200 seat hall; Fall/winter – various venues, from churches to libraries to 500-seat theaters. Submit complete score and tapes of piece(s). SASE. Reports in 1 month.
Music: "Good chamber music – any combination of strings, winds, piano." No "pop" music, new age type. "We like to see enough interest for the composer to come for a premiere and talk to the audience."
Performances: Ramon Zupko's *Folksody* (piano trio-premiere); Sebastian Carrier's *Vocalissimus* (soprano, 4 percussion, strings, winds, piano-premiere); and Donald Tovey's *Horn Trio*.
Tips: "Provide a resume and clearly marked tape of a piece played by live performers. We have received some recent tapes done by "synthesizer" sounds. Our director won't even listen to it unless it's been played by somebody."

GRAND TETON MUSIC FESTIVAL, P.O. Box 490, Teton Village WY 83025. (307)733-3050. Music Director: Ling Tung. Symphony orchestra and chamber music ensemble. Estab. 1962. Members are professionals. Performs 45 concerts/year. Commissions 1-3 new works/year. "Concerts are aimed at people interested in wide variety of classical music. Concert hall is an enclosed, all-wood structure seating approximately 700." Pays weekly honorarium plus travel expenses. Query first. Does not return unsolicited material. Reports in 6 months.

Music: "For the most part, the Festival performs standard repertoire. New music is usually restricted to small ensembles (less than 10 players), although occasionally, if a noted composer is involved, the orchestra will perform a large scale work. Generally less than 10 players, no restriction on difficulty. No musical theater or opera."

Performances: Joan Tower's *Petroushskates* (quintet: flute, clarinet, violin, cello and piano); John Harbison's *Woodwind Quintet*; and George Crumb's *Gnomic Variations* (solo piano).

GREAT FALLS SYMPHONY ASSOCIATION, Box 1078, Great Falls MT 59403. (406)453-4102. Music Director and Conductor: Gordon J. Johnson. Symphony orchestra. Estab. 1959. Members are professionals and amateurs. Performs 7 concerts (2 youth concerts)/year, including 2-3 new works. "Our audience is conservative. Newer music is welcome; however, it might be more successful if it were programatic." Plays in Civic Center Auditorium seating 1,850. Negotiable payment. Submit complete score and tapes of pieces. SASE.

Music: "Compositions should be for full orchestra. Should be composed ideomatically for instruments avoiding extended techniques. Duration 10-20 minutes. Avoid diverse instruments such as alto flute, Wagner tuben, saxophones, etc. Our orchestra carries 65 members, most of whom are talented amateurs. We have a resident string quartet and woodwind quintet that serve as principals. Would enjoy seeing a piece for quartet or quintet solo and orchestra. Send letter with clean score and tape (optional). We will reply within a few weeks."

Peformances: Bernstein's *Chichester Psalms* (choral and orchestra); Hodkinson's *Boogie, Tango and Grand Tarantella* (bass solo); and Stokes' *Native Dancer*.

Tips: "Music for orchestra and chorus is welcome. Cross cues will be helpful in places. Work should not require an undue amount of rehearsal time (remember that a concerto and symphony are probably on the program as well)."

THE GRINNELL ORCHESTRA, Dept. of Music, Grinnell College, Grinnell IA 50112. (515)269-3064. Assistant Professor of Music: Jonathan Knight. Chamber orchestra. Members are amateurs and college students. Performs 4-5 concerts/year. "Our audience includes students, faculty and staff of the college, members of the community of Grinnell and nearby towns; performances in Herrick Chapel, seating capacity about 700." Composers are not paid. Submit complete score and tapes of piece(s). SASE. Reports in 2-3 months.

Music: "We can perform scores for chamber-size orchestras: about 20 strings, pairs of woodwinds and brass, harp and keyboard instruments. Please avoid exotic percussion. I would consider any length or style, as long as the difficulty of the work did not exceed the ability of the group, which may be characterized as a fairly good undergraduate ensemble, but not as capable as a conservatory orchestra. No 'pops' music."

Performances: Schubert's *Symphony No. 6*; Lou Harrison's *Seven Pastorales*; and Charles Ives's *The Gong on the Hook and Ladder*.

Tips: "Composers may submit completed works to me, with or without tapes, for consideration. As the relative strengths of my orchestra change from year to year due to normal student turnover, it is difficult to give specific tips other than those above regarding size and difficulty of scores."

HASTINGS SYMPHONY ORCHESTRA, Fuhr Hall, 9th & Ash, Hastings NE 68901. (402)463-2402. Conductor/Music Director: Dr. James Johnson. Symphony orchestra. Estab. 1926. Members are professionals and amateurs. Performs 6-8 concerts/year, including 1 new work. "Audience consists of conservative residents of mid-Nebraska who haven't heard most of the classics." Concert Hall: Masonic Temple Auditorium (950). Pays commission or rental. Submit complete score and tapes of piece(s). Does not return unsolicited material. Reports in 2 months.

Music: "We are looking for all types of music within the range of an accomplished community orchestra. Write first and follow with a phone call."

Performances: Bernstein's *Candide Overture*; Richard Wilson's *Silhouette (1988)*; and Menotti's *Doublebass Concerto (1983)*.

Tips: "Think about the size, ability and budgetary limits. Confer with our music director about audience taste. Think of music with special ties to locality."

HIGH DESERT SYMPHONY ORCHESTRA, Dept. SM, P.O. Box 1255, Victorville CA 92392. (619)245-4271 ext. 387. Music Director: K.C. Manji. Symphony orchestra. Estab. 1969. Members are both amateurs and professionals. Performs 15 concerts/year, including 2 new works/year. Plays in a 500 seat auditorium. Community-based audience; middle class incomes. "Composers usually not paid." Submit complete score and tapes of piece(s). SASE. Reports back in 2 months.

Music: "Style: American nationalistic; length: up to 30 minutes. Level of difficulty must be intermediate/advanced, depending on amount of rehearsal time. Right now I would appreciate anything that would stress ensemble blending and be fairly tonal in color. This is an orchestra in the process of

rebuilding and going forward. Submit pieces 5-15 minutes in length, classical size orchestration (2,2,2,2,2,2,0,0) or small ensembles."
Performances: Villa-Lobos' *Fantasia for Sax* (concerto); Stravinsky's *8 Instrument Miniatures* (small ensemble); and J. Berger's *Overture for Strings* (string orchestra).
Tips: "Make the works accessible in difficulty, i.e., rhythm and instrumentation."

THE PAUL HILL CHORALE (AND) THE WASHINGTON SINGERS, 5630 Connecticut Ave., NW, Washington DC 20015. (202)364-4321. Music Director: Paul Hill. Vocal ensemble. Estab. 1967. Members are professionals and amateurs. Performs 8-10 concerts/year, including 2-3 new works. Commissions one new composer or work every 2-3 years. "Audience covers a wide range of ages and economic levels drawn from the greater Washington, DC metropolitan area. Kennedy Center Concert Hall seats 2,700." Pays by outright purchase. Submit complete score and tapes of pieces. SASE. Reports in 2 months.
Music: Seeks new works for: 1)large chorus with or without symphony orchestras; 2)chamber choir and small ensemble.
Performances: Argento's *Peter Quince at the Clavier*; Rorem's *An American Oratorio*; and Luboff's *A Choral Extravaganza*.
Tips: "We are always looking for music that is high quality and accessible to Washington audiences."

HOUSTON YOUTH SYMPHONY & BALLET, P.O. Box 56104, Houston TX 77256. (713)621-2411. Orchestra Operations Manager: Jesse P. Johnson. Symphony orchestra. Estab. 1947. Members are students. Performs 6 concerts/year. "Performs in Alice Pratt Brown Hall, Rice University, 800-seat concert hall for general audiences." Query first. SASE. Reports in 2 months.
Music: Uses string orchestra music suitable for players age 7-14. "Full orchestra music suitable for players 14-23."
Performances: Dzubay's *Ascension* (brass/percussion); and Turner's *Opening Night* (symphony).

HUNTSVILLE YOUTH ORCHESTRA, P.O. Box 7223, Huntsville AL 35807. (205)880-0622. Music Director: Dr. Chris Laaz. Chamber music ensemble and youth orchestra. Estab. 1961. Members are students. Performs 4-10 concerts/year, including 0-2 new works. Commissions 0-1 composers or new works/year. Receives 10 submissions/year. Audience is mainly family adults of performers, students, musicians and music educators. Perform at Von Braun Civic Center Concert Hall; 2,200 seats. "Acoustically excellent." Payment individually arranged. Submit complete score and tapes of piece(s) or send representative works, score and tape. "We prefer to keep copies of scores and tapes on file." Reports in 3 weeks initially; 6 months for final decision.
Music: No longer than 3-15 min; Instrumentation: 3-2(1)-2(1)-2, 4331, Perc (3) pno, strings. "Works possessing good rhythmic motion and drive; with dramatically contrasting sections. Areas of tonal centricity helpful. Good parts for all (when possible) and great parts for a few in typically strong instruments. NYSMA Grade 2-3 and 4-6. Must have relatively strong audience appeal on single listening."
Performances: Les Fillmer's *Finale from "Quodlibet"* (full orchestra); and Joann Forman's *Ballet in Progress* (full orchestra).
Tips: "Beautiful sounds that have something to say. Excitement, contrast; challenging, worthwhile parts for young players."

*I CANTORI DI NEW YORK, P.O. Box 4165, New York NY 10185-0035. (212)439-4758. Artistic Director: Mark Shapiro. Vocal ensemble. Estab. 1984. Members are professionals and amateurs. Performs 3 concerts/year. "Performs in Merkin Hall, St. Peter's Church and comparable spaces." Submit complete score and tape of piece(s). Does not return unsolicited material. Reports in 3 months.
Music: "Seeks a capella music or works with up to 7 instruments, performable by nonprofessional singers in terms of vocal and musical difficulties. We will consider various styles and lengths. I Cantori has 24 voices. Divisi should not exceed 8 parts. No pop or sacred music of inferior quality. We are especially interested in a dramatic work lasting 40 minutes or so with extensive use of the chorus, and no more than three or four difficult solo roles."
Performances: Daniel Pinkham's *Saint Mark Passion* (cantata); Frank Martin's *Le Vin Herba* (oratorio); and Franticek Tuma's *Stabat Mater* (cantata).
Tips: "Composer should have experience writing for *voices*. Notation should be without ambiguity."

IDAHO STATE—CIVIC SYMPHONY, P.O. Box 8099, Pocatello ID 83209. (208)236-3479. Music Director/Conductor: Dr. Thom Ritter George. Symphony orchestra. Estab. 1934. Members are professionals and amateurs. Performs 12 concerts/year, including 4 new works. "Audience varied, ranges from highly musically educated to little background in music; in general, prefer music with which they have some familiarity. The symphony performs in Goranson Hall, on the campus of Idaho State University—

seats 444, good acoustics. Pays by outright purchase or per performance. Query first. SASE. Reports in 1 month.
Music: "We consider works by composers scoring for full orchestra. The majority of our activities are oriented to the classical music audience." Does not wish "any kind of 'popular music'; music by living composers written in historic styles (e.g. Baroque; chamber music; opera)."
Performances: Prokofiev's *Romeo and Juliet*, Haydn's *The Creation*; and Peter Schmalz's *The Swans of Apollo* (tone poem Idaho premiere).
Tips: "Write a work which is structurally sound and scored idiomatically for the symphony orchestra."

INTER SCHOOL ORCHESTRAS OF NEW YORK, 207 E. 85th St., New York NY 10028. (212)288-0763. Music Director: Jonathan Strasser. Youth orchestra. Estab. 1972. Members are amateurs making up 5 youth orchestras on three levels. Performs 12-15 concerts/year. "Varied churches to major halls like Carnegie or Alice Tully. Varied audiences." Does not return unsolicited material.
Music: Orchestra of 70 (advanced) of 30 strings, horns and trumpets; full orchestra, intermediate group of 70; 3 beginner orchestras with 30-40 each. "Composers should realize that players are 18 and younger so works should not be outrageously complicated or difficult."
Performances: Gordon Jacob's *Concerto for Trombone* (full orchestra); Gail Kubik's *Gerald McBoing Boing* (narrated work with violas, celli, winds [single] 2 trumpets and 23 percussion instruments); and Samuel Barber's *Adagio for Strings*.
Tips: "Remember that we are an educational, music making organization seeking to give the youngsters in our orchestras the best learning and performing experiences possible. We wish to stretch their experience but not present them with impossibilities."

JACKSON SYMPHONY ORCHESTRA, P.O. Box 3429, Jackson TN 38303. (901)427-6440. Executive Director: Dr. Carol L. Quin. Symphony orchestra. Estab. 1961. Members are professionals. Performs more than 60 concerts/year, including 1 new work. Commissions 1 composer or new work/year. "The audience is a conservative group with an average age of 50. The hall seats 2,000. Four concerts on the season are 'classical,' three are 'Cabaret' with table seating and dinner." Composer is paid by prize for composition competition. Query first. SASE.
Music: "Music should be melodic, not complicated. No more than 60 performers. Do not send strange requests for instrumentation."
Performances: Jordan Tang's *Anniversary Fanfare* (fanfare opener premiere); William Grant Still's *Miniature Overture* (2nd premiere).
Tips: "Write a letter about the piece—send instrumentation list and description with length."

JOHNSON CITY SYMPHONY ORCHESTRA, P.O. Box 533, Johnson City TN 37605. (615)926-8742. Symphony orchestra. Estab. 1969. Members are professionals and amateurs. Performs 7 concerts/year, including 1 new work. Commissions 1 composer or new work/year. Pays $1,500 outright purchase. Query first. Does not return unsolicited material. Reports in 1 month.
Music: "We have done 3 minute pieces for strings, brass or winds; up to 45 minute pieces for full orchestras. We can perform pieces of moderate difficulty—strings 10-10-6-4-3, 2 oboes max, 1 English horn max, 3 trombones, 1 tuba. Preference has been given to Tennessee residents or composers with a strong connection to Tennessee."
Performances: Lewis Songer's *MacRae Meadow* (brass piece, 3 min.); Martin Herman's *Up a Tree* (storyteller and orchestra); and Alan Murchie's *Daen for Brass and Woodwinds*.
Tips: "Music should not be too atonal. Should be something with market interest and have local color."

KENTUCKY OPERA, 631 S. Fifth St., Louisville KY 40202-2201. (502)584-4500. Opera. Estab. 1952. Members are professionals. Performs 22 concerts/year. Performs at Whitney Hall, The Kentucky Center for the Arts, seating is 2,400; Bomhard Theater, The Kentucky Center for the Arts, 620; Macauley Theater, 1,400. Pays by royalty, outright purchase or per performance. Submit complete score and tapes of piece(s). SASE. Reports in 6 months.
Music: Seeks opera—1 to 3 acts with orchestrations. No limitations.
Performances: Daniel Dutton's *The Stone Man* (1 act opera); Philip Glass' *The Fall of the House of Usher* (2 act opera).

KITCHENER-WATERLOO CHAMBER ORCHESTRA, Box 937, Waterloo ON N2J 4C3 **Canada**. (519)744-3828. Music Director: Graham Coles. Chamber Orchestra. Estab. 1985. Members are professionals and amateurs. Performs 8 concerts/year, including some new works. "We perform at St. John's Lutheran Church (seats 500), Humanities Theatre, University of Waterloo (seats 1,200). We perform mainly baroque and classical repertoire, so that any contemporary works must not be too dissonant, long or far fetched." Pays by music rental and performing rights fees only. Submit complete score.

"It's best to query first so that we can outline what not to send. Include: complete CV—list of works, performances, sample reviews." SASE. Reports in 4 weeks.
Music: "Musical style must be accessible to our audience and players (3 rehearsals). Length should be under 20 minutes. Maximum orchestration 2/2/2/2 2/2/0/0 Timp/1 Percussion Harpsichord/organ String 4/4/3/3/1. We have limited rehearsal time, so keep technique close to that of Bach-Beethoven. We also play chamber ensemble works—octets, etc. We do not want choral or solo works."
Performances: John Weinzweig's *Divertimento I* (flute and strings); Peter Jona Korn's *4 Pieces for Strings* (string orch.); and Graham Coles *Variations on a Mozart Rondo* (string orch.).
Tips: "If you want a first-rate performance, keep the technical difficulties minimal."

*KNOX-GALESBURG SYMPHONY, Box 31 Knox College, Galesburg IL 61401. (309)343-0112, ext. 208. Music Director: Bruce Polay. Symphony orchestra. Estab. 1951. Members are professionals and amateurs. Performs 7 concerts/year including 1 new work. Commissions 1 composer or new work/ year. Middle age audience; excellent, recently renovated vaudeville theater. Pays by royalty. Submit complete score and tapes of piece(s). SASE.
Music: Moderate difficulty 3222/4331/T piano, harpsichord, celesta and full strings. No country western.
Performances: Polay's *Perspectives for Tape & Orchestra* (world premiere); Pärt's *Cantus in Memory of Britten*; and Finko's *2nd Symphony* (US premiere).

L.A. SOLO REPERTORY ORCHESTRA, 7242 Louise Ave., Van Nuys CA 91406. (818)342-8400. Music Director: James Swift. Symphony orchestra. Estab. 1968. Members are professionals and amateurs. Performs 6 concerts/year, including 7 new works. Commissions 1 composer or new work/year. "General audience. Hall of Liberty: 1,400 seats, Van Nuys Jr. High School auditorium: 800 seats." Pay is negotiated. Submit complete score and tapes of pieces. SASE. Reports in 2 months.
Music: "20th century symphonic, particularly with solo instruments. Many composers extend development to point of boredom, so we reserve right to cut or perform single movements. Use of odd instruments or greatly extended sections tends to inhibit performance. No hard rock—even when intended for large orchestra."
Performances: Samuel Adler's *To Celebrate a Miracle* (Hanukkah medley symphonia); Leon Levitch's *Elegy for Strings* (tone poem—premiere); Harvey Woolsey's *Concerto Corto for String Bass* (concerto premiere).
Tips: "Tapes are nice, but a good score is essential. Edit the work! Keep the moderately sophisticated audience in mind. Compose for audience enjoyment if you want your work repeated."

LAKESIDE SUMMER SYMPHONY, 236 Walnut Ave., Lakeside OH 43440. (419)798-4461. Contact: G. Keith Addy. Conductor: Robert L. Cronquist. Symphony orchestra. Members are professionals. Performs 8 concerts/year. Perform "Chautauqua-type programs with an audience of all ages (2-102). Hoover Auditorium is a 3,000-seat auditorium." Query first. SASE.
Music: Seeking "classical compositions for symphony composed of 50-55 musicians. The work needs to have substance and be a challenge to our symphony members. No modern jazz, popular music or hard rock."
Performances: Richard's Nanes' *Prelude, Canon & Fugue* (classical).

LEHIGH VALLEY CHAMBER ORCHESTRA, Box 20641, Lehigh Valley PA 18002-0641. (215)770-9666. Music Director: Donald Spieth. Symphony orchestra. Estab. 1979. Performs 35 concerts/year, including 1-2 new works. Members are professionals. Commissions 1-2 composers or new works/year. Orchestra has "1,000 subscribers for Friday/Saturday pairs of concerts. Also offers youth programs, pops, etc." Pays by outright purchase for commissioned work. Submit complete score and tape of pieces. Reports in 2 months.
Music: "Original compositions for chamber orchestra instrumentation: 2/2/2/2-2/2/1/0 percussion, strings (7/6/4/4/2); amateur of no interest. A composer should not write specifically for us without an agreement."
Performances: Libby Larsen's *Cold, Silent Snow* (flute and harp concerto); James Brown's *Symphony for Chamber Orchestra* (symphony in 3 movements); and Larry Lipkis's *Capprizio* (15 minute, one movement work).
Tips: "Send a sample type and score of a work(s) written for the requested medium."

*LEXINGTON PHILHARMONIC SOCIETY, 161 N. Mill St., Arts Place, Lexington KY 40507. (606) 233-4226. Music Director: George Zack. Symphony orchestra and chamber music ensembles. Estab. 1961. Performs 35-40 concerts/year including 12-15 new works. Members are professionals. Commissions 1-2 composers or new works/year. Series includes "8 serious, classical subscription concerts (hall seats 1,500); 15-outdoor pops concerts (from 1,500 to 5,000 tickets sold); 3-5 run-out concerts (½ serious/ ½ pops); and 10 children's concerts, 2 rock/pops concerts (hall seats 1,500)." Pays via ASCAP and

BMI, rental purchase and private arrangements. Submit complete score and tape of pieces. SASE.
Music: Seeking "good current pops material and good serious classical works. No specific restrictions, but overly large orchestra requirements, unusual instruments and extra rentals help limit our interest."
Performances: Zwillich's *Celebration* (overture); Crumb's *A Haunted Landscape* (tone poem); and Corigliano's *Promenade* (overture).
Tips: "When working on large-format arrangement, use cross-cues so orchestra can be cut back if required. Submit good quality copy, scores and parts. Tape is helpful."

LINCOLN YOUTH SYMPHONY ORCHESTRA, P.O. Box 82889, Lincoln NE 68501. (402)436-1631. Music Director: Dr. Brian Moore. Youth orchestra. Estab. 1956. Members are amateurs drawn from Lincoln public schools. Performs 3 concerts/year. "The audience is made up of parents, friends, University teachers and teachers from other schools and a general audience." Pays by outright purchase. Query first. SASE. Reports in 2 weeks.
Music: "Needs orchestral compositions of moderate difficulty—new music/contemporary styles are welcomed. Orchestra is full winds and strings."
Performances: Schubert's *Unfinished*; Percy Grainger's *Walking Song* (winds only); and Shostakovich's *Cello Concerto* (solo).
Tips: "Call and talk to us first."

*LINDENWOOD CONCERTS—THE GARY BEARD CHORALE, 40 E. Parkway S., Memphis TN 38104. Director: Gary Beard. Vocal ensemble and professional concert series. Estab. 1979-series, 1987-chorale. Members are professionals and amateurs. Performs 15+ concerts/year including 1 new work. "Our concerts are more of the MOR format, appealing to all ages and backgrounds; our standard concert hall has excellent acoustics, a PA system used for speaking purposes only, and seats approx. 1,000." Pays per performance. Submit complete score and tapes of piece(s). SASE. Reports in 3 months.
Music: "Choral selections preferred, with orchestral/piano accompaniment. Styles can vary, but do not wish any "avant" or non-tonal music. We are seeking music for 25 singers, access to 3 professional pianists, and orchestra for hire. Difficulty can be of varying quality. Works should not be over 45 minutes; prefer small works or single movements."
Performances: John Rutter's *Te Deum* (choral/orchestral; of the English genre); Craig's *Musicological Journey . . . 12 Days of Xmas* (satirical 12 mvts. through 12 periods of music history); Mozart's *Coronation Mass* (traditional mass setting; with orchestra).
Tips: "Submit well reviewed scores; easy to read; *extremely* organized. Submit tapes (audio and/or video) for review."

LITHOPOLIS AREA FINE ARTS ASSOCIATION, 3825 Cedar Hill Rd., Canal Winchester OH 43110. (614)837-8925. Series Director: Virginia E. Heffner. Performing Arts Series. Estab. 1973. Members are professionals and amateurs. Performs 5-6 concerts/year, including 1 or 2 new works. "Our audience consists of couples and families 35-85 in age. Our hall is acoustically excellent and seats 400. It was designed as a lecture-recital hall in 1925." Composers "may apply for Ohio Arts Council Grant under the New Works category." Pays 1-2% royalty, $66/performance. Query first. SASE. Reports in 3 weeks.
Music: "We prefer that a composer is also the performer and works in conjunction with another artist, so that they could be one of the performers on our series. Piece should be musically pleasant and not too dissonant. It should be scored for small vocal or instrumental ensemble. Dance ensembles have difficulty with 15' high 15' deep and 27' wide stage. We do not want avant-garde or obscene dance routines. No ballet (space problem). We're interested in something historical—national, or Ohio emphasis would be nice. Small ensembles or solo format is fine."
Tips: "Call me to see what our series is consisting of that year at (614)837-8925."

*LONG BEACH COMMUNITY BAND, 6422 Keynote St., Long Beach CA 90808. (714)527-0964. Music Director: John E. Hall III. Community band. Estab. 1947. Members are professionals and amateurs. Performs 15 concerts/year including 12 new works. Average age level of audiences. Performs mostly in outdoor venues such as parks. Pays by outright purchase. Submit complete score and tapes of piece(s). SASE. Reports in 1 month.
Music: 3-10 minutes pieces for concert band of medium difficulty. Looking for arrangements of film and TV music, songs of '70s to present.

*L.A. JAZZ CHOIR, 5759 Wallis Ln., Woodland Hills CA 91367. (818)704-8657. Chairman, Repertoire Committee: Barbara Keating. Vocal ensemble. Estab. 1980. Members are professionals. Performs 15 concerts/year; performs 4 new works per year. Commissions 1 composer/year. Performs in large concert halls (Los Angeles Music Center, Hollywood Bowl), small club venues (At My Place, Birdland West) and convention functions. Our audiences range from 18-60. Pays negotiable percentage or flat purchase fee. Query first. SASE. Reports in 3 weeks.

Music: "We are looking for more fusion-type music, with specific instruments are represented by voices. We are also desirous of obtaining original popular music, both in ballad and uptempo form. A capella or with rhythm section. 12 voices only, 6 male and 6 female. Level of difficulty must be of professional standard. Please do not submit '40's-style jazz standard or classical styles. If composer wishes, they can contact Barbara Keating for a sample packet including tapes and charts to see our scoring preference."

Performances: Milcho Leviev's *The Green House* (jazz cantata); and "Cole Porter Medley," arranged by Earl Brown (jazz medley).

THE LOUISVILLE ORCHESTRA, 609 W. Main St., Louisville KY 40202. (502)587-8681. Contact: Nan Herman. Symphony orchestra. Estab. 1937. Members are professionals. Performs 100 concerts/year, including 6 new works. Commissions 2 composers or new works/year. MasterWorks classical subscription concerts are performed in the 2,400-seat Whitney Hall of the Kentucky Center for the Arts. "Our audience varies in age from University students to seniors and comes from the areas surrounding Louisville in Kentucky and Indiana." Pays by commission. Submit complete score and tapes of piece(s). Does not return unsolicited material. Reports in months. Planning done year in advance of performance.

Music: "All styles appropriate to symphony orchestras. No chamber works, pop music or lead sheets." Orchestration for standard symphony orchestra. No pop music/pop vocal/New Age. Enclose a tape of performance or keyboard realization.

Tips: "For information on New Music Competition in conjunction with Indiana State University, contact Pat Jenkins. For score submission, contact Nan Herman."

THE LYRIC OPERA OF DALLAS, Suite 400, 8111 Preston Rd., Dallas TX 75225. (214)368-2183. Artistic Director: John Burrows. Music theater company. Estab. 1982. Members are professionals. Performs 3-4 productions/year, including 3 new works in 6 years. "The Majestic Theatre in downtown Dallas is a beautifully restored Victorian building, seating 1,500. There are excellent stage facilities and a good orchestra pit." Query first or submit complete score and tapes of piece(s). SASE. Reports in 3 weeks.

Music: "We welcome all styles of music and high performance demands. Submission length should not exceed 2 hours of music. We want stageworks for not in excess of 35 onstage performers, and 30 orchestra musicians. The only other limitation is that all performances are in English. We don't want works demanding exceptional scenic demands or very large forces. The Lyric Opera of Dallas is known for performing a high proportion of comedic material, and has no tradition of presenting esoteric works. Please do not send concert music. Musical theater/opera only."

Performances: Robert Rodriguez's *The Ransom of Red Chief* (one-act opera); Leonard Bernstein's *Candide* (comic operetta, SW premier of opera version); and Alan Strachan/Benny Green's *Cole* (revue of life and compositions of Cole Porter).

MANITOBA CHAMBER ORCHESTRA, 202-1317A Portage Ave., Winnipeg Manitoba R3G OV3 **Canada.** (204)783-7377. General Manager: Rita Manzies. Chamber orchestra. Estab. 1972. Members are professionals. Performs 9 concerts/year, including 2 new works. "Audiences are generally professionals—also many young people. We perform at Westminster Church (seats 1,000)." Pays by commission. Query first. SASE.

Music: Seeks "music for string orchestra and one solo instrument. Limitations: 22 strings; no pop music."

Performances: Gary Kulesha's *Concerto for Recorder and Small Orchestra* (Canada Council Commission world premiere); and Andrew McDonald's *Violin Concerto op. 22* (world premiere).

*****MEASURED BREATHS THEATRE COMPANY,** 193 Spring St., #3R, New York NY 10012. (212)334-8402. Artistic Director: Robert Press. Music-theater producing organization. Estab. 1989. Members are professionals. Performs 2 concerts/year. "Performances in small (less than 100 seats) halls in downtown Manhattan; strongly interested in highly theatrical/political vocal works for avant-garde audiences." Pays $500 for outright purchase. Query first. SASE. Reports in 1 month.

Music: "Traditionally, we have produced revivals of baroque or modern vocal works. We are interested in soliciting for new works by theatrically adept composers. Typical orchestration should be 7 pieces or less. Would prefer full-length works." Chamber-size, full-length operas preferred. At most 10 performers. Difficult works encouraged.

Performances: Lully's *Amadis* (opera, French; 1684); Monteverdi's *The Madrigals of Love & War* (opera, Italian; 1638); Handel's *Tamerlano* (opera, English; 1724). All works performed in English translation.

*****MID-AMERICA SINGERS AND CHILDREN' CHOIRS,** 305 E. Walnut #201, Springfield MO 65806. (417)863-7464. Managing Artistic Director: Charles Facer. Community chorus. Estab. 1967. Members are professionals and amateurs. Performs 5 concerts/year including 5 new works. Commissions 1 new

Close-up

Libby Larsen
Composer
Minneapolis, Minnesota

Libby Larsen has found there's no place like home to write
her music. Minnesota has provided many things for her: a
home, a school and a successful career that has produced
works from chamber music to opera. Her musical training
led to a doctoral degree from the University of Minnesota in
1978. The twin cities of Minneapolis-St. Paul, where Larsen
makes her home, have a strong tradition of performing con-
temporary music; the Minnesota Orchestra, the St. Paul Chamber Orchestra and the Minnesota Opera have all commissioned Larsen. She has also received awards from the National Endowment for the Arts, the Exxon/Rockefeller Foundation and was named the
Minnesota Woman of the Year in Arts.

Finding performances

Larsen believes a composer's hometown is a source for musical ideas and meaning, both
in music and in life. The community may also provide performance opportunities through
local schools, church and college choirs, orchestras, even recital programs. Larsen herself
has written choral pieces for many groups in her area, capitalizing on Minnesota's strong
college choral tradition. The composer's hometown may also be a source of performers for
an ensemble playing music written by the members of that group.

Finding a performer for your work is important. Larsen is now lucky enough to work
solely on commission. But when she was beginning her career as a composer, it was equally
important to have a specific performance and performer in mind. "It's a matter of choosing
and working with performers who will be compatible with your work. When I began to
think of myself as a composer, I began right away to work with performers. Both to learn
how to write and to perform the piece." Larsen also reminds composers that finding performances for their music may be easier among smaller ensembles. "The practical reason is
that there are many more venues for performances with smaller ensembles. The aesthetic
reason is that in writing for a smaller group of forces I can study the detail of my style in
a way I can't when I'm writing for larger forces."

Working directly with performers, even beginning a group to perform your music, can
provide another important tool in developing a reputation: fine performance, which is the
key to generating interest in your work. An exciting and fine performance of a work is like
"prairie fire," as Larsen describes it. "All of a sudden there's something going on, and
when people feel that something is going on, they want to know what it is. And that's where
it all begins."

Organizations

Composer organizations can be important contacts for the composer beginning a career. Larsen began the Minnesota Composers' Forum with fellow composer Stephen Paulus "so a young composer can say there is a community of composers." Although an organization may not be located in your city, you may be able to connect with another local

composer through membership in these organizations. (Look in the Organizations section of *Songwriter's Market* to find out how to contact and join some of these organizations.) These contacts may be a source for evaluation of your work or may make you aware of opportunities for performance of your work by a local group or soloist. Larsen identifies another function these groups serve; "It provides a sense of competition . . . a sense that people are out there working and 'By God, I'd better get busy!' "

Other musical organizations may also provide important contacts and compositional opportunities, whether they are contests, commissions or a call for new works. Larsen points out that the national conventions for organizations like Opera America, Chamber Music America, the American Choral Directors' Association and the American Symphony Orchestra League are important in finding a market for your music. Simply attending the conventions and being on the lookout for leads can be valuable. The conventions also provide an opportunity to learn what the needs and concerns of those particular performing groups are.

Disappearing opportunities

Technology has made staying at home to work much easier for the modern-day composer. The computer, desk top publishing capabilities, the fax, modem; all these have helped creators of music to present their music and encourage performance. On the other hand, technology has limited a traditional source of introducing music to a larger market: music publishing. With the development of music printing software, a composer can enter music from a keyboard and convert that information to a complete, easily-read score with a minimum of time and editing, in essence becoming a small publisher.

Another area of opportunity not open to aspiring composers is commissioning programs. The well-known commissioning and grant programs, like the National Endowment for the Arts (NEA), aren't good places for aspiring composers to look for support. Larsen says, "The notion of commissioning programs is kind of a myth in this country. The NEA has a commissioning program, but having sat on that panel on and off over the years [I know] what happens is 500 people apply and there's enough money for 12. It's not really a program, it's a crapshoot."

Where to from here?

Larsen stresses concentrating on achieving the finest performances as often as possible, not only to hear your music and develop a "compositional voice," but to develop an audience. The result? "That audience will feedback in all the areas. They'll help you articulate (about your music) by asking questions and expecting answers." They will also provide other possible contacts and help with networking. "But, first and foremost," Larsen says, "the music has to be good, and that takes practice." How can a composer make his work better? "In a creative life, the learning never ends. Keep current with technique, as good painters, sculptors and architects will. You never know everything you need. If you really feel that, and I've felt that at times, that's a signal to me that I ought to stop. Stop and re-evaluate."

—Michael Oxley

work every other year. "Next year we will move into a new 2,200 seat performing arts center. Audience is older students through seniors. Somewhat conservative tastes." Pays $400-800 per work. Query first. SASE. Reports in 3-4 weeks.

Music: SATB or 2 part children's or a combination with piano or small instrument ensemble or a cappella in singable style. Variety of lengths. 50 adults, 36 children.

Performances: Ariel Rameriz's *Misa Criolla* (SATB with percussion); Charles Facer's *Civil War Suite* (SATB, traditional); Ward Swingle's *Swingle Bells X* (SATB, traditional); and Bob Krogstad's *A Song for Spring* (SATB children and piano 4-hands).

Tips: "Contact us first and then tailor work to group."

THE MIRECOURT TRIO, #11M, 3832 Quail Pl., Waterloo IA 50701. (319)273-6073. Contact: Terry King. Chamber music ensemble; violin, cello, piano. Estab. 1973. Members are professionals. Performs 30-80 concerts/year, including 2 new works. Commissions 2 composers or new works/year. Concerts are performed for a "general chamber music audience of 100-1,500." Pays by outright purchase $1,000-3,000 or recording subsidy. Query first. SASE. Reports in 2 weeks to 6 months.

Music: Seeks "music of short to moderate duration (5-20 minutes) that entertains, yet is not derivative or cliched. Orchestration should be basically piano, violin, cello, occasionally adding soprano and/or clarinet. We do not wish to see academic or experimental works."

Performances: Lou Harrison's *Trio*; John Cooper's *Parameter*; and Vincent Persichetti's *Parable*.

Tips: "Submit works that engage the audience or relate to them, works that reward the players as well."

MISSOURI SYMPHONY SOCIETY, P.O. Box 1121, Columbia MO 65205. (314)875-0600. Artistic Director and Conductor: Hugo Vianello. Symphony orchestra, chamber music ensemble, youth orchestra and pops orchestra. Estab. 1970. Members are professionals. Performs 23 concerts/year, including up to 8 new works. Commissions one composer or new work/year. Receives 10-15 outside submissions/year. "Our home base is a 1,200-seat renovated 1928 movie palace and vaudeville stage. Our home audience is well-educated, including professionals from Columbia's five hospitals and three institutions of higher education. Our touring program reaches a broad audience, including rural Missourians and prison inmates." Pays through ASCAP and BMI. Submit complete score (and if available, tapes of pieces). SASE. Reports in 8 weeks.

Music: "We want good orchestral (chamber) music of any length—2222/2200/timp/strings/piano. There are no limitations on difficulty."

Performances: Norman Dello Joio's *New York Profiles* (chamber orchestra); Richard Nanes' *Symphony for Strings*; and Charles Hoag's *When the Yellow Dream Leaves Fell* (world premiere).

MOHAWK TRAIL CONCERTS, P.O. Box 75, Shelburne Falls MA 01370. (413)625-9511. Managing Director: Diane Bruno. Chamber music presenter. Estab. 1970. Members are professionals. Performs approximately 10 concerts/year, including 2-3 new works. "Audience ranges from farmers to professors, children to elders. Concerts are performed in churches and town halls around rural Franklin County, Massachusetts." Pays by performance. Query first. Does not return unsolicited material. Reports in months.

Music: "We want chamber music, generally not longer than 30 minutes. We are open to a variety of styles and orchestrations for a maximum of 8 performers. We don't want popular, rock or theater music."

Performances: Michael Cohen's *Fantasia for Flute, Piano and Strings* (chamber); William Bolcom's *Nes Songs* (piano/voice duo); and Arnold Black's *Laments & Dances* (string quartet and guitar duo).

Tips: "We are looking for artistic excellence, a committment to quality performances of new music, and music that is accessible to a fairly conservative (musically) audience."

*MORAVIAN PHILHARMONIC OLOMOUC, Nám. míru 23, Olomouc, CSSR 772 00 **Czechoslovakia**. Phone: 0042 68 28971. FAX: 0042 68 28511. Contact: S. Macura. Chamber music ensemble and philharmonic orchestra. Members are professionals. Performs 60 concerts/year including 20 new works. Commissions 1-2 composers or new works/year. "Audience of a university town of considerable historic tradition." Concerts are performed in a hall seating about 800, "neoclassicist style." Pays per performance in Czech crowns. Submit complete score with tapes of pieces. SAE and IRC. Reports in 3 weeks.

Music: Maximum 15 minutes, any style, large orchestra or interesting concerto music (soloist accompanied by large orchestra or chamber ensemble-strings). "Special emphasis on melody."

Performances: Vacek Miloš' *Symfonie č.2*, Matěj Josef's *Kytička*; and Parsch Arnošt *Poeme.Koncert pro cimbál*.

Tips: "Wait until the piece starts simmering in your mind; do not write just for the sake of writing something."

*MUSIC PROGRAMS: LOS ANGELES COUNTY MUSEUM OF ART, 5905 Wilshire Blvd., Los Angeles CA 90036. (213)857-6115. Music Programs Coordinator: Cheryl Tiano. Presenting organization. Estab. 1971. Members are professionals. Performs 100 concerts/year including 35 new works. "Usually, the audience is, to some extent, educated in either the classics or arts. The hall seats 600." Pays $350-12,000 per performance. Submit program proposal and tape. SASE. Reports in 3 months.
Music: "We want small groups, electronics, computers, chamber ensembles, outstanding solo classical artists and jazz. We require good credentials. We don't present dance music (usually). Rap, disco, pop, country, etc ... are not appropriate for this venue; however, sometimes there is a fine line between art and entertainment. Submit a written program proposal (what they would play), tapes of prior performances, and follow through with phone calls.
Performances: Stravinsky's *Four Russian Peasant Songs* (choral); Bussotti's *Veliera* (contemporary chamber work); Eliott Carter's *Triple Duo* (contemporary chamber work).
Tips: "Composers should submit their works to ensembles, as the ensembles generally pick their own repertoire."

NASHVILLE OPERA ASSOCIATION, 1900 Belmont Blvd., Nashville TN 37212. (615)292-5710. General Director: Kyle Ridout. Opera company. Estab. 1981. Members are professionals and amateurs. Performs 7 concerts/year. "Tennessee Performing Arts Center (Jackson Hall) has 2,400 seats and Tennessee Performing Arts Center (Polk Theatre) has 1,100 seats." Pays by outright purchase. Submit complete score and tapes of pieces. SASE. Reports in 1 month.
Music: Seeks opera and music theater pieces, sometimes accept one-acts."
Performances: Rogers & Hammerstein's *Carousel* (American Broadway musical); Bizet's *Carmen* (grand opera); Verdi's *Rigoletto* (grand opera).
Tips: "Be willing to work through the score by subjecting the work to readings/workshop."

NATIONAL ASSOCIATION OF COMPOSERS/USA, Nacusa P.O. Box 49652, Los Angeles CA 90049. (213)541-8213. President: Marshall Bialosky. Chamber music ensemble and composers' service organization. Estab. 1932. Members are professionals. Performs 5-9 concerts/year – all new works. Receives 20-30 outside submissions/year. Usually performed at universities in Los Angeles and at a mid-town church in New York City. Paid by ASCAP or BMI (NACUSA does not pay composers). Must join the organization to receive services. SASE. Reports in 6 weeks.
Music: Popular chamber music for five or fewer players; usually in the 5 to 20 minute range. "Level of difficulty is not a problem; number of performers is solely for financial reasons. We deal in serious, contemporary concert hall music. No 'popular' music."
Performances: Howard Quilling's *Sonata #1 for Violin and Piano*; David Soley's *Labertino for Solo Flute* and Byong-kon Kim's *Four Short Pieces for Piano*.

NEBRASKA CHAMBER ORCHESTRA, 749 NBC Center, Lincoln NE 68508. (402)477-0366. General Manager: Peggy Chesen. Chamber orchestra. Estab. 1976. Members are professionals. Performs 6 concerts/year, including approximately 6 new works. "We perform in two halls; one seats 850 and the other seats 2,250. Our audience is primarily 30 years or older in age, a minimum of a Bachelor's Degree in education and a minimum income of $25,000. Our audience comes from metropolitan Lincoln and surrounding areas." Pay by individual arrangements. Submit complete score and tape of piece(s). SASE. Reports in 6 months.
Music: "We want all styles appropriate to a chamber orchestra and accessible for the Nebraska audience. Lengths can vary but prefer no longer than 30 minute pieces. NCO standard instrumentation: 2-2-2-2 2-2 timpani, strings (65442). No excessively difficult works due to limited rehearsal time."
Performances: Loris Tjeknavorian's *Concerto for Guitar and Orchestra, "Zareh" Op. 39* (concerto); Russell Peck's *Amber Waves for Brass Quartet and Orchestra* (miniature classical symphony); and Michael Torke's *Ash (1988)*.
Tips: "Make it accessible to a general audience."

*NEBRASKA JAZZ ORCHESTRA INC., 3842 Garfield, Lincoln NE 68506. (402)486-1085. Executive Director: Dean Haist. Jazz band. Estab. 1988. Members are professionals. Performs 20-25 concerts/year including 5-10 new works. Commissions 5-10 composers and new works/year. "The audience is very diverse. They range in age from 10 years old on up. We perform in a ball room in the Hilton

 The asterisk before a listing indicates that the listing is new in this edition. New markets are often the most receptive to unsolicited submissions.

hotel. Capacity is about 400." Pays by outright purchase; $30 and up. Query first. Does not return unsolicited material. Reports in 1-2 weeks.
Music: "We want big band jazz with a length of less than 10 minutes. Orchestration: 2 alto, 2 tenor, 1 baritone, 4 trombones, 4 trumpets, bass, piano, guitar, and drum. Piece should allow for improvisation solos."
Performances: Tom Larson's *Pelicans* (jazz); Tom Larson's *Etude for 2 Basses* (jazz); and Rex Cadwallader's numerous compositions (jazz).

THE NEW YORK CONCERT SINGERS, Dept. SM, 401 East 80th St., New York NY 10021. (212)879-4412. Music Director/Conductor: Judith Clurman. Chorus. Estab. 1988. Performs 2-3 concerts/year, including new works. Commissions 1 composer or new work/year. "Audience is mixture of young and old classical music 'lovers.' Chorus performs primarily at Menkin Concert Hall, NYC." Pays at completion of work. Query first or send score and tape with biographical data. SASE.
Music: Seeks music "for small professional ensemble, with or without solo parts, a cappella or small instrumental ensemble. Not for large orchestra and chorus (at this stage in the group's development). Looking for pieces ranging for 7-20 minutes."
Performances: Ned Rorem's *Homer: Three Scenes from the Eliad* (30 minutes/chorus/soloist/8 instruments); Richard Hundley's *Ball* (12 minutes/chorus/soloists from chorus/4 hand PN.); and Leonard Bernstein's *Missa Brevis* (15 minutes/chorus/2 percussionsists).
Tips: "When choosing a piece for a program I study both the text and music. Both are equally important."

NORFOLK CHAMBER MUSIC FESTIVAL/YALE SUMMER SCHOOL OF MUSIC, 96 Wall St., New Haven CT 06520. (203)432-1966. Summer music festival. Estab. 1941. Members are international faculty/artists plus fellows who are young professionals. Performs 12 concerts, 14 recitals/year, including 3-6 new works. Commissions 1 composer or new work/year. "The 1,100-seat Music Shed (built in 1906 by architect Eric K. Rossiter) is lined with California redwood, with a peaked cathedral, which creates wonderful acoustics." Pays a commission fee (set fee). Submit complete score and tapes of piece(s). SASE. Reports in 1 month.
Music: "Chamber music of combinations, particularly for strings, woodwinds, brass and piano. There are 1-2 chamber orchestra concerts per season which include the students and feature the festival artists. Other than this, orchestra is not a featured medium, rather, chamber ensembles are the focus."
Performances: Joan Panetti's *Fanfare* (trumpet quartet premiere); Martin Bresnick's *String Quartet #4*; and Jacob Druckman's *Incenters* (13 players).

NORTH ARKANSAS SYMPHONY ORCHESTRA, P.O. Box 1243, Fayetteville AR 72702. (501)575-6385. Music Director: Carlton Woods. Symphony orchestra, chamber music ensemble, youth orchestra and community chorus. Estab. 1954. Members are professionals and amateurs. Performs 20 concerts/year, including 1-2 new works. "General audiences—will soon perform in Walton Arts Center (capacity 1,200) as well as in churches and schools in six area cities." Pays $500 or more/performance. Query first. SASE.
Music: Seeks "audience pleasers—rather short (10-15 minutes); and full orchestra pieces for subscription (classical) concerts. Orchestra is 60-70 members."
Performances: Robert Mueller's *Deep Earth Passing*; and Will Gay Bottje's *Sounds from the West Shore*.

OLD STOUGHTON MUSICAL SOCIETY, P.O. Box 794, Stoughton MA 02072. (617)344-5993. President: Joseph M. Klements. Music Director: Raymond Fahrner. Community chorus. Estab. 1786. Members are amateurs. Performs 2 concerts/year. "Audience is general public." Query first. Does not return unsolicited material. Reports in 6 weeks.
Music: Seeks "choral compositions by American (preferably New England) composers. We have an extensive collection of materials from early American singing schools but have broadened repertoire to early and modern American composers. Chorus size less than 40, with 1-20 accompanists. Level of difficulty should be geared to accomplished amateurs."
Performances: E.A. Jones' *Easter Oratorio*; Everett Titcomb's *Christmas Story* (cantata); and Leo Sowerby's (anthems).

OPERA ON THE GO, 184-61 Radnor Rd., Jamaica Estates NY 11432. (718)380-0665. Artistic Director: Jodi Rose. American opera chamber ensemble. Estab. 1985. Members are professionals. Performs about 30 operas/year; all new works. "We perform primarily in schools and community theaters. We perform only American contemporary opera. It must be lyrical in sound and quality as we perform for children as well as adults. We prefer pieces written for children based on fairy tales needing 4 to 6 singers." Pays $20 per performance. Submit complete score and tapes of piece(s). SASE. Reports ASAP if submissions are requested; if unsolicited, about 2-3 months.

Music: Need works in all age groups including adults. For older ages the pieces can be up to 60 minutes. Rarely use orchestra. "Keep the music as short as possible since we do a prelude (spoken) and postlude involving the children's active participation and performance. If it is totally atonal it will never work in the schools we perform in."

Performances: Edith Hemenway's *Goldilocks and the 3 Bears* (opera for N-3 grade); Mark Bucci's *Sweet Betsy From Pike* (opera for 6 grade-adult); and Seymour Barab's *Little Red Riding Hood* (children's opera).

Tips: "Be flexible. Through working with children we know what works best with different ages. If this means editing music to guarantee its' performance, don't get offended or stubborn."

*OREGON SYMPHONY, 711 SW Alder, Portland OR 97205. (503)228-4294. Director of Concert Operations: Peggie Schwarz. Symphony orchestra. Estab. 1896. Members are professionals. Performs 125 concerts/year including 3-4 new works. Commissions varying number of new works. "Classical concerts are attended predominantely by 35-60 year olds. Hall seats 2,776 – renovated vaudeville house." Pays by commission – flat fee negotiable. Submit complete score and tapes of pieces. SASE. Reports in 2 months.

Music: "Classical 10-20 min.: 16-14-12-10-8; pops: 12-10-8-10-4; jazz: 3333-5331 3 perc, 1 tmp, 1 harp, 1 keyboard. No country. Send a list of other orchestras with whom you have performed."

Performances: Schiff's *Slow Dance* (symphonic w/jazz flavor); and Singleton's *Shadows* (symphonic w/jazz flavor).

*PARAGON RAGTIME ORCHESTRA, Suite 2, 36 Embury Ave., Ocean Grove NJ 07756. (908)774-6515. Director: Rick Benjamin. Chamber music ensemble. Estab. 1986. Members are professionals.. Performs 30 concerts/year including 5 new works. Commissions 1 composer or new work/year. "We perform to a generally classical music audience with a growing number of college age attendees. This is a touring ensemble – theater venues vary." Pays by outright purchase. Query first. SASE. Reports in 2 months.

Music: "Short pieces for small orchestra (strings, flute, 2 clarients, 2 cornets, trombone, percussion and piano) rooted in, or flavored by American pop music of 1900-1925 period: Early jazz, ragtime, etc. Must be rooted or inspired by vintage American pop music."

Performances: S. Kent Goodman's "Storm Warning Rag" and "Mosquito Rag" (rag) and "Painting the Town Red, White, and Blue" (one step).

Tips: "We are looking for descriptive pieces for use at children's concerts."

PERRY COUNTY COUNCIL OF THE ARTS, P.O. Box 354, Newport PA 17074. (717)567-7023. Executive Director: Carol O. Vracarich. Arts organization presenting various programs. Estab. 1978. Members are professionals and amateurs and anyone who pays membership dues. Performs 5-7 concerts/year. "Performances are presented outdoors at a local state park or in a 500-seat high school auditorium. Outdoor area seats up to 5,000." Pays $50-2,000 per performance. Submit complete tapes (or videocassette if available) and background info on composer/performer. Does not return unsolicited material.

Music: "We present a wide variety of programs, hence we are open to all types of music (folk, rock, classical, blues, jazz, ethnic). Most programs are 1-2 hours in length and must be suitable as family entertainment."

PICCOLO OPERA COMPANY, 24 Del Rio Blvd., Boca Raton FL 33432-4737. (800)282-3161. Executive Director: Marjorie Gordon. Opera company. Estab. 1962. Members are professionals. Performs 5-50 concerts/year, including 1 new work. Commissions 1 composer or new work/year. Receives 3 or more outside submissions/year. Concerts are performed for a mixed audience of children and adults. Pays by royalty or outright purchase. Query or submit complete score and tapes of pieces. SASE.

Music: "Musical theater pieces, lasting about one hour, for adults to perform for adults and/or youngsters. Performers are mature singers with experience. The cast should have few performers (up to 10), no chorus or ballet, accompanied by piano or orchestra. Skeletal scenery. All in English."

Performances: Humperdinck's *Hansel & Gretel* (opera); Barab's *Little Red Riding Hood* (opera); Gilbert & Sullivan's *Festival of Highlights* (concert); and Martin Kalmanoff's *A Quiet Game of Cribble* (opera).

PLYMOUTH MUSIC SERIES OF MINNESOTA, 1900 Nicollet Ave., Minneapolis MN 55403. (612)870-0943. Managing Director: Jeanne Patterson. Choral orchestral performing society. Estab. 1969. Members are professionals and amateurs. Performs 5 concerts, including 1-2 new works. Audience is generally all ages from late 20s. Comes from entire Twin Cities metro area. "We perform in Ordway Music Theatre, Orchestra Hall, cathedrals in both Minneapolis and St. Paul." Pays commission fee. Query first. SASE. Reports in months.

Music: All styles appropriate to a choral/orchestral society except pop or rock. "Text used is of special concern. If the work is over ½ hour, the use of soloists is preferred."
Performances: Peter Schickele's *Oedipus Tex* (fully-staged opera); Libby Larsen's *Cóming Forth Into Day* (dramatic 1-hour work for narrator, baritone and soprano soloist, chorus and orchestra); and Aaron Copland's *The Tender Land* (semi-staged opera).
Tips: "Be patient. We have a very small staff and are constantly behind in reviewing scores. Tapes are very helpful."

PRO ARTE CHAMBER ORCHESTRA OF BOSTON, 1950 Massachusetts Ave., Cambridge MA 01240. (617)661-7067. Chairman, New Works Committee: Ann Black. Symphony orchestra. Estab. 1978. Members are professionals. Performs 8 concerts/year, including 4 new works. Commissions 2 composers or new works/year. "We have an average audience of about 700, approximately 340 subscription seats, age range attending is from 17 to 75, the average is 47, income categories in the middle to lower middle income range. Hall seats 1250, small stage, on university campus." Paid only if grant or individual support can be found. Query first. SASE. Reports in 6 months.
Music: "Styles range from baroque to modern, but original; some jazz, some minimalist, open to suggestions. Length of no longer than 15 minutes. Orchestration size of 2222 2200 tmp+1 perc. (moderate on percussion equipment capacity). Strings 7.6.4.3.2. Level of difficulty not a problem, forces to be utilized must be strictly enforced as stated above."
Performances: Linda Bouchard's *Fanorev* (short, minimalistic); Jay A. Gach's *I Ponentino* (medium length, somewhat dissonant); and Jan Swafford's *Chamber Sinfonietta* (concertino/ripieno utilized medium length, jazzy).
Tips: "Reasonable forces without lots of percussion, medium length, not too dissonant, no sound equipment, interesting individual style."

*RIVER CITY BRASS BAND, P.O. Box 6436, Pittsburgh PA 15212. (412)322-7222. Music Director: Robert Bernat. Professional brass band. Estab. 1980. Members are professionals. Performs 90 concerts/year including 10-20 new works. Commissions 6-8 composers or new works/year. Older audience (50-70), affluent, professionals and homemakers. Self-produced concert series (56 performances) in Carnegie Music Hall, (1,800 seats) university and high school auditoriums. Contracted performances (30-40 per year) in wide variety of venues. Pays $1,000-3,000 for outright purchse and normal publishing and performance royalties of work selected for publication by inhouse publishing firm, beginning late 1992. SASE. Reports in months.
Music: Seeks "Accessible, tonal works of 3-20 minutes duration for either American-style, 28-piece, brass band or 12-piece brass ensemble (4 cornets/trumpets, horn, baritone, euphonium, tenor trombone, bass trombone, tuba, 2 percussion). Must be performable with 2-3 hours of rehearsal by highly accomplished professional musicians. No post-Webern, academic avant garde, educational pieces or popular/commercial songs."
Performances: Philip Sparke's *A Pittsburgh Symphony* (4 movement piece for brass band; Joseph Jenkins' *Gateway West* (single movement piece for brass band); William Himes *Confluence* (single movement piece for brass band). "All 3 pieces were commissioned works; all received a minimum of 6 performances in the season of their premiere; all have been—or will be—performed in subsequent seasons."
Tips: "Have a good command of writing for brass band. Be able to use tonal materials imaginatively. Write with players' and audiences' enjoyment in mind."

*SACRAMENTO MASTER SINGERS, P.O. Box 215501, Sacramento CA 95821. (916)925-3159. Director: Ralph Hughes. Community chorus. Members are amateurs. Performs 4 concerts/year including 5-6 new works. "We perform at St. Frances Church—a large downtown church with acoustics favorable to choirs. Audience size 200-700 per concert." Pays by outright purchase. Submit complete score and tapes of piece(s). SASE. Reports in 1 month.
Music: "We perform music in the "classical" vein-medieval to avant-garde works appropriate for a chamber choir of 30-40 voices. Maximum forces—40 singers, 15 instrumentalists. Challenging scores are sought. No pop."
Performances: Benjamin Britten's *Ad Majorem Dei Gloriam* (cycle of part songs); Stephen Paulus's *Jesu Carols* (carol arrangements); Hugo Alfren's *Och jungfrun i gar i ringen* (Swedish folksong).

SALT LAKE SYMPHONIC CHOIR, Box 45, Salt Lake City UT 84110. (801)466-8701. Manager: Richard M. Taggart. Professional touring choir. Estab. 1949. Members are professionals and amateurs. Performs 4-15 concerts/year, including 1-3 new works. Commissions 1-3 new works or composers year. "We tour throughout U.S. and Canada for community concert series, colleges and universities." Pay is negotiable. Query first. Does not return unsolicited material. Reports in 3 months.
Music: Seeking "4- to 8-part choral pieces for a 100-voice choir—from Bach to rock."

SEAWAY CHORALE AND ORCHESTRA, INC., 2450 Middlefield Rd., Trenton MI 48183. (313)676-2400. Conductor, Executive Director: David M. Ward. Auditioned chorus and orchestra. Estab. 1975. Members are professionals and amateurs. Performs 5 major concerts/year, including 4 new works/year. Commissions 0-2 composers or new works/year. "We perform in halls, some church settings and high school auditoriums—large stage with orchestra pit. Our audience is ecumenically, financially, racially, socially, musically, multi-generation and a cross section of our area." Pays by negotiation. Submit score and tape of piece(s). SASE. Reports in 3 months.
Music: "We want 3-minute ballads for orchestra and chorus (for subscription concerts); sacred music, either accompanied or a cappella; Christmas music for chorus and orchestra. We have three performing groups: Voices of the Young—4th through 8th grades (40 members); Youth Sings—9th through 12th grades (a show choir, 24 members); Chorale—adults (70 members). Charismatic Christian music is not high on our priority list. Country music runs a close second. Our major concerts which draw large audiences utilize light selections such as show music, popular songs and music from movies. We present two concerts each year which we call Choral Masterpieces. These concerts include music from master composers of the past as well as contemporary. Our choral masterpieces concerts require Biblical or secular thoughts that are well-conceived musically."
Tips: "Don't settle for one musical avenue. Be as creatively prolific as possible. You may discover a lot about your own abilities and avoid redundancies as a result."

SINGING BOYS OF PENNSYLVANIA, P.O. Box 206, Wind Gap PA 18091. (215)759-6002. Director: K. Bernard Schade, Ed. D. Vocal ensemble. Estab. 1970. Members are professional children. Performs 120 concerts/year, including 2-3 new works. Commissions 1-2 composers or new works/year. "We attract general audiences: family, senior citizens, churches, concert associations, university concert series and schools." Pays by outright purchase $500-750. Submit score. SASE.
Music: "We want music for commercials, music for voices in the SSA or SSAA ranges sacred works or arrangements of American folk music with accompaniment. Our range of voices are from G below middle C to A (13th above middle C). Reading ability of choir is good but works which require a lot of work with little possibility of more than one performance are of little value. We don't want popular songs which are not arranged for SSA or SSAA choir. We sing very few popular songs except for special events. We perform music by composers who are well-known composers and do works by living composers, but ones who are writing in traditional choral forms. Works of music which have a full orchestral score are of interest. The orchestration should be fairly light, so as not to cover the voices. Works for Christmas have more value than some other, since we perform with orchestras on an annual basis."
Performances: Don Locklair's *The Columbus Madrigals* (opera).
Tips: "It must be appropriate music and words for children."

SUSQUEHANNA SYMPHONY ORCHESTRA, P.O. Box 485, Forest Hill MD 21050. (301)838-6465. Music Director: Sheldon Bair. Symphony orchestra. Estab. 1978. Members are amateurs. Performs 5 concerts/year, including 2 new works. "We perform in 2 halls. One is more intimate, 600 seats; the other is larger (999 seats) both with fine acoustics. Our audience encompasses all ages." Composers are normally not commissioned, just ASCAP or BMI royalties. Query first or submit complete score. SASE. Reports in 6 months.
Music: "We desire works for large orchestra any length, in a 'conservative 20th century' style. Seek fine, tonal music for chamber or large orchestra (large orchestra is preferable). We are a community orchestra, so the music must be within our grasp. Violin I to 7th position by step only; Violin II—stay within 3rd position, English horn and harp are OK. We don't want avant-garde music. Full orchestra pieces preferred."
Performances: Hutt's *Graphic Variations* (short character work); Unger's *Variations for Orchestra* (tonal variations); and Palmer's *Symphony #2* (neo-classic).

TORONTO MENDELSSOHN CHOIR, 60 Simcoe St., Toronto, Ontario M5J 2H5 **Canada**. Phone: (416)598-0422. Manager: Michael Ridout. Vocal ensemble. Members are professionals and amateurs. Performs 30 concerts/year including 1-3 new works. "Most performances take place in Roy Thomson Hall. The audience is reasonably sophisticated, musically knowledgeable but with moderately conservative tastes." Pays by royalty or by direct commission (does not result in ownership of the work).

Market conditions are constantly changing! If you're still using this book and it is 1994 or later, buy the newest edition of Songwriter's Market at your favorite bookstore or order directly from Writer's Digest Books.

Submit complete score and tapes of pieces. SASE. Reports in 6 months.

Music: All works must suit a large choir (180 voices) and standard orchestral forces or with some other not-too-exotic accompaniment. Length should be restricted to no longer than ½ of a nocturnal concert. The choir sings at a very professional level and can sight-read almost anything. "Works should fit naturally with the repertoire of a large choir which performs the standard choral orchestral repertoire."

Performances: Handel's *Messiah* (choral/orchestral); Mozart's *Requiem* (choral/orchestral)l; Mendelssohn's *St. Paul* (choral/orchestral).

UNIVERSITY OF HOUSTON OPERA THEATRE, School of Music, Houston TX 77204-4893. (713)749-4370 or 749-1116. Director of Opera: Buck Ross. Opera/music theater program. Members are professionals, amateurs and students. Performs 3-4 concerts/year, including 1 new work. Performs in a proscenium theater which seats 1,100. Pit seats approximately 40 players. Audience covers wide spectrum, from first time opera-goers to very sophisticated." Pays by royalty. Submit complete score and tapes of piece(s). SASE. Reports in 3 months.

Music: "We seek music that is feasible for high graduate level student singers. Chamber orchestras are very useful. No more than 2½ hours. We don't want serial pieces, aleatoric or children's operas."

Performances: Verdi's *Falstaff* (opera); Handel's *Alcina* (opera); Carlisle Floyd's *Bilby's Doll* (opera premiere of revised version).

*VANCOUVER CHAMBER CHOIR, 1254 W. 7th Ave., Vancouver BC V6H 1B6 Canada. Artistic Director: Jon Washburn. Vocal ensemble. Members are professionals. Performs 40 concerts/year; performs 5-8 new works/year. Commissions 3-4 composers or new works/year. Pays statutory SOCAN royalty. Submit complete score and tapes of piece(s). Does not return unsolicited material. Reports in 6 months.

Music: Seeks "choral works of all types for small chorus, with or without accompaniment, soloists. 'Serious' concert music only. Choir made up of 20 singers. Large or unusual instrumental accompaniments are less likely to be appropriate. No pop music."

Performances: Alice Parker's *That Sturdy Vine* (cantata for chorus, soloists and orchestra); R. Murray Schafer's *Magic Songs* (SATB a capella); and Jon Washburn's *A Stephen Foster Medley* (SSAATTBB/piano).

Tips: "We are looking for music that is performable yet innovative and choral music which has the potential to become "standard repertoire." Although we perform much new music it is only a small portion of the scores which are submitted."

*VANCOUVER YOUTH SYMPHONY ORCHESTRA SOCIETY, #204, 3737 Oak St., Vancouver BC V6H 2M4 **Canada.** Music Director: Arthur Polson. Youth orchestra. Estab. 1930. Members are amateurs. Performs 6-8 concerts/year. Generally family and friends of orchestra members. Perform in various venues from churches to major concert halls. Query first. SASE.

Music: "The Senior Orchestra performs the standard symphony repertoire. Programs usually consist of an overture, a major symphony and perhaps a concerto or shorter work. The Christmas concert and tour programs are sometimes lighter works."

Performances: Glen Morley's *Coquihalla Legends* (commissioned for 60th anniversary); Saint—Saens' *Symphony #3 (Organ)* (Symphony); and Benjamin Britten's *Men of Good Will.*

WARMINSTER SYMPHONY ORCHESTRA, 524 W. Pine St., Trevose PA 19053. (215)355-7421. Music Director/Principal Conductor: Gil Guglielmi, D.M.A. Community symphony orchestra. Estab. 1966. 12 "pros" and amateurs. Performs 4 concerts/year, including perhaps 1 new work. "We *try* to commission one composer or new work/year." Audience is blue collar and upper middle-class. The concert hall is a local junior high school with a seating capacity of 710. "We operate on a small budget. Composers are not paid, or paid very little (negotiable)." Composer should contact Dr. Guglielmi. Does not return unsolicited material. Reports in months.

Music: Romantic style. Length: 10 minutes to a full symphony. Orchestration: full orchestra with no sound effects, synthesizers, computers, etc. "We play from Mozart to Tschaikovsky." "Performers: we have a maximum of about 60 players. Level of difficulty: medium advanced—one grade above a good high school orchestra. We rehearse 2 hours a week so that anything written should take about 20 minutes a week rehearsal time to allow rehearsal time for the remaining selections. Our musicians and our audiences are middle-of-the-road." "The composer should write in *his* style and not try to contrive a piece for us. The orchestra has a full string section, 4 horns, 3 clarinets, 3 flutes, 2 bassons, 3 trumpets, 2 oboe, 1 English horn, 3 trombones, 1 tuba, 1 harp and a full percussion section."

Performances: Al Maene's *Perla Bella* (mini symphony); and David Finke's *The Wailing Wall* (tone poem).

Tips: "Do not expect the Philadelphia Orchestra. My musicians are primarily lay-people who are dedicated to the performance of good music. What they lack in expertise they more than make up or in practice, work and dedication."

*WAUKEGAN SYMPHONY ORCHESTRA, 39 Jack Benny Dr., Waukegan IL 60087. (312)244-1660. Director: Dr. Richard Hynson. Symphony orchestra. Estab. 1974. Members are professionals and amateurs. Performs 4 concerts/year including 1 new work. "We have a middle-aged and older audience, basically conservative. We perform in a 1,800 seat house." Paid through BMI and ASCAP. Query first. SASE. Reports in 3 months.
Music: "We want conservative music, especially regarding rhythmic complexities, four to ten minutes in length, orchestrated for wind pairs, standard brass, strings, etc., up to 4 percussionists plus timpani. The number of performers basically limited to 75 member orchestra, difficulty level should be moderate to moderately difficult, more difficulty in winds and brass than strings. We don't want aleatoric 'chance' music, pointillistic—to a large extent non-melodic music. We are always looking for beautiful music that speaks to the heart as well as the mind, music with a discernable structure is more attractive."
Performances: Sibelius' *Symphony No. 2*; Copland's *Appalachian Spring* and *Quiet City*.
Tips: "Write beautiful, listenable music. Make the composition an exercise in understanding the orchestral medium, not an academic exercise in rehearsal problems."

WAYNE CHAMBER ORCHESTRA, 300 Pompton Rd., Wayne NJ 07470. (201)595-2694. Managing Director: Sheri Newberger. Chamber orchestra. Estab. 1986. Members are professionals. Performs 4 concerts/year. Receives 2-3 outside submissions/year. Regional audience from North Jersey area. Attractive and modern concert hall seating 960 patrons. Query with bio first. SASE.
Music: "We are looking for new American music for a 40-piece orchestra. Our only method of funding would be by grant so music may have to tie in with a theme. Although we have not yet performed new works, we hope to in the future."
Performances: Victor Herbert's *Fall of a Nation*; Paul Creston's *Partita for Flute, Violin and Strings*; and Zwilich's *Prologue and Variations*, all orchestral works.

WHEATON SYMPHONY ORCHESTRA, 1600 E. Roosevelt, Wheaton IL 60187. (708)668-8585. Manager: Donald C. Mattison. Symphony orchestra. Estab. 1959. Members are professionals and amateurs. Performs 3 concerts/year, including 1 new work. Composers are paid $100/performance. Query first. SASE. Reports in 2 months.
Music: "This is a *good* amateur orchestra that wants pieces in a traditional idiom. Large scale works for chorus and orchestra. No avant garde, 12-tone or atonal material. Pieces should be 20 minutes or less and must be prepared in 3 rehearsals. Instrumentation is woodwinds in 3s, full brass 4-3-3-1, percussion, etc."
Performances: Jerry Bilik's *Aspects of Man* (4-section suite); Walton's *Variations on a Theme of Hindeminth's*; and Augusta Read Thomas' *A Crystal Planet*.

*WOMEN'S PHILHARMONIC, 330 Townsend St., San Francisco CA 94107. (415)543-2297. Director, NWCRC: Susan Rands. Philharmonic orchestra. Estab. 1980. Members are professionals. Performs 15 concerts—year; performs 6 new works/year. Commissions 3 composers or new works/year. "Audience median age is 39; urban professional. Performance space is downtown hall in prime retail district with 1,100 reserved seating." Pays by commission. Query first. SASE.
Music: Seeks symphonic/orchestral music with or without soloist by women composers."
Performances: Hilary Tann's *Open Field*; Chen Yi's *Duo Ye #2*; and Joan Tower's *Piano Concerto* (all orchestral).

ZION CHAMBER ORCHESTRA, Dowie Memorial Drive, Zion IL 60099. (708)872-4803. Orchestra Director: Donna Walker. Chamber orchestra. Members are professionals and amateurs. Performs 12 concerts/year, including occasional new works. Audience is "low-middle class—middle class mostly. 522-seat auditorium, modern, effective acoustically, but a little dry for music." Submit complete score and tape of pieces. Does not return unsolicited material.
Music: "Instrumentation for chamber group—full complement of brass, winds, strings. Not interested in dissonance at this time. Prefers medium level difficulty."
Performances: D. Dickering's *Our Inurement* (serial...anti-abortion); A. Koetz's *Sweet Hour of Prayer* (sacred, traditional); and Mendelsohn, Bach, Mozart, Brahms, Ives, Prokofiev, etc.

Fine Arts/'92-'93 Changes

The following markets appeared in the 1992 edition of *Songwriter's Market* but are absent from the 1993 edition. Most of these companies failed to respond to our request for an update of their listing for a variety of reasons. For example, they may have gone out of business or they may have requested deletion because they are backlogged with material. If we know the specific reason, it appears within parentheses.

Cabrillo Music Festival
Canadian Opera Company
Carson-Dominquez Hills Symphony (requested deletion)
Center for Contemporary Opera
City Summer Opera
Fine Arts Strings
Greater Nashville Arts Foundation
Israel Sinfonietta Beer Sheva
Lamarca American Variety Singers and Image
Manitoba Chamber Orchestra
Melodious Accord, Inc. (not accepting submissions)

Milwaukee Youth Symphony Orchestra
Music Today
New York City Opera Education Department (requested deletion)
Opera in the Schools
Orange County Opera Inc.
PFL Management
Philadelphia College of Bible
Phoenix Symphony Orchestra
Queens Opera
The Ridgefield Youth Orchestra
San Diego Symphony Orchestra

Sarasota Opera Association
Sault Ste. Marie Symphony Orchestra
Shaw Festival Theatre
The Singers Forum
Southwestern College/Winfield Community Orchestra
University of Southern Mississippi Symphony Orchestra
Utah Arts Festival
Valley Youth Orchestra Association
Vereinigte Buhnen/Opernhaus
Virginia Beach Orchestral Association
The Williamsburg Symphonia

Resources

Organizations

by Terry Miller

Let's look at what a songwriter organization is and what it does for its members. A songwriter organization is a support group, the membership usually consisting of lyricists and songwriters, that provides assistance to professional and amateur songwriters in the form of workshops, critique services and discounted instructional materials such as books, cassette tapes and videos. Other services include networking situations in which songwriters and lyricists may find collaborators and music publishing opportunities through the vehicle of song pitch sessions.

Most songwriter organizations publish monthly newsletters containing articles on songwriting and tips about publishers and record labels looking for material. Some large songwriter organizations like Los Angeles Songwriters Showcase and the Nashville Songwriters Association International provide a phone "hotline" members can call for help with everything from filling out a copyright form to how to pitch a song to a publisher.

The vast majority of songwriter organizations are nonprofit groups with membership open to anyone interested in songwriting. There may be more than one category of membership in the group with one category for amateurs and another for professional songwriters and lyricists. Members usually pay an annual fee for the privilege of being a member.

The advantages of belonging to national songwriting organizations are the many networking opportunities and resources that are made available to the songwriter. Songwriters who do not live in the cities where the national organizations are located miss out on interacting with other songwriters on a direct basis. Many of these songwriters choose to join or form smaller songwriter organizations in their own communities.

The groups provide the same services as their larger counterparts, but on a smaller scale. These associations may meet weekly or monthly to review and critique members' songs and to exchange news about publishers looking for material or information about new songwriting books. To find out if there is a local songwriter organization in your area, consult the following listings. If you find that there is no local songwriter organization in your area, you may want to consider beginning a new group.

Getting started

If you wish to keep the group small, say a dozen or fewer members, it will require less organization than a larger group. Small groups may not need the formalities of electing officers and charging dues. The group can meet in each member's home on a rotating basis.

Terry Miller is a published and recorded songwriter living in Houston, Texas. He has been instrumental in establishing several songwriter organizations in the Houston area including the Fort Bend Songwriter's Association, the North Channel Songwriter's Association, and the International Network of Lyricists and Songwriters. He currently works as a public relations advisor for the Songwriter's Network of Houston and as a songwriting and computer software consultant.

Occasionally, a representative from a small independent music publishing company or some other industry professional may be asked to speak to the group. (Consult the Music Publishers section for contact names, addresses and phone numbers of publishers in or near your town. Write or call to ask them to speak at your meetings. Most independent publishers will enjoy the chance to speak at your meetings.) Members may meet collaborators and assist each other with home recorded demos. The advantage in keeping the group small is that much more of the meeting time can be spent discussing songwriting techniques and styles as well as critiquing songs rather than handling the business affairs of a larger group. The disadvantage of belonging to a smaller group: networking possibilities with other songwriters are greatly limited because of the small number of members. An organizer who wants a larger group can locate potential members by sending public service announcements to the local media and posting announcements in public places like supermarkets, music stores, local clubs and studios.

If this type of organization begins to grow to over 20 members, the group may decide to become more formal by adopting a charter and seeking nonprofit status. You can prepare to do this by researching the potential for growth. In other words, are there more songwriters in the area who would be interested in joining a songwriting organization? A good basic indicator of potential membership is the local population. If the population of the area is 100,000 or more, it's likely the group can obtain up to 100 members. Another good indicator of interest in songwriting within your area is the number of small recording studios in your town. Also, note the number of night club and restaurant open mikes, songwriter nights and musician jams advertised in your local papers. In a city of 100,000, if there are two or more such events advertised weekly or two or more operating studios, then there are probably enough songwriters in your area who will be interested. Contact Los Angeles Songwriters Showcase, the National Academy of Songwriters or the Nashville Songwriters Association International; they may have other data pertinent to the group's potential for growth.

If there is interest in forming such an organization, a free or inexpensive meeting place must be found. The best places to check out are the local libraries, public schools, city or county halls, community civic centers, churches, community colleges, American Legion halls and any other civic or community meeting places. Some of these places may be used free of charge or the group may be charged a nominal clean-up and utilities fee. The chamber of commerce may also be able to provide you with the name of local businesses that would be willing to help. The important thing about the meeting place is that it should be centrally located so that the majority of the members do not have to travel long distances to attend. Also keep in mind the availability of the meeting place. If the group decides to establish a set time for its meetings, will the meeting place be available to the organization on a regular basis? The time of the meeting should also be set to insure the greatest attendance.

Song critique sessions

Song evaluation is one of the most important services a group provides. If one or more of the members has already had songs published and recorded, then those members should be sought out to give opinions during critique sessions. Persons inexperienced in critiquing songs should select their words of criticism carefully to prevent discouraging the less-experienced songwriter whose song is being critiqued.

The group may wish to seek the help of a local independent publisher to assist with the critique sessions. Many independent music publishers are extremely happy to attend critique sessions and offer their opinions on songwriters' material. An added advantage of having the publisher do the critiquing is that members are often more receptive to input from an outside source than they are to the critiques of their fellow members.

The organizers should research the publisher before approaching him to make sure the publisher is legitimately qualified to give opinions on songs. Some people calling themselves music publishers are really "song sharks" who ask for money to have songs published or recorded. (See The Business of Songwriting in the front of the book for more information.) To check out the publisher, call or write the performing rights organization the publisher belongs to and ask for information on the publisher. BMI, ASCAP and SESAC closely monitor their member publishers and deny or withdraw membership to any who use questionable consumer business practices.

Once the group has held several critique sessions and the members' songs have gone through the "creative grinder" of evaluation, rewriting and more evaluation, a representative from the group can call or write the A&R departments of a larger publishing company or label, asking them to send representatives to sit on a critiquing panel. It is more difficult to get regional A&R representatives to attend critique sessions; they may be unable to participate due to scheduling difficulties. Be sure to call these A&R people only when you know there are enough songwriters in your group with enough songs to be worth the A&R representative's time to attend. The group should stay informed about representatives who are coming to town for expositions, award presentations or other company business. If they are in the area, many A&R people will be happy to give a few minutes of their time to a group, if time is available.

One final source for getting evaluators for critique sessions is to consult this section for the names of organizations that may exist in towns that are within two or three hours driving time of your area. Also, small nonprofit songwriter organizations are usually happy to assist with the formation of other groups in other towns. These sister groups may provide panel members for critique sessions and help with other details. Finding panel members for critique sessions may take several weeks or even months, but good instructive critique sessions can do much to help the songwriters in the group improve their songs.

Other help and encouragement

Call the membership offices of ASCAP and BMI in New York, Nashville or Los Angeles and ask the regional membership directors for assistance in getting the songwriting group started. These two organizations work with both large and small songwriter organizations throughout the United States and will gladly assist anyone who shows a interest in promoting the growth of the songwriting industry.

Contact the local performing arts council or arts support group and ask for assistance with legal details and drawing up a charter. Your local or state Bar Association can provide names of attorneys who will provide free or low-cost legal advice. In Texas, an example of a group that provides these services to nonprofit groups for little or no fee is Texas Accountants and Lawyers for the Arts. See the listing in this section for Volunteer Lawyers for the Arts, another legal group providing advice to nonprofit organizations unable to afford private counsel.

The group should not be discouraged if the organization does not grow too quickly within the first couple of years. Things beyond the organizers' control, like differences in musical style preferences among the members as well as the outcropping of other songwriter organizations in the area may impede the group's growth in membership. Handling these situations as they turn up is the best method for solving them.

Most songwriters who stay with the craft tend to join one or more national songwriter organizations and perhaps one smaller local group. Belonging to the larger group gives the songwriter access to more educational and pitching resources than a smaller group can provide, while belonging to a smaller group gives a songwriter the interaction with other songwriters he needs to nurture creativity and to find collaborators.

The following section of listings will aid in finding contacts for help in organizing new groups, input for critique sessions and new industry information and will act as a larger support group for new songwriter organizations. Let them help guide you in the development of your local organization!

ACADEMY OF COUNTRY MUSIC, #923, 6255 Sunset Blvd., Hollywood CA 90028. (213)462-2351. Membership: David Young. Estab. 1964. Serves producers, artists, songwriters, talent buyers and others involved with the country music industry. Eligibility for professional members is limited to those individuals who derive some portion of their income directly from country music. Each member is classified by one of the following categories: artist/entertainer, club operator/employee, musician/trend leader, DJ, manager/booking agent, composer, music publisher, promotion, publications, radio, TV/motion picture, record company or affiliated (general). The purpose of ACM is to promote and enhance the image of country music. "The Academy is involved year round in activities important to the country music community. Some of these activities include charity fund raisers, participation in country music seminars, talent contests, artist showcases, assistance to producers in placing country music on television and in motion pictures and backing legislation that benefits the interests of the country music community. The ACM is governed by directors and run by officers elected annually." Also offers a newsletter. Applications are accepted throughout the year. Membership is $40/year.

AMERICAN CHORAL DIRECTORS ASSOCIATION, P.O. Box 6310, Lawton OK 73506. (405)355-8161. Estab. 1959. Serves musicians. "From college age students to the oldest senior adults. Members are those who are interested in learning, teaching, performing, composing and publishing choral music. Must be a student of, teacher of or conductor of choral music. We encourage the finest in choral music and promote its development in all ways, including performance, composition, publication and research. Provides an opportunity for songwriter to know names of potential markets. ACDA has membership of almost 16,000." Offers competitions, instruction, lectures, library, newsletter, performance opportunities, workshops and annual division or national conventions. Applications accepted year-round. Membership fees are: Active Member-$40, Retired Member-$10, Student Member-$10, Foreign Member-$60, Industry Member-$100, Institutional Member-$75 and Life Member-$1,000.

AMERICAN FEDERATION OF MUSICIANS (AFM), Suite 600, 1501 Broadway, New York NY 10036. (212)869-1330. Membership available to all qualified musicians and vocalists in the United States and Canada. "The American Federation of Musicians of the United States and Canada is the largest entertainment union in the world and exists solely for the advancement of live music and the benefit of its 250,000 members. In addition to enhancing employment opportunities for members, the AFM aids members in negotiating contracts; enforces employers' observance of working conditions and wage scales; processes traveling members' claims at no cost to members; protects musicians from unfavorable legislation at the federal, state and local levels; negotiates pension, welfare and retirement benefits; offers instrument insurance to members; offers free job referral service to members who are seeking employment with traveling groups; and keeps membership informed of happenings in the business through its publication, *International Musician*. Members also receive numerous benefits provided by each local chapter. Initiation fees and local dues vary; a small percentage of work dues are contributed by members. Write for further information or contact AFM local nearest you."

AMERICAN MUSIC CENTER, INC., Suite 1001, 30 W. 26th St., New York NY 10010-2011. (212)366-5260. Executive Director: Nancy Clarke. Estab. 1939. For composers and performers. Members are American composers, performers, critics, publishers and others interested in contemporary concert music and jazz. Offers newsletter, circulating library of contemporary music scores and advice on opportunities for composers and new music performers; disseminates information on American music. Purpose is to encourage the recognition and performance of contemporary American music. Members receive the twice-yearly *AMC Newsletter*, professional monthly "Opportunity Updates," eligibility for group health insurance and the right to vote in AMC elections.

AMERICAN MUSICIANS UNION INC., 8 Tobin Ct., Dumont NJ 07628. (201)384-5378. President and Treasurer: Ben Intorre. Estab. 1948. Serves musicians and vocalists of all age groups, all ethnic groups, music from gay 90's to contemporary, ballroom music, banquets, weddings, rock, disco, western, Latin, standards, etc. "We assist musicians in their efforts to perform and serve the public. We offer membership in a union, life insurance, meetings and union publication. "Applicant must be a musician, vocalist or manager. Disc-jockeys are not eligible." Offers newsletter and performance opportunities. Applications accepted year-round. Annual dues $27; $10 initiation. Services include life insurance ($2,000 to age 65, reduced insurance to age 70) and advertisements in *Quarternote* are usually free to members. "We have locals in the U.S., in New Jersey, Minnesota, Michigan, etc."

*AMERICAN ORFF-SCHULWERK ASSOCIATION INC., P.O. Box 391089, Cleveland OH 44139-8089. (216)543-5366. FAX: (216)543-4057. Executive Secretary: Cindi Wobig. Estab. 1969. Serves musicians and music educators; preschool, kindergarten and classroom teachers; music therapists; church musicians; college students and retired music educators. Offers workshops, annual conference and a quarterly publication. Chapters located in most states.

AMERICAN SOCIETY OF COMPOSERS, AUTHORS AND PUBLISHERS (ASCAP), 1 Lincoln Plaza, New York NY 10023. (212)621-6000. Director of Membership: Paul S. Adler. Membership Department Staff: Wanda LeBron, Jonathon Love, Debbie Rose, Lisa Schmidt, Dewayne Alexander, Marcy Drexler, Emilio Garcia and Michael Kerker. Members are songwriters, composers, lyricists and music publishers. Applicants must "have at least one song copyrighted for associate membership; have at least one song commercially available as sheet music, available on rental, commercially recorded, or performed in media licensed by the Society (e.g., performed in a nightclub or radio station) for full membership. ASCAP is a membership-owned, performing right licensing organization that licenses its members' nondramatic musical compositions for public performance and distributes the fees collected from such licensing to its members based on a scientific random sample survey of performances." Primary value is "as a clearinghouse, giving users a practical and economical bulk licensing system and its members a vehicle through which the many thousands of users can be licensed and the members paid royalties for the use of their material. All monies collected are distributed after deducting only the Society's cost of doing business."
Tips: "The Society sponsors a series of writers' workshops in Los Angeles, Nashville and New York open to members and nonmembers. Grants to composers available to members and nonmembers. Contact the membership department in New York or the following branch offices: 7920 Sunset Blvd., Suite 300, Los Angeles, CA 90046; Kingsbury Center, 350 W. Hubbard St., 2nd Floor, Chicago, IL 60610; 2 Music Square W., Nashville TN 37203; 52 Haymarket, London SW1Y4RP, **England**."

*ARKANSAS SONGWRITERS, 6817 Gingerbread, Little Rock AR 72204. (501)569-8889. President: Peggy Vining. Estab. 1979. Serves songwriters, musicians and lovers of music. Any interested may join. To promote and encourage the art of songwriting. Offers competitions, instruction, lectures, newsletter, performance opportunities, social outings and workshops. Applications accepted year-round. Membership fee is $15/year.
Tips: "We also contribute time, money and our energies to promoting our craft in other functions. Meetings are held on the first Tuesday of each month at 6:45 p.m."

AUSTIN MUSIC BUSINESS ASSOCIATION, (formerly Austin Music Industry Council), Box 1967, Austin TX 78767. (512)288-1044. Chairman: Martin Theophilus. Estab. 1983. "Serves all persons who are actively engaged in any music industry related business. Plus anyone who participates or supports the Austin Music Industry. (Board member must be in the business of music.)" Main purpose is to support and increase the success of the Austin Music Industry—through public relations, education, seminars and information. "Primary value for a songwriter is the opportunity to know significant business persons and be aware of opportunities in the music industry." Offers instruction, newsletter, performance opportunities, social outings and workshops. Applications accepted year-round. Membership fee is $30/year.

AUSTIN SONGWRITERS GROUP, P.O. Box 2578, Austin TX 78768. (512)442-TUNE. President: Steve Christopher. Estab. 1986. Nonprofit. Serves songwriters, musicians, producers, engineers and others in the music business. Members include beginning songwriters to published professionals; no age restrictions. All are welcome for membership. "Purpose is to educate songwriters in the areas of lyric development, musical structure, general songwriting skills, publishing, marketing and related music business activities. ASG also provides a networking forum for members to interact with other songwriters and industry professionals." Produces the annual Austin Songwriters *EXPO*, an annual statewide song contest, competitions, field trips, instruction, lectures, library, newsletter, performance opportunities and workshops. Offers discounts at local recording studios for A.S.G. members. Developing songwriter's library with books, magazines and newsletters of interest to songwriters. Applications accepted year-round. Membership fee is $35/year.

*BROADCAST MUSIC, INC. (BMI), 320 W. 57th St., New York NY 10019. (212)586-2000; 8730 Sunset Blvd, Los Angeles CA 90069; and 10 Music Square E., Nashville TN 37203. President: Frances W. Preston. Senior Vice President: Theodora Zavin. Vice President, California: Ron Anton. Vice President, Nashville: Roger Sovine. Performing rights organization representing over 85,000 creators of music: songwriters, composers and music publishers. "Applicants must have written a musical composition, alone or in collaboration with other writers, which is commercially published, recorded or otherwise likely to be performed. Purpose: BMI licenses the nondramatic performing rights of musical compositions to users of music which include radio and TV stations, hotels, night clubs, universities, colleges and the many other places in the US where music is publicly performed." Payment is secured for distribution to the copyright owners: songwriters, composers and publishers. Offers competitions, instruction, lectures, newsletter, performance opportunities, workshops, seminars and awards. Applications accepted year-round. No membership fee for songwriters; 1-time fee of $25 to affiliate a publishing company.

CALIFORNIA COUNTRY MUSIC ASSOCIATION, Box 6116, Fullerton CA 92631. (714)992-CCMA. Executive Director: Gary Murray. Serves songwriters, musicians and country music fans and business. "Our members are of all ages, from the very young to the very old. They come from a wide variety of vocations, talents and professions. Their common interest is country music. A preferred geographic location would be the state of California, although a member may live out of state. All musicians, artists, and songwriters are eligible to compete in our chapter and statewide award shows, as long they have not charted on a major chart list in the last two years. The main purpose of this organization is to support, sponsor, organize, inform, and promote all facets of country music and entertainment. Our organization works together with the aspiring artist. We recognize, support and award their talents throughout the state and within our chapters. This organization cooperates with and supports country music radio stations, country music publications, charitable organizations, and the country music industry. We are a non-profit organization and our motto is 'God, country and country music.' Country music people are our number one concern." Offers competitions, instruction, lectures, newsletter, performance opportunities, social outings, workshops, showcases and award shows. Applications accepted year-round. Membership fee is $20/year.

CANADA COUNCIL/CONSEIL DES ARTS DU CANADA, P.O. Box 1047, Ottawa, Ontario K1P 5V8 **Canada**. (613)598-4365/6. Information Officer: Lise Rochon. Estab. 1957. A federal organization serving songwriters and musicians. "Individual artists must be Canadian citizens or permanent residents of Canada, and must have completed basic training and/or have the recognition as professionals within their fields. The Canada Council's objectives are to foster and promote the arts in Canada by offering financial assistance to professional Canadian artists and arts organizations. The Canada Council offers grants to professional musicians to pursue their own personal and creative development through the Grants to Artists Program. There are specific deadline dates for the various programs we administer." Call or write for more details.

CANADIAN ACADEMY OF RECORDING ARTS & SCIENCES (CARAS), 3rd Floor, 124 Merton St., Toronto, Ontario M4S 2Z2 **Canada**. (416)485-3135. Executive Director: Daisy C. Falle. Serves songwriters and musicians. Membership is open to all employees (including support staff) in broadcasting and record companies, as well as producers, personal managers, recording artists, recording engineers, arrangers, composers, music publishers, album designers, promoters, talent and booking agents, record retailers, rack jobbers, distributors, recording studios and other music industry related professions (on approval). Applicants must be affiliated with the Canadian recording industry. Offers newsletter, performance opportunities and social outings, Canadian artist record discount program, nomination and voting privileges for Juno Awards and discount tickets to Juno awards show. Also promotional merchandise, benefit plans, discount on trade magazines and complimentary Juno Awards CD. "CARAS strives to foster the development of the Canadian music and recording industries and to contribute toward higher artistic standards." Applications accepted year-round. Membership fee is $45/year. Applications accepted from individuals only, and not from companies or organizations.

CANADIAN COUNTRY MUSIC ASSOCIATION, Suite 127, 3800 Steeles Avenue West, Woodbridge Ontario L4L 4G9 **Canada**. (416)739-5014. Executive Director: Sheila Hamilton. Estab. 1976. Members are songwriters, musicians, producers, radio station personnel, managers, booking agents and others. Offers newsletter, workshops, performance opportunities and annual awards. "Through our newsletters and conventions we offer a means of meeting and associating with artists and others in the industry. During our workshops or seminars (Country Music Week), we include a songwriters' seminar. The CCMA is a federally chartered, nonprofit organization, dedicated to the promotion and development of Canadian country music throughout Canada and the world and to providing a unity of purpose for the Canadian country music industry. Send for application.

*CANADIAN MUSICAL REPRODUCTION RIGHTS AGENCY LIMITED (CMRRA), 56 Wellesley St. W., Suite 320, Toronto, ON M5S 2S3 **Canada**. (416)926-1966. FAX: (416)926-7521. General Manager: David A. Basskin. Estab. 1975. Serves songwriters and copyright owners or administrators of musical compositions (composers, authors and music publishers). "Eligibility requirements a songwriter/musician must meet for membership: must own the copyright or have administration rights in one or more musical compositions for the territory of Canada. The organization's main purpose is to license the reproduction rights of copyright musical works and to collect and distribute the royalties collected to the rights owners on the basis of the licenses. The primary value in this organization for a songwriter is the administration and protection of their copyrights and the collection of royalties due to them." Applications accepted year-round. "There are no membership fees or annual dues. For administering the copyright owner's work, CMRRA retains a 5% commission on revenues collected for mechanical rights and 10% for synchronization rights. Where money is received from a foreign society, CMRAA distributes it to its member clients at a 3% charge. CMRRA is the principal mechanical rights agency in Canada. It was primarily responsible for securing passage of amendments to Canada's *Copyright Act* abolishing the compulsory licence and statutory rate for songs used by record companies. This action permitted the royalty rate for recorded songs to rise for the first time in over 64 years."

CONNECTICUT SONGWRITERS ASSOCIATION, Box 1292, Glastonbury CT 06033. (203)659-8992. Executive Director: Don Donegan. "We are an educational, nonprofit organization dedicated to improving the art and craft of original music. Founded in 1979 by Don Donegan, CSA has grown to become one of the best known songwriter's associations in the country. Membership in the CSA admits you to 16-24 seminars/workshops per year at 5 locations throughout Connecticut. Noted professionals deal with all aspects of the craft and business of music including lyric writing, music theory, music technology, arrangement and production, legal and business aspects, performance techniques, song analysis and recording techniques. CSA also offers showcases and concerts which are open to the public and designed to give artists a venue for performing their original material for an attentive, listening audience. CSA benefits have helped United Cerebral Palsy, Muscular Dystrophy, group homes, Hospice, world hunger, libraries, nature centers, community centers and more. CSA shows encompass ballads to bluegrass and Bach to rock. Our monthly newsletter, *Connecticut Songsmith*, offers free classified advertising for members, and has been edited and published by Bill Pere since 1980. Annual dues are $50. Senior citizen and full time students are $20. Organizations can join for $100. Memberships are fully tax-deductible as business expenses or as charitable contributions to the extent allowed by law."

COUNTRY MUSIC SHOWCASE INTERNATIONAL, INC., Box 368, Carlisle IA 50047. (515)989-3676 or 989-3748. President: Harold L. Luick. Vice President: Barbara A. Lancaster. "We are a nonprofit, educational performing arts organization for songwriters, recording artists and entertainers. The organization showcases songwriters at different seminars and workshops held at the request of its members in many different states across the nation. It also showcases recording artists/entertainer members at many Fair Association showcases held across the United States. When a person becomes a member they receive a membership card, newsletters, an educational information packet (about songwriting/ entertainment business), a question and answer service by mail or phone, a song evaluation and critique service, info on who's looking for song material, songwriters who are willing to collaborate, and songwriting contests. Members can submit 1 song per month for a critique. We offer good constructive criticism and honest opinions. Songs that meet our professional standards may be retained in our 'In House Song Bank,' or a songwriting contract may be offered to our member songwriter to represent it through our 'In House Publishing Company' for possible use in future recordings. The song bank and publishing company are membership owned and operated for the benefit of our paid members. For the recording artist/entertainer members we have in-house services, PR services, studio production services and promotion layout and mailing services. We maintain that a songwriter, recording artist or entertainer should associate himself with professional people and educators that know more about the business of music than they do; otherwise, they cannot reach their musical goals." Supporting Songwriter membership donation and Supporting Recording Artist/Entertainer membership donation are $40 per year; Supporting Band, Group or music related business membership donation is $60 per year. For free information, brochure or membership application send SASE to the above address.

DALLAS SONGWRITERS ASSOCIATION, 2932 Dyer St., Dallas TX 75205. (214)691-5318. President: Barbara McMillen. Estab. 1988. Serves songwriters and lyricists of Dallas/Ft. Worth metroplex. Members are adults ages 18-65, Dallas/Ft. Worth area songwriters/lyricists who are 18 years and older who are or aspire to be professionals. Purpose is to provide songwriters an opportunity to meet other songwriters, share information, find co-writers and support each other through group discussions at monthly meetings. To provide songwriters an opportunity to have their songs heard and critiqued by peers and professionals by playing cassettes and providing an open mike at monthly meetings and by offering contests judged by publishers. To provide songwriters opportunities to meet other music business professionals by inviting guest speakers to monthly meetings. To provide songwriters opportunities to learn more about the craft of songwriting and the business of music by presenting mini-workshops at each monthly meeting. "We offer a chance for the songwriter to learn from peers and industry professionals and an opportunity to belong to a supportive group environment to encourage the individual to continue his/her songwriting endeavors." Offers competitions, field trips, instruction, lectures, newsletter, performance opportunities, social outings and workshops. "Our members are eligible to join the Southwest Community Credit Union and for discounts at several local music stores and seminars." Applications accepted year-round. Membership fee is $25.

THE DRAMATISTS GUILD, INC., 234 W. 44th St., New York NY 10036. (212)398-9366. Membership includes over 7,000 playwrights, composers, lyricists and librettists nationwide. "As the professional association of playwrights, composers and lyricists, the Guild protects the rights of all theater writers, and improves the conditions under which they work. Additionally, the Guild encourages and nurtures the work of dramatists in the U.S. through its program of seminars and workshops. To be a member of The Dramatists Guild, you must have completed a dramatic work (a one-act or full-length play or component part- book, music or lyrics- of a musical) whether produced or not. The Guild offers many services and activities, including use of the Guild's contracts and a royalty collection service; The Hotline, a nationwide toll-free phone number for business or contract problems; an annual marketing directory with up-to-date information on grants, agents, producers, playwriting contests, conferences and workshops; two publications (*The Dramatists Guild Quarterly* and *The Dramatists Guild Newsletter*); access to group health insurance and access to Guild's newsroom."

THE FOLK ALLIANCE, P.O. Box 5010, Chapel Hill NC 27514. (919)542-3957. Contact: Art Menius. Estab. 1989. Serves songwriters, musicians and folk music and dance organizations. Members are organizations and individuals involved in traditional and contemporary folk music and dance in the USA and Canada. Members must be active in the field of folk music (singers/songwriters in any genre—blues, bluegrass, Celtic, Latino, old-time, etc.). Also must reside in USA or Canada. The Folk Alliance serves members through education, advocacy, field development, professional development, networking and showcases. Offers newsletter, performance opportunities, social outings, workshops and "database of members, organizations, presenters, folk radio, etc." Applications accepted year-round. Membership fee is $25/year/individual (voting); $75-350/year for organizational.
Tips: The Folk Alliance hosts its annual conference in late January/early February at different locations in the USA and Canada.

FORT BEND SONGWRITERS ASSOCIATION, 7010 FM 762, Richmond TX 77469. 713-563-9070. Info line: 713-CONCERT (Access Code FBSA). Coordinator: Dave Davidson. Estab. 1989. Serves "any person, amateur or professional, interested in songwriting or music. Our members write pop, rock, country, rockabilly, gospel, R&B; children's music and musical plays." Open to all, regardless of geographic location or professional status. The FBSA provides its membership with help to perfect their songwriting crafts by conducting workshops, seminars, publishing a monthly newsletter and holding songwriting and vocal performance competitions and showcases. The FBSA provides instruction for beginning writers and pubilshing and artist tips for the more accomplished writer." Offers competitions, field trips, instruction, lectures, newsletter, performance opportunities, workshops, mail-in critiques and collaboration opportunities. Applications accepted year-round. Full membership: $40; Associate Membership: $25. For more information send SASE.

GOSPEL MUSIC ASSOCIATION, 7 Music Circle North, Nashville TN 37203. (615)242-0303. Membership Coordinator: Clarke Beasley. Estab. 1964. Serves songwriters, musicians and anyone directly involved in or who supports gospel music. Professional members include advertising agencies, musicians, agents/managers, composers, retailers, music publishers, print media, broadcast media, and other members of the recording industry. Associate members include supporters of gospel music and those whose involvement in the industry does not provide them with income. The primary purpose of the GMA is to promote the industry of Gospel and Christian music, and provide professional development series for industry members. Offers library, newsletter, performance opportunities and workshops. Applications accepted year-round. Membership fee is $50/year (professional); and $25/year (associate).

THE GUILD OF INTERNATIONAL SONGWRITERS & COMPOSERS, Sovereign House, 12 Trewartha Rd., Praa Sands, Penzance, Cornwall TR20 9ST **England**. Phone: (0736)762826. FAX: (0736)763328. Secretary: C.A. Jones. Serves songwriters, musicians, record companies, music publishers, etc. "Our members are amateur and professional songwriters and composers, musicians, publishers, independent record publishers, studio owners and producers. Membership is open to all persons throughout the world of any age and ability, from amateur to professional. The Guild gives advice and services relating to the music industry. A free magazine is available upon request with an SAE or 3x IRC's. We provide contact information for artists, record companies, music publishers, industry organizations; free copyright service; *Songwriting & Composing Magazine*; and many additional free services." Applications accepted year-round. Annual dues are £20 in the U.K.; £25 in E.E.C. countries; £25 overseas. (Subscriptions in pounds sterling only).

*HAWAIIAN ISLANDS COUNTRY MUSIC, P.O. Box 75148, Honolulu HI 96836. Owner: Maitai. Estab. 1977. Serves songwriters, musicians and entertainers. Members are anyone who loves music. Main purpose is to promote the emerging aspiring artist. Offers competitions, lectures, performance opportunities, workshops and promotion/management. Applications are accepted year-round. Memberships fee is $20.

THE HYMN SOCIETY IN THE UNITED STATES AND CANADA, P.O. Box 30854, Texas Christian University, Fort Worth TX 76129. (817)921-7608. Executive Director: W. Thomas Smith. Estab. 1922. Serves hymn text and tune writers. "Our members are church musicians, clergy, hymn writers and institutional libraries. The main purpose is to promote hymn singing, sponsor hymn writing, and foster hymnological research. Members will acquire skills in writing congregational hymns." Offers competitions, lectures, library, newsletters, performance opportunites, workshops and annual conferences. Applications accepted year-round. Membership fee and annual dues: $35.

*IDAHO SONGWRITERS ASSOCIATION, P.O. Box 382, Firth ID 83236-0382. President and Founder: Jay Allen Congdon, Jr. Estab. 1991. "A nonprofit organization designed to promote Idaho songwriters by showing the world that Idaho has more than great potatoes, we have great talent too." Offers workshops, seminars, contests and showcases. ISA publishes a monthly newsletter and sponsors several songwriting contests a year. We are working to establish a network of connections in the music business to help members market their material. We offer a Partners Finder service for writers needing collaborators and a critique/review service for members' songs. Annual membership fees: Full membership $20, Limited membership $5 (Student and military full memberships $5 off). For more information send large SASE to the listed address.

INDIANAPOLIS SONGWRITERS, P.O. Box 44724, Indianapolis IN 46244-0724. (317)257-9200. Vice President: Liz Efroymson. Estab. 1983. Purpose is "to create an affiliation of serious-minded songwriters, promote the artistic value of the musical composition, the business of music and recognition for the songwriter and his craft." Sponsors quarterly newsletter, monthly meetings, periodic showcases and periodic seminars and workshops. "The monthly critiques are helpful for improving songwriting skills. The meetings offer opportunities to share information concerning publishing, demos, etc. In addition, it provides the opportunity for members to meet co-writers." Membership fee of $20 per year.

INTERNATIONAL COMPUTER MUSIC ASSOCIATION, (formerly Computer Music Association), 2040 Polk, San Francisco CA 94109. (817)566-2235. President: Larry Austin. Estab. 1978. Serves songwriters, musicians and computer music specialists. Membership includes a broad spectrum of composers, scientists, educators and hobbyists. The function of this organization is "to serve the interests of computer music practitioners and sponsor annual computer music conferences." Primary value in this organization is "music technology information." Offers lectures, performance opportunities, workshops and newsletters to members. Applications are accepted throughout the year. Membership fee is $50/year (individual); $15/year (student); $150/year (nonprofit organization); and $100/year (sustaining).

*THE INTERNATIONAL ENTERTAINMENT CLUB, P.O. Box 470346, Tulsa OK 74147. Estab. 1989. Serves individuals and companies involved in music and entertainment. Best known as the sponsors of the Southwest Music Expo (3-day convention) and SongSearch. Offers competitions, performance opportunities, showcases, administrative services and awards. Applications are accepted year-round. Write for membership information.

INTERNATIONAL LEAGUE OF WOMEN COMPOSERS, Box 670, Southshore Rd., Pt. Peninsula, Three Mile Bay NY 13693. (315)649-5086. Chairperson: Elizabeth Hayden Pizer. Estab. 1975. Serves (women) composers of serious concert music. "Members are women composers and professional musicians, music libraries, institutions and organizations. Full composer membership is open to any woman composer whose seriousness of intent has been demonstrated in one or more of the following ways: (1) by any single degree in composition (if the degree is not recent, some evidence of recent activity should be offered); (2) by holding a current teaching position at the college level, (3) by having had a serious work published; (4) by having had a work performed at a recognized symposium or by professional musicans; or (5) by submitting two compositions to the Executive Board for review, exhibiting competence in scoring for chamber ensemble. Admission is governed neither by stylistic nor regional bias; however, primarily educational music is not considered sufficient. The ILWC is devoted to creating and expanding opportunties for, and documenting information about, women composers of serious music. This organization will help composers stay informed of various career/performance opportunties; plus, allow them to participate in projects spear-headed by ILWC." Offers competitions, newsletter and performance opportunities. Applications accepted year-round. Annual dues are $25 for individuals; $15 for students/senior citizens; $35 for institutions/organizations.

INTERNATIONAL SONGWRITERS ASSOCIATION LTD., 37b New Cavendish St., London WI England. Phone: (01)486 5353. Membership Department: Anna M. Sinden. Serves songwriters and music publishers. "The ISA headquarters is in Limerick City, Ireland, and from there it provides its members with assessment services, copyright services, legal and other advisory services and an investigations service, plus the magazine for one yearly fee. Our members are songwriters in more than 50 countries worldwide, of all ages. There are no qualifications, but applicants under 18 are not accepted. We provide information and assistance to professional or semi-professional songwriters. Our publication, *Songwriter*, which was founded in 1967, features detailed exclusive interviews with songwriters and music publishers, as well as directory information of value to writers." Offers competitions, instruction, library and newsletter. Applications accepted year-round. Membership fee for European writers is £13.90; for non-European writers, it is US $20.

KERRVILLE MUSIC FOUNDATION INC., P.O. Box 1466, Kerrville TX 78029-1466. (512)257-3600. Executive Director: Rod Kennedy. The Kerrville Music Foundation was "founded in 1975 for the promotion and preservation of both traditional and new American music and has awarded more than $25,000 to musicians over the last 18 years through open competitions designed to encourage excellence in songwriting. 40 new folk finalists and six new folk Award Winners are annually invited to share 20 minutes of their songs at the Kerrville Folk Festival with one selected to perform on the main stage the next year." Opportunities include: The Emerging Songwriters Competition at Columbia Music Festival in Spokane, WA—August 1 (award winners on August 2); and The New Folk Concerts for Emerging Songwriters at the Kerrville Folk Festival.

KEYBOARD TEACHERS ASSOCIATION INTERNATIONAL, INC., 361 Pin Oak Lane, Westbury NY 11590. (516)333-3236. President: Dr. Albert DeVito. Estab. 1963. Serves musicians and music dealers/keyboards. "Our members are music teachers, music dealers, music publishers, especially keyboard/piano/organ. Active members must be teachers. We also have Friend Members who are not teachers. The main purpose of this organization is to keep keyboard teachers informed of what is happening in their field, students evaluation, teacher certification, etc. The primary value in this organization for a songwriter is being in contact with keyboard players, publishers and dealers." Offers evaluations of students, instruction, newsletter and workshops. Applications accepted year-round. Membership fee is $25.
Tips: "Each student in auditions receives a certificate according to grade level. It is a great experience for them with the encouragement given."

THE LAS VEGAS SONGWRITERS ASSOCIATION, P.O. Box 42683, Las Vegas NV 89116-0683. (702)459-9107. President: Betty Kay Miller. Estab. 1980. "We are an educational, nonprofit organization dedicated to improving the art and craft of the songwriter. We offer quarterly newsletters, monthly general information meetings, workshops three times a month and seminars held quarterly with professionals in the music business. Dues are $20 per year." Members must be at least 18 years of age.

THE LOS ANGELES SONGWRITERS SHOWCASE (LASS), Box 93759, Hollywood CA 90093. (213)467-7823. Showcase Hotline: (213)467-0533. Co-Directors: Len H. Chandler, Jr. and John Braheny. General Manager: Stephanie Perom. "The Los Angeles Songwriters Showcase (LASS), is a nonprofit service organization for songwriters, founded in 1971 and sponsored by Broadcast Music, Inc. (BMI). LASS also provides counseling and conducts classes and seminars. At our weekly Showcase, we feature Cassette Roulette™, in which a different publisher every week critiques songs submitted on cassette that night; and Pitch-A-Thon™, in which a different producer or record company executive every week screens songs for his/her current recording projects and/or acts for their labels. The Showcase takes place every Tuesday night in front of an audience of songwriters and the music industry guests; there is no prescreening necessary. LASS also produces an annual Songwriters Expo in October." General membership: $120/year. Professional membership: $150/year. Included in both "general" and "professional" membership benefits are: priorities to have tapes listened to first at Pitch-A-Thon™ sessions; discounts on numerous items such as blank tapes, books, demo production services, tapes of Songwriters Expo sessions and other seminars; discounts on admission to the weekly showcase; career counseling (in person or by phone) and a subscription to the LASS 'Songwriters Musepaper," a magazine for songwriters (also available to non-members for $19 bulk rate/$29 first class). Professional membership is available to general members by invitation or audition only and features special private pitch-a-thon sessions and referrals.
Tips: "Members may submit tapes to the weekly Cassette Roulette™ and Pitch-A-Thon™ sessions from anywhere in the world and be sent the recorded comments of the industry guests for that week. Most of the record companies, publishers and producers will not accept unsolicited material, so our Tuesday night showcase is the best way to get material heard by these music industry professionals."

LOUISIANA SONGWRITERS ASSOCIATION, P.O. Box 80425, Baton Rouge LA 70898-0425. (504)924-0804. Vice President, Membership: DuBois Daniels. President: Janice Calvert. Serves songwriters. "LSA is a support group of songwriters who are interested in helping each other and sharing their abilities. Our membership is not limited to age, music style, ethnic group or musical ability. We have members in their teens, as well as retired persons in our group. LSA was organized to educate and promote songwriting in Louisiana and help develop a market for our writers in Louisiana. We do have members outside of Louisiana, however. LSA has a membership of over 200. Have completed first songwriting contest, Louisiana Hot Sounds—Country Edition. We are currently sponsoring the Louisiana Hot Sounds Contest featuring "The Louisana Boys." If you are interested in songwriting you qualify to belong to LSA. Many of us are unable to relocate to major music centers due to responsibilities to jobs and families. Through songwriting organizations like LSA, we are able to work together as a group to establish a line of communication with industry professionals while developing economically a music center in our area of the country. Members must be interested in music and in developing ideas into a marketable format that can compete with other writers. However, if the writer is only interested in expressing himself/herself, that's very important too." Offers competitions, lectures, library, newsletter, performance opportunities, workshops, discounts on various music related books and magazines, and discounts on studio time. General membership dues are $25/year. "Our fiscal year runs June 1-May 31."

LOUISVILLE AREA SONGWRITERS' COOPERATIVE, P.O. Box 16, Pewee Valley KY 40056. President: Paul M. Moffett. Estab. 1986. Serves songwriters and musicians of all ages, races and all musical genres. "The Louisville Area Songwriters' Cooperative is a nonprofit corporation dedicated to the development and promotion of songwriting. Membership is open to any person in the Louisville area (and beyond) who is interested in songwriting. We offer a songwriter showcase on the first Saturday of each month, a series of tapes of songs by members of the cooperative, meetings, speakers, the LASC newsletter, a songwriting contest, referral for collaboration, promotion and song plugging to local, regional and national recording artists and occasional bookings for performing members." Applications accepted year-round. Dues are $25/year.

MEMPHIS SONGWRITERS' ASSOCIATION, 1857 Capri St., Memphis TN 38117. (901)763-1957. President: Juanita Tullos. Estab. 1973. Serves songwriters, musicians and singers. Age limit: 18 years and up. No specific location requirement. Must be interested in music and have the desire to learn the basics of commercial songwriting. "We instruct the potential songwriters on how to structure their songs and correctly use lyrics, commercially. We critique their material. We help them obtain copyrights, give them a chance to expose their material to the right people, such as publishers and A&R people. We hold monthly workshops, instructing members in the Commercial Music Techniques of songwriting. We have an annual Songwriters Showcase where their material is performed live for people in the publishing and recording professions and the general public. We have an annual Shindig, for bands and musicians and an annual seminar." Offers competitions, instruction, lectures, newsletter, performance opportunities and workshops. Applications accepted year-round. Annual dues: $25.
Tips: "Our association was founded in 1973. We have a charter, by laws and a board of directors (8). All directors are professionals in the music field. We are a nonprofit organization. No salaries are paid. Our directors donate their services to our association. We have a president, vice president, secretary, treasurer, music instructor and consultant, production manager, assistant production manager and executive director.

*MIAMI SONGWRITERS, #915, 9310 SW 137th Ave., Miami FL 33186. (305)386-1307. Workshop Coordinator: Elizabeth C. Axford. Estab. 1989. Serves songwriters and musicians. All ages, all occupations. "No eligibility requirements other than a sincere and genuine interest in promoting the art and craft of songwriting. Provides members an opportunity to get feedback from others, meet others in the music business and exchange information. Offers competitions, field trips, instruction, lectures, newsletter, performance opportunities, social outings and workshops. Local dues are $10/year.
Tips: "Every little bit of energy and support counts, no matter what business you're in. All input, suggestions and feedback are welcome. Participation is welcomed by all who are interested."

MIDWESTERN SONGWRITERS ASSOCIATION, 91 N. Terrace Ave., Columbus OH 43204. (614)274-2169. Vice President: Al Van Hoose. Estab. 1978. Serves songwriters. All interested songwriters are eligible—either amateur or professional residing in the midwestern region of U.S.A. Main purpose is the education of songwriters in the basics of their craft. Offers competitions, instruction, lectures, library, newsletter, weekly tip sheet, social outings and workshops. Applications accepted year-round. Membership fee is $20 per year, pro-rated at $5 per calendar quarter (March, June, September, December). "We are offering membership to BAND members at $30.00 per year."
Tips: "We do not refer songwriters to publishers nor artists—we are strictly an educational organization."

MISSOURI SONGWRITERS ASSOCIATION, INC., 693 Green Forest Dr., Fenton MO 63026. (314)343-6661. President: John G. Nolan, Jr. Serves songwriters and musicians. No eligibility requirements. "The MSA (a non-profit organization founded in 1979) is a tremendously valuable resource for songwriting and music business information outside of the major music capitals. Only with the emphasis on education can the understanding of craft and the utilization of skill be fully realized and in turn become the foundation for the ultimate success of MSA members. Songwriters gain support from their fellow members when they join the MSA, and the organization provides 'strength in numbers' when approaching music industry professionals." As a means toward its goals the organization offers: "(1) an extremely informative newsletter; (2) Annual Songwriting Contest; prizes include: CD and/or cassette release of winners, publishing contract, free musical merchandise and equipment, free recording studio time, plaque or certificate; (3) Annual St. Louis Original Music Celebration featuring live performances, recognition, showcase, radio simulcast, videotape for later broadcast and awards presentation; (4) seminars on such diverse topics as creativity, copyright law, brainstorming, publishing, recording the demo, craft and technique, songwriting business, collaborating, etc.; (5) workshops including song evaluation, establishing a relationship with publishers, hit song evaluations, the writer versus the writer/artist, the marriage of collaborators, the business side of songwriting, lyric craft, etc; (6) services such as collaborators referral, publisher contacts, consultation, recording discounts, musicians referral, library, etc. The Missouri Songwriters Association belongs to its members and what a member puts into the organization is returned dynamically in terms of information, education, recognition, support, camaraderie, contacts, tips, confidence, career development, friendships and professional growth." Applications accepted year-round. Tax deductible dues are $50/year.

*MUSIC MILL, P.O. Box 1341, Lowell MA 01853. (508)686-5791. President: Peter Keyes Burwen. Estab. 1985. Serves songwriters, musicians, producers and engineers. Members are active in New England's music industry 18 and over. Purpose is to "act as a 'networking clearing house' for the regional music/entertainment industry and to provide economic opportunities and promotion for artists and songwriters." Offers a newsletter, performance opportunities, workshops and networking referral. Applications accepted year-round. Contact for membership information. "The Music Mill is New England's only central communication link within the regional industry."

*MUSICIANS CONTACT SERVICE, 7315 Sunset Blvd., Hollywood CA 90046. (213)851-2333. Estab. 1969. For musicians and bands seeking each other in the greater Southern California area."Provides 24-hour computerized call-in gig line of working bands needing players. Also for composers and lyricists seeking each other for collaboration.

MUSICIANS NATIONAL HOT LINE ASSOCIATION, 277 East 6100 South, Salt Lake City UT 84107. (801)268-2000. Estab. 1980. Serves songwriters and musicians. "Members are musicians and those involved in related musical occupations. Our goal is to help musicians find bands to join, to help bands find musicians and gigs, and to help songwriters find work in a band or group." Offers newsletter (free advertising for members) and computer search file. Applications accepted year-round. Membership fee is $20/year.
Tips: "The Musicians National Hot Line Association is a nonprofit organization dedicated to helping musicians. Those interested in more detailed information may call (1-801-268-2000) or write (Musicians National Hot Line Association, PO Box 57733, Salt Lake City, UT 84157) for a free brochure."

NASHVILLE SONGWRITERS ASSOCIATION, INTERNATIONAL (NSAI), 15 Music Square West, Nashville TN 37203. (615)256-3354. Executive Director: Pat Rogers. Purpose: a not-for-profit service organization for both aspiring and professional songwriters in all fields of music. Membership: Spans the United States and several foreign countries. Songwriters may apply in one of four annual categories: Active ($55 - for songwriters who have at least one song contractually signed to a publisher affiliated with ASCAP, BMI or SESAC); Associate ($55 - for songwriters who are not yet published or for anyone wishing to support songwriters); Student ($25 - for full-time college students of for students of an accredited senior high school); Professional ($100 - for songwriters who derive their primary source of income from songwriting or who are generally recognized as such by the professional songwriting community). Membership benefits: music industry information and advice, song evaluations by mail, quarterly newsletter, access to industry professionals through weekly Nashville workshop and several annual events, regional workshops, use of office facilities and writers room, collaborators list, discounts on books and blank audio cassettes, discounts on NSAI's three annual instructional/awards events.

NATIONAL ACADEMY OF POPULAR MUSIC—SONGWRITERS' HALL OF FAME, 8th Floor, 875 3rd Ave., New York NY 10022. (212)319-1444. Managing Director: Christina Malone. Projects Director: Bob Leone. Estab. 1969. The main purpose of the organization is to honor great songwriters and support a Hall of Fame museum. Activities include: songwriting workshops, music industry panels and songwriter showcases. Offers newsletter. "Informally, our projects director helps members to network with each other. For example, publisher/members looking for material are put in touch with writer/members; collaborations are arranged. Nowhere else on the East Coast can a writer learn more about the craft of songwriting, the business of songwriting and the world of songwriting, in general. And nowhere are there more opportunities to meet with all types of music industry professionals. Our activities are available to all of our members, so networking is inevitable." Membership is open to everyone, but consists primarily of songwriters, publishers and other music industry professionals who are eligible to vote in annual inductee election. Annual awards dinner. Applications accepted year-round. Membership fee is $25/year.

NATIONAL ACADEMY OF SONGWRITERS (NAS), Suite 780, 6381 Hollywood Blvd., Hollywood CA 90028. (213)463-7178. Executive Director: Dan Kirkpatrick. A nonprofit organization dedicated to the education and protection of songwriters. Estab. 1973. Offers group legal discount; toll free hotline; *SongTalk* newspaper with songwriter interviews, collaborators network and tipsheet; plus Los Angeles based *SongTalk* seminar series featuring top names in songwriting, song evaluation workshops, song screening sessions, open mics and more. "We offer services to all songwriter members from street-level to superstar: substantial discount on books and tapes, song evaluation through the mail, health insurance program, and SongPitch service for qualifying members. Our services provide education in the craft and opportunities to market songs. The Academy is also active in addressing political issues affecting the profession. We produce the TV show *Salute to the American Songwriter*. Memberships: General—$75; Professional—$120; Gold—$200."

NATIONAL ASSOCIATION OF COLLEGE BROADCASTERS (NACB), 1 George St., 2nd Floor, Providence RI 02906. (401)863-2225. Executive Director: Glenn Gutmacher. Estab. 1988. Serves musicians, college radio and TV stations, broadcast/communications departments and others interested in the college media market. Members also include students, faculty members, record companies and manufacturers who want to tap into the college media market. Any songwriter/musician may join under Associate Member status. The primary benefits of membership in NACB are the music reviews in every issue of our magazine (which features major label, independent and unsigned acts in equal proportion). It reaches the stations most likely to play new music (audio and video). Also, several music programs on the satellite network give national exposure to new music—free. Offers conferences, instruction, lectures, newsletter, performance opportunities, workshops, magazine subscription, satellite network, station handbook, consulting hotline, legal advice and more. Applications accepted year-round. Membership fee is $25/year. "Our 'Guide Wire Radio' show on U Network radio has brought national fame to several unsigned musicians. Also, low-cost advertising in our magazine and newsletter lets your expose your music to all 2,000 U.S. college radio and TV stations—more than other publications. Our mailing list of all 2,000 college stations is available for purchase at low cost."

THE NATIONAL ASSOCIATION OF COMPOSERS/USA, Box 49652, Barrington Station, Los Angeles CA 90049. (213)541-8213. President: Marshall Bialosky. Estab. 1932. Serves songwriters, musicians and classical composers. "We are of most value to the concert hall composer. Members are serious music composers of all ages and from all parts of the country, who have a real interest in composing, performing, and listening to modern concert hall music. The main purpose of our organization is to perform, publish, broadcast and write news about composers of serious concert hall music—mostly chamber and solo pieces. Composers may achieve national notice of their work through our newsletter and concerts, and the fairly rare feeling of supporting a non-commercial music enterprise dedicated to raising the musical and social position of the serious composer." Offers competitions, lectures, performance opportunities, library and newsletter. Applications accepted throughout the year. $15 membership fee; $35 for Los Angeles and New York chapter members.
Tips: "99% of the money earned in music is earned, or so it seems, by popular songwriters who might feel they owe the art of music something, and this is one way they might help support that art. It's a chance to foster fraternal solidarity with their less prosperous, but wonderfully interesting classical colleagues at a time when the very existence of serious art seems to be questioned by the general populace."

*NATIONAL ASSOCIATION OF RECORDING MERCHANDISERS (NARM), Suite 140, 11 Eves Dr., Marlton NJ 08053. (609)596-2221. Executive Vice President: Pam Horovitz. Serves manufacturers, distributors, retailers of recorded music. Members are: major and independent record labels, major and independent distribution companies, rack jobbers, one stops, chain and independent retail outlets (who sell records, CDs, audiovisual cassettes), and companies which provide a product or service to the record industry (e.g., computer hard/software, fixtures, packaging, pressing plants). NARM markets music via merchandising/POP materials, provides educational seminars, has lobbyists in Washington, provides a forum for communication for the various segments of the music industry and has an annual convention."

*NATIONAL BAND AND CHORAL DIRECTORS HALL OF FAME, 519 N. Halifax Ave., Daytona Beach FL 32118. (904)252-0381. Director: Dr. Watie Riley Pickens. Estab. 1985. Serves band and choral directors. Members are "high school and college band and choral directors and other nationally recognized choral directors. The main purpose of our organization is to recognize, honor and promote the profession of Band and Choral Directors." Offers competitions; clearing house for band and choral directors. Applications are accepted by invitation only. There are no annual fees or dues.

*NATIONAL HIGH SCHOOL BAND INSTITUTE, 519 N. Halifax Ave., Daytona Beach FL 32118. (904)252-0381. Director: Dr. Watie Riley Pickens. Serves musicians. Members are high school band directors. "Professional high school band directors who have had national recognition are invited to submit their candidacy for nomination to the N.H.S.B.D. Hall of Fame. The main purpose of our organization is to recognize, honor and promote the profession of marching band directors." Offers competitions, instruction, lectures, library, newsletter, performance opportunities and National High School Band Directors Hall of Fame. Applications are accepted by invitation only. There are no annual fees or dues.

*NATIONAL JAZZ SERVICE ORGANIZATION, P.O. Box 50152, Washington DC 20004-0152. (202)347-2604. Contact: John Murph, Willard Jenkins or Sara Warner. Estab. 1985. Serves songwriters, musicians, jazz educators and programs. Members include jazz musicians, enthusiasts, related organizations, schools, jazz media and state arts agencies. The NJSO is a not-for-profit public benefit corporation founded in 1985. The purpose of NJSO is nuture the growth of and enhancement of jazz music as an American art form. The NJSO functions as a consultant and referral service for the jazz community. NJSO provides help through their Technical Assistance program. The songwriter would have untold access of resources available through out Technical Resource Program. His or her membership would further enhance the status of jazz as an art in the United States. Offers instruction, newsletter and Technical Assistance Program and subscription discounts to *Down Beat*, *The Wire*, *Jazziz* and *Jazz Times*. Membership fee $25-100. "We have a comprehensive jazz database of presenters, radio stations, record companies, managers/booking, press contacts, NJSO members and musicians."

*NATIONAL TRADITIONAL MUSIC ASSOCIATION, INC., P.O. 438, Walnut IA 51577. (712)784-3001. President: Robert Everhart. Estab. 1976. Serves songwriters and musicians. "Crosses all boundaries. They should be interested in traditional acoustic music." To preserve, perform and promote traditional acoustic music. Offers competitions, field trips, instruction, lectures, newsletter, performance opportunities, social outings and workshops. Applications accepted year-round. Membership fee is $12/year.
Tips: They (members) also receive *Tradition* magazine 6 times a year.

*NEW DRAMATISTS, 424 W. 44th St., New York NY 10036. (212)757-6960. Service organization dedicated to the development of playwrights. "We sponsor a composer-librettist studio each year where 5 of our member writers work with 5 selected composers." For information about playwright membership, the studio and New Dramatists call (212)757-6960.

NEW ENGLAND SONGWRITERS/MUSICIANS ASSOCIATION, 87 Lafayette Rd., Hampton Falls NH 03844. (800)448-3621 or (603)929-1128. Director: Peter C. Knickles. "Our organization serves all ages and all types of music. We focus primarily on the business of songwriting and overall, the music business. We have done various co-promotions of seminars with BMI in the past and may continue to do so in the future. Membership is free. Call to be on our mailing list and receive our free quarterly newsletter."

NEW JERSEY AND PENNSYLVANIA SONGWRITERS ASSOC., 226 E. Lawnside Ave., Westmont NJ 08108. (609)858-3849. President and Founder: Bruce M. Weissberg. Estab. 1985. Serves songwriters and musicians. Members are all ages 16-80, representing all types of music from Delaware, Philadelphia and North and South Jersey area. Must be serious about songwriting. Provides networking, information center and promotional center for workshops and guest speakers. "Primary value is that it enables musicians to network with other songwriters in the area." Offers lectures, library, newsletter, performance opportunities and workshops. Applications accepted year-round. $25/year (single), $35/year (band). After June 1st single membership will be $30. "Our group is always interested in new ideas, new interested guest speakers and a true professional type of atmosphere."

NORTHERN CALIFORNIA SONGWRITERS ASSOCIATION, Suite 211, 855 Oak Grove Ave., Menlo Park CA 94025. (415)327-8296. FAX: (415)327-0301, or (800)FORSONG (California and Nashville only). Executive Director: Ian Crombie. Serves songwriters and musicians. Estab. 1979. "Our 1,200 members are lyricists and composers from ages 16-80, from beginners to professional songwriters. No eligibility requirements. Our purpose is to provide the education and opportunities that will support our writers in creating and marketing outstanding songs. NCSA provides support and direction through local networking and input from Los Angeles and Nashville music industry leaders, as well as valuable marketing opportunities. We offer opportunities and education for songwriters. Most songwriters need some form of collaboration, and by being a member they are exposed to other writers, ideas, critiquing, etc." Offers annual Northern California Songwriting Conference, "the largest event in northern California. This 2-day event features 16 seminars, 50 screening sessions (over 1,200 song listened to by industry profesionals) and a sunset concert with hit songwriters performing their songs." Also offers monthly visits from major publishers, songwriting classes, seminars conducted by hit songwriters ("we sell audio tapes of our seminars — list of tapes available on request"), a monthly newsletter, monthly performance opportunities and workshops. Applications accepted year-round. Dues: $50/year.

Tips: "NCSA's functions draw local talent and nationally recognized names together. This is of a tremendous value to writers outside a major music center. We are developing a strong songwriting community in Northern California. We serve the San Jose, Monterey Bay, East Bay and San Francisco area and we have the support of some outstanding writers and publishers from both Los Angeles and Nashville. They provide us with invaluable direction and inspiration."

OPERA AMERICA, Suite 520, 777 14th St. NW, Washington DC 20005. (202)347-9262. Estab. 1970. Members are composers, musicians and opera/music theater producers. "OPERA America maintains an extensive library of reference books and domestic and foreign music periodicals, and the most comprehensive operatic archive in the United States. OPERA America draws on these unique resources to supply information to its members." Offers conferences. Publishes directories of opera/music theater companies in the US and Canada. Publishes directory of opera and musical performances world-wide and US. Applications accepted year-round. Membership fee is on a sliding scale. Please contact for more information.

PACIFIC NORTHWEST SONGWRITERS ASSOCIATION, Box 98564, Seattle WA 98198. (206)824-1568. "We're a nonprofit association, and have served the songwriters of the Puget Sound area since 1977. Our focus is on professional songwriting for today's commercial markets. We hold monthly workshops and publish a quarterly newsletter. Our workshops are a great place to meet other writers, find collaborators, critique each other's songs and share news and encouragement. Our members get immediate contact with hundreds of the biggest national artists, producers, publishers and record companies. Members also get free legal advice from our staff attorney. All this for only $35 per year. We welcome new members. If you have any questions, just give us a call."

PACIFIC SONGWRITERS ASSOCIATION, Box 15453, 349 W. Georgia, Vancouver, BC V6B 5B2 **Canada.** (604)872-SONG. Estab. 1983. Serves songwriters. All ages, from teens to retired people; writers of music, lyrics and both; also industry people interested in understanding the craft of songwriting. "To inform and promote songwriting and songwriters in the Pacific area; our main activity is a monthly song evaluation session called The Song Works, and 6 times/year we publish the magazine *Hook Line & Singer*. "Songwriting can be a very introverted process. P.S.A. encourages the sharing of frustrations, challenges, information, successes and opens the door to collaborations." Offers access to professional panels for song evaluation and information; opportunity to meet other writers and industry people; a resource place for information. Offers local business discounts to membership card holders (such as specified studios and instrument retailers)." Offers lectures and workshops. Offers liaison with Songwriters Association of Canada. Applications accepted year-round. Renewals are based on your 12-month anniversary. $40/year, includes subscription to *Hook Line & Singer*. Subscription only $10.

PENNSYLVANIA ASSOCIATION OF SONGWRITERS, COMPOSERS, P.O. Box 4311, Allentown PA 18105. (215)433-6788. President: John Havassy. Estab. 1979. Serves songwriters and musicians. "Teens to 40's, mostly rock, contemporary and country. Open to anyone interested in finding a better, easier, faster way to further needs of songwriters. We offer venues for original music performances." Applications accepted year-round. Dues are $15 yearly. "Any performing songwriters should send tape and bio and other promotional materials for consideration for bookings. We maintain a library of business and educational publications and copywright information."

PITTSBURGH SONGWRITERS ASSOCIATION, 408 Greenside Ave., Canonsburg PA 15317. (412)745-9497. President: Frank J. DeGennaro. Estab. 1983. Serves songwriters. "Any age group is welcome. Current members are from mid-20s to mid-50s. All musical styles and interests are welcome. Country and pop predominate the current group; some instrumental, dance, rock and R&B also. Composers and lyricists in group. Our organization wants to serve as a source of quality material for publishers and other industry professionals. We assist members in developing their songs and getting their works published. Also, we provide a support group for area songwriters, network of contacts and collaboration opportunities. We offer field trips, instruction, lectures, library and social outings. Annual dues are $25. We have no initiation fee."

POP RECORD RESEARCH, 17 Piping Rock Dr., Ossining NY 10562. Director: Gary Theroux. Estab. 1962. Serves songwriters, musicians, writers, researchers and media. "We maintain archives of materials relating to music, TV and film, with special emphasis on recorded music (the hits and hitmakers

1877-present): bios, photos, reviews, interviews, discographies, chart data, clippings, films, videos, etc." Offers library and clearinghouse for accurate promotion/publicity to biographers, writers, reviewers, the media. Offers programming, annotation and photo source for reissues or retrospective album collections on any artist (singers, songwriters, musicians, etc.), also music consultation services for film or television projects. "There is no charge to include publicity, promotional or biographical materials in our archives. Artists, writers, composers, performers, producers, labels and publicists are always invited to add or keep us on their publicity/promotion mailing list with career data, updates, new releases and reissues of recorded performances, etc. Fees are assessed only for reference use by researchers, writers, biographers, reviewers, etc. Songwriters and composers (or their publicists) should keep or put us on their publicity mailing lists to ensure that the information we supply others on their careers, accomplishments, etc. is accurate and up-to-date."

PORTLAND MUSIC ASSOCIATION, Box 6723, Portland OR 97228. (503)223-9681. President: Tony Demicoli. Serves songwriters, musicians, booking agents and club owners. Members are all ages — amateur and professional musicians, music industry businesses, technical support, personnel, music lovers and songwriters. "Main purpose is in the development and advancement of music and related business opportunities within our metro area and to the international music industry." Benefits include networking opportunities, educational seminars, contests, new talent showcase, local music awards and Musicians' Ball. Offers songwriter contest, lectures, newsletters, performance opportunities, social outings, workshops and songwriter/musician referral. Annual dues: General $20; band $25; business $50; association $50; corporate $100.

*PORTLAND SONGWRITERS ASSOCIATION, P.O. Box 5323, Aloha OR 97006. (503)645-0750. "The P.S.A. is a non-profit organization serving western Oregon and southwestern Washington. We are open to songwriters, musicians and lyricists. The association is centered around monthly workshops to help members develop their songwriting skills. All musical styles and interests are welcome. Members also have access to publishers, record companies and artists who are actively seeking new material. Annual dues are $35. Please feel free to attend several workshops; there is no obligation to join. We encourage new members. If you have any questions, please call."

RECORDING INDUSTRY ASSOCIATION OF AMERICA, Suite 200, 1020 19th St., NW Washington DC 20036. Director, Member Services: John H. Ganoe. Estab. 1952. Serves recording companies. RIAA membership is corporate. Members include U.S.-based manufacturers of sound recordings. "Membership in RIAA is not open to individuals. RIAA has extensive programs on behalf of our industry in the areas of government relations, public relations and anti-piracy enforcement. RIAA also addresses challenges facing the U.S. industry in the international market place. RIAA also coordinates industry market research and is the certifying body for gold and platinum records. We will provide, upon request, samples of RIAA publications, including our industry sourcebook, newsletter and annual statistical overview. Dues are corporate, and computed in confidence by an outside auditing firm."

SAN FRANCISCO FOLK MUSIC CLUB, 885 Clayton, San Francisco CA 94117. (415)661-2217. Serves songwriters, musicians and anyone who enjoys folk music. "Our members range from age 2 to 80. The only requirement is that members enjoy, appreciate and be interested in sharing folk music. As a focal point for the San Francisco Bay Area folk music community, the SFFMC provides opportunities for people to get together to share folk music, and the newsletter *The Folknik* disseminates information. We publish 2 songs an issue (6 times a year) in our newsletter, our meetings provide an opportunity to share new songs, and at our camp-outs there are almost always songwriter workshops." Offers library, newsletter, informal performance opportunities, annual free folk festival, social outings and workshops. Applications accepted year-round. Membership fee is $5/year.

SANTA BARBARA SONGWRITERS' GUILD, Box 22, Santa Barbara CA 93116. (805)687-5269. President: Gary Heller. Estab. 1981. "The Guild helps to open doors to music industry professionals which otherwise would be closed to them. We are a nonprofit organization for aspiring songwriters, performers, those interested in the music industry, and anyone interested in original music. Our members are able to meet other songwriters, to learn more about the craft of songwriting, to get their songs heard, and to network. The Guild sponsors monthly cassette tape presentations to L.A. publishers called Songsearches. We also sponsor workshops, classes and lectures on music in film and TV, studio recording, music business contracts and copyright law, record production, song marketing, music composition, lyric writing and vocal techniques, in addition to publishing a directory of local music services and organizations. Discounts available to members include the following: books that deal with a wide range of pertinent music industry information, studio time at local recording studios, equipment and supplies at local music stores." Membership is $35/year.

SESAC INC., 156 W. 56th St., New York NY 10019. (212)586-3450; 55 Music Square E., Nashville TN 37203. (615)320-0055 President and Chief Executive Officer: Vincent Candilora. Vice President: Dianne Petty, Nashville. Serves writers and publishers in all types of music who have their works performed by radio, television, nightclubs, cable TV, etc. Purpose of organization is to collect and distribute performance royalties to all active affiliates. "Prospective affiliates are requested to present a demo tape of their works which is reviewed by our Screening Committee." For possible affiliation, call Nashville or New York for appointment.

SOCIETY FOR THE PRESERVATION AND ENCOURAGEMENT OF BARBER SHOP QUARTET SING-ING IN AMERICA, INC. (S.P.E.B.S.Q.S.A., INC.), 6315 Third Ave., Kenosha WI 53143-5199. (414)656-8440. Membership Manager: Ron Rockwell. Estab. 1938. Serves songwriters, musicians and world's largest all male singing organization. "Members are from teenage to elderly. All are interested in vocal harmony (4 singing, barbershop style). The main purpose of this organization is to perpetuate and preserve the musical art form known as Barbershop Harmony. We are always looking for new songs that will adapt to barbershop harmonization and style." Offers competitions, instruction, lectures, library, newsletter, performance opportunities, social outings and workshops. "A week-long 'Harmony College' is presented each year, open to over 700 men. Instruction in all areas of music: vocal techniques, arranging, songwriting, show production, chorus directing, etc. A 'Young Men In Harmony' program is offered, especially designed to appeal to young high school boys. Approved by MENC and ACDA. Our publishing program, which at present offers over 600 songs, is arranged in the barbershop style. The Society offers the opportunity for songwriters to have their music arranged and published. We maintain a library of over 600,000 pieces of sheet music—most of which is turn of the century to the mid-late 20s." Applications accepted year-round. Membership is usually in local chapters with dues about $70 annually. A chapter-at-large membership, The Frank H. Thorne Chapter, is available at $70 annually.

SOCIETY OF COMPOSERS, AUTHORS AND MUSIC PUBISHERS OF CANADA (SOCAN), Head Office: 41 Valleybrook Dr., Don Mills, Ontario M3B 2S6 **Canada**. (416)445-8700. FAX: (416)445-7108. Chief Executive Officer: Jan Matejcek. (415)445-8700. Chief Operating Officer: Michael Rock (416)445-8700. In March, 1990, CAPAC and PROCAN merged to form a single, new Canadian performing rights society. The purpose of the society is to collect music user license fees and distribute performance royalties to composers, authors and music publishers. The SOCAN catalogue is licensed by ASCAP and BMI in the United States.

SONGWRITERS & LYRICISTS CLUB, %Robert Makinson, Box 023304, Brooklyn NY 11202-0066. Director: Robert Makinson. Estab. 1984. Serves songwriters and lyricists. Gives information regarding songwriting: creation of songs, reality of market, collaboration, disc jockeys and other contacts. Only requirement is ability to write lyrics or melodies. Beginners are welcome. The primary benefits of membership for the songwriter are opportunities to collaborate and assistance with creative aspects and marketing of songs through publications and advice. Offers newsletter and assistance with lead sheets and demos. Applications accepted year-round. Dues are $24/year, remit to Robert Makinson. Write with SASE for more information. "Plan and achieve realistic goals. If you have a great song, we'll make every effort to help promote it."

SONGWRITERS ASSOCIATION OF WASHINGTON, Suite 632, 1377 K St. NW, Washington DC 20005. (301)654-8434. President: Marcy Freiberg. Estab. 1979. "S.A.W. is a nonprofit organization committed to providing its members with the means to improve their songwriting skills, learn more about the music business and gain exposure in the industry. S.A.W. sponsors various events to achieve this goal, such as workshops, song swaps, seminars, meetings, showcases and the Mid-Atlantic song contest. S.A.W. publishes *S.A.W. Notes*, a bi-monthly newsletter containing information on the music business, upcoming events around the country, and provides free classifieds to its members. For more information regarding membership write or call.

THE SONGWRITERS GUILD OF AMERICA, Suite 306, 276 Fifth Ave., New York NY 10001. (212)686-6820. West Coast: Ste. 317, 6430 Sunset Blvd., Hollywood CA 90028. (213)462-1108. Nashville: United Artists Tower, 50 Music Square West, Nashville TN 37203. (615)329-1782. Founded as the Songwriters' Protective Association in 1931, name changed to American Guild of Authors and Composers in 1958, and expanded to AGAC/The Songwriters Guild in 1982. Effective 1985, the organizational name is The Songwriters Guild of America. "The Songwriters Guild of America is the nation's largest, oldest, most respected and most experienced songwriters' association devoted exclusively to providing songwriters with the services, activities and protection they need to succeed in the business of music." President: George David Weiss. Executive Director: Lewis M. Bachman. National Projects Director: George Wurzbach. West Coast Regional Director: Aaron Meza. Nashville Regional Director: Kathy Hyland. "A full member must be a published songwriter. An associate member is any unpublished songwriter with a desire to learn more about the business and craft of songwriting. The third class of membership comprises estates of deceased writers. The Guild contract is conceded to be the best available in the industry, having the greatest number of built-in protections for the songwriter. The Guild's Royalty Collection Plan makes certain that prompt and accurate payments are made to writers. The ongoing Audit Program makes periodic checks of publishers' books. For the self-publisher, the Catalogue Administration Program (CAP) relieves a writer of the paperwork of publishing for a fee lower than the prevailing industry rates. The Copyright Renewal Service informs members a year in advance of a song's renewal date. Other services include workshops in New York and Los Angeles, free Ask-A-Pro rap sessions with industry pros (see Workshops), critique sessions, collaborator service and newsletters. In addition, the Guild reviews your songwriter contract on request (Guild or otherwise); fights to strengthen songwriters' rights and to increase writers' royalties by supporting legislation which directly affects copyright; offers a group medical and life insurance plan; issues news bulletins with essential information for songwriters; provides a songwriter collaboration service for younger writers; financially evaluates catalogues of copyrights in connection with possible sale and estate planning; operates an estates administration service; and maintains a nonprofit educational foundation (The Songwriters Guild Foundation)."

SONGWRITERS OF OKLAHOMA, 211 W. Waterloo Rd., Edmond OK 73034. (405)348-6534. President: Harvey Derrick. Estab. 1983. Serves songwriters and musicians, professional writers, amateur writers, college and university faculty, musicians, poets and others from labor force as well as retired individuals. Age range is from 18 to 90. "Must be interested in writing and composing and have a desire to help others in any way possible. We have members from coast to coast. We offer workshops, critique sessions, contests, civic benefits, education of members on copyright, contracts, publishers, demos, record companys, etc., as well as a sounding board of peers, education, camaraderie and sharing of knowledge." Offers competitions, field trips, instruction, lectures, library, newsletter, performance opportunities, social outings and workshops. Applications accepted year-round. Membership fee is $15/year.

SONGWRITERS OF WISCONSIN, P.O. Box 874, Neenah WI 54957-0874. (414)725-1609. Director: Tony Ansems. Estab. 1983. Serves songwriters. "Membership is open to songwriters writing all styles of music. Residency in Wisconsin is recommended but not required. Members are encouraged to bring tapes and lyric sheets of their songs to the meetings, but it is not required. We are striving to improve the craft of songwriting in Wisconsin. Living in Wisconsin, a songwriter would be close to any of the workshops and showcases offered each month at different towns. The primary value of membership for a songwriter is in sharing ideas with other songwriters, being critiqued and helping other songwriters." Offers competitions, field trips, instruction, lectures, newsletter, performance opportunities, social outings, workshops and critique sessions. Applications accepted year-round. $10 subscription fee for newsletter.

SOUTHERN SONGWRITERS GUILD, INC., P.O. Box 6817, Shreveport LA 71136-6817. Public Relations Officer: Tommy Cassel. Estab. 1983. Serves songwriters, musicians and students. Members are multi-race, amateur/professional, all ages, with an interest in the entertainment business. Open membership. Purpose is to provide education in entertainment business and to provide scholarships. Offers competitions, instruction, lectures, newsletter, performance opportunities, social outings and workshops. Applications accepted year-round. Annual dues: $30 member, $100 organization, $500 or more Benefactor.

THE TENNESSEE SONGWRITERS ASSOCIATION, Box 2664, Hendersonville TN 37077. (615)824-4555. Executive Director: Jim Sylvis. Serves songwriters. "Our membership is open to all ages and consists of both novice and experienced professional songwriters. The only requirement for membership is a serious interest in the craft and the business of songwriting. Most of our members are local, but we also accept out-of-state memberships. Our main purpose and functon is to educate and assist the songwriter, both in the art/craft of songwriting and in the business of songwriting. In addition to education, we also provide an opportunity for camaraderie, support and encouragement, as well a chance to meet co-writers. Our members often will play on each others' demo sessions. We also critique each others' material and offer suggestions for improvement, if needed. We offer the following to our members: 'Pro-Rap' – once a month a key person from the music industry addresses our membership on their field of specialty. They may be writers, publishers, producers and sometimes even the recording artists themselves. 'Pitch-A-Pro' – once a month we schedule a publisher, producer or artist who is currently looking for material, to come to our meeting and listen to songs pitched by our members. Annual Awards Dinner – honoring the most accomplished of our TSA membership during the past year. Tips – letting our members know who is recording and how to get their songs to the right people. Other activities – a TSA summer picnic, parties throughout the year, and opportunities to participate in music industry-related charitable events, such as the annual Christmas For Kids, which the TSA proudly supports." Applications accepted year-round. Membership runs for one year from the date you join. Membership fee is $25/year.

THEATRICAL ENTERTAINMENT OF ACTORS & MUSICIANS, Box 30260, Bakersfield CA 93385. President: Judge A. Robertson. "Our purpose is to advance, educate, encourage, protect and promote overlooked creative talent. We help you help yourself to become a professionally paid artist by producing the creative aspects of songwriters, actors, and artists, and by providing performance opportunities. We notify publishers that demo tapes have been pre-screened by T.E.A.M. Our media showcase is in coproduction with Superstar Productions, Element Records, International Motion Pictures, Ltd., and Element Movie and Music (BMI)." Applications accepted year-round; one-time $55 fee and annual membership fee of $25.

TULSA SONGWRITERS ASSOCIATION, INC., P.O. Box 254, Tulsa OK 74101-0254. (918)437-SONG. President: Bryan Huling. Estab. 1983. Serves songwriters and musicians. Members are age 18-65 and have interests in all types of music. Main purpose of the organization is "to create a forum to educate, develop, improve, discover and encourage songwriting in the Tulsa area." Offers competitions, lectures, performance opportunities, field trips, social outings, instruction, newsletter and workshops. Applications accepted year-round. Dues are $30/year.
Tips: "We hold a monthly 'Writer's Night' open to the public for performance of original songs to expose the many talented writers in Tulsa."

VERMONT SONGWRITERS ASSOCIATION, RD 2 Box 277, Underhill VT 05489. (802)899-3787. President: Bobby Hackney. Estab. 1991. "Membership open to anyone desiring a career in songwriting, or anyone who seeks a supportive group to encourage co-writing, meeting other songwriters, or to continue their songwriting endeavors." Purpose is to give songwriters an opportunity to meet industry professionals at monthly meetings and seminars, to have their works critiqued by peers and to help songwriters learn more about the craft and the complete business of songwriting." Offers competitions, instruction, lectures, library, newsletter, performance opportunities, workshops. Applications accepted year-round. Membership fee is $30/year.
Tips: "We are a nonprofit association dedicated to creating opportunities for songwriters. Even though our office address in in Underhill, Vermont, our primary place of business is in Burlington, Vermont, where monthly meetings and seminars are held."

VICTORY MUSIC, P.O. Box 7515, Bonney Lake WA 98390. (206)863-6617. Estab. 1969. Serves songwriters, audiences and specifically local acoustic musicians of all music styles. Victory Music provides places to play, showcases, opportunities to read about the business and other songwriters, referrals and seminars. Produced 4 albums of NW songwriters. Offers library, newsletter, performance opportunities and workshops. Applications accepted year-round. Membership fee is $20/year (single); $50/year business; $28/year couple; $175 lifetime.

VOLUNTEER LAWYERS FOR THE ARTS, 3rd Floor, 1285 Avenue of the Americas, New York NY 10019. (212)977-9273. Estab. 1969. Serves songwriters, musicians and all performing, visual, literary and fine arts artists and groups. Offers legal assistance and representation to eligible individual artists and arts organizations who cannot afford private counsel. Also sells publications on arts-related issues. In addition, there are affiliates nationwide who assist local arts organizations and artists. Offers conferences, lectures, seminars and workshops.

WASHINGTON AREA MUSIC ASSOCIATION, 1690 36th St., N.W., Washington DC 20007. (202)337-2227. Membership Chairman: B.J. Cohen. Estab. 1985. Serves songwriters, musicians and performers, managers, club owners, entertainment lawyers; "all those with an interest in the Washington music scene." The organization is designed to promote the Washington music scene and increase its visibility. Its primary value to members is its seminars and networking opportunities. Offers lectures, newsletter, performance opportunities and workshops. Applications accepted year-round. Annual dues are $30.

*WESTERN NORTH CAROLINA SONGWRITER'S ASSOC. INC., P.O. Box 72, Alexander NC 28701. (704)683-9105. President: Henry C. Tench. Estab. 1991. Serves songwriters and musicians. Persons 18 years or older who want to write lyrics, songs and musicians both professional and amateur. Members are welcome from all states who are trying to learn or better the craft of songwriting in general. "Endeavors to assist those interested in becoming great songwriters through a series of meetings, critiques, workshops and other educational means available. We are serious but still have fun. Association with other songwriters, locally as well as a national organization. Serious songwriters need to study their craft as well as have them critiqued in a constructive way and make contacts in songwriting profession from other parts of the country. We take this to be serious business on our part and will handle it in a professional manner. Offers competitions, field trips, instruction, lectures, library, newsletter, performance opportunities, social outings and workshops. Applications accepted year-round. One time initiation fee of $20, then $24/year.

Tips: "Application must be approved by board. If you are serious about learning the craft of songwriting, come on and participate and support your local as well national songwriting organizations. We at WNCSA, Inc. will assist all who are sincere in their endeavor to excel in the songwriter's profession."

WHITEWATER VALLEY SONGWRITERS AND MUSICIANS ASSN., (formerly NSAI-WVSM Songwriters Association), RR #4, Box 112, Liberty IN 47353. (317)458-6152. Founder: Ann Hofer. Serves songwriters and musicians. Estab. 1981. "Our members are songwriters of all ages. Some are interested in all aspects of the music business and others just songwriting. We have artists, musicians, lyricists and melody writers. Our purpose is to assist our members with finding co-writers, keep them informed on publishers accepting material, help them make demo contacts, provide list of record companies, and to educate them on the ever-changing music and songwriting business. We are available to assist the songwriter in any way we can; we are dedicated to his/her needs. We believe that believing in yourself is the beginning of your dream coming true, and we want to encourage songwriters to do just that: believe in themselves." Offers competitions, instruction, lectures, library, performance opportunities, social outings and song critique sessions. For more information call Ann at (317)458-6152.

WICHITA SONGWRITERS GROUP, 2450 Somerset, Wichita KS 64204. (316)838-6079. Contact: David Kinion. Estab. 1988. Serves songwriters. Members include teenagers to retired people from the community. Members must live close enough to be present at meetings. Main purpose is to provide a sense of community for songwriters while helping them write better songs. Wichita Songwriters Group provides instruction, common support and a songwriter's network for placement of songs. Offers field trips, instruction, lectures, library, performance opportunities and workshops. Applications accepted year-round. Fee of $1 per meeting.

Tips: WSG meets on the first Monday of each month (except holidays) at 7:30 pm at Miller Music, 4235 West Central, Wichita, KS.

WYOMING COUNTRY MUSIC FOUNDATION, 1645 Sussex Road, Kaycee WY 82639. (307)738-2303 or 684-7305. President and Founder: Helen D. Ullery. Estab. 1983. Serves songwriters and musicians. Members include "youth, amateurs, professionals, pioneers, country and gospel/country songwriters, musicians and vocalists. No eligibility requirements. Our purpose is to promote country music and country music performers, showcase talent, educate members, and coordinate our annual festival each summer." Offers competitions, lectures, performance opportunities, social outings, newsletter, workshops and annual songwriters contest. "Our songwriter contest is held each spring. Contest deadline is April 15, 1993. Entry is $10/song; 50% of entry fees goes back as prizes to winners. Entrants can not have been in top 50 in charts in the last 10 years. Final review is done in Nashville." Membership fee is $25; festival registration is $15. For membership application and a copy of contest rules send SASE to WCMF address above.

Workshops

Evaluation, suggestions, feedback and motivation. All are important to the aspiring songwriter. A songwriting organization may provide these, but to gain an idea of how your music stacks up in the larger world of music, alternatives are needed. Conferences and workshops provide a means for songwriters to have songs evaluated, hear suggestions for further improvement and receive feedback and motivation from industry experts in a broader context. They are also an excellent place to make valuable industry contacts.

Usually these workshops take place in the music hubs: New York, Los Angeles and Nashville. In the past few years, major regional conferences have gained a lot of attention. Also, organizations exist that offer traveling workshops on just about every songwriting topic imaginable — from lyric writing and marketing strategy to contract negotiating. More small and mid-size cities with strong songwriter organizations are running their own workshops, drawing on resources from within their own group or bringing in professionals from the music centers.

A workshop exists to address every type of music. There are programs for songwriters, performers in all styles, musical playwrights and much more. Many also include instruction and suggestions on related business topics. The following list includes national and local workshops with a brief description of what each offers. For more information, write to the sponsoring organization.

ANNUAL NATIONAL CONFERENCE OF COLLEGE BROADCASTERS & REGIONAL CONFERENCES OF COLLEGE BROADCASTERS, 71 George St., 2nd Floor, Providence RI 02906. (401)863-2225. Association Director: JoAnn Forgit. Estab. 1988. "The purpose of these conferences is to bring top media leaders together with students from college broadcasting to learn and share ideas. Several sessions on music licensing, record company relations and alternative/new music programming trends are typically included. We conduct the National College Radio Awards and National TV Programming Awards (not open to songwriters). We also have a comprehensive awards/competitions listing every month in *College Broadcaster* magazine, many of which relate to musicians. The Annual Conference (November) and Regional Conferences (Spring) last 1-3 days at various host college campuses around the U.S. Participants include artists, producers, TV/radio program directors, amateur and professional songwriters, bands, composers and record label reps. "The National Conference Trade Show typically includes numerous record labels and programming syndicators. Participants are selected through submission of demo tapes and leads from college broadcasting stations. For information about dates and participation, call JoAnn Forgit at (401)863-2225. Closing date for application is September/October for the National Conference and one month prior to each regional conference. There is a $65 registration fee at National Conference, $25 at Regional Conferences. Lunches, receptions and refreshments throughout the day are included. A discount hotel package is available to attendees."

APPEL FARM ARTS AND MUSIC FESTIVAL, Box 888, Elmer NJ 08318. (609)358-2472. Artistic Director: Sean Timmons. Estab. Festival: 1989; Series 1970. "Our annual open air festival is the highlight of our year-round Performing Arts Series which was established to bring high quality arts programs to the people of South Jersey. Festival includes acoustic and folk music, blues, etc." Programs for songwriters and musicians include performance opportunities as part of Festival and Performing Arts Series. Programs for musical playwrights also include performance opportunities as part of Performing Arts Series. Festival is a one-day event held in June, and Performing Arts Series is held year-round. Both are held at the Appel Farm Arts and Music Center, a 176-acre farm in Southern New Jersey. Up to 20 songwriters/musicians participate in each event. Participants are songwriters, individual vocalists, bands, ensembles, vocal groups, composers, individual instrumentalists and dance/mime/movement. Participants are selected by demo tape submissions. Applicants should send a press packet, demonstration tape and biographical information. Application materials accepted year round. Faculty opportunities are available as part of residential Summer Arts Program for children, July/August.

APPLE HILL SUMMER CHAMBER MUSIC FESTIVAL, Apple Hill Center for Chamber Music, Box 217, E. Sullivan NH 03445. (603)847-3371. Student Recruitment and Special Projects Coordinator: Harriet Feinberg. "Apple Hill welcomes 45-50 students of all ages and abilities to each of 5 summer music sessions for coaching by the Apple Hill Chamber Players and distinguished guest faculty artists and opportunities to perform chamber music of all periods. Musicians may choose from 5 short sessions (10 days each), in which participants are assigned to 2 or 3 ensembles coached daily for up to 1½ hours. Programs are offered June-August. 55 musicians participate in each workshop. Participants are amateur and professional individual instrumentalists, singers and ensembles. Participants are selected by demo tape submissions. Send for application. Suggested application deadline: May 1st. There is an application fee. Total cost for the short sessions: $835-870. Programs take place on a 70-acre New England farm. Includes the Louise Shonk Kelly Concert Barn, home of countless rehearsals, student performances and festival concerts; general meeting place and dining hall/bathroom facilities; rehearsal barn; faculty and student cabins; tennis courts."

*ASH LAWN-HIGHLAND SUMMER FESTIVAL, Rt. 6, Box 37, Charlottesville VA 22901. (804)293-9539. Director of Programs: Judy Walker. Estab. 1978. 4 Music At Twilight programs—classical or contemporary concerts. Opera series in repertoire with orchestra. Summer only. June, July and August. Festivals last summer only in Charlottesville VA. 12 songwriters/musicians participate in each festival. Participants are amateur and professional individual vocalists, ensembles, individual instrumentalists and orchestras. Participants are chosen by audition. Auditions are held in February in New York and Washington D.C. Send for application. Closing date: January 15.

BMI-LEHMAN ENGEL MUSICAL THEATRE WORKSHOP, 320 W. 57th St., New York NY 10019. (212)830-2515. Director of Musical Theatre: Norma Grossman. Estab. 1961. "BMI is a music licensing company, which collects royalties for affiliated writers. We have departments to help writers in jazz, concert, Latin, pop and musical theater writing." Offers programs "to musical theater composers and lyricists. The BMI-Lehman Engel Musical Theatre Workshops were formed in an effort to refresh and stimulate professional writers, as well as to encourage and develop new creative talent for the musical theater." Each workshop meets one afternoon a week for two hours at BMI, New York. Participants are professional songwriters, composers and playwrights. "BMI-Lehman Engel Musical Theatre Workshop Showcase presents the best of the workshop to producers, agents, record and publishing company execs, press, directors for possible option and production." Call for application. Tape and lyrics of 3 compositions required with application.

BROADWAY TOMORROW PREVIEWS, % Broadway Tomorrow Musical Theatre, Suite 53, 191 Claremont Ave., New York NY 10027. Artistic Director: Elyse Curtis. Estab. 1983. Purpose is the enrichment of American theater by nurturing *new musicals*. Offers series in which composers living in New York City area present scores of their new musicals in concert. 2-3 composers/librettists/lyricists of same musical and 1 musical director/pianist participate. Participants are professional singers, composers and opera/musical theater writers. Submission by recommendation of past participants only. Submission is by audio cassette of music, script if completed, synopsis, cast breakdown, resume, reviews, if any, acknowledgement postcard and SASE. Participants selected by screening of submissions. Programs are presented in fall and spring with possibility of full production of works presented in concert. No entry fee.

*C-SC OPERA WORKSHOP, Culver-Stockton College, Division of Fine Arts, Canton MO 63435. (314)288-5221. Director of Opera Workshop: Dr. Carol Fisher Mathieson. "C-SC Opera Workshop provides students with experience in chamber opera through study and performance. We do one-act, small-cast chamber operas which require no chorus." Workshops offered annually, lasting 1 month (usually in February or March) with 1-4 performances. Performers are usually college students (3-8 per workshop) and occasional guests. "The new Mabee Theatre at Culver-Stockton College seats 150-200. It can be used as a thrust or arena stage. There is no curtain nor is there fly space. Lighting is state of the art. We will present the works of composers of chamber opera which are within the ability range of our students (undergraduate) and require a small cast with no chorus. Keyboard or small wind ensemble accompaniment is necessary. Ours is a small workshop which aims at introducing students to the art of chamber opera. Our students are undergraduates; Culver-Stockton College is a liberal arts college. If a work is useful to our workshop, it will also be marketable to other small colleges, undergraduate workshops at universities and some civic groups. We are a church-related school, affiliated with the Christian church (Disciples of Christ), and would provide a testing ground for works marketable to church dramatic groups, too."

DOULOS TRAINING SCHOOLS, Box 60341, Nashville TN 37206. Toll free: 1-800-235-1944. Estab. 1987. "Doulos Training Schools is a fully dedicated training center for Christian communicators, especially singers and songwriters. Separate 5 day schools for both performers and songwriters are held in Nashville every quarter in January, April, July and October (approximately 25-50 amateur and professional participants/session). The schools offer in-depth career development information to help both beginning and advanced songwriters, singers, bands, vocal groups, composers and ensembles get and stay on track. Each session is taught by recording artist and songwriter Russ Hollingsworth, and involves other major recording artists and songwriters from the Christian Music community. Past guests have included Steve Green, Steve Camp, Scott Wesley Brown, Kim Boyce and many more. Call or write for complete tuition information and description of curriculum. Entry fee ranges $675-875.

FOLK ALLIANCE ANNUAL CONFERENCE, Box 5010, Chapel Hill NC 27514. (919)542-3997. Contact: Art Menius. Estab. 1989. Conference/workshop topics change each year. Subjects covered at 1991 conference include "Survival on the Road," "Career Management" and "Grants for Folk Artists." Conference takes place late January/early February and lasts 4 days and take place at a different location each year. 150 amateur and professional musicians participate. "Offers songwriter critique session." Artist showcase participants are songwriters, individual vocalists, bands, ensembles, vocal groups and individual instrumentalists. Participants are selected by demo tape submission. Applicants should send 4 demo tapes and 4 copies of promotional material to "Showcase Committee" at above address. Closing date for application is July 1. Charges $50 on acceptance. Additional costs vary from year to year. For 1992 the cost is $88 in advance, which covers two meals, a dance, workshops and our showcase. Performers' housing is separate for the event, which is usually held in Convention hotel.

GREAT SMOKIES SONG CHASE & PERFORMING ARTISTS WORKSHOPS, Warren Wilson College, 701 Warren Wilson Rd., Swannanoa NC 28778. (704)298-3325. Director: Billy Edd Wheeler. Estab. 1988. "Offers seminars in lyric and melody writing, publishing, studio work, collaboration—almost all aspects of the creative and business side of music. Children's music seminars by award-winner Katherine Dines. This year's Performing category, aimed at songwriters and others who want to improve their voices, stage presence and performing abilities, will be directed by Ewel Cornett, founder of Actors Theatre of Louisville. For a brochure or further info contact Jim Magill, Director, The Swannanoa Gathering at the phone number/address above. $220 for weeklong day students, $445 for residents, that includes room and board and all fees and concerts. We also have a weekend rate for residents and day students." Program offered annually.

KERRVILLE FOLK FESTIVAL, Kerrville Festivals, Inc., Box 1466, Kerrville TX 78029. (512)257-3600. Founder/President: Rod Kennedy. Hosts 3-day songwriters school and new folk concert competition sponsored by the Kerrville Music Foundation. Programs held in late spring and late summer. Spring festival lasts 18 days and is held outdoors at Quiet Valley Ranch. Around 110 acts participate. Performers are professional instrumentalists, songwriters and bands. "Now hosting an annual 'house concert' seminar to encourage the establishment and promotion of monthly house concerts for traveling singer/songwriters to provide additional dates and income for touring." Participants selected by submitting demo tape, by invitation only. Send cassette, promotional material and list of upcoming appearances. "Songwriter schools are $100 and include breakfast, experienced professional instructors headed by Bob Gibson, camping on ranch and concert. Rustic facilities—no electrical hookups. Food available at reasonable cost."

*THE LEHMAN ENGEL MUSICAL THEATRE WORKSHOP, Suite 212, 1605 N. Cahuenga Blvd., Hollywood CA 90028. (213)465-9142. Co-Director: John Sparks. Estab. 1968. Held at Los Angeles Music Center 5 nights a week monthly (September through May), a series of workshops offered for development of musical theater authors and projects. "First-year members do assignments designed to develop creative and critical faculties by performing and critiquing each others' works. In subsequent years, composers, lyricists and book writers work on their own projects, bringing work in as often as they wish and as time allows for critique." Offers a multicultural showcase featuring work written by artists of color in public performances; and mini-musical project, an annual event for which writers create short (10-minute) musical theater works for a pre-selected cast of 6 actors and a production team—70 days from blank page to the stage. Size of group varies, with roughly 20 students and 60-80 ongoing professional members. Book writers, songwriters, composers, lyricists, solo instrumentalists, playwrights, poets, screenwriters and opera/musical theater writers are eligible. Members are amateur and professional and are selected from material submitted. Application fee is $25, which applies to dues ($100 per year), if accepted. Send for brochure and application. Deadline is first week of August. "We conduct readings of completed works using limited funds provided, in part by the NEA, to cover costs of copying scripts and music, fees for rehearsal pianists, etc."

*MUSIC BUSINESS FILE, P.O. Box 841, Gloucester MA 01930. (508)744-0477. Instructor: Peter W. Spellman. Estab. 1990. Purpose is "to empower independent songwriters and musicians with strategic business and industry information towards accelerating their careers. Applicable to all types of popular music." Offers instruction in "writing and implementing business plans. Targets marketing plans.

Offers national and international media contact lists and 'Tip Sheets for the Working Musician' covering practical music business matters." Offers programs year round. Workshops last anywhere from 5-15 hours. Workshops held at area colleges and universities. 15-20 amateur and professional songwriters, composers, individual vocalists and instrumentalists, bands, ensembles and vocal groups participate in each event. "Open to all. Send for free brochure describing our services. Specify music style(s) you work in. Prices vary according to length of workshop. We also offer management and promotion of world music acts including reggae, worldbeat, New Age and contemporary jazz. Booking into colleges, festivals, fairs and weddings."

MUSIC BUSINESS SEMINARS, LTD., 2 Roland Kimball Rd., Freeport ME 04032. (800)448-3621 and (207)865-1128. Director: Peter C. Knickles. "Now in its sixth year MBS, Ltd., presents 'Doing Music & Nothing Else: The Music Business Seminar.' The program is a two-day long, classroom style, multimedia educational experience that is presented in 24 major cities each year. Seminar is for all ages, all styles of music, bands and soloists, who are pursuing a career in original music songwriting, recording and performing. Learn how to establish goals, attract a songwriting or recording contract, book profitable gigs, raise capital and much, much more. Aftercare opportunities include toll free counseling with the instructor, A&R Tip Sheet/Showcase program and 2 free directories (A&R and T-100). Seminar is also available on 8 audio tapes with workbook. This is the only music seminar in US with a money back guarantee. Call for 2-year complimentary quarterly journal subscription and seminar brochure."

NATIONAL ACADEMY OF SONGWRITERS (NAS), Suite 780, 6381 Hollywood Blvd., Hollywood CA 90028. (213)463-7178. Staff Members: Dan Kirkpatrick and Steve Schalchlin. Estab. 1972. "Offers programs for songwriters including Publishers' Evaluation Workshops and SONGTALK seminar series, featuring top names in songwriting, lyric writing, demo production and more." Attendance: up to 30/workshop. Participants are amateur and professional songwriters, singers, bands and composers. Length: 2-4 hours/workshop. Membership is $75/year, professionals $125/year; Gold membership $200/year. Call hotline for application: 1-800-826-7287. "NAS is a nonprofit membership organization dedicated to the protection and education of songwriters. NAS also provides a bimonthly newsletter containing tipsheet (*Open Ears*) and collaborators' network."

NATIONAL MUSIC THEATER CONFERENCE, 234 West 44th St., New York NY 10036. (212)382-2790. Artistic Director: Paulette Haupt. Estab. 1978. Sponsored by the Eugene O'Neill Theater Center. 8-10 songwriters/musicians participate in each event. Participants are professional composers, opera/musical theater writers, lyricists, playwrights in collaboration with composers. "The Conference offers composers, lyricists and book writers the opportunity to develop new music theater works of all forms during a 2-5 week residency at the O'Neill Theater Center in Waterford, Connecticut. Some works are given publicly staged readings; others are developed in private readings during the conference with artistic staff and dramaturgs. All works selected are developed over at least a 2-3 month period. A professional company of approximately 20 singer/actors provides the writers with daily musical and dramatic readings during the Conference period. Staged works are read with script in hand, with minimal lighting and no physical properties, to allow flexibility for day-to-day rewrites. The Conference is held in August of each year. Participants are selected by Artistic Director and a panel of theater professionals. Composers and writers selected receive room, board and a stipend." Charges entry fee of $20. Send SASE for application.

*ORFORD FESTIVAL, Orford Arts Centre, Box 280, Magog, Quebec J1X 3W8 **Canada**. (819)843-3981. Artistic Director: Agnès Grossman. Estab. 1951. "Each year, the Centre d'Arts Orford produces up to forty concerts in the context of its Music Festival. It receives artists from all over the world in both classical and popular or jazz music." Offers programs for songwriters, musicians, musical playwrights or other artists related to the music industry. Programs offered during summer only. Workshops last 6 weeks and take place at Orford Arts Centre during July and August. 40 songwriters/musicians participate each year. Participants are professional songwriters, individual vocalists, bands, ensembles, vocal groups, individual instrumentalists, orchestras, opera/musical theatre writers and classical music. Participants are selected by invitation or demo tape submissions. Send for application. Closing date for application is six months before festival. Charges entry fee of $6-22.

SONGCRAFT SEMINARS, 441 East 20th Street, New York NY 10010-7512. (212)674-1143. Estab. 1986. Year-round classes for composers and lyricists conducted by teacher/consultant Sheila Davis, author of *The Craft of Lyric Writing* and *Successful Lyric Writing*. "The teaching method, grounded in fundamental principles, incorporates whole-brain writing techniques. The objective: To express your unique voice. All courses emphasize craftsmanship and teach principles that apply to every musical idiom—pop, theater, or cabaret. For details on starting dates, fees and location of classes, write or call for current listing."

Successful Lyric Writing: A 3-Saturday Course. Three 6-hour classes on the fundamental principles of writing words for and to music. Required text: *Successful Lyric Writing*. Held 3 times a year at The New School. Limited to 12.

Successful Songwriting: A one-day seminar/workshop/critique designed for composers as well as lyricists. Topics covered include: music forms, melody writing, plot development, guidelines on figurative language and whole-brain writing. Attendees receive "Keynotes on Successful Songwriting," a digest of seminar theory. Sponsored by colleges and songwriting associations around the country.

Song by Song by Sondheim: A one-day seminar focused on the elements of fine craftsmanship exemplified in the words and music of Stephen Sondheim, America's pre-eminent theater writer. Significant songs are played and analyzed from the standpoint of form, meter, rhyme, literary devices, and thematic development. Attendees are helped to apply these elements to their own writing. Held in April and November at The New School.

Whole-Brain Creativity: A five-week workshop that puts you in touch with your thinking/writing style through an understanding of split hemispheric specialization. While having fun doing exercises to access each quadrant of the brain, you'll acquire new tools for increased creativity and successful songwriting. Limited to 10.

Successful Lyric Writing Consultation Course: This course, an outgrowth of the instructor's book, covers the same theory and assignments as The Basics Course. Participants receive critiques of their work by the book's author via 1-hour phone sessions.

THE SONGWRITERS ADVOCATE (TSA), 47 Maplehurst Rd., Rochester NY 14617. (716)266-0679. Director: Jerry Englerth. "TSA is a nonprofit educational organization that is striving to fulfill the needs of the songwriter. We offer opportunities for songwriters which include song evaluation workshops to help songwriters receive an objective critique of their craft. TSA evaluates tapes and lyric sheets via the mail. We do not measure success on a monetary scale, ever. It is the craft of songwriting that is the primary objective. If a songwriter can arm himself with knowledge about the craft and the business, it will increase his confidence and effectiveness in all his dealings. However, we feel that the songwriter should be willing to pay for professional help that will ultimately improve his craft and attitude." Membership dues are $10/year. Must be member to receive discounts or services provided.

THE SONGWRITERS GUILD OF AMERICA, Suite 1002, 6430 Sunset Blvd., Hollywood CA 90028. (213)462-1108. West Coast Director: B. Aaron Meza. Estab. 1931.
ASK-A-PRO: "2-hour music business rap session to which all writers are welcome, held on the first Tuesday of each month at 7 p.m. Features industry professionals fielding questions from songwriters." Each session lasts 2 hours. Free to all Guild members, $2 for non-members. Reservations necessary. Phone for more information.
Jack Segal's Songwriters Guild Supershop "Creating Your Career Song, Your Market Breakthrough": This very successful workshop focuses on working a song through to perfection, including title, idea, re-writes and pitching your songs. Please call for more information regarding this very informative workshop. Dates to be announced.
Song Critique Sessions: Held on the last Tuesday of the month at 7 p.m., SGA members are given the opportunity to present their songs and receive constructive feedback from industry professionals and peers. There is a limit on the number of songs critiqued, and reservations are required. Call the SGA office for more information.
Supershop: SGA professional writers explore the marketing aspects of songwriting. Over 7 sessions, the group meets with music industry professionals. Supershop is a unique experience in networking.

THE SONGWRITERS GUILD OF AMERICA, 276 Fifth Ave., New York NY 10001. (212)686-6820. National Projects Director: George Wurzbach. Estab. 1931.
Ask-A-Pro: "2-hour bi-weekly music business forum to which all writers are welcome. It features industry professionals—publishers, producers, A&R people, record company executives, entertainment lawyers, artists—fielding questions from new songwriters." Offered year-round, except during summer. Charge: free to members, $2 for nonmembers.
Song Critique: "New York's oldest ongoing song critique. Guild songwriters are invited to either perform their song live or present a cassette demo for feedback. A Guild moderator is on hand to direct comments. Non-members may attend and offer comments. Free to members, $2 charge for non-members.
The Practical Songwriter: This is a 10 week nuts and bolts seminar dealing with song re-writing, demo production, industry networking, song marketing, contracts and publishing. Sessions are highlighted by visits from industry professionals. Instructor is songwriter/musician George Wurzbach. Fee: $130 for SGA members, $175 for non-members.

Pro-Shop: For each of 6 sessions an active publisher, producer or A&R person is invited to personally screen material from professional Guild writers. Participation is limited to 10 writers. Audition of material is required. Coordinator is producer/musician/award winning singer, Ann Johns Ruckert. Fee; $75 (SGA members only).

Writing For The Nashville Market: An important 4 session workshop for any writer considering writing for the expanding market of country/pop music. Developed to give writers a realistic approach to breaking into this market. Instructor is hit songwriter, author of *How To Pitch and Promote Your Songs* (Writer's Digest Books), Fred Koller. Fee; $60 for SGA members, $80 for non-members.

Other Courses And Workshops Will Include: Music Theory for Songwriters, Pop Music Workshop, Understanding MIDI, Lyric Writing, Saturday Afternoon Live (one day, selected topics) and Artist/Songwriter Career Development. Other workshops presented in Nashville (615)329-1782 and Los Angeles (213)462-1108.

GET YOUR WORK INTO THE RIGHT BUYERS' HANDS!

You work hard... and your hard work deserves to be seen by the right buyers. But with the constant changes in the industry, it's not always easy to know who those buyers are. That's why you'll want to keep up-to-date and on top with the most current edition of this indispensable market guide.

Keep ahead of the changes by ordering *1994 Songwriter's Market* today. You'll save the frustration of getting your songs returned in the mail, stamped MOVED: ADDRESS UNKNOWN. And of NOT submitting your work to new listings because you don't know they exist. All you have to do to order the upcoming 1994 edition is complete the attached post card and return it with your payment or charge card information. Order now, and there's one thing that won't change from your *1993 Songwriter's Market* - the price! That's right, we'll send you the 1994 edition for just $19.95. *1994 Songwriter's Market* will be published and ready for shipment in September 1993.

Don't let another opportunity slip by...get a jump on the industry with the help of *1994 Songwriter's Market* .
Order today!
You deserve it!

(See other side for more books to help you write and sell your songs)

To order, drop this postpaid card in the mail.

☐ Yes! I want the most current edition of *Songwriter's Market*. Please send me the 1994 edition at the 1993 price - $19.95.* (NOTE: *1994 Songwriter's Market* will be ready for shipment in September 1993.) #10342

Also send me these books to help me write and sell my songs:

_____(#10320) The Songwriters Idea Book $16.95 $14.50* (available NOW)
_____(#10287) 88 Songwriting Wrongs & How to Right Them $17.95 $15.25* (available NOW)
_____(#10195) Music Publishing: A Songwriter's Guide $18.95 $16.10 * (available NOW)
_____(#10220K) The Songwriter's Workshop $24.95 $9.99* (available NOW)

*Plus postage and handling: $3.00 for one book, $1.00 for each additional book. Ohio residents add $5^1/2\%$ sales tax.

Credit card orders call toll-free 1-800-289-0963

☐ Payment enclosed (Slip this card and your payment into an envelope)
☐ Please charge my: ☐ Visa ☐ MasterCard

Account #_____Exp. Date_____
Signature _____Phone ( )_____
Name_____
Address_____
City _____State _____Zip _____
(This offer expires May 1, 1994)

Save Over $14.00 On These Great Titles!

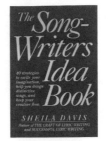
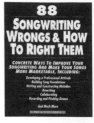

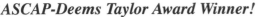

Contests and Awards

A songwriter should approach a contest, award or grant just as he would a music publisher or record company: with care, thorough research and professionalism. Treat your contest submission as you would any other; appropriate marketing techniques shouldn't be disregarded. Remember, you're still selling yourself and your work—and you always want both presented in the best light possible.

Participation in contests is a great way to gain exposure for your music. Winners receive cash prizes, musical merchandise, studio time and perhaps a recording deal. It can lead to performances of the work for musical theater and concert music composers. Even if you don't win, valuable contacts can be made. Some contests are judged by music publishers and other music industry professionals, so your music may reach the ears of important people. The bottom line is there is a chance that a beneficial relationship could result from entering.

Be sure to do proper research to ensure that you're not wasting your time and money on less-than-legitimate contests. We have confidence in the contests listed in this edition of *Songwriter's Market*. But, if you are considering entering an unlisted contest, be aware of several things. After obtaining the entry forms and contest rules, be sure you understand the contest stipulations BEFORE signing your name or sending an entrance fee. If a publishing contract is involved as a prize, don't give away your publishing rights. If you do, you're endangering possible future royalties from the song; this is clearly not in your best interest. In evaluating any contest, you must weigh what you will gain against what you will give up. Be particularly wary of exorbitant entry fees. And if you must give up any of your publishing rights or copyright, it's almost always a good idea to stay away.

Contests listed in this section encompass all types of music and all levels of competition. Read each listing carefully and contact the sponsoring organization if the contest interests you. Remember: when you receive the contest information, read the rules carefully and be sure you understand them before entering.

*ALEA III INTERNATIONAL COMPOSITION PRIZE, 855 Commonwealth Ave., Boston MA 02215. (617)353-3340. Executive Administrator: Synneve Carlino. For composers. Annual award.
Purpose: To promote and encourage young composers in the composition of new music.
Requirements: Composers 40 years of age and younger may apply; one score per composer. Works may be for solo voice or instrument or for chamber ensemble up to 15 members lasting between 6 and 15 minutes. All works must be unpublished." Deadline: March 15. Send for application. Samples of work required with application. "Real name should not appear on score; a nome de plume should be signed instead. Sealed envelope with entry form should be attached to each score."
Awards: ALEA III International Composition Prize: $2,500. Awarded once annually. Between 8-10 finalists are chosen and their works are performed in a competition concert by the ALEA III contemporary music ensemble. One grand prize winner is selected by a panel of judges.
Tips: "Emphasis placed on works written in 20th century compositional idioms."

*AMERICAN BULLET MAGAZINE SONGWRITER CONTEST, (formerly Indie Bullet Magazine Songwriter/Artist Contest), 2006-B East Rusk St., Jacksonville TX 75766. Estab. 1987. Send SASE for further information and entry blanks. Contest held each year.
Songwriter Contest: For songwriters of country music. Annual award. Two different deadlines for finalist selection each year: June 30 and November 30.
Requirements: Submit 1 country song in demo form on cassette with lyric sheet. Song must not have been nationally charted in *American Bullet* prior to entry or during contest. Enclose SASE for acknowledgment of entry. Entry fee of $25 with entry. Entries will be judged on lyric, tune and

commercial value by industry professionals to determine 12 finalists. The 12 finalists' demos will be copied on cassette (alphabetically by song title) and lyric sheets copied. Contest cassettes will be sent to all paid *American Bullet* subscribers for voting for the 4 top songwriter's songs. Winners will be notified by *American Bullet Magazine* within 30 days following voting deadline.

Awards: The four (4) winners will each receive the following: Master recording session in one of the top Nashville studios produced by one of the top independent record producers; single release on compact disk (with the other winners) on one of the top independent record labels; telephone promotion by two of the top independent record promoters; full page advertisements (shared with other winners), tracking services, overseas promotion, publicity service and 200 CDs for the winner's own use.

AMERICAN MUSICAL THEATRE FESTIVAL/NATIONAL CONTEST FOR NEW AMERICAN MUSICALS, % California Music Theatre, #400M, 2500 E. Colorado Blvd., Pasadena CA 91107. (818)792-0776. Contact: C.R. Coddington. For songwriters, composers and musical playwrights. Annual award.
Purpose: The National Contest for New American Musicals is designed to give creators of new musicals a forum for further creative work and exposure to musical theatre professionals.
Requirements: Entries must be full length, previously unproduced musicals with commercial potential. Deadline: December 30. Send for application. Samples of work required with application. Initial submissions must include 2 songs, 2 scenes and a synopsis with application and a $15 fee.
Awards: The winning entrant receives a $2,000 grand prize and a possible workshop or production.

*ASCAP FOUNDATION GRANTS TO YOUNG COMPOSERS, ASCAP Bldg., 1 Lincoln Plaza, New York NY 10023. (212)621-6327. Contact: Frances Richard, ASCAP Foundation Grants to Young Composers.
Purpose: To provide grants to young composers to encourage the development of talented young American composers.
Eligibility: Applicants must be citizens or permanent residents of the United States of America who have not reached their 30th birthday by March 15. Original music of any style will be considered. However, works which have earned awards or prizes in any other national competition or grant giving program are ineligible. Arrangements are ineligible.
Requirements: Each applicant must submit a completed application form; one reproduction of a manuscript or score; biographical information listing prior music studies, background and experience; a list of compositions to date; and one professional recommendation to be mailed by the referee directly to ASCAP under separate cover. A cassette tape of the composition submitted for the competition may be included if it is marked with the composer's name, the title of the work and the names of the performers. Tapes of electronic music must also be accompanied by written information concerning source material and electronic equipment used. A composition that involves a text must be accompanied by information about the source of the text with evidence that it is in the public domain or by written permission from the copyright proprietor. Deadline: All materials must be postmarked no later than March 15.
Awards: ASCAP Foundation awards grants of $500-2,500. Length: 1 year. Applications judged by screening-panel of composers.

BALTIMORE OPERA COMPETITION FOR AMERICAN OPERATIC ARTISTS, 101 W. Read St., Baltimore MD 21201. (410)727-0592. Competition Coordinator: James Harp. For performing artists. Annual award.
Purpose: "Prizes are awarded to talented operatic artists in order to further their development in the study of languages, voice and acting."
Requirements: Singers must be between the ages of 20 and 35, inclusive, and must be citizens of the United States. They must present two letters of recommendation from recognized musical authorities." Deadline: May 15. Send for application. Singers must audition in person.
Awards: 1st Prize: $10,000; 2nd Prize $8,000; 3rd Prize $5,000; Steber Award $2,500; Puccini Award $2,000; Janowski Award $1,000; Collinge Memorial Award $1,000; $150 stipends to all semifinalists. Prize may be renewed upon audition. Singers are judged by a panel of internationally recognized judges eminent in the field of opera.
Tips: "The purpose of the competition is to encourage young operatic talent on the verge of a career. Singers must demonstrate potential in singing, fluency in languages and histrionic capability."

*BMI AWARDS TO STUDENT COMPOSERS, 320 W. 57th St., New York NY 10019. (212)586-2000. Director: Barbara Petersen. Estab. 1951. For student composers under the age of 26 who are permanent residents of the Western Hemisphere and who are engaged in the serious study of music. Annual.

Purpose: "To identify outstanding young composers and make cash awards for furthering their musical education."
Requirements: Applicants must not have reached their 26th birthday by Dec. 31 of the year preceding the February 10th contest deadline. "Applicant must be a citizen or permanent resident of the Western Hemisphere enrolled in an accredited public, private or parochial secondary school, in an accredited college or conservatory of music, or engaged in private study with recognized music teachers." Deadline: early February. One entry per student. Judged under pseudonyms. Send for free application and rules. Rights retained. Entries returned (winning scores are retained for BMI Archives). SASE required.
Awards: BMI Awards to Student Composers: "prizes totaling $15,000 ranging from $500 to $2,500 may be given to winning students, by check, with certificate of honor." Contest judged by "outstanding composers, performers, music publishers and musicologists."

CINTAS FELLOWSHIP, I.I.E 809 UN Plaza, New York NY 10017. (212)984-5564. Program Officer: Vanessa Palmer. For composers and musical playwrights. Annual award. Estab. 1964.
Purpose: "Fellowships awarded to persons of Cuban citizenship or lineage for achievement in music composition (architecture, painting, sculpture, printmaking, photography and literature); students wishing to pursue academic programs are not eligible, nor are performing artists. Applicants must be creative artists of Cuban descent who have completed their academic and technical training." Deadline: March 1. Send for application. Samples of work required with application. "Send complete score and a cassette tape. Compositions submitted must be serious classical works. Popular songs and ballads will not be accepted."
Awards: Cintas Fellowship: $10,000 per grantee. Fellowship is good for 12 months. Applicant may receive an award no more than twice. Selection committee reviews applications.

COLUMBIA ENTERTAINMENT COMPANY'S JACKIE WHITE MEMORIAL PLAYWRITING CONTEST, 309 Parkade Blvd., Columbia MO 65202. (314)874-5628. Chairperson, CEC Contest: Betsy Phillips. For musical playwrights. Annual award.
Purpose: "We are looking for top-notch scripts for theater school use, to challenge and expand the talents of our students, ages 10-15. We want good plays with large casts (20-30 characters) suitable for use with our theater school students. Full production of the winning script will be done by the students. A portion of travel expenses, room and board offered to winner for production of show."
Requirements: "Must be large cast plays, original story lines and cannot have been previously published. Please write for complete rules." Deadline: June 30. Send for application; then send scripts to address above. Full-length play, neatly typed. No name on title page, but name, address and name of play on a 3×5" index card. Cassette tape of musical numbers required."
Awards: $250 first prize and partial travel expenses to see play produced. Second place winner gets no prize money but receives production of the play by the theater school plus partial travel expenses. This is a one-time cash award, given after any revisions required are completed. "The judging committee is taken from members of Columbia Entertainment Company's Executive and Advisory boards. At least eight members, with at least three readings of all entries, and winning entries being read by entire committee. We are looking for plays that will work with our theater school students."
Tips: "Remember the play we are looking for will be performed by 10-15 year old students with normal talents—difficult vocal ranges, a lot of expert dancing and so forth will eliminate the play. We especially like plays that deal with current day problems and concerns. However, if the play is good enough, any suitable subject matter is fine. It should be fun for the audience to watch."

*CONCERT ARTISTS' GUILD, 850 7th Ave., New York NY 10019. (212)333-5200. For performing artists. Annual award.
Requirements: Send for application.
Awards: Concert Artists Guild—Free management leading to recitals and solo appearances. Sponsored New York recital, commissioned work from a composer of the winner's choice $2,500.

*CONCOURS OSM COMPETITION, 85 St. Catherine St. West, Montreal Quebec H2X 3P4 **Canada**. (514)842-3402. For performing artists. Annual award alternates between winds and strings, and voice and piano.
Requirements: Contestants must be Canadian citizens or landed immigrants. Age requirements: Piano and Strings, Class A: 18-25; Piano and Strings, Class B: 17 and under; Winds: 16-25; Voice: 18-30. Send or phone for application.
Awards: Grand total of prizes of 10,000£ given in various categories. First prize winners perform as soloists with l'Orchestre Symphonique de Montréal in concert. Total of 10 prizes. Judged by jury during three eliminations.

*CORPUS CHRISTI YOUNG ARTISTS' AWARD, Corpus Christi Young Artists' Competition Inc., Box 81243, Corpus Christi TX 78468-1243. For performing artists. Annual award.
Purpose: "Providing opportunities for competing in the exercise of musical knowledge and skills before adjucative panel of high acclaim." Send for application.
Requirements: "Standard concerto with one additional solo number, and in piano solo division two contrasting solos." Deadline: December 15, 1992. Samples of work required with application. Send for application. Recording on cassette tape.
Awards: Young Artists' Award—$1,000 plus opportunity to perform with Corpus Christi Symphony Orchestra, four first place awards of $500 each—Pre College and College in Piano and Instrumental concerto, Second and Third place awards also. First, second and third prize awards in pre-college piano solo divisions. Applications are judged by committee for acceptance in competition.
Tips: "All contestants will receive advice and critique from panel and derive benefit from public stage performances."

*CRS NATIONAL COMPOSERS COMPETITION, 724 Winchester Rd., Broomall PA 19008. (215)544-5920. Administrative Assistant: Caroline Hunt. For songwriters, composers and performing artists. Annual award.
Requirements: Send for application. Samples of work required with application. Audio or video recording of composition.
Awards: 1st Prize: Commercial recording grant. Applications are judged by panel of judges including: Yo-Yo Ma, Lydia Walton Ignacio, William Smith, George Crumb and John Russo.

*EAST & WEST ARTISTS INTERNATIONAL AUDITIONS, for New York Debut, 310 Riverside Dr., #313, New York NY 10025. Phone/FAX: (212)222-2433. Executive Director/Founder: Miss Adolovni Acosta. For performing artists. Annual award.
Requirements: "Open to all classical instrumentalists, singers and ensembles of any nationality who have not given a New York recital debut." There is no age limit. Deadline: February 15, 1993. Send SASE for information and application forms.
Awards: "A fully subsidized solo debut at Weill Recital Hall at Carnegie Hall; cash awards."

ECKHARDT-GRAMATTÉ NATIONAL MUSIC COMPETITION FOR THE PERFORMANCE OF CANA-DIAN MUSIC, Queen Elizabeth II Music Bldg., Room 2-11, 270 - 18th St., Brandon Manitoba R7A 6A9 Canada. (204)728-8212. Administrative Officer: Mrs. Lynne Bailey. For performing artists. Annual competition alternating each year between voice, piano, and strings.
Purpose: To encourage young musicians to perform the works of modern (especially but not exclusively Canadian) composers.
Requirements: Must be citizens of Canada or resident in Canada for 2 years, under 30 years for piano and strings, and under 35 for voice. Deadline: October. Send for application. Samples are not required.
Awards: 1st Prize: $2,500 and national recital tour. 2nd Prize: $1,500. 3rd Prize: $1,000. Best performance of imposed piece: $700. Preliminaries: Tape recordings are forwarded to jurors to mark. The tapes are numbered, not named. Semi-finalists: Attend competition in May where 4 jurors listen and compare. Finalists: Same as semi-finals.

*FIRST BAR/INNER CITY CULTURAL CENTER'S COMPETITION FOR COMPOSERS & SONGWRIT-ERS, 1308 S. New Hampshire Ave., Los Angeles CA 90006. (213)387-1161. Executive Director: C. Bernard Jackson. For songwriters, composers and musical playwrights. Annual award.
Purpose: "The primary purpose of the competition is to bring songwriters, composers and those who perform original music into contact with those in the music and entertainment industry who are in a position to hire them, and to bring to public prominence the role played by creators of original music."
Requirements: "One entry per participant, maximum length 20 minutes. Participant must have a sponsor, entry must be performed live, may not have been previously published. Deadline: May. Send for application. Samples are not required.
Awards: "Guaranteed publication, future professional performance plus $1,500 (1st place), $1,000 (2nd place), $500 (3rd place). Additional prizes to be announced at time of competition. Criteria: 1. Originality 2. Overall presentation (performance) 3. Thematic development 4. Structural unity 5. Fullfillment of functional intent. Judges are recruited from the ranks of music industry professionals. Members of the audience cast ballots during a series of three elimination rounds to determine which entries proceed to the final round.
Tips: "Have a sponsor capable of providing the support necessary to gather resources needed to make an effective performance presentation (performers, transportation to competition site, rehearsal space, on-site accommodations, special equipment, etc.). This is done LIVE! Competition is open to all. There are NO categories or distinctions made based on genre (classical, jazz, country western, reggae, etc.). Lyrics or librettos may be in any language. There is no citizenship or U.S. residency

requirement. Compositions designed to support other media (dance, film, etc.) must be presented in their original context. Keep in mind that the goal of the competition is to develop employment opportunities for gifted writers and to bring attention to the craft in all of its diversity. The competition is divided into 2 divisions: Adult (over 18) and youth (under 18). Youth division prizes normally consist of scholarship awards. ICCC has successfully conducted competitions resulting in professional employment and production for actors over the past seven years as well as for playwrights."

FULBRIGHT SCHOLAR PROGRAM, COUNCIL FOR INTERNATIONAL EXCHANGE OF SCHOLARS, Suite 5M, 3007 Tilden St., NW, Washington DC 20008-3009. (202)686-7877. Estab. 1946. Director, Academic & University Liaison: Steven A. Blodgett. For songwriters, composers, performing artists, musical playwrights and scholars/artists in all disciplines. Annual award.
Purpose: "Awards for university lecturing and advanced research abroad are offered annually in virtually all academic disciplines including musical composition."
Requirements: "U.S. citizenship at time of application; M.F.A., Ph.D. or equivalent professional qualifications; for lecturing awards, university teaching experience." Application materials for the competition become available in March each year, for grants to be taken up 1½ years later. Application deadlines: June 15-Australia, U.S.S.R., South Asia. August 1-Africa, Northeast and Southeast Asia, Eastern Europe, Western Europe, Latin America and the Caribbean, Middle East, Canada. Send for application. Samples of work are required with application. Applicant should refer to checklist in application packet.
Awards: "Benefits vary by country, but generally include round-trip travel for the grantee and for most full academic-year awards, one dependent; stipend in U.S. dollars and/or local currency; in many countries, tuition allowance for school age children; and book and baggage allowance. Grant duration ranges from 2 months-1 academic year. Applications undergo a two-stage peer review by CIES advisory committees; first by subject matter specialists and then by an interdisciplinary group of geographic area specialists. After nomination, applications are sent to the J. William Fulbright Scholarship Board and the host countries for final review."
Tips: "The Applicant's Handbook, which is included in the application packet, provides suggestions on preparing a competitive application, as well as in-depth information about the review committee structure, etc."

HARVEY GAUL COMPOSITION CONTEST, The Pittsburgh New Music Ensemble, Inc., Duquesne University School of Music, Pittsburgh PA 15282. (412)261-0554. Conductor/Executive Director: David Stock/Eva Tumiel-Kozak. For composers. Biennial.
Purpose: Objective is to encourage composition of new music. Winning piece to be premiered by the PNME.
Requirements: "Must be unpublished and unperformed compositions—new works scored for 6 to 16 instruments drawn from the following: flute, oboe, 2 clarinets, bassoon, horn, trumpet, trombone, tuba, 2 violins, cello, bass, 2 percussion, piano, harp, electronic tape." Deadline: April 15. Send for application. Samples of work are required with application. "Real name must not appear on score—must be signed with a 'nom de plume'." Entry fee: $10.
Awards: Harvey Gaul Composition Contest: $1,500.

*GILMAN & GONZALEZ-FALLA THEATRE FOUNDATION MUSICAL THEATER AWARDS, 109 East 64th St., New York NY 10021. (212)734-8001. Contact: C. Kempler (Miss). For composers, musical playwrights any composer/lyricist/creative team with a produced musical to his/her/their credit. Annual award.
Requirements: Send for application.
Awards: $25,000.

*GREATER MIAMI OPERA ASSOCIATION YOUNG PATRONESSES OF THE OPERA VOICE COMPETITION, 1200 Coral Way, Miami FL 33145. (305)854-1643. For performing artists only. Biannual award (1993 next competition).
Purpose: To provide financial aid to young singers who are pursuing careers in opera as solo artists.
Requirements: Open to students age 18-29 seriously pursuing a career in opera. Send for application. Samples of work are required with application.
Awards: Judy George Award: $2,500. Young Patronesses of the Opera Award: $1,500. Additional awards totalling $6,000. Competition judged by recognized authorities in the field of opera.
Tips: "Be proficient in the language you are singing in. Do not be overly ambitious in the choice of selections."

HEMPHILL-WELLS SORANTIN YOUNG ARTIST AWARD, Box 5922, San Angelo TX 76902. (915)658-5877. For performing artists. Annual award. Estab. 1959.
Purpose: "There are 3 divisions of competition: Vocal, Instrumental and Piano. All candidates will be judged by the highest artistic standards, in regard to technical proficiency, musicianship, rhythm, selection of repertoire and stage presence. Objective: to further the career of the young artist."
Requirements: Piano/instrumental: not reached their 28th birthday by competition. Vocal: not reached their 31st birthday by competition. All contestants will perform all repertoire from memory. Deadline: October 25. Send for application. Judged on performance contest weekend.
Awards: A winner and runner-up will be declared in each division. The division winner will receive a cash award of $500; the runner-up will receive $250. An overall winner will be selected to appear with the San Angelo Symphony Orchestra on February 6, 1993, and will receive an additional $1,500 cash award. $500 to be paid at time of selection and $1,000 on February 6, 1993. Title held as winner of that year. Printed on all future information. Contest held every year. Can only win once. No limit on number of times you may enter. This is a competition for the young artist; highest priority will be placed on artistry, communication and stage presence.

HENRICO THEATRE COMPANY ONE-ACT PLAYWRITING COMPETITION, Box 27032, Richmond VA 23273. (804)672-5100. Cultural Arts Coordinator: J. Larkin Brown. For musical playwrights. Annual award.
Purpose: Original one-act musicals for a community theater organization.
Requirements: "Only one-act plays or musicals will be considered. The manuscript should be a one-act original (not an adaptation), unpublished, and unproduced, free of royalty and copyright restrictions. Scripts with smaller casts and simpler sets may be given preference. Controversial themes should be avoided. Standard play script form should be used. All plays will be judged anonymously, therefore, there should be two title pages; the first must contain the play's title and the author's complete address and telephone number. The second title page must contain only the play's title. The playwright must submit two excellent quality copies. Receipt of all scripts will be acknowledged by mail. Scripts will be returned if SASE is included. No scripts will be returned after the winner is announced. The HTC does not assume responsibility for loss, damage or return of scripts. All reasonable care will be taken." Deadline: September 15. Send for application first.
Awards: 1st prize $250.

*HOUSTON OPERA STUDIO VOICE COMPETITION, 510 Preston, Houston TX 77002. (713)546-0227. Manager: Shauna Bowman Unger. For performing artists. Annual award.
Purpose: A program for the development of young professional singers in Opera/Music Theater.
Requirements: Singers must have major operatic potential and demonstrate thorough musical and theatrical training. Deadline: October. Send for application.
Awards: Awards include membership in the Houston Opera Studio and cash prizes totalling $9,000. Membership is good for one-year with a three-year option.

INTERMOUNTAIN SONGWRITING COMPETITION, Box 71325, Salt Lake City UT 84107. (801)596-3058 or (801)451-2831. Estab. 1987. For songwriters. Annual award by Utah Songwriters Association.
Purpose: First place winner receives an all-expense paid trip to Nashville, Tennessee to attend Nashville Songwriters Association International Spring Symposium in March or to the LASS Expo in Los Angeles in October.
Requirements: All amateur songwriters may enter. Deadline: December 31. Send SASE for application to enter. One song per tape. Contest runs from October 15 to December 31 each year. Entry must be postmarked by December 31. Entry fee: $10 for first song, $5 each additional song.
Awards: First prize is a trip to Nashville or Los Angeles, or cash award of $500 (out of the United States may receive cash award only).
Tips: "Submit a well-written song on a quality demo tape. Lyric sheets should be typed or legibly hand written. Noisy cassettes should be avoided. Radio deejays are among the judges, so they listen for commerciality. We look for songs that say something important, and songs with a good hook."

*INTERNATIONAL NEW MUSIC COMPETITION, 9374 Jones St., Omaha NE 68114. Chairman 1992 Competition: Mrs. Sarah Carver. For composers. Annual award.
Requirements: Send for application.
Awards: International New Music Competition: $2,000. Premiere performance by Omaha Symphony Chamber Orchestra.

KENNEDY CENTER FRIEDHEIM AWARDS, Kennedy Center for the Performing Arts, Washington DC 20566. (202)416-8000. Estab. 1978. For American composers. Annual award. For symphonic instrumental compositions in even-numbered years; for instrumental compositions for 1-13 instruments (chamber music) in odd-numbered years.

Purpose: Annual award for new music by an American. "Our goal is to bring high level public recognition and honor to contemporary American composers. Award may be used as composer wishes."

Requirements: Requirements for application: American citizenship or permanent residency status; composition must have had American premiere performance within 2 year period, July 1-June 30 in year of composition. May not include voices unless used as an instrument—must be without words. Deadline: July 15th. Send or call for application. 3 tapes and 1 score with application plus $20 fee.

Awards: 1st prize: $5,000; 2nd prize: $2,500; 3rd prize: $1,000; 4th prize: $500. Applications are judged by a 3-person jury: 1) each receives copy of taped performance; 2) jury gathers to listen collectively to all compositions and examine score. They then nominate 10 semi-finalists; 3) jury members individually study scores (of 10) with tape; 4) these works are performed for final ranking. Prizes awarded at the conclusion of performance.

Tips: "Get a top quality recording by a fine chamber group if possible."

*THE KOSCIUSZKO FOUNDATION CHOPIN PIANO COMPETITION, 15 E. 65th St., New York NY 10021. (212)734-2130. Director: Monika Jasinski. For performing artists.

Purpose: "To encourage young pianists to further their studies and to perform the works of great Polish composers."

Requirements: Deadline: April 15. Send for application.

Awards: First prize: $2,500; second prize: $1,500; third prize: $1,000. "Scholarship monies may be awarded in the form of shared prizes." First prize is non-renewable. Other contestants may re-apply. Contestants judged on performance of the required repertoire.

*McCLAREN MEMORIAL COMEDY PLAYWRITING COMPETITION, 2000 W. Wadley, Midland TX 79705. (915)682-2544. Chair: Mary Lou Cassidy. For musical playwrights. Annual award.

Purpose: "Awards a comedy script with presentation in reader's theater at a community theater in Texas in memorium to Mike McClaren, a very funny guy." Deadline: January 31, 1993. "Send script, only returned if SASE included."

Awards: $400 plus plane fare to Midland, TX for rehearsal period and production of reader's theater production of the play. Awarded in April. Reader's theater production of play in June or July of the same year.

Tips: *"Must be funny.* No limit to number of scenes, scenery, number of characters."

MARIMOLIN COMPOSITION CONTEST, 207 N. Grove S., Bowling Green OH 43402. (419)352-0269. For composers. Annual award.

Purpose: To encourage the creation of works for the combination of marimba and violin.

Requirements: Open to all composers. Deadline: July 1. Send for application. A completed new work for violin and marimba. 2 scores, or 1 score and parts. "Winners announced by August 1. Prize of $600 awarded to up to 3 composers."

Awards: "Up to 3 winners will be selected. A total of $600 will be awarded at the judges' discretion. The winning work(s) will be premiered during the following season."

*MAXIM MAZUMDAR NEW PLAY COMPETITION, One Curtain Up Alley, Buffalo NY 14202-1911. (716)852-2266. Dramaturg: Joyce Stilson. For musical playwrights. Annual award.

Purpose: Alleyway Theatre is dedicated to the development and production of new works. Winners of the competition will receive production and royalties.

Requirements: May request guidelines or submit directly.

Awards: Full length winners receive $300 prize plus royalties and first production. One-Act winners receive $100 prize. Also receive air fare and lodging for final week of rehearsal. Applications are reviewed by artistic staff and are given at least two reads.

Tips: Entries may be of any style, but preference will be given to those scripts which take place in unconventional settings and explore the boundaries of theatricality. No more than ten performers is a definite, unchangeable requirement.

MID-SOUTH PLAYWRIGHTS CONTEST, 51 S. Cooper, Memphis TN 38104. (901)725-0776. Executive Director: Jackie Nichols. For musical playwrights. Annual award. Estab. 1983.

Requirements: Send script, tape, SASE. "Playwrights from the South will be given preference." Open to full-length, unproduced plays. Musicals must be fully arranged for the piano when received. Deadline: April 1.

Awards: Grants may be renewed. Applications judged by 3 readers.

MIXED BLOOD VERSUS AMERICA PLAYWRITING CONTEST, 1501 S. 4th St., Minneapolis MN 55454. (612)338-0937. Script Czar: Dave Kunz. For musical playwrights. Annual award. Estab. 1983.
Purpose: To encourage emerging playwrights (musical playwrights).
Requirements: "Send previously unproduced play (musical) resume, cover letter stipulating contest entry." Deadline March 15. Send SASE for copy of contest guidelines. Samples are not required.
Awards: Winner: $2,000 and full production of winning play/musical.
Tips: "Professionalism is always a plus. Surprise us. All subject matter accepted. Political satires and shows involving sports (baseball, golf etc.) always of interest."

MUSEUM IN THE COMMUNITY COMPOSER'S AWARD, Box 251, Scott Depot WV 25560. (304)757-2509. Contest Administrator: Trish Fisher. For composers. Biennial.
Purpose: The Composer's Competition is to promote the writing of new works by Americans for full orchestra of 5-10 minute duration.
Requirements: Work must not have won any previous awards nor have been published, publicly performed or used commercially. Requires 3 copies of the original score, clearly legible and bound. Title to appear at the top of each composition, but the composer's name must not appear. Entry forms must be filled out and a SASE of the proper size enclosed for return of entry. Enclose $25 entry fee (non-refundable). Send for application.
Awards: Museum in the Community Composer's Award First place: $5,000. "Up to 3 honorable mentions will be awarded at the discretion of the judges." Jurors will be 3 nationally known musicologists. Winning composer will be awarded $5,000 prize and a premiere concert of the composition at a West Virginia Symphony Orchestra subscription concert. Transportation to the premiere from anywhere in the continental United States will be provided by the Museum.
Tips: Read *and* follow rules listed in Prospectus. Neatness still counts!"

*MUSIC CITY SONG FESTIVAL, Box 17999-SW, Nashville TN 37217. (615)834-0027. Founder and Executive Director: Roy E. Sinkovich. Estab. 1979. "Prizes in 1989 totaled over $250,000. Sponsors for the 1989 competition included Atari Computer, Magnavox, Peavey, Shure, Smith Corona, TASCAM and Technics. The Music City Song Festival has eight divisions: Professional Song, Amateur Song, Novice Song, Vocal Performance, Professional Lyric, Amateur Lyric, Novice Lyric and Lyric Poem. Musical categories available are: Pop/Rock, Country, MOR/Adult Contemporary, R&B/Soul/Blues, Gospel/Contemporary Christian, Novelty/Miscellaneous (except for Vocal) and Musical Theater/Standards (Vocal only). Entrants submit cassette tapes to be judged by active music industry professionals (publishers, recording artists, producers, record company executives, radio personalities, managers, promoters, etc.) Entry fee varies, depending on level of competition (Professional, Amateur or Novice). All entries must be accompanied by an official MCSF entry form."
Awards: "433 prizes of cash, merchandise and cash plus merchandise are awarded to First through Tenth place in *each* musical category of each division. The Top Six Lyric Poem entries are published in *SoundMakers*, MCSF's free educational magazine distributed annually in conjunction with the competition. Finalist Certificates are awarded to the top 25 finalists in each musical category of each division. Honorable Mention Certificates are awarded to the top 10 percent in each musical category of each division. *SoundMakers* magazine is distributed free of charge to everyone on the MCSF mailing list regardless of whether they enter the competition. To be added to MCSF's mailing list for free entry information and *SoundMakers* magazine, contact the MCSF offices. NOTE: Entering the Music City Song Festival does not tie up your material in any way. You are free to continue pitching your songs throughout the competition. Entering the competition or winning an award does not give the MCSF any publishing or promotional rights to your song."
Tips: "Read the MCSF entry information very carefully. All tapes should present your songs so that words, music and vocals can be clearly heard and understood. Be sure to include a typed or neatly printed lyric sheet with tapes of original songs. Listen to the tape to be sure it is a good copy, then rewind it to the beginning of the song. For the purposes of the MCSF competition, each song must be submitted on a separate cassette labeled with song title only. Lyric sheets should be printed on 8½×11 *white* paper (so they can be photocopied for judging) and labeled with song title only. For more details, write to MCSF at the above address or call between 9:00 a.m. and 5:00 p.m. Central time."

*MUSICIANS' CLUB OF NEW YORK YOUNG ARTISTS AWARDS, Suite 19G, 20 W 64th St., New York NY 10023. (212)877-2127. Chairman of Young Artist Awards: Constance Mensch. For performing artists. Annual award.
Purpose: To further careers of young artists.
Requirements: Send for application.

NACUSA YOUNG COMPOSERS' COMPETITION, NACUSA, Box 49652 Barrington Station, Los Angeles CA 90049. (213)541-8213. President, NACUSA: Marshall Bialosky. For NACUSA members 18-30 years of age. Annual award.

Purpose: Goal is "to encourage the writing and performance of new American concert hall music."
Requirements: Must have NACUSA membership and meet age restrictions. Samples are not required. Write for information.
Awards: Judged by a committee of composers.

NEW FOLK CONCERTS FOR EMERGING SONGWRITERS, Box 1466, Kerrville TX 78029. (512)257-3600. Attn: New Folk. For songwriters and composers. Annual award.
Purpose: "Our objective is to provide an opportunity for unknown songwriters to be heard and rewarded for excellence."
Requirements: Songwriter enters 2 previously unpublished songs on same side of cassette tape — $6 entry fee per tape; more than one tape may be entered; 6-8 minutes total for 2 songs. No written application necessary; no lyric sheets or press material needed. Deadline: April 15th. Call or write for detailed information.
Awards: New Folk Award Winner. 40 writers invited to sing the 2 songs entered during The Kerrville Folk Festival. 6 writers are chosen as award winners. Each of the 6 receives a cash award of $150 and performs at a winner's concert during the Kerrville Folk Festival. Initial round of entries judged by the Festival Producer. 40 finalists judged by panel of 3 performer/songwriters.
Tips: "Make certain cassette is rewound and ready to play. Do not allow instrumental accompaniment to drown out lyric content."

OMAHA SYMPHONY GUILD NEW MUSIC COMPETITION, 310 Aquila Court, Omaha NE 68102. (402)342-3836. Contact: Chairman, New Music Competition. For composers with an annual award. Estab. 1976.
Purpose: "The objective of the competition is to promote new music scored for chamber orchestra."
Requirements: "Follow competition guidelines including orchestration and length of composition." Deadline: usually May 15. Send for application or call (402)342-3836. Each fall new guidelines and application forms are printed. Scores are due by May 15.
Awards: "Monetary award is $2,000. Winner has an optional premiere performance by the Omaha Symphony Chamber Orchestra. Applications are screened by Omaha Symphony music director. Finalists are judged by a national panel of judges."
Tips: "This is an annual competition and each year has a new Symphony Guild chairman; all requests for extra information sent to the Omaha Symphony office will be forwarded. Also, 1,700-1,800 application information brochures are sent to colleges, universities and music publications each Fall."

PAINTER MUSIC TOP TALENT SEARCH, Box 738, Ridgetop TN 37152-0738. (615)851-6860. FAX: (615)851-6857. President: Richard Allan Painter.
Purpose: To discover and develop outstanding talent for a sustained and successful musical career.
Requirements: Send SASE for entry forms and information. Entry forms are available during July and August. All entrees are due by the end of September and final results are announced with prizes awarded in October. Samples of work on cassette and lyric sheet (properly labeled) are required for entry with completed entry form and entry fee of $25 with SASE. All inquiries must be by mail with SASE. No phone calls, please. Entering or winning the Painter Music Top Talent Search does not tie up and does not give PMTTS any publishing or promotional rights to your work or material.
Awards: Prizes in 1990 totaled over $7,000. There are 3 top divisions: Top Female Talent, Top Male Talent and Top Group Talent. Judging is done by active music industry professionals.
Tips: "Read and follow the instructions on the entry form. This will help you make your best first impression. The PMTTS exists to help you. When you do things right the first time, you will help others to help you."

PULITZER PRIZE IN MUSIC, 702 Journalism, Columbia University, New York NY 10027. (212)854-3841. Administrator: Robert C. Christopher. For composers and musical playwrights. Annual award.
Requirements: "The piece must have its American premiere between March 15 and March 14 of year it is submitted for consideration." Deadline: March 1. Samples of work are required with application and $20 entry fee. "Send tape and score."
Awards: "1 award: $3,000. Applications are judged first by a nominating jury, then by the Pulitzer Prize Board."

THE QUINTO MAGANINI AWARD IN COMPOSITION, 37 Valley View Rd., Norwalk CT 06851. Contest Coordinator: Russell Cooper. For composers.
Requirements: The competition is open to all American composers. Entries should be submitted anonymously, with Social Security Number as identification and appropriate return envelope and return postage. In an accompanying sealed envelope, composer should give name, address, social security number, and brief resume. The composition is to be scored for standard symphonic orchestra,

and should not exceed 15 minutes in length; no soloists or concerti. Write for more information. Deadline January 31, 1993.

Awards: The recipient will receive a cash award ($2,500) and will have the composition performed in world premiere by the Norwalk Symphony Orchestra under the direction of Jesse Levine, Musical Director, during the 1992-93 season.

ROME PRIZE FELLOWSHIP, 41 East 65th St., New York NY 10021. (212)517-4200. Contact: Fellowships Coordinator. For composers. Annual award.

Purpose: "A center for artistic creation and for independent study and advanced research in the humanities, the academy provides living and working space for artists and scholars atthe Academy's ten-building, eleven-acre campus in Rome."

Requirements: "U.S. citizens only may apply. B.A. required in field of musical composition." Deadline: Nov. 15. Send or call for application. Samples of work are required with application. Tapes and scores.

Awards: "Rome Prize Fellowships—2 available in musical composition: $7,000 stipend, $500 European travel, $800 travel allowance, room, board, studio. One year in Rome. Judged by independent juries of professionals in the field."

Tips: "Write a good proposal explaining why a year in Rome would be invaluable to your development as a composer. Explain what you would do in Rome."

LOIS AND RICHARD ROSENTHAL NEW PLAY PRIZE, % Cincinnati Playhouse, P.O. Box 6537, Cincinnati OH 45206. (513)345-2242. Contact: Literary Manager. For musical playwrights. Annual award.

Purpose: The Rosenthal Prize was established to encourage the production of new work in the theater and to give playwrights the opportunity to see their work through all stages of production.

Requirements: A full-length work of any style or scale including plays, musicals or collaborations. Must not have received a full-scale professional production and must be unpublished at time of submission. Deadline: Jan. 15, 1993. Format should be complete, neatly typed, securely bound script with tape, if musical.

Awards: Lois and Richard Rosenthal New Play Prize—$1,500 stipend, residency expenses and appropriate royalties. The prize is awarded by May; production of the show in winter or spring of following season. Each submission is read and evaluated by a member of the Playhouse Literary staff; finalists are judged by Artistic Director.

Tips: "Follow submission guidelines carefully, and make sure script is securely bound. Prefer works of timely interest and a theatrical nature. Works with previous readings or workshop productions are encouraged. No submissions accepted before October 15, 1992."

SONGWRITERS ASSOCIATION OF WASHINGTON MID-ATLANTIC SONG CONTEST, Suite 632, 1377 K St. NW, Washington DC 20005. (301)654-3434. Contact: Director. Estab. 1982. Gives awards to songwriters and/or composers annually.

Purpose: "Contest is designed to afford *amateurs* the opportunity of receiving awards/exposure/feedback of critical nature in an environment of peer competition. Applicants must send for application; rules and regulations explained—amateur status is most important requirement. Samples of work are required with application: cassette, entry form and 3 copies of lyrics.

Awards: "Awards usually include free recording time, merchandise (for category winner) and cash and air fare (for grand prize winner). Awards vary from year to year." Awards must be used within one calendar year."

Requirements: Applications are judged by a panel of 3 judges per category, for 4 levels, to determine top winners in each category and to arrive at the grand prize winner. Reduced entry fees are offered for SAW members. Membership also entitles one to a newsletter and reduced rates for special events/seminars."

Tips: "Please check to see that you have followed *all* the rules, cue song to beginning—make lyric sheets legible and neat, no long introductions."

SONGWRITERS NETWORK OF HOUSTON SONGWRITING AND LYRIC WRITING CONTEST, (formerly Fort Bend Songwriters Assoc. Songwriting and Lyric Writing Contest), Box 1342, Friendswood TX 77546-1342. (713)264-4330. Contact: Sybrina Durant, Terry Miller, Tom Mulnix. For songwriters and lyricists. Annual award.

Purpose: Objective is to promote the growth of songwriting by providing an arena of competition for amateur writers and lyricists and to recognize works of more accomplished writers.

Requirements: Applicants in the amateur division must be of amateur status, must not have ever received royalties from ASCAP, BMI or SESAC, and must not have ever been or currently be signed to a *national* record label. Deadline: April 30. Send for application. Samples of work required with application. "One song on a cassette with neatly printed or typed copy of the lyrics. Label lyric sheet

and tape with name of song, songwriter, address and phone number. Cue tape before sending. Entry forms may be ordered by phoning (713)264-4330."
Awards: Songwriting category: Grand prize is $100 plus recording time and/or merchandise from sponsor as made available. Judged by impartial personnel from the music industry.
Tips: "Our judges have made the following comments about past entries in our contests. Use word economy but make each word count. Have a 'pay off' in your song, i.e. an unexpected or surprise ending. 'Marry' your lyrics to your music by not 'shoving' words together within the bars of music. Pick topics that will appeal to the majority of your audience. Use idioms and word play to make your lyrics more interesting. Maintain a consistent time progression, i.e. morning, noon, night or past to present. Don't 'jump around' in time. Select a point of view, first person, second person, etc. and stick with it throughout the song."

THE JULIUS STULBERG AUDITIONS, INC., Box 107, Kalamazoo MI 49005. (616)375-2808. Business Manager: Mrs. Zoe Forsleff. For performing artists. Annual award.
Purpose: "To encourage continued excellence in musical education and accomplishment for young string players studying violin, viola, cello and double bass."
Requirements: Must be 19 year of age or younger. There is a $30 application fee. Send for application. Prefers cassette tape, not to exceed 10 minutes in length. "Music on tape must be from standard concert on repertoire, and accompanied."
Awards: 1st place: $3,000 solo performance with Kalamazoo Junior Symphony and a solo performance with the Battle Creek, MI Symphony during the 93-94 season; 2nd place: $1,500 and recital performance with Fontana Concert Society; 3rd place: $1,000.
Tips: The cassette tapes are screened by a local panel of judges, from which 12 finalists are selected to compete in live competition. An outstanding panel of three judges is engaged to choose the winners. The 1990 judges were Sir Yehudi Menuhin, Maestro Catherine Comet and internationally-known violist, Csaba Erdelyi. The 1992 live competition will be February 29, 1992.

TALENT SEARCH AMERICA, 273 Chippewa Dr., Columbia SC 29210-6508. For songwriters, composers, poets and lyricists. Awards given quarterly.
Purpose: "To discover and award new songwriters and lyricists."
Requirements: Deadlines are February 1, May 2, August 3, and November 4. Send SASE for entry forms and information. Samples of work on cassette and lyric sheet are required for entry *with entry form*. "All inquiries must be by mail. No phone calls, please. Many entrants have gained contracts and other interests with many music and creative writing companies. Winners' lists are sent to winners only. Talent Search America is co-sponsored by selected companies in the music and creative writing businesses. Talent Search America is a national nonprofit contest partnership. Entrant information will not be returned or disclosed without written permission from winning entrants. Proper postage must be sent to gain entry forms. Entrants from around the world are welcome. All inquiries must include *first class postage for each entry form* desired. Non-published/unpublished lyrics and music accepted."
Awards: 6 awards given every quarter: 3 for songwriters, 3 for lyricists (cash awards and award certificates). Entries are judged on creativity, commercial appeal and originality.

MARVIN TAYLOR PLAYWRITING AWARD, Box 3030, Sonora CA 95370. (209)532-3120. Estab. 1980. For musical playwrights.
Purpose: To encourage new voices in American theater.
Requirements: Mail script with SASE. "We accept phone calls or written inquiry." No application form or fee. Submissions must be full-length, typewritten. SASE if manuscript is to be returned. Prefers cassette to written score with original submissions. No more than 2 prior productions of script. Deadline: August 31.
Awards: Marvin Taylor Playwriting Award: $500 and full staging. Applications are judged by a committee of the theater's artistic staff.

SIGVALD THOMPSON COMPOSITION AWARD COMPETITION, Fargo-Moorhead Symphony Orchestra, Box 1753, Fargo ND 58107-1753. (218)233-8397. Acting Executive Director: Nancy R. Jones. For "American citizens." Biennial award.
Purpose: "To select an orchestral composition by an American composer to be premiered by the Fargo-Moorhead Symphony. The objective of this award is to stimulate and encourage the writing and performance of works by American composers."
Requirements: "Manuscript must be of medium length. Only manuscripts written or completed during the past 2 years and which have not been performed publicly will be considered. Scoring should be for standard symphonic or chamber orchestra instrumentation and should not include soloist." Deadline: September 30, of even-numbered years. Send manuscript with composer's name, address, telephone number and date of composition on cover sheet. Samples are not required.

Awards: Sigvald Thompson Composition Award Competition: one award of $2,500 will be made, plus the premiere performance of the winning entry by the Fargo-Moorhead Symphony Orchestra. "Compositions will be screened by a local panel, and the finalists will be submitted to national judges for review and recommendation."
Tips: "Only manuscripts written or completed during the past 2 years and which have not been performed publicly will be considered. Date of composition must be included on cover sheet."

*ELIZABETH HARPER VAUGHN CONCERTO COMPETITION, Kingsport Symphony Orchestra, 1200 East Center St., Room 311, Kingsport TN 37660. (615)392-8423. General Manager: Barbara S. Gerwe. For performing artists. Annual award.
Purpose: To further the careers of young professional musicians.
Requirements: Send for application. Deadline: Dec. 31. Samples of work are required with application. Cassette tape of concerto or musical composition to be performed.
Awards: Honorarium of $1,000 and opportunity to perform with Kingsport Symphony Orchestra the following season. Judged by jury of peers – accredited professors of music in college.

VOCAL SONGWRITER'S CONTEST, P.O. Box 34606, Richmond VA 23234. (804)733-5908 and (804)541-3333. President: Gary Shaver. Song Contest Director: Robert (Chan) Laughlin. For songwriters and composers. Annual award with 14 categories.
Purpose: "To recognize good songs and lyrics as well as the writers of same."
Requirements: "Original songs, lyrics, compositions only." Deadline: March 31. Send for application. Samples of work are required with application. "Send cassette tape for songs; lyrics should be typed or neatly printed." Vocal Song Contest entries should be sent to: Vocal Song Contest, Box 2438, Petersburg, VA 23804.
Award: Grand prize $100. 1st, 2nd and 3rd place and honorable mention entries in each category receive certificates.
Tips: "Be sure to use a clean, fresh tape to record your entry. Listen to the entry to be sure it's not distorted or too low in volume. A decent sounding tape stands a much better chance. The judges can only grade based on what they hear. Don't over produce your entry. It will take away from the song itself. Fill out the entry form completely and follow all rules of the contest. You could be disqualified. Lyric entries should be typed or printed neatly. Mail your entry early. If postmarked after March 31st of the contest year we will not accept it. Entries received more than 45 days after the contest closing date will not be accepted."

WEST COAST ENSEMBLE–MUSICAL STAIRS, Box 38728, Los Angeles CA 90038. (213)871-8673. Artistic Director: Les Hanson. For composers and musical playwrights. Annual award.
Purpose: To provide an arena and encouragement for the development of new musicals for the theater.
Requirements: Send a copy of the script and a cassette of the score. Send script and score to West Coast Ensemble, P.O. Box 38728, Los Angeles, CA 90038.
Awards: The West Coast Ensemble Musical Stairs Competition Award includes a production of the selected musical and $500 prize. The selected musical will be part of the 1993 season. Panel of judges read script and listen to cassette. Final selection is made by Artistic Director.
Tips: "Submit libretto in standard playscript format along with professional sounding cassette of songs."

WYOMING COUNTRY MUSIC FOUNDATION ANNUAL SONGWRITING CONTEST, 1645 Sussex Road, Kaycee WY 82639. (307)738-2303 or 836-2939. Estab. 1983. Executive and Promotional Director: Helen Ullery or Floyd Haynes. For songwriters, composers and performers. Annual award.
Purpose: "To promote and encourage upcoming talent both in songwriting and the performing arts."
Requirements: Applicants can be from any geographical area. Deadline: April 15 1993. Send for application (include SASE). Samples are not required. Annual membership fee: $25; entry fee per song: $10. For gospel song entries and information, contact Helen D. Ullery, Sussex Rt., Kaycee, WY 82639; for country songs and information, contact Floyd Haynes, P.O. Box 132, Guensey, WY 82214.
Awards: "Top 10 country and Top 5 gospel songs are sent to Nashville for review; 50% of entry fees go back to the top winners. Contestants cannot have been in the top 50 in national charts in the last 10 years."

*YOUNG ARTIST COMPETITION, Fort Collins Symphony, Box 1963, Fort Collins CO 80522. (303)482-4823. Office Manager: Merrilee Pouliot. For performing artists. Annual award.
Purpose: To encourage young people to pursue excellence in the study and mastery of orchestral instruments.
Requirements: Deadline: Feb. 1. Send for application.
Awards: Senior Division: First Place, The Adeline Rosenberg Memorial Prize $2,000. Second Place: $500. Third Place: $250. Junior Division: Piano First Place: $250. Second Place: $50. Instrumental First Place: $250. Second Place: $50. Senior Division: Panel of judges listen to tapes in Round I, select

semi-finalists to play before judges for Round II, who select 3 finalists to perform with symphony and be judged in Round III. Junior Division: Panel of judges listen to all applicants in a recital-type environment. Winners selected the same day.
Tips: "The first round is judged on the strength of your tape. The tape and your performance must be with accompaniment."

ANNA ZORNIO MEMORIAL CHILDREN'S THEATER PLAYWRITING AWARD, Dept. of Theater and Dance, Univ. of NH, Durham NH 03824-3538. Annual award.
Purpose: Playwriting contest for new plays and musicals, with an award of up to $250 to a winning playwright(s), and a guaranteed production by the UNH Theater For Youth Program. The award will be administered by the Directors of the UNH Theater Resources For Youth Program. This faculty will reserve the right to withhold the award if, in their opinion, no plays merit the award. Production of the prize-winning script will be scheduled by the UNH Theater Resources for Youth Program during the 1992-93 academic year.
Requirements: The contest is open to all playwrights in the United States and Canada. The contest is for new plays, with a maximum length of 60 minutes, suitable for young audiences. Plays submitted must not have been: previously published; previously produced by a professional Equity company; a previously produced winner of an award or prize in another playwriting contest; and must not be under contract for publication before UNH's announcement of the award winner. Playwrights may submit more than one play, but not more than three. Deadline: April 24, 1992. Send for rules of entry for a complete list of requirements.
Awards: Anna Zornio Award: $250 and production of the play/musicals.

Publications of Interest

Knowledge about the music industry is essential for both creative and business success. Staying informed requires keeping up with constantly changing information. The "Age of Information" provides, in print and electronically, constant updates in the form of music magazines, music trade papers and books. There is a publication aimed at almost every type of musician, songwriter and music fan, from the most technical knowledge of amplification systems to the gossip about your favorite singer. These publications can enlighten and excite you and provide information vital in helping you become a more well-rounded, educated and, ultimately, successful musical artist.

Contained within this section are all types of magazines and books that may strike your fancy. From music magazines to how-to books, there will be something listed here that you'll enjoy and benefit from.

Periodicals

AMERICAN BULLET, (formerly Indie Bullet Magazine), Country Music Magazine, 2006-B East Rusk St., Jacksonville TX 75766. (903)586-7575. Publisher/Editor: Roy L. Haws. 12 monthly issues per year of 44 or more pages. Subscription price: $50/year bulk or $75/year for 1st class. "Includes: interviews with up-and-coming independent acts. 'Hot' new act discoveries and artist spotlights of the future stars in country music; guest articles and editorials pertaining to country music; and insider information in regard to 'what's really happening in country music today.' " Features a top 50 independent label chart and "All American Hot 100+" chart of Independent & Major product. Includes names, addresses and phone numbers of industry related companies and record labels in each monthly reference issue.

ASCAP IN ACTION, published by ASCAP—American Society of Composers, Authors & Publishers, One Lincoln Plaza, New York NY 10023. Editor, *ASCAP In Action*: Murdoch McBride. Quarterly (semi-annual) magazine; 44 pages. Free to ASCAP members and music industry, this has been ASCAP's membership magazine for several years. *ASCAP In Action* is ASCAP's premiere publication. The magazine features news about ASCAP members, events sponsored by the Society (ASCAP Pop Awards, Film and Television Awards, showcases and workshops) and a variety of articles on leading songwriters. Topics of interest to composers, lyricists and publishers are also covered at length along with summaries on ASCAP legislative efforts. ASCAP members can have their career updates published in the *Steppin' Out* section of the magazine: Send notices to *Steppin' Out*, % Editor, *ASCAP In Action*, One Lincoln Plaza, New York, New York 10023. *Steppin' Out* notices must come directly from the ASCAP member and should be written in the style used in that section of the magazine. Space limitations preclude more than one listing per member in each issue.

*ASCAP PLAYBACK, published by ASCAP-American Society of Composers, Authors and Publishers, One Lincoln Plaza, New York NY 10023. (212)621-6322. Editor: Murdoch McBride. A semi-annual supplement to *ASCAP in Action*, ASCAP *PlayBack* features photo coverage of numerous ASCAP events, member news and related music industry activities. 8-12 pages.

AWC NEWS/FORUM, American Women Composers, Inc., Suite 409, 1690 36th St. NW, Washington, DC 20007. (202)342-8179. Annual; 20 pages. Subscription price: $13.50. Estab. 1976. "*AWC News/ Forum* is an annual publication which is mailed free of charge to members and is subscribed to by numerous colleges and universities throughout the US. It contains articles of interest to women, about women, notices of performances of women composers, information about composition competitions, etc. The News/Forum is supplemented bi-annually with the AWC News-Update."

*BANZAI, Jim Kilroy, P.O. Box 7522, Overland Park KS 66207. (913)642-0406. Contact: Banzai Subscription. Bi-monthly periodical; 40 pages. Subscription price: $12/year. Estab. 1986. "*Banzai* is a heavy metal mag that is distributed free in 6 midwestern states. We run live, recorded and demo reviews as well as interviews, features and scene reports. We feature bands/acts that play their own material."

BUZZ MAGAZINE, P.O. Box 3111, Albany NY 12203. (518)489-0658. Contact: George Guarino. Monthly magazine; 32 pages; Subscription price: $6 for 6 issues. Estab. 1985. "Music magazine. College radio focus — ⅓ interviews/profiles, ⅓ record reviews, ⅓ on location reviews. *Buzz* offers an alternative focus, which includes the 'edges' of metal, world beat, dance and rock. Also supplies readers with many contact numbers and addresses."

CANADIAN MUSICIAN, 3284 Yonge St., Toronto, Ontario M4N 3M7 **Canada.** (416)485-8284. Special Projects Coordinator: Penny Campbell. Published 6 times/year; 70 pages; $21/year. Estab. 1979. "We provide musicians and music makers with in-depth, inside information that they can put to use in furthering their musical endeavors. Through regular columns on many aspects of playing and performing, we keep readers up-to-date and in touch with the Canadian music scene. Feature articles on successful Canadian songwriters provide young musicians with valuable information and insight. Columns on songwriting, arranging and publishing, usually written by musicians, producers or music publishers, offer pointers and advice on the music-making process and the business of songwriting."

*CARAS NEWS, CARAS, 124 Merton St., 3rd Fl., Toronto ON M4S 2Z2 **Canada.** Phone: (416)485-3135. Coordinator: Katie White. Quarterly newsletter; 2 pages. Subscription price: $45 (Canadian). A quarterly newsletter to keep songwriters, musicians, etc. abreast of current industry news.

*COUNTRY CHART ANALYST, Johnny Bond Publications, 1007 17th Avenue S., Nashville TN 37212. (615)320-5719. Publisher and Editor: Sherry Bond. Monthly; 20 pages. Subscription price: $50 for 12 issues. Estab. March 1987. *Country Chart Analyst* is an in-depth look at the top 50 songs on the *Billboard* and *Radio and Records* country charts. "Each month CCA provides the address and phone number of every producer, publisher and record company on the chart. Also each month, CCA interviews one new artist on the chart to find out how they were able to get their record deal; all songwriters on the chart for the very first time; a professional manager of a publishing company; and a producer. Other monthly columns include: a listing of all songwriters and the songs they are most noted for; an album analysis which tells how the producer and the artist picked songs for their current album; and a feature article on one of Nashville's support organizations."

COUNTRY MUSIC MAGAZINE, Silver Eagle Publishers, Suite 1, 329 Riverside Ave., Westport CT 06880. (203)222-5800. Bi-monthly magazine; 72 pages. Subscription price: $13.98. Estab. 1972. *Country Music Magazine* focuses on current performers, their professional and personal lives and the industry which sustains them. Each issue includes features on stars, industry news and extensive record reviews including reissues. *The CMSA Newsletter*, an additional publication included with higher priced subscriptions, focuses on fans and stars of the past.

*COUNTRY MUSIC — USA, P.O. Box 24922, Nashville TN 37202-4922. Ten issues per year; 32 pages. $19.95/year. Estab. 1980. Fan magazine with 200,000 readers. *Billboard* charts are published each month. "CM-USA is published monthly, except January and July, and is written with the purpose of keeping our readers informed about what's going on in the country music industry."

*COUNTRY SONG ROUNDUP, Country Song Roundup Publications, Inc., 40 Violet Ave., Poughkeepsie NY 12601. (914)454-7420. Contact: Subscription Department. Published monthly; 56 pages. Subscription Price: $25/(12 issues). Estab. 1949. "In-depth stories and interviews with country music artists and songwriters plus the lyrics to more than 30 top songs."

*DIRTY LINEN, Dirty Linen, Ltd., P.O. Box 66600, Baltimore MD 21239. (410)583-7973. Contact: Susan Hartman. Magazine published 6 times/year; 80 pages. Subscription price: $20/year U.S., $24 (overseas, surface), $30 (overseas, airmail). Estab. 1983. "Dirty Linen is the magazine of folk, electric folk, traditional and world music. Each issue contains articles or interviews on major performers in a variety of styles. Also, news, new releases listings, extensive reviews of recordings, videos, books, etc. Comprehensive tour schedule listing."

*GAJOOB MAGAZINE, P.O. Box 3201, Salt Lake City UT 84110. (801)355-8946. FAX: 355-5552 Editor: Bryan Baker. Triannually; 80 pages. Subscription price: $10. Estab. 1988. "*Gajoob Magazine* has the unique distinction of focusing exclusively on independent recording and cassette distribution. Each issue reviews over 200 independently produced tapes, along with articles and interviews by and about the people behind these tapes. *Gajoob* effectively offers its pages as an international forum for independent recording artists, songwriters and musicians."

*HEARTSONG REVIEW RESOURCE GUIDE, Wahaba Heartsun, P.O. Box 1084, Cottage Grove OR 97424. Biannual; 56 pages. Subscription price: $8/year, $15 for 2 years. Estab. 1986. "As a consumer's resource guide for socially and spiritually conscious music, we review New Age music of many styles; including vocal and instrumental, children's, chanting, folk, world/fusion, electronic/space and quiet relaxation. Our goal is to encourage consciousness expansion through music. "Free music samplers accompany each issue to all subscribers. We publish a list of radio stations requesting play copies. We write descriptive reviews of little known, independently published albums which would have a hard time getting attention elsewhere."

*HIT PARADER, Hit Parader Publications, Inc., 40 Violet Ave., Poughkeepsie NY 12601. (914)454-7420. Monthly magazine; 96 pages. Subscription price: $29.50. Contains articles and interviews on rock music personalities, information about trends in the music industry and rock music in particular. Also rock song lyrics, record and book reviews, new product reviews and reader mail.

*THE INSIDER, T.O.G.™, P.O. Box 4542, Arlington VA 22204. (703)685-0199. Publisher: T.O.G. Every other month; 20 or more pages. Subscription price: $5 for 6 issues. Estab. 1989. "We highlight live local music and review almost all cassettes received."

*KREATURE COMFORTS, Shangrila, Inc., 1916 Madison Ave., Memphis TN 38104. (901)274-1916. Subscription Department: Kreature Comforts. Bimonthly; 20 pages. Subscription price: $12/year. Estab. 1988. "We review all manner of music—especially independent label rock 'n roll. Heavy emphasis on psychedelia, garage and other extraordinary efforts. Features regular music reviews."

LIVING BLUES, Center for the Study of Southern Culture, University of Mississippi, University MS 38677. (601)232-5574. Circulation Director: M. Brooks Tyler. Bimonthly—6 times per year magazine; 64 pages. Subscription price: $18/year. Estab. 1970. "*Living Blues*—'Everything you want to know about America's musical legacy to the world—the blues. I have subscribed and I hope you do, too.'—B.B. King"

*LOUISVILLE MUSIC NEWS, Louisville Music News (Jean Metcalfe and Paul M. Moffett), 7400 Cross Creek Blvd., Louisville KY 40228. (502)231-5559. Editor: Jean Metcalfe. Monthly; 20-28 pages. Subscription price: $7.99 bulk mail/13.99 first class. Estab. 1989. "*Louisville Music News* is dedicated to promoting music and musicians, songwriters, etc. in Louisville and surrounding areas. It publishes concert, record, book and recording studio reviews, as well as features on local musicians, groups and people connected with the music business. National acts are also covered when they appear in the area. Contains the newsletter of the Louisville Area Songwriters' Cooperative."

*MARYLAND MUSICIAN MAGAZINE, Maryland Musician Magazine Inc., 7510 Harford Rd., Baltimore MD 21234. (410)444-3776. FAX: (410)444-1807. President: Susan E. Mudd. Monthly; 56 pages. Subscription price: $18. Estab. 1984. "A monthly publication which covers all genres of music: rock, blues, country, jazz, classical, metal. We also review local and national releases as well as rock and metal demos."

MUSIC BUSINESS DIRECTORY, Ray McGinnis. P.O. Box 120675, Nashville TN 37212. (615)255-1068. Published every 6 months, May and November; 96 pages. Subscription price: $13.95. Estab. 1983. " 'A Complete Guide To The Nashville Music Industry' with listings of song publishers, booking agents, artist managers, record companies, recording studios, etc. All with names, phone numbers and addresses. A great source of information for new writers and singers."

*MUSIC CONNECTION MAGAZINE, 6640 Sunset Blvd., Hollywood CA 90028. (213)462-5772. Contact: Subscription Dept. Biweekly magazine; 56-100 pages. Estab. 1977. "*Music Connection Magazine* is a musicians'/songwriters' trade publication. Departments include a gig guide connecting musicians and songwriters with agents, producers, publishers and club owners; a free classified section; music personal ads; interviews with music industry executives and major artists; and articles on songwriting, publishing and the music business. We cover current news, stories and interviews with up-and-coming music business people as well as established industry executives and major artists. *Music Connection*

Market conditions are constantly changing! If you're still using this book and it is 1994 or later, buy the newest edition of Songwriter's Market at your favorite bookstore or order directly from Writer's Digest Books.

Magazine connects musicians, songwriters, producers and other music business personnel with each other. Our 'cutting edge' cover stories have included Poison, Guns N' Roses and the Bangles prior to their great successes. A must read publication for anyone in the music business. Every issue of *Music Connection* contains a 2-page editorial spread which includes: Songworks—current activities of music publishers, songwriters and record company signings; and Publisher Profile—an in-depth spotlight on a music publisher." Subscription rate is $40 for one year/25 issues; $65 for two years/50 issues.

*MUSIC MAKERS, The Sunday School Board of the Southern Baptist Convention, 127 9th Ave. N, Nashville TN 37234. (615)251-2000. Contact: Church Music Dept. Music Editor: Sheryl Davis Tallant. Quarterly magazine; 32 pages. Cost is 93¢. Estab. 1970. Publishes music for use by lst, 2nd and 3rd graders in choir at church. Includes 12 pages of spiritual concept, musical concept and fun songs, 20 pages of stories, activities, musical games, art activities and puzzles. *Music Makers* magazine is an example of quality music education for children in the church choir setting. We provide opportunity for publication of spiritual concept songs, as well as fun/activity songs; there are also an accompanying recording and cassette which contain some of the printed songs.

MUSIC ROW MAGAZINE, Published by Music Row Publications, Inc. 1231 17th Ave. S., Nashville TN 37212. (615)321-3617. FAX: (615)329-0852. Magazine published 23 times a year; 28 pages. Price: $50/year. Estab. 1981. "*Music Row Magazine* is a music industry trade tip sheet for Nashville. We supply information about producers and publishers, and interviews with key players and writers. Subscription includes *In Charge: Music Row's Decision Makers*, a book updated yearly. Book includes photos, phone, fax and mini-bios on over 325 Nashville music executives, producers, publishers and more."

*THE MUSICAL QUARTERLY, Oxford University Press, 200 Madison Ave., New York NY 10016. Manager, Customer Service: Gloria Bruno. Quarterly magazine; 180 pages. Subscription price: $34 US—£23 UK and $48 rest of the world. Estab. 1915. "*The Musical Quarterly* is a journal written for professional musicians as well as dedicated amateurs. Articles feature all types of music, from the most ancient to the most recent, and cover a range of topics as diverse as the musical world it has chronicled for 75 years. Articles include analysis of musical scores providing an insight as to how our greatest composers and musicians created and performed music."

*THE NOISE, T Max, 74 Jamaica St., Jamaica Plain MA 02130. (617)524-4735. Publisher/Editor: T Max. Monthly (except Aug.); 24 pages. Subscription price: $12. Estab. 1981. "The Noise covers the alternative music scene in the greater Boston area (New England) with feature stories, record reviews, live reviews, tape reviews, gossip column, pictorials and cartoons."

*OLD TIME COUNTRY, Center for the Study of Southern Culture, University of Mississippi, University MS 38677. (601)232-5574. Circulation Director: M. Brooks Tyler. Quarterly magazine; 32 pages. Subscription price: $10/year. "*Old Time Country* covers all aspects of traditional acoustic country music, and discusses the late, great and current songwriters and artists in the industry."

PROBE AND CANADIAN COMPOSER, Society of Composers, Authors and Music Publishers of Canada (SOCAN), 41 Valleybrook Dr., Don Mills, Ontario M3B 2S6 **Canada**. (416)445-8700. Editor: Rick MacMillan. Published through the SOCAN public relations department: Nancy Gyokeres, Director. PROBE is a monthly 8-page newsletter. It is incorporated in Canadian Composer (24 pages), the quarterly magazine of SOCAN. Estab. 1990. Advertising is not accepted. "The publications are published by SOCAN to publicize the activities of composer, author and publisher members and to keep them informed of music-industry activities, both foreign and domestic." Cost: $10 annually to cover postage and handling.

*REJOICE!, Center of the Study of Southern Studies, University of Mississippi, University MS 38677. (601)232-5574. Circulation Director: M. Brooks Tyler. Bimonthly magazine; 32 pages. Subscription price: $12. Estab. 1988. "*Rejoice!* Covers the world of gospel music with an awareness of and respect for its history and diversity. It helps readers understand more fully gospel music, the source and mirror of American music."

*SING OUT! THE FOLK SONG MAGAZINE, Box 5253, Bethlehem PA 18015-5253. Contact: Subscription Department. Published quarterly; 120 pages. $18/year (US). Estab. 1950. "*Sing Out!* is a folk music magazine for musicans or music lovers dedicated to bringing its readers a diverse and entertaining selection of songs and information about traditional and contemporary folk music. We print about 20 songs and tunes in each issue. Some are traditional, some are newly written; most are solicited, some are not. We print songs in lead sheet format: first verse and chorus with chords and complete lyrics. We publish many new songwriters. Best form of song submission is on cassette with lyric and lead sheet."

SONG PLACEMENT GUIDE, 4376 Stewart Ave., Los Angeles CA 90066-6134. (310)285-3661. Publisher: M. Singer. Monthly newsletter; 2 pages; $6 introductory, $65/year. Estab. 1980. "A 12-year old endorsed Los Angeles tipsheet for music publishers/songwriters. The Song Placement Guide is designed to educate songwriters about craft and business—editorial is not the thrust however—it's the "tips" on who's looking for songs for recording. Includes monthly list of artists and producers looking for hit songs. In addition to inside information on who's looking for what material and where to submit. We provide an InnerView with an industry pro, or write a column to educate and inspire readers. Also small classified and news flash section."

*SONGTALK, Suite 780, 6381 Hollywood Blvd., Hollywood CA 90028. (213)463-7178. Editor: Paul Zollo. Quarterly journal; 52 pages. Subscription price: $30/2 years. Estab. 1985. "*SongTalk* is the publication of the National Academy of Songwriters. It covers all aspects of the art and craft of songwriting. We feature interviews with the world's most influential songwriters, delving deeply into the specifics of creating songs, as well as articles on the business and marketing of songs."

*SONGWRITER MAGAZINE, International Songwriters Association Ltd., P.O. Box 46 Limerick City, Ireland. Phone: (061)28837. Subscription Manager: Anna Sinden. Annual yearbook, monthly newsletter, number of pages varies. "A publication for songwriters and music publishers, featuring exclusive interviews with top American and European writers and publishers, and recording artists. Readers can avail of unlimited free advice, song assessment, song copyright and other services. Readers in 61 countries worldwide. Correspondence in English, French, Spanish and Italian." UK office: 37b Cavendish Street, London W1, UK. Phone (071) 486 5353.

*SONGWRITING AND COMPOSING MAGAZINE, The Guild of International Songwriters & Composers, Sovereign House 12 Trewartha Rd., Praa Sands, Penzance Cornwall TR20 9ST **United Kingdom.** Phone: (0736)762826. FAX: (0736)763328. Subscription Secretary: Carole A. Jones. Quarterly; 20 pages. Estab. 1986. Membership subscriptions: £18-United Kingdom; £20 E.E.C. countries; £25 overseas non-E.E.C. countries. Free to all members of the Guild of International Songwriters and Composers. "An international magazine for songwriters, composers, music publishers, record companies and the music industry. *Songwriting and Composing* features interviews and biographies of artists, publishers, songwriters, record companies and other music industry personnel and organizations. Lists details of artists, publishers, producers, record companies looking for songs. Lists publisher and other music industry contacts. Readers have access to unlimited free advice, free copyright service, free collaboration service, free song assessment service, and numerous other services on an international basis. Readers worldwide. A free news magazine is available upon request with an SAE or 2× IRC's."

*SOUNDMAKERS, Music City Song Festival, P.O. Box 17999-SW, Nashville TN 37217. (615)834-0027. Simply call or write the MCSF offices. Pubilcation is free. Once a year; 56 pages. Free upon request. Estab. 1985. *SoundMakers* magazine is published as a free educational service of the Music City Song Festival music competition. The magazine includes informative articles by music industry pros on a variety of music-related topics. *SoundMakers* magazine and Music City Song Festival entry information are free upon request. There is no obligation to enter the music competition to receive the free magazine.

*THE STAR MAGAZINE, published by Jellee Works, Inc., P.O. Box 16572, Kansas City MO 64133. (816)358-2542. Editor: James E. Lee. Monthly magazine; 20-24 pages. Subscription price: $24/year. Estab. 1990. Purpose is "to educate the aspiring songwriter about the industry. Includes 'how to' articles every month on the craft, business and legal issues an aspiring songwriter must face and deal with. Offers contests to help promote the songwriter and features stories on grassroots to successful songwriters."

*SYNTHESIS, Jason Marcewicz, 219 Napfle St., Philadelphia PA 19111. (215)725-1686. Managing Editor: Jason Marcewicz. Quarterly; 8 pages. Subscription price: $5/year. Estab. 1989. "*SYNTHESIS* exists as a 'forum for musicians and fans of electronic music (EM)' . . . i.e., music that is predominantly synthesizer, keyboard, or computer based. New releases on cassette, album, and CD are listed, if not reviewed, artists are interviewed, and various articles and editorials are written. Through interviews and reviews of their music, we grant musicians exposure and give feedback about their current releases. Addresses of the artists, for fan correspondence, are *always* printed."

*TEXAS BEAT MAGAZINE, Keith Allan Ayres, P.O. Box 4429, Austin TX 78765-4429. (512)441-2242. Publisher/Editor: Keith Ayres. Monthly; 32 pages. Subscription price: $20/12 issues. Estab. 1989. "Arts and entertainment monthly with primary focus on Texas music as well as the industry infrastructure. Includes features, interviews, live reviews (local and national acts), record reviews (local and national acts). Monthly studio activity report from Dallas, Austin, Houston, and San Antonio. Quarterly Texas Music Industry Guide gives comprehensive industry contacts."

*TRUSTY INTERNATIONAL NEWSLETTER, 8771 Rose Creed Rd., Nebo KY 42441. (502)249-3194. Publisher: Elsie Childers. Monthly; 1 page. Subscription price: $30/year (12 issues). "Overseas orders add $6.50/year." Estab. 1974. "Names and addresses of artists and producers and publishers needing new songs for recording sessions. Items of subscribers' song placements given. Also gives readers where and when to send songs for possible recordings. Send 25¢ for current issue of tip sheet plus 29¢ SASE (stamped envelope with your return address on front)."

WASHINGTON INTERNATIONAL ARTS LETTER, Allied Business Consultants, Inc., P.O. Box 12010, Des Moines IA 50312. (515)255-5577. FAX: (515)255-5577. Founder: Daniel Millsaps, III. Publisher: Nancy A. Fandel. Magazine published 10 times/year; 6-8 pages. Institutional rate $124/year. Special Individual Rate $55/year. "WIAL concentrates on discovering sources of funding for the arts and keeping up with policy changes in funding by governments, private foundations, and businesses which give out grants to institutions and individual creative and performing artists. In addition, we publish the Arts Patronage Series, which are directories where all information is under one cover and updated periodically. We are the major source of information about funding for the arts in the US. Songwriters and composers can get grants for their work through our information and keep informed about congressional actions which affect their lives. Areas covered include problems of taxation, etc., as well as how to get money for projects."

*WHITE THRONE, P.O. Box 20577, Castro Valley CA 94546. (510)537-5545. Publisher: Dave Johnson. Quarterly; 68 pages. Subscription price: $7. Estab. 1987. "*White Throne* covers the styles of Christian music young people want to hear (rock, alternative, rap, heavy metal, thrash) — maximum Christian rock 'n' roll. A lot of information about the music industry is revealed in the interviews. *White Throne* is a place where songwriters who are musicians can send demos and receive an honest review by an expert in the field."

*WIRE MAGAZINE, Tansy Publishing/Denis W. Toomey, 2319 N. 45th, No. 143, Seattle WA 98103. (206)789-4112. Contact: Wire Subscriptions. 6 per year; 40 pages. Subscription price: $9.50 domestic and Canada; $12.00 international. Estab. 1982. "*Wire* is published as an alternative viewpoint in the Seattle marketplace for music/art/politics. The scope is local to national with music/video reviews from tape projects to major releases. All types of music are considered for reviews and articles. 12,000 copies distributed mostly in Seattle area."

*YOUNG MUSICIANS, The Sunday School Board of the Southern Baptist Convention, 127 9th Ave. N., Nashville TN 37234. (615)251-2000. Contact: Church Music Dept. Music Editor: Sheryl Davis Tallant. Quarterly magazine; 52 pages. Cost: $1.36. Publishes music for use by 4th, 5th and 6th graders in church choirs. Includes spiritual and musical concept songs, activities, games, hymn studies and author/composer studies; plus 15-page music insert containing four or five anthems. There is also an accompanying Young Musicians Cassette and Young Musicians Recording containing music in the 15-page insert and other appropriate recorded material. "This is an excellent publication to which songwriters whose interests and skills lie in the area of composing for children may submit their original manuscripts."

Books

*ATTENTION: A&R, 2nd edition, by Teri Muench and Susan Pomerantz, Published by Alfred Publishing Co., Inc., Box 10003, Van Nuys CA 91410-0003. (818)891-5999. "Order from a music dealer or bookstore. If it cannot be located write to Alison Jordan, Customer Service Dept." Revised 1990. 116 pages. Price: $16.95 (paperback). "This invaluable book by Teri Muench (former A&R Director for Contemporary Music — RCA Records) and Susan Pomerantz (hit songwriter and publisher) provides a step-by-step guide for approaching record industry executives who can help bring you closer to breaking into the music business. Includes the do's and don'ts of submitting your tape; recording, distributing and publishing deals; a listing of prominent management companies and colleges with music business courses, plus much more!"

*BEGINNING SONGWRITER'S ANSWER BOOK, by Paul Zollo. Published by Writer's Digest Books, 1507 Dana Ave., Cincinnati OH 45207. (800)289-0963. Attention: Book Order. Published 1990; 128 pages. Price: $16.95, paperback. Zollo has collected and answered 218 questions most often asked by songwriters calling the National Academy of Songwriters telephone hotline. "You'll find terms and techniques explained with plenty of helpful illustrations, and you'll gain insight into the working methods of successful songwriters and musicians."

*THE CRAFT AND BUSINESS OF SONGWRITING, by John Braheny. Published by Writer's Digest Books, 1507 Dana Ave., Cincinnati OH 45207. 1-800-289-0963. Attention: Book Order. Published 1988; 322 pages. Price: $19.95 hardcover. A powerful, information-packed—and the most up-to-date— book about the songwriting industry that thoroughly covers all the creative and business aspects songwriters need to know to maximize their chances of success.

*THE CRAFT OF LYRIC WRITING, by Sheila Davis. Published by Writer's Digest Books, 1507 Dana Ave., Cincinnati OH 45207. 1-800-289-0963. Attention: Book Order. Published: 1985. 350 pages. Price: $19.95 hardcover. Davis, a gold-record lyricist, identifies and illustrates the elements that shape successful popular songs. The book contains the complete lyrics to the great standards by such writers as Larry Hart, Ira Gershwin, Oscar Hammerstein, Johnny Mercer, Lennon & McCartney, Paul Simon, Harry Chapin, Joni Mitchell, Jim Webb, and Sting, along with Davis' analysis of those qualities of craftsmanship that produce Grammy, Tony and Oscar winners. A highly-praised reference work that defines and illustrates over 100 literary terms and devices. ASCAP calls it "Required reading for anyone who aspires to a career in songwriting."

*GETTING NOTICED: A Musician's Guide to Publicity & Self-Promotion, by James Gibson. Published by Writer's Digest Books, 1507 Dana Ave., Cincinnati OH 45207. (513)531-2222. (800)289-0963. Attention: Book Order. Published 1987; 240 pages. Price: $12.95 (paperback). "Gibson shows musicians how, with just a few simple secrets and very little cash, to create attention-getting publicity materials, then use them to make more money with their music. Includes a wealth of business information on press releases, letter writing, and handling unpaid bills and broken contracts."

HOW TO OPEN DOORS IN THE MUSIC INDUSTRY—THE INDEPENDENT WAY, by Frank Fara/Patty Parker. Published by Autumn Gold Publishing; distributed by Starfield Press, Suite 114, 10603 N. Hayden Rd., Scottsdale AZ 85260. FAX: (602)951-3074. Published: 1987. 110 pages. List price: $8.95; $10 mail order. Book written from the "viewpoint of an unpublished writer or writer/artist needing to know the ground rules for succeeding in today's marketplace. Topics covered include song pitching, record promotion, international music markets, importance of a studio producer, independent record labels and how they can promote artist masters, and how to find the right publisher or record label. Also, where to work from: home or a music center, and the most frequently asked questions and answers on royalties, production, record sales and publishing. Popular music myths dispelled."

*HOW TO PITCH AND PROMOTE YOUR SONGS, by Fred Koller. Published by Writer's Digest Books, 1507 Dana Ave., Cincinnati OH 45207. (800)289-0963. Attention: Book Order. Published 1988; 114 pages. Price: $12.95 paperback. This book shows how to make a living as a full-time songwriter— exactly what it's like to be self-employed in the music industry and how to set up a step-by-step business plan to achieve your goals, including getting started: sources of motivation, how to expose your work through professional associations, seminars and support groups; running a business: basic supplies, expenses and accounts, legalities and financial considerations; planning to succeed: creation, protection and exploitation of new songs as well as older material, where the money comes from, how often and from whom; publishing: the difference between writing for a major publisher and self-publishing, advantages/disadvantages of co-publishing.

THE MUSIC BUSINESS HANDBOOK, by Jojo St. Mitchell. Published by Amethyst Press, 273 Chippewa Dr., Columbia SC 29210-6508. Published 1987; $16.95 paperback. "A brief overview of the music business for the newcomer with over 100 contacts in the music business, all in plain English for the inexperienced. A motivational tool to read over and over. Helps to give confidence, direction and a better understanding of how to view the music business. Discusses investors, booking, video, promotion and more. Easy to understand and affordable."

MUSIC DIRECTORY CANADA '92, Edited by Shauna Kennedy. Published by CM Books, 3284 Yonge St., Toronto Ontario M4N 3M7 **Canada.** (416)485-1049. FAX: (416)485-8924. Marketing Coordinator: Penny Quelch. Published 1992; 700 pages. Price: $29.95. "The most comprehensive and complete resource guide to the Canadian music industry available anywhere. The new sixth edition of the directory compiles over 6,000 entries in 60 categories. Contacts for record companies, management companies, music publishers and more are at your fingertips, keeping you up-to-date on the dynamic and ever-changing Canadian music scene."

*MUSIC PUBLISHING: A SONGWRITER'S GUIDE, by Randy Poe. Published by Writer's Digest Books, 1507 Dana Ave., Cincinnati OH 45207. (800)289-0963. Attention: Book Order. Published 1990; 144 pages. Price: $18.95 paperback. Poe describes the modern world of music publishing in depth, and gives advice on getting the best publishing deals for your songs. Winner of the 1991 ASCAP Deems-Taylor Award.

*PLAYING FOR PAY: HOW TO BE A WORKING MUSICIAN, by James Gibson. Published by Writer's Digest Books, 1507 Dana Ave., Cincinnati OH 45207. (800)289-0963. Attention: Book Order. Published 1990; 160 pages. Price: $17.95 paperback. Gibson shows you how to develop a well-organized and strategic "Personal Music Marketing System" that will help you make money with your music.

SOME STRAIGHT TALK ABOUT THE MUSIC BUSINESS, 2nd edition, by Mona Coxson. 3284 Yonge St., Toronto, Ontario M4N 3M7 **Canada.** (416)485-1049. FAX: (416)485-8924. Marketing Coordinator: Penny Quelch. Published 1989; 207 pages. Price: $19.95. "The book's sixteen chapters show the musician how to make the right career choices, how to get started and progress, and how to reach goals and avoid pitfalls. The book discusses all facets of the music business including music publishing and song demos. Coxson, a freelance consultant, writer and college music teacher, has taken nothing for granted and has outlined each step of the way so that every musician can avoid unnecessary mistakes." The book is especially valuable to those interested in the growing Canadian market. Published by CM Books.

SONGWRITERS CREATIVE MATRIX, by Carl E. Bolte, Jr. Holly Productions, 800 Greenway Terrace, Kansas City MO 64113. (816)444-8884. Published 1975. 25-page workbook. Price $11.50. A unique matrix/guideline for composers/lyricists including examples, instructions and 25 blank forms. "This unique guideline is 'a musical road map,' as well as a checklist regarding the composer's song form, chords, words, rhyme schemes, range, key signature and more. It makes one promise: to help songwriters compose better songs more easily."

THE SONGWRITER'S DEMO MANUAL AND SUCCESS GUIDE, by George Williams. Music Business Books. Box 935, Dayton NV 89403. (800)487-6610. Revised 1992. 200 pages. Price: $12.95. "A practical guide to selling songs and landing a record contract. Teaches how to work in the studio to prepare songs for professional presentation. Tells who the important people are and how to contact them. The author is a recording studio owner, jingle writer and producer with twenty years experience in the Los Angeles music business."

THE SONGWRITER'S GUIDE TO CHORDS AND PROGRESSIONS, by Joseph R. Lilore. Box 1272, Dept. WD, Clifton NJ 07012. Published: 1982. 48-page method/instruction book and 90 minute cassette. Price: $14.95. "Gives songwriters ideas for new and commercially proven chords and progressions. There are 58 individual song outlines with complete directions for creating thousands of songs in any style. The accompanying cassette allows songwriters to hear each new idea as it is introduced andhelps them compose anywhere, anytime." Available at your local music store. "Special offer to Writer's Digest readers - get **both** the songwriter's guide to "Melodies" and to "Chords and Progressions" for only $20.00 plus $1.50 postage and handling."

*THE SONGWRITER'S GUIDE TO COLLABORATION, by Walter Carter. Published by Writer's Digest Books, 1507 Dana Ave., Cincinnati OH 45207. 1-800-289-0963. Attention: Book Order. Published 1988; 198 pages. Price: $12.95 paperback. Devoted entirely to the subject of co-writing, this guide covers everything from finding a partner and sharing writing responsibilities to splitting the costs and royalties. As an added feature, top-name songwriters tell how they worked together to write their songs and get them recorded. Songwriters will learn: the mechanics of a writing relationship—how to complement lyric- or melody-writing strength, increase exposure and advance reputation by working with a better-known writer; the legal aspects of collaboration; how to deal with publishers, co-produce demos and plan pitching strategy; where to give credit when credit is due, and tips on sharing the glory (or rejection).

*SUCCESSFUL LYRIC WRITING, A STEP-BY-STEP COURSE AND WORKBOOK, by Sheila Davis. Published by Writer's Digest Books, 1507 Dana Ave., Cincinnati OH 45207. 1-800-289-0963. Attention: Book Order. Published: 1988. 292 pages. Price $19.95 paperback. Modelled after the author's noted classes at The Songwriters Guild of America, this companion to *The Craft of Lyric Writing* presents the first complete textbook on writing professional lyrics for every genre—from country to cabaret. Davis guides the reader in taking each vital step in the lyric writing process with a series of 45 warmup exercises and 10 graduated assignments that develop writing skill as they reinforce theory. Features include: diagrams of music forms, lyric time frames and viewpoint; an illustrated ten-point guideline for figurative language; a primer on right-brain/left-brain writing; and a blueprint for conducting songwriting critique sessions.

SUCCESSFUL SONGWRITING, by Carl E. Bolte, Jr. Published by Holly Productions, 800 Greenway Terrace, Kansas City MO 64113. Published 1988; 206 pages. Price: $11.50 paperback. "In 34 chapters, from inspiration through publication, *Successful Songwriting* will guide your musical creative ability, whether you are a full-time professional or a fun-time hobbyist. Contains guidelines, statistics and how other songwriters found success. Learn about song topics, titles, lyric quantity, song forms, melody composition, key signatures, rhythm and time values, songwriter organizations. Explains why songs don't get published. This how-to book is fun and easy to read, with clear directions for making a song a hit song."

SUCCESSFUL SONGWRITING AND MARKETING, by Glenn Ray and David Leary. Published by Greater Songs Publications, P.O. Box 38, Toowong, Brisbane, QLD **Australia** 4066. (011)61-7-870-7078. FAX: (011)617-870-5127. Sales Manager: Cathy Jacobs. Published 1989; 220 pages. Price: US $24.95 hardback. "Covers all aspects of songwriting including lyrics, accompaniment, melodies and marketing. The authors have adopted a completely new approach to explaining music theory relevant to songwriting in a way that requires no formal musical training. Each section is followed up with creative practice exercises to reinforce what has been explained. Topics covered include song forms, lyric writing techniques, chord progressions, modulation, chromatic chords, analysis and song marketing. Recommended by the Australian Government Sponsored National Music Research Project."

*THIS BUSINESS OF ENTERTAINMENT AND ITS SECRETS, by Gregory J. Reed. Published by New National Publishing Co., Box 2645, Detroit MI 48236. (313)961-3580. Contact: Diane Brown. Published 1985; 300 pages. Describes many aspects of the entertainment business including managers, booking agents, financial planning, promotions, contracts and tax documents.

Glossary

A&R Director. Record company executive in charge of the Artists and Repertoire Department who is responsible for finding and developing new artists and matching songs with artists.

A/C. Adult contemporary music.

ACM. Academy of Country Music.

Advance. Money paid to the songwriter or recording artist before regular royalty payment begins. Sometimes called "up front" money, advances are deducted from royalties.

AFM. American Federation of Musicians. A union for musicians and arrangers.

AFTRA. American Federation of Television and Radio Artists. A union for performers.

AIMP. Association of Independent Music Publishers.

Air play. The radio broadcast of a recording.

AOR. Album-Oriented Rock. A radio format which primarily plays selections from rock albums as opposed to hit singles.

Arrangement. An adaptation of a composition for a performance or recording, with consideration for the melody, harmony, instrumentation, tempo, style, etc.

ASCAP. American Society of Composers, Authors and Publishers. A performing rights organization.

A-side. The side of a single which is considered to have "hit" potential and is promoted as such by the record company.

Assignment. Transfer of rights of a song from writer to publisher.

Audiovisual. Refers to presentations which use audio backup for visual material.

Bed. Prerecorded music used as background material in commercials.

Beta. ½″ videocassette format. The Beta System uses a smaller cassette than that used with the VHS system.

BMA. Black Music Association.

BMI. Broadcast Music, Inc. A performing rights organization.

B-side. The flip side of a single promoted by a record company. Sometimes the B-side contains the same song as the A-side so there will be no confusion as to which song should receive airplay.

Booking agent. Person who solicits work and schedules performances for entertainers.

Business manager. Person who handles the financial aspects of artistic careers.

b/w. Backed with. Usually refers to the B-side of a single.

C&W. Country and western.

CARAS. Canadian Academy of Recording Arts and Sciences. An association of individuals involved in the Canadian music and recording industry.

Catalog. The collected songs of one writer, or all songs handled by one publisher.

CD. Compact Disc (see below).

Chart. The written arrangement of a song.

Charts. The trade magazines' lists of the best selling records.

CHR. Comtemporary Hit Radio. Top 40 pop music.

CIRPA. Canadian Independent Record Producers Association.

CMA. Country Music Association.

CMPA. Church Music Publishers Association.

CMRRA. Canadian Musical Reproduction Rights Association. A mechanical rights agency.

Collaborator. Person who works with another in a creative endeavor.

Compact disc. A small disc (about 4.7 inches in diameter) holding digitally encoded music that is read by a laser beam in a CD player.

Co-publish. Two or more parties own publishing rights to the same song.

Copyright. The exclusive legal right giving the creator of a work the power to control the publishing, reproduction and selling of the work.

Cover record. A new version of a previously recorded song.

CRIA. Canadian Recording Industry Association.

Crossover. A song that becomes popular in two or more musical categories (i.e. country and pop).

Cut. Any finished recording; a selection from an LP. Also to record.

DAT. Digital Audio Tape. A professional and consumer audio cassette format for recording and playing back digitally-encoded material. DAT cassettes are approximately one-third smaller than conventional audio cassettes.

Demo. A recording of a song submitted as a demonstration of writer's or artist's skills.

Distributor. Marketing agent responsible for getting records from manufacturers to retailers.

Donut. A jingle with singing at the beginning and end and instrumental background in the middle. Ad copy is recorded over the middle section.

Engineer. A specially trained individual who operates all recording studio equipment.

EP. Extended play record (usually 12") containing more selections than a standard single, but fewer than a standard LP.

Evergreen. Any song that remains popular year after year.

Exploit. To seek legitimate uses of a song for income.

Folio. A softcover collection of printed music prepared for sale.

GMA. Gospel Music Association.

Harry Fox Agency. Organization that collects mechanical royalties.

Hip-hop. A dance oriented musical style derived from a combination of disco, rap and R&B.

Hit. A song or record that achieves top 40 status.

Hook. A memorable "catch" phrase or melody line which is repeated in a song.

House. Dance music created by DJ's remixing samples from other songs. Also called freestyle or techno.

IMU. International Musicians Union.

Indie. An independent record label, music publisher or producer.

ips. Inches per second; a speed designation for tape recording.

IRC. International reply coupon, necessary for the return of materials sent out of the country. Available at most post offices.

Jingle. Usually a short verse set to music designed as a commercial message.

Label. Record company, or the "brand" name of the records it produces.

LASS. Los Angeles Songwriters Showcase.

Lead sheet. Written version (melody, chord symbols and lyric) of a song.

Leader. Plastic (non-recordable) tape at the beginning and between songs for ease in selection.

LP. Designation for long-playing record played at 33⅓ rpm.

Lyric sheet. A typed or written copy of a song's lyrics.

Market. A potential song or music buyer; also a demographic division of the record-buying public.

Master. Edited and mixed tape used in the production of records; a very high-quality recording; the best or original copy of a recording from which copies are made.

Maxi-single. The cassette equivalent of a 12" single. Also called Maxi-cassettes or Maxi-plays. (See 12" Single.)

Mechanical right. The right to profit from the physical reproduction of a song.

Mechanical royalty. Money earned from record, tape and CD sales.

MIDI. Musical instrument digital interface. Universal standard interface which allows musical instruments to communicate with each other and computers.

Mix. To blend a multi-track recording into the desired balance of sound.

MOR. Middle of the road. Easy-listening popular music.

Ms. Manuscript.

Music jobber. A wholesale distributor of printed music.

Music publisher. A company that evaluates songs for commercial potential, finds artists to record them, finds other uses (such as TV or film) for the songs, collects income generated by the songs and protects copyrights from infringement.

NAIRD. National Association of Independent Record Distributors.

NARAS. National Academy of Recording Arts and Sciences.

NARM. National Association of Record Merchandisers.

NAS. National Academy of Songwriters, formerly Songwriters Resources and Services (SRS).

Needle-drop. Use of a prerecorded cut from a stock music house in an audiovisual soundtrack.

NMPA. National Music Publishers Association.

NSAI. Nashville Songwriters Association International.

One-off. A deal between songwriter and publisher which includes only one song or project at a time. No future involvement is implicated. Many times a single song contract accompanies a one-off deal.

One-stop. A wholesale distributor of records (and sometimes videocasettes, blank tapes and record accessories), representing several manufacturers to record stores, retailers and jukebox operators.

Overdub. To record an additional part (vocal or instrumental) onto a basic multi-track recording. To sweeten.

Payola. Dishonest payment to broadcasters in exchange for airplay.

Performing rights. A specific right granted by US copyright law that protects a composition from being publicly performed without the owner's permission.

Performing rights organization. An organization that collects income from the public performance of songs written by its members and then proportionally distributes this income to the individual copyright holder based on the number of performances of each song.

Personal manager. A person who represents artists, in numerous and varying ways, to develop and enhance their careers. Personal managers may negotiate contracts, hire and dismiss other agencies and personnel relating to the artist's career, screen offers and consult with prospective employers, review possible material, help with artist promotions and perform many services.

Piracy. The unauthorized reproduction and selling of printed or recorded music.

Pitch. To attempt to sell a song by audition; the sales talk.

Playlist. List of songs that a radio station will play.

Plug. A favorable mention, broadcast or performance of a song; to pitch a song.

Points. A negotiable percentage paid to producers and artists for records sold.

Producer. Person who supervises every aspect of recording a song or album.

Product. Records, CDs and tapes available for sale.

Production company. Company that specializes in producing jingle packages for advertising agencies. May also refer to companies that specialize in audiovisual programs.

Professional manager. Member of a music publisher's staff who screens submitted material and tries to get the company's catalog of songs recorded.

Program director. Radio station employee who screens records and develops a playlist of songs that station will broadcast.

PRS. Performing Rights Society of England.

PSA. Public Service Announcement: a free broadcast "advertisement" for a nonprofit service organization.

Public domain. Any composition with an expired, lapsed or invalid copyright.

Publish. To reproduce music in a saleable form and distribute to the public by sale or other transfer of ownership (rent, lease or lending).

Purchase license. Fee paid for music used from a stock music library.

Query. A letter of inquiry to a potential song buyer soliciting his interest.

R&B. Rhythm and blues.

Rack jobber. A wholesaler of records, tapes and accessories to retailers and mass-merchandisers not primarily in the record business (e.g. department stores).

Rate. The percentage of royalty as specified by contract.

Release. Any record issued by a record company.

Residuals. In advertising or television, payments to singers and musicians for subsequent use of a performance.

RIAA. Recording Industry Associations of America.

Royalty. Percentage of money earned from the sale of records or use of a song.

RPM. Revolutions per minute. Refers to phonograph turntable speed.

SAE. Self-addressed envelope (with no postage attached).

SASE. Self-addressed stamped envelope.

Self-contained. A band or recording act that writes all their own material.

SESAC. A performing rights organization.

SFX. Sound effects.

Shop. To pitch songs to a number of companies or publishers.

Single. 45 rpm record with only one song per side. A 12″ single refers to a long version of one song on a 12″ disc, usually used for dance music.

SOCAN. Society of Composers, Authors and Music Publishers of Canada. A performing rights organization formed in 1990 by the merger of CAPAC and PROCAN.

Solicited. Songs or materials that have been requested.

Song plugger. A songwriter representative whose main responsibility is promoting uncut songs to music publishers, record companies, artists and producers.

Song shark. Person who deals with songwriters deceptively for his own profit.

The Songwriters Guild of America. Organization for songwriters, formerly called AGAC.

Soundtrack. The audio, including music and narration, of a film, videotape or audiovisual program.

Split publishing. To divide publishing rights between two or more publishers.

Standard. A song popular year after year; an evergreen.

Statutory royalty rate. The maximum payment for mechanical rights guaranteed by law that a record company may pay the songwriter and his publisher for each record or tape sold.

Subpublishing. Certain rights granted by a US publisher to a foreign publisher in exchange for promoting the US catalog in his territory.

Synchronization. Technique of timing a musical soundtrack to action on film or video.

Synchronization rights. Rights to use a composition in film or video.

Take. Either an attempt to record a vocal or instrumental part, or an acceptable recording of a performance.

Top 40. The first forty songs on the pop music charts at any given time. Also refers to a style of music which emulates that heard on the current top 40.

Track. Divisions of a recording tape (e.g., 24-track tape) that can be individually recorded in the studio, then mixed into a finished master.

Trades. Publications that cover the music industry.

12″ Single. A twelve inch record containing one or more remixes of a song, originally intended for dance club play.

U/C. Urban contemporary music.

Unsolicited. Songs or materials that were not requested and are not expected.

VHS. ½″ videocassette format. The VHS system uses a larger cassette than that used with the Beta system.

Work. To pitch or shop a song.

Index

Can't find a listing? Check the end of each market section for the '92-'93 Changes lists. These lists include any market listings from the 1992 edition which were either not verified or deleted from this edition.

Can't find a listing? Check the end of each market section for the '92-'93 Changes lists. These lists include any market listings from the 1992 edition which were either not verified or deleted from this edition.

Can't find a listing? Check the end of each market section for the '92-'93 Changes lists. These lists include any market listings from the 1992 edition which were either not verified or deleted from this edition.

Can't find a listing? Check the end of each market section for the '92-'93 Changes lists. These lists include any market listings from the 1992 edition which were either not verified or deleted from this edition.

Can't find a listing? Check the end of each market section for the '92-'93 Changes lists. These lists include any market listings from the 1992 edition which were either not verified or deleted from this edition.

OTHER BOOKS TO HELP YOU MAKE
MONEY AND THE MOST OF
YOUR MUSIC TALENT

The Songwriter's Idea Book
Sheila Davis
Noted songwriter/teacher/music author Sheila Davis takes you step by step through the songwriting process covering 40 proven songwriting strategies—guaranteed to spark your imagination and keep the creative flame burning. 240 pages/$16.95, hardcover

88 Songwriting Wrongs & How to Right Them
Pat & Pete Luboff
Professional songwriters Pat and Pete Luboff give you 88 ways to spot what's wrong with your song, then give you expert instruction on how to fix it. 160 pages/$17.95, paperback

Making It In the New Music Business
Revised & Updated!
James Riordan
Music industry expert James Riordan (co-author of *The Platinum Rainbow*) shows you how to build your own path to success in today's music business—no matter what type of music you're interested in. 374 pages/$22.95, hardcover

The Songwriter's & Musician's Guide to Nashville
Sherry Bond
This indispensable book of key information and contacts will help you open the doors along Nashville's Music Row. 176 pages/$18.95, paperback

Songwriters on Songwriting
edited by Paul Zollo
31 successful songwriters, including Carole King, Paul Simon, and Madonna, share solid writing instruction as well as the techniques they use to find success. 196 pages/$17.95, paperback

Singing for a Living
Marta Woodhull
As a singer, do you dream of becoming a professional performer or recording artist? Marta Woodhull explores the ever-growing options available to you, and shares secrets of top professionals in the business. 160 pages/$18.95, paperback

Music Publishing: A Songwriter's Guide
Randy Poe
You know that "success" in the music business means getting your songs published—but what *is* music publishing? Here Randy Poe explains the industry, and shows you how to make the best deals for you and your songs. 144 pages/$18.95, paperback

Making Money Making Music (No Matter Where You Live)
James Dearing
This new edition is thoroughly revised with updated pricing structures and trends! Dearing outlines *scores* of ways to make a profitable living with your musical talent—in any community, including performing solo or with a group, writing music for jingles, teaching music, organizing a home recording studio, and more. 192 pages/$18.95, paperback

Beginning Songwriter's Answer Book
Paul Zollo
An essential guide for the aspiring musician, this book provides answers to the 218 questions most often asked the National Academy of Songwriters. 128 pages/$16.95, paperback

The Craft & Business of Songwriting
John Braheny
A powerful, information-packed book about the songwriting industry which thoroughly covers all the creative and business aspects that you need to know to maximize your chances of success. 322 pages/$19.95, hardcover

The Craft of Lyric Writing
Sheila Davis
Davis, a successful lyricist, composer, and teacher, presents the theory, principles, and techniques that result in lyrics with timeless appeal. 350 pages/$19.95, hardcover

Successful Lyric Writing:
A Step-by-Step Course & Workbook
Sheila Davis
A practical, self-contained lyric writing course, complete with exercises and lyric writing assignments designed to stimulate your creativity and build writing skills. 292 pages/$19.95, paperback

A complete catalog of all Writer's Digest Books is available FREE by writing to the address shown below. To order books directly from the publisher, include $3.00 postage and handling for one book, $1.00 for each additional book. Ohio residents add 5½% sales tax. Allow 30 days for delivery.

To take advantage of your 15% discount, simply mention #6300 when placing your order!

Writer's Digest Books
1507 Dana Avenue
Cincinnati, Ohio 45207

Credit card orders call TOLL-FREE
1-800-289-0963

Prices subject to change without notice

Songwriter "Do's and "Don'ts"

Do:

1. Read contracts carefully and have them reviewed by a music industry attorney.

2. Read song contest rules and procedures carefully.

3. Research before signing contracts with companies asking for payment in advance.

4. Ask companies for supporting material or samples of successful work.

5. Ask questions if you don't understand!